Sleeping price codes

LL	$250 and over
L	$175-249
AL	$120-174
A	$80-119
B	$50-79
C	$25-49
D	under $25

Prices are in New Zealand dollars ($). Price codes refer to the cost of two people sharing a double room (usually with en-suite bathroom) during the high season. Cheaper rooms are often available with shared bathrooms. Many places, especially hotel chains, offer low season and weekend specials.

Eating price codes

♨♨♨	Over $30
♨♨	$25-30
♨	Under $25

Prices are in New Zealand dollars ($). Codes refer to the cost of a main course for one person, excluding drinks or service charge.

Footprint story

It was 1921

Ireland had just been partitioned, the British miners were striking for more pay and the federation of British industry had an idea. Exports were booming in South America – how about a handbook for businessmen trading in that far away continent? The Anglo-South American Handbook was born that year, written by W Koebel, the most prolific writer on Latin America of his day.

1924

Two editions later the book was 'privatized' and in 1924, in the hands of Royal Mail, the steamship company for South America, it became The South American Handbook, subtitled 'South America in a nutshell'. This annual publication became the 'bible' for generations of travellers to South America and remains so to this day. In the early days travel was by sea and the Handbook gave all the details needed for the long voyage from Europe. What to wear for dinner; how to arrange a cricket match with the Cable & Wireless staff on the Cape Verde Islands and a full account of the journey from Liverpool up the Amazon to Manaus: 5898 miles without changing cabin!

1939

As the continent opened up, the South American Handbook reported the new Pan Am flying boat services, and the fortnightly airship service from Rio to Europe on the Graf Zeppelin. For reasons still unclear but with extraordinary determination, the annual editions continued through the Second World War.

1970s

Many more people discovered South America and the backpacking trail started to develop. All the while the Handbook was gathering fans, including literary vagabonds such as Paul Theroux and Graham Greene (who once sent some updates addressed to "The publishers of the best travel guide in the world, Bath, England").

1990s

During the 1990s the company set about developing a new travel guide series using this legendary title as the flagship. By 1997 there were over a dozen guides in the series and the Footprint imprint was launched.

2000s

The series grew quickly and there were soon Footprint travel guides covering more than 150 countries. In 2004, Footprint launched its first thematic guide: *Surfing Europe*, packed with colour photographs, maps and charts. This was followed by further thematic guides such as *Diving the World, Snowboarding the World, Body and Soul escapes, Travel with Kids and European City Breaks*.

2010

Today we continue the traditions of the last 89 years that have served legions of travellers so well. We believe that these help to make Footprint guides different. Our policy is to use authors who are genuine experts who write for independent travellers; people possessing a spirit of adventure, looking to get off the beaten track.

New Zealand Handbook

Darroch Donald

P ut Charles Darwin, Claude Monet and JRR Tolkien in a room with six bottles of vodka and some recreational drugs and, combined, they still couldn't come close to the concept of New Zealand. If nature had a design studio, full of her most surreal and stupendous ideas, on the mantelpiece would be New Zealand or, as the Maori call it, 'The Land of the Long White Cloud'.

The country is living proof that small can not only be beautiful but also incredibly diverse and complex. The two main islands, North Island and South Island, are quite different. North, which is less mountainous, is home to more than two-thirds of New Zealanders, or 'Kiwis', who live life to the beat of a faster rhythm than their countrified neighbours to the south. For the tourist, North Island generally holds less aesthetic appeal than South Island, but few miss, or indeed forget, the expansive views across Auckland from its hypodermic Sky Tower, the dramatic displays of Maori culture in Northland, or the brooding and colourful thermal features in and around Rotorua.

South Island, however, is said to offer the 'true essence' of New Zealand. To travel through it is like a fun-filled lesson in geography and guarantees to have the digital camera running on overload. It's packed with vast empty beaches where you feel guilty leaving a single set of footprints; endless mountain ranges blanketed in snow and rainforest; pristine lakes, waterfalls and fiords; giant glaciers; vast limestone caves and arid natural springs and fizzing hot pools. New Zealand, although it may seem at the end of the Earth, but it's certainly heaven upon it. It is like making an appointment with Doctor Nature and her able assistant nurse Adrenaline. And now is the time to 'take the cure'.

New Zealand highlights

1 Experience history and culture at Waitangi National Reserve, the birthplace of the nation. ▶▶ page 155.

2 Admire the vistas, climb the mast or even jump from Auckland's hypodermic Sky Tower. ▶▶ page 73.

3 Explore the impressive Waitomo limestone caves. ▶▶ page 223.

4 Call in at the devil's home at the Wai-o-tapu Thermal Reserve. ▶▶ page 247.

5 See some tremendous tectonics along the Tongariro Crossing. ▶▶ page 298.

6 Bombard the senses at Te Papa museum, the nation's most celebrated museum. ▶▶ page 393.

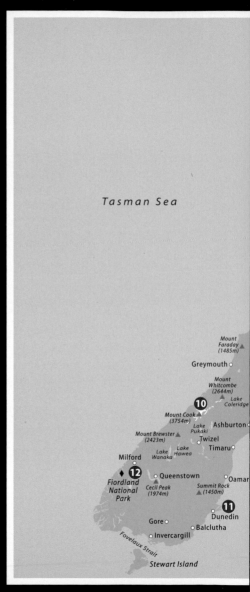

Tasman Sea

Mount Faraday ▲ (1485m)

Greymouth ○

Mount Whitcombe ▲ (2644m)

Lake Coleridge

10

Mount Cook ▲ (3754m)

Lake Pukaki

Ashburton ○

Mount Brewster ▲ (2423m)

Twizel

Lake Hawea

Timaru ○

Lake Wanaka

Milford

12

Fiordland National Park

Cecil Peak ▲ (1974m)

○ Queenstown

Summit Rock ▲ (1450m)

○ Oamar

11

Gore ○

○ Dunedin

○ Balclutha

○ Invercargill

Foveaux Strait

Stewart Island

Auopori Peninsula

1

Dargaville ○ ○ Whangarei

Great Barrier Island

Hauraki Gulf

Auckland ○ **2** ○ Whitianga
Papakura ○
Pukekohu ○ ○ Whangamata

Tauranga

Hamilton ○ *Bay of Plenty*
Cambridge ○ Whakatane ▲ *Hikurangi (1752m)*

3 ○ Tokoroa ○ Rotorua
4

New Taumarunui ○ *Lake Taupo* ○ Taupo ○ Gisborne
Plymouth
▲ Mt Egmont ○ Wairoa

▲ Mt Ruapehu **5** ○ Napier
Waverley ○ ○ Hastings
Wanganui ○ Waipukurau

○ Palmerston North

7 Paraparaumu ○
Porirua ○ ○ Masterton
Nelson ○ Picton **6**
Blenheim ○ WELLINGTON
8 *Cook Strait*
▲ Mount Franklin (2,339m) ○ Kaikora
9

Christchurch ○

Pacific Ocean

N

200 km
200 miles

7 Find solitude at Wharariki Beach and feel guilty about leaving footprints. ▶▶ page 463.

8 See white, red, then a bit fuzzy, touring the vineyards of Marlborough. ▶▶ page 422.

9 Spot whales or dolphins off the Kaikoura Coast. ▶▶ page 501.

10 Go glacier walking on Franz Josef or Fox glaciers. ▶▶ page 573.

11 Admire the grace of the albatross, or the charm of a penguin, on the Otago Peninsula. ▶▶ page 601.

12 Watch keas dismantle your hire car on the majestic Milford Road. ▶▶ page 666.

Top Wharariki Beach.
Above Te Papa museum.
Right Fox glacier.

Title page Sign at Kiwi Encounter.
Pages 2-3 Rangitoto Island.

Left Marlborough vineyards .
Below Whale watching, Kaikoura Coast.
Bottom Otago Peninsula.

Top Tongariro Crossing.
Above Waitangi.
Right Sky Tower, Auckland.

Left Kia watching tourists, Milford Road.
Below Waitomo limestone caves.
Bottom Wai-o-tapu Thermal Reserve.

The iconic cone of Mount Ngauruhoe peeks above early morning mist on the Central Plateau of the North Island. It is the youngest vent in the Tongariro National Park and last erupted in 1977.

Best photo locations

New Zealand is one of the most photogenic places in the world. Just walk in to any souvenir shop and the small forests of postcard racks and shelves laden with pictorials are testament to the country's awesome natural beauty.

Of course, a few years ago you may have been happy to settle for the odd book or postcard sent home with the old 'wish you were here' scrawled on the back. But now, with the digital revolution well and truly upon us, you are no doubt suitably armed and ready for action.

You may be the proud owner of a new digital compact or the latest DSLR. Regardless of your equipment or whether you're a pro, a keen amateur or a happy snapper, on your travels around New Zealand all you'll really want is to secure some great images and most importantly have a good idea of where to do so?

For most professionals and keen amateurs the pursuit of good imagery is an obsession. Indeed, it has to be. Taking great images is an art and always will be. But as already hinted, this is not about the profession, making money, the photographic revolution, or the obsession. It's not about in-depth techniques and not about whether your spiffy camera has an adjunct drinks cabinet (with ice). It's about getting to the right places and seeing New Zealand better. Making a few good images from precious moments in time and recording your memories with what you have and the most vital tool of all – your eyes.

Tip…

For 20 top tips for better photography and to view a comprehensive list of New Zealand's best photo locations refer to the author's website, **darrochdonald.com**.

Left Two yellow-eyed penguins courting, Otago Peninsula.

Below left Maori carving, Rotorua.

Below right Detail from paua shell casing.

Bottom A canoeist at Kaituna River, Rotorua.

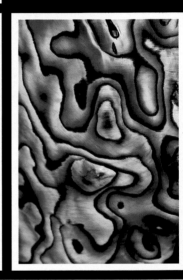

A traditional and intricately carved Maori whare (meeting house), is the centerpiece of the marae (sacred courtyard) in the historic village of Ohinemutu in Rotorua. A few distant descendants of the original iwi (tribe) still live around the marae.

The stunning view across Lake Pukaki in the Mackenzie Basin (Canterbury), with New Zealand's highest peak Mount Cook (Aoraki) in the distance. The remarkable azure colour of the water is due to the effects of glacial salts held in suspension.

Contents

Contents

Footprint features

Essentials

Planning your trip

New Zealand is everything you have heard about it, and an awful lot more. If you can only go for two to three weeks, unless you stay put in one area, or visit just a few places, it is going to be an exercise in frustration. Three weeks is pushing it, six is better and eight weeks is about right, short of actual emigration. That said, providing you are selective with your itinerary and do enough research, New Zealand's size and infrastructure mean that you can cram a surprising amount in to a relatively short period of time without necessarily blowing your wig off.

If New Zealand presents an irresistible lure, you are probably a nature-friendly, active and independent person. Start planning well in advance. You will find full sight and activity listings throughout this book. The web is also a major source of information. It's a good idea to secure your own transport on arrival, or even before. New Zealand is small and relatively easy to get about, but independence is a major advantage. If you are in a group consider the many campervan options (see page 39). The country is well geared up for this type of travel.

You might also consider buying a car (see box, page 41). Second-hand cars are relatively cheap in New Zealand and, provided they're still in one piece, you can usually sell them again when you have completed your journey. If you cannot afford your own wheels, then both islands are well set up for coach travel (see page 38). Information on public transport can be found in the 'Ins and outs' and 'Listings' sections of each chapter and also on the websites for each town or region.

The weather will be discussed in detail later in this chapter (see page 24) but early on in your planning you must take it into consideration. As a general rule, prepare for the fact that, even in summer, around 50 percent of the time it will be cloudy, perhaps raining and that many outdoor activities will be off the agenda. Remember this is not Australia – your fetching new Billabonk board shorts and flip flops (or jandles as they are called Downunder) will decorate little except your suitcase.

Where to go

Two weeks: North Island

Most international travellers arrive in the North Island and **Auckland** – home to the main international airport. Although the Auckland region has a lot to offer, only spend a day there, then move on quickly. Auckland is a great city – but a city nonetheless. It is modern and in many ways is not at all typical of New Zealand. Take a look from the top of the Sky Tower, stop by the Auckland Museum, and then head over to Devonport (including a walk to North Head) or one of the west coast beaches. Then the following day set off for Northland and the **Bay of Islands**, where there are numerous options for cruising the islands or dolphin watching. Don't miss Russell (the first significant European settlement) and Waitangi (where the Maori/Pakeha Treaty was signed). In the evening, the Maori performance at the Treaty grounds is recommended. The following day take a one-day trip to **Cape Reinga**, the northernmost tip of New Zealand. Then return to Auckland and dine down at the Viaduct Basin or in Ponsonby. The next day head southwest, for a couple of days in the **Coromandel**. If you do not have your own transport consider the cruise from Auckland (everyday except Monday and Wednesday) with **360 Discovery Cruises** ① *T0800-3603472, www.360discovery.co.nz*, or an organized road tour with one of the

Packing for New Zealand

New Zealand is a well-developed nation and anything you will need, from pharmaceuticals to camping gear, is readily available throughout the country. Given the favourable dollar rate if you are coming from Europe or North America, it might be better to travel light and buy as you go. Auckland can supply just about all your needs including quality maps and travel books. Backpackers, naturally, are advised to bring a good sleeping bag and a bed sheet. These are not always provided in hostels and certainly not available in the backcountry tramping huts. A good pair of boots and a large rucksack is a good idea if you are intending to hike. Also remember to bring an electrical adapter plug. Binoculars are recommended as are a sun hat, sunscreen and sunglasses.

Auckland-based operators like **Coromandel Explorer Tours** ① *T07-8663506, www.coromandeltours.co.nz*. If you have your own transport in the 'Coro' don't miss Coromandel township (including the Driving Creek Railway), Colville, Cape Colville and Cathedral Cove. From Coromandel head to **Rotorua** for two days of volcanic scenery and a multitude of activities. From Rotorua head southwest to **Taupo**, being sure not to miss the Wai-o-tapu Thermal Reserve on the way. Make sure you see the Huka Falls and relax and enjoy a hot pool at De Brett's Thermal Resort. If the weather is fine the following day and with an early start attempt 'The Tongariro Crossing', a full-day walk (moderate fitness required), or take a cruise on Lake Taupo, followed by a skydive from 12,000 ft, if your nerves can stand it. Alternatively from Taupo, get underground with a day trip to the **Waitomo Caves**. From Taupo take one of two recommended routes south. Either head south on SH1, taking SH47 at Taurangi around the western side of the **Tongariro National Park**. If you can, take the chairlift up the slopes of Ruapehu accessed from Whakapapa Village, or better still a scenic flight above the mountains. Another option is to drive up the Mountain Road from **Ohakune**. Stay in Ohakune. The next day travel to **Wellington** as early as possible. Alternatively, head southeast to **Napier** and the **Hawkes Bay**. Enjoy Napier itself or visit a winery or the gannets (seabirds) of Cape Kidnappers and take some time to enjoy the view from Te Mata Peak in **Havelock North**. From Havelock head south through the **Wairarapa** stopping at Mount Bruce Wildlife Centre and, if you have time, take in the coast at Castlepoint. The following morning try to visit the remote **Cape Palliser**, the southernmost tip of the North Island. Once in **Wellington**, take a trip up the Cable Car, see the view from Mount Victoria and check out 'Te Papa' – New Zealand's multimillion dollar national museum. For lunch or dinner muse the menus on and around Courtney Place. The following day drive back to Auckland (nine hours) or head across early by ferry or plane for a week in the South Island.

Two weeks: South Island

By ferry or plane from Wellington, try to arrive in **Picton** early in the day so you can join one of the trips out into the **Marlborough Sounds** – either dolphin watching, kayaking or a half-day walk to Ship Cove. The following day drive to Blenheim and visit one or two of the vineyards before heading through Havelock, making your way to **Nelson**. Enjoy the rest of the day in Nelson then head off to Motueka. The next day take a day-walk or kayak trip in the **Abel Tasman National Park**. Then continue to the west coast and **Franz Josef**. In Franz Josef be sure to take a scenic flight around Mount Cook, or at the least a glacier walk on the

Franz. The following day, drive from Franz Josef, stopping at Ship Creek and Haast to reach **Wanaka** by evening. The following day go canyoning, skydiving or for a walk up to the Rob Roy Glacier from Raspberry Creek. Alternatively, take a scenic flight to Milford Sound. Head for **Queenstown** and spend the day having a small nervous breakdown counting your dollars and deciding what to do. The bungee jump is the obvious attraction as is the Shotover Jet and the views from the gondola. Spend another day visiting **Milford Sound** – it's best to bus in (to see Te Anau and the Milford Road) and fly out.

For the following three days there is an alternative: head directly to Christchurch or travel via Dunedin. For Christchurch drive from Queenstown to **Mount Cook** village. Spend the rest of the day taking in the scenery by foot, by bike or with a scenic flight. If you are up to it, climb up to the Muller Hut for the night. The next day drive to Christchurch for a look at Tekapo and the McKenzie Country, arriving in **Christchurch** late evening. Alternatively, you could spend the first two days in **Dunedin** and the Otago Peninsula with the following day in the northern sector of the **Catlins**. After a day in Christchurch, head for **Kaikoura** where you can take a whale-watching or swimming with dolphins excursion, leaving yourself enough time to catch the late ferry from **Picton** that night.

Three weeks: North Island

Add to the above these following options. In Auckland try to get out on the **Hauraki Gulf**, visit **Tiritiri Matangi Island** (highly recommended), **Rangitoto** or **Great Barrier Island**. Another option is to try your hand at sailing aboard a former NZ America's Cup yacht with **Sail NZ** (see page 29). Alternatively, spend some time exploring the Waitakeres and the west coast beaches. In the city visit Kelly Tarlton's Underwater and Antarctic Encounter and/or the Waterfront and the Maritime Museum. Adrenaline seekers should consider the controlled bungee from the observation deck of the **Sky Tower**.

In Northland on the way to the Bay of Islands, don't miss the **Whangarei Heads** (Ocean Beach) and/or the **Tutakaka Coast**. While there consider diving the **Poor Knights Islands**. In the Bay of Islands consider a two-day kayak trip on and around the islands or walk to **Cape Brett**. Bruise your bum on the fast boat to the 'Hole in the Rock'. Heading north, take a peek at historic **Kerikeri** and the delights of the scenic coast road to Whangaroa. After visiting the Cape head southwest to the **Hokianga**. Just south of the Hokianga don't miss 'Tane Mahuta', the 1500-year-old kauri in the magnificent **Waipoua Forest**. Then learn more about the great trees at the **Kauri Museum** in Matakohe. Heading south from Auckland, spend a couple more days exploring the Coromandel. Go fishing from **Whitianga** or spend a day on **New Chums Beach**. Don't miss the Driving Creek Railway in Coromandel Township.

From Coromandel head to the Bay of Plenty. Spend a day enjoying one of the many activities in **Tauranga** or Mount Maunganui. Perhaps try staying upright on a surfboard. There is plenty to detain you in the **Tongariro National Park** and you could also consider a kayaking trip down the Wanganui River in the neighbouring **Wanganui National Park**, before heading south to Wellington. North from Rotorua you can negotiate the **East Cape** via Whakatane. While in **Whakatane** visit the active volcano White Island or swim with dolphins. If you head west from Rotorua or Taupo, a day underground in the **Waitomo Caves** is recommended. If at all possible and you can afford it, try the '**Lost World**' trip, see page 230. From Waitomo you can follow the coast to **Taranaki** and spend some time around the mountain and the **Mount Egmont National Park** – arguably the most beautiful mountain in the country. From New Plymouth, which is a great town in itself, you could take in **Wanganui** and a trip on the Wanganui River before heading south to **Wellington**.

If you head west from Rotorua or Taupo, spend time in **Napier** and consider staying at **Lake Waikaremoana** in the Urewera National Park. Then, from Napier head south via **Havelock North** through the Wairarapa taking in the scenery of Castlepoint, the Waiohine Gorge and **Cape Palliser** as well as the vineyards around Martinborough. From all these directions you will end up in Wellington and can spend more time in the city. For a superb day trip visit the wildlife paradise of **Kapiti Island**. From Wellington it is a nine-hour drive via SH1 back to Auckland, though the flight on a clear day – with Mount Taranaki on one side and Ruapehu on the other – is a delight.

Three weeks: South Island

Added to the above itinerary for the South Island, there are many additional excursions and activities. In Nelson and Marlborough consider an extra day or two in the Marlborough Sounds. Do part of the **Queen Charlotte Track**, or the lesser-known **Nydia Track**, a full-day cruise, a multi-day kayak trip from Havelock or **Picton**, or better still, spend a day or two getting to **French Pass**. From Nelson consider doing the **Abel Tasman Coast Walk** or a multi-day kayak trip. The more adventurous should take the controls of a Pitts Special for the ride of your life, with Uflyextreme (see Motueka activities page 447). From Motueka, venture over Takaka Hill to **Golden Bay**. Visit the Pupu Springs, Farewell Spit and the beautiful **Wharariki Beach**. While in Golden Bay consider doing the **Heaphy Track** or exploring the northern sector of the Abel Tasman or Kahurangi national parks.

Returning to Motueka, head for the west coast via the Nelson Lakes National Park. Consider the **Angelus Hut Walk** in the Nelson Lakes then head to **Westport** via the Buller Gorge. From Westport venture north to **Karamea** and see the incredible karst scenery of the **Oparara Basin**. Walk part of the Heaphy Track coastal stretch. From Karamea head south down the west coast to **Franz Josef**, taking in the arts and crafts of **Hokitika**, the **white heron colony** near Whataroa and the secluded delights of **Okarito**. Then give yourself an extra two to three days around the Glacier Region. As well as the glaciers, take in **Lake Matheson** (at dawn or dusk) and the wild coastline.

Heading south to Haast, stop at **Munroe Beach** and Ship Creek. Spend at least two days around **Haast**, take a jet-boat trip and explore further south to **Jackson's Bay** and the **Cascade Saddle**. Having negotiated the Haast Pass to **Wanaka** spend some time enjoying the scenery and activities, particularly the local walks. From Wanaka head for **Queenstown** via the Cardrona Road and lose yourself in the incredible range of activities.

For a break from the chaos head north and explore the **Glenorchy/Paradise** areas (featured heavily in *Lord of the Rings*), **Arrowtown** or climb to the top of the **Remarkables**. From Queenstown drive to **Te Anau**, consider the Kepler, Routeburn or Milford Tracks (book well ahead) or a multi-day kayak trip on **Milford** or **Doubtful Sound**. Be sure to make the scenic drive to **Milford Sound** and give yourself an extra day there. Great day or half-day walks include **Key Summit** or **Lake Marian**. Just south of Te Anau, take in the stunning scenery and atmosphere of **Lake Manapouri** and Doubtful Sound. From Manapouri negotiate the Southern Scenic Route to **Dunedin**, and en route consider doing the **Humpridge Track**, visiting **Stewart Island** (to see the diurnal kiwi) and certainly give yourself three days exploring the **Catlins Coast**. Spend two to three days in Dunedin allowing at least one on the **Otago Peninsula**. Take a tour to see the **albatross colony** and the **yellow-eyed penguins**.

From Dunedin head north to Oamaru then inland to **Mount Cook** spending some time exploring the area and its activities. If you are fit spend a night up in the Mueller Hut. Via **Tekapo** and the McKenzie Country, then head to Christchurch giving yourself more time in the city. While in Christchurch spend a day exploring the **Banks Peninsula**. West of Christchurch consider the scenic drive to Mount Sunday and Mount Potts Station used for the set for Edoras in *Lord of the Rings*. North of Christchurch, as an adjunct to Kaikoura, head inland to enjoy a hot pool and perhaps a mountain bike ride in **Hanmer Springs**. From Hanmer Springs and Kaikoura enjoy the stunning coastal road that will deliver you back to **Picton** via the **vineyards** of Marlborough.

When to go

For travellers from the northern hemisphere spending Christmas Day on the beach, sunbathing while digesting a hearty barbecue, or seeing Santa parade around in shorts under cloudless skies, is really quite a bizarre experience. The summer or **high season**, from **November** to **March**, is of course the busiest time of year and at these times you'll be joining battalions of Kiwis also on holiday (that's the people as opposed to the birds!). Over Christmas and for the whole of January, almost the entire country heads to the beach or the mountains. Accommodation is at a premium and the roads to the major tourist destinations can be busy. But again, 'busy' roads in New Zealand, especially in the more remote parts of the South Island, is a relative thing.

The months of late spring (**September/October**) or early autumn (**March/April**) are often recommended, as you are almost guaranteed accommodation and the weather is still pretty favourable. It is also cheaper. The winter or **low season** is from **April/May** to **August/September**. During this period prices are often reduced with plenty of special deals, especially at weekends and mid-range establishments. Bear in mind that some places are closed in winter but generally speaking, tourism is a year-round affair in New Zealand. Also bear in mind that some places like Queenstown (the principal tourist destination in the South Island) are as busy in the winter months with skiing activities as they are with general activities in summer. Taking all the above into account, the best months to visit, unless you enjoy the tourist/holiday buzz, are **October/November** or **March/April**.

Climate → *For detailed weather information consult www.metservice.co.nz or www.metvuw.com*
New Zealand has what is called an 'ocean temperate' climate, which to the layman means that it is generally agreeable. As the country is fairly elongated and lying very much at a north to south angle, the weather varies greatly. The north and east of both islands are consistently a few degrees warmer than the south and west. Predictably, the warmest region of the country is generally Northland and the coldest Southland, but some inland areas of Otago and the east of the North Island also see higher temperatures. However, in recent years, there have been unusual weather patterns and plenty of inconsistencies. In 2006 for example a small flotilla of large icebergs came within 'flightseeing' distance of Southland and Otago. Once a rare phenomenon it may prove more common thanks to global warming and its effect on the Antarctic Ice Shelf. In summary, like any temperate climate you can rely on one thing – unpredictability.

In Auckland the winter (June to August) and summer (December to March) average temperatures are 8-15°C (48-59°F) and 14-23°C (57-74°F) respectively and in Dunedin 4-12°C (39-53°F) and 9-19°C (48-66°F) respectively. But this can be misleading: not too far inland from Dunedin, Alexandra is quite often the hottest spot in the country. When it comes to sunshine, various regions compete closely for the title of 'sunniest place'. For several years now it has been Nelson and Marlborough in the South Island. But next year it could just as easily be Napier on the relatively dry and sunny east coast of the North Island, or even Whakatane in the Bay of Plenty. Wellington and Auckland, too, boast a lot of sunshine with Auckland being far more humid. Wellingtonians also suffer from wind – quite severely too (thankfully not of the beans variety). The west coast and Fiordland in Southland also have their extremes of wind and rain. But having said that, the beauty of a place like New Zealand is that, even in winter, it doesn't rain for long periods. In summary, the weather is generally favourable here; you can swim in the sea, wear shorts in summer and will not be forced indoors for days on end. One other word of advice: thanks to ozone depletion, the sun in New Zealand is dangerous, so always wear a hat and the strongest possible sun block. ▸▸ *See Health, page 54.*

What to do

Birdwatching

Much of the wildlife in New Zealand is of the feathered variety. Thanks to human intervention, the mainland is certainly not the place it once was. However, there are still plenty of opportunities to see the country's incredible birdlife first hand. Offshore island reserves such as Tiritiri Matangi Island north of Auckland (see page 118) and Kapiti Island north of Wellington (see page 408), protect unique and endangered species that were wiped out from the mainland. The birds are naturally very tame allowing you to get up close.

DoC's Mount Bruce Wildlife Centre in the Wairarapa (see page 355), or the penguin viewing tours and Albatross Centre on the Otago Peninsula (see page 601) are recommended. The city zoos are also great places to see captive native wildlife at close range.

Perhaps the best and most comical of New Zealand's birds is the **kea** or mountain parrot. Very intelligent and hopelessly delinquent they are an endless source of entertainment, or annoyance, depending on your point of view. Another notable character is the **takahe**, an ancient and admirably laid-back species that looks like a large prehistoric purple chicken. Only about 200 remain. Then of course there is the **kiwi** – that remarkable nocturnal bird with no wings, an awfully long beak and an ability to lay an egg the size of a small melon. There are many commercial nocturnal houses where you will get a good view of one, however, to see one in the wild you will either have to be exceptionally lucky or go on a specialist trip to Stewart Island (see page 684). Sadly, the kiwi is fast heading for extinction on the mainland.

Other species to look out for include the rare Yellow-eyed penguin, the kokako and the industrial sized Royal Albatross. For further information, see the Background chapter.

For specialist wildlife operators, see page 63. The **Royal Forest and Bird Protection Society**, www.forestandbird.org.nz, has further information.

Bungee jumping

The strange practice of attaching a rubber band to your ankles and diving off a very high bridge has now become synonymous with a visit to New Zealand. The concept was developed by A J Hackett, who jumped from the Eiffel Tower in 1986 and from the Sky Tower in Auckland (see page 73) in 2000. Jumps vary from 'tasters' of around 40 m (from bridges) to the 134 m 'Nevis' near Queenstown. Most are in Queenstown in the South Island, where you can do it from a bridge, high above a canyon, or even at night. Folk have jumped in tandem, in canoes, on bikes and, of course, butt naked. At $130-250, a jump is far from cheap but it's a once-in-a-lifetime experience. Of course AJ Hackett's mighty 134-m Nevis near Queenstown is recommended.

Caving

The underground world of the Waitomo Caves (see page 223) is a renowned playground. There are over 360 mapped caves, the longest of which is 14 km. Most have rivers which carve a wonderland of caverns, pools, waterfalls and rapids. These are negotiated with a headlamp, in a wetsuit, attached to a rubber ring. Added to that, there's a 300-m abseil into the 'Lost World' as well as the spectacle of glow-worms. There is a huge range of activities; almost all involve getting wet. Prices range from a 4-hr trip at around $120 to a 7-hr trip at around $400.

Cricket

Given the nation's colonial roots, cricket has long been a well-established spectator sport in New Zealand, with the national team, The Blackcaps, hosting visiting nations and touring overseas each summer. Cricket does not inspire quite the same fanatical following as rugby, but they share a healthy distain for their greatest foes – Australia. Test matches are held at the main provincial stadiums (see Rugby, page 29).

Fishing

New Zealand is fishing heaven and noted as one of the best and most unspoilt **trout fishing** locations in the world. All levels of experience are catered for with numerous boat charters and guides, from the relatively affordable $80 an hour to the all-mod-cons trips at around $200 an hour.

Fishing licences cost $21 for 24 hours and $105 for a season and are available online from **New Zealand Fish and Game**, www.fishandgame.org.nz, and most fishing tackle outlets. May fishing related tourism operators also supply licences.

The warm Pacific waters that grace the North Island's shores attract a huge range of saltwater species from snapper to massive marlin, providing some superb sea and **big-game fishing**. And in New Zealand it's not just the preserve of the idle rich. Costs vary from the 3-hr novice trip to the highly organized but still affordable 3-day 'Hemingway' trips to catch that prize marlin. It's an unforgettable experience as you watch the seabirds, the occasional dolphin (sometimes even a whale) and the amazing flying fish erupting from the water, then suddenly the line from your rod and barrel-sized reel goes off like the wheels of a formula one car at the start of a race, and your jaw drops as you see a huge marlin sail out of the water at incredible speed, and the fight is on. It might sound like hard work, but you don't have to be the Incredible Hulk to do it. The cost of big game fishing varies between operators and depends on the vessel and the services on offer. Expect to pay between $1000 and $4000 a day for a full charter.

Flightseeing and aerobatics

For a real insight into what flying is all about, not to mention the stunning views, a flight in a **fixed-wing** aircraft or a **helicopter** is highly recommended. There are endless locations throughout the country and at around $100 for a 10- to 15-min flight in a helicopter or a 30-min flight in a small fixed-wing, it's well worth it. If you can only afford one flight, make it the helicopter flight around the glaciers and summit of Mt Cook. Most operate out of Franz Joseph or Fox glaciers. This 30-min trip (around $275) on a clear day is truly breathtaking.

If you fancy having a go yourself, it's possible to take the controls of a Pitts Special aerobatic biplane with Uflyextreme in Motueka (see page 447). It is the only operation in New Zealand where you actually fly the aircraft. Of course the aircraft is a twin open cockpit and you are accompanied and under the close scrutiny of the pilot. But in essence it is safe, remarkably easy, good value (at around $300 for 20 minutes) and extreme fun.

At several locations around the country you can also take tentative control of a small training helicopter (again accompanied and under close scrutiny, on a 30-min flight). Together these single training flights are one of the most exhilarating experiences of a lifetime (and arguably even better than bungee jumping and tandem skydiving).

For a more sedate ride you could consider a trip by **hot-air balloon** which, although not so common and more expensive (around $300), is available in a number of locations. Or, for the full 'Biggles' experience, you can don the goggles and scarf and get strapped into a biplane.

There are numerous operators in Wanaka, Queenstown, Te Anau and Milford. See www.flightseeing.co.nz, www.touristflightoperators.co.nz and www.airmilford.co.nz.

Golf

New Zealand is blessed with hundreds of golf courses, from those that require a cute wedge shot to avoid sheep to others with well-manicured greens fit for an open championship. In Taupo and Rotorua you can even play on a steaming golf course; from little fumaroles on the fairways to bursts from the ground.

Green fees vary from $50-400 and it's usually possible to hire clubs. If you go early and in the off-season, it can be rare to even see another player. Attitudes to golfing etiquette are much less strict than in Europe or North America, so don't be surprised if you a group of Kiwi lads drop their trousers on the 18th tee to play a 'provisional', just accept it – it's tradition apparently.

See the following for further information: www.nzgolf.org.nz, www.golfguide.co.nz, www.golfnewzealand.co.nz, www.golftoursnz.net and www.nzgolf.net.

Horse trekking

The New Zealand landscape is ideal for horse trekking; there are a wealth of operators and horse riding is available throughout the country. All levels are well catered for and it will only cost around $50 for 2 hours. Other equestrian options include thoroughbred stud tours in the Waikato (see page 232).

See www.ridingholidays.com/newzealand_aus1.htm. The **International League for the Protection of Horses**, PO Box 10-368 Te Rapa, Hamilton, T07-849 0678, www.horsetalk.co.nz, publishes a very informative leaflet.

Jet boating

You have probably seen it. A red boat packed with tourists, all wearing the same 'well isn't this fun' expression, while thinking 'get me out of here now'. It is quite an unnerving experience whizzing down a river, heading straight at some rocks at insane speeds and closing your eyes in the face of inevitable death, only to open them again to find yourself still, remarkably, alive. Then, as a last hurrah, to be spun about in a 360° turn, just to make sure you are *completely* wet. Not all are adrenaline-pumping trips with some (especially in the North island) being more scenic affairs. Prices are reasonable, with a 30-min trip costing around $110. See the following: www.dartriver.co.nz, www.shotoverjet.com, www.hukajet.co.nz and www.riverjet.co.nz for further information.

Kayaking

New Zealand is a renowned playground for kayaking whether on river, lake or sea – even fiord. For novices, kayaking just takes just a wee bit of time to get used to, but before you know it, you'll be off and paddling before you can say *'Deliverance'*. A word of warning – never share a canoe with a loved one. Within 5 mins there will be a major argument about technique, threats of violence and floods of tears. If you find it to your taste (the silence, the solitude and the scenery can be heart-warming) then consider a multi-day trip. The best of these are in the Bay of Islands (page 167), Abel Tasman National Park (page 459) and, most recommended, Fiordland (from Te Anau, page 665). Inland try Whanganui National Park (page 379). The coastal scenery is often best taken in by kayak and there are some great guides out there. You never know, you might even come across a friendly dolphin or fur seal. Costs again vary slightly but you can hire your own kayak for about $25 per hr; a 3-hr trip will cost about $120; a 4-day affair from $550.

See (among many other operators) www.alpinekayaks.co.nz, www.seakayaknz.co.nz, www.abeltasmankayaks.co.nz, www.seakayaknewzealand.com, www.nzkayakschool.com.

Mountain biking
New Zealand is, as you might expect, a paradise for the avid mountain biker. With its wide range of magnificent landscapes, the country offers numerous tracks, both long and short and mainly through native bush or commercial forest and in summer on the ski fields. Bike hire is readily available and quite cheap, so give it a go. Whether you go down vertical rock faces and submerge yourself in mud pools, or stick to the straight and not so narrow, is up to you.

Cycle Touring Company New Zealand, Whangarei, T09-436 0033, www.cycletours.co.nz, specializes in self-led cycling adventures on routes all over Northland from 2-21 days. Food and lodging included. See also www.mountainbike.co.nz, www.bike-nz.com, www.vorb.org.nz, www.planet bike.co.nz and www.bikenz.org.nz.

Mountaineering
It would take a lifetime to climb all the major peaks in New Zealand. Mt Cook at 3753 m is the country's highest. Although not especially high, the New Zealand peaks are spectacular, challenging and potentially dangerous. Many of the most accessible peaks are in the South Island, however Mt Taranaki in the North Island is the country's most-climbed mountain. To look at it on a clear day is to stand in awe. Its symmetry and isolation just beckons you up its precarious slopes.

If you are new to mountaineering, this is the perfect country in which to start. You are, after all, in Sir Edmund Hillary's back garden. Once you scale that first peak and feel the sense of achievement, you will almost certainly be hooked. If you are a novice seek advice and go well prepared; check the weather forecast and tell someone where you're going. Many tourist lives have been lost through sheer stupidity and over-confidence. There are numerous guided trips available especially around Taranaki and Mt Cook.

NZ Alpine Club, Christchurch, T03-377 7595, www.alpineclub.org.nz. Specialist enquiries. **NZ Mountain Guides Association**, www.nzmga.org.nz. Good source of information, contacts and weather reports. The following are also useful: www.alpinere creation.co.nz, www.adventure.co.nz and www.alpinismski.co.nz.

Paraflying and tandem parapenting
What is the difference? One is done from the back of a speedboat over water, the other around hills and coastal slopes. It's basically a bit like glorified kite flying with you attached to the kite. Paraflying is the easier and more commercial of the two and is practised at many coastal resorts. You are strapped to a cradle below a special parachute and kept in the air by a speedboat. Parapenting (or paragliding) takes time to master. Like skydiving the novice is taken in tandem with an expert. It's great fun and will have you screaming like a banshee

and gesticulating wildly to your highly amused compadres. A boat tow paraflight of around 10 minutes costs about $100 and tandem land-based paragliding around $175.

Contact the **New Zealand Hang Gliding and Paragliding Association**, www.nzhgpa.org.nz, for further information and see also the following websites: www.nelsonparagliding.co.nz, www.skyout.co.nz and www.extremeair.co.nz.

Rafting

This is another 'must do' activity. The rapids are graded from I to VI. Although the 45-minute trips at about $100 are packed with adrenaline-pumping moments, the real experience only comes with a multi-day trip (4 days costs around $800). The 4-day trip down the wild and remote Motu in Eastland or Landsborough in South Island are recommended. The trips are well organized and safe; most even do the campfire cooking for you. If the multi-day trip is beyond your budget or timeline then the best experience is the 45-minute trip down the Kaituna Rapids near Rotorua (page 258). The highlight of this trip is the 7-m drop down the Okere Falls, the highest commercially rafted falls in the world.

See the following: www.nz-rafting.co.nz, www.raft.co.nz, www.wetnwildrafting.co.nz, www.whitewaterrafting.co.nz and www.queenstownrafting.co.nz.

River sledging

This is the ludicrously simple but superb concept of rafting down a river on a bodyboard with little except a wet suit, flippers, a crash helmet and a PhD in silliness. A good dunking will cost you from $100-285. See www.kaitiaki.co.nz and www.frogz.co.nz.

Rock climbing

This is on the increase in New Zealand. Contact the following for further information: www.climb.co.nz, www.alpineclub.org.nz, www.mojozone.co.nz, www.wanakarock.co.nz and www.indoorclimbing.com.

Rugby

Rugby is the most popular spectator sport in New Zealand, with the mighty All Blacks assuming an almost religious status. Every winter, the All Blacks host teams from abroad and tour overseas demanding huge respect if not a modicum of disguised fear. The All Blacks are, in essence, the crème de la crème of national talent derived from the Super-14 tournament (which includes teams from New Zealand, Australia and South Africa) as well as the NPC, or National Provincial Cup, both of which precede the All Blacks test season.

With major matches staged at the high profile stadiums in Auckland (Eden Park); Wellington (The Westpac Stadium); Christchurch (Jade Stadium) and Carisbrook (often dubbed the 'House of Pain') in Dunedin, it is often possible for visitors to go along and see what all the fuss is about – provided of course you can secure tickets.

Sailing

New Zealand, and Auckland in particular, is famous for sailing. Indeed, from 1995-2003 the Kiwis were the proud holders of the world's biggest sailing trophy – the America's Cup – and despite the loss are still considered not only the best sailors in the world but also the best designers and speed racers. Auckland is not called the 'City of Sails' for nothing. An estimated 1 in 4 of its inhabitants owns a recreational boat of some kind and this trend is echoed throughout the country.

At least a few hours out on the water are recommended but, if you can, try a multi-day trip. This will give you an insight into what sailing is all about. There are numerous opportunities to get out on the water in a proper yacht, even an ex America's Cup yacht, though if you plan a longer trip there must be someone present with the relevant experience; 'tickets' and the Sir Peter Blakes of this world don't come cheap.

Explore NZ (Sail NZ), Viaduct Basin, Auckland, T0800 397 567, www.sailnz.co.nz; **Charter Link**, Bayswater Marina, Auckland, T09-445 7114, www.charterlink.co.nz; **CharterNZ**, www.charternz.co.nz; and **Sail Connections**, T09-358 0556, www.sailconnections.co.nz, will all be able to provide more information.

Scuba diving

New Zealand has some world-class diving venues with superb marine reserves all around the country. The Poor Knights is where most budding Jacques Cousteaus gravitate to, for its combination of geology, marine life and water clarity. With up to 80 m of visibility you can go head to head with a huge grouper or clench your rubbers at the sight of a shark. There is also some fine wreck-diving available with the old navy frigates *Tui*, *Canterbury* and *Waikato* deliberately sunk for the benefit of divers off the east Northland coast. Another fine trip is the one to pay homage to the Greenpeace vessel *Rainbow Warrior* that was laid to rest off Matauri Bay; it was bombed in Auckland by French terrorists in 1985. If you're not already qualified, local operators will often take you for a full- or half-day first dive experience for around $250 including gear hire. If the thought of all that is too much you can also go snorkeling, which gives you a great insight into the wonders of the deep for minimum effort. Try the following websites for more information: www.scubadiving.co.nz, www.divenz.com, www.splash.co.nz, www.globaldive.net.

Shark encounters

While the vast majority of the human race still have nightmares at the mere suggestion of a fin surfacing above the water, it appears there is a lunatic fringe who actually wish to have a picnic with them. If you are one of these people and wish to encounter these fascinating creatures in their own habitat from the relative safety of a cage, you can do so in New Zealand. Sadly, thanks to commercial as opposed to recreational human activity, operators are finding it increasingly difficult to locate these ancient and toothy denizens of the deep. A 4-hour trip will cost about $250, prosthetic limbs extra.

Skiing and snowboarding

New Zealand is the principal southern hemisphere skiing and snowboarding venue and although it is of course seasonal (May-August), the slopes are highly accessible. The average cost of hire for skis, boots and poles is around $40, snowboard and boots $50. A lift pass will cost around $85 per day, with concessions for students and children. Packages are available that include lift pass, equipment hire and one or more lessons. There may also be 'Lift and Ski Hire Packages' which cost from $85. A group lesson (2 hours) will cost about $50 while a private lesson (1 hour) will cost about $85. See www.nzski.com, www.snow.co.nz, www.brownbear.co.nz and www.nzsnow.com for further information

Surfing

New Zealand is a world-class surfing venue with an almost religious following, but in such close proximity to Australia it is often overlooked by the surf set and so remains pretty uncommercial. You can get excellent and cheap tuition in many places (especially in Taranaki, Mount Maunganui and Raglan). If you want a beginner's taste of what surfing is like, try boogie boarding or bodysurfing. Boogie boards are about half the size of a surfboard and made of compressed foam, and are cheap to buy or hire. With this and a pair of flippers you can then go pseudo-surfing and take out the difficult bit – standing up. See www.surf.co.nz, www.surfingnz.co.nz and www.newzealandsurftours.com.

Tandem skydiving
Adrenaline aside, the beauty of taking the jump in New Zealand is the scenic factor. Once you have recovered from that falling feeling, the view of the land below hurtling towards you at 150 kph is unforgettable. There is some scant instruction before the actual jump but you are in very safe hands and you can come away with a DVD of the experience as well as a smile like 'Garfield'. Jumps range in height from 9000-15,000 ft. The latter will give you about 40 seconds of free-fall. Jumps cost from $285 and the price increases the higher you go, but it is well worth it. Most commercial operators will not take first timers beyond 15,000 ft.

Tramping
Even before the *National Geographic* proclaimed the Milford Track as 'the world's best walk', New Zealand could, without doubt, claim to be the tramping (or hiking) capital of the world. Not only is it one of the principal pastimes for many New Zealanders, it is also the reason many visitors come to the country. There is a vast network of routes and literally thousands of kilometres of track the length and breadth of the country, from the well-formed and trodden highway of the famed Milford Track, to the sporadic trail and markers of the lesser-known and challenging Dusky Track. The range of habitats is immense, from remote coastlines and island traverses to rainforests, volcanic lakes and mountain peaks, with most penetrating national parks.

Other than the sheer scenic beauty and scope of opportunities in New Zealand, what makes tramping so popular is the ease of access and good condition of the tracks. Under the administration and advocacy of the Department of Conservation (DoC) all advertised tracks are clearly marked, well maintained and have designated campsites and huts offering clean water, basic accommodation, cooking facilities and toilets. Add to that the wealth of detailed information available, from route descriptions and access to up-to-date weather forecasts, it is little wonder that tramping is perhaps New Zealand's biggest and most uniquely precious tourist asset. Even safety is well managed, with the tracks classified by type and fitness required. Guided trips are available for the more inexperienced and an 'intentions sheet' system is used for major excursions. All this for as little as $6 per tent or nightly hut fees.

You are advised to consult the local DoC office before embarking on any of the major tramps regardless of experience and weather conditions and, if required, fill in an intentions sheet. Always make sure you are well prepared, equipped and of the required level of fitness. Unless you are experienced, tramping on the more remote and quieter tracks alone is not advisable.

The most famous track is, deservedly, the magnificent Milford Track, a 54-km 4-day trek that combines lake and mountain scenery. Also in the Te Waipounamu World Heritage Park are the Routeburn, Kepler, Dusky, Greenstone, Hollyford and Hump Ridge tracks. But these are only a few of the many tasty options. It would be easy just to recommend the likes of the Milford, Kepler and Abel Tasman, but a word of warning: many of the tracks are very busy and are now not so much tracks as public highways. The Milford, Kepler, Heaphy and Abel Tasman are considered the worst in this respect. Of course that does not mean that they should be avoided. They are still worth doing, and no

Tramping – it's no walk in the park

If you have never been tramping before and intend to embark on one that involves a number of days, you need to be warned that it will be a challenge. A challenge not only to your physical, but also your mental self. Tramping is not walking the dog or even a long and congenial afternoon jaunt. Tramping is all about nature: nature's extremes, and your own. You can, and will, get extremely tired, hot, wet, thirsty, hungry and in, New Zealand, bitten alive. But the rewards are immense. Not only will you experience nature at its best (or worst), your senses will be bombarded by all the immensity and richness that it offers, from stunning views, to the quiet chuckle of mountain streams – that you could swear are sometimes laughing at you. In many ways it is also a test. You are pitching yourself not against nature, but alongside it, and for many, this is a new and foreign experience, well out of their comfort zone. There will be no lattes, no email, no warm duvets or clean, flush toilets. There will be no hi-fi, no pubs, no dot-coms, stocks and shares, no fingernail polish or powder puff. You're going to get wet and you're going to smell. Again, although your companions may care, nature doesn't – that's natural. You're going to wake up tired because you were sharing a dorm with what sounded like a small family of warthogs (now that can't be natural!). Everyday you are out there, you are going to eat a meagre breakfast, put those wet boots on again, what feels like a small house on your back, and not for the first time, set off thinking 'what the hell am I doing here?' And again nature doesn't care. Instead, and only if you are receptive to it, somewhere along that track that day, nature will remind you exactly why you are there. There is also another welcoming and rare factor – appreciating the simple things in life. Once the day's walking is done and you have reached your shelter it is the simple things and simple cravings that really matter – a log fire for warmth or a cup of tea. And let's face it, almost all of us need to feel a lot more of that! So, in essence, you are either going to love it or hate it, but you are going to have to accept the challenge and take the risk to find out which. Above all, like any challenge or any risk, it is the best way to learn a bit more about yourself and others. One word of advice – travel light. I mean really light. Forget the butter, put your toothpaste in a film cartridge, anything to lighten the load, and in the South Island, don't forget to take lots of heavy duty insect repellent.

less spectacular, but if you like a bit of solitude with your tramp, consider other options or at the very least go towards the start or the end of the tramping season (October-April). To give you some idea of how busy they are, the Milford now hosts about 10,000 trampers annually and the Abel Tasman up to 300 a day in mid-summer. This not only means a lot of company, it also means you must book accommodation sometimes weeks in advance.

Information, booking and safety Hut fees vary depending on category and the services and facilities provided. The general fee range per person is as follows. **Great Walks Huts (GW)** $10-45 per night. GW huts have bunks with mattresses, basic cooking facilities, usually a log fire plus a clean water supply and long-drop toilets. **Serviced Huts (SV)** $10 (Serviced Alpine Huts $20-35) offering similar to more basic facilities to the above. **Standard Huts (ST)** $5-$10. These are mere shelters with just water and toilets, some are very basic or just bivvies and are free of charge. Campsites associated with huts cost $15. An annual Hut Pass can be purchased for $90. All Great Walk Huts must be pre-booked, sometimes weeks in advance, and all huts (except those run by guided walk companies) operate on a first come first served basis. **Camping** is permitted at some huts ($15) or at designated campsites. DoC campsites come under 3 categories; 'serviced', 'standard' and basic and cost $5-15. Camping is free for children under 5.

VICs and DoC field centres stock excellent leaflets for each track ($1), maps and can provide up-to-date track and weather reports as required. For detailed information about all the major tramping tracks and 'Great Walks', accommodation bookings and other information, contact the local DoC Field Centre or visit the website www.doc.govt.nz.

Tramping track classifications All DoC managed and maintained walks from 5-minute boardwalks to mountain traverses have a classification, as follows:

Path Easy Generally low-lying and well formed. Suitable for all ages and levels of fitness. No walking boots required.

Walking Track Easy and well formed. Can involve short or steady climbs. Suitable for all ages and the reasonably fit. Shoes are okay, but proper walking boots preferable.

Tramping Track Requires relevant skill and experience. Generally continuous track but may be vague in parts. Expect a full range of topographies up to scrambling. Suitable for people of average fitness. Walking boots required.

Route Requires a high degree of skill and route-finding experience. The track may only have markers as guidance. A high level of fitness and equipment (including maps) is required.

Walking
The walking opportunities are endless. New Zealand is a walker's paradise and most VICs or regional DoC offices compile lists of the most notable long and short walks in each region. There is everything from coastal or bush walks to historical trails. Multi-day walks enter the realm of tramping, the New Zealand term for hiking. The country is world-famous for this, offering some of the best tramping trails in the world (see box, page 32).

Whale watching and swimming with dolphins
The New Zealand coast is world famous for its rich variety of marine mammals. Pods of dolphin can regularly be seen, from the large, common bottlenose to the tiny and endangered Hector's dolphin. New Zealand is also on the main whale migration routes, making it relatively easy to encounter them. Just off Kaikoura on the South Island's northeast coast a deep coastal trench attracts whales close to the shore, making it one of the world's best whale-watching spots. Huge pods of dolphin frolic in the surf and seem to delight in investigating any clumsy human who ventures into the water. Encounter success rates are high (around 95%) and operators offer a refund, or another trip, if the whales/dolphins do not turn up. A 2½-hr whale-watching trip costs around $145, $60 for children. A 2-hr dolphin-swimming experience (30 mins in the water) will cost around $165, $150 for children (spectators $80). Dolphins can be seen year-round, however summer is the best time if you want to swim with them. The endangered Hector's dolphin can also be viewed from Curio Bay in the Catlins, Southland and around Banks Peninsula in Canterbury. See the following websites for further details: www.whaledolphintrust.org.nz, www.dolphinsafari.co.nz, www.dolphin.co.nz, www.whalewatch.co.nz, and www.whales.co.nz.

How big is your footprint?

Ultimately when it comes to being a responsible eco-tourist it is of course your own attitude that is crucial. Much of the Environmental Code advocated by the **DoC** (see www.doc.govt.nz) is common sense. Over all, the entire concept can be summed up with two words: respect and awareness; and an age-old cliché: 'take nothing but pictures, leave nothing but footprints'. Given the unbelievable damage we humans have already inflicted on New Zealand's unique and ancient biodiversity, surely that attitude is not only poignant, but also demanded. Eco-tour operators are listed on page 63 and in the listings section of each relevant chapter.

The independent organization New Zealand Royal Forest and Bird Society, 90 Ghuznee St, Wellington, T04-385 7374, www.forest-bird.org.nz, produces an excellent quarterly magazine. The monthly Wilderness Magazine ($7) or bi-monthly New Zealand Geographic ($15), are also good, containing comprehensive outdoors and eco-activity information and are available in most newsagents and bookshops. For other magazines available in New Zealand see www.nzmagazineshop.co.nz.

Wine tours

New Zealand is world renowned for its wines and associated restaurants and accommodations play a big role in the tourism industry. Specialist tour operators are commonplace especially on Waiheke Island off Auckland and in the Hawke's Bay, Wairarapa, Marlborough, Nelson and Queenstown regions. Routes are well publicized with the excellent www.classicwinetrail.co.nz recommended. For details, see Eating and drinking, page 48.

Zorbing

Last and by no means least is zorbing. This is a most bizarre concept that could only be the creation of incredible Kiwi ingenuity. Described as a 'bi-spherical momentous experience', it involves climbing into a clear plastic bubble and rolling down a hill. Sadly, the organized venture involves a short hill that takes about 10 seconds to roll down and relieves you of about $50 – a bit of a rip-off. But what you could do with your own zorb blows the mind. Incidentally, you can also do a wet run – joined inside the bubble by a bucket of water.

Responsible tourism

For the vast majority of tourists it is New Zealand's environment and nature that are its greatest attraction. Yet regardless of your interest or your intention, the moment you set foot in New Zealand you are by definition an **eco-tourist**. Be aware that although your hosts may not demand it, the environment does. There is no doubt whatsoever that the environment is the biggest and brightest jewel in the tourism crown and a resource that is not only precious but requires considerable protection.

Yet one could argue that environmentalism and tourism are a contradiction in terms. Surely what makes New Zealand so special, so attractive, is the very lack of humanity and its areas of virtually inaccessible wilderness. There is no doubt this is true, but thankfully, the New Zealand psyche is such that it seems to successfully marry tourism and environmentalism and bestow upon the union a blessing that has so far resulted in a congenial, if naturally imperfect relationship. So good in fact, that the country has earned the reputation as one of the best eco-tourism destinations in the world. Part of this success is due to the vast area that is protected as forest parks, national parks, nature and marine reserves – almost a quarter of the entire country – all coming under the committed, yet under-resourced advocacy and administration of the **Department of Conservation** (**DoC**), www.doc.govt.nz.

Before you arrive you can avail yourself of a wealth of information on its excellent website, www.doc.govt.nz, and throughout your travels you will find dedicated information centres and field stations in all cities, major provincial towns and national parks. If you intend to go walking or to embark on a longer tramp then you will find DoC invaluable; its system of huts and campsites is an essential part of the experience.

Given the country's natural resources New Zealand, not surprisingly, is on the cutting edge of eco-tourism. The sheer choice and quality of activities, let alone the location in which they can be experienced, are superb from whale watching at Kaikoura or tramping in Fiordland to exploring the island sanctuaries of Kapiti or Tiritiri Matangi. New Zealand is one of very few countries where you can see rare or endangered species (especially birds) at close hand and in solitude. For many this is a new and welcome experience and in deep contrast to the constraints of a being in a busy hide or being surrounded by an orgy of twitchers all falling over each other to compare the size of their telescopes.

Getting there

Air

Airport information → *For airlines see Auckland, page 68.*
There are six airports in the country which handle international flights, but Auckland and, to a lesser extent, Christchurch are the principal international airports. Wellington, Palmerston North and Hamilton in the North Island and Dunedin and Queenstown in the South Island also receive regular flights from eastern Australia.

For information on negotiating Auckland International Airport, see page 68, or visit the website www.auckland-airport.co.nz. Other airports' websites include: **Wellington**, www.wellington-airport.co.nz, and **Christchurch**, www.christchurch-airport.co.nz.

Buying a ticket
With the effects of the global financial crisis on the airline industry it has never been cheaper to fly to Australasia from Europe or North America. Attractive and highly competitive fares abound. But how long this may last remains debatable.

There are now enormous numbers of high-street phone and internet outlets for buying your plane ticket. This can make life confusing but the competition does mean that dogged work can be rewarded with a very good deal. Fares will depend on the season, with prices much higher during December to January unless booked well in advance. Mid-year tends to see the cheapest fares. **Air New Zealand**, www.airnewzealand.com, is New Zealand's main international airline and flies from a considerable number of capitals and major cities. **Qantas**, www.qantas.com.au, also offers regular flights via New Zealand en route to or from Australia. Other airlines worth looking at are **Emirates**, www.emirates.com, and **Cathay Pacific**, www.cathaypacific.co.nz.

The internet is the best way of finding a bargain ticket, but can be frustrating unless you just want a straight return or single fare to a single destination. If you are considering a multi-destination journey it is worth checking with two or three agents in person.

One-way flight tickets are not necessarily much more expensive than half a return fare. If you are contemplating a lengthy trip and are undecided about further plans, or like the idea of being unconstrained, then a single fare could be for you. Note that immigration officials can get very suspicious of visitors arriving on one-way tickets, especially on short-term visas. Anyone without long-term residency on a one-way ticket will need to show proof of substantial funds – enough for a stay and onward flight. Discuss this with your local New Zealand Embassy or High Commission before deciding on a one-way ticket. **Round-the-World** (RTW) tickets can be a real bargain if you stick to the most popular routes, sometimes working out even cheaper than a return fare. RTWs start at around £900 (€1027) or US$1400, depending on the season.

When trying to find the best deal, make sure you check the route, journey duration, stopovers, departure and arrival times, restrictions and cancellation fees. Many cheap flights are sold by small agencies; most are honest and reliable, but there are some risks involved when buying tickets at rock-bottom prices. Do not pay too much money in advance and check with the airline directly to confirm your reservation.

From Europe

The main route, and the cheapest, is usually via Heathrow or Frankfurt and the USA (Los Angeles), though fares will also be quoted via other US cities and Asia. Either route usually takes from 20 to 30 hours including stops. There are no non-stop routes, so it's worth checking out what stopovers are on offer: this can be a good opportunity to see Kuala Lumpur or LA. A 30-hour journey, only stopping in airports to refuel is, in a word, gruelling and stopovers of a few nights do not usually increase the cost of the ticket substantially. The cheapest return flights, off-season, will be around £700 (€800), rising to at least £1000 (€1150) around Christmas. Mainstream carriers include **Air New Zealand** and **Qantas** (west via the USA); and **Singapore Airlines**, www.singaporeair.com, or **Thai Air**, www.thaiair.com (east via Asia).

From Australia

As you might expect there is a huge choice and much competition with trans-Tasman flights. Traditionally most flights used to go from Cairns, Brisbane, Sydney and Melbourne to Auckland but now many of the cheaper flights can actually be secured to Wellington, Christchurch, Dunedin and Queenstown. At any given time there are usually special deals on offer from the major players like **Qantas** (JetStar), **Virgin Blue** and **Air New Zealand** so shop around. Prices start from AUS$400 return. From Australia you are likely to be interested in 'open-jaw' tickets that will allow you to fly in to one city and depart from another. This will almost certainly be more expensive and, given the many restrictions and conditions imposed, they are often hard to secure at a good price. Always be careful to check the conditions of the cheaper 'temporary' deals with regard to your minimum or maximum allowed length of stay, cancellations, refunds etc. The flight time between Sydney and Auckland is three hours, Melbourne three hours and 45 minutes.

From the Americas

There are direct **Air New Zealand** and **Qantas** flights from Los Angeles (LAX) to Auckland. Sadly, one of the cheapest carriers, **United**, succumbed to recent financial strains and has had to cut services to New Zealand, but still flies to Australia. The cost of a standard return in the low season from LAX starts from around US$1050, from New York from US$1500 and Chicago from US$1450. In the high season add about US$800 to the standard fare. **Air**

Canada, www.aircanada.com, and United, www.united.com, connect with Alliance partners at LAX from Vancouver, Toronto and Montreal. Prices range from CAN$1150-2700. Singapore Airlines, www.singaporeair.com flies direct to Auckland daily from LAX stopping in Singapore. There are also direct flights from Buenos Aires to Auckland with Aerolineas Argentinas, www.aerolineas.com.ar, flying out of New York and Miami. The flight time between LAX and Auckland is around 12½ hours.

Discount travel agents

Australia

Flight Centres, T133133, www.flightcentre.com.au

STA Travel, T134782, www.statravel.com.au, T1300-130482, www.travel.com.au.

North America

Air Brokers International, 323 Geary St, Suite 4111, San Francisco, CA 94102, T1800-8833273, www.airbrokers.com. Consolidator and specialist in RTW and Circle Pacific tickets.

Discount Airfares Worldwide On-Line, www.etn.nl. Discount agent links.

STA Travel, T1800-7814040, www.statravel.com. Discount/youth travel company.

Trailfinders, T0845-058 5858, www.trailfinders.com. Popular and well established.

Travel CUTS, T18662469762, www.travelcuts.com. Specialists in student discount fares, IDs and other travel services.

Travelocity, www.travelocity.com. Online consolidator.

UK and Ireland

Austravel, T0800 988 4676, www.austravel.com. Specialists in Australasian travel itineraries and discounts.

Ebookers, www.ebookers.com. Comprehensive travel booking website.

Expedia, www.expedia.co.uk. Online travel site, with lots of background information.

STA Travel, 6 Wrights Lane, London, T0871-2300040, www.statravel.co.uk. Specialists in student discount fares and IDs.

Trailfinders, 194 Kensington High St, London W8 6FT, T0845-0585858, www.trailfinders.com. Excellent tailor-made itineraries.

Usit Campus, 19 Aston Quay, Dublin 2, T01-6021906 www.usit.ie. Student/youth specialists in Ireland.

Getting around

Public transport in all its forms (except rail) is generally both good and efficient. All the main cities and provincial towns can be reached easily by air or by road. Although standard fares, especially air tickets, can be expensive there are a vast number of discount passes and special seasonal deals available, aimed particularly at the young, independent traveller. Although it is entirely possible to negotiate the country by public transport, for sheer convenience you are advised to get your own set of wheels. Many of the country's delights are only to be seen off the beaten track and are certainly a long walk from the nearest bus stop. You will also free yourself of organized schedules. Long-term vehicle hire or temporary purchase is generally viable (especially if the costs are shared) and whether you go the way of a standard vehicle or campervan, you will find the country is well geared up for this mode of travel. Having said that, petrol costs are expensive and need to be taken into account.

Domestic air travel in New Zealand is in an almost constant state of flux due to the highly competitive nature of air travel in general and especially within Australasia. Currently **Air New Zealand** and **Qantas Link** are the principal domestic air carriers providing services between Auckland, Christchurch and Wellington and most regional centres. Thankfully, the relative lack of competition has not adversely affected prices. On the contrary, bookings made well in advance over the web with **Air New Zealand** or **Qantas** can see you flying from Auckland to Christchurch for as little as $100.

Worse still is the state of rail travel. In 2002, **TranzRail** closed all domestic routes except the Auckland/Wellington (**Northerner**), the Christchurch to Greymouth (**Tranz- Alpine**) and the Christchurch to Picton (**TranzCoastal**). Again only time will tell whether these survive. It seems that even in New Zealand, modern society is becoming so obsessed with speed and the increased pace of life that trains are just too slow.

Air

As well as the principal international airports of Auckland, Wellington and Christchurch, New Zealand has many smaller provincial town airports that are mainly well served. **Air New Zealand Link**, T0800-737000, www.airnewzealand.co.nz, **Qantas**, T0800-808767, www.qantas.co.nz, **Jet Star**, T0800 800 995, www.jetstar.com, and **Pacific Blue**, T0800-670000, www.www.flypacificblue.co.nz, all offer domestic services. All are generally efficient and you will rarely have problems with delays or service.

Apart from the major domestic operators there are many smaller companies with scheduled services. These include: **Great Barrier Airlines** (Great Barrier, Coromandel and Northland), **SoundsAir** (offering a viable alternative to the ferry between the North and South Islands) and **Southern Air** (between Invercargill and Stewart Island). All these companies are listed in the relevant sections. Note that flying anywhere in New Zealand is, on a clear day, a scenic delight and often well worth the expense.

Discount fares If you can, book domestic flights well in advance on the internet or through a travel agent. Most discounted fares can only be purchased in New Zealand and are subject to 12.5% GST (tax). There are always a number of dynamic deal schemes available that will make considerable savings depending on season and availability. For more information ask your travel agent or see the website, www.air newzealand.co.nz.

Road

Bus

National bus travel in New Zealand is well organized and the networks and daily schedules are good. Numerous shuttle companies service the South Island and there are also many local operators and independent companies that provide shuttles to accommodation establishments, attractions and activities. These are listed in the Transport sections of the main travelling text.

The main bus companies are **Intercity**, www.intercitycoach.co.nz, and **Newmans**, www.newmanscoach.co.nz. They often operate in partnership. For information and reservations call the following regional centres: Auckland T09-623 1504; Rotorua T07-348 0999; Wellington T04-385 0512; and Christchurch T03-365 1114. Intercity operates in both the North and South Islands, while Newmans operate throughout the North Island, except in Northland where **Northliner Express**, T09-307 5873, www.northliner.co.nz, co-operates with Intercity. The latest coach company is **Nakedbus.com**, which uses the same model of low overheads and internet-only booking service that the cheap airlines do. It has managed to undercut the long-established companies. And no, contrary to the clever brand name, it's not clothing optional.

Other companies in the North Island are: **Coromandel Explorer Tours**, T07-866 3506, www.coromandeltours.co.nz, a small company that recently began offering services around Coromandel; and **White Star**, T06-759 0197, who serves the route between New Plymouth and Wellington, taking in Wanganui and Palmerston North. For luxury sightseeing tours throughout New Zealand contact **Great Sights**, T0800-028 7913, www.greatsights.co.nz. ▸▸ *For Backpacker buses and coach tours, see page 62.*

Concession fares All the bus companies offer a variety of concessions. With **Intercity** and **Newmans** infants less than three years travel free. Children less than 12 years, travellers over the age of 60 and backpackers are all eligible for discounts. Check the website for the last fare deals and structures. Economy fare cancellations must be made up to two hours in advance to avoid a loss of 50% on the ticket price.

Bus passes The **Intercity Flexi-pass and Travelpas**s offer a range of 'hop-on/hop-off' routes throughout both the North and South Islands and nationally. They can often work in combination with ferry and rail and range from $600 to around $1200. Tickets are valid for 12 months. Consult the website for details, www.intercity.coach.co.nz.

Campervans → *See also Car, below.*
New Zealand is well geared up for campervan hire and travel and there's an accompanying glut of reputable international companies. Being a fairly compact country it is certainly a viable way to explore with complete independence. Although hire and petrol costs may seem excessive, once you subtract the costs of accommodation, provided you are not alone and can share those costs, it can work out cheaper in the long run. You will find that motorcamps are available even in the more remote places and a powered site will cost $20-35 per night for two people. Note that lay-by parking is illegal and best avoided. If in doubt ask the local I-Site. Again, like car rental rates, campervan rates vary and are seasonal. Costs are rated on a sliding scale according to model, season and length of hire. The average daily charge for a basic two-berth/six-berth for hire over 28 days, including insurance is $200/300 in the high season and $85/150 in the low season. Although there are fewer risks involved with campervan hire, the same general rules apply as with car hire. You generally get what you pay for but shop around and check the small print. The average campervan works out at about 14-16 litres per 100 km in petrol costs.

The most popular rental firms are **Britz**, T0800-831900/T09-275 9090, www.britz.co.nz; **Maui**, T0800-8008 0009/T09-2753013, www.maui-rentals.com; and **Kea Campers**, T0800-520052/T09-441 7833, www.keacampers.com. For more unconventional vehicles take a look at **Spaceships** 31 Beach Rd, Auckland, T0800-SPACE SHIPS, T09-309 8777, www.spaceships.tv. Motorhomes can be booked through **Maui Motorhome Rentals & Car Hire** T0800-8008 0009/T09-275 301, www.maui.co.nz.

Car
Other than a campervan this is by far the best way to see New Zealand. Petrol is expensive (around $1.80 per litre or $6.60 per gallon), but it will give you the flexibility and freedom needed to reach the more remote and beautiful places. Outside the cities traffic congestion and parking is rarely a problem. In many remote areas, especially in the South Island, the roads are single track and unsealed, so a little more driving skill is required. Generally, keep the speeds and gears low while on these roads. Also, in most rural areas, you will almost

Travelling times and distances from Auckland

	Distance	Car	Bus/Coach	Train	Air
Wellington	647 km	8 hrs	9 hrs	10 hrs	1 hr
Christchurch	1000 km	2 days	2 days	2 days	1 hr
Dunedin	1358 km	2-4 days	2-4 days	3 days	2 hrs
Queenstown	1484 km	2-4 days	2-4 days	-	2½ hrs
Bay of Islands	241 km	3 hrs	4 hrs	-	50 mins
Rotorua	235 km	2 hrs	3 hrs	4 hrs	45 mins

certainly encounter livestock of all shapes and sizes along the road verges, so be careful. At night you should of course take extra care and though there are very few mammals in New Zealand, one thing you will encounter is the cat-sized and brush-tailed possum. But with 70 million of the little critters denuding the countryside of its native vegetation and to the ruination of native wildlife, no one will mind the occasional road kill.

Rules and regulations In New Zealand you drive on the left. The 'give way to the right' rule applies except when turning left; i.e. the oncoming car has right of way. This will seem rather strange for the UK driver who, if unaware of this rule, will end up on the receiving end of much abuse, all the time thinking they have done nothing wrong and coming to the rapid conclusion this beautiful little nation is, tragically, populated by nothing but belligerent, wildly gesticulating nutters. So, make sure you familiarize yourself with the rules before setting out (*NZ Road Code* booklets are available from AA offices).

The accident rate in New Zealand is high, so be extra vigilant. The speed limit on the open road is 100 kph and in built-up areas it is 50 kph. Police patrol cars and speed cameras are omnipresent so if you speed you will almost certainly be caught. A valid driving licence from your own country or an international licence is required to get behind the wheel in New Zealand and certainly must be produced if you rent a vehicle.

Parking In the cities parking can be very expensive. Do not risk parking in restricted areas or exceeding your time allotment on meters. Alas, in the major towns it feels like there is a traffic warden round every corner and up every tree. Most meters take gold and silver coins so take a supply. The **New Zealand Automobile Association** 99 Albert St, City, Auckland, T0800-500444, www.aa.co.nz; breakdowns, T0800-500222, is the principal motoring organization in New Zealand. It has offices in most provincial towns. It also provides a great range of maps and travelling information as well as the usual member benefits. If you have bought a vehicle and intend to travel extensively throughout New Zealand, the basic annual membership fee of around $80 (which provides the basic breakdown assistance) is recommended. If you intend travelling down the west coast and to Fiordland and to a lesser extent Southland in the South Island, breakdown cover is highly recommended. Members of equivalent motoring organizations in other countries may qualify for reciprocal benefits.

Car hire Almost all the major companies (like **Avis**, **Budget** and **Hertz**) are represented in New Zealand and you will find offices at airports as well as the major airports, cities and provincial towns (listed in the Directory sections throughout the guide). There are also many local operators, which you can support as opposed to the big corporates, but if you intend to travel extensively you are advised to stick with one of the major companies as

Buying a car

Having a set of wheels to see New Zealand is highly recommended. Given the fact that second-hand cars are cheap and readily available it is worth some serious thought. Even on a low budget it's possible to buy a car, share running costs then resell on leaving. Auckland is a good place to buy but choose carefully.

Buying procedure and legalities

Automobile Association membership costs around $89 per annum. It covers emergency breakdown service or towing to the nearest garage. You also get free maps, information and insurance discounts. Auckland AA, 99 Albert St, T09-966 8919/ T0800-500555, open Mon-Fri 0830-1700; breakdown, T0800-500222.

→ **Change of ownership** The buyer and seller must fill in a MR13A, which can be obtained and submitted at any New Zealand post office. For details refer www.nzta.govt.nz/vehicle/

→ **Credit check** Have the car's legalities checked before purchase. AA Auto Report on the web ($25) or T0800-500333. Quote chassis and licence plate numbers.

→ **Highway/Road Code** There are a few subtle differences in New Zealand road rules (right of way while turning right is a prime example). You are advised to familiarize yourself with the NZ Road Code booklet available from the AA centres or major bookshops, $15.

→ **Insurance** Not compulsory but Third Party is recommended. The AA offer good rates along with breakdown membership.

→ **Licence** A current international or accepted driver's licence is essential.

→ **Registration** Registration can be gained with legal ownership and a valid WOF certificate for six months (about $112) or 12 ($217).

→ **Vehicle inspections** The AA does a thorough inspection as do a number of companies found under 'Vehicle Inspection Services' in the Yellow Pages; cost $165 (members $140). It is highly recommended, T0800-500333, www.aa.co.nz/motoring/Pages/default.aspx

→ **WOF (Warrant of Fitness)** All cars need a safety certificate to be legally on the road and to obtain registration. Most garages and specialist 'drive-in/drive-out' Vehicle Testing Stations (VTS) do a WOF test (about $50) which if passed will last six months (see 'Warrant of Fitness' in the Yellow Pages). If you buy a car with a WOF make sure it is not more than 28 days old. For more information refer www.nzta.govt.nz/vehicle/

Where to buy a car

There are a number of auto magazines available at newsagents but the major daily newspapers (New Zealand Herald, Wednesday and Saturday) and the auctions are also recommended. Backpacker noticeboards and the hot new website 'Trade Me' www.trade me.co.nz are also worth a look.

→ **Backpacker car markets** There are car markets at 20 East Street, Auckland, T09-377 7761; and 33 Battersea Street, Christchurch, T03-377 3177. The website, www.backpackerscarmarket.co.nz, is a good place to look and for re-sale, but be sure to have a full vehicle inspection done before purchase.

→ **Car auctions** Turners Car Auctions, corner of Penrose and Leonard Roads, Penrose, T09-5251920, www.turn ers.co.nz. Budget CarAuctions, 212 Great South Rd, Manurewa, T09-266 3780, www.budget carauction.co.nz. Check the websites for viewing and category auction days.

→ **Car fairs** Ellerslie Racecourse, Greenlane, www.car fair.co.nz, Sunday 0900-1200; Manakau Car Market, Manakau City Centre Car Park, Sunday 0900-1300.

they generally offer better cars, have more extensive networks as well as sound insurance and accident coverage. You must be over 21 and have a valid driver's licence to hire a vehicle; insurance premiums for the under 25s can be high. Small, older and, typically, Japanese cars (1600 cc) start at about $70 per day but rates vary depending on season, kilometres covered and the length of time you have the car (getting cheaper the longer you rent it). A medium-sized 2000 cc car will cost around $90 per day with unlimited kilometres. Without unlimited kilometres you are looking at around $0.35 per kilometre.

There are of course cheaper deals out there (up to 50%) but not without risk and you will also find that many companies advertise rates below $50 a day but do not include insurance and mileage costs. You can also rent a vehicle in one of the major cities (Auckland being the cheapest) and drop it off at another. This will almost certainly involve a drop-off fee of around $150-175 but may be worth it for the convenience. In the summer high season, if you are returning to Auckland, it is worth bargaining since many operators have a glut of cars needing to be driven back north.

Overall, the choice is vast so you are advised to shop around, but beware of cowboy operators and always read the small print before you sign. Some of the cheaper companies have an insurance excess of $750 even on minor repairs, so be careful. Always go over the car with a company representative and get them to acknowledge and list any dents or scratches that you see on the vehicle. Also take a few pics of your own and at the same time they do. This may avoid considerable frustration trying to prove you were not to blame. If you do not have a credit card you may have to leave a substantial cash deposit of between $500 and $1,000. Although it comes at extra cost, a 'Collision Waiver' can often be secured, which means you do not automatically lose this deposit in the event of an accident. Note also you may not be covered on certain roads. You will certainly not be covered if you venture onto any of the 'sand highways' on the coast, like Ninety Mile Beach.

There are a few motorcycle rental firms in Auckland and although not cheap, it can be a superb way to see the country, especially in the South Island.

Car-pooling An option worth considering if funds are restricted is sharing travel costs by car-pooling, ride-sharing and lift-sharing. Ask at the backpackers in the main centres for details and local contacts.

Cycling
Touring New Zealand by bike is highly recommended and becoming increasingly popular, especially in the South Island. Although it is not exactly flat, it is 'topographically manageable'. Cycle hire companies are listed in the Transport section of each town. Other companies are listed under Specialist activity tours on page 63.

Ferry
Other than a few small harbour-crossing vehicle ferries and the short trip to Stewart Island from Bluff in Southland, the main focus of ferry travel is of course the inter-island services across Cook Strait. The two ports are Wellington at the southern tip of the North Island and Picton in the beautiful Marlborough Sounds on the South Island.

There are currently two services: the Interislander, Wellington Railway Station, T0800-802802/T04-498 3302, www.interislander.co.nz; and the smaller of the two companies Bluebridge, T0800-844844/T04-4716188, www.bluebridge.co.nz.

Generally speaking, all vessels have plenty of deck access with good views. For amenities go for the Interislander's 'Kaitaki' and for more traditional ferry experience go

Combination travel passes

The **New Zealand Travel Pass**, T0800-339966, www.travelpass. intercity.co.nz, offers a wide range of route specific passes both nationally and throughout both islands. The national passes include the ferry crossing. A full 'Aotearoa Adventure'tour from north to south will cost around $1,220 has a minimum of 14 days travel and is valid for 12 months. The 'Alpine Discovery' pass that takes in all the main centres of the South Island including Milford Sound and the West Coast costs around $600 and includes a cruise on Milford Sound.

TranzScenic offers the **Scenic Rail Pass**, T04-495 0775/T0800-277 482, www.tranzscenic.co.nz, which combines travelling by train with the inter-island ferry crossing. They offer a 7-day all services with one ferry journey, from $409, child $286; a 14-day all services with one ferry journey, from $517, child $394 and a 7-day TranzAlpine, TranzCoastal services (South Island), from $301, child $211.

for the **Bluebridge**. For details on the inter-island crossing, see box page 409; for Stewart Island services, see page 684.

Hitching

Hitching is still quite heavily practised in New Zealand but not entirely safe. As ever, it is not advised for those travelling alone, especially women. If you do decide to take the risk, keep to the main highways and don't hitch at night. The usual common sense rules apply and if in doubt, don't. Another good tip is never take off a rucksack and put that or a bag in the car first. For the opportunist thief this can be like Christmas; as they speed off with your gear, you will be left standing there like a proper Charlie.

Train

The rail network in New Zealand is in a seemingly incessant state of flux and has struggled to maintain anything other than a core network between its main population centres. However, that said, the trains in themselves are pretty comfortable, the service is good and the stunning scenery will soon take your mind off things. Within the **North Island** there is a daily service between Auckland and Wellington known as the 'Overlander'. Within the **South Island**, the daily services between Picton and Christchurch (the 'TranzCoastal') and Christchurch to Greymouth (the 'TranzAlpine'), are both world-class journeys. Also, designed specifically as a tourist attraction, the **Taieri Gorge Railway** runs from Christchurch to Middlemarch and back.

All fares are of a single class, but prices range greatly from 'standard' to 'super saver' so check carefully what you are entitled to and what deals you can secure. Reservations and timetables from the Auckland or Wellington railway station information centres, accredited Visitor Information Centres (I-Sites) or travel agents throughout New Zealand: **TranzScenic**, T0800-872467/T04-495 0775, www.tranzscenic.co.nz, 0700-2200. For further information on TranzScenic's 'Scenic Rail Pass', see box, page 43.

Maps

Detailed urban and rural maps are readily available throughout New Zealand. **Wises**, www.wises.co.nz, produces a range of handbooks and fold-out city maps; its provincial town maps for both the North and South Islands are invaluable and are stocked in most large bookshops. Most information centres provide free leaflet maps and the coverage is generally excellent. The **Department of Conservation** (DoC) offices (see page 34) are very well stocked with national park and rural maps. For really detailed maps the **Land Information New Zealand** offices can provide for all your needs. **Mapworld**, T0800-627967, www.mapworld.co.nz, in Christchurch is an excellent outlet and also stocks complete CD-ROMs of all New Zealand national, regional and town maps. In the UK, **Stanfords**, www.stanfords.co.uk (consult the website for your nearest store), has a good choice and is recommended.

Sleeping

Besides actually getting there, accommodation in New Zealand will be your biggest expense. There is a wealth of choice and, though you will rarely end up without a bed for the night, you are advised to book ahead during the high season. At present the New Zealand Tourist Board are heavily plugging homestay/farmstay options. You are advised to try this at least for a few nights to encounter real Kiwi hospitality and general Kiwi life.

Visitor Information Centres (I-Sites) are a great help with accommodation and generally stock all the highly illustrated leaflets. They can also offer plenty of good advice regarding the range of options and sort out bookings. The web is also a major source of information with almost all reputable establishments now having at least an email address. There are also many books available including the *AA Accommodation Guides*, www.aaguides.co.nz; *Jason's Motels and Motor Lodges Guide*, www.jasons.co.nz; *The New Zealand Bed and Breakfast Guide*, www.bnb.co.nz; and *Friars B&B Guide*, www.friars.co.nz; as well as numerous motorcamps, motels, campsites and backpacker guides (most of which are free).

Hotels
Hotels in New Zealand can generally be listed under one of the four following categories:

Large luxury hotel There are a surprising number of large, modern and luxurious (four- to five-star) hotels in the major cities, particularly in Auckland. There are so many luxury rooms and apartment blocks in the city centre it's amazing they can all survive. These major hotels tend to be part of major international or trans-Tasman chains and the prices range from $250-600 per night. As you would expect, all rooms are equipped with the latest technology including laptop plug-in ports and Sky TV. They also have restaurants and leisure facilities including swimming pools, spa pools and gyms.

Standard chain hotels These range in age and quality and include names such as **Quality Hotels**, **Novotel** and **Copthorne Hotels**. Found in all major cities and the larger provincial towns, their standard prices are $95-300 but they have regular weekend or off-season deals. Most have restaurants and facilities such as a heated pool.

Boutique hotels These vary in size and price but tend to be modern and of a luxurious standard. The smaller, more intimate boutique hotels are overtaking the major chains in popularity. On average double rooms here can cost anything from $175-400.

Traditional pub and budget hotels Many of the rural towns have kept the traditional wooden hotels. Don't be fooled, however; some of these may look grand from the outside, but often the interior doesn't match up. However, a basic cheap and comfortable room can still be found here generally. Beware of the bars in many of these places, unless

Hotel price codes

Prices are based on a double room (usually with en suite bathroom) during high season. Cheaper rooms are often available with shared bathrooms. Many places, especially hotel chains, offer low season and weekend specials. Prices are in New Zealand dollars.

LL	$250 and over
L	$175-249
AL	$120-174
A	$80-119
B	$50-79
C	$25-49
D	under $25

you're quick on the draw – or know the age of the All Black fly-half that scored in the last minute of the Bledisloe 27 years ago at exactly 1500. Also note that prices are often dropped at weekends and during the off-season.

Lodges and B&Bs

There are a growing number of luxury **lodges** throughout the country and most sell themselves on their location or classic 'bush setting' as much as their architecture, sumptuous rooms, facilities and cuisine. Prices tend to be high, ranging from $200 to a mind-bending $2600 per night (which equates to almost eight months in a well- equipped campsite). **B&Bs** are not as common in New Zealand as they are in Europe, but can still be found in most places. They vary greatly in style, size and quality and can be anything from a basic double room with shared bathroom and a couple of boiled eggs for breakfast to a luxurious en suite or self-contained unit with the full breakfast. Again prices vary, with the standard cost being as little as $75-100. Some of the more luxurious, however, are extortionate. When looking at prices bear in mind a full breakfast costs at least $20 in a café or restaurant. Many lodges and B&Bs also offer evening meals. The average Kiwi B&B has still got a long way to go, but you will find most hosts to be very congenial and helpful folk.

Homestays and farmstays

Generally speaking if an establishment advertises itself as a homestay it will deliberately lack the privacy of the standard B&B and you are encouraged to mix with your hosts. The idea is that you get an insight into Kiwi life, but it may or may not be for you depending on your preferences and personality. Other than that they are very similar to B&Bs, with breakfasts as standard and an evening meal often being optional.

Farmstays of course give you the added agricultural and rural edge, and are generally recommended. Accommodation can take many forms from being in-house with your hosts or fully self-contained, and breakfasts and evening meals are often optional. You may find yourself helping to round up sheep or milking a cow and if you have kids (farmstays usually welcome them) they will be wonderfully occupied for hours.

Both homestays and farmstays tend to charge the same, or slightly lower, rates as B&Bs. **New Zealand Farm Holidays**, T09-412 9649, www.nzfarmholidays.co.nz, based near Auckland, produces a helpful free catalogue listing about 300 establishments. For farmstay options in Southland (considered the hub of agriculture in New Zealand) contact the very helpful **Western Southland Farm Hosting Group**, T03-225 8608, www.farmhost.co.nz. Visitor Information Centres (I-Sites) can help you find homestays or farmstays and the New Zealand Tourist Board website, www.purenz.com, also has a detailed list. If you're interested in working on a farm, **Farm Helpers (FhiNZ)**, 31 Moerangi

St, Palmerston North, T06-354 1104, www.fhinz.co.nz, has a very useful website. A booklet listing over 190 associate farms is also available on line for $25.

Motels

Motels are the preferred option of the average Kiwi holidaymaker. They vary greatly, from the awful 1950s love shacks to the new and luxurious condos with spa pool. There is usually a range of rooms available and almost all have at least a shower, kitchen facilities and a TV. Most are clean and comfortable and well appointed, while in others you may find yourself trying to sleep next to the main road. Prices vary from studio units at about $75-100, one-bedroom units from $85-120 and suites accommodating families and groups for an additional charge for each adult. Many of the bigger and better establishments have a restaurant and a swimming pool. Many also make the most of the country's thermal features and have spas, sometimes even in your room.

Hostels

New Zealand is well served with hostels and budget accommodation. Naturally, they vary greatly in age, design, location and quality. Some enjoy a busy atmosphere in the centre of town while others provide a quiet haven of sanctity in the country. They also have a range of types of beds on offer, with many having separate double and single rooms as well as the traditional dormitory. Dorms are usually single sex but sometimes optionally mixed. Camping facilities within the grounds are also common. Generally, hostels are good places to meet other travellers, managers are usually very knowledgeable and helpful; pick-ups are often free. Bikes, kayaks or other activity gear can often be hired at low cost or are free to use. Wherever you stay you will have access to equipped kitchens, a laundry, games or TV room, plenty of local information and, of course, phones and the internet. Prices vary little for a dorm bed and start from $20 depending on season. Single rooms and doubles tend to start around $55, or about $25 per adult. In the high season and especially over Christmas through to March you are advised to pre-book everywhere at least three days in advance.

YHAs

The **Youth Hostel Association NZ**, T0800-278299/T03-3799970, www.yha.co.nz, is part of a worldwide organization with over 4500 hostels in 60 countries. There are about 70 establishments throughout New Zealand; the vast majority are associates as opposed to YHA owned and operated. Being part of a large organization, most are on a par if not better than the independent backpacker hostels. They all offer very much the same in standard of accommodation and facilities. They are also to be congratulated on their eco-friendly policies with recycling not only provided in most hostels, but actively and enthusiastically embraced.

YHAs are only open to members but you can join in your home country (if YHA exists) or in New Zealand for an annual fee of $40 ($30 for renewals). Non-members can also stay at hostels for an additional charge of $3 per night if you wish accruing a stamp for their Downunder Card system. With 15 stamps you get a full one year membership. YHA membership cards are very handy even if you do not intend to stay consistently at YHA hostels. They entitle you to a number of discounts on travel and activities. There are a number of associate YHA hostels where no membership card is required but where members get a small discount. Pick up the YHA *Accommodation and Hostel Guide* at any major VIC (I-Site).

Backpacker organizations

There are several other major backpacking membership organizations in New Zealand which provide hostel listings and discounts, including a dollar off each night's stay and reductions on transport and activities.

Budget Backpacker Hostels Ltd (BBH), T03-379 3014, www.bbh.co.nz, has around 350 member establishments that must meet certain minimum quality criteria. These are listed in its *Blue Book* (free from VICs) along with handy descriptions, contact details and location maps of each hostel.

If you choose, you can purchase a BBH Club Card ($45, with $20 free phone card) that guarantees the listed prices. Recommended.

Other trans-Tasman chain/brand backpackers include **Base**, T0800227369 and **Nomads**, T(61)02-9299 7710, www.nomads world.com

Motorcamps and cabins

New Zealand's fairly compact size and quality road network lends itself to road touring. Given that so many visitors and Kiwis take the campervan or camping option, New Zealand is very well served with quality motorcamps and campsites. In fact, it is hailed as one of the best in the world. Motorcamps can be found almost everywhere and not necessarily just in towns. The hub of many a remote beach, headland or bay is often the great Kiwi motorcamp. The quality and age does of course vary. Some are modern and well equipped while others are basic. Almost all motorcamps are equipped with laundry facilities and a few will charge a small fee ($0.20-$1) for hot showers. Prices range from $12-18 per person (child half price) for powered sites. Non-powered sites are often the same price or marginally less.

Most motorcamps have a range of cabins from dog kennels to well-appointed alpine-type huts. They vary in price staring with a 'standard cabin' with little more than a bed and electric socket for a mere $35 to a better facilitated cabin for up to $75 per night (for two) with an additional charge of $12-15 per person after that.

The **Top Ten**, www.top10.co.nz, chain have almost 50 camps nationwide. They charge up to $3 per night more than the average motorpark but offer consistently good and above average facilities. Bear in ming that you may also find yourself bumping into the same people, which can be great or, conversely, an utter nightmare.

DoC campsites and huts

The **Department of Conservation**, www.doc.govt.nz, has over 100 basic campsites all over the country with many being in prime locations. They tend to provide clean running water, toilet facilities and BBQ areas, but rarely allow open fires. The national parks in particular are all excellently equipped with comfortable huts. There is usually a nightly fee of $2-10. Fees for huts are anything from $5-45 per night depending on category and location. If you plan to use DoC campsites and huts you are advised to research their locations, fee structures, rules and regulations and book well in advance.

Holiday homes and cottages (baches)

This is one accommodation option very often overlooked by visitors. The country has a wealth of holiday homes and 'baches' (seaside huts, cottages or mansions), which are available for rent throughout the year. While in summer they will most probably be frequented by the owners, in the off-season you can sometimes find a real bargain. The best place to look is in the national newspapers, travel or house rental sections. The regional VICs can also often be of assistance. Most operate on a minimum weekend or week stay basis and costs vary depending on quality and location. If you are travelling with a family or group, this option is well worth looking into.

Restaurant price codes

All the places listed are recommended as offering relatively good value, quality and standards of service within their respective price category. Some are also noted for having particularly pleasant or unusual surrounds.

Prices are in New Zealand dollars.
Eateries are divided into three categories:

TTT	$30 and over for a main course
TT	$25-30 for a main course
T	under $25 for a main course

Eating and drinking

Food

Budget-permitting you are in for a treat. The quality of food in New Zealand is superb. Although there are many types of traditional cuisine and restaurants in evidence, the principal style is 'Pacific Rim'. It dips into the culinary heritage of many of the cultures of the Oceania region, with inspiration and influences from Thailand, Malaysia, Indonesia, Polynesia, Japan and Vietnam as well as further afield like Europe. For dishes that have a distinctly Kiwi edge look out for the lamb (arguably the best in the world), pork, venison and freshwater fish like salmon and eel. Despite its reputation as perhaps the best trout-fishing country in the world, you cannot buy trout commercially. Although this is a shame, it does provide the added incentive to go and catch your own; many restaurants will be happy to cook it for you.

As you might expect there is a heavy emphasis on fine seafood. The choice is vast with many warm-water fish like snapper, kingfish, hoki, hapuka and orange roughie. Catching these yourself and cooking them on a BBQ fresh off the boat will provide a memorable culinary experience. Other seafood delights include crayfish (the South Pacific equivalent to the lobster), oysters (the best being from Bluff in the South Island), paua (abalone), scallops and the famous green-lipped mussels. These mussels are very substantial, delicious and should not be missed. They are also relatively cheap and readily available. There are also some treats in store from below the ground. The kumara (sweet potato) will shed a whole new light on the humble 'spud', while many of the international vegetables like asparagus and broccoli come cheap (especially while in season) and are always fresh. From the tree the fruit of choice is of course the succulent kiwi fruit or 'Chinese gooseberry' which although not exclusively grown in New Zealand is deservedly celebrated. Other fine fruits include feijoa and tamarillo. The celebrated dessert in New Zealand is the pavlova; a sort of mountainous cake made of meringue and whipped cream. For a real traditional feast try a Maori *hangi* (see box, page 49). Prepared properly and without ketchup you will be amazed at just how good and different fish, meat and vegetables can taste when cooked underground.

If you intend to do your own cooking, supermarkets offer a wide choice of fare. The main chains are **Big Fresh**, **Woolworths** and **New World**, with **Pac-n-Save** and **Countdown** being marginally cheaper. For fresh fruit and vegetables, stick to the numerous roadside or wholesale fruit markets where the difference in price and quality can be astonishing.

Drink

Other than **L&P** (a fairly unremarkable soft drink hailing from Paeroa) New Zealand lacks a national drink. If there is one, it is the highly sub-standard and over-rated beer called **Lion**

The *hangi*

Pronounced 'hungi', this is the traditional Maori and Pacific Island feast or method of cooking. To the uninitiated, the concept of cooking your dinner in the ground may seem a bit odd, but it is actually incredibly efficient and produces a certain taste and texture in the food that is extraordinarily good. *Hangis* were designed for the masses and were as much a social occasion as anything else. Traditionally the men would light a large fire and place river stones in the embers. While the stones are heating a pit is dug in the earth. Then the stones are placed in the pit and sacking placed upon them (before sacking it was suitably fashioned plant material). Then, presumably, the boys went off for a beer while the good ladies of the tribe prepared the meat. Nowadays this includes chicken, wild pig and lamb, but was formerly moa, pigeon and seafood. Vegetables are added too, particularly the traditional sweet potato, kumara. Once cleaned and plucked the smaller items are wrapped in leaves (now foil) and the whole lot placed in a basket (traditionally woven leaves from the flax plant, now wire-mesh) and then the whole affair is covered with earth. Then the ladies joined the men for a beer and a chat. Meanwhile, the steam slowly cooks the food and the flavours are sealed in. Then a couple of hours later it is all dug up and *voilá!* – it's 'pig-out' time. The succulence and smoked flavours of the food are gorgeous.

Although due to modern-day health and safety requirements it is not really possible to sample a proper *hangi* the commercial offerings by the Maori tourist concerns can still be very tasty and well worth the experience. Rotorua is the principal venue (see page 254). If you ever have the opportunity of a real one, do not pass it up.

Red. This and a number of other equally watery relations are drunk not so much by the pint as the jug, and are all backed by a very 'Kiwi-bloke' image, which is regularly promoted with less-than-PC advertising. Rest assured, however, that all the main internationally well-known bottled beers are available, as are some good foreign tap ales like Caffrey's and Kilkenny. Depending on the pub and how it is kept and poured, you can also get a good Guinness.

Beer and lager is usually sold by the 'handle', the 'glass' (pint) or the 'jug' (up to three pints). Half-pints come in a 12-fl oz (350 ml) glass. Rarely is a pint a proper imperial pint, it's usually just under. Drinks generally cost $7-8 for a pint, about $4-5 for a jug of New Zealand brand beers and up to $8 for a double shot. Alcohol is much cheaper in rural pubs and RSAs (Retired Servicemen's Associations), where you can usually get yourself signed in. The minimum drinking age has just been reduced from 21 to 18. Liquor shops (off licences) are everywhere and alcohol can generally (in most places) be bought seven days a week. There is a thriving coffee culture almost everywhere in the main towns and cities, so you will not go without your daily caffeine fix.

New Zealand wine

New Zealand's rich diversity of climates and soil types has borne an equally rich array of wines and after over a century of development the country now boasts many of internationally recognized standards. Wine is produced the length and breadth of the country but the Hawkes Bay and Nelson/Marlborough areas are the principal wine producing regions. New Zealand Sauvignon Blanc is rated throughout the world as one of the best, but there is also recognition for its Chardonnay, Pinot Noir, Methode Traditionelle sparkling wine, Riesling, Cabernet Sauvignon and Merlot. Fruit wines, including the unusual 'kiwi fruit wine', are also evident. The choice is vast and whether a connoisseur or a novice you are advised to experiment. If you can, visit one of the many vineyards that offer tastings and cellar sales. For more information about New Zealand wines see www.nzwine.com, www.winesnewzealand.co.nz and www.classicwinetrail.co.nz.

Eating out

There are eateries to suit every taste and budget from the ubiquitous fast-food joints to world-class seafood restaurants. Auckland and Wellington (which has more cafés and restaurants per capita than New York) are particularly rich in choice with a vast selection of cafés, café-bars, brasseries and specialist international restaurants giving added puff to the celebrated 'Pacific Rim'. There is often a fine line between cafés and restaurants. **Cafés** perhaps provide a more informal atmosphere with an emphasis on a broader range of cheaper light meals during the day, happily simmering on into the night with more substantial dishes. They also almost always serve coffee, breakfast or brunch, are licensed (or at the very least BYO) and often provide outdoor seating. **Restaurants** are similar with few expecting formal attire. You can find upmarket, snooty eateries if you wish, but they will not provide the celebrated, laid-back, food-centred focus of the vast majority. Many of the top hotels, motels and lodges are open to non-residents and provide fine dining at affordable prices. Most cities and major towns have at least one Irish or old English-style pub offering 'pub-grub' from the 'Full-Monty' breakfast and Irish stew to good old fish and chips – all for under $20. **Vegetarians** are generally well catered for in the main centres and provincial towns, while the more remote corners of New Zealand still offer the 'half cow on the barbie'. Ask for a vegetarian dish in a South Island backcountry station and you'll most probably be shown the door.

Eating out in New Zealand is generally good value, especially for those visitors revelling in the more than favourable dollar exchange rates. Even backpackers on a strict budget should be able to treat themselves occasionally. The vast majority of eateries fall into the 'mid-range' bracket ($20-30 for a main).

Most cafés open for breakfast between 0700 and 0900 and stay open until at least 1700, and often until late into the evening or the early hours. This usually applies seven days a week with special Sunday brunch hours provided. Most mid-range restaurants open their doors daily for lunch (often 1100-1400) and dinner (from 1800). The more exclusive establishments usually open for dinner from about 1800, with some (especially in winter) only opening some weekday evenings and at weekends.

Entertainment

Most cities are blessed with numerous venues hosting first-class concerts and shows. Theatre, orchestral concerts, ballet, dance, comedy, rock and jazz are all well represented. Many international rock stars now include at least one gig in Auckland in their itinerary. On a smaller scale you will find a vibrant nightlife in New Zealand cities and major provincial towns. Although not necessarily world class, the nightclubs, cabarets, pubs and local rock concerts will certainly have you 'shaking your pants'. There's even Country and Western and line dancing. New Zealand boasts two large, modern, 24-hour casinos in

Christchurch and Wellington. **Ticketek** are the national administrators for information and ticketing and a full listing of shows and events can be sourced from their website, www.ticketek.co.nz or www.nzlive.com.

Pubs, bars and clubs

The pub scene has come on in leaps and bounds over the last decade with new establishments opening up almost everywhere. Before the 1990s the vast majority of pubs in New Zealand were the archetypal male bastions – establishments where ashtrays were built into the tables, pictures of the local hairy rugby team adorned the walls and the average Saturday night consisted of a good argument about sport, a band playing Deep Purple's *Smoke on the Water*, followed by a fight, copious wall-to-wall vomiting and a failed attempt to get home. Of course such places still exist, but generally speaking pubs and bars are now a much more refined and classy affair yet still retain that congenial and laid-back 'traditional pub' atmosphere. Now you can enjoy a good beer and conversation over an open fire in winter or under the sun in summer. New Zealand has also caught on to the 'Irish pub' fad and although some are gimmicky, others are very good, offering fine surroundings and beer to match. Many drinking establishments are also now attached to restaurants and cafés with outdoor seating. If you really must sample the old-fashioned Kiwi pub you will find them often in the hotels or main streets of the rural towns. While not all bad, do not walk round in a pair of pink shorts, or without knowing what an 'All Black' is.

In December 2004 it became illegal to smoke in all pubs, restaurants and cafés in New Zealand, though many still provide segregated (legal) areas outside.

Pubs and bars are generally open from 1100-2230 with many having an extended licence to 2400 and sometimes even 0300 at weekends.

Festivals and events

There are a huge range of events and festivals held throughout the year, ranging from the bizarre **Great Naked Tunnel Run** in Fiordland to the huge, spectacular **Opera in the Park** in Auckland. One of the more obscure events is the **Wildfoods Festival** on the South Island's west coast, an extravaganza of gourmet 'bush tucker' based on natural (or highly unusual) food resources from the land and sea. The many regional and provincial town **Food, Arts and Wine Festivals** are usually held in summer and provide a fitting and lively celebration of the country's wealth of creations. There are also many traditional (if a little commercial) **Maori cultural performances** in the main centres and particularly in Rotorua.

New Zealand hosted the UK and Ireland **Lions Tour** in 2005. Despite all the pre-tour hype resulting from the English team's success at the Rugby World Cup in Australia 2003 and the Welsh Grand Slam of the Six Nations Tournament in 2005, the tour proved something of a disappointed for the Lions, with convincing victories for the All Blacks in all three test matches. But the celebrations were short-lived. With the 'mighty' All Blacks once again falling short at the 2007 Rugby World Cup hosted in Europe the nation once again went in to protracted mourning. But with New Zealand set to host the 2011 Rugby World Cup expectations are once again on the rise and it seems yet another failure in lifting the trophy would be tantamount to a national disgrace.

Local VICs have listings of events and the NZTB website, www.purenz.com, or www.nzlive.com both have detailed nationwide events listings. Regional and city events are listed in the relevant sections.

Shopping

Although on first acquaintance you might be forgiven for thinking it is all fluffy sheep or rugby jerseys, shopping in New Zealand can be a rewarding and interesting experience. For a country so sparsely populated there is a surprising wealth of quality goods on sale, from international designer label clothing to traditional arts and crafts.

Arts and crafts

Beyond the international and the kitsch, New Zealand arts and crafts consist of a vast array of South Pacific, Maori and contemporary Kiwi styles and influences. Much of the art is very colourful, reflecting the beautiful bright blues and greens of the environment, while two-dimensional works are often beautifully carved panels, figures, bowls and furniture made of native woods like kauri and rimu.

Pottery and ceramics abound. There are Maori pendants (*tiki*) carved from whale bone and greenstone (*pounamu*). These have been made and worn by the Maori for centuries and often depict sacred animals or spirits. If you buy one, it is customary to offer it as a gift. They are also often associated with *mana* (power or standing) and fertility. There are many cheap and nasty versions on sale, especially in the city souvenir shops, so if you want quality, look in specialist arts and craft or museum shops. Almost everywhere you will also see the stunning hues of the abalone shell (or *paua*). The *paua* is harvested naturally under strict controls and the shells are utilized as a by-product. You can buy the best quality half shells polished and varnished for about $25 or choose from the many jewellery pieces created or inlaid with colourful fragments.

Also proving popular are possum fur products. Though not quite in the same league as wool it can make an eminently fetching pair of cosy gloves with matching furry hat. One enterprising outlet in the South Island has even gone so far as to venture into the rather up and down business of possum fur nipple warmer production.

Clothing

On the clothing front look out for the famous red or blue plaid Kiwi 'swandrie'. It's a sort of thick woollen shirt/jacket and offers the best protection from the cold. You will also see the world-famous All Black rugby jerseys all over the place. Although the real thing is now made by Adidas (in a much less appealing synthetic material) the 'Canterbury' rugby tops have to be the best cotton-made tops in the world and last for years. Make sure the one you buy is made by the Canterbury Clothing Company (CCC). For modern fashion look out for some award-winning Kiwi labels, like Zambesi, NomD, Karen Walker and World.

Essentials A to Z

Accident & emergency

For **police, fire or ambulance**: T111. Make sure you obtain police/medical reports required for insurance claims. For legal advice contact the **Citizen's Advice Bureau** in Auckland, 305 Queen St, Auckland, T09-3773314 T0800-367222.

Children

New Zealand is very child- friendly and replete with all the usual concessions for travel and activities. With so many outdoor activities safety is a natural concern, but this is nothing common sense can't take care of.

There are a few hotels that will not accept children especially some of the 'higher end' boutique B&Bs or lodges. Check in advance.

A good resource is **Kidz Friendly New Zealand**, www.kidsfriendlynz.com. Also, in Queenstown/Wanaka look out for the independent magazine *Kidz Go*, www.kidz go.co.nz, available from the VIC (I-Site).

Customs & duty free

Customs

New Zealand's environment and highly unique biodiversity has been decimated by unwelcome and non-native wildlife and vegetation. Not surprisingly it has imposed strict bio-security laws. Be extra vigilant about not carrying any fruit, animal or plant matter of any kind without prior permission. Heavy fines are imposed on those who flout the rules. The New Zealand Customs Service website, www.customs.govt.nz, provides comprehensive advice for travellers including details of restricted items. The usual rules and regulations are also in force regarding pets or any live animals, drugs and firearms.

Duty free

Apart from your personal effects and as long as you are over 17 years of age you are allowed the following importation concessions: 200 cigarettes or 250 g of tobacco or 50 cigars, or a mix of all three weighing no more than 250 g; 4½ litres of wine or beer and one 1125 ml bottle of spirits, liqueur or other libation. Goods up to a total combined value of NZ$700 are duty and tax free. New Zealand duty free liquor is some of the cheapest in the world.

Disabled travellers

Most public facilities are well geared up for wheelchairs, however older accommodation establishments and some public transport systems (especially rural buses) are not so well organized. It is a requirement by law to have disabled facilities in new buildings. The larger airlines like **Air New Zealand** and **Qantas** are well equipped. Disabled travellers usually receive discounts on travel fares and some admission charges. Parking concessions are also available for the disabled and temporary cards can be issued on production of a mobility card or medical certificate.

For more information within New Zealand contact: **Enable**, T0800-171981/ T06-3535800, www.enable.co.nz; and **New Zealand Disability Resource Centre**, 14 Erson Av, PO Box 24-042 Royal Oak, Auckland, T09-625 8069, www.disabilityresource.org.nz.

Accessible Kiwi Tours Ltd, T07-362 7622, www.toursnz.com, is a specialist tour company acting specifically for the disabled, based in Rotorua in the Bay of Plenty.

Electricity

The New Zealand supply is 230/240 volts (50 hertz). Plugs are either 2- or 3-pronged with flat pins. North American appliances require both an adapter and a transformer; UK an adaptor only; Australian appliances are the same. Adapters and transformers are widely available at hardware stores or the airport.

Embassies and consulates

For further information on visas and immigration, page 63. See also www.mfat.govt.nz.

Foreign consulates in New Zealand
Auckland
Australia 7th floor, Price WaterHouse Coopers Tower , 188 Quay St, City, T09-921 8800. **Canada** 9th floor, 48 Emily Pl, City, T09-309 3690. **Denmark** 273 Bleakhouse Rd, Howick, T09-537 3099. **Germany** 90-92 Hobson St, Thorndon, Wellington, T04-4736063. **Ireland** 7th floor, Citibank Blg, 23 Customs St East, City, T09-977 2252. **Japan** Level 12, ASB Bank Centre, 135 Albert St, City, T09-303 4106. **Korea** Level 11, ASB Bank Tower 2 Hunter St, Wellington, T04-4739073 **Netherlands** Level 1, 57 Symonds St, City, T09-379 5399. **Sweden** 13th floor, 13 O'Connell St, City, T09-373 5332. **UK** IAG House, 151 Queen St, City, T09-303 2973. **USA** 29 Flitzherbert TerraceThordon, Wellington, T04-4626000.

New Zealand embassies abroad
See also www.nzembassy.com.
Australia High Commission Commonwealth Av, Canberra, ACT 2600, T+61-(0)2-6270 4211. **Consulate General** Level 10, 55 Hunter St, Sydney, PO Box 365, NSW 2001, T+61-(0)2-8265 2000.
Canada High Commission Suite 727, 99 Bank St, Ottowa, Ont K1P 6G3, T+1-613-238 5991. **Consulate General** Suite 1200, 888 Dunsmuir St, Vancouver, BC, V6C 3K4, T+1-604-684 7388. **France** Embassy 7 Rue Leonard de Vinci, 75116, Paris, T+33-01-45 01 43 43. **Germany** Embassy Friedrichstrasse 60, 10117, Berlin, T+49-30-206210-0. **Netherlands** Embassy Eisenhowerlaan 77n,

2517KK, The Hague, T+31-70-346 9324. **UK** High Commission New Zealand House, 80 Haymarket, London SW1Y 4TQ, T+44-(0)20-7930 8422. **USA** Embassy Observatory Circle NW, Washington DC, 20008, T+1-202-328 4800. **Consulate General** 2425 Olympic Blvd, Suite 600E, Santa Monica, CA 90404, T+1-310-566 6555/T+1-310-460 4424.

Gay & lesbian travellers

Homosexuality is generally well accepted in New Zealand and indeed in some parts it is flourishing. Auckland has a thriving gay and transvestite community heavily focused around the Ponsonby and Karangahape Road (K'Road) areas, where there are many gay and gay-friendly clubs, cafés and pubs. There are also a number of specialist publications and independent groups, see the Auckland chapter, page 98. Each Feb Auckland hosts the popular 'Hero Parade' – the national gay event of the year. The festival involves a street parade and entertainment in the Ponsonby area. Although not quite on the scale of the world famous Sydney 'Mardi Gras', it is enjoyed by thousands, both gay and straight.
New Zealand Gay and Lesbian Tourism Association (GALTA) PO Box 638, Queenstown, T021-762796, www.gay pages.co.nz, provides information on gay and lesbian New Zealand. Also check www.pinkpagesnet.com, www.gaynewzealand.com and www.gaytravel.net.nz.

Publications to look out for in the main centres include the long-established *Gay Express*, www.gayexpress.co.nz.

Health

The standards of public and private medical care are generally high, but unless you have a genuine accident these services are not free. Health insurance is recommended. A trip to the doctor will cost around $60 with prescription charges on top of that. Dentists and hospital services are expensive.

Safety precautions

There are few dangerous creatures in New Zealand. An exception is the **Katipo Spider**. Small and black, about 25 mm from leg tip to leg tip, it is found on beaches, under stones and in driftwood throughout the North Island and parts of the South. It is not uncommon and can be fatal, with agonizing pain around the bite. Antivenin is readily available in hospitals.

Although not poisonous, the dreaded **sandfly** is found everywhere, but particularly common in the wetter and coastal areas of Fiordland. These black, pinhead sized 'flying fangs' can annoy you beyond belief. There are numerous environmentally friendly repellants available such as: *Shoo*, *Botanica* and *Repel*.

Giardia is a water-borne bacterial parasite on the increase in New Zealand which, if allowed to enter your system, will cause wall-to-wall vomiting, diarrhoea and rapid weight loss. Don't drink water from lakes, ponds or rivers without boiling it first.

The **sun** is dangerous and you should take care. Ozone depletion is heavy in the more southern latitudes and the incidence of melanomas and skin cancer is above average. Burn times, especially in summer, are greatly reduced so get yourself a silly hat and wear lots of sun block.

New Zealand's **weather**, especially at higher elevations, is changeable and can be deadly. If you are tramping, or going 'bush' make sure you are properly clothed, take maps, a first-aid kit a compass and on particularly remote locations a mountain radio and/or a GPS emergency beacon. Above all inform somebody of your intentions.

Volcanic eruptions and **earthquakes** are a rare but exciting factor and can prove fatal. In the event of an earthquake, stand in a doorway, get under a table and if you are in the open, get indoors or keep away from loose rock formations and trees. Apparently, all the major existing volcanoes in New Zealand are well 'overdue'.

Should you come across any **injured wildlife** call the nearest DoC office and try to ensure the animal is taken to one of the few local wildlife rehabilitators. Provided the animal is not on the 'Don't touch' list (ask DoC) and you use common sense, capture the animal and put it in a dark, fully enclosed box with some ventilation holes. Then find out the location of the nearest rehabilitator and take it there yourself. If in doubt, leave it alone. If you come across a **whale stranding** or an obviously sick seal on the beach call DoC immediately or, in the South Island, **Marine Watch**, T02-535 8909.

Insurance

Although New Zealand honours its reputation as clean and green it has a dark side and crime rates are high, especially when it comes to theft – for which tourists are an obvious target. Full travel insurance is advised, but at the very least get medical insurance and cover for expensive personal effects. The **New Zealand Accident Compensation Scheme** covers visitors to New Zealand for personal injury by accident. Benefits include some emergency medical expenses, but do not include loss of earnings.

There are a wide variety of policies to choose from, so shop around. Always read the small print carefully. Check that the policy covers the activities you intend or may end up doing. Also check exactly what your medical cover includes, i.e. ambulance, helicopter rescue or emergency flights back home. Also check the payment protocol. You may have to cough up first (literally) before the insurance company reimburses you. Dig out all the receipts for expensive personal effects like jewellery or cameras. Take photos of these items and note down all serial numbers. It will also almost certainly be necessary to extend the premium and pay more to cover individual items worth more than NZ$500. In recent years there have been a number of high profile cases of tourists trying to rip off their insurers. New Zealand police are pretty savvy to such fraud especially in the main centres so be extra vigilant with paperwork and when a crime has occurred report it immediately, preferably with an independent witness.

Insurance companies
In North America
Young travellers can try the **International Student Insurance Service (ISIS)**, available through STA Travel, (USA) T1-800-7814040, www.statravel.com. Other companies include: **Access America**, T1-800-284-8300, www.access america.com; **Travel Assistance International**, T1-800-8212828, www.travelassistance.com; **Travel Insurance Services**, T1-800-9371387, www.travelinsure.com; and **Travel Guard**, T1-800-8264919, www.travelguard.com.

In the UK
STA Travel, www.statravel.co.uk, offer good-value policies. Other companies that specialize in travel for those under 26 include: **Columbus**, T0870-033 9988, www.columbusdirect.com; **Direct Line**, T0845-246 8702, www.directline.com; and **Flexicover Group**, T0800-093 9495, www.flexicover.co.uk. Some companies will not cover people over 65 years old, or may charge higher premiums. Specific policies for older travellers are offered by **Co-op Insurance**, T0800-917 1431, www.co-operativeinsurance.co.uk.

Internet

New Zealand had one of the highest per capita internet access rates in the developed world. Internet cafés and terminals are everywhere and if you are among the many who start walking funny or dribbling if you do not get your daily 'email-inbox-fix' you should be fine. As well as internet cafés, libraries and VICs (I-Sites) are a good bet, they charge standard rates of $6-12 per hr. Due to growing competition, rates are getting cheaper (as little as $3 per), but you are advised to shop around.

Wireless internet hot spots
New Zealand is well up to speed with the rapid development of wireless technology and the demand for hand held wireless capable devices and laptop connectivity. Your own service provider may offer international roaming within New Zealand but you will certainly pay for it.

As yet there are few service providers within New Zealand that offer short-term non-contract policies that allow only a few weeks of activity. One is **Vodafone**, though you will have to purchase a USB data card, see www.vodafone.co.nz. If you are travelling as a couple it may be worth looking at a package that includes two cheap mobile phones and a short-term wireless internet policy using the same sim card for the laptop, but bear in mind if you intend using your own data-card it will have to be compatible with that service – many lock the data cards so you can only use that company's service.

Both coverage and speed is generally good throughout the country though obviously in a land replete with many a mountain range, don't expect miracles.

For Wi-Fi hotspots try the local libraries or refer to the websites www. jahoog.org/wifi/, www.wi-fihotspotlist.com or www.zenbu.co.nz

Language

English is of course the principal language spoken in New Zealand. Maori is the traditional. See also page 723 and Glossary of Maori words on page 738.

Laundry

Most towns, villages and accommodation establishments have launderettes. They tend to operate with $1 or $2 coins. A full wash and dry will cost about $8.

Media

Although not blessed with the same choice as countries like the UK, the **newspapers** in New Zealand are pretty good, featuring fairly comprehensive and factual sections on local, national and international news as well as sport, business and travel. The main dailies are the *New Zealand Herald*, www.nzherald.co.nz (Auckland and upper North Island), the *Dominion* (Wellington and lower North Island) and the *Press* (Christchurch and central South Island). The *Sunday Star Times* is available nationally. The website www.nzstuff.co.nz, is good for national and regional news.

National **magazines** of interest include *North and South*, which covers a wide range of traditional and contemporary issues; *New Zealand Geographic*, the quality New Zealand version of the great US national icon; *New Zealand Wilderness*, a glossy outdoor activity magazine; and *New Zealand Outside*, a similar effort. These are readily available at bookshops.

Although New Zealand radio is quite good, **television** is a shocker; the 4 principal terrestrial channels have little to offer. Except for good news and current affairs programmes you are bombarded with the usual UK or US soaps, reality TV or game shows. Most New Zealanders have now subscribed to Sky TV. Perhaps most aggravating of all is the advertising. It is not unusual to get the same advert every 10 mins for days.

Money

The New Zealand currency is the dollar ($), divided into 100 cents (c). Coins come in denominations of 5c, 10c, 20c, 50c, $1 and $2. Notes come in $5, $10, $20, $50 and $100 denominations.
Exchange rates Due to the global financial crisis exchange rates are erratic but as of mid-2010 they were as follows:
US$1 = NZ$1.41; UK£1 = NZ$2.14;
€1 = NZ$1.79; AUS $1 = NZ$1.24.

Traveller's cheques (TCs)
The safest way to carry money is in TCs. These are available for a small commission from all major banks. **American Express** (Amex), **Visa** and **Thomas Cook** cheques are widely accepted. Most banks do not charge for changing TCs and usually offer the best exchange rates. Keep a record of your cheque numbers and keep the cheques you have cashed separate from the cheques themselves, so that you can get a full refund of all uncashed cheques. It is best to bring NZ$ cheques to avoid extra exchange costs.

Credit cards, ATMs and EFTPOS
All the major credit cards (**Visa, MasterCard, Amex, JCB** and **Diners**) are widely accepted. Most hotels, shops and petrol stations use EFTPOS (Electronic Funds Transfer at Point of Sale), meaning you don't have to carry lots of cash. It is best suited to those who have a bank account in New Zealand, but credit cards can be used with the relevant pin number. If you intend to stay in New Zealand for a while you may be able to open an account with one of the major banks and secure an EFTPOS/ATM card and PIN. ATMs are readily available in almost all towns. Credit cards can of course be used and some banks are linked to foreign savings accounts and cards by such networks as **Cirrus** and **Plus**.

Banks
Almost all towns and villages have at least one of the major bank branches. The main banks are the **Bank of New Zealand**, the **National Bank of New Zealand**, the **ASB Bank**, **Post Bank** and **Countrywide Bank**, with other trans-Tasman banks, like **Westpac Trust** and **ANZ** also in evidence. Bank opening hours are Mon-Fri 0900-1630 with some city branches opening on Sat until 1230. Exchange offices like **Thomas Cook**, **Travelex** and **American Express** tend to

have longer opening hours, sometimes staying open until 2100 in the cities.

Money transfers

If you need money quickly or in an emergency the best way is to have it wired to you via any major bank with **Western Union** (NZ) T1800-325 6000, www.westernunion. com; or via **Thomas Cook** and **Moneygram** (NZ) T0800-872893, www.moneygram.com. The transfer can take less than an hour or up to a week depending how much is being transferred and how much you are willing to pay (sending GBP100 for example will incur a fee of GBP12). Charges are on a sliding scale; it will cost proportionately less to wire out more money. Most post shops can assist with money transfers.

Cost of living/travelling

With the recent strengthening of the Australasian currencies as a result of the global financial crisis you will find less worth in your tourist buck, especially if travelling from the US or UK. That said those travelling from both North America and Europe will find most things generally cheaper, with other consumables like beer costing about the same. For accommodation and restaurants, see pages 45 and 48. Petrol is around $1.80 per litre ($6.66 per gallon).

The minimum budget required, if staying in hostels or campsites, cooking for yourself, not drinking much and travelling relatively slowly is about $75 per person per day, but this isn't going to be much fun. Going on the occasional tour, travelling faster and eating out occasionally will raise this to a more realistic $100-120. Those staying in modest B&Bs, hotels and motels as couples, eating out most nights and taking a few tours will need to budget for $200-300 per person per day. Costs in the major cities will be 20-50% higher. Non-hostelling single travellers should budget on spending around 60-70% of what a couple would spend.

See also student travellers, page 59, for discounts available.

Opening hours

Most government offices are open 0830- 1630. Weekday business hours are usually 0900-1700. Most retail outlets close at 1730 and in the larger towns many are also open at the weekend. The modern malls open daily with at least one late shopping night a week, usually Thu or Fri. Also, in the main centres, the larger supermarket chains are open in the evenings. Almost every town and village has the iconic Kiwi corner 'dairy' which are often open until 2000 and sometimes until 2300. Petrol (gas) stations are open until about 2300 with some open 24 hours; many now sell a substantial range of supermarket type items.

Post

Post offices (most often called 'Post Shops') are generally open Mon-Fri 0900-1700, Sat 0900-1230. Within New Zealand standard (local) post costs $0.50 for medium letters and postcards (2-3 days); $1 for airmail (fast post) to domestic centres (1-2 days); $1.80 for airmail letters and postcards to Australia and postcards worldwide and $2.30 for standard overseas airmail letters to Europe, North America, East Asia, Australia and South Pacific. Domestic mail takes 1-2 days, perhaps longer in rural areas. When sending any cards or letters overseas be sure to use the free blue 'Air economy' stickers. Books of stamps are readily available as are pre-paid envelopes and a range of purpose-built cardboard boxes. Average international delivery times vary depending on the day of the week posted, but a standard letter to the UK can take as few as 4 days (scheduled 6-12 days). North America is scheduled 4-12 days and Australia and the South Pacific 3-8 days. For details see www.nzpost.co.nz.

Poste restante

Mail can be sent to 'Post restante', CPO (Chief Post Office) in the main centres, where it will be held for up to 30 days. If you are being sent any mail make sure the sender marks your surname in capitals and underlines it. The principal pick-up points are:

Auckland Bledisloe Bldg, 24 Wellesley St, 1010, T09-3796714, Mon-Fri 0730-1730.

Christchurch 736 Colombo St North, 8011, Cathedral Sq, T03-3775414, Mon-Fri 0830-1730, Sat 1000-1400.

Dunedin Dunedin Post Shop, 243 Princess St, 9016, T03-4773517, Mon-Fri 0830-1730, closed Sat/Sun.

Nelson 209 Hardy St, 7020, T03-5467631, Mon-Fri 0800-1700, Sat 0930-1230.

Queenstown Main Post Office, 15-19 Camp St, 9300, T03-4224972, Mon-Fri 0830-1730, Sat 0900-1600.

Rotorua 1189 Hinemoa St, 3010 T07-349 2393, Mon-Fri 0800-1730, Sat 0830-1400.

Wellington 43 Manners St, 6011, T04-499 7469, Mon-Fri 0800-1730, Sat 0900-1300.

Public holidays

If you are a tourist, public holidays can be an inconvenience since shops and banks close and cohorts of Kiwis join you. School holidays are particularly bad with Jan and Feb being the worst months. During these times you should book accommodation and activities well ahead. Bear in mind this also applies to the winter season at the major ski resorts like Tongariro, Wanaka and Queenstown.

Jan 1-2 New Year; **Feb 6** Waitangi Day; Good Fri; Easter Mon; **Apr 25** Anzac Day; **1st Mon in Jun** Queen's Birthday; **4th Mon in Oct** Labour Day; **Dec 25** Christmas Day; **Dec 26** Boxing Day.

Anniversary Day varies between the provinces: **Jan 17** Southland; **Jan 22** Wellington; **Jan 29** Auckland; **Feb 1** Nelson.

Safety

Tourists are rarely targeted for anything other than petty crime but you still need to be

careful. Theft, especially in Auckland, is rife and tourist accommodation establishments are not exempt. Cars and their contents are also regularly targeted. Do not relax your guard; keep money safe and out of sight. Keep your vehicle locked at all times and put valuables in the boot (trunk). It may sound ridiculous but you also need to be wary of other tourists. Having suitable insurance cover is also wise. Drink driving and speeding laws are very strict in New Zealand: do not even think about driving while under the influence, and keep your speed down. Speed cameras and patrol cars are omnipresent. Drug laws are also strict so don't get caught in possession.

Smoking

It is illegal to smoke in bars, restaurants and the workplace, except in segregated sections, if provided. It is also banned on public transport.

Student travellers

If you are a student (and can prove it) you will enjoy discounts on public transport and specialist tourist travel, tourist attractions and tourist-based activities throughout New Zealand. There are also some savings to be made on insurance, restaurants, shopping and accommodation. However, if you are backpacking note that the main discounts are best secured through the affiliation and membership of one or more of the specific backpacker chains (i.e. **YHA**, **BBH**, or **Nomad**). See Backpacker organizations, page 46.

The **International Student Identity Card** (ISIC), www.isiccard.com, is the most widely accepted form of ID and far more effective and hassle-free than an institution-specific identity card. ISIC cards are also available from **STA travel**, www.statravel.co.uk. The **International Student Travel Confederation** (ISTC), www.isic.org, is the principal administrator of the scheme. Consult their website for specific contacts within your own country. For information on student visas, see Visas and immigration, page 63.

Taxes

There is a 12.5% GST (Goods and Services Tax) placed on almost every bought item in New Zealand. Prices quoted almost always include GST, but on bigger quotes or services it pays to check.

Telephone

Within New Zealand there are 5 area codes: Auckland and Northland **09**; Bay of Plenty, Coromandel, Taupo, Ruapehu and Waikato **07**; Eastland, Hawkes Bay, Wanganui and Taranaki **06**; Wellington **04**; South Island **03**. All telephone numbers in this book include the area code.

Telecom payphones are found throughout the country and are colour coded. Although there are both coin (blue) and credit card (yellow) booths available, the vast majority are 'phone-card only' so you are advised to stock up. Cards come in $5, $10, $20 and $50 and are available from many retail outlets, visitor information offices and hostels. Unless you want to see just how fast digital numbers can disappear on screen, do not use these Telecom cards for anything other than domestic calls within New Zealand.

There is a wealth of cheap international calling cards and call centres available. The cards vary in price from $10-$50 and can be bought from many retail outlets and on the net (look for the E Phone flag signs outside the shops). They can be used from any landline telephone. Voice instructions will tell you what to do and how much credit you have available before each call.

Local non-business calls are free from standard telephones in New Zealand, so it is not too offensive to ask to use a friend's domestic (non-business) telephone. 0800 or

occasionally 0508 precede toll-free calls. Try to avoid 0900 numbers as they are usually very expensive. The 2 major **mobile** service providers are **Telecom**, www.telecom.co.nz and **Vodafone** , www.vodafone.co.nz.

If you intend to use a mobile check with your service provider on the cost of international calls. Sometimes it is cheaper to sign up with a New Zealand company and buy a new phone and go pre-paid if you intend to be in the country for a few weeks.

Time

New Zealand Standard Time (NZST) is 12 hrs ahead of GMT. So at 1200 in New Zealand it is 1000 in Sydney, 0900 in Japan, 1900 yesterday in New York or 2400 in the UK. Allow for daylight saving: from the 1st Sun in Oct to the 3rd Sun in Mar the clock goes forward 1 hr.

Tipping

Tipping in New Zealand is at the customer's discretion. In a good restaurant you should leave a tip of 10-15% if you are satisfied with the service, but the bill may include a service charge. Tipping is appreciated in pubs and bars and taxi drivers also expect some sort of tip; on a longer journey 10% is fine. As in most other counties, hotel porters, bellboys, waiters and waitresses should all be tipped to supplement their meagre wages.

Toilets

Public toilets are readily available and very rarely are you charged for the privilege of using them.

Tourist information

The official New Zealand Visitor Information Network is made up of around 100 accredited

Visitor Information Centres (VICs) nationally known as I-Sites.

National I-Sites are based in Auckland and Christchurch as well as the main tourist centres, like Rotorua and Queenstown. Open 7 days a week, they provide a comprehensive information service as well as accommodation bookings and domestic airline, bus and train ticketing. Souvenir shops and occasionally other retail outlets, currency exchange and cafés are often attached.

Regional I-Sites are found throughout the country. There may be more than one in each region. They provide a general information booking service usually 7 days a week and there is also a huge amount of free material.

Local I-Sites can be found almost anywhere, providing local information as well as assistance in accommodation and transport bookings. They are open at least 5 days a week, but are subject to varying seasonal and weekend hours.

Useful websites
Accommodation and transport
www.aatravel.co.nz Useful general New Zealand travel and sleeping information.
www.auckland-airport.co.nz and **www.christchurch-airport.co.nz** Worth a quick look before you enter the country.
www.backpack.co.nz Comprehensive guide to hostels in New Zealand.
www.intercitycoach.co.nz Intercity bus information and additional news about fare concessions and package deals.
www.interislander.co.nz and **www.bluebridge.co.nz** The principal websites for the inter-islander ferry services.
www.jasons.co.nz Useful information on transport, accommodation and activities.
www.orbitz.com Good general travel site with broad information and competitive airfares for New Zealand.
www.travel-library.com Detailed general travel site packed with good tips on buying flight tickets.
www.tranzscenic.co.nz Provides all your rail information needs.

www.travelplanner.co.nz Useful visitor information and good links.
www.yha.org.nz One of the principal backpacker travel organizations.

Photography
www.andrisapse.co.nz and **www.craigpotton.co.nz** Some of the best photographers, photographs and pictorial references of New Zealand.
www.darrochdonald.com The author's website with comprehensive photographic coverage of New Zealand and advice on best photo locations.

General information
www.destination-nz.com Useful tourist/ visitor based sites with good links.
www.doc.govt.nz The invaluable website of the Department of Conservation provides detailed information on national parks, tramping and short walks.
www.ecotours.co.nz Good site outlining reputable eco-tours throughout the country.
www.mapworld.co.nz Best map supplier in New Zealand including CD-ROMS.
www.newzealandvacations.co.nz and **www.nzcity.co.nz** Regional news and a superb weather satellite picture.
www.nzembassy.com Lists all the overseas New Zealand embassies and some other useful immigration links.
www.nzherald.co.nz Excellent website of the Upper North Island's main daily newspaper, with national and international news, as well as sport, weather and travel.
www.purenz.com Official website of the New Zealand Tourism Board packed with useful information, listings and contacts.
www.searchnz.co.nz One of the country's best national search engines.
www.tourism.net.nz Directory of tourism and travel companies.
www.trademe.co.nz New Zealand's version of eBay has over 1 million members and around 50,000 online at any one time.
www.yellowpages.co.nz Useful for any national telephone and address listings.

History and culture

Comprehensive sites worth looking at include: **www.maori.org.nz**, **www.nzhistory.net:nz**, **www.nzlive.com** and **www.teara.govt.nz**

Tour operators

Although New Zealand is very much the domain of the independent traveller there are a number of specialist tour operators. As you might expect most of these are either eco- or activity-based. The New Zealand Tourism Board has detailed operator listings on its website, www.purenz.com. Other tour operators are listed in the Activities and tours sections throughout the book.

In the UK

Australian Pacific Touring (UK), T020-88797444, www.aptouring.co.uk. Escorted tours or fully independent packages.
AATKings (UK), T20 8225 4220, www.aatkings.com/uk. Solid reputation for premium or low cost escorted tours.
Explore Worldwide, T0870-3334002, www.exploreworldwide.co.uk. Special interest trips such as cycling, walking or family holidays.
High Places, T0114-275 7500, www.high places.co.uk. Specialists in mountain trekking and adventure travel.
Kuoni Worldwide, T01306-741111, www.kuoni.co.uk. Tailor-made itineraries.
Travelmood, 214 Edgware Rd, London, W2 1DH; also at 1 Brunswick Court, Bridge St, Leeds, LS2 7QU; and 16 Reform St, Dundee, DD1 1RG, T0871-226 6151, www.travel mood.com. 25 years' experience as a top travel specialist in adventure and activity trips.

In North America

Abercrombie and Kent, T1-800-5547016, www.abercrombiekent.com. Well-established US company offering a diverse range of luxury guided trips of 9-13 days, with other longer trips in combination with Australia.

Newmans South Pacific Vacations, T1-800-342 1956, www.newmansvacations.com. Lots of tours or fully independent itineraries.
Swain Tours, T1-800-22-SWAIN, www.swain tours.com. Tailor-made or group tours of around 14 days, from approximately US$8500.
Tauck, T1-800-788 7885, www.tauck.com. Australia and New Zealand combos, or a 9-day NZ tour taking in the best of Auckland, Rotorua, Queenstown and Milford from $3000.

In New Zealand
Backpacker bus companies

The principal backpacker bus companies offer good value flexible routes and options.
Bottom Bus, T03-434 7370, www.bottom bus.co.nz. Runs along the Southern Scenic Route between Dunedin and Milford Sound.
Contiki, 1st floor, 15-17 Day St, Newton, Auckland, T1300-2668454, www.contiki.com.
Flying Kiwi, T0800-693296/T03-5470171, www.flying kiwi.com. Eco/activity-orientated.
Kiwi Experience, T09-3364286, www.kiwiexperience.com. **Magic Travellers**, T09-358 5600, www.magicbus.co.nz.
Stray, 31 Beach Rd, Auckland City, T09-5262140, www.straytravel.co.nz.

Coach tours

Great Sights, 180 Quay St, Auckland, T0800-744487/T09-583 5790, www.greatsights. co.nz. A wide range of tours throughout the country, from day city tours to 2-11 day excursions as well as a 3 to 12-day hop-on/ hop-off option.
Guthreys Tours, T09- 4431945, www.guthreys .co.nz. Tours from Auckland to Rotorua, Taupo, Waitomo and Bay of Islands a speciality.
Scenic Pacific Tours, T0800-500388/T03-359 3999, www.scenicpacific.co.nz. Well-established company offering de luxe (yet good value) coach trips with the emphasis on activities as much as sightseeing.
Thrifty Tours, T09-359 8380, www.thrifty tours.co.nz. Budget-conscious tours with flexibility. Range of options from 2-16 days in both islands. Thrifty specials to Waitomo, Rotorua and the Bay of Islands.

Eco-tourism operators

Adventure South, PO Box 33, 153 Christchurch, T03-942 1222, www.advsouth.co.nz. Eco-based 5-23 day cycling and hiking trips.
Catlins Wildlife Trackers, Papatowai, Owaka, Southland, T03-415 8613, www.catlins-ecotours.co.nz. Eco-tours and conservation holidays in New Zealand.
Elm Tourism, Elm Lodge Backpackers, Dunedin, Otago, T03-454 4121/T0800-356563, www.elmwildlifetours.co.nz. Award-winning company offering excellent nature tours of the Otago Peninsula, Catlins and Southern Scenic Route.
Heritage Expeditions, 53B Montreal St, Christchurch, Canterbury, T03-365 3500, www.heritage-expeditions.com. Guided birdwatching trips and expeditions in New Zealand, Sub-Antarctic Islands and Antarctica.
Kiwi Wildlife Tours, 346 Cowan Bay Rd, Warkworth, Auckland, T09-422 6868, www.kiwi-wildlife.co.nz. 1- to 20-day guided birdwatching trips locally and nationally.
Miranda Shorebird Centre, 283 East Coast Rd, Pokeno, Tiritiri Matangi Island, Auckland, T09-232 2781, www.miranda-shorebird. org.nz. Specialist wader field centre on internationally significant site, accommodation available.

Nature safaris

Hiking New Zealand, T0800-697232/ T03-384 3706, www.hikingnewzealand.com. Popular, with a wide range of trips to suit all fitness levels, including the Great Walks as well as some 'off the beaten track' adventures.
Manu Tours New Zealand, 106 Ocean Beach Rd, Tairua, T07-864 7475, www.nz birding.co.nz. Great for avid twitchers with a national hunt to see as many endemic species as possible in 17 days.
Nature Quest New Zealand, Dunedin, T03-489 8444, www.naturequest.co.nz. South Island based company offering guided trips or independent custom designed itineraries.

Specialist activity tours

Active Earth, T0800-201040, www.active earthnewzealand.com. Good guided activity

tours of the North Island, from 5-10 days.
New Zealand Pedaltours Ltd, PO Box 37-575, Parnell, Auckland, T0800-302 0968/T09-585 1338, www.pedaltours.co.nz. Specialist cycle tours and eco-tours.
Pacific Cycle Tours, 14 Kennaway Rd, Christchurch 8023, T03-9829913, www.bike-nz.com. Offer both hike and bike options.

Vaccinations

There are no vaccinations required to enter New Zealand but as with any country, you are advised to get a tetanus injection or ensure that your boosters are up to date. See also Health, page 54.

Visas and immigration

For embassies and consulates, see page 54. Visa information is also available from **New Zealand Immigration Service (NZIS)**, Private Bag, Wellesley St, Auckland, T0508-558855/ T09-914 4100, www.immigration.govt.nz.

All visitors must have a passport valid for 3 months beyond the date you intend to leave the country. Australian citizens or holders of an Australian returning resident visa can stay in New Zealand indefinitely. UK citizens do not need a visa and are automatically issued with a 6-month **visitor permit** on arrival. All visitors making an application for a visitor permit require: (a) a passport that is valid for at least 3 months after your departure from New Zealand; (b) an onward or return ticket to a country you have permission to enter; (c) sufficient money to support yourself during your stay (approximately NZ$1000 per month). The sufficient funds factor can be waived if you have a friend or relative in New Zealand (citizen) who agrees to sponsor you by guaranteeing to support you financially during your stay. If you have to apply for a **visitor visa** go to your nearest New Zealand Embassy or by downloading the relevant forms from the website.

Longer stays and work visas

It is illegal to work on a visitor permit. Non-residents (with the exception of Australian citizens) must obtain a **work visa** which allows you to enter the country, then a **work permit** which allows you to work upon arrival. Applications for both are best made well before arrival. The NZIS website has details and application forms to download. An exception to this rule is the **working holiday visa** which is available for those aged 18-30 from a number of countries (including Canada, Japan, Ireland, Germany, France and the UK) and entitles you to work for 12 months; conditions apply. See also Working in New Zealand, below. **Student visas** come under a separate category. You can also get extensions on your visitor permit for up to 9 months but you must meet certain criteria. For detailed information contact the NZIS direct and their web page www.immigration.govt.nz/migrant/stream/work/workingholiday.

For a **residence visa** an application must be made from your own country. It involves a points system relating to factors such as age, education and occupation. The target number required fluctuates depending on the perceived demand for immigrants and, to a degree, politics. For details, consult the 'Migration' section on the website or contact the NZIS direct. Be warned – you will need endless supplies of patience. Once a residence visa is secured you can apply for **citizenship** after 3 years' residency in New Zealand.

Weights and measures

The metric system is used throughout. Distances are in kilometres, petrol is in litres. Ask for a pint in a pub, however, and you will not be looked at in a funny way.

Women travellers

There are few specific problems that especially affect women or single female travellers in New Zealand. However, that said, the country is not immune to the usual crime and social problems so all the normal common sense levels of vigilance and precaution should be adopted. **Bushwise Women**, T+61-2-6684 0178, www.bushwise.co.nz. For trips especially designed for women.

Working in New Zealand

See also Visas and immigration, page 63. Vineyards, orchards and farmstays (see page 45) are often on the lookout for casual labour but like any 'casual situation' be careful and protect your own rights . Given the ever-increasing development of tourism in Queenstown you are just about guaranteed to find a job in both the summer and winter high seasons. One organization that will help you locate these is **Farm Helpers (FhiNZ)**, 16 Aspen Way, Palmerston North, T0800- 327681/T06-355 0448, www.fhinz.co.nz. Its website is a fine place to start and a booklet listing over 190 associate farms is also available on line for $25.

Other useful contacts include: **Seek**, T0508-733569, www.seek.com.au, which is a recruitment specialist with offices in Auckland, Wellington and Christchurch ; and the excellent website **www.seasonal work.co.nz**, which offers job listings and a host of other information. Do not expect to be paid premium hourly rates. The minimum wage is around NZ$12 per hour.

There is also an option of working voluntarily through **Willing Workers on Organic Farms (WWOOF)**, PO Box 1172, Nelson, T03-544 9890, www.wwoof.co.nz. Reports of this network are good and as a member ($30 joining fee) you can get free comfortable accommodation in return for a few hours' daily work. You receive a comprehensive booklet with operator listings upon receipt of membership.

Contents

Footprint features

Auckland

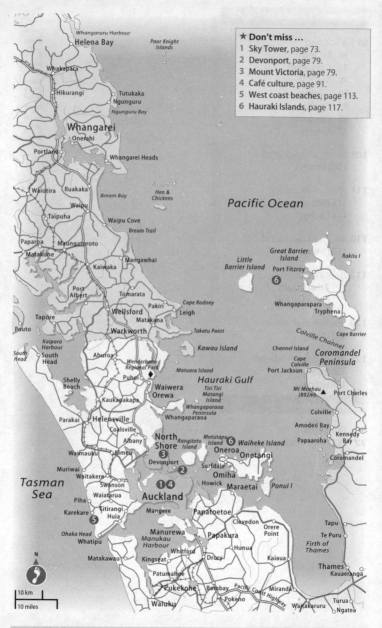

★ **Don't miss ...**
1 Sky Tower, page 73.
2 Devonport, page 79.
3 Mount Victoria, page 79.
4 Café culture, page 91.
5 West coast beaches, page 113.
6 Hauraki Islands, page 117.

Whangaruru Harbour
Helena Bay
Poor Knight Islands
Whakapara
Hikurangi
Tutukaka
Ngunguru
Ngunguru Bay
Whangarei
Onerahi
Portland
Whangarei Heads
Waiotira
Ruakaka
Bream Bay
Hen & Chickens
Waipu
Taipuha
Waipu Cove
Bream Trail
Paparoa
Maungaturoto
Matakohe
Kaiwaka
Mangawhai
Port Albert
Tomarata
Wellsford
Pakiri
Cape Rodney
Tapora
Matakana
Leigh
Pouto
Kaipara Harbour
Ahuroa
Warkworth
Takatu Point
South Head
Wenderholm Regional Park
Puhoi
Kawau Island
Shelly Beach
Waiwera
Orewa
Motuora Island
Hauraki Gulf
Kaukapakapa
Tiri Tiri
Matangi Island
Helensville
Whangaparaoa
Whangaparaoa Peninsula
Coalsville
Parakai
Albany
North Shore
Rangitoto Island
Motutapu Island
Waiheke Island
Waimauku
Kumeu
Devonport
Oneroa
Onetangi
Muriwai
Waitakere
Surfdale
Omiha
Piha
Swanson
Auckland
Howick
Maraetai
Waiatarua
Mangere
Karekare
Titirangi
Huia
Papatoetoe
Clevedon
Ohaka Head
Whatipu
Manurewa
Manukau Harbour
Papakura
Orere Point
Hunua
Matakawau
Kingseat
Whitford
Drury
Kaiaua
Patumahoe
Pukekohe
Bombay
Pacific Coast Highway
Miranda
Waiuku
Pokeno
Waitakaruru
Turua
Ngatea

Pacific Ocean

Great Barrier Island
Rakitu I
Little Barrier Island
Port Fitzroy
Whangaparapara
Tryphena
Colville Channel
Cape Barrier
Channel Island
Cape Colville
Coromandel Peninsula
Port Jackson
Mt Moehau (892m)
Port Charles
Colville
Amodeo Bay
Kennedy Bay
Papaaroha
Coromandel
Tapu
Te Puru
Ponui I
Firth of Thames
Thames
Kauaeranga

Tasman Sea

N

10 km
10 miles

With a population of one and a quarter million, Auckland is Polynesia's largest city and by far the biggest in New Zealand. Thanks to its spacious suburban sprawl, Auckland covers more than 500 sq km – twice that of London and close to that of Los Angeles – but because the city is built on an isthmus and constantly fragmented by coastline, you are never far from water. As a result, the sea pervades almost every aspect of Auckland life, from recreation to cuisine. The city has more recreational boats per capita than any other in the world, earning it the affectionate nickname of 'City of Sails' and most sailing is done in Auckland's backyard – the beautiful aquatic playground and island-studded waters of the Hauraki Gulf, one of the most beautiful sailing venues in the world.

For the vast majority of visitors, Auckland will be their arrival point and their first introduction to the country. Many will treat it merely as a gateway to better things, but they may be pleasantly surprised by what it has to offer. As well as sailing, you can go fishing, swimming or surfing within minutes of the city centre and, in some places, have the beach to yourself. The city also boasts some impressive man-made attractions such as the stunning 360° views from the hypodermic Sky Tower, and its bustling city centre streets and trendy suburbs are home to a thousand high quality restaurants.

Auckland → Colour map 1, C4 Population: 1,320,000.

It is of course standard procedure to arrive in the largest city of any country by air, but somehow, when it is Auckland so very far from home, it presents its own dilemma. For a start you will almost certainly be feeling like death warmed up and look a bit like you've just walked out of the 'bad guys' make-up section on a 'Lord of the Rings' film set. Then, add to that all the preconceptions surrounding New Zealand – the inevitable expectations of sweeping mountain ranges, an empty land not unduly worried about the global population explosion – and poor 'young' Auckland can be a little disappointing. However, put the jet lag aside and New Zealand's largest city will prove to be a pleasant, if transitory, surprise. Here, from the top of the great hypodermic Sky Tower you can marvel at how a metropolis almost the size of Los Angeles can really be so beautiful. ▶▶ *For Sleeping, Eating and other listings, see pages 87-108.*

Ins and outs

Getting there

Airport information Most visitors arrive by air (see page 35). Auckland International Airport (**AKL**) ⓘ *20 km south of centre, T0800-247767, www.auckland-airport.co.nz*, is a relatively small gateway to the nation. On the ground floor there is an **Airport I-Site Information Centre**, T09-2756 467/T0800-282552, open from 0500 until the last flight, which provides transport details, baggage storage and can help book hotels. The hospitality ambassadors (smiley folk in bright blue jackets) or customer service officers (red jackets and splendid hats) can also offer assistance. Airport facilities include shops, food outlets, mailboxes, internet, crèche, free showers (towel hire from the Airways Florist shop on the ground floor) and telephones. Phone cards are sold at the information kiosk and most major outlets on the ground floor. There are also day rooms for hire that contain a bed, desk, TV, coffee, tea and shower facilities, from $30 for four hours (tickets at Airways Florist). Showers are free. ▶▶ *For airline offices, see page 105.*

Transport from the airport Auckland airport is 21 km southwest of the CBD and transport to and from the airport is straightforward. The **Airbus**, T0508-247287, www.airbus.co.nz, is a cheap option leaving the airport every 20-30 minutes from 0600-2200 (from the city 0435- 2250), $15, child $6 one-way. Taxis wait outside the terminal and charge about $40 to the centre. The **Super Shuttle**, T0800-748885, www.supershuttle.co.nz, provides a door-to-door service from $30 one-way. There are no train services.

To get to the city by car from the airport, take the main exit road (George Bolt Memorial Drive) to the intersection with SH20. Follow signs for Auckland City and take the motorway to Queenstown Road exit. Turn right into Queenstown Road and continue straight ahead, through the roundabout into Pah Road which becomes Manukau Road (SH12). Follow Manukau Road and turn right at the traffic lights (before Newmarket) into Alpers Avenue. At the end of Alpers Avenue, turn right into Gillies Avenue then almost immediately left to join SH1 motorway. The last exit to the city centre is Nelson Street.

Getting around

Bikes, scooters and motorcycles These are a brave option in Auckland, given the way people drive. Unless you are an experienced city cyclist, it's safest to stick to walking, buses or a car. However, outside the city centre and major suburbs, bike and motorcycle touring can be a joy. ▶▶ *For rental companies, see Transport, page 106.*

Bus Public transport is a major bone of contention in Auckland as traffic congestion clogs the city's roads and pollutes the air. Although adequate for the average visitor, it is generally poor and improvements are not happening fast enough.

Most central and suburban buses stop at the Britomart Transport Centre (BBT), centrally located between Customs and Quay streets near the waterfront (bottom of Queen Street). Information can be obtained from the terminal itself, all major tourist information offices and by contacting **MAXX**, T09-3666400/T0800-103080, www.maxx.co.nz. This website also offers a convenient journey planner. There are several tourist oriented passes, a 1-day 'Discovery Pass' allowing unlimited travel on bus, ferry and train for $13, or a 3-day 'Rover Pass' for $25 that includes the North Shore ferries.

The excellent hop-on hop-off Auckland City Loop 'Link' bus (lime green) is an ideal way to get about the city centre and charges a flat fare of $1.60 for each journey. The national bus terminal is at the **Sky City Travel Centre**, 102 Hobson Street, Auckland, CBD (below the Sky Tower), T09 5835780, www.intercity.co.nz. Office hours (for sales) are 0700-1950 daily. ▸▸ *For further details, see Transport, page 105.*

Car Most of the major sights and attractions are centrally located and can be accessed on foot or by bus or ferry. For longer stays a car is recommended due to the urban sprawl. Car ownership per capita in Auckland is one of the highest in the world and you will quickly see that Auckland is not only a 'City of Sails' but also a 'City of Wheels'; driving can be hazardous and rush hour is best avoided. Metered and multi-storey parking costs up to $6 an hour and traffic wardens are omnipresent. There are more car rental companies than you could shake a gear stick at, ranging from fully insured, nearly-new cars, to dodgy looking rent-a-dents. ▸▸ *For car rental companies, see Transport, page 106.*

Ferry and water taxi Almost all ferries depart from the historic Ferry Building on the waterfront, at Quay Street. A limited commuter service to some waterside suburbs has been developed, but the vast majority of ferry traffic is tourist-based and operated by **Fullers**, T09-3679111, www.fullers.co.nz. There are many excellent island or harbour locations, trips and tours to choose from.

Taxi All Auckland taxi drivers are required to belong to a registered taxi company. This sets certain standards, but that is no guarantee of good English or not being taken via 'the scenic route'. Typical rates are around $2.75 base charge and then about $2 per kilometre. Taxis are widely available and can be flagged down, ordered by phone or picked up at numerous city centre ranks. ▸▸ *For taxi companies, see Transport, page 106.*

Train Auckland has a scant suburban rail network operating out of the Britomart Terminal between Customs and Quay streets near the waterfront. For local suburban rail information contact **MAXX**, T09-366 6400, www.maxx.co.nz. The Auckland to Wellington 'Overlander' service is operated by **TranzScenic**, T04-495 0775/T0800- 872467, www.tranzscenic.co.nz, which also runs from the Britomart Terminal. Further information about routes and timetables can be obtained from VICs and the terminal itself. Reservations can be made at all mainstream travel agents.

Tourist information
There are Visitor Information Centres (i-SITES) at both airport terminals and two main i-SITES in the CBD: **Atrium** ① *Sky City, corner Victoria and Federal sts, T09-3676009/*

T0800-AUCKLAND, www.aucklandnz.com, daily 0800-2000; and the quieter **Viaduct Harbour** ⓘ next to the Maritime Museum, corner Quay and Hobson sts, T09-3676009, Nov-Apr daily 0800-1700, May-Oct 0900-1730.

If you venture north across the bridge, there are VICs at **North Shore** ⓘ 49 Hurstmere Rd, Takapuna, T09-486 8670, www.northshorenz.com, Mon-Fri 0830- 1700, Sat-Sun 1000-1500, or **Devonport** ⓘ 3 Victoria Rd, T09-446 0677, www.north shorenz.com, daily 0830-1700. All provide piles of free leaflets and many can book accommodation. Don't miss the readily available Auckland A to Z, Auckland What's On, I-Tag Visitors Guide, TNT Magazine and the Backpackers' News – all excellent, up-to-the-minute publications. The New Zealand Herald is the main Auckland and North Island daily, www.nzherald.co.nz. For all things

1 Greater Auckland

environmental and ecological, including nature walks, get yourself to the **Department of Conservation** (DoC) ① *Information Centre, 137 Quay St, Princes Wharf, Downtown, T09-379 6467, www.doc.govt.nz, Mon-Fri 0900-1700, Sat 1000-1500, Sun closed.*

Maps Perhaps your first purchase in Auckland should be a map. The **Auckland Map Centre** ① *National Bank Building, 209 Queen St, T09-309 7725*, has a fine selection of national and local maps, as does **Speciality Maps** ① *Albert St*, and **Whitcoulls** ① *corner of Queen and Victoria sts.* Whitcoulls also has a national travel guide sections, as does **Borders** ① *291 Queen St.*

Various free tourist handouts have some colourful maps of the city, but if you are serious get the *Wises Auckland Compact Handi Map Book* ($25), or at the very least the

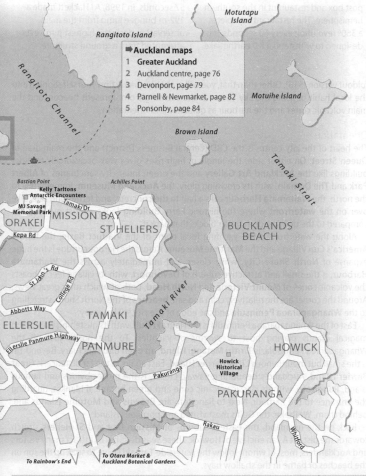

➡ **Auckland maps**
1 **Greater Auckland**
2 Auckland centre, page 76
3 Devonport, page 79
4 Parnell & Newmarket, page 82
5 Ponsonby, page 84

Sky Tower – some statistics

The Sky Tower was opened in 1997 and took two years and eight months to build. At 328 m tall it is the tallest man-made structure in the southern hemisphere and 23 m taller than the AMP Tower in Sydney. The tower's shaft measures 12 m in diameter and its foundations reach 15 m into the earth. It houses the highest weather station, post box and restaurant in the southern hemisphere. The restaurant completes a 360° revolution every 60 seconds. It is designed to withstand a 8.0 earthquake and 200 kph winds. Such winds would only create a 1-m sway of the entire structure. During construction, the tower was kept absolutely vertical using complex telemetry including three global satellite positioning systems. There are 1257 steps to the Sky Deck. The fastest recorded ascent during the annual 'Sky Tower Vertical Challenge' is five minutes, 57 seconds. In 1998, AJ Hackett made a 192-m bungee jump from the main observation deck, the highest jump ever attempted from a ground structure.

foldout version ($16). Other than that, you will probably quickly find yourself slipping into the local habit of using the Sky Tower as the seemingly omnipresent beacon, and the main volcanic cones and the harbour as guidance and orientation.

Orientation

The heart of the city centre is the **CBD** (Central Business District) and the main drag of **Queen Street**. On either side, the jungle of high-rises gives way occasionally to older buildings like the **Auckland Art Gallery** and the green inner city sanctuaries of **Albert Park** and **The Domain**, with its crowning glory, the **Auckland Museum**. Immediately to the north, the **Waitamata Harbour** calls a halt to the concrete, and ferries and sails take over on the **waterfront** where the historic **Ferry Building** looks almost out of place compared to the ugly, modern tower blocks that back it.

Along the waterfront is the yachting focal point of the **Viaduct Basin**, the former **America's Cup Village** and the **Maritime Museum**. Across the Harbour Bridge is the huge expanse of **North Shore City**, while closer, and immediately across the **Waitamata Harbour**, is the small and attractive suburb of **Devonport**, with its village feel. It boasts the volcanic cones of **Mount Victoria** and **North Head**, both of which offer great views. Around the corner are the relatively calm and safe **beaches** of the North Shore, stretching to the **Whangaparaoa Peninsula** and the edge of the city, 40 km away.

East of the Whangaparaoa Peninsula is the **Hauraki Gulf**, with its glistening waters and magical islands playing host to swarms of yachties. To the north, just off the Whangaparaoa Peninsula, is **Tiritiri Matangi Island**, an open bird sanctuary. Beyond Tiri is the small but mountainous **Little Barrier Island**. East again, in the far distance, is **Great Barrier Island**, Auckland's beautiful getaway. Closer, is the most obvious and famous island, **Rangitoto**, with its classic volcanic cone and green botanical blanket, guarding the entrance to the harbour. Next to Rangitoto are **Browns** and **Motuihe islands** and, behind them, **Waiheke**, the Gulf's most visited and populous island.

Back on the mainland, the eastern suburbs of **Mission Bay** and **St Heliers** stretch towards the distant Asian enclave of **Howick**. These seaside suburbs attract many visitors and Aucklanders, most of whom follow the waterside **Tamaki Drive** to soak up the sun on the beaches or bathe in the shallow bays.

Dominating the southern horizon are two of the most well-known volcanic mounts in the city, **Mount Eden** and **One Tree Hill**. South from these impressive landmarks, the low-income suburbs of South Auckland spread unceasingly to the southern city limits of the **Bombay Hills**. Within these suburbs are the **Auckland Botanical Gardens**. Thankfully, nature has called a halt to city expansion to the west in the impressive form of the bush-clad **Waitakere Ranges**. The lower-income suburb streets of **Henderson** and **Glendene** give way to the expensive dwellings of **Titirangi**. The inner western suburbs host the **Auckland Zoo** and **Museum of Transport and Technology (MOTAT)**, both of which border the pleasant lakeside park of Western Springs.

Finally, the best place to find your bearings is the observation decks of the amazing **Sky Tower**, especially on a clear day.

City centre

Sky Tower, Sky City and the Casino
① *Corner of Victoria and Federal sts, T0800-759 2489, www.skycityauckland.co.nz. Observation levels open Sun-Thu 0830-2230, Fri-Sat 0830-2330, $28, child $11. Restaurant open lunch 1000-1500, dinner from 1730, weekend brunch 1000-1500, T09-3636000. SkyJump/SkyWalk, T09-3681835, www.skyjump.co.nz.*

It took almost three years for the Auckland skyline to sprout its great 328-m hypodermic needle, opening in 1997 to a hail of publicity and – back then – a rather skeptical public. But Aucklanders have grown to love their Sky Tower – perhaps because it acts like a beacon and can be seen from as far away as the Coromandel Peninsula. It's an awesome sight and, unless you hate heights, you just have to go up it. It has spacious viewing decks and a revolving restaurant from which you can enjoy the full 360° views. In recent years, perhaps inevitably, it has also become the focus for some lunatic activities including a 192-m controlled bungee known as the 'Sky Jump', and the 'Sky Walk' which involves a leisurely stroll round a 1.2 m-wide platform. ▶▶ *For further details see Activities and tours, page 102.*

The tower's rather nondescript 'grow-bag' is called **Sky City** and claims to be Auckland's largest multi-faceted entertainment and leisure destination. The main casino provides all kinds of gambling and gaming opportunities, restaurants, bars and live entertainment 24 hours a day. Even if you are not a gambler it is well worth a look. Less intimidating is the Sky City Theatre, a 700-seat, state-of-the-art entertainment venue, staging national and international events and productions. As well as the tower's Orbit restaurant (see page 92) there are five other eateries offering everything from Pacific Rim to Chinese, traditional buffet or café-style options.

The waterfront and America's Cup Village
The once sandy beaches of the waterfront have now become cliffs of glass and concrete as the city has grown relentlessly outwards and upwards over the last 150 years. Radiating from the historic **Ferry Building**, built in 1912, the waterfront is the place where the city of concrete becomes the 'City of Sails' and where the locals would say it takes on its proper and distinct character. The waterfront has always been a focus of major activity. In the early years it was the point where exhausted immigrants first disembarked to begin a new life in a new land. Later, the immigrant ships gave way to the fleets of log-laden scows bringing kauri to the timber mills. Today, recreation has taken over, as modern ferries come and go and lines of expensive yachts rock gently together at the **Westhaven Marina**, the largest in the southern hemisphere.

The waterfront has seen perhaps the most rapid development of all, centred around the **Viaduct Basin** – until recently the hallowed home of the America's Cup Village. Even before New Zealand took the cup from the USA's tight grasp in 1995, the Viaduct Basin was a stopover point for the Whitbread Round the World Race (also won by New Zealand in 1994) and the place has become an aquatic stadium of profound celebration. New Zealanders are proud of their yachting heritage and, even outside the fierce competition of the yachting trophy wars, this is reflected on the waters of the Viaduct Basin. Much debate has raged, since the somewhat embarrassing loss of the America's Cup in February 2003, over what will become of the Viaduct Basin and the site of the former syndicate headquarters but, seven years on, it has ballooned with modern development while at the same time maintaining much of its social and aesthetic allure.

New Zealand National Maritime Museum

① *Corner of Quay and Hobson sts, on the waterfront and within easy walking distance of the centre or Britomart Transport Centre, T0800-725897/T09-3730800, www.nzmaritime.org; daily 0900-1700; $16, child $8. Guided tours 1030 and 1300. 'Ted Ashby Heritage Cruise' (1½ hrs) in summer Wed-Sun, $26, child $13 (includes museum entry).*

Even if you are a committed landlubber the New Zealand National Maritime Museum (Te Huiteananui-a-Tangaroa) is a wonderful museum and well worth a visit. Based on the waterfront it depicts a very important aspect of New Zealand's history and the maritime flavour of the 'City of Sails'. Laid out chronologically, you begin with early Maori and Polynesian exploration and arrival before moving through to European maritime history, including immigration. Here, in the replicated living quarters of an early immigrant ship, complete with moving floor and appropriate creaking noises, you cannot help but empathize with the brave souls who made the journey. It is certainly a long way from reclining in an Airbus 380 with a gin and tonic, iTunes and the latest Hollywood movie.

Moving on, you emerge into the galleries of New Zealand's proud yachting history, including the stories of New Zealand's participation and triumphs in the Louis Vuitton Cup, the Whitbread Round the World Yacht Race and, of course, the much-lauded America's Cup. Much of this story is the personal résumé of the late Sir Peter Blake, New Zealand's most famous sailing son who was so tragically murdered in the Amazon in 2002. The centerpiece for the exhibition is the 1995 America's Cup-winning boat NZL32 – *Black Magic*.

A number of cruises are also available from the museum, including the popular 'Ted Ashby Heritage Cruise', aboard the 57-ft traditionally built scow *Ted Ashby* and weekend excursions aboard the unfortunately named but nonetheless charming *SS Puke* – 'The loveliest Little Steamboat Around'. All the vessels are beautiful replicas or originals and it is an ideal opportunity to get out on to the water. Note you can also experience a cruise on board former Americas Cup yachts with **SailNZ** (see page 104).

The museum also houses the scenic and relaxed **Big Boat Café** as well as a maritime shop with nautical gifts and memorabilia.

The Domain → *To get to the Domain, see Auckland Museum, below.*

① *T09-379 2020, Winter Gardens and Fernz Fernery, 0900-1730, free.*

The Domain is one of Auckland's less obvious volcanic cones and New Zealand's oldest park. Originally another enclave and early Maori *pa*, it was formally put aside as a reserve by Governor Hobson in 1840. Within its spacious grounds are a number of historic features including the **Bledisloe** and **Robert Burns Memorial statues** and its crowning glory, the **Auckland Museum** and **War Memorial** (see below). Other points of interest include the **Winter Garden** and **Fernz Fernery** where you can take in the scents of various blooms or study the 300 species of fern on display. The Formal Garden within the Domain was once the site of the Auckland Acclimatisation Society where exotic trees, birds and fish were kept before being released to wreak havoc on indigenous species. The park also has a number of quiet inner city bush walks, some with alluring names such as 'lovers walk', which would fool you into the belief you are far from the city, were it not for occasional glimpse of the Sky Tower through the branches. If you get hungry during your wanderings then the **Domain kiosk** (daily 1000-1500) by the duck pond serves basic snacks and refreshments.

Auckland Museum (Te Papa Whakahiku)

ⓘ *T09-3067067, www.aucklandmuseum.com, daily 1000-1700, $5 donation. Maori performance Jan-Mar 1100, 1200, 1330, 1430; Apr-Dec 1100, 1200, 1330; $25, child $12.50 (includes entry). Guided tours daily 1030, $10, child $5. Most city tour buses stop at the museum, as does the Link bus from the CBD. The museum is also on the 'Coast to Coast' walkway.*

The Auckland Museum, an impressive edifice that crowns the spacious surroundings of the Auckland Domain, houses some wonderful treasures, displayed with flair and imagination. Its most important collection is that of Maori *taonga* (treasures) and Pacific artifacts which, combined, is the largest such collection in the world. Other special attractions include an award-winning Children's Discovery Centre, Social and Settlement History Sections, Natural History Galleries, and 'Scars on the Heart', the story of New Zealanders at war, from the Maori Land Wars in the late 1800s to the campaigns in Gallipoli and Crete in the two world wars of the 20th century. The museum also houses a major national **War Memorial** and hosts the traditional dawn gathering of veterans on Remembrance (Anzac) Day on the forecourt. The most recent addition to the building is 'The Dome' described as a four-storey suspended bowl, clad in Fijian Kauri that hangs over the auditorium and events centre, crowned in copper and glass. This and its surrounding infrastructure increased the footprint of the museum by 60% and it certainly forms a striking first impression from the museum's south entrance.

If you are short of time make sure you see the **Maori Court**, a fascinating collection of pieces from woven baskets to lethal hand weapons carved from bone or greenstone, all centred round the huge 25-m Te Toki a Tipiri war canoe (*waka*) and a beautifully carved meeting house (*hotunui*). A commercial yet entertaining Maori concert is held three to four times daily and guided tours are available.

In the **Natural History Galleries** pay particular attention to the 'Human Impacts' section, which will give you a frightening reality check of how New Zealand has been systematically raped of the vast majority of its once huge indigenous biodiversity from the first day man set foot on the shores of this unspoilt paradise. The **Children's Discovery Centre** is a 'sensory learning feast' that you and the kids might find it hard to drag yourselves away from. There are computers, games and plenty of things to jump on, look through, poke or prod. The museum café is on the ground floor, and there is a well-stocked museum shop.

Auckland Art Gallery (Toi-O-Tamaki)

ⓘ *Corner Wellesley and Lorne streets, T09-3791349, www.aucklandartgallery.co.nz, daily 1000-1700, free, $7 for temporary exhibitions; guided tours at 1400. Both galleries are in close proximity and within easy walking distance from Queen St. The 'Link' bus stops right outside the gallery every 10-20 mins.*

The Auckland Art Gallery is essentially two buildings: one in Kitchener Street and the other

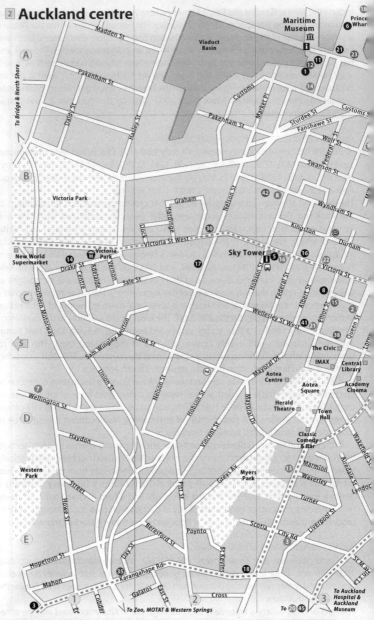

Madden St

Viaduct
Basin

Maritime
Museum

Prince
Wharf 6

A

Pakenham St

18

i

m

1

12 11

21

23

14

To Bridge & North Shore

Daldy St

Hadley St

Customs St

Market Pl

Pakenham St

Sturdee St

Fanshawe St

Wolf St

Federal St

Swanson St

B

Victoria Park

Graham

Hardinge

Dock St

Nelson St

Wyndham St

Kingston

Durham

42 8

30

Victoria St West

Sky Tower

i 5

16

16

New World
Supermarket

14 M

Victoria
Park

Vernon

Safe St

Drake St

Adelaide

Centre

17

Hobson St

Federal St

Albert St

Victoria St

22

8

15

2

Wellesley St West

41

21

Elliot St

Queen St

38

C

Northern Motorway

5

Sam Wingley Morton

Cook St

Union St

Nelson St

Hobson St

Mayoral Dr

The Civic

IMAX

Central
Library

Academy
Cinema

7

Wellington St

Haydon

Aotea
Centre

Aotea
Square

Herald
Theatre

Town
Hall

D

Vincent St

Mayoral Dr

Classic
Comedy
& Bar

Western
Park

Howe St

Street

Pitt St

Grey Av

Myers
Park

13

Marmion

Waverley

Turner

Liverpool St

Airedale St

Lyndo

Scotia

City Rd

3

Hopetoun St

Mahon

Beresford St

Day St

35

Poynto

Karangahape Rd

St Kevins

18

To Auckland
Hospital &
Auckland
Museum

3

Galatos

1

Cobden

East St

2

Cross

St M. a

E 13 St.

To Zoo, MOTAT & Western Springs

To 20 45

→Auckland maps

Queens Wharf

Fullers Ferries

DoC Office

Ferry Building

Quay St

Britomart Rail & Bus Terminal

Waitemata Harbour

To Kelly Tarltons Underwater World

Gore St

Gore La

Commerce St

Fort St

Shortland St

Shortland St

Emily Pl

Anzac Av

Chancery

Eden Cres

Bowen Av

Waterloo Quadrant

Parliament

Princes St

Kitchener St

Albert Park

Alfred

Symonds St

Alten Rd

Auckland Art Gallery

Wellesley St East

Grafton Rd

St Paul St

Mount St

Stanley

Auckland Domain

Grafton Rd

Karl

Moehau

High St

N

200 metres
200 yards

Sleeping

Aspen House **5** *B5*
Auckland City
  YHA **3** *E3*
Base Backpackers **2** *C3*
Bond Street
  Lodge **20** *F2*
Columbia **15** *E4*
Elliott St
  Apartments **21** *C3*
Empire
  Backpackers **1** *E4*
Freemans B&B **7** *D1*
Heritage **8** *B3*
Hilton & White
  Restaurant **18** *A3*
Princetown
  Backpackers **17** *D4*
Quay West **12** *B3*
Quest Auckland **13** *D3*
Sebel **14** *A3*
Sky City Grand **16** *C3*
Surf & Snow **22** *C3*

Eating

Cin Cin **4** *A4*
Euro **6** *A3*
Food hall on Atrium
  on Elliot **8** *C3*
French Café **9** *D4*
Gallery Café **10** *D4*
Harbourside Seafood
  Bar & Grill **4** *A4*
Joy Bong **3** *F1*
Kermadec **11** *A3*

Mecca **2** *C4*
Mexican Café **16** *C3*
Middle East Café **41** *C3*
O'Connell Street
  Bistro **29** *B4*
Orbit & Observatory
  (Sky Tower) **5** *C3*
Rakinos **13** *C4*
Sake Bar Rikka **14** *C1*
Soul **1** *A3*
Toto **17** *C2*
Verona **18** *E2*
Vertigo at Mercure
  Hotel **7** *A4*
Vulcan **19** *B4*
White Lady **20** *B4*
Wildfire
  Churrascaria **21** *A3*

Bars & clubs

Belgian Beer
  Café **22** *B4*
Club 4:20 **35** *E1*
Danny Doolans **12** *A3*
Deschlers **27** *C4*
Empire **30** *B2*
Galbraith's Ale
  House **45** *F2*
London **38** *C3*
Margaritas **15** *C3*
Minus 5 **23** *A3*
Muddy Farmer **42** *B3*

Link bus route - - -

on the corner of Wellesley Street and Lorne Street in the city centre. They combine to form the largest and most comprehensive collection of art in the country. The first building The Main Gallery (Kitchener Street) is over 100 years old and is currently undergoing major reconstruction. In the meantime, the New Gallery (corner of Wellesley and Lorne streets) hosts all the exhibitions from the permanent collections. These include some of the better-known international masters, particularly 17th-century works, but from a national perspective it is the works by Charles Goldie and Gottfried Lindauer that are of particular interest. Goldie and Lindauer were early European settlers who specialized in oil landscapes and portraits of Maori elders in the 18th and 19th centuries. The works of Goldie are impressive to say the least, with their almost Pre-Raphaelite detail bringing the portraits to life, particularly the detail of the moko (Maori facial tattoos). However, one has to be a little wary of the romanticism of the depictions of Maori life as seen through early European eyes: the warrior savages being civilized by those who think they know better. Also look out for works by Colin McCahon one of the nation's more contemporary artists and hugely respected. *Reuben Café* ⓘ *weekdays 0700-1600, Sat/Sun 0900-1530*, is situated next to the New Gallery, with indoor and outdoor seating overlooking Khartoum Place.

Albert Park
Behind the art gallery, Albert Park is the informal lunchtime escape for city suits and university students. The park was formerly another Maori *pa* and later, during the Second World War, the site of concrete bunkers. Manicured flowerbeds, statues, a floral clock and old spider-like fig trees have now thankfully replaced these sites. It's a great place to bring a sandwich, escape the noise and look up at the Sky Tower.

North Shore

North Shore City, better known as the North Shore, is most famous for the miles of coastline and pretty bays that fringe its quiet eastern suburbs. Many British immigrants reside north of the bridge and in summer you will find them on one of the many sheltered beaches enjoying the sun and aquatic delights they never could back home. The commercial centre is **Takapuna**, with its attractive range of modern shops, popular restaurants and bars; but it is **Devonport** with its history, city views and village feel that deservedly attracts most tourists.

Ins and outs
Getting there Devonport is 12 km from the city centre across the Harbour Bridge. By car, take the Takapuna off ramp, turn right on Lake Road and just keep going. Alternatively, take Bus 813 from the BBT. The North Shore can also be accessed by boat, **Fullers Ferry** ⓘ *Ferry Building, Quay St, T09-367 9111, www.fullers.co.nz, Mon-Thu every 30 mins 0615-2030, then hourly until 2300, Fri-Sun every 30 mins 0610-0030, last sailing 0100; $10 return, child $5.*

The **Devonport Explorer Tour** ⓘ *T09-357 6366, www.devonporttours.co.nz, daily, every hour 1025-1525, 2 hrs, $30*, is a combination of ferry, bus and walking which is personally guided and includes North Head and Mount Victoria. It also offers a tour option with a buffet lunch at McHughs of Cheltenham (departs 1100, from $50) and a dinner option at the Watermark Restaurant (departs 1800, from $70).

Devonport VIC (I-Site) ⓘ *3 Victoria St, T09-446 0677, www.northshorenz.com, daily 0800-1700*, is almost next door to the historic Esplanade Hotel. The centre and its friendly staff will provide information on historic sights, the best short walks and places to stay.

Devonport, Mount Victoria and North Head

The heart of North Shore City is in **Devonport**. This is the area's oldest and most popular settlement, lying on the shores of its southernmost edge. Devonport's greatest asset is the fact that it is so near yet so far from the city centre, creating a distinct village feel. A 10-minute ferry ride from the city centre, or a 12-km drive across the Harbour Bridge, brings you to the heart of this picturesque little suburb. Victorian villas, craft shops, cafés and pleasant short walks all lie in wait, dominated by its two volcanoes, Mount Victoria and North Head, both of which offer great views. For a longer stay try one of its many bed and breakfast hideaways.

According to Maori tradition the great ancestral canoe, Tainui, rested here on its coastal explorations in or around the 14th century, before both Mount Victoria and North Head were, not surprisingly, settled by the Maori and used as *pa*. A village called Flagstaff on the western side of Mount Victoria was one of Auckland's earliest European settlements before land sales expanded in all directions to eventually form the suburb and naval base called Devonport – after its namesake in southwest Devon, England.

If time is short take the short walk to **North Head** which guards the entrance to Waitemata harbour. Follow the shore east along the pohutukawa-lined King Edward Parade for views of the harbour, alive with all manner of craft, from jet skis to supply ships. From there you can climb up and all around North Head and enjoy the commanding views back across the city and the Hauraki Gulf. The warren of underground tunnels and bunkers built amidst the hysteria of various potential invasions during both world wars provide added interest.

From North Head climb down to **Cheltenham Beach**, a popular swimming and sunbathing spot in summer and one that gives the most spectacular and almost surreal view of the volcanic island of **Rangitoto**. It is a particular delight at sunrise. On your return to the village, if you are feeling energetic, try to include a climb to the summit of **Mount**

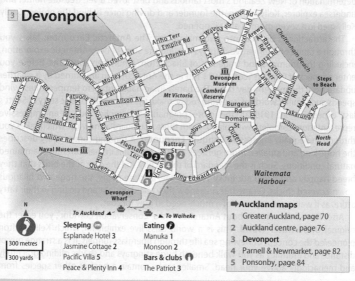

③ Devonport

Sleeping 🛏
Esplanade Hotel 3
Jasmine Cottage 2
Pacific Villa 5
Peace & Plenty Inn 4

Eating 🍴
Manuka 1
Monsoon 2

Bars & clubs 🍸
The Patriot 3

To Auckland ◄ To Waiheke ►

300 metres
300 yards

➡ **Auckland maps**
1 Greater Auckland, page 70
2 Auckland centre, page 76
3 **Devonport**
4 Parnell & Newmarket, page 82
5 Ponsonby, page 84

Victoria. Equally stunning views of the city can be had from here; its slopes retain the remnants of the Maori *pa*. From there you can wander to Victoria Road for lunch or some shopping before catching a ferry back to the city.

The **Naval Museum** ① *Spring St, T09-445 5186, daily 1000-1630, free,* is best left to those with a specific interest. The recently renovated **Devonport Museum** ① *31a Vauxhall Rd, T09-445 2661, Sat-Sun 1400-1600, free,* in the Cambria Reserve, is small but still worth a look.

Devonport is famous for its resident artists and there are a number of quality galleries. **Art of this World** ① *Queen's Parade, across the road from the wharf, T09- 446 0926,* is the best, but the **Flagstaff** ① *30 Victoria Rd, T09-445 1142,* and **Art by the Sea** ① *King Edward Parade, T09-445 6665,* are also worth a look.

The **Devonport Food Wine and Music Festival** is held every February. Shopping in the village is a delight and there are a number of interesting craft shops, but you may be hard pressed to drag yourself away from the two excellent second-hand bookshop: **Evergreen Books** on Victoria Road.

City East

Kelly Tarlton's Antarctic Encounter and Underwater World

① *23 Tamaki Drive, T09-5315065, www.kellytarltons.co.nz, daily 0900-1800, $29, child $15. Kelly Tarlton's operates a free shuttle between Sky City Atrium and Kelly Tarlton's daily between 0900-1700. Or, it is a scenic 6-km walk along the waterfront and Tamaki Drive.*

A 10-minute drive east of the city centre along Tamaki Drive is Kelly Tarlton's Antarctic Encounter and Underwater World. The development is housed within the walls of Auckland City's old disused sewage holding tanks beneath the car park and Tamaki Drive itself. It is a fascinating concept, and typical of the imagination, ingenuity and determination of New Zealand's most famous and best-loved diver, treasure hunter and undersea explorer, Kelly Tarlton, the founder and driving force behind the project. Sadly Kelly died just seven months after it opened.

The attraction is divided into two main parts. The **Antarctic Encounter**, takes you through a range of informative displays relating the story of early Antarctic exploration, including the triumphs and tragedies of Shackleton, Amundsen and Scott. Before you enter a replica of Captain Scott's 1911 hut in the Antarctic, you are primed by a weather update from the modern-day base. The barely imaginable sub-zero temperatures, wind speeds and familiar words of 'snowing today' make the famous and tragic story of Scott's last expedition in 1910 all the more poignant. The replica hut is an impressive representation, complete with piano. From there you board a snow cat which takes you through the equally impressive **Penguin Encounter**. A running commentary describes the huge king and smaller, more genteel, gentoo penguins in their carefully maintained natural conditions. Such is the standard of the facility and the care of the birds that they breed happily and if you are lucky you will see, at close range, the huge and hilarious down-covered chicks. On the freezing snow they stand upright and dozing in their tatty attire, as if waiting in a queue for a much-needed new fur coat.

After more information about Antarctica and a 'Conservation Corridor', you enter the original **Underwater World**. This is a world-class live exhibit for which Kelly Tarlton pioneered the concept of viewing sea life through fiberglass tunnels. It is a strange mix of distance and intimacy as you walk beneath huge stingrays and sharks gliding gracefully and menacingly above your head. Smaller tanks contain a host of other species from beautiful sea horses to ugly moray eels and the highly poisonous scorpion fish. Open rock pools provide a tremendous learning experience for kids. For the more adventurous there are opportunities to dive with sharks from $155 or enter a glorified 'Shark cage' from $50.

Tamaki Drive, Mission Bay and St Heliers

On a sunny afternoon, especially at the weekend, there is almost no better place to be in central Auckland than somewhere along Tamaki Drive. All along its 9-km length it is both a buzz of activity and a haven of relaxation. Round every corner the view of Rangitoto and yachts plying the harbour predominate. You will see people roller- blading, walking, jogging and cycling, leaving the road to the vintage cars and city posers. Bike and rollerblade hire is readily available along the route for $8-12 per hour.

If you have time, take the short walk up the hill to the **M J Savage Memorial Park**, from where the view of the harbour mouth and Rangitoto is wonderful. This is a rather elegant memorial to the nation's first Labour prime minister. It was here, at Bastion Point, where one of the most serious recent altercations occurred between Maori and *Pakeha* in the late 1970s. The matter, as ever, concerning land ownership and sale, was eventually settled after a 17-month stand-off between police and the local Nga-Whatua, whose fine *marae* (sacred courtyard) sits on the southern edge of the park. There are many fine cafés and restaurants along Tamaki, and in **Mission Bay** and **St Heliers**, from which to sit back and watch the sun set before perhaps taking in a movie at the art deco **Berkley Cinema** ① *Mission Bay, T09-521 9222*. **Achilles Point**, at the very end of Tamaki Drive, with its secluded beach, is a favourite spot for lovebirds and naturist bathers, and has wonderful views over the gulf and back towards the city.

Parnell and Newmarket → *See map page 82.*

Trendy Parnell, 2 km east of the city centre, was once a rather run-down suburb, but in recent years it has undergone a dramatic transformation which has seen it almost overtake Devonport and Ponsonby in the popularity and fashion stakes. It has the same 'village within a city' feel as Devonport, with tiny brick-paved lanes and boutique style outlets, and boasts some of Auckland's finest galleries, shops and restaurants.

At the top of Parnell Rise is the recently finished **Auckland Cathedral of the Holy Trinity** ① *T09-303 9500, www.holy-trinity.org.nz, Mon-Fri 1000-1600, Sat and Sun 1300-1700, free*, whose angular structure is aesthetically interesting but nothing compared to the beautiful stained-glass windows and 29-ton organ within. Guided tours and an audio-visual display are both available. The older **Cathedral of St Mary** ① *same opening hours*, which now rests in its big sister's shadow, is one of the largest wooden churches in the world and its wonderfully peaceful interior is a delight. The stained-glass windows are beautiful, as is the entire wooden construction. There is usually a volunteer guide on hand who will proudly explain the 110-year history and show you pictures of how the grand old building was moved to its present site from across the road in 1984. The café (daily from 0700) on the cathedral forecourt has some great food and is an excellent place to sit and admire its unusual architecture.

Around the corner in Ayr Street you will find **Kinder House** ① *2 Ayr St, T09-379 4008, Tue-Sun 1100-1500, $4*, a recently renovated, two-storey building originally built in 1856 as the home of pioneer churchman and artist John Kinder. It displays some of his art works. A little further down Ayr Street is **Ewelme Cottage** ① *14 Ayr St, T09- 379 0202*,

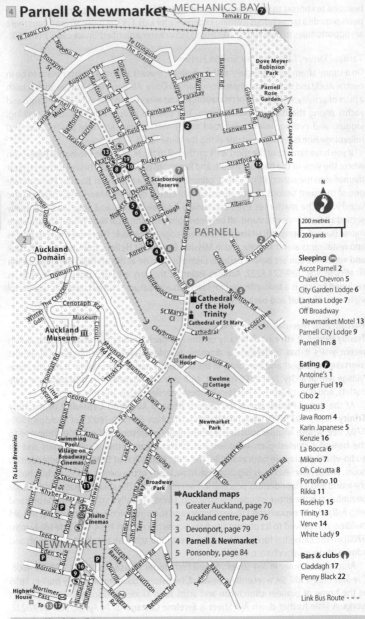

MECHANICS BAY

Tamaki Dr

Te Taou Cres

Te Uringutu
The Strand

Dove Meyer
Robinson
Park

Parnell
Rose
Garden

To St Stephen's Chapel

Kenwyn St

Balfour Rd

Cleveland Rd

Stanwell St

Avon St   Avon La

Stratford St

Ruskin St

Scarborough
Reserve

PARNELL

Scarborough
La

Auckland
Domain

Auckland
Museum

Cathedral
of the Holy
Trinity

Cathedral of St Mary

Cathedral
Pl

Kinder
House

Ewelme
Cottage

Newmarket
Park

Broadway
Park

To Lion Breweries

Swimming
Pool/
Village on
Broadway
Cinemas

Rialto
Cinemas

Highwic
House

NEWMARKET

N

200 metres
200 yards

Sleeping
Ascot Parnell **2**
Chalet Chevron **5**
City Garden Lodge **6**
Lantana Lodge **7**
Off Broadway
  Newmarket Motel **13**
Parnell City Lodge **9**
Parnell Inn **8**

Eating
Antoine's **1**
Burger Fuel **19**
Cibo **2**
Iguacu **3**
Java Room **4**
Karin Japanese **5**
Kenzie **16**
La Bocca **6**
Mikano **7**
Oh Calcutta **8**
Portofino **10**
Rikka **11**
Rosehip **15**
Trinity **13**
Verve **14**
White Lady **9**

Bars & clubs
Claddagh **17**
Penny Black **22**

Link Bus Route · · ·

➡ **Auckland maps**
1 Greater Auckland, page 70
2 Auckland centre, page 76
3 Devonport, page 79
4 **Parnell & Newmarket**
5 Ponsonby, page 84

Wed-Sun 1030-1200 and 1300-1630, $7.50 (joint ticket with Highwic House in Newmarket), built in 1863 as the Auckland home of the family of Archdeacon Vicesimus Lush. It was altered in 1882 but has remained largely unchanged and contains a collection of colonial furniture and household effects.

Back towards the harbour in Judges Bay is the very cute **St Stephen's Chapel**, one of a number of examples designed by Frederick Thatcher, the favourite architect of the former prominent missionary bishop, George Selwyn. It was one of Auckland's first churches. Although it is not generally open to the public you can have a peek in the window. Access to the park is off Gladstone and Judges Bay Roads. **Parnell Rose Gardens** nearby are a charming escape with rows of scented varieties.

South of the cathedral, Parnell merges into the more modern commercial centre and suburb of **Newmarket** (www.newmarket.net.nz) which is best known for its shops, restaurants, cafés and entertainment (see pages 93and 97). Historians may be interested in the grand **Highwic House** ① *40 Gillies Av, T09-524 5729, Wed-Sun 1030- 1200 and 1300-1630, $7.50, the former home (in the 1860s) of 'colonial gentleman of property' Alfred Buckland*.

Howick

Further east beyond the rather seedy suburb of Panmure is Howick, the largest Asian enclave in Auckland. The suburb is a concrete jungle but it has a pleasant centre with some interesting shops. The biggest attraction in these parts is the award-winning **Howick Historical Village** ① *Bells Rd, Lloyd Elsmore Park, Pakuranga, T09-576 9506, www.fencible.org.nz, daily 1000-1600, $14, child $7; Howick and Eastern buses run a regularly from the city centre, T09-366 6400*. This is a fine example of a restored 'Fencible settlement'. Fencibles were pensioned British soldiers re-enlisted to defend the sites against the Maori and the French in the early years of Auckland settlement and expansion. The village is a 'living museum' where staff in period clothing entertains. The **Homestead Café**, with its suitably historic theme, is also on site.

City West

Ponsonby and Herne Bay

Although offering little in the way of conventional tourist attractions, a wander round Ponsonby and Herne Bay does present an example of upmarket Auckland living and culture. For the last two decades the back streets of both postcodes have steadily developed as the reserve of the well-off, as rows of renovated villas and designer homes attest. But, of course, in Ponsonby any elitism is challenged by Ponsonby's main drag, which is itself as cosmopolitan and up beat as it ever has been. There you can be well-off, well-on, or a little out of order, it matters not.

Auckland Zoo

① *T09-360 3819, www.aucklandzoo.co.nz, daily 0930-1730, $18, child $9, 5 mins' drive from the centre; from the Great Western Motorway take the Western Springs off ramp and follow signs, free car parking. Or take Explorer Bus or Bus 045 from the city centre.*

Set in pleasant parkland next to Western Springs and 6 km west of the city centre is New Zealand's premier wild animal collection. It has kept pace with the more conservation-minded function of zoos and is worth a visit. The zoo claims to be leading the way in the breeding of native species including **kiwi** and **tuatara** – both of which are

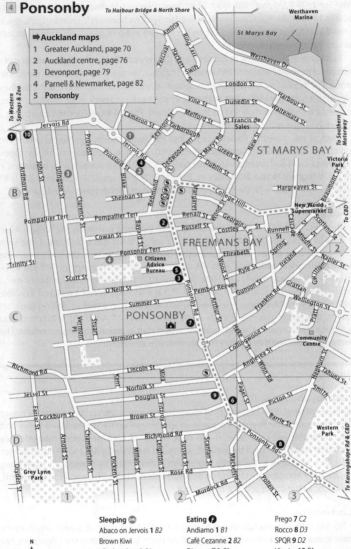

To Harbour Bridge & North Shore

Westhaven Marina

St Marys Bay

➡ Auckland maps
1 Greater Auckland, page 70
2 Auckland centre, page 76
3 Devonport, page 79
4 Parnell & Newmarket, page 82
5 Ponsonby

ST MARYS BAY

FREEMANS BAY

PONSONBY

Community Centre

Western Park

Citizens Advice Bureau

Grey Lynn Park

N

200 metres
200 yards

Sleeping
Abaco on Jervois **1** *B2*
Brown Kiwi
  Backpackers **2** *B2*
Colonial Cottage **3** *B1*
Great Ponsonby
  B&B **4** *C1*

Eating
Andiamo **1** *B1*
Café Cezanne **2** *B2*
Dizengoff **3** *C2*
Fusion Café **4** *B2*
GPK **5** *C2*
Ponsonby Fresh Fish
  & Chip Co **6** *D2*

Prego **7** *C2*
Rocco **8** *D3*
SPQR **9** *D2*
Vinnies **10** *B1*

Link Bus Route - - -

on display. All the old favourites are also there – elephants (sometimes taken on walkabout around the zoo), giraffes, hippos, tigers and orangutans.

Auckland Zoo has gradually developed some imaginative themed exhibits with sponsorship from corporate New Zealand. The huge walk-through aviary, alive with the song of native bird life, is a must-see, as is the 'Newstalk ZB Rainforest' where you feel more captive than the obscenely laid-back spider monkeys. More recent additions include 'Pridelands', the spacious home of the giraffe, lion and zebra with its adjoining 'Hippo River' and a new state-of-the-art seal and penguin exhibit. 'KidZone' provides the usual touchy-feelies with rabbits and other assorted furry friends. Several tours (from $150, T09-3604700) are also offered including the increasingly popular behind-the-scenes animal encounters.

Museum of Transport, Technology and Social History
ⓘ T09-815 5800, www.motat.org.nz, daily 1000-1700, $14, child $7. By car, follow the Western Springs Motorway, taking the Western Springs turning; or take Bus 045 from Customs St in the city centre, every 15 mins, 30-min journey.

The Museum of Transport, Technology and Social History (MOTAT) is on the Great North Road, 4 km west of the city next to the attractive parklands of Western Springs and near the Auckland Zoo. It was opened in 1967 and is sadly showing its age. A mish-mash of tired-looking buildings over two sites houses many and varied exhibits, from vintage cars, fire engines and motorcycles to telephone boxes and printing presses. It is in great need of a major revamp, but trainspotters, and those looking for somewhere else to take the kids on a rainy day, may find it worth a visit.

The second site, the **Sir Keith Park Memorial Site** (named after New Zealand's most famous war time aviator) concerns all things to do with aviation, rail and the military, including a restored flying boat. The sites are connected by a tramline, which passes Western Springs Park and stops at the zoo on the way.

City South

Mount Eden
At 196 m Mount Eden, the closest volcano to the city centre, provides a spectacular view and the vast, almost surreal crater gets your imagination running wild as you picture it 'going off'. The best time to come here is at dawn, especially on misty winter mornings, when it can be a photographer's delight, and you can avoid the coach-loads of visitors.

At the southern base of Mount Eden, **Eden Gardens** ⓘ 24 Omana Av, T09- 638 8395, daily 0900-1630, $6, child free, concessions available, café 1000-1600, is a great place for lovers of all things green that grow. It is an all-seasons garden with a fine variety of flowering shrubs and New Zealand natives. Mount Eden village itself is worth a look, boasting some interesting shops and a number of fine cafés and restaurants. Mount Eden is a long walk from the city centre, and given the climb you might be better off taking Bus 274 or 275 from the BBT in the CBD.

Cornwall Park and One Tree Hill
ⓘ Cornwall Park Visitor Centre, T09-630 8485, www.cornwallpark.co.nz, 1000-1600, free. Café and free 'points of interest' trail leaflet available.

Just to the south of Mount Eden, and 5 km south of the Sky Tower, is Cornwall Park, a great escape from the hustle and bustle of city life, as the hordes of joggers and picnic-carrying locals will testify. It's most famous for its crowning glory, "One Tree Hill" (now minus said tree) but also the well-preserved remains of Maori *pa* on and around the summit. Kiwi Tamaki, the great chief of the Nga Marama, lived here during the mid-18th century with his thousands of *whanau* (family) and followers, attracted by the rich pickings of the region's coast and its fertile soils. His claim to the region ended after being routed by sub-tribes from the north and his people being decimated by a smallpox epidemic introduced by the Europeans. Around the summit, if you look carefully, you will see the grass-covered terraces on which sat dwellings and the 'kumara pits' scattered beside them. With the land essentially vacant when the first European settlers arrived, it was the Scot, Logan Campbell, the most powerful and well-known of the new capital's residents, who eventually took ownership. Shortly before his arrival, a single Totara tree stood proudly on the summit. This had already given rise to the hill's Maori name, *Te-Totara-a-Ahua*, meaning 'Hill of the single Totara'. Early settlers rudely cut down this tree in 1852 and it was Campbell who planted several trees in its place, including the lonesome pine you could see until its demise in 2001. The prosperous Campbell, mayor and 'Father of Auckland', donated his estate (now the park) to the people of New Zealand to commemorate the visit in 1901 of the heirs to the throne, the Duke and Duchess of Cornwall – hence the name.

At the base of the hill is a visitor centre in **Huia Lodge**, Campbell's original gatekeeper's house. It houses some interesting displays and a video surrounding the natural and human history of the park. Across the road is the simple and faithfully restored **Acacia Cottage** ① *dawn till dusk, free,* in which Campbell himself lived, though the building itself originally stood in the city centre and was relocated here in the 1920s.

Also within the park boundary at its southern end is the **Auckland Observatory** ① *T09-624 1246, www.stardome.org.nz, times and events vary; standard viewing session with show $16, child $8. To get there by car: from SH1 take the Greenlane off ramp, the main entrance to the park is off Green Lane West. By Bus: 302, 305 or 312 depart regularly from the city centre.* This is the official home of Auckland's star gazers, and also contains the **Stardome Planetarium**, a cosmic multimedia experience played out on the ceiling for the general public. Outdoor telescope viewing sessions and special events are also held, depending on what the weather and the heavens are up to. You can even 'adopt a star', an interesting concept that will probably have you trying to find it again, for the rest of your life.

Rainbow's End

① *Near the Manukau Shopping complex, corner of Great South and Wiri Station Rd, Manukau, T09-262 2030, www.rainbowsend.co.nz, daily 1000-1700. All day unlimited rides $45, children $35, spectator only $16. By car, head south and take the Manukau off ramp from SH1, it is a further 500 m. Buses 327, 347, 447, 457, 467, 487 or 497 from the city centre.*

Rainbow's End is advertised as '23 acres of fun'. It's New Zealand's largest theme park and has rides and attractions with such alluring and stomach-churning names as the 'Corkscrew Rollercoaster', 'Power Surge' and 'The Invader'. Along with these are old favourites like dodgems, go-karts, bumper boats, mini golf and an interactive games arcade. Even small kids and cowardly parents are catered for in the more sedate 'Land Castle'.

Auckland Botanical Gardens

① *T09-267 1457, daily 0800-dusk, free. Visitor Centre: Mon-Fri 0900-1600, Sat and Sun 1000-1600; café 0830-1630. By car, head south, take the Manurewa off ramp from SH1, turn left into Hill Rd. Stagecoach buses (Papakura, Pukekohe or Drury) leave from the BBT every 15 mins; alight in Great South Rd, Manurewa, just before Hill Rd.*

In Manurewa, 20 minutes south of the city centre, are the Auckland Botanical Gardens. Since planting first began in 1974 an extensive 64-ha, 10,000-plant collection has sprouted, consisting mostly of New Zealand natives. There is also an ornamental lake, a nature trail and a handsome and wonderfully fragrant display of New Zealand-bred roses. The gardens also have an interpretative visitor centre, an attractive café and a library. The annual Ellerslie Flower Show, which is the southern hemisphere's most illustrious gardening and horticultural event, was held here for a number of years but, thanks to its huge popularity, it has now been relocated to Christchurch (see page 489).

Otara Market
ⓘ T09-274 0830, every Sat 0600-1100. By car, head south and take the Otara off ramp from SH1. Buses 487/497 from the BBT, 1 hr.

The southern suburbs are the poorest part of the city. They can be dangerous and are not a place to stray, especially at night. However, they are definitely the place to experience the atmosphere of urban Maori or Pacific Island living. The Otara Market, held every Saturday morning in the Otara town centre car park, 18 km south of the city centre, is ideal for this and is thought to be the largest Maori and Polynesian market in the world. Like most street markets there is always a lot of nonsense for sale but some of the clothes, fabrics and certainly the fruit and vegetables are weird, wonderful and reasonably priced. Try some yams or *taro* – a type of vegetable and traditional staple diet for many native Polynesians.

⊙Auckland listings

For Sleeping and Eating price codes and other relevant information, see Essentials pages 44-50.

⬤ Sleeping

As you might expect of the country's largest city and principal arrival point, Auckland is not short of accommodation. Most of the major hotels are to be found in the city centre, particularly on the waterfront or on either side of Queen St. There are also hundreds of B&Bs and homestays available, but these tend to be concentrated in the better-known suburbs like Parnell and Ponsonby. There are lots of motels throughout the city, mostly in the suburbs of Greenlane and in Manukau and Mangere, the latter 2 being near the airport. Self-catering can be readily found in all types of accommodation, but the city centre plays host to a number of plush apartment buildings, most at the higher range of the market. If you are travelling alone and intend to stay longer than a few days, a flatshare is undoubtedly the best and cheapest option; check the Sat listings in the *New Zealand Herald*, but start hunting early. With New

Zealand being such a huge backpacker destination, there are many hostels, from the awful to the plush, and the rowdy to the sedate. They, too, are mostly in the city centre or the more happening suburbs like Parnell. The popular and professional YHA, www.yha.co.nz, has 2 hostels in Auckland and although perfectly functional they do not reflect the aesthetic quality of many other finer establishments throughout the country.

Be warned: there aren't many motorcamps in Auckland and most campsites are where they should be – amid the beauty of the surrounding countryside parks and on the many islands of the Hauraki Gulf. The main VICs will help you find what you are looking for and provide a booking service (see page 69).

Campsites
Auckland Regional Parks Campsites, T09-3662000, www.arc.govt.nz/parks/ our-parks/stay-in-a-park/camping-pass.cfm. There are 22 regional parks in and around Auckland and 39 have basic facility vehicle and backpack campsites. An annual campsite

pass is $30, child $12. DoC also has many regional campsites and administer almost all the Hauraki Island campsites. For information contact **DoC**, T09-379 6479.

Motels

There are lots on Kirkbride Rd and McKenzie Rd in Mangere, near the airport. There are also a huge number on Great South Rd; they are similar in style and price and include:

AL Oak Tree Lodge, (104), T09-524 2211, www.oaktree.co.nz.

A Hansen's Cottage Motel, (96), T09-520 2804, www.ascotstar.co.nz.

A Greenlane Manor, (353), T09-571 2167, www.greenlanemanor.co.nz.

Motorcamps

All the following are in the **B-D** price range.

Avondale Motor Park, 46 Bollard Av, Avondale, T09-828 7228, www.auckland motorpark.co.nz. Four-star, 15 mins from the centre, with all the usual facilities plus a gaggle of friendly ducks. Close to the metro train station.

Manukau Top Ten Holiday Park, 902 Great South Rd, Manukau City, T09-266 8016, www.manukautop10.co.nz. Handy for the airport or for those heading south.

North Shore Motels and Top Ten Holiday Park, 52 Northcote Rd, Takapuna, T09-418 2578, www.nsmotels.co.nz. The most popular holiday park in the city offering lodges, motel and cabin accommodation as well as the usual reliable Top Ten motorcamp facilities. 5 mins to the beach.

Remuera Motor Lodge and Inner City Camping Ground, 16 Minto Rd, Remuera, T09-524 5126, remlodge@ihug.co.nz. The only traditional-style motorcamp near the centre. Quiet bush setting, standard facilities.

Self-catering

Many hotels also offer self-catering. The following are modern establishments located in the city centre.

L Quest Auckland, 62 Queen St, T09-3669680/T0800-456647, www.questapartments.com.au.

AL Elliott St Apartments, corner of Elliott and Wellesley sts, T09-308 9334, www.esapts.co.nz.

City centre *p73, map p76*

L Heritage Hotel, 35 Hobson St, T09-379 8553, www.heritagehotels.co.nz. With more rooms than any other hotel in the country, the Heritage is more like a village complex. It offers a wide range of luxury and standard en suite options, most of which have great views. The indoor and outdoor recreation areas are fantastic.

L Hilton Hotel, Princes Wharf, 147 Quay St, T09-978 2000, www.hilton.com. Making its mark during the America's Cup, the Hilton sits in an enviable position on Princes Wharf, overlooking the harbour on both sides, and only a short stroll from the city centre. Contemporary, luxury and boutique in style the service is naturally first class, but for many it is the in-house restaurant, **White**, which really exceeds expectations. Classy yet informal it offers memorable views across the harbour. In-house health and beauty spa.

L Quay West, 8 Albert St, T09-309 6000/ T0800-507903, www.mirvachotels.com.au. Standard well-established, 5-star option in the CBD. Rooms are spacious and exquisite, the views even better; the Roman pool and spa are so cute you will probably spend most of your stay there. Facilities include internet and a reputable in-house bar and restaurant offering contemporary New Zealand cuisine. Off-street parking.

L The Sebel Suites, corner of Hobson St and Customs St West, T09-978 4000/ T0800-937373, www.mirvac hotels.com.au. Ideally situated overlooking the Viaduct Basin and former America's Cup Village. It offers high standards of suite-style accommodation.

L Sky City Grand Hotel, corner of Victoria and Federal sts, T09-363 7000, www.skycity auckland.co.nz. One of the most popular 5-star offerings, right in the heart of the city and very handy for facilities within the Sky City complex. It offers an impressive marriage of luxurious quality and modern style with elegant standard or executive suites and premium self-contained rooms, all with the usual 5-star features. In-house facilities include a heated lap pool, gym, health and beauty spa, sauna and a rather noisy sun deck.

AL-A Columbia Apartment Hotel, 15 Whitaker Pl, T09- 963 8600, www.columbiahotel.co.nz. Modern multi-storey with an almost minimalist retro feel. 1- to 2-bedroom units and budget studios, some with internet port and all with en suite, Sky TV. Very clean, good facilities, and within a short walk of Queen St.

AL-A Freemans B&B, 65 Wellington St, T09-376 5046, www.freemansbandb.co.nz. Long-established and best known for its handy location than anything else. B&B and self-contained options within walking distance of the centre.

B-C Aspen House, 62 Emily Pl, T09-379 6633, www.aspenhouse.co.nz. A no-nonsense cheaper and eco-conscious hotel, well placed, comfortable and clean. Standard or connecting rooms with TV. Some rooms are small which is reflected in the price. Wi-Fi, free breakfast and undercover parking $10 per night. The 'CityHop' car service enables guests to hire immensely cute little cars by the hour – a fine short-term alternative to car hire. Recommended.

B-D Surf and Snow, corner of Victoria St and Albert St, T09-363 8889, www.surfand snow.co.nz. A new hostel set in a historic building with high ceilings and polished floors. Good, modern facilities, spotless standard or en-suite singles/doubles and dorms. Good location and the service is pretty polished too.

C Auckland City YHA, corner of City Rd and Liverpool St, T09-309 2802/T0800-278299, yhaauck@yha.org.nz. One of 2 YHAs in Auckland, the other is just around the corner, at 5 Turner St, T09-302 8200/T0800-278299. Both are reliable with modern and clean facilities, good kitchen, pleasant friendly atmosphere, in-house bistro. 4- and 5-star Qualmark ratings respectively.

C-D Base Auckland Central Backpackers (ACB), corner of 229 Queen St and Darby St,

T09-358 4877, www.acb.co.nz. The busiest and most high-profile of the central backpacker hostels (now part of the Base chain of hostels). Simple clean accommodation, 24-hr reception, security, café, bar, internet and a travel shop attached. The travel shop staff are very knowledgeable and helpful. There's always a buzz of activity and it's the perfect starting point for socialites.

C-D Empire Backpackers, 21 Whitaker Pl, Grafton, T09-9509000, www.auckland backpackers.co.nz. Backpacker hostel-cum-budget hotel. Modern, centrally located multi-storey with a range of good-value en suite units (with kitchenette) sleeping up to 4. Perfect for couples and small groups looking for a bit of privacy. Facilities include internet, TV and a café-bistro and bar on site. No off-street parking. They also have two similar, affiliate premises: **C-D The Princetown**, 30 Symonds St, T09-9508300; and **C-D The Columbia**, 15 Whitaker Place, T09-9508600.

North Shore *p78, map p79*

LL-L Peace and Plenty Inn, 6 Flagstaff Terr, Devonport, T09-445 2925, www.peace andplenty.co.nz. A top B&B on the waterfront offering luxury accommodation and fine food. 7 beautifully presented individually decorated rooms with every attention to detail.

L-AL Emerald Inn, 16 The Promenade, Takapuna, T09-488 3500, www.emerald-inn.co.nz. Wide range of options with suites, units, a cottage and villas, close to the beach and all amenities.

L-AL Esplanade Hotel, 1 Victoria Rd, Devonport, T09-445 1291, www.esplanade hotel.co.nz. One of Auckland's oldest hotels, dominating the promenade with fine views of the harbour. Due to its position (15 mins from the city centre by car, or a 10-min ferry ride from the CBD) it's a good place to get away from the centre and enjoy Devonport's village-within-a-city atmosphere. All rooms are en suite, the spacious 'harbour view' suites being the most sought after. Sky TV and Wi-Fi. Classy in-house restaurant with an open fire in winter adds to the charm. Tariff includes breakfast.

L-AL The Spencer on Byron, 9-17 Byron Av, Takapuna, T09-916 6111, www.spencer byron.co.nz. The highest building on the North Shore so it is never short of good views. Overall a reliable option close to the 'Shore's' major centre and a pleasant alternative to the city centre (8 km).

L-AL Pacific Villa, 41 Bartly Terr, Devonport, T09-445 0537, www.pacificvilla.co.nz. Two-storied 1910s villa in a quiet location. Fully self-contained with three very tastefully decorated bedrooms and facilities with the added attraction of abundant, quality artworks from local artisans. Modern kitchen and private balcony.

A Jasmine Cottage, 20 Buchanan St, Devonport, T09-445 8825, www.photo album.co.nz/jasmine. Lovely courtyard cottage in quiet garden setting, queen en suite with tea and coffee making facilities. Exceptional hosts.

City East *p80, map p82*

L Aachen House, 39 Market Rd, Remuera, T09-520 2329, www.aachenhouse.co.nz. Well-regarded boutique hotel in an Edwardian mansion full of antiques. Not everyone's cup of tea, but the rooms are spacious with en suite bathroom, and the beds themselves are magnificent. Fine in-house cuisine.

AL Ascot Parnell, 4/32 St Stephens Av, Parnell, T09-309 9012, www.ascotparnell. com. A historic and characterful house with huge rooms. Terrific breakfast included.

AL Chalet Chevron, 14 Brighton Rd, Parnell, T09-309 0290, www.chaletchevron.co.nz. Older style 3-storey residence with plenty of character and a gracious homely feel. Double and single rooms available all with private bathrooms. Generous breakfast included. Fast internet.

AL-A Off Broadway Newmarket Motel, 11 Alpers Av, Newmarket, T09-529 3550/ T0800-427623, www.offbroadway.co.nz. Modern, reliable motel with stylish studios or suites with spa, within walking distance of Newmarket shops and restaurants.

A Parnell Inn, 320 Parnell Rd, Parnell, T09-358 0642/T0800-472763, www.parnellinn. co.nz. 16 clean and comfortable executive and standard studio units with kitchenettes. Right on Parnell Rd but still quiet. Funky and Licensed café onsite.

A Parnell City Lodge, 2 St Stephens Av, Parnell, T09-377 1463, www.parnellcitylodge. co.nz. Good-value long-established option perfectly situated in the heart of Parnell Village and just a short bus ride from the CBD. 2-storey residence offering standard studios and Edwardian or modern apartment style studios. Off-street parking. Plenty of restaurants nearby.

C-D City Garden Lodge, 25 St George's Bay Rd, Parnell, T09-302 0880, www.citygarden lodge.co.nz. A huge mansion of a place with wooden floors and Kauri staircase. Clean, comfortable and friendly with all the necessary facilities. Emphasis is on offering a quiet location in which to escape the city pace or recover from your arduous travels. Recommended.

C-D Lantana Lodge, 60 St George's Bay Rd, Parnell, T09-373 4546, www.lantana lodge.co.nz. A quiet but smaller option with various room types and free internet. Clients are well looked after.

City West *p83, map p84*

L Waitakere Park Lodge, 573 Scenic Drive, Waitaura, T09-814 9622, www.waitakere estate.co.nz. Off the beaten track, set in 80 acres of bush at the base of the Waitakere Ranges. Close to the vineyards and west coast beaches. 17 suites with bush and city views. A la carte restaurant.

AL Great Ponsonby B&B, 30 Ponsonby Terr, Ponsonby, T09-3765989, www.great pons.co.nz. Undoubtedly one of the best in the city, this B&B is a restored villa in a quiet location only a short stroll to the 'funky' Ponsonby Rd. Has a range of tastefully decorated en suite rooms and studios with a colourful Pacific influence. Enthusiastic, knowledgeable owners, a friendly dog and cat and Sky TV.

A Abaco on Jervois, 59 Jervois Rd, Ponsonby, T09-376 0119, www.abaco.co.nz.
Contemporary, comfortable and conveniently situated for Ponsonby and the city centre. Within walking distance of 30 restaurants. Spa rooms available. Internet, off-street parking.
A Colonial Cottage, 35 Clarence St, Ponsonby, T09-3602820. Old kauri villa with plenty of character and charm. Alternative health specialists and organic emphasis.
C-D Brown Kiwi Backpackers, 7 Prosford St, Ponsonby, T09-378 0191, www.brown kiwi.co.nz. The best backpacker hostel west of the city. Good reputation and full of character. Close to Ponsonby Rd and link bus service.

City South p85

L Jet Inn, 63 Westney Rd, Mangere, T09-2754100, www.jetinn.co.nz. 3 km from the airport, 16 km from the city. Modern and well facilitated. Ideal for a pre/post-flight sleep.
A-AL Bavaria Guest House, 83 Valley Rd, Mt Eden, T09-6389641, www.bavariaband bhotel.co.nz. 100-year old villa. Spacious and comfortable with 11 suites, nice deck and garden. German spoken.
A Hotel Grand Chancellor, corner of Ascot and Kirkbride Rds, Airport Oaks, T09-275 7029, www.grandhotelsinternational.com. A safe bet if you need to be near the airport. All the trimmings, such as a pool and restaurant.
B Bond Street Lodge, 77 Bond St, Kingsland, T09-846 4585, www.bondstlodge.co.nz. Modern 3-storey budget accommodation on the fringe of the city centre and in the fast developing suburb of Kingsland. A fine alternative to the CBD and only 5 mins' walk from Eden Park. Tidy rooms (with internet ports), shared bathrooms and kitchen. Spacious lounge. Off-street parking.
C-D Oaklands Lodge Backpackers, 5a Oaklands Rd, Mt Eden, T09-638 6545, www.oaklands.co.nz. A good budget choice on the fringe of the CBD, Victorian villa with a relaxed atmosphere and a tempting short walk to the summit of Mt Eden.

Eating

When it comes to eating, Auckland is said to be on a par with New York and London. With almost 1000 restaurants in the city it is not surprising to learn that 'dining out' is New Zealand's 3rd biggest retail spend. Note that restaurants and cafés are essentially the same thing, with the latter perhaps just being a bit more casual. The cafés listed separately below are some of the traditional favourites; those particularly noted for their character, ambience and/or coffee.

The city centre offers waterside dining indoors and out, with spacious brasseries, intimate silver service, or romantic balconies overlooking the viaduct and harbour. Elsewhere, in High St and Vulcan Lane, you can find a more casual setting in the many streetside cafés. Many of the pubs also offer a decent meal for a reasonable price (see Bars and clubs, below). To the west of the city centre, Ponsonby (Ponsonby Rd) has for years managed to hold on to its reputation as the culinary heart of the city, with Parnell coming a close second. Service is generally good and refreshingly friendly. Tipping is not essential but appreciated. BYO means bring your own (bottle).

City centre p73, map p76

Cin Cin, Ferry Building, 99 Quay St, T09-307 6966, www.cincin.co.nz. Daily from 1000. Established as one of Auckland's top restaurants for years, Cin Cin has changed hands a number of times. With its location right next to the ferry docks it is very much a happening place, serving Pacific cuisine to the highest standard. The service here is outstanding, as is the wine list. Licensed, outdoor dining available.
Euro, Shed 22, Princes Wharf, Quay St, T09-3099866. Daily for lunch and dinner, brunch Sat-Sun from 1030. A waterfront restaurant designed to capture the sailing crowd, with a boast of being the 'best of the best'. It has a very luxurious, clean interior with a large mesmerizing clock projected

onto the wall, and offers new and imaginative cuisine in the revered Pacific Rim style. Licensed, outdoor dining available.

Harbourside Seafood Bar and Grill, 1st floor, Ferry Building, T09-3070486, www.harboursiderestaurant.co.nz. Daily from 1130, licensed. Located right above Cin Cin, it is advertised in all the tourist publications and seems to live up to all the praise. This is a good opportunity to try New Zealand snapper or green-lipped mussels.

Kermadec, 1st floor, Viaduct Quay Building, corner of Lower Hobson St and Quay St, T09-3090412, www.kermadec.co.nz., Mon-Fri for lunch and dinner. Perhaps the best restaurant in town, and arguably the best seafood venue. Here you can tickle your taste buds with the many delights of the Pacific Ocean as well as more traditional fare. There are 2 private rooms in a Japanese-style decor that contain small ponds. Don't miss the seafood platter. Licensed and BYO.

Orbit Restaurant, Sky Tower, corner Victoria and Federal sts, T09-3636000. Brunch Sat/Sun 1000-1500, lunch Mon-Fri 1130-1430, dinner daily 1730-2230, licensed. Over two-thirds of the way up the Sky Tower, this restaurant has the best view of any in the city, if not the entire hemisphere. The restaurant itself revolves of course, apparently once every 60 mins (a bit more frequently would be far more fun). Contemporary Pacific Rim cuisine and extensive NZ wine list. (The Observatory is the other option in the Sky Tower and offers buffet-style fare. Open for dinner daily and lunch Thu-Sun.)

White, Hilton Hotel, Princes Wharf, 147 Quay St, T09-978 2000, www.white restaurant.co.nz. Breakfast Mon-Fri 0630-1030, Sat-Sun 0700-1100, lunch Mon-Sun 1200-1500, dinner Mon-Sun 0600-1030. Since the America's Cup, White has earned a reputation that now places it among the very best of Auckland's offerings. There is no doubt the views across the water and classy atmosphere have as much to do with that as the food and the service. **Bellini**, the hotel's self-styled cocktail bar, is an added attraction.

Wildfire Churrascaria, Princes Wharf, Quay St, T09-353 7595, www.wildfire restaurant.co.nz. Daily from 1130. Wildfire has reinvented itself as a 'Brazilian BBQ' restaurant focusing on South American-style skewered meats generously dished out by Churrasco waiters' on a set menu. It's an interesting concept and if half a cow isn't your thing then fear not, à la carte comes to the rescue with seafood and vegetarian options. There's live Brazilian music at weekends. Licensed, outdoor dining available.

The French Café, 210 Symonds St, T09-377 1911, www.thefrenchcafe.co.nz. Lunch Fri, dinner Tue-Sat, licensed. Well-established favourite that has stood the test of time. Fine starters available as main courses, excellent fresh fish dishes.

Joy Bong, 531 Karangahape Rd, T09-377 2218, www.joybong.co.nz. Daily from 1700, licensed. Once part of the notoriously competitive Ponsonby restaurant family this relocated Thai restaurant known affectionately as the 'bong' continues to enjoy a solid reputation. Good value.

O'Connell Street Bistro, 3 O'Connell St, T09-377 1884, www.oconnellstbistro.com. Dinner daily, lunch Tue-Fri, licensed. An intimate, tiny venue serving fine examples of Pacific Rim with a legendary wine list. Express menu for theatre-goers.

Sake Bar Rikka, 19 Drake St, Victoria Park Market, T09-377 8239. Lunch and dinner Tue-Sun, licensed. Some say Sake is now past its best but it remains for now one of the best Japanese restaurants in town. Fine seasonal dishes in a wood-beamed warehouse, in character with the Victoria Park Market.

Soul Bar and Restaurant, Viaduct Harbour, T09-3567249, www.soulbar.co.nz. Daily for lunch and dinner. Much to the chagrin of the local competition, owner and chef Judith Tabron ensured that Soul was the place to be during the America's Cup and its reputation lives on. Doubtless, the open-air decks overlooking the harbour had much to do with that and of course the bar is the main attraction, but the food is also excellent and affordable. Occasional internationally renowned 'guest' chefs add to its appeal.

Toto, 53 Nelson St, T09-302 2665. Lunch, Mon-Fri, dinner daily. Licensed, outdoor dining and private rooms available. Lavishly decorated Italian-style restaurant offering some of the finest Italian food in the city.

Vertigo, top floor, **Mercure Hotel**, 8 Customs St, T09-302 9424, www.vertigorestaurant.co.nz. Daily breakfast, lunch and dinner, licensed. A bit more down-to-earth than the **Orbit** restaurant in the Sky Tower, but still an impressive view and good modern dishes to go with it.

Food Hall on Atrium on Elliot, Elliot St. A convenient, cheap daytime venue.

Mexican Café, 67 Victoria St West, T09-373 2311. Lunch Mon-Fri from 1200, dinner daily. A favourite cheap and cheerful café that has been around for years (no mean feat in Auckland).

Middle East Café, 23a Wellesley St, T09-379 4843, www.middleeastcafe.co.nz. Daily 1100-1300 and 1715-2100. For many years this tiny café has become a sanctuary for office workers and shoppers eager to absorb its cosy ambience, brimming character and legendary 'shawarmas' (strips of lamb in bread packet with a delightful garlic and tomato dip). All sorts of quirky Middle Eastern artefacts adorn the walls. It's hard to imagine you're still in Auckland.

White Lady, 18 Commerce St, open all night. Believe it or not this is a caravan that looks more like a train, which seems to appear from nowhere each night, towed by an old tractor. Within its battered walls are 2 battered-looking gentlemen, serving various items of battered food, which taste amazing (as do most things at 0300). It's the best 'post-drink munchies' venue in the city and is open until the sun rises.

Cafés

Gallery Café, 1st floor, Auckland Art Gallery, corner of Wellesley St East and Kitchener St, T09-377 9603. A great café, even without all the in-house artworks.

Mecca, Chancery Mall, Chancery Lane, CBD, T09-356 7028. Daily 0700-late. Café/ restaurant/bar combo worth a mention due to its location in the heart of the chic Chancery Centre – a haven for fashion shops and designer labels. Decent coffee, attractive menu and a good spot for people-watching.

Rakinos, 1st floor, 35 High St, T09-358 3535, www.rakinos.com. Hard to find but worth it. Great coffee and traditional café fare.

Verona, 169 Karangahape Rd, T09-307 0508. Daily 1000-late. Perhaps The K'Rd's favourite café, colourful in character and clientele.

Vulcan, Vulcan Lane, T09-377 9899. Mon-Fri 1100-late, Sat 1200-late. Unpretentious old favourite with live entertainment or DJs Fri/Sat.

North Shore p78, map p/9

Manuka, 49 Victoria Rd, Devonport, T09-445 7732. Daily for breakfast, lunch and dinner, licensed. The pick of the bunch in Devonport with its much-loved wood- fired pizzas and laid-back atmosphere.

Monsoon Thai, 71 Victoria Rd, T09-4454263, www.monsoonthai.co.nz daily dinner. Reliable, value Thai/Malaysian option offering both eat-in and takeaway.

City East p80, map p82

Antoine's, 333 Parnell Rd, Parnell, T09-379 8756, www.antoinesrestaurant.co.nz. Dinner Mon-Sat, lunch Wed-Fri, licensed. Parnell's best and on a par with anything in the city. French cuisine with some firm favourites with the regulars – the venison is exquisite. Very professional.

Cibo, 91 St Georges Bay Rd, T09-303 9660, www.cibo.co.nz. Lunch Mon-Fri, dinner Mon-Sat. A long established favourite located in-of all things-an old chocolate factory. There is no doubting the class here, the smooth service or culinary talents of lauded chef Kate Fay. Good wine list and great outdoor seating.

Hammerheads, 19 Tamaki Dr, Orakei, T09-521 4400. Daily from 1200, www.hammer heads.co.nz, licensed. A tourist favourite. Right next to Kelly Tarlton's Underwater World, with decent seafood and fine harbour views.

Mikano, 1 Solent St, Mechanics Bay, T09-309 9514. Mon-Fri 1130-late, Sat 1730-late, Sun

1000-late, licensed. A bit out the way, next to the helicopter base and container wharves, but with a great view across the harbour and serving a very high standard of mainly Asian-inspired fare. Well worth the trip. Has maintained a good reputation for years.

Iguacu, 269 Parnell Rd, Parnell, T09-358 4804, www.iguacu.co.nz. Mon-Fri 1200-0100, Sat-Sun 1100-0100. Licensed. Parnell's 'place to be seen', especially with the younger set. Not for the casually dressed or happily single female, but still immensely popular. Menu from snack-size to feast. Top breakfast spot.

Java Room, 317 Parnell Rd, Parnell, T09-366 1606. Dinner Mon-Sat 1800-late, licensed and BYO. Fine selection of Asian and Pacific Rim cuisine at affordable prices.

Karin Japanese, 237 Parnell Rd, Parnell, T09-356 7101. Daily lunch 1200-1400, dinner 1800-2200. Parnell's Japanese offering with all the traditional favourites. Fast efficient service.

Oh Calcutta, 151 Parnell Rd, Parnell, T09-3779090, www.ohcalcutta.co.nz. Lunch Wed-Fri 1200-1400, dinner daily from 1730. Up against stiff opposition in the city, Oh Calcutta consistently ranks as one of the finest in all departments from food quality to ambience and service. Right in the heart of the Parnell restaurant strip.

Rikka, 73 Davis Cres, Newmarket, T09-522 5277. Mon-Fri 1200-1430, Sat 1800-2230. An offshoot of the city centre branch and no less popular. Fantastic interior. The Tenshin section of the menu is more expensive but highly recommended if you are new to Japanese food. Licensed.

Tonino's, 35 Tamaki Dr, T09-528 8935, daily lunch and dinner, licensed and BYO. A good value Italian choice in Mission Bay, with generous pasta dishes and standard pizza choices. Dine-in or takeaway.

Burger Fuel, 187 Parnell Rd, T09-377 3345. One of several in a chain fast reproducing around the city which is a sure sign that their generous range of burgers from half-cow to veggie are going down exceptionally well.

La Bocca, 251 Parnell Rd, Parnell, T09-375 0083, www.labocca.co.nz. Dinner Mon-Sat

1800-late (summer only), licensed. A fine laid-back café especially noted for its seafood.

Portofino, 156 Parnell Rd, Parnell, T09-373 3740. Daily for lunch and dinner. Long-standing favourite now with nine outlets throughout the country. Reliable and affordable Italian style – let's just hope that quality does not become compromised by the rapid expansion. Licensed and BYO.

Verve, 311 Parnell Rd, Parnell, T09-379 2860. Daily from 0730, dinner Tue-Sat, licensed. A great 'all rounder' in every way both day and night. Always busy and a top breakfast spot.

White Lady, corner of Broadway and Remuera Rd, Newmarket, open all night. The sister of the infamous **White Lady** in the city centre. It sees its fair share of loonies in the wee hours trying to read the extensive menu, but the stalwart owners remain in control.

Cafés
Kenzie, 17a Remuera Rd, T09-522 2647. Good 'chill over a coffee and watch the world go by' establishment on the edge of busy Broadway.

Rosehip, 82 Gladstone, Parnell, T09-369 1182. A bit pricey, but remains a popular haunt, well-situated next to the rose gardens and away from busy Parnell Rd. Good coffee.

Trinity, 107 Parnell Rd, Parnell, T09-3003042. Prompt no-nonsense service and a good hearty breakfast. Fine coffee.

City West *p83, map p84*
Prego, 226 Ponsonby Rd, Ponsonby, T09-376 3095, lunch and dinner daily, licensed. A favourite with the locals who know they will get good food and service. Italian-style menu. Great wood-fired pizza and fish.

Andiamo, 194 Jervois Rd, Herne Bay, T09-3787811, www.andiamo.co.nz. Mon-Fri from 1130-late, Sat-Sun from 1000-late, licensed. Always busy, with a particularly fine all-day breakfast selection.

GPK, 262 Ponsonby Rd, Ponsonby, T09-360 1113, www.gpk.co.nz. Mon-Fri 1100-late, Sat-Sun 0900-late, licensed. One of Auckland's most successful restaurants, with other branches in Takapuna and Albany.

Always busy with a lively atmosphere. The bar is as popular as the menu.

Rocco, 23 Ponsonby Rd, Ponsonby, T09-360 6262, www.rocco.co.nz. Dinner only Tue-Sat from 1730. Enjoys a reputation for consistently good Spanish and Italian inspired dishes with a specialization in game and seafood. Cosy private dining upstairs.

Vinnies, 166 Jervois Rd, Herne Bay, T09-376 5597, www.vinnies.co.nz. Daily from 1830, licensed. This is considered to be one of Auckland's finest, now under the care of ex-Hilton (White Restaurant) executive chef, Geoff Scott. A special menu is available allowing you to sample a wide variety of dishes. Professional in style, quality and presentation. Book ahead.

Dizengoff, 256 Ponsonby Rd, Ponsonby, T09-360 0108. Daily 0700-1700, unlicensed. A fine counter service operation offering takeaway or sit-in items that attract a wide-ranging clientele, making it a great spot for people-watching. Light food with a Jewish influence. The breakfasts (especially the salmon and eggs on toast) are delicious.

Ponsonby Fresh Fish and Chip Co, 127 Ponsonby Rd, Ponsonby, T09-378 7885. Daily 1100-2130. A Ponsonby institution. Although the portions have gradually decreased in size, the quality has pretty much stayed the same. Try the local Pacific fish. Always busy, and it is takeaway only, so expect to place an order then return about 20 mins later. Good vegetarian burgers.

Café Cezanne, 296 Ponsonby Rd, Ponsonby, T09-3763338. Very popular with students and backpackers. Good hearty fare with the classic Ponsonby atmosphere.

Fusion, 32 Jervois Rd, Ponsonby, T09-378 4573. Local favourite, especially for breakfast, with good garden seating.

SPQR, 150 Ponsonby Rd, Ponsonby, T09-360 1710. Mon-Fri 1100-late, Sat-Sun 1000-late, licensed. One of the oldest and trendiest places in Ponsonby, a favourite with many for food and beverages and deservingly so. More mince than a butcher's dog and a very high posing quotient to boot.

City South *p85*

Roasted Addiqtion, 487 New North Rd, Kingsland, T09-815 0913. Mon 0700-1600, Tue-Fri 0700-2200, Sat-Sun 0800-1700 Increasingly popular both for its fine coffee, music and highly imaginative evening menu.

Sitar Indian Restaurant, 397 Mount Eden Rd, Mt Eden, T09-630 0321. Dinner Tue-Sun from 1730, lunch Tue-Fri 1200-1400, licensed and BYO. The most popular Indian restaurant south of the city centre.

Crucial Traders, 473 New North Rd, Kingsland, T09-846 3288. Laid-back café favourite for those tired of the Ponsonby scene.

Frazers, 434 Mount Eden Rd, Mt Eden, T09-630 6825. A popular spot for locals, students and backpackers. Good selection of cheap light meals and fine coffee.

Pubs, bars and clubs

Sadly, when it comes to good pubs, Auckland is really not in the same league as most other cities of its size. Only in the last decade has the city, and New Zealand as a whole, woken up to the fact that the 'ashtray built into the table, rugby boys and jugs of insipid beer until you're sick' establishments were not everybody's 'pint of ale'. However, whether you are an ardent trendsetter, an avid Guinness drinker or cocktail specialist it can still perhaps provide a pub that will suit your needs. With the arrival of the new millennium you can at least find most things, from gay venues to quiet intellectual establishments and, on occasions, even good beer. Pubs are well distributed around the city but are concentrated mainly in the city centre with High St, Vulcan Lane and The Viaduct Basin being the main focus. On the fringes, the trendy suburbs of Parnell, Newmarket and Ponsonby are all stalwarts with the occasional desirable establishment lying further afield. The Waterfront and Viaduct Basin in particular has developed rapidly in recent years and is now arguably 'the' place to go in the city.

Most nightclubs in Auckland are based in the city centre on Queen St, Vulcan Lane,

High St and Karangahape Rd (or 'K' Rd – noted especially for its gay and transvestite scene). Some venues in Ponsonby and Parnell, although not considered clubs, also remain open well into the wee hours. For the most up-to-date information surrounding venues and gigs refer to the free *Auckland Grove Guide*, available from the VIC, www.grooveguide.co.nz. Most of the clubs are open nightly, warming up towards the end of the week before going off at the weekend. Venues usually have a cover charge of about $10-15, and drinks will be at least $8. Dress codes often apply. Pubs vary greatly with their attempts at last orders, but generally speaking the solid drinking stops from midnight to 0300, and from then on it's clubbing till dawn.

City centre *p73, map p76*

Belgian Beer Café (Occidental), 6-8 Vulcan Lane, T09-300 6226, www.belgian-beer-cafe.co.nz. With Queen St clubs and a number of major backpacker hostels nearby, this bar rages well into the night; popular by day and serves a fine lunch. Tries hard to push the Euro feel with favourable results.

Danny Doolans, on the Viaduct Basin, T09-358 2554, www.dannydoolans.co.nz. Considered by many to be the best Irish pub in the city. Goes off like a rocket at weekends. Particularly good for live music.

Deschlers, 17 High St, T09-379 6811, www.deschlers.co.nz. Also close to Queen St, this is a cocktail lounge with lounge lizard music. A big favourite at the weekend with trendy young things with wandering eyes.

The Empire, corner of Nelson and Victoria sts, T09-373 4389, www.theempire.co.nz. A fine-looking establishment and a real party spot at weekends, offering live music at night and a decent espresso by day in its either frantic or peaceful courtyard.

Minus 5, Princess Wharf, T09-377 6702, www.minus5.co.nz. An extraordinary concept in trendy cocktail bars, Minus 5 is one of two in the country (the other is in Queenstown) that takes 'cool' to the literal level with a bar made of ice.

The decor (all of it bar the bottles) is all fashioned from ice and includes some impressive sculptures. Obviously it is not a place to linger too long and it is touted more as a one-off experience. Tours last about 30 mins and come replete with a loan of cosy jackets and gloves. Entry from $27 (includes one drink).

The Muddy Farmer, 14 Wyndham St, T09-336 1265, www.themuddyfarmer.co.nz. Similar in size, popularity and decor as **Danny Doolans** but not so well placed. The bar is great but the beer is expensive.

Clubs

On K' Rd, although most of the clubs are essentially gay orientated, they are very welcoming and popular with all comers. **Ibiza**, 253 K' Rd; **Club 4:20** (at 373); and **Rising Sun** (also at 373), are popular spots and the dance music can be excellent especially if you go around 2400. Later on, as it gets busy, don't be surprised (or indeed offended) if a large gentleman called Dina, in an amazing scarlet number, high heels and a huge fruit filled hat, gives you a cheeky squirt with his large water pistol – it's all done in the best possible taste.

For more traditional options, head down to the bottom of Queen St and join the queues outside venues around Princess and Viaduct Wharf High St and Vulcan Lane. **Khuja Lounge**, 536 Queen St, is popular. Khuja Lounge has Latino, hip-hop and funk from DJs and live percussionists. **Margaritas**, 18 Elliot St, T09-302 2764, is also popular especially being so close to the Base Backpackers.

North Shore *p78, map p79*

The North Shore has its fair share of pubs and there are a number of favourites that deserve to lure locals and visitors across the bridge. Devonport is your best bet with Takapuna serving the trendier crowd. Further afield (and for a real experience) try the Puhoi Hotel.

The Patriot British Pub, 14 Victoria Rd, Devonport, T09-4453010. Sure, 'When in Rome' as the saying goes… but if you are European and weary of all things new, want a good beer, or a hearty breakfast or rapport with ex-pats, then head here on a sunny Sunday or weekend evening.

Puhoi Hotel and Tavern, just north of Orewa, 40 km north of the city, in the tiny settlement of Puhoi, T09-422 0812. More an experience than a watering hole. Very popular in summer and a favourite haunt of bikers on Sun afternoons. Basic, but richly decorated with a historic interior and interesting clientele.

City East p80, map p82

There are a number of bars nestled in among the cafés and shops of Parnell Rd, which are, along with those in Ponsonby, considered to be the trendiest drinking spots in the city.

The Claddagh, 372 Broadway, T09-522 4410. Despite the ever-growing competition, this remains one of the most popular Irish pubs in the city. Opened in 1997 by the much-loved Noel and Margaret, originally from Limerick (and essentially the founders of Irish bars in Auckland) it is a wonderful homely Irish pub and a favourite haunt of Irish and Scottish immigrants. Throughout the day it is quiet and welcoming, but as the evening draws in and the locals start to arrive, it gets busier and busier, till eventually (especially at weekends) it is jumping to the sound of Irish music late into the night. Serves a fine pint of Guinness.

Iguacu, 269 Parnell Rd, T09-358 4804. The old favourite and the kick-off venue for others. From there just follow the designer clothing and the clickity-clack of high heels.

The Penny Black, corner of Khyber Pass Rd and Broadway, T09-529 0050. An old favourite and one of a number of pubs in Newmarket, near Parnell.

City West p83, map p84

The main drinking venue west of the city centre is Ponsonby, which is similar to Parnell. Here trendy young things parade up and down the pavements and in and out of the many cafés and bars which fringe them.

City South p85

Galbraith's Ale House, 2 Mount Eden Rd, Mt Eden, T09-379 3557, www.alehouse.co.nz.

Used to be the old Grafton library and is perhaps the only notable pub south of the city centre. Within its grand exterior a fine range of foreign and home-brewed ales are available (at slightly elevated prices) as is a fine menu. Further south of here beyond Mt Eden and into the depths of South Auckland the pubs are not generally recommended.

⦿ Entertainment

The after-sunset scene in Auckland has improved greatly in recent years and now boasts some fine venues for dancing, comedy or huge outdoor summer events in the Auckland Domain; the *New Zealand Herald*, www.nzherald.co.nz, or www.events auckland.com and www.nzlive.com. The free publication *What's Happening* is also a very useful guide, again available from information centres. For gigs and clubbing check out www.muzic.net.nz and www.eventfinder .co.nz. For up-to-the-minute information and comment tune in to BFM's gig guide on the radio or net, www.95bfm.co.nz.

The Edge, T0800-3573355/T09-3573355, www.the-edge.co.nz, is a conglomerate of Auckland's main venues offering the top international performance events. It combines the **Aotea Centre**, **The Civic**, the **Auckland Town Hall**, and **Aotea Square**. The regularly updated event schedule leaflets is available from all the main information centres.

Cinemas

There are many cinema complexes throughout the city. New Zealand often receives films before Europe due to film distribution arrangements. For a daily guide to all venues and films consult the *New Zealand Herald* entertainment section, especially in the weekend edition. Admission is around $10, cheap nights are usually Tue.

Academy, 44 Lorne St, T09-373 2761, www.academycinemas.co.nz. Specialist films.

Skycity Cinemas, 291-297 Queen St, T09-369 2400. Has 12 screens.

Rialto, 169 Broadway, Newmarket, T09-369 2417.

Comedy clubs

There is a healthy comedy scene in Auckland, and stand-up New Zealand humour (on stage) can be very similar to that found in the US and Europe. See the *New Zealand Herald* weekend edition for details. There is also an **Annual Comedy Festival** held in late Apr at various venues throughout the city www.comedyfestival.co.nz. The main venues for comedy are: **The Classic**, 321 Queen St, T09-373 4321, www.comedy.co.nz; and **Silo Theatre**, 108 Quay St, T09-366 0339, www.silotheatre.co.nz.

Gay and lesbian

The Auckland gay scene is kept up to date with the *Express Magazine* ($2.50) which can be bought from the magazine outlets **Magazzino** (see Shopping, page 100). This publication and the local gossip can also be sought at the **Pride Centre**, www.pride.org.nz, or in the predominantly gay cafés and clubs. The main club venues are listed above in the clubbing section. The Auckland Gayline/Lesbian line is T09-3033584.

Useful websites include www.gaynz.com, www.gaytravel.net.nz, and www.pride.org.nz.

Music venues

Auckland is well served with local, national and international gigs and venues. Most major concerts take place (usually just for one night in New Zealand) at the **Aotea Centre** (www.the-edge.co.nz), **Vector Arena** (www.vectorarena.co.nz), or **Ericsson Stadium**. Although New Zealand is isolated, it's not unusual to hear the likes of Coldplay or to find oneself throwing one's knickers at an ageing Tom Jones. The traditional local music venues are described below. The best bet for schedules is the *New Zealand Herald*, www.nzherald.co.nz.

General and Irish folk and rock

The Claddagh, 372 Broadway, Newmarket, T09-522 4410. 'Diddly dee' jam session Mon nights, regular bands most others.
Danny Doolans, 204 Quay St, T09-358 2554.
Devonport Folk Music Club, The Bunker, Mt Victoria, Devonport, T09-445 2227. Mon night.

Jazz and Rhythm'n'Blues

Waiheke is the best venue for jazz after hosting the former annual jazz festival. For details see www.waihekejazzandblues.co.nz. In the city occasional gigs are hosted in several inner city bars and clubs including:
Iguacu, 269 Parnell Rd, Parnell, T09-358 4804.
Ivory Bar, 412 Parnell Rd, T09-373 3328, live entertainment most nights.

Rock

Galatos, 17 Galatos St, T09-303 1928, Wed-Sat.
King's Arms, 59 France St, Newton, T09-373 3240.
Masonic Tavern, 29 King Edward Parade, Devonport, T09-445 0485, every Fri night.
Safari Lounge, 116 Ponsonby Rd, T09-3787707.

Theatres

For listings see the entertainment section of the *New Zealand Herald*, particularly at the weekend. Tickets can be booked through **Tiketek**, www.premier.ticketek.co.nz. For further information contact **Auckland Theatre Company**, T09-309 0390, www.atc.co.nz.
Bruce Mason Theatre, corner of Hurstmere Rd and the Promenade, Takapuna, North Shore, T09-488 2940.
Maidment Theatre, corner of Princess St and Alfred St, at the university, T09-308 2383, www.maidment.auckland.ac.nz.
Silo Theatre, 108 Quay St, T09-366 0339, www.silotheatre.co.nz. 'Off-the-wall' theatre.
Sky City Theatre, Sky City, corner of Victoria and Federal sts, T09-912 6000/ T0800-759 2489, www.skycityauckland.co.nz.

❀ Festivals and events

Auckland has a dynamic range of annual events, some annual, some biannual and many one offs. For details see, www.aucklandnz.com and www.nzlive.com.
Feb Auckland Anniversary Weekend Sailing Regatta, www.regatta.org.nz, held on the Waitemata Harbour in the first week of the month. **Auckland Pride Festival**, see www.gaynz.com. New Zealand's oldest and biggest gay-fest. Not quite in the same league as Sydney's Mardis Gras but colourful and entertaining none the less with events like 'drag aerobics with Buffy and Bimbo' and 'wigs on the waterfront'. **Devonport Food Wine and Music Festival** (3rd week), T09-353 4026, www.devonportwinefestival.co.nz. **Mission Bay Jazz and Blues Streetfest** (last Sat), www.jazz andbluesstreetfest.com. **Sky City Starlight Symphony** (last week). A free open-air event held annually (sometimes with a different name) in the Auckland Domain, attracts over 300,000.
Mar Pasifika Festival (2nd week), www.aucklandcity.govt.nz/pasifika. New Zealand's largest Pacific culture festival with food, arts, crafts and music performances. **Round the Bays Fun Run**, www.roundthe bays.co.nz, a charitable event that attracts over 7000 competitors. **AK08 Festival** (2nd week biannual), www.aucklandfestival.co.nz, since its inception in 2004, this multifarious arts event has promised an impressive line up of international stars as well as local artists. The next is in 2011
Mar-Apr Royal Easter Show, www.royaleastershow.co.nz.
Apr Sky Tower Vertical Challenge, competitors from 10 years old and up, race up and down the Sky Tower with mixed results. **Rally of New Zealand**, www.rallynz.org.nz, part of the world series; 25 stages start and finish in the city.
Jun New Zealand Boat Show, www.boatshow.co.nz.
Jul Auckland International Film Festival (1st week), www.enzedff.co.nz.

Sept Start of the Rugby World Cup, the nation's biggest and most hyperbolic event since the America's Cup. Auckland's Eden Park stadium will host various fixtures.
Oct New Zealand Fashion Week, www.nzfashionweek.com, an increasingly high profile event and the annual showcase for established and up and coming designers. Plenty of hype, pretension, vacuous models and mass back-stabbings offstage.
Dec Christmas in the Park (4th week), a popular and free precursor to the Starlight Symphony, again held in the Auckland Domain and hugely popular.

O Shopping

If you fancy some serious retail therapy then Auckland should not disappoint. And given the currency exchange rates, if you are coming from Europe or the US, you are in for a treat. Whatever you're after, Auckland has it all. The most popular shopping spots are to be found in the city centre, and also in Parnell and Newmarket to the east, and Ponsonby to the west. Most major suburbs have the ubiquitous mall that provides both quality and quantity.

If you are looking for products specific to New Zealand, whet your appetite by visiting the **New Zealand Trade Centre**, 26 Albert St, City, T09-366 6879, www.nztc.co.nz. Although you cannot actually buy things here, it will give you an insight into what is available. The *Official Auckland Shopping Guide* and individual leaflets are available from VICs, and there are even a few specialist shopping tours available.

Art

There are plenty of quality art galleries in the city, and if you are serious about buying or viewing get the detailed *Auckland Gallery Guide* or the *Auckland Art Precinct Map* from the main VICs and allow a full day. Many Auckland artists reside in the western suburbs in and around Titirangi and the Waitakeres. The VIC can supply the relevant brochures should you wish to investigate in detail. Pacific and especially New Zealand art is unique, appealing and colourful – reflecting the very nature of New Zealand itself. The best gallery venues are Parnell (ask about the **Parnell Arts Trail**), Devonport, Titirangi and the city centre.

Books

Borders, 291-297 Queen St, T09-309 3377, open until 2100, dwarfs the largest of the more traditional stores like **Dymocks**, 344 Ponsonby Rd, T09-3784860, or **Whitcoulls**, 210 Queen St, T09-356 5400. These majors should meet all your traditional needs, along with **Paper Plus** and **Books and More**, which also have smaller outlets in most major suburbs and shopping malls. For smaller, more personal outlets try:
Auckland Map Centre, National Bank Building, 209 Queen St, City, T09-309 7725.
The Children's Bookshop, corner of Jervois and St Mary Rds, Ponsonby, T09-376 7283. Travel books and maps.
Hard to Find (But Worth the Effort), 171 The Mall, Onehunga, T09-634 4340. Has a delightful rabbit warren-like interior and is (hard to find your way out) an experience in itself.
Magazzino, 123 Ponsonby Rd, T09-376 6933. Magazines.
Unity Bookshop, 19 High St, Auckland City, T09-307 0731.
The Woman's Bookshop, 105 Ponsonby Rd, Ponsonby, T09-376 4399.

Camping and tramping gear

Although there is a good selection of camping and tramping clothes, boots and equipment to be found in Auckland and New Zealand, there does not seem to be the range or the quality available in Europe or the US. However, the best places to try are:
Bivouac Outdoor, 210 Queen St, City, T09-366 1966, and 302 Broadway, Newmarket, T09-529 2298.
Katmandu, 151 Queen St, City, T09-309 4615, and 200 Victoria St West, City, T09-377 7560.
Tent Town, 399 New North Rd, Kingsland, T09-846 1076.

Clothing

Most of the leading international brands and labels can be found in the city centre especially in the new **Chancery Mall** on Chancery Lane (off High St, CBD). **O'Connell** and **High St** in the CBD are also famous for designer fashions – look out for Feline, Tanya Carlson, World, Karen Walker, and Morrison Hotel. Newmarket and Ponsonby are also other favourite spots. There are specialist boutiques on Ponsonby Rd including **Sabine**, **Wallace Rose** and **State of Grace**. The best factory shops are in the **Dressmart** outlets in suburban Onehunga. For listings get hold of a copy of the *Auckland Fashion Guide* from the VIC. To source a comprehensive list of clothing stores and other shops in Newmarket visit www.newmarket.net.nz.
Atrium on Elliot, Queen St, T09-358 3052.
Barkers, 4a High St, T0800-808700. Menswear.
Country Road Clothing, 277 Broadway Newmarket, T09-529 1987.
George Harrison, Atrium on Elliott, T09-366 7788. Menswear.
Kate Sylvester, High St CBD and Newmarket, T09-307 3282. Womenswear.
Little Brother, 5 High St, T09-377 6536. Menswear.
Rodd and Gun, 75 Queen St and throughout the city, T09-309 6571. Menswear.
Saks, 254 Broadway, Newmarket, T09-520 7630. Menswear.
Zambesi, Vulcan Lane, CBD, T09-377 7220, and outlets throughout the city.
Zebrano, Newmarket, T09-523 2500. Womenswear.

Gifts, jewellery and souvenirs

Auckland city centre has souvenir shops everywhere packed with everything from cute furry kiwis in All Black shirts to the omnipresent bone or greenstone Maori pendants – which, traditionally you are supposed to buy for someone else, not yourself. Parnell and K' Rd are also recommended. But, the more discerning buyer should wait to see the smaller more provincial souvenir shops which tend to offer

more specialist, unique stock. If you like the look of Kauri or other wood crafts and are heading for Northland wait and buy there, it may well be better quality and also cheaper.
Aotea New Zealand Souvenirs, Lower Albert St, City, T09-379 5022.
Artisanz, Victoria Park Market, Victoria Park, City, T09-303 1113.
Craftworld, T09-831 0277, 15 mins from the city centre, in West Auckland in **Westgate Shopping Centre**, Fernhill Drive, Massey. One of the largest craft shops.
The Elephant House, 237 Parnell Rd, Parnell, T09-309 8740. One of the best craft shops.
Great Kiwi Yarns, 107 Queen St, T09-308 9013. For original knitwear.
The Great New Zealand Shop, Downtown Shopping Centre, Queen St, T09-377 3009. For the classic Kiwi souvenirs.

Markets

The most famous market in Auckland is the **Victoria Park Market**, opposite Victoria Park, just a few mins' walk west of the city centre, www.victoria-park-market.co.nz. It provides 7 days a week shopping with a variety of outlets from shops to stalls that expand into the car park on Sat. There are a wide variety of products with a market theme, a number of good cafés, a food hall and a pub, all in pleasant surroundings.

K'Rd (Karangahape Rd), at the southern-most end of Queen St, is an excellent area for unusual shops, particularly Polynesian clothing and craft items. The Sat morning market on the bridge over the motorway can also produce the odd unusual bargain.

If you would prefer a less commercial, raw Polynesian feel then an excursion to the **Otara Market** in the rather dodgy suburb of Otara in South Auckland is interesting and good for a wander (see page 87).

Photography

Digital camera equipment is readily available throughout the city, but for specialist equipment try **Camera and Camera**, 162 Queen St, City, T09-303 1879.

PCL, 30 Karaka Street, Eden Terr, T09-309 8090.
The Photo Warehouse, 154 Queen St, City, T09-309 0715.

Shopping malls

Downtown Shopping Centre, 11-19 Customs St, City, T09-978 5265.
Manukau Shopping Centre, corner of Great South Rd and Wiri Station Rd, Manukau City, T09-978 5300. The largest shopping centre in New Zealand.
The Plaza Pakuranga, Main Highway, Pakuranga,T09-572 0264.
St Luke's Shopping Centre, 80 St Luke's Rd, Mt Albert, T09-978 6000.
Shore City Galleria, corner of Lake Rd and Como St, Takapuna, T09-978 6300.
Westgate Shopping Centre, 1 Fernhill Dr, Massey North, T09-8310200.
West City Shopping Centre, Catherine St, Henderson, T09-978 6700.

Sports

Quality sports stores can be found throughout the city and suburbs, but in this land of rugby and for that world-famous sporting souvenir – the All Blacks Jersey – head no further than:
Canterbury Clothing Company (CCC), corner Quay and Hobson sts, CBD, T09-307 2699.
Maritime Museum Shop, on the waterfront, page 74. For all things nautical, and for the America's Cup souvenir and clothing range.

▲ Activities and tours

Bridge climb

For anyone who has been to Sydney and seen the Sydney Harbour Bridge, let alone made the ascent of that world famous 'Bridge Climb', the mere sight of Auckland's equivalent will bring about a wry smile if not the full 'paah'. However, this is Auckland, not Sydney, and besides, the views are still amazing. Night trips can also be arranged.

Harbour Bridge Experience (Bridge Climb), Westhaven Reserve, T09-3612000, www.ajhackett.com. 1½ hrs from $120.

Bungee jumping and sky walking

A J Hackett, T09-3612000/T0800-462 8649, www.ajhackett.com. The newest jump opportunity, from the Harbour Bridge, from $120, minimum age is 10. Spectators can do the 'express climb' to the jump platform for $35. Operated by the leaders in the field, it may not be the highest but it is still a lot of fun.
Sky Jump, T0800-759586, www.skyjump. co.nz, from $195 (maximum weight 125 kg). This is the original and much talked about jump from just above the restaurant of the Sky Tower. But there is a 'catch' (thankfully, or sadly, depending how you look at it). Given the incredible jump height of 192 m, not to mention all that nasty hard concrete and people watching you below, it is not possible to jump conventionally with an elastic cord attached to the ankles and to do the 'yoyo' bit. Obviously if you did, in this scenario, you would probably end up like Garfield the ginger cat plastered against somebody's office window. So be advised, watch what is involved first and note that it is a cable-controlled descent in the horizontal, not vertical, position. That said, at 20 seconds and 75 kph it is should still get the adrenaline pumping.
Sky Walk, T0800-759586, www.skyjump. co.nz. Sky Walk the latest Sky Tower adventure that involves walking around the tower's pergola (or ring) on a narrow walkway with 192-m drop and nothing but thin air on either side. An overhead safety tether travels above. From $135, combo $260.

Canyoning

Although Wanaka is generally considered the country's canyoning capital, the streams and waterfalls of the Waitakere Ranges (Piha) west of the city and the Coromandel Peninsula provide some exciting opportunities.
Awol Adventures, T0800-462965, www.awol adventures.co.nz. Half- or full- day trips, with overnight excursions, from $135.

Canyonz, T0800-422696, www.canyonz.co.nz. 3-hr excursions with beach visit from $175 and an extended 5-hr trip to Coromandel from $235.

Climbing

See www.climb.co.nz or www.indoor climbing.co.nz for details. Auckland has plenty of opportunities, both indoors and outside. **Mt Eden Quarry** offers excellent climbing on basalt rock cliffs.
Extreme Edge, T09-574 5677, www.extremeedge.co.nz. One of the largest indoor rock climbing walls in New Zealand.
University of Auckland Recreation Centre, 17 Symonds St, T09-373 7599 (ext 88386), www.auckland.ac.nz/recreation. Has a cutting edge indoor climbing wall.

Cruises

A cruise around the inner harbour, or better still, out into the Hauraki Gulf, gives you the opportunity to experience Auckland's 'other-and-far-more-attractive-half' and is highly recommended. Once out there you will see why Auckland is considered such a yachties' heaven. The waterfront and Viaduct Basin is the place to 'cruise shop'.
360-Discovery (Kawau Kat) Cruises, T0800-360 3472/T09-307 8005, www.360discovery.co.nz, or ask at the VIC. A range of harbour cruise options as well as day trips to Kawau Island and the Coromandel Peninsula. The day trip to Tiritiri Matangi Bird Sanctuary is particularly recommended.
Explore NZ Dolphin and Whale Safaris, T09-357 6032/T0800-397567, www.dolphinsafari.co.nz. Trips depart from the Viaduct Harbour daily (Oct-Apr) at 1330 (year round), cost $150, child $100. 5-hr whale- and dolphin-watching trips are often in conjunction with university research projects, so there is no shortage of knowledge. Although there is reputedly a 90% success rate, the Hauraki is not generally as productive as many other sites around New Zealand like the Bay of Islands, Whakatane or the great sea mammal capital, Kaikoura. What is guaranteed, however, is

stunning scenery and an entertaining day-long cruise.

Fullers, Fullers Cruise Centre, Ferry Building, waterfront, T09-367 9111, www.fullers.co.nz. The main operator offering everything from a 2-hr harbour cruise (taking in the Viaduct Basin, Devonport, the Harbour Bridge etc) from $35, child $18, to island transportation and stop-overs (see Hauraki Islands, page 117).

Golf

Auckland, like much of New Zealand, is a golfer's heaven. Green fees are very reasonable ($35-50). Club hire is available at most courses. Mid-range, reasonably quiet and scenic courses include **Hauapi**, Riverhead, West Auckland, T09-412 8809; **Murawai**, west coast beaches, T09-411 8454; and **South Head**, West Auckland, Kaipara Heads, T09-420 2838; the latter is a good 45-min drive, but the course is a delight.

For more expensive, high-profile courses try: **Formosa**, Beachlands, South Auckland, T09-536 5895; **Gulf Harbour**, Whangaparaoa Peninsula, T09-428 1380, www.gulf-harbour. co.nz; or **Titirangi**, West Auckland, T09-827 5749.

Horse trekking and stud visits

Horse trekking operations are generally focused on the west coast beaches particularly around Murawai or Parakai. **South Kaipara Horse Treks**, T09-420 2835, www.horserides.co.nz. Half or full day and overnight from $85.
Tasman Rides, T09-420 8603, www.tasmanrides.co.nz. 1-4 hrs from $45.

Hot air ballooning

Although Christchurch and the Canterbury Plains is considered 'ballooning central' in New Zealand Auckland can still offer some fine city and harbourscapes during the 1-hr standard dawn runs, from $320.
Balloon Expeditions, T09-416 8590, www.balloonexpeditions.co.nz.
Balloon Safaris, T09-415 8289, www.balloonsafaris.co.nz.

Kayaking

Fergs Kayaks, 12 Tamaki Drive, T09- 5292230, www.fergskayaks.co.nz. Based in the city itself, long established and owned by Olympic champion Ian Ferguson. A range of trips on offer including the deservedly popular day or night guided trips to Rangitoto Island ($120). Independent hire available.

Given Auckland's proximity to Waiheke Island (page 120) and the beautiful, varied coastline it is no surprise to find several operators based there, including the following who offer a range of half- to full-day or overnight guided trips from $85-250. Independent hire also available. Try **Ross Adventures**, T09-372 5550, www.kayakwaiheke.co.nz.

Leisure centres

Village on Broadway Cinemas, Broadway, Newmarket, T09-520 0806. Olympic pools and fitness centre, next to the cinema complex.

Quad biking and 4WD

It would be rude not to have a quad bike operator and some 4WD adventures somewhere around the city and the west coast beaches and forest trails lend themselves to the pursuit.
4 Track Adventures, Woodhill Forest, T0800-487225, www.4trackadventures.co.nz. Half- to full-day trips covering 15-55 km, from $155.
Extreme 4WD Adventures, Helensville, T0800-493238/T09-420 3050, www.extreme 4wd.co.nz. Self-drive, $90 for 2 hrs.

Rugby

Eden Park Stadium, Reimers Av, Kingsland, T09-8155551, www.edenpark.co.nz. New Zealand's largest stadium, hosting up to 48,000 spectators for major rugby and cricket matches and the principal stadium for the final of the 2011 Rugby World Cup.

Sailing

Naturally, there are many opportunities to experience the Hauraki in the best possible way – by sail. Options range from catamarans to racing yachts. The VIC has full listings. 2 of the most popular vessels are the former America's Cup racing yachts of SailNZ and the tall ship *Soren Larsen*.

SailNZ, T09-359 5987, www.sailnz.co.nz, offers cruises and match races between authentic America's Cup racing yachts, the *NZL 40* and *NZL 41*. A basic, yet exhilarating 2-hr sailing trip costs from $150, child $110; the full-on race between the 2, during which you have the opportunity to participate, costs $195, child $175. This is without a doubt the most 'Auckland' of activities, the crew are always entertaining and it is recommended.

SailNZ also offer a *Whale/Sail Eco Adventure* on the Hauraki (7hr from $225); a *Dolphin/Sail Eco Adventure* of around 8 hours for a very reasonable $155.

There are also all-inclusive sailing trips to the Bay of Islands with one offering 'the ultimate coastal maxi adventure' with a 2-night excursion on board the *Lion New Zealand*, once owned by Sir Peter Blake. Given the location and the history, this is the ideal opportunity to indulge.
Soren Larsen, T09-817 8799, www.soren larsen.co.nz. This vessel has been gracing the gulf for a number of years and starred in the TV hit series *The Onedin Line*. There are a number of multi-day sailing options where you can take the helm or help raise sails, or simply kick back and watch. 5-night voyages to the Bay of Islands from around $500.

Skiing and snowboarding
Snowplanet, Small Rd, Silverdale, T09-4270044, www.snowplanet.co.nz, daily 1000—2200. Indoor skiing, snowboarding and air- boarding (a high-tech air filled bodyboard for snow), day-pass $54 child $42. Lessons available. Also has a neat café overlooking the slope.

Surfing
The best surfing is on the west coast beaches. The Piha breaks are internationally renowned.
Surf and Snow Tours, T0800-787386/ T09-828 0426, www.newzealandsurf tours.co.nz. A reputable outfit offering surfing trips and lessons to the west coast beaches from $99.

Swimming
Birkenhead on the Shore, T09-418 3560; **Olympic Pool**, Newmarket, 77 Broadway, T09-522 4414; the **Tepid Baths**, Viaduct Basin, 100 Customs St West, T09-379 4745 and the thermal complexes at Parakai and Waiwera.

Tour operators
There are many coach tours to key locations including the Bay of Islands, Waitomo and Rotorua, ranging from simple day tours to activity and accommodation packages. Shop around and compare prices. The VIC has full details. Good local tour companies include:
Auckland Wine Tasting Tours,
T09-6301540, www.winetrailtours.co.nz. Explore the ever-increasing range of vineyards and vintages springing up around the region, from $105 (includes lunch).
Bush and Beach, T09-837 4130/ T0800-423 224, www.bushandbeach.co.nz. Specializing in insightful and flexible eco-trips to the west coast beaches and Waitakeres, from $135.
Coromandel Explorer Tours, T07-866 3506, www.coromandeltours.co.nz. For those short of time, or without their own wheels. 1 to 4-day tours of the peninsula from $250. Recommended.
Potiki Adventures, T09-845 5932, www.potikiadventures.co.nz. Excellent Maori-themed adventure tours, with a range of fixed or custom activities from hiking to Marae stays. Their 'Auckland Orientation Trip' (8 hrs from $145) is a fine introduction to the city, region and country from the Maori perspective. Recommended.

Walking
The best walking opportunities in the region are to be found at the **Wiatakeres** and **west coast beaches**, see the relevant areas for details. Regional parks and islands like **Rangitoto** and **Tiritiri Matangi** also offer

excellent walking opportunities. See Hauraki Islands section page 117, or consult the VIC. **Arataki Information Centre**, Scenic Drive, Titirangi, T09-817 0077, is a fine place to gather information before a walk.

⊖ Transport

Air
Air New Zealand, T0800-737000/T09-357 3000, www.airnewzealand.co.nz. **Qantas**, T0800-808767, www.qantas.com.au/travel/ airlines/home/nz/en. **JetStar**, T0800-800995, www.jetstar.com/nz/en. **Virgin Blue**, T0800-670000, www.virginblue.com.au. All fly regularly to most provincial centres including **Wellington** (10 daily, 1 hr, $100-240), and **Christchurch** (18 daily, 1 hr 20 mins, $80-190). Tickets are best secured in advance on the internet.

Bicycle
Adventure Cycles, 9 Premier Av, Western Springs, T09-940 2453, www.adventure-auckland.co.nz. For bike hire. Great service with a free helmet provided, lock, tool kit and water bottle, plus maps and tips. Prices range from about $35 a day to $200 a month. Also offers a 50% buy-back for up to 6 months, which equates to the rental rate for 1 month when an inexpensive bike is purchased, and is a good deal.

Bus
Local
MAXX, T0800-103080/T09-366 6400, www.maxx.co.nz. Has a detailed telephone information service on all major local city transport carriers' routes, prices and connections with ferry services.
Stagecoach, T09-366 6400, www.nzbus.co.nz. Publishes an *Auckland Busabout Guide*, available from the bus terminal and all major VICs, showing routes and departure points for the main city attractions. Fares are on a staged system 1-8 and range between $1.60-9.70. They offer a

'Discovery Pass' allowing unlimited travel on board bus/ferry/train for $13; 7-day $40.
'City Circuit' is an environmentally friendly electric red bus providing a free service around the immediate city centre every 10 mins, daily 0800-1800.
The **Auckland City Loop 'Link'** is a good way to get around the city centre. Each journey costs $1.60 and buses run every 10 mins on weekdays 0600-1900, every 15 mins evenings and weekends 0700-1800. You will feel like a sardine at rush hour. The route (which goes both ways) runs from the city centre (Britomart)-Quay Park-Parnell-Newmarket-Hospital-University-AUT-Library-Myers Park-K'Rd-Ponsonby-Victoria Park-Casino/Sky City-Mid Queen St-Britomart. For further details and information, see www.maxx.co.nz.
The **Double Decker 'Explorer'**, T0800-439756, www.explorerbus.co.nz, bus has all day sightseeing with commentary; $35 day pass, $20 for 1hr ride.

Long distance
The 2 main players providing standard coach travel from Auckland to destinations throughout New Zealand day and night are: **Intercity Coach Lines**, www.intercitycoach.co.nz; and **Newman's**, www.newmanscoach.co.nz. All coaches arrive/depart from the **Sky City Coach Terminal**, 102 Hobson St, City (round the corner from the Sky Tower), T09-583 5780, Open daily 0700-1930. **Northliner Express**, T09-307 5873, www.northliner.co.nz, offers a valued service to a number of North Island destinations, especially Northland. Concession fares apply. Buses also arrive and depart from the Sky City Coach Terminal.

Car
For those interested in buying a car or campervan, see Essentials, page 41. If you own a car and have been drinking, there is a wonderful service in Auckland called **Dial-a-Driver**, T0800-382438/T09-828 6398. A sober employee drives you and your car to your chosen destination while another driver

follows in a company car. The drivers are generally friendly and immensely stoic.

Car hire

Take time to find a good deal through the main VICs. A new, fully insured car without mileage costs from around $75 a day.

For a cheap, no nonsense deal, try Scotties (see below). Ask about the 'buy-back deals' and drop-off arrangements with its sister operation in Christchurch. For the numerous office locations contact the company direct.

A2B Rentals, T0800-222929, www.a2brentals.co.nz.
Action Rent-a-Car, T09-277 4422, www.action-rent-a-car.co.nz. Free pick-up, 24-hr service.
Affordable Rental Cars and Vans, T0800-454443/T09-630 1567, www.car-rental.co.nz.
Alternative Rental Cars, T09-373 3822, www.hireacar.co.nz.
Apex Rental Cars, T0800-939597, www.apexrentals.co.nz.
Avis, 17/19 Nelson St, City, T09-526 3256/ T0800-284722, www.avis.co.nz.
Big Save Car Rentals, T0800-502277.
Budget Rent A Car, T0800-283438/ T09-5297784, www.budget.co.nz.
Hertz, T09-2568690, www.hertz.co.nz.
Rent-a-Dent, T0800-736823/T09-275 2044.
Scotties, 27 New North Rd, Eden Terr, T09-303 3912.
Thrifty Car Rental, Airport, T0800-737070/ T03-3592720, www.thrifty.co.nz.

Campervan hire

Adventure Campervans, 2 Beach Rd, Otahuhu, T09-276 7100/T0800-123555, www.nzmotorhomes.co.nz.
Backpacker Campervan Rentals, 36 Richard Pearse Dr, Mangere (3 km from Auckland Airport) T09-275 0200/ T0800-422267, www.backpackercamper vans.com. Offices in Wellington, Christchurch and Queenstown.
Britz Motorhomes, 36 Richard Pearse Drive, Mangere, T09-255 3984/ T0800-831900,

www.britz.com. Offices in Auckland, Wellington, Christchurch and Queenstown.
Kea Campers, 36 Hillside Rd, T0800-520052/T09-441 7828, www.keacampers.com. Offices throughout the country.
KiwiKombis, 96 Uxbridge Rd, Howick, T09-533 9335, www.kiwikombis.com. The iconic if slow old favourite.
Maui Motorhomes, 36 Richard Pearse Drive, Mangere, T09-255 3983/ T0800-651080, www.maui-rentals.com.
Spaceships, 50 Fort St, CBD, T09-5262130/ T0800-772237, www.spaceships.co.nz. 'Kick-ass' campervans at the top end of the scale, equipped with everything you might need.
Tui Campers, 142 Robertson Rd, Mangere East, T03-359 7410, www.tuicampers.co.nz.

Ferry

For further information about ferry services, contact the VIC.
Fullers, ground floor of the Ferry Building, T09-367 9111, www.fullers.co.nz. The main ferry company.
Auckland Water Taxi, Viaduct Basin, T09-4258006, www.aucklandescape.co.nz. Not quite as popular as in Sydney Harbour, but these are a good way of zipping over to the North Shore or the eastern suburbs.

Scooter and motorcycle

NZ Motorcycle Rentals and Tours, 72 Barry's Point Rd, Takapuna, T09-486 2472, www.nzbike.com. An award-winning national company. It hires out a range of bikes from the 50 cc sensible sewing machines to the 1100 cc scary monsters, all at reasonable rates.

Taxi

Alert Taxis, T09-309 2000.
Auckland Taxi Co-op, T09-300 3000.
Citicabs, T09-300 1111.
Corporate Cabs, T09-377 0773.
Discount Taxis, T09-529 1000.

ⓘ Directory

Banks
There are numerous outlets along Queen St and within the CBD. **American Express Currency Exchange**, 105 Queen St, City; also at NZ Cup Village, Quay St, City; and 67-69 Symonds St, City. **ANZ Banking Group**, 126 and 268 Queen and Victoria St, T04-472 7123/T0800-269296, www.anz.co.nz. **ASB Bank Ltd**, corner of Queen and Wellesley sts, T0800-803804/T09-306 3011, www.asbbank.co.nz. **Bank of New Zealand**, 80 Queen St, T09-375 1300/T0800-240000, www.bnz.co.nz. **National Bank of New Zealand**, 205 Queen St, T09-359 9826/T0800-181818, www.nationalbank.co.nz. **Travelex**, 32 and 157 Queen St, T0800-4401100. **Westpac Trust**, 79 Queen St, T09-302 4200/T0800-400600, www.westpac.co.nz.

Disabled facilities
Auckland Disabilities Resource Centre, 14 Erson Av, Royal Oak, T09-6258069, www.disabilityresource.org.nz. **Enable**, T0800-362253, www.enable.co.nz.

Embassies and consulates
Australia 7th floor, Price Waterhouse Coopers Tower, 188 Quay St, City, T09-921 8800. **Canada** 9th floor, 48 Emily Pl, City, T09-309 3690. **Denmark** 273 Bleakhouse Rd, Howick, T09-537 3099. **Germany** 90-92 Hobson Street, Thorndon, Wellington, T04-4736063.**Ireland** 7th floor, Citibank Blg, 23 Customs St East, City, T09-977 2252. **Japan** Level 12, ASB Bank Centre, 135 Albert St, City, T09-303 4106. **Korea** Level 11, ASB Bank Tower 2, Hunter Street, Wellington, T04-4739073. **Netherlands** Level 1, 57 Symonds St, City, T09-379 5399. **Sweden** 13th floor, 13 O'Connell St, City, T09-373 5332. **UK** IAG House, 151 Queen St, City, T09-303 2973. **USA** 29 Flitzherbert Terrace, Thorndon, Wellington, T04-4626000.

Gay and lesbian
Express Magazine available from outlets of **Maggazzino** (see Shopping, page 100). **Pride**, T09-302 0590, www.pride.org.nz.

Internet
Readily available in the CBD including: **Auckland City Library**, 44-46 Lorne St, City, T09-377 0209. **High Tech**, 63 Wakefield St, T09-368166. **Big World Internet Café**, 102/76 Wakefield St, T09-3695999 and 43 Cook St, T09-5504582, **Bros**, 28 Fort St, T09-3090798. **Cyberdate**, 320 Queen St, City, T09-3770320.

Laundry
Suds Laundromat, 18 Fort St, T09-358 4370, Mon-Sat 0900-2000.

Left luggage
Auckland International Airport, T09-275 6467, daily 0600-2300.

Libraries
Central City Library, 44-46 Lorne St, City, T09-377 0209, Mon-Fri 0900-2000, Sat/Sun 1000-1600.

Medical services
Accident and medical centres
Ponsonby Accident and Emergency, 202 Ponsonby Rd, T09-376 9222.

Hospitals Auckland Hospital, Park Rd, Grafton, T09-367 0000. Greenlane Hospital, Greenlane Rd West, Greenlane, T09-367 0000. Middlemore Hospital, Hospital Rd, Otahuhu, T09-276 0000. North Shore Hospital, Shakespeare Rd, Takapuna, T09-486 8930. Waitakere Hospital, Lincoln Rd, Henderson, T09-839 0000.

Police
Emergency Dial 111. Main police station is at the corner of Cook and Vincent sts, City, T09-302 6400.

Post offices
Main post office and post restante, 24

Wellesley St West, City, T09-379 6710, Mon-Fri 0800-1700. Additional branches at: 23 Customs St, T09-302 1059; 167 Victoria St West, T09- 367 9617; and Downtown Shopping Centre, Queen St, T09-309 6343.

Supermarkets
There are Night Owl or Star 24-hr grocery stores on Queen St and the waterfront. Foodtown, 76 Quay St.

New World, 2 College Hill, City (near Victoria Park on the Link bus route), daily until 2400.

Travel agents
Backpackers World Travel, at Base Backpackers 229 Queen St, City, T09-358 4871.
STA Travel, 267 and Level 10 220 Queen St, City, T0800-474400 / T09-356 1550.

North of Auckland → *Colour map 1, 4A.*

The Kaipara Harbour, with a combined coastal length that exceeds 3200 km, is one of the biggest natural harbours in the world. It was of huge economic significance in the Kauri logging and export days of the mid- to late-1800s, with the ports of Helensville to the south and Dargaville to the north being of particular importance. Some 40 km north of the city centre (but a mere stone's throw from the northern edge of it) is the Hibiscus Coast – a coastline dominated by the 3-km beach adjacent to the main town, Orewa. Around Orewa there are the more sheltered bays of the Whangaparaoa Peninsula to the south and the Wenderholm Regional Park and Puhoi River to the north. ⏵⏵ See Sleeping, Eating and other listings, pages 110-111.

Ins and outs
Getting there For city northbound bus services MAXX T0800-103080/T09-366 6400, www.maxx.co.nz, offers a regular daily service to and from Orewa and the Whangaparaoa Peninsula from Auckland. By car, take SH16 off the Great Western Motorway in the city.

Tourist information **Hibiscus Coast VIC (I-Site)** ① *on the main drag, 214a Hibiscus Coast Highway (HCH), next to Orewa Beach Holiday Park, T09-426 0076, www.orewa-beach.co.nz/www.rodneynz.com, Mon-Sat 0900-1700, Sun 1000-1600,* can fill you in on what local activities are available and where to stay. Book accommodation well ahead in summer.

Southern Kaipara, Helensville and Parakai
The **VIC (I-Site)** ① *27 Commercial Rd, T09-420 8060, www.helensville.co.nz, Mon-Fri 1000-1700, Sat 1000-1400,* will help with activity and accommodation bookings.

Looking at Helensville today, it is hard to imagine it as a bustling port; these days it is a rather dull place, with little to attract you except perhaps a reminder of yesteryear in the **Pioneer Museum** ① *Commercial St, T09-420 7881, Wed, Sat-Sun 1300-1530 or by arrangement, $5, children free.* Most other sights and activities are water-based.

Nearby, **Parakai** is famous for its hot pools at **Aquatic Park Parakai Springs** ① *150 Parkhurst Rd, T09-420 8998, www.parakaisprings.co.nz, $16, child $8, daily 1000- 2100.* A long soak is particularly welcome after a horse trek on the beach.

Hibiscus Coast and the Whangaparaoa Peninsula
Whangaparaoa Peninsula At the ever-expanding northern fringe of Auckland City is the Whangaparaoa Peninsula. It is essentially a rather unexciting enclave for the northern Auckland suburbanites. However, the scenery is good and there are some attractions worth

considering. **Snowplanet** ⓘ *Small Rd, Silverdale, T09-427 0044 www.snowplanet.co.nz, daily 1000-2200, day-pass $54, child $42,* is a new snow-sports facility offering indoor skiing, snowboarding and air- boarding (a high-tech air-filled bodyboard). Lessons are also available, and there's a café overlooking the slope. Elsewhere, kids and rail buffs might enjoy a visit to the **Whangaparaoa Narrow Gauge Steam Railway** ⓘ *400 Whangaparaoa Rd, Stanmore Bay, T09-424 5018, www.rail.co.nz, Sep-Jun Sat-Sun 1200-1600, $6.*

There's also the **Gulf Harbour** ⓘ *www.gulf-harbour.co.nz,* with its posh marina village and international standard golf course. In 2006 it hosted the New Zealand Open Golf Tournament, but if you have ventured this far out and left your golf clubs at home, then you would be better off heading for the **Shakespeare Regional Park**. Here, beyond Gulf Harbour, you will encounter fine views, a few walks and the occasional quiet beach. Alternatively, if your timing is right, take the Fuller's ferry from the Gulf Harbour Marina to the beautiful open bird sanctuary of **Tiritiri Matangi Island** (see page 118).

Orewa Although the coastal resort of Orewa is not essentially part of Auckland City it has, with the recent motorway and ever-encroaching housing developments, become a satellite town. But Orewa is still a staunchly independent community. It boasts a fine beach which lures the city slickers and visitors in increasingly healthy numbers in summer, but otherwise there is not a great deal on offer, except perhaps a coffee and snack before heading north. The focus of the town is **Hillary Square**, which boasts a statue of the great man himself. Sir Edmund Hillary is New Zealand's best-known explorer and climber, the first to conquer Mount Everest.

Orewa to Warkworth At the northern end of Orewa you will pass the scenic **Red Beach** before winding your way to Waiwera Thermal Spa Resort ⓘ *21 Main Rd, T09-427 8800, www.waiwera.co.nz, Sun-Thu 0900-2200, Fri-Sat 0900-2230, $25, child $15, family $60.* It's a small resort built around natural hot springs, where you can laze about in a purpose-built resort that has large pools, spas and water slides for the kids, and even a separate covered pool where you can take in a movie – presumably to emerge afterwards looking like a walnut. Their new and well-facilitated spa complex 'Infinity' offers all the usual body treatments with a private spa costing around $40 per hour, and massage from $65 for 30 minutes.

About 1 km north of Waiwera is **Wenderholm Regional Park**. This is one of the region's most handsome regional parks, sited on a sand spit deposited by the Puhoi River and now grassed over and dominated by beautiful large pohutukawa trees. The beach is often wild and windswept and offers a wonderful view of the small offshore islands and the mountainous Little Barrier Island to the north. The park has some excellent walking tracks ranging from 20 minutes to 2½ hours. There is a choice of coastal walks, or the more challenging headland walks, where you may see, or hear, the fluid song of the tui and clattering wings of the keruru or native pigeon. If history is your preference, the park's administration block is dominated by the 1860s colonial homestead, **Couldrey House** ⓘ *T09-366 2000, Sat-Sun only 1300-1600; bus 895 terminates here on Sun in summer.*

The small and picturesque village of **Puhoi** is just off SH1, 5 km north of Wenderholm. It has an intriguing history as a Catholic Bohemian settlement established in 1863. Although most of the memories are focused in the **Puhoi Historical Society Museum** ⓘ *in the former convent school, www.puhoihistoricalsociety.org.nz, open Christmas to Easter, over weekends and during school holidays 1300-1600, donation,* much of the story is evident in the historic

Puhoi Tavern. It is a fascinating little pub full of historic clutter and characters. Provided no one is playing pool you can read all about the early settlers and sympathize with their desperate cause. It is a depressing and unhappy story of a seemingly never-ending struggle with the land, hunger and desperation. Despite the awful stories the pub is very appealing and on the second Friday of each month a local Bohemian band play their toe-tapping tunes. On a fine summer Sunday afternoon the river can be a fine place to be, as you gently wind your way downstream to Wenderholm Regional Park in a canoe or Canadian kayak.

◉ North of Auckland listings

For Sleeping and Eating price codes and other relevant information, see Essentials pages 44-50.

● Sleeping

Helensville and Parakai *p108*
A Kaipara House B&B, corner of SH16 and Parkhurst Rd, Helensville, T09-420 7462, www.kaiparahouse.co.nz. 4 spacious rooms with period furnishings, and a separate summerhouse.
A Malolo House, 110 Commercial Rd, Helensville, T09-420 7262, malolo@xtra.co.nz. Comfortable villa-style B&B and backpacker accommodation. Centrally located.
C-D Point of View, Te Makiri, Helensville, T09-420 7331, www.pointofview.net.nz. Pleasant and alternative backpacker farmstay run by local poet/songwriter.

Campsites
D Parakai Hot Pools, Parkhurst Rd, Parakai, T09-420 8998. Basic caravan and campsites, standard facilities. Reduced entry to the pools.

Hibiscus Coast and Whangaparaoa Peninsula *p108*
LL The Gulf Harbour Lodge, 164 Harbour Village Drive, Gulf Harbour, Whangaparaoa Peninsula, T07-428 1118, www.gulfharbour lodge.com. One of the main luxury options in the area with the added bonus of free access to the Gulf Harbour Country Club facilities. Cheaper weekend rates.
A Coach Trail Villas and Beach Cottages, 1 Waiwera Rd, Waiwera, T09-426 4792,

www.kiwistay.co.nz. Offers comfortable accommodation in villa or self-contained waterfront cottages within walking distance of the hot pools, should you need to hang yourself out to dry overnight in Waiwera.
A Waves, corner of Hibiscus Coast Highway and Kohu St, T09-427 0888, www.waves.co.nz. Modern small and good quality hotel option close to the beach.
C-D Marco Polo Tourist Lodge, 2D Hammond Av, Hatfields Beach, Orewa, T09-426 8455, www.marcopolo.co.nz. Comfortable backpacker hostel with full range of room types, a relaxing garden and palm tree-painted bedroom walls.
C-D Pillows Travellers' Lodge, 412 Hibiscus Coast Highway, Orewa, T09-426 6338, www.pillows.co.nz. Another budget option with value double en suites with TV.

Motels
Motels dominate the northern end of Orewa and almost all of them can be found on either side of the main drag – the Hibiscus Coast Highway.
A Anchor Lodge Motel, 436, T09-427 0690, www.anchorlodge.co.nz.
A Beachcomber Motel, 246, T09-426 5973, www.beachcombermotel.co.nz.
A Hibiscus Palms Motel, 416, T09-426 4904, www.hibiscuspalms.co.nz.

Motorcamps
Orewa Beach Top 10 Holiday Park, 265 Hibiscus Coast Highway, T0800-673921/ T09-426 5832. 4-star facilities including camp kitchen.

● Eating

Helensville and Parakai *p108*

McNutts Farm and Café, 11 km north of Parakai, 914 South Head Rd, South Head, T09-420 2501, www.macnut.co.nz. A good alternative, in combination with a macadamia nut orchard tour ($5). Congenial and friendly.

Ginger Crunch Station Café, 2 Railway Rd, T09-420 9133, Wed-Sun 0900-1500. Based at the historic rail station and-as the name suggests-a purveyor of fine Ginger Crunch as well as all day breakfasts, light meals, home made baking and good coffee.

Hibiscus Coast and Whangaparaoa Peninsula *p108*

There are numerous small cafés and takeaways in Orewa.

Muldoon's Irish Bar, Unit 8/9 Westpac Plaza Moana Av, T09-427 8000. Small, family oriented pub.

The Sahara Café, 336 Hibiscus Coast Highway, right on the waterfront, T09-426 8828, daily. Offers quality, convenience and a hearty all-day breakfast.

Walnut Cottage Café, Orewa House, 498 Hibiscus Coast Highway, T09-427 5570, Mon-Thu 0930-1630, Fri-Sun 0930-1800. BYO and licensed. Situated in congenial grounds.

▲ Activities and tours

Helensville and Parakai *p108*

Several tours leave from Helensville to link up with others in Dargaville, see page 182.

South Kaipara Horse Treks, T09-420 2835, www.horserides.co.nz.

Tasman Rides, T09-420 8603, www.tasmanrides.co.nz.

Taylor Made Tours, T09-4391576, www.taylor madetours.co.nz. Great range of options from touring on the remote and extensive Ripiro Beach, from $95.

Hibiscus Coast and Whangaparaoa Peninsula *p108*

Puhoi River Canoe Hire, 84 Puhoi Valley Rd, T09-422 0891, www.puhoirivercanoes.co.nz. $40 for the full river adventure or $20 per hr.

West of Auckland → *Colour map 2, A1.*

From the centre of the city the Great Western Motorway straddles the inner inlets of the Waitemata Harbour before taking you to the western suburbs of Auckland. From these western fringes of the city, the Waitakere Ranges rise to form a huge area of bush with an extensive network of walking tracks. These seemingly endless hills eventually reach the sea and the west coast beaches that offer a huge contrast to the quiet Pacific beaches of the Hauraki Gulf. **▸▸** *For Sleeping, Eating and other listings see pages 114-115.*

Ins and outs

Getting there Public transport to the Waitakeres and especially the west coast beaches is limited. Hiring a car or taking an organized tour are your best options. Alternatively **Veolia**, www.maxx.co.nz, has a rail service from the city to Henderson and Waitakere; a workable option if you hire a bike. From Titirangi village it is a 27-km ride to Whatipu. **Piha Surf Shuttles**, T09-627 2644, www.surfshuttle.co.nz, offers a daily service to Piha (taking in Karekare) Dec-Feb departing the city at 0830 and returning at 1600, from $40 one-way, $60 return. **Bush and Beach**, T09-575 1458, www.bushandbeach.co.nz, includes Muriwai in its tours, see Auckland Activities and tours page 104.

Waitakere City

West Auckland, or Waitakere City, is made up of a number of diverse suburbs. Te Atatu, Swanson, Henderson, New Lynn and Glendene are relatively low-income areas of little note, except for being home to the 'Westie', a peculiar type of Aucklander who dresses predominantly in black, loves rock 'n' roll, does not believe in hair salons, and simply loves anything on wheels that goes fast, burns rubber and makes lots of noise. The **Great Western Motorway** pays homage to this almost nightly, with nearly every dawn presenting a trail of abandoned vehicles that never made it home.

Further west and south is **Titirangi** where, on the slopes of the ranges around **Scenic Drive**, the more well-to-do citizens enjoy their secluded, often beautiful, bush dwellings with wonderful views across the city. Titirangi, 'the gateway to the Waitakeres', is a very pleasant little village that is worth a visit in itself, with a number of pleasant cafés, interesting shops and a good art gallery, **Lopdell House** ⓘ *corner of Titirangi and South Titirangi Rds, T09-817 8087, www.lopdell.org.nz, daily 1000-1630, free*. Overall, Waitakere City is most famous for its liberal attitudes, art, vineyards and orchards and its spectacularly wild unspoilt bush and beaches. It has, as a result, proclaimed itself Auckland's 'Eco-City' with the Kumeu area being known as the 'Gannet and Grape district'.

The Waitakeres

The 'Waitaks', as they are affectionately known, are one of the region's biggest and most attractive regional parks, offering a 200-km network of walking tracks, many of which hide such scenic delights as large kauri trees, waterfalls and large dams. Before embarking on any activities in the area, visit the **Arataki Information Centre** ⓘ *on the hill at the southern end of Scenic Drive, 6 km from Titirangi, T09-817 0089/ T09-817 0077, www.arc.govt.nz/parks/our-parks/arataki-visitor-centre/, daily 0900- 1700 (1600 in winter)*. It is a modern centre that provides a vast amount of information, interesting interpretative displays, an audio-visual display, nature trail, education centre and, dominating the scene, an impressive Maori *pou* (carving), which lost its rather impressive 'manhood' a few years ago (though another was duly carved, and the glint in his little paua shell eye restored). From here make sure you take detailed advice on walks and buy the relevant maps. The Waitakeres have seen their fair share of lost trampers over the years. Don't forget to pick up the *Welcome Out West, Art Out West, Artists' and Artisans' Trail* and *Accommodation Out West* leaflets, as well as numerous walking maps and options from the centre, all free.

Sights The 28-km **scenic drive** is the best way to get an impression of the area as it winds along the eastern fringe of the Waitakeres, offering stunning views across the city both by day and by night. One of the best views can be seen from the garden of **Hellaby House** ⓘ *515 Scenic Dr, gardens daily 1300-1600, Sun, 1100-1700, free*, just below the TV masts. Its elderly owner, Rose, who loved the Waitakeres with a passion, donated Hellaby House to the city; given the view from her backyard this is not surprising.

West Auckland is one of the best-known wine-producing areas of the country, containing nearly 20 **wineries** with such famous names as Corbans, Coopers Creek, Matua Valley, Nobilo and Babich. The northern areas of Waitakere City host most of these, especially in the Kumeu area. Most wineries offer tastings. **Soljans** ⓘ *SH16, Kumeu, T09-412 5858, www.soljans.co.nz, daily 0900-1730, shop and café*, is recommended. Copies of the official *Wine Trail* and *Wineries of Auckland* leaflets can be found at the **Kumeu and District VIC (I-Site)** ⓘ *Main Rd, Huapai, T09-412 9886, www.kumeudistrict.co.nz*, and main city VICs. ▸▸ *See Activities and tours, page 115*.

One of the most unusual attractions in the area is the **Watercare Rain Forest Express** ⓘ *T09-302 8028, www.watercare.co.nz, $25 (twilight $28), child $12 ($14), regular trips on Sun 1400, 'glow-worm special' 1800 in summer, booking essential,* a fascinating and fun 2½-hour trip on the small gauge railway train that still plies the numerous lines and tunnels to service and maintain the local dams. **Bush and Beach** run tours, see page 115.

Wild west coast beaches ⏺⏸ ➤ *pp114-115.*

Whatipu

If you are looking for solitude and a real sense of wilderness, without doubt one of the best places to go in the region is Whatipu. Situated 45 km from the city centre, at the southernmost tip of the Waitakere Ranges, its huge expanse of sand in part forms the narrow mouth of the **Manukau Harbour**. At the terminus of the winding, unsealed road, past the picturesque little settlements of **Huia** and **Little Huia**, is a small cluster of buildings that make up **Whatipu Lodge**. The lodge is the last sign of habitation and chance of accommodation before you head north along the 6-km-long beach that stretches all the way to Karekare. If you can pull yourself away from the sound of the surf, head inland across the 700 acres of sand dune and wetland. Hidden in the undulations of dune grasses and cabbage trees are extensive wetlands that are home to noisy paradise shelduck, delicate pied stilts and elegant black swans. At the foot of the bush-clad hills are the remains of the **Parahara Railway** that once hauled huge kauri from Karekare in the 1870s. A boiler and a small tunnel still remain, even though the sand has long swallowed the tracks.

If you are on foot you can head north to Piha. Just before the road falls down the hill to Whatipu, take the Donald McLean Road up to the summit of **Mount Donald McLean**. The summit itself is a short 10-minute walk from the road end, and the view across the Waitakeres, the harbour and back across to the tiny Sky Tower is magnificent.

Karekare

Like most of the west coast beaches, the bush-clad hills of the Waitakeres fall dramatically into the sea and form a natural amphitheatre of vegetation and cliff, with the beach as its stage, the wind its song and the surf its applause.

There are a number of short walks and tracks around Karekare, some of which head inland or south to join the extensive Waitakere network. For long inland excursions, make sure you carry a map and supplies. The short walk up the Taraire Track to **Karekare Falls** is worthwhile, especially if you intend to swim in the pool beneath it. Another is the **Colman's Track** from the end of Watchmans Road, where the path creeps up the hill at the northern point of Karekare beach and terminates with a magnificent view. Looking south you can see well past Karekare beach to the huge expanse of Whatipu beach beyond, as well as the tiny, inaccessible Mercer Bay, immediately below and north. If you are feeling energetic, keep going along the track which follows the coast to meet Te Ahahu Road eventually, at Piha.

Piha

It is very hard to spend the day at Piha beach without contemplating packing it all in to live here. Piha has been luring dreamers and surfers for years and is, along with Muriwai, one of the west coast's most popular beaches. And as you climb down the windy road you will quickly realize that, for a few lucky souls, the dream has become reality. Although it can be very busy in summer, it still retains a distinctly isolated charm perhaps due to the lack of public transport. When you get fed up with sunbathing, swimming or trying to hold on to your surfboard in the fierce surf, there are two things you must do. The first and most obvious is to climb **Lion Rock** (a strenuous 30-minute walk), the guardian of the beach that looks with menace out to the ocean; from the summit you can look down on the surfers bobbing about in search of the perfect wave. The other thing to do, especially in a wild winter storm or at sunset, is to take the **Tasman Lookout Track** at the south end of the beach to **The Gap**. Here you can sit and watch in awe at the power of the breakers as they pound and crash into the narrow gap.

There is also an interesting, if less dramatic, walk at the northern end of Piha Beach, which leads to the isolated and beautiful **White's Beach**. If you have time, also try to see the **Kitekite Falls** from the Kitekite Track down Glen Esk Road behind the main camping ground. If you swim at Piha you can do so in relative safety, but always stay between the flags and in sight of the lifesavers. Piha has been the watery grave for many shore fishermen and uninitiated swimmers. If you get into trouble, raise an arm and keep it aloft – you will be in an inflatable rescue boat before you know it.

Muriwai

Muriwai, 15 km north of Piha and 45 km west of the city centre, is the west coast's most visited beach. On summer weekends it plays host to locals and visitors, who nestle down in the black sands to soak up the sun, surf, fish, play, or look over the **gannet colony**. These angry-looking birds have taken up residence on the flat rock outcrops at its southern end to breed, forming a small seabird city. It is a delight in spring, when the stomachs of the fluffy white chicks being kept full by the comings and goings of their bad-tempered parents. Muriwai boasts the only major North Island colony, after Cape Kidnappers on the east coast, near Napier.

Muriwai is well-serviced for locals and tourists and boasts a fine golf course (T09-411 8454). If Muriwai beach is too busy for you then try **Maori Bay**, another favourite surf spot just south of Muriwai, reached via Waitea Road. If you find the huge stretch of beach a bit daunting, a good way to explore is on horseback; try **Muriwai Beach Homestay and Horse Riding** (see Sleeping, below).

◉ West of Auckland listings

For Sleeping and Eating price codes and other relevant information, see Essentials pages 44-50.

● Sleeping

For local B&B and farmstay options contact the **Arataki Information Centre**, T09-817 0089, or consult the free *Staying Out West* leaflet available from all VICs.

The Waitakeres *p112*
C Aio Wira, T09-810 9396, www.airwira.org.nz. A peaceful simple retreat set in 4 ha of mature native bush.

Whatipu *p113*
B-D Whatipu Lodge, T09-811 8860, whatipu lodge@xtra.co.nz. Book a cabin or a tent site which will give you plenty of time to explore before heading back to the city the next day.

Piha *p113*
AL Piha Lodge, 117 Piha Rd, T09-812 8595, www.pihalodge.co.nz. Award winner with 2 self-contained units. Large pool and spa.
A Piha Cottage, T/F09-812 8514, www.piha cottage.co.nz. A secluded self-contained cottage in quiet bush surroundings.

Motorcamps

B-D Piha Domain Motor Camp,
T09-812 8815. In the heart of the village, tent
sites and cosy huts, camp kitchen. Bookings
advisable.

Muriwai *p114*

**B Muriwai Beach Homestay and Horse
Riding**, 781 Muriwai Rd, T09-411 7111,
www.farmstayauckland.co.nz. Offers the
choice of queen, twin or single in a country
setting only 2 km from the beach. Base for
horse trekking, about $70 for 2 hrs.

Motorcamps

B-D Muriwai Beach Motor Camp, T09-
411 9262, www.muriwaimotorcamp.co.nz.
Powered and non-powered sites and camp
kitchen, but no cabins.

⑦ Eating

Piha *p113*

The **RSA**, 3 Beach Valley Rd, T09-812 8138,
across the river from the motorcamp, and
Surf Club, 23 Marine Parade, T09-812 8896, at
the southern end of the beach, offer great
value meals, but you will have to ask a
member to sign you in. Opening times vary.

Other than that there are the usual
sad-looking pies to be had at the general
store near the motorcamp, or burgers and
the ubiquitous fish and chips at the burger
bar, next to the Surf Club (summer only).

Muriwai *p114*

The **Waterfront** general store serves light
meals and refreshments.

🍴 **Wuz's Café**, 185 Motutara Rd, Muriwai
Beach T09-411 8624. Open daily for breakfast,
lunch and dinner.

▲▲ Activities and tours

The Waitakeres *p112*
Canyoning

Although Wanaka is generally considered the
country's canyoning capital, the streams and
waterfalls of the Waitakere Ranges (Piha)
west of the city and the Coromandel
Peninsula provide some exciting
opportunities.

Awol Adventures, T0800-462965,
www.awoladventures.co.nz. Half- or full- day
trips, with overnight excursions, from $135.
Canyonz, T0800-422696,
www.canyonz.co.nz. 3-hr excursions with
beach visit from $175.

Tour operators

Bush and Beach, T09-837 4130/T0800-423
224, www.bushandbeach.co.nz. Specializing
in insightful and flexible eco-trips to the west
coast beaches and Waitakeres, from $135.
Potiki Adventures, T09-845 5932,
www.potikiadventures.co.nz. Excellent
Maori-themed adventure tours, with a range
of fixed or custom activities from hiking to
Marae stays. Their 'Auckland Orientation Trip'
(8 hrs from $145) is a fine introduction to the
city, region and country from the Maori
perspective. Recommended.

Wine tours

Auckland Wine Trail Tours, T09-630 1540,
www.winetrailtours.co.nz. Excellent half- and
full-day tours concentrating on vineyards, or a
combination of vineyards and general sights
in the Wiatakeres, from $95.
NZWinePro, T09-575 1958, www.nzwine
pro.co.nz. Offers one of the best wine tour
packages available (half or full-day from $129).

South of Auckland → Colour map 2, B1.

With so much to see elsewhere and usually limited time to do so, there is little to attract the international visitor to South Auckland. However, if you have ample time or want to take an alternative route to the Coromandel Peninsula, the scenic coast road via Miranda is recommended. Along the way the Shorebird Centre and Miranda Hot Pools on the shores of the Firth of Thames can make an interesting and soothing stop. Within the city itself Rainbow Springs is a fine place to take the kids and it can perhaps be combined with a walk in the Hunua Ranges Regional Park. ►► *For Sleeping and Eating, see page 117.*

Sights

Once you leave the city southbound through the **Manukau City** and **Franklin District** the SH1 climbs over the Bombay Hills then falls to meet the Waikato River towards Hamilton. The **Franklin VIC (I-Site)** ① *Mill Rd, Bombay, T09-236 0670, www.tourism franklin. co.nz*, can recommend excursions or detours in the area. South of Auckland

If you are heading to the Coromandel Peninsula, the best way is to follow the **Pacific Coast Highway** via **Howick** and **Whitford**. The route is generally well marked (with the Pacific Coast Highway logo) and has a number of interesting stops on the way. Just before you hit the coast proper you pass the **Omana Regional Park**. This small park offers outstanding views of the gulf across to Waiheke and a pleasant beach with a rock platform that provides safe and shallow swimming at high tide and is ideal for kids.

Further south and inland again, is the farming town of **Clevedon**, home to **Auckland's Polo Club**, T09-292 8556, which has games on Sundays in the summer. There are also a number of cafés in which to grab a cup of tea. South of Clevedon (but a diversion off the Pacific Coast Highway) is **Hunua**, on the edge of the **Hunua Ranges Regional Park**. These bush-clad ranges contain the watersheds for a number of dams that supply Auckland with most of its water. Although the park and the ranges are not in the same league as the Waitakeres west of Auckland, there are a number of interesting walks – the best of which is an all-day hike that takes in the Wairoa River, Cossey's Dam and the 30-m **Hunua Falls**. For information visit the **Hunua Ranges Park Visitor Centre** ① *Hunua, T09-366 2000, daily 0800-1630*.

Back on the Pacific Coast Highway east of Clevedon you will hit the coast again. It is a very pleasant drive framed by pohutukawa trees and an area famous for its bird life. Christened the **Seabird Coast**, it is well worth stopping at the **Miranda Shorebird Centre** ① *Pokeno, T/F09-232 2781, www.miranda-shorebird.org.nz, daily, 0900-1700*, home of the **Miranda Naturalists' Trust**. The Firth of Thames offers an internationally important habitat and stopover point for thousands of migrating wading birds. The 'target' birds at Miranda (for study not shooting) are the native wrybill – a strange little wader with a crooked beak designed for specialist feeding – and the rare New Zealand dotterel. Both join the near 60 other transitory species that stop over for a short time in spring and autumn to refuel for migration. The godwit, a medium-sized wader that breeds in Alaska, makes the journey to spend the southern hemisphere winter in New Zealand. Recent studies suggest that they do this journey non-stop, in a week. They fly at 4000-6000 m and reach speeds of 60-70 kph. Just a few kilometres south of the Shorebird Centre are the **Miranda Hot Pools** ① *T07-867 3055, www.mirandahotsprings.co.nz, Mon-Thu 0900-2130, Fri-Sun 0800-2230 all year, $12.50, child $6*. Private spas are also available.

For Sleeping and Eating price codes and other relevant information, see Essentials pages 44-50.

● **Sleeping**

South of Auckland *p116*
LL Umoya Lodge, Mount Rataroa, Pokeno, T09-232 7636, www.umoyalodge.co.nz. Stunning, luxury lodge in an elevated position overlooking the coast. Spacious suite and self-contained lodge. Superb in-house cuisine.
L The Inverness Estate, Ness Valley Rd, Clevedon, T09-292 8710, www.inverness.co.nz. Luxury accommodation in a country setting with fine food and its own estate wine.
A The Miranda Holiday Park, 595 Front Miranda Rd, T0800-833144/T09-867 3205, www.mirandaholidaypark.co.nz. Wonderful facilities including its own hot pools.

C-D Miranda Shorebird Centre, T09-232 2781. Bunk, single/double room and self-contained accommodation available from $20-60. Great value, offers a fine roost.

Camping
Omana Regional Park, T09-303 1530. The region's campsite.

❶ **Eating**

South of Auckland *p116*
▼ **Kaiaua Fishery**, T09-232 2776. Fish and chip shop on East Coast Rd in Kaiaua, north of Miranda, has a great reputation.
▼ **Bayview Hotel**, Kaiaua, T09-232 2717, daily from 1700. Offers takeaways and snacks as well as a restaurant serving mainly seafood.

Hauraki Islands → *Colour map 2, A2*

The Hauraki Gulf is famed for its picturesque islands, which range in size from the 179-ha Motuihe to the 93-sq-km Waiheke. There is significant contrast in their use and character as well as their geography. Close to the city Waiheke is by far the most populated, so much so that it is often labelled 'just another suburb' of Auckland. Famed for its vineyards and blessed with a number of fine beaches, it has for decades been a favourite and convenient escape from the city for both residents and visitors. Perhaps most obvious among the island family is Rangitoto with its volcanic cone that dominates the horizon and, although now fully clad in bush, reveals some fascinating lava flows upon closer inspection. Second largest in the group is Great Barrier, which is 90 km from the city, offering a true island escape and some superb scenery, walks and beaches. Two other islands in the Hauraki are the world-renowned wildlife reserves of Tiritiri Matangi near the Whangaparaoa Peninsula on the city's northern fringe, and the mountainous Little Barrier, which can be seen on a clear day to the north. Tiri is the most accessible and offers visitors an insight into what New Zealand used to be like, with abundant bird life and such enchanting avian odysseys as the takahe and spotted kiwi. Little Barrier is home to a few precious and well-looked after kakapo – a large flightless parrot that, with only around 100 remaining in the wild, is one of the rarest birds in the world.

Ins and outs
Getting there To Rangitoto, **Fullers**, T09-367 9111, www.fullers.co.nz, runs ferries from the Ferry Building on Quay Street, daily at 0915 and 1215, $25, child $12.50. It also offers a ferry/tour package with the 'Rangitoto Explorer' – a carriage pulled by a tractor that winds its way around the island, with an interesting commentary, $55, child $27.50. Booking is essential for all trips. Take plenty of water, sun block and a hat – the black scoria can

emanate terrific heat. **Fullers** also runs a ferry to Motuihe at weekends in conjunction with the Rangitoto ferry. Additional sailings in summer.

To Tiritiri Matangi, **360-Discovery (Kawau Kat)**, T0800-888006, www.360discovery. co.nz, runs a service from Auckland from Pier 4 (next to the Ferry Building) Wed-Sun at 0900, $66, child $29; or the same ferry from Z Pier, Gulf Harbour on the Whangaparaoa Peninsula, 45 mins later, $39, child $19.50. Trips return by 1645.

Rangitoto Island

Rangitoto seems to dominate your views of the Hauraki Gulf from almost every vantage point in the city, so it is only a matter of time before its classically shaped cone lures you across the water to take a closer look. Rangitoto first emerged from the sea in a series of eruptions about 600 years ago, when Maori were known to be inhabiting the area. One Maori myth suggests that the eruption occurred after a casual dispute between the gods of fire and volcanoes, but many years later science put it all down to being the latest of the many eruptions to take place in the area over the millennia. It is only a 30-minute journey by ferry to take a closer look and to enjoy one of the island's walks.

Most of these walks culminate at the summit from where there is a 360° view of the gulf and the city and you can peer down into its bush-clad crater. The vegetation of the island is of international importance with the recent botanical blanket boasting 200 species of native tree (the most prolific and famous being its pohutukawa) and flowering plants, 40 kinds of fern, some orchids and, of course, many lichens. All this is interspersed with the ankle-breaking mounds of loose laval scoria.

There are a number of **walking** options, all neatly presented in DoC's guide to the island – available from the DoC office in the Ferry Building. If you have time and want to get away from the crowds that immediately make for the summit (two hours), follow the tracks from the wharf to the summit via McKenzie Bay. It can take six hours but gives you a great feel for the island and its plant life, and provides great sea-level views.

Motutapu Island – the contrasting island connected to Rangitoto by a short causeway – has a few interesting Maori archaeological sites but is best visited as part of the extensive winter replanting programmes that are taking place in conjunction with DoC. As you can see from Rangitoto, Motutapu needs it.

Tiritiri Matangi Island

Even if you are not particularly interested in wildlife 'Tiri' (as it is affectionately known) is well worth a visit. This jewel in the Hauraki is one of the few 'open bird sanctuaries' in New Zealand and has become an internationally famous conservation success story. Situated 4 km off the Whangaparaoa Peninsula, north of the city centre, the 220-ha island was originally leased for farming from 1855 to 1971, during which time the native forest was reduced to 6% of its former glory. Thankfully, the island was recognized by the New Zealand Wildlife Service (now DoC) as having great potential as a wildlife sanctuary. A nursery was set up in 1983 and from 1984 volunteers became involved in planting over 250,000 trees and shrubs, and the island is now 70% regenerated. A vital poison drop rid the island of rats making it predator free and ready for the arrival of most of its current avian residents. Now Tiri has become the safe haven for numerous rare and endangered species including the famous takahe, little spotted **kiwi, kokako**, whitehead, saddleback, North Island robin, kakariki, stitchbird and brown teal. Being an open sanctuary, members of the public can visit and experience what New Zealand used to be like, with the bush alive with the sound of birdsong. The **takahe** – those big friendly purple chickens with red beaks – are perhaps the most famous of its current tenants. These amazing, almost prehistoric birds, were thought to be extinct until a small group was rediscovered in the wild Fiordlands of the South Island. Since then a successful breeding programme has increased numbers and, given there are only about 200 of these birds left in the world, seeing them is an unforgettable experience.

The island has a numerous and varied network of **walks** on which you are almost certain to 'encounter' takahe and other species. The coastal scenery and sea views are magnificent. Do not miss the little blue penguin boxes near the wharf or the 'Wattle Track'. Kiwi are nocturnal so don't expect to see one unless you stay at the bunkhouse overnight. Ray and Barbara are excellent hosts, as are the highly committed volunteers of **Supporters of Tiritiri Matangi** ① *T09-479 4490, www.tiritirimatangi.org.nz.* Contact them for details of volunteer work. A guided tour costs $6. There is a souvenir shop on the island, but no food, so take a packed lunch. Snacks are available on the ferry.

Other islands in the Hauraki

Motuihe
This small unusually shaped island of 179 ha lies between Motutapu and Waiheke. There is archaeological evidence that suggests the island was inhabited and used extensively by Maori before it was purchased and farmed by European pioneer W H Fairburn in 1839. Ownership changed hands again a few times before the Crown finally bought it in 1872 and used it as a quarantine station. This station would be used as a prisoner of war camp in the First World War (prisoners included the infamous German Captain Felix von Lucker), an emergency hospital during the influenza epidemic in 1918, and a naval training base in the Second World War. In 1967, when the Hauraki Gulf Marine Park was established, the island came under the control of the Auckland City Council. Today, although the island is still farmed and is a DoC reserve, it is essentially a recreation venue, popular for swimming, fishing and escaping the city. There are a number of walks of up to three hours taking in a number of geological formations, archaeological sites, and the graves of those who died during the influenza epidemic. For detailed information about Motuihe and the ongoing conservation projects being undertaken refer to the website www.motuihe.org.nz.

Little Barrier Island
On a clear day it is just possible to see the mountainous bush-clad peaks that make up Little Barrier Island from the city. Little Barrier lies 90 km north of Auckland and 18 km west of her big sister, Great Barrier. This island is a plant and wildlife reserve of international value and significance. Being predator-free, it is sanctuary to a host of native birdlife, such as black petrel, cooks petrel and brown teal (all endangered). Other unusual inhabitants include the tuatara (a prehistoric native reptile), rare skinks and New Zealand's only bat (and native mammal) – the short-tailed bat. There are also 350 species of native plant on the island. But perhaps the most famous inhabitants are the **kakapo**. These flightless heavyweights (up to 3.5 kg) are the rarest parrot, and one of the most endangered birds, in the world. At present only 62 known individuals remain in captivity or on protected off-shore islands around New Zealand.

Waiheke Island → Colour map 2, A2.

At 93 sq km, Waiheke is the largest island in the gulf and, at only 20 km from the city (a 35-minute ferry ride), also the most visited and heavily populated. It has plenty of beaches, activities, easy access, fine restaurants and accommodation, but if you are looking for a real 'island experience' then you are far better off going to Great Barrier. The main village and focus of attention on Waiheke is Oneroa at the western end of the island, just a short walk from the Matiatia Wharf. From Oneroa east, the settlements generally fade after Palm Beach and Onetangi, until the occasional holiday home and residential property gives way to farmland. ► *See Sleeping, Eating and other listings, pages 122-125.*

Ins and outs
Getting there **Fullers**, T09-367 9119, offers a passenger-only service from the Auckland Ferry Building every two hours Mon-Fri 0520-2345, Sat 0630-2345, Sun 0700-2130; $32, child $16. There is also a service from Halfmoon Bay in the eastern suburbs and a number of tour packages (see page 124). Passenger and car ferries are also run by **Sealink**, T09-300 5900/T0800-732546, www.sealink.co.nz, almost hourly daily from Halfmoon Bay to Kennedy's Point, 0600-1830, $130 car only, passengers $30 return. Bookings essential.

Getting around **Fullers**, T09-369 79111, offers a four-route service to and from the main Matiatia wharf and connects with all ferries. **Route One** runs to and from Onetangi taking in Oneroa, Blackpool, Surfdale and Ostend. **Route Two** goes from the wharf to Oneroa, Little Oneroa, Hauraki Store, Palm Beach and Ostend to Rocky Bay and back. **Route Three** runs from the wharf to Oneroa, Blackpool, Surfdale, Hauraki store, Palm Beach, Ostend, Onetangi to Rocky Bay and back. **Route Four** runs to Oneroa, Surfdale, Ostend to Onetangi and back. Tickets and $15 hop-on/hop-off day passes available on the bus. 'Bus and Boat' specials are also often available. Fullers offer bicycle tours or you may wish to hire your own on the island, try **Waiheke Bike Hire** T09-372 7937 www.waihekebikehire.co.nz.

Tourist information **Waiheke VIC (I-Site)** ① *2 Korora Rd, in front of the Artworks Complex, Oneroa, T09-372 1234, Mon-Sun 0900-1700, waiheke.aucklandnz.com, www.tourism waiheke.co.nz and www.gotowaiheke.co.nz.* Other than the island map ($2), publications to look out for are the *Gulf News*, www.waihekegulfnews.co.nz (Thu), the free *Gulf Islander* and the *Waiheke Marketplace*. For walks, *Waiheke Island Walkways* is comprehensive; for vineyard details ask for the *Waiheke Island of Wine*.

Oneroa and around
Near the wharf and sandwiched between the popular Oneroa Bay and Blackpool beaches is the main settlement of Oneroa – a well-known creative haunt. Waiheke has been home to arty types for years and boasts some well-known artists, poets and writers, including the internationally renowned Zinni Douglas, Barbara Bailey and ceramist Hilary Kerrod. The VIC can provide information about art outlets and studios. Situated just behind the VIC, the **Artworks Complex** is a small conglomerate with a cinema, a library, restaurant and the **Whittakers Musical Museum** ① *T09-372 5573, www.musical-museum.org, closed Tue, $3; entry and performance $12.50, child $5,* which displays over 100 musical instruments dating back 500 years, and which has live (1½-hour) performances at 1300.

Vineyards

Within a few kilometres of Oneroa are two examples of Waiheke's other claim to fame: vineyards. **Mudbrick Vineyard** ① *2 km west of Oneroa, Church Bay Rd, T09-372 9050, www.mud brick.co.nz*, is open daily 1030-1700 in summer; see also Eating, page 123. Although their reign is now threatened, traditionally the two most famous vineyards on

Waiheke Island

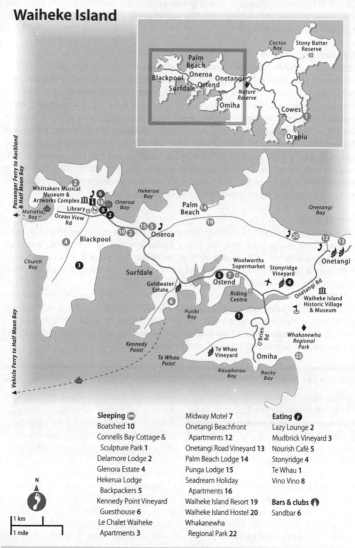

Sleeping
Boatshed **10**
Connells Bay Cottage &
  Sculpture Park **1**
Delamore Lodge **2**
Glenora Estate **4**
Hekerua Lodge
  Backpackers **5**
Kennedy Point Vineyard
  Guesthouse **6**
Le Chalet Waiheke
  Apartments **3**

Midway Motel **7**
Onetangi Beachfront
  Apartments **12**
Onetangi Road Vineyard **13**
Palm Beach Lodge **14**
Punga Lodge **15**
Seadream Holiday
  Apartments **16**
Waiheke Island Resort **19**
Waiheke Island Hostel **20**
Whakanewha
  Regional Park **22**

Eating
Lazy Lounge **2**
Mudbrick Vineyard **3**
Nourish Café **5**
Stonyridge **4**
Te Whau **1**
Vino Vino **8**

Bars & clubs
Sandbar **6**

Waiheke are: **Goldwater Estate** ① *18 Causeway Rd, Putiki Bay, T09-372 7493, www.goldwater wine.com, visits by appointment*, and, heading east, **Stonyridge Vineyard** ① *80 Onetangi Rd, T09-372 8822, www.stonyridge.co.nz, tastings daily 0900-1700, tours at weekends at 1130, $10*, which produces one of the world's most sought-after Cabernets-Larose. South of Onetangi is **Te Whau Vineyard** ① *218 Te Whau Dr, Rocky Bay, T09-372 7191, www.tewhau.com*, one of the newest on the island and noted for its fine labels, superb views and a classy café. You can visit the vineyards on the island on an organized tour (see page 124).

Onetangi and around
Within walking distance east of Oneroa along **Oneroa Bay** and up through the pleasant reserves and back roads is **Palm Beach** (two hours), with its small collection of houses and lovely sandy beach, which has a secluded spot for naturists. There is also a **General Store** that offers bike, boogie board and snorkelling gear hire. From Palm Beach it is about 3 km to **Onetangi**, the site of Waiheke's longest and perhaps most popular beach. The Onetangi Beach Store hires out equipment for watersports. The **Waiheke Island Historic Village and Museum** ① *165 Onetangi Rd, T09-372 5168, Mon, Wed, Sat-Sun (daily during school holidays) 1200-1600, free*, is overlooked by a 700-year-old Maori *pa* and has cottages and a small museum with collections of farm machines, engines and bric-a-brac. Also close by on Waiheke Road is the Forest and Bird Society's **Nature Reserve** which may, if you are lucky, produce the odd tui or native pigeon amidst its native tree plantations.

Further afield
East of Onetangi, the habitation diminishes and farmland, the odd vineyard and secluded bay takes over. If you have time the **Stony Batter Reserve**, on the islands northeast headland, is worth a visit (1½-hour walk from the delightful **Cactus Bay**). It consists of an underground complex linked by a series of tunnels which, like others in Auckland, were built in the Second World War in fear of foreign invasion.

At the far south eastern corner of the island amidst some of its most stunning views is The **Connells Bay Sculpture Park** ① *Cowes Bay Rd, T09-372 8957, bookings only (mid-Oct to mid-Apr)*. A stunning private collection of installations by some of New Zealand's best-known sculpture artists, all in a sublime garden setting with great views. There is no café but you are welcome to take a picnic. Recommended.

⊚ Waiheke Island listings

For Sleeping and Eating price codes and other relevant information, see Essentials pages 44-50.

● Sleeping
Given its popularity and proximity to the city, Waiheke is very well served with lodging, but in recent years the focus seems to be mainly on vineyard accommodation luring couples or honeymooners. **Fullers**, Ferry Building on Quay St, T09-336 79111, www.fullers.co.nz, provides packages with accommodation included. **Waiheke Unlimited**, T09-372 7776,

www.waihekeunlimited.co.nz, also acts as an agent for self-contained accommodation. There are also a number of lodges, motels, hostels and over 100 B&Bs to choose from, many with the ever-inviting 4-poster beds.

Oneroa and around *p120, map p121*
LL Boatshed, corner of Tawa and Huia sts, Little Oneroa, T09-372 3242, www.boat shed.co.nz. Neat architecture incorporates modern individual boatshed-style units and an elevated 'lighthouse' all luxuriously decked

out for clients' comfort and relaxation. Expensive but certainly different.

LL Delamore Lodge, 83 Delamore Dr, Owhanake Bay, west of Oneroa, T09-372 7372, www.delamorelodge.com. 4 stunning luxury suites with private patios and panoramic views of the Hauraki Gulf. A fine example of how well luxury and good architecture can combine.

L Glenora Estate, 160 Nick Johnstone Dr, Church Bay, T09-372 5082, www.glenora estate.co.nz. Nestled within 3 ha of land, this 17th-century style farmhouse and barn offers wonderful en suite rooms – ideal for couples.

AL-A Punga Lodge, 223 Ocean View Rd, Little Oneroa, T09-372 6675, www.ki-wi.co.nz/punga.htm. Comfortable but conventional self-contained or B&B units in garden and bush.

A Le Chalet Waiheke Apartments, 14 Tawa St, Oneroa, T09-372 7510. Self-contained apartments with decks and fine views in a quiet bush setting, further out from the beach.

A Seadream Holiday Apartments, 35 Waikare Rd, Oneroa, T09-372 8991, www.seadream.co.nz. Close to the beach, 2 well-appointed units, a studio and a larger unit with lounge.

B-D Hekerua Lodge Backpackers, 11 Hekerua Rd, Little Oneroa, T09-3728990, www.hekerualodge.co.nz. Describes itself as an oasis of tranquility, offering fine doubles (1 en suite) twins, singles and dorms, an unusual pool and spa, all surrounded by native bush. Bike hire, internet.

Onetangi and around p122, map p121
L Palm Beach Lodge, 23 Tiri View Rd, Palm Beach, T09-372 2680, www.essenceof waiheke.co.nz. Spacious Mediterranean-style suites with fine views. Also has other equally good properties on the island, refer to website.

L-AL Waiheke Island Resort, 4 Bay Rd, Palm Beach, T09-372 0011, www.waiheke resort.co.nz. One of Waiheke's better-known luxury establishments with a wide range of options from villa and chalet accommodation for up to130 people. Fine restaurant and swimming pool. Good venue for socialites.

AL Onetangi Beachfront Apartments, 5 Fourth St, Onetangi, T09-372 0003, www.onetangi.co.nz. Self-contained luxury apartments, BBQs, spas and free use of kayaks.

AL Onetangi Road Vineyard, 82 Onetangi Rd, T09-372 1014, www.onetangiroad.co.nz. Offers a self-contained set-up for 2 in a private vineyard cottage.

C-D Waiheke Island Hostel, 419 Seaview Rd, Onetangi, T09-372 8971, www.waiheke hostel.co.nz. Newly refurbished and friendly, offering a cheaper option with plenty of choice including en suite doubles, family and twin bunk rooms with fine views, Sky TV lounge, BBQ and mountain bikes available.

South of Oneroa p122, map p121
LL Kennedy Point Vineyard Guesthouse, 44 Donald Bruce Rd, Ostend, T09-372 5600, www.kennedypointvineyard.com. Well-appointed suites in a vineyard retreat.

A The Midway Motel, 1 Whakarite Rd, Ostend, T09-372 8023, www.waihekemotel.co.nz. Has small and large units, an indoor heated pool, spa and spa room suites.

Campsites
Whakanewha Regional Park, T09-366 2000. If you have a tent, you can have your own 110-ha retreat with fine views for $10.

Further afield
LL Connells Bay, Cowes Bay Rd, T09-372 8957, www.connellsbay.co.nz. A charming 100-year-old, luxury self-contained guest cottage just metres from the beach on a 25-ha property featuring the classy sculpture park (see page 122). Minimum 2-night stay.

❶ Eating

Oneroa and around p120, map p121
❦❦❦ Mudbrick Restaurant, attached to the vineyard, T09-372 9050, www.mudbrick.co.nz, daily, bookings essential. Great set menus, à la carte and, of course, a fine wine list.

¶¶ **Vino Vino Restaurant**, 3/153 Ocean View Rd, Oneroa, T09-372 9888, www.vinovino.co.nz. Mediterranean fare in relaxed surrounds overlooking the bay. Try the mussels.

¶¶ **The Lazy Lounge**, 139 Oceanview Rd, T09-372 5132. Outdoor decks with fine views across the Gulf and a fine choice for that lazy breakfast or brunch.

South of Oneroa *p122, map p121*

¶¶ **Nourish Café**, 3 Belgium St, Ostend, T09-372 3557. Recommended for fresh light meals, snacks and good coffee.

The following vineyards are recommended.

¶¶ **Veranda Café at Stonyridge**, 80 Onetangi Rd, Ostend, T09-372 8822, open daily for lunch 1130-1700, and for dinner in Jan.

¶¶ **Te Whau**, 218 Te Whau Drive, Te Whau Point, T09-372 7191, daily except Tue 1100-1630, and for dinner Fri-Sat in summer.

❶ Bars, pubs and clubs

Oneroa and around *p120, map p121*

Sandbar, 153 Oceanview Rd, Oneroa, T09-372 9458, www.sandbar.co.nz. Arguably the best on the island, with a relaxed atmosphere and decks overlooking Oneroa Beach. Extensive wine and cocktail list and regular live entertainment.

❷ Entertainment

Oneroa and around *p120, map p121*

Live music

For live music on summer weekends, try at a number of low-key eating venues.

Artworld Complex, Oneroa (behind the VIC), 2 Korora Rd, T09-372 4240. Cinema decked out with comfy sofas donated by residents which, after a day wine tasting, can be sleep-inducing.

Sandbar, 153 Ocean View Rd, Oneroa, T09-372 9458, www.sandbar.co.nz. Regular live entertainment especially jazz.

Lazy Lounge Café, 139 Oceanview Rd, Oneroa, T09-372 5132, www.thelazylounge.co.nz.

Vino Vino, 3/153 Ocean View Rd, Oneroa, T09-372 9888, www.vinovino.co.nz.

▲ Activities and tours

Fullers, T09-3679111, www.fullers.co.nz. Offers a number of tour packages inclusive of ferry fare: the Island Explorer Tour ticket (departing at 1000) includes an all-day bus pass, from $48, child $24; the **Vineyard Tour** (departs 1100) takes in 3 of the island's best, plus an all-day bus pass for $115.

Out-There Surf and Skate, 21 Belgium St, Ostend, T09-372 6528. Hires out dive gear, surfboards, body boards and skates.

Ross Adventures Sea Kayaking, Matiatia, T09-372 5550, www.kayakwaiheke.co.nz. Half- (4 hrs), full- or multi-day trips, from $70.

Flying Carpet Sailing, 104 Wharf Rd, Ostend, T09-3725621, www.flyingcarpet.co.nz. A pleasant 6½-hr day cruise including lunch on a spacious catamaran, $160 a 2-hr scenic cruise for $65 and a 3-hr dinner cruise Fri-Sat $120.

Vineyard tours

Other than the popular Fullers Tours (see above) you might like to try **Waiheke Island Adventures Ltd**, T09-372 6127, www.waihekeislandadventures.com. A local operator offering a more personal service and flexible itineraries.

❸ Transport

Bicycle hire

Available at the Matiatia Wharf, T09-372 7937, from around $35 per day.

Car hire

Waiheke Auto Rentals, T09-372 8998, www.waihekerentals.co.nz. Operates a fleet of cars, station wagons, 4WDs, scooters and a minibus from $50 per day.

Waheke Rental Cars, T09-372 8635, www.waihekerentalcars.co.nz. Rent cars (from $50 a day) and minibuses.

Taxi
Taxi Co-op, T09-372 8038 or **Island Taxis**, T09-372 4111.

Great Barrier Island → *Colour map 2, A2.*

Unlike Waiheke, Great Barrier (or the 'Barrier') has not yet been spoilt by the influences of the city and still offers the visitor a true island adventure. The ferry to the Barrier is a joint island service that at first is packed with commuters and visitors before it empties dramatically at Waiheke and you are left among the Barrier locals, the fishing rods and rucksacks of the occasional intrepid backpacker. Great Barrier is the second largest island in the gulf and lies almost 90 km northeast of Auckland. It used to be part of what is now the Coromandel Peninsula and in a way shares the same isolated, under-developed feel, with rugged hills, numerous bays and beautiful quiet beaches. The Barrier is 'possum free' so a precious habitat for some rare and endangered species – the brown teal and New Zealand's largest skink, the cheveron – being the most notable. For those out to do some diving, fishing, tramping, surfing, sailing and relaxing it is unsurpassed in the region. » *For Sleeping, Eating and other listings, see pages 127-131.*

Ins and outs

Getting there by air The main airfield is at Claris in the centre east of the island about 17 km from Tryphena's Shoal Bay Wharf. Another airfield is at Okiwi, north of Claris. **Great Barrier Airlines**, offices at the Auckland Domestic Terminal (and at the airfield on the Barrier at Claris), T09-275 9120, T0800-900600, www.greatbarrierairlines.co.nz, is the main carrier; it offers an efficient service to the island from Auckland and North Shore airports, as well as connecting flights to the Coromandel (Whitianga) and Whangarei in Northland. There are 2-4 flights daily from Auckland and extra flights in summer on demand. A standard one-way costs around $109. Fly-Boat option costs $169. Surfboards $35 return, bikes $35. These prices are cheap considering the scenic extravaganza on offer. The airline also offer pick-up/drop-off shuttle services throughout the island (see Getting around, below).

Getting there by sea Ferry services access the island mainly at Tryphena but also Whangaparapara and Port Fitzroy. **Fullers**, T09-367 9111, www.fullers.co.nz, offers regular passenger ferry services from the city (2 hrs), from $69, child $39 one-way; book ahead. **Sealink** (Subritzky Shipping), T0800-732546/T09-300 5900, www.sealink.co.nz, offers a vehicle and passenger service on the *MV Sealink*, from Wynyard Wharf in Auckland. Sailings daily except Mon, Wed and Sat (three hours); extra sailings in summer. Vehicles from $350 return, passenger $120, child $80 return. Fly/boat options from $169.

For a day package including flights try **Bush and Beach**, T09-8374130, www.bushandbeach.co.z, from $575.

Getting around A network of roads (mostly unsealed) connects the main settlements. Public transport around the island is well organized. **Great Barrier Airlines (GBA)** provide shuttles to and from the airport. A swarm of vehicles will be at Tryphena Wharf (Shoal Bay) or Claris Airport. Many hotels provide pick-ups but, if you have not yet booked, the shuttles will take you to the VIC in Tryphena or beyond. Hitching is generally safe – don't be surprised if you find yourself on a quad bike or steamroller. **Great Barrier Travel** T0800-426832 runs a daily service around the main centres and meets incoming aircraft 0800-1520. A one-way fare to Tryphena costs $15; hop-on/hop-off passes available. vehicles can be hired from **GBI Transfer and Shuttles**, T09-429 0062. ▶▶ *See Transport, page 131.*

Tourist information **Great Barrier VIC (I-Site)** ① *in the post shop in Claris, T09-429 0767, www.greatbarrier.co.nz, daily 0900-1700.* Also useful is www.greatbarrierisland.co.nz. Take detailed maps if you intend to explore the island's wild interior. Free handouts are available from the **Fullers** information centre and DoC offices at the Ferry Building in Auckland, or the **DoC** ① *Port Fitzroy, T09-429 0044, www.doc.govt.nz, Mon-Fri 0800-1630,* or the VIC in Claris. The DoC leaflets are detailed and informative.

Sights

Great Barrier is an activities destination, from lounging on the beach to multi-day tramps in the huge **Great Barrier Forest**, which is where you will find the most notable 'sights', both natural and historical. There are numerous walks or tramps and the best source of information on these is the DoC office in Port Fitzroy. The *Essential Guide to Great Barrier* highlights the best walks and routes. Most tramps start or finish from various access points on the road between Port Fitzroy and Whangaparapara. The most popular starting point is Port Fitzroy, where supplies and information can be gathered at the wonderfully stocked general store and DoC office.

Tryphena and the south
Tryphena is the main arrival point (by sea) and centre of population on Great Barrier. It is split into three areas or bays: **Shoal Bay** where the wharf is, **Pa Beach** and **Mulberry Grove**. In Pa Beach and Mulberry Grove you will find most of what you need petrol to accommodation. Most shops are in the Stonewall Complex in the heart of Tryphena.

About 4 km north, **Needle Rock** (270 m) is a fine place to start exploring the island. It is a rough 20-minute scramble to the summit, which offers a great view back to Tryphena and the Coromandel to the south and all that awaits you to the north.

Medlands Beach is perhaps the most popular beach, especially with surfies, but it is also a fine place to swim, fish, sunbathe or take a walk around the headlands.

Around Claris
North of Claris is a crossroads. Head directly north for about 3 km, and you will arrive at the access point for the **Kaitoke Hot Springs** – a flat, easy one-hour walk past the Kaitoke Swamp to a series of pools in which you can relieve tired limbs.

Some 2 km along and south of the Whangaparapara Road on the Te Ahumata track, the concrete foundations are all that remain of the **Orville Stamping Battery**. It once crushed quartz from the Te Ahumata gold field. From Whangaparapara Harbour are the remains of the Barrier's old **whaling station**. The oceans around the Barrier were the killing fields for thousands of whales from the 1950s before operations thankfully ceased in the 1960s.

Heading east from the Claris crossroads, cross the river and continue up around the headland to **Palmers Beach** with its shroud of pohutukawa trees falling chaotically to the beach. This is a fine beach but access is not easy. The far more accessible **Awana Bay** is also a fine spot, popular for surfing.

Port Fitzroy and the north
The path to **Windy Canyon Lookout** starts at the Palmers Track entrance on the summit (330 m) of Whangapoua Hill/Aotea Road (15 minutes). It then climbs 100 m through Windy Canyon to the central ridge and offers good views of the Okiwi Basin and Kaitoke. The Palmers Track then follows the ridge and climbs steeply to the summit of Mount Hobson (three hours one way). At 621 m, **Mount Hobson (Hirakimata)** is the island's highest point. On a clear day its 360° view of the island and beyond is unsurpassed. The summit is the principal nesting site for the rare black petrel. Only about 4500 remain and they are only found on Great and Little Barrier Islands. They spend most of their life out at sea and are nocturnal on land, so don't expect to see any. They also nest in burrows so make sure you keep to the paths. From the summit the track splits – The Kaiarara track offering a route west to **Port Fitzroy** (with some remains of kauri dams on the way) or south via the Peach Tree Track that ends at the Kaitoke hot springs. The well preserved remains of a **kauri dam** can be seen along the Kaiarara Track. Kauri dams were used by loggers to drive large numbers of kauri down- stream, allowing access to remote areas of bush. The lower one at Kaiarara was one of the largest driving dams to be built in New Zealand and is one of its best examples.

The *SS Wairarapa* was one of many ships wrecked on the island and the most tragic, with the loss of 130 lives. It ran ashore near Miner's Head in 1894. The 30-minute walk along Whangapoua Beach to Tapuwai Point takes you to one of two graveyard sites on the island – the other being at Onepoto Beach at Katherine Bay on the west coast.

The **Whangapoua Estuary** is a top spot for wildlife and is home to many interesting coastal and wetland species including spotless crake, banded rail and brown teal. If you spot a brown teal – a rather nondescript little brown duck – consider yourself very lucky as there are only 1200 left in the world. Great Barrier is home to 80% of these.

◉ Great Barrier Island listings

For Sleeping and Eating price codes and other relevant information, see Essentials pages 44-50.

● Sleeping
Great Barrier is remote and basic, with no mains power, street lights, reticulated water supply or extensive road network. However, when it comes to accommodation you can enjoy that simplicity or be spoilt. Book in advance in summer. Contact the island's VIC, or check out www.great barrier.co.nz and www.great barrierisland.co.nz. **Fullers**, Ferry Building, Auckland, T09-367 9111, www.fullers.co.nz, offers accommodation packages and advice from its office on the mainland. **Island Accommodation**, T09-429 0995, www.island accommodation.co.nz, is the local agent.

Tryphena and the south *p126, map p128*
LL Earthsong Lodge, 38 Medland Rd, Tryphena, T09-429 0030, www.earthsong lodge.co.nz. A popular 5-star luxury option overlooking Tryphena Harbour. The fine cuisine is reflected in the price.
LL Oasis Lodge, Tryphena, T09-429 0021, www.barrieroasis.co.nz. Set in a vineyard, this is an old favourite. Luxury and cheaper cottage options available, meals included.
L-AL Tipi and Bob's Waterfront Lodge, Puriri Bay Rd, Tryphena, T09-429 0550, www.water frontlodge.co.nz. An old favourite with 6 tidy self-contained units, close to amenities.
AL Pigeon's Lodge, 179 Shoal Bay Rd, Tryphena, T09-429 0437, www.pigeons lodge.co.nz. A fine B&B with rooms with

Great Barrier Island

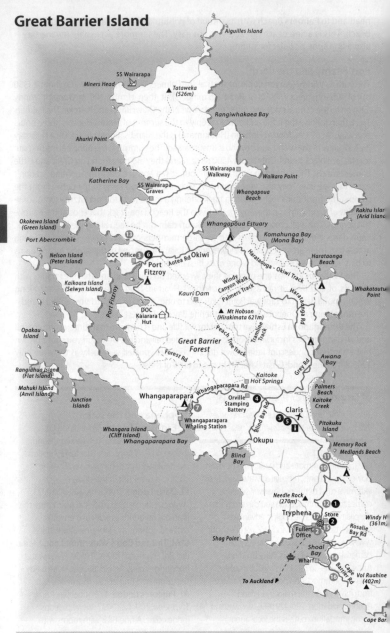

Aiguilles Island

SS Wairarapa
Miners Head
▲ Tataweka
(526m)

Rangiwhakaea Bay

Ahuriri Point

Bird Rocks
Katherine Bay
SS Wairarapa
Graves

SS Wairarapa
Walkway
Waikaro Point

Whangapoua
Beach

Rakitu Island
(Arid Island)

Okokewa Island
(Green Island)
Port Abercrombie

Whangapoua Estuary
Komahunga Bay
(Mona Bay)

Harataonga
Beach

Nelson Island
(Peter Island)

DOC Office ③⑥
Port
Fitzroy

⑬
Aotea Rd Okiwi

Harataonga - Okiwi Track

Whakatatutu
Point

Kaikoura Island
(Selwyn Island)

Windy
Canyon Walk
Palmers Track
Kauri Dam

Harataonga Rd

Port Fitzroy

DOC
Kaiarara
Hut

▲ Mt Hobson
(Hirakimata 621m)

Opakau
Island

Peach Tree Track

Tramline Track

Great Barrier
Forest
Forest Rd

Awana
Bay

Rangiahua Island
(Flat Island)

Kaitoke
Hot Springs

Palmers
Beach

Kaitoke
Creek

Mahuki Island
(Anvil Island)

Whangaparapara
▲

⑦

Whangaparapara Rd

Orville
Stamping
Battery

Grey Rd

④
Claris
③⑤
🛈

Pitokuku
Island

Junction
Islands

Whangaparapara
Whaling Station

Blind Bay Rd

Memory Rock
Medlands Beach

Whangara Island
(Cliff Island)
Whangaparapara Bay

Okupu

Blind
Bay

⑪

⑩

Needle Rock
(270m) ▲

Tryphena

⑫ ①
Store
②

⑰
📧
②
⑮

Windy H
(361m,

Rosalie
Bay Rd

Fullers
Office

Shag Point

Shoal
Bay
Wharf ⚓

To Auckland ▶

⑭

⑯

Cape
Barrier Rd

Vol Ruahine
(402m)

Cape Bar

bathrooms and set in quiet bush.

AL Medlands Beach Bach, T021-367771, www.greatbarrier.co.nz. Mid-range self-contained option and one of the original beach baches set right on the surf beach.

A-D Medlands Beach Backpackers and Motel, T09-429 0320, www.medlands beach.com. Excellent range of budget accommodation for couples and families. Chalet and villa as well as a 4-bunk lodge. It is remote so stock up with food. Surfies' favourite.

A Pohutukawa Lodge, Pa Beach, Tryphena, T09-4290211, www.currachirishpub.com. 5 en suite rooms, close to shops, restaurants and pubs.

A-D Stray Possum Lodge, 64 Cape Barrier Rd, Tryphena, T09-429 0109, www.straypossum .co.nz. Excellent backpacker hostel near the wharf, offering dorms, doubles, self-contained chalets and camping in a lovely bush setting. Bar, Sky TV, internet and pizza café. Friendly management and staff. Tours available, bikes, boogie boards and wet suits for hire.

Around Claris *p126, map p128*

A Great Barrier Lodge, Whangaparapara, T09-429 0488, www.greatbarrierlodge.com. Accommodation is in cottages in the grounds and, being out of the way, just about all you need is available. Car, bike and equipment hire, bar and restaurant. Close to the hot pools.

Port Fitzroy and the north *p127, map p128*

AL Fitzroy House, T09-429 0091, www.fitz royhouse.co.nz. Self-contained cottage in a wonderful setting with heaps of activities. Tramp and Sail package available.

A Orama Christian Community, near Port Fitzroy, T09-429 0063, www.orama.org.nz. Self-contained flats and cottage, guestroom, cabin and bunkroom, in a very scenic spot. Has its own library, shop and laundry.

Camping

There are several DoC campsites and 1 DoC hut available (The Whangaparapara hut having burnt to the ground recently). Bookings are advised and current charges

N

| 2 km |
| 2 miles |

Sleeping ●
Earthsong Lodge **2**
Fitzroy House **3**
Great Barrier Lodge **7**
Medlands Beach
  Backpackers & Motel **10**
Medlands Beach Bach **11**
Oasis Lodge **12**
Orama Christian
  Community **13**
Pigeon's Lodge **14**
Pohutukawa Lodge **15**
Stray Possum Lodge **16**
Tipi & Bob's
  Waterfront Lodge **17**

Eating ●
Angsana Thai **5**
Barrier Oasis **1**
Claris Texas Café **3**
Curragh Irish Pub **2**
Great Barrier Island Sports
  & Social Club **4**
Port Fitzroy Boating Club **6**

(average $6) are available on enquiry at the main DoC office is in Port Fitzroy, T09-429 0044. The campsites are at Akapoua Bay (Port Fitzroy), Whangaparapara, Medlands, Whangapoua, Harataonga and Awana. For convenience **Akapoua Bay** is advised, and the best of the more secluded campgrounds is Harataonga; there is also a guest lodge sleeping 8. The **Kaiarara Hut**, T09-429 0044, $10, has 24 bunks, a wood stove, toilet and cold water.

Private campgrounds are also available at **The Stray Possum** (see above); **Orama Christian Community** $10, (see above); and **Mickey's**, Awana Valley, T09-429 0170, probably the most entertaining camping venue on the island and all for under $10.

● Eating

There are very few restaurants on the Barrier; most are attached to hotels. Food can be bought in Tryphena at: **Stonewall Village Store**, T09- 429 0451; **Mulberry Grove Store and Café**, 1 Mulberry Grove, T09-429 0909; in Whanga parapara at **The Claris Store**, T09-429 0852, and **Great Barrier Lodge**, T09-429 0488; and at **Port Fitzroy General Store**, T09-429 0056.

Tryphena and the south *p126, map p128*
♥♥♥ **Barrier Oasis**, Stonewall, Tryphena, T09-429 0021. Top quality cuisine for guests and visitors, lunch and dinner. Booking essential.
♥♥ **Curragh Irish Pub**, Stonewall Complex, Tryphena, T09-429 0211. Good pub food with a wicked seafood chowder.
♥♥ **Earthsong Lodge**, Tryphena, T09-429 0030. Excellent French cuisine. Bookings essential.
♥ **Stray Possum Lodge**, Tryphena. Pizza.
♥ **Tipi and Bob's**, Tryphena, T09-429 0550. Menu includes fish and chips and takeaways.

Around Claris *p126, map p128*
♥♥ **Angsana Thai Restaurant**, 63 Gray Rd, Claris, T09-429 0292 Excellent Thai and Kiwi cuisine, vegetarian dishes. Bookings advised.
♥♥ **Claris Texas Café**, Claris, T09-429 0811,

daily 0800-1600. Fine food all day and from 1800 Thu-Sun. Best coffee on the island.
♥♥ **Great Barrier Lodge**, Whangaparapara, T09-429 0488. Restaurant and bar.
♥ **Great Barrier Island Sports and Social Club**, Claris, T09-429 0260. Open Wed, Fri, Sat. Good value bar meals and takeaways.

Port Fitzroy & the north *p127, map p128*
♥ **Port Fitzroy Boating Club**, T09-420 0072. Thu-Sat from 1600, from 1000 in summer.

● Pubs, bars and clubs

On the mainland there are 2 fine places to drink: **Curragh Irish Pub**, at the Pohutukawa Lodge, T09-429 0211. Live entertainment with an unusual Kiwi/Irish flavour.
The Stray Possum Lodge, T09-429 0109. Has a delightful little bar, where the occasional wild party sometimes ensues.

▲ Activities and tours

Boat hire
GBI Adventure Rentals, Mulberry Grove, Tryphena, T09-429 0062, www.greatbarrier island.co.nz. A wonderland awaits you.

Fishing
The VIC has information on local charters. Some of the best land-based spots are Lighthouse Point (Shoal Bay, Tryphena), Cape Barrier, Shag Point, 'Shark Alley' (south headlands of Medlands Beach) and Haratoanga.

Kayaking
The Barrier is a sea kayaking paradise. Circumnavigation of the island takes about 5 days and is an awesome trip needing careful planning and local help.
Aotea Kayaks, T09-429 0664, trips from $40.
Fitzroy House Outdoor Centre, T09-429 0091. Hire only.
Great Barrier Lodge, T09-429 0488. Independent hire costs about $45 a day.

Mountain biking
This is a great way to explore the island; both airlines and ferry operators are bicycle-friendly. For environmental reasons most tracks are off limits, but a fine track that is accessible is the DoC forest 4WD track off Whangaparapara Rd. Companies include: **GBI Hire**, Claris, T09-429 0471; **Great Barrier Lodge**, Whangaparapara, T09-429 0488; and **Paradise Cycles**, Tryphena, T09-429 0311.

Scuba diving
Great diving can be found all around the island, but preferred spots are Tryphena Harbour, around Port Fitzroy and off Harataonga Bay. **Hooked on Barrier**, 89 Hector Sanderson Rd, Claris, T09-429 0740. Also offers refills. **Mobile Dive Centre**, Tryphena Wharf, T09-429 0628. Dive gear for hire.

Swimming
Swimming (especially for kids) is best kept to sheltered west coast bays, but the big eastern beaches are fine for adults if you are vigilant. Take flippers and a boogie board.

Tour operators
Barrier Tour Co, T09-429 0062, www.gbi nz.com/tours. Small-group guided tours. **Discover Great Barrier**, T021-420935, www.discovergreatbarrier.co.nz. Also offers tours for small groups.

Walking/tramping
1 day From the start of Palmers Track at the top of Okiwi Hill take a look at Windy Canyon before continuing to the top of Mt Hobson. From there take the Peach Tree Track to the springs with pick-up from Whangaparapara Rd. The Harataonga – Okiwi Track (5 hrs) and Rosalie Bay Rd end to Claris (5 hrs) are also fine walks.
2 days Follow the above, but from Mt Hobson, check out the kauri dam remains before continuing along the track and staying the night at the Kaiarara Hut (see Sleeping). The next day take the Forest Rd and Tramline Tracks to finish at Kaitoke Hot Springs. Arrange a pick-up from the Whangaparapara Rd access point.

⊖ Transport

Bus
Great Barrier Travel, T0800-426832/T021-715858, runs a bus from Tryphena to the main centres 5 times daily in summer. Day pass ($50), 5-day pass ($99), hop-on/hop-off.

Car hire
Petrol and diesel available at Tryphena (Mulberry Grove), Claris, Port Fitzroy and Whangaparapara. Gas: refills at Claris Motors, **Port Fitzroy Store** and 428 Shoal Bay Rd, Tryphena. **Aotea Rental Cars**, T09-429 0474. **GBI Rental Cars**, Mulberry Grove, Tryphena, T09-4290062, full range including mokes. **Great Barrier Lodge**, Whangaparapara, T09-429 0488. All companies offer a range of vehicles from hatchbacks to mokes, from $55. **Medlands Rentals**, Kaitoke, T09-429 0861, www.medlandsrentals.co.nz.

Taxi
The typical fare from Tryphena to Claris is around $15. **Great Barrier Travel** (see Bus, above), offers transfers on demand.

● Directory

Banks There are no banks but EFTPOS is available in most shops, cafés, hotels and restaurants. **Internet** Claris Texas Cafe, daily 0800-1600, T09-429 0811. **Laundry** Claris Fuel and Laundromat, T094-290075. **Medical services** Health Centre, Claris, T09-429 0356. Pharmacy: Claris, T09-429 0006. **Police** Claris, T09-429 0343. **Post office** Outpost, Tryphena (Stonewall Complex), T09-429 0610. Port Fitzroy Store, T09-429 0056. You can even send a message by pigeon at the **Pigeon Post**, Claris, T09-429 0242. **Public toilets** Shoal Bay, Whangaparapara, Port Fitzroy Wharves, Mulberry Grove and Pa Beach Tryphena, Medlands, Claris and the Airfield. **Telephone** Available at main centres.

Contents

Northland

Footprint features

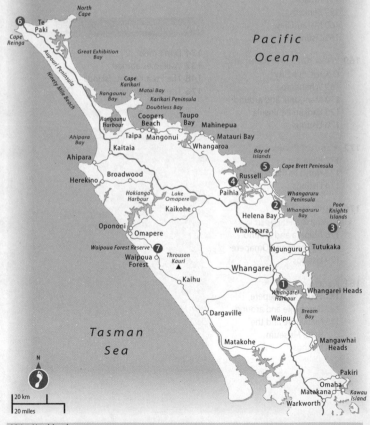

Pacific Ocean

North Cape

Te Paki

Cape Reinga

Great Exhibition Bay

Aupouri Peninsula

Ninety Mile Beach

Cape Karikari

Matai Bay

Rangaunu Bay

Karikari Peninsula

Doubtless Bay

Coopers Beach

Taupo Bay

Mahinepua

Rangaunu Harbour

Taipa

Mangonui

Matauri Bay

Ahipara Bay

Kaitaia

Whangaroa

Ahipara

Bay of Islands

Herekino

Broadwood

Cape Brett Peninsula

Russell

Hokianga Harbour

Lake Omapere

Paihia

Kaikohe

Whangaruru Peninsula

Helena Bay

Whangaruru Bay

Poor Knights Islands

Opononi

Omapere

Waipoua Forest Reserve

Waipoua Forest

Throuson Kauri ▲

Whakapara

Ngunguru

Tutukaka

Kaihu

Whangarei

Whangarei Harbour

Whangarei Heads

Dargaville

Bream Bay

Waipu

Tasman Sea

Matakohe

Mangawhai Heads

Pakiri

Omaha

Matakana

Kawau Island

Warkworth

N

20 km
20 miles

Northland is often called the 'birthplace of the nation' and 'the 'winterless north'. The region is rich in history, has a fine climate and boasts some of the most stunning coastal scenery in the country. It was here that the first Maori set foot in New Zealand, about AD 1000, followed by the first European settlers over 800 years later. It was also here, in the Bay of Islands in 1840, that the Treaty of Waitangi was signed – the document that launched the relationship between two deeply contrasting peoples. This relationship is reflected in the calms and the storms of unsettled ocean currents that unite uneasily at New Zealand's northernmost point, North Cape. Lost in time in the Waipoua Forest, making all that human history seem like yesterday, stands one of the few remaining 'ancient' kauri trees: the centuries-old 'Tane Mahuta'.

All in all, for the modern day visitor, although the fine weather label does not always hold true, Northland must feature as one of the most aesthetically and historically interesting regions to visit in New Zealand. Most of what it has to offer is signposted and detailed as the aptly named and celebrated 'Twin Coast Discovery'.

Warkworth and Kowhai Coast → *Colour map 1, C4.*

Although not geographically within Northland, Warkworth is for most a starting point and a gateway to the region. Most travellers, in their haste to reach Whangarei or the Bay of Islands (on SH1), miss it out altogether, while others stop for lunch or a coffee by the river before taking the slower and more scenic route north, along the Kowhai Coast, via the vineyards of Matakana, then on to the scenic coastal settlements of Leigh, Mangawhai and Waipu. Whatever your intention, Warkworth and the pleasant coastal bays, peninsulas and islands to its east, are certainly worthy of a stop. When it comes to tourism and its associate services, the district is developing at a phenomenal rate.

The Kowhai Coast extends from Wenderholm Regional Park, just north of Waiwera, to Pakiri Beach and contains three regional parks, Kawau Bay, including Kawau Island, the Marine Reserve at Goat Island and over 26 accessible beaches popular for boating, fishing, diving and walking. ▸▸ *For Sleeping and Eating and other listings, see pages 140-143.*

Warkworth ●❷❸ ▸▸ *pp140-143.*

Although of some historic significance as a former kauri-milling town, Warkworth is now essentially a farming and tourism service centre set in the heart of Rodney District and on the banks of the Mahurangi River, 70 km north of Auckland.

Ins and outs
Intercity in collaboration with **Northliner**, T09-385 5780, arrive outside **Warkworth VIC (I-Site)** ① *1 Baxter St, T09-425 9081, www.warkworth-information.co.nz, Mon-Sat 0830-1730, Sun 0900-1500.*

Sights
Much of the local history is presented in the **Warkworth and District Museum** within the **Parry Kauri Park** ① *Tudor Collins Drive, on the southern outskirts of the town, T09-425 7093, www.wwmuseum.orconhosting.net.nz, daily 0900-1500, $8, child $2.* The museum falls under the shadow of two impressive 600- to 800-year-old kauri trees (the tallest on the east coast of Northland), and explores, in a number of rooms, the life of the early pioneers and the influence of the kauri industry upon them. There is also a small but pleasant nature trail.

Four kilometres south, and in stark contrast, is the **Warkworth Satellite Station**, which is the Telecom NZ national base for international satellite communications. Although the unmanned visitor centre has now closed, the two huge satellite dishes may lure still you off the main road for a closer look. Back on SH1 again, and less than 1 km further south, you can get back to nature and all things sweet and communal at the **Honey Centre** ① *7 Perry Rd, T09-425 8003, www.honeycentre.co.nz, daily 0900- 1700, free.* It provides an interesting insight into the industry and a close-up look at a resident hive, and provides an ideal opportunity to buy a tub of the golden stuff for the kids to spread gratuitously all around the hire car. There is also a café on site.

About 4 km north of Warkworth is **Sheepworld** ① *T09-425 7444, www.sheep world.co.nz, daily 0900-1700, shows at 1100 and 1400, $14 (with show $24), child $7/$8.* If the foot falls heavy on the accelerator at the very prospect of such a place, then just hold off. It is actually quite entertaining and worthy of the stop. Although chasing them is rightly frowned upon, you are allowed to feed the lambs and get involved in some shearing. The souvenir shop more than caters for the remainder of your visit; there's also a café.

Wallabies abroad

In the sporting arena Australians are often called Wallabies and New Zealanders, of course, Kiwis. But when it comes to the influence of playing home or away, this story takes the biscuit. In the late 1800s the then-governor of New Zealand, Sir George Grey, shipped, along with several zebra, antelope and kookaburras, a group of South Australian tammar wallabies to his privately owned Kawau Island, near Auckland. Although the antelope and zebra soon perished, the wallabies survived, indeed thrived, reaching pest proportions. The Department of

Conservation would quietly love to have seen their total eradication, were it not so controversial. This was further exacerbated given the fact that the wallabies had become a tourist attraction, and were proving popular with day visitors from which they sought considerable camaraderie especially when eating. Ironically, meanwhile, in Australia, that specific genetic strain of tammar wallaby had become extinct. Now, remarkably rediscovered, it is hoped a small group of the Kiwi wallabies can be shipped back to South Australia to resurrect the species.

A further 3 km north is the **Dome State Forest**, which provides a number of walks ranging from 40 minutes to three hours. The best walk takes 1½ hours and involves climbing to the Dome Summit from where you can spot the Auckland Sky Tower on a clear day. All the walks start at the top of the **Dome Café**, which is open daily.

To the east of Warkworth, on the scenic Mahurangi Peninsula, are the popular coastal holiday venues of **Snells Beach** (with the **Salty Dog Tavern**, see page 142), **Algies Bay** and **Martins Bay**, the latter having the best beach, and **Sandspit**, from where the ferry departs to **Kawau Island** (see below).

Short river trips by steamboat ($15) and self-guided or guided tours of the Matakana vineyards are also on offer from Warkworth; contact the VIC for information.

Kawau Island ● ➤➤ *pp140-143.*

Kawau Island is a popular holiday resort 8 km off the coast on the Mahurangi Peninsula. In summer its sheltered bays are almost more popular than terra firma, as yachties from far and wide drop anchor to enjoy the surroundings, fish, swim, dive or party long into the wee small hours. In pre-European times the island was the headquarters of Maori raiders who made numerous attacks on surrounding tribes from their villages and *pa*.

Ins and outs

Getting there There is a seasonal cruise to Kawau run by **Rubens** ① *T0800-111616, www.reubens.co.nz, departs daily from Sandspit at 1030 from, $65.* Rubens also operate water taxis from Sandspit. There is no public transport to Sandspit from Warkworth. For a taxi call T09-425 0000.

Around the island

European ownership dates back to 1837 when the island became the focus for mining activities – first manganese, then copper – with operations ceasing in 1869. There are still remnants of copper mines a short walk from the wharf. In 1862 Sir George Grey, in his second term as Governor of New Zealand, purchased the island for a mere £3500 and began a 26-year stay in Bon Accord Harbour, where he created perhaps the biggest modern day tourist draw, the **Mansion House** ① *T09-422 8882, daily 1000-1530, $5, child $2*. Grey was fascinated by botany and zoology, developing a small collection of exotic animals and plants and also using the island as an acclimatization centre. He even had a pair of zebra brought from Africa to pull his carriage, which resulted in their death shortly after. Sadly, George was also blissfully unaware of the monumental environmental damage he was unleashing on the increasingly threatened New Zealand native wildlife and vegetation. To this day the odd wallaby hops through the bush, accompanied by the laughing of the Australian kookaburra (see box, page 137).

In 1967, 79 years after Sir George Grey went home to England, the island became part of the **Hauraki Maritime Park**. Some 176 ha were put aside as public domain, the Mansion House turned from guesthouse to museum and the rest of the island went to farmers and the wallabies.

North of Warkworth◉● ▸▸ *pp140-143.*

Matakana and around
Blink and you may miss Matakana, 8 km north of Warkworth on the main Warkworth to Leigh Road, but the surrounding countryside is famous for its **vineyards**. Heron's Flight **Vineyard** ① *49 Sharp's Rd, T09-422 7915, www.heronsflight.co.nz, daily 1000-1800; tours and tastings available, café on site*, is one of a number producing fine merchandise. Others include: **Ascension** ① *T09-422 9601, www.ascension vineyard.co.nz;* **Hyperion** ① *T09-422 9375, www.hyperion-wines.co.nz;* **Matakana Estate** ① *T09-425 8446, www.matakana ,estate.co.nz;* **Ransom** ① *T09-425 8862, www.ransomwines.co.nz;* and a few other labels around Mahurangi. The VIC (I-Site) in Warkworth, see page 136, can provide details.

Also of interest is the **Morris and James Country Pottery and Café** ① *Tongue Farm Rd, T09-422 7116, www.morrisandjames.co.nz, 1000-1700; café daily 0900-1500*. It uses clay sourced from the Matakana River to produce a wonderful array of terracotta pots and tiles that have become famous throughout the country. There are free weekday pottery tours and the café serves delicious food and local wines in a relaxed garden setting.

Tawharanui
If you have time, do not miss the biggest countryside and northernmost coastal park in the region, Tawharanui (pronounced 'Ta-fara-nui'). It takes some getting to via Takatu Road just north of Matakana, but is well worth the effort. Even before you reach the park you are afforded spectacular views of Kawau Island and beyond. Being so isolated, it is quieter than most other parks and offers beaches, walks and scenery unrivalled in many other eastern coastal parks. A haven for native birds, you are almost sure to see noisy paradise shelduck, together with pied stilts and variable oystercatchers. Plans are afoot to turn Tawharanui into a 'mainland island' protected with predator-free fences: an exciting prospect. The two main beaches are ideal for relaxing or swimming and look out across Omaha Bay to Leigh. Extended walks out to the headland offer even better views. Permits are available for camping.

Leigh and the Goat Island Marine Reserve
The original name for Leigh was Little Omaha – common sense given its position on the west of Omaha Cove, 13 km from Matakana. However, to avoid confusion with its sister settlement of Big Omaha, slightly inland, the name was changed to Leigh. Why 'Leigh' remains a mystery. Whatever, Leigh is a small fishing community the nature of which is

best summed up by its rather mundane street names like 'Wonderview', 'Barrierview', 'Grandview' and, yes, even 'Seaview'.

Matheson's Beach is 1 km to the west of the village and is a popular spot in summer for all beach and aquatic pursuits, but by far the main focus of attention lies 4 km north of Leigh, around **Goat Island** and its associate **marine reserve**. Although the island itself, 300 m offshore, is fairly nondescript, the waters that surround it are very special. In 1975, these waters were established as New Zealand's first marine reserve. Treated essentially like any reserve on land, the entire aquatic flora and fauna is fully protected, and no angling or shell fishing is allowed. Basically, nothing can be taken except photographs and scientific samples. The result is an astonishing abundance of marine life that brings hordes of divers to the area all year round. The added allure is that you do not need to be Jacques Cousteau to enjoy it. From the shore, swimmers and snorkellers can (particularly in summer) find themselves surrounded by shoals of inquisitive fish looking for an easy meal. In the early days it was possible to feed the fish, but it quickly became obvious a diet of cheese slices and crisps was not conducive to their good health. Indeed a sign just before the beach now states: 'Do not feed the fish, it can make them sick'.

Dive gear can be hired from **Goat Island Dive** ① *142a Pakiri Rd beside the Sawmill Café, T0800-348369, www.goatislanddive.co.nz.*

On the surface, the glass-bottom boat **Aquador** ① *T09-422 6334, www.glassbottomboat.co.nz,* offers a number of trips around the island lasting up to 45 minutes ($20), with a commentary and good views of the fish and abundant marine life below. Trips are weather dependent and can be subject to seasonal schedules. Call first.

Pakiri

The main road north of Leigh splits in to a series of metalled roads that begin to give the first raw impressions of rural Northland life. About 10 km north of Leigh is the very pleasant and fairly isolated beach at Pakiri. Pakiri is also one of the best bases for horse trekking in the North Island. **Pakiri Beach Horse Treks** ① *Taurere Park, Rahuikiri Rd, Pakiri Beach, T09-422 6275, www.horseride-nz.co.nz,* is a popular outfit offering a huge range of trekking options from one-hour to seven-day safaris and twilight rides. It also provides a range of basic or more comfortable homestay accommodation and a café.

Mangawhai Heads

From Pakiri the metalled roads wind their way up to Mangawhai, a short distance from the sweeping coast and beaches of the Jellicoe Channel. Slightly inland the rather exposed **Spectacle** and **Tomorata Lakes** play host to local water-skiers and jet-skiers. The best spot at which to access the beach and coastal views is at **Te Arai Point**, just north of Spectacle Lake. There is little in the way of habitation here, which adds to the peace and isolation. North along the beach from Te Arai there is a wildlife refuge that takes in the impressive sand spit of the **Mangawhai Harbour**, but this is best accessed just south of Mangawhai village on Bull Road (off Black Swamp Road).

Some 10 km north of Te Arai is **Mangawhai**, a small farming village which offers a limited range of motel and motorcamp accommodation. Mangawhai Heads, a short distance to the north of the village, is basically a scattering of holiday houses frequented by the wealthy in summer. The beaches around both villages are popular with surfers and beach-goers, and 'The Heads', as it is better known, is also a good base for deep-sea and game fishing.

There is no information centre in Mangawhai but there is an information booth next to the main drag, Molesworth Drive, near the golf club. The website, www.mangawhai

heads.co.nz, is also useful. Here you can see the various accommodation options and local activities available. The leaflet *Magical Mangawhai* is comprehensive and available from regional tourist offices, local shops and motor parks.

Waipu and around ●❶❷❀ ➤ pp142-143.

North of Mangawhai the road negotiates the headland and falls to the beautiful shoreline settlements of Lang's Beach and Waipu Cove at the southern end of Bream Bay, before turning inland to the proudly Scottish enclave of Waipu. The small community is very proud of its Scottish heritage and no visit to Waipu would be complete without a look inside the **Waipu Museum and Heritage Centre** ⓘ *T09-432 0746, www.waipumuseum.com, 0930-1630, $8, child $3*, with its large Nova Scotian flag outside – a flag that combines the ancient Scottish Saltire and Lion Rampant designs. Inside the museum, walls are decked with photographs, and faces of early immigrants look down on cases full of personal effects from spectacles to spinning wheels. Logbooks listing the immigrant arrivals and the ships on which they arrived are being continuously updated. It is little wonder that many Nova Scotians come to Waipu to trace their ancestors and at times find family heirlooms amongst the treasured pieces. There has been so much interest over the years that the new heritage centre was added to house more modern resources with which the public can now trace their lineage. The staff in the museum are very knowledgeable.

Every New Year's Day since 1871 the **Waipu Highland Games** – the largest and longest-running in the southern hemisphere – gets into full swing with highland dancers, pipe bands and kilted, caber-tossing men, who descend on the village from far and wide. ➤ *See Festivals and events, page 143.*

At the **Waipu Wildlife Refuge** you can see a variety of native shorebirds in an easily accessible area situated around the mouth of the Ruakaka River. The **Waipu Caves**, 13 km to the west of Waipu (via Shoemaker Road), offer a great opportunity to see glow-worms through a 200-m passage, part of an extensive limestone cave system. The cave has free access, so caution is advised. Going alone is not recommended and do not enter without a torch and appropriate footwear. A map giving directions is available in the museum and the cave is signposted from Waipu Caves Road.

North of Waipu and back on SH1 you follow the edge of Bream Bay (the beach is best accessed at Uretiti 6 km north of Waipu) before turning inland towards Whangarei. At the northern end of Bream Bay and the entrance to Whangarei Harbour is the unsightly **Marsden Oil Refinery** ⓘ *T09-432 8194, daily 1000-1700*. This is where all of New Zealand's crude oil is imported. Sadly, even with all the best technology in the world, the refinery and its tanker traffic poses a significant threat to Northland's pristine coastline and remains a potential environmental disaster. However, see if the **visitor centre** at the refinery can persuade you otherwise.

◉ Warkworth and Kowhai Coast listings

For Sleeping and Eating price codes and other relevant information, see Essentials pages 44-50.

● Sleeping

Warkworth and around *p136*
Warkworth offers plenty of country B&B

options. The VIC (I-Site), www.warkworth-information.co.nz, has full listings.
LL Uhuru Lodge, 390 Pukapuka Rd, Mahurangi West, T09-422 0585, www.uhurulodge.co.nz. A spectacular, spacious house in farm and bush setting over a private bay. Superb pool.

L Saltings B&B, 1210 Sandspit Rd, T09-425 9670, www.saltings.co.nz. Luxury B&B with classy suites and rooms and self-catering accommodation in a fine vineyard setting.
A Central Motel, 24 Neville St, Warkworth, T09-425 8645, www.centralmotel.co.nz. Basic and affordable option.
A Willow Lodge B&B, 541 Woodcocks Rd, T09-425 7676. Tidy self-contained units 3 mins from the town in a quiet setting, friendly, knowledgeable hosts.
A-D Sheepworld Caravan Park and Backpackers, SH1 (4 km north of Warkworth), T09-425 9962, www.sheepworldcaravan park.co.nz. Next to the sheep farm, with full facilities including café and spa pool.

Kawau Island *p137*
There is a wide range of options in the satellite coastal villages. The VIC (I-Site) in Warkworth has extensive listings and will arrange bookings, see Warkworth, above.
A Coppercabanas Cedar Lodge, Smelting House Bay, T09-4228700, www.coppercabanas.co.nz. Self-contained waterfront units.
A-D Kawau Lodge , North Cove, T09-422 8831, www.kawaulodge.co.nz. 4-star lodge in a tranquil location. Recommended.

Matakana *p138*
Camping permits are available for Tawharanui.
LL The Castle Matakana, 378 Whitmore Rd, T09-422 9288, www.the-castle.co.nz. Fine country living, food and wine in a modern designer home with rural and sea views. 3 tastefully decorated luxury guest rooms including the sumptuous 'Tower Suite' all replete with contemporary NZ artworks.
LL Sandpiper Lodge, Takatu Rd Peninsula, T09-422 7256, www.sandpiperlodge.co.nz. Near the beautiful Tawharanui Regional Park. Very classy. Pool and restaurant attached.
B Matakana House Motel, 975 Matakana Rd, T09-422 7497, www.matakana house.co.nz. Mid-range and very tidy.

Leigh and Goat Island *p138*
LL-L Tera del Mar, 140 Rodney Rd, Leigh, T09-422 6090, www.teradelmar.co.nz. A rambling Victorian villa offering all mod cons. One room has a 4-poster bed and open fire.
A-C Leigh Sawmill Café Accommodation, 142 Pakiri Rd, Leigh, T09-422 6019, www.leighsawmillcafe.co.nz. A more affordable option in the village offering tidy rooms with en suite bath and also bunks.
C-D Goat Island Campground, Goat Island Rd, Leigh, T09-422 6185. Budget option with powered camping sites, may close in winter.
C-D Whangateau Holiday Park, 559 Leigh Rd, Whangateau, T09-422 6305, www.whangateauholidaypark.co.nz. On the beachfront and friendly.

Pakiri *p139*
AL Miller's Ark, just north of Pakiri, T09-431 5266, www.pakiriretreat.co.nz. A rather intriguing homestay or self-contained option.
A-D Pakiri Holiday Park, on the beach, T09-422 6199, www.pakiriholidaypark.co.nz. Some decent cabins, luxury cottages, camp kitchen and kayak hire.

Mangawhai Heads *p139*
AL Mangawhai Lodge, 4 Heather St, T09-4315311, www.seaviewlodge.co.nz. Best B&B in the area and good value.
A Hidden Valley Chalets, corner of Te Arai Point and Mangawhai Rd, (15 km off SH1), T09-431 5332, www.hiddenvalley.co.nz. Good self- contained chalets, peaceful area. Outdoor spa.
A Milestone Cottages, Moir Point Rd, Mangawhai, T09-431 4018, www.milestone cottages.co.nz. An award-winning self-contained option, near the beach. Pool, kayaks.
B-D Coastal Cow Backpackers, 299 Molesworth Drive, T09-431 5246, www.mangawhaibackpackers.com. The best budget backpacker option in the area. Just 16 beds, cosy, spotlessly clean and run by enthusiasts with an obvious fondness for all things bovine.

Motorcamps
B-D Mangawhai Heads Motor Camp, 2 Mangawhai Heads Rd, T09-431 4675.
B-D Riverside Holiday Park, 41 Black Swamp Rd, Mangawhai, T09-431 4825. Close to the beach and the sand spit wildlife refuge.

Waipu and around *p140*
There are a number of good B&Bs and lodges in the area mainly in Waipu Cove or Lang Beach to the south of Waipu village.
L Royal Palm Lodge, 19 Highland Lass Pl, Lang's Beach, T09-432 0120, www.royalpalm lodge.co.nz. A modern villa with a range of well-appointed rooms and en suite baths, a spa and excellent cuisine.
A Flower Haven B&B, 53 St Ann Rd, Waipu Cove, T09-432 0421, www.flowerhaven.com. Self-contained apartment with sea views and close to the beach.
A Stone House B&B, Cove Rd, Waipu, T09-432 0432, www.stonehousewaipu.co.nz. Self-contained 2-bedroom stone cottage, cabin and budget 'loft'-style accommodation, all a short stroll to the beach. Recommended.

Motels
A Waipu Clansman Motel, 30 Cove Rd, Waipu, T09-432 0424, www.waipuclansman motel.co.nz. Standard facilities.
A Waipu Cove Resort, 891 Cove Rd, T09-432 0348, www.waipucoveresort.co.nz. Eleven units by the beach.
A-D Waipu Cove Cottages and Camping Ground, Cove Rd, T09-432 0851, www.waipucovecottages.co.nz. Tidy and popular.
C-D Waipu Wanderers Backpackers, 25 St Mary's Rd, T09-432 0532,. Small, cosy and conveniently located.

● Eating

Warkworth *p136*
Most people staying in the Warkworth area head for the local vineyards for fine dining. There are restaurants at **Ascension**, T09-422 9601,

www.ascensionvineyard.co.nz; and **Heronsflight**, T09 422 7915, www.herons flight.co.nz. Also try **Morris and James Country Pottery and Café**, Tongue Farm Rd, T09-422 7116, www.morrisandjames.co.nz. 1000-1700; café daily 0900-1500. The café serves delicious food and local wines in a relaxed garden setting.
♈ Sandpiper Lodge, see Sleeping above, T09-422 7256. The best option for fine dining. Bookings essential.
♈ Warkworth Pizza Company, Neville St, T09-425 7373. Daily 1100-1500, 1700-late. A local favourite.
♈ Salty Dog Inn, Snells Beach, T09-425 5588. An old English-style pub with good beer and pub grub, just like back home.

Cafés
Duck's Crossing Café, Riverview Plaza, T09-425 9940, daily 0730-1630.
Queens St Corner Café, opposite the VIC, T09-425 8749, daily.

Leigh and Goat Island *p138*
♈ Sawmill Café, 142 Pakiri Rd, T09-422 6019. Summer daily, 0930-late; winter Thu-Sun late. The place to go for fresh light meals, good coffee and occasional live music.
♈ Leigh Fish and Chips, Cumberland St, T09-422 6035. Daily 1100-1930 Sun-Thu (-2000 Fri-Sat).

Mangawhai Heads *p139*
♈ Naja Garden Café, Molesworth Dr, T09-431 4111, www.najagarden.co.nz. Daily 0830-1700, dinner Thu-Sat in winter. Licensed. Modern food, all-day breakfast attached to a Garden Centre.
♈ Sail Rock Café, 12 Wood St, T09-431 4051, www.sailrockcafe.co.nz. Daily in summer. A la carte plus a range of pizzas and café lunches, bar and BYO.
♈ Karvana Cafe, 7 Wood St, T09-431 5587. Good for a quick coffee, or a nice cool beer.

Waipu and around *p140*
♈ Clansman Motel and Restaurant, 30 Cove

Rd, Waipu, T09-432 0424.
Pizza Barn and Bar, 2 Cove Rd, Waipu,
T09-432 1011.
Food45, 45 The Centre, T09-432 0254. Daily
in summer.

games.co.nz. For details contact the Waipu
Caledonian Society, T09-432 0746.

❻ Directory

❀ Festivals and events

Waipu and around p140
1 Jan Highland Games, www.highland

Warkworth p136
Internet At the library next to the VIC. Mon-
Thu 0900-1700, Fri 0900-2000, Sat 0900-1200.

Whangarei and around → Colour map 1, B4 Population: 45,000.

Given the obvious allure of the Bay of Islands to the north, with its promise of stunning scenery and a whole host of activities, few visitors pay much attention to Northland's largest town. However, if you do choose to linger here a while, you will find that it has quite a lot to offer – not only in aesthetics (just take a look at the Town Basin) but also in some lesser-known gems only a short drive away. One such pearl is Ocean Beach at Whangarei Heads – the perfect place to sit just after a storm or watch the sun rise. ►► *For Sleeping, Eating and other listings, see pages 148-153.*

Ins and outs

Getting there **Onerahi airport**, T09-437 0666, is 9 km west of the city and is linked to the city centre by shuttle bus, $10. The district is serviced by **Air New Zealand Link**, T0800-737000, www.airnewzealand.co.nz. **Great Barrier Airlines**, T09-275 9120, www.greatbarrierairlines.co.nz, also run a Fri and Sun service from Whangarei to Claris (on Great Barrier Island) from $129 one-way.

The **bus station** is in Rose St, T09-438 2653, downtown Whangarei, but they can also stop at the VIC at the southern approach to town. **Intercity** and **Northliner**, T09-583 5780, has a daily coach service to and from Auckland and destinations further north. If you are arriving by car, take extra care on the stretch of road from Waipu to Whangarei.

Getting around Whangarei has a fairly comprehensive bus service. Timetables are available from the VIC or **Citylink Whangarei**, T09-4381079; the standard city fare is $3. **Kiwi Cabs**, T09-438 2299, provides a 24-hour taxi service. There is no public transport for getting to Whangarei Heads (page 145), but cycling is an option. For local bike hire information try the **Town Basin Hire**, Jetty One, T09-437 2509, $25 a day or contact Paul at the locally based **The Cycle Touring Company**, T09-4360033, www.cycletours.co.nz

Tourist information The main **VIC (I-site)** ⓘ *Tarewa Park, 92 Otaika Rd, T09-438 1079, www.whangareinz.com, Mon-Fri, 0830-1700, weekends 0930-1630, extended hours in summer,* is just as you come into the town (northbound). The staff are very friendly and helpful and there is a café attached. The new toilets are also worth a sneaky muse. The regional **DoC office** ⓘ *Ka Ka St, T09-470 3304, www.doc.govt.nz,* can provide a useful pamphlet called *Whangarei District Walks*; also available from the VIC.

Sights

A good place to start your tour of Whangarei's sights is with a fine view of the city and the harbour itself. **Mount Parahaki** on Memorial Drive (off Riverside Drive) is 241 m high and was once the site of New Zealand's largest Maori *pa*. Today it is crowned with a war memorial and a rather tacky red cross that glows at night. You can also walk up Parahaki (one hour) via the **Mair Park**, a peaceful park of native bush and well-marked trails. There is an old gold mine and remnants of Maori fortifications within it.

The jewel in Whangarei's scenic crown is the congenial **Town Basin**, where expensive nautical hardware bobs and squeaks on the glistening waters of the marina. The Basin is an award-winning waterfront development which houses a number of interesting attractions including the Clapham's Clocks Museum, art galleries, craft shops and a café and restaurant. There is also a small **information booth** ⓘ T09-438 1315, beside Clapham's Clocks Museum (see below) to help you find your way around.

Without doubt the best attraction, other than the atmosphere of the Basin itself, is **Clapham's Clock Museum** ⓘ T09-438 3993, www.claphamsclocks.com, daily 0900- 1700, $8, child $4, a highly entertaining and ever-growing collection of timepieces from all around the world. The best thing to do is to take a guided tour, otherwise the collection, which is the biggest in the southern hemisphere, is a bit daunting.

There are two good art galleries at the Basin. The historic colonial **Reyburn** House ⓘ Tue-Fri 1000-1600, Sat-Sun 1300-1600, (the oldest in Whangarei), features displays of local art. West of the Town Basin, in the peaceful and pleasant **Cafler Park and Rose Gardens**, is the small modern **Whangarei Art Museum** ⓘ Water St, T09-430 4240, www.whangareiartmuseum.co.nz, Tue-Fri 1000-1630, Sat-Sun 1200-1600, donation, which shows the best of local art past and present and also hosts touring national exhibitions. A short walk will take you to the **Fernery, Conservatory and Cacti House** ⓘ T09-438 4879, daily 1000-1600, free. The Fernery houses New Zealand's largest collection of ferns, while the Conservatory is filled with ever-changing displays of flowers. Near the park on Rust Avenue is the **Forum North Cultural Complex** (see Entertainment, page 152).

On the outskirts of town at the end of Selwyn Avenue is the celebrated creative haven of the **Northland Craft Trust** (**Quarry Arts Centre**) ⓘ daily 0930-1630, free. It's an impressive collective of working artists and crafts people producing an array of works from pottery and lithographs to traditional Maori carvings – worth a visit.

Further west and 6 km out of town, in the suburb of Maunu, is the **Whangarei Museum, Clarke Homestead** and **Kiwi House** ⓘ T09-438 9630, www.whangareimuseum.co.nz, daily 1000-1600, adult $10, child $5 all sites. It is an indoor/outdoor complex with a colonial farming block and homestead and a modern building housing a number of significant Taonga or Maori treasures, including kiwi feather capes and a musket that belonged to the great northern warrior Hone Heke. The display is deliberately indigenous in content and perspective. 'Live Days' are held regularly during the summer with special events like bullock riding, vintage car displays and horse-drawn carriages. The Kiwi House is one of the better examples in the country with exhibits of native flora and live kiwi. Note that there is usually only one. This is deliberate as kiwi are solitary birds and fiercely territorial.

Next to the museum is the **Whangarei Native Bird Recovery Centre** ⓘ T09-438 1457, www.whangareinativebirdrecovery.org.nz. Although not freely open to visitors you may be allowed to visit by prior arrangement and for a donation. This charity has the main centre in the north for wild bird rehabilitation and an excellent and successful kiwi egg incubation facility. To the south of the city on SH1 is the **Paper Mill** ⓘ T09-438 2652, www.papermill.co.nz,Mon-Sat 1000-1500, donation; small charge to make paper. This tourist attraction is growing in popularity and deservedly so. It gives the visitor an insight into traditional craft papermaking using recycled materials in an historical setting, and you can even try to make some yourself. Just 1 km further south is the **Longview** Winery ⓘ *T09-438 7227, www.longviewwines.co.nz, Mon-Sat 0830-1800 in summer, 0830-1730 in winter*, a 30-year-old estate producing popular and award-winning wines.

To the north of the city on Ngunguru Road, Tikipunga, are the slightly over-rated 23-m **Whangarei Falls**, which are worth a peek if you are passing. (Perhaps a better way to experience them is to abseil down them with **Northland Outdoors**, T09-430 3474.) The **AH Reed Memorial Kauri Park** on Whareora Road is the pick of the local parks with some fine examples of native Kauri trees up to 3 m in diameter and 500 years old. They are impressive, but nothing compared to the 1500-year-old Tane Mahuta on the west coast (see page 181), which in turn is nothing, compared to some monsters that once were. The park has short walks and tracks and a very pleasant waterfall thrown in for good measure.

Although they are hard to find and a bit out of town, the **Abbey Caves** are worth a visit. If you take a right off Memorial Drive (up Mount Parahaki) on to Old Parua Bay Road and on to Abbey Caves Road you will, with a little difficulty, find a DoC sign next to the road. Provided you have adequate footwear, a torch and are not alone (or have kids in tow), then follow the footpath and signs past the weird and wonderful limestone foundations that lead to the caves. Do not venture too far into the caves without a guide. If you are brave, switch off your torch and amidst the sound of trickling water, enjoy the small galaxy of glow-worms above. It is easy to get lost in and around the caves so the best option is to join a guided tour from **Bunkdown Lodge**, T09-438 8886 (see Sleeping, page 149).

Whangarei Heads

Ocean Beach is one of Northland's best: it's quiet, beautiful and, in a raging easterly wind, a place where the senses are bombarded with nature at its best. On the way you will begin to notice the prevalence of evocative Scots place names like McLeod's and Urquart's Bay and street names like McDonald Road – all family names of the 'overspill' Scots settlers from the Bream Bay and Waipu enclaves. Above these quiet communities and scenic bays are the towering peaks of **Mount Manaia**, the base of which can be accessed from the car park next to the Manaia Club. It is an excellent, but steep walk through bush that takes about three hours return. You cannot climb to the peak summits themselves – they are *tapu* (sacred and off limits) – steeped in Maori legend. Other coastal walks are to **Peach Cove** (three hours) and **Smugglers Cove** (one hour) both reachable from **Urquart's Bay**.

Tutukaka Coast

Tutukaka is on the loop road that also takes in Ngunguru and Matapouri before turning inland again back to SH1 and Whangarei. By car from the city suburb of Tikipunga, take the Ngunguru Road past Whangarei Falls. On the outskirts of the city in Glenbervie the roads become lined by drystone walls giving the area a distinctly British countryside feel (no doubt a legacy of the early settlers) before New Zealand bush takes over once again and you hit the coast at Ngunguru.

Even if fishing and scuba diving did not exist, the Tutukaka coastline would still deserve to be one of the finest coastal venues in Northland. But its rugged scenic bays are best known throughout New Zealand and beyond as the gateway and safe harbour to some of the best **deep-sea fishing** and **diving** in the world. The **Poor Knights Islands** (see box, page 148), which lie 25 km offshore, are internationally significant both above and below the waterline, with a wide range of wildlife and vegetation. Here the

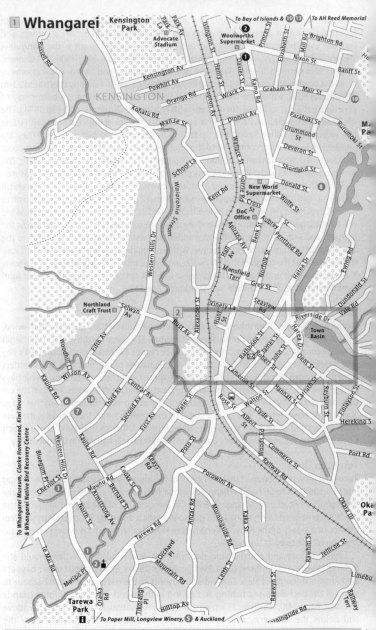

Whangarei

Kensington Park

To Bay of Islands & ⑩ ⑬   To AH Reed Memorial

Park La

Islington St

Princes St

Woolworths ②
Supermarket

Elizabeth St

Kamo Rd Rd

Brighton Rd

Advocate
Stadium

Russell Rd

①

Davies St

Nixon St

Banff St

Henry St

Wrack St

Graham St

Mair St

Kensington Av

Powhiri Av

Lupton Av

Oranga Rd

Kohatu Rd

Dinniss Av

Parahaki St

⑲

KENSINGTON

Manse St

Wallace St

Drummond
St

Rurumoki St

Ma
Pa

Deveron St

School La

Shortland St

Waiarohia Stream

Gorrie Rd

Donald St

Kent Rd

New World
Supermarket

Wolfe St

⑧

Cross
St

Western Hills Dr

Doc
Office

Aubrey
St

Apirana Av

Bank St

Pentland Rd

Hall St

Hatea Dr

Ewing Rd

Northland
Craft Trust

Selwyn
Av

Mansfield
Terr

Norfolk St

Grey St

Dundonald St

Vinery La

Seaview
Rd

Vale Rd

Fifth Av

Rust Av

Alexander St

Hunt St

Riverside Dr

Hatea Dr

Town
Basin

Woodhill

Wilson Av

Central Av

Rathbone St

James St

Robert St

John St

Dent St

Reyburn St

Fintayson St

Kauika Rd

⑥ ⑱

Third Av

Water St

Cameron St

Hannah St

Carruth St

⑦

Second Av

Rose St

Walton St

Herekino S

First Av

Clyde St

Albert
St

Port Rd

Poto St

Commerce St

Keays
Rd

Woods Rd

Railway Rd

Cooke St

Porowini Av

Blagburn St

Maunu Rd

Bernard St

Anzac Rd

Morningside Rd

Kaka St

Oka
Pa

Chelfot St

Armstrong Av

North St

Tarewa Rd

Rawhiti St

Okara Dr

Te Mai Rd

Orchard
Pl

Jellicoe St

① To Whangarei Museum, Clarke Homestead, Kiwi House
& Whangarei Native Bird Recovery Centre

Mountain Rd

Leith St

Raewyn St

Limebu

②

Matiqo Rd

Otaika Rd

Tikorangi
Pl

Hilltop Av

Morningside Rd

Railway
Terr

Tarewa
Park

ℹ To Paper Mill, Longview Winery, ⑤ & Auckland

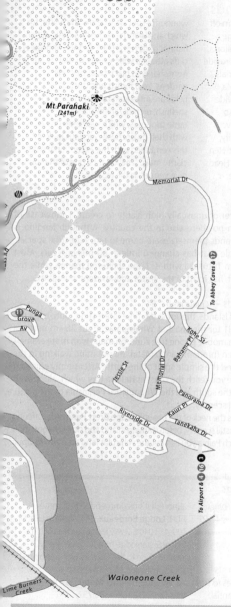

Tutukaka Coast, Whangarei Falls & **9** **14** **15**

Mt Parahaki
(241m)

Memorial Dr

➡ **Whangarei maps**
1 Whangarei
2 Whangarei centre,
  page 149

300 metres
300 yards

To Abbey Caves & **17**

Punga
Grove
Av

Kohe St

Jessie St

Bahama Pl

Memorial Dr

Panorama Dr

Riverside Dr

Kauri Pl

Tanekaha Dr

To Airport & **4** **16** **3**

Sleeping 🛏
Alpha Motel & Holiday Park **5**
Avenue Heights Motel **7**
Bunkdown Lodge **1**
Channel Vista **4**
Cherry Court Motor Lodge **2**
Cheviot Park Motor Lodge **3**
Graelyn Villa **14**
Kamo Springs Caravan Park **13**
Kingswood Motor Inn **10**
Little Earth Lodge **17**
Lodge Bordeaux **18**
Lupton Lodge **9**
Pohutukawa Lodge **6**
Settlers **8**
Totaranui B&B **16**
Whangarei Falls Backpackers
 & Holiday Park **15**
Whangarei Manaakitanga YHA **11**
Whangarei Top Ten Holiday Park **19**

Eating 🍴
A Deco **2**
Adriatic Fisheries **1**
Topsail Café **3**

Waioneone Creek

Lime Burners
Creek

The Poor Knights Islands

The Poor Knights Islands, lying 24 km off Tutukaka, are the remnants of a large volcano, which erupted over 10 million years ago. The islands themselves provide a predator-free refuge for land animals like tuatara, native lizards, giant weta, flax snails, giant centipedes and a wide variety of rare seabirds. They are also home to several species of distinctive plants, including the Poor Knights lily, found only on 'The Knights' and the Hen and Chicken islands off Whangarei Heads. But it is the marine reserve, and the wonderful spectacle below the water, for which the islands are most famous. A rich habitat of caves, arches, tunnels and sheer cliffs attract a wide variety of marine life from sharks to black coral. Sponge gardens, kelp forests and gorgonian fields are inhabited by a myriad of fish, shellfish, urchins, anemones and even tame groupers, which welcome divers with their distinctively vacuous look. All this combined with the exceptional water clarity make 'The Knights' one of the top dive venues in the world.

nutrient-rich currents meet in water of unusually high clarity to create a showcase of marine life much of which is seen nowhere else in the country. Although landing is forbidden without a permit, the islands themselves are home to rare terrestrial species, like the prehistoric tuatara, a reptile that has changed little in 60 million years. Most activity in the area takes place from Tutukaka with its large sheltered marina while the village of **Ngunguru**, 5 km before it, has most of the visitor and resident amenities.

Whangarei to the Bay of Islands → *Colour map 1, B4.*

Most people take SH1 to the Bay of Islands, though a far more interesting route is via the **Old Russell Road** which leaves SH1 for the coast at Whakapara, about 26 km north of Whangarei. Here you are entering a mobile phone free zone, on roads with more animals than cars, and on which the children (predominantly Maori) do not mind walking in the rain. Welcome to rural Northland and the simple spirit of the north. After simply enjoying the countryside and its atmosphere you reach the coast at **Helena Bay** which, along with Whananaki and Mimiwhangata to the south and the Whangaruru Peninsula to the north, offers remote and beautiful coastal scenery.

From Whangaruru the road passes the neck of the beautiful **Cape Brett Peninsula**, offering great walking in equally stunning coastal scenery, before turning inland and slowly negotiating its way to Russell. If you intend to reach Paihia you can get the vehicular ferry at Okaito to Opua (last ferry 2050, except Friday 2150).

Whangerei & around listings

For Sleeping and Eating price codes and other relevant information, see Essentials pages 44-50.

● Sleeping

Whangarei *p143, maps p146 and p149*
Whangarei has a wide variety of places to stay and pre-booking is generally not essential, although it's recommended in summer.
LL-L Lodge Bordeaux, 361 Western Hills Dr, T09-438 0404, www.lodgebordeaux.co.nz. Classy 5-star lodge motel conveniently located close to the CBD. 15 well-appointed suites, fast internet, pool and spas.
AL Avenue Heights Motel, 355 Western Hills Dr (SH1), T09-438 2737,

www.avenueheights.co.nz. New motel, conveniently located, with 10 luxury units.

AL Channel Vista, 254 Beach Rd, Onerahi, T09-436 5529, www.bnbwhangarei.co.nz. 2 fully self-contained and traditional bedrooms with great harbour views.

AL Kingsgate Hotel, 9 Riverside Dr, T09-438 0284, www.kingsgatewhangarei.co.nz. Well-established hotel overlooking the marina and Town Basin. Modern rooms with standard 3-star facilities. In-house bar/ restaurant offers à la carte and buffet-style dining. Indoor pool, spa pool and sauna. Off-street parking.

AL-A Lupton Lodge, 555 Ngunguru Rd, Glenbervie, T09-437 2989, www.luptonlodge.co.nz. Traditional Kiwi villa in peaceful surrounds. Friendly owners. En suite or shared bathroom, pool.

A Cherry Court Motor Lodge, 35 Otaika Rd, T09-438 3128, www.cherrycourt.co.nz. Swimming pool, laundry and licensed restaurant nearby.

A Cheviot Park Motor Lodge, corner of Cheviot St and Western Hills Dr, T09-438 2341, www.cheviot-park.co.nz. Modern and friendly.

A Kingswood Motor Inn, 260 Kamo Rd, T09-437 5779. 5 mins' north of the city centre, disabled facilities, laundry, spa.

A Pohutukawa Lodge, 362 Western Hills Dr, T09-430 8634, www.pohutukawalodge.co.nz. Modern studios, some with spas.

A Settlers Hotel, Hatea Dr, T09-438 2699/ T0800-666662, www.settlershotel.co.nz. In a nice setting overlooking the river and within walking distance of the Town Basin. Bedrooms with en suite bath, laundry, pool and private spas, licensed à la carte restaurant.

C-D Bunkdown Lodge, 23 Otaika Rd, T09-438 8886, www.bunkdownlodge.co.nz. Large, modern, more like a B&B and even has a bath. Very helpful, friendly hosts who have an information centre attached. In-house tours to Abbey Caves and strong links with local activity operators. Popular so book ahead.

C-D Little Earth Lodge, 85 Abbey Caves Rd (6 km from town centre), T09-430 6562, www.littleearthlodge.co.nz. Small, purpose-built and well-facilitated in peaceful rural setting and close to Abbey Caves. Full range of rooms, classy and clean replete with Balinese decor. Recommended.

C-D Whangarei Falls Backpackers and Holiday Park, 12 Ngunguru Rd, Tikipunga, T0800-227222/T09-437 0609. A great back-packer hostel that doubles as a motorcamp with all mod cons plus a pool, spa and TV room.

2 Whangarei centre

➡Whangarei maps
1 Whangarei, page 146
2 Whangarei centre

Town Basin

Library
Forum North Cultural Complex
Whangarei Art Museum
Cafler Park & Rose Gardens
Fernery, Conservatory & Cacti House
Clapham's Clock Museum
Reyburn House

N

100 metres
100 yards

Sleeping
Kingsgate 1

Eating
Bob 1
Caffeine Espresso Café 10
Dickens Inn 2
Killer Prawn 3

Mondos Café 7
Reva's on the Waterfront 4
Water Street Brasserie 6

C-D Whangarei Manaakitanga YHA, 52 Punga Grove Av, T09-438 8954, www.yha.org. nz. Set in peaceful surroundings and spacious grounds overlooking the harbour and Tower Basin, 5-min walk from the town centre. Dorms and doubles with all the usual facilities. Dive trips to the Poor Knights Islands can be arranged as well as guided walks to Abbey Caves.

Motorcamps and campsites
A-D Whangarei Top Ten Holiday Park, 24 Mair St, T09-437 6856, www.whangareitop 10.co.nz. This is the best of the bunch.
B-D Alpha Motel and Holiday Park, 34 Tarewa Rd, T09-438 6600, www.alphaholidaypark.co.nz.
B-D Kamo Springs Caravan Park, 55 Great North Rd, T09-435 1208, www.kamosprings.co.nz.

Whangarei Heads *p145*
There is little in the way of accommodation at the heads beyond McLeod's Bay but the small communities of Parua Bay just before it, and Pataua and Taiharuru a few kilometres north, have a number of options.
A Tide Song, Taiharuru Estuary, Beasley Rd, T09-436 1959, www.tidesong.co.nz. Self-contained in a bush and seaside setting.
A Totaranui B&B, 205 Owhiwa Rd (20 km east), T09-436 5170, www.totaranui.co.nz. Laid-back, good value B&B/homestay set in an elevated position in the bush. 2 cosy en suite doubles, and good views across the harbour. Friendly hosts are a dab hand at making fresh homemade bread. Generous breakfast.

Motorcamps and campsites
A-D Treasure Island Trailer Park, Pataua South, T09-436 2390, www.treasureisland nz.co.nz. Motorcamp with a beachfront campsite, camp kitchen.

Tutukaka Coast *p145*
AL Oceans Resort and Hotel, Marina Dr, Tutukaka, T0508-623267, www.oceanshotel. co.nz. Modern resort-style hotel with a nautical theme. Rooms or suites available,

in-house à la carte restaurant not surprisingly with a seafood edge, local activity bookings and all the usual bells and whistles.
AL Waipouri Lodge, Tutukaka, T09-434 3696, mckillop@extra.co.nz. Self-contained 3-bedroom home with private beach access.
A Bluewater Cottages, T09-434 3423, www.bluewaterparadise.co.nz. Halfway between Tutukaka and Matapouri (35 km from Whangarei), smart cottage-style accommodation, with memorable sea views.
A Dreamstay, 1350 Matapouri Rd, Sandy Bay, T09-434 3059, www.bed-and-breakfast. co.nz. B&B, homestay or self-contained.
A Malibu Mals Divestay, Tutukaka Block Rd, Kowharewa Bay, T09-434 3450, www.mali bumals.co.nz. Self-contained units or B&B handy to the marina.
A Pacific Rendezvous Motel, Tutukaka, T09-434 3847, www.oceanresort.co.nz. The most celebrated motel in the area with great views across the Tutukaka Harbour.
A The Sands Motel, Whangaumu Bay, Tutukaka, T09-434 3747, www.sandsmotel.co.nz. Spacious self-contained units.

Motorcamps and campsites
B-D Tutukaka Holiday Park, T09-434 3938, www.tutukaka-holidaypark.co.nz. Opposite the marina, self-contained and standard cabins, powered and non-powered sites, standard facilities including camp kitchen.

Whangarei to the Bay of Islands *p148*
Accommodation is basic and sparse with the exception of a few luxurious retreats.
C-D Farm Backpackers and Homestay, near Whangaruru, T09-433 6894, www.thefarm. co.nz. Comfortable and friendly, with a warm welcome, but perhaps the biggest attraction are the activities, including horse trekking, use of quad and mountain bikes and even yacht racing. Recommended.

Motorcamps and campsites
There are basic motorcamps mainly at Oakura (just north of Helena Bay).

C-D Oakura Motels and Caravan Park,
Oakura Bay, T09-433 6803. Beachside camps with units, cabins, powered or non-powered sites.
C-D Whangaruru Beachfront Camp,
Whangaruru, T09-433 6806. An alternative.
D Mimiwhangata Bay and Coastal Park,
bookings can be made through the **Tarewa Park Visitor Centre,** T09-430 2133. DoC's relatively cheap facilities with a self-contained lodge, cottage, beach house (book well in advance) and a campsite.

Basic DoC camping facilities are also available at **Whananaki** and **Whangaruru;** contact DoC, T09-430 2007.

❶ Eating

Whangarei *p143, maps p146 and p149*
In addition to the eateries listed below, there is a supermarket, **New World,** at 167 Bank St, T09-470 1090.
♥♥♥ A Deco, 70 Kamo Rd, T09-459 4957. As the name suggests, an art deco property housing an award-winning restaurant said by many to be the best in Northland. Imaginative and beautifully presented Pacific Rim cuisine. Good wine list.
♥♥♥ Killer Prawn, 28 Bank St, T09-4303333, www.killerprawn.co.nz. A swish and busy restaurant/bar considered the best eatery in town, offering a wide selection of traditional and specialist seafood options. Try the namesake 'Killer Prawn' – a small pond of seafood in which to bathe your taste buds.
♥♥♥ Reva's on the Waterfront, Quayside Town Basin, T09-438 8969, www.revas.co.nz. Quality international cuisine in pleasant surroundings, great pizza, licensed. Live music.
♥♥♥ Topsail Café, 1st floor, Onerahi Yacht Club, Beach Rd, Onerahi, T09-436 0529. Mon-Sat from 1800, Sun brunch 1000-1500. Serves continental-style cuisine and is a local seafood favourite.
♥♥♥ Water Street Brasserie, 24 Water St, T09-438 7464. Tue-Sat, BYO. Fine traditional cuisine in modern surroundings.

♥♥ BOB, 29 Bank St, T09-4380881. Laid back, popular café and a favourite for breakfast.
♥♥ Caffeine Espresso Café, 4 Water St, T09-438 1116. Arguably the best café in the city centre.
♥♥ Dickens Inn, corner of Cameron and Quality sts, T09-430 0406, www.dickens inn.co.nz. One of Whangarei's most popular pubs. Pub-style cuisine, breakfast, lunch, dinner and snacks, children's menu.
♥♥ Mondos Café, 14 Quayside, Town Basin, T09-430 0467. One of the best cafés in the city overlooking the marina it's a very relaxed venue and particularly popular for lazy breakfasts, brunches or the infamous 'Blokes Burger'
♥ Adriatic Fisheries, Kensington, 91 Kamo Rd, T09-437 3874. Best fish and chippy in town.

Whangarei Heads *p145*
If you want to cook for yourself, the **Taurikura General Store,** just west of Ocean Beach, is a traditional and interesting place to stock up, also has a café in summer. You can also get supplies at the supermarket in the **Onerahi Shopping Centre.**
♥♥ Flames International Hotel, Waverley St, Onerhai, T09-436 2107.

Tutukaka Coast *p145*
♥♥♥ Oceans Resort Tutukaka, Marina Rd, Tutukaka, T0508-623267. Daily, licensed. Resort restaurant with a nautical theme and a seafood edge.
♥♥ Marina Pizzeria, Tutukaka T09-434 3166, www.marinapizzeria.co.nz. Quality pizzas.
♥♥ Schnappa Rock Cafe, Marina Rd, Tutukaka, T09-434 3774. Daily til late. Café bar that forms the main focus for the Tutukaka community and occasional live bands.

❶ Pubs, bars and clubs

Whangarei *p143, maps p146 and p149*
There are a number of trendy bars and nightclubs in Whangarei. **The Killer Prawn** and the **Bacio Bar,** on Bank St, are the local places to be seen. While the **Frings**

Brauhaus, 104 Dent St, is a microbrewery bar with a fine beer garden. For the full 'shake of the pants' try **Heaven** or **Danger Danger** on Vine St, and **Rynoz**, Cameron St, all of which are pretty lively but, as you would expect, have that small town atmosphere. **Dickens Inn**, on Cameron St, is better for something a little quieter.

🎬 Entertainment

Whangarei *p143, maps p146 and p149*
The main cinema is the **Sky City Cinemas**, James St, T09-438 8550. The **Forum North Cultural Complex**, Rust Av, T09-438 3815, www.forumnorth.co.nz, is a well-equipped space and one of the best in the country for cultural and performing arts.

⛰ Activities and tours

Whangarei *p143, maps p146 and p149*
Bush safaris
The Bushwacka Experience, Highway 14, Maungatapere, T09-434 7724. Thrilling trips in a 4WD, BBQ and abseiling. Daily 4-hr trip $85, 2-hr $55. Recommended.

Cycling
Cycle Touring Company New Zealand, 100 Church St, Whangarei, T09-436 0033, www.cycletours.co.nz. Self-guided cycling adventures on routes all over Northland from 2-9 days. Accommodation and food included.

Dolphin, seabird and whale watching
Although viewing success rates are far lower than Kaikoura in the South Island, sightings of a number of whale species are possible. Dolphin trips are also better catered for in the Bay of Islands but if time is short and you do not intend to head north, **Bream Bay Charters**, T09-4327484, www.breambaycharters.co.nz, offers trips locally.

Fishing
The harbour and more especially the Tutukaka Coast offers excellent sea fishing. Big game fishing charters are available at Tutukaka with record catches in summer. **Bream Bay Charters**, Ruakaka, T09-432 7484, offers good trips locally.

Kayaking
Pacific Coast Kayakas, T09-436 1947, www.nzseakayaking.co.nz.
Town Basin Hire, Jetty One, Riverside Dr, Town Basin, T09-437 2509, hires out bikes, rollerblades and leisure craft including kayaks.

Scuba diving
See also Tutukaka Coast, below.
Dive HQ, 41 Clyde St, T0800-102102/T09-438 1075, www.divenow.co.nz.
Knight Diver Tours, 30 Heads Rd, T0800-766756, www.poorknights.co.nz.
Pacific Highway Charters, Tutukaka, T09-434 3762, www.divenz.co.nz.

Tutukaka Coast *p145*
Adventure sports
Jet-skiing, mountain biking, kayaking and surfing available from:
Ngunguru Holiday Park, T09-434 3851.
Tutukayax, Marina Beach, T09-4377442.
Water Sport Hire, 14 Kopipi Cres, Ngunguru, T09-434 3475.

Cruising
Cave Rider, T0800-288882/T09-434 3867, www.caverider.co.nz. High speed 2½-hr jet boat trips to the Poor Knights Islands taking in what is reputed to be the biggest sea cave in the world, Riko Riko, from $90, child $45.

Fishing
Fishing is not allowed in the marine reserve of the Poor Knights but the surrounding ocean has some of the best deep-sea fishing in the world, with numerous species like shark and marlin. The 'big game' season runs Dec-Apr. A day trip costs at least $250 a head. Most companies are based in Tutukaka:

For more information on charters contact the **Whangarei Deep Sea Anglers Club**, T09-4343818, www.sportfishing.co.nz.

Golf
Whangarei has some fine golf courses, including: **Northland Golf Club**, Pipiwai Rd, Kamo, T09-435 0042; **The Pines**, Parua Bay, T09-436 2246; **Sherwood Park**, Millington Rd, Maunu, T09-434 6900; and **Whangarei Golf Club**, Denby Cres, T09-437 0740 (the best).

Horse treks
Whananaki Trail Rides, Whananaki, T09-433 8299, www.hostrekin.co.nz. Trekking in local kauri forests and on the beach, from $40 (free camping and budget accommodation).

Rugby
The ITM Stadium in the city is the venue for local and provincial games as well as international test matches.

Scuba diving
Tutukaka is the main dive base. Companies offer personalized tours and equipment hire. Most boats leave for the Poor Knights Islands about 0830 and return at 1600. As well as the Poor Knights, wreck dives to the sunken navy frigate *Tui* just offshore from Tutukaka, and the *Waikato*, another warship sunk in 2000. A 2-dive trip costs about $200-250 including full gear hire. Tuition, snorkelling and kayaks are also available for the novice.
Dive Tutukaka, T0800-288882/ T09-434 3867, www.diving. co.nz. The main dive company, now internationally recognized, runs a very professional outfit from its base on the marina. It offers over 10 'world-class' site dives with names as 'The Labyrinth' and 'Maomao Arch' as well as dive courses, snorkelling, kayak, and whale- and dolphin-watching activities. Full day from $129. Recommended.

Skateboarding
The Skateboard Park, William Fraser Memorial Park, Riverside Dr, has a modern 1500-sq-m facility.

Swimming
Whangarei Aquatics, Ewing Rd (near the Town Basin), T09-438 7957, daily, $6. Olympic-size outdoor pool and a large indoor heated pool, spas and sauna.

Walking
One of the best walks in the area is at Tutukaka Head. To reach the car park take the 'right of way' sign right off Matapouri Rd, 400 m past the marina turning. It is marked private but actually it isn't. From there, the track goes over the headland before falling to a small beach and a series of small rock stacks. After negotiating the stacks (beware at high tide), climb the hill to the light beacon (2 km; 1 hr return), from where there are magnificent views along the coast. A few km north of Tutukaka, before the road turns inland again, are a number of small settlements and attractive bays and beaches. Matapouri and Whale Bay, 1 km to the north, are worth a stop.

Whangarei to the Bay of Islands *p148*
Oakura Bay Cruises, Oakura Bay (just north of Helena Bay), T09-433 6669.

⊖ Transport

Whangarei *p143, maps p146 and p149*
Car hire
Avis, 14 Hannah St, T09-438 2929. **Budget**, 22 Hannah St, T09-438 7292. **Rent-a-Cheapy**, 69 Otaika Rd, T09-438 7373.

① Directory

Whangarei *p143, maps p146 and p149*
Banks Most major branches can be found on Bank St. **Internet** Available at the library; the VIC; BOB Cafe (see above). **Library** The library is on Rust Av, T09-430 7260. **Medical services** Primecare, 12 Kensington Av, T09-437 9070. 0830-2200. **Post office** 16-20 Rathbone St, T09-430 2761. Open Mon-Fri 0830-1700, Sat 0900-1300.

Bay of Islands → *Colour map 1, B4.*

Paihia is the main launching point for the Bay of Islands; if you arrive here by road you may be disappointed because all you can see is one very little island just offshore. However, what you will certainly see are plenty of 'no vacancy' signs, boats (including a ferry that crosses the bay to the small village of Russell) and ticket offices. But don't worry, they are out there – all 150 of them. The Bay of Islands is one of the major tourist draws in the country, offering the visitor numerous water-based activities and superb coastal scenery. The area is also of huge historic significance in that it is the site of the first European settlement and the signing of the Treaty of Waitangi – the document that began the uneasy 'voyage' of New Zealand's bicultural society. While the islands themselves are the main attraction, most are uninhabited and you can only stay at designated campsites. Most visitors stay on the mainland and take cruises to the islands. You can also explore them by kayak, yacht or sailing boat; go big game fishing for marlin or shark; dive amid shoals of blue maomao; swim with the dolphins; bask in the sun; or jump out of a plane. ▶▶ For Sleeping, Eating and other listings, see pages 161-169.

Ins and outs

Getting there The **Bay of Islands airport** (also known as Kerikeri airport) is just outside of Kerikeri. Flights to and from Auckland take around 40 mins via **Air New Zealand Link**, T0800-737000. **Paihia Cabs and Shuttles**, T09-407 9515, operate a shuttle service between Paihia and Kerikeri via the airport, $15 one way. There are car hire companies at the airport and in town. The principal bus companies include **Intercity/Northliner**, T09-583 5780, www.intercity.co.nz and **Nakedbus**, www.nakedbus.com. Both run regular daily coach services to the Bay of Islands from Auckland and all major points on the SH1. The journey from Auckland takes about 4 hrs. In Paihia all buses arrive outside the Maritime Building on the wharf. Book at the VIC (I-Site) on the waterfront. Most people ,arrive at Paihia by car on the SH1 from Whangarei. A more scenic route is along Old Russell Road will bring you in via Russell.

Russell is served by 2 ferry services: one is a passenger-only service running directly from Paihia, the other is a vehicle ferry operating from the wharf at Opua, 9 km to the south (see page 157 for details).

Tourist information and orientation Paihia is the main resort town in the Bay. Its focus is on the waterfront where many activities on or around the islands and Bay of Islands Maritime and Historic Park can be booked and boarded. For the best of land-based attractions head to Russell or to the Waitangi National Reserve, possible diversions along the way include the collection of fierce looking Maori *pou* (carvings) and the 1917 sailing ship the *Tui* along the way. The **tourist office** ① *The Wharf, Marsden Rd, T09-402 7345, www.visitfarnorthnz.com, www.northlandnz.com, www.paihia.co.nz, daily 0800-2000 (reduced hours in winter)*, is on the waterfront by the wharf. Look out for the useful *Northland Visitors Guide*, free.

Paihia and Waitangi ⊜❼❶❀▲❸❶ ▶▶ pp161-169.

Paihia was the site of New Zealand's first church and missionary centre, but unless you have an inexplicable fetish for motels there is little in the way of sights, with the town acting primarily as an accommodation and amenity centre for tourists. **Waitangi** is a short walk north of Paihia and is a pleasant contrast. It's a site of celebrated national heritage as the Treaty of Waitangi was signed here in 1840 at the Treaty House, which is now a national museum and visitor centre for the Waitangi National Reserve.

Waitangi National Reserve

① *T09-402 7437, www.waitangi.net.nz, daily 0900-1700, $20, child $5 ($35 including tour).*
A little further along, across the bridge, is Waitangi and the very impressive Waitangi Visitor Centre and Treaty House set in the **Waitangi National Reserve**. This is the heart of New Zealand's historical beginnings. The haunting sound of piped Maori song leads you into the visitor centre where your first stop should be the audio-visual display before taking the pleasant walk around the reserve. It's well done but does give you a rather politically correct outline of events that led to the signing of the Treaty of Waitangi in 1840 and the significance of the document right up to the present day (see page 711). The main focus of the reserve is the beautifully restored **Treaty House**. It was built in 1833-1834 and was once the home of British resident, James Busby, who played a crucial role in the lead-up to the treaty signing. The house is full of detailed and informative displays that help clarify the quite confusing series of events surrounding the creation of the treaty. Near the Treaty House the reserve boasts perhaps the most visited **Whare Runanga** (Maori meeting house) in the country. To call this, or any *whare*, merely 'a house' is rather an understatement. They are essentially artworks, with all the meaning, soul and effort therein and the Whare Runanga at Waitangi is a fine example.

In front of the Treaty House and Whare Runanga is a spacious lawn overlooking the bay to Russell. From the lawn it is a short walk down to the shore where the **war canoe** *Ngatokimatawhaorua*, is housed. This impressive 35-m-long craft is named after the canoe in which Kupe, the great Maori ancestor and navigator, discovered Aotearoa (New Zealand), and was commissioned along with the Whare Runanga as a centennial project commemorating the signing of the treaty. The *Ngatokimatawhaorua* continued to be launched every year as part of the high profile **Waitangi Day** commemoration ceremonies hosted on and around the national reserve. However, in recent years, after attracting protesters, Waitangi Day was scrapped and there was a call for a more progressive and low-key 'New Zealand Day'.

There are daily half-hour *kappa haka* **Maori performances** at 1030, 1130, 1330 and 1430, $15, child $5 (excludes entry). A recent addition to the Waitangi experience is the **Culture North Treaty of Waitangi Night Show** ① *T09-402 5990, www.culturenorth. co.nz, $60 all-inclusive, free pick-up*, which is staged most evenings and is highly recommended. It is genuine and so far lacking in the commercialism so rife in other tourist areas. This is the one 'must-do' beyond the islands themselves. While visiting Waitangi try brunch or a coffee at the Waikokopu Café in the Treaty Grounds. It's better than most in Paihia.

The **Huia Creek Walkway**, which begins near the Treaty House, is an easy walk (two hours) through the reserve to the unremarkable **Haruru Falls**, taking in a fine example of mangrove habitat on the way. Running adjacent to the reserve is the **Waitangi Golf Course**, which along with **Mount Bledisloe**, 3 km away, commands fine views across the bay.

Around Paihia

You might think it ridiculous to recommend a public convenience as a major attraction but if you have time, visit the **Kawakawa 'Hundertwasser' Public Toilets** in the centre of Kawakawa, 17 km south of Paihia. This marvellous and colourful creation of local artist Friedrich Hundertwasser who died in 2000, is now something of an icon and a monument. South of Kawakawa the **Kawiti Glow Worm Caves** ① *T09-404 0583/ T09-403 7887, daily 0830-1630, $12, child $6, tours hourly on the hour*, are also well worth a visit. Local Maori guides give a very interesting and genuine tour that provides insight into their natural and human history.

Paihia & Waitangi

Sleeping

Abri Apartments **1**
Admirals View Motel **14**
Allegra House **13**
Aloha Garden Seaview
  Resort Motel **2**
Base Bay of Islands **11**
Bay Adventurer & Bay
  View Apartments **11**
Bay Cabinz **3**
Bay of Islands Lodge **20**
Captain Bob's **12**
Copthorne Hotel
  & Resort Bay of Islands **6**
Dolphin Motel **7**
Haruru Falls Resort
  Panorama **18**
Heartland **4**
Kingsgate Autolodge **19**
Mousetrap **9**
Paihia Beach Resort & Spa **10**
Peppertree Lodge **17**
Saltwater Lodge **11**
Twin Pines **8**
Waiora **5**

Eating

35 Degrees **4**
Café Over the Bay **2**
Only Seafood **1**
Ruffino's **6**
Swiss Café & Grill **3**
Sugarboat **5**
Waikokopu Café **7**

Bars & clubs

Beachhouse **8**
Mako Bar **9**

Russell ◑❶❷ ↦ pp161-169.

About 2 km across the bay from Paihia, still on the mainland, is the contrasting settlement of Russell which enjoys a village feel and a rich history that eludes its frenetic, tourism-based neighbour. With the advent of the first European settlement, Kororareka quickly grew to be the base for whalers, sealers and escaped convicts and earned the sordid and notorious reputation as 'the hellhole of the Pacific'. The earliest missionaries tried their best to quell the unholy mob with mixed results. When the Treaty of Waitangi was signed in 1840, although it was the largest European settlement in New Zealand, William Hobson, the then governor, decided it was not a good marketing ploy to give it capital status and instead bought land in what is now Auckland. To make matters worse, the treaty was seen by local Maori as a fraud and not as beneficial as was promised, with financial benefits in particular failing to materialize. Their scorn (led by the infamous chief Hone Heke) was focused on the Flagstaff near Russell, which proudly flew the Union Jack. Heke and his men duly cut it down, not once but four times, the last felling causing a major battle in which Kororareka was sacked and the first Maori Wars began. Once relative peace returned the authorities decided to make a new beginning and lose the notorious label, calling it Russell.

Today Russell, along with Kerikeri (also in the Bay of Islands), is flaunted as the most historic village in New Zealand and, although it bustles with transitory tourists in the summer and is inundated at New Year, it manages admirably to maintain a sedate and close community feel, which if you stay, can warm the heart.

Ins and outs

Getting there Russell can be reached by **passenger ferry** ① *Paihia Wharf, T09-4027421 Oct-Mar every 30 mins 0720-2230, less in winter, $6, child $3;* or there is a **vehicle ferry** ① *every 10 mins from Opua, 9 km south of Paihia, daily 0650-2200, car and driver $10, campervan $16, passenger $2 one way.* Most of the Paihia-based tours pick up in Russell on their way out to the islands. For more information contact the VICs.

Russell

To ❺ ❿ & Tapeka Point Reserve (1km)

Flagstaff Hill

Kororareka Bay

To Paihia

Fullers/ Bradley's

Russell Mini Tours

Supermarket

Russell Museum 🏛

Anglican Church

DoC Visitor Centre

Pompallier 🏛

Bay of Islands

To Long Beach

To ⑦, Omata Estate Vineyard & Opua Car Ferry (11 km)

Hope Av

Florence Av

Matauwhi Bay

N

500 metres
500 yards

Sleeping ◑
Arcadia Lodge 1
Duke of Marlborough
  & Restaurant 2
Eagles Nest 5
Orongo Bay Homestead 11

Ounuwhao Harding House 7
Pukeko Cottage B&B
  & Backpackers 8
Pukematu Lodge 10
Russell Top Ten
  Holiday Park 6
Triton Suites 3

Eating ❶
Gables 4
Kamakura 3
York St Café 2

Tourist information There is no official tourist centre in Russell but the **Russell Booking and Information Centre** ① *on the Wharf, T09-4038020, www.russellinfo.co.nz,* will certainly suffice, or visit the Paihia VIC (I-Site) beforehand. **»** *For further details, see Activities and tours, page 166.*

Sights

For a detailed historic indulgence head for the **Russell Museum** ① *corner of Pitt and York sts, T09-403 7701, daily, Jan 1000-1700, Feb-Dec 1000-1600, $7.50, child $2.* It has an interesting collection of early settler relics and, having being built to commemorate the bicentenary of Captain Cook's visit in 1769, features a host of information about the explorer including a very impressive 1:5 scale model of Cook's ship *The Endeavour.*

A short distance south along the shore from the museum is **Pompallier** ① *T09-403 9015, daily 1000-1700, $7.50, child $3.50.* This historic 1842 dwelling was originally set up by the early missionaries as a printing works. It later served as a tannery and a private home before becoming a small museum in 1990. On the corner of Church Street and Robertson Street is the 1836 **Anglican Church** which was one of the few buildings to survive the 1840s sacking and Maori war (bar a few visible musket ball holes) and remains the oldest church in New Zealand. For a grand view it is worth the steep climb to **Flagstaff Hill** (*Maiki*). Parts of the current pole were erected in the late 1850s over a decade after Hone Heke's attempts at clear felling. One kilometre north, the earth terraces of the ancient *pa* on the **Tapeka Point Reserve** make a pleasant walk.

Long Beach, 1 km behind the village, is also a pleasant spot and a fine venue on a hot summer's day. If the history of Russell is of particular interest the *Heritage Trails* leaflet from the DoC visitor centre is useful or you might like to join the excellent Maori guided tour on offer with **Fernz Eco Tours** ① *T09-403 7887, www.fernzecotours.co.nz, half or full-day.*

Cape Brett Walk

This is one of the finest walks in Northland following the ridge of Cape Brett to the lighthouse and DoC Cape Brett Hut. With a clear view across the Bay of Islands it provides some spectacular coastal scenery. The well-formed track starts near Rawhiti, 29 km from Russell in Oke Bay (secure parking is available at **Hartwells**, Kaimaramara Bay, end of Rawhiti Road, T09-403 7248). It will take an entire day (about eight hours) to walk the 20 km to the hut. If you cannot face the return journey, book a water taxi back to Rawhiti (from just below the hut) or Russell (contact the VIC for operators).

To attempt the walk and stay in the hut you must first pay a hut fee of $10 and a track fee of $30. Track and hut fees can be paid at the **Russell Bookings and Information Centre**, on the Wharf, Russell, T0800-633255/T09-4038020, www.russellinfo.co.nz. Essential maps and all the relevant information are available from there. Basic camping is available near the start of the track in Rawhiti, T09-403 7044. The track is on Maori Trust land so stick to the rules.

Perhaps the best way to tackle the walk is with the reputable **Cape Brett Walkways** ① *T09-403 8823, www.capebrettwalks.co.nz,* which offers a number of attractive alternatives for doing the walk either way, in a day, including transport from Russell and Paihia or from Rawhiti (inclusive of track fees). Contact them direct for the latest fees and itineraries for guided or self-guided tour options.

You have never tasted a mandarin until you have been to Kerikeri. Travelling north from Paihia the rolling hills give way to corridors of windbreaks that hide the laden trees of citrus, grape and kiwifruit for which the area is famous. The word *keri* means 'dig', and it was here, in pleasant little 'Dig Dig', that the first plough cut into New Zealand soil in 1820. Along with Russell, Kerikeri is rich in Maori and early European history with the Kerikeri Basin, 2 km northeast of the present town, being the nucleus of New Zealand's first European colonization.

Ins and outs

Getting there and around Kerikeri is 22 km north of Paihia just off SH1. The **Bay of Islands airport** is just outside Kerikeri (see page 154). Both **Intercity** and **Northliner** coaches stop in the centre of town on Cobham Road. Several tour shuttles can get you to Kerikeri for the day including **Kerikeri Tours**, T09-407 9904, www.kerikeritours.co.nz, from around $20 one way. **Paihia Cabs and Shuttles**, T09-407 9515, operate a shuttle service between Paihia and Kerikeri via the airport, $15 one way, and **Kerikeri Taxi Shuttle Service**, T09-407 9515, www.kerikeritaxis.co.nz, also operate a shuttle from $15 one way, providing drop-off or pick-up to and from the airport along the way.

Tourist information The independent **Kerikeri Visitor Centre** ① *library complex, Cobham Rd, T09-407 9297, www.kerikeri.co.nz, Mon-Fri 0900-1700, Sat 1000-1200*, can provide general local information. The **DoC information office** ① *34 Landing Rd, T09-407 0300*, can provide advice on walks in the Puketi Forest.

Sights

For a sense of history and atmosphere head straight for the **Kerikeri Basin** past the main commercial centre. There the road falls to meet the babbling Kerikeri River and the dominant and attractive **Stone Store** ① *daily 1000-1700, $3.50*. This was New Zealand's first stone building and was completed in 1835. It was used by the first Anglican bishop George Selwyn as a library in the early 1840s and later as an ammunition store during conflicts between Ngapuhi chief Hone Heke, before assuming its intended purpose as a general mission store. Today it is neatly laid out as testimony to that function with a museum on its top floor.

Almost immediately next door is the two-storey Kemp House or **Mission House** ① *daily 1000-1700, $5, combined entry with Stone Store $7.50, children free*. Built in 1822, this is the oldest surviving building in New Zealand. It was established by pioneer missionary Samuel Marsden on land offered to him by the great local Maori warlord Hongi Hika, who accepted 48 felling axes for the land and also offered Marsden and his staff protection from invading tribes. In 1832 it became the home of catechist-blacksmith, James Kemp, and his family – generations of whom lived in the house until 1974, when it was passed over to the nation as an historic site. The house is now packed with Kemp family relics.

Overlooking both buildings is the more ancient **Kororipo Pa** which was chief Hongi Hika's more basic domain (until, not surprisingly, he had a European-style house built nearby in the 1820s).

The **Kerikeri Basin** offers a number of pleasant short walks along the river, the most notable of which takes in the 27-m **Rainbow Falls** (also accessible 3 km north from

Waipapa Road; leaflet available from DoC). You can also take a 1 hr heritage steamboat cruise aboard the *SS Eliza Hobson* ① *T09-4079229 www.steamship.co.nz, Sun-Fri 1400, $30 child $15*.

Another fine short walk is to **Ake Ake Point and Pa**, accessible from the pretty Opito Bay, 20 km east of the city.

As well as its fruit, Kerikeri is also famous for its **arts and crafts**. The free leaflet *Kerikeri Art and Craft Trail* lists a number of venues. Worth a visit is '**Kaleidoscopes**' ① *256 Waipara Rd, T09-407 4415*. The **Kauri Workshop** ① *just as you come into town on Kerikeri Rd, T09-407 9196*, has a quality range of kauri and other native wood products. From there you can take a stroll next door to the **Makana Chocolate Factory** ① *T09-407 6800, daily 0900-1730*, where you can watch the stuff being made while wondering why all the employees are not the size of small houses. If natural beauty and skin products are your thing then you can't get more natural than the terrific range on offer from **Living Nature** ① *Bulls Gorge Kerikeri turning on SH10, T09-407 7895, www.livingnature.com, 0900-1800*. Beauticians and therapists are available on site.

On an ecological theme is the excellent **Aroha Island Ecological Centre** ① *Kurapari Rd, 12 km east of the town, T09-407 5243, www.arohaisland.co.nz (see Sleeping below), daily but may be closed 1 month in winter*. Aroha Island and the neighbouring **Rangitane Scenic Reserve** are important remnant habitats of the brown kiwi. The island is kept predator-free and therefore offers a small but valuable sanctuary for a few birds. Alas, with the kiwi being nocturnal, daytime visitors will only be able to see interpretative material in the visitor centre. However, if you stay overnight you may get the opportunity to see, and certainly hear, the birds after dark on a guided tour.

Kerikeri to Kaitaia

Provided you have your own transport, the roads that branch off SH1 to the coast north of Kerikeri offer stunning coastal scenery and some secluded beaches that are well worth visiting. About 15 km north of Kerikeri the road loops to the coast taking in the small settlements and peaceful hideaways of **Matauri Bay**, **Te Ngaire**, **Wainui**, **Mahinepua** and **Tauranga Bay** before rejoining SH1 again near Whangaroa. From there you meet the sweeping shores of **Doubtless Bay** with its mainly retirement communities of **Mangonui**, **Coopers Beach** and **Cable Bay**, before cutting across the picturesque **Karikari Peninsula** on your way to the last significant northern outpost and predominantly Maori enclave of **Kaitaia**.

Matauri Bay ⊜▲ ↦ *pp161-169*.

The views above Matauri Bay are stunning, with the numerous **Cavalli Islands** offering a sight that almost surpasses that of the Bay of Islands. Captain Cook named the islands after travalli (a species of fish) bought by Cook from local Maori. The **Samuel Marsden Memorial Church** in Matauri Bay commemorates New Zealand's pioneer missionary who first preached the gospel in the Bay of Islands on Christmas Day 1814.

The area remains a top venue for **deep-sea fishing** and **scuba diving**. Matauri Bay has always been a popular holiday spot, but assumed additional national fame when the wreck of the Greenpeace vessel *Rainbow Warrior* was laid to rest off the Cavallis in 1987. The famous flagship was bombed by French secret service through a ludicrous act of terrorism in Auckland in 1985. The idea was to prevent her leading a protest flotilla to the French nuclear test grounds on the Pacific atoll of Mururoa. Her sunken hull, 3 km offshore, provides the poignant home to a myriad of sea creatures while an impressive memorial on the hill overlooking the islands near the beach pays tribute to the ship, her crew (one of which was killed) and the continuing cause for a nuclear-free region. The incident sparked an international outcry and New Zealanders are in no hurry to forget, or forgive. There is an echo of Maori history, spirit and support in the Bay with the *waka* (war canoe) *Mataatua II* located near the campground. The history of this legendary canoe led to the local tribe, the Ngati Kura, offering the remains and the *mana* of the modern day *Rainbow Warrior* a final resting place.

North to Whangaroa

From Matauri Bay the road follows the coast to the picturesque bays and settlements of **Te Ngaire** and **Wainui**. A branch road, just past Wainui, will take you to **Mahinepua Bay**, which provides a classic touch of seclusion, scenery and the only campsite (DoC). From there the road climbs again, offering fine views inland at Radar Heights (an old radar station), before temporarily leaving the coast towards Tauranga Bay and Whangaroa.

◉ Bay of Islands listings

For Sleeping and Eating price codes and other relevant information, see Essentials pages 44-50.

● Sleeping

Paihia *p154, map p156*
Paihia is well-served with accommodation to suit all budgets. There are motels all over town, most are centrally located, as well as numerous backpacker hostels. King St is the main focus and is home to the most modern, lively hostels. With so much competition in these parts all of them have to maintain good standards so you can't go far wrong. There are also a number of self-contained options.

Despite a wealth of beds, remember that the Bay of Islands is also the favoured holiday spot for hundreds of New Zealanders. It is essential to book ahead in summer, especially over Christmas. If you are looking for peace and quiet you would be better staying across the water in Russell where you will find the best lodges and B&Bs.
LL Bay of Islands Lodge, SH11, Port Opua, T09-402 6075, www.bayofislandslodge.co.nz. Luxurious 5-star cedar-clad lodge set in an elevated position and amid private bush, commanding views across Opua Bay. There are 4 spacious well-appointed rooms with all the bells and whistles and, to top it all, a small infinity pool.

L-AL Abri Apartments, 10 Bayview Rd, T09-402 8003, www.abri-accom.co.nz. 2 delightful modern stand-alone self-contained studio apartments. Peaceful location.
L-AL Allegra House, 39 Bayview Rd, T09-402 7932, www.allegra.co.nz. Conveniently located in the heart of Paihia with fine views across the bay to Russell and beyond, this modern home offers the choice of B&B accommodation or a spacious self-contained apartment with an extra en suite if required. There are 2 B&B rooms that can accommodate single, twin or double. Both have TV, tea and coffee making facilities and a fridge. Owners are fluent in both German and French. Internet and off-street parking. Minimum 2-night stay.
L-AL Heartland Hotel Beachcomber, 1 Seaview Rd, T09-402 7434, www.heartlandhotels.co.nz. A popular hotel resort with New Zealanders, at the southern end of town. Studios and family suites. Right next to the beach. Fine buffet breakfast.
L-AL Kingsgate Hotel Autolodge Paihia, Marsden Rd, T09-402 7416, www.millenniumhotels.com. Central and reliable with views directly across the bay.
L-AL Paihia Beach Resort and Spa, 116 Marsden Rd, T0800-870111/T09-402 0111, www.paihiabeach.co.nz. Studios and suites with good views, spa facilities and treatment rooms on site.

L-AL Waiora, 52 Puketona Rd (northern end of town), T09-402 6601, www.waiora-valley.co.nz. A fine peaceful option, 4-star with in-house health spa.

L-A Aloha Garden Seaview Resort Motel, 32-36 Seaview Rd, T09-402 7540, www.aloha.co.nz. At the top of the range, has a good reputation.

AL Copthorne Hotel and Resort Bay of Islands, Tau Henare Dr, T09-402 7411, www.copthornebayofislands.co.nz. The largest hotel located right on the waterfront and within the Waitangi Reserve. Modern, recently refurbished rooms with standard facilities. There is an in-house café/restaurant, and the independent **Waikokopu Café** only a few mins away in the reserve grounds is also recommended. Large and unusual outdoor pools and spas. Spacious grounds and only a short stroll from the Waitangi Reserve and Waitangi Golf Course.

A Admirals View Motel, 2 McMurray Rd, T0800-247234, www.admiralsview lodge.co.nz. 5-star rated accommodation with cheaper and popular garden studios.

A Bay Cabinz, 32-34 School Rd, T09-402 8534, www.baycabinz.co.nz. Cosy cedar cabins sleeping 1-4.

A Dolphin Motel, 69 Williams Rd, T09-402 8170, www.paihiamotel.co.nz. Mid-range option, quiet location, plus private spa pool.

A-D Bay Adventurer and Bay View Apartments, 28 Kings Rd, T0800-112127/ T09-4025162, www.bayadventurer.co.nz. One of the most modern backpacker additions. An award-winner that marries self-contained apartments with modern standard backpacker facilities. Pool, spa, internet and off-street parking.

B-D Base Bay of Islands, 18 Kings Rd, T0800-227369/T09-4027111, www.stayatbase.com. An old stalwart now taken over by the Base chain. Great selection of value options from bunks to doubles. There's a popular bar attached, which is the main focus and meeting venue for travellers in town, as well as the haunt of a few good-value locals. Off-street parking.

B-D Saltwater Lodge, 14 Kings Rd, T09-402 7075/T0800-002266, www.saltwaterlodge. co.nz. The most popular and the busiest hostel with an impressive range of facilities, as you might expect from its rare 5-star rating. Immaculately clean, very tidy rooms and bathrooms, from dorm to double, incredible kitchens, sky TV, internet, gym, kayak and bike hire and even disabled facilities. Off-street parking. Recommended.

C-D Cap'N Bob's, 44 Davis Cres, T09-402 8668, www.capnbobs.co.nz. A perfectly adequate hostel, away from the Kings Rd hype.

C-D Mousetrap, 11 Kings Rd, T0800-4028182/ T09-402 8182, www.mousetrap.co.nz. A quieter hostel and very arty.

C-D Peppertree Lodge, 15 Kings Rd, T09-402 6122, www.peppertree.co.nz. Again a quieter hostel, with free bike and kayak hire.

Motorcamps and campsites

L-D Haruru Falls Resort Panorama, 6 km northwest of Paihia on the Old Wharf Rd T0800-757525, www.harurufalls.co.nz. Has powered sites and camping facilities as well as motel units and a pool. The Haruru Falls are directly in view.

A-D Twin Pines, 340 Puketona Rd (a short walk up the hill), T09-402 7322, www.twinpines.co.nz. Improving steadily under new management with all the usual facilities including a camp kitchen.

Russell *p157, map p157*

Russell has the widest selection of B&Bs north of Whangarei.

LL Eagles Nest, 60 Tapeka Rd, T09-403 8333, www.eaglesnest.co.nz. One of the best lodges in the country. Impressive architecture, sumptuous beautifully appointed suites and self-contained villas, pool, spa, superb cuisine and just about everything a body needs.

L Pukematu Lodge, Flagstaff Hill, T09-4038500, www.pukematulodge.co.nz. Perched high on the hill this modern B&B offers spectacular views across to the Waitangi Reserve and Paihia. The hosts (one of which is of local Maori descent and the village policeman) go the extra mile to make sure your stay is memorable and enjoyable. The cosy, stylish suites furnished in recycled rimu wood, offer plenty of privacy and a huge deck provides the perfect venue for a generous breakfast. Evening meals including a Maori *hangi* BBQ are available on request. In-house tours of the village with plenty of fascinating historical and personal insight. Credit cards welcome. Recommended.

L-AL The Duke of Marlborough Hotel, T09-4037829, www.theduke.co.nz. Right on the waterfront and oozing all the gracious charm its 150-year location deserves, 'The Duke', as it is affectionately known, offers some welcome relief from the tourist hype of Paihia. The recently refurbished modern rooms perhaps deflect from its historic charm, but there is no denying the quality, with some affording fine bay views and a large bath or spa. The cosy bar and à la carte restaurant offers a fine place to relax. When you're here, it's difficult to believe, the village was once called the 'Hell Hole of the Pacific'. Continental breakfast included, cooked breakfast extra.

L-AL Orongo Bay Homestead, Aucks Rd, T09-403 7675, www.thehomestead.co.nz. Beautiful rooms in what used to be New Zealand's first American Consulate (1860). Organic gourmet dinners can be arranged, boom in advance. Recommended.

L-AL Ounuwhao Harding House, Matauwhi Bay, T09-403 7310, www.bedandbreakfastbayofislands.co.nz. A good B&B or self-contained option in historic surrounds. Closed Jun-Jul.

L-AL Triton Suites, 7 Wellington St, T09-4037473, www.tritonsuites.co.nz. Boutique motel units in the centre of the village.

A Arcadia Lodge, 10 Florence Av, Matauwhi Bay, T09-403 7756, www.arcadialodge.co.nz. Lovingly restored, historic Tudor house with 3 characterful, spacious suites, and two rooms, great breakfast. Recommended.

B-D Pukeko Cottage B&B and Backpackers, 14 Brind Rd, T09-403 8498, www.pukeko cottagebackpackers.co.nz (book well ahead). Small and cosy.

C-D Wainui Lodge Backpackers, 92D Te Wahapu Rd, T09-403 8278, www.pelnet.org/wainui. Set in an idyllic waterfront location between Okaito (3km) and Russell (5km). 2 doubles, 2 twin and dorms. Fine relaxed atmosphere. Closed May-Sep. Recommended.

Motorcamps and campsites
A-D Russell Top Ten Holiday Park, Long Beach Rd, T09-403 7826, www.russelltop10.co.nz. Range of motels, flats, cabins and backpacker rooms. Reliable and fairly modern.

Kerikeri *p159*
Accommodation in Kerikeri is plentiful and generally less expensive than Paihia. Although not as busy, you are still advised to book ahead, especially at Christmas and in Jan. Hostels also tend to fill up Apr-Aug due to the fruit-harvesting season.

LL-L The Summerhouse B&B, 424 Kerikeri Rd, T09-407 4294, www.thesummer house.co.nz. A deservingly popular B&B set in a 1-ha citrus orchard, only 2 mins from Kerikeri. Contemporary New Zealand art complements a choice of 2 modern en suites, or a self-contained suite with its own private entrance. Legendary breakfast.

L-D Pagoda Lodge, 81 Pa Rd, T09-407 8617, www.pagoda.co.nz. Unusual property once the domain of an eccentric Scotsman with an obsession with all things Asian. Self-contained units in the pagoda building, self-contained cottage or villa, a boathouse, luxury tents, powered and non-powered sites. Not exactly typically Kiwi, but all very unique and certainly memorable. Kayak and bike hire. Recommended.

L Buddha Lodge, 1608 E State Highway 10, T09-407 7780, www.buddhalodge.co.nz. Another countryside retreat with some fine organic cooking.

L Kerikeri Village Inn, 165 Kerikeri Rd, T09-407 4666, www.kerikerivillageinn.co.nz. B&B in a contemporary Santa Fe-style house. Fine views and sumptuous breakfast.

A Kauri Park Motel, 512 Kerkeri Rd, T09-407 7629, www.kauripark.co.nz. Relatively new and set in sub-tropical garden setting. Large nicely appointed units, some with private spa.

B Aroha Island Ecological Centre, Kurapari Rd, T09-407 5243. Cottage-style lodge (sleeps 5), B&B, campervans and campsites. Kayaks available, kiwi-watching at night.

C-D Hone Heke Lodge Backpackers, 65 Hone Heke Rd, T0800-339922/T09-407 8170, www.hone heke.co.nz. Named after the William Wallace-style Braveheart of local Maori history, offering dorms, twins and doubles, some with en suite bath, tent sites. Excellent hosts.

Motorcamps and campsites

There are also campsites at **Hone Heke Lodge Backpackers** (above).

B-D Kerikeri Top Ten Holiday Park, Aranga Rd, T09-407 9326, www.kerikeritop10.co.nz. Modern motorcamp, centrally located next to the river.

Matauri Bay p160

The area, like the Bay of Islands, is very popular so book in advance.

LL Cavalli Beach House, Mahinepua Rd, T09-405 1049, www.cavallibeachhouse.com. Luxurious accommodation in a fine setting and an unusual beachfront house. Fine cuisine.

Motorcamps and campsites

C-D Matauri Bay Holiday Park, T09-405 0525, www.matauribay.co.nz/camp.html. Right on the beach in the shadow of the *Rainbow Warrior* memorial hill (which sadly affects the view). All the usual facilities for camping and campervans but no units.

North to Whangaroa p161

Tauranga Bay hosts a scattering of options.

A-B Tauranga Bay Motel, 34 Tauranga Bay Beach Road, Kaeo,T09-405 0222. Basic with 5 units, 100 m from the beach.

B-D Tauranga Bay Holiday Park, T09-405 0436, www.taurangabay.co.nz. New self-contained beachside log cabins. Many come here to join **Northland Sea Kayaking**, T09-405 0381, www.northland seakayaking.co.nz, a popular sea kayaking outfit offering $85 day trips with an extra $20 for accommodation. It can provide shuttle pick-ups from the main bus route at Kaeo.

🍴 Eating

Paihia and Waitangi p154, map p156

As you would expect, there are plenty of choices in Paihia, most serving fresh local fish and seafood. The **Discount 4** supermarket is on Williams Rd while **Woolworths**, with all mod cons, is more of a trek at the northern end of town (500 m west of the roundabout) on the Puketona (KeriKeri) Rd, daily 0700-2200.

♦♦♦ Sugarboat, Waitangi Bridge, T09-402 7018, www.sugarboat.co.nz daily from 1700. Mediterranean dishes with Pacific Rim influence on board a retired tallship, with bar.

♦♦ Only Seafood, 40 Marsden Rd, T09-402 6066, daily from 1700, licensed. A well-established choice with a good reputation for seafood.

♦♦ 35 Degrees South Aquarium Restaurant, 69Marsden Rd, T09-402 6281. Daily 0730-2300. Without doubt the best placed restaurant in the town set right on the waterfront overlooking bay. Open for breakfast, lunch and dinner. Generally areliable option for the cuisine with its seafood edge

♦♦ Swiss Café and Grill, Marsden Rd, T09-402 6701, licensed. Good for traditional European fare.

Cafés

Café over the Bay, right on the waterfront, T09-402 8147, breakfast from 0800. Has a nice

healthy variety of snacks, good coffee and a small deck overlooking all the action.
Ruffino's, 39 William's Rd, T09-402 7964, daily from 1730, licensed. Good if you're just looking for a pizza snack in a central location.
Waikokopu Café, Waitangi National Reserve, T09-402 6275, daily 0900-1700. BYO and licensed. Undoubtedly one of the best places for daytime eating with pleasant surroundings and a highly imaginative menu including the sumptuous 'Whalers Breakfast'.

Russell *p157, map p157*
There are some good restaurants along the waterfront (Strand). The supermarket is centrally located on Cass St, daily 0800-1900.
♥♥♥ **Duke of Marlborough Hotel** (see Sleeping, page 163), open for lunch and dinner. For a bit of tradition the restaurant here is an old favourite, with a great atmosphere and outdoor seating overlooking the bay.
♥♥♥ **Gables**, T09-403 7670, www.gables restaurant.co.nz. On the waterfront. Romantic atmosphere, fine Mediterranean cuisine and a good wine list, but it's a tad expensive.
♥♥♥ **Kamakura**, waterfront (Strand), T09-403 7771, www.kamakura.co.nz. One of the area's best restaurants, it's worth a muse of the menu.
♥♥ **York St Café**, York St, T09-403 7360. Daily 1000-2100. Great pizzas, seafood and breakfasts. Licensed.

Kerikeri *p159*
The New World **supermarket** is on Kerikeri Rd in the town centre. Keri Pies are widely available – try one of Northland's finest here.
♥♥ **The Black Olive**, 308 Main Rd, T09-407 9693. Tue-Sun 1700 till late. BYO. Fantastic pizza. Sit in or take away.
♥♥ **Landing Restaurant and Bar**, Kerikeri Basin, T09-4078479. Daily 0900-2100. In a great setting across the road from the stone store. English pub-style lunch and fine dining in the evening. Beautiful on a sunny day. Sometimes has live music.
♥ **Café Cinema**, Hobson Av, T09-4079121. Perfect before a film at the Cathay (T09-407

4428, from $12). The cinema also has lots of character.
♥ **Café, Jerusalem**, Cobblestone Mall, T09-407 1001. Mon-Fri 1100-2300, Sat 1500-2300. Cheap Middle Eastern food, sit-in or take away. Vegetarian snacks.
♥ **Kerikeri RSA**, Cobham Rd, T09-4078585. Mon-Sat 1300-2200, Sun 1500-2200. Cheap food and lots of it, in the local RSA, bridge and tennis club.

⊙ Pubs, bars and clubs

Paihia *p154, map p156*
The best pubs in town are along Kings Rd among the backpacker establishments.
Beachhouse, next door to Saltwater Lodge, is the place to be. Other than that try the **Maco Beach Bar**, on Marsden Rd, or **Base Pipi Patch Backpackers**, 18 Kings Rd. Most popular with the younger crowd.

⊛ Festivals and events

Paihia and Waitangi *p154, map p156*
Feb Waitangi Day, New Zealand's 'national day' held at the Waitangi Reserve. The most genuine display of Maori culture and largest gathering in the country.
Aug Jazz and Blues Festival, T09-404 1063, www.jazz-blues.co.nz. A popular 3-day event attracting over 50 acts that include street performances in both Paihia and Russell.
Sep Taste Bay of Islands Festival. Over 30 winemakers and brewers gather together at the Copthorne Hotel and Resort near Paihia to offer the very best regional fare.

Russell *p157, map p157*
May Country Rock Festival, www.country-rock.co.nz. In its 11th year, the Country Rock Festival is held in various locations in Paihia and Russell. It's a fairly low-key but entertaining event hosting mainly New Zealand based acts.
Aug See Jazz and Blues Festival, above.

▲ Activities and tours

Paihia and Waitangi *p154, map p156*
The minute you arrive in Paihia you are under pressure to book, book, book and buy, buy, buy. Competition is fierce as the huge range of tour and activity operators vie for your attention and dollar. The booking offices open daily 0700-2130, until 1830 in winter. The best thing to do is to take your time and to take advice from the unbiased VIC before venturing into the 'booking mall' on the waterfront to be mauled by the sales sharks. It is better not to book ahead as you will lose much freedom of choice. The 2 main players are:
Fullers Great Sights, T0800-653339/ T09-402 7421, www.fullers-bay-of- islands.co.nz (not the same company as the ferry operators in Auckland); and
Explore NZ, T0800-397567/T09-4028234, www.explore.co.nz.
Both offer similar tours around the islands with Cape Brett's famous 'Hole in the Rock' and the local dolphins being the main highlights. Trips generally involve combinations of activities from simple sightseeing to island stops, lunch cruises and swimming with dolphins. Prices start at about $90. Entertaining day trips to Cape Reinga with sand tobogganing and a return via Ninety Mile Beach are another popular option – good if you have your own transport but limited time (from $139).

Cruising
A huge choice, again in combination with sightseeing, dolphin encounters and the 'Hole in the Rock' – a massive natural arch in a rock outcrop at the very tip of Cape Brett through which the cruise boats navigate the ocean swell. Trips range from 3 hrs ($85, child $45) to 8 hrs ($155, child $95). Some cruise options take in a stop on **Urupukapuka Island**, a favourite haunt of Zane Grey (www.zane grey.co.nz), the famous American author and big-game fisherman. The bay at Otehei is beautiful and if you wish to stay on the island to take in the atmosphere, sights,

archaeological walks (see DoC leaflet) and would prefer to pick up a later ferry, there is the **Otehei Bay Resort**, T09-4028234, or **DoC campsites**. The resorts restaurant in front of the lodge will see you right for a decent meal. See also under Sailing, below.

Also very popular (especially in high swell) is the bone-crunching, high speed 'Hole in the Rock' trips in the **Mac Attack**, T09-402 8180, www.mackattack.co.nz, from $85, child $40. The 'Mac' prides itself on actually threading its way through the Hole, but given the heavy swell this is never guaranteed. You can take a camera but you will probably return with blurred pictures of the posterior of the person in front of you. And forget wearing specs unless fitted with automatic wipers.

The Rock, T0800-762527, www.rocktheboat.co.nz. For the more traditional, holistic approach, The Rock offers an excellent 24-hr cruise on board its own purpose-built craft, from $178. It is proving deservedly popular offering a whole host of activities from snorkelling to dolphin watching. The vessel itself is comfortable and well-kitted out with shared (twin or quad) or private cabins, bar and dining area. Meals are inclusive and the experience is a lot of fun. The layout also lets you be as social or as private as you like.

R Tucker Thompson, T09-402 8430, www.tucker.co.nz. For a more traditional approach, try polishing your best hook and exploring the bay aboard this tall ship. It's a popular and laid-back cruise with island stopover, BBQ lunch and some memorable swing diving from the yardarm, from $135.

Dolphin watching
The Bay of Islands is a top spot for dolphins, orca and the occasional migratory whale and there is much debate about the impact of tourist activities on the creatures, though the jury is still very much out. Only 3 companies are allowed actively to approach the dolphins, and all offer a similar experience of observation and encounter, including a

scenic trip around the islands and the 'Hole in the Rock'. Limited numbers are allowed in the water at a time, so it can be slow and frustrating, but the animals come first. All 3 companies have high success rates and will take you out again the following day for free if you don't find any dolphins.

Dolphin Discoveries (ExploreNZ), T09-402 8234, www.dolphinz.co.nz. Offer 2 trips daily at 0900 and 1330, a 4-hr 'Discover the Bay' sightseeing/watching trip for $89, child $45, and specific dolphin swimming trips for about the same price.

Fullers Great Sights, T09-402 7421, www.fullers-bay-of-islands.co.nz. Similar trips from Oct-Apr, depart daily at 0800, returning at 1200 and 1230-1620 from $89, child $45.

Fishing

The Bay and the upper Northland Coast is the best sea angling and big-game fishing venue in the country and one of the best in the world. A trip can be just about affordable for the average Joe at $250-350 a day. It is a very exciting experience, especially if you are 'in the chair' when you hook a big one. There are numerous reputable charter boats operating from Paihia and Russell. Contact the Paihia VIC for details. For beginners and standard sea-fishing options (including diving) try:

Captain Bucko's, T09-402 7788, www.captainbucko.co.nz. From $98 (4 hrs).

Golf

Waitangi Golf Club, Tau Henare Dr, T09-402 7713. Above the Treaty Grounds in Waitangi and overlooking the bay. When it comes to aesthetics this has to be one of the finest courses in the country. Visitors welcome.

Horse trekking

Horse Trek'n, T09-407 7151, www.horsetrekn.co.nz. Forest trails and good ocean views, from $95.

Kayaking

Bay Beach Hire, on the waterfront opposite Kings Rd, T09-402 6078, www.baybeach

hire.co.nz. Offers freedom hire of single and double kayaks and half or full-day guided trips that explore the shore or outer islands. Prices start from $60.

Coastal Kayakers, T09-402 8105, www.coastal kayakers.co.nz. Offers half- or full-day guided trips (some up river to Haruru Falls) and also the excellent 2 or 3-day experiences. 3 days on a remote bay with a kayak to explore the islands can be a great adventure, and is a fine chance to encounter dolphins. All equipment and food provided. Half-day trip $75, full day $95, 3-day from around $500; independent hire available for $40 per day.

Sea Kayak Adventures, T09-402 8596, www.seakayakingadventuresnz.com. Offers an excellent service, 3-, 6- and 10-day trips at around $200 per day, occasional specials for backpackers. All equipment and food provided.

Parasailing and jet skiing

Flying Kiwi Parasail, T0800-359691/ T09-402 6068, www.parasail-nz.co.nz. A far more sedate option to the tandem skydive which operates along the foreshore in Paihia; 800 ft from $79, 1200 ft (reputedly New Zealand's highest) from $89.

Jet ski hire, Ask at the i-Site for latest operators (Oct-Apr).

Sailing

There are numerous independent sailing charters and options in the bay, contact the Paihia VIC for advice and details. A day on the water will cost about $90-150.

ExploreNZ, T0800-365744, www.explorenz.co.nz. Offer an 8-hr dolphin swimming and sailing (fast catamaran) combo from $155, child $95.

Bay of Islands Sailing (*Gungha II*), T0800-478900, www.bayofislandssailing.co.nz. Departing Paihia and Russell daily, the $90 trip features fresh snacks and lunch, snorkel gear, kayaks and fresh lunch.

Ecocruz, T0800-432627, www.ecocruz.co.nz. Excellent 3-day trip around the islands on the

72ft ocean-going yacht *Manawanui*. The focus is on native marine wildlife with the aid of the 'bathyscope', with more traditional activities thrown in, including kayaking, snorkelling and fishing, from $595. Recommended.

Great Escape Yacht Charters, Opua, T09-402 7143, www.greatescape.co.nz. Hire your own yacht, from $160 per day.

Scenic flights and skydiving

BOI Sky-Hi Tandem Skydive Ltd, T0800-427 593, www.nzskydive.co.nz. The customary 'But, but, but… what if' here in the Bay of Islands is based at the airport and all perfectly safe. Standard jumps of 6000-12,000 ft from a good value $200-$300.

Salt Air, T09-4028338, www.saltair.co.nz. A range of spectacular fixed wing and helicopter scenic flights from a 30-min local jaunt to a top-of-the-range flight to Cape Reinga and back, with a stop and some 4WD. Expensive at $395, but worth it.

Scuba diving

The bay is a fine dive venue and trips are also available for the Greenpeace 'Rainbow Warrior Wreck Dive'. See also **Captain Buckos** under Fishing.

Dive North, T09-402 5369, www.divenorth.co.nz, specializes in *Rainbow Warrior* trips.

Paihia Dive, T09-402 7551, www.divenz.com. Has a very tidy purpose-built launch and offers a 2-dive trip with all gear from around $200. They also dive 'The Warrior'.

Tours

Paihia acts as base for a number of full-day coach trips to the far north and Cape Reinga. The trips vary a little but usually entail a number of stops to view kauri in the Puketi Forest, the lighthouse at the cape and a dune surfing experience, whereby you throw yourself down huge sand dunes on a boogie board. Both **Fullers Great Sights** and **ExploreNZ** (see page 166) offer the trip for around $120.

Awesome Adventures, T0800-653339/T09-402 6985, www.awesomenz.co.nz. Also offer a day-trip and can perhaps being a little less commercial can offer a more personalized service. Recommended.

Walking

One of the best coastal walks in the North Island is nearby in the very scenic form of the Cape Brett Walk (see Russell, page 158). Recommended.

Cape Brett Walkways, T09-403 8823, www.capebrettwalks.co.nz. Packages for the Cape Brett and other walks in the region.

Adventure Puketi, T09-401 9095, www.forestwalks.com. Informative half, full-day or twilight walks in the Puketi Forest and Manganinganinga Kauri Reserve with Ian Candy, a local resident who has immersed himself in its innate natural wonders for over 40 years, $90-$150.

Kerikeri *p159*

Eco-tours

Aroha Island Ecological Centre, PO Box 541, Kerkeri, T09-407 5243, www.aroha.net.nz. Peaceful island where overnight visitors can see the North Island Brown Kiwi in its natural surroundings. Activities include walking, kayaking and workshops.

Fruit picking

If you intend to find work in the orchards of Kerikeri, the hostels will provide advice and occasionally transport.

Walking

For details on camping and walks contact DoC in Kerikeri, T09-4078474.

As well as the attractive short walks along the river from the Basin reserve, further afield (northwest of Kerikeri) the **Puketi** and **Omahuta forests** can be accessed between Waipapa and Kapiro on SH1. These forests contain a number of impressive Kauri trees linked by a boardwalk. A brief stop here is usually included on the agenda for most of the Cape Reinga coach tours from Paihia.

Adventure Puketi, T09-401 9095,
www.forestwalks.com. Informative half-,
full-day and twilight walks.

Matauri Bay *p160*
Golf
Kauri Cliffs Golf Course, Kauri Cliffs, Matauri
Bay Rd, T09-405 0010, www.kauricliffs.com.
One of the most scenic golf courses in the
country, but expensive at least $400 a round.

Scuba diving
The *Rainbow Warrior* is a well-known and
popular wreck. A number of companies offer
trips from Whangarei, Tutukaka and Paihia
(see pages 160 and 168).
Matauri Bay Charters, Matauri Bay Holiday
Park, T09-405 0525. The local company.

⊖ Transport

Paihia *p154, map p156*
Bicycle hire
Bay Beach Hire, T09-402 6078, at the
southern end of the beach opposite Kings Rd.
Bikes from $40 per day.

Taxi
Haruru Cabs, T09-402 6292, or **Paihia Cabs**,
T09-402 9515.

⊕ Directory

Paihia *p154, map p156*
Internet Internet and cheap overseas calls
available at **Boots Off**, Selwyn Rd, T09-402
6632, or the Waterfront Booking Centre. **Post
office** 2 Williams Rd, Paihia, T09-402 8623,
Mon-Fri 0830-1730, Sat 0900-1300. **Medical
services** Selwyn Rd, T09-402 8407.

Whangaroa Harbour & Doubtless Bay →*Colour map 1, B3.*

Although most visitors are by now a little drunk on bays and coastal scenery, Whangaroa Harbour and the wide sweep of Doubtless Bay add that last little tipple of pleasant aesthetics before the sandy mass of the Aupouri Peninsula and Cape Reinga heralds the end of the nation's terra firma – next stop Hawaii. The small settlement of Whangaroa is best known for its sea fishing; while Mangonui (to the transitory visitor anyway) is known for its fish and chips. Completing the arc of Doubtless Bay, is the Karikari Peninsula, a wonderfully quiet spot with some memorable and deserted beaches on which to proudly make a solitary line of footprints. ►► For Sleeping, Eating and other listings, see pages 170-172.

Whangaroa ⊖❼▲ ►► *p170-172.*

Whangaroa, on the eastern shoreline of the Whangaroa Harbour, has more the feel of an inland lake than a coastal settlement due to the hills and the subsequent hidden narrow harbour entrance. It is a modern-day base for a number of deep-sea fishing charter companies and boasts the historic claim as the site where the sailing ship *Boyd* was sunk after a *Pakeha*/Maori disagreement in 1809. A small **gallery** based in the well-stocked general store will enlighten you. Whangaroa was also home to the first **Wesleyan Mission**, which was established in 1823, and is where the infamous Maori chief Hone Heke died in 1828. The settlement is dominated by the almost globular volcanic plug, **St Paul**, which provides a great view. It is a short but stiff climb best accessed from the top of Old Hospital Road.

Mangonui and around ⊜❷▲ ➤ *p170-172.*

Although historically noted as a port for whaling ships and kauri export, today the congenial waterfront community of Mangonui is most famous for its fish and chips.

Ins and outs
All the main Doubtless Bay settlements are serviced by **Intercity/Northliner** coaches, which stop in Mangonui. There is an independent **VIC (I-Site)** ① *waterfront, Mangonui, T09-406 2046, www.doubtlessbay.co.nz, daily 0930-1700 (winter hours vary)*. The free *Doubtless Bay Visitors Directory* has a host of local information.

Sights
Just beyond Mangonui are the small beachfront settlements of **Coopers Beach** and **Cable Bay** (a former terminus for ocean cable), now the habitat of the rich retiree with great views across **Doubtless Bay**. A little further along the coast at **Taipa** is the spot where Maori legend proclaims Kupe, the discoverer of Aotearoa, first landed. Now his honourable footprints are followed by the bucket and spade brigade, who descend in their hundreds in summer. The 1840s **Butler House, Gardens and Whaling Museum** ① *Butler Point, towards HiHi, T09-406 0006 (phone ahead), www.butlerpoint.co.nz*, is worth a visit if you are interested in the local history.

Karikari Peninsula ⊜❷ ➤ *p170-172.*

The temptation is to miss the Karikari Peninsula and head straight for Kaitaia or the cape but, if you have time, visit the area; its isolated and remote beaches have considerable appeal. This T-shaped peninsula separates Doubtless Bay and the mangrove swamps of **Rangaunu Harbour**, with the broad empty sweep of **Karikari Bay** to the north. This bay is a natural danger zone for whale strandings. The last, in 1995, involved over 100 beached pilot whales. **Whatuwhiwhi** is the main settlement on the peninsula and is serviced by a shop, service station, takeaway and the **Whatuwhiwhi Top Ten Holiday Park**, itself is worthy of investigation for its fine location near the beach. There is a popular DoC campsite and coastal walkway at Maitai Bay. Rock-fishing here is said to be excellent. Karikari Beach can be accessed from a number of marked points along the way. Also of note on the peninsula is the **Karikari Estate vineyard** ① *based at the Carrington Club (see Sleeping, page 171), T09-408 7222, www.carringtonclub.co.nz*, the country's most northerly. It is open for tastings and only complements the place as an ideal spot for a 'special' lunch or luxury stay.

◉ Whangaroa Harbour & Doubtless Bay listings

For Sleeping and Eating price codes and other relevant information, see Essentials pages 44-50.

⊜ Sleeping

Whangaroa *p169*
LL Butterfly Bay, T09-405 0225, www.butter flybay.co.nz. Luxurious self-contained hideaway with its own beach. Fine seafood.
L Kingfish Lodge, T0800-100546/

T09-405 0164, www.kingfishlodge.co.nz. This is a famous, 50-year-old establishment that is a favourite isolated haven for sea anglers and only accessible by boat. Has 12 fully serviced en suites, silver service cuisine, gym, sauna and a well-stocked bar (also open to visitors).
AL-D Sunseeker Lodge, Old Hospital Rd, T09-4050496, www.sunseekerlodge.co.nz. Peaceful, friendly backpacker accommodation with 2 motel units and doubles. Internet.

AL Whangaroa Lodge Motel, Church St, T09-4050222, www.whangaroalodgemotel.co.nz. Self-contained units with views across the water.

B-D Kahoe Farms Hostel, SH10, Whangaroa, T09-405 1804, www.kahoefarms.co.nz. Small, delightful backpacker hostel on a working farm offering a fine relaxing base. Spotless doubles, twins and dorms, kayak hire and sublime homemade pizza. Buses stop outside.

Motorcamps and campsites
B-D Whangaroa Harbour Motor Camp, Whangaroa Rd, T09-405 0306, dyleewhangaroa@xtra.co.nz. Usual facilities. Arranges dive and fishing trips and charters.

Mangonui and around *p170*
LL-L Coopers Beachfront Suites, 18 Bayside Drive, Coopers Beach, T09-406 1018, www.coopersbeach.net. 2 luxury self-contained suites in a quiet location, with great sea views.

AL-L Old Oak Inn, Waterfront Rd, Mangonui, T09-406 1250, www.theoldoak.co.nz. Newly restored, characterful historic kauri hotel with a good range of rooms from luxury to standard, all very well presented. Caring and enthusiastic owners.

AL Carneval, 360 SH10, Cable Bay, T09-4061012, www.carneval.co.nz. Perched on a hill overlooking Doubtless Bay this modern B&B provides a fine base to just kick back and relax, or from which to explore the Aupouri Peninsula to Cape Reinga. Fresh en suites with contemporary decor offering either garden or ocean views. The Swiss-German owners have created a fine marriage of European and Kiwi hospitality and memorable cuisine. A sauna and log burning fire add to the appeal. Organized trips to Cape Reinga and a range of other aquatic based activities can be arranged.

AL Waterfront Motel Apartments, Waterfront, Mangonui, T09-406 0347, www.mangonuiwaterfront.co.nz. Lovely themed, self-contained apartments ideal for couples and conveniently located in the heart of the village. The **Waterfront Café** is so close you can smell the coffee.

A Mangonui Motel, 1 Colonel Mould Dr, T09-406 0346, www.mangonuimotel.co.nz. Set in a peaceful location 1 min from the village with good views across the bay, 6 self-contained units.

Motorcamps and campsites
B-C HiHi Beach Holiday Camp, HiHi Beach Rd, HiHi, off SH10, 7 km south of Mangonui, T09-406 0307. Peaceful beachfront location.

Karikari Peninsula *p170*
LL-A Carrington Club, Maitai Bay Rd, T09-408 7222, www.carringtonclub.co.nz. Luxurious modern lodge or villa option and a host of activities including horse riding, its own 18-hole golf course, vineyard and private beach. The restaurant is also excellent.

A Reef Lodge Motel, Rangiputa Beach, T09-408 7100, www.reeflodgemotel.co.nz. Self-contained 1 or 2 bedroom studios and conventional units next to the beach, well off the beaten track, spa pool.

A White Sands Motor Lodge, Rangiputa Beach, T09-408 7080. Modern units and 1 studio in a beachside location, on site store.

Motorcamps and campsites
A-C Whatuwhiwhi Top Ten Holiday Park, Whatuwhiwhi Rd, T0800-142444/ T09-408 7502, www.whatuwhiwhitop10.co.nz. Peaceful holiday location next to the beach.

There's also a popular **DoC** campsite located at Maitai Bay.

🍴 Eating

Whangaroa *p169*
🍴 **Marlin Hotel**, T09-405 0347. Provides some rather unremarkable fare.

🍴 **Whangaroa Big Game Fish Club**, across the road, T09-405 0399, www.whangaroabig gamefishclub.co.nz. Has a restaurant and pleasant veranda bar, winter hours are limited.

Mangonui and around *p170*

There are a number of cafés scattered along the waterfront offering fine local seafood.

♔ **Waterfront Café**, Beachfront Rd, T09-406 0850, daily 0830-late. A good bet.

♔ **Mangonui Fish and Chip Shop**, just north of the village on Beach Rd, T09-406 0478. 0800-2100. Everything revolves around the delights of this popular licensed chippy.

Karikari Peninsula *p170*

♔♔ **Carrington Club Restaurant**, Maitai Bay Rd, T09-408 7222, www.carringtonclub.com. It is a bit of a drive to this luxury resort on the Karikari Peninsula, but the food, wine and scenery are worth it. Bookings advised.

▲ **Activities and tours**

Whangaroa *p169*

Fishing

There are a number of fishing charters available from the marina beside the **Whangaroa Big Game Fish Club**, T09-405 0347, and quality, good-value trips aboard the yacht **Snow Cloud**, T09-405 1663, from $90 a day (minimum 2).

Mangonui and around *p170*

Many of the Paihia-based Cape tour operators also pass through Mangonui and bookings can be made direct, or through the VICs (I-Sites) in Paihia or Mangonui.

A-Z Diving, T09-408 3336, www.atozdiving.co.nz. Local and *Rainbow Warrior* wreck dives from $135.

Paradise Connection, T0800-494392 T09-406 0260, www.paradisenz.co.nz. Offers the local Cape Reinga day excursion, and its sister operation **4x4 Exclusive Tours**, takes the personalized approach with day or multi-day tours to the cape and other local attractions.

Aupouri Peninsula → *Colour map 1, B3 Population: 5000.*

The Aupouri Peninsula forms the northernmost tip of New Zealand and satisfies that strange human desire to reach the very end of everything. Like some long sandy pier, people naturally gravitate and rush as if late for an appointment for an obligatory photo with the lighthouse and a signpost to famous cities with distances that bend the mind. And to further satisfy that sense of 'okay, what now?' an organized trip is made truly memorable with a blast down Ninety Mile Beach on the peninsula's western flank. It is, in fact, less than 90 miles and nearer to 90 km. Clearly, whoever first measured it was northbound and in a bit of a rush. ▶▶ *For Sleeping, Eating, and other listings, see pages 174-176.*

Kaitaia ⊜❷❸▲❶ ▶▶ *pp174-176.*

Kaitaia is the main rural service centre for the Far North. It is predominantly Maori with an interesting smattering of Dalmatian blood – mainly Croats who came during the kauri gum boom years of the late 1800s. For the tourist it provides a gateway to the Aupouri Peninsula, with its famous, uninterrupted sweep of **Ninety Mile Beach** to **Cape Reinga** and **North Cape**, the northernmost tip of New Zealand.

Ins and outs

Kaitaia airport ⓘ *6 km north*, is served daily by Air New Zealand Link, T0800-737000. Northliner and Intercity coaches drop off outside the **Far North VIC (I-Site)** ⓘ *Centennial Park, South Rd, T09-408 0879, www.visitnorthland.co.nz, daily 0830-1700.*

Sights

The **Far North Regional Museum** ⓘ *next to the VIC, T09-408 1403, daily 1000-1600, $6*, is worth a peek. It boasts a number of important exhibits and Maori *Taonga* including the Kaitaia Carving (one of the earliest Maori carvings in existence) and a very impressive 1500 kg anchor left by de Surville in 1769. Other collections include some Moa remains and modern remnants from the *Rainbow Warrior*. There is also the regulation collection of kauri gum and digging items that feature heavily in every museum in Northland. The **Okahu Estate** ⓘ *corner of Okahu Rd and the Ahipara/Kaitaia highway, 3½ km from Kaitaia, T09-408 2066, www.okahuestate.co.nz, 1000-1700 (closed winter weekends)*, is one of New Zealand's northernmost wineries. It is in pleasant surrounds and offers free tastings.

Further field **Gumdiggers Park** ⓘ *Heath Rd, off SH1, 13 km north of Awanui, T09- 406 7166, www.gumdiggerspark.co.nz, daily 0900-1700, from $10, child $5*, is well worth a look. The result of a local John Johnson's passion to recreate a little piece of family history, it is a faithful representation of a gumdigger's village around 1900 and depicts what must have been a hard and basic existence. A lot less impressive and far more commercial is the **Ancient Kauri Kingdom** ⓘ *Awanui, 8 km north of Kaitaia, T09-406 7172, www.ancientkauri.co.nz, daily, free*, which lures in the coach loads with its range of kauri furniture and crafts. The shop is perhaps worth a muse but what makes a stop here really worthwhile is the impressive 50-tonne log centrepiece, the old kauri logs drying in the car park, and the date scones in the café.

North to the cape ⊕⊘ ▶▶ *pp174-176.*

Human nature being what it is, one is naturally drawn up the Aupouri Peninsula to reach the northernmost tip of New Zealand. The peninsula itself, which is bounded by **Ninety Mile Beach** to the west and **Great Exhibition Bay** and the **Rangaunu Bay and Harbour** to the east, used to be covered in kauri forest, but today mainly consists of dune systems and swamps, interspersed with commercial forestry. Although the dunes that back Ninety Mile Beach impress, it is the white silica sands of **Kokota** – the huge sand spit on the Parengarenga Harbour – that stands out the most. This peninsula offers one of the best coastal walks in the country and in spring and autumn is alive with flocks of migratory wading birds. The highest point south of the cape is the 236-m **Mount Camel** near Houhora. Sadly, access is some distance from the north and to enjoy its view is a major hike. From Houhora you pass the village of **Pukenui** before winding your way towards the remote and highly spiritual lands and landscapes of the cape itself with **Cape Reinga** to the west and **North Cape** – the true northernmost point, to the east.

Ins and outs

Getting there With your own wheels it will take about 1½ hrs to reach the cape from Kaitaia. The road is sealed all the way to the cape but watch your speed – many a budding rally driver in their Maui campervan has come to grief along this stretch. Although Ninety Mile Beach is classified as a highway, you are not advised to take anything other than a 4WD vehicle onto the sand. For those in rental cars (which are not insured on the sand) who cannot resist the temptation to do so, be warned: it will probably all end in tears. If you are short of time the best way to see the peninsula is to join the many coach tours from Paihia, Mangonui or Kaitaia. ▶▶ *See Activities and tours, page 166.*

Pukenui and further north

Pukenui is the last major settlement on the way to the cape, so it may pay to grab some petrol or a coffee at the café and general store, or on your return quench your thirst at New Zealand's northernmost pub the **Houhoura Tavern**. About 25 km north of Pukenui you reach the small Maori enclave of **Te Kao**. This is the best place to park up and access the **Kokota Sand Spit**. The forestry gate is about 1 km up the road but vehicular access is forbidden. Ensure you have maps and a compass since the forestry roads to reach the sand spit and bluff are difficult to negotiate. Eventually you will emerge, preferably on the beach to the west. From there walk north to the sand bluff and dunes which are wild, remote and stunning. Allow eight hours.

Cape Reinga

From Te Kao the road passes through the basic motorcamp at Waitiki Landing before entering the huge **Te Paki Station and Recreation Reserve** towards North Cape, Cape Reinga and the lighthouse. This reserve has a total area of 23,000 ha and contains some of the most extraordinary landforms in New Zealand. The Maori call this area *Te Hiku o te Ika* (tail of the fish) from the legend that tells how the giant fish (North Island) was pulled from the sea by Maui from his canoe (South Island). Geology posits a more prosaic theory. The rocks that form the cape were formed 60 million years ago and later separated from the mainland. Then around two million years ago sand moved northwards from Kaitaia forming a huge tombolo and the peninsula we see today. The area supports a wide variety of coastal scenery from cliffs to wide sweeping beaches. There is a great network walks in the area (information from DoC) but access may be denied, or permission required, T09-409 7831. Local Maori own almost a quarter of the land, and areas around North Cape are particularly sacred. The tip of North Cape, the northernmost point of New Zealand, is a scientific reserve with limited access.

For most visitors, sadly, the visit to this amazing area will be all too brief and revolve around Cape Reinga and the **lighthouse**. The views from the hill above the lighthouse are stunning and in stormy weather you can see the Tasman Sea and Pacific in an uneasy union, and as far as the Three Kings Islands, 57 km offshore. The northland coastline has claimed over 140 vessels and many lives since 1808, with the majority falling foul around the cape. The lighthouse was built in 1941 and contains the lens from the original lighthouse built on Motuopao Island to the south. Beside the lighthouse is the obligatory multi-destination signpost for that vital memento.

⊚ Aupouri listings

For Sleeping and Eating price codes and other relevant information, see Essentials pages 44-50.

⊜ Sleeping

Kaitaia *p172*
L The Northerner Motor Inn, corner of North Rdand Kohuhu St, T0800-334422/ T09-408 2800, www.northerner.co.nz. Consider the closest to a hotel with all the standard facilities including spas, bar and restaurant.
A Wayfarer Motel, 231 Commerce St, T09-408 2600, www.wayfarermotel.co.nz. Centrally located.

C-D Main Street Lodge Backpackers, 235 Commerce St, T09-408 1275, www.tall-tale.co.nz. A lively and friendly place, Maori-operated with en suite rooms. Cape activities arranged.
C Endless Summer Lodge, 245 Foreshore Rd, Ahipara (14km west of Kaitaia) T09-409 4181, www.endlesssummer.co.nz. Restored 1880 villa full of characterand ideally located at the base of 90 Mile Beach. Consistently gets good reviews. Free boogie boards/sand boards, surfing lessons and board hire, internet

Cape Reinga p174

The accommodation north of Kaitaia is fairly basic, with Houhoura, Pukenui and Waitiki Landing offering the best base (the latter being the last available beds before the cape).
A Houhora Chalets Motor Lodge, corner of Far North and Houhoura Heads Rd, T09-409 8860, www.houhora.co.nz. Ageing but adequate A-frame units near the Wagener Museum.
A-D Pukenui Lodge Motel and Youth Hostel, SH1, 42 km north of Kaitaia and 68 km south of Cape Reinga, Pukenui, T09- 409 8837, www.pukenuilodge.co.nz. Tidy self-contained motel units with satellite TV and backpacker accommodation in a former post office store overlooking the Houhora Harbour. Spa and bike hire. Organized trips to the cape and Ninety Mile Beach. Small supermarket opposite. Standard 2-bedroom motel studios, twin double and shared budget hostel rooms.

Motorcamps and campsites
B-D Pukenui Holiday Camp, Lamb Rd, T09-409 8803. Better facilities than the very basic, but more scenic Houhora equivalent.
B-D Waitiki Landing, SH1, only 20 km from the cape, T09-409 7508. Tent sites, bunks and ensuite cabins. Restaurant and bar on site.
There are DoC campsites, T09-408 6014 at Rarawa on the east coast just south of Te Kao; at Kapowairua next to the beautiful Spirits Bay; and at Tapotupotu Bay, near the cape.

① Eating

Kaitaia p172
†† Beachcomber Restaurant, The Plaza, 222 Commerce St, T09-4082 010. Mon-Fri 1100-1430, Mon-Sat 1700-late.
†† Birdies, 14 Commerce St, T09-408 4935. Daily from 0700. Arguably the best café with traditional Kiwi fare and good coffee.
† Bushman's Hut Steak House, corner of Bank St and Puckey Av, T09-408 4320. Tue-Sun 1700-2100. Live music and good value.

Cape Reinga p174
The café in Pukenui and the restaurant at Waitiki Landing are your only hope.

⊛ Festivals and events

Kaitaia p172
Mar Te Houtaewa Challenge, www.newzealand-marathon.co.nz, is a gruelling 60-km run up Ninety Mile Beach with added 5-person relay, 42-km marathon, 21-km half marathon and a leisurely 6-km walk for the lazy. The Festival of Maori arts and crafts runs in parallel with the Te Houtaewa Challenge.

▲ Activities and tours

Kaitaia p172
A number of quality day trips leave Kaitaia for the Cape Reinga/Ninety Mile Beach circuit. They are really good value and generally offer more time at the cape and various other stops than their distant counterparts operating out of Paihia. All stop at the Ancient Kauri Kingdom or Gumdiggers Park, the cape and the Te Paki Stream sand dunes (for dune surfing) before running almost the entire length of Ninety Mile Beach. Note that tours run in either direction depending on tides.
Cape Reinga Adventures, T09-4098445, www.capereingaadventures.co.nz. Offers a range of activity packages including kayaking, fishing, horse trekking and 4WD adventures around the peninsula. Half or full day from $85.
Far North Outback Adventures, T09-408 0927, www.farnorthtours.co.nz. Offers a more personalized luxury 4WD tour of the cape. Flexible itinerary, friendly, great food and great value, from $400.
Harrison's Cape Runner, 123 North Rd, Kaitaia, T09-408 1033, www.ahipara.co.nz/caperunner. Leaves daily from Kaitia at 0900, returning about 1700, $45, child $25, lunch included. Harrison's also operates a more personalized '4x4 Reef Runner' tour, which takes in a half-day of

The souls departing

The northern tip of New Zealand is steeped in Maori legend and tradition. The name Reinga means 'Place of Leaping' and it is here, according to Maori lore, that the souls of the dead depart Aotearoa to the afterlife. After travelling up the west coast to Spirits Bay, the dead are believed to descend the slopes of the headland to the roots of an old, lone pohutukawa tree, before falling into the sea. From there they are said to re-emerge on Ohaua, the highest point of the Three Kings Islands, where, still within view of Aotearoa, they bid their last farewell, before returning to the lands of their ancestors – Hawaiki.

4WD driving, spectacular views and sand tobogganing. Twin tour discounts apply. **Sand Safaris**, 221 Commerce St, T09-408 1778/T0800-869090, www.sandsafaris.co.nz. A full-day tour with all the usual stops and activities including the Gumdiggers Park (see page 173). Departs Kaitia daily 0900, returning 1700, $60, child $30 (includes entry to the park).

Surfing
At the southern end of 90 Mile Beach, the long left-hand break at **Shipwreck Bay** is one of the best in the country, if a little fickle. On the plus side, it's usually uncrowded, and so far north that the water is considerably warmer than the rest of the country.

Walking
For details about local walking and mountain biking routes consult the *Kaitaia Area Walks* leaflet, available from the VIC (I-Site), $1.

❻ Directory

Kaitaia *p172*
Internet VIC (I-Site) or Hackers Internet Café, 84 Commerce St, Kaitaia, T09-4084999. Mon-Wed 0900-2100, Thu-Sat 0900-late, Sun 1000-2100. The VIC (I-Site) is cheaper.

South to the Hokianga Harbour → *Colour map 1, B2.*

With the vast majority of visitors joining organized trips to the cape from the Bay of Islands, most miss out on the western side of Northland; but if you have your own transport it is well worth heading back south via SH12 and the Hokianga, Waipoua Forest and Dargaville. Other than the palpable sense of being well off the beaten track, the attraction and highlights are the dunescapes of the Hokianga Harbour opposite Opononi and, further south in the Waipoua Forest, with its mighty and ancient kauri trees. Sadly, very few of these giants remain to make a mockery of our human longevity, but you can get a true sense of their former glory, if not their sad fate, at the excellent Kauri Museum, before SH12 rejoins SH1 to Auckland. ▶▶ *For Sleeping, Eating and other listings, see pages 179-180.*

Ahipara and around ⊜❼▲ ▶▶ *pp179-180.*

Ahipara forms the southern extremity of Ninety Mile Beach and is 14 km west of Kaitaia. Formerly a 2000-strong gum-digging community it is now a shadow of its former self but still a scenic spot offering a number of beach-based activities. The VIC (I-Site) in Kaitaia will provide all the relevant information (see page 172). The website www.ahipara.co.nz, is also useful. The hill at the far end of town has fine views up Ninety Mile Beach.

South to Rawene

From Ahipara the road turns south to **Herekino**, through Broadwood and **Kohukohu** to **Narrows Landing** on the **Hokianga Harbour**. There you meet the ferry to **Rawene** and the heart of Hokianga. This road is fairly tortuous and once again the familiar Northland Mobile-Phone-No-Service-Zone country sights apply. There is little of interest on the road itself but two venues in the area are of particular note. First is the **Golden Stairs Walkway** on the southern shore of the mouth of the **Whangape Harbour**. If you can muster the courage and tackle the sealed route to the little settlement of Pawarenga, this walk is well worth it. The mouth of the Whangape Harbour is like a small fjord and out of character with the other larger harbours along the west Northland coast. The walk is fairly short but steep and culminates at the northern tip of the vast and wild beach. From here you could continue down the beach to Mitimiti, where there is a fine and remote backpacker hostel (see below). The following day could be spent exploring the coast before being dropped off at the end of the Golden Stairs Walkway again, from where you negotiate the return to retrieve your car. Be sure to secure all belongings out of sight and lock the car.

The second venue is actually **Mitimiti** and the wild **Warawara Forest**, which is the second largest kauri forest in New Zealand, still containing some whoppers. The 41-km road to get to Mitimiti from Narrows Landing is quite arduous but worth the drive simply for the views and remote nature of the Northland countryside, not to mention the broad stretch of coast and wild beach at its terminus. If you stay at the **Manaia Hostel** at Mitimiti you can just about have 50 km of beach to yourself for fishing, walking or (careful) swimming. The Maori owner of the hostel will happily take you for a tour of the beach, and while doing so give you a fascinating insight into the area's Maori history. The **Tree House** is another fine youth hostel located near the Narrows Landing Ferry. ►► *See Sleeping, page 179.*

Rawene and Kaikohe

Rawene is essentially the gateway to the heart of Hokianga from the north, but has a heart of its own that seems strangely broken. The **Rawene Ferry** ⓘ *T09-405 2602, daily 0730-1930, light vehicles/campervans $16-$30, foot/car passengers $4),* runs across the inlet. Even in the earliest years of Maori and European settlement, when a large sawmill and shipyard was established in the area, Rawene saw its fair share of conflicts, both internally and externally. However, these days it is a relatively quiet place with potential. There is little to hold the visitor, except the laid-back **Boatshed Café and Gallery** ⓘ *T09-405 7728,* and the historic 1868 **Clendon House** ⓘ *T09-405 7874, Nov-Apr Sat-Mon 1000-1600, $2,* both on the waterfront. Clendon House is the former residence of James Clendon, a local dignitary who was, amongst other things, the former Hokianga district magistrate.

To the east of Rawene and 14 km north of the small settlement **Taheke** (off SH12) is one of Northland's newest natural tourist attractions, though at almost three million years old, new is hardly an apt description. The **Wairere Boulders** ⓘ *McDonnell Rd, Horeke, T09-401 9935, www.wairereboulders.co.nz, daily, $10, child $5,* can loosely be described as a valley of ancient basalt rocks formed by ancient pyroclastic flows that have since eroded and become stacked upon one another, creating a strange geological labyrinth, or 'stream of rocks'. A well-formed path with boardwalks winds through the conglomerate to give the best views. Allow three hours.

Just south of Rawene you join the SH12 to Opononi and Omapere and all points south to Dargaville. East of here is the small town of **Kaikohe** just before SH1. **Kaikohe Hill** offers a good view, perhaps followed by a soak in the wooden hot tubs of the **Ngawha Springs Waiariki Pools** ⓘ *southeast of town, T09-4052245,daily 0700-1930, $3.* These very basic and non-commercial springs are said to cure some rheumatic, lumbago, arthritic and skin conditions. The old Maori warrior Hone Heke recognized the remedial power of the springs, bringing his wounded here for treatment after the British assault on his fortified Ohaeawai pa.

Opononi and Omapere ●❷▲▶ *pp179-180*.

These two converging waterfront villages are the main resorts in the Hokianga. The villages and the harbour entrance are dominated by the impressive bare sand dunes that grace its northern shore. They rise to a height of 100 m and at sunset glow with an orange radiance. It was here in the Hokianga Harbour, in the 10th century, that the great Polynesian explorer Kupe first set foot in Aotearoa (New Zealand) from his homeland of Hawaiki. After a short stay he went home again leaving a small group behind. Although Kupe himself never returned his ancestors did and it was christened *Hokianganui- a-Kupe* meaning 'the place of Kupe's great return'. The area is also known as *Te Kohanga o Te Tai Tokerau* or 'the nest of the northern tribes'. Indeed, it remains the centre point from which most Northland Maori trace their ancestry. Both Opononi and Omapere were somewhat insignificant until the appearance of a solitary wild dolphin in 1955. Opo, as she was christened, won the hearts of the nation and subsequently put little Opononi on the map.

Ins and outs
Intercity runs a service through Omapere in conjunction with Kaitoke Bus Co. **Magic Bus** also offers services 5 days a week. Contact and book at the **VIC (I-Site)** ① *on the main road (SH12) roughly halfway between the two communities, T09-405 8869, www.hokianga tourism.org.nz.* They also have internet facilities.

Sights
Most activity in Opononi and Omapere revolves around the two hotels, particularly the **Copthorne Hotel and Resort** with its deck over looking the harbour and mountainous sand dune. Supposing you do nothing else, a meal, a coffee or a cold beer here is memorable especially at sunset.

The small **Omapere Museum** ① *0930-1630, free*, housed above the information centre, has some interesting historical stories, pictures and items, of which the original and highly entertaining 'Tally Ho' video about Opo the dolphin stands out.

For a fine coast walk head for the southern edge of Omapere and the **Arai-Te-Uru** headlands. The tip of the headland supported a signal station that for many years used to help ships negotiate the tricky harbour entrance. The headland offers a great view across to the sand spit (North Head) or *Niua* to give it its Maori name. The **Ocean Beach track** takes you down to the rocky coast below, where a blowhole and cave can be explored (turn left and watch the tide). The **Coastal Walkway** also starts here and winds its way round to the remote and beautiful beaches to the south. **Pakia Hill** at the southern end of Omapere also offers spectacular views of the harbour and the dunes. The **Labyrinth Woodworks and the Amazing Maize Maze** ① *along Waiotemarama Gorge Rd next to the Kauri Forest Walk, T09-405 4581, www.nzanity.co.nz*, is worth a look and has all sorts of other puzzles to baffle the brain. The **Kauri Forest Walk** is a pleasant 10-minute amble that takes in a waterfall, or you can go the full hog with a six-hour hike up to Mount Haturu.

⊚ South to the Hokianga harbour listings

For Sleeping and Eating price codes and other relevant information, see Essentials pages 44-50.

⊜ Sleeping

Ahipara and South to Rawene *p176*
L Beachfront, 14 Kotare St, Ahipara, T09-4094007, www.beachfront.net.nz. Tidy, beachside self-contained accommodation promising 'surf views from every pillow'. Hosts also operate a fishing charter boat.
L-A Ahipara Bay Motel, 22 Reefview Rd, T09-409 4888, www.ahipara.co.nz. Attractive motel overlooking the end of Ninety Mile Beach, with standard and luxury units, restaurant and bar. Can advise you about and book activities.
AL Beach Abode, 11 Korora St, Ahipara, T09-409 4070, www.beachabode.co.nz. Wide range of modern 4-star self-contained accommodation options. Recommended.
AL Mitimiti Beach House, West Coast Rd,Kohukohu T09-409 5347, mitimiti@xtra.co.nz/www.beach-house.co.nz. Great self-catered accommodation, 2 queen bed rooms, in a truly remote Northland location. Internet. Recommended.
C Endless Summer Lodge, 245 Foreshore Rd, Ahipara (14km west of Kaitaia), T09-409 4181, www.endlesssummer.co.nz. Restored 1880 villa full of characterand ideally located at the base of Ninety Mile Beach. Consistently gets good reviews. Free boogie boards/sand boards, surfing lessons and board hire, internet
B-D Tree House, 168 West Coast Rd, Kohukohu, T09-405 5855, www.treehouse.co.nz. Remote gem located off the beaten track and alongside the Hokianga Harbour (6 km south of Kohukohu and 2 km west of the Hokianga car ferry. No public transport, but pick-ups available). Set in 7 ha of bush and orchards it offers basic but characterful cabins and dorms in the main building, as well assheltered camping with one powered site. Limited food supplies.

Motorcamps and campsites
A Ahipara Motor Camp and Backpackers, 168 Takahe St, T0800-888988/T09-409 4864, www.ahiparamotorcamp.co.nz. Best option for campervans and tents. Handy to all amenities, sheltered location and a camp kitchen.

Rawene *p177*
A Old Lane's Store Homestay, 9 Clendon Esplanade, Rawene, T09-405 7554. Self-contained lodging in villa, just past Clendon House and not far from the café.
B Masonic Hotel, Parnell St, I09-405 7822. Simple, affordable accommodation and food.
B-D Rawene Motor Camp, 1 Marmot St, T09-405 7720, www.rawenemotorcamp.co.nz. Small but adequate with camping and campervan sites. Swimming pool.

Opononi and Omapere *p178*
AL Hokianga Haven, 226 SH12, Omapere, T09-405 8285, www.hokiangahaven.co.nz. A fine beachside B&B, with a cosy guestroom. Friendly art-oriented hosts, dogs and a hammock. Recommended.
A Copthorne Hotel and Motel, SH12, Omapere, T09-405 8737, www.millenniumhotels.co.nz. A fine spot right next to the beach and the wharf. Well-equipped and recently refurbished units are available. Heated pool, nice lawns, restaurant and bar.
B-D Globe Trekkers, SH12, Omapere, T09-405 8183, www.globetrekkerslodge.com. Small, friendly beachside outfit with a range of rooms, tent sites and organized activities.
C-D Okopako Wilderness Farm, 140 Mountain Rd (1½ km off SH12), South Hokianga (5 km south of Opononi), T09-405 8815. Spacious lodge with doubles, twin and family rooms and on-site caravans. Open-plan living area with open fire. Farm activities and horse trekking. Magic Bus drops off at the door. Pick-ups from Opononi.

🍴 Eating

Ahipara and around *p176*

🍴🍴 **Bayview Restaurant**, at the Ahipara Bay Motel (see Sleeping, page 179). Daily from 0600, Fri-Sat 1900, Sun 1600.

🍴 **Waterline Café**, on the waterfront in Kohukohu, T09-405 5552, Tue-Thu 0930-1630, Fri-Sat 0930-late, Sun 0930-1600.

Rawene *p177*

🍴 **Boatshed Café**, Clendon Esplanade, T09-405 7728, daily 0830-1630. A welcome stop before or after the ferry crossing. Varied selection of light snacks, good coffee and harbour views. Colourful arts and crafts from local artisans adorn the walls and spaces with some available for purchase.

Opononi and Omapere *p178*

Four Square supermarket in Opononi.

🍴🍴🍴-🍴🍴 **Copthorne Hotel** (see Sleeping, above) has a good restaurant offering the traditional New Zealand fare.

🍴 **The Opo Beach Takeaway**, next to the Opononi Hotel, T09-405 8065. Daily 1000-2100. Great fish and chips.

⛰ Activities and tours

Opononi and Omapere *p178*

Crossings Hokianga, Opononi, T09-405 8207, www.crossingshokianga.co.nz. Offers an enjoyable 3-hr cruise across to the sand dunes (10 min stop), then the Mangungu Mission House (site of the largest signing of The Treaty of Waitangi) and Kohukohu (an artists haven), from $70, child $40. Also hourly departures from Opononi Wharf across to the dunes for walk or sand tobogganing, from $25

Footprints Waipoua, T09-405 8207, www.footprintswaipoua.co.nz. A range of Maori guided trips to the Waipoua forest offering a unique insight in to the natural world of the giant kauri Tane Mahuta. Twilight Trip, from $85, child $25, basic 40-min trip from $15 and a visit to Tane followed by an overnight stay on a Marae (POA).

Hokianga Express Charters, T09-405 8872. Trips to the dunes to explore or go sand-boarding ($25). Also fishing and dive trips.

Fern River Horse Treks , 953 Waiotemarama Gorge Rd, Opononi , T09-405 8344, www.fernriver.co.nz. from $45.

Kauri Coast → *Colour map 1, B3.*

Just south of Omapere you bid farewell to the coast and the Hokianga and enter 'kauri country'. Waipoua, Mataraua and Waima forests make up the largest remaining tract of native forest in Northland, and the Waipoua and Trounson Kauri forests contain 300 species of tree including the great kauri with two of the finest examples and living monuments to these magnificent and awe inspiring trees. The mighty kauri forests used to blanket much of the upper North Island but, thanks to the activities of man, those forests have been plundered and raped and remain a mere suggestion of their former selves. The Waipoua Forest is home to the largest remaining individuals, including the much-loved and ancient Tane Mahuta or 'Lord of the Forest'. For lovers of life and for those who have a healthy respect for nature, to visit this great tree is something of a pilgrimage. For those who have never really thought about it, it is a fine place to start. ▸▸ *For Sleeping, Eating and other listings, see pages 184-185.*

South of Omapere ◉ ▸▸ *pp184.*

Waipoua Kauri Forest and around
The 15,000-ha Waipoua Forest includes the 9105-ha Waipoua Sanctuary of which 2639 ha contain mature kauri trees. The original block of forest was bought from the local Maori chiefs for $4400 in 1876 and, although the original intention was to use the land for 'settlement purposes', most of the forest was reserved for government forestry purposes in 1906. Thankfully, due to much local and national pressure, which came to a head in 1952 with a 70,000-strong petition, the forest is now safely under the administration of DoC. The 20-km drive through the forest is appealing in itself, with roadside kauri and umbrella-like ponga ferns giving you just a hint of what Northland and much of the entire country used to be like.

Walking tracks at the northern end of the forest, immediately next to the highway, give access to the two largest known kauri specimens, **Tane Mahuta**, or 'Lord of the Forest' and **Te Matua Ngahere**, the 'Father of the Forest'. Tane Mahuta can be reached within five minutes and is an awesome sight, with a trunk height of 17.7 m, girth of 13.8 m and total height of 51½ m. It is estimated to be over 1500 years old. Two kilometres south of Tane Mahuta is a car park where you pay a $2 security fee (such is the level of car theft from the most destructive of New Zealand's introduced mammals – the human). From here, there are a number of short or long walks. Te Matua Ngahere, the second largest tree, can be reached in about 20 minutes, while the **Four Sisters**, a stand of four trees growing together like a huge botanical oil rig, are only 100 m from the car park. The Yakas Track is 6 km in length and takes in another monster, the **Yakas Kauri**, before emerging at the visitor centre. A lookout point, 1½ km from the park's southern boundary, is worth a look on the one-hour trek from the visitor centre.

The **Waipoua Forest Visitor Centre** (DoC) ⓘ *off SH12 towards the southern end of the park. T09-439 3011, www.doc.govt.nz, daily 0900-1700*, contains an interesting museum and can provide all walking or sundry information.

Trounson Kauri Park and Kaihu
There is also a smaller but impressive kauri forest in the 450-ha **Trounson Kauri Reserve**, which is 17 km south of Waipoua. The road is signposted about 40 km north of Dargaville and goes through Donelly's Crossing, which has everything bar the saloon and stagecoach. A 'tipi' site is available, and facilities include hot showers and a communal

cookhouse ($7); powered sites are also available. In summer at night there are **guided tours** ① T09-439 0621, Oct-May, $20, child $12, see Kauri Coast Top Ten Holiday Park, Sleeping, page 184, to hear the kiwis. The forest has a healthy population of North Island browns because of its isolation from other predator-rich forests by a sea of farmland. The camp (T09-439 3011) is closed in winter.

Just south of Trounson is the settlement of **Kaihu**. The Nelson's **Kaihu Kauri** (0900-1700 Mon-Sat) is a good quality retail outlet for quality kauri crafts.

Kai Iwi Lakes

About 30 km south of Waipoua and 10 km towards the coast is the aquatic summer playground of the Kai Iwi Lakes. This is a favourite Northland holiday spot for those wanting to enjoy the combination of endless beach and surf, together with the more sedate inland waters of the three main lakes – **Kai-iwi**, **Taharoa** and **Waikere**. Here, mainly in summer, you can enjoy sailing, windsurfing, water-skiing, jet skiing and fishing. Lacking much cover and being so close to the beach, bear in mind the lakes can be a little exposed at times.

Dargaville and around ⊜❼▲❶ ➤ pp184-185.

Dargaville, located on the banks of the **Wairoa River** (the Kaipara Harbour's largest and longest tributary) has become a shadow of its former self, due to the exhaustion of the kauri forests. It was founded in 1872 by Irish timber merchant Joseph Dargaville, when the district was already the enclave of a large group of Dalmatian settlers. Kauri timber was the name of the game and for many years Dargaville was an important export centre. The rivers north of the bustling port were choked with kauri being worked downstream, and it was from here that much of Northland's kauri was shipped to Australia and elsewhere. With the myriad tributaries of the Northern **Kaipara Harbour** inundating the region, access in those days was only possible by boat from the port and timber-milling town of Helensville, on the south of Kaipara Harbour, north of Auckland.

Today Dargaville is a main service centre for the farms with their barren fields on which the great kauri once stood, and the river nearby transports little except ducks. The region as a whole is also known as the 'Kumara Capital' of the country producing the best of this sweet potato introduced by the early Polynesian navigators.

Ins and outs

Intercity and **Mainline**, T09-278 8070, www.maincoachline.co.nz, have connecting services to Auckland (from $48). **Magic Bus**, T09-3585600, www.magicbus.co.nz, runs an Auckland to Paihia service and back via Dargaville and Opononi every day except Wed. Buses stop on Kaipa Street. Information and ticketing is available from the **Kauri Coast VIC (I-Site)** ① 4 Murdoch St, T09-439 8360, www.kauricoast.co.nz, daily in summer 0830-1800, winter 0830-1700, Sat-Sun 1000-1600.

Sights

Although generally considered as the principal gateway to the Kauri Coast, and an important supply or overnight stop on the developing and popular Twin Coast Highway, there are some significant things to see in Dargaville. A number of tour operators and local activities are also based here. The information centre has put together an **Historic River Walk**, with an interesting free leaflet; it is 5 km and takes about an hour. One of the highlights is the **Dargaville Museum** ① *T09-439 7555, daily 0900-1600, $6*, which bears the remnants and relates the sorry tales of the many ships wrecked trying to negotiate the notorious Kaipara Bar. It also has a collection of Maori *taonga* and pioneer exhibits and, at 84 kg, the largest piece of kauri gum in the world (just a few grams more than a similar piece in the Kauri Museum at Matakohe).

The useful *Kauri Coast* brochure from the VIC (I-Site) details the various attractions including galleries and outlets at which to see kauri and other native woods being crafted, on display or for sale. This is your best chance to buy quality kauri products at competitive prices. One 'working' studio, the **Woodturners KauriGallery** ① *4 Murdoch St, T09-439 4975, www.thewoodturnersstudio.co.nz, daily*, is run by Rick Taylor, who has been turning and chipping away at kauri for over 26 years.

It is worthwhile taking a look at the coast near Dargaville and the ridiculously long **Ripiro Beach** – if only to see what 104 km of almost uninterrupted sand looks like. It is accessible at a number of places, the best serviced being **Baylys Beach**, 14 km west of Dargaville. But if you fancy a look at the local countryside (and the locals) followed by a truly remote walk to the disused 1884 **Kaipara Lighthouse** and the seemingly endless sand dunes of the **Kaipara Heads**, then take the road to the tiny outpost village of **Poutu**. It is a strangely disconcerting 69 km south from Dargaville and gives an inkling of the staggering length of the Kaipara Harbour's shoreline; at 3000 km it is one of the longest natural harbour coastlines in the world.

If you are not on a tour or cannot be bothered with the 69 km to the Kaipara Heads and the remote walk to the Kaipara Lighthouse then there are three interesting peaks to conquer in the vicinity, all of which offer interesting views of the vast Kaipara Harbour. **Mount Tutamoe** is a four- to five-hour walk; the 221-m **Mangaraho Rock** (11 km south of Dargaville) is 45 minutes around base and 30 minutes to summit; and the very knobbly **Toka Toka Peak** (17 km south) is a 20-minute walk. For directions and more information call at the VIC.

Matakohe and the Kauri Museum ●❹ ›› p185.

The village of Matakohe, 45 km south of Dargaville, is the home of the **Kauri Museum**. The museum is one of the finest in the country and provides a fitting finale to the Twin Coast Discovery Highway before the SH12 meets the main SH1 at Brynderwyn and heads back south to Auckland. The museum is on SH12, 26 km from SH1 at Brynderwyn, which is 114 km north of Auckland. All major coach companies that take the Twin Coast Discovery Highway stop at the museum.

Sights
The **Kauri Museum** ① *Church Rd, T09-431 7417, www.kauri-museum.com, daily 0900-1700, $15, child $3*, houses a number of highly imaginative displays that offer a detailed insight into the natural history of the kauri and man's exploitation and love affair with the great tree. Starting in the Volunteer Hall one cannot fail to be impressed with the 22½-m section of the Balderston kauri, a local specimen that was killed by lightening. It is a massive example but a relative youngster. On the wall at its base this is dramatically highlighted with life-size circumference outlines of larger recorded trees. The largest outline, depicting a tree that once grew in the Coromandel, has a diameter of 8½ m, which makes the Balderston slice seem like a piece of cress and even dwarfs Tane Mahuta. Around the edges of the hall there are some exquisite examples of kauri furniture and finely crafted models of some of the many kauri scows that used to ply the Kaipara Harbour.

Next to the Volunteer Hall is the **Steam Sawmill**. This is a good working mock-up which takes you through the complex and ingenious methods used to cut the huge logs. Additional displays in the **Smith Wing** outline examples of wood types and ages, the extraction of kauri gum and include some monstrous moving equipment and saws that show what a task it was get the tree from bush to mill. That effort and detail is cleverly and subtly highlighted right down to a bead of sweat from a mannequin's nose.

Other wings of the museum display mock-up pioneer family rooms, machines hall, chainsaw displays, fine kauri furniture, timber panels and carvings. Downstairs is the world's best kauri gum display with some fine (and some not so fine) carvings, busts and ornaments, all carefully fashioned from the tree's resin or sap. This 'amber' (its other name) is of varying ages, some of it hundreds of thousands of years old. Within the museum grounds there are some nicely restored examples of kauri buildings, including the 1867 Pioneer Church and 1909 Post Office. A well-stocked souvenir shop offers a great opportunity to purchase some finely crafted pieces of kauri including some 'Swamp Kauri' pieces, which are tens of thousands of years old.

The museum is well worth a visit and stands as a wonderful tribute to man's imagination and sheer hard work in the extraction and use of the kauri. If there has to be some criticism it is that there is not enough to echo the fact that man's love affair with this great native tree has been an incredibly damaging and unsustainable affair.

◉ Kauri coast listings

For Sleeping and Eating price codes and other relevant information, see Essentials pages 44-50.

● Sleeping

Waipoua Kauri Forest and around *p181*
LL Waipoua Lodge, SH12, T09-439 0422, www.waipoualodge.co.nz. 5-star luxury in a former wool shed and stables. Restaurant attached for in-house cuisine.
A Solitaire Homestay, SH12, 6 km north of the forest, T09-405 4891, solitairehomestay@ xtra.co.nz. Comfortable B&B in traditional kauri villa. En suite rooms and standard doubles.
B-D Kaihu Farm Backpackers, Kaihu, 20 km south of Waipoua, bus stops outside, T09-439 4004, www.kaihufarm.co.nz. Backpacker rooms and twin/double.

Motorcamps and campsites
A-D Kauri Coast Top Ten Holiday Park, Trounson Park Rd, Kaihu, T09-439 0621, www.kauricoasttop10.co.nz. Powered sites and cabins in a very pleasant site next to the river. Clean, modern and quite homely. Guided night tours to Trounson Kauri Reserve

in summer to hear kiwi (if you're lucky) but certainly to see glow-worms and native eels, $20. Recommended.
C-D Waipoua DoC, Waipoua, T09-439 0605. Cabins for 2-4 available. Hot and cold showers and some with cooking facilities. Campsites and campervan sites.

Kai Iwi Lakes *p182*
A Country Cottage, Kai Iwi Lakes Rd, T09-439 0303, www.kaiiwilakes.co.nz. 5 self-contained cottages near the lakes. Also has jet skis for hire.
A Hilltop Studio, SH12, T09-439 6351, rwatt@igrin.co.nz. Single self-contained unit in bush setting, about 10 km from the lakes.

Campsites
Basic facilities available at **Pine Beach** on the shores of Taharoa, and **Promenade Point**, $6, T09-439 8360. Book at the Dargaville VIC (I-Site), see page 182.

Dargaville and around *p182*
L Kauri House Lodge, Bowen St, Dargaville, T09-439 8082, www.kaurihouselodge.co.nz.

Spacious kauri-built house with comfortable rooms with en suite bath.

L Lighthouse Lodge, Pouto Point, T09-439 5150, www.lighthouse-lodge.co.nz. A remote and luxurious hideaway at the end of the northern Kaipara Peninsula at Kaipara Heads, a long drive and probably not a 1-night stay, but worth the journey. Fishing trips and quad bikes.

AL-A Awakino Point Boutique Motel, Awakino Point, Dargaville, T09-4397870, www.awakinopoint.co.nz. Quiet and central.

A Parkview Motel, 36 Carrington St, Doraville, T09-439 8338, www.parkviewdargaville.co.nz. Pool spa and children's play area.

C-D Greenhouse Backpackers, 15 Gordon St, Dargaville, T09-439 6342. Former primary school with spacious dorms, units ideal for couples.

Motorcamps and campsites

B-D Baylys Beach Holiday Park, 24 Seaview Rd, Baylys Beach, T09-439 6349, www.baylysbeach.co.nz. Small and functional near the beach. Also offers quad bike hire.

B-D Dargaville Campervan Park and Cabins, 18 Gladstone St, T09-439 8479, www.dargavilleaccommodation.co.nz. Central location opposite Woolworths, usual facilities including camp kitchen and internet.

Matakohe p183

A Matakohe House, 24 Church Rd, T09-431 7091, www.matakohehouse.co.nz. 50 m from the museum. Comfortable modern double and twin rooms. Communal lounge, evening meals. Café and art gallery next door. Overall convenience and good value.

C-D Old Post Office Guest House, corner SH12 and Oakleigh, Paparoa, 6 km east of the museum, T09-431 6444. Homestead with Old World character and charm, with one room an ex-prison cell

Motorcamps and campsites

C-D Matakohe Top Ten Motor Camp, 350 m from the museum, T09-431 6431, www.matakohetop10.co.nz. Fairly modern, tent sites, camp kitchen and fast internet.

🍴 Eating

Dargaville and around p182

In Dargaville itself there is not a huge selection beyond the usual takeaways. **Woolworths** is on Victoria St, T09-439 3935, daily 0700-2200.

🍴 **Blah, Blah, Blah Café and Bar**, 101 Victoria St, T09-439 6300. Breakfast, blah blah, blah.

🍴**Funky Fish Café**, 34 Seaview Rd, Baylys Beach, T09-439 8883. Daily 1100-late. The best place in the area. Well worth the drive.

🍴 **New Asian Restaurant**, 73 Victoria St, T09-439 8388. Daily 1100-2200. Palatable local Chinese.

🍴 **Steakhouse and Bar**, corner of Victoria and Gladstone sts, T09-439 8460. Good family venue.

Matakohe p183

🍴 **Matakohe House**, 50 m from the museum, doubles as a café. Smorgasbord on Sat.

🍴 **Sahara**, corner of Franklin Rd and SH12, 7 km from Matakohe in the historic former BNZ bank, T09-431 6833. Wed-Sun from 1100. Tidy restaurant and bar with friendly hosts.

▲ Activities and tours

Dargaville and around p182

There is a range of options available including scenic beach excursions by 6WD coach or 4WD along Ripiro Beach, harbour cruises, quad bike tours and fishing. Ask at the I-site for details.

Kaipara Cruises, T09-4208466, link to Helensville on the Southern Kaipara Harbour just north of Auckland as well as Cruise options from $60 or a 4WD Sand Safari Tour from $60.

🛈 Directory

Dargaville and around p182

Internet Internet at the VIC (I-Site) or **Kauri Computers**, 79 Victoria St, Mon-Fri 0900-1730, Sat 0900-1230. **Police** T09-439 3400. **Post Office** 80 Victoria St, T09-439 6051, Mon-Fri 0800-1700.

Contents

Coromandel Peninsula

N

10 km
10 miles

Channel Island
Cape Colville
Fletcher Bay
Stony Bay
Port Jackson
Coromandel Peninsula
Cuvier Island
Mt Moehau (893m)
Port Charles
Great Mercury Island
Red Mercury Island
Colville
Amodeo Bay
Kennedy Bay
Papa Aroha
Whangapoua
Matarangi
Opito Bay
Opito
Coromandel
Kuaotunu
Te Rerenga
Pacific Ocean
Mercury Bay
Whitianga
Hot Water Beach
Hahei
Cooks Beach
Kereta
Coromandel Range
The Alderman Islands
Tapu
Shoe Island
Tairua
Te Puru
Pauanui
Firth of Thames
Coromandel Forest Park
Slipper Island
Thames
Kauaeranga
Opoutere
Puriri
Whangamata
Waitakaruru
Turua
Ngatea
Karepehi
Whiritoa
Mayor Island
Kaihere
Pacific Coast Hwy
Piako River
Waihou River
Paeroa
Waihi
Waikino
Waihi Beach

In many ways the Coromandel Peninsula is like a compact and easily accessible mix of Northland and Great Barrier Island. It offers varied and spectacular coastal scenery, rugged mountain bush and a relaxed lifestyle, which together make it the main attraction on the Pacific Coast Highway.

The west coast, bounded by the Firth of Thames, is the most undeveloped side of the peninsula. It has a ragged coastline of islands and pebble beaches, lined with some of the best examples of pohutukawa trees in the country. For three weeks in December the olive evergreen leaves that crown the gnarled trunks, flower in a radiant mantle of crimson, earning them the label of New Zealand's Christmas tree.

In contrast, the east coast is a plenitude of beautiful bays and sandy beaches, with Cathedral Cove and Hot Water Beach being two of the most celebrated in New Zealand. Here you will find most of the development, activity and population, from the transitory tourist in the holiday townships of Whitianga and Whangamata to the rich retiree in the rather sterile resorts of Matarangi and Pauanui.

Between the two coasts a dominating backbone of bush-clad mountains make up the Coromandel Forest Park, with its wealth of walks and historic logging and mining remains. In summary, if you have the time, put the 'Coro' firmly on the travelling agenda.

Thames to Coromandel → *Colour map 2, B2 Population: 10,000.*

From Thames, the SH25 negotiates a seemingly endless number of headlands and a string of small coastal communities before climbing inland towards the township of Coromandel – the main focus of the peninsula's west coast. After numerous tricky bends, this latter section of road offers a welcome relief and some stunning vistas of what the Coromandel is all about with its numerous bays, small offshore islands and mountain ranges, not to mention the occasional smug-looking bovine, happily chewing the cud. ▸▸ *For Sleeping, Eating and other listings, see pages 192-193.*

Ins and outs

Getting there **Great Barrier Airlines**, T0800-900600, www.aircoromandel.co.nz, operate a twice-daily service to and from Auckland (around $129, child $86), for Whitianga and Matarangi. There are also scheduled flights to and from Great Barrier Island and Whangarei in Northland. You can also visit Coromandel Township on a day-cruise from Auckland Tue, Thu, Fri and Sat with **360 Discovery**, T0800-888006, www.360discovery.co.nz. From $89, child $49, full tour $136.

Getting around The Coromandel Peninsula is the premier destination on the North Island's 'Pacific Coast Highway' tourist route that links Auckland to the north, with Napier and Hawkes Bay to the east. Like the 'Twin Coast Discovery' in Northland, the route is well signposted, with free leaflets and maps readily available at all VICs (I-Sites). Throughout the peninsula there is a combination of sealed roads (linking the main towns) and unsealed roads (linking west to east and the further up the north of the peninsula), which results in difficult and time-consuming driving. All the roads are scenic but very windy and are often affected after heavy rain. The best way to deal with this is to relax and take your time. If you have hired a campervan, intend to head south via the Coromandel Peninsula and want to miss the Aukland altogether, try The Miranda Holiday Park (see page 193) 1hr south east of Auckland, 50 mins from Auckland Airport.

There are regular **Intercity** offers coach services to and from the Coromandel; it is also a feature of their Wellington or Rotorua North Island Pass schedule. The VIC (I-Site) in Thames act as agents, T07-868 7284. A number of bus tour companies offer shuttle, personalized or specialist tour options, including: **Go Kiwi Shuttles**, T07-8660336, www.go-kiwi.co.nz, Auckland to Thames from $42, Whitianga from $65, shuttle plus tours and charter; and **Coromandel Explorer Tours**, T07-866 3506, www.coromandeltours.co.nz, day-tour from $250, 2-day from $420 (plus accommodation), 4-day from $820 (plus accommodation).

Tourist information There are VICs (I-Sites) throughout the Coromandel for free and comprehensive information on all that 'the Coro' has to offer as well as places to stay. They also book travel and sell tickets for local attractions. Details of the VICs are given under the relevant town. You'll find them in Thames, Coromandel Town, Whitianga, Tairua, Whangamata and Waihi. The principal website is www.thecoromandel.com.

Thames ●❶❷●❸ ▸▸ *pp192-193.* → *Colour map 2, B2.*

Thames is at the western base of the Coromandel Peninsula at the mouth of the Waihou River and fringe of the Hauraki Plains. Behind the town rise the bush-clad hills of the **Coromandel Forest Park**. Thames serves as the gateway to the peninsula, either north to

Coromandel town and the west coast, or across the heart of the forest park to Tairua and the east coast. Thames is the largest town on the Coromandel and was one of the largest towns in New Zealand during the peak of the kauri logging and gold mining eras of the late 1800s, though you would not guess it now. Other than essential services there is little in the town to hold the tourist back, except perhaps a few historic buildings and the old **Gold Mine and Stamper Battery**. On its doorstep, the **Kauaeranga Valley**, the main access point to the Coromandel Forest Park, is well worth a visit.

Ins and outs

Tourist information Most of the town's amenities are on Pollen Street, which runs the length of the town from south to north. The **VIC (I-Site) and bus terminal** ① *206 Pollen St, T07-868 7284, www.thamesinfo.co.nz, Mon-Fri 0830-1700, Sat-Sun 0900- 1600*, provides free street maps. The DoC office is at the **Kauaeranga Valley Visitor Centre** ① *T07-867 9080, www.doc.govt.nz, daily 0800-1600*.

Sights

Perhaps the best place to start and to get your bearings is the **War Memorial Monument Lookout** on Waiotahi Creek Road, at the northern end of the town. From there you can get a fine view of the town and across the Hauraki Plains and Firth of Thames. Also at the northern end of town, on Pollen Street, is the **Thames Gold Mine and Stamper** Battery ① *T07-868 8514, www.goldmine-experience.co.nz, daily 1000-1600, $15, child $5*. It offers regular 45-minute tours which take in the impressive ore-crushing stamper, various horizontal tunnels and a small-gauge railway all with an informative commentary about the process and history of gold mining along the way. You can try your hand (and your luck) at gold panning.

Along the same mining and mineral theme, the **Thames School of Mines and Mineralogical Museum** ① *corner of Brown and Cochrane sts, T07-868 6227, Wed-Sun 1100-1600, $3.50, child free*, has a varied and interesting collection of rocks and minerals from around the world. Given the significance of the area for both kauri logging and gold mining the small **Thames Historical Museum** ① *corner of Pollen and Cochrane sts, T07-868 8509, daily 1300-1600, $4, child $2*, is worth a peek.

Other places of interest that may (or may not) tickle your fancy include: the **Matatoki Cheese Farm** ① *Wainui Rd, off SH26, 7 km south of Thames, T07-868 1284, www.matatokicheese.co.nz, daily 0900-1630*; the very leggy inhabitants of the **Piako Ostrich Farm** ① *311 Piako Rd, Turua, south off SH25, T07-867 5326, www.ostrichfarm.co.nz*, or the wonderfully aromatic products on sale at the **Eco People and Natural Soap Factory** ① *corner of Grey and Pollen sts, T07-868 3830*.

There are also a number of notable gardens, walks and art and craft galleries in the area including: **Lyndell and Rapaura Gardens**; the **Twin Souls and Mahara Garden Pottery**; the sculpture park and the **Maori craft gallery** (Te Whare Whakairo) and the **Historic Grahamstown Trail**. Details of these can be obtained from the VIC (I-Site).

Coromandel Forest Park (Kauaeranga Valley) ● ▶▶ pp192-193 Colour map 2, B2.

The Coromandel Forest was, in the late 1800s, one of the most extensive kauri logging areas in the North Island. At the head of the **Kauaeranga Valley**, there is a fine **DoC Kauaeranga Visitor Centre** ① *13 km east of Thames, T07-867 9080*, set in a very pleasant recreation area, accessed via Parawai Road at the southern end of town. A fascinating audio-visual display gives you an insight into the life and times of the early pioneer loggers. (If you do not have your own wheels the **Sunkist Lodge**, see Sleeping page 193, in Thames offers a shuttle service to the park; from $35 return, T07-868 8808.) From here there are a number of fine walks spread through the forest park. These vary from a few hours to a few days, taking in some of the best scenery the park has to offer and a few remnants of the old logging days, including the impressive **Dancing Creek Dam**. The **Kauaeranga Kauri Trail** (leaflet from the Visitor Centre) is the most popular walk taking trampers to the interesting Pinnacles rock formation.

Thames Coast and north to Coromandel Town ⊜ ➤ pp192-193.

The coast road to Coromandel township is scenic but very windy and quite dangerous, so take your time. On the way, the **Rapaura Watergardens** ⓘ *6 km up the Tapu-Coroglen Rd, T07-868 4821, www.rapaurawatergardens.co.nz, 0900-1700, admission charge*, are worth a look, with numerous paths and lots of 'Monet-like' lily ponds. After your explorations you can enjoy a cuppa and a snack in the **Koru Café**, or even stay the night in the self-catering lodge or cottage.

Just east of the gardens, a little further up the road and along a fairly steep track, is the impressive **'Square Kauri'** estimated to be over 1000 years old. Ask at the gardens for detailed directions. Another pleasant garden with the added attraction of butterflies is the **Butterfly and Orchid Garden** ⓘ *3 km north of Thames, T07-868 8080, www.butterfly.co.nz, daily summer 1000-1600, winter 1000-1500, admission charge, café and shop*. If you haven't seen a Monarch yet, this may be your chance.

Just north of Kereta the SH25 climbs, turns inland and at the crest of the hill, offers a magnificent view of the northern part of the Coromandel Peninsula.

⊕ Thames to Coromandel listings

For Sleeping and Eating price codes and other relevant information, see Essentials pages 44-50.

⊜ Sleeping

Thames *p190*
There are also some pleasant B&Bs out of town and ideally placed near the forest park in the Kauaeranga Valley.
L-AL Cotswold Cottage, Maramarahi Rd, T07- 868 6306, www.cotswoldcottage.co.nz. A restored villa set in spacious grounds with a range of rooms. Local cuisine a speciality.
AL Grafton Cottage, 304 Grafton Rd, T07-868 9971, www.graftoncottage.co.nz. 5 very smart chalets with fine views, B&B or self-contained. Pool and spa.
AL-A Coastal Motor Lodge, 608 Tararu Rd, T07-868 6843, www.stayatcoastal.co.nz. Overlooking the Firth of Thames, just north of

the town offering self-contained chalets, spa and Sky TV.
AL-C Brian Boru Hotel, 200 Richmond St, T07-868 6523, brianboru@xtra.co.nz. The best hotel option, established in 1868, provides affordable, traditional hotel and standard motel-style accommodation, double spas.
A Brookby Motel, 102 Redwood Lane, T07-868 6663, www.brookbymotel.co.nz. A newly renovated motel option with Sky TV and just a short walk from the town centre.
A Huia Lodge, 589 Kauaeranga Valley Rd, T07-868 6557, www.thames-info.co.nz/huialodge. 2 units with en suite.
A Tuscany on Thames, corner of Jellicoe Crescent and Banks St, T07-868 5099, www.tuscanyonthames.co.nz. Spotless motel units with double spa baths. Pool and free Wi-Fi.
B-D Dickson Holiday Park , 3 km north of Thames, T07-868 7308,

www.dicksonpark.co.nz. Pleasant streamside rooms with shared facilities and en suite bathrooms with TV, plus all the usual facilities. The 3-hr return 'Home of the Butterfly and Orchid gardens' and 'Rocky's Goldmine Trail' begin from here.

C-D Sunkist Lodge, 506 Brown St, T07-868 8808, www.sunkistbackpackers.com. Well-established and friendly alternative, housed in one of the oldest buildings in the town. 4-star rating with spacious doubles, twins and dorms, large well-equipped lounge and kitchen, 24-hr internet, travel desk, organized BBQs and regular shuttles to the Coromandel Forest Park from $35 (return).

C-D Wolfies Lair, 11 Firth View Rd, Te Puru (14km north of Thames) , T07-868 2777. Small (6-bed), cheap and comfortable hostel opposite the beach in Te Puru. Within walking distance of local store. Fishing trips a speciality. Pick-ups available from Thames.

Motorcamps and campsites
B-D Miranda Holiday Park, 595 Front Miranda Rd, 30 km west of Thames, T0800-833144/T07-867 3205, www.mirandaholidaypark.co.nz. Although some distance from Thames this is an excellent motorpark with above average facilities, plus the added attraction of its own hot pool. Guaranteed to get your visit to the Coromandel off to a good start.

Coromandel Forest Park p191
There is a DoC campsite near the visitor centre and 7 others throughout the park (from $9, child $2).
D Pinnacles Hut, on the park track, T07-867 9080. Run by DoC, a fine place to stay; beds (80) must be booked in advance, $15.

Thames Coast and north to Coromandel Town p192
If you are beginning to feel dizzy trying to negotiate all the bends in the road, this stretch of coast has some fine accommodation in which to recover. It is also a good place to base yourself to explore the peninsula.

A-AL Te Mata Lodge, off Te Mata Creek Rd, 20 km north of Thames, T0800-420868/ T07-868 4834, www.tematalodge.co.nz. Self-contained cottages and cabins in the valley, yet within walking distance of the coast.

Motorcamps and campsites
C-D Tapu Motor Camp, 18 km north of Thames, T07-8684837. Popular but fairly basic beach/riverside location.

🍴 Eating

Thames p190
Thames has yet to produce a truly reputable restaurant so don't expect a food feast.
🍴 **Food For Thought**, 574 Pollen St, T07-868 6065. Mon-Fri 0730-1530. Good value.
🍴 **Old Thames Restaurant**, 705 Pollen St, T07-868 7207. Good value with a loyal local following, day and evening menus. Licensed.
🍴 **Sola Café**, 720b Pollen St, T07-868 8781,. Tue-Sun 0900-1600 and 1800-2100 Wed-Sat. New and already perhaps the most popular café in town with good vegetarian options and the best coffee.

🚌 Transport

Thames p190
Bicycle hire Paki Paki Bike Shop, Goldfields Shopping Centre, T07-867 9026. **Car** hire Saunders Motors, 201 Pollen St, T07-868 8398, or **Ultimate**, 400 Pollen St, T07-868 6439. **Taxi** Thames Taxis, T07-868 3100.

🏢 Directory

Thames p190
Internet Available at the VIC (I-Site), 206 Pollen St. **Laundry** World-Wide-Wash, 742 Pollen St, T07-868 7912. Mon-Fri 0830-2100, Sat-Sun 1000-2100.

Coromandel Town and around → Colour map 2, A2.

Coromandel Town, with a population of only around 2,000, has a wonderful bohemian village feel and a warm atmosphere. The locals, many of whom are artists, are friendly and contented souls who walk about with a knowing smile, as if they are well aware they have come to the 'right' place. It is refreshingly free from the drearily ubiquitous high street chains or rows of unsightly advertising hoardings, and only a lamp-post opposite the road junction as you arrive in the heart of the town bears any signs or place names. The village, and indeed the whole peninsula, derives its name from the visit, in 1820, by 'HMS Coromandel', which called in to load kauri spars. Again, gold and kauri in the late 1800s were the attraction, and some old buildings remain, though sadly not the beautiful native bush that once cloaked the hills. Just north of the town one of New Zealand's most famous potters, Barry Brickell, has created – along with many fine works from his kiln – a quirky Driving Creek Railway. ➤➤ For Sleeping, Eating, and other listings, see pages 196-199.

Ins and outs
Tourist information VIC (I-Site) ① 355 Kapanga Rd, T07-866 8598, www.coromandel town.co.nz, Mon-Fri 0900-1700, Sat-Sun 1000-1300 (extended summer hours). In keeping with the village the staff are very friendly and helpful. The same office also provides DoC information and internet facilities.

Sights
The **Coromandel Mining and Historic Museum** ① 841 Rings Rd, T07-866 7251, daily in peak season 1000-1600, winter Sat-Sun 1330-1600, small admission charge, is a fairly small affair but provides a worthy insight into the rapacious days of gold mining, when the town had three times the population it does now. The 100-year-old operational **Coromandel Gold Stamper Battery** ① 410 Buffalo Rd, T07-866 7933, daily, summer 1000-1700, tours $6, child $3, gold panning $5, is set in very pleasant surrounds with a waterwheel and stream in which you can try your hand at gold panning.

The **Driving Creek Railway** ① T07-866 8703, www.drivingcreekrailway.co.nz, trains run daily at 1015, 1400, also 1245 and 1515 in summer, $23, child $13, family $59, created by Kiwi sculptor Barry Bricknell, is well worth the visit. Barry has lived in Coromandel for years and his artistic creations, open-air studio and railway line all ooze character and charm. Building began on the narrow gauge railway in 1975 as a means of transporting clay to the kilns at the base of the hill. Now 25 years on, the line winds its way almost 2 km up the hill through regenerating bush to the expansive views from the ridge-top terminus (New Zealand's 'Eiffel Tower'). It is a delight and a construction of budget engineering genius, together with artistic creativity and environmental sensitivity. Tunnels and embankments built of empty wine bottles (the fuel of the railway builders), together with some of Barry's evocative – and at times quite erotic – sculptures, decorate the route. There is an entertaining and informative commentary along the way with the occasional stop (one of which is to see some impressive creepy crawlies). There are plans to build a predator-free bush area and museum near the present base terminus, which is housed in the old brickworks (where all the bricks used along the railway were made). As it stands this area, the kilns and the shop are all fascinating.

The one-hour short walk at **Long Bay Scenic Reserve**, west of Coromandel, is very pleasant, taking in bush and beach (for the beach turn right to Tucks Bay on reaching the road). It begins at the end of Long Bay Road and is accessed at the **Long Bay Motor Camp.**

The view from the short walk to the **Tokatea Lookout**, at the crest of the hill, up Kennedy Bay Road (via Driving Creek Road) is well worth it.

Don't miss the **craft shops** along Coromandel's main street. The **Weta Design Store** ① *46 Kapanga Rd, www.wetadesign.co.nz*, is particularly good. The VIC (I-Site) and the free *Coromandel Craft Trail* leaflet will point the way to others.

South on the 309 road → *Colour map 2, A2.*

The old 309 road, which starts just south of Coromandel Town, winds its way 22 km to Whitianga and has a number of fine attractions along the way. The other route to Whitianga is along the SH25.

The first stop on the 309, 4½ km from Coromandel, is the charming **Waiau Waterworks** ① *T07-866 7191, www.waiauwaterworks.co.nz, daily 0900-1800 (1600 in winter, $15, child $10*, which is a garden full of fascinating whimsical water sculptures and gadgets. Like the Driving Creek Railway, it is Kiwi ingenuity and imagination at its wonderfully eccentric best. Great for kids.

A short distance up the road from the waterworks there is a track on the left that takes you a further 2 km to the start of the Castle Rock Walk (standard cars will be fine). The aptly named **Castle Rock** (490 m) is a very knobbly-looking volcanic plug that commands a wonderful view of the northern end of the peninsula. It is a stiff climb and one to two hours return depending how fit you are. Take suitable footwear as the track is more like a stream in winter, but the view is worth the effort.

Just over 7 km up the 309 are the **Waiau Falls**. It is a 15-minute walk to a very pleasant glade where the falls crash over a rock face. Less than a kilometre further up the road is the **Kauri Grove**, a stand of ancient kauri, some of the very few left alone and protected, and all the more impressive for it. The walk takes about 20 minutes. From here you can return to Coromandel Town or carry on to Whitianga.

North to Colville and the Cape → *Colour map 2, A2.*

North of Coromandel Town, the Colville Road rejoins the coast at **Papa Aroha** (Land of Love) and **Amodeo Bay**. From these charming bays you will be able to feast your eyes once again on Mount Moehau and what is called the **Pohutukawa Cape**. These wonderfully old and gnarled *pohutas* that grace the shoreline are some of the best examples in the country, and in December flower in a gorgeous crimson mantle. From this point you are entering perhaps the most remote and scenic area of the Coromandel Peninsula with an atmosphere all of its own. The beach at **Waitete Bay**, 5 km north of Amodeo Bay, is a cracker and a favourite haunt in summer. From here the road climbs over the hill and falls again to the historic settlement of **Colville**, with its amazingly well-stocked **general store** ① *T07-866 6805, Mon-Thu 0830-1700, Fri 0830-1800, Sat 0900-1700, Sun 0930-1700*. Next door, the **Colville Café** is a great place for a snack.

Just north of Colville you can cross the peninsula northeast on the Port Charles Road to Port Charles or back down southeast to Kennedy Bay, then back to Coromandel. **Port Charles** is the northernmost settlement on the east side of the peninsula and has a great bay and beach. **Kennedy Bay** is less well endowed than Port Charles in both scenery and amenities, but gives the passer-by an insight into real peninsula life. Note the St Paul's Anglican Church, which must have a very small congregation.

The **Port Jackson Road**, which heads north of Colville, is an absolute delight with the Moehau Range looming on your right and pebble beaches to the left. The road itself becomes almost completely shrouded by huge gnarled pohutukawa trees. About 13 km north of Colville you reach the small Te Hope Stream and the beginning of the Mount Moehau Track (temporarily closed). **Mount Moehau** is 893 m and the highest peak anywhere near Auckland. Indeed, on a clear day the Moehau range is visible from the city. Mount Moehau is a superb climb, but somewhat frustrating, because the last few hundred metres to the summit (and what must be incredible views) is sacred to the Maori and out of bounds. So if you do make the climb, show suitable respect and settle for nearly reaching the top. The first 2 km of the walk, which follows the river, are still superb with numerous clear pools (sadly swimming is prohibited) and small waterfalls to enjoy. The track, before it starts to make a serious ascent, is a delight and you are almost certain to see native wood pigeon and hear tui. At the time of going to press the track was closed due to the potential spread of a fungus that is killing the native Archey's frog.

After negotiating numerous idyllic pebble bays, the road eventually climbs round the northern tip of the cape and falls steeply to **Port Jackson** and **Fletcher Bay**, where the road ends. From here you can enjoy great views of Great Barrier Island, seemingly only a stone's throw away across the Colville Channel. Fletcher Bay marks the beginning of the popular **Coromandel Walkway**, which connects Fletcher Bay with Stony Bay and effectively the east coast road and all points south; information about the walkway is available at the VIC (I-Site). There are two tracks about 7 km in length and they take about three hours one way. The steeper of the two tracks offers better views and also doubles as a fine mountain biking route.

SH25 to Whitianga
From Coromandel Town the SH25 winds its way east, over the ranges, offering fine views, before descending steeply to Te Rerenga and Whangapoua Harbour. **Whangapoua village**, 4 km north of the junction at Te Rerenga, is essentially a conglomeration of holiday homes and baches that come alive in the summer months. A 30-minute walk north from the road end in Whangapoua is **New Chums Beach**, which is one of the best beaches in the Coromandel. The fact that you cannot drive there and have to negotiate the headland by foot seems to protect its beauty, enhance its character and make it a truly magical place. Even in bad weather it is worth the walk.

Back on SH25, heading east, is the sterile real estate settlement of **Matarangi**, which is saved only by its sweeping beach and great golf course. About 6 km further on at the end of the beach is **Kuaotunu**, a pleasant spot, especially for swimming. Kuaotunu also acts as the gateway to **Opito Bay** via the scenic and intriguingly named Black Jack Road. Opito has a lovely beach with magnificent views across to the Mercury Islands and numerous other small Islands. In summer this is a great spot to escape the crowds. (Yeah – who does own that house at the end of the beach?)

⊙ Coromandel Town and around listings

For Sleeping and Eating price codes and other relevant information, see Essentials pages 44-50.

● Sleeping

Coromandel Town *p194*
There is a good range of accommodation in and around Coromandel Town, mainly in the form of B&Bs, motels, motorcamps and backpacker hostels. The VIC (I-Site) has

comprehensive information about B&Bs. In summer you are advised to book ahead everywhere.
LL-L Buffalo Lodge, 860 Buffalo Rd, T07-866 8960, www.buffalolodge.co.nz. Closed May-Sep. Tasteful, 5-star luxury in a bush setting with sweeping views. Fine cuisine.
AL Karamana Homestead, 84 Whangapoua Rd, T07-866 7138, www.karamana homestead.com. A 1872 semi-rural kauri villa

with French, Victorian and colonial themed rooms and a separate cottage for more privacy. Plenty of antiques.

L-D Anchor Lodge Resort, 448 Wharf Rd, T07-866 7992, www.anchorlodge coromandel.co.nz. A modern motel in the heart of town and very tidy, offering 14 luxury units, pool, spa, 24-hr internet, off-street parking and also backpacker rooms.

AL-A Coromandel Colonial Cottages, 1737 Rings Rd, T07-866 8857, www.corocottages motel.co.nz. Self-contained cottage-style motel units with large grounds and a swimming pool.

AL-A Coromandel Court Motel, 365 Kapanga Rd, T07-866 8402, www.coromandel courtmotel.co.nz. Modern, well- equipped and very central, behind the VIC.

AL-A The Green House B&B, 505 Tiki Rd, Coromandel, T07-866 7303, www.thegreen housebandb.co.nz. Tidy B&B with 2 en suite rooms. The friendly hosts volunteer at the VIC so they are very well informed.

AL-A Pottery Lane Cottage, 15 Pottery Lane, T07-866 7171, www.coromandelcottages.co.nz. 2 good-value, self-contained cottages in a peaceful garden setting and within a short stroll from the village. One has a separate double and twin room while the other is smaller and open-plan. Both have plenty of character and are tastefully decorated in the classic cottage-style. Off-street parking.

A Jacaranda Lodge, 3195 Tiki Rd, SH25, T07-866 8002, www.jacarandalodge.co.nz. Big farmstay with 6 rooms (2 en suite), just south of the village. Home-grown produce adds to the appeal.

A Te Kouma Harbour Farmstay, SH25, T07-866 8747, www.tekouma.co.nz. If you are looking for a farmstay, although it is some distance back towards Thames, then this offers great value self-contained cottages and a whole host of activities beyond mere animal patting.

A-D Tidewater Tourist Park and YHA, 270 Tiki Rd, T07-866 8888, www.tidewater.co.nz.

Offers YHA backpacker accommodation. Sauna and camp kitchen.

C-D Lion's Den Backpackers, 126 Te Tiki St, T07-866 8157, www.lionsdenhostel.co.nz. Small, homely, with friendly owners who can offer lots of sound advice about exploring the region. A short walk from the village centre. Excellent homemade pancakes.

C-D Tui Lodge, 60 Whangapoua Rd, T07-866 8237, www.coromandeltuilodge.co.nz. A bit further out, but has a good range of accommodation with en suite bathrooms, a sauna, tent sites in a large garden.

Motorcamps and campsites
A-D Coromandel Holiday Park, 636 Rings Rd, T07-866 8830, www.coromandel holidaypark.co.nz. Central and has good facilities and modern cabins.

B-D Long Bay Motor Camp, 3200 Long Bay Rd, to the west of town, T07-866 8720.

C-D Shelly Beach Top Ten Motels and Holiday Park, Colville Rd, T07-866 8988, www.shellybeachcoromandel.co.nz. North of town on the beach. Usual facilities including camp kitchen and internet café.

North to Colville and the Cape *p195*
A-D Anglers Lodge, Amodeo Bay, T07-866 8584, www.anglers.co.nz. Offers excellent motel units and a campsite, with swimming pool, spa, shop, kayak hire and charter boat (water taxi), all on site.

A-D Colville Farm, 2140 Colville Rd, T07-866 6820, www.colvillefarmholidays. co.nz. Camping, backpackers, on-site caravans, bush lodges and housesall on a working farm. Horse trekking. Internet? Yes, even here!

C-D Mahaudra Centre, T07-866 6851, www.mahamudra.org.nz. Popular Buddhist retreat with a fine range of accommodation from shared to separate rooms and cabins. Meditation courses available.

C-D Fletcher Bay Camping and Backpackers, T07-8679180, www.fletcherbay.co.nz. The northernmost backpacker hostel and campsite, offering a remote but welcome overnight stop if you have done the Coromandel Walkway. The campsite has no camp kitchen but it does have fireplaces and drinking water.

Motorcamps and campsites
The DoC operates 5 campsites with basic facilities at Fantail Bay, Port Jackson, Fletcher, Stony and Waikawau Bays. For information and availability, T0800-455466. $9, child $2. Bookings are essential at Waikawau Bay in summer, T07-866 1106/T07-8679080. Fletcher BayT07-8679180

C-D Papa Aroha Holiday Park, Papa Aroha (11km north of Coromandel), T07-866 8818, www.papaaroha.co.nz. A good place to camp or park up with the van. Motel units, cabins, chalets fishing charters/trips (from $80 for 1 hr), water taxi service, boat and kayak hire.

SH25 to Whitianga *p196*
L-AL Kuaotunu Bay Lodge, SH25, Kuaotunu, T07-866 4396, www.kuaotunu bay.co.nz. A great purpose-built lodge a stone's throw from the beach with twin/ double or self-contained unit with a good reputation, owned by long-term and friendly residents.
A Drift In B&B, 16 Gray's Av, Kuaotunu T07-866 4321, www.coromandelfun.co.nz/ driftin/. A good value B&B with great views.
AL-A Kaeppeli's, 40 Gray Av, Kuaotuna, T07-866 2445, www.kaeppelis.co.nz. Popular and well-established B&B run by a Kiwi/Swiss family and chef. Renowned for its cuisine. Recommended.
B-D Black Jack Lodge, Chalet and Backpackers, 201 SH25, at the river mouth, eastern end of Kuaotunu Beach, T07-866 2988, www.black-jack.co.nz. Modern, beachside hostel with lodge and chalet options, tidy en suite doubles and dorms. Camping available. Free use of kayaks and bike hire.

Motorcamps and campsites
There is a DoC campsite at Whangapoua (Hamiora), T09-3796476, and a general store that can also assist in organizing bach rentals, T07-866 8274.

There are 2 holiday parks at Kuaotunu (and a well-stocked store), including:
B-D Kuaotunu Motor Camp, T07-866 5628, www.kuaotunumotorcamp.co.nz.

🍴 Eating

Coromandel Town *p194*
The main eateries are on Kapanga Rd.
🍴 **Coro Smoking Co**, 70 Tiki Rd, T07-866 8793, www.corosmoke.co.nz. Daily 0800-1800. Smoke your own catch of the day or choose from a range of fresh, locally caught seafood.
🍴 **Peppertree Restaurant and Bar**, T07-866 8211,www.peppertreerestaurant.co.nz. Daily from 0900. Award-winning fine dining with a lunch and mainly seafood dinner menu. It has a pleasant interior, bar and outdoor eating area. On summer evenings book in advance.
🍴 **Success Café**, T07-866 7100. Fine light meals on offer during the day (includes good-value cooked breakfasts) and a more comprehensive menu in the evening year round. Again seafood is the speciality (try the mussels or lamb). Licensed and BYO.
🍴 **Umu Restaurant and Café**, 22 Wharf Rd (opposite the BNZ), T07-866 8618. Daily 0930-late. Good pizza and vegetarian options.
🍴 **Coromandel Takeaway**, 24 Wharf Rd (opposite the BNZ), T07-866 8438. Daily from 1100-2100. Fish and chips.

North to Colville and the Cape *p195*
🍴 **Colville Store and Café**, daily 0930-1600, Fri-Sun 1800-2000. This well-stocked place will more than do, considering the location.

🏔 Activities and tours

Coromandel Town *p194*
Activity operators seem to come and go in Coromandel and you are advised to call in at the VIC (I-Site) for the latest listings.
Argo Adventure Gold Miners Tour, T07-8668658/T022-6004174. Tours to mining

sites, wetas and tame eels, from $65.
Coromandel Kayak Adventures,
T07-866 7466, www.kayakadventures.co.nz.
Kayak rental and tours 3hr from $75.
Papa Aroha, 11km north of Coromandel,
T07-866 8818, www.papaaroha.co.nz. Fishing
or scenic tours (around $80); kayak hire.
Mussel Barge Snapper Safaris, T07-866 7667.
Offers fishing and scenic cruising, from $50
(departs from the Town Wharf daily 0700, 1230
and 1600). Book at the VIC.
Strongman Coaches, T07-866 8175,
www.coromandeldiscovery.co.nz. For those
who enjoy walking, Strongman offers a
6-pack shuttle service to the Coromandel
Coastal Walkway (far north between Fletcher
Bay and Stony Bay 3-4 hrs, for a manly $90.
White Star (Colville), T07-866 6820,
www.colvillefarmholidays.co.nz. Horse
trekking.

⊖ Transport

Coromandel Town *p194*
Bicycle hire
Bikes are available from **Tide Water Tourist
Park**, 270 Tiki Rd, T07-866 8888.

Bus
Intercity runs a service to and from **Thames**
and a daily service to **Whitianga** stopping in
the town centre. For information and tickets
contact the VIC (I-Site).

❶ Directory

Coromandel Town *p194*
Internet VIC (I-Site), 355 Kapanga Rd,
T07-866 8598; also at **Star and Garter Saloon
Bar**, 5 Kapanga Rd, T07-866 8503.

Whitianga and the east coast → *Colour map 2, A2.*

*Whitianga is a small but very popular holiday town on the shores of beautiful Mercury Bay, which
was given its planetary name by Captain Cook during a spot of astronomy on his brief visit in 1769.
'Whiti' (pronounced 'fitty') – as it is affectionately known – has much to offer, including a number of
fine beaches within walking distance of the town. It also acts as a convenient short-cut access point,
across the narrow Whitianga Harbour entrance and Ferry Landing, to two fine smaller resorts –
Cooks Beach and Hahei. Although there is an abundance of leisure activities to choose from, Whiti is
perhaps most famous as a sea- and big-game fishing base and, like the Bay of Islands, a trip on the
water is highly recommended. In summer and especially at Christmas and New Year, Whiti's
growing resident population increases dramatically, resulting in excellent tourist services and
amenities year round.* ▸▸ *For Sleeping, Eating and other listings, see pages 203-208.*

Ins and outs

Getting there and around Whitianga airport is 3 km south of the town and is serviced
from Auckland by **Great Barrier Airlines**, T0800-900600/T09-275 9120, from $129 one
way. **Intercity** buses drop off and pick up outside the VIC (I-Site) in the centre of town and
service the local area. Other smaller shuttle companies operate to and from Auckland,
Hamilton or Rotorua and tour around the peninsula (see also page 190). **Go Kiwi**,
T0800-446549, www.go-kiwi.co.nz, offers shuttles from Auckland (from $54) and some
recommended tour options. Contact the VIC (I-Site) for operators offering a full-day
hop-on/hop-off service from Ferry Landing to Cooks Beach, Cathedral Cove, Hahei and
Hot Water Beach. All buses can be booked at the VIC (I-Site).

The passenger-only ferry to Ferry Landing takes 5 mins and operates continuously in
summer 0730-2300, less frequently in winter; $2, child $1, T07-8665472. **Cook Beach**

Minibus, T0274-432329/T07-8662644, offers shuttles to Hahei (Cathedral Cove) and Hot Water Beach from $35.

The ferry to Pauanui, T027-497 0316, leaves from Tairua Wharf on Wharf Road, hourly

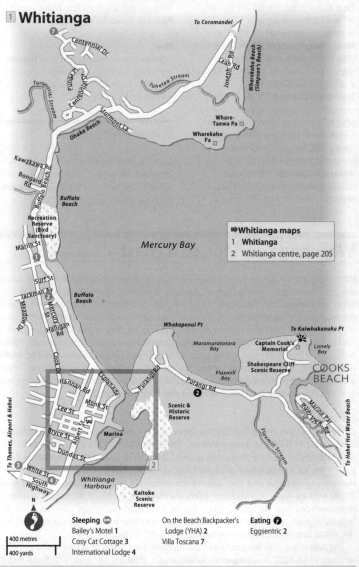

1 Whitianga

Whitianga maps
1 Whitianga
2 Whitianga centre, page 205

Sleeping 🛏
Bailey's Motel 1
Cosy Cat Cottage 3
International Lodge 4

On the Beach Backpacker's
Lodge (YHA) 2
Villa Toscana 7

Eating 🍴
Eggsentric 2

400 metres
400 yards

in summer and every two hours in winter 0900-1700, $6 return. Good-value cruises are also offered in summer. Tairua is the main gateway to Alderman, Shoe, Slipper and Mayor Islands. Opoutere can be reached by bus from Whangamata, T07-865 8340.

Tourist information **'Whiti' VIC (I-Site)** ① *66 Albert St, centre of town, T07-8665555, www.whitianga.co.nz, daily 0900-1800, Sat-Sun 0900-1600*, can provide information about the many fine craft shops around Whitianga. **Tairua VIC (I-Site)** ① *Main St, T07-864 7575, www.tairua.info, summer daily 0930-1600, winter, 1000-1400*, can assist with finding accommodation or book water-based activities or island trips. **Whangamata VIC** (I-Site) ① *616 Port Rd, T07-865 8340, www.whangamatainfo.co.nz, Mon-Sat 0900-1700, Sun 1000-1600*. **Waihi VIC (I-Site)** ① *Upper Seddon St, T07-863 6715, www.waihi.org.nz, daily 0900-1700 in summer, 0900-1630 in winter*. Ask for the very useful *Discover Waihi* brochure.

Sights

The **Mercury Bay Museum** ① *on the Esplanade, daily summer 1000-1600, Tue, Thu, Sun winter, $5, child $0.50*, is fairly small, but does a good job of showcasing the area's rich human history which goes back over 1000 years, when Maori explorer Kupe made landfall here. Cook's visit is also documented. The main waterfront beach is called **Buffalo Beach**, named after *HMS Buffalo* which was wrecked here in 1840. It is a fine beach but gets a little hectic in summer. **Flaxmill Bay**, across the water just beyond Ferry Landing, and better still **Lonely Bay**, at the eastern base of the Shakespeare Cliff Scenic Reserve, are often a better bet.

Even if you do not intend to go as far as Cooks Beach and Hahei, the short ferry ride across to **Ferry Landing** is worthwhile. The wharf itself was built in 1837 and, though it is one of the oldest in New Zealand, is less than attractive with its concrete coating. However there is a nice café and a number of fine **coastal walks** nearby. Immediately to the right of the wharf is the Whitianga Rock Walk (20 minutes) which takes in a Maori *pa* and offers a great view back over Whiti. The Maramaratotara Bay Walk (40 minutes) joins the Rock Walk and also has good views. A little further down the road, opposite the **Flaxmill Bay Resort**, is the access point to the **Shakespeare Cliff Scenic Reserve**. Climb the path to the right then cross the hill to the viewpoint where you are rewarded with a wonderful view across the bay.

Whiti has a couple of excellent **bone carving studios**, which offer the opportunity to carve your own bone pendant – traditionally from whale bone but now typically from beef bone. **Bay Carving** ① *next to the museum on the Esplanade, T07-866 4021, www.dreamland.co.nz/baycarving, 0900-1600, evenings by appointment*, is very well equipped and provides expert tuition ($50-100). You choose your own design then test your skills. The other company that offers all-day tuition is the **Bone Carving Studio** ① *6B Bryce St, T07-866 2158, www.carving.co.nz*, which offers more comprehensive full-day courses from $100 and acts as a showpiece for the professional trade.

East coast ●❷▲ ↠ *pp203-208*.

Hahei, Cooks Beach and Hot Water Beach → *Colour map 2, A3*.

Hahei is a wonderful little unspoiled coastal settlement, 35 km by road from Whitianga. A shorter route is via the ferry from Whitianga. Both Hahei and Cooks Beach have wonderful beaches in their own right, especially **Hahei Beach** that looks over a wealth of islands and rock outcrops. But the real jewel in the region's crown, indeed perhaps for the whole peninsula, is the amazing **Cathedral Cove**, which guards the **Te Whanganui-A-Hei Marine Reserve**; watching the sunrise here is unforgettable. Access is by boat or a half-hour walk. The track starts from a glorious lookout point just north of Hahei on Grange Road. Tracts of native bush and pine have to be negotiated before the path falls, almost literally, to the beach. It is actually two beaches connected by a natural rock arch (negotiable at low tide). There are sandstone pinnacles on both beaches, with the highest pinnacle, Sail Rock, on the western beach. Although the beach can get very busy it offers great sunbathing, swimming and scenery, and it is very difficult to drag yourself away.

About 15 km south of Hahei is **Hot Water Beach** where you can dig a hole in the sand to access natural hot water. You can only do this for about two hours each side of low tide. Once filled, you can settle in to read a book or watch the surfers doing what you can't. The beach in itself is very pleasant, but be warned: it is also very dangerous with notorious rips. The **Hot Water Beach Store** hires out spades for $5. Once suitably boiled or if you did not time the tides right, then pop your head into the **Moko Art Gallery** ① *24 Pye Pl*, just opposite the main car park. The arts and crafts are reasonably priced, very Kiwi and top class.

Tairua and Pauanui → *Colour map 2, B3.*
Only the Tairua Harbour and a resulting 20-km road trip separate these deeply contrasting communities. **Tairua**, which was settled as a milling and farming town, is the older, smaller and more accessible of the two, situated on SH25. **Pauanui**, in contrast, is full of expensive holiday and retirement homes with fussy gardens, 4WDs and luxury watercraft. It's a place where men wear polyester shorts and knee-length nylon socks with fawn-coloured dress shoes, and the women sport the latest clinical blue-rinse hairdo. Not exactly the haunt of the happy-go-lucky traveller. Perhaps the best thing about the two towns is the setting and the memorable view from **Paku Hill** which dominates the harbour entrance. It can be accessed from the end of Tirinui Crescent off Paku Drive.

Opoutere
Opoutere is one of the Coromandel's best-kept secrets. It has a quiet and magical atmosphere with gorgeous sweeping white-sand **Ocean Beach**, guarded by the Wharekawa Harbour and a narrow tract of forest. At the tip of the sand spit is the **Wharekawa Wildlife Refuge**, where oystercatchers and rare New Zealand dotterel breed in summer. Special care should be taken not to enter this area and disturb the birds (dogs are strictly forbidden). The beach can be accessed from the car park around the corner from the **Opoutere Youth Hostel** (YHA), see page 205. While you are in the area it is also well worth your while visiting the unusual artworks of Guity and David Evelyn at the **Topadahil Studios** ① *Opoutere Rd, T07-865 7266.*

Whangamata
Whangamata is a very popular holiday spot and the main **surfing** venue on the Coromandel. Well-serviced with luxury and budget accommodation, eateries and mainly water-based activities, it acts as a magnet to youngsters, especially at New Year. There are a number of good short coastal walks, while south of the town the **Wentworth and Parakiwai valleys** offer longer walks taking in remnants of the gold mining years and waterfalls. The often busy beach at Whangamata is over 4 km long, while the quieter **Whiritoa Beach** and lagoon, 12 km south of Whangamata, also offers a lovely bush walk, heading north. There is a quality **art and crafts trail** in the area (see VIC for details) and,

like Tairua, Whangamata is also a base for trips to the outer islands, including **Mayor Island**. Before you leave Whangamata (from the north) be sure to duck in to Whangamata Traders, 114 Port Road, for second-hand and antique goods.

Waihi

Although gold mining once flourished all around the Coromandel, Waihi was in many ways the capital of operations, with 1200 mines producing half of the country's gold. The scale of operations earned Waihi the reputation as the most famous mining town in New Zealand. The town itself, although well-serviced, is nothing remarkable, but it boasts a heart of gold and seems to retain a sort of Wild West feel.

The most impressive evidence of the town's mining history is the enormous **Martha Mine** ① *Waihi Gold Mining Company, Barry Rd, T07-863 9880, www.marthamine.co.nz, guided tours most weekdays from $6*, which sits like a huge, but strangely discrete bomb crater right in the centre of town. The Martha Mine was one of the originals that reopened after a brief redundancy in the mid-1900s and is reputed to currently produce over NZ$1 million of gold and silver a week. Today, from a lookout behind the VIC, you can watch huge earth-moving trucks relentlessly winding their way in and out of the massive terraced hole.

The very reasonable admission charge aside, the **Waihi Museum and Art Gallery** ① *54 Kenny St, T07-863 8386, www.waihimuseum.co.nz, Thu-Sun 1000-1500, $5, child $3*, is well worth a look. It displays an array of mining memorabilia and interesting working models, including a miniature stamping battery. Inevitably you leave a lot wiser about the incredible systems and network of tunnels that insidiously lies beneath your feet.

Nearby, the Ohinemuri River winds its dramatic way west, through the **Karangahake Gorge**, where there are a number of interesting walks and mining relics (DoC leaflet available from the VIC). A vintage steam train, the **Goldfields Railway** ① *T07-863 9020, www.waihirail.co.nz, trains leave from Wrigley St, daily at 1000, 1145, 1345, 1500, $15 return, child $8; café at Waikino station, daily 1000-1600*, runs 6.5 km (30 minutes) into the gorge from Waihi to **Waikino**.

There are also two wineries in the area, two golf courses and a generous collection of gardens, including the pretty **Waihi Waterlily Gardens** ① *Pukekauri Rd, T07-863 8267, daily in summer 1000-1600, admission charge*. If you want to go to the beach, head for the popular surfers' hangout at **Waihi Beach**, 11 km to the east. A pleasant 45-minute coastal walk at the northern end of the beach will take you to the very pretty **Orokawa Bay**.

◉ Whitianga and the east coast listings

For Sleeping and Eating price codes and other relevant information, see Essentials pages 44-50.

● Sleeping

Whitianga *p199, maps p200 and p205*
There is a huge range of accommodation in Whitianga to suit all tastes and budgets. The VIC has all the information and can pre-book, which is highly recommended in summer.
LL Villa Toscana, Ohuka Park, T07-866 2293, www.villatoscana.co.nz. A superb villa set in an elevated position on 2 ha of native bush near the town. Enormous, self-contained designer suite has a distinct Italian feel, with 2 bedrooms and a deck that commands memorable views across the bay, and a spa pool. In-house gourmet Italian cuisine, a legendary breakfast and personal wine cellar adds to the appeal.
LL-L Crows Nest Apartments, 5 Victoria St, T07-8695979, www.crowsnest whitianga.co.nz. New luxury apartment over-looking the beach.
L-A Bailey's Motel, 66 Buffalo Beach Rd, T07-866 5500, www.baileysmotel.co.nz. At the

higher end of the market but comfortable, on the beachfront and close to town.

AL-C International Lodge, 4 White St, T07-8660544, www.internationallodge.co.nz. Purpose-built lodge offering 12 tidy, spacious rooms, some en suite and all the standard facilities including free internet.

B Cosy Cat Cottage, 41 South Highway, T07-866 4488, www.cosycat.co.nz. A tidy cottage with a distinctly feline theme offering both B&B en suite rooms and a separate self-contained option. No dogs allowed!

C-D Cat's Pyjamas, 12 Albert St, T07-866 4663, www.cats-pyjamas.co.nz. The smallest of the backpackers in Whiti and a fine one to boot. Located in the heart of town with all the usual choice of rooms (some en suite), as well as a cosy lounge with open fire and a spa pool.

C-D On the Beach Backpacker's Lodge (YHA), 46 Buffalo Beach Rd, T07-866 5380, www.yha. org.nz. Overlooking the bay, standard and en suite doubles and dorms. Bike and kayak hire.

Motorcamps and campsites

Given the rapacious development that has happened in recent years, the town is surprisingly short of motor park facilities.

B-D Mercury Bay Motor Camp, 121 Albert St, T07-866 5579, www.mercurybayholiday park.co.nz. Long-established, family orientated, convenient to town centre. Camp kitchen.

B-D Mill Creek Bird and Campervan Park, 365 Mill Creek Road, Whitianga, T07-8660166, www.halcyonheights.co.nz. If you love animals and/or have kids this is an ideal option. Peaceful and friendly with over 400 birds of 40 species to view, even the odd hedgehog and donkey with many tame. Located a few kilometres south of Whitianga. Powered sites and B&B rooms with ensuite.

Hahei *p201*

LL-AL Island View Villas , 11 Christine Terr, T07-866 3247, www.islandviewapartments. co.nz. On the hill on the southern end of the village, the range of self-contained apartments are immaculate and the views

unforgettable. Swimming pool and spa. Recommended.

AL Spellbound B&B, 77 Grange Rd, T07-866 3543, www.spellboundhahei.co.nz. At the northern end of the village, with equally good views as Island View Villas, above. 2 king/twin rooms and 1 queen, all en suites.

AL The Church, 87 Beach Rd, T07-866 3533, www.thechurchhahei.co.nz. As the name suggests this accommodation/restaurant combination is set in and around a former village church. Accommodation takes the form of wooden studio units, separate studio or self-contained cottages surrounding the church (restaurant) and surrounded by gardens. 2 of the 11 self-contained cottages have an open fire. The licensed restaurant is a local favourite.

A-D Hahei Holiday Resort, Harsant Av, T07-866 3889, www.haheiholidays.co.nz. Right on the beach is this fine and spacious facility with self-contained (beachfront) lodges and backpacker accommodation. Camp kitchen.

A-D Tatahi Lodge, Grange Rd, T07-866 3992, www.tatahilodge.co.nz. Excellent motel and backpacker hostel with a cottage, 5 units and backpacker lodge all with modern facilities and a short stroll from the beach.

Hot Water Beach *p201*

L Hot Water Beach B&B, 48 Pye Pl, T07-866 3991, www.hotwaterbedand breakfast.co.nz. Modern home looking right across Hot Water Beach, with spa.

A Auntie Dawn's Place, 15 Radar Rd, T07-866 3707, www.auntiedawn.co.nz. A cheaper and friendly option with a couple of self-contained flats and in-house B&B.

Tairua and Pauanui *p202*

LL Puka Park Lodge, Pauanui Beach, T07-864 8088, www.pukapark.co.nz. Luxurious accommodation on the peninsula. Private bush chalets with a restaurant and bar in the main lodge house. Spa, pool and organized activities.

LL-D Slipper Island Resort, T021-776977, www.slipper.co.nz. An opportunity to escape the mainland to a private island with lodge, self-contained chalets, tent sites and activities.

L Dellcote, T07-864 8142, www.dellcote. co.nz. An attractive, peaceful homestay lodge set amidst an organic orchard and gardens in the Rewarewa Valley. 3 very attractive rooms with en-suites, guest lounge. In-house cuisine.
AL-A Pacific Harbour Lodge, Main Rd, T07-864 8581, www.pacificharbour.co.nz. Centrally located with a good restaurant.
AL-A Pauanui Pines Motor Lodge, 174 Vista Paku, Pauanui Beach, T07-864 8086, www.pauanuipines.co.nz. A fine award-winning motel in Pauanui.
C-D Pinnacles Backpackers, 305 Main Rd, T07-864 8448, www.pinnaclesbakpak.co.nz. A reputable alternative that also offers tent sites.
C-D Tairua Beachhouse Backpackers, 342A Main Rd, Tairua, T07-864 8313, www.tairuabeachhouse.co.nz. Centrally

located with spa and internet. One ensuite double.

Opoutere *p202*
B-D Opoutere Youth Hostel (YHA), 389 Opoutere Rd, T07-865 9072, www.yha.org.nz. A fine, peaceful place to stay with great facilities, short walks nearby, and a lovely view across the harbour. Considered the best backpacker hostel in the region. Recommended.

Whangamata *p202*
Consult the VIC (I-Site) and book in advance in summer and New Year.
LL Brenton Lodge, 2 Brenton Pl, T07-865 8400, www.brentonlodge.co.nz. A gorgeous bijou country retreat with 2 romantic cottages, 1 en suite and lots of pampering.
LL Bushland Park Lodge, 444 Wentworth Valley Rd, T07-865 7468, www.bushlandpark lodge.co.nz. Another fine establishment in a

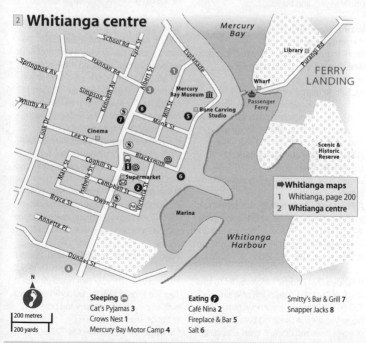

2 Whitianga centre

Mercury Bay

Library

FERRY LANDING

School Rd
Fire St
Esplanade
Springbok Av
Hannan Rd
Albert St
Purangi Rd
Whitby Av
Simpson Pl
Kenneth Av
Wharf
Mercury Bay Museum 🏛
Passenger Ferry
Whitby Av
Mill St
Bone Carving Studio
Cook Dr
Lee St
Monk St
Cinema
Scenic & Historic Reserve
Mary St
Coghill St
Blacksmith
Isabella St
Campbell St
Supermarket
Bryce St
Owen St
Victoria St
Annette Pl
Marina
Dundas St
Whitianga Harbour

➡ **Whitianga maps**
1 Whitianga, page 200
2 **Whitianga centre**

N

200 metres
200 yards

Sleeping 🛏
Cat's Pyjamas 3
Crows Nest 1
Mercury Bay Motor Camp 4

Eating 🍴
Café Nina 2
Fireplace & Bar 5
Salt 6

Smitty's Bar & Grill 7
Snapper Jacks 8

lovely location, European in style, emphasis on health and a quality restaurant attached.
AL-A Palm Pacific Resort, 413 Port Rd, T07-865 9211, www.palmpacificresort.com. A large modern motel in the centre of town with tidy de luxe and standard units, restaurant, pool, spas and sauna.
AL-A Pipinui Motel, 805 Martyn Rd, T07-865 6796, www.pipinuimotel.co.nz. A modern motel set away from the main road and, accordingly, quieter than the larger resorts.

Motorcamps and campsites
There is a basic **DoC** campsite at Wentworth Valley, Wentworth Valley Rd ($9), T07-865 7032.
B-D Settlers Motor Camp Park, 101 Leander Rd, T07-865 8181. Usual facilities with kitchen.
B-D Whangamata Motor Camp Park, Barbara Ave, T07-865 9128, www.whangamata.co.nz. Kitchen cabins, powered sites and bunks.

Waihi, Waihi Beach and Karangahake *p203*
Waihi and Waihi Beach, 11 km to the east, are well-serviced with the full range of accommodation options.
AL Falls Retreat, 25 Waitawheta Rd, Karangahake Gorge, T07-212 8087. Popular with honeymooners, two rustic self-contained cottages handy if you are coming or going through the gorge to Waihi. Great value.
A Sea Air Motel and Motor Park, 127 Emerton Rd, Waihi Beach, T07-863 5655, www.sea air.co.nz. Relatively new standard motel.
A Trout and Chicken B&B, 2 km from town, 9137 SH2, Waihi, T07-863 6964, www.trout andchicken.co.nz. Peaceful, modern B&B and self-contained barnset in a blueberry orchard.
B Chez Nous B&B, 41 Seddon St, T07-863 7538. Central and good value.
B Golden Owl Lodge, 3 Moresby Rd (6 kms south of Paeroa, 10kms north of Waihi), T07-862 7994, www.goldenowl.co.nz. Small, homely lodge run by caring owners. 2 tidy doubles, twin and dorm. A great change from

the larger commercial backpackers. Recommended.

Motorcamps and campsites
A-D Waihi Beach Top Ten Holiday Park, 15 Main Beach Rd, Waihi Beach, T0800-924448/T07-863 5504, www.waihibeach.com. Has some fine beachside cabins and sheltered campsites.
B-D Athenree Hot Springs and Holiday Park, Athenree Rd, T07-863 5600, www.athenreehotsprings.co.nz. A little further field and offers all the usual with the added attraction of the natural (public) hot springs.
B-D Waihi Motor Camp, 6 Waitete Rd, T07-863 7654. Newly developed with chalets, log cabins, tent sites and camp kitchen. Good value.

● Eating

Whitianga *p199, maps p200 and p205*
Whiti is well-served with fine eating establishments; most offer a variety of fresh seafood; the best are along the Esplanade.
♥♥ Café Nina, behind the VIC (I-Site) at 20 Victoria St, T07-866 5440, from 0800 and 1730 for dinner. The finest café in town. Small and bustling, it covers a great range of healthy and imaginative dishes.
♥♥ Fireplace Restaurant and Bar, T07-866 4828. Wed-Sun for dinner. On the Esplanade, aesthetically the best with a lovely fire. Pizza and lamb a speciality.
♥♥ Salt Restaurant, Whitianga Marina Hotel, 1 Blacksmith Lane, T07-866 5818. Daily from 1100. Overlooking the marina with outdoor seating. Specializes in Pacific Rim and Thai cuisine.
♥ Eggsentric Café and Restaurant, Purangi Rd, Flaxmill Bay (1 km east of Ferry Landing), T07-866 0307. Daily for lunch and dinner Tue-Sun (closed in Aug). Colourful and lively, with musical performances and poetry readings. Licensed and BYO.
♥ Snapper Jacks, 26 Albert St, T07-866 5482.

Daily from 1100. Reputedly the best fish and chips in town.

¶ **Smitty's Bar and Grill**, 37 Albert St, T07-866 4647. For decent pub grub this is a good bet.

Hahei p201

¶¶ **The Church**, 87 Beach Rd, T07-866 3797, www.thechurchhahei.co.nz. Thu-Tue. Better say 'Grace' in this one. Unusual venue that is as memorable for the cuisine as well as its ecclesiastical character.

¶ **Café Luna**, nearby at 1 Grange Rd, T07-866 3016. Daily in summer from 0900 until late, reduced hours in winter. Great breakfast.

Tairua and Pauanui p202

¶¶¶ **Puka Park Lodge**, see Sleeping, page 204, bookings advised. The area's fine dining option.

¶¶ **Colenso Country Café**, SH25, 12 mins north of Tairua, T07-866 3725. 1000-1700. A top spot for partaking in fine food.

¶¶ **Shells Restaurant**, Main Rd, Tairua, T07-864 8811. Tue-Sat. Convenient for dinner.

¶ **Out of the Blue Café**, Main Rd, Tairua, T07-864 8987. 0800-1600. Serves good coffee, imaginative lunches and snacks, and breakfast.

Whangamata p202

¶¶¶ **Bushland Park Lodge**, see Sleeping, page 205. Cosy, fine dining with a creative edge using specially created glass tableware.

¶¶ **Oceanas**, 328 Ocean Rd, T07-865 7157. A little more upmarket and the place to head for those who like seafood and Pacific Rim cuisine.

¶ **Vibes Café**, 638 Port Rd, T07-865 8494. Light lunches and the best coffee in town.

Waihi p203

¶¶ **Chambers Wine Bar and Restaurant**, 22 Haszard St, T07-863 7474. 1100-late. Housed in the 1904 Council Chambers building, offering a mix of Mediterranean and Antipodean dishes.

¶¶ **Ti Tree Café**, 14 Hazard St, T07- 863 8668. A local favourite.

¶¶ **Waitete Orchard Café**, Waitete Rd, off SH2,

T07-863 8980. Daily 0830-1730. Great lunch venue with organic flair, wine and ice cream.

¶¶-¶ **The Porch**, 23 Wilson Rd, T07-863 1330. Daily lunch and dinner. Funky, South Pacific-style café bar with cosy open fire.

▲ Activities and tours

Whitianga p199, maps p200 and p205
Cruising, fishing and scuba diving
There are numerous charters of all shapes and sizes offering a wide range of trips from fishing and diving to speedboat cruising out into Mercury Bay and beyond. Bare in mind that most coastal fishing charters charge per boat rather than per person, so group bookings are best, or be prepared to join others. The best bet for fishing is to call at the VIC (I-Site) and ask who is going out on any particular day.

The stunning coastal explorations with **Hahei Explorer** is also well worth considering (see Hahei page 208).
Cathedral Cove Dive, T07-866 3955, www.hahei.co.nz/diving. Offers trips for certified divers to the Te Whanganui-A-Hei Marine Reserve off Cathedral Cove. The scenery above water is equally stunning.
Cave Cruzer, T0800-427893/T0274-427893, www.cavecruzer.co.nz. The *Cave Cruzer* is a rigid inflatable that can take you on a range of tours around the bay from 1-2.5 hrs ($50/$75), taking in the main coastal sights including a stop at Cathedral Cove and an evening trip with a spot of live music. Alternatives include older sailing vessels and glass-bottomed boats to luxury speedboats. The VIC can assist with the details.
Seafaris Glass Bottom Boat, T07-867 1962, www.glassbottomboatwhitianga.co.nz. 2-hr eco-tours to Cathedral Cove and around with underwater viewing from $85, child $50.

Golf
Whitianga has a fine golf course about 4 km south of town, T07-866 5479. **Matarangi**, north of Whitianga, is also an excellent course, T07-866 5394.

Horse treks
Rangihau Ranch, Rangihau Rd, Coroglen, T07-866 3875, www.rangihauranch.co.nz. Conventional treks from $40.
Twin Oaks Riding Ranch, 9 km north of Whitianga, T07-8665388, www.twinoaks ridingranch.co.nz. Treks depart daily at 0930, 1330 and 1800, 2 hrs from $50.

Kayaking/windsurfing/watersports
The coast, with its sandstone scenery and pohutukawa trees is ideal for sea kayaking, and a trip in calm conditions is recommended.
Banana Boat, T07-866 0166. This yellow inflatable that speeds around the bay, with you trying to hold on is a laugh. There many trip options including the 'Hell Bender', the 'Thrill' and 'Kiddies Ride'. Ask at the VIC for details.
Cathedral Cove Sea Kayakings, T07-8663877, www.seakayaktours.co.nz. Based in Hahei, offers kayak hire and half- or full-day kayak trips at $85. Courtesy transport to/from Whitianga Ferry.

Ropes course
High Zone, south of Whitianga near the 309 Rd turning, T07-866 2113, www.highzone. co.nz. 14-m adventure ropes course. From $15-70.

Hahei *p201*
A trip here can combine with your own explorations of Cathedral Cove by foot, followed by some swimming and sunbathing.
Hahei Explorer Tours, T07-866 3910, www.glassbottomboatwhitianga.co.nz. Daily trips to Cathedral Cove on board an inflatable $65, child $40, for 1 hr, departs 1000 and 1400. Also takes in caves and a blowhole.

Tairua and Pauanui *p202*
Water-based activities operate mainly out of Tairua, a beach at Pauanui and the *Broken Hills Recreation Area* walks (leaflet from VIC (I-Site).
Dive Tairua, Tairua, T0800-348382, www.divetairua.co.nz. Good-value dive trips to the Alderman Islands, courses and lodging. Also offers independent kayak hire from $20 per hour, or $60 per day.

Whangamata *p202*
Whangamata VIC can book the numerous water-based trips and activities on offer.
Kiwi Dundee Adventures, T07-865 8809, www.kiwidundee.co.nz. A well-established operator offering an extensive and imaginative range of eco-tours from 1-5 days, taking in natural sights and gold mining remnants.

Surfing
Whangamata's oldest surf shop **Saltwater Surf Co**, 505 Port Rd, T07-865 8666 and the **Whangamata Surf School**, T07-865 6879, are the focus for surfers' gossip and board hire.

Waihi *p203*
Surfing
Learn to Surf, T07-863 4587. The local outfit providing the very entertaining opportunity of learning to stand on a surf board for more than 3 nanoseconds.

⊖ Transport

Whitianga *p199, maps p200 and p205*
Bicycle hire
Bike Man, 16 Coghill St, Whitianga, T07-866 0745. From $40 per day.

Taxi and shuttles
Paradise Cabs, Whitianga, T09-869 5555. Cook Beach Minibus, T0274-432329/ T07-8662644, offers shuttles to Hahei (Cathedral Cove) and Hot Water Beach from $35. Go Kiwi Shuttles, T0800-446549/ T07-866 0336, www.go-kiwi.co.nz, offers tours and shuttles to Hahei and Hot Water Beach from $35.

⊕ Directory

Whitianga *p199, maps p200 and p205*
Internet Bartley Graphics, 706 Port Rd, Whangamata, T07-865 8832. **Inter Earth**, Shop 14, Blacksmith Lane, Whitianga, T07-866 5991, www.interearth.co.nz. Mon-Fri 0900-1700, Sat 1000-1600 (extended hours in summer).

Contents

Footprint features

The Waikato

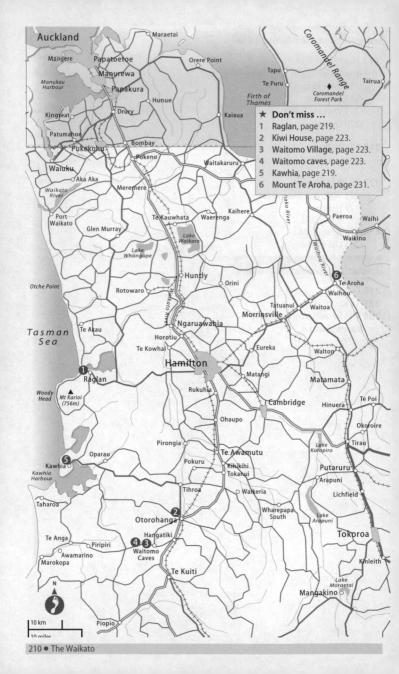

★ **Don't miss ...**
1 Raglan, page 219.
2 Kiwi House, page 223.
3 Waitomo Village, page 223.
4 Waitomo caves, page 223.
5 Kawhia, page 219.
6 Mount Te Aroha, page 231.

The Waikato is one of the country's richest agricultural areas, where the eponymous river – the longest in the country – snakes its way through a landscape of green rolling hills and fields. The Waikato, the homeland of the Tainui people – one of the largest tribes in the land – is rich in Maori history, as well as being home to the current Maori queen and head of state. The first Maori king was elected here in 1858 and the subsequent formation of the Maori King Movement, in direct opposition to rule under the British monarchy, led to much bloodshed. After almost a year of fierce battles and confrontation the British finally quashed the Kingites, who fled to southern Waikato, which is now also known as King Country. Today, peace reigns but the memory lives on.

Waikato also boasts New Zealand's fourth largest city, Hamilton, which despite being an unremarkable commercial centre, is increasingly seen as an alternative base to Auckland. Although not a major tourist destination, the Waikato is a region with considerable diversity from the famous surf beaches on its coast to the jewel in the crown of the King Country, the Waitomo District – a wonderland of limestone caves and subterranean activities that deservedly make it one of the North Island's premier tourist attractions. Also of note, since the abiding success of the film *Lord of the Rings*, is the small agricultural town of Matamata, where local farmland was used to create the set of 'Hobbiton', home of Frodo and friends. Although very little remains, it is still the first stop on the 'tour of homage' for *Lord of the Rings* fanatics.

Hamilton and Waikato North → *Colour map 2, B2.*

Perched on the serpentine banks of the famous Waikato River, 129 km south of Auckland, Hamilton, with a population of around 120,000, is the main service centre for the rich fertile agricultural region of the Waikato. Being so close to the major tourist destinations of Auckland and Rotorua, the city struggles to keep visitors for any length of time as it has few major attractions. It is, however, ideally located for explorations around the Waikato Region and can be used as base for exploring the North Island. Hamilton is also a university town and plays host to some major national events including the annual National Agricultural Field Days in June and the colourful Balloon over Waikato in April. Visitors stopping briefly in the city can enjoy a ride down the Waikato on the MV Waipa Delta paddleboat and visit the celebrated museum, gardens and 'Free-flight Aviary' of Hamilton Zoo.
▸▸ *For Sleeping, Eating and other listings, see pages 216-218.*

Ins and outs

Getting there and around

Air Hamilton has a busy international **airport** ⓘ *15 km south of the city, T07-8489027, www.hamiltonairport.co.nz.* **Pacific Blue**, T0800-670000, www.flypacificblue.com.au, and **Jetstar**, T0800-800995/T03-93470103, both fly regularly from eastern Australia; **Air New Zealand**, T0800-737000/T07-839 9835, www.airnewzealand.co.nz, serves the major domestic destinations. A shuttle to the city costs about $15, T0800-748885, taxi T07-8477477.

Road Hamilton is on the SH1 and is well served north and south by **Intercity** and **Newmans**, T09-5835780. For internet fares throughout the North Island try **Nakedbus.com**. **BOP Shuttle**, T0800-700727/T07-3481364, offer a shuttle service to Rotorua and Taupo from the airport. Other services include **Dalroy's**, T06-759 0197/T0508-465622, www.dalroytours.co.nz, to Auckland or Taranaki. All buses arrive and depart from the **Transport Centre** ⓘ *corner of Bryce and Anglesea sts, T07-9585960, Mon- Fri 0830-1700, Sat-Sun 0930-1530.* It has a café, internet and also is home to the VIC (I-Site). For information on local bus services, contact **Busit/GoBus**, T0800-4287 5463, www.busit.co.nz. Hamilton has a free central city shuttle that leaves every 10 mins, Mon-Fri, 0700-1800 and Sat 0900-1300. The shuttle travels in a one way loop from the new Knox St car park, north along Victoria and Liverpool sts and then south along Anglesea St, into Caro, Alexandra, Hood, Anglesea and then Bridge St.

   Both SH1 and the main Auckland to Wellington trunk rail line run through the heart of the Waikato. An alternative route south is SH27, which branches off SH1 just south of Auckland at the Bombay Hills and also accesses Waikato East. SH27 passes through Matamata before rejoining SH1 again at Tirau. The principal signposted touring route is called the 'Thermal Explorer Highway', from Auckland via Hamilton, Rotorua and Taupo to Napier. A free touring map is available from all major VICs, www.thermalnz.co.nz.

Train Hamilton is on the main trunk 'Overlander' rail line with services daily to Auckland, Wellington, Rotorua and Tauranga, T0800-872467, www.tranzscenic.co.nz. The **train station** is on Fraser St, in Frankton.

Tourist information and orientation

Hamilton VIC (I-Site) ① *Hamilton Transport Centre, corner of Bryce and Anglesea sts, T07-958 5960, www.visithamilton.co.nz, www.waikatonz.co.nz, Mon-Fri 0900-1730, Sat-Sun 0930-1530.* **DoC** ① *5 Northway St, T07-858 1000.*

Hamilton ⊜❼🏃❀⊛⊜☎❻ ➤ *pp216-218.*

The modern **Waikato Museum of Art and History** ① *1 Grantham St, (south end of Victoria St), T07-838 6606, www.waikatomuseum.org.nz, daily 1000-1630, (admission charge for special exhibitions)*, overlooks the river. It presents a wide-ranging programme of both permanent and temporary exhibitions, including a balance of contemporary and historical art of regional significance and national importance. The history of Hamilton is explored with a particularly impressive collection of Tainui Maori *taonga* (treasures). The highlight of the collection has to be the beautiful, carved and decorated *waka*, 'Te Wainika', given to the museum in 1973 by Te Arikinui Dame Te Atairangikaahu, the Maori Queen. There is also an adjunct science and technology centre, which offers all the usual whizz-bang earthquake simulation stuff. It's great for little kids and big kids alike. There is also a fine café/restaurant, selling interesting fare such as ostrich antipasto and kangaroo loin, amongst other things. **Arts Post Galleries** ① *120 Victoria St, T07-838 6928, daily 1000-1630*, runs in conjunction with the museum and focuses on existing and emerging local artists with three exhibition spaces.

While near the river it is worth taking a stroll to soak up the almost English atmosphere, with its rowboats and pleasant gardens.

Just south of the city centre and east of Cobham Bridge are the celebrated **Hamilton Gardens** ① *T07-856 3200, 0730-sunset, visitor centre 1000-1600, free.* These are a conglomerate of Japanese, Chinese and English flower gardens, mixed with numerous smaller and more traditional themed displays. The gardens also have a popular café/restaurant. The VIC (I-Site) has a free and comprehensive *Heritage Trail* leaflet, another outlining *Hamilton's Walkways* and the *Waikato Vintage Wine Trail*.

Hamilton Zoo ① *T07-838 6720, www.hamiltonzoo.co.nz, daily 0900-1700, extended hours in Jan, $14, child $7*, is 8 km from the city centre (take the SH23 Raglan Road, turn right onto Newcastle Road, then go straight ahead down Brymer). Modern and progressive in its outlook, the zoo not only acts as a major attraction, but also attempts to mix a considerable collection of native New Zealand species with others important to international conservation breeding programmes. The highlight is the 3800 sq m, walk-through 'free-flight aviary', which houses 10 species of indigenous, rare and endangered New Zealand birds within a native bush setting. Other attractions include the Sumatran tigers, and the 'Waikato Wetlands' and 'Out of Africa' exhibits. Moto to the white rhino, has won many hearts, although not quite as many perhaps as the very grumpy Kune pig in the centre of the park.

Waikato North

Ngaruawahia ➤ *Colour map 2, B1.*

Around 19 km north of Hamilton, Ngaruawahia is the Maori capital of New Zealand. It is home of the Maori Queen, Te Atairangikaahu (first queen and sixth person to hold office), and one of the best and most significant *maraes* in the country: the **Turangawaewae**

Hamilton

N

200 metres
200 yards

marae, beside the river on River Road, and only open once a year in March, during the annual regatta, when a number of *waka* (canoes) are displayed on the river. (The town is located where the Waipa meets the mighty Waikato.)

Another point of interest in Ngaruawahia is the **Mahinarangi House**, built in 1929. It is beautifully carved both inside and out, with the royal coat of arms on the giant doors, entitled 'Te Paki o Matariki', announcing the hope of peace and calm between Maori and *pakeha*. Next door is the Queen's official residence. Ngaruawahia also has a number of good walks including the **Hakarimata Walkways** and **Taupiri Mountain**, the site of the Waikato's most sacred burial ground. If you fancy a well-deserved hot soak after your walk or explorations of the town you might like to head 23 km west to the **Waingaro Hot Springs** ① *T07-825 4761, www.waingaro hotsprings.co.nz, 0900-2130, $10*, featuring large thermal mineral pools and spas. Motor park accommodation is also available.

Huntly and around

With its power station and the slow-moving muddy waters of the Waikato, Huntly is not a pretty place. The underground coal reserves are the largest in New Zealand and the power station produces 20 per cent of the country's needs. However, the **Waikato Coalfields Museum** ① *26 Harlock St, T07-828 8128*, displaying local and national mining history, may tempt you to linger. A new and much larger museum is on the drawing board.

In direct contrast to the man-made gloom of Huntly are the numerous lakes and wetlands that surround the town. These are popular for water sports and bird watching. For a detailed description of the lakes and walks ask for the DoC leaflet *Waikato Wetlands* at the Huntly VIC or DoC in Hamilton. If you have kids and can bear it, **Candyland** ① *75 Henry Rd, 15 mins southeast of Huntly in Taupiri, T07-824 6818,*

Barzurk Pizza Bar **3**
Iguana **11**
Museum Café/Restaurant **2**
Sahara Tent Café & Bar **4**
Scott's Epicurean **5**

Bars & clubs 🍸
Biddy Mulligan's **7**
Easy Tiger **9**
Fox & Hounds **8**
Outback, Loft & Diggers **10**

www.candyland .co.nz, daily 1000-1700, is the largest sweet shop in New Zealand. Candy making shows are offered on weekends at 1030 and 1300, adult $8, child $5.

Te Kauwhata → *Colour map 2, B2.*

The main attraction in this mainly grape-growing area is the **Rangiriri Battle Site Heritage Centre** ① *T07-826 3663, 0900-1500, free,* which sits just off the SH1 next to the Rangiriri Hotel (a congenial, old-fashioned country pub that offers a fine pub lunch). Although the place seems to function more as a roadside café than anything else, there is some memorabilia and an information office where you can arrange to see an audio- visual display. The battle that took place in Rangiriri in 1863 was one of the bloodiest of the Maori Land Wars and involved a small group of Maori who made a brave stand against the numerically superior British forces. The remains of the redoubts from which they fought still survive, as does the cemetery.

◉ Hamilton and Waikato North listings

For Sleeping and Eating price codes and other relevant information, see Essentials pages 44-50.

● Sleeping

Hamilton *p212, map p214*
Hamilton has plenty of mid-range options and it is not usually necessary to pre-book. Ulster St, just north of the city centre, is the main motel drag and there is certainly plenty of choice. But there are not many B&Bs in Hamilton. The VIC (I-Site) has full listings.
LL-L Novotel Tainui Hotel, 7 Alma St, T07-838 1366, www.accorhotels.co.nz. The city's best located hotel is great value for money. Standard 4-star facilities. Some rooms have views across the river. The in-house café/ restaurant offers indoor and outdoor à la carte dining, again with pleasant views. Spa and sauna. Secure, valet parking.
L Narrows Landing, 431 Airport Rd, Tamahere, T07-858 4001, www.thenarrows landing.co.nz. Near the airport, offers self-contained accommodation, with country views and a fine restaurant attached.
L-A Ambassador Motor Inn, 86 Ulster St, T07-839 5111, www.silveroaks.co.nz. A short walk from the river, with a restaurant attached.
L-A Barclay Motel, 280 Ulster St, T07-838 2475, www.barclay.co.nz. All mod cons including spa facilities.
L-A Chloe's, 181 Ulster St, T07-839 3410, www.chloes.co.nz. Has a restaurant adjacent.

L-A Sails Motel, 272 Ulster St, T07-838 2733, www.sails-motorinn.co.nz. Spa facilities.
AL-A Ventura Inn and Suites, 23 Clarence St, T07-838 0110, www.venturainns.co.nz. Located in a quiet position, on the fringe of the CBD. Standard rooms, de luxe studios (king-sized bed and spa) and standard suites (king-sized bed, pull-out sofa and kitchenette) available. No in-house restaurant, but some of the city's best are within a short stroll.
B Cedar Lodge, 174 Ulster St, T07-8395569, www.cedarlodge.co.nz. One of the cheapest on Ulster St.
C-D Colts and Fillies Backpackers , 37 Smith Rd, T07-825 9809, www.ktt.co.nz. Tidy backpacker place attached to a horse trekking outfit and the Karamu Trail Track, an off-road trail bike track. Accommodation consists of 2 family rooms sleeping up to 5 people and dorm rooms. Facilities include free internet, open fire and Sky TV. The horse treks are great value and start from only $20.
C-D Eagles Nest Backpackers, 937 Victoria St, T07-838 2704, www.eaglesback packers.co.nz. A relatively new establishment that seems to enjoy a good reputation. Centrally located and spotless.
C-D J's Backpackers, 8 Grey St, T07-856 8934, www.jsbackpackers.co.nz. A long-established suburban offering with comfortable dorms, twins and doubles. Also organizes trips.

Motorcamps and campsites

There are 2 basic motorcamps with camping facilities in East Hamilton, 3 km from town: **C-D Hamilton City Holiday Park**, 14 Ruakura Rd, T07-855 8255,. www.hamiltoncityholidaypark.co.nz; and **C-D Hamilton East Motor Camp**, 61 Cameron Rd, T07-856 6220. Camp kitchen.

🍴 Eating

Hamilton *p212, map p214*
Hamilton boasts an amazing number of café/restaurants (mainly along the southern end of Victoria St), all trying to outdo each other in interior design, theme and cuisine.
₩₩₩ **The Bank Bar and Brasserie**, corner of Hood and Victoria sts, further south, T07-839 4740. Sun-Thu 1100-2300, Fri-Sat 1100-0300. A local favourite, especially with the suits at lunchtime and trend-setters at night. Generous servings.
₩₩₩ **Iguana**, 203 Victoria St, T07-834 2280, www.iguana.net.nz. Mon-Wed 1000-late, Thu-Sun 1000-0300. A well-established, spacious favourite, with a wide-ranging mainly Pacific Rim menu and excellent gourmet pizza. The bar is popular which adds to the establishment's lively atmosphere.
₩₩ **Café Alma**, in the Novotel Tainui Hotel, see Sleeping page 216.
₩₩ **Museum Café/Restaurant**, Grantham St, T07-839 7209. Daily from 1030, Tue-Sat dinner from 1800. You can't go far wrong here, with an eclectic menu. Jazz on Thu.
₩₩ **The Sahara Tent Café and Bar**, 254 Victoria St, T07-834 0409. A Middle Eastern-style eatery, which is worth seeing, never mind eating in.
₩₩ **Scott's Epicurean**, 181 Victoria St, T07-839 6680. A funky little café with a highly imaginative lunch/brunch menu.
₩ **Barzurk Pizza Bar**, 250 Victoria St, T07-834 2363. Daily, 1200-late. Recommended for gourmet pizza.

🍷 Pubs, bars and clubs

Hamilton *p212, map p214*
With so many trendy bars and restaurants Hamilton enjoys a lively and friendly social scene and if you mingle with the locals it will probably be a long and interesting night.

For a traditional Irish pub with live bands at the weekend **Biddy Mulligan's**, 742 Victoria St, T07-834 0306, is a good bet. Other popular conventional venues includethe **Fox and Hounds**, corner Victoria and Alama sts. **The Bank**, corner of Hood St, or **Easy Tiger**, 186 Victoria St.

For more traditional Kiwi pub atmosphere and for younger crowds, try **Outback**, **Loft** or **Diggers Bar**, all on Hood St.

🎭 Entertainment

Hamilton *p212, map p214*
Casino
Hamilton has succumbed and now has its own casino, the main focus within the flash **Sky City Hamilton Riverside Entertainment Centre**, 346 Victoria St, T07-834 4900, www.skycityhamilton.co.nz, daily 1100-0300. Minimum age 20, smart casual dress.

Theatres
For information and bookings contact the VIC (I-Site) or Theatre Services, T07-838 6600. **The Founders**, 221 Tristram St, T07-838 6600, www.hamiltontheatres.co.nz. Opera, ballet/dance and musicals.
Meteor, 1 Victoria St, T07-838 6600. The smallest. Drama, dance, bands and comedy.
Clarence Street Theatre, 59 Clarence St, T07-838 6600. Drama, ballet/dance, concerts, musicals and comedy.

🎪 Festivals and events

Hamilton *p212, map p214*
Mar Ngaruawahia Maori Regatta, 12 km north of Hamilton. Held annually for over 100

years, the regatta celebrates Maori culture. Replicas of *waka* are rowed by Maori in native dress, attracting 30,000 people.

The **Balloons over Waikato Festival** is also held over 5 days in late Mar with around 80,000 attending the colourful 'Nightglow'.

Jun Fieldays Agricultural Show, www.fieldays.co.nz. Held middle weekend.

O Shopping

Hamilton *p212, map p214*
Shopping centres include: **Hamilton Central Shopping Centre**; **Westfield Shopping Centre**, corner of Hukanui and Comries Rd, Chartwell; **Downtown Plaza**; and Centreplace Shopping Centre.
New Zealand World, 24 Garden Pl. For New Zealand souvenirs.

▲▲ Activities and tours

Hamilton *p212, map p214*
The Waikato countryside lends itself to hot-air ballooning
Kiwi Balloon Company, T07-8438538, www.kiwiballooncompany.co.nz. The main operator in the region, with flights from $290.

⊖ Transport

Hamilton *p212, map p214*
Car hire Rent-A-Dent and First Choice, 383 Anglesea St, T07-839 1049. **Waikato Car Rentals**, Brooklyn Rd, T07- 855 0094.
Taxi Hamilton Taxi Society, T0800-477477.

❶ Directory

Hamilton *p212, map p214*
Banks The main banks are found on Victoria St, most offer foreign exchange. **Internet** Numerous locations. Also the VIC (I-Site) and the library on Garden Pl. **Medical services** Victoria Central Medical Clinic, 750 Victoria St, T07-834 0333. **Post office** 36 Bryce St, T07-838 2233, Mon-Fri 0800-1700, Sat 0900-1200.

Waikato Coast → *Colour map 2, B1.*

With the well-advertised attractions of Waitomo and its caves, the Waikato Coast seldom features very high on the average travelling agenda. Indeed, after some unique subterranean adventures most simply pass through the Waikato on their way south, or east to the capital of all things thermal – Rotorua. But for those with more time, who wish to ride a world-class 'left-hand break', or who simply wish to get off the beaten track, then the Waikato Coast offers some pleasant surprises. The small laid-back coastal village of Raglan, 50 km west of Hamilton, offers a palpable sense of relaxation, not to mention plenty of the aforementioned and near legendary surf breaks. Further south, a diversion off SH1 to the remote coastal village of Kawhia, and back via the Marakopa Falls to Waitomo, can be a relaxing, scenic and often solitary highlight. ►► *For Sleeping, Eating and other listings, see pages 220-221.*

Ins and outs

Getting there and around The drive to Kawhia from anywhere is quite arduous but scenic. If you are peckish be sure to stop for a homemade pie at the **Oparau Roadhouse** (T07-871 0683, 0600-2200). Raglan is 48 km from Hamilton. The commuter-orientated **Hamilton Busit**, T07-847 5343/T0800-4287 5463, offers daily services (three times daily Mon-Fri, twice daily at weekends) to Raglan, departing from Hamilton Transport Centre for $7 return (first at 0830). In Raglan, buses stop at the VIC. For a taxi in Raglan, T07-825 0506.

Tourist information **The Kawhia Museum** ① *T07-871 0161, www.kingcountry.co.nz, www.kawhia.co.nz/www.kawhiaharbour.co.nz*, operates as a VIC. The **Raglan VIC** ① *4 Wallis St, T07-825 0556, daily 0900-1700, www.raglan.net.nz, www.raglan.org.nz*, is small but highly efficient.

Kawhia → *Colour map 2, B1.*

Outside the summer influx of mainly domestic holidaymakers, when the population almost triples, Kawhia (pronounced 'Kafia') is a sleepy, fairly unremarkable, coastal village on the shores of the Kawhia Harbour southwest of Hamilton. But perhaps due to its remote location and nature's rich pickings, Kawhia seems in no hurry to announce itself as anything more spectacular, and has the contented atmosphere of a place entirely happy with its lot. And it would seem that this has always been the case. Kawhia (which actually translates as 'place of abundance') was home to the Tainui people who first arrived here some 750 years ago. So happy were they with the place and its natural provision, that it took them over 300 years before heading inland to settle other parts of the Waikato. Even then, it was only through inter-tribal disputes, which ironically were over the abundant fishing grounds.

Most of Kawhia's points of interest are on the shoreline in the town and extending around to the harbour entrance and **Ocean Beach**. This is the most popular beach with summer visitors and it is best accessed through the Tainui Kawhia Forest Track southwest of the town centre. Ocean Beach boasts the **Puia Hot Springs** (a far less commercial echo of Hot Water Beach in Coromandel). Here, too, you can dig your own 'spa bath' in the sand, but it's difficult to know where exactly to do this, especially in the off-season. It is perhaps best to join a local tour to access the best spots (see page 221). Back in town if you want to immerse yourself in Kawhia's interesting history and learn more about the Tainui landing, the small **Kawhia Museum** ① *T07-871 0161, www.kawhia.co.nz, Oct-Apr Wed-Sun 1200-1600, or by appointment, free*, which sits next to the wharf, will proudly oblige. The *Best of the West* Heritage leaflet will pinpoint and explain specific sites.

When the Tainui people first made landfall they tied their canoe to a pohutukawa tree and named it **Tangi-te-Korowhiti**. Although the specific tree is not marked, it is one of a small grove at the northern end of Kaora Street. What is marked is the site of its burial with two stones – **Hani** and **Puna** – which can be seen behind the **Maketu marae** about 500 m south of the landing site (ask for permission at the *marae* to see them).

Raglan → *Colour map 2, B1.*

Raglan is the Waikato's main seaside resort and is internationally renowned for its fine surfing. So when you arrive in the heart of the village, with its palm trees and laid-back cafés, don't be surprised if you end up being sandwiched in a queue or sharing your lunch table with a colourful length of fibreglass with 'Ride 'em Baby', 'The Big Phallus' or 'No Fear' written on it. In Raglan these strange, almost religious objects seem to make up half the population. The village itself is on the quiet Raglan Harbour with all the surf action on beaches a short drive away heading west. One of those beaches – Manu Bay – has apparently one of the best left-hand breaks in the world.

The main attractions around Raglan are its beaches, the most convenient and safest for swimming being **Te Kopua**, which borders the Raglan campground. Access is via the camp access road west, or across the footbridge at the end of Bow Street in the centre of the village. All the main surf beaches are west of town. **Ocean Beach** is the first and as well as surfing, it is also popular for swimming and the view across the 'Raglan Bar' (harbour entrance). Access is off Wainui Reserve Road via a walking track. Surf lifesavers operate in summer and, as always, you must swim between the flags. The next beach is **Manu Bay**, with its famous left-hand break, the best spot to surf or spectate. Further still is **Whale Bay**, which is a great spot for both surfers and the uninitiated, but it can only be accessed over rocks.

For wild coastal scenery **Ruapuke Beach** is popular but remote. Follow the old coast road (taking in the impressive **Te Toto Gorge** on the way), then follow Ruapuke Beach Road and walk from there. Other beaches near the town that are safe and child-friendly include **Cox's Bay** (accessible from Bayview Road and Daisy Street or the walkway along Government Road) and **Puriri Park** (Aro Aro Bay) at the end of Wallis Street.

If you are interested in local history the small **Raglan and District Museum** ① *22 Kaitoke St, T07-825 7195, weekends 1300-1530, donation*, has mainly European material. Further afield on SH23 are the aptly named 55-m **Bridal Veil Falls**, which are a bit of a trek but worth it, particularly after heavy rain. If the 756-m summit of **Mount Karioi** beckons it is best accessed from Te Toto Gorge, 12 km southwest (see above). There are fine views from the top; allow six hours. It is known by the Maori as 'the sleeping lady', the reason for which is obvious if you study its outline.

◉ Waikato Coast listings

For Sleeping and Eating price codes and other relevant information, see Essentials pages 44-50.

● Sleeping

Kawhia *p219*
B Blue Chook Inn, Jervois St, T07-871 0778. A congenial little place with 2 self-contained units and a 3-bedroom villa.
B Kawhia Motel, corner of Jervois and Tainui sts, T07-871 0865. Basic but central.

Motorcamps and campsites
B-D Kawhia Beachside S-Cape, 225 Pouewe St, as you come into town, T07-871 0727, www.kawhiabeachside scape.co.nz. The usual range of motorcamp accommodation including a self-contained cottage and backpacker facilities overlooking the harbour. Bike and kayak hire. Good camp kitchen.
B-D Kawhia Camp Ground, 73 Moke St, T07- 871 0863, www.kawhiacampingground.co.nz. Reputable and popular motor/camping ground, it has cabins as well as powered, non-powered sites and internet access. Also offers 4WD trips to the hot springs.

Raglan *p219*
Raglan has plenty of options with many self-contained and pitched at the quiet retreat/weekend getaway market. Ask at the VIC or visit www.raglan.net.nz. Note that the surf school and horse trekking operators offer accommodation packages.
LL-A Rohi Mahu, 26 Rose St, T07-8258957, www.rohimanu.co.nz. Portal to a wide range of options from beach baches to lodges.
LL-AL Ocean House and Bach, Whale Bay, T03-442 8696, www.oceanhouse.co.nz. Ideal for keen surfers, this tasteful modern eco-oriented lodge and bach is in the perfect position overlooking Raglan's famous surf break. The lodge is fully self-contained, while the bach has motel unit facilitation.
AL-D Solscape Eco-retreat (YHA), 7 km west of the village centre at 611 Wainui Rd, T07-825 8268, www.solscape.co.nz. If you're looking for something completely different this really is the only place to stay in Raglan. The owners have gone to great pains to relocate and renovate an array of railway wagons as colourful accommodation units from dorm to self-contained. Smaller cabooses (cabin houses) and a choice of 3 fully self-contained cottages (2 with open fires) are also available, plus tent sites. The

entire property enjoys views across the bay. Massage treatments also available. Good value and recommended.

A-B Raglan Sunset Motel, 7 Bankart St, T07-825 0050, www.raglansunsetmotel.co.nz. Popular modern motel in the heart of the village and close to the beach, with studios and family units, some with spa. Pleasant and peaceful alfresco area adds to the appeal.

B Harbour View Hotel, 14 Bow St, T07-825 8010. A traditional Kiwi hotel in the centre of town, worth mentioning because it is nicely renovated, cheap, clean and has a good restaurant attached.

B-D Raglan Kopua Holiday Park, Marine Parade, T07-825 8283, www.raglanholiday park.co.nz. Almost on an island of its own, with a beach and linked to the village by a short bridge.

C-D Raglan Backpackers and Waterfront Lodge, 6 We Nira St, T07-825 0515, www.raglanbackpackers.co.nz. The main backpacker hostel in the village is quite small but purpose-built and well situated. Popular of course with the surfing set. Kayak and bike hire. Recommended.

❼ Eating

Kawhia p219
🍴 **Annie's Café**, T07-871 0198. Wed-Sun 1000- 1600 and Fri, Sat 1800-late. Traditional fare.
🍴 -🍴 **Kawhia Hotel**, Powewe St, T07-871 0700. Basic meals.
🍴 **Kawhia Fisheries**, on the wharf. The best bet, serving fish and chips.

Raglan p219
Four Square supermarket, 16-18 Bow St, Mon-Fri 0730-1700, Sat-Sun 0730-1600.
🍴 **Black Sand Cafe**, 17 Bow St, T07-825 8588. The local's favourite. Live music at weekends.
🍴 **Tongue and Grove Café**, 9 Bow St, T07-8250 027. Daily 0830-late. Another popular and affordable eatery. Good size value breakfasts.

🍴 **Verandabah**, Harbour View Hotel (see Sleeping), T07-825 8010. Standard pub fare.
🍴 **Vinnies**, 7 Wainui Rd, T07-825 7273, 1000-late, Sat-Sun from 0800-1100. Popular, traditional cuisine with a seafood edge.
🍴 **Raglan Fresh Fish and Takeaways**, 35 Bow St. Good fish and chips, but service not so great unless you are a local or are attached to a surfboard.

▲ Activities and tours

Kawhia p219
Sand Rover Tour, operates out of the Kawhia Camping Ground, T07-871 0863, www.kawhiacampingground.co.nz. The friendly and enthusiastic 4WD tour includes fishing and a picnic at the Te Puia Hot Springs.

Raglan p219
There are several fishing and harbour cruise charters. In summer you can try paragliding, kayaking and kitesurfing. Ask at the VIC.
Gag Raglan, 9a Bow St, T07-825 8702, www.gagraglan.com. State-of-the-art surf shop, surfboard hire and conditions reports.
Magic Mountain, 30-min drive south of Raglan, T07-825 6892, www.magic mountain.co.nz. Horse treks in great scenery, including the Bridal Veil Falls. Day trips from $80.
Raglan Harbour Cruises, T07-825 0556, from $20. Trips to see the unusual Pancake Rock formations (no description necessary!).
Raglan Surfing School, T07-825 7873, www.raglansurfingschool.co.nz. 2-3 hr lesson costs around $89. It also offers independent board rentals and accommodation packages.

❶ Directory

Raglan p219
Internet At the library and the video shop, which are all on Bow St. **Police** Nero St, T07-825 8200.

Waikato South → Colour map 2, B/C2

Heading south, beyond the gentle meanderings of the Waikato River and the uninspiring urban vistas of Hamilton, the rest of the Waikato is typical of the North Island countryside with deliciously green, gently rolling hills replete with plump and contented dairy cows. However, in these parts, perhaps more than anywhere else in the country, looks are deceiving since beneath the hooves and the haystacks exists a very different world more suited to the stuff of mystical dreams and wild adventures. As Rotorua is to bubbly mud or Kaikoura is to whales, then southern Waikato and Waitomo is to subterranean caves, rivers and glow-worms. There is easy access to a labyrinth of incredible limestone caves and underground river systems and to all the unique activities that go with them. Where else, for example, can you abseil 100 m into the 'Lost World' or float through the 'Haggas Honking Holes'?➤➤ *For Sleeping, Eating and other listings, see pages 227-230.*

Ins and outs

Getting there **Intercity**, T09-638 5700, www.intercitycoach.co.nz and **Nakedbus.com** are among several bus companies that run a regular service north and south to Te Awamutu, Otorohanga, Te Kuiti and Waitomo from Hamilton. Otorohonga and Te Kuiti are also on the main Auckland to Wellington rail line, T0800-872467. For transport to the **Waitomo Caves**, see page 224.

Information **Otorohanga VIC (I-Site)** ① *on the main SH3 drag at 21 Maniapoto St, T0800-122665/T07-873 8951, www.otorohanga.co.nz, Mon-Fri 0900-1730, Sat-Sun 1000-1600*, can provide internet access. **Te Kuiti VIC (I-Site)** ① *Rora St in the centre of town, T07-8788077, daily 0900-1700 (reduced hours in winter)* and **Te Awamutu VIC (I-Site)** ① *1 Gorst Av, T07-871 3259, www.teawamutuinfo.com, daily 0900-1700 (reduced hours in winter)*, can both assist with bus information, tickets and accommodation options in the area. There is also a VIC (I-Site) at the Waitomo **Museum of Caves**, see page 225.

Te Awamutu → Colour map 2, B2.

Te Awamutu is in the heart of Waikato dairy farming country and the Waipa District, which also takes in Cambridge to the east. It is most famous for its **Rose Gardens** ① *Gorst Av, across the road from the VIC*. The gardens contain hundreds of varieties which are best seen during the **Rose and Cultural Festival** held in the first two weeks of November. Local activities worth looking at here include rock climbing, with the region offering some of the North Island's best. Quad biking and horse trekking are other reliable options.

The **Te Awamutu District Museum** ① *135 Roche St, T07-872 0085, www.tamuseum.org.nz, Mon-Fri 1000-1600, Sat 1000-1300, Sun 1300-1600, free*, is a bizarre leap of time, culture and theme, with some fine examples of local *Maoritaonga* mixed with a celebration of the town's two best-loved sons – Neil and Tim Finn, of the rock bands Split Enz and Crowded House.

You can hang around – literally – at the **Wharepapa Rockfields**, about 20 km southeast of the town. The crags include the 'Froggatt Edge', which is considered the best sport-climbing crag in the North Island, with over 115 climbs. The VIC (I-Site) will give you information and directions to the fields, as will 'base', **Bryce's Wharepapa Outdoor Centre** ① *1424 Owairaka Valley Rd, T07-872 2533, www.climb.co.nz*, and the aptly named **Boulderfield Café.**

There are numerous walks around Te Awamutu, and the town also acts as the gateway to the **Pirongia Forest Park**. Dominated by the 959-m Mount Pirongia, the park offers some fine long and short walks, including the seven-hour summit track, which rewards you with great views. Again the VIC (I-Site) will provide directions and information (which is best described in the *Go Bush* leaflets or DoC's own *Pirongia Forest Park*). Alternatively, pay a visit to the home of the **DB Clydesdale Team** ⓘ *T07-871 9711, www.clydesdales.co.nz*, an impressive team of Clydesdale horses.

Otorohanga → *Colour map 2, C2.*

The small agricultural service town of 'Oto', as it is better known, is so close to Waitomo with its famous caves that it struggles to attract anything other than occasional passing tourist. However, it does fancy itself as the gateway to the caves and boasts one of the best kiwi houses and displays of native New Zealand birds in the country. If you happen to be in Oto on the second Saturday in March you may catch the **Great Kiwiana Festival**, when the streets are decked with flower baskets and the gumboot-clad locals have fun celebrating anything and everything 'kiwi'. It's worth looking at the Kiwiana Displays at various points along the main street. They are very well presented and chronicle a range of kiwi icons, heritage and heroes from Sir Edmund Hillary to rugby and pavlova. The VIC (I-Site) has a locations leaflet.

Established in 1971, the **Otorohanga Kiwi House and Native Bird Park** ⓘ *Alex Telfer Drive, T07-873 7391, www.kiwihouse.org.nz, daily 0900-1630, $16, child $4*, is one of the oldest native bird and reptile parks in the country, housing over 50 species, including three of the four known species of kiwi. It maintains the delicate balance of visitor attraction and conservation activity, attracting thousands of people each year, yet behind the scenes, successfully breeding more than 65 kiwi since 1975. The park's main attraction is the unique double nocturnal house where you are almost certain to see a kiwi going about its fascinating and comical hunt for food. Back outside, once your eyes have readjusted to daylight, you can go on to see a number of raptors, waterfowl and reptiles, including the prehistoric tuatara and cheeky native parrot, the kea. The walk culminates with a large walk-in aviary where other rare birds can be spotted. Throughout the park there are also some fine examples of native trees.

Te Kuiti → *Colour map 2, C2.*

Te Kuiti is fairly unremarkable but is often used as a base for the Waitomo Caves, 19 km to the north. It is a small provincial town known as the sheep-shearing capital of New Zealand (witness the rather grotesque statue at the southern end of town). For a number of years it was home and refuge to the rebellious east coast Maori chief Te Kooti who built the highly aesthetic **Te Tokanganui-o-noho marae** at the south end of Rora Street. Also on Rora Street is the magnificent **Te Kuititanga-o-nga- Whakaaro Millennium Pavilion**, which is next to the railway, near the VIC (I-Site). Its carvings and stained and sandblasted window designs are great works of art. The big event of the year is the annual **Te Kuiti Muster** in April when the town celebrates its reputation with sheep-shearing championships, the 'bloated sheep race' and street celebrations. There are some fine gardens in the area, outlined in the free *King Country Gardens* leaflet available from the VIC (see page 222).

Waitomo and the caves ●●▲ ▸▸ *pp227-230.*

The district of Waitomo ('wai' water and 'tomo' hole), with its underground wonder-world of limestone caves, is the region's (and one of the North Island's) biggest tourist attractions. Above ground, the typical farmland and the tourist village itself almost completely belie what is hidden below. Although only the geologically trained eye would suspect it, there is an astonishing network of over 360 recorded caves in the area, the longest over 14 km. If you don't mind getting wet, you should promise yourself that you will try at least one of the amazing underground activities, beyond the highly commercial tour of Glow-worm Cave. Wherever you go, it is pretty unforgettable.

Ins and outs

Getting there To get to the Waitomo Caves by bus, the **Waitomo Shuttle Caves Connection**, T07-873 8279, $10 one way, operates a regular service from 0900-1730, between Otorohanga's bus depot, train station, motels, backpacker hostels, motorparks and Waitomo. The **Waitomo Wanderer**, T03-4779083, www.waitomotours.co.nz, $40 ($68 return), runs a daily service from Rotorua. It departs Rotorua at 0730 and arrives in Waitomo at 1000, departing Waitomo again at 1545. **Intercity**, **Newmans**, T09-583 5780 and **Great Sights**, T0800-744487, all offer highly commercial day trips to the Glow-worm Cave from Auckland and Rotorua; shop around for the best deal. **Magic Traveller Buses** and **Kiwi Experience** (see Essentials, page 62) allow more flexibility than the day-trip option. The best idea is to get to Otorohanga on a standard Intercity bus and get to Waitomo independently from there. If coming by car, note there is no fuel available in Waitomo Village.

Tourist information Waitomo Museum of Caves VIC (I-Site) ① T0800-474839/ T07-878 7640, www.waitomo.org.nz and www.waitomo-museum.co.nz, daily 0845- 1930, (reduced hours in winter) $6, child free, is at the heart of operations in the small tourist village of Waitomo. Almost all the above-ground attractions, below-ground activity operators, booking offices and tourist amenities are within walking distance. Although compact it can be confusing, so the best bet is to absorb the information at the VIC (I-Site) and take your time. There are numerous and often very similar activities on offer. Let the staff book on your behalf, or go to the relevant tour operator for more information. There is a village store attached to the **Waitomo Adventures** booking office (next to the VIC/I-Site), that sells limited supplies. The VIC (I-Site) has stamps, internet access, ATM and currency exchange.

Sights

Glow-worm Cave ① 39 Waitomo Caves Rd, 8 km, T0800-456922/T07-878 8227, www.waitomo caves.co.nz, tours every 30 mins 0900-1700, arrive early, $39, child $18, cave combo ticket (Glow-worm and Aranui) $65, child $28, is Waitomo's biggest attraction, but it is also the most commercial. During the day, lines of buses park outside and group after group are herded underground. A local Maori, Tane Tinorau, and English surveyor, Fred Mace, first extensively explored the caves in 1887. Further explorations eventually led to the opening of the cave to tourists in 1889. They now attract almost 250,000 visitors annually. The highlight of the 45-minute tour – the silent, almost religious homage to see the glow-worm galaxy by boat – is well worth it, especially if you have never seen these amazing insect larvae before.

Aranui Cave ① 3 km west of Glow-worm Cave near the Ruakuri Scenic Reserve, tours hourly 1000-1500 and limited to groups of 20, $39, child $18; cave combo ticket (Aranui and Glow-worm), $65, child $28; book at Glow-worm Cave or the VIC, offers a far more realistic experience. With effective lighting, the colour and variety of the stalactites and stalagmites, and the sound of a thousand drips of water, you can let your imagination run wild and emerge satisfied that you have experienced a real limestone cave.

Te Kooti

Te Kooti – or Rikirangi Te Turuki – (1830-1893) could arguably be considered the William Wallace (Braveheart) of Maoridom.

Born near Gisborne, of a good family but of no particular chiefly rank, he was given a sound education at the Waerenga-a-hika Mission School before becoming a horse-breaker and later a seaman on a small schooner trading the east coast of the North Island. During the Maori uprising and siege of Waerenga-a-hika in 1865, Te Kooti actually supported the pakeha, but was accused of supplying the Hauhau Maori rebels with ammunition and intelligence regarding the positions of colonial Government troops.

Without trial and after being essentially set up by a local pakeha-allied Maori chief, he was exiled to the Chatham Islands with a group of Hauhau rebels in 1866. Te Kooti had constantly protested his innocence, but his claims were ignored. During his two years on the Chathams Te Kooti studied the New Testament and, after claiming he had experienced a Divine revelation, established the tenets of his own 'Ringatu' faith. Convinced that the government had no intention of releasing him, Te Kooti and a small group of other exiles captured a ship and forced the crew to take them back to the east coast of the North Island. Now a fugitive and considered dangerous, he was immediately pursued by government forces. Again, after writing to the government and claiming his innocence, his protestations were ignored. Given little choice, Te Kooti had to fight and, gathering considerable support, he did so with a vengeance.

In a fierce battle at Matawhero against a large force commanded by Colonel Whitmore, he and his men killed 33 Europeans and 37 allied Maori. Still outnumbered and closely pursued he retreated to the Urewera Forest. Ropata Wahawaha, who was a Maori chief allied to Whitmore, executed 120 of Te Kooti's men. For the following three years Te Kooti was relentlessly pursued and harried not only by government forces, but also European colonials and allied Maori tribes. In 1872 he sought refuge in the Waikato where the Maori 'King Movement' had been established by fellow Maori rebels. There he spent much time peacefully, still proclaiming his original innocence as well as consolidating and spreading the word of his Ringatu religion.

Te Kooti was finally pardoned in 1883 and died back on the east coast, 10 years later – a free man. To this day his Ringatu religion lives on in the Bay of Plenty and his memory in the hearts of all Maori.

Sights and activities above ground A fine insight into the area can be found at the **Museum of Caves** ① VIC (I-Site), T07-878 7640, www.waitomo-museum.co.nz, daily 0830-1700, 1730 in summer, $6, child, free entry with some activities. Considered the best limestone cave museum in the world, it offers interesting and highly informative displays about cave formation, the history surrounding the local caves and the natural history, including the spectacular and intriguing glow-worms. If you are claustrophobic and shudder at the very thought of going underground then there is also an audio- visual display and even a fake cave to crawl through.

The **Waitomo Walkway** (three hours return), begins opposite Glow-worm Cave and follows the Waitomo Stream, taking in a number of limestone features before arriving at the

The formation of limestone caves (karst)

Limestone is a fossil rock made from the layered remains of countless marine animals. The limestone around Waitomo was therefore formerly the seabed, formed about 30 million years ago. Over the millennia these layers have been raised by the action of the earth's plates. In some places the limestone is over 200 m thick. Through its gradual uprising the limestone bends and buckles creating a network of cracks and joints. As rainwater drains into these cracks it mixes with small amounts of carbon dioxide in the air and soil forming a weak acid. This acid slowly dissolves the limestone and the cracks and joints widen. Over time small streams flow through converging cracks and eventually form underground caves.

Once these caves are created, the same acidic water seeps from the cave walls or drips from the roof, leaving a minute deposit of limestone crystal. Slowly these deposits form stalactites, stalagmites and other cave features. The size and rate of their formation depends on the rate of flow. Stalactites form from the drips falling from the ceiling of the cave and stalagmites grow up as the drips fall to the floor. When the two join, pillars are formed; when they spiral around they are called helictites.

Various minerals in the soil like iron oxide can add colouration to the formations. The growth rates of caves and limestone features vary considerably according on topography, vegetation, and of course the weather. It is also important to realize that, like everything else, the caves have a 'lifespan', eventually collapsing to form gorges, holes or arches. The 'Lost World' near Waitomo is a fine example of part of a cave system that collapsed in on itself. These caves are also home to a unique range of plants and animals of which the New Zealand glow-worm is the most spectacular example.

Ruakuri Scenic Reserve. This reserve encompasses a short walk that is hailed as one of New Zealand's best. Although it does not deserve quite that billing, it is well worth it, with a circular track taking in interesting caves and natural limestone bridges, hidden amongst lush, native bush. At night, just before the path crosses the stream, you can see a small 'scintilla' of glow-worms. These are the only glow-worms you'll see around here for free, so take a torch.

Another popular walk is the **Opapaka Pa Walk**, which takes about 45 minutes return and is 1 km east of Waitomo. The view is memorable and there are interpretation points explaining about the *pa* and the medicinal uses Maori made of surrounding flora.

Woodlyn Park ① *T07-878 6666, www.woodlynpark.co.nz, shows are staged on demand, book first, $25, child $15*, is the above-ground entertainment 'must see' in Waitomo, if not the region. Like the Driving Creek railway in the Coromandel it is a typical example of Kiwi ingenuity. The 'show', hosted by ex-shearer Barry Woods or staff, is an informative and interactive interpretation of old and modern-day Kiwi country life.

About 500 m north, down Waitomo Valley Road from Woodlyn Park, in Waitomo Village, is the **Shearing Shed** ① *T07-878 8371, shows daily at 1245, free, shop daily 0900-1630*, where cute Angora bunnies are cuddled to within an inch of their little lives and then given a short back and sides so that their highly-prized fur can be used for knitting. Still on the animal theme, the **Altura Garden and Wildlife Park** ① *4 km south of Waitomo village on Fullerton Rd, T07-878 5278/T027-2000091, www.alturapark.co.nz daily* *summer 1000- 1700, $12, child $5*, provides a diversion if you have kids or wish to stay above ground. Horse trekking is available from $50 for half an hour to $80 for 1½ hours.

Waitomo to Kawhia

The **Marokopa Road**, which winds its way to Te Anga and the small coastal town of Marokopa, before heading north to Kawhia, is a long but pleasant trip with a number of worthwhile stops on the way. If you have your own wheels the first stop should be the slight diversion to see the impressive view looking back towards Waitomo from 3 km down Waipuna Road. The road is on the left, 11 km from Waitomo. Once back on the main road sit back and enjoy the scenery until you reach the **Mangapohue Natural Bridge Scenic Reserve**. Here a short streamside walk (10 minutes) will take you to an impressive natural limestone arch, complete with unusual stalagmites. This arch was once part of a large cave and it is hard to imagine that the rather inconspicuous little stream essentially created it all. About 5 km further on are the **Piripiri Caves**, accessed by a short but stiff climb up a boardwalk. These caves are in stark contrast to the well-lit, tourist-friendly offerings in Waitomo. They are dark and forbidding, and the path into them is steep and quite dangerous. If you are alone do not venture far and take a torch.

A little further on and about 35 km from Waitomo are the beautiful 32-m **Marokopa Falls**, which have to rate as amongst the best in the North Island, though due to their remote location they are not well known. A 15-minute walks descends to a lookout. If you go beyond the lookout to take photos prepare to get very muddy. From the falls it is a short distance to the small settlement of **Te Anga** where there is a tavern for lunch.

From Te Anga you have the choice of a very scenic road heading north to Kawhia or carrying on to the coast and **Marokopa**, a small, remote fishing village with black-sand beaches. From Marokopa you can to drive to **Awakino**, another small coastal settlement, on the main SH3 New Plymouth road, but it is long, unsealed and fairly arduous.

⊚ Waikato South listings

For Sleeping and Eating price codes and other relevant information, see Essentials pages 44-50.

⊜ Sleeping

Te Awamutu *p222*

Te Awamutu and the southern Waikato is considered the farmstay capital of New Zealand and there are over 500 B&Bs and farmstay beds in the area. It is therefore a great place to experience New Zealand rural life, see Essentials, page 45. The VIC has listings of these and some modern local motels.

B-D Road Runner Motel and Holiday Park, 141 Bond Rd, T07-871 7420, www.roadrunneraccommodation.co.nz.

Otorohanga *p223*

Accommodation in is limited; ask at the VIC.

A Palm Court Motel, corner of Clarke and Maniapoto sts (SH3), T0800-686764, T07-8737122. Modern, clean and comfortable.

C-D Oto-Kiwi Backpackers, 1 Sangro Cres, T07-873 6022, http://otokiwibakpak.tripod.com/home.html. Has a good reputation. Facilities include campsites and internet. Also offers farm tours and trips, including to the caves and back and some in-house fun with a karaoke studio.

Motorcamps and campsites

D Otorohanga Holiday Park, 12 Huiputea Dr, T07-873 7253, www.kiwiholidaypark.co.nz. Full range of facilities including a camp kitchen.

Te Kuiti *p223*

The VIC lists local B&Bs and farmstays.
C-D Casara Mesa Backpackers, Mangarino Rd, T07-878 6697, casara@xtra.co.nz. Comfortable with good en suite doubles as well as the usual share options. Breakfasts, transport and bike hire available.

Motorcamps and campsites
C-D Te Kuiti Camp Ground, Hinerangi St, T07-878 8966.

Waitomo and the caves *p223*

There is a wide range of accommodation here, but in summer pre-booking is essential.
AL-A Waitomo Express, Hobbit Motel and **The Waitanic**, 1177 Waitomo Valley Rd, T07-878 6666, www.woodlynpark.co.nz. If it is the unusual you are looking for, look no further than Barry Woods at Woodlyn Park (1 km down Waitomo Valley Rd) and his converted train carriage, hobbit motel, or ex-WWII aircraft accommodation. The latest is a boat.
AL-D Waitomo Caves Hotel, T07-878 8240, www.waitomocaveshotel.co.nz. On the hill overlooking the village this historic, if somewhat staid, hotel offers a wide range of comfortable standard, en suite or family rooms and has a restaurant attached.
A Abseil Inn B&B, 709 Waitomo Caves Rd, T07-878 7815. The aptly named Abseil Inn is up an 'exciting' driveway within walking (or climbing) distance of all amenities. Tidy, clean and classy decor. En suite double and queen rooms.
A Te Tiro, 970 Caves-Te Anga Rd, T07-878 6328, www.waitomocavesnz.com. 2 modern self-contained timber frame cottages (sleeping 1-5) in the picturesque hills 10 km west of Waitomo. Good value.
A-B Caves Motor Inn, on SH3 (728), just south of Waitomo Caves turning T07-873 8109, www.cavesmotorinn.co.nz. Fine motel choice with a good restaurant/bar.
B-D YHA Juno Hall Backpackers, T07-878 7649, www.junowaitomo.co.nz. This is a great log-cabin style hostel 1 km from the village, with a pool and log fire. Courtesy van.

B-D Kiwi Paka Waitomo, behind the VIC and Tavern, T07-878 3395, www.yha.co.nz. The best backpacker hostel with an emphasis on providing quality budget accommodation rather than bunks and dorms. There is a full range of rooms and some separate chalets on offer, from double to shared, some with en suite. Facilities are above average with a hot pool and a fine in-house pizzeria/café.

Motorcamps and campsites
A-D Waitomo Caves Top Ten Holiday Park, T07-878 7639, www.waitomopark.co.nz. A modern, convenient and very friendly motorcamp right in the heart of the village. Spacious, great facilities including internet, pool and spa. Possibly the best showers of any park in the country! Recommended.

Waitomo to Kawhia *p227*
B-C Marokopa camping ground, Marokopa, T07-876 7444. Basic campsite with cottages, backpacker cabins, powered sites, a very basic shop and good showers.

🍴 Eating

Te Awamutu *p222*
🍴 **The Alehouse Bar and Cafe**, 32 Arawata St, T07-871 8761. Locally recommended.
🍴-🍴 **Ngaroto Nurseries Café**, 208 Ngaroto Rd, 5 km north of town, T07-871 5668. Provides a pleasant rural lunch or coffee option.

Otorohanga *p223*
🍴-🍴 **Thirsty Weta**, Maniapoto St, T07-873 6699. Daily. Generous pub grub.
🍴-🍴 **The Little Tart**, 13 Maniapoto St, , T07-873 6611. Mon-Fri0700-1500, Sat 1000-1400. With a name like that it's hard not to ignore! Outdoor seating.

Te Kuiti *p223*
There are numerous rather forgettable cafés and eateries on Rora St and the best bet is:
🍴 **Riverside Lodge Café Bar and Restaurant**, east down King St, then turn

right before the bridge, T07-878 8027, Tue-Sun 1230-late.

Waitomo and the caves *p223*
There is a village store next door to Waitomo Luminosa, open until 1900, but you are advised to stock up before arriving.

Caves Motor Inn, 8 km east of Waitomo Village (see Sleeping). Good value for dinner.

Roselands Restaurant, 3 km from Waitomo Village up Fullerton Rd, T07-878 7611. Daily in summer 1100-1400. The best place for lunch, specializing in hearty BBQs and salads in a lovely garden setting.

Waitomo Caves Hotel, see Sleeping, page 228. Decent à la carte traditional cuisine.

Waitomo Tavern, near the VIC, T07-878 8448. The place for cheap and basic pub grub and a pint with the locals.

Cafés
Morepork Pizzeria and Café, at the Kiwi Paka (see Sleeping, above). The best- value evening meal in town (especially pizza).

There are 3 other cafés in Waitomo run by the operators: the Waitomo Adventures' **Cavelands**, village centre; Legendary Black Water Rafting Company's **Long Black**, 2 km east, which does a fine breakfast for around $12; and **Glow-worm Caves Café**, just west of the village. All are open daily from 0800-1730 (later in summer).

▲ Activities and tours

Te Awamutu *p222*
Castle Rock Adventures, 1250 Owairaka Valley Rd, T07-8722509, www.castlerock adventure.co.nz. Full or half-day climbing tuition, abseiling and self-guided mountain bike hire. Also has a campsite with full facilities.

Waitomo and the caves *p223*
There is a wide range of choice and competition is fierce; research the options carefully and take your time. Whatever activity or operator you choose, it will usually

be money well spent. Note that there are also price reductions for combinations with some also offering free museum entry. A combination of trips that offer value for money and a high level of safety and professionalism is the Lost World Epic followed by the Haggas Honking Holes.

Legendary Black Water Rafting Company, T0800-228464, www.waitomo.com offer two options:

Black Abyss, 5 hrs, 2½ hrs underground, $193, price includes museum, showers, soup and bagels – this is one of the more adventurous trips, involving a 30-m abseil; and **Black Labyrinth**, 3 hrs, 1 hr underground, $99. Price includes museum entry, showers, soup and bagels. This trip involves floating down a subterranean river by a waterfall, the cave formations and glow-worms.

Rap, Raft 'n' Rock, T0800-228372/ T07-8739149, www.caveraft.com. Offer 5 caving adventures in one 5-hr tour taking in a 27-m (80 ft) abseil into a cave, then a float through a river system, some rock climbing and a great display of glow-worms. Altogether excellent value.

Waitomo Adventures, T0800-Waitomo/ T07-8787788, www.waitomo.co.nz, offer the following trips:

Haggas Honking Holes, $194, 4 hrs, 2 hrs underground, this trip involves an abseil, rock climbing and an intimate encounter with a waterfall, as well lots of crawling and scenery.

St Benedict's Cavern, $130, 3½ hrs, 1½ hrs underground, this cave was discovered in 1962 but was only opened commercially in 2003, said to be the prettiest cave in the region and had parts of it christened 'The Hobbit Holes' long before *Lord of the Rings* was filmed in New Zealand – exploration of the cave involves 2 abseils and a flying fox.

Tumu Tumu Toobing, $130, 4 hrs, about 2 hrs underground, ideal trip if you are limited for time, this is the least strenuous of Waitomo Adventures' tours and involves a highly entertaining walk, swim and float down an underwater stream with glow-worms and interesting rock formations.

Lost World Epic, dinner included, $355, 7 hrs, 5 hrs underground (or 4 hrs, 2 hrs underground). This has to be one of the best and most unusual full-day activity trips in NZ. It involves a descent into a gaping hole and is followed by the exhilarating and highly entertaining 3-hr negotiation of the cave system and underground river. It involves walking, climbing, swimming, wading, jumping and even racing, with the final stage a quiet reflection on the trip under a galaxy of glow-worms, before emerging, like some intrepid latter-day explorer, at the river entrance. If you can splash out, it's a once-in-a-lifetime trip.

Spellbound, T0800-773552, www.spellbound.co.nz. Offer a mainly eco-based adventure for those who want to remain dry, with a trip into a cave system, 2-3 hrs, 2 hrs underground, $50, child $25 (includes museum entry).

Caveworld, 277 Te Anga Rd, T07-878 6577/ T0800-228396, www.caveworld.co.nz. Offers its own range of options such as the exclusive 'Baby Grand' and also a night glow abseil from $175.

Waikato East → *Colour map 2, B2.*

The English-looking countryside of the eastern Waikato is among the most lucrative areas in New Zealand; over the decades, many a fortune has been secured through its fertile soils. However, other than the hot pools in Te Aroha or horse studs surrounding the pleasant town of Cambridge, there was always a paucity of major tourist attractions, until, that is, a character called 'Frodo' arrived. In 1999 at the behest of 'Lord of the Rings' director Peter Jackson, location researchers scoured the area for a plot of land that suited the universal image of Tolkien's 'Hobbiton'. Near the quiet agricultural service town of Matamata, a discreet plot was secured and it proved to be the perfect setting for one of the most complex sets created for the film trilogy. Despite the fact that almost nothing remains, the much hyped 'Tours to Hobbiton' remain a major draw. ▶▶ *For Sleeping, Eating and other listings, see pages 233-234.*

Ins and outs
Getting there Busit Services, T0800-4287 5463, links Hamilton and Thames (via Paeroa) most days, arriving at Thames VIC (I-Site). **Intercity**, T09-913 6100, offers services to Matamata from Hamilton or Tauranga stopping outside the Matamata VIC (I-Site). Most of the main bus operators heading north or south on SH1 stop in Cambridge. For local bus information and services to/from Hamilton contact **Busit** or the VIC (i-Site).

Tourist information Paeroa VIC (I-Site) ① *2 Seymour St, T07-862 8636, www.pae roa.org.nz, Mon-Fri 0900-1700, Sat-Sun 0930-1430*. **Te Aroha VIC (I-Site)** ① *in the original Te Aroha Hot Springs Domain, ticket office at 102 Whitaker St, T07-8848052, www.tearohanz.co.nz, Mon-Fri 0930-1700, Sat-Sun 0930-1600*. The enthusiastic, friendly but under-resourced staff will provide all your local information needs including maps and advice about accommodation. **Matamata VIC (I-Site)** ① *45 Broadway, T07- 888 7260, www.matamatanz.co.nz, Mon-Fri 0830-1700, Sat-Sun 1000-1500*, can assist with transport and accommodation enquiries or bookings, has internet facilities and also acts as agents for the 'Hobbiton' tour. **Cambridge VIC (I-Site)** ① *corner of Queen and Victoria sts, T07-8233456, www.cambridgeinfo.co.nz, Mon-Fri 0900-1700, Sat-Sun 1000-1600*, takes travel bookings and offers bike hire. Don't leave without the free *Cambridge Welcomes You* booklet. **Tirau VIC (I-Site)** ① *next to the Big Sheep in the Big Dog, T07-883 1202, www.tirauinfo.co.nz, daily 0900-1700*, and **Tokoroa VIC (I-Site)** ① *SH1, T07-886 8872, www.southwaikatonz.com*, can both can assist with enquiries, bookings and details about local walks and attractions.

Paeroa → *Colour map 2, B2.*
Aside from being home to 'Lemon and Paeroa' (L&P), New Zealand's national soft drink, this old, once thriving port has little to offer. There's the **L&P Café and Bar** ① *corner of SH2 and Seymour St, T07-862 7773, www.cafeandbar.co.nz,* for a light lunch, an ice cream or a coffee, **Primrose Hill**, for views back across the Hauraki Plains, and, if you're here on the third Sunday in February, there's the '**Battle of the Streets**', a popular annual event attracting bikers from far and wide. In the same month is the **Pipe Band Tattoo**.

Te Aroha → *Colour map 2, B2.*
In 1875 Te Aroha was little more than a single house in the shadow of the mountain, occupied by Irish pioneer Charlie Lipsey, and subsequently known as 'Lipseytown'. With the discovery of gold nearby in 1880 the settlement expanded, but only temporarily, as the mining returns proved relatively poor. Later, with the discovery of the hot soda water geyser, the Hot Springs Domain were born and today this remains the jewel in the crown of this mainly agricultural service town. Incidentally, Mount Te Aroha in Maori means 'Mountain of Love', and comes from the story of a Bay of Plenty Maori chief who once made those utterings in relief after getting lost and seeing the glorious views south, homewards towards his *pa*.

There are two major attractions in Te Aroha, **Mount Te Aroha** and the **Hot Springs Domain**. The four- to five-hour return climb up the 952-m summit can be rewarded with a dip in the pools, providing the perfect marriage of the two. The mountain path is accessed at the rear of the Domain. The Whakapipi or **Bald Spur Lookout** about halfway up is easily reached after about 45 minutes and offers a fine view west. But, if you can, carry on to the summit and take in the spectacular 360° view, north across the Coromandel and south to the Bay of Plenty. For track information see the *Te Aroha Mountain Tracks* leaflet from the VIC (I-Site). There is also a popular 12-km mountain bike track (circuit) adjacent to the springs, but no bike hire outlet in town. However, the YHA offers free bike hire to its guests.

On your return by foot or pedal you can fall straight into the **Te Aroha Leisure Pools and Spa** ① *near the track entrance, T07-884 8717, www.tearohapools.co.nz, daily 1000-2200, from $6, private pools available.* The pools, which were originally created in the late 1800s, are the world's only naturally flowing hot soda spa pools.

Behind the pools is the **Mokena Geyser**, which is one of very few soda water geysers in the world. Named after the Maori chief and benefactor of the land on which the Domain now stands, the geyser shoots 3-m high about every half-hour.

Also on the Domain is the **Te Aroha Museum** ① *T07-884 4427, www.tearoha-museum.com, daily 1200-1500, $3.* Housed in the original bathhouse (which was once said to be possibly the most attractive building in the country and 'the sanatorium of New Zealand'), it now contains some interesting displays on the mining and agricultural development of the town. Also of historical interest, but not housed in the museum, is the 1712 Queen Anne pipe organ in **St Mark's Church** ① *T07- 884 8052.* The town has a fairly unremarkable arts and crafts trail, and a gardens and heritage trail; ask for leaflets at the VIC (I-Site). For a pleasant easy grade short walk there is the wildlife-rich **Howarth Memorial Wetlands Walk**, on the banks of the Waihou River. The VIC (I-Site) can give you directions and a leaflet.

Matamata → *Colour map 2, B2.*
Matamata lies in the heart of Waikato's rich and fertile agricultural landscape and is the epitome of affluent rural Kiwi life. Large ranches and spacious farmsteads would seem to suggest that the domestic and export agricultural worth of New Zealand is alive and well.

Although it is pleasant enough, there was never a great deal here to attract the tourist – that is until a film about a little hobbit called Frodo came along.

Long before *Lord of the Rings* hit the world's movie screens, a small plot of private farmland close to Matamata was being transformed into the magical village of **Hobbiton**, home to two of the film's key characters Frodo and Sam. Although there was a lot of hype about the set you must be under no illusions as to what remains. As with all the 'Rings' sets throughout the country there were strict conditions set in place to ensure almost all traces were removed. There are some remnants, the highlight being over-grown 'Hobbit Holes' but now, in essence, a trip to Peter Jackson's Hobbiton is more an exercise in the imagination than reality. But that said, particularly for stalwart fans, the guides do a good job of answering questions and setting the scene and over all the scenery and experience is certainly memorable. ① *Rings Scenic Tours depart regularly from the VIC, T07-888 6838, www.hobbitontours.com, from $58, child $26*

Elsewhere in Matamata a few of the old, low-key attractions remain. The historic and well-armoured landmark **Firth Tower**, on Tower Road, was built in 1882 by Yorkshireman Josiah Firth, and is the town's other main attraction. The tower is the centrepiece of the **historical museum** ① *T07-888 8369, daily 1000-1600, $5, child $1*, which explains the intriguing history. About 6 km from Matamata, the **Opal Hot Springs** ① *T07-888 8198*, are a popular spot, and compete with Te Aroha's Domain, with a pool complex of mineral and private spa pools.

Cambridge → *Colour map 2, B2.*

Also on the Waikato River, 20 km south east of Hamilton on SH1, is the pleasant country town of Cambridge, a popular stop while heading south to Taupo or beyond and recognized nationally as a centre for thoroughbred horse studs, antiques, arts and crafts.

The VIC (I-Site) has some excellent leaflets outlining the numerous antique, art and craft outlets in the town. The most famous is the **Cambridge Country Store** ① *92 Victoria St, T07-827 8715, Mon-Sat 0830-1700, Sun 0900-1700*, which is housed in an old church. It has a wide range of crafts including native New Zealand wood pieces, ceramics, knitwear, Maori carvings, wine and food. The **All Saint's Café** attached serves fresh snacks and home baking. For horse and pony fanatics the **Cambridge Thoroughbred Lodge** ① *SH1, Karapiro, 6 km south of the town, T07-827 8118, www.cambridgethoroughbredlodge.co.nz, daily 1000-1500, $12, child $5*, puts on an entertaining hour-long 'New Zealand Horse Magic Show' where a range of horse breeds are shown and perform to order with much horsey humour and audience participation. Call to confirm show times. For a more thorough equestrian insight you might like to consider a 'Thoroughbred Stud Tour' with **Barry Lee Bloodstock Ltd** ① *T07-827 5910, www.barrylee.co.nz, book at the VIC*. The tour costs $120 for up to four people and lasts an hour taking in four studs, so it's good value.

The small **Cambridge Museum** ① *Victoria St, Mon-Sat 1000-1600, Sun 1000-1400*, is housed in the old courthouse. There are a number of good walks in and around Cambridge. For a short walk, the **Te Koutu Lake** on Albert Street is very picturesque, while the tramp up **Maungatautari Mountain** (at the terminus of Maungatautari and Hicks Road, off SH1, a few kilometres south of town) is a more strenuous affair rewarded with fine views of the river and beyond. The mountain is also a very important spot for native wildlife after the creation of 'Warrenheip' – an ecological 'island' of native bush, fenced off and cleared of introduced predators before being left to regenerate and being restocked with native birds, including kiwi. For more information, contact the **Maunga Trust** ① *T07-823 7455, www.maungatrust.org*.

Tirau → *Colour map 2, B2.*

Tirau is at the junction of SH1 and SH27 – the two main routes south – making it a popular coffee stop. The highlight of the town is not hard to miss and comes in the form of a giant corrugated iron sheep and a dog on the Main Road. Its popularity has led to the creation of other **corrugated iron art** by local artist Steven Clothier. The sheep houses the **Big Sheep Wool Gallery** ① *T07-883 1954*, which sells an array of New Zealand-made woolly products and kitsch sheep souvenirs. There is a range of other tourist-orientated shops on Main Street selling various New Zealand products.

Putaruru and Tokoroa → *Colour map 2, B-C3.*

Tokoroa is a major forestry base and takes its name from a Maori chief who was killed during the Maori Land Wars of the mid 1800s. The main attraction here are the various walks and mountain biking tracks in the surrounding forest. **Hatupatu Rock** is an interesting place steeped in Maori legend. In Putaruru the **Timber Museum** ① *3 km south of the village on SH1, T07-883 7621, daily 0900-1600, $8, child $3*, is the main draw. It has a steam engine and some very ancient native logs.

Waikato East listings

For Sleeping and Eating price codes and other relevant information, see Essentials pages 44-50.

● Sleeping

Te Aroha *p231*

Accommodation is fairly limited in Te Aroha.
AL Aroha Mountain Lodge, 5 Boundary St T07-884 8134, www.arohamountainlodge.co.nz. A lodge-style B&B with 6 luxury en suite rooms or the fully self-contained Miners Cottage with 3 double rooms right next to the spas and starting point for the mountain walks.
B Te Aroha Motel, 108 Whitaker St, T07-884 9417, www.tearohamotel.co.nz. The town's lone motel.
B-D Te Aroha Holiday Park and Backpackers, 217 Stanley Rd, T07-884 9567. Basic facilities and a mineral pool.
C-D Te Aroha YHA Hostel, Miro St, T07-884 8739. Friendly 11-bed hostel where cooking is a speciality. Free bikes.

Matamata *p231*

B-D Lazy Tramper, 282 Old Kaimai Rd St, T07-543 3185, www.thelazytramper.co.nz. Tidy, rural-based backpacker hostel set in a former schoolhouse, large living area with

open fire, well-equipped kitchens and all the usual room configurations.

Cambridge *p232*

LL Maungatautari Lodge, 844 Maunga-tautari Rd (6 km south of Cambridge, 3 km off SH1), T07-827 2220, www.malodge.com. Modern purpose-built boutique hotel on a working farm and thoroughbred breeding operation in the heart of the Waikato. A choice of suites or individually decorated villas with 5-star facilities. Extensive gardens and a swimming pool. In-house restaurant offers innovative and contemporary Kiwi cuisine with an organic edge. Horse riding, massage and beauty therapies also available.
L Houseboat, T07-827 2195, www.house boatescape.co.nz. For something different consider a self-drive houseboat, from $600 for 2 nights excluding fuel.
L Thornton House B&B, 2 Thornton Rd, T07-827 7567, www.thorntonhouse.co.nz. A very tastefully renovated historic 1902 villa with 2 well-appointed rooms. Central.
A Bubble Lodge Homestay, 64 Cowley Drive, T07-823 4046, www.bubble lodge.co.nz. Intriguingly named and good-value operation in suburban Cambridge, with modern tasteful decor, run

by a friendly, cat-crazy couple.
A Cambridge Mews, 20 Hamilton Rd,
T07-8277166, www.cambridgemews.co.nz.
Perhaps the best motel in town.
A No1 Motels on Victoria, 87-89 Victoria St,
T07-823 1467, www.no1motels.co.nz. New
and affordable centrally located motel.

Motorcamps and campsites
B-D Cambridge Motor Park, 32 Scott St,
T07-827 5649, www.cambridgemotor
park.co.nz. Only 1 km from town. Camp
kitchen.

Tokoroa *p233*
**B-D Tokoroa Motor Camp and
Backpackers**, 22 Sloss Rd, T07-886 6642,
www.tokoroamotorcamp.co.nz. If you are
looking to park up for the night this is your
best bet.

🍴 Eating

Te Aroha *p231*
🍴 **Ironique Café and Bar**, 159 Whitaker St,
T07-884 8489. Daily from 1000. This place
stands out for its traditional à la carte menu,
light lunches and good coffee.

Matamata *p231*
🍴 **Workmans Café and Bar**, 52 Broadway,

T07-888 5498. The best place in Hobbiton,
open for breakfast, lunch and dinner Tue-Sun.

Cambridge *p232*
🍴-🍴 **Frans Café**, 62 Victoria St, T07-827 3946.
Mon-Sat. Worth trying for lunch or dinner.

Tirau *p233*
🍴 **Loose Goose**, 7 Main Rd, T07-883 1515.
Closed Tue. More impressive on the outside
than inside but still a good choice.

⛰ Activities and tours

Cambridge *p232*
The Boatshed Café, on the shores of Lake
Karapiro, south on SH1 then right on Gorton
Rd and right again on Amber, T07-827 8286,
www.theboatshed.net.nz. Offers kayak hire,
3 hrs from $20.

ⓘ Directory

Te Aroha *p231*
Internet Te Aroha Library, Rewi St,
T07-889 5689.

Cambridge *p232*
Internet All Saints Café, 92 Victoria St.

Contents

Footprint features

Bay of Plenty

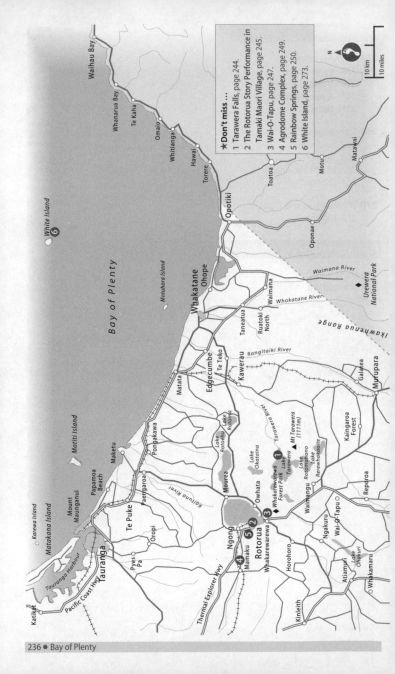

★ Don't miss ...

1 Tarawera Falls, page 244.
2 The Rotorua Story Performance in Tamaki Maori Village, page 245.
3 Wai-O-Tapu, page 247.
4 Agrodome Complex, page 249.
5 Rainbow Springs, page 250.
6 White Island, page 273.

N

10 km
10 miles

Bay of Plenty

White Island
6

Waihau Bay
Whanarua Bay
Te Kaha
Omaio
Whitianga
Hawai
Torere
Opotiki
Toatoa
Motu
Matawai
Oponae

Motuhora Island

Whakatane
Ohope
Waimana
Whokatane River
Waimana River
Urewera National Park
Ikawhenua Range

Edgecumbe
Te Teko
Kawerau
Rangitaiki River
Galatea
Murupara

Matata
Ponpakawa
Maketu
Lake Rotoma
Lake Rotoehu
Lake Rotoiti
Mourea
Owhata
Lake Rotorua
Lake Okataina
Lake Tarawera
Tarawera River
Mt Tarawera (1111m)
Lake Rotomahana
Lake Rerewhakaaite
Kaingaroa Forest
Repuroa

Papamoa Beach
Mount Maunganui
Te Puke
Paengaroa
Kaituna River
Whakarewarewa Forest Park
Waimangu
Waiotapu
Ngakuru
Wai-O-Tapu

Motiti Island
Karewa Island
Matakana Island

Tauranga
Tauranga Harbour
Pacific Coast Hwy
Katikati
Pyes Pa
Oropi
Mamaku
Ngong
Rotorua
Whakarewarewa
Horohoro
Atiamuri
Lake Okaro
Lake Ohakuri
Whakamaru
Kinleith
Thermal Explorer Hwy

1
2
3
4
5

236 ● Bay of Plenty

When Captain James Cook explored this particular stretch of the country's coast in the 18th century he christened it the Bay of Plenty. Back then a mere stretch of the legs on terra firma was no doubt enough to attain such a label. But now, for us modern-day navigators, the obvious question remains – so, is it?

Well, if statistics are anything to go by the answer is categorically yes. By population, the Bay of Plenty is the North Island's fastest-growing region, with the real estate figures of Tauranga now generally accepted as being a barometer to the health of the national economy. The region is also the most visited tourist destination in the North Island and is where the very idea of New Zealand tourism began.

Rotorua, or 'Roto-Vegas' as it is known, is the thermal and volcanic capital of New Zealand, with geysers, hot pools and vents of bubbling mud. The city also has a rich and fascinating human history. Tauranga – along with its close neighbour Mount Maunganui – is another tourist hot spot and considered the capital of the region. Its sunny climate and beaches as well as its proximity to Coromandel and Auckland, attract visitors by the bus load. Even the cruise ships have started visiting this busy port. The outlying towns, too, get their turn on the tourist merry-go-round. Proud Whakatane offers not only a lovely coast and congenial atmosphere but also its own distinct attractions. One minute you can be swimming with dolphins, the next reeling in a marlin, and the next staring down the steaming barrel of White Island's volcanic crater.

Rotorua → *Colour map 2, C3 Population: 70,000.*

Rotorua – alias 'Sulphur City' – can sometimes be smelled before it's seen, though they say you get used to it. Of all the places in the Bay of Plenty, nature has indeed given Rotorua 'plenty'. The natural thermal wonders first attracted the Maori in the 14th century and later the Europeans, though nature has not always been so kind. The violent eruption of the Tarawera volcano in 1886 led to the loss of 150 lives.

Rotorua is deserving of its 'most visited' tourist status. The city and the region probably offer more unusual sights and activities than anywhere else in New Zealand. And although, like Taupo, it is particularly famous for its thermal and volcanic features, lakes and fishing, the region offers a multitude of other activities. Here you can join in a Maori concert or gorge yourself at a Maori hangi (feast), throw yourself down a 7-m waterfall in a raft, jump out of planes, bike, walk or shop till you drop. ▸▸ *For Sleeping, Eating and other listings, see pages 251-259.*

Ins and outs

Getting there
Air **Rotorua airport** ⓘ *10 km from the town centre, on the eastern shores of Lake Rotorua, T07-345 6176, www.rotorua-airport.co.nz*, is served by **Air New Zealand Link**, T0800-737000, www.airnewzealand.co.nz, with daily flights from Auckland, Wellington and other principal domestic centres. They also offer a Sydney service. **Super Shuttle**, T0800-748885, and the main taxi companies, T07-3482444 and T07-3481111, provide transfers to and from the airport; shuttle $16 one way, taxi $25. The international airport in Hamilton (see page 212) runs a shuttle service.

Road Rotorua is reached via SH5, which branches off SH1 at Tirua from the north and Taupo from the south. It is a major destination on the signposted 'Thermal Explorer Highway' tourist route. **Intercity**, T09-583 5780, and **Nakedbus.com**, are two of several bus companies that service Rotorua daily and stop outside the VIC (I-Site) on Fenton St. The **Waitomo Wanderer**, T03-4779083, www.waitomotours.co.nz, $40 ($68 return), runs a daily service from Rotorua. It departs Rotorua at 0730 and arrives in Waitomo at 1000, departing Waitomo again at 1545, see page 224. There is a specialist **travel centre** ⓘ *T07-348 5179, www.rotoruanz.com*, within the VIC (I-Site), which handles enquiries and bookings.

Getting around
Around town **Baybus**, T0800-422 9287, www.baybus.co.nz are the principal local bus company, the main stop being on Pukuatua St. Several local shuttles vie for business in providing daily transportation to the Tamaki Maori Village, Waimangu Volcanic Valley, Waiotapu Thermal Wonderland and Waikite Valley Thermal Pools, with scheduled and flexible non-scheduled pick-ups and drop-offs available, from around $25 return. The **Geyser Link**, T0800-0004321, www.gyserlink.co.nz, leaves for most major attractions several times daily and the fare usually includes entry. Contact the VIC (I-Site) for other local operators. For a taxi, call T07-348 1111. ▸▸ *For specific tour buses, see Activities and tours, page 258.*

Tourist information
Tourism Rotorua Travel and Information ⓘ *1167 Fenton St, T07-348 5179/T0800-768678, www.rotoruanz.com, daily 0800-1800*, is one of the oldest and busiest tourist offices in the country. It is the principal base for all local information, as well as the bus

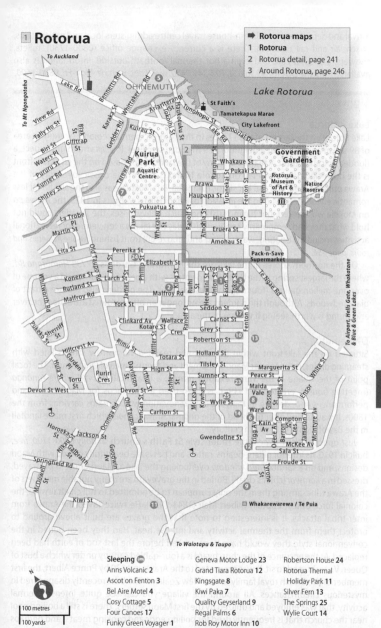

To Auckland

Lake Rd

Bennetts Rd

OHINEMUTU

St Faith's

Lake Rotorua

Tamatekapua Marae

City Lakefront

Memorial Dr

Queens Dr

To Mt Ngongotaha

View Rd

Tally Ho St

Biri St

Glittrap St

Blak St

Geddes Rd

Karaka St

Whittaker Rd

Ariariterangi St

Haukotuku St

Totohi St

Tunohopu St

Lake Rd

Waters Pl

Pururu St

Sunset Rd

Shirley St

Kuirau St

Kuirua Park

Aquatic Centre

2

Whakaue St

Rangiuru

Pukaki St

Arawa

Tutanekai

Fenton St

Hinemaru St

Rotorua Museum of Art & History

Government Gardens

Nature Reserve

Tarewa Rd

Pukuatua St

Haupapa St

La Trobe Pl

Martin St

Lita St

Pererika St

Elizabeth St

Tawa St

Whakaturu St

Ranolf St

Amohia St

Hinemoa St

Eruera St

Amohau St

Pack-n-Save Supermarket

Te Ngae Rd

To Airport, Hells Gate, Whakatane & Blue & Green Lakes

Whitworth Rd

Konene St

Rutland St

Malfroy Rd

Ann St

Philip St

Larch St

James St

King St

Ruihi

Victoria St

Eason St

Toko St

Union St

Herewini St

Seddon St

Fenton St

Pukeko St

Sheriff St

York St

Clinkard Av

Kotare St

Wallace Cres

Ranolf St

Miller St

Carnot St

Grey St

Robertson St

Holland St

Tilsley St

Sumner St

Marguerita St

Peace St

Maida Vale

Gibson St

Hilda St

White St

Ensor St

Hilcrest Av

Garden Pl

Huia St

Toru St

Puriri St

Rimu St

Totara St

High St

Arthur St

Ashley St

Kowhai St

McLean St

Wylie St

Ward St

Kain Av

Trigg Av

Compton Av

Barrott St

Obere Av

Jameson Av

McIntyre Av

Devon St West

Davidson St

Devon St

Duncan St

Carlton St

Sophia St

Gwendoline St

McKee Av

Sala St

Froude St

Tyrone St

Horogeka St

Jackson St

Oronga Rd

Old Taupo Rd

Goodwin Av

Nikau St

Galbraith Av

Springfield Rd

McDowell St

Kiwi St

Whakarewarewa / Te Puia

To Waiotapu & Taupo

100 metres
100 yards

Sleeping	
Anns Volcanic **2**	Geneva Motor Lodge **23**
Ascot on Fenton **3**	Grand Tiara Rotorua **12**
Bel Aire Motel **4**	Kingsgate **8**
Cosy Cottage **5**	Kiwi Paka **7**
Four Canoes **17**	Quality Geyserland **9**
Funky Green Voyager **1**	Regal Palms **6**
	Rob Roy Motor Inn **10**

Robertson House **24**
Rotorua Thermal Holiday Park **11**
Silver Fern **13**
The Springs **25**
Wylie Court **14**

arrival and departure point. The in-house travel centre administers local and national bus, coach, air and rail ticketing. There is a currency exchange office (0800-1730), toilets, showers, a shop, a café and even a hot thermal footbath outside. Information is also available from the **DoC** ① *99 Sala St, T07-349 7400, www.doc.govt.nz. Mon-Fri, 0800-1600.*

Sights

Lake Rotorua

Lake Rotorua is the largest of the 17 lakes in the Rotorua thermal region, covering an area of 89 sq km and sitting at a height of 279 m above sea level. It is, as you might expect, a flooded volcanic crater. A feature of many of the launch trips based on the city's lakefront is the bush-clad nature reserve of **Mokoia Island**, scene of the classic love story of the Arawa princess Hinemoa and her suitor Tutanekai. But Mokoia was also the site for far less romantic encounters. During the invasion of Hongi Hika's warriors in 1823, the Arawa *pa* on Mokoia was sacked, but having sustained such heavy losses, the invaders could not hold what they had temporarily conquered. Today the lake is a top venue for recreational activities including boating, water skiing and, above all, trout fishing. ▶▶ *See Activities and tours, page 256.*

On the northern shores of the lake are the **Hamurana Gardens** ① *733 Hamurana Rd*, where the largest spring in the North Island erupts with a beautiful clarity and a volume of over one million gallons (four million litres) an hour. The gardens also feature a tract of giant redwoods. Although the gardens are no longer an official tourist attraction the river and spring is worth seeing if you are in the area.

Ohinemutu

Situated on the lakefront within the city, and reached via narrow streets lined with steaming drains, is the former Maori settlement and thermal area of Ohinemutu. The focal point of the village is the **Tamatekapua marae**, a beautifully carved *whare runanga* (meeting house), erected in 1939. It is often used as the focus for Maori events and performances and, despite its fairly modern renovation, still contains carvings from the 1800s. It was named after the head of the original Arawa canoe which first made landfall in the Bay of Plenty in the 14th century.

Just opposite the *marae* is the Tudor-style **St Faith's Church** ① *daily 0800-1700, free*, built in 1910. Its interior pillars, beams, rafters and pews are beautifully carved with Maori designs, and on a sandblasted window overlooking the lake a 'Maori Christ' is portrayed, dressed in a *korowai* (chief's cloak). Buried in the graveyard are many notable members of the Arawa tribe, among them the only European to be admitted to full chieftainship, the colonial force officer Captain Gilbert Mair (1843-1923). He twice saved the Arawa from inter-tribal attacks. It is interesting to note that the graves are built above ground to protect them from the thermal activity and intense heat. Had they been buried in the conventional style they would have been cooked before the last sod of earth had been replaced. At the entrance of the churchyard is a four-gabled canopy under which a bust of Queen Victoria used to sit. It was presented to the Arawa in 1870 by Prince Albert, the first member of the British royal family to visit New Zealand. The bust recently disappeared in mysterious circumstances. All around the village you can see quite intense thermal activity, that was enjoyed and utilized by the first Maori settlers. There is still a boiling pool near the church that is frequently used for boiling eggs and cooking meat – and perhaps the occasional member of the British monarchy.

Government Gardens and Rotorua Museum of Art and History

ⓘ *T07-349 4350, www.rotoruamuseum.co.nz, daily, summer 0900-2000, winter 0930- 1700, $12, child $5.50. Guided tours daily at 1100 and 1400. Shop and a café on site.*

Just west of Ohinemutu and fringing Lake Rotorua are the elegant and beautifully maintained **Government Gardens**. They form a stark and attractive setting for the museum, with the well-manicured bowling greens and croquet lawns, ponds and scented roses, creating a distinctly Edwardian, colonial atmosphere.

The **Rotorua Museum of Art and History** itself is housed in the once-famous **Bath House**. Built in 1908, it was designed along the lines of the European spas and attracted hundreds of clients the world over who hoped to take advantage of the thermal waters' therapeutic and curative powers. At the time the soothing waters were thought to be a cure for any ailments, as diverse as anxiety and even obesity. Its popularity for 'taking the cure', together with the added volcanic features and attractions surrounding the city,

Rotorua detail

➡ **Rotorua maps**
1 Rotorua, page 239
2 **Rotorua detail**
3 Around Rotorua, page 246

Sleeping
Ambassador
 Thermal Motel **1** *A2*
Base Backpackers **6** *C2*
Central Backpackers
 3 *B1 & B2*
Crash Palace **4** *C2*
Eaton Hall **5** *C2*
Millennium Rotorua,
 Nikau Restaurant
 & Zazu Bar **8** *C3*
Princes Gate **9** *B2*
Regent Flashpackers **7** *A1*
Royal Lakeside
 Novotel **10** *A2*
Treks YHA Backpackers **2** *B1*

Eating
Bistro 1284 **1** *C1*
Blue Baths **8** *B3*
Capers Epicurean **15** *C1*
Fat Dog **2** *A2*
Freos **3** *A2*
Lewisham's **6** *A2*
Lovely India **7** *A2*
Pig & Whistle **9** *B2*
Relish **5** *A2*
Rendezvous **10** *C1*
Zanelli's **13** *B1*

Bars & clubs
Hennessey's **4** *B2*
Lava **14** *B1*

made the Bath House the focus of the New Zealand government's first major investment in the new concept of tourism. In one wing of the museum you can see some of the original baths, changing rooms and equipment, together with photographs. Given the rich local Maori history it is not surprising to find a superb collection of Te Arawa *taonga* (treasures) which contrast interestingly with collections of modern artworks by local Maori artists. There are also displays that feature the great Tarawera eruption of 1886 as well as touring exhibitions and more modern dynamic offerings. Not to be missed is the excellent audio-visual display entitled *Rotorua Stories*. It screens every 20 minutes and is a 15-minute introduction to the great historical legends and stories of the area. It comes complete with shuddering pews during the fascinating account and depiction of the Tarawera eruption.

A short distance from the museum are the **Blue Baths** (Blueys) ① *T07-350 2119, daily, 1000-1600 in winter, pools open till 1900 in summer, from $11, child $6*. Built in the Spanish Mission style during the Great Depression of 1933, the pools soon flourished as one of the major social and recreational venues in the city, and were one of the first public baths to offer 'mixed' bathing. Due to competition and social change, the Blueys' were closed in 1982. However, still much loved, they were restored and re-opened in 1999 as functional hot pools, museum and tearooms. There is an entertaining video presentation relating the story of the pools, and the museum displays are imaginatively set in the former male and female changing room cubicles.

Behind the Blue Baths is the highly popular **Polynesian Spa complex** ① *T07-3481328, www.polynesianspa.co.nz, daily 0800-2300, from $20, child $15*. Rain or shine this is a Rotorua 'must do' and, although often very busy, it is a delight. There is a luxury spa complex and hot springs and pools, private spa pools, a family spa, shop and café. A range of massage treatments are also available. If you cannot afford the luxury spa then the therapeutic adult hot springs will not be a disappointment. Until recently the main baths, which range in temperature from 33°C to 43°C, were set outside in timber-style tubs overlooking the lake and although they still remain a new complex has recently been added to address the ever-increasing visitor numbers. Progress aside, it is a great place to ease the aches and pains of your active tourist pursuits and to mix with the locals, though the omnipresent tour groups can make it all very chaotic. The best times to go are at lunch and dinnertime when the tour buses are elsewhere.

Whakarewarewa/Te Puia
① *Fenton St (3 km south of the city, just head for the steam), T07-3489047, www.tepuia.com, summer daily 0800-1800, winter 0800-100, $40, child $20, guided tours depart hourly. Maori concerts 1015, 1215, 1515, tour and concert $50, child $25. Te Po evening performance and feast, $95, child $47.50. General admission and Te Po $130, child $65. There is a shop and a café on site.*
'Whaka' (pronounced, rather unfortunately, 'Fuckka') is the most famous and historic of the region's thermal reserves. The entire complex has recently undergone a face-lift and been re-branded under the banner of **Te Puia**, which relates to the former fortified 'pa' that protected the resident tribe. With the new name and, naturally, the new prices, it claims to be New Zealand's premier Maori cultural centre and is certainly the most commercial. The complex includes the Rotowhio Marae, the Mai Ora Village (a replica of the former Te Arawa Maori settlement) and the modern and thriving Maori Arts and Crafts Institute. The complex also hosts a number of natural thermal attractions. The star attraction is the much-celebrated Pohutu, the country's largest geyser, but as well as the great spout there are also boiling pools, silica terraces and, of course, the obligatory bubbling mud.

On entering you have the option of self-guided or Maori-guided tour (recommended) around the reserve. A series of paths branch out from the main visitor block and take in a strictly 'showpiece' nocturnal kiwi house before passing the large and at times, fairly inert Ngamokaiakoko ('Leaping Frog') mud pool, before the path delivers you at the geyser formations. There used to be around 60 geysers in Whaka, but now there are essentially two. The famed **Pohutu** or 'Big Splash' goes off like a broken water hydrant 10 to 25 times a day (more recently for days on end), to a height of over 30 m, while the more impotent Prince of Wales (sorry Charles) geyser nearby, is less spectacular.

The tracks then negotiate the small mud pools and volcanic features of the valley before arriving back near the entrance and the **Rotowhio Marae**. There are many features in this functional *marae*, including a banquet and weaving house and a *waka* (canoe). The *marae* also hosts daily **cultural performances** that feature a traditional *powhiri* (welcome), demonstration of the *taiaha* (warrior's weapon), *haka* (posture dance), *poi* (women's dance) and a range of traditional Maori songs. A longer performance entitled 'Mai-Ora' in the evenings also includes a *hangi* (feast). There is a deliberate element of interactivity with visitors, but it is generally well balanced and if you're feeling shy you won't be forced to join in.

The **Maori Arts and Crafts Institute** was established in 1963 to ensure that the traditional artist aspects of Maori culture are not lost. A viewing platform allows visitors to see students at work in the woodcarving studio before taking them through galleries and display areas where pieces of completed work can be seen and are for sale.

Whakarewarewa Forest Park

On the southern outskirts of Rotorua is the recreational playground of the Whakarewarewa Forest Park, well known for its excellent walking and mountain biking opportunities. The best way to choose from those opportunities is to visit the **Fletcher Challenge Information Centre** ① *<Long Mile Rd, off Tarawera Rd, just off SH30 heading east, T07-350 0110, Mon-Fri 0830-1730, Sat-Sun 1000-1600*. It has a number of interesting interpretative displays as well as all track information and colour-coded track maps. The walks range from 20 minutes to eight hours, with the shortest taking in a tract of giant **Californian Redwoods** (along Long Mile Road) and the longest taking in the shores of the Blue and Green lakes. ▶▶ *See Activities and tours, page 258.*

Kuirua Park

If you arrive in the city from SH4 north, the steam that issues from the thermal features in Kuirua Park will be your first sight and smell (if not taste) of the city's volcanic activity. The park is 25 ha, with gardens linked by tracks to a number of low-key thermal pools and features, as well as the cutely named 'Toot and Whistle' miniature steam railway, which is perfect for kids. There is also a miniature golf course and the city's **Aquatic Centre** ① *0600-2100*. While in the vicinity of Kuirua take a short drive down Tarawera Road. On the left heading south, you will see two fenced-off sections that are billowing steam. These were – believe it or not – former properties until 1998, when new boiling springs literally erupted in the driveway. Under a system of government volcanic damage compensation the families were forced to move and the land given back to nature.

If you want a great view of the city and surrounding area, then **Mount Ngongotaha** to the west of the city is easily accessible by car. From SH5 heading north, take Clayton Road at the crossroads with the Old Taupo Road. After about 3 km Mountain Road is signposted off Clayton to the right. The **Aorangi Peak Restaurant** is near the summit, though if you intend to go to the Skyline Complex (see below) then the views are just as good from there.

Blue and Green lakes → *Colour map 2 ,C3.*

Southeast of the city, off SH30, Mount Tarawera Road takes you to some of the most celebrated lakes of the Rotorua region. The road runs adjacent to the Whakarewarewa Forest Park, before arriving at the Blue and Green lakes. **Blue Lake** (Tikitapu) has a very cheery atmosphere and is good for boating and swimming, with a very pleasant walking track that circumnavigates its shores, while **Green Lake** (Rotokakahi) is *tapu* (sacred) and off limits to all recreational activities.

Buried Village

Past the Blue and Green lakes, the road enters the Te Wairoa Valley, home of the Buried Village. Prior to the 1886 eruption, the Te Wairoa Valley was the focus for Maori-guided tourist trips to see the pink and white terraces at the foot of Mount Tarawera. The sudden eruption of Tarawera on the evening of 10 June 1886 was witnessed by the tourists staying at the village hotel. Sadly for them and many of the settlers, this sight of the mountain was their last. Much of the area, including the village and its hotel, was laid waste with a blanket of rock and ash falls. Interestingly it was the Maori *whare* (houses) that fared better due to their stronger construction and sloping roofs. There is a small **museum** ① *T07-362 8287, www.buriedvillage.co.nz, daily 0900-1730, $30, child $8*, which relates the tale, complete with everyday items excavated from the ash almost a century later. Of particular interest is the treatment of the poor Maori elder who, hours before the eruption, made the prediction that it was about to blow. After the interior displays of the museum, a walk takes you around the remains of some of the original buildings. To complete the main walk you have the option of a 10-minute extension on a new boardwalk above the 80-rn **Te Wairoa Falls** that offers views across the lake. You can take a guided or a self-guided tour of the village. There's a shop and café on site – not to mention the occasional ghost.

Lake Tarawera → *Colour map 2, C3.*

Lake Tarawera is almost the same size as Lake Rotorua and lies at the slightly higher elevation of 315 m. With a shoreline that is sparsely populated and almost entirely rimmed with bush, the lake has a pleasant atmosphere, dominated by the slopes of the jagged volcanic ridge of Mount Tarawera on its western shore. The lake has been altered in both shape and depth by Tarawera's eruptions over the centuries.

It was on Lake Tarawera on 31 May 1886 that two separate boat loads of tourists, on their way to see the then world-famous Pink and White Terraces (since obliterated), caught sight of a fully-manned *waka* (war canoe) in the mists. Both the Maori and the *pakeha* knew there was no such *waka* in the region and, due to the fact it was seen by so many independent eyewitnesses, it was taken as a bad omen. Just 11 days later Tarawera erupted and the whole area was laid waste with the loss of 150 lives. Today the lake is an almost deceptive picture of serenity and is the venue for fishing and other water-based recreational activities. **Hot Water Beach** on its southern edge is a popular spot where thermal activity creates an area of warm water, which is pleasant for bathing.

There are three DoC campsites and numerous walking opportunities around Lake Tarawera, including the excellent **Tarawera Falls Track**. The best way to visit the beach and to take in the atmosphere and learn more of the area's diverse and, at times, violent history, is on one of the three tours available, see page 257, for details. The **Landing Café**, T07-362 8502, opposite the jetty, just off Lake Tarawera Road, is a fine place for a meal or snack.

Mount Tarawera

Standing at 1111 m, with a 6-km converging gash of craters, is the dormant volcano Mount Tarawera. In looks it is very different to the higher, classic snow-capped cones of Ngauruhoe and Ruapehu in central North Island. It is essentially a conglomerate of three mountains: **Wahanga** to the north, **Ruawahia** in the centre and **Tarawera** to the south. All were naturally very different in appearance prior to their eruption in 1886.

A number of scenic helicopter flights and 4WD tours provide the opportunity to see its colourful interior, but generally speaking it is hard to access independently and is on Maori Reserve Land. Indeed, there is no public transport for miles around and independent access is actively discouraged. Guided tours by 4WD are available with **Mount Tarawera NZ Ltd**, see page 258. For mountain activity operators, see page 256.

Tarawera Falls

ⓘ *To access the forest you need a permit, obtainable from the Fletcher Challenge Forests Redwood Grove Visitor Centre, Long Mile Rd, Rotorua, T07-346 2082; or from the Kawerau VIC in the Bus Terminal on Plunket St (turn right at the BP station when coming into town), T07-3237550. The permit costs $2 and is valid for 2 weeks. They will give you directions on how to access the forest itself and negotiate the unsealed tracks to the falls car park.*

The Tarawera Falls and walkway are set in the heart of the **Tarawera Forest**, where the Tarawera River flows from the eastern shores of Lake Tarawera and northern slopes of Mount Tarawera. The falls are remote and hard to access, but this is part of their charm, and the effort is definitely worthwhile. The walkway, complete with waterfalls, a disappearing river, beautiful native bush and swimming holes, has to rate as one of the North Island's best short to medium walkways. The falls are of particular interest because the river first disappears underground before reappearing from a sheer cliff face. The track can be tackled either from above or below the falls.

There are three or four ways to get there. By car it is a 70-km drive (one way) from Rotorua via SH30 and the forestry township of Kawerau. Although the roads through the forest are very straight, do not go fast, and keep your headlights on at all times. Once you reach the falls car park it is a 10-minute walk to the base of the falls past the crystal-clear waters of the river. From the falls the track then zig-zags up behind them, through native bush with huge ponga ferns before arriving at the point where the river disappears underground. Then you can continue past a series of other beautiful falls and a swimming hole before emerging at the head of Lake Tarawera. The walk to the lake is about 4 km (2½ hours one way). You can also access the track via the Eastern Okaitania Walkway, but in total this involves an enjoyable two-day tramp.

Tamaki Maori Village

About 10 km south of Whakarewarewa, on SH5, is the base for award-winning **Tamaki Heritage Experience** ⓘ T0508-826254/T07-349 2999, www.maoriculture.co.nz, daily shows at 1730, 1830 and 1930, from $100, child $58. There are now dozens of traditional Maori performances on offer in Rotorua, some good, some not so good, and almost all highly commercial. But what is generally well accepted is that for over 20 years it has always been Mike and Doug Tamaki who have led the way. Since their mock-up 'Maori village' and associated performance was first created in 1990 the spectacle has steadily morphed and grown in stature to become the most sophisticated and professional in the country. Now, entitled *The Chronicles of Uitara* it is a performance of two parts. The first, 'The Rotorua Story', is staged here near Rotorua, while the second part 'Lost in Our Own

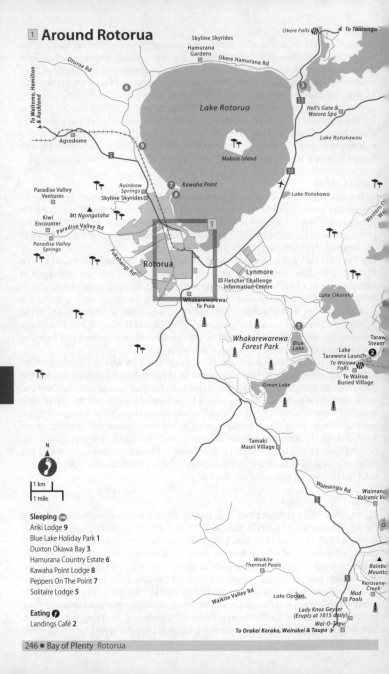

Okere Falls ▶ To Tauranga

Skyline Skyrides

Hamurana Gardens

Okere Hamurana Rd

Oturoa Rd

6

To Waitomo, Hamilton & Auckland

5

Agrodome

Lake Rotorua

Hell's Gate & Waiora Spa

3

Lake Rotokawau

9

Mokoia Island

Lake Rotokawa

30

Paradise Valley Ventures

Rainbow Springs
Skyline Skyrides

7 Kawaha Point

8

Western C...
Wa...

Kiwi Encounter

Mt Ngongotaha

Paradise Valley Rd

Lake Rotokawa

Taraw...

Paradise Valley Springs

Pukehangi Rd

Rotorua

1

Lynmore

Fletcher Challenge Information Centre

Lake Okareka

Whakarewarewa/ Te Puia

Whakarewarewa Forest Park

Blue Lake

Lake Tarawera Launch
Te Wairoa Falls

Taraw...
Steam...

2

Te Wairoa Buried Village

Green Lake

N

1 km
1 mile

Tamaki Maori Village

Waimangu Rd

Waiman...
Volcanic V...

Sleeping
Ariki Lodge **9**
Blue Lake Holiday Park **1**
Duxton Okawa Bay **3**
Hamurana Country Estate **6**
Kawaha Point Lodge **8**
Peppers On The Point **7**
Solitaire Lodge **5**

Waikite Thermal Pools

Rainb... Mounta...

Kerosene Creek

Eating
Landings Café **2**

Waikite Valley Rd

Lake Opouri

Mud Pools

Lady Knox Geyser
(Erupts at 1015 daily)
Wai-O-Tapu
To Orakei Korako, Wairakei & Taupo ▶

Rotorua maps
1 Rotorua, page 239
2 Rotorua detail, page 241
3 Around Rotorua

Land' is staged at a sister site in Christchurch. In the backdrop of a traditional village 'The Rotorua Story' is set well before the arrival of the Europeans when the Maori culture was still developing. You are guided through a 3½-hour re-enactment (the first chapter of the warrior Uitara's story) that in essence depicts the daily life and drama of the times, including the ancient ceremonies of welcome and of farewell, all culminating in a traditional *hangi* (or feast). All in all it is an impressive, unique and memorable experience, and you will, of course, be tempted to see Part II in Christchurch (see page 481).

Wai-O-Tapu

ⓘ *29 km south of Rotorua Off SH5 (29 km south of Rotorua and not to be confused with Waimangu Thermal Valley 4km before it), T07-3666333, www.geyserland.co.nz, daily 0830-1700, $30, child $10. Geyser Link Shuttles, T0800-000 4321, also offers transport from Rotorua (VIC at 0930) for around $30 or contact the VIC (I-Site) for other operators.*

Wai-O-Tapu is, without doubt, the best thermal park in the region, with an almost surreal and colourful range of volcanic features, from mud pools and silica terraces to the famous and beautiful 'Champagne Pool'.

If you can, time your arrival with the daily 1015 eruption with the **Lady Knox Geyser**, which is signposted on the Wai-O-Tapu Loop Road (off SH5). If ever there was a spectacle of tourism hype gone completely nutty then this is it. It is actually more interesting to witness the whole event as just that – a human spectacle rather than a natural one. Arrive early, get a good seat at the back then watch the people come and go like one mass flock of sheep all armed with their digital cameras.

Just before the geyser, again on the Loop Road, are a number or globulous mud pools that are separate from the park itself. Without the hordes of expectant tourists they offer a far better spectacle, with their melodic, impressive and unpredictable flatulence. The thermal park proper is at the southern end of the Loop Road. The full self-guided walk around the park will take about two hours. Along the first section of track there are a number of features including steaming caverns, mud pools and cavernous holes, with evocative names like **Devil's Home** (very photogenic), the **Devil's Ink Pots** and **Thunder Crater**. The track then arrives at a lookout across the aptly named **Artist's Palette**, a multi- coloured silica field. It really is a wonderful sight to behold with pastel shades of yellow, green and blue, fading in and out of swathes of billowing white steam. A boardwalk takes you across the silica fields, where you can either go on to investigate a silica waterfall, some 'alum cliffs', 'frying pan flat' and some colourful lakes, or (more likely) get entirely engrossed with the **Champagne Pool**. This is hard to describe, but essentially is a bright orange-edged, steaming, fizzing pool of about 60 m in diameter. What you are looking at is in fact a 62-m deep flooded volcanic vent, the base of which boils the water to a surface temperature of around 74°C. Hot stuff, and without doubt the highlight of the park. From the Champagne Pool it is a short meander past more steaming, gurgling crevasses and a pastel green lake, before returning to the visitor centre, shop and café.

Kerosene Creek

Between the Waiotapu and Waimangu Thermal Reserves is the dormant 'volcanoette' **Rainbow Mountain**, which although commanding a fine view from the summit requires a 4WD and considerable guile to get there. Far less stressful is a visit to the natural hot waters of **Kerosene Creek** that emanates from the lakes at its base. DO NOT swim in the lakes. It is not a good idea to do so, as a rather sad-looking white cross with dishevelled flowers suggests. Instead, go past the lakes down Old Waiotapu Road (signposted off SH5) to the marked Kerosene Creek parking area. The rest is all towels and 'Oooohh that's good'. One word of warning however: you will very probably not be alone, especially in summer, and the car park is often hit by thieves, so do not leave valuables in the car and make sure you lock it. The best time to go is around 1000 when everyone is 'flocking' to the Lady Knox Geyser.

Waimangu Volcanic Valley

ⓘ *26 km south of Rotorua, off SH5, T07-366 6137, www.waimangu.com, daily 0830- 1645. There are self-guided, guided walk-only, or walk and cruise options from $33, child $10. Geyser Link Shuttles, T0800-000 4321, offer transport from Rotorua (VIC at 0930) for around $30 or contact the VIC (I-Site) for other operators.*

The volcanic features in the Waimangu Volcanic Valley are all very recent and were created as a result of the 1886 eruption of Tarawera. Lake Rotomahana is essentially a water-filled crater which, before the eruption, was once the site of the famed pink and white silica terraces. Sadly, both of the terraces were completely obliterated by the eruption, but what was created in their place was the lake and a number of new volcanic features around it. These include the **Waimangu Cauldron** – the world's largest boiling lake – the **Inferno Crater Lake** that rises and falls up to 10 m a month, steaming cliffs, and numerous boiling springs and steaming fumaroles. At the turn of the last century the now inactive **Waimangu Geyser** used to be the largest in the world, spouting water to a staggering 500 m. The park is self-guided and you can see it partly on foot and partly by boat but there are a number of options.

The **Waikite Thermal Pools** ⓘ *between Waimangu and Wai-O-Tapu, from SH5 turn west onto Waikite Valley Rd at Waiotapu Tavern, the pools are about 4 km on the right, T07-333 1861, www.hotpools.co.nz, daily 1000-2130, $12, child $6,* consist of large family and adult hot pools fed by a local hot spring. This is a gem of a place and the perfect spot to relax and escape the crowds. Also, with a small motorpark attached, it is a great place to stay for a night or two. An impressive adjunct to the park is a short nature trail that takes you upstream to a massive spring that is in a constant state of angst – and has been for centuries. Its clarity, mind-bending temperature and billowing steam is utterly mesmerizing.

Hell's Gate and the Waiora Spa → Colour map 2, C3.
ⓘ 15 km from Rotorua, SH30, Tikitere (15 km from Rotorua), T07-3453151, www.hellsgate.co.nz, daily 0900-2030, from $30, child $15. Park entry, mud bath and spa from $115, massage from $80. A shuttle is available from town for the most expensive attraction packages, otherwise contact the VIC (I-Site) for latest independent shuttle operators .

If you can ignore the very saucy looking, scantily clad couple daubing each other in mud on all the promotional material, the aptly-named Hell's Gate thermal reserve and Waiora Spa, will not disappoint. It is not the most colourful of the reserves, but certainly one of the most active, and a thoroughly steamy affair. The 10 ha are set on two levels separated by a tract of bush, yet subtly connected by a warm thermal stream, complete with steaming waterfall. The pools of bubbly mud and water on the lower levels, with such evocative names as 'Sodom and Gomorrah' and 'The Inferno', hiss with menace and are quite scary, reaching temperatures well over that required to boil your potatoes.

The upper level of the reserve is much of the same, with steaming lakes and myriad tiny steaming vents, scattered with features including mini mud volcanoes and cauldrons of boiling water. Best of all is the **Devil's Cauldron**, a small pit that is home to a lively globular mud pool which makes the most wonderfully disgusting noises. Thankfully the entire reserve is connected with a boardwalk, from which you are encouraged not to stray.

With all that mineral rich bubbly mud about it would seem rude not to create a **mud spa** and this is indeed Hells Gate's latest venture. There are a number of options from massage or sulphur spas, to the wonderfully messy and therapeutic mud facials, scrubs and (best of all) private mud baths. After all that, the small shop and café seem a little mundane.

Agrodome complex
ⓘ 10 km north of Rotorua on SH5, T07-357 1050, www.agrodome.co.nz, www.zorb.com, daily 0830-1700. Shows at 0930, 1100 and 1430, show $26, child $13 (farm tour $6 extra). Try to attend the busiest show: mid-morning or mid-afternoon.

The Agrodome complex is one of the principal tourist draws on the Rotorua circuit and, although highly commercial, a lot of fun. It has a wide array of attractions from the full-on **bungee jump** to some more sedate farm activities. The focus of the complex and its principal feature attraction is the **sheep show**. If the very thought of such an event leaves you cold, then think again. This ovine spectacular features over 19 breeds of sheep – all of which are highly domesticated, wonderfully tame and very co-operative. Before the show starts the 'stars' are available for copious stroking and perhaps an autograph if you're lucky. The actual animal show is very informative, entertaining and professional. There is much audience participation and the opportunity to bottle-feed the lambs. As for the audience, well, they are almost as entertaining as they attempt to video and photograph the entire proceedings.

Surrounding the Agrodome there are a scattering of sundry attractions including a **woollen mill** and a **chocolate factory**. Activities abound including a **farm tour** (optional extension to the sheep show); Freefall Extreme bodyflying (from $49, child $35); helicopter rides ($89-885); jet boat trips ($45, child $35); as well as the 'Swoop' ($45 child $35), 'Shweeb' and 'Zorbing'. The **Freefall Extreme** involves a lot of wind and a very fetching suit, all in order to simulate a freefall experience from about 5 m. Frankly, the real tandem skydiving experience is far better, but as a taster it is perhaps worthwhile. A word of warning, however: if you have more than one chin, don't even go there, unless you relish the propect of lamentable portraits on your Facebook page. The **Swoop** is a glorified swing, where you are strapped into a harness then dropped from a height of 40 m. Apparently somewhere on the way down you reach over 130 kph, with a G-force of three, which, roughly translated, means your kidneys attempting to seek an unexpected and rapid exit out of your back passage. However, it all seems to go down very well. The **Shweeb** is the world's first human-powered monorail racetrack. It consists of two 200-m long overhead rail circuits that vary in height between two and four meters above the ground. Under the tracks hang high performance pedal powered vehicles in which, well, you pedal like the clappers. **Zorbing** (the site for which is located a short distance away) is described as a 'biospherical monumentous disturbance' and is the unique New Zealand invention of rolling down a hill in a large clear plastic bubble. It can, if you so wish, be filled, with a bucket or six of water. It is highly entertaining but a bit of a rip-off as the entire episode lasts about 10 seconds and costs $49. What will they think of next? Once flush with adrenaline you can then sample the souvenir shop and café on site.

Trout Springs and Kiwi Encounter

The Rotorua region is rich in freshwater springs, the streams from which are home to thousands of brown and rainbow trout. Trout are not native to New Zealand and were introduced to the region in the 1800s. Some of these springs have been developed into tourist resorts where you can observe wild and captive trout above and below the water or feed the swirling masses. Some streams are also home to the huge native New Zealand eels.

The largest and most popular springs resort is **Rainbow Springs** ① *5 km from the city centre on SH5 north, T07-350 0440, www.rainbowsprings.co.nz, 0800-2100 (later in summer), $26, child $15*. Here the attraction of the trout is combined with other wildlife treats, including some very tame native birds in a free-flight aviary. The underwater viewing area is particularly popular and a fine reminder of what fish should look like as opposed to piled up on a platter in a fish shop or supermarket counter with that 'Oh my God' expression on their faces. There are also fluffy farm animals for the kids to stroke and regular guided tours of the park, farm animal shows and a café on site.

There are also the smaller but quite charming **Paradise Valley Springs** ① *11 km from the city along Claydon Rd, which is straight on at the Koutu Corner intersection as you head north out of the city on the Old Taupo Rd, T07-348 9667, www.paradisevalley.co.nz, daily 0800-dusk, $26, children $13*. This attraction is very similar to Rainbow Springs with the same features (plus added lions) but, provided there are no coach tours, it enjoys a quieter, more congenial atmosphere. There is also a small bottling plant which utilizes the pure spring water. The Geyser Link, T0800-000 4321, offers regular shuttle services from $25.

Opposite the Rainbow Springs complex is the **Kiwi Encounter complex** ① *T07-350 0440, www.kiwiencounter.co.nz, 1000-1700, $27.50, child $17.50*. As the name suggests the attraction comes in the form of that truly enigmatic creature and national icon, the kiwi. There are of course a number of well-established tourist operations that display kiwi throughout New Zealand and some fine ones too, but this is undoubtedly one of the best. Here, right from the outset they seem to strike a fine balance between pleasing people and making money but not doing so to the detriment or exploitation of the birds themselves. All the display material is impressive enough, but it is the fact that it is a working hatchery that holds eminent appeal. You will certainly see live kiwi and be bemused at their hilarious natural antics, ie scuttling about like old men in big fur coats with their hands firmly in their pockets, or fussing about for food like a short-sighted old seamstress rummaging in a box of buttons. Surely if any animal should have evolved supporting a pair of bifocal spectacles, this is it. But that aside, the experience is only augmented by a view through to the husbandry area where you can see staff tending to incubating eggs, or, if you are very lucky, chicks (November to March). Needless to say the latter is a sight that would render a very large, menacing looking gentleman astride a Harley Davidson to a tearful dribbling mess.

Skyline Skyrides
ⓘ *Fairy Springs Rd, T07-3470027, www.skylinesskyrides.co.nz, daily 0900-late. Gondola $24, child $12; gondola and 3 luge rides $45, child $35.*
If you are physically able, everyone who visits Rotorua should call into the Skyline Skyrides to take a ride up the mountain in the gondolas and have a go on the infamous luge, which basically involves throwing yourself down a concrete course on a plastic tray with wheels and primitive brakes. Sounds mad? It is, and apparently keeps the casualty department of Rotorua Hospital very well attended. However, don't let that deter since, like anything, a little daring it is utterly addictive and a lot of fun. Perhaps part of its appeal is the fact that once down, and if still alive, you can then hitch a ride on a secondary chairlift to repeat the operation time and again. You are given brief instructions, a plastic helmet and a chance to try the 'family' course first, just to get the hang of it. This is very slow – so much so that you can have a conversation with complete strangers, if not tea and cakes on the way down – and once completed you can attempt the main course with its savage turns and precipitous jumps. As well as the luge and scenic gondola there is also a Sky Swing that will reputedly fly you (and two others) through the air at 120 kph, from $40. Other more conventional activity options include helicopter trips, mountain biking and then once the adrenaline has settled there is always the scenic restaurant, with its memorable views across the city and the lake.

Whirinaki Forest Park
ⓘ *90 km southwest of Rotorua on SH38, T07-3661080. For detailed information of how to access this excellent forest park contact DoC in Rotorua, or better still call in at the DoC field centre on the main road in Murupara, at the northern edge of the park.*
Whirinaki Forest Park is one of New Zealand's finest remaining podocarp forests, aptly described by one famous botanist as a 'dinosaur forest'. The park is off the beaten track but that is part of its charm. There are a number of excellent **walking tracks** taking in the diverse remote forest landscape with giant trees, waterfalls, river valleys and lagoons. If you are short for time try the short walk to the **To Whaiti Nui-a-Toi Canyon**. The entrance to the park (and the canyon) is past Minginui village and up River Road to the Whirinaki carpark. There are DoC campsites and huts within the park to allow longer multi-day tramps.

◉ Rotorua listings

For Sleeping and Eating price codes and other relevant information, see Essentials pages 44-50.

● Sleeping

Rotorua *p238, maps p239 and p241*
There are over 13,000 tourist beds in Rotorua, so the choice is huge. Many of the main hotel chains are here and there are lots of motels on either side of Fenton St, between the centre of town and Whakarewarewa. Pre-booking is advised throughout the year. Whatever you do and wherever you end up, make sure there is an accessible hot pool in-house or nearby.

Hotels and B&Bs

LL The Springs, 16 Devon St, T07-348 9922, www.thesprings.co.nz. Purpose-built luxury B&B in a quiet central location. 4 attractive en suites, off-street parking.

L-AL The Princes Gate, 1057 Arawa St, T07-348 1179, www.princesgate.co.nz. Conveniently located between the city centre and Government Gardens, the 1897 Princes Gate advertises itself as one of the country's leading boutique hotels. Whether it actually honours that heady claim is debatable, but there is no denying its character. There is a wide range of rooms, some self-contained, replete with 4-poster beds and (a rarity these days) a proper bath. An elegant in-house bar/restaurant, sauna and the obligatory private thermal pools all add to the hotel's appeal.

LL-AL Grand Tiara Rotorua, corner of Fenton and Sala sts, T07-349 5200, www.grandtiara.co.nz. Fully renovated, this is one of Rotorua's best and most expensive hotels. Close to Te Puia (Whakarewarewa) thermal reserve, it has a pool, spas, gym, café, excellent cuisine specializing in Japanese and seafood and an in-house bar attached. Maori concert and feasts nightly.

LL-AL Royal Lakeside Novotel, lake end of Tutanekai St, T07-346 3888, www.novotelrotorua.co.nz. In the heart of town, near Lake Rotorua and Government Gardens. Good reputation with in-house spas, and a popular restaurant and bar. It also offers one of the best hotel Maori concerts and *hangis*.

AL Millennium Rotorua, corner of Eruera and Hinemaru sts, T07-347 1234, www.millennium rotorua.co.nz. Popular chain hotel just metres from the Polynesian Spa (discounts to guests). The modern rooms and suites have plenty of style with marble floored bathrooms and residential-style decor, Sky TV and internet access. The fine in-house bar and restaurant, Nikau, is considered one of the city's best. Although the Polynesian Spa is the best place to go, there is a spa and fitness centre on site, with massage, beauty and body treatments.

AL Quality Hotel Geyserland, 424 Fenton St, T07-348 2039, www.regalgeyserland.co.nz.

Famed for its location overlooking the Whakarewarewa (Te Puia) Thermal Reserve. You can literally hear the Pohutu geyser going off and look down on a pool of bubbling mud. Refurbished in recent years (though from the outside you wouldn't guess it) it has all the usual facilities and in-house hot pools.

AL-A Kingsgate Hotel, Fenton St, T07-348 0199, www.kingsgaterotorua.co.nz. Recently refurbished, comfortable, no-nonsense option with good facilities including a restaurant specializing in simple kiwi fare, a pool, spa and gym.

AL Robertson House, 70 Pererika St, T07-343 7559, www.robertsonhouse.co.nz. Lovingly restored colonial villa with plenty of character in a quiet location. 4 tidy, spacious en suites (twin and double) with standard facilities. A good mid-range B&B option.

A-B Eaton Hall, 1255 Hinemaru St, T07-347 0366, www.kiwiasguesthouse.co.nz. Basic but good value B&B, close to the Polynesian Spa.

Motels

There are almost 100 motels in Rotorua, most on Fenton St, so the choice is vast. Most are modern and very much the same and, given the fierce competition, you will rarely be let down. The best bet is to take a drive down Fenton and take your pick. The following are just a few of the most recommended or well-situated.

L-AL Regal Palms, 350 Fenton St, T07-350 3232/T0800-743000, www.regalpalms.co.nz. The Regal is one Rotorua's newest motels and is certainly one of the best. Very classy decor and attention to detail throughout, which goes well beyond what you might expect from a motel, even with its 5-star rating. Superior and executive suites and apartments all with spa. Facilities also include a sauna, internet and guest lounge and bar.

AL Four Canoes, 273 Fenton St, T07-348 9184/T0800-422663, www.fourcanoes.com. Hotel/motel that uses the Maori theme and an evening Maori performance and *hangi* to attract custom. Wide range of suites with spa pools and a buffet restaurant.

AL Silver Fern, 326 Fenton St, T07-346 3849, www.silverfernmotorinn.co.nz. Hailed as one of the city's best. Range of suites with spa pools.

AL-A Ambassador Thermal Motel, corner of Whakaue and Hinemaru sts, T07-347 9581, www.ambassrotorua.co.nz. Ideal waterfront location close to the Polynesian Spa.

AL-A Geneva Motor Lodge, 299 Fenton St, T07-348 6033/T0800-333002, www.genevamotorlodge.co.nz. 14 tidy suites and 2 units with spas and spa pool.

AL-A Wylie Court, 345 Fenton St, T0800-100879/T07-347 7879, www.wyliecourt.co.nz. 36 suites, with pool and a restaurant. Free wireless internet

A Ascot on Fenton, 247 Fenton St, T07-3487712, www.ascotonfenton.co.nz. Spas in all units.

A Bel Aire Motel, 257 Fenton St, T07-3486076. Older and good value.

B Anns Volcanic, 107 Malfroy Rd, T0800-768683/T07-3471007, www.rotoruamotel.co.nz. Offers good rates and a first rate personable service.

B Rob Roy Motor Inn, 291 Fenton St, T07-3480584, www.robroymotel.co.nz. Offers good rates and has a thermal mineral pool.

Hostels

B-D Regent Flashpackers, 1181 Pukaki St, T07-3483338, www.regentflashpackers.co.nz. A smart new establishment that claims to cater for the 'business class flashpacker'. Although somewhat lacking in character it is certainly stylish, with all mod cons, including shared and private rooms as well as women only shared rooms, private thermal pools, bar, fast internet and perhaps most importantly, secure onsite parking.

B-D Funky Green Voyager, 4 Union St, T07-346 1754, www.funkygreenvoyager.com. One of the city's smallest and best backpacker hostels. Well-established and eco-friendly offering 4 doubles, 8 twins and dorms. Good kitchen facilities, plenty of local information and close to the supermarket. Parking a bonus.

B-D Kiwi Paka, 60 Tarewa Rd, T07-347 0931, www.kiwipaka.co.nz. A popular establishment,

with a fine range of accommodation including dorm, unit, motel, campervan and campsite options. The staff are on the ball and the amenities are excellent. There's a large kitchen and sitting room, a bar and café and a thermal pool. Activities arranged. It is a bit out of town but most operators provide pick-ups.

B-D Treks YHA Backpackers, 1278 Haupapa St, T07-349 4088, www.treks.co.nz. A fine establishment recently taken over by the YHA. Purpose-built in 2004, it's layout is carefully considered and there's an exceptional kitchen and living area. Offers all the usual room layouts, fast internet and good security. Recommended.

B-D Base Backpackers, 1286 Arawa St, T0800-227369/T0/-3488636, www.stayatbase.com. Formerly the well-established Hot Rock backpackers and Lava bar and now resurrected by the national Base chain, this is a popular place for the social crowd and backpacker buses. Sits overlooking Kuirau geothermal park and is within a short walk of the town centre. Two mineral hot pools and a large heated outdoor pool and yes the old Lava Bar with a new lease of life add to its appeal.

C-D Central Backpackers, 1076 Pukuatua St, T07-349 3285. A congenial, friendly and more historic establishment that is deservedly growing in popularity. Beds not bunks, single rooms, an in-house spa and off-street parking.

C-D Crash Palace, 1271 Hinemaru St, T07-3488842, www.crashpalace.co.nz. Head here for quieter, more homely, treatment.

Motorcamps and campsites

B-D Cosy Cottage, 67 Whittaker Rd, T07-348 3793, www.cosycottage.co.nz. An excellent motorcamp just north of the city centre, almost lakeside. It is one of the only motorcamps in the world that can boast a 'naturally heated' campsite. It has a wide range of cabins, good amenities and spa pools.

B-D Rotorua Thermal Holiday Park, Old Taupo Rd, T07-3463140, www.rotoruathermal.co.nz. Well-maintained, spacious and sheltered motorpark with a wide range of accommodation options from standard self-contained units to standard and en suite log cabins, powered and non-powered sites. There is a good camp kitchen for self-caterers, a comfortable TV lounge, internet, small shop, a fine licensed café and free hot pools on site. Within walking distance of the Whakarewarewa (Te Puia) Thermal Reserve.

Around Rotorua *p244, map p246*
Rotorua and the surrounding area is exceptionally well-endowed when it comes to luxurious rural lodges, boutique hotels and B&Bs. Most are lakeside and offer peace and quiet with all the usual 5-star mod cons. The VIC in Rotorua has full listings.
LL Hamurana Country Estate, 415 Hamurana Rd, Ngongotaha, T07-332 2222, www.hamuranalodge.com. Luxurious mansion, recently fully refurbished, with 12 luxury en suites, the best of which overlook Lake Rotorua. Beautifully appointed and well regarded for its cuisine.
LL Peppers On The Point, 214 Kawaha Point Rd, Rotorua, T0800-275373/ T03-3601063, www.onthepoint.co.nz. Beautifully refurbished, spacious 1930s lodge set in an elevated position overlooking Lake Rotorua. Sumptuous, tasteful interior design incorporating 7 en suites with spa. In-house fine dining, health treatments and a gym. Pure class.
LL Solitaire Lodge, 16 Ronald Rd, Lake Tarawera, T07-362 8208, www.solitairelodge.co.nz. Highly celebrated hideaway on the shores of Lake Tarawera. Excellent service, fine attention to detail in the Kiwi-faceted decor, and a great range of facilities. A choice of spacious, luxurious suites, some with spa, private decks and lake views. Of added appeal is the cuisine at the in-house restaurant and a collection of art showcasing some stunning original artworks by, among others, celebrated New Zealand wildlife artist Raymond Ching. Various charter boats and fishing guides are available from the lodge.
LL Kawaha Point Lodge, 171 Kawaha Point Rd, lakeside, T07-346 3602, www.kawaha lodge.co.nz. Classy kauri lodge with 8 en suite doubles, 2 with spa baths, garden with pool.

L Duxton Okawa Bay, SH33, Mourea, Lake Rotoiti, T07-362 4599, www.amorahotels.com/DuxtonRotorua/. A good mid-luxury hotel option out of town, in an idyllic lakeside setting. Full amenities including restaurant and private beach.
L-AL Ariki Lodge, 2 Manuariki Av, Ngongotaha, T07-357 5532, www.ariki lodge.co.nz. Spacious, well-appointed and lakeside, Ariki offers a good mid-range option north of the city.

Motorcamps and campsites
B-D Blue Lake Holiday Park, on the banks of Blue Lake on Tarawera Rd, T07-362 8120. If you are looking for a quiet country spot, look no further. There is a beach across the road for swimming, kayak hire and a lovely walk around the lake.

🍴 Eating

Rotorua *p238, maps p239 and p241*
There are more than 50 restaurants in Rotorua offering a wide range of cuisine to suit all budgets. Most of them are on or around Tutanekai St towards the lake. Consider sampling one of the many Maori *hangis* available. Few of them are truly authentic, having neither the time nor the health and safety go-ahead to dig earth pits and cook the food underground, they will still give you just a taste of how good a Maori *hangi* can be.
🍴 **Lewisham's Café and Restaurant**, 1099 Tutanekai St, T07-3481786. Daily 0930-2200. Has a good reputation, offering traditional European dishes with a definite Austrian edge. The venison and wiener schnitzel are recommended.
🍴 **Nikau Restaurant**, in the **Millennium Rotorua** hotel (see Sleeping, page 252), T07-347 1234. A good reputation for traditional European and Kiwi-style fine dining without being too formal. The bar, **Zazu**, is also popular.
🍴 **The Rendezvous**, 1282 Hinemoa St, T07-348 9273. Daily from 1800. A popular award-winning restaurant offering fine

Pacific Rim dishes in very congenial surroundings. There is venison, quail and even emu on the menu.

¶¶¶ **Zanelli's**, 1243 Amohia St, T07-3484908. Tue-Sun from 1730. Touted as the best Italian restaurant.

¶¶ **Freos**, lake end of Tutanekai St, T07-346 0976. Daily from 0830. A busy little café/ restaurant that offers traditional Kiwi fare and has a loyal following.

¶¶ **Landings Café**, Spencer Rd, Lake Tarawera, T07-362 8502. Daily from 0900. Book for dinner. A fine, affordable and friendly spot with a distinctive Scots flavour.

¶¶ **Lovely India**, corner Tutanekai and Pukaki sts, T07-348 4088. Daily from 1130. Perhaps the best Indian eatery in the city and good value.

¶¶ **The Pig and Whistle**, corner of Haupapa and Tutanekai sts, T07-347 3025. Daily 1130-2130. Great pub food washed down with their own brews.

¶¶ **Relish**, 1149 Tutanekai St, T07-343 9195. Mon-Tue 0700-1600, Wed-Fri 0700-late, Sat 0800-late, Sun 0800-1600. Usually busy with a fine atmosphere and locally recommended for pizza.

¶ **Bistro 1284**, 1284 Eruera St, T07-364 1284. Tue-Sat from 1800, booking advised. Congenial little place causing something of a stir locally since having won the city's best restaurant award several years running. Crispy skinned chicken with smoked mushroom sausages is the signature dish and lamb is another speciality. Recommended.

¶ **Fat Dog**, 1161 Arawa St, T07-347 7586. Mon-Fri 0900-late, Sat-Sun 0800-late. Consistently rated as the best café in town, always busy and friendly with a mixed clientele. Imaginative blackboard menu.

¶ **Capers Epicurean**, 1181 Eruera St. Daily from 0730. An old faithful and a consistent local award-winner with an imaginative lunch and dinner menu, some of the best coffee in town and locally recommended for breakfast. Doubles as a deli.

⊙ Pubs, bars and clubs

Rotorua *p238, maps p239 and p241*
Hennessey's, 1206 Tutanekai St, T07-343 7901. Popular Irish pub. Good beer and live music.

Lava Bar, at the Base Backpackers, 118 Arawa St, T07-347 9469. Especially popular with travellers and a younger crowd.

Pig and Whistle, corner of Haupapa and Tutanekai sts, T07-347 3025. Nicely decorated, brews its own ales and has a congenial atmosphere. It also has bands on weekends.

Zazu Bar, in the Millennium Rotorua hotel (see Sleeping, page 252), T07-347 1234. The classy place where the locals are apparently secretly hanging out. Happy hours on Fri at 1930 and Sat at 1730 are especially popular.

⊛ Festivals and events

Rotorua *p238, maps p239 and p241*
Mar Rotorua Tagged Trout Fishing Contest (3rd week), catch the tagged trout in Lake Rotorua and become a rich fisher-person.
May Rotorua Marathon (last week), 42-km run around Lake Rotorua. **Cateye Moonride**, www.moon ride.co.nz, a night time mountain biking event held in the Whakarewarewa Forest Park (unfortunately lights are allowed).
Sept Rugby World Cup, Rotorua Stadium will host several matches.
Dec New Year's Eve Mardi Gras, wild shenanigans down at the waterfront.

○ Shopping

Rotorua *p238, maps p239 and p241*
As you might expect, there are lots of souvenir shops in Rotorua. Most are on Fenton St.

Maori Arts and Crafts Institute, at the Whakarewarewa Thermal Reserve, SH5, is worth looking at for Maori Art.

Outdoorsman Headquarters, 6 Tarawera Rd, T07-345 9333, www.outdoorsman.co.nz.

Outdoor/camping equipment and sound advice regarding venues.
The Souvenir Centre, 1231 Fenton St. One of the better ones.

▲ Activities and tours

Rotorua *p238, maps p239 and p241*
In New Zealand, only Queenstown – the reputed activity capital of the world – can claim to have more activities than steamy Rotorua. As the country's second most visited tourist destination 'Roto Vegas' can certainly satisfy just about everyone, from adrenaline junkies keen to fly upside down in a bi-plane or raft down a waterfall, to those in search of some therapy in the form of a delightfully messy mud bath or a soothing mineral spa.

But before parting with any cash take a long hard look in the VIC to see the vast range on offer and ask about the various combo deals that can save both time and money.

Agrodome
Agrodome complex, just north of Rotorua on SH5, T07-357 1050, www.agrodome.co.nz. Offers a wealth of activities including bungee jumping, jet boating, 'The Swoop', 'Free Fall' 'Shweeb' and the infamous Zorb (see page 249).

Climbing
The Wall, 1140 Hinemoa St, T07-350 1400, www.basementcinema.co.nz, daily. An impressive 20-m climbing wall, from $16.

Eco-tours
Nature Connection, based in the city, T07-347 1705, www.natureconnection.co.nz. Offers a range of excellent fully-guided, fully-equipped half- to full-day trips to local sights and the Whirinaki Forest Park.
Whirinaki Rainforest Guided Walks, T07-377 2363, www.rainforest-treks.co.nz. Offers 1- to 3-day fully-catered treks led by professional Maori guides, starting at Rotorua and Taupo. The 3-day trek includes 2 nights at a safari-style camp in the rainforest,

complete with hot showers. Prices range from $155 for the 1-day eco-cultural walk, from $285 for 1-day privately guided walk; from $745 for the 3-day Rainforest Trek.

Fishing
As you might expect there are numerous guided and self-guided charters that mainly operate on Lake Rotorua or Lake Tarawera. Reputable charters include:
Clearwater (Lake Tarawera), T07-362 8590, www.clearwater.co.nz. Luxury launch.
Ernie Scudder, T07-332 3488, www.trout fly.co.nz. Big Ern' offers a great trip on the *Silver Hilton*, $90 per hr plus licenses for both boats (up to 4 people) and fly fishing (up to 2 people) with a minimum of 3 hrs on the boat and 4 hrs fly fishing. Special full day rate for both is $600 plus licenses, and includes lunch.
Rotorua Trout Safaris, T07-362 0016, www.wildtrout.co.nz.

4WD and quad bikes
Off Road NZ, 193 Amoore Rd (off SH5 north), T07-332 5748, www.offroadnz.co.nz. A range of thrills and spills in a range of 4WD vehicles and buggies. From their base near the city you can go uphill and down dale (including a monstrous 15-m 'luge' drop) and through some very large mud pools. There is also clay bird shooting and archery available. Guided tours (you drive) daily 0900-1700, from $90.

Golf
Arikikapakapa Course, Rotorua Golf Club, at the southern end of Fenton St, T07-348 4051. The best in the area.
Government Gardens, T07-3489126. Has a range and a short 9-hole course.

Health treatments and spas
There is an increasing number of health treatment facilities in addition to the busy, high-profile spas and thermal reserves.
QE Spa, Whakaue St, T0800-734325/ T07-348 0189, www.qehealth.co.nz. Mon-Fri 0800-2200, Sat-Sun 1400-2200. Massage from $60, mud bath from $60. Recommended.

Jet-boating
Kawarau Jet, City Lakefront, Memorial Dr, T07-343 7600/T0800-5387746, www.nzjetboat.co.nz. Fast jet boat trips with the usual action as well as a range of longer trips to a variety of locations including the Manupirua Hot Springs or Mokoia Island, from $69. There are also self-drive speed boats available for hire – but alas, a lot slower.

Horse trekking
Paradise Valley Ventures, 679 Paradise Valley Rd, T07-348 3300, www.paradisetreks. co.nz. Horse trekking (from 1 hr, $65) 15 mins from the city in a typical North Island rural setting.
The Farmhouse, Sunnex Rd (off Central Road), T07-3323771, www.thefarmhouse. co.nz. Also offers B&B accommodation/trekking packages from $150 per night), trekking from 1 hr $40. Good value.

Kayaking and waka experience
Adventure Kayaking, T07-5332634, www.adventurekayaking.co.nz. Extensive range of half- or full-day tours to a number of lakes and rivers in the region, as well as fishing trips and twilight paddles, from $70. Independent hire available from $40 per day.
Go Kayaking, T07-362 4222. Offers similar trips with more emphasis on teaching the beginner; from $75. Independent hire also available.
Mana Adventures, T0800-463925, www.mana adventures.co.nz. A Maori oriented operator offering a range of mainly water-based adventures and one of only 2 commercial operations in New Zealand that provides the opportunity to paddle a *waka* (Maori war canoe). Naturally the experience is augmented with lots of Maori tradition and interactive protocols. Lake Rotorua experience 45 mins from $48 (weather permitting).
Kaituna Kayaks, T07-362 4486, www.kaitunakayaks.com. Half-day from $149 (group $99). Full-day course $290 (190), 2-day from $149 per day. Recommended for river kayaking and some very good professional tuition. They also offer a tandem trip down the rapids of the Kaituna including the notorious 7-m falls (from $149). Recommended.

Lake Tarawera tours
See Lake Tarawera, page 244.
Lake Tarawera Water Taxis, The Landing, T07-362 8502, www.thelandinglake tarawera.co.nz. The most flexible company offering shuttle services to Hot Water Beach and The Lake Tarawera Track on demand.

Maori concerts and hangis
A trip to Rotorua is not complete without the Maori cultural experience of a concert and/or *hangi* (feast). There are numerous options, some good, some not so good. The major hotels almost all offer *hangis* and concerts, but these tend to be less grand affairs than the above and very commercial. A hotel *hangi* and concert will cost you $65-90. The following are recommended:
Te Po, based at Whakarewarewa (Te Puia), T07-349 9047, www.tepuia.co.nz. Fine cultural performances with entertaining interaction and an all-you-can-eat *hangi*, from $99, child $50 (see page 242). Expect up to 100 people.
Matariki Hangi and Concert, at the Royal Lakeside Novotel, T07-346 3888. Daily at 1830, one of the best on offer, from $65.
Mitai, based at Rainbow Springs off SH5, T07-343 9132, www.mitai.co.nz. The performance is said to be raw and authentic incorporating a short bush walk and *hangi* (90-100 people), $99 including transport.
Tamaki Heritage Experiences, T07-3492999, www.maoriculture.co.nz. A well-renowned Maori operator that has developed their product over the years with their latest offering being the most impressive so far. Witness the 'The Chronicles of Uitara – The Rotorua Story Performance'. Pick-ups from your accommodation are provided.

Others include: **Grand Tiara**, T07-349 5200; **Sudima Lake Plaza**, T07-348 1174; and **Kingsgate**, T07-348 0199.

Mountain biking

Whakarewarewa Forest Park is just one of many popular and challenging venues for mountain biking around Rotorua, with over 30 km of trails (see page 243). For track and operator information, contact T07-346 1717, www.bikerotorua.co.nz.

Planet Bike, T07-346 1717, www.planet bike.co.nz. Offers organized trips. Try the kayak and bike combo trips from $90. Independent bike hire also available, from $35 for 2 hrs, $55 per-day.

Rafting and whitewater sledging

Rotorua is the capital for rafting adventures in the North island with a number of rivers providing all the action from Grades II-V. The most popular and recommended trip is the 45-min blast down a stretch of the Kaituna (between Lake Rotorua and Lake Rotoiti) which negotiates 14 falls. The largest of these is the famous and highly entertaining 7-m drop down the Okere Falls – the highest commercial rafted falls in the world. Beyond that the Rangitaikei, Wairoa and Motu also offer some memorable rapids and are particularly good for multi-day trips. The Motu, that winds its way through the wilderness regions of the East Cape, is especially well worth considering for a multi-day trip. With much of it inaccessible by road it gives one a real sense of escape and adventure. Whitewater sledging is the new and exciting concept of doing all you do in a raft, on a Grade V river except alone on a type of 'head-first' water toboggan. With several companies vying for your attention and offering similar trips you will find prices are pretty much standard throughout and any real difference is in the finer detail like combo offers, facilities, cultural edge etc. They all have to be of a high standard.

If the thought of descending a 7-m waterfall in a 'rubber-dingy-thingie' seems like your idea of hell, but you like the idea of the schadenfreude involved in watching others do it, then head for the car park at the Otere Falls anytime from around 1000-1600. From a lookout deck high above the river you will regularly see them coming down

with the inevitable hysterics and – eventual – celebration.

Kaitiaki Adventures, T0800-338736/ T07-357 2236, www.sledge-it.com. Sledging and rafting trips, with the opportunity to learn about Maori culture on the way (from $99).

Raftabout, T0800-723822/T07-343 9500, www.raftabout.co.nz. Consistently receives good reviews as a very professional, safe and experienced company that offers a range of whitewater rafting on the Kaituna, Rangitaiki Wairoa rivers from its purpose-built riverside base. Trips start at $89 and there are various combo packages with everything from skydiving to the infamous luge. Like Kaitiaki (above) they also offer a sledging option on the rapids of the lower Kaituna Gorge, from $110.

Kaituna Cascades, T0800-5248862/ T07-345 4199, www.kaitunacascades.co.nz. Good outfit offering similar trips to **Raftabout**, above, ranging from $82 (Kaituna River 50 mins) to $385 (Motu). You get a photo of the drop down the falls (Kaituna).

River Rats, T0800-333900/T07-345 6543, www.riverrats.co.nz. A similar company offering a wider range of multi-activity adventure packages that include jet boating, bungee jumping, 4WD, luge, bikes and more. Also offers a more sedate rafting trip aimed at families and kids, starting at the Aniwhenua Falls before negotiating a gorge with a few gentle grade 2 falls.

Wet-n-Wild, T0800-462 7238/ T07-348 3191, www.wetnwildrafting.co.nz. Reputable company that has been around for many years offering all the local trips but also specializing in multi-day trips on the Motu and Mohaka rivers. From $95.

Sightseeing tours

There are a wealth of independent operators and the VIC offers reductions and package deals. For eco-tours, see page 256.

Mount Tarawera NZ Ltd, T07-349 3714, www.mt-tarawera.co.nz. One of the few operators licensed to take tours on to the mountain to see the dramatic Tarawera craters (or 'gash') left by the violent eruption of 1886.

The sight leaves you in no doubt about the ferocity of the explosion. There's a wide range of options including a guided half-day Volcano Adventure from $155, a fly/drive option from $435 and heli-biking from $610. **Rotorua Duck Tours**, T07-345 6522, www.ducktours.co.nz. The amphibious yellow duck shuttles the camera-toting masses to Kuirua Park and the lakefront followed by 'splash-down' at Sulphur Point, Lake Okareka and the Blue Lake. It is of course highly commercial but the combination of its novelty, the scenery and the entertaining commentary make it worthwhile. Tours last 90 mins and depart from the VIC, from $62.

Scenic flights

Most scenic flight operators are based at either the airport, Whakarewarewa, the Lake Rotorua waterfront near the town centre (float planes) or at the Agrodome. Flights range from city and Mt Tarawera fly-overs to extended trips to the volcanically active White Island in the Bay of Plenty. **Volcanic Air Safaris**, based at the airport and the waterfront, T07-348 9984, www.volcanicair.co.nz. Has a fleet of fixed-wing and float plane aircraft as well as helicopters that take in all the local sights and go as far as White Island from $75-845.

Skyline skyrides

Accessed by a scenic gondola there are a number of activities available on the slopes of Mt Ngongotaha. These include the infamous luge, a flying fox, flight simulator and helicopter trips, T07-347 0027.

Tandem skydiving

NZone, operates from the airport, T0800-376796/T07-3457569, www.nzone.biz. Highly professional, with jumps daily, depending on weather conditions. From 9500 ft for $249 (15,000 ft, $399).

Walking

DoC/VIC has information on the wealth of opportunities in the region, which range from a short walk around **Government Gardens** and the waterfront, to the **Tarawera summit** climb, the 20-min to 8-hr walks through the **Whakarewarewa Forest Park** (see page 243), and the superb **Tarawera Falls** walk (see page 245). Other excellent walking tracks are to be found around Lake Okataina in the **Lake Okataina Scenic Reserve**; these are best accessed from SH30 at Ruato (Lake Rotoiti) or Lake Okareka (Tarawera Falls Rd). The **Okere Falls** walk (30 mins) is accessed from SH30 east and then SH33 (16 km) and worth the trip, while a great view can be had from the summit of **Rainbow Mountain** (2 hrs) which is accessed off SH5, 26 km south of Rotorua. A little further afield is the **Whirinaki Forest**, which is lauded as having an almost prehistoric appearance.

⊙ Transport

Rotorua *p238, maps p239 and p241*
Bicycle hire Planet Bike, 30 Clouston, T07-346 1717, 2 hrs $35, full-day from $55; Rotorua Cycle Centre, 1111 Hinemoa St, T07-348 6588. **Car hire** Budget, 1230 Fenton St, T07-348 8127; Rent-A-Dent, 316B Te Ngae Rd, T07-349 3993.

❶ Directory

Rotorua *p238, maps p239 and p241*
Banks All major branches on Hinemoa St. Money exchange: **Travelex**, VIC, T07-348 0640, T0800-200232, daily 0830-1800.
Internet Numerous outlets including: Cyber Shed, 1176 Pukuatua St, T07-3494965, open Mon 0900-2200, Tue-Sat 0900-1700, Sun 0900-1700; Cyber World, 1174 Haupapa St, T07-348 0088. **Medical services** Accident and Urgent Medical Care Centre, Cnr Arawa andTutanekai sts, T07-348 1000, Mon-Sat 0800-2200, Sun 0800-2330 (also 24 hr duty doctor). **Police** Fenton St, T07-348 0099. **Post office** 1159 Pukuatua St, T07-3492397, Mon-Fri 0800-1700, Sat 0900- 1600 (Post Restante).

Tauranga → *Colour map 2, B3 Population: 66,000.*

Tauranga has enjoyed tremendous growth in recent years. So much so that it is used as a barometer of the general state of the economy and national real estate prices. As well as its thriving commercial and business centre, busy port (the name means 'sheltered anchorage') and rich horticultural farmland, it seems Tauranga is also proving the ideal place in which to enjoy the archetypal Kiwi lifestyle. With the combination of location, climate, attractive beaches and the many associated activities, as well as its proximity to the delights of Rotorua, it has much to offer both the native and the tourist. Dominating the scene is the harbour and the volcanic dome of Mount Maunganui to the north, which guards its precarious entrance. Nowadays there are almost as many cruise liners as there are merchant ships, and the town's tourist allure seems almost set to overtake its popularity with the locals. ➤➤ *For Sleeping, Eating and other listings, see pages 264-270.*

Ins and outs

Getting there

Tauranga, 210 km southeast of Auckland and 83 km north of Rotorua, is a major destination on the Pacific Coast Highway, which connects Auckland with Napier in the Hawke's Bay region. **Tauranga airport** ① *4 km east of the city centre, www.tauranga-airport.co.nz,* is served daily by **Air New Zealand Link**, T0800-737000. A taxi to the centre costs about $20, T07-575 0999 or T07-578 6086.

Intercity and **Newman's** buses operate services from most North Island destinations arriving at the VICs (I-Sites) in the city and Mount Maunganui; both handle bookings and ticketing. **Nakedbus.com**, offers internet deals, and **Go Kiwi Shuttles**, T07-866 0336, www.go-kiwi.co.nz, offers services from Auckland via Thames, Whitianga and Rotorua.

Getting around

Tauranga city centre is fairly compact and easily negotiable by foot. **Bay Hopper**, T0800-422 9287/T07-578 3113, www.baylinebus.co.nz, the local suburban bus company, operates regular daily services to Mount Maunganui and east as far as Opotiki. Buses depart from the corner of Wharf and Willow Streets beside the VIC (I-Site); day pass $6. For car rental and taxi companies, see Transport, page 270. **Kiwi Coast Cruises**, The Strand Reclamation Pontoon, T07-5791325, www.kiwicoastcruises.co.nz, connects Tauranga with Mount Maunganui and offers five sailings daily (summer only) 0900-1700, $8 one way.

Tourist information

Tauranga VIC (I-Site) ① *95 Willow St, T07-578 8103, www.bayofplentynz.com or www.tauranga.govt.nz, Mon-Fri 0830-1730, Sat-Sun 0900-1700.* For quick reference be sure to avail yourself of the free *What's to See and Do* leaflet. DoC information is also available here. **Mount Maunganui VIC (I-Site)** ① *Salisbury Av, T07-575 5099, Mon-Fri 0900-1700, Sat-Sun 0900-1600, closed weekends in winter.*

Sights

The main historical attraction in Tauranga is the **Elms Mission House** ① *T07-577 9772, www.theelms.org.nz, Wed, Sat, Sun 1400-1600, $5,* set amid pleasant grounds on Mission Street on the Te Papa Peninsula, on the site of the original mission. Nearby in **Robbins**

Tauranga orientation

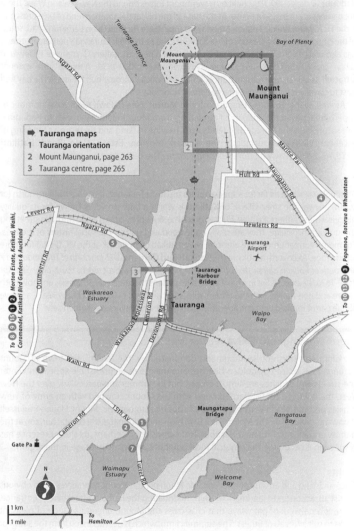

➡ **Tauranga maps**

1 Tauranga orientation
2 Mount Maunganui, page 263
3 Tauranga centre, page 265

Bay of Plenty

Tauranga Entrance

Ngatai Rd

Mount Maunganui

Mount Maunganui

Marine Par

Hull Rd

Maunganui Rd

To Papamoa, Rotorua & Whakatane

Levers Rd

Ngatai Rd

Hewletts Rd

To Morton Estate, Katikati, Waihi, Coromandel, Katikati Bird Gardens & Auckland

Otumoetai Rd

Tauranga Airport

Waikareao Estuary

Waikareao Expressway

Cameron Rd

Devonport Rd

Tauranga

Tauranga Harbour Bridge

Waipo Bay

To Papamoa, Rotorua & Whakatane

Waihi Rd

15th Av

Turret Rd

Cameron Rd

Gate Pa

Maungatapu Bridge

Rangataua Bay

Waimapu Estuary

Welcome Bay

N

1 km
1 mile

To Hamilton

Sleeping 😴
Ambassador Motor Inn **1**
Beach Front Villas **13**
Beach House Motel **10**
Bell Lodge **3**

Cosy Corner Motor Camp **4**
Fantail Lodge & Villas **15**
Just the Ducks Nuts
   Backpackers **5**
Matahui Lodge **9**

Ridge Country Retreat **8**
Silver Birch Holiday Park **7**
Top Ten Papamoa
   Beach Holiday Resort **12**
Touranga Tourist Park **2**

Eating 🍴
Bluebiyou **3**
Mills Reef Winery **1**
Somerset Cottage **2**

Park on Cliff Road on the eastern side of the peninsula are the remnants of the **Monmouth Redoubt** ① *daily 0900-1800*, built by government forces during the New Zealand Wars. There are gardens and a begonia house. At the base of the hill, at the southern end of Dive Crescent, is the **Te Awanui Waka**, a replica Maori war canoe. **Gate Pa Church** on Cameron Road, south of the city centre, marks the spot of the Battle of Gate Pa in 1864. Tauranga's perpetual growth has also reached the fine arts with the creation of a new **art gallery** ① *corner of Willow and Wharf sts, T07-5787933, www.artgallery.org.nz, daily 1000-1630*. Although the exterior attracted its fair share of remonstration, it has become a welcome hub for arts in the bay and host to travelling national and international exhibitions.

As well as the obvious attraction of **'the Mount'** (see below), there are a number of superb **beaches** in the area, most stretching from Mount Maunganui east to Papamoa. Not surprisingly the climate also lends itself to wine making and there are a scattering of excellent **vineyards** including the lauded **Morton Estate Main Road Katikati** ① *T07-552 0795, www.mortonestatewines.co.nz*. The cellar door is open daily.

Excursions

Although perhaps a bit far for a special return trip from Tauranga, if you are heading north (or south) anyway the small village of **Katikati** is worth a brief stop. It is known for its quality historical murals (there are now 23) that grace the sides of buildings along the main street and throughout the village. They are really quite good and portray the social history of the area. For more information visit the website, www.katikati.co.nz, or ask at the VIC (I-Site) for more information. Also worth a look are the **Katikati Bird Gardens** ①*25 km north of Tauranga and 7 km south of Katikati, signposted off SH2, T07-549 0912, www.birdgardens.co.nz, daily Sep-Apr 1000-1630, $9, child $4*. Set in 4 ha of attractive gardens there are over 50 species on show both native and non-native, with the undeniable 'stars' (as ever) being the 'cheeky kea' – a native alpine parrot imbued with considerable intelligence and delinquent tendencies.

Mount Maunganui ◎❼▲ ▶ *pp264-270.*

Six kilometres north of Rautanga and dominated by 'the Mount', the town of Mount Maunganui is graced by golden beaches and maintains an irresistible appeal. In winter the streets and beaches are almost empty, but in summer and particularly over the New Year, the town is a tourist battleground with the Mount crowned with an army of view junkies and the beach with battalions of soporific sunbathers. Mount Maunganui itself (known as 'Mauao' or 'The Mount') is 232 m high and dominates the coastal horizon at the narrow entrance to Tauranga Harbour. Not surprisingly, perhaps, its sheer presence has resulted in it becoming the physical focal point of culture and heritage in the region.

Sights

Once an island and an almost impregnable Maori *pa*, the Mount now serves as an obvious tourist attraction and a landmark for ships negotiating the harbour's treacherous entrance. There is a network of pathways that criss-cross the Mount, offering a range of pleasant walks to suit all levels of fitness. The summit climb, which is best accessed from the south of the motorcamp, takes about 45 minutes one way and is rewarded with a memorable view. The 3½-km base track walk is a less demanding option and also has some great views.

From the narrow neck of the Mount, **Ocean Beach** begins a stretch of sand that sweeps, almost uninterrupted, east to the cape. Just offshore from Ocean Beach are the two small islands **Moturiki** and **Motuotau**. Moturiki can be reached from the shore, has a blowhole and is a popular spot for fishing, while Motuotau is important for its wildlife. Other than the Mount and the beaches the town's major attraction are the **Mount Maunganui Hot Salt Water Pools** ① *at the base of the mount, Adams Av, T07-575 0868, Mon-Sat 0600-2200, Sun 0800-2200, from $9, child $6*. Here, therapeutic salt water is heated to 39°C in a number of large communal and private pools.

Even if you cannot stay up on a board for more than a nanosecond, the **Mount Surf Shop and Museum** ① *139 Totara St, T07-927 7234, $6, daily 1000-1500*, is worth a look if only to see the huge collection of boards and the intriguing 'shrine' to Malibu surfing guru 'Da Cat'.

② Mount Maunganui

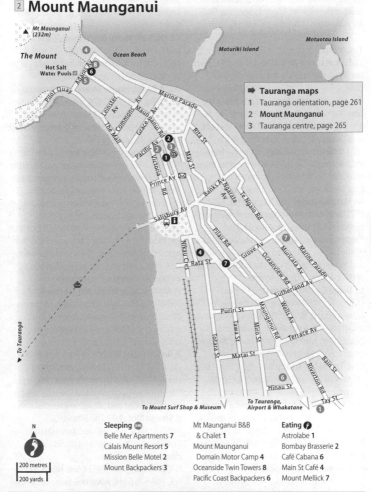

➡ **Tauranga maps**
1   Tauranga orientation, page 261
2   **Mount Maunganui**
3   Tauranga centre, page 265

Sleeping 🛏
Belle Mer Apartments 7
Calais Mount Resort 5
Mission Belle Motel 2
Mount Backpackers 3
Mt Maunganui B&B
& Chalet 1
Mount Maunganui
Domain Motor Camp 4
Oceanside Twin Towers 8
Pacific Coast Backpackers 6

Eating 🍴
Astrolabe 1
Bombay Brasserie 2
Café Cabana 6
Main St Café 4
Mount Mellick 7

For Sleeping and Eating price codes and other relevant information, see Essentials pages 44-50.

⊜ Sleeping

There is plenty of choice in Tauranga itself and Mt Maunganui, but it's best to book ahead in mid-summer when the area is hugely popular with Kiwi holidaymakers. Most of the region's luxury lodges and B&Bs are northwest of the city towards Katikati.

Tauranga *p260, maps p261 and p265*
LL Fantail Lodge and Villas, 117 Rea Rd, 35 km north of Tauranga, near the small village of Katikati, T07-549 1581, www.fantail lodge.co.nz. This popular country lodge estate offers a fine base from which to explore the Bay of Plenty and the Coromandel Peninsula. Set in beautiful rural surroundings it offers luxury suites and self-contained garden villas. Additional features include a reputable European-influenced guest restaurant, an in-house spa complex and informative and entertaining eco-tours.
LL Matahui Lodge, 187 Matahui Rd, T07-571 8121, www.matahui-lodge.co.nz. A stunning property in a tranquil spot overlooking Tauranga's Inner Harbour and Matakana Island. All the facilities and comforts you might expect and friendly hosts with a passion for fine food and wine. Dinner by arrangement.
LL Ridge Country Retreat, 300 Rocky Cutting Rd, Welcome Bay, T07-542 1301, www.rcr.co.nz. Beautifully appointed suites and an overall emphasis on health and beauty with a full range of in-house therapies on offer. You simply won't want to leave.
LL-L The Sebel Trinity Wharf, 51 Dive Cres, T07-577 8700, www.mirvachotels.com.au. The newest hotel in the city – and an impressive one at that – built over 3 former piers at Trinity Wharf. As such, the beautifully appointed suites offer excellent views across the harbour and you will have access to all the usual bells and whistles.
L-AL Hotel on Devonport, Devonport Towers, 72 Devonport Rd, T07-578 2668,

www.hotelondevonport.net.nz. Quality boutique hotel with all the bells and whistles right in the heart of town. Designed with business people in mind but still a fine convenient place to indulge yourself.
L-AL Puriri Park Boutique Hotel, 32 Cameron Rd, T07-577 1480, www.puriri park.co.nz. Well-established and equipped centrally located hotel. Self-contained suites. Good weekend and winter specials.
AL Durham Motor Inn, corner of Cameron Rd and Harrington St, T07-577 9691, www.durham. co.nz. One of the better motels in the city centre. 20 clean modern units, pool and spas.
AL-A Beach House Motel, 224 Papamoa Beach Rd, T07-572 1424, www.beachhouse motel.co.nz. Modern, award-winning and unusual beachside motel in Papamoa with 18 luxury units, spa, Sky TV.
AL-A Harbour City Motor Inn, 50 Wharf St, T07-571 1435, www.taurangaharbour city.co.nz. One of the city's newest upper-range motels, ideally located in the heart of Tauranga. Its stylish design and the attention to detail are striking. Modern features and an almost minimalist aspect to the decor make it look and feel more like an Auckland boutique hotel than a provincial motel. Both studio and 2-bedroom units have spa baths. General facilities also include Sky TV and secure parking.
A Ambassador Motor Inn, 9 Fifteenth Av, T07-578 5665, www.ambassador-motorinn. co.nz. Modern 4-star rated motel at the estuary end of the avenue. Wide range of units, spa and heated pool.
A Beach Front Villas, 535 Papamoa Beach Rd, T07-572 0816, www.papamoabeach. co.nz. Although a few miles from Tauranga in Papamoa, this complex and the villas are on the beachfront and are recommended.
B Strand Motel, 27 The Strand, T07-578 5807, www.strandmotel.co.nz. Comfortable, basic, budget motel located close to all amenities.
B-D Bell Lodge, 39 Bell St, SH2 North (Waihi Rd), T07-578 6344, www.bell-lodge.co.nz. Very

smart purpose-built complex located 4 km the city, in park surroundings. Large kitchen and comfortable en suite rooms or dorms, open fire, tent sites and off-street parking. Free pick-ups and free trips to 'The Mount'.
D Loft109 Backpackers, 109 Devonport Rd, T07-5795638, www.loft109.co.nz. Centrally located with some interesting artwork that adds the character so often missing in other modern 'boutique' establishments. Dorms, doubles, twins and triples and all the usual

facilities including free bike hire. Caring and friendly hosts.
B-D Harbourside Central Backpackers, 105 The Strand, T07-5794066, www.back packtauranga.co.nz. Large hostel right in the heart of the action, popular with socialites and fruit pickers who have benefited from the in-house job finding service. Double and twin rooms with shared bathrooms (or en suites) and dorms, some of which have harbour views. Good rooftop garden, free bike hire.

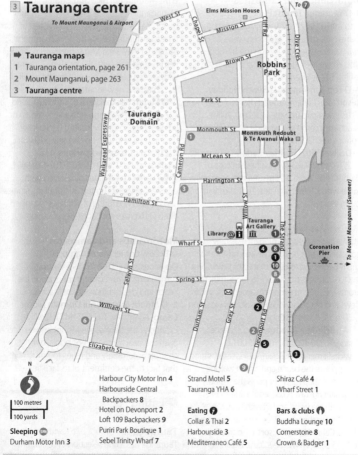

3 Tauranga centre

To Mount Maunganui & Airport

➡ **Tauranga maps**
1 Tauranga orientation, page 261
2 Mount Maunganui, page 263
3 **Tauranga centre**

West St
Chapel St
Elms Mission House
Mission St
Cliff Rd
Dive Cres
To 7
Brown St
Robbins Park
Park St
Tauranga Domain
Monmouth St
Monmouth Redoubt & Te Awanui Waka
McLean St
Walkaread Expressway
Cameron Rd
Harrington St
Hamilton St
Willow St
Tauranga Art Gallery
Library @
Wharf St
The Strand
Coronation Pier
To Mount Maunganui (Summer)
Selwyn St
Spring St
Williams St
Durham St
Grey St
Devonport Rd
Elizabeth St

N
100 metres
100 yards

Sleeping 🛏
Durham Motor Inn **3**

Harbour City Motor Inn **4**
Harbourside Central Backpackers **8**
Hotel on Devonport **2**
Loft 109 Backpackers **9**
Puriri Park Boutique **1**
Sebel Trinity Wharf **7**

Strand Motel **5**
Tauranga YHA **6**

Eating 🍴
Collar & Thai **2**
Harbourside **3**
Mediterraneo Café **5**

Shiraz Café **4**
Wharf Street **1**

Bars & clubs 🍸
Buddha Lounge **10**
Cornerstone **8**
Crown & Badger **1**

C-D Tauranga YHA, 171 Elizabeth St, T07-578 5064, yhataur@yha.org.nz. Well-established hostel in a quiet, central location. Friendly and comfortable with twin, double (one en suite), dorm and camping options.

D Just the Ducks Nuts Backpackers, 6 Vale St, T07-576 1366, www.justtheducks nuts.co.nz. Small, but popular and (despite the name) laid-back hostel located about 2 km from the city centre with the usual facilities including a log fire and free bike hire.

Motorcamps and campsites

A-D Tauranga Tourist Park, 9 Mayfair St (off 15th Av), T07-5783323, www.tauranga touristpark.co.nz. An excellent, well maintained little park beside the harbour, with above average facilities and value cabins. Recommended.

A-D Top Ten Papamoa Beach Holiday Resort, 535 Papamoa Beach Rd, T07-572 0816, www.papamoabeach.co.nz. A fine beachfront camp with a wide range of options and facilities.

B-D Silver Birch Holiday Park, 101 Turret Rd, SH2, T07-578 4603, www.silverbirch.co.nz. Harbourside location, en-suite or basic cabins some with kitchen facilities. Tent sites with camp kitchen.

Mount Maunganui *p262, map p263*
Mt Maunganui is becoming increasingly popular as a true resort-style holiday location and is beginning to have that mini-Gold Coast feel to it. So, apartment blocks predominate, all promising the usual modern amenities, ocean views and of course, location, location, location … The VIC has full listings.

LL-AL Belle Mer Apartments, 53 Marine Parade, T0800-100235/T07-575 0011, www.bellemer.co.nz. Again, well located, sitting just opposite the beach and within walking distance of shops and hot pools the 3-storey block offers luxury 2-3 bedroom apartments most with sea views and all with spas, fully equipped kitchen, Sky TV and private balcony.

LL-AL Calais Mount Resort, 6 Adams Av, T07-575 3805, www.calais.co.nz. Again, close to

all amenities and modern 4-star, but with the added attraction of an in-house bistro/bar.

LL-AL Oceanside Twin Towers, 1 Maunganui Rd, T07-575 5371, www.oceanside.co.nz. Luxury apartments with all the standard amenities, commanding the finest views and just opposite the hot water pools.

AL Mission Belle Motel, corner of Victoria Rd and Pacific Av, T0800-202434/ T07-575 2578, www.missionbellemotel.co.nz. Modern, Spanish-style motel and a more affordable option located in the heart of town.

B Mt Maunganui B&B and Chalet, 463 Maunganui Rd, T07-575 4013, www.mount bednbreakfast.co.nz. Has stood the test of time, surrounded as it is by new apartment blocks, so they are doing something right. Refurbished and centrally located, 5 rooms with shared bathrooms, with breakfast, all good value. A new separate chalet sleeps 6.

C-D Mount Backpackers, 87 Maunganui Rd, T07-575 0860, www.mountbackpackers.co.nz. Smaller, more centrally located backpacker hostel. They help with finding seasonal work.

C-D Pacific Coast Backpackers, 432 Maunganui Rd, T0800-666622/T07-574 9601, www.pacific coastlodge.co.nz. Lively with excellent range of comfortable doubles, singles and bunks. Wide range of activities organized, often with price reductions. Recycling policy.

Motorcamps and campsites

C-D Cosy Corner Motor Camp, 40 Oceanbeach Rd, T07-575 5899, www.cosy corner.co.nz. A quiet camp, further along the beach and cheaper than Mount Maunganui.

C-D Mount Maunganui Domain Motor Camp, Adams Av, T07-575 4471. Ideally located at the base of the Mount and next to both the beach and the hot pools, but charges accordingly and relies too much on that fact to the detriment of its facilities.

❷ Eating

Tauranga *p260, maps p261 and p265*
Tauranga has a fine selection of restaurants

and cafés to suit all tastes and budgets. Most are on or around the Strand overlooking the harbour. Pick up the free and comprehensive *Dine Out* guide from the VIC (I-Site).

♥♥♥ The Bluebiyou, 559 Papamoa Beach Rd (city east), T07-572 2099. Daily from 1100. Right next to the beach in Papamoa. Great if you want to get away from the city.

♥♥♥ Harbourside Restaurant, T0800- 721714, www.harboursidetauranga.co.nz. 1130-late. Enjoys a loyal following and a reputation as Tauranga's best restaurant. Located as much on the water as beside it, at the southern end of the Strand, it offers an excellent and imaginative all-day blackboard and à la carte menu, with an emphasis on local seafood.

♥♥♥ Mills Reef Winery and Restaurant, 143 Moffat Rd (city west), T07-576 8800, www.millsreef.co.nz. Daily from 1000. Another out-of-town option for lunch and dinner is this renowned (but expensive) restaurant, specializing in seafood and fish delights. Live music on Sun.

♥♥♥ Somerset Cottage Restaurant, away from the city centre, at 30 Bethlehem Rd (city west), T07-576 6889, www.somerset cottage.co.nz. A small, congenial place serving a classic range of international cuisine to suit a wide range of tastes. Fine reputation and an excellent wine list. Bookings essential.

♥♥ Collar and Thai, Goddards Centre, 21 Devonport Rd, T07-577 6655. Mon-Fri 1130-1400, Mon-Sun 1730-late. For Thai food you can't go wrong here, good value.

♥♥ Wharf Street Restaurant, Upstairs 8 Wharf St, T07-578 8322. Daily, open till late. Another award-winner with a wide-ranging menu including vegetarian. Once again seafood dominates. Fine harbour views.

♥ Mediterraneo Cafe, 62 Devonport Rd, T07-577 0487. New café proving popular with the locals for a good vibe, coffee or value breakfast.

♥ Shiraz Café, 12 Wharf St, T07-577 0059. Mon-Sat from 1100. A great range of lunchtime snacks (try a shwarma or falafel) and value breakfast.

Mount Maunganui *p262, map p263*

♥♥ Astrolabe, 82 Maunganui Rd, T07-574 8155. The combination restaurant, bar and café facilities here are to be recommended. It offers breakfast, lunch and dinner with a range of fine and imaginative traditional dishes. Live bands often play at weekends.

♥♥ Bombay Brasserie, 77 Maunganui Rd (almost directly opposite Astrolabe), T07-575 2539. Daily from 1800. An excellent, affordable Indian restaurant that seems to be getting the thumbs up from discerning British curry aficionados.

♥♥ Cafe Cabana, below the Twin Towers on Adams Av, T07-572 1109. Daily. Modern and trendy and popular mainly for its position just opposite the beach and hot pools.

♥♥ Mount Mellick, 317 Maunganui Rd, T07-574 0047. Daily 0900-2200. Irish pub good for traditional European fare with an all-day roast on Sun, live music Fri-Sat.

♥ Main St Café, just south of the roundabout at 262 Maunganui Rd. From 0700. Locals head here for a good, cheap breakfast.

⊙ Pubs, bars and clubs

Tauranga *p260, maps p261 and p265*
Cornerstone, The Strand. Has a distinctly European feel and is a popular spot, especially on sunny evenings when the clientele spills out on to the street.
Crown and Badger, corner of Strand and Wharf sts, T07-571 3038. Also popular, again with an English Pub theme with a good range of beers and pub grub.
Buddha Lounge, 61B The Strand, T07-928 1216. Thu-Sat until 0300. Reputed to be the best place to go in the wee hours.

⊛ Festivals and events

Tauranga *p260, maps p261 and p265*
Jan Brightstone Blues Brews and Barbecues, outdoor performances with national and international celebrities, mixed

with boutique brewery products and BBQs, www.bluesbrews.co.nz.

Apr Montana National Jazz Festival, considered (after Waiheke Auckland perhaps) to be the country's premier jazz event, performed in the Baycourt Theatre, bars and cafés, www.jazz.net.nz.

Nov Garden and Arts Festival, a biannual event held over a weekend early in the month. It alternates between a **Garden festival** where regional gardens are opened to the public, and an **Arts festival**, where visual art exhibitions are staged throughout the city.

▲ Activities and tours

Tauranga and Mount Maunganui
p260 and p262, maps p261, p265 and p263
Abseiling and climbing
Rock House, 9 Triton Av (opposite the Mount Action Centre), in Mt Maunganui, T07-572 4920, www.therockhouse.co.nz. Tue-Fri 1200-late, Sat-Sun 1000-1800, $16, child $12. A rock wall that's proving very popular. Instruction provided.

Cruising and sailing
Blue Ocean Charters, Corporation Wharf, Tauranga, T0800-224278/T07-578 9685, www.blueocean charters.co.nz. Offers a wide range of half- day, full-day or evening, scenic harbour, island and fishing trips from $80.
South Sea Sailing Company, T07- 5786444, www.southseasailing.com. Offers day- and multi-day eco-cruises aboard its luxury catamaran and is licensed to offer dolphin watching and swimming. Day trips from $120.

Dolphin watching
Butler's Swim with the Dolphins, Tauranga, T07-578 3197, www.swimwith dolphins.co.nz. $125, child $95. With over 15 years' experience of providing dolphin watching and swimming eco-trips on its 18-m sailing ship *Galaxsea*. Departs daily for an all-day trip at 0900 from the port at Tauranga and 0930 from Mt Maunganui. All gear provided, take your own lunch.

Dolphin Seafaris, Birth D5 Tauranga Bridge Marina, T0800-3268747/T07-5770105, www.nzdolphin.com. Offers a similar 3- to 4-hr trip on board a fast 50ft catamaran from$120, child $80.
Dolphin Blue, Sulphur Point Marina, Tauranga or Salisbury Wharf, Mount Maunganui, T07-5764303, www.dolphinblue.co.nz. Offers a smaller group, more personalized 6-hr dolphin watching and swimming trip on board a luxury launch, from $165, child $120, includes lunch.

Fishing
There are numerous fishing charters (including big game) available and the VIC has full listings and prices.
Blue Ocean Charters, Wharf St, Tauranga, T07-578 9685, www.blueoceancharters.co.nz. Wide range of opportunities including diving, dolphin watching and fishing, from $80.
Tauranga Marine Charters, Pier D34, Bridge Marina, T07-552 6283, www.taurangamarine charters.co.nz. Lots of local knowledge.

4WD and quad biking
U-Drive (Longridge Park), Te Puke, T0800-867386/T07-5331515, www.adventure4wd.co.nz. One of the region's best 4WD activity operators and is based at the Longridge Park complex in Te Puke. It has over 3 km of track and a wide range of vehicles. Suitable for all levels, from $55, child $35. Also offers jet-boating up the Kaituna River from $95, child $45.

Helicopter flights
Aerius, Te Puke, T07-533 1838, www.aerius.co.nz. Flights in a cute little red number, from $190, White Island from $570.
Kiwikopters, Tauranga airport, T07-572 4077, www.kiwicopters.co.nz. For the iconic Bell 47s (à la M.A.S.H TV series) that has its own MASH medical camp to land in.

Horse trekking
Briar's, 22A Otimi St, Te Puke, T07-533 2582, www.briarshorsetrek.co.nz. Beach and coastal rides with great views, from $70, 3hr $120.

World of Horses, SH2 between Tauranga and Katikati (14 km), T07-5571754, www.horsesinc.co.nz. Offers not only horse trekking but also display, corral, show stables and a café.

Jet boating and jet skiing

Longridge Park, Te Puke, T07-533 1515. Among its many attractions is a thrilling jet-boat ride, $95, child $45.

Kayaking

Oceanix, Mt Maunganui, T0800-335800, www.oceanix.co.nz. Offers a range of excursions that take in very different environments from New Zealand's largest port and the Maunganui Heads to the McLaren Falls Park. Sunset and moonlight trips are also an option.
Waimarino Adventure Park, Bethlehem, Tauranga, T07-576 4233, www.waimarino.com. Also offers a range of guided and self-guided day trips on Tauranga Harbour and local rivers with one taking in a glowworm canyon, from $120.

Mountain biking

Oropi Grove, 3 km up Oropi Rd from SH28, accessed off Joyce Rd (off Pyes Pa Rd), Tauranga, T07-577 3055. Considered the best track in the area.

Parasailing and kite surfing

Assault Kite Surfing, 24 Pacific Ave, Mt Maunganu, T07-5757831, www.assault.co.nz. One-on-one lessons from $50 per hour.

Rafting

The **Wairoa**, **Kaituna** and **Rangitaiki** rivers near Tauranga are major venues for white-water rafting. For operators, see page 258.

Scenic flights and flight simulator

Flight Experience, Tauranga airport, Dakota Way, T07-574 3737, www.flightexperience.co.nz, from $135, 90 min, $295. If taking the controls of a commercial airliner takes your fancy, then this flight simulator will bring the reality that little bit closer.

Tauranga Aero Club, Aerodrome Rd, T07-575 3210. Scenic flights and hands-on trail flight from $100.

Scuba diving

The 2 main operators in the city offer dive and snorkelling tours around Mt Maunganui and to local wrecks and Mayor Island.
Dive Tauranga/Earth2Ocean, 50 Cross Rd, Tauranga, T07-571 5286, www.earth2ocean.co.nz
Dive HQ, 213 Cameron Rd, T07-578 4050, www.divehqtauranga.co.nz.

Sightseeing and wine tours

The VIC (I-Site) has a full listing of local day trip operators in the area.
Tasting Tours, Ohauiti, Tauranga, T07-544 1383, www.tastingtours.co.nz. An entertaining day of beer and wine tasting with lunch at the very congenial **Mills Reef Vineyard Restaurant**, from $130.

Surfing

Matakana Island is a short boat trip (or long paddle) from Mt Manganui and offers some of the most pristine tubes in the country. The island doesn't break as often as some of its east coast counterparts and scoring the right combination of wind and tide is tricky, but once you've sampled a Makatana tube you'll be wanting more.

Tandem skydiving

Tauranga Tandem Skydiving, at the airport, T07-576 7990, www.tandemskydive.co.nz, from $245.

Thermal pools

There are numerous hot pools in the area, with the most popular being the **Mount Maunganui Hot Pools** (see page 263). There are also hot springs at:
Athenree, Athenree Rd, north of Tauranga, on SH2, T07-863 5600, daily 0900-1700.
Fernland Spa Mineral Hot Pools, 250 Cambridge Rd (SH29), Tauranga, T07-578 3081, daily 1000-2200.

Walking

The *Tauranga Walkways* booklet is free from the VIC and outlines a number of local walks. The walks around **Mt Maunganui** and to its summit are the main attraction, but the **McLaren Falls Park** (about 10 km south of the city on SH29, T07-543 1099, Wed-Sun), and the **Rerekawau Falls (Kaiate Falls)** tracks (signposted from Welcome Bay Road) have other short walking opportunities. In McLaren Falls Park there are also some interesting animals including very hairy Tibetan yaks. The **Kaimai Ranges**, just to the west of the city, also offer numerous longer and more strenuous walks.

⊖ Transport

Tauranga *p260, maps p261 and p265*
Car hire Avis, Tauranga Airport, T07-5741840; **Budget**, Tauranga Airport, T07-5742299; **Rent-A-Dent**, 19 Fifteenth Av, T07-578 1772; **Rite Price Rentals**, 25 Totara St, Mt Maunganui, T0800-250251. **Taxi** Taxi Cabs, T07-575 4054; **Tauranga Mount Taxis**, T07-578 6086.

❶ Directory

Tauranga *p260, maps p261 and p265*
Banks Major branches and ATMs in the city centre. **Internet** Gateway, Shop 18, Goddard Centre, Devonport Rd, T07-571 1112; Maunganui Library, Maunganui Rd; **Mount Internet**, 87 Maunganui Rd, T07-575 0860, 0900-2000; Tauranga Library, Willow St. **Medical services** Baycare, 10th St, T07- 578 8000. 1700-0800; Hospital, Cameron Rd, T07-579 8000. **Post office** 536 Cameron Rd, T07-5711690, Mon-Fri 0800-1700, Sat 0900-1200.

Whakatane and Opotiki → *Colour map 2, B4.*

Whakatane is the principal town in the eastern Bay of Plenty, at the mouth of the Whakatane River. It has a vibrant atmosphere that is often lacking in many New Zealand towns of the same size. There is just something about it – something that can warm the heart. Opotiki, 60 km southeast of Whakatane, near the mouths of the Waioeka and Otara rivers, is a small seaside town with some fine beaches and, like Whakatane, is rich in Maori history, with settlement taking place before the great migrations of the 14th century. It was the base of the Hauhau – a semi-religious sect of Maori rebels who were fierce enemies of the early Pakeha. ▶▶ *For Sleeping, Eating and other listings, see pages 272-274.*

Ins and outs

Getting there and around **Whakatane airport** ① *just northwest of the town off SH2*, is served by **Air New Zealand Link**, T0800-737000. The airport shuttle will get you into town for about $20, T07-5474444. For taxis T07-3080222. **Intercity** and **Naked Bus** buses run to Whakatane from around the country; the VIC (I-Site) acts as a booking agent. The Bay of Plenty company **Bay Bus**, T0800-368267, runs services to and from Tauranga daily except Sunday and Opotiki on Mon and Wed. You can connect with the East Cape and Opotiki shuttle from Whakatane. For shuttle buses going around the East Cape (SH35), see page 326.

Tourist information **Whakatane VIC (I-Site)** ① *corner of Quay Drive and Kakahoroa Drive (east of the centre), T0800-942528/T07-308 6058, www.whakatane.com, Mon-Fri 0800-1700, Sat-Sun1000-1600 (reduced hours in winter)*, also has DoC information. **Opotiki VIC** (I-Site) ① *corner of St John and Elliot sts, T07-315 3031, www.opotikinz.com, daily 0800-1700*. The **DoC** ① *T07-315 1001*, is an adjunct to this office. The free booklet *Opotiki and East Cape Free Holiday Guide* is a must for anyone touring the area.

Whakatane

The major attraction of Whakatane is as a gateway to visit the active volcano **White Island**, which can, on a clear day, be seen 50 km offshore, steaming away merrily. The other major activities are swimming with dolphins, fishing and, to a lesser extent, walking in the **Urewera National Park**, **Whirinaki Forest Park** and **Tarawera Falls** areas. The town also enjoys some of the highest annual sunshine hours in the country.

If you have your own transport, perhaps the best thing to do first is to get your bearings. To do this take Hillcrest Road south from the centre of town and the road over the hill west towards Ohope Beach. At the crest of the hill turn left and follow the signs to the **Kohi Point Scenic Reserve**. At the headland (which was the *pa* site of the first Maori settlers) you will get a grand view of the town, the coast and White Island. From here you can also embark on a number of short or long scenic coastal walks.

The island close to shore is **Moutohora Island**, also known as **Whale Island** (it does indeed look like a whale from the side). Moutohora is another less active volcano which has some hot springs and a number of historic *pa* sites. It is privately owned and a wildlife refuge administered by DoC. Although generally off limits, DoC does offer occasional guided tours in the summer months; contact the VIC (I-Site) for details.

Back in the town centre another natural feature is the **Pohaturoa**, a large rock outcrop located at the corner of the Strand and Commerce Street. For some six centuries this was used by the Maori as a meeting place and was also where the local Ngati Awa tribe signed the Treaty of Waitangi in the 1840s. While the summit was used as a sacred place for the bones of early chiefs, the newborns were given a form of baptism and dedicated to the gods in a stream at its foot. More local information can be gleaned at the **Whakatane District Museum and Gallery** ⓘ *Boon St, T07-306 0505, www.whakatanemuseum.org.nz, Mon-Fri 1000-1630, Sat-Sun 1100-1500, donation*. As well as a wealth of historical displays and a fine dynamic gallery space, it houses a collection of over 20,000 photographs.

No trip to Whakatane would be complete without a short drive west along to the harbour entrance to see sculpture of **Wairaka** – a fine tribute to the town's roots. There is a **mural** on the wall at the corner of the Strand and the Quay. It depicts a scene of Maori and *Pakeha* (whites). Look closely and you will see the head of Captain Cook has been defaced a number of times (strong feelings still exist here over bicultural and land issues).

Ohope

Just 8 km over the hill from Whakatane, heading east, is the 11-km-long sandspit called **Ohope Beach**, guarding the entrance to the Ohiwa Harbour. Principally a beach resort, it is a fine place to while away a few hours in the sun, swimming, sunbathing or just watching White Island billow with steam in the distance.

Opotiki

The **Hukutaia Domain** is about 6 km from the town and signposted to the left after the Waioeka Bridge. It is a hectare of bush with many New Zealand native trees, including a historic 2000-year-old puriri tree called 'Taketakerau', with a girth of about 22 m and a height over 23 m. The hollow in this tree was used by the local Iwi to store the preserved bones of their dead, in an elaborate ritual and as protection from enemy desecration. Also of historical interest is the **Church Of Hinoa** (St Stephen's Anglican Church) at the north end of Church Street. It was originally built for the Church Missionary Society and the Reverend Karl Volkner, who first arrived in 1859. Sadly, given local bad feeling towards the *Pakeha*, he was considered a government spy and killed by Hauhau emissaries in 1865. There naturally followed much unrest in the region.

For Sleeping and Eating price codes and other relevant information, see Essentials pages 44-50.

◉ Sleeping

Whakatane *p271*

AL Motuhora Rise B&B, 2 Motuhora Rise (off Waiewe) St, T07-307 0224, www.motuhorarise. com. Fine B&B on the outskirts of town. En suites, open fire and spa. Dinners on request.

AL-A Barringtons Motor Lodge, 34 Landing Rd, T0800-830130/T07-308 4273, www.barringtonsmotorlodge.co.nz. Modern units, some with spa and disabled facilities.

AL-A Pacific Coast Motel, 41 Landing Rd, T07-308 0100, www.pacificcoastwhakatane. co.nz. A modern option with luxury 1-bedroom or studio units, and spa.

AL-A White Island Rendezvous, 15 Strand East, T0800-733529/T07-308 9588, www.whiteisland.co.nz. Part of the **Pee Jay White Island** tour operation. Modern waterfront motel with a full range of units from standard to de luxe with spa, a fully self-contained apartment and cottage. Sky TV and internet ports. Café open 0630-1700. Recommended

A Briar Rose, 54 Waiewe St, T07-308 0314. Charming cottage in bush setting close to town. Double, single and studio en suite. Good value.

A Clifton Manor Motel and B&B, 5 Clifton Rd, T0800-307214/T07-307 2145, www.cliftonmanorwhakatane.co.nz. B&B in a spacious home and self-contained units within walking distance of town centre. Pool.

B-D Karibu Backpackers, 13 Landing Rd, T07-307 8276, www.karibubackpackers.co.nz. Friendly no-nonsense suburban house hostel in central location. Tent sites. Free bike use.

B-D Lloyds Lodge Backpackers, 10 Domain Rd, T07-307 8005, www.lloydslodge.co.nz. A small, friendly option in a centrally located 1930s villa. Owned by a Maori couple who add a memorable cultural aspect to your stay. Doubles and dorms, off-street parking.

C-D Whakatane Holiday Park, McGarvey Rd, T07-308 8694. Spacious with good

facilities next to the river and only a short stroll from the town centre.

Ohope *p271*

There are numerous motels on the waterfront.

LL-AL Beachpoint Resort, 5 West End, waterfront, T0800-232247, www.beach point.co.nz. Smart modern apartments and pool overlooking the beach.

A The Ocean View, 18 West End, waterfront, T07-312 5665, www.oceanviewmotel.co.nz. 3 units without the 'resort' feel, quiet, broadband.

A-B Jody's on the Beach, 31 West End, waterfront, T07-312 4616, www.jodysbeachfrontmotels.co.nz. Five spacious ground floor units fronting the beach.

A-B The Rafters, 261A Pohutukawa Av, T07-312 4856, the_rafters_ohope@xtra.co.nz. Single apartment with sea views and full cooking facilities. Good value.

Motorcamps

C-D Ohope Beach Top Ten, 367 Harbour Rd, T07-3124460, www.ohopebeach.co.nz. A good motorcamp in a quiet spot at the west end, right on the beach.

Opotiki *p271*

L-AL Ohiwa Lodge and Day Spa, 215 Ohiwa Beach Rd via SH2, T07-315 4838, www.ohiwalodge.co.nz. A 'coastal hideway' just off SH2 between Whakatane and Opotiki. The lodge is set amid bush in an elevated position overlooking the beach. 5 suites, all with balcony and sea views, and full kitchen facilities. One suite has a private spa pool set into its balcony. Packages can include bed and breakfast and spa treatments. Recommended.

AL Capeview Cottage, 167 Tablelands Rd via SH35, T07-315 7877, www.capeview. co.nz. Peaceful, modern cottage B&B in country setting, 5 km from town.

C-D Central Oasis Backpackers, 30 King St, T07-315 5165, www.centraloasis backpackers.co.nz. A small traditional cottage in the heart of town with doubles, twins and

White Island

White Island (Whakāri) is one of New Zealand's most active cone volcanoes, built up by continuous volcanic activity over the past 150,000 years. What makes it more remarkable is that about 70 percent of the volcano is under the sea, making this massive volcanic structure one of the largest in New Zealand.

It also has an intriguing human history that revolves principally around a sulphur mining venture begun on the island in 1885. In 1914 part of the crater wall collapsed and the resulting landslide destroyed both the sulphur mine and the miners' village, along with twelve lives. What remains of the buildings from that era are now a major tourist attraction. The island became a private scenic reserve in 1953. Daily tours allow more than 10,000 people to visit

White Island every year and GeoNet constantly monitors volcanic activity. The most recent eruption was in 2000 when a new vent developed and began to emit ash. An eruption then occurred late in July, which covered the crater area in scoria, also displacing the main crater lake and forming a new crater 150 m across. Of course these days although subtle changes can occur at any time and you can never say never, it is perfectly safe to visit although all visitors must wear a hard hat.

You can visit the island by boat or by helicopter. The principal (and very good) water based tour company is **Pee Jays** (see page 274).

To see a live webcam of White Island's crater log on to www.geonet.org.nz/volcano/activity.

---

dorm. Free use of body boards and bikes and will assist with East Cape transport bookings.
C-D Opotiki Beach Backpackers, Appleton Rd, T07-315 5117, www.opotikibeach house.co.nz. A small, laid-back, beachside backpacker hostel 5 km west of the town enjoying a good reputation with doubles, twins, singles and dorms. Free use of body boards and kayaks. Pick ups from town. Closed Jun-Aug. Recommended.

Motorcamps
C-D Opotiki Holiday Park, Potts Av, T07-315 6050. The only motorcamp within the town – basic but adequate.

❷ Eating

Whakatane *p271*
There is a decent choice of eateries, and all are pretty affordable. The **New World** super-market is on Kakahora Dr. Daily 0800-2000.
⑪⑪⑪ The Wharf Shed, Strand East, T07-308 5698. Daily from 1100. Has an imaginative,

mainly seafood menu. Try the chowder.
⑪⑪ Wally's Fish and Chips, next to the Wharf Shed, Strand East. The best option for fish and chips and a chat with Wally, the parrot.
⑪⑪-⑪ The Bean, 76 Strand. Head here for a snack, and a global range of quality beans.
⑪⑪-⑪ Ground Zero Café, 163 The Strand T07-308 8548. Daily 0800-1700. Good coffe.

Ohope *p271*
⑪⑪ Sea Thai Restaurant and Bar, Fisherman's Wharf, T07-312 4005. Standard Thai fare and especially good for families. Harbour views.
⑪⑪ The Quay Café and Restaurant, 22 Pohutukawa Av, T07-312 4675. Mon-Wed 0830-1700, Thu-Sun 0830-2130. Relaxed, conveniently located with a good reputation.

Opotiki *p271*
The **New World** supermarket is at the western end of Bridge St as you head out of town.
⑪ Hot Bread Shop Café, on the main road (SH2) opposite the **Eastland Pacific Motel**, T07-315 6795. Daily 0500-1700. Wide selection of light meals, good coffee. Internet.

◑ Pubs, bars and clubs

Whatakane *p271*
The Craic, in the Whakatane Hotel. A superb small, cosy Irish pub.

▲Activities and tours

Whakatane *p271*
Dolphin watching
The bay is rich with playful dolphin. Encounters with pods of over 1000 are not uncommon.
Whale Island Tours/Dive Works, 86 The Strand, T0800-3085896/T07-3085896, www.whaleislandtours.com. Offers a weather-dependent, 3-4-hr trip to White Island with dolphin swimming and snorkelling from $150, or a 2-hr eco-cruise from $85, child $65. If you find a pod of dolphins (highly likely) you can either observe or get in the water. Several trips daily in summer. Booking essential.
Whales and Dolphins, 96 The Strand, T07-3082001, www.whalesanddolphin watch.co.nz. Offer similar trips at 0830 and 1330, from $150 (swim), $110 watch only.

Horse trekking
Tui Glen Farm, 2 km from Kawerau (25 min-drive from Whakatane), T07-323 6457, www.tuiglen.net.nz. 1 hr from $50, cattle muster $150.

Hot pools
Awakeri Hot Springs, 16 km away, just off SH30 to Rotorua southwest of the town, T07-304 9117, $5. The nearest hot pools to Whakatane. Basic but relaxing, with a motorpark and camping available.

Jet boating
Kiwi Jet Tours, T07-3070663, www.kiwijet boattours.com. Quality 20-min trips down the Rangitaiki taking in the 'Weeping Gorge', $70.

Scuba diving and snorkelling
Whale Island and White Island in particular offer some excellent diving.
Dive White (Island), Sportsworld, 186 Strand, T0800-348394, www.divewhite.co.nz. The principal operator in the area offering dive trips and snorkel trips off White Island from $180 (snorkel), $325 dive (gear included).
Diveworks (see also Dolphin watching above). Dive trips and snorkelling.

Tours to White Island and scenic flights
Air Discovery, based at Whakatane airport, T07-308 7760, www.airdiscovery.co.nz. Fixed-wing trips over White Island (1 hr 30 mins from $399).
Pee Jays, 15 Strand East, T07-308 9588, T0800-733529, www.whiteisland.co.nz. The principal (and very good) company offering excellent guided 5-6 hr trips to White Island with around 2 hr on the island. Lunch and refreshments provided. It will often deviate off schedule if dolphins are spotted, $175. Bookings essential. Recommended
Vulcan Helicopters, Whakatane airport, T0800-804354, www.vulcanheli.co.nz. 3-hr tour, 1 hr on the island, from $455.

Opotiki *p271*
Motu River Jet Boat Tours, T07-325 2735, www.motujet.co.nz. The main operator for the remote Motu River. 2 hrs, $95, child $55.
Wet 'n' Wild, T07-348 3191, www.wetnwild rafting.co.nz. Offers one of the North Island's best wilderness rafting expeditions, the multi-day trip down the remote Motu River. Provided the river levels are good, this is an unforgettable experience that will cost around $850. Recommended.

◐ Directory

Whakatane *p271*
Bike hire From Dive Works on the Strand.
Internet At the VIC and Simply Computers, 96 The Strand T07-3071209, daily 0900-1700.
Post office Corner of Commerce St and The Strand, Mon-Fri 0830-1700, Sat 0900-1200.

Contents

Footprint features

Taupo & Ruapehu

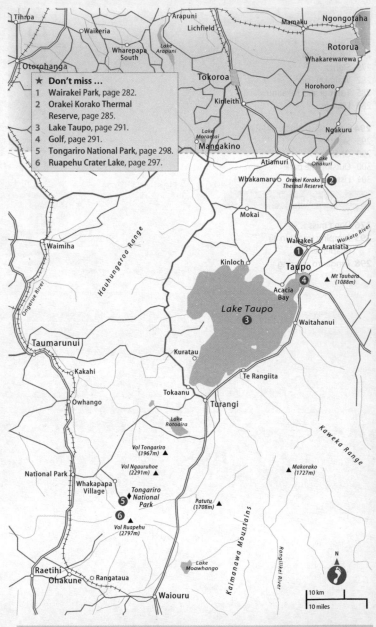

Tihroa
Waikeria
Arapuni
Lichfield
Mamaku
Ngongotaha

Wharepapa South
Lake Arapuni
Rotorua
Whakarewarewa

Otorohanga
Tokoroa
Horohoro

Kinleith
Ngakuru

Lake Maraetai
Mangakino
Atiamuri
Lake Ohakuri

Whakamaru
Orakei Korako Thermal Reserve ②

Waimiha
Mokai
Wairakei ①
Waikato River
Aratiatia

Kinloch
Taupo
Mt Tauhara (1088m) ▲

Hauhungaroa Range
Acacia Bay ④

Ongarue River
Lake Taupo ③
Waitahanui

Taumarunui
Kuratau

Kakahi
Tokaanu
Te Rangiita

Owhango
Turangi
Kaweka Range

Lake Rotoaira

Vol Tongariro (1967m) ▲

Vol Ngauruhoe (2291m) ▲
Makorako (1727m) ▲

National Park
Whakapapa Village ⑤
Tongariro National Park

⑥
Patutu (1708m) ▲

Vol Ruapehu (2797m) ▲

Kaimanawa Mountains

Raetihi
Lake Moawhango

Ohakune
Rangataua

Waiouru

Rangitikei River

N

10 km
10 miles

From space, Lake Taupo, the largest lake in New Zealand, looks like a large bullet-hole shot through the heart of the North Island. This is perhaps fitting given that its placid waters, now world famous for trout fishing, mask a frightening heritage of volcanoes and thermal activity – one that is the trademark of the Taupo and Ruapehu region. Here are the remains of the largest volcanic eruption in the last 5000 years.

Now, during its dormancy, Lake Taupo is home to a bustling tourist town, Taupo, renowned not only for its fishing, but for a host of other activities from rafting and mountain biking to tandem skydiving; you can even fly a helicopter here. But what is of added appeal in this popular volcanic hotspot is that after exerting yourself, all the aches and pains can be soothed away in the town's popular and wonderfully relaxing hot pools.

Evidence of ancient and ongoing volcanic activity is apparent throughout the region, but nowhere more so than in the Tongariro National Park. Steeped in Maori legend and spirituality, New Zealand's oldest national park boasts the still active volcanoes of Ngauruhoe and Ruapehu – the North Island's highest peak, which erupted in spectacular fashion as recently as 1996. When the mountains are in a less aggressive mood the park provides excellent skiing, tramping and walking opportunities, including the great Tongariro Crossing, a walk full of volcanic wonder and considered one of the best day hikes in the country.

Taupo and around → Colour map 3, A4 Population: 20,000.

For those heading south, Taupo is really the first place that begins to satisfy the imagination in terms of what New Zealand is 'supposed' to look like: wide open spaces with snow-capped mountains and clear blue lakes. As you come over the hill into the town on a clear day, the scene hits you like the first sip of a fine wine, with the huge expanse of Lake Taupo dwarfing the distant snow-tipped volcanoes of the Tongariro National Park. Take a while to enjoy it from the roadside lookout above the town before merging into the picture in the sure knowledge that it gets even better from here.

Because of its position in the centre of the North Island, Taupo is the commercial headquarters for the central districts of Taupo and Ruapehu, as well as a major tourist resort. The town is very pleasant, busy, friendly and well set out, nestled close to the source of the Waikato River (the longest in the country), and lies on the northernmost bank of the huge lake, once a mighty volcanic crater. The region has a multitude of activities to enjoy. Fishing is, of course, the main attraction, but you can also try the more adrenaline-pumping pursuits of bungee jumping and tandem skydiving, as well as mountain biking, golf, sailing and walking. One of the latest activities is the fairly unique opportunity to take the controls of a helicopter. Beyond the town and its lake, the glorious mountain peaks of the Tongariro National Park provide an irresistible lure with that omnipresent edge of fear that maybe, just maybe, another volcanic eruption will strike. ▸▸ *For Sleeping, Eating and other listings, see pages 286-294.*

Ins and outs

Getting there

Air **Taupo airport** ① *just off SH1, 8 km south of the town, T07-378 7771, www.taupo airport.co.nz*, receives direct daily flights from Auckland and Wellington with **Air New Zealand Link**, T0800-737000, www.airnewzealand.co.nz, with connections from the South Island. Shuttles and taxis usually meet incoming flights at the airport. **Taupo Taxis**, T07-378 5100, operates an airport shuttle service from $20. Shuttles can also be booked with **Taupo Top Cabs**, T07-378 9250.

Road Taupo is on the SH1, 280 km south of Auckland and 80 km from Rotorua; it is a major stop on the tourist 'Thermal Explorer Highway'. By bus Taupo is served daily by **Newman's**, **Intercity** and **Nakedbus.com**, which arrive and depart from the **Travel Centre** ① *16 Gascoigne St, T07-378 9032.*

Turangi is well served by both **Newman's**, **Intercity** and **Nakedbus.com** which stop near the VIC (I-Site) on the corner of Ngawaka Rd and Ohuanga St. The VIC (I-Site) also acts as bus ticketing agents.

Getting around

Tongariro Expeditions, T07-377 0435, www.thetongarirocrossing.co.nz, offers daily services via Turangi to Tongariro Alpine Crossing in summer, or Whakapapa in winter.

The **Alpine Hot Bus**, T0508-468287, www.alpinehotbus.co.nz, offers transport to the track and pick-ups from your accommodation. See Tongariro National Park, page 294, for details.

In Taupo itself the **Lake Taupo Hot Bus**, T0508-468287, www.hotbus.co.nz, is a hop-on/hop-off service that links most major attractions including the hot pools, Huka Falls and the Craters of the Moon, with an hourly service 1000-1600, $15 return day pass to one attraction then an extra $5 for each attraction after that.

In Turangi, beyond the Taupo services (above), **Mountain Shuttle**, T0800-117686, www.tongarirocrossing.com, offers a Tongariro Alpine Crossing shuttle service at 0545, 0730 from $35. For taxis, bike hire and car rental see Transport, page 294.

Tourist information

Taupo VIC (I-Site) ① *30 Tongariro St, SH1, T07-376 0027, www.laketauponz.co.nz, daily 0830-1700*, has all the usual information and a good range of maps. It also handles DoC enquiries and offers specialist information available on the Tongariro Crossing (see box page 298) with up-to-date weather forecasts.

Turangi VIC (I-Site) ① *Ngawaka Pl, just off SH1, T07-386 8999, www.laketaupo nz.com, www.ruapehunz.com, daily 0830-1730*, sells fishing licenses ($21 for 24 hours) and provides information about where to catch the 'big ones'. Internet is available and there is information on other activities in the Kaimanawa Forest Park and Tongariro National Park. Hut bookings and ski passes can also be arranged. All the local DoC information is held at the VIC (I-Site).

Sights

Taupo's natural sights are mostly outside the town itself (see below and Tongariro National Park, page 294). The most immediate and dominant sight in town is of course the huge expanse of **Lake Taupo** itself – 619 sq km. On a calm day it can be mirror-like, disturbed only by the wakes of boats and ducks. But it wasn't always like this and the origin of the lake itself will make you quake in your walking boots: Lake Taupo is in fact the tranquil remains of one of the biggest volcanic eruptions the planet has created in the last 5000 years. The latest occurred in AD 186 spewing out over 30 cu km of debris at up to 900 kph (about 30 times more than Mount St Helens spewed out).

The now placid waters are famous for copious trout and are the domain of the serious angler. The lake is used for numerous other water-based activities including sailing, cruising, windsurfing and waterskiing. Most of the longer cruises take in the remarkable **Maori rock carvings** (a huge face complete with *moko* or tattoos), which can only be seen from the water and adorn an entire rock face in Mine Bay, 8 km southwest across the lake. Although remarkable, they were only created in recent years, which does somewhat dampen the excitement. For cruising and other lake activities, see Activities and tours, page 290.

Near the oriental-style trout statue is the **Taupo Museum and Art Gallery** ① *Story Pl, T07-376 0414, daily 1030-1630, donation $5*. There are some interesting photos and artworks that focus on the early days of the region, and a gallery that features regular exhibitions. Just a little further west the **Waikato River** begins its 425-km journey to the Tasman Sea and winds its merry way north behind the town towards **Wairakei Park** (see below).

On a cliff edge, carved out over the millennia by the river, is the headquarters for **Taupo Bungy** ① *202 Spa Rd, T0800-888408, www.taupobungy.co.nz*, which might be your first opportunity to get an elastic band tied to your ankles before throwing yourself over a 45 m cliff. Masochistic adrenaline junkies will be delighted to hear that the ones in the South Island are at least twice this height. A jump in Taupo will cost from $109, which includes a video and some photos with which to terrify the folks back home. You can also jump again for $55. Good practice!

The **AC Baths** ① *top of Spa Rd, T07-3760305 www.taupovenues.co.nz/ac baths.asp, daily 0600-2100, $6.50, child $2.50*, is one of two large thermal pool complexes in Taupo. Here you can soak away all your troubles in a range of recently renovated outdoor, indoor and private spa pools while the kids do their thing on the hydro-slide. Next door, the

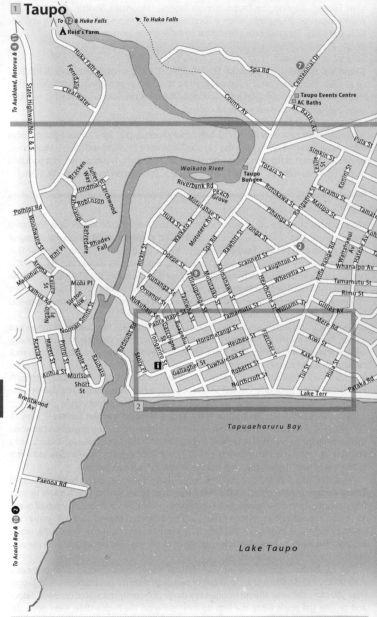

To ⑫ & Huka Falls

▼ To Huka Falls

▲ Reid's Farm

To ⑪

To Auckland, Rotorua & ④

State Highway No 1 & 5

Huka Falls Rd

Ferndale

Clearwater

Spa Rd

⑦

Centennial Dr

County Av

Taupo Events Centre

AC Baths

AC Baths Av

Pula St

Bracken

Jules' St

Larchwood

Hindmarsh

Robinson

Kahuang

Belvedere

Rhodes Fall

Waikato River

Riverbank Rd

Peach Grove

Totara St

Taupo Bungee

Rotokawa St

Tongariro Rd

Matipo St

Kohm

Simkin St

Castle St

Karamu St

Tamate

Poihipi Rd

Woodward St

Rini Pl

Motuahae St

Huka St

Waikato St

Motutere Av

Spa Rd

Rawhiti St

Tonga St

Pihanga St

②

Whanaipo Av

Koha

Tai

Whitianaui Av

Hatepe Rd

Rickit St

Odene St

Runanga St

Ortamui St

Nukuhau St

Tuiraone St

Motuariki St

Scannell St

Laughton St

Heuchroft St

Wherena St

Tamamutu St

Rimu St

Arama St

Kaimu Rd

Mahunui St

Kaimu Rd

Green

Simon Row

Norman Smith St

Mohi Pl

Redoubt Rd

Raubato

Story Pl

Paora Gascoigne St

Hape St

Tongario St

Tuiraone St

Ruapehu St

Horomatangi St

Tamamutu St

Williams St

Gilles Av

Mere Rd

Kiwi St

Tui St

Paraka St

Kaka St

Hula St

Pitroi St

Marei St

Acacias St

Noble St

Morison

Short St

ℹ️

Gallagher St

Tuwharetoa St

Heuheu St

Roberts St

Northcroft St

Peche St

Lake Terr

Brentwood Av

Anhia St

②

Tapuaeharuru Bay

To Acacia Bay & ⑩②

Paenoa Rd

Lake Taupo

➡ Taupo maps
1 Taupo
2 Taupo centre, page 287
3 Wairakei Park, page 283

400 metres
400 yards

Sleeping
Anchorage Resort Motel **1**
Berkenhoff Lodge **2**
Hilton Lake Taupo **5**
Huka Lodge **12**
Lakeland **6**
Lake Taupo Lodge **10**
Lake Taupo Top Ten
  Holiday Park **7**
Rainbow Lodge
  Backpackers **9**
Wairakei Resort **4**
Wairakei Thermal Valley
  Motor Camp **11**

Eating 🍴
L'Arte Music Café
  & Sculpture Garden **2**
Ploughmans Pub **1**

Taupo Events Centre ⓘ *T07-376 0350, www.taupoevents centre.co.nz*, hosts major sporting tournaments, exhibitions and trade shows. It also has a quality 12-m **climbing wall**, see Activities and tours, page 290.

The other thermal complex is the excellent and recently refurbished **Taupo Hot Springs** ⓘ *next to De Brett's just off SH5 (which heads west from SH1, along the lake front at the southern edge of town), T07-377 6502, www.taupohotsprings.com, daily 0730-2130, $15, child $6*. This is the better of the two complexes with all the usual facilities including a massage and beauty treatment centre, hydro-slides and private pools. It's a fine place to relax and mix with the locals. **Hot Bus**, T07-377 1967, offers a return shuttle to the pools for $15.

Wairakei Park ●▲ ▸▸ *pp286-294.*

Huka Falls
ⓘ *Signposted from the SH1, accessed via the Huka Falls Rd, www.hukafalls.com. There is an information kiosk in the car park at the falls.*
No visit to Taupo would be complete without seeing the mighty Huka Falls. In the heart of the Wairakei Park north of the town, these falls are arguably the most spectacular in the country. From a sedate steady flow roughly 100 m across, the waters of the Waikato River are forced through a cleft of solid rock only 15 m wide, before falling 7 m into a cauldron of aquatic chaos and foam. From the car park a bridge crosses the rapids before joining a walkway down to the waterfall where, depending on the flow (regulated at Lake Taupo for electricity generation), the falls can be up to 11 m in height with a staggering volume of 220,000 litres per second.

The **walking tracks** that lead both north and south along the river from here are worthy of a trek on foot or mountain bike. Just up river is the exclusive retreat of **Huka Lodge** (see Sleeping, page 286), an exorbitant luxury pad that hosts the filthy rich and visiting dignitaries.

Honey Hive
ⓘ *T07-3748553, www.honeyhivetaupo.com, daily 0900-1700, free.*
Carrying along the Huka Falls Loop Road (north) you can take a small diversion to admire the view looking back at the falls, before passing **Helistar Helicopters** (see page 292) and arriving at the Honey Hive. For honey monsters this is the 'place to bee' with some interesting interpretative displays, a working glass-fronted hive and the **Honey Hive Café**. There is also a shop where you can purchase a tub of Manuka honey, the most delectable toast spread on earth.

Volcanic Activity Centre
ⓘ *T07-374 8375, www.volcanoes.co.nz, daily 1000-1700, $9.50, child $5. The fascinating website provides the latest status reports on national earthquakes and eruptions.*
The next attraction along the road is the Volcanic Activity Centre and its geological delights. It's well worth a peek, if only to get an inkling of the scale and magnitude of the natural powers that lie beneath your feet. The Taupo district is in the heart of one of the most active volcanic zones in the world, the details of which are well presented in the centre. There are models and displays, all with appropriate shaking and rumbling noises.

Prawn Park
ⓘ *T07-374 8474, www.prawnfarm.co.nz, daily 0900-1630, from $15, child $10.*

Carrying along Huka Falls Road you pass **NZ Woodcraft** (a glorified native wood souvenir workshop) before reaching the road end and the riverbank. Here you will find Prawn Park. Hailed as the world's only geothermal prawn farm, you can join an informative tour of the nursery and hatchery (to meet 'em), or fish for a few (catch 'em) and then tuck into a few (and eat 'em), in the **Prawn Farm Restaurant**. After all that you can perhaps understand

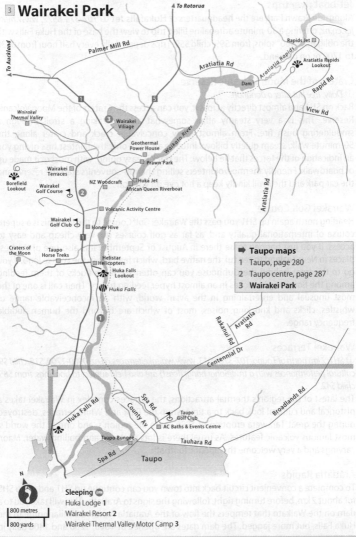

3 **Wairakei Park**

⇨ Taupo maps
1 Taupo, page 280
2 Taupo centre, page 287
3 Wairakei Park

Sleeping 🛏
Huka Lodge 1
Wairakei Resort 2
Wairakei Thermal Valley Motor Camp 3

800 metres
800 yards

why their star captive was called 'Grumpy' – apparently the largest prawn in captivity. Now, alas, it seems an unfortunate sweaty person in a prawn suit with googly eyes (yet amusingly half blind), wandering the premises trying not to walk in to tables and chairs has taken the limelight. Somehow, you have to admire the effort. Prawnless meals are also available in the restaurant for those of a sensitive disposition.

Jet-boat river trips
Alongside Prawn Park are the headquarters of **Hukafalls Jet** ① *T07-374 8572, www.huka jet.co.nz*, offering a 30-minute adrenaline filled trip to view the base of the Huka Falls with the obligatory 360° spins, from $99, child $59. Trips depart daily every half hour from 0830 to 1700 or on demand.

Craters of the Moon Volcanic Reserve
① *Daily, free but offer a donation.*
Back on SH1 and almost directly across it, you can access the Craters of the Moon Volcanic Reserve. This is a very steamy affair somewhat akin to taking a stroll through a smouldering bush fire. From almost every conceivable crack and crater along the 50-minute walk, steam quietly billows into the air, with only the faintest hiss giving you an indication of the forces that lie below. The track is easy going, with most of it made up of boardwalk. Friendly thermo-volunteers selling thermo-souvenirs staff the reserve and the car park and they will kindly keep a hot eye on your car.

Wairakei Golf Course
Heading north again up SH1 you pass the Wairakei Golf Course to the left. This is a superb course of international quality and, as far as golf courses go, very cheap and easy to access. If you just happen to be there in August or September it is also one of the best places in New Zealand to see **tui**, the native bird, which features in the course logo. If you go to the trees behind the clubhouse you can often see large flocks of them feeding among the flowering branches in an almost hyper feeding frenzy. Their call is one of the most unusual and entertaining in the avian world, with an inconceivable range of whistles, clicks and knocking noises, most of which are beyond the human audible frequency range.

Wairakei Terraces
① *SH1, 7 km north of Taupo, T07-378 0913, www.wairakeiterraces.co.nz, 0900-1700, $18, child $9; cultural performances with a traditional hangi (feast) are also held subject to bookings, from $85, child $42.*
The latest of the region's thermal attractions, the terraces complex in Wairakei takes a historical and cultural look back to a time when the Pink and White terraces, destroyed during the great Tarawera eruption of 1886, were the region's, and one of the world's, most famous volcanic features. As usual there is lots of steam and boiling water, Maori carvings and a very welcome therapeutic footbath.

Aratiatia Rapids
To complete a convenient circuit back into town you can continue up SH1 and on to SH5 for about 2 km, before turning right, following the signs to Aratiatia. This will take you to a dam on the Waikato that tempers the flow of the Aratiatia rapids, a similar gorge to the Huka Falls, but more jagged. The dam gates are opened at 1000, 1200 and 1400 daily in

winter (plus 1600 in summer); all openings depend on water levels. You can see the rapids from a viewpoint just beside the dam or from a hilltop lookout about 1 km further up the road. From here it is a short drive back into Taupo via the Taupo Golf Club on Spa Road. **Rapids Jet** ① *T0800-727437/T07-374 8066, www.rapidsjet.com, from $90, child $50*, is at the base of the falls on Rapids Road. It's an entertaining trip beginning with a spin upstream to the base of the controlled rapids and power station, then downstream through a series of rapids with plenty of 360° spins along the way.

Orakei Korako Thermal Reserve
① *Head north from Taupo on SH1 for 27 km, turn right onto Tutukau Rd for 13 km, then left on to Orakei Korako Rd, T07-378 3131, www.orakeikorako.co.nz, 0830-1630 (hours vary according to demand), $34, child $14.*
About 40 km north of Taupo is one of the least visited, but best thermal parks in the country. Even without the thermal park, this tranquil lakeside spot, formed by another dam on the Waikato, offers the visitor sanctuary from the hustle and bustle of Taupo and its busy tourist attractions. From the lakeside visitor centre and **Geyserland Resort Lodge** only plumes of steam and a strange colourful silica terrace across the water give any indication of the numerous interesting volcanic features awaiting you. Once delivered at the terraces by boat you are free to roam the self-guided tracks of the reserve. There is a bit of everything here including colourful algae-covered silica terraces, boiling pools, geysers and lots of bubbling mud. Added to that, a short boat trip takes you to the fascinating Ruatapu Cave which descends into the earth, with the warm Waiwhakaata Pool (Pool of Mirrors) at its base. Apparently, if you put your left hand in the pool and make a secret wish, it will come true. The cave itself is about 40 m deep and from its depths you can look heavenwards towards its gaping entrance and the daylight, shrouded by fronds of silhouetted silver fern. You can stay as long as you like in the reserve before re-boarding the boat back to the visitor centre. If you have any questions about the reserve ask local guide Chris, an entertaining and knowledgeable 'geyser'.

Pureora Forest Park
This little-known forest park to the west of Taupo offers a number of easy short walks as well as the more demanding climb to the summit of **Mount Pureora** (1165 m). The park is also the focus for the successful reintroduction of the **kokako**, a native bird with a beautiful haunting song. Most of the main park sights can be taken in on a scenic drive that starts from Kakaho Road, south of the intersection of SH32 and Poihipi Road, to emerge again at Mangakino. For maps and more information see the Taupo VIC (I-Site), see page 279.

Turangi and Tokaanu ☺🛈⛰👣 *pp286-294.* → *Colour map 3, A3 Population: 4000.*

① *SH1, 50 km south of Taupo, 4 km inland from the southeastern edge of Lake Taupo.*
Turangi is a small, pleasant village, world famous for the trout fishing on the scenic Tongariro River that flows past its eastern edge before quietly spilling into the huge expanses of the lake. The village is well served with accommodation and amenities and is often used as a base for exploring the Tongariro National Park.

The village would not be content without proudly displaying some live trout somewhere and the **Tongariro National Trout Centre** ① *3 km south of Turangi on SH1, T07-386 8085, daily 1000-1600, free*, tries hard. Although there is some way to go before it could be called a major attraction, you can at least see a trout hatchery in operation, huge swirling shoals of adult fish in a large pool and some others in an underwater viewing area. There is also an interpretive centre where you can muse upon some displays and learn about their interesting life cycle.

The neighbouring village of Tokaanu, 5 km to the west along SH41, also provides accommodation, amenities, and basic **thermal pools** ⓘ *Mangaroa St, T07-386 8575, 1000-2100, $8*, as well as fishing and boat access to Lake Taupo.

⦿ Taupo and around listings

For Sleeping and Eating price codes and other relevant information, see Essentials pages 44-50.

● Sleeping

Taupo *p278, maps p280, p283 and p287*
There is a wealth of motels with the best being the 'lake view' options on or around Lake Terrace and the waterfront. The cheaper options tend to be a bit 'time warped' and are in the town's western suburbs. There are also many luxury lodges, B&Bs, homestays and farmstays available, mainly around town and in Acacia Bay to the east of Taupo. For full details contact the VIC (I-Site).
LL Huka Lodge, Huka Falls Rd, T07-378 5791, www.hukalodge.com. Luxury at its most lucrative, in quiet seclusion beside the river. Mingle with heads of state and visiting stars. Watch your money evaporate.
LL Lake Taupo Lodge, 41 Mapara Rd, Acacia Bay, T07-378 7386, www.laketaupo lodge.co.nz. Another top establishment offering total luxury in 4 suites with dining room, reading gallery, open fire. Includes exquisite cuisine.
L Hilton Lake Taupo (formerly Debretts Hotel), 80 Napier-Taupo Highway, T07-378 7080, www.terraceshotel.co.nz. First established in 1889 this renovated hotel on the edge of the town has rooms, studio suites and apartments, bar and restaurant that combined offer both class and character. The added attraction of course is the **Hot Springs and Spa Resort** only a short stroll away.
L-AL Copthorne HotelTaupo, 100-102 Lake Terr, T07-376 0116, www.taupo caboose.co.nz. A luxury establishment with a

'colonial African' theme. The lodge, which sits on the waterfront overlooking the lake, offers log cabin-style architecture with an attractive range of premium suites. In-house facilities include spas, pool, and a restaurant/bar and staff can assist in arranging local activities with fishing 'safaris' a speciality.

L-AL Quest Taupo (Aspen Villas), 9-11 Tui St, T07-378 7487, www.questtaupo.co.nz. Immaculate 4-star fully self-contained units with spa 50 m from the lakefront.
AL Lakeland, 282 Lake Terr, Two Mile Bay, T07-378 3893, www.lakeland.co.nz. Mid-range comfort next to the lake. Restaurant and bar, spas and pool.
AL-A Tui Oaks, corner of Lake Terr and Tui St, T07-378 8305, www.tuioaks.co.nz. One of the best motels in the mid-range, great views across the lake. Pool, restaurant and bar.
A Anchorage Resort , Lake Front, Two Mile Bay, T07-378 5542, www.taupo motel.co.nz. Good facilities including pool, spas and gym.
A Ascot, 70 Rifle Range Rd, T07-377 2474, www.ascotattaupo.co.nz. Comfortable modern motel within walking distance of town.
A Catelli's Motel, 23-27 Rifle Range Rd, T07-378 4477, www.catellis.co.nz.

Backpacker hostels
C-D Action Downunder YHA Hostel, 56 Kaimanawa St, T07-378 3311, www.yha.co.nz. A very tidy 86-bed YHA associate with great modern rooms and facilities including family and double en suites with personal computer and internet – a rare find. Off-street parking, impressive kitchen facilities, outdoor

big-screen movies, spa, gym and bike hire. All in all one of the best YHAs in the North Island.

C-D Berkenhoff Lodge, 75 Scannell St, T07-378 4909, www.berkenhofflodge.co.nz. Slightly out of the centre but has a fine rambling atmosphere and is friendly and well kept. An added attraction is the basic in-house bar (locally popular), café, spa and free bikes.

C-D Rainbow Lodge Backpackers, 99 Titiraupenga St, T07-378 5754, www.rainbow lodge.co.nz. Well-established, popular and congenial backpacker hostel that has been satisfying clients for many years. Good dorms and excellent doubles. Recommended.

C-D Tiki Lodge, 104 Tuwharetoa St, T0800-845456/T07-377 4545, www.tikilodge.co.nz. A modern purpose-built hostel in the heart of town. Excellent facilities include spacious double en suites, spa, internet and off-street parking. The excellent staff will ensure you have a comfortable stay. Recommended.

C-D Urban Retreat, 65 Heuheu St, T07-378 6124, www.tur.co.nz. Another modern, purpose-built party-oriented hostel right in the heart of town. Full range of rooms centered around a happening social area and bar that is

the focus for early evening action before heading out on the town. Good facilities throughout. A great place to meet others and be social, but not if you intend to catch up on some sleep and gather your thoughts.

Motorcamps and campsites

A-D De Brett's Thermal Resort, Napier/Taupo Highway (SH5), T07-378 8559, www.debrettsresort.co.nz. A well-facilitated 5-star motorpark located right opposite the best hot pools complex in the town. Standard and self-contained cabins, studio and family units and lodges. Powered and non-powered sites, camp kitchen and TV lounge. Concession rates to thermal pools are an added incentive. Recommended.

B-D Lake Taupo Top Ten Holiday Park, 28 Centennial Dr, T07-378 6860. An adequate if not overly spacious alternative, closer to town and opposite the newly renovated AC Thermal Baths.

B-D Wairakei Thermal Valley Motor Camp, Wairakei, T07-3748004. Basic camping with powered sites and camp kitchen 9 km north of Taupo and 1.5 km from SH1. The appeal here is the peaceful location and the small

2 Taupo centre

Lake Taupo

200 metres
200 yards

Sleeping
Action Downunder
YHA Hostel 1

Ascot 9
Catelli's Motel 3
Copthorne Hotel Taupo 2
Quest Taupo (Aspen Villas) 8
Tiki Lodge 5
Tui Oaks 7
Urban Retreat 6

Eating
Burbury 7
Creative Café 6
Friends 1
Lotus Thai 3
Mr India 5
Mulligan's 4
Pimento's 12
Plateau 2

➡ **Taupo maps**
1 Taupo, page 280
2 **Taupo centre**
3 Wairakei Park, page 283

Bars & clubs
Finn MacCauls 11
Jolly Good Fellows 13

menagerie of visitor loving animals roaming free. Missing your pets? Here is the solution.

Wairakei Park *p282, map p283*
LL-L Wairakei Resort, 7 km north of town on SH1 and right in the heart of all the Wairakei Park attractions, T07-374 8021, www.wairakei.co.nz. One of the few conventional-style hotel resorts in the area, and right in the heart of all the Wairakei Park attractions. It is well appointed and laid out with good facilities especially for the sporty, with tennis, golf and squash, plus a spa, pool and sauna in which to relax after all the activity.
B-D Wairakei Thermal Valley Motor Camp (see above), Wairakei, T07-3748004.

Turangi and Tokaanu *p285*
LL River Birches, T0800-102025/ T07-386 0445, www.river birches.co.nz. Very classy boutique fishing lodge with 3 sumptuous en suites. Breakfast included, 3-course dinner available for $80. Geared up for anglers, but recommended for any discerning traveller.
LL Tongariro Lodge, Grace Rd, T07-386 7946, www.tongarirolodge.co.nz. Fine lodge on the banks of the river. Range of very luxurious chalets, some with kitchen facilities. Again, geared up for anglers with its own resident fishing guides. Restaurant and bar.
AL-A Anglers Paradise Resort, corner of SH41and Ohuanga Rd, T07-386 8980, www.anglersparadise.co.nz. Well-appointed motel with swimming pool and spas.
A-B Creel Lodge Motel, 183-187 Taupahi Rd, T07-386 8081, www.creel.co.nz. Popular due to its position backing on to the Tongariro River, peaceful atmosphere and good value.
A-B Parklands Motorlodge, corner of SH1 and Arahori St, T07-386 7515, www.parklands motorlodge.co.nz. Modern and comfortable, close to the Rafting Centre. Pool, spa, sauna, restaurant and bar, activities organized.
B-D Extreme Backpackers, 26 Ngawaka Pl, T07-386 8949, www.extremebackpackers. co.nz. Very tidy lodge-style accommodation with private and shared rooms. Café with

open fire, climbing wall and internet. Recommended.
B-D Riverstone Backpackers, 222 Tautahanga Rd, T07-386 7004, www.riverstoneback packers.co.nz. 'Purpose-renovated boutique' backpacker hostel, 4 mins from the town centre. Standard room types with shared or private bath. Spacious and well equipped, with indoor and outdoor log fires that add to a relaxed and cosy atmosphere. Equipment hire.

Motorcamps and campsites
There are two well equipped motorparks in Turangi and another (arguably the best) in Tokaanu 4 km west of here.
C-D Club Habitat, Ohuanga Rd, T07-386 7492, www.clubhabitat.co.nz. Large motel, motorcamp and campsite with good facilities.
C-D Turangi Cabins and Holiday Park, Ohuanga Rd, T07-386 8754, www.turangi cabins.co.nz. Again good facilities and handy to the town centre.
C-D Oasis Motel and Caravan Park, SH41, Tokaanu, T07-386 8569, www.oasismotel.co.nz. A very peaceful little motorpark with the adequate facilities and the added attraction of some ageing but functional hot pools – perfect after tackling the Tongariro Crossing.

Eating

Taupo *p278, maps p280 and p287*
There is a wide selection of restaurants, cafés and brasseries in Taupo, most are in the many motels and in the heart of town, around the waterfront. If you have been looking forward to sampling a big fat juicy trout, you will be disappointed. Under the conservation act it is illegal to buy or sell trout. However, if you have had a successful fishing trip most restaurants will be delighted to cook your catch for you. There is a plethora of mid-range eateries along the waterfront and Robert St, all claiming to have the best menus and views.

There are 2 supermarkets: **Woolworths**, corner Spa and Tongariro sts, T07-349 7040; and **Pak-N-Save**, Ruapehu St, T07-377 1155.

¶¶¶ **The Brantry Restaurant**, 45 Rifle Range Rd, Taupo, T07-3780484. Owned and operated by local sisters Prue and Felicity Campbell the Brantry is fast earning a reputation as one of Taupo's best. Set in a stylishly refurbished 1950s townhouse you can enjoy the intimacy of the cellar room or the buzz of alfresco in summer. Beautifully presented and affordable contemporary NZ cuisine and an extensive wine list. Perhaps try the set 3-course option and for sweet the divine Tiramisu.

¶¶¶ **The Lotus Thai Restaurant**, 137 Tongariro St, T07-376 9497. Daily 1200-2100, closed Tue. Good Thai fare.

¶¶¶ **Mr India**, 30 Tuwharetoa, T07-377 1969. Mon-Sat 1100-1430 for lunch and from 1730 for dinner. Reliable Indian option.

¶¶¶ **Pimento's**, 17 Tamamutu St, T07-377 4549. From 1800 (closed Tue). A firm local favourite offering an imaginative Pacific Rim menu and tidy aesthetics.

¶¶¶ **Plateau**, 64 Tuwharetoa St, T07-377 2425. Daily from 1130. If you are looking for a good traditional beef or lamb dish look no further. An imaginative menu and congenial surroundings including a great open fire.

¶¶¶ **HiltonHotel Restaurant**, Napier-Taupo Highway, T07-378 7080, www.terraces hotel.co.nz. Historic hotel with a classy restaurant. A fine option and a good evening out especially when combined with a visit to the **Hot Springs and Spa**, a short stroll away.

¶ **L'Arte Mosaic café and Sculpture Garden**, 225 Marapa Rd (2.5 km off Acacia Bay Rd right on to Marapa Rd), Acacia Bay, Taupo T07-3782962. Open Wed-Sun 0900-1600. A magical little café that has grown around the work and imaginations of local clay artist Judi Brennan. Her signature quirky clay garden decor adorned with colourful mosaics and the work of other local artists are a delight and the food and coffee is also well worth the trip. Try the famous 'eggs benny'.

¶ **Friends**, 42 Roberts St, T07-3787798. Good waterfront location. Always busy and offers a fine selection of quick snacks and breakfasts.

¶ **Mulligan's**, 17 Tongariro St, T07-376 9100. Decent pub grub in quiet surroundings.

¶ **The Ploughmans Pub**, 43 Charles Cres, T07-377 3422. A pleasant and peaceful English-style pub just off SH1 heading south out of town offering good pub grub.

¶ **Creative Café**, 85 Heuheu St, T07-3770261. A good option in inclement weather, here you can combine an extended coffee fix with painting ceramics, stringing beads, or making candles. Plenty of help on hand and a good atmosphere.

Turangi and Tokaanu p285

Though you can't buy trout in New Zealand, most eateries will cook your catch for you.

¶¶ **Angler's Café**, in the **Angler's Paradise Resort**, T07-386 8980. Daily from 1800. Good food at affordable prices.

¶¶ **Parklands Motorlodge** (see Sleeping, page 288). Good, reasonably-priced food.

¶¶ **Red Crater Cafe**, at the Extreme Backpackers, 26 Ngawaka Place. Good value and has an open fire.

¶¶ **Valentino's**, in the town centre, T07-386 8821, from 1830. A popular Italian joint.

ⓝ Pubs, bars and clubs

Taupo p278, maps p280 and p287

Most of the action emanates from Tongariro and Tuwharetoa sts (waterfront) and their connecting blocks in the heart of town, which is where the best pubs are to be found.

Finn MacCauls, Tuwharetoa St, T07-378 6165. This pseudo Irish offering is a good venue and has bands at the weekends.

Jolly Good Fellows, 80 Lake Terr, T07-3780457. Fine lake views and a congenial atmosphere.

Mulligan's, 17 Tongariro St, T07-376 9100. A fine establishment with a relaxed atmosphere and the best place to mix with both locals and travellers. It tends to go off like a rocket towards the end of the evening especially at weekends when the occasional red or yellow cards are presented to anyone in imminent danger of making a Charlie of themselves. **Ploughmans**, Charles Cres, T07-377 3422, at the southern edge of the town. Good for a quiet pint and traditional pub food.

⊛ Festivals and events

Taupo *p278, maps p280 and p287*
Great Lake Relay, taking place almost immediately after the arts festival, is a 160-km relay around the lake, www.relay.co.nz.
Feb Mar The biennial **Lake Taupo Arts Festival** (1st and 2nd weeks) swings into action, attracting local and national artists and exhibitions. The street performances are excellent, T07-377 1200, www.taupo fest.co.nz.
Apr Lake Taupo International Trout Fishing Tournament (around the 3rd week).
Aug Taupo half-marathon (1st week in Aug).
Sep Day-Night Thriller (mid-Sep), mountain bikers from far and wide descend on the town for a 12-hr 5-person lap race, www.daynightthriller.co.nz.
Nov Great Lake Cycle Challenge (late Nov), T07-378 1546.

⊙ Shopping

Taupo *p278, maps p280 and p287*
Kura, 47A Heuheu St, T07-377 4068. For interesting New Zealand art and crafts.

⚠ Activities and tours

Taupo *p278, maps p280, p283 and p287*
Bungee jumping
Taupo Bungy, just off Spa Rd, T0800-888408/T07-377 1135, www.taupobungy.com. From $109 (tandem $218) for a 45-m jump.

Charter boats
As you might expect there are numerous boat charters plying the lake. The marina office in Taupo, at the Boat Harbour, along Storey Place, has all the information.
Chris Jolly Outdoors, T07-378 0623, www.chrisjolly.co.nz (see Cruising, below).
Sailing Centre, 75 Kurupae Rd, 2 Mile Bay, T07-378 3299, www.sailingcentre.co.nz.

Climbing
Events Centre Climbing Wall, corner of Spa Rd and AC Baths Av, T07-376 0350. Mon-Fri 1700-2100, Sat-Sun 1200-2100. Excellent climbing-wall, from $9-15.
Rock and Ropes, Karetoto Rd, Wairakei (SH1), T07-374 8111, T0800-244508, www.rocknropes.co.nz. A challenging low and high ropes course with a giant 15-m swing, which combined offers a fine alternative to more traditional activities especially if dependent on fine weather. Half-day course from $65.

Cruising
There are numerous opportunities to cruise the lake in all types of craft from the sedate to the ridiculous. Most day trips leave regularly from the Boat Harbour on Storey Place and are run by **Fish Cruise Taupo (Taupo Launchmen's Association)**, T07-378 3444, www.fishcruisetaupo.co.nz. Almost all take in the 10-m Maori rock carvings at Mine Bay, 8 km southwest of the town (only accessible by boat or kayak).
The Barbary, T07-378 3444. A fine 50-ft ocean-going yacht that was (apparently) once owned by Errol Flynn. Daily at 1030 and 1400 and 1700; 2½ hrs $40, child $10.
Cruise Cat , T07-378 3444, daily 1030 and 1400, 1½ hrs trips to see the Maori rock carvings and the picturesque Whakaipo Bay, from $40, child $16 (Sun Brunch Cruise from $58, child $34).
Ernest Kemp, T07-378 3444. A small and delightfully cute replica steamboat that leaves from the Boat Harbour daily at 1030 and 1400 (1700 in summer). Again it takes in the Maori rock carvings – albeit very slowly. $40, child $12.

Fishing

Guides charge from $60 per hr for up to 2 people with a full day costing anything from $250 per head. The obligatory licence is $18.50 per day. A minimum 3-hr trip is recommended to give you at least a chance, especially for beginners. For full listings see the VIC (I-Site), the following are all well-established operators.
Greg Catly, T07-377 0035, www.nzflyfish.co.nz.
Mark Aspinall, T07-378 4453, www.markaspinall.com.
Paddy Clark, T07-378 2336, www.nzfly fishing.co.nz. Fly-fishing specialist.
TroutLine, T07-378 0895, www.troutline nz.com. The best value option for the casual visitor with a fully guided lake trip on board the 45-ft *MV Loloma*, 3 hrs from $100-$150 depending on numbers. This trip in particular creates the perfect balance between comfort, fun and expert local knowledge and includes a light meal, free tea and coffee and/or your catch cooked on board. Overnight trips are also an option. Recommended.

Gliding

Taupo Gliding Club, Centennial Dr, T07-378 5627, www.taupoglidingclub.co.nz. Tandem trail flights, mainly at weekends, with more regular schedules in summer, weather permitting, from $120.

Golf

Taupo is one of the best golfing venues in the country.
Taupo Golf Club, Spa Rd, then Centennial Drive, T07-378 6933, www.taupogolf.co.nz. One of the very few 'steaming' courses in the world. Green fees from $45.
Wairakei 9 Hole Course, on SH1 adjacent to the Wairakei Resort (north), T07-374 8021. If you are a complete novice, this place is 'hacker friendly'. Green fees from $15.
Wairakei Golf Club, SH1 North, T07-374 8152, www.wairakigolfcourse.co.nz.

Horse trekking

Taupo Horse Treks, Karapiti Rd, Wairakei

(near 'Craters of the Moon' reserve), T07-378 0356, www.taupohorsetreks.co.nz. 1- to 2-hr treks, from $60.

Kayaking

Wilderness Escapes, T07-378 3413, www.wildernessescapes.co.nz. Reputable local operator offering a wide and successful range of kayaking trips in combination with cruises and walking with a kayak only trip to the Maori Rock carvings from $85.
Kayaking Kiwi, T0800-353435/ T07-3787902, www.kayakingkiwi.com. Excellent half-day kayak and launch eco-adventures including the Maori Rock Carving from $108.
Kiwi River Safaris, T07-377 6597/T0800-723 8577, www.krs.co.nz. Relaxed kayak trips on the Waikato. Includes a soak in the hot pools, from $45. Departs 0900 and 1300.

Motorsport

Formula Challenge, T07-377 0338, www.fcr.co.nz. This company offers the chance to drive an authentic Formula Challenge racing car or V8 – the dream of many a petrol head. 10 laps from $290.

Mountain biking

There are some excellent tracks nearby, including the recommended riverside track that goes all the way to the Aratiatia Rapids from Spa Rd or the Craters of the Moon. See also Transport, below, for bike hire.
Kaimanawa Helibiking, T07-384 2816, www.kaimanawahelibiking.co.nz. The luxury option with a 4-hr trip that begins with a scenic flight to a remote 10-km track with a 2500-ft descent, from $395.
Rapid Sensations, T0800-227238, www.rapids.co.nz. Guided trips including the Craters of the Moon (1½ hrs), from $75. Freedom hire half-day from $45.

Parasailing and jet skiing

Regular flights along the waterfront from $85 (spectator ride on the boat from $20). Jet-ski hire from $85 per 30 mins. Ask at the I-Site for latest operators.

Quad biking

Taupo Quad Adventures, T07-377 6404, www.4x4quads.com. Offer the usual thrills and spills across local farmland, also taking in native bush and forest trails, from $95.

Rafting

See also Turangi, below, where many of the major companies are based.
Kiwi River Safaris, T0800-7238577, www.krs.co.nz. Raft the Rangitaiki as opposed to the more famous Tongariro (2 hrs from $110).

Scenic flights

Helistar Helicopters, Huka Falls Loop Rd, T0800-435478, www.helistar.co.nz. Flights vary from a quick 5-min trip hovering near the falls, to several hours taking in the Tongariro National Park, from $99-650.
Taupo's Floatplane, based at Boat Harbour, T07-378 7500, www.tauposfloatplane.co.nz. Float plane trips from $75-590.

Town tours

Paradise Tours, T07-378 9955, www.paradise tours.co.nz. Twice daily 3-hr tours around town or further on request. From $99.

Walking

The much-celebrated, 1-day (16 km) **Tongariro Alpine Crossing**, across the volcanic slopes and landscapes of the Tongariro National Park, is accessible from Taupo (see page 298). There are various ways of tackling the walk, with either the independent option using local transport operators and the range of accommodation around the park, or with specialist guides. The VIC (I-Site) can also help with information and hut bookings.
Tongariro Expeditions, T07-377 0435, www.thetongarirocrossing.co.nz. Recommended for 'all in' packages. See also Getting around, page 294.

Orakei Korako Thermal Reserve *p285*

You can hire kayaks at the visitor centre, T07-378 3131, www.orakeikorako.co.nz.
NZ Riverjet, in the visitor centre, T07-3337111, www.riverjet.co.nz. Interesting 3-hr jet-boat trips taking in some lovely lake and river scenery. From $145, child $75.
Paradise Tours, Taupo, T07-378 9955, www.paradisetours.co.nz. Offers specialist tours to the reserve.

Turangi and Tokaanu *p285*
Climbing

Extreme Backpackers, 26 Ngawaka Pl, T07-386 8949. Has an international standard climbing-wall open to the public.

Fishing

Taupo and the Tongariro River is New Zealand's premier trout-fishing region. Provided you have a licence ($21 a day available from the VIC or DoC) you can fish all year round, though summer is considered the best time for brown trout, and winter for the rainbow variety. There are numerous boat charters and guided trips (from $60 per hr, gear included) based in and around Turangi (consult the VIC) and tackle can be hired from tackle shops on Taupehi Rd, including **Greig Sports**, 59 Town Centre, T07-386 6911.

Mountain biking

Tongariro River Rafting, see Rafting, below. Guided trips or guidance on walking some excellent local tracks including the **42 Traverse**, considered the best track in the North Island. Independent hire available.

Rafting

The Tongariro River is up to Grade III and has over 50 rapids. Further afield, the Rangitaiki is up to Grade IV, providing a bit more action.
Rock and River (Wai Maori), 203 Puanga St, Tokaanu, T0800-865226, www.raftingnew zealand.com. Entertaining 3½-hr trips down the Tongariro, from $119. Recommended.
Tongariro River Rafting, Atirau Rd, Turangi, T0800-101024, www.trr.co.nz. Tours on the

Jumping into thin air

Taupo is now considered the premier jump site for tandem skydiving in the North Island; given the scenery and professionalism of operations here it is not difficult to understand why. During the peak season it is not unusual for up to 300 jumps to be made over the lake in one day.

There are three companies that compete for business and all are based at the airport at the southern edge of the town. The only differences between the companies are the aircraft, the numbers jumping at any one time and how your jump is recorded. The rest is minor detail like the mode of transport to the airport.

Jump heights and prices vary little between companies and escalate depending on whether you have photos, a video, a T-shirt and so on: a jump from 9000 ft without all the bells and whistles will cost about $200; 12,000 ft around $219; and 15,000 ft (Taupo Tandem) $314. You can even go higher, with oxygen assistance, if you have the money and prior experience. Also note the weight limit is 100 kg.

Don't go for anything less than 12,000 ft jump or it will be all over far too quickly. If you have gathered the courage to get up there at all, you might as well go as high as you possibly can.

There are two recording methods used for that essential keepsake of your jump depending on the company. You have the choice of being filmed by a 'third jumper', or alternatively by your own jump master with a audio-digital camera attached to his wrist. Either way, you will be presented with a fully edited video or DVD only minutes after landing as a highly entertaining (or embarrassing) record of your jump.

Cancellations due to inclement weather happen regularly of course so it pays to look at the long range weather forecast before booking (see www.metservice.co.nz). In the event of cancellation all the operators are happy to re-book or book an alternative jump for you elsewhere. They also all offer transportation to and from the airport.

The three companies are as follows and all are recommended. So, have a look at what has to offer, then put your best underwear on and make the call. **Great Lake Skydive**, T0800-373 335/ T07-3784662, www.freefall.net.nz; **Skydive Taupo**, T0800-586766, www.skydive taupo.co.nz; **Tandem Skydive Taupo**, T0800-586766/ T07-377 8300, www. skydivetaupo.co.nz.

Tongariro, with the choice of a relaxing scenic trip (1½ hrs) or a more exhilarating challenge down some Grade II sections.

Walking

One of the best short walks around Turangi is around **Lake Rotopounamu**, which is just off SH47, 9 km south of the intersection of SH47 and SH41 towards National Park Village. It is a pleasant 2-hr stroll through native bush around the lake. Sadly, there are no views from here south to the volcanoes. For a good view north you can climb **Mt Maunganamu** in about 25 mins. This walk starts at the Scenic

Reserve along a track turning right after the Tokaanu Tailrace Bridge on SH41. The VIC in Turangi has details of other walks in the area.

⊖ Transport

Taupo p278, maps p280 and p287
Bicycle hire Rent-a-Bike, 11 Kereru St T025-322 729; Life Cycles, Oranui St, T07-3786117, or the YHA, corner Kaimanawa and Tamamutu sts, T07-378 3311. **Car hire** Avis, 61 Spa Rd, T07-378 6305; Budget, Spa Rd and Pihanga St, T07-378 9764;

Rent-A-Dent, 7 Nukuhau St, T07-378 2740.
Taxi Taupo's Top Cabs, T07-378 9250;
Taupo Taxis, T07-378 5100.

⊙ Directory

Taupo *p278, maps p280 and p287*
Banks All the major banks have branches
and ATMs in central Taupo. **Internet**
Internet Outpost, 11 Tuwharetoa St, T07-376
9920, open daily til late; **Log On**, 71 Tongariro

St, opposite the VIC (I-Site), T07-376 5901,
until 2200. **Library** Story Pl, T07-376 0070.
Medical services Hospital, Kotare St,
T07-3761000; Taupo Medical Centre, corner
of Heuheu and Kaimanawa sts, T07-378 4080;
Main Street Open Late pharmacy, Main St,
67 Tongariro St, T07-378 2636, 0900-2030.
Police Story Pl, T07-378 6060. **Post
office** 42 Horomatangi St, T07-378 9090,
Mon-Fri 0900-1700, Sat 0900-1400. **Useful
addresses** AA, 3 Tamamutu St, T07-378
6000.

Tongariro National Park → *Colour map 3, A3.*

*Tongariro National Park is New Zealand's oldest national park, and the fourth oldest in the world. In
1887 Horonuku Te Heuheu Tukino, the then paramount chief of Ngati Tuwharetoa, gave the central
portion – essentially the volcanoes of Ruapehu, Ngauruhoe and Tongariro – to the nation. In more
recent years the park has been substantially increased in size to cover an area of 75,250 ha, taking in
the forest, tussock country and 'volcanic desert'. As well as its stunning scenery, Tongariro National
Park offers some excellent walking opportunities, including the Tongariro Northern Circuit,
considered one of New Zealand's great day hikes. The Tongariro Crossing (part of the circuit) is
hailed as one of the best one-day walks in the country. In winter, skiing is the principal activity here.*
▸▸ *For Sleeping, Eating and other listings, see pages 301-306.*

Ins and outs

Getting there
Tongariro Expeditions, T07-377 0435, www.thetongarirocrossing.co.nz, offers an early
bird and economy service between Taupo and Tongariro Crossing in summer; or Taupo
and Whakapapa in winter. The standard service departs Taupo 0620, Turangi 0700 and
returns from the mountain at 1530, arriving Turangi 1700, Taupo around 1730. This will
have you on the track at around 0745. In summer, the early bird departs Taupo 0540,
Turangi 0620, returning at the same time; this service will have you on the track at about
0700. The return fare is $55 Taupo, $40 Turangi one-way.

The **Alpine Hot Bus**, T0508-468287, www.alpinehotbus.co.nz, also offers transport to
the track and pick-ups from your accommodation. They leave Taupo at 0615 and Turangi
0700 and pick up from the Ketetahi Car Park at 1600. Their early bird service leaves Taupo
at 0530, Turangi at 0615 and picks-up at 1500, from $45, Turangi $35.

In Turangi most backpacker hostels offer their own track transport. From National Park
Village, most accommodation options also offer shuttles, including **Howard's Lodge**,
T07-892 2827, www.howardslodge.co.nz, to Whakapapa Village and the start of the
Tongariro Crossing for $30 return. Beware of cowboy operators in the region and try to
stick to well-publicized companies. For the latest weather conditions over Ruapehu and
Ngauruhoe log on to the 'live' webcam during daylight hours, www.geonet.org.nz and
www.metservice.com. See also individual village Getting there sections, below.

A word of warning. The Tongariro Crossing is becoming a victim of its own popularity and on a clear summer's day it can look like an army of ants following a honey trail. By far the best way to tackle the crossing is backwards (from north to south) and starting your ascent about an hour before dawn, which will see you at the summit before most are setting off from the southern car park. Then spend the day around the summit before returning the same way. At least then you will have a little solitude before the hoards arrive. Of course this will require your own transport arrangements, and a good head torch!

Getting around

The park is bordered along its north and western sides by the SH47, with the principal settlements of Turangi, National Park Village and Ohakune, and to the east by SH1 – the famous Desert Road. The small township of Waiouru is to the southeast. Whakapapa Village, at the northern base of Ruapehu, serves as the park's main headquarters. All the surrounding townships are served by **Intercity**, with Turangi also being served by **Newman's**. The main Auckland/Wellington **TranzScenic** rail line runs through Ohakune and the national park. A number of local shuttle bus operators provide access to Whakapapa Village and major tramping drop-off/pick-up points around the park.

Tourist information **DoC Whakapapa** ⓘ *Whakapapa Village on SH48, T07-892 3729, www.doc.govt.nz, www.whakapapa.co.nz, www.ruapehunz.com, daily 0800- 1700*, has a wealth of information on the park, interesting displays, maps and weather reports. It also an excellent summer programme of organized and guided walks, which usually start from the Whakapapa VIC, see page 297. Don't miss the excellent displays, especially the seismograph, monitoring the fickle moods of the Ruapehu.

Park hut bookings/fees are administered here. If you are planning a longer tramp or summit climb you are advised to fill in an intentions sheet at the centre. For sleeping and eating within and surrounding the park see Whakapapa Village, National Park, Turangi and Ohakune listings. DoC hut bookings can be made at all major DoC field centres and the Whakapapa Visitor Centre. Campsites have been established near each of the huts. Hut fees are from $15 for basic backcountry huts to $45for the Great Walks ($15-$25 for Northern Circuit or Tongariro Crossing Huts). Camping fees are from $4-10 depending on the type of site.

Sights

All of the national park's sights are, of course, natural and dominated by the three majestic volcanic peaks of Ngauruhoe, Ruapehu and Tongariro. Although all three mountains are active volcanoes they are quite different in size and appearance. For a live webcam of Ngauruhoe or Ruapehu visit www.geonet.org.nz/volcano/animations/ngauruhoe.html and www.geonet.org.nz/volcano/animations/ruapehu.html.

Ngauruhoe

The symmetrical cone of Ngauruhoe (2291 m) is the youngest of the three volcanoes. Its classic cone shape is due to its relative youth, but also because it has a single vent, unlike Ruapehu and Tongariro. Although Ruapehu and White Island (Bay of Plenty) have been far more active recently, Ngauruhoe has, over the years, been considered the most continuously active, frequently venting steam and gas and, occasionally, ash and lava in spectacular displays of pyroclastics. Its last significant eruption occurred in 1954. There is plenty of evidence of these eruptions, the most obvious being the old lava flows on its slopes. The Tongariro Crossing Track skirts the eastern flank of Ngauruhoe, while another popular three- to four-day tramp is the **Northern Circuit Track**, one of New Zealand's great walks encompassing both Ngauruhoe and Tongariro.

Ruapehu
About 16 km south of Ngauruhoe is the majestic shape of Ruapehu, with its truncated cone, perpetually snow-covered **summit peaks** and **crater lake**. It is the North Island's highest mountain, at 2797 m, and over the course of the last century has seen the most violent activity of all the three volcanoes. Between 1945 and 1947, due to a number of eruptions blocking the overflow, the waters of the crater lake rose dramatically. On the stormy Christmas Eve of 1953, without warning, the walls of the crater collapsed and a mighty lahar (volcanic rock and water debris) rushed down the Whangaehu River, wiping out the rail bridge near Karioi. The night train to Auckland arrived moments later and 153 lives were lost. It erupted more recently in September 1995, miraculously without loss of life, and the same thing happened a year later, wiping out the possibility of a ski season for both Whakapapa and Turoa. Ruapehu attracts thousands of visitors each year who come to ski or climb, or enjoy its numerous tramping tracks. The longest track is the **Round-the Mountain Track** which takes five to six days with overnight stays at a number of DoC huts on the way. Ruapehu is home to three ski fields: **Whakapapa** on its northern flank (serviced by Whakapapa and Iwikau Villages), **Turoa**, on the southern flank (serviced by Ohakune); and **Tukino**, the smallest and least popular of the three on the eastern slopes.

Tongariro
Tongariro, at the northern fringe 3 km north of Ngauruhoe, is a fairly complex, flat-topped affair and the lowest at 1968 m. Of the three mountains it is the most benign with only a few mildly active craters, some hot springs, lakes, fumaroles and pools of boiling mud. From a purely aesthetic point of view its most attractive features are the aptly named **Red Crater** (which is still active) and the small **Emerald Lakes** at its base. Nearby are the contrasting **Blue Lakes** of the central crater and the **Ketetahi Springs**, which emerge on its northern slopes. All of these interesting features are included on the **Tongariro Crossing**, which can be completed in a day and is considered one of New Zealand's best one-day walks (see box, page 298).

Whakapapa Village → *Colour map 3, A3.*
Whakapapa Village is essentially the headquarters and information base for the Tongariro National Park and the gateway to the Whakapapa Ski Field. It is also home to the magnificent **Bayview Chateau Hotel**, built in 1929. As well as the chateau itself there are a number of accommodation and eating options available in the Whakapapa Village. There is also a store, the DoC field centre and, believe it or not, a golf course. Don't miss the excellent displays in the Whakapapa DoC Visitor Centre, especially the seismograph, monitoring the fickle moods of the mighty Ruapehu, which, lest you forget, is an active volcano that last let rip in the mid-1990s.

Getting there and around There is only shuttle bus transportation available to Whakapapa Village (**Intercity** service Turangi and National Park). For shuttle services to Whakapapa Village and the start of the Tongariro Crossing see Tongariro Park Ins and outs above and book at the DoC Visitor Centre. There is a shuttle bus service to the ski fields

(Top-o-the-Bruce) from outside the VIC (I-Site) at 0830 and 1230 (returning 1530 and 1630), $6 return. Again, enquire at the DoC Visitor Centre in Whakapapa.

Tourist information The **Whakapapa DoC Visitor Centre** ① *SH48, T07-892 3729, www.doc.govt.nz, www.whakapapa.co.nz, daily 0800-1800*, offers a broad range of information on the park with many displays and an audio-visual theatre for rainy days ($5). The staff are expert in advising on walks. DoC's organized walks start from here, see page 295.

National Park Village → *Colour map 3, A3*

The small, unremarkable and almost barren village of National Park is set overlooking Mount Ruapehu and Ngauruhoe, at the junction of SH4 (which links Taumaranui and Wanganui) and SH47. It is also on the main Auckland–Wellington railway line. Graced only by its convenient location to both Tongariro and Wanganui national parks, it has a numbered **Northern Circuit** and the **Round-the-Mountain Track**. Most of the shorter walks are accessed from Whakapapa Village and the Ohakune Mountain Road, which connects Ohakune with the Turoa Ski Field. Note that a number of local activity operators also offer guided walks, as does the DoC in Whakapapa Village (page 295). ▸▸ *See also Activities and tours, page 305.*

Northern Circuit The Tongariro Northern Circuit winds its way over Mount Tongariro and around Mount Ngauruhoe passing through unusual landforms and volcanic features including lakes, craters and glacial valleys. Taking three to four days to complete (with overnight accommodation provided in DoC huts), it is listed as one of New Zealand's great walks. The track officially starts from Whakapapa Village and finishes at the Mangatepopo Road just off the SH47, but can also be accessed from Ketetahi Road (north) or Desert Road (east). Detailed information can be obtained from the Whakapapa Visitor Centre (see above), where you can also arrange hut bookings and are advised to fill in an intentions form. The DoC website, www.doc.govt.nz, also provides excellent details. If you do not have your own transport, the local shuttle operators will provide transportation (see Getting there, page 294, and in the relevant towns below). If you have your own vehicle do not leave valuables in it.

Round-the-Mountain Track The Northern Circuit can be combined with the full Ruapehu Round-the-Mountain Track to create a mighty six-day tramp around all three mountains. Again comfortable accommodation is available in DoC huts along the way. The track can be accessed from Whakapapa Village or the Ohakune Mountain Road. For information and hut bookings contact the Whakapapa Visitor Centre (see below) or the DoC field centre on Ohakune Mountain Road, Ohakune (see page 300).

Ruapehu Crater Lake Both the summit and Crater Lake of Ruapehu are popular climbs in both summer and winter and are, in part, easily accessible via the Whakapapa Ski Field chairlift. The climb to the crater and back takes about seven hours (four hours if you use the chairlifts). Once you reach the snowline it is tough going and can be dangerous. Ice axes and crampons are essential kit in winter and recommended even in summer. Whatever your intentions, always obtain all the necessary information before attempting this climb and let DoC know your plans. Ruapehu has claimed many lives (a close eye is also kept on the mountain's seismic activity, and at the slightest sign of any action, an exclusion zone is placed around the crater). A few local operators offer guided walks to the crater; enquire at DoC in Whakapapa, see page 297.

Tongariro Crossing

This excellent hike with its views and varied volcanic features is hailed as one of the best one-day hikes in the country. At about 16 km in length with some steep climbs and the odd bit of scrambling, it can take up to 10 hours, in winter it can be impassable and even in summer it can be dangerous, so despite what you may have heard, don't underestimate it.

The walk can be tackled from either north or south, with a number of diversions on the way. The usual recommendation is to start from the **Mangatepopo Car Park** (off SH47 on the park's western edge), walk the 10 km north to **Ketetahi Hut**, stay the night (all part of the 'package'), then either descend from the Ketetahi Hut to SH47A (walk terminus), or return the 10 km back to Mangatepopo. There is a hut at the Mangatepopo end but it has neither the character nor the view of the Ketetahi. If you have your own transport try the walk in part reverse to the conventional route described below (i.e. north to south, not south to north) spending the day around the summit before returning to Ketetahi. If you set off from the Ketetahi Car Park with a head torch about 1½ hours before sunrise you can reach the top just after dawn and well before the 'ant trail' of people coming from Mangatepopo arrive. Then return to Ketetahi.

From Mangatepopo the track makes a gradual ascent towards the southern slopes of Tongariro, while the steep slopes and lava flows of Ngauruhoe loom to the northwest. Sandwiched between the two mountains the track is then forced to make a steep ascent up the **Mangatepopo Saddle**. Before this ascent there is the choice of a short diversion to the **Soda Springs** – a series of cold springs which emerge from beneath an old lava

flow, surrounded by an oasis of greenery. Once you have negotiated the Saddle you enter Tongariro's **South Crater**. The views of Ngauruhoe from here are excellent (and the especially fit can take in the summit diversion from here). A short climb then leads to the aptly named **Red Crater** and the highest point on the crossing (1,886 m). Following the rim of this colourful (and, in the odd place, steaming) crater you are then treated to a full artist's palette, with the partial descent to the **Emerald Lakes**. (The minerals from Red Crater create the colours in the water.) Just beyond Emerald Lakes the track branches right to **Oturere Hut**, or continues to Ketetahi Hut across the Central Crater and alongside **Blue Lake**, another water-filled vent. The track then straddles the North Crater taking in the stunning view north across Lake Taupo, before making a gradual zigzag descent to the Ketetahi Hut. The hut sits alone on the slopes at an altitude of about 1,000 m. (It is the busiest and most popular hut in the park. If you have booked your stay in the hut bear in mind it operates on a first come first served basis, so get there early.) The huts all have mattresses, gas cookers (summer only), water supplies and toilet facilities. In the busy seasons wardens can provide information and weather reports. The hot Ketetahi Springs are on private Maori land only a few hundred metres away. Until recently a soak in the pools of the stream armed with a gin and tonic was a highlight of the walk. But sadly disagreements between DOC and the local Iwi mean the springs and stream are now out of bounds.

From Ketetahi it is a two-hour descent through native bush to the SH47A access point. For more information contact the Whakapapa Visitor Centre, page 297.

The pleasant little ski resort of Ohakune (meaning 'place to be careful'), near the southern edge of Tongariro National Park, changes its mood according to the season. In winter when (and if) the snows arrive, it attracts skiers in droves. But when winter brings little snow, or when spring arrives and the snow fades, it falls silent. So pretty little Ohakune is unpredictable, but whatever the season or the weather, it is worth lingering.

The main centre of Ohakune is on Clyde Street (SH49, where you arrive into the town) and this is the base for the VIC (I-Site), the main cafés, restaurants and amenities. The other 'centre' is of the après-ski variety and is about 2 km northwest, towards the mountain, up Goldfinch Street and Mangawhero Terrace. Here the focus is the **Powderhorn Chateau** (principal the après-ski base), with the railway station, the mountain access point (Ohakune Mountain Road) and the DoC field centre also here. The **Turoa Ski Field** is 17 km up the Ohakune Mountain Road.

Getting there Ohakune is served by **Intercity** buses every day except Sat, which stop in the centre of town at the VIC (I-Site). The daily Auckland-Wellington train also stops here, T0800-872467, www.tranzscenic.co.nz. For all booking and ticketing contact the VIC (I-Site).

Tongariro Crossing

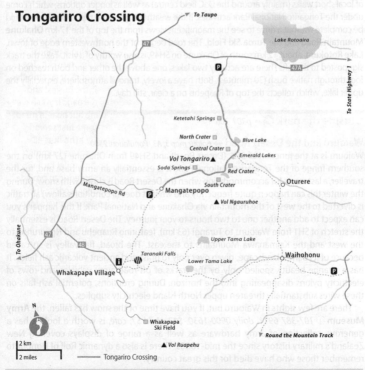

To Taupo

Lake Rotoaira

47

47A

To State Highway 1

Ketetahi Springs

North Crater

Blue Lake

Central Crater

Vol Tongariro ▲

Emerald Lakes

Soda Springs

Red Crater

South Crater

Oturere

Mangatepopo Rd

Mangatepopo

P

▲ Vol Ngauruhoe

To Ohakune

47

Upper Tama Lake

48

Taranaki Falls

Waihohonu

P

Lower Tama Lake

Whakapapa Village

i

N

2 km
2 miles

Whakapapa
Ski Field

▲ Vol Ruapehu

Round the Mountain Track

——— Tongariro Crossing

Getting around Although it has essentially two centres, and shuttling between them is awkward, everything in Ohakune is within walking distance. Shuttles operate up and down the Ohakune Mountain Road (to the Turoa Ski Field) or elsewhere within the Tongariro National Park, pretty much on demand. Check with the VIC (I-Site) for latest schedules and prices. **Matai**, 61 Clyde St, T06-385 8724, www.tongarirocrossingtransport.co.nz, offers a shuttle service to the Tongariro Crossing from $35 return. The **Ohakune Top Ten Motorpark** also offers a service on demand, T06-385 8561

Tourist information **Ruapehu VIC (I-Site)** ① *54 Clyde St, T06-385 8427, www.oha kune.info, www.visitruapehu.com, daily 0900-1700*. **DoC Ohakune field centre** ① *at the base of the Ohakune Mountain Rd, T06-385 3809, Mon-Fri 0900-1500*, has some excellent displays (including video footage of the 1995 Ruapehu eruption), up-to-date weather forecasts and maps, and can advise on any aspect of park activities including local short walks. For information on the **Turoa Ski Field**, contact T06-385 8456, www.ruapehu.com, www.snow.co.nz or www.oha kune.info. For local weather and regular snow updates in winter listen to Peak FM 95.8 FM, or Ski FM 96.6 FM; snow phone, T0832-22182

Sights All of Ohakune's 'sights' are essentially natural and revolve around **Mount Ruapehu** and its associate activities: skiing and walking being the principal pursuits. There are a number of local short walks (mainly around the DoC field centre) as well as longer options, which come under the Tongariro National Park activities. If the weather is good, no trip to Ohakune would be complete without a drive to see the magnificent views from the top of the 17-km **Ohakune Mountain Road** and the **Turoa Ski Field**. The road begins at the northwestern edge of town. **Lake Rotokura**, about 12 km south of Ohakune on SH49, is also worthy of a visit. Take the track signposted to the left. There are actually two lakes, one above the other and both reached on foot through native bush (30 minutes). Both have a lovely, tranquil atmosphere, especially the upper lake, which reflects the top of Ruapehu on a clear, still day.

Outside the park ⊜ ⇨ *p301-306.*

Waiouru and the Desert Road → *Colour map 3, A3 Population: 2500*
Waiouru is at the junction of SH1 (Desert Road) and SH49 from Ohakune (27 km) on the southern fringe of the Tongariro National Park. It is essentially an army base and, for the traveller, a last resort for accommodation when the Desert Road is closed with snow. During the winter this can happen quite frequently and when it does (if conditions allow) all traffic is diverted to the west of the mountain via Ohakune and National Park. If this happens you can expect to add another one to two hours to your journey. The Desert Road is essentially the stretch of SH1 from Waiouru to Turangi (63 km), featuring Ruapehu and Ngauruhoe to the west and the Kaimanawa Mountains to the east. The broad, flat valley is so called because of its barren landscape, given over only to grass and ancient volcanic ash fields. It has a strange beauty spoiled only by the tracks of off-road army vehicles and rows of electricity pylons disappearing into the horizon. During eruptions, potential ash-falls on these wires substantially threaten upper North Island electricity supplies.

There are few sights in Waiouru but, if you have time or the snow has fallen, the **Army Museum** ① *T07-387 6911, daily 0900-1630, $12, child $7, café*, is worth a look. It has a generous collection of army hardware as well as a range of displays covering New Zealand's military history since the mid-1800s. There is also a dynamic Roll of Honour to remember those who have died for this great country.

Taumarunui → *Colour map 3, A3 Population: 5000*

Taumarunui is a small agricultural service town lying at the confluence of the Ongarue and Whanganui rivers, on the western fringes of the Ruapehu District. Although nothing to write home about, it is often used as an overnight base for skiing in the Tongariro National Park, and as a base for kayak, canoe and jet-boat tours of the Whanganui River and the Whanganui National Park. For Whanganui River activity operators based in Taumarunui see Whanganui National Park section, page 379.

Getting there Taumarunui is served by **Intercity** and **Newman's** and is also on the main Auckland-Wellington rail line. The VIC (I-Site) administers bookings and tickets.

Tourist information Taumarunui VIC (I-Site) ⓘ *at the train station on Hakiaha St, the main drag through town, T07-895 7494, www.taumarunui.co.nz/www.visit ruapehu.com, Mon-Fri 0900-1630, Sat-Sun 1000-1600*, has an interesting working scale model of the 'Raurimu Spiral' (see below).

Sights The major attraction around Taumarunui is the **Raurimu Spiral**, an impressive feat of railway engineering on the main north-south trunk line, devised by the late RW Holmes in 1908. The track falls (or rises) 213 m at an incline of one in 50, by means of a complete circle, three horseshoe curves and two tunnels, which double the distance travelled. Check it out from the lookout, 37 km south of the town on SH4, or the working model in the VIC (I-Site).

There are a number of walks around the town for which the VIC (I-Site) has details. For the very energetic there is the climb to the summit of the flat-topped **Mount Hikurangi** (770 m) behind the town. For detailed directions, and to confirm permission with the local landowner, ask at the VIC (I-Site). The 155-km **Taumarunui to Stratford Heritage Trail** (scenic drive) begins or ends here, taking you through the Wanganui and Taranaki regions to Stratford. The highlight of this trip is the tiny settlement of **Whangamomona**, which, after a run-in with regional bureaucracies in 1995, declared itself a republic. It is an unremarkable little place with a population of less than 100. The village opens its borders on the anniversary of the great uprising in October each year, when there is a weekend of celebrations. No passport control or baggage checks necessary, just a pint glass. There is also an alternative scenic route from Taumarunui, across the hills via Ohura and SH40 to SH3 and New Plymouth. This is a rugged trip over remote country so make sure you are stocked up.

◉ Tongariro National Park listings

For Sleeping and Eating price codes and other relevant information, see Essentials pages 44-50.

● Sleeping

Whakapapa Village *p296*
All prices rise in winter, and opening and closing times vary. Booking ahead is necessary in winter, and advisable in summer.
LL-AL Bayview Chateau, T07-892 3809, www.chateau.co.nz. Perhaps the most famous hotel in the North Island, the Bayview

provides traditional luxury in a grand location. Visible for miles around, the hotel sits like a beacon in the heart of the national park and in the shadow of 2 of New Zealand's most famous volcanoes – Ngauruhoe and Ruapehu. Whether just relaxing and enjoying its traditional comforts or using it as a base from which to ski, or walk the world-renowned Tongariro Track (special packages available), it offers a level of elegance in keeping with its age (1929) combined with traditional modern facilities, including an excellent restaurant, a bar, café, pool and even a small golf course. Ask about special packages in summer.

AL-A Skotel Alpine Resort, T07-892 3719, www.skotel.co.nz. A good-value establishment with modern facilities, luxury and standard hotel rooms or self-contained chalets. Restaurant and bar with great views towards Ngauruhoe. Spa, sauna, gym, internet and tramping gear hire.

C-D Discovery Lodge, on SH47, 1 km from the Whakapapa turning, T0800-122122/T07-8922744, www.discovery.net.nz. Overlooking the mountains, with a good range of accommodation options and facilities, including a bar and restaurant. Tongariro Crossing Track transport at 0545, which allows customers to be among the first on the track.

C-D Whakapapa Holiday Park, T07-892 3897, www.whakapapa.net.nz. Backpacker accommodation with basic facilities but set in the heart of the village and riverside, close to all amenities.

D DoC Huts, T07-892 3729. There are 9 DoC huts in the park with foot access only. Fees $10-25.

National Park Village *p297*

All accommodation in National Park Village is in high demand in the winter ski season, when prices also rise. Booking is advised.

AL-D Howard's Lodge, 11 Carroll St, T07-892 2827, www.howardslodge.co.nz. A fine establishment with a wide range of comfortable rooms. Spa. Well geared up for local activities especially skiing, tramping and mountain biking. Breakfast and transport service available.

AL-D The Crossing Backpackers, Erua Road East (off SH4, 6km south of National Park Village), T07-892 2894, www.thecrossingbackpackers.co.nz. Well equipped establishment, clean, warm and friendly. Breakfast and transport service available. Paintball on-site.

AL-D Pukenui Lodge, corner of SH4 and Miller St, T07-892 2882, www.tongariro.cc/.

Modern single-storey lodge. Various rooms, quad, double or single, some en suite. Spa and cosy open fire in winter.

A-B Mountain Heights Lodge, SH4, T07-892 2833, www.mountainheights.co.nz. B&B, self-contained, motorcamp and camping just south of National Park Village. Bike hire.

A-D Plateau Lodge, Carroll St, T07-892 2993, www.plateaulodge.co.nz. Self-contained units, double en suites and comfortable backpacker accommodation available. Activities and transport pick-ups.

B-D National Park Backpackers, Findlay St, T07-892 2870, www.npbp.co.nz. Modern establishment with dorms and doubles with en suite bathrooms, tent sites and internet. Climbing wall from $12. Activities and transport to Tongariro Crossing arranged.

B-D Ski Haus, Carroll St, T07-892 2854, www.skihaus.co.nz. Family and multi-share rooms, spa pool and bar. Activities and transport arranged.

Ohakune *p299*

As a main ski resort, Ohakune offers a wide range of accommodation, though it operates on a seasonal basis. In winter, especially at weekends, you are advised to book well in advance. If you are stuck or want to avoid the high winter prices, the far less salubrious village of **Raetihi**, 11 km to the east, has a number of cheaper options. For information, options and bookings contact the Raetihi VIC, 46 Seddon St, T06-385 4805.

LL Whare Ora, 1 Kaha St, Rangataua, 5 km from Ohakune, T06-385 9385, www.whareora lodge.co.nz. Beautiful, renovated, 2-level wooden house originally built in 1910. One en suite with spa and sitting room, 1 attic en suite room. Luxuriously appointed with great cuisine.

AL Powderhorn Chateau, corner of Mangawhero and Thames sts, T06-385 8888, www.powderhorn.co.nz. Considered the best-equipped hotel in Ohakune, the Alpine-style Powderhorn Chateau has always proved popular as a base for skiing in winter, and advertises itself as the place where Elijah

Wood (Frodo) and other key members of the cast stayed during filming in 2001. To add to the undeniably warm and lively atmosphere of the bar and 2 in-house restaurants, there is a fine choice of lodge-style suites, an apartment, a heated swimming pool and a small casino. Ski and bike hire is also available with the former subject to season and snow conditions.

AL-A Cairnbrae House 140 Mangawhero River Rd, 7 km southwest of Ohakune, T06-385 3002, www.cairnbraehouse.co.nz. Lovely rural homestay with immaculate en suite rooms. Private guest lounge, Sky TV and internet, not to mention the occasional deer in the garden. Dinner on request.

AL-A Tairoa Lodge, 144 Magawhero Rd, T06-385 4882, www.tairoalodge.co.nz. Modern, spacious single-storey farm/ homestay lodge beside the Magawhero River and 30 km from the ski field. Range of en suite rooms, open fire and outdoor spa pool. Activities arranged.

AL-A Waireka B&B, 11 Tainui St, T06-385 8692, www.waireka.co.nz. Friendly B&B, with local photographer and qualified naturopath.

A Hobbit Motor Lodge, corner of Goldfinch and Wye sts, T06-385 8248, www.the-hobbit.co.nz. Good in-house restaurant.

A Peaks Motor Inn, corner of Mangawhero Terr and Shannon St, T06-385 9144, www.thepeaks.co.nz.

A-D Alpine Motel Lodge, 7 Miro St, T06-385 8758, www.alpinemotel.co.nz. A cheap, central motel with backpacker accommodation. Bistro attached. Spa pool.

B Sunbeam Motel and Lodge, 4 Foyle St, T06-385 8470, www.sunbeammotels.co.nz. Bar and restaurant, spas and tours.

C-D Matai Lodge YHA, corner of Clyde and Rata sts, T06-385 9169, www.maitailodge. co.nz. Central location, recently renovated, good range of rooms and dorms. Bike hire. Free pick-up from Waiouru, National Park and Whakapapa and in-house transport service for the Tongariro Crossing. Open year round.

D Station Lodge, 60 Thames St, T06-385 8797, www.stationlodge.co.nz. Basic, laid-

back and close to all the nightlife with in-house ski shop and rental. Spa. Winter-only.

Chalets
There are numerous self-contained chalet-style options in town.

AL-A Ruapehu Chalet Rentals, 23 Clyde St, T06-385 8149, www.ruapehu.co.nz.

A Ossie's Chalets and Apartments, corner of Tainui and Shannon St, T06-385 8088, www.ossies-ohakune.co.nz.

B Ruapehu Cabins, 107 Clyde St, T06-385 8608, www.ruapehucabins.co.nz.

B-D Rimu Park Lodge and Chalets, 27 Rimu St, T06-385 9023, www.rimupark.co.nz. Also offers backpacker accommodation.

Motorcamps and campsites
C-D Ohakune Top Ten Holiday Park, 5 Moore St, T06-385 8561, www.ohakune. net.nz. An excellent facility with spotless amenities near the town centre and next to the Mangateitei Stream. Tongariro Crossing shuttle service available. Spa.

D DoC Mangawhero Campsite, Ohakune Mountain Rd, T06-385 8578. Book with DoC. Basic facilities for purist campers.

Taumarunui *p301*
There is not a huge range of choice, but the VIC can advise.

B-D Taumarunui Holiday Park, near SH4 and next to the river, 4 km south of town, T07-895 9345, www.taumarunuiholiday park.co.nz. The best motorpark in town. Camp kitchen.

❶ Eating

Whakapapa Village *p296*
Whakapapa Camp Store, in the village has light snacks and sells groceries at elevated prices, so stock up before you go.

🍴🍴🍴 **Bayview Chateau**, see Sleeping, above. Fine, traditional à la carte dining.

🍴🍴 **Pihanga Café and Bar**, attached to the Bayview Chateau (see Sleeping, above) with good coffee and the best and most varied café menu in the village. Brunch and dinner from 1030 daily.

Skotel Resort, T07-892 3719 (see Sleeping, above). Good restaurant and bar with expansive views across to Ngauruhoe. Open to non-guests for breakfast, lunch and dinner.

Fergusson's Café, opposite the chateau, 0800-1530. Great for a light, cheap snack.

Knoll Ridge Café, up the Top of the Bruce Rd (take the chairlift), T07-892 3738. Chairlift $23, child $14, 0900-1600 (last lift up 1530 in summer). A good place to head if you fancy a coffee with a view.

National Park Village p297

There is no supermarket in the village. The BP Station on Carroll St, T07-892 2879, 0730-1900, stocks basic supplies.

BaseKamp, Carroll St, T07-892 2872. Daily. Excellent gourmet burgers and pizza.

Eivin's Café, on the corner of Carroll St and SH4, T07-892 2844. Daily from 0830. Pleasant enough and serves traditional pub-style fare, including pizza.

Schnapps Hotel, Findlay St, T07-892 2788. Daily from 1100.

Ski Haus, see Sleeping, page 302. In-house restaurants offering breakfast, lunch and dinner to non-guests.

Station café, T07-892 2881. Daily 1000-late. Set in the historic National Park Railway Station, which does not see many passenger trains these days. Cosy atmosphere and friendly staff.

Ohakune p299

A number of motels have reputable mid-range restaurants including **The Hobbit**, corner of Goldfinch and Wye sts, T06-385 8248; and **Turoa Ski Lodge Restaurant**, 10 Thames St, T06-385 8274, licensed, open daily; cosy and great value steak.

The Matterhorn and **Powderkeg** restaurants, in the Powderhorn Chateau, corner of Mangawhero and Thames St, T06-3858 888. Both very popular with a fine range of traditional dishes. The Matterhorn is

open daily year round; the Powderkeg restaurant is closed in summer.

Alpine Wine Bar and Restaurant, opposite the **Ohakune Hotel** on Clyde St, T06-385 9183. More formal dining, open year-round from 1800.

Ohakune Hotel's O Bar, 72 Clyde St, T06-385 8268. Good traditional pub food both day and evenings throughout the year.

Sassi's Bistro, Miro St, T06-385 8758. Open for breakfast from 0700 and dinner from 1800 every night, year round. Has an intimate, congenial atmosphere.

Utopia Café, 47 Clyde St, T06-385 9120, 0900-1600 (extended hours in winter). Good coffee and an altogether better class of snack.

◑ Bars and clubs

Ohakune p299

Suggested bars include: **Mountain Rocks**, Clyde St, in the centre of town; **Powderkeg Bar**, in the Powderhorn Chateau, Thames St, is without doubt the place to go – it is spacious, nicely decked out in an Alpine style, very popular and has a great open fire.

◉ Entertainment

Ohakune p299

Ohakune Cinema, 17 Goldfinch St, T06-385 8488.

▲ Activities and tours

Whakapapa Village p296
Mountaineering

Whakapapa provides the most accessible routes to the Ruapehu summit(s) and the Crater Lake. You can ride 2 chairlifts 2020 m above sea level to the Knoll Ridge Chalet ($23), from where you can reach either the Crater Lake and/or the summits; 6 km, 4 hrs (9 km, 7 hrs minus chairlift). The highest summit is **Tahurangi** (2797 m) on the southwest fringe of the crater. The Dome hut, which took a pummelling during the 1990s eruptions, is easily accessible at the crater's northern fringe. As always, make sure you are well-equipped and leave details of your intentions with DoC at the visitor centre (see also Ruapehu Crater Lake Walk, page 297).

Scenic flights
Mountain Air Scenic Flights, on SH47 at the junction to Whakapapa Village and the Grand Chateau (pick-ups from Turangi), T07-892 2812, www.mountainair.co.nz. Operates excellent and affordable flights over the park and beyond. From $110-265.

Skiing
Whakapapa, T07-892 3738, www.whaka papa.co.nz, www.snow.co.nz, or Snowphone T0900-99333/T083-222182. The Whakapapa ski field, on the northwestern slopes of Mt Ruapehu, is New Zealand's largest ski area. An all-day lift pass costs from $86, child from $52. Full-day ski, boot and pole hire costs from $38, child from $28 (snowboard and boots from $46). Various day and beginner packages are available as well as lessons (from $45) and a sightseeing package (lift only) from $23 (winter and summer). There are ski school and crêche facilities available on the mountain as well as a café at Knoll Ridge (a ridge above the village).

Walking
A number of short walks can be accessed from Whakapapa, as well as the longer tramps of the **Tongariro Crossing**, **Tama Lakes**, **Northern Circuit** and the **Round the Mountain** tracks (see Walking, page 297). The **Whakapapa Nature Walk** (1 km, 30 mins) is an easy and pleasant stroll which starts near the visitor centre; the **Taranaki Falls Walk** (6 km; 2 hrs) crosses low-lying tussock to the 20-m falls of the Wairere stream; and the **Silica Rapids Walk** (7 km; 2½ hrs), is a loop track that follows another stream through beech forest to some coloured silica terraces.

Note that a number of local activity operators also offer guided walks and the DoC runs an excellent summer programme of organized and guided walks, which usually start from the Whakapapa Village VIC, T07-892 3738, from around $85.

National Park Village p297
There are a number of activity operators based in the village, most connected to the various lodges and backpacker hostels. Walking equipment (including boots) can be hired from **Howard's Lodge**, **Pukenui Lodge** and the **Ski Haus** (see Sleeping, page 302).

Climbing
National Park Backpackers, Findlay St, T07-892 2870, daily 0900-2100. An 8-m climbing wall open to non-guests, $12.

Kayaking, canoeing and rafting
National Park is used as a base for Wanganui river trips; the main lodges and backpacker hostels will assist in arranging trips. For operators see Whanganui National Park, page 379.

Mountain biking
The **42 Traverse** is a 46-km (3- to 7-hr) track and the major biking attraction in the area. Companies that provide guided trips, information or independent bike hire, include:
Howard's Lodge, T07-892 2827. With transport, from $35, hire from $60 per day.
Pukenui Lodge, T07-892 2882.

Scenic flights
Mountain Air Scenic Flights, on SH47 at the junction to Whakapapa Village and the Bayview Chateau, T0800-922812, www.moun tainair.co.nz. Excellent and affordable flights over the park and beyond. From $110.

Skiing
For information log on to www.snow.co.nz. Equipment hire is available from **Eivin's**, SH4, T07-892 2844; **Howard's Lodge**, T07-892

2827; **Pukenui Lodge**, T07-892 2882; and **Ski Biz**, 10 Carroll St, T07-892 2717, www.skibiz.co.nz.

Walking
Adrift Guided Outdoor Adventures,
T07-892 2751, www.adriftnz.co.nz. Guided trips of the Tongariro Crossingincluding a pre-dawn trip from $195, as well as kayaking and canoe adventures.

Ohakune p299
Kayaking, canoeing and rafting
Ohakune is a popular base for river activities on the Whanganui River. For tours, see page 383.

Mountain biking
The area is excellent for mountain biking of all grades of difficulty. For information on what tracks are available and bike hire call into the DoC field centre or VIC (I-Site).

Skiing
Turoa, southwestern slopes of Mt Ruapehu, www.whakapapa.co.nz. Serviced by the town of Ohakune, the ski field of Turoa is preferred by many to Whakapapa. Both Turoa and Whakapapa have both suffered in recent years due to the Ruapehu eruptions in the mid-1990s and a lack of fresh winter snow, but when conditions are right there is no doubt Turoa can offer some of the best skiing in the North Island. There are numerous ski equipment hire shops in Ohakune as well as at the base of the ski field itself. An all-day lift pass costs from $86, child from $52. Full-day ski, boot and pole hire costs from $38, child from $28 (snowboard and boots from $46). Various day and beginner packages are available from $100: A group lesson on the mountain will cost about $40 while a private

lesson will cost from $110. For further information on skiing see Whakapapa and National Park Activities and tour sections, page 304. Also try to source the *Turoa 2010* booklet. For transport services up the mountain see page 299.

Walking
The Ohakune Mountain Rd provides short and long walks, some of which join the Tongariro National Park's major walking circuits.

There are 2 very pleasant short walks which depart from the DoC field centre at the edge of town. The 15-min **Rimu Track**, with its interpretative information posts, is wonderful, even in the rain, while the 1-hr **Mangawhero Forest Walk** follows the river valley up towards the mountain.

A further 12 km up the road, the 1-hr **Waitonga Falls Track** is popular, as is the longer (5-hr) **Lake Surprise** tramp, which starts about 16 km up the road. The less active can try the 10-min **Mangawhero Falls Walk**, also accessed off the Mountain Rd.

For details, maps and the latest on weather call in at the DoC field centre, T06-385 8578. The **Tongariro Crossing** is also accessible from Ohakune. For information see box, page 298. For shuttle transport see page 294.

⊕ Directory

Ohakune p299
Internet Peppatree Design and Print, 45 Clyde St, T06-385 9320. The Video Shop, 53 Clyde St. 1000-2030. **Police** 10 Clyde St, T06-385 0100. **Post office** 5 Goldfinch St, T06-385 8645, Mon-Sat 0700-1700.

Contents

Footprint features

Taranaki

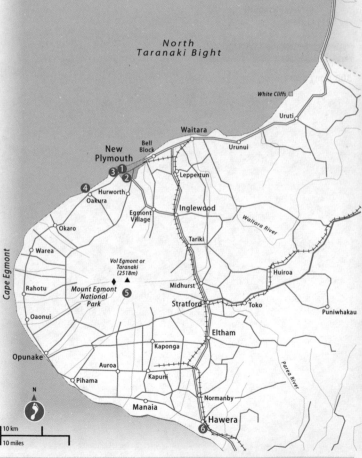

North Taranaki Bight

Awakino

Mokau

White Cliffs

Uruti

Waitara

Bell Block

Urunui

New Plymouth

Leppertun

Hurworth

Oakura

Egmont Village

Inglewood

Waitara River

Okaro

Tariki

Cape Egmont

Warea

Vol Egmont or Taranaki (2518m)

Huiroa

Rahotu

Mount Egmont National Park

Midhurst

Stratford

Toko

Puniwhakau

Oaonui

Eltham

Porea River

Opunake

Kaponga

Auroa

Kapuni

Pihama

Normanby

Manaia

Hawera

N

10 km

10 miles

In many ways Taranaki is more mountain than region. The awesome 2518-m snow-capped volcanic cone of the same name seems to dominate everything and, even shrouded in mist, it is strangely omnipresent. Although many have enjoyed the volcano, it has also caused a number of deaths, and they say it is due for another eruption. However, whether you look at it with reverence or fear, it will always be the region's one defining feature.

The mountain has two names, Taranaki and Egmont, both official, but in a way controversial. Taranaki is the original Maori name, while Egmont is the result of Captain Cook's habit of renaming anything in sight during his explorations in 1770.

The largest town is New Plymouth, a proud, prosperous and modern centre that lies in the shadow of the great mountain on the northwest coast. Although a little bit out of the way, those who make the effort to visit the region will not be disappointed. As well as the superb scenery and range of activities on or around the mountain itself, the region boasts a fascinating history, fine parks, gardens, arts and crafts and a coastline internationally recognized for its excellent surfing.

New Plymouth → *Colour map 3, A1   Population: 67,000*●

Based on resources of rich agricultural land and natural gas and oil supplies, lively New Plymouth enjoys considerable prosperity and is the main service town and population base of the Taranaki Region. The town, and the entire district, is dominated by the mountain, which seems to dictate the general mood, like some huge meteorological barometer. On a clear day, when the mountain radiates, its sheer size and stature are mirrored proudly in the town and the region. But, when shrouded in mist and rain, the area feels dull and sombre. As well as being a fine base from which to explore the recreational delights on and around the mountain and the region as a whole, New Plymouth itself has an excellent art gallery, some interesting historic buildings and a fine marine and public park. ►► *For Sleeping, Eating and other listings, see pages 315-318.*

Ins and outs

Getting there
New Plymouth airport ① *12 km north of the town*, is served by **Air New Zealand Link**, T0800-737000. For shuttles to and from the airport T0800-373001 from $20 one way. By road, New Plymouth is a little out of the way: 254 km from Hamilton and 172 km from Wanganui, which is roughly halfway between Auckland and Wellington. SH3 links New Plymouth to Hamilton, is notorious for slips and is in a constant state of upgrading, while its continuation to Wanganui is a little better, but still quite slow. **Intercity**, **Newman's**, **Nakedbus** and **Dalroy Express/White Star**, 7 Erica Pl, T06-759 0197/T0508-465622, www.dalroytours.co.nz, run regular bus services to New Plymouth from Auckland and Hamilton to the north and Wanganui, Palmerston North and Wellington to the south. The major operators stop at 19 Ariki St in the city centre. For bookings and information contact the VIC (I-Site) or the **Travel Centre**, 19 Ariki St, T06-759 9039.

Getting around
New Plymouth's central grid of streets has a very confusing one-way system, so a certain amount of patience is required. The local bus company is **Citylink Services**, T06-7657127, www.trc.govt.nz/bus-information. **Taranaki Tours**, T06-7579888/T0800-886877, www.taranakitours.com, runs a service to the mountain from $35.

Tourist information
New Plymouth VIC (I-Site) ① *at the Puke Ariki Museum and Library, near the waterfront, 65 St Aubyn St, T06-759 6060, www.newplymouthnz.com or www.taranaki.co.nz, Mon, Tue, Thu, Fri 0900- 1800, Wed 0900-2100, Sat-Sun 0900-1700.* The VIC can give details of a number of Heritage Trails, including an interesting two-hour walk in town starting at Puke Ariki Landing, a park with sculptures and the lofty 'wind wand' by the shoreline. **DoC** ① *55A Rimu St, T06-759 0350.*

Sights

One of the town's most celebrated institutions is the **Govett-Brewster Gallery** ① *corner of Queen and King sts, T06-759 6060, www.govettbrewster.com, daily 1000-1700, free.* Although it opened 35 years ago you could be forgiven for thinking the paint was still wet. The interior is on three levels and looks very modern, befitting its reputation as the premier contemporary art gallery in the country. Although perhaps not to everyone's taste, the mainly three-dimensional and highly conceptual pieces are well worth a look. The gallery doyen is Len Lye, a poet, writer and multimedia artist who specialized in pioneering animation work in the 1930s. His mainly abstract films are regularly shown.

For contemporary works by local artists, stop by at the **Real Tart Gallery** ① *19 Egmont St, T06-756 5717, daily 1100-1600, free.* The rather flash **Taranaki Museum and Library (Puke Ariki)** ① *Egmont St, T06- 759 6060, www.pukeariki.com, Mon, Tue, Thu, Fri 0900-1800, Wed 0900-2100, Sat-Sun 0900-1700, free (temporary exhibitions $6),* is worth a visit and houses an interesting collection of Maori artifacts and displays, mixed with the usual pioneer exhibits and wildlife specimens. The quaint little **Richmond Cottage** ① *Ariki St, Sat-Sun 1100-1530,* now almost absorbed by the museum, is a furnished colonial cottage built in 1853. There are some other notable historic buildings and sites in the city including the oldest stone church in the country, **St Mary's**, on Vivian Street. The original church was built in 1846. The interior contains some lovely Maori carvings and stained-glass windows. The cemetery echoes the military theme, with the graves of several soldiers testifying to the area's colourful and, at times, bloody past.

The **Fitzroy Pole** (Pou Tutaki) which stands proudly at the northern end of town on the corner of Devon Street East and Smart Road was erected by the Maori in 1844. It commemorates Governor Fitzroy's decision to question the legalities of white settlers and forbid their acquisition of huge tracts of land. Although not the original, the carving speaks for itself. In distinct contrast and far more contemporary is the **'Wind Wand'** on the waterfront near the museum. Created for the 2000-millennium celebrations by local multimedia artist Len Lye it is a 45-m, 900-kg kinetic sculpture that is designed to sway gently in the breeze. The bulb at the end is lit at night to enhance this effect.

New Plymouth is famous for its parks, the oldest and finest of which are **Pukekura** and **Brooklands**, which merge. They are best accessed via Fillis Street, just east of the town centre. Pukekura, opened in 1876, is a well-maintained 20 ha of lakes and assorted gardens, with a cricket ground, fernery and tearoom serving refreshments and light meals daily except Tuesday. From here, on a clear and calm day, you will see the reflection of Mount Taranaki across the main lake, which is crossed by a Japanese-style bridge. Brooklands has an outdoor amphitheatre, ponds studded by lily pads, English-style rhododendron gardens, an historic colonial hospital museum/gallery and a 2000-year-old puriri tree. There is also a small **children's zoo** ① *daily 0900-1700,* with all the usual inmates, including kune-kune pigs, goats and miniature horses, as well as red pandas, monkeys and a fine collection of parrots and parakeets.

Near the ugly towers of the power station and the busy port is the **Sugar Loaf Island Marine Park**, with its eroded, volcanic rock islands. Designated in 1986, the park is home to New Zealand fur seals and a variety of nesting seabirds. Boat trips to visit the park and view the wildlife are available. The shoreline of the park is part of an interesting 7-km Coastal Walkway, the highlight of which is the climb up **Paritutu Rock** – if you can. The climb requires considerable effort and involves pulling yourself up by a steel cable, but the view (though spoilt slightly by the power station and oil storage tanks) is worth the effort, with the ever-present Taranaki cone to the east and the town to the north, and Ruapehu and Ngauruhoe just visible on a clear day. Then you're faced with the descent, which is not so much a scramble, as an abseil. If the climb is too daunting, a fine view can also be had from Marshland Hill, off Robe Street, which was formerly the Pukaka *pa.* ▸▸ *See Activities and tours, page 317.*

Around New Plymouth 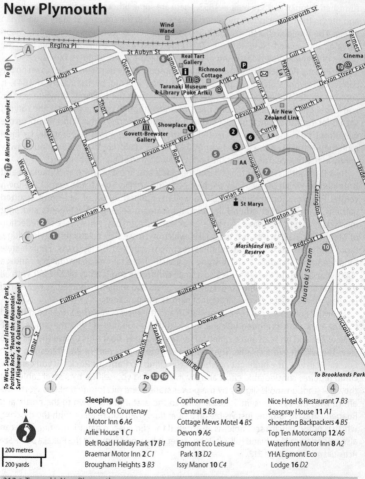 » p316.

North on SH3

There are a few attractions, walks and viewpoints along this road that are definitely worth a visit; pick a copy of the free *Scenic Highway 3* leaflet and the more detailed *Walks in north Taranaki* ($1) from the DoC or the VIC (I-Site) in New Plymouth.

Heading north past Waitara and Urenui, which have some popular beaches in themselves, is the **White Cliffs Brewing Company** ① *487 Main North Rd, Urenui, T06-752 3676, daily 1000-1800*, a boutique organic beer brewery offering tastings and sales of some fairly heady brews. The **Whitecliffs Walkway** is the most celebrated in North Taranaki. The Whitecliffs

New Plymouth

Sleeping
Abode On Courtenay
  Motor Inn **6** *A6*
Arlie House **1** *C1*
Belt Road Holiday Park **17** *B1*
Braemar Motor Inn **2** *C1*
Brougham Heights **3** *B3*

Copthorne Grand
  Central **5** *B3*
Cottage Mews Motel **4** *B5*
Devon **9** *A6*
Egmont Eco Leisure
  Park **13** *D2*
Issy Manor **10** *C4*

Nice Hotel & Restaurant **7** *B3*
Seaspray House **11** *A1*
Shoestring Backpackers **4** *B5*
Top Ten Motorcamp **12** *A6*
Waterfront Motor Inn **8** *A2*
YHA Egmont Eco
  Lodge **16** *D2*

N

200 metres
200 yards

(named after the famous Dover cliffs in England), although not on the same scale or grandeur as their namesake, are nonetheless quite impressive and dominate the shore for some 7 km. The track can be accessed from the south at the Pukearuhe Historic Reserve at the end of Pukearuhe Road, north of Urenui. The track's length totals 9.5 km, terminating at the northern access point, on Clifton Road at the mouth of the Tongaporutu River. Much of the track is along the shoreline, so make sure you check the tides.

The immediate coastline either side of the **Tongaporutu River** is scattered with rock towers, caves and arches, though they are not easily accessed (low tide only). For a superb view of them head just north of the Clifton Road, across the bridge and up the hill on the other side. Turn left onto Cemetery Road. From the end a short walk across an accessible field will take you to the headland. There is also a fine view of the Whitecliffs from there.

Just north of Tongaporutu are **Mokau** and **Awakino**. Both are popular but remote holiday spots especially good for coastal walks and fishing. For canoe trips and cruises on the Mokau River see Activities and tours, page 317.

A lengthy diversion off SH3 along SH40 will take you to the 74-m **Mount Damper Falls**, the highest waterfall in the North Island. From SH40 take the Okau Road to the Mount Damper Falls car park, which is well marked. The 15-minute walk will take you to a lookout platform. The falls are best viewed after heavy rain.

Carrington Road

Carrington Road (off Victoria Road) heads southwest out of New Plymouth towards the mountain. It has a number of sights including **Hurworth Cottage** ① *906 Carrington Rd, T06-7568606, Sat-Sun 1100-1500*, which was originally built in 1856 by young lawyer Harry Atkinson, who was also New Zealand's Prime Minister, not once, but four times. Young Harry and his family had to flee the house and the area during the Taranaki Wars in 1860. The house today is a well-renovated tribute to the family.

The highlight on the Carrington Road is the **Pukeiti Rhododendron Trust Gardens** ① *2290 Carrington Rd, T06-752 4141, www.pukeiti.org.nz, daily 0900-1700, winter 1000-1500, $15 ($12 in winter).* This is a 4-sq-km garden surrounded by bush that is world renowned for its beautiful displays of 'rhodies' and azaleas, which are

To ⑨ ⑫, North, Airport & Fitzroy Pole

Gover St

State La ❸ ⑥

Courtenay St

Woolworths Supermarket

Elliot St

Leach St

P

New World supermarket

Gover St

Cameron St

Lemon St ❹

Pendarves St

To South (SH 3), Mt Egmont National Park & Around the Mountain Circuit

Gilbert St

Fillis St

Gover St

Pukekura Park

⑤

Eating ❼
Agra 1 *A5*
Andre
L'Escargot 6 *B3*
Chaos 2 *B3*
El Condor 3 *A5*
GCR & Bar 5 *B3*

⑥

Peggy Gordon's
Celtic Bar 11 *B2*

Bars & clubs ❶
Crowded House 10 *A4*

best viewed in the spring/summer and especially during the Rhododendron Festival in late October. There is a restaurant, and a shop selling plants and souvenirs.

If you continue on Carrington Road you will join the network of roads that surround the mountain. There is a fine walk and views of the mountain on the **Stony River** and **Blue Rata reserves**. From Carrington take a left onto the Saunders Road dirt track and follow it to the end. From there, by foot, negotiate your way through the bush following the sound of the river. You will emerge onto the Stony River boulder field. From here you can walk carefully east or west, under the shadow of the mighty mountain. The large Blue Rata, from which the reserve takes its name, is hard to find, about 100 m into the bush, on the riverside of the track, about halfway up its length.

Before rejoining SH45 and heading north or south, take a discreet peek at the memorial to the great man, prophet and Maori chief, Te Whiti, which is at **Parihaka Pa**, on Mid-Parihaka Road (signposted).

Lake Mangamahoe
There is something you simply must do on your visit to New Plymouth (weather permitting) and that is to soak up the beauty and serenity of Lake Mangamahoe. Just 10 km southeast on SH3, this scenic reserve is one of the very best places where you can see a reflection of the mighty mountain on water. After enjoying the lake itself, with its numerous swans, ducks and geese, head to the road end and take the right hand track up the steps to the lookout point. From here at sunset, or anytime when the mountain is clear, the view is magnificent. Take your camera.

'Surf Highway 45'
If you fancy doing the 175-km trip around the mountain, it involves at least a full day via the 'Surf Highway 45' and SH3. But on a clear day the mountain will be good company throughout, and there are a number of interesting places to see and visit on the way.

Heading south from New Plymouth the view of the mountain is shielded by the Kaitake and Pouakai ranges for a short while, then you arrive in **Oakura**, famous for its surf, windsurfing and swimming beach. There is also an interesting craft shop called the **Crafty Fox** in the heart of town next to the main road. Various local art and craft pieces are for sale and there is a railway wagon café next door.

While in the area you may like to visit the **Emacadamia Nut Orchard** ① *219 Surrey Hill Rd, T06-752 7793, www.emacadamia.co.nz, tours available on Sun 1330-1630, free*, where you will get a fascinating insight into the great nut and its associated products.

Lucy's Gully, 3 km south of Oakura, is a pleasant picnic spot with exotic trees, including redwoods, and ferns. There are also walking tracks into the Kaitake Range. Around the small settlement of **Okato** the mountain comes back into view and the road edges its way closer to the coast. You can satisfy your desire to see it again at the **Cape Egmont Lighthouse**, about 3 km down Cape Road. Although the lighthouse is closed to visitors it is still of interest. It seems strangely out of place, standing in a field with a huge mountain in the background. Just south of Cape Road back on SH45 is Mid-Parihaka Road. Two kilometres up is **Parihaka Pa**.

Back on SH45, you can enjoy the scenery or explore the many side roads until you reach **Opunake**, which has a fine surf and swimming beach and a 7-km walkway, starting at Opunake Lake, which takes in lake, beach and river scenery. Visit the **VIC** ① *in the library, Tasman St, T06-761 8663, Mon-Thu 0930-1700, Fri 0930-1830*, for accommodation options.

The next settlement south of Opunake is **Manaia** which is the place to leave SH45 if you want to get a bit more intimate with the mountain at **Dawson Falls**. There is not a lot in Manaia itself, a small settlement of about 1000, named after a Maori chief. Country and Western fans might like to pop into the **Taranaki Country Music Hall of Fame** ⓘ *11 Surf Highway, T06-274 8442, Sat-Wed 1000-1600.*

◉ New Plymouth listings

For Sleeping and Eating price codes and other relevant information, see Essentials pages 44-50.

● Sleeping

New Plymouth *p310, map p312*
For full listings contact the VIC (I-Site) or www.accommodationtaranaki.co.nz. For mountain accommodation see page 320.
L The Nice Hotel, 71 Brougham St, T06-758 6423, www.nicehotel.co.nz. A small, 2-storey, luxury boutique hotel well placed for the town centre and all amenities. Each of the 8 rooms is themed according to its outlook and reflects the town's history or contribution to the arts. Examples include the 'Redcoats' room relating to the former British army barracks near the town, or 'The Wind Wand', relating to Len Lye's kinetic sculpture on the waterfront. As well as stylish design, the rooms offer all the comforts, such as a spa bath and large comfortable armchairs. The popular, in-house **Table Restaurant** is intimate and relaxed, offering excellent contemporary Pacific Rim cuisine. Also offers nice tours.
L-A Waterfront Motor Inn, 1 Egmont St, T06-769 5301, www.waterfront.co.nz. One of the newest offerings in the town centre, with a contemporary feel. The location and views are hard to beat.
AL-A Abode on Courtenay Motor Inn, 155 Courtenay St, T06-769 5465, www.abodemotorinn.co.nz. One of the newest, centrally located.
AL-A Airlie House, 161 Powerham St, T06-757 8866, www.airliehouse.co.nz. A historic villa B&B, centrally located and very tastefully renovated, with 2 en suite rooms and a self-contained studio, fast internet. Recommended.
AL-A Brougham Heights, 54 Brougham St,

T06-757 9954, www.broughamheights.co.nz. Well-located, modern and comfortable motel that seems to absorb some of the niceties from the **Nice Hotel** across the road.
AL-A Copthorne Grand Central Hotel, 42 Powerham St, T06-758 7495, www.grand centralhotel.co.nz. Conveniently placed standard hotel with a solid reputation, spa rooms and in-house restaurant.
AL-A Devon Hotel, 390 Devon St, T0800-843338/T06-759 9009, www.devonhotel. co.nz. The best in this range, along with **Grand Central**, above.
AL-A Issy Manor, 32 Carrington St, T06-758 2375, www.isseymanor.co.nz. Classy, contemporary boutique accommodation in a renovated former 1857 coach house. Centrally located next to Pukekura Park. 4 good value rooms, spa, internet and off-street parking.
A Braemar Motor Inn, 152 Powerham St, T06-758 0859, www.breamarmotorinn.co.nz. Well-established 3-star motel, fairly modern with an in-house restaurant.
B Cottage Mews Motel, 48 Lemon St, T06-758 0403, www.cottagemews.net.nz. Suites attached to **Shoestring Backpackers**, below. Immaculate, good value and run by fine folk.
B-D Shoestring Backpackers, 48 Lemon St, T06-758 0404. A large traditional villa with a range of rooms and fine facilities. Friendly folk, sauna and fast internet.
B-D Seaspray House, 13 Weymouth St, T06-759 8934, www.seasprayhouse.co.nz. Immaculate 14-bed hostel, centrally located with doubles, twins, one single and 4 or 3 share rooms with beds not bunks, shared bathroom. Recommended.
B-D YHA Egmont Eco Lodge, 12 Clawton St, T06-753 5720, www.taranaki-bakpak.co.nz. Small, very friendly and set in a quiet location

a 15-min walk from town (taxi fare refunded). Full range of rooms including motel-style en suites to tent sites. An added attraction here is the free introduction to some large and rapacious local river inhabitants.

C-D EcoInn Backpackers Hostel, 671 Kent Rd, T06-752 2765, www.ecoinn.co.nz. Eco-friendly and relaxed backpacker hostel, 3 km from the Egmont National Park. Solar, hydro and wind-powered property with doubles and share, hot tub, internet.

Motorcamps and campsites

There are several options in town.

B-D Belt Road Holiday Park, 2 Belt Rd, T06-758 0228, www.beltroad.co.nz. Near the water and well equipped, overlooking the port.

B-D Egmont Eco Leisure Park, 12 Clawton St, T06-753 5720, www.egmont.co.nz. Set in native bush with lodge, cabins powered and tent sites, fully equipped camp kitchen. A short walk from the town centre.

B-D New Plymouth Top Ten Motorcamp, 29 Princess St, Fitzroy, T0800-758256/T06-758 2566, www.nptop10.co.nz. Small and central.

North on SH3 *p312*

A Mokau Motel, SH3 T06-752 9725. 4 basic, but comfortable units.

C-D Palm House, 1 Reanga St, T06-752 9081, www.egmont.co.nz/retreat/mokau. A good backpacker hostel, affiliated with the **Taranaki** Experience accommodation conglomerate, with the full range of rooms and a quiet relaxing atmosphere.

Motorcamps and campsites

C-D Seaview Motorcamp, Awakino, just before SH3 turns inland heading north, T06-752 9708. Excellent, right on the beach, with camp kitchen and a café attached.

Carrington Road *p313*

A Patuha Farm Lodge, 575 Upper Pitone Rd, Okato, T06-7524469, www.patuha lodge.co.nz. This 10-bedroom working farm lodge is well placed in a quiet bush setting on the edge of the Pukeiti Rhododendron Trust Gardens. En suites and in-house spa. Overall a fine relaxing retreat and guests have the opportunity to join in daily farm activities.

'Surf Highway 45' *p314*

L-AL Ahu Ahu Beach Villas, 321 Ahu Ahu Rd, Oakura, T06-752 7370, www.ahu.com. Rustic award-winning architecture in the form of 2 villas housing 4 fully self-contained units overlooking the ocean. Cosy and highly individual. Recommended.

A Oakura Beach Motel, 53 Wairau Rd, Oakura, T06-752 7680, www.oakurabeach motel.co.nz. Standard self-contained units 3 mins from the beach.

Motorcamps and campsites

C-D Oakura Beach Camp, 2 Jans Terr, Oakura, T06-752 7861, www.oakurabeach.com. Basic but has a store and is across the road from the beach.

Eating

New Plymouth *p310, map p312*

There is a Countdown supermarket on Leach St and a Pack-n-Save on Gill St.

TTT Andre L'Escargot 37-43 Brougham St, T06-758 4812. Mon-Sat from 1700. This is an old favourite offering award-winning, fine French-style cuisine in a congenial setting.

TTT The Nice Hotel's Table Restaurant, 71 Brougham St. Mon-Sat from 1600. Fine à la carte with superb desserts and a good wine selection. Well it couldn't be horrible, could it?

TTT Salt Restaurant, Waterfront Hotel, 1 Egmont St, T06-769 5304. Daily 0700-2200. Modern, trendy and overlooking the ocean.

TT Flame, 151 Devon St, T06-758 0030. Daily from 1630-late. A small, good-value Indian diner deserving of its loyal following.

TT GCR Restaurant and Bar, 40 Brougham St, T06-758 7495. Mon-Fri from 0630-0930 and from 1800, Sat-Sun from 0730-1030 and from 1800. A modern restaurant and bar specializing in gourmet pizzas.

Peggy Gordons Celtic Bar, corner of Devon and Egmont sts, T06-758 8561. Daily from 0700. Good pub grub.

Daily News Cafe, Puke Ariki Library, T06-769 5386. The library café that offers a nice escape from the main street buzz with the added attraction of a newspaper or six.

Chaos, 36 Brougham St, T06-759 8080. Popular organic café with good coffee and a wide range of snacks. Good breakfast venue.

El Condor, 170 Devon St East, T06-757 5436. Tue-Sat from 1700. Good-value Argentine pizza joint.

Pubs, bars and clubs

New Plymouth *p310, map p312*
Crowded House, 93 Devon St, T06-759 4921. About the size of a football field and claims to be the official bar of the famed Taranaki rugby team supporters.

Peggy Gordon's, corner of Devon and Egmont sts, T06-758 8561. The town's Irish-style offering.

Entertainment

New Plymouth *p310, map p312*
Cinema and theatre
Cinema 5, 125 Devon St East, T06-759 9077.
New Plymouth Operatic Society, 76 King St, T06-758 4958. Excellent annual shows.
TSB Showplace, 92 Devon St, T06-7596712. Regular national and international acts.

Festivals and events

New Plymouth *p310, map p312*
See www.taranaki.co.nz for details.
Feb Taranaki Wine and Food Festival usually held at one of the top vineyards and with the added attraction of live music.
Mar WOMAD, www.womad.co.nz. A 3-day celebration of World music with over 400 artists from around the world.

Jul-Aug Taranaki Festival of the Arts, www.artfest.co.nz. A biennial festival (next held in 2011) of international and New Zealand artists and performers. Theatre, contemporary music, fine music, choirs, literature, dance, visual arts, film and cabaret.
Oct Taranaki Rhododendron Festival, www.rhodo.co.nz. Various events and tours take place at various major gardens.
Dec-Feb New Plymouth Festival of Lights, held in Pukekura Park, involves the illumination of trees, waterfalls and fountains with additional staged events.

Shopping

New Plymouth *p310, map p312*
There are numerous excellent arts and crafts galleries and outlets in the region, for details see the VIC.
Rangimarie Maori Art and Craft Centre, near Paritutu Rock on Centennial Dr, T06-751 2880. Mon-Fri 0900-1500.
Real Tart Gallery, 19 Egmont St, T06-756 5717. Wide range of local contemporary art.

Activities and tours

New Plymouth *p310, map p312*
For mountain activities see Mt Egmont (Taranaki) National Park, page 320. New Plymouth offers many of the usual activities, along with dam-dropping (see under Hawera, page 322) and tandem-surfing.

Fishing, scuba diving and cruising
Taranaki Outdoor Adventures, T06-7527876, www.toa.co.nz. Offer a range adventures from dam dropping and canyoning, to kayaking and mountain biking.
Mokau River Cruises, T06-752 9036, www.mokauriver.co.nz. River cruising on the Mokau north of New Plymouth (Nov-Apr), departs 1100, 3 hrs from $45.

Horse trekking

There are several operators so shop around. **Gumboot Gully Horse Treks**, 1034 Piko Rd, Okoki, T06-756 5809. From 2 hrs to 5-day hill country treks on horses that featured in the film *The Last Samurai*, from $40.

Okau Horse Treks, 1282 Okau Rd, Urenui (30 mins east of New Plymouth), T06-752 5990, www.okauhorsetrekstaranaki.com. Bush and coast treks from 2 hrs to a full-day, views of Mt Taranaki, from $35.

Kayaking

Canoe and Kayak Taranaki, 6/631 Devon Rd, T0508-529256, www.canoeandkayak. co.nz/Taranaki. Various regional whitewater and coastal options, from $70.

Chaddy's Charters, T06-758 9133. Kayak hire. Shoreline and marine park explorations.

Mineral pools

Mineral Pool Complex, 8 Bonithon Rd, T06-759 1666. Mon-Fri 0900-2000, Tue 0900-1700, Sat-Sun 1200-2100, bookings essential. This modern complex offers both communal and private pools (4 people) with a range of professional massages and health treatments. The pools cost $15. This is on a 'per pool' basis and they are freshly filled for each client. Very therapeutic.

Mountaineering and climbing

The following will see you safely up and down the mountain from around $350. Other activities include trekking and abseiling. **MacAlpine Guides**, T06-765 6234, www.mac alpineguides.com; and **Top Guides**, T0800-448433, www.topguides.co.nz.

Scenic flights

Heliview Taranaki, T06-753 0123, www.heliview.co.nz. Mountain specials from $125.

Surfing and windsurfing

The Taranaki or Egmont Coast is one of the best surfing places in the country. The so-called 'Surf Highway 45' which hugs the coastline between New Plymouth and Wanganui has some fine surf beaches, particularly at **Oakura** and **Opunake**. Particular gems also include **Ahu Ahu Road**, the **Kumara Patch** and **Stent Road**. In town, **Footsore Beach** is one of the favourites.

Companies offering trips and lessons come and go as much as the surf, for the most recent listings contact the VIC (I-Site). **Sirocco**, 605 Main St, Oakura, T06-752 1363, www.siroccosurf.com. Board hire and wave information.

Vertigo, Oakura, T06-752 7363, www.vertigosurf.com. Surf board hire and also offers windsurfing lessons.

Tours

Taranaki Tours, T06-757 9888, www.taranakitours.com. Offer tours of the region with emphasis on the mountain with a full-day 'Round the Mountain' from $225, shuttle service from $55 return.

⊖ Transport

New Plymouth *p310, map p312*
Bicycle hire Cycle Inn, 133 Devon St East, T06-758 7418. Raceway Cycles, 207 Coronation Av, T06-759 0391. **Car hire** Avis, Airport, T06-755 9600. **Budget**, T0800-283438. **Taxi** New Plymouth Taxis, T06-757 3000.

ⓘ Directory

New Plymouth *p310, map p312*
Banks Most main branches can be found on Devon St. Currency exchange at TSB Centre, 120 Devon St East, T06-759 5375. **Internet** Computer Corner, Shop 8, Richmond Centre (Egmont St) is the cheapest. Also at: New Plymouth Library, Brougham St. **Medical services** Pheonix Accident and Medical Clinic, 95 Vivian St, T06-7594295, Mon-Fri 0900-1800, Sat-Sun 0900-1600. **Police** Powerham St, T06-759 5500. **Post office** 21 Currie St, Mon-Fri 0800-1730, Sat 0900-1300.

Mount Egmont (Taranaki) National Park

Weather permitting, no trip to Taranaki would be complete without getting close to the mountain. At 2518 m, Mount Taranaki is not only at the heart of Egmont National Park, but metaphorically it is the heart. This classically shaped, dormant volcano was formed by the numerous eruptions of the last 12,000 years. The most recent happened 350 years ago and they say she is now 'overdue', with the potential to 'go off' at any time. Fatham's Peak, on the southern slopes, is a parasitic outcrop from the main vent, while the Pouakai and Kaitake ranges to the west are older andesite volcanoes and have eroded for much longer than Taranaki. ▶▶ *For Sleeping, Eating and other listings, see page 320.*

Ins and outs

Getting there The main access points to the park and the mountain are at North Egmont (Egmont VIC), Stratford (East Egmont) and Manaia (Dawson Falls). East Egmont is accessed via Pembroke Rd, which heads 18 km towards the mountain from Stratford. Dawson Falls is at the end of Upper Manaia Rd, via Kaponga on the southern slopes of the mountain, 24 km from Stratford. **Taranaki Tours**, T06-757 9888, www.taranakitours.com, offer shuttle services to the mountain from New Plymouth (particularly Egmont VIC), from $55 return.

Tourist information Before attempting any walks on the mountain you should read all the relevant information. The VIC (I-Site) in New Plymouth (see page 310) can provide basic information particularly about getting there, while the DoC office (both in town and on the mountain) can fill in the detail with walking information, maps and weather forecasts. **DoC Egmont VIC** ⓘ *16 km from North Egmont Village, at the end of Egmont Rd (which heads towards the mountain), T06-756 0990, egmontvc@doc.govt.nz, daily 0800-1630.* **DoC Dawson Falls VIC** ⓘ *Manaia Rd, T027-443 0248, Mar-Dec Wed-Sun 0800-1630, Jan-Feb daily.*

▲▲ Walks

The 140-km of walks take from 30 minutes to four days and are well maintained by DoC. The tracks vary in difficulty, but all are easily accessible from the main access points and information centres above. The forest and vegetation is called 'goblin forest' (due to its miniature 'hobbit-style' appearance as the altitude increases) and the entire mountain is drained by myriad babbling streams. Beware that the higher you go, obviously, the more dangerous it gets. In winter the slopes are covered in snow and ice, so climbing boots, crampons and an ice axe are essential. Even in summer crampons are advised on the summit, though the main enemy underfoot is loose scree. Guides can supply crampons as part of their service, but otherwise you will need your own.

To the uninitiated, **Mount Taranaki** looks deceptively easy, however the weather is highly unpredictable and many people have lost their lives on its slopes, so you must be well prepared. DoC produces a number of leaflets: *Around the Mountain Circuit* and *Short Walks in Egmont National Park* are both excellent. The VICs around the mountain can also advise on routes, hut accommodation, prices and bookings. At Dawson Falls two of the best short-walk options include the track to the falls which can be accessed via the **Kapuni Loop Track** (one hour). This walk offers some good photo opportunities along the way, as does the **Wilkie's Pools Track** (one hour), which takes in some very pretty 'goblin forest' and a series of plunge pools, formed by sand and gravel running over the lava.

At North Egmont, the 45-minute walk from the park entrance to the Waiwhakaiho River has some beautiful base native bush, while the **Ngatoro Loop Track** (1 hour) takes in some beautiful 'goblin forest', and the **Veronica Loop Track** (2 hours) some excellent views. Both of these tracks start from the top of the road.

⊙ Mount Egmont (Taranaki) National Park listings

For Sleeping and Eating price codes and other relevant information, see Essentials pages 44-50.

● Sleeping

Mount Egmont National Park *p319*
For all mountain hut bookings contact and pre-book with DoC.
L Dawson Falls Tourist Lodge, Manaia Rd, Dawson Falls, T06-765 5457, www.dawson-falls.co.nz. An Alpine-style lodge, comfortable suites, log fire and all mod cons, restaurant.
AL Anderson's Alpine Lodge, 922 Pembroke Rd, East Egmont, T06-765 6620. Swiss-style chalet with 3 guestrooms.
C-D Konini Lodge, Upper Manaia Rd, Kaponga, Dawson Falls, T027-4430248. A poor relation of the above, but comfortable nonetheless. DoC owned.
C-D Missing Leg Backpackers, 1082 Junction Rd, Egmont Village, North Egmont, T06-752 2570, www.missinglegbackpackers. co.nz. Very friendly and relaxed backpacker hostel with doubles and dorms, log fire, bike hire and shuttle service up the mountain. The 'missing leg' refers to 'journey' as opposed to shark attacks or poor travel planning. Recommended.
C-D The Mountain Café, DoC North

Egmont VIC, T06-756 9093. Daily 0900-1530. Located within the visitor centre with a good all day selection.

▲ Activities and tours

Mount Egmont National Park *p319*
Mountain guides
If you want some experienced company and some great information en route then the 3 main operators below offer guided summit treks and other walks. All will see you safely up and down the mountain from around $170-300 per day. Other activities include climbing, abseiling and low-level hikes.
Adventure Dynamics, T06-751 3589, www.adventuredynamics.co.nz. **MacAlpine Guides**, T025-417042, www.macalpine guides.co.nz. **Top Guides**, T0800-448433, www.topguides.co.nz.

Skiing
The only ski field on Taranaki is **Manganui** on the Stratford Plateau, 20 km from Stratford. For information contact the **Stratford Mountain Club**, T027-280 0860; or call the ski field direct, T06-765 5493, www.snow.co.nz.

Hawera and around → *Colour map 3, A2*

Hawera, an interesting little town with many architecturally significant buildings, is the largest of the southern Taranaki townships and is on the coast at the confluence of SH45 and SH3. It's a good place to stop for a break and take in a few sights and attractions. From here it is about 70 km to complete the circuit around the mountain, north to New Plymouth. For Sleeping, Eating and other listings, see page 322.

Ins and outs
Hawera VIC (I-Site) ① *55 High St (just head for the water tower), T06-278 8599, visitorinfo@stdc.govt.nz, Mon-Fri 0830-1700, Sat-Sun summer 1000-1500*, also acts as travel and accommodation booking agent.

Sights

The most obvious one is the **water tower** ① *open to climb daily 1000-1400, $2, child $1*, built in 1914. The VIC has a *Historic Hawera* heritage trail leaflet that details the major buildings. The **Tawhiti Museum** ① *401 Ohangai Rd, T06-278 6831, www.tawhitimuseum.co.nz, Fri-Mon 1000-1600, open daily in Jan, Sun only Jun-Aug, $10, child $3*, is a private museum that uses realistic life-size exhibits and scale models to capture Taranaki's past. There is also a narrow gauge railway. Equally unusual is the **Elvis Presley Memorial Room** ① *51 Argyle St, phone for appointment, T06-278 7624, www.digitalus.co.nz/elvis, donation*, where avid collector and fan Kevin Wasley has amassed memorabilia and 2000 of 'The King's' records.

SH3 from Hawera to New Plymouth ⊜🕖▲ ⊮ *p321*.

Eltham

Eltham is well known for its dairy products, especially its production of cheese, but for the tourist the main attraction is its surrounding lakes. **Lake Rotokare** (Rippling Lake), 11 km southeast on Sangster Road, is in a pretty setting with a one-hour walk and picnic sites. Further afield, **Lake Rotorangi** on Glen Nui Road (via Rawhitiroa Road) is 40 km in length and was formed by the damming of the Patea River. It is popular for watersports and fishing. For more information see the local library on the High Street.

Stratford

A glance at the street names in Stratford will soon confirm your suspicion that this rural service centre and eastern gateway to the Egmont National Park was named after Shakespeare's birthplace in England. There's little to detain you beyond a meal, a coffee and perhaps a look at the **glockenspiel** (playing clock) on the clock tower in the centre of town with its Romeo and Juliet theme, or the **Taranaki Pioneer Village** ① *SH3, T06-765 5399,www.pioneervillage.co.nz, daily 1000-1600, $10, child $5*. It consists of 50 re-sited buildings on 4 ha, all faithfully equipped to depict the Taranaki of the early 1900s. For more information on accommodation and local attractions, contact **Stratford VIC (I-Site)** ① *Broadway, T06-765 6708, www.stratfordnz.co.nz, Mon-Fri 0830-1700, Sat-Sun 1000-1400*. It also acts as a travel agent.

◉ Harewa and around listings

For Sleeping and Eating price codes and other relevant information, see Essentials pages 44-50.

⊜ Sleeping

Hawera *p320*
L Kingfisher Cottage, 483 Skeet Rd (north, between Hawera and Eltham), T06-2726630, www.kingfishercottage.co.nz. Well-appointed self-contained cottage with great views and good fishing nearby.
A-B Kerry Lane Villas Motel, 2 Kerry Lane, T06 278 1918, www.kerrylanemotel.co.nz. A good modern option in a quiet rural setting 5

mins from town.
C-D Wheatly Downs Farmstay Backpackers, Ararata Rd, T06-278 6523, www.taranaki- bakpak.co.nz. Well-equipped and entertaining farmstay backpacker lodge, 2 km from town.

Motorcamps and campsites
B-D King Edward Park Motorcamp, 70 Waihi Rd, T06-278 8544. 1 km from the town centre, camp kitchen. Next door to a heated public swimming pool.

Stratford *p321*

C-D The Heritage Lodge, 103 Miranda St, Stratford, T06-756 7482, www.eastern-taranaki.co.nz. 'Flashpacker' styled accommodation with quality tours. A good option if attacking the mountain from the east.

Motorcamps and campsites

B-D Stratford Holiday Park, 10 Page St, T06-765 6440, www.stratfordtoptown holidaypark.co.nz. The closest motorcamp to the mountain.

🍴 Eating

Hawera *p320*

The Tawhiti Museum (see page 321) also has café attached .

🍴🍴 🍴 Il Chefs Steakhouse, 47 High St St, T06-278 4444. Best bet for fine dining.

🍴 Anderson's Pies, 142 Princess St. Simple but good value.

Stratford *p321*

🍴🍴–🍴 Urban Attitude Café and Wine Bar, Broadway, T06-765 6534. Considered one of the best eateries.

▲ Activities and tours

Hawera *p320*
Dam-dropping

Another 'Kiwi unique' adrenaline offerings. This time you throw yourself down a dam outlet with a boogie board. Full-river run taking in 9 rapids, from $100, child $80. Minimum age is 8 years.
Kaitiaki Adventures, based in Okato, T06-752 8242, www.damdrop.com.

Contents

East Coast

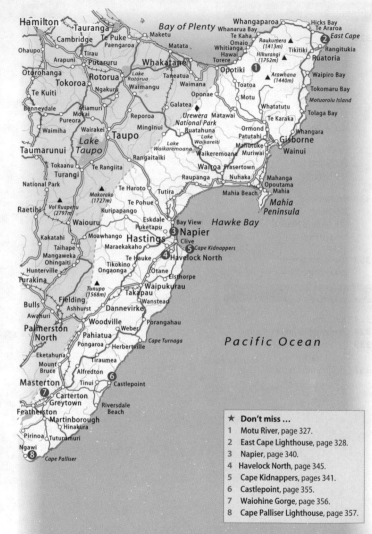

Hamilton
Tauranga
Cambridge
Te Puke
Paengaroa
Maketu
Bay of Plenty
Whangaparaoa
Whanarua Bay
Te Kaha
Omaio
Whitianga
Hawai
Torere
Hicks Bay
Te Araroa
East Cape

Ohaupo
Arapuni
Putaruru
Matata
Raukumera ▲ (1413m)
Tikitiki
Rangitukia

Otorohanga
Rotorua
Ngakuru
Whakatane
Taneatua
Waimana
Opotiki
Hikurangi (1752m) ▲
Ruatoria

Tokoroa
Te Kuiti
Atiamuri
Mokai
Reporoa
Waimangu
Waimana
Oponae
Motu
Toatoa
Arawhana (1440m) ▲
Waipiro Bay

Benneydale
Pureora
Wairakei
Minginui
Urewera National Park
Matawai
Whatatutu
Te Karaka
Tokomaru Bay
Motuoroiu Island
Tolaga Bay

Waimiha
Taupo
Ruatahuna
Lake Waikaremoana
Lake Waikareiti
Ormond
Patutahi
Whangara

Taumarunui
Lake Taupo
Rangaitaiki
Waikaremoana
Manutuke
Muriwai
Gisborne
Wainui

Tokaanu
Turangi
Te Rangiita
Te Haroto
Raupanga
Frasertown
Nuhaka
Mahanga
Opoutama
Mahia

National Park
Makorako (1727m) ▲
Te Pohue
Tutira
Wairoa
Mahia Beach
Mahia Peninsula

Raetihi
Vol Ruapehu (2797m) ▲
Waiouru
Kuripapango
Eskdale
Puketapu
Bay View
Hawke Bay

Kakatahi
Moawhango
Maraekakaho
Napier ❸
Clive
Cape Kidnappers ❺

Taihape
Mangaweka
Ohingaiti
Te Hauke
Tikokino
Ongaonga
Hastings
Havelock North ❹

Hunterville
Tunupo (1568m) ▲
Otane
Elsthorpe

Turakina
Fielding
Takapau
Waipukurau
Wanstead

Bulls
Awahuri
Ashhurst
Danneverke
Pahiatua
Weber
Pongaroa
Pohrangahau
Cape Turnaga

Palmerston North
Woodville
Herbertville

Eketahuna
Mount Bruce
Alfredton
Tiraumea
Pacific Ocean

Masterton ❼
Tinui
Castlepoint ❻

Carterton
Greytown
Featherston
Riversdale Beach

Martinborough
Hinakura

Pirinoa
Tuturumuri

Ngawi ❽
Cape Palliser

★ **Don't miss ...**

1 **Motu River**, page 327.
2 **East Cape Lighthouse**, page 328.
3 **Napier**, page 340.
4 **Havelock North**, page 345.
5 **Cape Kidnappers**, pages 341.
6 **Castlepoint**, page 355.
7 **Waioine Gorge**, page 356.
8 **Cape Palliser Lighthouse**, page 357.

N

30 km
30 miles

The east coast of the North Island is all about sun, wine and remote coastal scenery. The East Cape (the 'heel' of the 'upside-down boot') is where you can witness the day's first warming rays and, a little further south, the coastal town of Gisborne prides itself on being the first place Captain Cook set foot in New Zealand in 1769.

Inland from Wairoa (south of Gisborne) and the enchanting Mahia Peninsula, are the dense forests of the Te Urewera National Park, a place of almost spiritual beauty and particularly famous for its 'Great Walk', which circumnavigates its most scenic jewel, Lake Waikaremoana. Back on the coast you enter the wine country of northern Hawke's Bay and the pretty coastal town of Napier, almost completely flattened by an earthquake in 1931 and now reborn as an international showpiece for its art deco buildings.

Further south, on the bleached cliffs that caress Hawke's Bay, is the largest gannet colony in the country, at Cape Kidnappers. Continuing southwards is one of the most stunningly beautiful and remote parts of the North Island, the Wairarapa, where, from Castlepoint to the lighthouse at Cape Palliser – the southernmost tip of the island – the peace and isolation is unsurpassed anywhere in the North Island.

East Cape to Wairoa → *Colour map 2, B4.*

Those with a healthy imagination and good sense of geography will recognize East Cape as the 'heel' of the 'upside-down boot' that is New Zealand. Along with the Wairarapa, East Cape is the least-visited area in the North Island. This is due not so much to its isolated location as its geography. Almost the entire peninsula is sparsely populated, remote and mountainous. Much of the Raukumara Range, which makes up most of its interior, remains impenetrable by road, with only rivers like the Motu and Mata carving their way through the wilderness. ▸▸ *For Sleeping, Eating and other listings, see pages 333-336.*

Ins and outs

Getting there

Air **Gisborne airport** ⓘ *2 km west of town centre*, is served by **Air New Zealand Link**, T0800-737000, several times daily from Wellington and Auckland. **Eastland Taxis** operates an airport shuttle, T06- 867 6667, $15.

Road Gisborne is linked with all major points south to Wellington (550 km), and north to Opotiki (147 km) and Auckland (504 km) by SH2. Gisborne is a major stop on the well-signposted 'Pacific Coast Highway', which includes SH35. This 330-km trip terminates at Opotiki, where SH35 rejoins SH2.

Both Opotiki and Gisborne are served by **Intercity** buses, T06-868 6139. Beyond those places getting around the East Cape by public transport is possible, but unpredictable. Before travelling you are advised to contact the VIC (I-Site) Opotiki or Gisborne for the latest information. Your best bet is with **Polly's Passenger and Courier Services**, T06- 864 4728, T06-8686139, which runs a service from Gisborne to Hicks Bay, Hicks Bay to Opotiki/Whakatane and return. Departs Gisborne VIC (I-Site) 1300 weekdays. **Cook's Couriers**, T06-864 4711, T027-437 1364, cook.teararoa@xtra.co.nz, also offers a service from Gisborne to Hick's Bay and back, departing Gisborne VIC (I-Site) Mon-Fri 1400 and Sat 1230, from $40 one way. Couriers to take you from Hick's Bay to Opotiki and Whakatane can also be arranged. Always check with the VIC (I-Site) for any changes to schedule and price. **Matakaoa Coastline**, T0800-628252/T07-3153031, offers a service from Opotiki to Hick's Bay and back. The backpacker-oriented national operator **Kiwi Experience**, T09-366 9830, www.kiwiexperience.com, offers four-day trips from Rotorua and Taupo departing Mon, Wed and Fri. Always check with the VIC (I-Site) for any changes to schedule and price.

Getting around

The best way to explore the Cape is to drive the 334 km of SH35 from either Opotiki to Gisborne or vice versa. Although the trip can be done comfortably in two days, taking longer will allow you time to soak up the laid-back atmosphere and explore the numerous bays and beaches as you go, or to climb Hikurangi, the North Island's fourth highest peak. From this legendary summit, on a clear day, the entire East Cape is laid out before you.

Tourist information

Gisborne VIC (I-Site) ⓘ *209 Grey St, T06-8686139, www.gisbornenz.com, Mon-Fri 0830-1730, Sat-Sun 0900-1730*, and **Opotiki VIC (I-Site)** ⓘ *corner St John and Elliott sts, T07-315 3031, www.opotikinz.com, daily 0800-1700*, provide information for the East

Cape. The latter (see page 270) has two free handbooks, the *Opotiki and East Cape Holiday Guide* and the *Eastland Visitor Guide*, both essential pieces of kit for the trip. **Gisborne DoC** ① *63 Carnarvon St, T06-869 0460*, and **Wairoa VIC (I-Site)** ① *corner of SH2 and Queen St, T06-838 7440, www.wairoanz.com, Nov-Mar daily 0900-1700, Apr-Oct Mon-Fri 0900-1700*, acts as bus booking agents, can help organize transport to Waikaremoana and has internet.

Opotiki to East Cape Lighthouse 🚌 ⏩ *pp333-336.*

The cape road, SH35, begins at Opotiki (see page 271) and you will soon begin to feel that you are entering another world. Change your watch to 'Coast Time', which really means taking the batteries out. Maori influences are also apparent in the first small settlement of **Torore** (24 km) and the beautiful carvings which adorn the gates to its school.

With the coast now your guide and the steaming volcanic White Island offshore as companion you continue past **Hawai** and make your way around the mouth of the **Motu**

East Cape

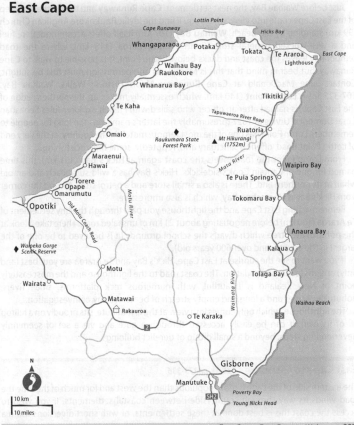

River (49 km). Here, when there has been little rain, the expansive boulder fields of the Motu riverbed can make it look like an insignificant trickle. But don't be deceived, at times this river can be a raging torrent spewing forth from its mountain wilderness and leaving huge piles of driftwood as evidence of its fury. On this part of the coast, there often seems to be more tangled wood on the beach than there is rock and sand. **Omaio**, the next settlement, has one such beach and is renowned for its good fishing. Just around the corner from the Motu River mouth keep your eyes open for the **Whitianga Marae** at Whitianga Bay (51 km), which is beautifully carved.

After Omaio is **Te Kaha** (70 km) with its shallow rocky coast and popular beaches. Te Kaha is pleasant and offers the first really credible place to stop for supplies or accommodation. **Whanarua Bay** (88 km), a mere 20 minutes north of Te Kaha, also offers real serenity and is another fine spot to spend your first night on the cape. As the road climbs into the tiny village take the track on the left (easily missed) that falls abruptly to the beach. This small secluded bay is stunning. Whanarua has a fine backpacker hostel and a basic camping ground about 1 km past the village.

Just before Waihau Bay, the next settlement, **Cape Runaway** and the northern sweep of the East Cape come into view, where you'll find the idyllic **Raukokore Anglican Church** (99 km) standing by the beach. **Waihau Bay** (107 km) itself offers accommodation, fuel and a well-stocked general store. From **Whangaparoa** (118 km), where the road temporarily leaves the coast and ducks below Lottin Point, it is possible to walk to Cape Runaway, but bear in mind that this is Maori land and permission must first be sought. Contact June MacDonald at **Cape Runaway Maori Historic Walks**, Waihau Bay, T07-325 3697. **Lottin Point** (140 km), which essentially makes up the northern edge of the East Cape, is named after an officer who sailed with French explorer Jules Sebastian Cesar Dumont d'Urville in 1827 (presumably the latter's name was too long for people to remember). Lottin Point has one of the most remote motels in the country, at the very end of Lottin Point Road, offering sanctuary and, reputedly, some fine rock fishing.

From Lottin Point the road meets the coast again at **Hick's Bay** (151 km), this time named after one of Captain Cook's sidekicks. Hick's Bay has a wild surf beach and an old wharf at its northern end. There is also a small store and a petrol stop. Around the corner from Hick's Bay is **Horseshoe Bay**, which is also impressive.

Before reaching East Cape and the lighthouse you pass through the tiny settlement of **Te Araroa** (160 km) before negotiating about 21 km of unsealed road. There take a look at the **pohutukawa tree** which dwarfs the school grounds (it is believed to be one of the largest in the country and over 600 years old).

If you want to see the sunrise at East Cape, Hick's Bay and Te Araroa are your best (and only) options for accommodation. The coast road to the lighthouse and the most easterly point of New Zealand is beautiful, with numerous rock platforms, small rivers, pohutukawa trees and a long and empty stretch of beach worthy of investigation.

The **lighthouse**, which only comes into view at the last minute, sits proudly on a hilltop all of its own. It can be easily accessed through a gate and via a set of seemingly never-ending steps, beyond a small group of derelict buildings.

East Cape to Gisborne ●▲ ⇥ *pp333-336.*

The eastern side of the cape is more populous than the west and for much of the time the road winds its way through countryside between coastal settlements. If you wish to access the coast this is best done at these settlements, or with short diversions using a

Climbing Mount Hikurangi

Hikurangi is an attractive mountain but does not look the 1,752 m that makes it the fourth highest (and highest non-volcanic mountain) in the North Island. The name Hikurangi means 'Sky Peak' and refers to the well-loved peak in Hawaiki, the ancient ancestral home of the Maori. It is relatively accessible and a delightful climb but bear in mind that the summit return will take at least nine hours (13 km) – so give yourself plenty of time. If you follow the Tapuwaeroa River Road almost to the end you will see an iron bridge that crosses the boulder fields of the Tapuwaeroa River to several farm buildings on the hill. At the far side of the bridge a sign will remind you that you are on Maori (private) land, but once you park your car down the side road towards the river, you can still use the track that heads up and past the houses, over the hill and beyond, towards the summit. Once you reach the top of this first hill you will clearly see the climb that lies before you. Follow your nose and the stiles up a well-formed sheep station track that goes almost two thirds of the way to the summit. It terminates at Hikurangi's 'well-kept secret' – the

detailed map. From Te Araroa you head south and gain the first sight of Mount Hikurangi before arriving in **Tiki Tiki**. Here, the Anglican church with some fine Maori designs is worth a visit. It was built in 1924 as a memorial to local Iwi tribesman (Ngati Porou) who died in the First World War.

Just before the Mata River crossing is the turning to **Mount Hikurangi** (see box, page 329). Even if you do not intend to climb the mountain it is worth the short diversion to enjoy the river and mountain views. The road, which flirts with the Tapuwaeroa River, is a bit of an obstacle course as you dodge stray pigs, chickens, horses, sheep and cattle. Back on SH35 it is only a short distance to **Ruatoria**, the main administrative base of the predominant East Cape Iwi, the *Te Runanga O Ngati Porou*. It has a food store and petrol station where you can have a light-hearted chat with the locals.

Turning your back on the mighty Hikurangi, the next stop is **Te Puia Springs** ① *T06-864 6755, open to non-residents but hours are seasonal*, whose eponymous hot thermal pools are behind the hotel. The village also has a store and a petrol station. A short

Millennium Maori Pou (carvings). These are beautifully crafted pieces that stand in a circle to greet the sunrise. From here head upwards and locate the white bunkhouse. From behind the bunkhouse things start to get difficult. Climb up the scree slope to the rock outcrops and the path that leads you through a tract of mountain bush. Keep your eyes open for Tom Tit – a native black and white bird that looks like a robin and is particularly fearless. Beyond the bush it is a hard slog to the summit – the main summit is only reached after several almost equally high 'false summits'. On a clear day the view is spectacular. To the north the empty bush-cloaked peaks of the Raukumara Ranges dominate and offshore to the north, White Island's active crater can be seen steaming away.

For more information on the mountain, hut accommodation ($5) and guided tours ($70) contact the local Iwi (tribe), Ngati Porou, T06-8679960, www.ngati porou.iwi.nz. You must inform Ngati Porou that you intend to climb the mountain and seek official permission. If you join a tour it will save a lot of climbing and if the weather turns nasty it provides added security.

diversion from Te Puia is scenic **Waipiro Bay** with its three *marae*. The beachside holiday resort of **Tokomaru Bay** is next, where you can find accommodation and food. Between Tokomaru and Tolaga Bay is **Anaura Bay**, a 7-km diversion from SH35, where there's a very pleasant, relatively easy two-hour coastal walk.

Tolaga Bay is the largest coastal town and resort on the east coast. Worth a visit is the 660-m-long wharf (reputed to be the longest in the southern hemisphere) which can be accessed down Wharf Road to the south of the town. Also here is **Cook's Cove** where the intrepid explorer stopped to make repairs and gather supplies; the ship's naturalists Banks and Solander were particularly interested in the coastal scenery and unusual rock formations which can now be seen on a three-hour walkway.

For decades the sleepy little settlement and beach at **Whangara**, 29 km north of Gisborne (then 5 km east), was seldom visited by tourists. All this has changed due to the success of the film *Whale Rider*, in which the location (particularly the beach), was extensively featured. There is no disputing its beauty or spirituality, but local Iwi are now worried is that its popularity may well prove to be its demise.

From Tolaga Bay the road leaves the coast for a while before reuniting at Tatapouri and Makorori, both well known as fine surfing spots. **Wainui** is essentially a beachside suburb of Gisborne with all the attendant amenities. From Wainui you have just about reached your East Cape journey's end (or beginning) and Gisborne.

Gisborne ⊜⊖⊘⊕⊛▲⊖⊕ ➤➤ *pp333-336*.

The busy agricultural service town, port and coastal resort of Gisborne attracts many visitors in search of the sun, eager to jump on a surfboard or explore the East Cape. Being the most easterly city in the country, Gisborne prides itself on being the first city in the world to see the sunrise. It is also the first place that Captain Cook set foot in New Zealand. On top of that, it boasts an almost subtropical climate with long hours of sunshine and rich fertile plains. You'd be forgiven for expecting the place to be brimming with pride and vitality, yet somehow Gisborne seems a little tired.

Sights

After the VIC (see page 326) your first stop should be **Cook's Landing Site and National Historic Reserve** next to the main port and the base of Titirangi (Kaiti Hill). To get there, cross to the east bank of the river, which flows through the centre of the town. The reserve marks the spot where Cook first set foot, on 9 October 1769, to a hostile response from local Maori. Above the reserve the **Titirangi Domain** or **Kaiti Hill** provides great views across the city and the second of three Cook memorial edifices. At the summit of the hill is the **Cook Observatory** ⓘ *T06-867 7901*, *Tue only at 1930* – which has seen better nights.

Set in trees at the foot of the hill to the east is the **Te Poho-O-Rawiri marae** ⓘ *T06-868 5364*, which was built in 1930 and is one of the largest carved meeting houses in the country. Nearby is the **Toko Toru Tapu Church** ⓘ *T06- 867 2103*.

Before re-crossing the river it is worth taking a look at the Inner Harbour Area. There are a number of good cafés and restaurants here and next to the **Wharf Café** is a wall colourfully adorned with children's self portraits.

Head to the beachside reserve on the southern bank of the river to see another **Cook memorial**. A little further along is a statue of Cook's cabin boy, Young Nick, who is credited as being the first to sight land. He was rewarded by having the promontory, **Young Nick's Head** (which forms the southern edge of Poverty Bay), named in his honour. He also apparently won himself a bottle of rum, the customary reward for the first able seaman to see land. These statues are of particular interest simply because of their location with the backdrop of the port and huge steel-hulled cargo ships, which prove we have come a long way since the tall ships and crow's nests.

To learn more about Young Nick and the region's history head for the small but effective **Gisborne Museum (Tairawhiti)** ⓘ *Stout St, T06-867 3832, www.tairawhiti museum.org.nz, Mon-Sat 1000-1600, Sun 1330-1600, donation*. It houses all the usual stuff with a particular bent towards the fascinating Maori history and, of course, that man Cook. There are also ever-changing exhibitions of national and international contemporary art. Attached to the museum (quite literally) is the wheel-house of *HMS Canada*, which foundered at the base of Kaiti Beach in 1912. It forms part of the maritime section of the museum.

There is one other, less remarkable museum in the city, of particular interest to transport and technology buffs, the **East Coast Museum of Technology** ⓘ *Main Rd, Makaraka, T06-868 8254, daily 1000-1600, $5, child $1*.

There are an increasing number of **vineyards** around the region producing the notable vintages. Names to look out for include **Kirkpatrick Estate (KEW)** ⓘ *569 Wharekopae Rd, T06-862 7722, www.kew.co. nz*; **TW Chardonnay** ⓘ *Back Ormond Rd, T021-864818, www.twwines.co.nz*; **Lindaur** ⓘ *Solander St, T06-868 2757, www.montana wines.co.nz*; **Bushmere** ⓘ *166 Main Rd, T06-868 9317, www.bushmere.com*, and the organic **Wrights Wines** ⓘ *202 Wainui Rd, T06-868 0967, www.wrightswines.co.nz*. Most offer tastings. Contact the VIC (I-Site) for details or visit www.gisbornewine.co.nz.

If wine is not your tipple fear not, as usual, boutique **breweries** are also in evidence and fill the niche admirably. Try the lauded Gisborne Gold at the **Sunshine Brewing Company** ⓘ *109 Disraeli St, T06-867 7777, www.gisbornegold.co.nz*.

South to Wairoa ●● ➻ *pp333-336.*

From Gisborne, SH2 climbs the **Wharereta Hills** offering great views back across Poverty Bay. On the southern slopes are the **Morere Hot Springs** ⓘ *60 km south of Gisborne, T06-837 8856, www.morerehotsprings.co.nz, daily summer 1000-2100, winter 1000-1700, $6, child $3*, where public and private thermal pools are set among a pleasant bush setting, with a number of good short walks. There is accommodation and a café across the road.

At the tiny junction settlement of **Nuhaka**, 8 km south of the springs, a scenic coastal road leaves SH2 towards the **Mahia Peninsula**. The Mahia is a barren, windswept peninsula, 21 km long and about 12 km wide, which marks the coastal boundary between the Pacific and Hawke's Bay. The Mahia used to be an island and is now joined to the mainland by a sandspit, or tombolo. Almost totally devoid of trees, infested by sheep and deeply rutted by eroded green valleys, the peninsula has a strange appeal. One of the great Maori migration *waka* (canoes), the *Takitimu*, made landfall here in the 14th century, after circumnavigating the northern and eastern coasts from its first landfall at Awanui near Ninety Mile Beach. Some of its crew never left and the peninsula was also home to one of the North Island's biggest whaling stations.

Today, at the neck of the peninsula, is the small holiday village of **Mahia Beach** which forms a link between two beaches: **Mahanga Beach**, lying to the east, is exposed to the elements of the open ocean and a popular surf spot; **Opoutama Beach**, on the Hawke's Bay side (west), is much more sheltered and therefore better for swimming. On the eastern edge of the peninsula are the settlements of **Oraka** and **Mahia**, connected by a rows of holiday baches which hug the shore like a string of pearls. In summer the peninsula is a very

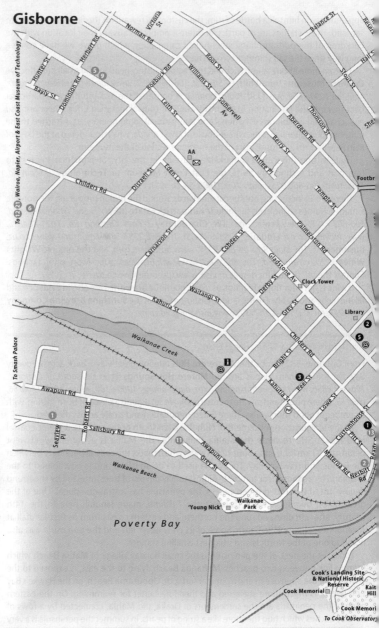

Gisborne

Norman Rd
Victoria St
Balance St
Hall St
Souts St
Hebert Rd
Hunter St
5 **9**
Bayly St
Dominion Rd
Roebuck Rd
Williams St
Root St
Somervell Av
Thornton St
Aberdeen Rd
Berry St
Leith St
Attlee Pl
AA
Footbr
Childers Rd
Disraeli St
Eden La
Temple St
Palmerston Rd
Carnarvon St
Cobden St
Gladstone Av
Waitangi St
Derby St
Clock Tower
Kahutia St
Grey St
Library
Waikanae Creek
Childers Rd
2
5 @
Bright St
Peel St
3
i
@
Kahutia St
Lowe St
6
To Smash Palace
Awapuni Rd
Custonhouse St
Roberts Rd
Salisbury Rd
Seaview Pl
1
11
Awapuni Rd
Grey St
Materoa Rd
Nesbitt Rd
Pitt St
Reads
1
13
Waikanae Beach
'Young Nick'
Waikanae Park
Poverty Bay
Cook's Landing Site
& National Historic
Reserve
Cook Memorial
Kaiti
Hill
Cook Memorial
To Cook Observator

To Wairoa, Napier, Airport & East Coast Museum of Technology

Sleeping

Teal Motor Lodge **5**
Tekura B&B **3**
Waikanae Beach
　Holiday Park **11**
White Heron **9**

Al Fresco Motor Lodge **12**
Beachcomber **1**
Cedar House B&B **4**
Colonial **21**
Flying Nun Backpackers **6**
Gisborne YHA **7**
Portside **2**
Senator Motor Inn **13**
Tatapouri Camp Ground **19**

Eating

Café Ruba **1**
Fettucine Brothers **2**
Gordon Gecko **8**
Irish Rover **3**
Three Rivers Marina **4**
Verve Café **5**
Wharf Café **6**
Works **7**

popular spot for surfing, windsurfing, swimming and fishing, but year-round it enjoys the erstwhile island atmosphere, which makes it an idyllic spot in which to get away from it all. You will need your own transport. From Mahia it is a 44-km drive to Wairoa past farmland and coastal lagoons renowned for their birdlife.

Wairoa → *Colour map 3, A5 Population: 5200.*
Wairoa is the eastern gateway to the Te Urewera National Park and sits on the coast at the junction of SH2 and SH36, roughly halfway between Gisborne (98 km) and Napier (118 km). Strategically built on the banks of the Wairoa River, it was once a thriving port. These days, however, it has little to hold the visitor except perhaps a brief peek at the relocated and reconstructed 1877 **lighthouse** which once shone on the Mahia Peninsula. The town has a number of shops in which to stock up, and small takeaways to grab a snack before heading north, south or inland to **Waikaremoana** via SH36. There is limited accommodation available in town; the VIC (I-Site) has details.

◉ East cape to Wairoa listings

For Sleeping and Eating price codes and other relevant information, see Essentials pages 44-50.

◉ Sleeping

Opotiki to East Cape Lighthouse *p327*
Torere, Te Kaha and Whanarua Bay
AL Tui Lodge B&B, Copenhagen Rd, T07-325 2922, www.tuilodge.co.nz. Spacious modern home with tidy twins and doubles, shared facilities. Excellent cuisine.
A Waiwaka B&B, 2 km north of Te Kaha and 12 km from Whanarua Bay, T07-325 2070, www.waikawa.net. 2 attractive self-contained options in a beautiful peaceful spot.
L-AL Te Kaha Resort, T07-325 2830, www.tekahabeachresort.co.nz. New resort overlooking the bay with a modern range of apartments. Bar/restaurant serves lunch and dinner. Recommended for local seafood.

B-D Te Kaha Holiday Park, Motels and Cafe, T07-325 2894. Modern amenities and popular backpacker accommodation.

D Maraehako Camp Ground, 1 km past the holiday park, T07-3252047. Beachfront.

Waihau Bay and Lottin Point

AL Waihau Bay Homestay, T07-325 3674, www.waihaubayhomestay.co.nz. Self-contained unit and a double overlooking the beach. Free use of bikes and kayaks.

A Lottin Point Motel, T06-864 4455. Given its remote ocean-side location, a great sense of escape is assured. A licensed restaurant complements simple self-contained units. Activities including in-house fishing charters to some of the cape's best spots are available.

A Oceanside Apartments, far end of Oruaiti Beach, 3 km northeast of Waihau, T07-325 3699, www.waihaubay.co.nz. Two spacious motel units. Fishing charters a speciality.

B-D Waihau Bay Holiday Park, T07-325 3844. Opposite the beach. Full range of options, camp kitchen, store and a café.

Hick's Bay and Te Araroa

B-D Hick's Bay Motel Lodge, up the hill past the village, T06-864 4880, www.hicks baymotel.co.nz. Licensed restaurant.

B-D Te Araroa Holiday Park, at the end of the bay, west of the village, T06-864 4873, www.teararoaholidaypark.co.nz. Modern facilities, store and off-licence.

C-D Mel's Place, Onepoto Beach Rd, T06-864 4694, www.eastcapefishing.co.nz. Cosy and friendly, next to bay. Popular with surfers. Recommended.

East Cape to Gisborne *p328*

B-D Tolaga Bay Motor Camp, 167 Wharf Rd, Tolaga Bay, T06-862 6716. A bit tired and basic but the only one for miles.

C-D Brian's Place, Potae St, Tokomaru Bay, T06-864 5870. Intimate and relaxed backpackers with friendly host. Loft rooms, fresh crayfish and horse trekking an added bonus. Recommended.

Gisborne *p330, map p332*

Gisborne is a popular summer resort so book ahead in the high season. The VIC has full listings of B&Bs and holiday rentals, the best of which are to be found at Wainui Beach. Most of the motels are on Gladstone Av, which is the main drag (SH35), and Salisbury Rd, which is centrally located near the beach.

LL Cedar House B&B, 4 Clifford St, T06-868 8583, www.cedarhouse.co.nz. Centrally located Edwardian-style boutique B&B with spacious rooms, en suite or private bathrooms. Dinner on request.

LL-AL Portside Hotel, 2 Reads Quay, T0800-767874, www.portsidegisborne.co.nz. Gisborne's newest hotel set in centrally located waterfront position. Studio rooms and suites, broadband, pool and gym.

LL-AL Te Kura, 14 Cheeseman Rd, T06-8633497, www.tekura.co.nz. Quality and good value B&B on the banks of the Waimata River and only 10-min walk from the town centre. Pool, free internet and full breakfast.

AL Senator Motor Inn, 2 Childers Rd, T06-868 8877, www.senatormotorinn.co.nz. New and harbourside.

AL-A Al Fresco Motor Lodge, 784 Gladstone Av, T06-863 2464, www.alfrescolodge.co.nz.

AL-A Teal Motor Lodge, 479 Gladstone Av, T06-868 4019, www.teal.co.nz.

A Beachcomber, 73 Salisbury Rd, T06-868 9349, www.nzmotels.co.nz/beachcomber.

A Colonial, 715 Gladstone Av, T06-867 9165, www.gisbornecolonial.co.nz.

A White Heron, 474 Gladstone Av, T06-867 1108.

C-D Flying Nun Backpackers, 147 Roebuck Rd, T06-868 0461, yager@xtra.co.nz. Colourful and comically ecclesiastical from the outside, and although perhaps not the best in town, the interior is modern enough and the place certainly has character. Cable TV.

C-D Gisborne YHA, near the inner harbour, 32 Harris St, T06-867 3269, www.yha.co.nz. Friendly, well-maintained and just a short walk from the town centre. Full range of rooms and all the usual facilities, Including tent sites.

Motorcamps and campsites

B-D Waikanae Beach Holiday Park, Grey St, T06-867 5634, www.gisborneholidaypark.co.nz. This is the best equipped and most centrally located motorcamp in town. Short walk to the beach and the VIC (I-Site).

D Tatapouri Camp Ground, 5 Innes St, T0800- 828276. A good camping option 15 mins north of the town, right by the beach.

South to Wairoa *p331*

Booking ahead is advisable in summer.

AL The Quarters Te Au Farmstay, Te Au Farm, Nuhaka (Mahanga), T06-837 5751, www.quarters.co.nz. Modern isolated farmstay/self-contained cottage overlooking the ocean. Plenty of peace and quiet.

A Cappamore Lodge, 435 Mahia East Coast Rd, T06-837 5523, www.cottagestays.co.nz/cappamore/cottage. This is like Scandinavia by the sea. The log cabin has one double and a twin with full self-catering facilities and a great view across the ocean.

A-D Morere Hot SpringsLodge and Cabins, Morere, T06-837 8824, www.morerehotsprings.co.nz. Tidy self-contained cottage and cabins located across the road from the hot springs.

Motorcamps and campsites

B-D Mahia Beach Motel and Holiday Park, 43 Moana Drive, Mahia Beach, T06-837 5830, T0800-383262. The centre of activity on the peninsula, with café and camp store.

Eating

Gisborne *p330, map p332*

There are 2 supermarkets: **Woolworths**, corner of Gladstone Rd and Carnarvon St, daily 0700-2200, and **Pak-n-Save**, Childers Rd, daily 0800-2100.

YYY **Gordon Gecko Restaurant and Bar**, No1 Wharf Shed, on the Esplanade, T06-868 3257. 1100-late. Relatively new and locally very popular offering a varied Pacific Rim menu.

YYY **The Wharf Café**, 60 The Esplanade, The Wharf, T06-868 4876. Daily 0900-late. This is not very expensive but still at the high end, very popular, with wide-ranging menu with European, Pacific Rim and Asian combinations.

YY **The Fettuccine Brothers Restaurant**, 12 Peel St, T06-8631285. Daily 1800-late. Decor and food is Mediterranean. Locally popular.

YY **The Three Rivers Marina Restaurant**, Vogel St, T06-868 5919. Well-established and popular eatery next to the marina. Fine international cuisine and the rather unique opportunity to sample locally grown Perigord Black Truffles – something of an obsession with the restaurant's 3 chefs. Good wine list.

YY **The Works**, The Esplanade, Inner Harbour, T06-863 1285. 1130-late, wine-tasting 1000-1500. Home of **Longbush Wines** so no need to recommend the wine list. Good for lunch.

Y **Café Ruba**, 14 Childers Rd, T06-868 6516. Chic award winner with fine coffee.

Y **The Irish Rover**, Peel St, T06-867 1112. The best pub and pub grub in town.

Y **Verve Café**, 121 Gladstone Rd. Value light meals and internet.

South to Wairoa *p331*

Y **Café Mahia**, 476 Mahia East Coast Rd, Mahia Beach, T06-837 5094.

Y **Sunset Point Sports Bar and Bistro**, Newcastle St, Mahia Beach, T06-837 5134.

Pubs, bars and clubs

Gisborne *p330, map p332*

The Irish Rover, Peel St, T06-867 1112. The town's offering to the mighty leprechaun is especially good during happy hours (1700-1900) and on Fri evening. Regular live bands.

Sandbar, Oneroa Rd, Wainui, T06-868 6828. The hub of nightlife north of the town, frequented by tousled surfies. Live music at weekends and free shuttles to town.

⊛ Festivals

Gisborne *p330, map p332*
Dec Rhythm and Vines, www.rhythmand vines.co.nz. New Year's Eve music festival.

▲ Activities and tours

East Cape to Gisborne *p328*
Horse trekking
Given its relative inaccessibility and grass-roots way of life, let alone its aesthetics, the East Cape lends itself to perambulations on 4 legs. Horse treks start from an hour for $60.
Eastender Horse Treks, Rangitukia, Tikitiki, T06-864 3033, www.eastenderhorse treks.co.nz. 2-hr bush and beach rides with memorable views and a cultural edge. Accommodation available.
Coastal Country Horse Trekking, Hicks Bay, T06- 864 4780,.

Maungaroa Station Horse, Maungaroa Access Rd, just north of Te Kaha, T07-325 2727, www.maungaroa.co.nz. Bush and beach rides. Group accommodation available.

Rafting
The Motu River offers a memorable multi-day wilderness adventure. For information contact:
Wet'n Wild Rafting Company, T07-348 3191, www.wetnwildrafting.co.nz.

Gisborne *p330, map p332*
Surfing
Wanui Beach is a 2-km stretch open to a variety of swell from the north right around to the south. For the latest surf reports call T06-868 1066, or listen out for radio 89 FM after 0700 news and ZG90.9 FM after 0800 news.
Chalet Surf Lodge, 62 Moana Rd, Wainui, T06-868 4475, www.chaletsurf.co.nz. Get a taste of the region's fine surf beaches with lodging and board hire available.
Gisborne Surf School, T06-8683484,

www.gisbornesurfschool.co.nz. Offers lessons.
Wainui Surf School, T06-863 3912, magoo140@hotmail.com. Also offers lessons.

Tour operators
Air Gisborne, T0800-866006, www.airgis. co.nz. Everything from short scenic flights around the bay to Lake Waikaremoana.
Dive Tatapouri, T06-868 5153, www.dive tata pouri.co.nz. Seal and dolphin encounters in the Te Tapuwae o Rongokaka Marine Reserve. Accommodation available.
New Zealand Safari Adventures, Tangihau Station Enterprise, Rere, T06-867 0872, www.nzsafari.co.nz. An interesting venture offering a range of Station life experiences from basic farm tours and shepherd's muster, to ATV quad bike tours and deer hunting.
Paradise Leisure Tours, T06-868 6139. Local winery tours.
Surfit Charters, T06-867 2970, www.surf it.co.nz. A chance to encounter those persecuted denizens of the deep; shark cage encounters $300. Fishing half-day $150.
Whalerider Tours, T06-868 6139. Visit film locations, see the props and learn about local Maori culture with Hone Taumaunu, cultural adviser to the movie *Whale Rider*. From $50.

⊖ Transport

Gisborne *p330, map p332*
Taxi Eastland Taxis, T06-867 6667.

❶ Directory

Gisborne *p330, map p332*
Banks All the major banks have branch offices on Gladstone Rd. **Internet** Available at **Verve Café**, 121 Gladstone Rd. **VIC (I-Site)**, Grey St. **Police** Corner of Childer Rd and Peel St, T06-869 0200. **Post office** 127 Gladstone Rd, T06-8603046, Mon-Fri 0830-1700, Sat 0900-1300.

Te Urewera National Park → *Colour map 2, C4.*

Te Urewera is daunting and mysterious; a place of almost threatening beauty. The national park encompasses the largest area of native bush in the North Island and is the fourth largest national park in the country. The main focus of the park is Lake Waikaremoana, the 'Sea of Rippling Waters', while the track, which circumnavigates it, the Lake Waikaremoana Circuit, is one of the most popular walks in the country. The vast park is home to a wealth of wildlife: some native and welcome including kiwi, kaka and kokako (one of New Zealand's rarest and most endangered birds); others introduced and very unwelcome, such as the omnipresent possum, stoats, goats, rats and feral cats. The park is also a favourite haunt for pig hunters, though, thankfully, there are few known banjo players. ►► For Sleeping, Eating and other listings, see page 338.

Ins and outs

Getting there and around Frasertown to Waikaremona is about 50 km; Waikaremoana to Murupara is another 75 km. Access to Lake Waikaremoana and the heart of the park is via the hardy SH38. This almost completely unsealed highway links Murupara on the western boundary of the park with Frasertown, near Wairoa to the east. It is pretty heavy going: very windy, often subject to fallen trees and, if you break down, you're on your own. The park and all the amenities of Lake Waikaremoana are best accessed from the east via Wairoa and Frasertown. This will allow you to get intimate with the park on foot from Waikaremoana before building up the strength to explore the western part. **Big Bush Holiday Park**, in Wairoa, T06-837 3777, www.lakewaikaremoana.co.nz, offers a regular shuttle service to and from Wairoa ($30) depending on demand. It also runs a water taxi service on Lake Waikaremoana taking trampers to and from the trailheads, from $30 one way.

Tourist information **DoC Aniwaniwa Visitor Centre** ⓘ *SH38 at Lake Waikaremoana, T06-837 3803, teurewerevc@doc.govt.nz, daily 1000-1700*, has modern displays, an audio-visual show ($2) and a gallery, which is entrusted to care for and display the controversial **Urewera Mural** by Colin McCahon. Staff can assist with the limited but surprisingly good accommodation options and also handle walk information, fees and hut bookings. If accessing the park from the west (Rotorua) contact **DoC Murupara** ⓘ *SH38, T07-366 1080.*

Sights

Beautiful Lake Waikaremoana was created 2000 years ago when the Waikaretaheke River was dammed by a huge landslide between the Ngamoko and Panekiri ranges. One section of that landslide is thought to have been 3 km long by 1 km wide. This relatively new addition to the landscape sits beautifully with the equally impressive bush that cloaks its indented shores. The main activities on the lake are trout fishing and boating, but it is most famous for the network of excellent walks around its shores.

▲▲ Walks

Most of the short walks radiate from the main settlement of **Waikaremoana**, which is little more than a scattering of DoC buildings and a motorcamp at the northeastern end of the lake. There are two waterfalls within 15 minutes of the DoC visitor centre. The first, the

Aniwaniwa Falls, is less than 1 km from the centre and is accessed from a track right beside it. The slightly higher and more impressive **Papakorito Falls** are up a short track opposite the centre (or by car to within a five-minute walk). The 2-km **Black Beech Track** (30 minutes) is a pleasant track connecting the visitor centre with the motorcamp.

If you fancy something more demanding and scenic, the **Ngamoko Track** (2½ hours), south of the motorcamp, climbs the mountain through a delightful tangle of native bush before emerging at a 1099 m trig and viewpoint. Better still is the four-hour tramp to see the idyllic **Lake Waikareiti**, which is a smaller body of water formed in the same way as Lake Waikaremoana. Set 300 m above Lake Waikaremoana, it is almost like a lost world with a magical atmosphere and shores entirely cloaked by bush. The DoC **Sandy Bay Hut** is available for an overnight stay (book at the visitor centre, $20) and there is also boat hire. Most serious trampers, however, come to Lake Waikaremona to experience the scenic **Waikaremoana Circuit Track**, a national tramping top 10 (see box, page 339).

There are numerous other walks and huts in the park including the three to five-day **Whakatane River Round Trip**, the three-day **Manuoha-Waikareiti Track** and the two-hour **Onepoto Caves Track**. For more information and bookings contact DoC or call at the Aniwaniwa Visitor Centre (see page 337).

◉ Te Urewera National Park listings

For Sleeping and Eating price codes and other relevant information, see Essentials pages 44-50.

● Sleeping

Te Urewera National Park *p337*
Accommodation is available at Waikaremoana or the settlements of Kaitawa and Tuai at the southeast entrance to the park. Booking is advised in summer.
A-B Big Bush Holiday Park, Onepoto (4 km from the start of the track), T06-837 3777, www.lakewaikaremoana.co.nz. Full range of accommodation at the eastern entrance to the park. Transport and water taxi services.
A-B Whakamarino Lodge, Tuai, T06-837 3876, www.lakelodge.co.nz. Comfortable self-contained units, 5 km from Waikaremoana.
D DoC Sandy Bay Hut, booking from DoC office, SH38 at Lake Waikaremoana, T06-837 3803, urewerainfo@doc.govt.nz.

Motorcamps and campsites
B-D Waikaremoana Motorcamp, T06- 837 3826, www.lake.co.nz. Well situated right next to the lake near most of the major short walks and the visitor centre. Modern range of lodges, chalets, cabins and backpacker beds, powered and non-powered tent sites, petrol and a well-stocked store. Recommended.

▲ Activities and tours

Te Urewera National Park *p337*
Fishing, boat and kayak hire
There are many activities based on and around the lake. Fishing, fishing licences, hunting trips, and cruises are available from **Big Bush**, T06-837 3777, bigbush@ paradise.co.nz; and **Waikaremoana Motorcamp**, see Sleeping, above.

The Waikaremoana Circuit Track

The Circuit Track, a 46-km walk of moderate difficulty, completely circumnavigates the lake. It can usually be completed in three to four days taking in a variety of bush types, full of birdlife and rocky or sandy bays ideal for fishing and swimming. Most of the route is fairly easy going except for ascent of the 900 m Panekiri Range, which offers a spectacular view across the lake and national park. There are five modern, comfortable DoC huts and five designated campsites along the route which provide basic amenities. The walk can be tackled in either direction from the southern access point at Onepoto (which climbs Panekiri first), or from the most popular starting point, Hopuruahine, on the lake's northern shores. Although there is parking at both access points most people leave their vehicles at the Waikaremoana Motorcamp ($6) and take the water taxi to either starting point (from $25-$35). The taxi will also pick up or drop off from various designated points along the way, which is ideal for those who only wish to walk part of the circuit. Weather can be very changeable throughout the year and downright ugly in winter, so, as always, go well equipped. The walk is very popular in summer, so late spring or early autumn is advised. Bookings is essential. The huts cost $25 per person per night, child free. Campsites are $12. For all information, maps, and bookings contact the DoC Aniwaniwa Visitor Centre, T06-8373803 (see page 337). For web bookings and information log on to www.doc.govt.nz (Great Walks).

Napier and around → Colour map 3, A5 Population: 56,500

Napier is a bright, dynamic place with the pleasant vibe of a Mediterranean coastal town. On the surface it enjoys the perfect relationship with nature: the rich fertile land and the warming sun making it the wine-producing capital of the North Island. However, it paid a heavy price in 1931 when an earthquake almost razed the town. Undeterred, the proud and determined people used this to their advantage and set about its rebuilding with an internationally recognized collection of art deco buildings thought to be among the finest in the world. Now, well into the new millennium, Napier seems in the best of health. ▸▸ *For Sleeping, Eating and other listings, see pages 346-353.*

Ins and outs

Getting there **Napier airport** ⓘ *just north of the town on SH2*, is served by **Air New Zealand Link**, T0800-737000, with regular daily flights from Auckland, Wellington and Christchurch and other principal national destinations. The **Airport Shuttle**, T0800-748885, costs around $16 one way.

By bus, Napier is served by **Intercity**, **Newman's** and **Nakedbus**. Buses arrive and depart from the **Napier Travel Centre** ⓘ *train station, Munroe St, T06-835 2720, 0830-1700*. All major buses companies serve Hastings too. The VIC (I-Site) act as ticketing agents.

By car, Napier is on SH2, 321 km north of Wellington. The junction with SH5 and SH2 is about 6 km north of the town and from there it is 117 km to Taupo and 397 km to Auckland. Napier is the premier east coast destination on the 'Classic New Zealand Wine Trail', www.classicwinetrail.co.nz.

Getting around Much of the city is negotiable on foot and, given the architectural appeal, is best appreciated from the street. The local suburban bus company is **GoBay**, T06-8358833, www.hbrc.govt.nz. It operates Mon-Sat only and offers a service to Hastings and Havelock North. For car rental companies, cycle hire and taxis, see page 353.

Tourist information Napier VIC (I-Site) ⓘ *100 Marine Parade, T0800-847488/ T06-834 1911, www.VisitUs.co.nz, daily 0900-1700*, has information and leaflets on local and regional heritage walks, food and wine, gardens and art and craft trails. **DoC** ⓘ *59 Marine Parade, T06-834 3111, napier-ao@doc.govt.nz, Mon-Fri 0900-1615*. It has information about Cape Kidnappers Gannet Colony (plus tide times), as well as Te Urewera and Ruahine national and forest parks. **Hastings VIC (I-Site)** ⓘ *Westerman's Building, corner of Russell and Heretaunga sts, T06-873 5526, www.hawkesbaynz.com and www.hastings.co.nz, Mon-Fri 0830-1700, Sat-Sun 0900-1700*, has internet access and can help with transport booking.

Sights

The main attraction of Napier is its famous **art deco architecture**. On foot, the two central streets, Emerson and Tennyson, have many examples. On Emerson Street is the **ASB Bank** with its incorporated Maori designs and fine doorway, while on Tennyson Street the highlights are (from east to west) the **Daily Telegraph Building**, restored **Municipal Theatre** and the **Deco Centre** (art deco shop).

Further afield is perhaps the most attractive building of all, the façade and entrance of the 1932 **National Tobacco Company** at the corner of Bridge and Ossian streets. Although somewhat distant from the town centre (in the port area of Westshore), it is worth the diversion. The building is even more impressive at night, when it is beautifully and imaginatively lit. During the day it is possible to have a look at the interior which hosts just as much attention to detail. For a more modern example of art deco take a wander inside the pharmacy at the southern end of Emerson Street. ▸▸ *For tours of the art deco buildings, see Activities and tours, page 350.*

Marine Parade

Marine Parade creates an impressive perspective with its long promenade lined with **Norfolk Pines** and old wooden houses (the few that survived the earthquake). The **Marine Parade Walkway and Cycleway** starts at the northern end of Marine Parade. It features a number of art deco sculptures in a beachside garden setting and links several waterfront attractions that combine to create an almost English/Mediterranean ambience. First up, at the northern end heading south is the **Ocean Spa complex** ⓘ *T06-835 8553, www.oceanspa.co.nz, Mon-Sat 0600-2200, Sun 0800-2200, $8, child $6, private spa $10, massage 1hr from $60*. It has hot pools, private spas, health and beauty therapies, and a café and gymnasium.

Almost immediately to the south of the spa complex gardens again predominate with a **floral clock**, the **Tom Parker Fountain** (no Elvis connections here) and **'Pania of the Reef'** statue. The fountain is just your average garden fountain by day but by night comes alive with a multi-coloured aquatic light show. 'Pania' is a small, attractive statue of a Maori maiden, with her legend of love described accordingly in a shower of the fountain's mist.

Heading south is the art deco **Colonnade** and **Sound Shell**. The Colonnade was once used for dancing and skating. Opposite the Sound Shell, which is occasionally used for open-air concerts, is the **Hawke's Bay Museum and Art Gallery** ⓘ *9 Herschell St, T06-835*

7781, www.hbmag.co.nz, daily 1000-1800, $10, children free, which offers a wide range of exhibits relating to the history and art of the region in modern surroundings. *Nga Tukemata* (The Awakening) presents the art and *taonga* of the local Maori and a rare presentation of evidence that dinosaurs once existed in New Zealand. Special attention is afforded to the earthquake of 1931. Relics from the rubble accompany audio-visual descriptions and touching memories of survivors. Recommended.

Dominating the corner of Emerson Street and Marine Parade are the **Art Deco Tower** (The Dome), which is nicely lit at night, and the art deco **Masonic Hotel**.

Back on the seaward side of Marine Parade past the modern VIC (I-Site) and Mini Golf Park are the **Sunken Gardens**, complete with ponds of water lily and a lazy waterwheel.

Opossum World ① *157 Marine Parade, T06-835 7697, www.opossumworld. co.nz, daily 0900-1700, free*, bills itself as 'creating useful products from an ecological nightmare'. If the aesthetically appealing Australian import was a native species and not the infamous pest and destroyer of native plants and animals that it is in New Zealand, such a tourist oriented shopping and educational concept would be actively frowned upon. But as it stands it is worth popping your head in here to learn just how easily man's ill-conceived ideas can cause such permanent and ongoing ecological havoc, before perhaps furnishing said head with a fetching furry hat, or taking the plunge with set of matching nipple warmers.

Continuing south you then encounter the intriguing **Millennium Sculpture** created by local artist, David Trubridge. The work is carefully lined up to where the sun rose at the dawning of the new millennium. One can only wonder if it will still be standing for the morning of 1 January 3000 and if so, what on earth will be reflected in its steel discs.

The **National Aquarium of New Zealand** ① *T06-834 1404, www.national aquarium.co.nz, 0900-1700, $16, child $8, behind the scenes tours $32, child $16, tank dives from $68*, hosts an eclectic mix of native and non-native water and land creatures, from the enchanting seahorse to the iconic kiwi. The design of the building is quite clever, creating the impression that one is descending into the depths. 'Izzy', a remarkably toothy Singaporean import, will also have any unsuspecting crocodilaphobes breaking into a cold sweat.

Around Napier 🏨🍴🎡⛺🎯 ❱❱ *pp346-353.*

Cape Kidnappers' gannet colony → *Colour map 3, B5.*
① *All trips are subject to season and tide times. There is a shuttle between Napier and Clifton or Te Awanga, from $30. Contact the VIC (I-Site) for details, T0800-847488.*

Cape Kidnappers is the jagged white peninsula that marks the southern boundary of Hawke Bay. It gets its name from another rather unfortunate incident involving Captain Cook and the local Maori. Believing Cook's Tahitian interpreter was being held against his will, the Maori sent a *waka* to bring him back to shore. Doubtless a little confused, the Tahitian captive escaped back to the Cook's ship, which promptly weighed anchor and left, leaving only a name behind – Cape Kidnappers.

The cape is famous for its colony of gannets. These large, elegant seabirds have lots of attitude and, weighing in at about 2 kg with deadly 6-inch beaks designed to spear fish, they have every right to it. They hunt by gliding high over the surface of the water and diving at tremendous speed with wings folded back to catch the unsuspecting fish beneath. In the summer months up to 15,000 gannets gather at Cape Kidnappers to breed, forming the biggest mainland colony in New Zealand, and one of the biggest in

Napier

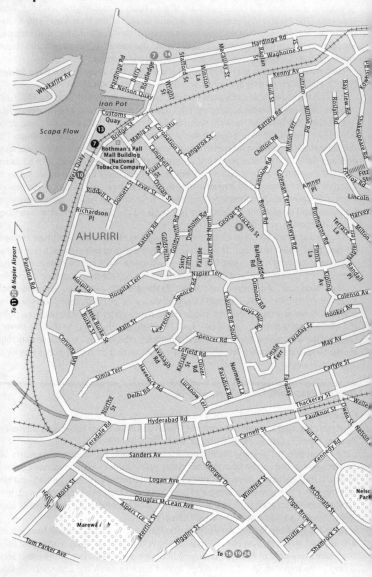

Whakarire Av

Iron Pot

Customs Quay

Scapa Flow

Rothman's Pall Mall Building (National Tobacco Company)

West Quay

Riddell St

Richardson Pl

AHURIRI

Hardinge Rd

H Nelson Quay

Batty

Routledge

Stafford St

Macaulay St

Raglan St

Hardinge Rd

Waghorne St

Winton St

Wright St

Kenny Av

Bull St

Outram

Milton Terr

Bay View Rd

Roslyn Rd

Shakespeare Rd

Battery Rd

Bridge St

Mahia St

Coronation St

Tu

Campbell St

Stuart St

Ossian St

Lever St

Tangaroa St

Chilton Rd

Lambton Rd

Coleman Terr

Amner Pl

Fitzroy St

Fitz St

Lincoln

Harvey

Milton

Donett St

Battery Rd

Goldsmith Terr

Sixty Fifth

Dexholm Rd

Parade

Chaucer Rd North

George St

Bracken St

Burns Rd

Selwyn Rd

Burlington Rd

Terrace La

Randall Pl

Napier Terr

Balquhidder Rd

Ormond Rd

Finnis La

Kipling

Colenso Av

Hospital Terr

Napier Terr

Spencer Rd

Chaucer Rd South

Guys Hill Rd

Faraday St

Hooker Av

To Napier Airport

Pandora Rd

Hospital La

Little Burke St

Burke St

Main St

Lawrence

Spencer Rd

Smale Terr

May Av

Carlyle St

Coruma Bay

Simla Terr

Kavanagh Rd

Enfield Rd

Kelsall St

Oliver Rd

Normans La

Paradise Rd

Faraday

Havelock Rd

Delhi Rd

Lucknow Terr

Thackeray St

Owen St

Welles

Northe St

Teradale Rd

Hyderabad Rd

Faulknor St

Jull St

Nelson

Carnell St

Sanders Av

Logan Ave

Georges Dr

Winifred St

Kennedy Rd

McDonald St

Nelson Park

Henry St

Morse St

Alpers Tce

Douglas McLean Ave

Herrick St

Vigor Brown St

Marewa

Tom Parker Ave

Higgins St

Thistle St

Shamrock St

To 16 19 24

Napier detail

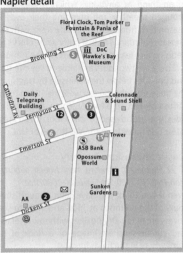

Floral Clock, Tom Parker
Fountain & Pania of
the Reef

Browning St

DoC
Hawke's Bay
Museum

Daily
Telegraph
Building

Colonnade
& Sound Shell

Tennyson St

Emerson St

ASB Bank

Opossum
World

Tower

Sunken
Gardens

AA

Dickens St

Breakwater Rd

Bluff Hill

Hornsey Rd

Seapoint Rd

Karaka Rd

Thompson Rd

Lighthouse Rd

Cobden
Cres

Cobden Rd

Cobden
La

Elizabeth Rd

Priestley Terr

Elizabeth Terr

France Rd

Priestley Rd

Lucy Rd

Thompson Rd

Centennial
Gardens

Coore Rd

Hadfield
Terr

Hukarere

Gladstone Rd

Clyde Rd

Ocean
Spa

Corry Av

Seaview
Terr

Onslow Rd

Brewster

Byron St

Shakespeare Rd

Cameron Rd

Shakespeare Terr

Cameron Terr

Browning St

DoC

Heschell St

Municipal
Theatre

Market
St

Deco
Centre

Shelley St

Tennyson St

Emerson St

Supermarket

Clive Sq

Clive Sq

Craven St

Dickens St

Albion St

Station St

Faulknor

Dalton St

Library

Vautier St

Raffles St

Bower St

Munroe St

Marineland

Hastings St

Edwards St

Millennium
Sculpture

Marine Parade

Swan St

Travel Centre

Hall St

Sale St

Wellesley Rd

Latham St

Morris St

National Aquarium
of New Zealand

To Hastings, Havelock
North & Cape Kidnappers

N

200 metres

200 yards

Sleeping
Anchorage 1
Archies Bunker
  Backpackers 21
Ballina 24
Beach Front 3
Bluewater 4
Cobden Villa 10
County & Churchill's Bar 5
Criterion Backpackers 6
Crown 14
Deco City Motor
  Lodge 19
Dome 15
Harbour View Motor
  Lodge 7
Kennedy Park Top Ten
  Motel & Holiday Park 16
Masonic Art Deco 17

Master's Lodge 8
McHardy Lodge 9
Napier Prison
  Backpackers 18
Napier YHA 11
Rocks 20
Scenic Circle Te Pania 22
Sea Breeze B&B 12
Shoreline Motel 13
Wally's Backpackers 23

Eating
Breakers Café & Bar 3
Café Ujazi 12
Ocean Boulevard
  Foodcourt 2
Provedore 13
Shed 2 7
Soak Café 6
Take Five Jazz Bar 4
Westshore Fish Café 11

Bars & clubs
Rosie O'Gradys 9
Thirsty Whale 10

the world. Perhaps given their attitude and armoury, gannets are not particularly fearful of anything or anybody, which makes them very approachable, particularly when grouped together and guarding their own little breeding patch. The tourist visiting season runs from October to late April, with the best time to view being early November and late February. The first fluffy white chicks hatch in early November with the last chicks fledging and leaving the colony for their migration to Australia during May.

There are two tours available to see the gannets. One operator negotiates the beach and the tides below the peninsula by tractor, the other goes overland by 4WD. Provided the tides are right you can walk the 10 km to the colony yourself. The walk starts from the **Clifton MotorCamp** (see Sleeping, page 348) but given the time restrictions due to the tides, you are advised to join a tour. If you are determined to go it alone, you can get the latest tide times from the VIC (I-Site) or DoC.

Classic Sheepskins Tannery
ⓘ *22 Thames St, Pandora, near Napier airport, T06-835 9662, www.classicsheep skins.co.nz, Mon-Fri 0730-1700, Sat-Sun 0900-1600, free.*
Even if you think you have seen enough sheep, the Classic Sheepskins Tannery offers tours of the premises at 1100 and 1400 to see just how those hearth rugs and car seat covers are made. Drying lines with row after row of stretched sheepskins is a bizarre sight and conjures up an image of a flock of naked, highly embarrassed sheep hiding somewhere in the fields beyond.

Hawke's Bay vineyards
Given the climate and the soil in the Hawke's Bay area, it was inevitable that it would not take long for the first grapevine to be planted by the first Europeans settlers. Since that first harvest, the vines and the industry have boomed, making Hawke's Bay second only to Marlborough as the country's top wine-producing region. The two regions combined produce a range of wines to can compare with the world's best. Hawke's Bay offers a particularly wide variety due to the composition of the land and diverse 'sub regions'. Two such established 'sub-regions' are Gimblett Gravels Ngatarawa Triangle and the Esk Valley. There are over 60 wineries in the area so, unless you are a connoisseur, knowing which to visit can be a dilemma. Thankfully the free *Hawke's Bay Winery Guide* leaflet gives details of what each vineyard offers. Some have stunning architecture, some are particularly famous or more established, others have fine restaurants or cafés. Most offer sales and tastings. You can either embark on a tour according to your own choice and itinerary, or join a number of organized tours. If you know little about wines, and New Zealand wine in particular, an organized tour is advised.

Hastings → *Colour map 3, B5 Population: 50,000.*
Hastings is a lively, sprawling, mainly agricultural service centre 21 km south of Napier and, like Napier, it was devastated by the 1931 earthquake, with the loss of 93 lives. In rebuilding the town the architects echoed Napier's art deco and Spanish Mission styles, much of which can clearly be seen in the town centre. The two best examples are the **Westerman's Building** that now houses the VIC (I-Site) on Russell Street and the recently refurbished **HB Opera House** on Hastings Street. The prominent art deco **clock tower**, right in the centre of town, was erected in 1935 to house the bells from the old 1909 Post Office Tower which collapsed in the quake; architect Sydney Chaplin won 25 Guineas ($52) for its design. During the summer the town is a blaze of colour for the annual

Blossom Festival, when row upon row of hanging baskets line the streets providing a tourist attraction in itself and winning the town much praise around the country.

Modern-day attractions in Hastings include the **Hastings City Art Gallery** ⓘ *20 r Eastbourne St, T06-871 5095, daily 1000-1630, usually free depending on exhibitions*. It has undergone a new lease of life in recent years and is now considered a premier arts venue offering a varied programme forlocally recognized and emerging artists, as well as the occasional national touring exhibition.

Given the dangerous nature of some beaches in the region, **Splash Planet** ⓘ *Grove Rd, T06-873 8033, www.splashplanet.co.nz, daily 1000-1800, from $25, child $19.50*, a modern themed water park, is proving very popular. There are hot pools and the inevitable slides and rides to keep the kids happy for hours. If wine tasting doesn't whet your appetite, the **Pernel Fruitworld** ⓘ *1412 Pakowhai Rd (north towards Napier), T06-878 3383, www.pernel.nzliving.co.nz, daily 0900-1730, tours from $15, child $7.50*, might. It offers an interesting orchard tour and experience, fruit tastings and small animal farm for kids. It is especially good in spring when the trees are in blossom. There's a café on site.

If your visit to the town coincides with a Sunday the weekly **Farmers' Market** ⓘ*Hawke's Bay Showgrounds, Kenilworth Rd, 0830-1230 rain or shine*, provides an ideal opportunity to meet locals and purchase fresh produce.

Havelock North → *Colour map 3, B5 Population: 9000.*
Havelock North is a very pleasant little village nestled amongst vineyards and orchards towards the coast and in the shadow of the 399-m **Te Mata Peak**. The view from the summit of Te Mata on a clear day is a 'must see' and it is easily reached by car via the village and Te Mata Peak Road. Weather permitting, it is also a popular spot for paragliding.

As well as the wineries surrounding Havelock North it is also home to another one of nature's great delights, honey. **Arataki Honey Ltd** ⓘ *66 Arataki Rd, T06-877 7300, www.aratakihoneyhb.co.nz, Mon-Sun 0900-1700, free*, was established in 1944 and is one of the largest bee-keeping enterprises in the southern hemisphere, with a staggering 30,000 hives. There is a shop and the spectacular 'wall', with its army of 40,000 live and very busy bees.

The **Village Growers' Market** ⓘ *at the Black Barn (Lombard) Vineyard, every Sat in summer 0900-1200*, is worth a visit and is where the locals stock up on fresh produce and the latest gossip, T06-8777985.

Central Hawke's Bay south to the Wairarapa → *Colour map 3, B4.*
From Hastings, SH2 winds its way through Central Hawke's Bay towards the stunning region of the Wairarapa, before arriving in Wellington. On SH2 there are a number of small towns including **Waipawa**, **Waipukurau**, **Dannevirke** and **Norsewood** (the latter two having obvious Scandinavian links). Although these settlements have little to offer the visitor there are plenty of activities available in the area including ballooning and tramping. The wild **Kaweka** and **Ruahine ranges** have some fine tramping but you are advised to plan carefully and go well prepared. DoC (Napier) or the field station in the historic village of **Ongaonga** ⓘ *T06-856 6808, 15 km west of Waipukurau*, will provide all the necessary information and leaflets. The **VIC (I-Site)** ⓘ *Waipukurau railway station (southern end of town), T06-858 6488, www.centralhawkesbay.co.nz, Mon-Fri 0900-1700, Sat 0900-1300*, can assist with activity and accommodation bookings.

Before leaving Hawke's Bay region proper, there is one other place worth visiting. However, bear in mind it is on the 'alternative' route into the back country of the rarapa and involves a bit of a hike. For the sake of it, it is worth the trip to see the dicrously latitudinous sign that points at a distinctly unremarkable hill (252 m) called aumatawhakatangihangakoauauotamateaturipukakapikimaungahoronukupokai **whenuakitanatahu** and declares it as having the longest place name in the world (85 letters). Roughly translated, it means 'The place where Tamatea, the man with the big knees, who slid, climbed and swallowed mountains (known as land eater) played his flute to his loved one'. As you carefully contemplate both sign, place and meaning, you can be sure of one thing – old Tamatea may have been a big eater and thought of himself as a bit of a sexy monkey, but he was a lousy lover if this was his idea of a romantic spot. To get to the sign from Waipukurau, take the coast road towards Porangahau (SH52). The sign is located on the right heading south and roughly halfway between Porangahau and Wimbledon. From Wimbledon it is well worth taking a look at the coast and Cape Turnagain at Herbertville. If you have time it is one of those lovely remote places you can end up staying at for a week. Back on SH52 from Wimbledon you can undertake the alternative route to the Wairarapa, re-emerging on SH2 at either Eketahuna or Masterton. This will also allow you to take in the stunning and equally remote Castlepoint on the way.

◉ Napier and around listings

For Sleeping and Eating price codes and other relevant information, see Essentials pages 44-50.

● Sleeping

Napier *p339, map p342*
Napier is a popular holiday spot, in summer you are advised to book ahead.
LL The Dome, corner of Marine Parade and Emerson St, T06-835 0707, www.thedome. co.nz. Two contemporaryluxury apartments on the top floors of the iconic 1937 art deco T&G building. Ocean views and onsite spa facilities.
LL Cobden Villa, 11 Cobden Rd, T06-835 9065, www.cobdenvilla.com. Stylish and tastefully decorated art deco accommodation that gives a nice reminder of the local style without being over the top.
LL Master's Lodge, 10 Elizabeth Rd, Bluff Hill, T06-834 1946, www.masterslodge.co.nz. An exceptional centrally located lodge offering 2 luxury private suites, solarium, in-house museum and veranda with commanding views. This all comes at a price, however. Quality cuisine with in-house chef Lisa Frater.
LL McHardy Lodge, 11 Bracken St, Hospital Hill, T06-835 0605, www.mchardylodge.com. One of Napier's oldest estates, central, with 4

suites and 2 rooms. Luxuriously appointed with fine dining and panoramic views.
LL-L Crown Hotel, cnr Bridge St and Hardy Rd, Ahuriri, T06-833 8300, www.thecrown napier.co.nz. One of Napier's newest hotels offering premier accommodation on the waterfront in Ahuriri. Stylish rooms ranging from studio to 2-bedroom suites. Restaurant.
LL The County Hotel, 12 Browning St, T06-835 7800, www.countyhotel.co.nz. Restored art deco Edwardian hotel in the centre of town and one of the few original buildings to survive the 1931 earthquake. There are 18, spacious, individually decorated suites, named after New Zealand birds, ranging from 2 bedrooms with private lounge, spa bath and balcony, to a standard double. All have Sky TV and internet. Popular **Chambers Restaurant** and **Churchill Bar** attached. No off-street parking.
LL-L Scenic Circle Te Pania Hotel, 45 Marine Parade, T06-833 7733, www.scenic-circle.co.nz. Named after Te Pania, a legendary Maori maiden of the sea, this modern 6-storey block sits on the waterfront like a human aquarium and seems a little clinical in appearance. It is certainly far removed from the art deco theme of the city. Character aside, however, the rooms, which range from the executive to

family, are quite spacious, fresh and offer sea views. There is a restaurant and bar on the ground floor. An added bonus is the **Ocean Spa complex** (see page 340) which is directly opposite. Secure parking.

AL Bluewater Hotel, 10 West Quay, Ahuriri, T06-835 8668, www.bluewaterhotel.co.nz. A modern hotel in a pleasant location overlooking the Westshore Marina. Spas, restaurant and bar.

AL-A Masonic, corner Tennyson St and Marine Parade, Waterfront, T06-835 8689, www.masonic.co.nz. When in Rome as they say. This establishment prides itself on being the largest original art deco hotel and is in the perfect position on the waterfront and in the heart of the city. Clean, freshrooms and suites with ocean views and all the standard comforts at a reasonable price.

Motels

There are many motels in Napier, especially in Auriri (Westshore) and along the promenade.
A Ballina Motel, 393 Gloucester St, Taradale, T06-8450648, www.ballina motel.co.nz. Located in a quiet residential area close to Taradale shops and cafés.

AL Deco City Motor Lodge, 308 Kennedy Rd, T06-843 4342, www.decocity.co.nz. Modern and well-equipped with shades of art deco style, especially popular during the art deco weekend.

A The Anchorage, 26 West Quay, T06-834 4318, www.anchorage.net.nz. Modern and well-appointed, overlooking the harbour.

A The Beach Front, 373 Marine Parade, T06-835 5220. Modern and the best on this street, along with **Shoreline Motel**, below.

A Harbour View Motor Lodge, 60 Nelson Quay, Westshore, T06-835 8077, www.harbourview.co.nz.

A The Rocks, 27 Meeanee Quay, Westshore, T06-835 9626, www.therocksmotel.co.nz. Perfect if you are hankering after an old-fashioned bath in your motel.

A Shoreline Motel, 337 Marine Parade, T06-835 5222, www.shorelinenapier.co.nz. Attractive location next to the beach and just

a few mins' walk from the centre of town.
A-B Sea Breeze B&B, 281 Marine Parade, T06-835 8067, seabreeze.napier@xtra.co.nz. Tidy guesthouse with themed rooms and plenty of character, right on the promenade.

Backpacker hostels

C-D Archies Bunker Backpackers, 14 Herschell St, T06-833 7990, www.archies bunker.co.nz. A good, centrally located option set in an historic building. Full range of rooms, internet, bike hire, Sky TV and secure parking.

C-D Criterion Backpackers, 48 Emerson St, T06-8352059, www.criterionartdeco.co.nz. A former hotel with spacious rooms and above average amenities right in the heart of the city.

C-D Napier Prison, 55 Coote Rd, T06-835 9933, www.napierprison.com. Here you can 'do time' in the old prison complex. The cells are comfortable enough but it is the jail tour that is the attraction.

C-D Napier YHA, 277 Marine Parade, T06-835 7039, Comfortable and friendly, overlooking the beach.

C-D Wally's Backpackers, 7 Cathedral Lane, T06-833 7930, www.wallysbackpackers. co.nz. Centrally located within a listed art deco building. Spotless and well facilitated with a choice of double en suite, standard double/twin, single or dorm, internet. Recommended.

Motorcamps and campsites

AL-D Kennedy Park Top Ten Motel and Holiday Park, Storkey St, T06-843 9126, www.kennedypark.co.nz. For campervans and tents this is a popular and well-established motorpark offering a wide range of options. Recommended.

Cape Kidnappers *p341*

For self-contained options refer to www.capeaccommodation.co.nz.

C-D Gannet Cottage, 77A School Rd, Clive, T06-870 1222, gannetcottage@paradise. net.nz. Backpackers need look no further than this small cottage although group bookings are taken so book well ahead.

Motorcamps and campsites

B-D Te Awanga Holiday Park, 52 Kuku St, Te Awanga, T06-875 0334. Can accommodate campervans and tent sites.

C-D Clifton Motor Camp, Clifton Beach (road terminus) T06-875 0263. Offer adequate beachside accommodation near the cape.

Hastings p344

LL Cardoness Lodge, 2543 Roy's Hill Rd, SH50, Ngatarawa, T06-879 8869, www.cardoness.co.nz. Contemporary rural B&B in the heart of the vineyard region. Classy en suites, lounge with open fire, swimming pool. Full cooked breakfast and dinner on request.

LL Hawthorn Country House, 420 SH2, T06-878 0035, www.hawthorne.co.nz. Award-winning luxury B&B again in a country setting. Spacious rooms. Sumptuous breakfasts.

L-AL Cumberland CourtMotel, corner Omahu and Maraekakaho rds, T06-8786190, www.cumberlandcourt.co.nz. Modern, centrally located luxury motel with spas and indoor pool.

C-D Travellers' Lodge, 608 St Aubyn St West, T06-878 7108, ask@tlodge.co.nz. One of several budget options in Hastings, locally recommended, with purpose-built facilities, spacious doubles, singles and dorms, sauna, internet, free bike hire and assistance finding seasonal fruit picking work (Feb-Apr).

Motorcamps and campsites

A-D Hastings Top Ten Holiday Park, 610 Winsor Av, T06-878 6692, www.hastings top10.co.nz. Wide range of options and good facilities. Within walking distance of Splash Planet so ideal for kids.

Havelock North p345

There are a number of magnificent traditional and modern 'country house style' B&Bs and lodges in the area. For full listings contact the VIC (I-Site).

LL Black Barn Private Retreat, Havelock North, T06-877 7985, www.blackbarn.com.

Luxury self-contained lodges set in the heart of the vineyard and a large homestead situated on Summerlee Station, which incorporates Cape Kidnappers and the Beach House at Waimarama Beach.

LL Mangapapa Petit Hotel, 466 Napier Rd, Havelock North, T06-878 3234, www.manga papa.co.nz. A world-famous small luxury hotel in 100-year-old refurbished country house. Magnificent range of accommodation and fine in-house restaurant.

LL Lawn Cottages, 527 Lawn Rd, East Clive, T06-870 0302, www.lawncottages.co.nz. 3 excellent stand alone, private, and stylish 2 bedroom self-contained cottages overlooking ponds amid 3 acre of park-like grounds. Full facilities including Sky TV and wireless internet. Breakfast included. Good luxury option if visiting the Gannet Colony.

LL Toms Cottages, 116 Matangi Rd, Havelock North, T06-874 7900, www.tomscottages.co.nz. Equally excellent luxury self-catering cottages for two to four people nestled between the Tuki Tuki River and Te Mata Peak. Superb views and a truly memorable outdoor bath.

L-AL Brompton Apartments, 39 Havelock Rd, T06-877 0117, www.brompton.co.nz. Modern self-contained apartment complex in the heart of the village. Classy decor and spas.

L-AL Harvest Lodge, 23 Havelock Rd, T0800-119030/T06-877 9500, www.harvest lodge.co.nz. New 5-star rated boutique motel centrally located with spas.

L-AL Te Mata Lodge, 21 Porter Dr, Havelock North, T06-877 4880, www.tematalodge motel.co.nz. Comfortable, self- contained and centrally located in the village, spas.

AL-A Village Motel, corner of Te Aute Rd and Porter Dr, T06-877 5401, www.village motel.co.nz. Modern motel, centrally located with very tidy units, spas, Sky TV and internet.

Motorcamps and campsites

B-D Arataki Motel and Holiday Park, 139 Arataki Rd, Havelock North, T06-877 7479, www.nzmotels.co.nz. Peaceful location, good facilities including a heated indoor pool.

❶ Eating

Napier *p339, map p342*

Given the region's love affair with food and wine there is plenty of choice when it comes to eating out. In the town itself there are essentially 2 main areas, the CBD (especially Marine Parade) and the waterfront and wharf within the suburb of Ahuriri, 2 km to the north. Both are equally good. Beyond that, if time and funds allow, it is well worth considering the numerous vineyard restaurants and cafés. Useful websites: www.savourhawkesbay.co.nz and www.hawkesbaywinemakers.co.nz.

There is a small foodcourt in the **Ocean Boulevard Mall**, off Dickens St.

₹₹₹-₹₹ Breakers Café and Bar, corner of Tennyson St and Marine Parade, T06-835 8689. Central location, perhaps a bit over the top on modern 'neon' aesthetics but fine food, again with an emphasis on seafood.

₹₹₹-₹₹ Shed 2, West Quay, Ahuriri, T06-835 2202. Daily from 1830. Waterfront location, imaginative international menu including ostrich, good seafood.

₹₹ Provedore, 60 West Quay, T06-834 0189, the latest offering at West Quay. Stylish surroundings, Euro-influenced menu complemented by local fare.

₹ Take Five Jazz Bar,189 Marine Parade, T06-835 4050. Daily from 1800. Local favourite with emphasis on organic cuisine. The works of local artists adorn the walls, there is live jazz at weekends and of course an admirable wine list.

₹ Westshore Fish Café, 112a Charles St, T06-834 0227. Tue-Sun 1130-late. The best fish and chips in town.

Cafés

₹ Café Ujazi, 28 Tennyson St, T06-835 1490. Daily from 0800. Good coffee and some imaginative vegetarian dishes.

₹ Soak Café, in the Ocean Spa complex, 42 Marine Parade, T06-835 7888.

A good option offering an eclectic range of food and wine and of course the inevitable lure of the spas.

Cape Kidnappers *p341*

₹ Clifton Bay Café and Bar, T06-875 0096. Daily in summer, Wed-Sun in winter, 1000-1600. In a convenient location near the entrance to the motorcamp and overlooking the beach.

Hawke's Bay vineyards *p344*

You are advised to try at least one lunch or dinner at one of the vineyards (see page 352). For more detail and a map ask at the VIC (I-Site) for the *Hawke's Bay Food Trail* leaflet. Recommended vineyards with fine restaurants include: **Brookfields**, **Crab Farm**, **Craggy Range**, **Mission Estate**, **Te Awa Winery** and **Vidal Estate Winery**.

Hastings *p344*

For fine dining near Hastings see **Vidal** vineyards pages 344 and 352. There is a **Countdown** supermarket on Queen St, Mon-Fri 0800-2100, Sat-Sun 0800-2000.

₹₹ Corn Exchange, 118 Maraekakaho Rd, T06-870 8333. Daily for lunch and dinner. A stylish modern café in the old corn exchange building. Gourmet pizza a speciality.

₹ Rush Munro's, 704 Heretaunga St West. Old and famous place serving fine ice cream.

Havelock North *p345*

₹₹ Peak House Restaurant, Te Mata Peak Rd, T06-877 8663, www.peakhouse.co.nz. Wed- Mon 1200-1400 for lunch and Wed-Mon 1000-1200 and 1400-1600 for morning or afternoon tea, licensed. Magnificent view, but be sure to book ahead and ask for a table by the window.

₹₹ ₹ Pipis, 16 Joll Rd, Havelock North, T06-877 8993.Daily from 1600-2200. Good option for pizza.

₹₹ Rose and Shamrock, corner of Napier Rd and Porter Dr, T06-877 2999. Daily from 1030, lunch 1200-1400 and dinner 1800-2130. A

spacious and delightful Anglo-Irish-style pub in the centre of the village with fine ale and good pub food. For a good breakfast on a Sat head for the farmers' market (see page 345).
❦ **The Olive Tree**, 17 Joll Rd, T06-877 0222. Serves snacks and good coffee.
❦ **The Post**, in the old village post office on Havelock Rd, T06-8771714. Dinner Thu-Mon from 1830. Affordable Mediterranean dishes with a good blackboard wine list.

❶ Pubs, bars and clubs

Napier p339, map p342
Rosie O'Grady's on Hastings St is a popular venue and has been there for many years

Gintrap and the bar restaurant combos of **The Thirsty Whale** (no 62) and **Provedore** (no 60) all on West Quay Ahuriri, are the trendy places to be seen at the moment. The former in particular is like a cross between a wool shed and NASA's mission control centre with music that may well result in 'lift off'.

Back in the centre of town **Churchill's Bar**, below the County Hotel in Browning St is great if you want to have a bit of fun. The staff are well used to merry clients doing awful Churchill impersonations but quite rightly draw the line when it gets to… 'Never, in the field of human drinking…'

❷ Festivals and events

Napier and Hawke's Bay p339, map p342
Here, in hedonistic Napier it seems food, wine and all things convivial are the one constant and the very core of the region's lifestyle. A useful source of information is www.hawkesbaynz.com/events.
Feb Harvest Hawke's Bay Wine Festival, www.harvesthawkesbay.co.nz, is a weekend of fun and games celebrating the region's wine production. Apparently, grown men race around a park in wine barrels before dispersing

for a spot of lunch – tremendous stuff.
International Mission Estate Concert, is an outdoor concert at the Mission Estate Winery drawing increasingly large crowds, truckloads of picnickers and some famous (if ageing) performers. Over the last few years they have included Dionne Warwick, the Beach Boys and Cliff Richard. **Art Deco Weekend** (3rd weekend), is Napier's biggest and most popular event celebrating the art deco-style. It involves vintage cars, period costume, parades, Devonshire teas on the promenade and a spot of 'wineglass wanders'. **Weta Wine and Food Fest**, offers time to relax after a hectic month, with some more food and wine.
Mar The **Horse of the Year Show**, is the largest horse show in the southern hemisphere attracting over 1000 riders and a small army of well-fed spectators.
Jun Winter Arts Festival/Winter Solstice Fire Festival, is a celebration of the arts, with theatre, restaurant theatre and vocal arts all enhanced by a spectacular fire show at the Sound Shell. **Matariki (Maori New Year)** Festival, has traditional events, performances and copious *hangis* (feasts).
Oct Kelt Capital Stakes is New Zealand's most glamourous horse races.
Nov Month of Wine and Rose is a series of private garden tours with a little music and, naturally, lots (and lots) of food and wine.

❸ Shopping

Napier p339, map p342
Art Deco Shop and Information Centre, 163 Tennyson St (old fire station building), T06-835 0022. Good selection of quality gifts and souvenirs related to Napier's art deco architecture, and to the style in general.

🔺 Activities and tours

Napier p339, map p342
Art deco or earthquake walks
There are several guided or self-guided tour

options available. The **morning walk** (1 hr, $15) leaves daily from the VIC at 1000; the **afternoon walk** (2 hrs, $20) leaves at 1400 from the Art Deco Shop, 163 Tennyson St. In summer there is an additional walk at 1730 ($18)All the tours are hosted by the Art Deco Trust, an organization set up in 1985 to help preserve and promote art deco in the region. Included in the morning and afternoon walks is an audio visual and free refreshments at the **Art Deco Shop**, www.artdeconapier.com.

If you wish to see the buildings on your own, or are pushed for time, pick up a copy of the excellent *Art Deco Walk* leaflet ($5) from the VIC. There are also *Art Deco Scenic Drive* maps available. These walks encompass the history and events surrounding that fateful day in 1931 when an earthquake measuring 7.8 on the Richter scale hit the city. If on a self-guided walk, a pre-emptive tremor musing upon the relevant exhibits in the museum is recommended.

Swimming
The main beach in Napier is pebble, deeply shelved and too dangerous for swimming. However, there are more sheltered bays namely Westshore, Waipatiki and Waimarama (the VIC can provide directions). There is also a small lap pool and hot pools at the **Ocean Spa Complex**, Marine Parade. See page 340.

Tour operators
Airplay, Havelock North, T06-845 1977/ T025- 512886, www.airplay.co.nz. Paragliding around Te Mata Peak from $140.
Bay Tours and Charters, T06-845 2736, www.baytours.co.nz. Local and regional sightseeing and winery tours from $65.
Early Morning Balloons, T06-879 4229. Hot air balloon rides from $325.
Grant Petherick Fly Fishing, T06-876 7467, www.flyfishingwinetours.co.nz. Fishing trips and wine tours. Recommended.
Kiwi Adventure Company, 58 West Quay, T06-834 3500, www.kiwi-adventure.co.nz. Canoeing, kayaking and climbing trips and

hire. Climbing-wall open Tue and Thu 1500-2100, Sat-Sun 1000-1800, from $15.
Long Island Tours, T06-877 0977, www.longislandtoursnz.com. A wide range of local and regional sightseeing tours.
Mountain Valley (Mohaka River), T06-834 9756, www.mountainvalley.co.nz. Rural adventure centre offering a range of activities including horse treks, kayaking and rafting, accommodation available.
Napier Prison Tours, T06-835 9933, www.napierprison.com. Visit the local prison reputed to be the oldest in New Zealand, daily 0930 and 1500, from $20.
Out of the Blue, T06-875 0188, www.outoftheblueboatcharters.co.nz. Customized ocean and trout fishing trips.
Whana Valley Walk, T06-874 2421, www.whanawalkhawkesbay.co.nz. Walk and accommodation packages on the renowned coastal and country tracks, from $80.
Wine Country Cat, West Quay, Ahuriri, T06-877 7850/T0800-946338, www.hb winecountrycat.co.nz. It was only a matter of time before the sampling of local wine and produce took to the high seas. Luxury 3½-hr catamaran cruises leave daily at 1100, from $50; a 6-hr smorgasbord dinner cruise at 1830 costs from $65.
Waimarama Maori Tours, Waimarama Road, Clive, T021-057 0935, www.waimaramamaori.com. Based at the Hakikino Reserve near Clive where Maori traditions began more than 700 years ago. You can see the archaeological remains of the village, walk the reserve and learn about the Maori, their myths and legends. Tours range from 2 to 3 ½ hrs, from $60. Recommended.

Cape Kidnappers *p341*
Gannet colony
The big attraction on the cape is the gannet colony (the largest in the North Island). Several operators run tours.
Gannet Beach Adventures, T06-875 0898, T0800-426638, www.gannets.com. The oldest company. This 4-hr tour leaves daily (Oct-May) from Clifton Beach by tractor and allows about

1½ hrs with the gannets, from $38, child $23. Shuttles available from the main centres. Given the unique use of tractors this tour is understandably the most popular. The guides offer a very entertaining commentary. Overall it is a great experience. Highly recommended.
Gannet Safaris Overland, at the Summerlee Station on the cape (near Te Awanga), T06-875 0888, www.gannetsafaris.co.nz. Go overland by shuttle bus or 4WD, which involves very little walking. The 3-hr tours depart daily Sep-May at 0930 and 1330, from $65. Transport from Napier $22.

Golf
Cape Kidnappers Golf Course, 448 Clifton Rd, Te Awanga, T06-875 1900, www.cape kidnappers.com. A challenging course with stunning views – but at $400 for visitors ($300 low season) – it comes at a price.

Hawke's Bay vineyards *p344*
Vineyards
A useful source of information is www.hawkesbaywinemakers.co.nz.
Black Barn Vineyards, Te Mata Rd, T06-877 7985, www.blackbarn.com. Daily 1000-1700. Excellent accommodation, underground cellar and host to the village growers' market every Sat morning in summer.
Church Road, 150 Church Rd, Taradale, T06-845 9137, www.churchroad.co.nz. Daily 0900-1700. Formerly the McDonald Winery. Owned by the internationally famous Montana Estates. Winemaking museum and restaurant. Hosts excellent jazz concerts.
Clearview, 194 Clifton Rd, Te Awanga, Hastings, T06-875 0150, www.clearview estate.co.nz. Daily 1000-1700. One not to miss if you are visiting Cape Kidnappers. Quality not quantity with a classy Mediterranean-style café.
Craggy Range, 253 Waimarama Rd, Havelock North, east of the village, T06- 873 7126, www.craggyrange.com. One of the most celebrated wineries in the region, in the shadow of Te Mata Peak. All the grandeur and self-promotion is perhaps a bit over the top.

Classy restaurant that could make more of the view. Lunch from 1200 and dinner daily.
Elephant Hill Estate and Winery, 86 Clifton Road Te Awanga, T06-873 0400, www.elephanthill.co.nz. Daily 0900-1700. One of the region's newest and noted for its contemporary architecture and ocean views as well as its hand picked vintage. Restaurant open daily for lunch and dinner Wed-Sat.
Mission Estate, Church Rd, Taradale, T06-8459350, www.missionestate.co.nz. Mon-Sat 0900-1700, Sun 1000-1630. The oldest vineyard in New Zealand. Famous labels, restaurant and established tours.
Sileni, Maraekakaho Rd, Hastings, T06-879 8768, www.selini.co.nz. 1100-1700. Stunning modern architecture is as much the draw here as quality wine. Located 34 km from Napier on the Maraekakaho Rd (via SH50), it is worth the journey.
Te Awa, 2375 SH50, T06-879 7602, www.tea wa.com. Daily 0900-1700. Interesting building, fine labels and good restaurant.
Te Mata Estate, Te Mata Rd, T06-877 4399, www.temata.co.nz. Mon-Fri 0900-1700, Sat 1000, Sun 1100. Another architectural stunner. Reputable label.
Vidal Estate, 913 St Aubyn St East, T06-876 8105, www.vidal.co.nz. Daily 0900-1700. Excellent restaurant for lunch and dinner daily.

Wine tour operators
Most of the tours available are flexible, and will cater for your needs.
Bay Tours, T06-843 6953, www.bay tours.co.nz. Locally recommended and good value with a flexible itinerary, from $65.
Bike About Tours, T06-845 4836, www.bikeabouttours.co.nz. Explore the vineyards by bicycle from $35.
Bike D'Vine, T06-833 6697, www.bikede vine.com. Tours are flexible, usually self-guided and sometimes include other less intoxicating destinations. Lunch is often provided as well as maps, cell phones and even pick-ups, should you get too tired or weighed down with purchases. Prices start at a very reasonable $40 per day.

Grant Petherick Wine Tours, T06-876 7467, www.flyfishingwinetours.co.nz. High quality, entertaining and informative, customized tours. Recommended.

Hawkes Bay in a Glass, T06-836 7427, www.qualityhb.co.nz. A quality operator offering flexible tours arranged to your own time schedule and tastes. Price varies.

OdysseyNZ, 219 Kenilworth Rd, Hastings, T0508-639 773, www.odysseynz.co.nz. Quality tours of up to 7 local vineyards with platter, lunch or dinner options, from $85. Recommended.

On Yer Bike Winery Tours, Hastings, T06-879 8735, www.onyerbikehb.co.nz. The energetic option, by bike from $50 (requires supreme coordination and orientation skills towards the end of the day).

Vince's Vineyard Tours, T06-836 6705. Personalized tour with friendly, local, knowledgeable guide. In operation for 10 years. Flexible itineraries from $50.

Hastings and Havelock North *p345*
Airplay, T025-512886, www.airplay.co.nz. For those wishing to take to the sky, paragliding flights and courses are available from $140.
Grant Petherick Wine Tours, T06-876 7467, www.flyfishingwinetours.co.nz. Offers high-quality, entertaining and informative tours.

⊖ Transport

Napier *p339, map p342*

Car hire Hertz, T06-835 6169; Xpress, T06-835 8818. **Taxi** Napier Taxi, T06-835 7777; **Star**, T06-835 5511.

❶ Directory

Napier *p339, map p342*
Internet Cybers, 98 Dickens St, T06-8350125. Mon 0830-2100, Tue-Fri 0830-2400, Sat 0900- 2400, Sun 0900-2000. **Email Espresso** 6 Hastings St, T06-8336920. **Library** Station St, T06-8344180. **Police** 77 Station St, T06-8310700. **Post office** 151 Hastings St. Mon-Fri 0800-1700, Sat 0930-1230.

Hastings *p344*
Internet Hectic Netway, 1/123 Heretaunga St, Hastings. 1000-2200 and at the VIC (I-Site). **Medical services** Hawke's Bay Regional Hospital, Omahu Rd, Hastings, T06-878 8109. **Post office** Hastings, 100 Market St, T06-8703205. Mon-Fri 0830-1800, Sat 1000-1300.

The Wairarapa → *Colour map 3, C3.*

The Wairarapa is one of the least-visited regions in the North Island. Most visitors miss it out in their rush to reach Wellington via SH1, which lies to the west beyond the natural barrier of the Ruahine and Tararua ranges. If that simple fact is not appealing enough, the remote and stunning coastal scenery and relaxed atmosphere will, if you make the effort to visit, confirm that this is a place worth getting to know. The highlights, other than the delights of rural towns like Martinborough, which lie like a string of pearls along SH2, are the ever-increasing number of quality vineyards, a terrific range of country B&Bs and the coastal splendour of Castlepoint and Cape Palliser, the North Island's most southerly point. ⏭ *For Sleeping, Eating and other listings, see pages 359-362.*

Ins and outs

Getting there Metlink, T0800-801700, www.metlink.org.nz, runs a daily rail service linking Wellington with the Wairarapa towns of Masterton, Carterton, Greytown and Featherston, connecting with local bus services to Martinborough. Trains depart at intervals throughout weekdays with a limited weekend service. Scheduled **InterCity** coach services also run from Palmerston North to Masterton via Woodville.

Getting around **Wairarapa Coachlines** offers a regular weekday and limited weekend services between Masterton, Martinborough and Featherston and connect with all **Metlink** train services, T0800-666355/T06-308 9352, www.waicoach.co.nz. There is no public transport to Castlepoint. However, you may be able to hook up with the holiday park or hotel staff on supply trips to Masterton.

Tourist information **Masterton VIC (I-Site)** ① *Cnr Bruce and Dixon sts, T06-370 0900, www.wairarapanz.com, Mon-Fri 0900-1700, Sat-Sun 1000-1600*, and **Martinborough VIC (I-Site)** ① *18 Kitchener St, T06-306 5010, www.wairarapanz.com, daily 0900-1600*, are the two main accredited VIC (I-Sites) in the region. They hold comprehensive information about sights and activities, as well as the wealth of B&B beds throughout the Wairarapa region. Other non-accredited, volunteer manned VICs are to be found in **Greytown** ① *110 Main St, T06-304 9008, Fri-Sun 1000-1600*, and **Featherston** ① *in the Old Courthouse (SH2) in the village, T06-308 8051, daily 1000-1500*. Walks information can be secured at the I-Sites or **DoC Masterton Field Centre** ① *220 South Rd (continuation of Queen St), T06-377 0700*.

Masterton → *Colour map 3, C3 Population: 18,000*.

Given its relative geographical isolation (thanks to the Tararua Ranges), Masterton was not settled to any great degree until the late 1850s, but with rich fertile soils and a favourable climate, when settlement came, growth was rapid. Today, the town is the chief commercial centre for the Wairarapa Region. Masterton also gives Te Kuiti in the Waikato (the 'sheep-shearing capital of New Zealand') a run for its money in the big woolly event stakes. The **Golden Shears** is the major date in the local young farmers' calendar, held at the beginning of March.

Just opposite the VIC (I-Site) is the **Aratoi Wairarapa Museum of Art and History** ① *T06-370 0001, www.aratoi.co.nz, daily 1000-1630, donation*, which showcases many aspects of the area's social, cultural and natural history, as well as rapidly blossoming into the main focus for local contemporary artists. The museum also hosts visiting national exhibitions. There's also a good in-house café. Alongside Aratoi is the new **Shear Discovery National Shearing and Wool-handling Museum** ① *12 Dixon St, T06-378 8008, www.sheardiscovery.co.nz, daily 1000-1600, $5, child $2*. Developed in two relocated former woolsheds it offers 'a fine round-up' of the shearing and weaving process and showcases the champions of the prized annual 'Golden Shears' contest.

Also within walking distance of the VIC (I-Site) and town centre is the much-loved and celebrated **Queen Elizabeth Park**. First planted in 1878, today it boasts a lake (with boats for hire), sports grounds, a miniature railway, swing bridge, aviaries, a deer park and the usual tracts of manicured herbaceous borders. A little further out of town, on Colombo Road, is **Henley Park**, with lakes offering fishing and lakeside walks.

Masterton has a number of interesting gardens and **Heritage Trail Walks** (one to two hours) which are part of an eight-walk Regional Heritage Trail. Information and leaflets for all can be obtained from the VIC (I-Site). Be sure to check out the bronze statue and charming story of **Russian Jack**, the erstwhile Wairarapa 'swag' man, on Queen Street.

For recreational walks the **Mount Holdsworth** area offers access to the Tararua Range with short and long walk options. Details are outlined at the car park. To get there take Norfolk Road just south of the town (17 km).

Mount Bruce → *Colour map 3, C3*.

The main focus of Mount Bruce, 30 km north of Masterton on SH2, is the **Pukaha Mount Bruce National Wildlife Centre** ① *T06-375 8004, www.mtbruce.org.nz, daily 0900-1630, $15, child $4.* This centre is the flagship of DoC's conservation and endangered species breeding programme. Although much of what happens at Mount Bruce takes place behind the scenes (and involves dedicated staff acting as surrogate mothers), the public can see many species otherwise rarely seen, such as the takahe (a charming prehistoric-looking purple bird, not dissimilar to a large chicken), stitchbird and kokako.

There is a nocturnal kiwi house that rates among the best in the country and leaves you in no doubt as to the numerous threats which this national icon faces in the modern world. Other highlights include the eel feed at 1330 and the kaka feed at 1500. The wild eels live in the stream running through the reserve and gather beneath the bridge at feeding time in a swirling mass. This particular species, native to New Zealand, is far larger than the average eel and lives up to at least 80 years. The kaka is a cheeky and at times raucous native bush parrot. There is a small colony at Mount Bruce that have been bred in captivity and now live wild in the area. They all have names and will quite happily nibble your hair or your ear before cracking open a peanut with their powerful beaks. If you go to the feeding area just before 1500 they will usually be hanging about in the trees, available for interviews and photographs. Within the main building there are some fine displays, a shop and a café.

Castlepoint → *Colour map 3, C4*.

It is a major diversion to get to this remote coastal settlement (65 km from Masterton) but the trip is well worth it. Castlepoint is considered to be the highlight on the Wairarapa's wild and remote coastline and it certainly deserves the honour. At the eastern end of the main beach a stark rocky headland, from which sprouts the **Castlepoint Lighthouse**, sweeps south to enclose a large lagoon. The picturesque bay, which is itself a popular spot with surfers and swimmers, is dominated at its southern entrance by the aptly named 162-m **Castle Rock**, which can be accessed from the southern end of the bay. The lighthouse can be accessed across the sand tombolo which connects it to the mainland via a boardwalk. Just below the lighthouse there is a cave that can be explored at low tide, but beware – Maori legend has it that it is the hiding place of a huge menacing octopus. One word of warning: a small memorial stone testifies to the number of people who have drowned while exploring the offshore reef, so take care. On its eastern side, huge ocean waves can catch you unawares. While contemplating the memorial stone, look closely at the rocks that surround it and you will see hundreds of fossil shells embedded therein.

Riversdale Beach and Flat Point

The small coastal resort of Riversdale is 35 km northeast of Te Wharau which is itself east of Masterton (130 km round trip). The beach is long and sandy and as it's patrolled in summer offers safe swimming as well as surfing, fishing and diving. The Flat Point to Honeycomb Rock section of coast is wilder than Riversdale with interesting rock formations and an old shipwreck.

Carterton → *Colour map 3, C3*.

Carterton acts as a secondary service town to Masterton and is famous in spring for its daffodils (first planted in 1920). Although not as aesthetically pleasing as its neighbouring settlements, it is perhaps worth a stop to see the Paua Shell Factory and use the town as an access point to the Mount Dick Viewpoint and the Tararua Forest park at Waiohine Gorge.

The **Paua Shell Factory** ⓘ *54 Kent St, T06-379 4222, www.pauashell.co.nz, daily 0800-1700, free*, is one of the few places in the country that converts the stunningly beautiful paua (abalone) shells into jewellery and souvenirs. It is possible to see how the shell is crafted and to watch a video about the paua itself, with complimentary coffee or tea. This is all cleverly designed to get you into the shop, where there is a vast range of paua shell items on sale, some of which are painfully kitsch.

You can then go and see one of the best views in the Wairarapa, from **Mount Dick**. At the southern end of town turn into Dalefield Road which heads straight towards the hills like a never-ending runway. At the very end of the road keep going and just before its terminus look for a farm track on the left. This track, which is negotiable without a 4WD (just), goes about 3 km up to a viewpoint; 14 km total.

The trip to **Waiohine Gorge** (22 km) at the entrance to the **Tararua Forest Park** is well worth it for the scenery itself, let alone the walks on offer and the heart-stopping **swing bridge**, one of the longest in New Zealand. The road is signposted just south of the town on SH2. Eventually an unsealed road connects you with the riverbank which gradually rises high above the river gorge. At the road terminus you can embark on a number of walks from one hour to several days, almost all of which involve the initial negotiation of the swing bridge which traverses the gorge at a height of about 40 m. If you do nothing else at Waiohine, a few trips back and forth on the bridge is great fun.

About a 10-min drive southeast of Carterton is one of the country's most unusual – if a little misplaced – attractions. The **Stonehenge Aotearoa** ⓘ *Ahiaruhe Rd, T06-377 1600, www.astronomynz.org.nz, Wed-Sun 1000-1600, $15, child $6*, is a full-scale working adaptation of the original Stonehenge in England. The main aim of the creators of Stonehenge Aotearoa has been to explain what stone circles are about and to offer 'a window into the past where the visitor can rediscover the knowledge of their ancestors, by incorporating ancient Egyptian, Babylonian and Indus Valley astronomy, Polynesian navigation, and Celtic and Maori starlore'.

Greytown → *Colour map 3, C3.*

Greytown, along with Martinborough, is the prettiest of the Wairarapa settlements and is best known for its antiques, art and craft shops and roadside cafés. It's also a great spot to stop and wander around the old buildings and quaint shops. Given its historic village feel it is not surprising to learn that Greytown was one of the first places settled in the area. Settlement began in earnest in the 1850s on land purchased by Sir George Grey, one of New Zealand's first governors and after whom the town is, of course, named. The **Cobblestones Museum** ⓘ *169 Main St, T06-304 9687, daily 0900-1630, $3, child $1*, is a collection of buildings and memorabilia from the early settler days.

Martinborough → *Colour map 3, C3.*

Martinborough is located towards the coast from SH2, 16 km southeast of Greytown. First settled by a nationalistic Briton, John Martin in the late 1880s, the **village square** and the streets running off it form the shape of the Union Jack. With names like Kansas, Texas and Ohio, it is clear that Martin had as much a love of the US as he did his homeland. Described as a unique 'wine village', with 20 vineyards within walking distance of the square, and blessed with as many charming B&Bs, it is a favourite romantic haunt for Wellingtonians in search of a quiet weekend. Of local historical interest is the **Colonial Museum** ⓘ *on the square, T06-306 9736, Sat-Sun 1400-1600, donation*, which was itself the former village library built in 1894. It is furnished with all the usual early settler artifacts. The *Vintage*

Shelling out for paua

The Maori have long valued paua, as a source of both food and decoration. To protect paua as a sustainable resource, strict quotas are in place in New Zealand and no paua harvesting is allowed with compressed air. This makes their collection, with only a snorkel, often in cold southern waters over 12 m in depth, quite an art. Dives of up to two minutes are not uncommon. What comes up from those depths is not the radiant casing t... you see in the souvenir shops, but a drab coralline coated shell, that once removed of its flesh, must be ground down to reveal the beautiful patterning beneath. The paua industry – for both the food and the shell – is well established in New Zealand. You will encounter the huge range of jewellery designs using it in almost every souvenir shop throughout the land.

Village Heritage Walk leaflet available from the VIC will pinpoint other sites of historical interest like the rather grand and recently restored **Martinborough Hotel**. Again there are a number of 'open gardens' for which the VIC will point the way.

The **Patuna Chasm** ⓘ *Patuna Farm, Ruakokopatuna Rd, book through the VIC or T06-306 9966, www.patunafarm.co.nz*, is an interesting limestone gorge featuring stalactites, fossils and waterfalls and a host of native wildlife. The chasm is on private land but guided walks are available from $15. Along a similar theme the nearby **Ruakokopatuna glow-worm caves** are also on private land but can be accessed with instruction from the VIC (I-Site); take a torch and your gumboots. About 20 km southeast of the village are the busy white propellers of the **Hau Nui Wind Farm** on White Rock Road. Although you are not free to wander among them there is a viewing platform provided. From there you might consider going all the way to the remote coast at **Tora** or **White Rock** which offers some great walks and coastal scenery.

The main attraction is of course the **vineyards** and most offer tastings and tours, but note that not all of them are open year-round. The most noted labels tend to be Sauvignon Blanc, Riesling and Pinot Noir. The popular **wine centre** ⓘ *in the heart of the village, T06-306 9040, www.martinboroughwinecentre.co.nz*, is a good place to get a feel for what is available and ask about tours. *The Martinborough Wairarapa Wine Trail* leaflet, available from the VIC (I-Site), will also get your tour started. The website www.nzwine.com is useful. The **Ata Rangi Vineyard** ⓘ *T06-306 9570, www.atarangi.co.nz, Sep-Mar, Mon-Fri 1300-1500, Sat-Sun 1200-1600*, is one of the better known, producing a Pinot Noir, for which the village is now famous. There are a number of local tour operators who can arrange specialist wine tours, including **Wairarapa Coachlines Tours**, T0800-666355. If you are around in November, your visit may coincide with the immensely popular **Toast Martinborough** celebrations, a festival of fine wine and food.

Cape Palliser, Ngawi and Lake Ferry → *Colour map 3, C3.*

The day-long drive to see the Cape Palliser Lighthouse epitomizes the region and is highly recommended. On the way you can take in the bizarre rock formations of the Putangirua Pinnacles that featured in the film trilogy *Lord of the Rings*, the charming coastal fishing village of Ngawi and a colony of fur seals, before the road terminates at the steps of the lighthouse. To get there from Featherston or Martinborough make your way down Lake Ferry Road, towards Lake Ferry. Just before the village turn left for Ngawi. From here the lighthouse is about 40 km. Once the road joins the coast and if it is a clear day, you may be able to see the snow-capped Kaikoura Ranges of the South Island.

about 15 km look out for the **Putangirua Pinnacles** car park. The pinnacle ~ions are a series of gravel spires and turrets. They are about an hour's walk down a ~n bed, so take proper footwear. Once you reach the entrance to the pinnacles (on ~left, after about 30 minutes) you have the choice of climbing a steep path through ~ash to a viewpoint (30 minutes), or entering the pinnacles stream bed and going into ~heart of the formation. Don't miss the viewpoint but both trips are worth it.

From the car park the road continues, hugging the cliffs before opening out across a wide coastal plain, with a beautiful shore of rock and sand, well known for its excellent surfing. The coastal village of **Ngawi** soon comes into view and you will be struck by the collection of old tractors and bulldozers on the beachfront with rigs supporting a raft of fishing boats of all shapes and sizes. It is worth a stop here to take a closer look and watch as one of the dearly loved machines is used to launch a boat.

From Ngawi the red and white tower of the lighthouse can be seen. On the rocks just before it is a colony of New Zealand **fur seals**, though you have to look carefully so as not to miss them. Like fat, brown barrels they doze the day away amongst the boulders. All they're missing is a TV, a can of beer and a remote control. By all means take a closer look, but do not go nearer than 10 m. If you do, their soporific attitude will evaporate in an explosion of rippling blubber as they charge towards the surf.

From the seal colony it is only a short distance to the **lighthouse**, with its steep climb of steps and rewarding views. This is the southernmost tip of the North Island. Once you return to Lake Ferry Road it is worth the short diversion to see **Lake Ferry** itself.

Featherston → *Colour map 3, C3.*

Featherston is the southern gateway to the Wairarapa (or the last settlement depending on which way you came) and sits in the shadow of the Rimutaka Range that was, and continues to be, the 'great divider' between the Wairarapa and Wellington. Featherston is best known as the 1870s base of operations, in the mammoth task of connecting the Wairarapa and Wellington by rail.

The main attraction in Featherston is the **Fell Engine Museum** ⓘ *Fitzherbert St, T06-308 9379, Mon-Fri 0930-1600, Sat-Sun 1000-1600, donation.* It houses the beautifully restored Fell Engine (the only one of its type in the world) that used to climb the steep 265-m slopes of the Rimutaka Incline. The railway line now goes through a tunnel and the **Rimutaka Incline** has been opened up as a walkway, which starts at the end of Cross Creek Road, 10 km south of Featherston. It takes a whole day to reach the summit or cross the ranges to Kaitoke (17 km).

As you leave the Wairarapa by road (or indeed arrive) a fine departing (or introductory) view can be seen from the **Rimutaka Trig** (725 m) at the crest of the ranges road. The track (one hour return) starts beside the road, just below the summit café, on the Wellington side. From the top you will get a great view of **Lake Wairarapa** and the coast.

◉ The Wairarapa listings

For Sleeping and Eating price codes and other relevant information, see Essentials pages 44-50.

◉ Sleeping

Masterton *p354*

The Wairarapa is renowned for its ever-increasing number of B&Bs, which comfortably cater for the Wellingtonians who cross the hills into the Wairarapa in droves on summer weekends and during the holiday periods. Given the sheer number of beds, standards are generally high and competition is fierce. The choices around the vineyards of Martinborough are particularly good (if a little pricey).

AL Copthorne Solway Resort, High St South, T06-370 0500, www.solway.co.nz. A standard, fairly unremarkable hotel, but with an attractive range of amenities including pools, spas, squash courts and solarium. Good for families.

AL-A Masterton Motor Lodge, 250 High St, T06-378 2585, www.masterton-motor lodge.co.nz. Wide range of top quality units, pool, spa, in-house restaurant and bar.

C The Hut, off SH2, Mt Bruce, T06-375 8681, www.thehut.co.nz. Excellent, small and cosy self-contained option set high over the valley (near the Mt Bruce National Wildlife Centre) with spectacular views across to the Tararua Ranges. Log burner, outside heated bath. Great value and recommended.

B Empire Lodge, 94 Queen St, T06-377 1902. The town's main budget hotel, with basic rooms (with bathroom) and restaurant.

Motorcamps and campsites

B-D Mawley Park Motor Camp, 15 Oxford St, T06-378 6454. All the usual basic amenities (from cabins to tent sites) situated close to town and beside the river.

Castlepoint *p355*

Motorcamps and campsites

A-D Castlepoint Holiday Park and Motels,

T06-372 6705, www.castlepoint.co.nz. Well off the beaten track in a stunning, wild coastal location. Old, yet well-maintained, spacious motorpark with adequate amenities right next to the beach and overlooking the lighthouse and headland. Wide range of accommodation options from tent sites to tourist flats. Additional, modern self-contained motel units are also available in the village.

Riversdale Beach and Flat Point *p355*

Riversdale Beach is 65 km from Masterton. There is a store, a motorcamp and a few accommodation options.

A Cobwebs Cottage, Orui Station, T06-372 3445, www.cobwebscottage.co.nz. Tidy self-contained cottage overlooking the beach. Ideal for couples.

Motorcamps and campsites

C-D Riversdale Beach Holiday Park, T06-372 3889, holidaypark@inspire.net.nz. Cabins and sites.

Carterton *p355*

There are numerous friendly B&Bs available. For the full range contact the VIC (I-Site).

AL Carrington Cottages, T06-379 7039, www.carringtoncottages.co.nz. Nearer Carterton, an option worth considering.

B Matador Motel, 187 High St, T06-379 8058, www.matadormotel.co.nz. Not as dodgy as the name suggests and the town's only motel.

Motorcamps and campsites

B-D Carterton Holiday Park, Belvedere Rd, T06-379 8267. Powered and non-powered sites, standard cabins, self-contained units and camp kitchen.

Greytown *p356*

Greytown and the immediate area has its fair share of lovely B&Bs, details of which are available at the VICs.

LL-L Briarwood, 21 Main St, T06-304 8336, www.briarwood.biz. Boutique B&B in a renovated historic homestead with 2 tidy suites with claw-foot baths, guest lounge with open fire and just about everything else a body needs to guarantee a relaxing stay. Dinner on request.

LL-AL White Swan Country Hotel, Main St, T06-304 8894, www.thewhiteswan.co.nz. The White Swan has an interesting history being a relocated and fully renovated former railway building from Wellington. It offers a choice of 7 tasteful luxury, individually designed rooms from the Asian 'Bombay' to the English 'George'. There are also cheaper modern suites and studios in a separate wing to the rear of the hotel. Restaurant and bar.

L-A Oak Estate Motor Lodge, corner Main St and Hospital Rd, T06-304 8188, www.oakestate.co.nz. Modern luxury suites with spa and Sky TV.

Motorcamps and campsites

There is a basic campsite (**D**, Kuratawhiti St, T06-304 9837), but campers and motor homes are better facilitated at Carterton or Martinborough.

Martinborough p356

Martinborough has a huge selection of B&Bs and self-contained cottages very similar in design and focusing on the romantic weekend market, in a region becoming internationally renowned for its quality vineyards. You are advised to visit or call the VIC to choose and book.

LL Peppers Martinborough Hotel, The Square, T06-306 9350, www.peppers.co.nz. The historic 1882 Martinborough Hotel adds character and sophistication to this Wairarapa village. The elegant, luxury en suite rooms are individually designed and named after some of the region's first settlers. Attractive features include French doors, which open on to either the hotel veranda or garden, and large claw-foot baths.

LL Wharekaukau Country Estate, Western Lake Rd, Palliser Bay, T06-307 7581, www.wharekaukau.co.nz. Pronounced 'forry-coe-hoe', this is one of the country's top

luxury lodges. Located in a quiet corner of the Wairarapa, part of its appeal is the surrounding land (the lodge is based in a 2000-ha working sheep station overlooking the ocean), where you can relish the feeling of getting away from it all. Accommodation is in individual, fully self-contained cottage suites, designed and decorated with natural elements including clay tiles, an open fire and New Zealand wool carpeting. The cuisine is superb with a French/Italian influence and comes with the added allure of top local wines. On-site activities include horse riding, 4WD safaris and clay pigeon shooting, which can, if you wish, be followed by professional spa treatments.

L Petit Hotel, 3 Kitchener St, T06-306 8086, www.petithotel.co.nz. Well-appointed suites with 'plump beds and rich furnishings', bound to attract any couple for a lively weekend. Very discreet hosts. There are numerous romantic self-contained cottages.

LL-AL The Old Manse, 19 Grey St, T06-306 8599, www.oldmanse.co.nz. Spacious and fully renovated Presbyterian manse overlooking a vineyard and within walking distance of the village centre. 6 tasteful en suites, spa pool.

AL Duckback Cottage, 9 Broadway St, T06-306 9933, www.duckbackcottage.co.nz. Renovated 1890s self-contained cottage with open fire, 3 bedrooms, and bathroom with claw-foot bath. Again within walking distance of all amenities.

AL-A La Petite Valle Carriage, T06-306 9767, www.lapetite.co.nz. Something different in the form of an authentic hand-crafted carriage with all mod cons, including en suite and pot belly stove, set on a working sheep farm 13 km east of Martinborough. Cottage and B&B options are also available.

AL The Claremont, 38 Regent St, T0800-809162/T06-306 9162, www.claremont-motels.co.nz. A motel in one of the few places in New Zealand where a motel is hard to find! This higher-end establishment seems to live up to its near singular standing.

A-D Kate's Place, 7 Cologne St, T06-306 9935, www.katesplace.co.nz. Small, friendly backpacker-homestay with dorms and one en suite double.

Motorcamps and campsites
D**Martinborough Village Camping**, on the corner of Princess and Dublin sts, T0800-780909/T06-306 8919, www.martinborough camping.com. Quality motorpark with all the usual facilities. Bike hire.

Cape Palliser *p357*
AL **Lake Ferry Hotel**, Lake Ferry Rd, T06-307 7831. Five very pleasant double and 2 twin rooms with shared bathroom facilities, and one double room with ensuite. Good restaurant and bar attached.

Motorcamps and campsites
DoC administers a campsite at the Putangirua Pinnacles, T06-307 8230.
Self registration.
B-D **Lake Ferry Motorcamp**, Lake Ferry Rd, T06-307 7873. Busy, basic and waterside. Within walking distance of the hotel and beach.

🍽 Eating

Masterton *p354*
♦♦ **Café Cecille**, in the heart of Queen Elizabeth Park (eastern end of Park Av or from Memorial Drive off Dixon St), T06-370 1166. Good choice for either lunch or dinner. Licensed.
♦♦ **Dish Cafe**, 10 First St, T06-377 7531, Wed-Sun 0800-1630. Locally recommended and licensed.
♦♦ **Plaza India**, 3 Perry St, T06-370 5177. Does an above-average curry.
♦ **Café Strada**, 232 Queen St, next to the Regent Theatre, T06-3782070. Daily 0800-late. Locally recommended.

Castlepoint *p355*
Beyond the village store T06-372 6823, the **Berley Pot Restaurant and Bar**, on Jetty Rd, T06-372 6944, is your best bet.

Carterton *p355*
♦♦ **Buckhorn Bar and Grill**, 20 Memorial Sq, T06-379 7972. Dinner daily from 1800, lunch Wed-Mon. Pub grub in nice surroundings.
♦ **Wild Oates Bakery and Deli Cafe**, 127 High St, T06-379 5580. Open from 0630.

Greytown *p356*
♦♦ **Main St Deli**, 88 Main St, T06-304 9022. Sun-Thu 0800-1800, Fri-Sat 2000. Considered the best café in the region it has a large outdoor eating area and offers excellent fare for breakfast, lunch and dinner along with some great snacks and coffee, good value.
♦♦ **Wakelin House**, 123 Main St. Wed-Mon from 1100. Very congenial and a favourite throughout the region for both lunch and dinner. Recommended.
♦ **Salute**, 83 Main St, T06-304 9825. Tue-Sun for lunch and dinner and weekends for brunch. Imaginative Middle Eastern/ Mediterranean cuisine with alfresco seating and a fine range of sweets.

Martinborough *p356*
As you might expect, Martinborough is not short of choice.
♦♦ **Peppers Martinborough Hotel**, T06-306 9350. 0800-late. Popular for breakfast, lunch and dinner.
♦♦ **The Circus Cinema Restaurant and Bar**, 34 Jellicoe St, T06-306 9442. Daily except Tue 1600-late. As the name suggests a boutique cinema, restaurant and bar that offers a fresh seasonal menu including pizzas. It has indoor seating around an open fire and a pleasant courtyard for al fresco summer dining. The films range from art house to mainstream and you can of course take a coffee or a wine in with you.

Cafés
There are a number of good vineyard cafés.
♦♦ **The Old Winery Café**, on the **Margrain** Estate, corner Ponatahi Rd and Huangarua Rd, T06-306 8333. Summer daily for lunch in summer, Fri-Sat dinner; winter Thu-Sun for lunch, Fri-Sat dinner. One of the most popular.

¶ **Village Café**, Martinborough Wine Centre, Kitchener St, T06-377 7251. Wed-Sun till late. Convenient with an eclectic range of locally grown produce and good organic coffee.

Featherston *p358*
¶ **Tin Hut Hotel**, Tauherenikau, T06-308 9697. Mon-Fri 1000-1700, Sat-Sun 0830-1800. Country pub with local produce a wine. Ask at the VIC for a map and directions.

❀ Festivals and events

Masterton *p354*
Mar Golden Shears, www.golden shears.co.nz. See page 354. Sheep-sheering competition.

▲ Activities and tours

Masterton *p354*
Genesis Recreation Complex, Dixon St. Heated indoor and outdoor swimming pools.
The Kaiwhata Walk, Ngahape Rd, T06-372 2772, www.kaiwhatawalk.co.nz. Well-organized 3-day walk on private land towards the coast from the Ngahape Valley. Accommodation, food and transport arranged, from $130.
Mount Bruce National Wildlife Centre, RD1, Masterton, T06-375 8004, www.mt bruce.org.nz. Wildlife viewing and eco-tours in the Wairarapa.
Tranzit Coachlines, T06-370 6600, www.tranzit.co.nz. Offer good value daily sightseeing and vineyard tours throughout the region, from $95.

Castlepoint *p355*
Legionnaires Charters, T06-372 6613, www.legionnaire-charters.co.nz. Fishing trips, competitions in summer.

Carterton *p355*
Early Morning Balloons, T06-879 4229. Will take you up, up and away (if the weather is settled) for an early morning 2- to 3-hr flight for about $330, breakfast included.

Martinborough and Featherston *p356*
In an effort to lure the well-heeled Wellingtonians there is an increasing range of activity operators around Martinborough. You have the choice of canoeing, clay-bird shooting, jet boating and of course vineyard tours (see page 357), among other acitivities. The VIC (I-Site) will fill you in with all the details and book on your behalf.
McLeods Adventures, Hautotara, White Rock Rd, Martinborough, T0800-494335, www.mcleodsadventures.co.nz. Entertaining 1½- to 3½-hr guided quad bike trips (with river crossings) in the hill country surrounding Martinborough. Ideal wet weather activity, from $120-180. Also offers accommodation and clay pigeon shooting, from $35.
Patuna Farm Adventures, 17 km southeast of Martinborough, T06-306 9966, www.patunafarm.co.nz. Offers a range of activities including horse trekking (from $40), pole to pole ropes course (4 hrs, $60), and guided walks to the Patuna Chasm from $15. Accommodation available.
Tora Walks, T06-307 8115, www.toracoastal walk.co.nz. Offers an interesting and varied 3-day coastal tramp with an equal variety of accommodation types. $375 (all inclusive).

❂ Transport

Bicycle hire Christina Estate Vineyard, T06-306 8920, or **Martinborough Village Camping**, on the corner of Princess and Dublin sts, T06-306 8919.

❶Directory

Internet Library, 50 Queen St, Masterton T06-378 9666, Mon-Tue 0900-1730, Wed 1000-1730, Thu 0900-2000, Fri 0900-1800, Sat 0930-1300. **Police** Masterton, T06-370 0300.

Contents

Footprint features

Wanganui & Manawatu

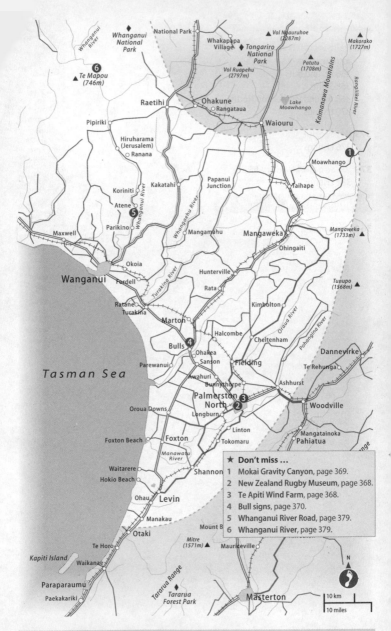

★ Don't miss ...
1 Mokai Gravity Canyon, page 369.
2 New Zealand Rugby Museum, page 368.
3 Te Apiti Wind Farm, page 368.
4 Bull signs, page 370.
5 Whanganui River Road, page 379.
6 Whanganui River, page 379.

Stretching from south of Levin to just north of Taumarunu, from Wanganui on the west coast across to Cape Turnagair, east, is the Wanganui/Manawatu Region, scythed almost in ha the Whanganui River, the longest navigable river in the North Island. Steeped in history, and supporting a rich watershed of remote hills adorned with native bush, much of the region is protected within the boundaries of the Whanganui National Park.

Settlement began with groups of Maori moa hunters between 1400 and 1650, who were in turn followed by the first Europeans – whalers from Kapiti Island. The rich agricultural lands have now made the region the sixth most populous in New Zealand with almost half of it contained within the urban boundaries of Palmerston North and Wanganui. Palmerston North, home to New Zealand's largest university, is an important national seat of learning. Although not blessed with the tourist bounty of other parts, the region has much to offer and provides a good base for exploring the lower North Island and surrounding national parks. The Whanganui National Park is especially popular with kayakers and trampers, who are able to leave civilization behind for days on end.

...nks of the Manawatu River and in the heart of flat, rural Manawatu, is the pleasant university *...ricultural service town of Palmerston North. Although set away from SH1 and not exactly blessed ...a wealth of tourist attractions, 'Palmy', with a population of around 75,000, can provide a good base ...m which to explore the southern half of the North Island and is an important gateway west, through ...he impressive Manawatu Gorge, to the Wairarapa and Hawkes Bay. Other than Massey University, which is the second largest in the country, the town is perhaps most famous for its rugby museum, a place of almost spiritual significance, where many New Zealand rugby fanatics come on a pilgrimage to pay homage to their All Black heroes.* ▶▶ For Sleeping, Eating and other listings, see pages 370-373.*

Ins and outs

Getting there

By air Palmerston North airport ① *4 km northwest of the city, T06-351 4415, www.pn airport.co.nz,* receives regular flights from most domestic centres with **New Zealand Link,** T0800-737000, www.airnewzealand.co.nz. A taxi to the centre costs around $20.

By road Palmerston North is about 30 km west of SH1, 140 km from Wellington and 546 km from Auckland. It is the main gateway to the Wairarapa and Hawke's Bay via SH3 to SH2 at Woodville. The town is serviced by **Intercity, Newmans,** T06-355 5633; **Nakedbus.com** and **Dalroy/White Star,** T0508-465622. The latter runs a regular service from Wanganui and stops at the Courthouse, Main St, while the others run from Wellington, Auckland and Napier and stop at the **Palmerston Travel Centre** ① *corner of Main and Pitt sts, T06-355 5633.*

By train Palmerston North is on the main north south rail line. **TranzScenic,** T0800-872467, operates only one service through the region, the 'Overlander' to Auckland. This is currently the only service between Auckland and Wellington. The station is about 2½ km from the town centre off Tremaine Av.

Getting around

Be warned: 'Palmy' is a nightmare for getting lost in because it is so flat. Stray too far from the central square and visible tall buildings without a street map and you will be lost in a world of fast food and chain retail outlets. Most of the town's sights are within walking distance. **Horizon Tranzit,** T0508-800800, is the local bus service; standard fare $3. The VIC (I-Site) has timetables. **Madge Buses (Uzabus),** T06-356 4896, www.madge.co.nz, runs a local service to Feilding and Levin from outside Farmers on King St.

Tourist information

Palmerston North and Destination Manawatu VIC (I-Site) ① *The Square, T06-350 1922, www.manawatunz.co.nz, daily 0900-1700.* **Palmerston North DoC** ① *717 Tremaine Av, T06-350 9700.* **Feilding and District VIC (I-Site)** ① *10 Manchester Sq, Feilding, T06-323 3318, Mon-Fri 0900-1600, Sat 1000-1300.* **Nature Coast VIC (I-Site)** ① *93 Oxford St, Levin, T06-367 8440, www.naturecoast.co.nz, Mon-Fri 0900-1730, Sat-Sun 1000-1500,* **Rangitikei (Taihape) VIC (I-Site)** ① *Town Hall, Hautapu St, Taihape, T06-388 0604, www.rangitikei.com, daily 0900-1700.* **Bulls VIC (I-Site)** ① *113 Bridge St, T06-322 0055, www.unforgetabull.co.nz, www.rangitikei.com, daily 0900-1700.*

Palmerston North

To Railway Station, Wanganui & DOC Office

Palmerston North Hospital

To Airport

New Zealand Rugby Museum

The Square

Plaza Shopping Centre

Regent Theatre

Cinema

Abbey Theatre

Travel Centre

Te Manawa Science Centre, Museum & Art Gallery

Square Edge Centre

Supermarket

Centrepoint Theatre

To Levin & Wellington (SH 56)

To Massey University & Tararua Wind Farm

City Rock

Ongley Park

Manawaroa Park

Victoria Esplanade Gardens

Manawatu River

N

200 metres
200 yards

Sleeping
Boulder Lodge **11** *B3*
Coachman Motel &
  Suites **2** *C2*
Colonial Court **3** *E3*
Cornwall Motel **10** *C2*
Fairway Woods **4** *D3*
Fitzherbert Regency **1** *E3*
Kingsgate **9** *C2*
Nikau Loft **5** *D1*
Palmerston North
  Holiday Park **6** *E2*
Peppertree
  Backpackers **7** *B2*
Plum Trees Lodge **8** *A3*

Eating 🍴
Bella's Café **1** *C2*
Café Cuba **2** *B1*
Déjeuner **5** *B2*
Downtown on
  Broadway Mall **6** *B2*
Elm Café &
  Brasserie **7** *E3*
India 2Nite **4** *C1*
Moxies **3** *C2*
Pompeii **14** *B1*
Spostato **15** *B1*

Bars & Clubs 🍸
Flying Fish **16** *B2*
Highflyers **9** *B2*
Murphy's Law
  Irish Bar **17** *B2*

Sights

The best-known attraction in 'Palmy' is the **New Zealand Rugby Museum** ① *87 Cuba St, T06-358 6947, www.rugbymuseum.co.nz, Mon-Sat 1000-1200 and 1330-1600, Sun 1330-1600, $5, child $2*. Established in 1969, it was the first of its kind in the country and contains the largest collection of rugby memorabilia including shirts, caps, photographs and programmes. There are also videos and detailed accounts of every All Black game since 1870 available for specialist research. If you have a particular question there is a wealth of fanatics on hand to fill you in on every pass, ruck and maul.

The **Te Manawa Science Centre, Museum and Art Gallery** ① *326 Main St, T06-355 5000, www.temanawa.co.nz, daily 1000-1700, free entry to some galleries*, is a progressive and modern centre that integrates the usual social, cultural and artistic heritage with hands-on science displays. It is split into three main parts, the museum, gallery and science centre, all of which are worth visiting. There are the some interesting Maori *taonga* and a few nationally significant artworks by contemporary gurus like Colin McCahon and Ralf Hotere. The gallery often hosts important national touring exhibitions.

If you head west towards the university and the river (Fitzherbert Avenue, then Park Road) you can access the **Victoria Esplanade Gardens** ① *dawn to dusk*, a very pleasant mix of bush, lawn and gardens that grace the banks of the river. There are numerous walking tracks and a large play park.

As usual there are leaflets available from the VIC (I-Site) outlining other city walks and gardens. From a historical perspective, the **Regent Theatre** is of particular note and a main feature of the city's heritage walk. Elsewhere, horticultural properties feature under the banner of 'Health, Herbs and Honey'. The **Pohangina Valley Tourist Route**, which takes in a combination of rural scenery, gardens, craft outlets and the market town of Feilding (see page 368) is also worth considering, best broken up with an overnight stay. On a rainy day, the active can head for the climbing wall at **YMCA ClimbingRock** ① *217 Featherston St, T06-357 4552, Tue-Thu 1530-2200, Fri 1530-1830, Sat 1000-1900, Sun 1200-1900, $11*, which has a 10-m-high top rope and boulder wall.

Well before arriving in 'Palmy' you will no doubt have seen the small forest of white blades that make up the **Te Apiti and Tararua Wind Farms** on the ranges east of the town. With almost 200 turbines combined this is one of the largest wind farm sites in the southern hemisphere and a great testimony to clean, renewable energy in New Zealand. It is well worth going to take a closer look and you can do so in the heart of the Te Apiti site via the town of Ashhurst. From Palmerston North, turn off SH3 at Ashhurst and follow the Saddle Road signs. A visitor car park underneath one of the turbines has views of the wind farm and an information display. The 55 turbines of Te Apiti are 70-metres in height and the blades 35-metres, combined they create enough power for 45,000 homes. f you do not have your own transport you can join a quad or mountain bike tour.▶ *See Activities and tours, page 372.*

Around Palmerston North ⊜❼▲ ▶ *pp370-373.*

Feilding → *Colour map 3, A6.*
Feilding sits in the heart of the Manawatu 'flatlands' on the banks of the Oroua River. Named after Colonel William Fielding (a former Director of Emigrants and Colonists Aid Corporation in Australasia), it is a pretty, relatively prosperous town, well known for its gardens. Indeed, their careful nurturing has played a key role in the town's run of success

in the nation's 'Most Beautiful Small Town Awards', which it has won a rem... times. Although there is not a huge amount to see or do, Feilding is a pleasant stop for a wander, with a scattering of small museums (traction engines b speciality), craft outlets and of course, gardens. Better still, take a tour by horse and c watch the local farmers bidding at the stock sales on a Friday. Guided tours are availa by locals at 1100, $5 (book at the VIC I-Site), T06-3233318. The **Saleyards Cafeter** ① *Manchester St, T06-3237036, is the place to go to get a real taste of rural North Island.*

Levin and Foxton → *Colour map 3, B3.*

Levin and **Foxton**, both southwest of Palmerston North, lie in the heart of the Horowhenua Region. This narrow strip of land, bordered by the Tararua Ranges to the west and the Tasman Sea to the east is, known for its rich alluvial soils and fruit and vegetable growing properties. Earlier industries included flax milling and timber exports.

The **Tokomaru Steam Engine Museum** ① *SH57, T06-329 8867, Mon-Sat 0900- 1530, Sun 1030-1530, $10, child $5,* is the highlight (if not the sum total) of Tokomaru Village, 32 km north of Levin. The museum offers the enthusiast or the layperson the chance to see the country's largest collection of working steam engines. There are a number of static displays and the occasional 'steam ups'.

The **Lake Papaitonga Scenic Reserve**, 4 km southwest of Levin, offers a delightful 30-minute walk through superb native bush, before reaching two viewpoints across the lakes. The atmosphere here, particularly at sunset, is magical. The area is rich in both Maori history and birdlife, details of which are outlined at the park's entrance.

Himatangi Beach, which is off SH1 between Foxton and Sanson, is considered the region's best. The sand dunes here are up to 19 km wide and make up New Zealand's largest expanse of sand country. This sense of wilderness, together with the driftwood strewn along the tide line, make a trip well worth while.

Taihape → *Colour map 3, B3 Population: 2000.*

North of 'Palmy' on SH1, in the odd little region of **Rangitikei**, is Taihape, a fairly nondescript town quietly serving the local dairy farming industry. At first sight, there appears to be little of interest, other than a few cafés, motels and shops; but there are some notable activities in the area, with fishing leading the way, and some of the major river adventure companies are based in the town. The VIC (I-Site) can provide information about a number of garden visits and heritage tours and, of course, Taihape's famous and very silly **World Gumboot Festival**, which formerly brought some life and 'sole' to the town. Given the town's love of footwear, it would be rude not to take a closer at the giant **corrugated gumboot** beside SH1 at the northern entrance to town.

Mokai Gravity Canyon

① *T0800-802864, www.gravitycanyon.co.nz. From $120 for one activity and $270 for all three.*
Although a good 20 min drive east of SH1 (turn east off SH1 7km south of Taihape), it is well worth taking the diversion to witness, or indeed partake in, the adrenaline pumping (and frankly lunatic) antics at Mokai, an 82-m canyon cut into the landscape by the Hautapu (Rangitikei) River. There are three adventure activities on offer, a 1-km Flying Fox, an 80-m bungee and a 50-m freefall bridge swing. After spectating for a while (which is in itself very entertaining), many cannot resist trying all three activities. But if you were to choose just one the Flying Fox is highly recommended. The other two you can do elsewhere in New Zealand, but the flying fox is unique and a truly memorable (and very

You start 175 m above the canyon and travel the 1 km right through the middle speed of up to 160 kph. It really is like flying.

gaweka → Colour map 3, B3.

ngaweka is best known for its **DC-3**, which sits next to SH1 and houses a café. It is also the ase for **Mangaweka Adventure Company** and **River Valley**, which operate a variety of adventure packages on the river with kayaking a speciality. There is a basic camping ground in the village and local walks established by DoC. ▶▶ See Activities and tours, page 373.

Bulls → Colour map 3, B3 Population: 3,898.

The small agricultural service town of Bulls stands off the junction of SH3 and SH1, midway between Wanganui and Palmerston North. Blink and you'll miss it, but take a closer look and you may be surprised to learn that the township was not named after our four-legged friends, but after James Bull, who was one of the first settlers in 1858. By all accounts he was quite the entrepreneur and created so much of the town's infrastructure that in 1872 the government approved the replacement of the original name for the settlement – Rangitikei – with Bulls. However, our James has a lot to answer for. In the desperate effort to put Bulls on the map, the community has gone to ridiculous lengths to incorporate its name into every one of its amenities. Take a look around and you'll find the VIC (see page 366) named 'Inform-a-Bull', the chemist 'Dispense-a-Bull', the fire station 'Extinguish-a-Bull', the police station 'Const-a-Bull' – and the church, predictably, is 'Forgive-a-Bull'. There are a few omissions, however, including, as you head out on SH3, a sign saying 'Antiques and Collectibles' – clearly owned by the black sheep of the town. Some may find Bulls entertaining, others may find such taste 'Question-a-Bull'.

◉ Palmerston North and around listings

For Sleeping and Eating price codes and other relevant information, see Essentials pages 44-50.

● Sleeping

Palmerston North p366, map p367
Most of the motels are along Fitzherbert Av or the Pioneer Highway.
L Fairway Woods, 17A Montgomery Terr, T06- 356 1854, www.fairwaywoods.co.nz. Large modern homestay overlooking the Manawatu Golf Course. Two luxury en suite rooms and excellent cuisine. Breakfast included, dinner $60 extra.
L-AL Fitzherbert Regency, 250 Fitzherbert Av, T06-355 5155, www.fitzherbertregency. co.nz. New, luxury motor lodge with classy suites, some with spa, broadband.
L-A Kingsgate Hotel, 110 Fitzherbert Av, T06- 356 8059, www.kingsgatepalmerston. co.nz. One of 'Palmy's' few hotels, but doesn't

let the side down. Restaurant, bar, spa and sauna.
AL Cornwall Motel, 101 Fitzherbert Av, T06-354 9010, www.cornwallmotorlodge. co.nz. Modern and well-located. Enjoys a good reputation.
AL Nikau Loft, 93 Monrad St, T06-354 0561, www.nikauloft.co.nz. Very classy self-contained loft, in a quiet area at the southern fringe of the city. Great value.
AL-A Coachman Motel and Suites, 134 Fitzherbert Av, T06-356 5065, www.coach man.co.nz. Pleasant and well appointed, with café, gardens and an open fire.
A Colonial Court, 305 Fitzherbert Av, T06-359 3888, www.colonialcourtmotel.co.nz. A decent option, worth considering.
A Plum Trees Lodge, 97 Russell St, T06-358 7813, www.plumtreeslodge.com. The former coach house and solid timer beams give this B&B an Old English ambience.

Well-appointed and self- contained apartment.

B Boulder Lodge, Pohangina Valley West Rd, Ashhurst, T06-329 4746, www.boulder-lodge.co.nz. Some distance from Palmerston North, this is a popular and isolated self-contained wooden lodge and cabins complex. You arrive by 4WD and can have a bath outside in an open fire heated tub under the stars. It has no electricity but LPG which provides heating and hot showers. Good value.

C-D Peppertree Backpackers, 121 Grey St, T06-355 4054. Old rambling, single storey house close to the town centre. Excellent facilities, open fire and garden.

Motorcamps and campsites
C-D Palmerston North Holiday Park, 133 Dittmer Dr, T06-358 0349, www.holiday parks.co.nz/palmerstonnorth. Rather tired but next to the river and the Esplanade Park.

Taihape *p369*
Ask the VIC about good farmstays in the area.
AL-B Mairenui Rural Retreat, Ruahine Rd, T06-382 5564, www.mairenui.co.nz. Good-value B&B and self-contained options.
A Aspen Court Motel, SH1, Mataroa Rd North, T06-388 1999, www.aspencourt.co.nz. One of the most modern in town, with good facilities.
B Taihape Motels, Kuku and Robin sts, T06-388 0456, www.taihapemotels.co.nz. An older, cheaper option with adequate facilities and close to the centre.
C-D River Valley Lodge, Mangahoata Rd, Pukeokahu, T06-388 1444, www.rivervalley. co.nz. An excellent low to mid-range option in a prime rural location. Full range of rooms including some lovely en suites, tent sites, restaurant/bar and even a sauna and spa. All manner of activities are available from rafting and kayaking to horse trekking and fishing. Various packages available. Recommended. See Activities and tours, page 373.

Motorcamps and campsites
C-D Riverview Holiday Park, Old Abattoir Rd, 3 km north of town, T06-388 0718. Cabins, campervans and tent sites. Camp kitchen.

🍴 Eating

Palmerston North *p366, map p367*
'Palmy' has more restaurants and cafés per head than anywhere else in New Zealand. Most of the high profile eateries are on Cuba St, Broadway Av and George St, just off the main square. Many of the pubs offer good affordable grub. There are various fast food outlets in the Downtown on Broadway mall.
¶¶¶ Bella's Café, 2 The Square, T06-357 8616. Lunch Tue-Sat from 1100, dinner Mon-Sat 1800-late. A popular choice offering a mix of Italian, Thai and traditional Pacific Rim dishes. Cosy atmosphere and great service.
¶¶¶ Dejeuner, 159 Broadway. T06-952 5581, www.dejeuner.co.nz. Mon-Sat 1800-late. A small well-established restaurant offering an imaginative blackboard menu.
¶¶¶ Spostato, 213 Cuba St, T06-952 3400. Daily 1800-late. Italian-style restaurant, at the top end of the Cuba St offerings.
¶¶ Elm Café and Brasserie, 283 Fitzherbert St, T06-355 4418. Daily 0900-1700, Wed-Sat 1830-late. Away from the centre, but worth the effort. Traditional cuisine in rather grand Tuscan-style surroundings.
¶¶ Indian 2Nite, 22 George St, T06-353 7400. From 1730. Arguably the best Indian option with a loyal following.
¶¶ Moxies, 67 George St, T06-355 4238. Daily from 0730. A popular spot for breakfast, lunch and dinner offering an interesting blackboard menu.
¶ Cafe Cuba, 236 Cuba St, T06-356 5750. Mon-Sat. Has mixed reviews but always busy which speaks for itself.
¶ Murphy's Law , see Pubs, bars and clubs, below. Pub lunches in plush surrounds.
¶ Pompeii, 163 The Square, T06-952 5575. Daily from 1700 (deliveries available). For a pizza you can't go far wrong here.

hape *p369*

...here are a number of eateries on Hautapu St.
The Brown Sugar Café, Huia St, T06-388
1880. Daily 0900-1700, Fri-Sun until 2030. The
best café in town with good coffee, breakfasts
and an open fire.
Al Centro, 105 Hautapu St, T06-388 0593.
Tue-Sun from 1700. Decent Italian fare.

🍺 Pubs, bars and clubs

Palmerston North *p366, map p367*
Flying Fish, Regent Arcade, T06-354 7215. A
hip sushi and cocktail bar going off like a
rocket. For discerning locals this is the place
to be seen.
Highflyers, corner of The Square and Main St,
T06-357 5155. For trendsetters and
modernists.
Murphy's Law Irish Bar, 505 Main St,
T06-355 2337. The best bet for traditionalists.

😎 Entertainment

Palmerston North *p366, map p367*
For most performances in the town you can
get more information and book with
Ticketek, Convention Centre, Main St,
T06-358 0000.
Abbey Theatre, 369 Church St, T06-355
4165, www.abbeymusicaltheatre.co.nz. Hosts
mainly musical (rock and pop) events.
Centrepoint Theatre, corner of Pitt and
Church sts, T06-354 5740, www.centre
point.co.nz. Established in 1974, this is one of
the few North Island theatres that can boast its
own full-time professional theatre company.
There are regular shows, many of national
importance, from comedy to classic dramas,
with an emphasis on New Zealand plays.
Downtown Cinemas, Downtown Shopping
Arcade, Broadway Av, T06-355 5656, www.dt
cinemas.co.nz. The city's mainstream cinema.
Regent Theatre, on Broadway,
T06-350 2100, www.regent.co.nz. Formerly
the 'Picture Palace' built in 1929, and

reinvented several times, this latest rebirth is
very impressive. Officially opened in 1998 and
with a seating capacity of almost 1500 it
hosts events such as ballet, musicals,
orchestras and comedy.

🛍 Shopping

Palmerston North *p366, map p367*
Munchkins, 51 Broadway Av, T06-356 4615.
Handmade chocolates, fudges and other
delectable goodies.
Square Edge Creative Centre, corner of The
Square and Church St, www.pncac.org.nz.
Various shops and galleries offering mainly
New Zealand arts and crafts.
Taylor Jensen Gallery, 39 George St, T06-
355 4278, www.finearts.co.nz. For fine art.

🏔 Activities and tours

Palmerston North *p366, map p367*
Brookfields, Te Matai Rd, T06-358 0749. Golf
course.
Feilding Airfield, Taonui, T06-323 8389. Local
gliding club, flights at weekends.
Feilding Golf Course, Feilding, T06-323 8636.
Golf course.
Go 4 Wheels, Ballance, T0800-353122/
T06-3767040, www.go4wheels.co.nz.
One-hour to overnight adventures with trips
to the wind farm a speciality.
Helipro, T06-357 1348, www.helipro.co.nz.
Offers a range of scenic flights including the
City Panorama, $95, 10 mins, and the
Windfarm Wizzer, $210, 20 mins.
Lido Aquatic Centre, Park Rd, T06-357 2684.
Pool open Mon-Thu 0600-2000, Fri 0600-
2100, Sat-Sun 0800-2000. Swimming $2.50.
Timeless Horse Treks, Gorge Rd, Ballance,
T06-376 6157, www.timelesshorsetreks.co.nz.
1- to 2-hr trips including Tararua Wind Farm.

Taihape *p369*
Mokai Gravity Action, based at Mokai Bridge
(off SH1) south of Taihape, T0800-802864,

www.gravitycanyon.co.nz.
Adrenaline-sapping operations include North
Island's highest bungee (80 m, from $120),
New Zealand's longest Flying Fox (1 km) from
$120. See also page 369.
Tarata Fishaway, T06-388 0354,
www.tarata.co.nz. Fly fishing trips on the
Rangitikei. Accommodation available.

Mangaweka *p370*
Mangaweka Adventure Co, Main Rd,
Mangaweka, T0800-655747/T03-382 5744,
www.rra.co.nz. Good river trips including
rafting, kayaking, overnight campouts and
wilderness safaris, half-day from $65, full day
taking in the 80-m canyons of the Rangitikei
(used in the *Lord of the Rings* film trilogy) from
$180. Suitable for families.
River Valley Lodge, T06-388 1444,
www.river valley.co.nz. A wide range of
activities including whitewater rafting ($165),
horse trekking ($105) and inflatable kayaking
($165, hire from $35) and spa (from $20).

Shuttle from Taihape $30 return, excellent
on-site lodging.

Transport

Palmerston North *p366, map p367*
Car hire Rent-a-Dent Car Centre, 133 Cuba
St, T06-357 6694. **Taxi** Taxis Palmerston
North, T06-355 5333.

Directory

Palmerston North *p366, map p367*
Internet Alpha Internet Café, 92 Princess
St; iCafé, 49 Broadway Av; **Library**, 4 The
Square. **Medical services** City Health, 22
Victoria Av, T06-355 3300. Palmerston North
Hospital, Southern Cross, 21 Carroll St,
T06-356 9169. **Police** 400 Church St,
T06-313 600. **Post office** 328 Church St,
Mon-Fri 0830-1730, Sat 0930-1300.

Wanganui → *Colour map 3, B2 Population: 43,300.*

*Wanganui lies at the mouth of the Whanganui River roughly halfway between New Plymouth and
Wellington. Proud of its river and once a bustling port, Wanganui is now principally an agricultural
service town and the southern gateway to the Whanganui River National Park. The town boasts a
rich heritage and retains some fine buildings as well as a reputable museum and many parks and
gardens. In summer the main street is ablaze with a thousand hanging baskets of flowers and
throughout the year the restored steamboat Waimarie plies the great river, reminding both locals
and visitors of days gone by.* ▸▸ *For Sleeping, Eating and other listings, see pages 376-378.*

Ins and outs

Getting there Wanganui airport ① *5 km southwest of town*, is served by **Air New
Zealand Link**, T0800-737000. Flights are met by **Wanganui Taxi**, T06-343 5555. By car,
Wanganui is on the main SH3 coastal route 162 km southwest of New Plymouth and
196 km north of Wellington (via SH1 which joins SH3 at Bulls). SH4 from Te Kuiti (250 km)
ends in Wanganui. **Newmans** and **Intercity** buses stop at The VIC (I-Site). **Dalroys/White
Star**, T0508-465622, operates a service between New Plymouth and Wellington (via
Palmerston North). The VIC (I-Site) facilitates all national bus bookings.

Getting around Wanganui has four looped bus routes run by **Tranzit Citylink (Horizons)**,
T06-345 4433, www.horizons.govt.nz, Mon-Fri (weekends vary), standard fare $3. The
routes start at Maria Place in the centre of town, off Victoria Av, and link the main suburbs,
including Castlecliff on the coast; pick up a timetable from the VIC (I-Site). There is also a

Mail Run service to Pipiriki and the Whanganui National Park via the Whanganui River Road (see page 379).

Tourist information **Wanganui VIC (I-Site)** ① *101 Guyton St, T06-349 0508, www.wanganui.com, www.destinationwanganui.com, www.rivernz.com, Mon-Fri 0830-1700, Sat-Sun 0900-1500*, has details about the Wanganui Heritage Walk and local Arts Trail. **DoC Wanganui Conservancy Office** ① *Ingestre Chambers, 74 Ingestre St, T06-349 2100.*

Sights

Queen's Park was a former British stockade site during the New Zealand Wars of the 1860s and is east of Victoria Avenue. It is essentially the cultural heart of the city and home to the Wanganui Regional Museum, the War Memorial, the Alexander and District Libraries and the Sarjeant Gallery.

The **Wanganui Regional Museum** ① *T06-349 1110, www.wanganui-museum.org.nz, daily 1000-1630, $7.50*, is of particular note due to the rich local history and the influence of the river. There is a fine collection of Maori *taonga* (treasures) in the *Te Atihaunui-a-Paparangi* (Maori Court) including an inevitable collection of *waka* (canoes), the finest of which is the beautifully carved *Te Mata-o-Houra*. Also of interest also is the range of displays showing the ingenious methods and traps the early Maori used to catch fish on the river and birds in the bush. Upstairs there is a large, tired-looking collection of wildlife exhibits, including numerous native birds and moa bones. Temporary galleries feature a programme of changing exhibitions.

A short distance away from the museum, proudly crowning Queen's Park Hill, is the **Sarjeant Gallery** ① *T06-349 0506, www.sarjeant.org.nz, daily 1030-1630, donation*, set in a grand building and reputed to be one of the best in the country. Home to over 4000 permanent artworks, there is an ever-changing programme of local and national touring exhibitions and occasional international shows.

The **Wanganui Riverboat Centre** ① *Taupo Quay, T0800-7832637/T06-347 1863, www.riverboat.co.nz, Mon-Sat 0900-1600, Sun 1000-1600; The Waimarie sails Mon-Fri at 1400 (2 hrs), Sat-Sun 1400 (3 hrs); from $45, child $15, in summer there may be additional lunch and dinner cruises, from $48*, has been a hive of activity in recent years as committed enthusiasts have been hard at work fully restoring the old paddlesteamer *The Waimarie*. This steamer worked the river for 50 years, carrying a wide variety of cargoes and tourists, before she came to grief and sank at her moorings in 1952. In 1993 she was removed from the mud and over the next seven years faithfully restored to be relaunched on the first day of the 21st century. Now, she is sailed proudly up the river daily with a loving crew and cargo of admiring tourists. Although the riverboat centre no longer houses *The Waimarie* there are displays of photographs and memorabilia from the river era. If you do go for a trip be sure to ask if you can take a look at the restored steam engine that pumps the pistons below decks. It is quite a sight and testimony to the loving care and attention that is now bestowed upon the old girl since she was pulled from the mud.

In 2006, another vessel, *The MV Wairoa*, began her second life on the Wanganui. Like *The Waimarie* she served for many years as a passenger and goods vessel back and forth from the city to Pipiriki, before sinking in 1955. Salvaged in 1987 she was lovingly restored and is now used for scheduled picnic cruises to Hipango Park 25 km upstream, from $50, child $20. Consult the centre for the latest cruise schedule.

Immediately across the road from the riverboat centre are the **Moutoa Gardens** which, though unremarkable, are famous as the spot where the deed was believed to be signed

between the New Zealand Company and the Maori for the dubious land deals of
This notoriety and the continued displeasure felt by Maori regarding land deals led t
occupation of these gardens in 1995. High profile court battles followed and an u
confrontation with police was only avoided by face-to-face meetings and thankfully
peaceful end to the 83-day occupation.

Cook's Gardens, which grace the western heart of the town on St Hill Street, are home
to the 1899 colonial-style **Opera House**, the modern **Trust Bank Stadium** (with its
wooden cycling velodrome) and the **Ward Observatory** ① *T025-245 8066, open for
public viewing Fri 2000-2130*. This observatory was originally built in 1901 and houses the
largest telescope of its kind still in use in the country.

Just across the bridge from Taupo Quay is the unusual access to the **Durie Hill** and the
War Memorial Tower. Almost immediately across the bridge, a tunnel takes you 200 m
into the hillside where you can take the **Earthbound Durie Hill Elevator** ① *Mon-Fri
0730-1800, Sat 0900-1700, Sun 1000-1700, $1*. From the top you can then climb the Durie
Hill War Memorial Tower, built of fossilized rock. The view from the top is rather engaging

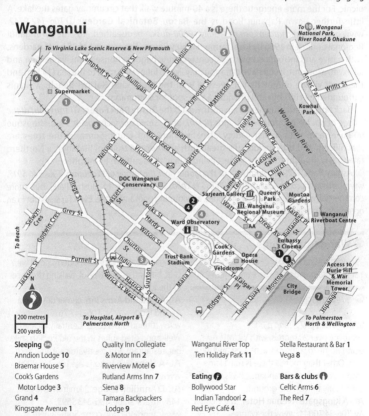

Wanganui

Sleeping	Quality Inn Collegiate	Wanganui River Top	Stella Restaurant & Bar 1
Anndion Lodge 10	& Motor Inn 2	Ten Holiday Park 11	Vega 8
Braemar House 5	Riverview Motel 6		
Cook's Gardens	Rutland Arms Inn 7	**Eating**	**Bars & clubs**
Motor Lodge 3	Siena 8	Bollywood Star	Celtic Arms 6
Grand 4	Tamara Backpackers	Indian Tandoori 2	The Red 7
Kingsgate Avenue 1	Lodge 9	Red Eye Café 4	

a clear day can include Mount Taranaki and Ruapehu, but don't expect to get any photographs of Ruapehu, unless you want a water tower in the way.

There are a number of good parks and gardens in the town and surrounding area. At the top end of Victoria Avenue up the hill is the **Virginia Lake Scenic Reserve** with the usual lake, themed gardens and aviary. There is a nice walk that goes around the lake and once completed you can celebrate by setting off the coin-operated lake fountain.

If you have kids the star attraction in Wanganui has to be the excellent **Kowhai Park** on the eastern bank of the river just across the bridge to Anzac Parade. Here you can find a wonderful array of interactive attractions including a dinosaur slide, a pirate ship, a flying fox, roller beetles and sea serpent swings, as well as the traditional bike and skateboard tracks, all of which will keep them happy for hours.

Wanganui to Hawera

About 5 km northwest of Wanganui, down Rapanui Road (towards the sea) is **Westmere Lake**. Set aside as a wildlife refuge with native bush, it provides a pleasant spot for a picnic. For the more energetic there is a 40-minute walk that circumnavigates the lake. A little further down Rapanui Road is the **Bason Botanical Gardens** ① *T06-342 9742, www.basonbotanicgardens.org.nz, daily 0800-dusk*, bequeathed to the Wanganui Regional Council in 1966 by local farmer Stanley Bason. They consist of 25 ha of gardens, with native and introduced plants, a conservatory, begonia house, camellia garden and lake with a lookout. If you have time you may like to follow the road to the sea (14 km) and the small village of Mowhanau, blessed with the black-sand **Kai Iwi Beach**, which is surrounded by cliffs but still provides a safe spot for swimming.

Back on SH3 and a further 20 km northwest is the **Bushy Park Forest** ① *turn right at the village of Kai Iwi and follow the signs (8 km), daily, small entry charge*. It's a picturesque 90-ha reserve with a rich variety of native flora and fauna. Some of the trees are magnificent and they include the great girth and twisted trunk of 'Ratanui', a Northern rata that is thought to be the largest living rata in the southern hemisphere.

Ashley Park ① *29 km northwest of Wanganui near the village of Waitotara, T06- 346 5917, www.ashleypark.co.nz, daily 0900-1700, $4, child $2*, is similar to Bushy Park, but more commercial, with farm animals, pony rides, a swimming pool and a café. Even fur seals put in an occasional appearance.

◉ Wanganui listings

For Sleeping and Eating price codes and other relevant information, see Essentials pages 44-50.

⊜ Sleeping

Wanganui *p373, map p375*
There are over 20 motels, with Victoria Av being home to some of the newest and the best. Other than motels there is not a large amount of choice in Wanganui; B&Bs are particularly thin on the ground.
AL-A Kingsgate Avenue Hotel, 379 Victoria Av, T06-349 0044, www.theavenue

wanganui.com. Glorified modern motel with café, bar and outdoor pool, walking distance to the town.
AL-A Rutland Arms Inn, corner of Victoria Av and Ridgeway St, T06-347 7677, www.rutland-arms.co.nz. Centrally located. Well-appointed suites in the old English style. Bar, restaurant and courtyard café attached.
AL-A Siena, 355 Victoria Av, T06-345 9009, www.siena.co.nz.
AL-D Anndion Lodge, 2 km from the CBD, 143 Anzac Parade, T06-343 3593, www.anndionlodge.co.nz. Somewhere

between a modern backpacker hostel and a motel this rates as one of the best places in the North Island. It offers modern and tidy riverside accommodation, with rooms ranging from super-king to dorms at reasonable prices. Well equipped with spa, internet, off-street parking. Recommended.
A Cook's Gardens Motor Lodge, corner of Guyton and Purnell sts, T06-345 6003, www.cooksgardens.info.
A Quality Inn Collegiate Hotel and Motor Inn, 122 Liverpool St, T06-345 8309, www.collegiatemotorinn.co.nz.
A Riverview Motel, 14 Somme Parade, T06-345 2888, www.wanganuimotels.co.nz.
AL-B Grand Hotel, corner of St Hill and Guyton sts, T06-345 0955, www.thegrand hotel.co.nz. A 1920s hotel in the heart of town. Nothing spectacular but good value with, spa, bar and good restaurant attached. Internet.
C-D Braemar House YHA, 2 Plymouth St, T06-348 2301, www.braemarhouse.co.nz. YHA affiliate, large renovated villa and round the corner from the **Tamara**. Comfortable and more sedate, off-street parking.
C-D Tamara Backpackers Lodge, 24 Somme Parade, T06-347 6300, www.tamaralodge.co.nz. Closer to the CBD than **Braemar** and well established. Very good backpacker hostel with a l ocally streetwise manager, set in a large 2-storey villa overlooking the river. A range of older rooms or units with own bathroom. Large garden, free bike hire, internet, off-street parking. River trips organized.

Motorcamps and campsites
C-D Wanganui River Top 10 Holiday Park, 460 Somme Parade, T06-343 8402, T0800-272664, www.wrivertop10.co.nz. A bit out of the centre but worth the drive. Quiet, modern facilities next to the river, spa, kayak hire.

Wanganui to Hawera p376
A-D Bushy Park Homestead, T06- 342 9879, www.bushypark-homestead.co.nz. Built in 1906, this homestead provides grand B&B and budget accommodation.

B-D Ashley Park, SH3, Waitotara, T06-346 5917. Motel, B&B, farmstay and campsite.

🍴 Eating

Wanganui p373, map p375
🍴 **Bollywood Star Indian Tandoori Restaurant**, 88 Guyton St, T06-345 9996. Lunch Tue-Sun 1100-1500, daily for dinner from 1800. Licensed. The best Indian in town.
🍴 **Vega Restaurant**, overlooking the river, 49 Taupo Quay, T06-349 0078. Lunch Tue-Sun, daily for dinner. Licensed. Classy establishment set in a converted warehouse that has quickly earned a reputation as the city's finest, especially for seafood. Excellent wine list.
🍴 **Stellar Restaurant and Bar**, 2 Victoria Av, T06-345 7278. Fri-Sat from 0800-1400, Sun-Thu 0800-2300. Popular sports bar and nightclub with live music that also enjoys a good reputation for traditional New Zealand fare.
🍴 **Red Eye Café**, 96 Guyton St, T06-345 5646. Tue-Sat 0830-late. Live jazz 1st Sun of the month 1000-1500. Has a loyal following and serves a good coffee.

🍺 Pubs, bars and clubs

Wanganui p373, map p375
For the inevitable Irish-style offerings try **Rosie O'Grady's**, attached to the Grand Hotel, Guyton St; and **Celtic Arms**, 437 Victoria Av, T06-3477037.
The Red, Anzac Parade. Along with the **Rutland Arms**, this is one of the main pubs in town, also offering à la carte dining.
Rutland Arms Inn, see above. Seems to attract a friendly clientele.

🎭 Entertainment

Wanganui p373, map p375
Embassy 3 Cinema, 34 Victoria Av, T06-345 7958. For details about other up-and-coming performances contact the VIC.

Royal Wanganui Opera House, on the edge of Cooks Gardens, St Hill St, T06-349 0511, www.royaloperahouse.co.nz. Small but very grand and a regular venue for touring shows.

⊛ Festivals

Wanganui *p373, map p375*
Dec-Mar Wanganui in Bloom. The streets are adorned with 1000 hanging baskets of flowers. The highlight is the festival and **Heritage Weekend** in Mar, when there are various events including a raft race, vintage car procession and street bands.
Mar Wanganui Artists Open Studios Weekend (last 2 weekends). This nationally recognized festival offers a fine opportunity to sample the (considerable) local talent in the towns fine galleries. The *Arts Trail* leaflets from the VIC provide information. **Wanganui Arts Festival** is a more high profile biennial event that takes place over the course of a week; next held end Mar 2012.

▲ Activities and tours

Wanganui *p373, map p375*
For all river activities based in or around Wanganui, see page 383. Note that there is a **Mail Run Tour** service operating to Pipiriki and the Whanganui National Park via the Whanganui River Road (see page 379).

Mountain biking
As well as being the main gateway to the national park, Wanganui is known for its excellent mountain biking. Favoured tracks include **Lismore Forest, Hylton Park, Bushy Park Loop, Whanganui River Road** and **Pauri Village Forest**. The VIC can provide details. **Wanganui Pro Cycle Centre**, 199 Victoria Av, T06-345 3715. Bike hire and advice.

⊖ Transport

Wanganui *p373, map p375*
Car hire Avis, 192 Guyton St, T06-348 7528. Rent-a-Dent, 26 Churton St, T06-345 1505.
Taxi Wanganui Taxis, T06-343 5555.

❶ Directory

Wanganui *p373, map p375*
Internet Available at the VIC (I-Site) and the library, Queen's Park, T06-349 1000, Mon-Fri 0900-2000, Sat 0900-1630. **Post office** 226 Victoria Av (between Ingestre and Plymouth sts), T06-345 4103, Mon-Fri 0830-1730, Sat 0900-1300. **Medical services** After Hours, 163 Wicksteed St, T06-348 0333. Wanganui Hospital, Heads Rd, T06- 348 1234. **Police** Bell St, T06-349 0600.

Whanganui National Park → Colour map 3, A3.

*Springing from high on the volcanic slopes of Tongariro National Park, the Whanganu.
its 290-km journey to the sea, carving its way through some of the most remote and ir.
country in the North Island. At its most remote mid to lower reaches, it cuts deep in to the s.
and mudstone and is joined by tracts of intact lowland forest, which form the heart .
Whanganui National Park. Although the river is not the longest in the North Island (that hor.
goes to the Waikato) it has been the longest navigable river for generations. As a result the river .
rich in both Maori and European history, from the first days of early exploration and settlement
through to the river's renaissance as a tourist and recreational attraction. Although the entire area is
hard to access (which is undoubtedly part of its charm), there is the opportunity to explore the
historical sites of the river and enjoy its atmosphere. You can do this, in part on its banks by road and
walking tracks, or on the river itself by jet boat or kayak. ▸▸ For Sleeping, Eating and other listings, see
pages 382-384.*

Ins and outs

Getting there and around The three principal gateway settlements to the river are
Taumarunui to the north, **Raetihi** to the northwest and **Wanganui** to the south. Physical
access to the river and the park is from six main access points: from the north, **Ohinepane**,
21 km downriver from Taumarunui; from the east, **Whakahoro** (linked to SH4 by roads from
Owhango and Raurimu), **Pipiriki** (accessible from Raetihi), and **Ohura Road** (from SH4
north of Raetihi); from the south via the **River Road** off SH4 (just north of Wanganui) to
Pipiriki; and from the west via way of **Stratford/Ohura Road** (SH43) where Brewer Road and
Mangaehu Road lead on to Kohi Saddle and the Matemateaonga Track. As well as the **Mail
Run** service from Wanganui to Pipiriki, T06-347 7534, www.whanganuitours.co.nz, most
tour operators provide transport in and out of the park for $60 return. Other than that you
are on your own.

Both the backroads, tracks and the river itself are subject to slips and flooding so
always consult the **DoC** before attempting a major excursion. Summer is the busiest and
safest time to visit the park. During this time you are advised to pre-book all
accommodation.

Tourist information Before heading into the park stock up on all the information available
at the **DoC** offices in Wanganui, 74 Ingestre St, www.doc.govt.nz. They deal with all
information enquiries and hut/campsite bookings and fees. There are a number of good
books available about the river and the park (available from main DoC offices) while DoC
produces detailed leaflets, including the helpful *In and Around Whanganui National Park*
and the *Whanganui Journey*. They also stock the recommended publication *Guide to the
Whanganui River* ($10).

Whanganui River Road

Due to its inaccessible nature it takes some effort, and almost certainly a trip on the river
itself, to get a proper feel for the park and the river (see Activities and tours, page 383).
However, if you are short of time or if you don't fancy getting your feet wet, the best way
to make your acquaintance with the park is via the Whanganui River Road.

This windy scenic road branches off SH4 15 km north of Wanganui and follows the river
to Pipiriki, before turning inland to Raetihi where it rejoins SH4. The entire trip is 106 km

road is slow and for the most part unsealed, it can be done comfortably
...urs. As well as the scenery itself, there are a number of small historically
...ttlements, specific historic sites, *marae* and some fine short- to
...gth walks along the way.

...outh to north after the Aramoana Walkway and Lookout (now closed) the road
...e river proper. The first specific point of interest is the *Pungarehu Wharenui*
...ng house), just before the settlement of **Parikino**, which used to be located on the
...er side of the river and now occupies a former Maori village. Just after Parikino the
...ad cuts into a series of **Oyster Shell Bluffs** (once seabed) before reaching **Atene**
(Athens), the first of a number of mission settlements created in the 1840s by the
Reverend Richard Taylor. Just before the village is the access point to the **Atene Skyline
Track**. This recently upgraded DoC track crosses farmland before climbing to take in
rewarding views of the entire region before continuing to rejoin the River Road further
north (viewpoint 1½ hours return; full walk six to eight hours).

The next settlement and former mission settlement is **Koriniti** (Corinth). Formerly the
Maori settlement of Otukopiri, it still retains a *marae* that welcomes visitors. The Anglican
Church dates back to 1920. Keep your eyes open here too for flood markers, one of which
is half way up a barn, providing a reminder of the dangers of the river. The **Operiki Pa**, just
north of Koriniti, was the original home of the Koriniti Maori and the site of the first
Anglican Church built in 1840. About 6 km further north is the **Kawana Flour Mill**, a
restored example from 1854. Both the mill and the cottage are a short walk from the main
road and well worth a quick look. **Ranana** (London) is the next settlement. Ranana was
one of the largest former mission settlements first established in the 1890s and its church
is still in use today.

After Ranana is **Hiruharama** (Jerusalem) the most picturesque of all the former
missions. Originally a larger Maori village known as Patiarero, it was once home to famous
New Zealand poet James Baxter and French Sister Mary Aubert whose Catholic mission
still remains to this day. You can visit the church that was built in the late 1800s. From here
the road climbs to a fine viewpoint and the **Omorehu Waterfall Lookout** before
delivering you at **Pipiriki**. Pipiriki used to be the major tourist destination at the turn of
the century, complete with a large hotel. These days, although not so blessed with
luxurious accommodation, it is still an important settlement, serving as the main
southern gateway to the heart of the national park via the river itself. Although the large
hotel, Pipiriki House, that once stood here has long since burnt down, a former **Colonial
House** ① *summer 1000-1600, $1, child $0.50*, remains and serves as a small museum and
information centre, as well as a reminder of the former glory days.

The small DoC office in Pipiriki can assist with information and also provides overnight
parking. On the way you will pass the rather sorry remains of the former 1903 steamer *MV
Ongarue*, which plied the river until the late 1950s. Although restored in 1983 and placed
high and dry on the hill for all to see, she is clearly much in need of some attention and a
new lick of paint. From Pipiriki the road then turns inland and winds its way for 27 km to
the small township of Raetihi, where it rejoins SH4.

One of the major man-made 'sights' within the park is the very aptly named '**Bridge to
Nowhere**'. Built in 1936 to provide access for a remote rural pioneer settlement, it never
really served its intended purpose after the project was abandoned with the advent of the
Second World War. Regenerating bush quickly covered the track and the bridge is all that
remains. It is located about 30 km upstream from Pipiriki and can only be reached from
the river by jet-boat, canoe or by a three-day walk.

Whanganui National Park

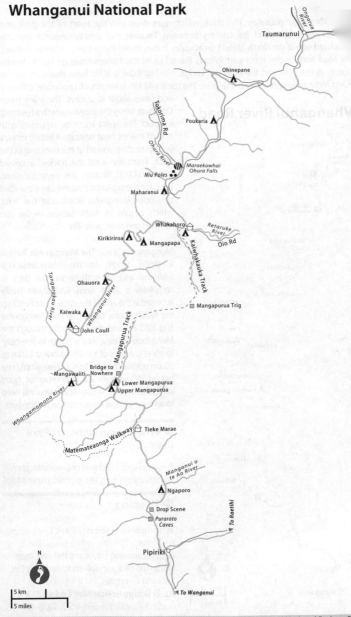

Taumarunui

Ongarue River

Ohinepane

Tokorima Rd

Poukaria

Ohura River

Maraekowhai
Ohura Falls

Niu Poles

Maharanui

Whakahoro

Retaruke River

Oio Rd

Kirikiriroa

Mangapapa

Kaiwhakauka Track

Tangarakau River

Ohauora

Whanganui River

Kaiwaka

John Coull

Mangapurua Trig

Mangapurua Track

Bridge to Nowhere

Mangawaiiti

Lower Mangapurua
Upper Mangapurua

Whangamomona River

Matemateaonga Walkway

Tieke Marae

Mangui o te Ao River

Ngaporo

Drop Scene

Puraroto Caves

To Raetihi

Pipiriki

N

5 km
5 miles

To Wanganui

ping

...ateaonga Walkway This track, which goes deep into the heart of the park and
...es thick bush-clad hill country between Taranaki and the Whanganui River, is
...idered one of the North Island's great walks. It uses an old Maori trail and former settlers'
...y road and for the most part follows the ridges of the Matemateaonga Range before
...riving at the river and the Ramanui Lodge. The highlight is a 1½-hour diversion up the
...730-m Mount Humphries for a fine view. The track is 42 km in length, of 'moderate' difficulty

Whanganui River Road

and takes about four days. There are three
DoC huts along the way for which a fee must
be paid. Transport must be arranged with
one of the jet boat operators either to pick
you up or drop you off at the river end of the
track. From the west the track is accessed
from SH43 at Strathmore, near Stratford.
Look for the signpost that indicates the road
to Upper Mangaehu Road and the track
which begins at Kohi Saddle. ▸▸ See also
Activities and tours, page 384.

Mangapurua Track The Mangapurua Track is
a similar length to the Matemateaonga
Walkway and takes three to four days to
complete. It starts from Whakahoro (easily
accessed at the end of the Whakahoro Road) up
the Kaiwhakauka Valley past the Mangapurua
Trig (663 m) and then descends through the
Mangapurua Valley, via the 'Bridge to Nowhere'
to meet the river at the Mangapurua Landing,
30 km upstream from Pipiriki. There is only one
hut at Whakahoro but a number of good
campsites along the way. Again, you will need
to arrange jet boat transportation back to base.

◉ Whanganui National Park listings

*For Sleeping and Eating price codes and other
relevant information, see Essentials pages 44-50.*

⊜ Sleeping

Whanganui National Park *p379, maps
p381 and p382*
Both the walking tracks and the river itself
within the park are well-endowed with DoC
huts and campsites.
AL-D Bridge to Nowhere Lodge, 21 km
north of Pipiriki, T06-385 4622, T025-480308,

www.bridgetonowhere.co.nz. In addition to the DoC facilities and the *marae*, this is a very popular option. Set in a very remote spot on the riverbank in the heart of the park, access is either by boat or on foot, which makes the place very special. There is B&B (and dinner if required), cabin and campsite accommodation, along with a bar and positively exquisite home cooking. Guided tours to the 'bridge' via jetboat are also available via Pipiriki, from $115.

Whanganui River Road *p379, maps p381 and p382*
A Rivertime Lodge, Parikino, T06-342 5595, www.rivertimelodge.co.nz. 1000-ha hill farm with self-catering homestay. One en suite and 2 twins with shared facilities. The lodge is only 4 km from the Atene Skyline Track.
B Flying Fox, Koriniti, T06-342 8160, www.theflyingfox.co.nz. The Flying Fox is on the western bank of the river and is only accessible by an exciting aerial cableway or by jet boat. The accommodation is full of character and consists of 2 self-contained cottages and campsites. There is a very cute outdoor wood-fired bath, some fine 'home brew' to sample and the home cooking is superb. Recommended.
B Kohu Cottage, 3154 Whanganui River Rd, T06-342 8178, kohu.cottage@xtra.co.nz. Renovated and peaceful riverside cottage sleeps 3-4.
B Operiki Farmstay, Operiki, T06-342 8159 operiki@xtra.co.nz. Traditional single storey house farmstay close to the river. One double and one twin, dinner on request. Friendly hosts and good value.
D Koriniti Marae, Koriniti, T06-342 8198 www.koriniti.com. An ideal opportunity to stay at an authentic *marae*. A traditional *hangi*, flax weaving lessons and *waka* (canoe) cruises under the banner of the full 'Marae Experience' is available from $190. Recommended.

Campsites
D DoC, Pipiriki, T06-385 5022.
D Kauika Campsite, near Ranana, T06-342 8061.

▲ Activities and tours

Whanganui National Park *p. p381 and p382*
There are numerous options available exploring the river from simple indepen and self-guided canoe hire, to single- or multi-day kayak trips, jet-boat trips and mur. day tramps. The various operators can supply all the necessary equipment (including camping gear). As well as the designated DoC huts and campsites along the way there is a comfortable B&B Lodge (Ramanui) in the heart of the park. Note that if you do go it alone, especially tramping, the tracks essentially end at the river and pick-ups will have to be arranged. If you are alone this may be costly, so careful logistics are sometimes necessary to time your arrivals and departures with scheduled tour trips.

Kayaking
The Whanganui is very popular with kayakers and canoeists due to its sheer length – and the 239 listed rapids along the way. But it is fairly unique in this sense, in that for almost its entire length the rapids are of a grade suitable for beginners. There are a wide range of trips available from 5 days (Taumarunui to Pipiriki) to just a few hours. There are designated DoC huts and campsites with basic amenities, throughout the park for use by kayakers and trampers. Note fees apply and bookings are required. Kayaking trips can be done independently or with the various tour operators, most of whom access the river from the north. The best time to embark on a major trip is in the summer, though more experienced canoeists sometimes tackle the river after winter rains. Costs vary but standard independent canoe or kayak (Canadian) hire starts at about $75. A trip with a tour operator, which includes all equipment, will cost you about $85-110 per day. DoC charges the Great Walks Hut and Campsite Pass fee of $45 for hut and campsite use in peak season 1 Oct-30 Apr. In the off season standard backcountry hut/campsite rates apply.

Taumarunui, T07-895 5261, www.blazingpaddles.co.nz. ...ay trips. Canadian or kayak. ... from $250 for full 5-day trip. ...ptional.

...to Nowhere, Bridge to Nowhere ...e, T06-348 7122, ...w.bridgetonowhere.co.nz. 1- to 2-day ...etboat in, canoe back' options.

Canoe Safaris, Ohakune, T06-385 9237, www.canoesafaris.co.nz. Canoe and rafting trips throughout the area, fully guided and catered. Whanganui 2- to 5- day guided trips from $365, all-inclusive.

Wade's Landing Outdoors, Whakahoro, T06-895 5995/T0800-226631, www.whanganui.co.nz. Canoe, kayak and jet-boat trips (including combinations thereof), tramping drop-offs. Flexible itineraries.

AwaTours, Ohakune, T06-385 8297, www.wakatours.com. 3-day guided Canadian canoe trip with a Maori cultural and environmental edge, including a stay and *hangi* at the Koriniti Marae from $650.

Yeti Tours, Ohakune, T0800-322388/ T06-385 8197, www.canoe.co.nz. Luxury or economy 2- to 10-day trips, from $375. Recommended for the longer excursion.

Jet boating
Since the 1980s, jet boats have been the principal fast transport link up and down the river. There are various operators providing sightseeing trips from 15 mins to 2 days (including the drop-off for the 40-min 'Bridge to Nowhere' walk) and pick-ups from the river

ends of the Matemateaonga Walkway and Mangapurua Track. Again costs vary but a 5-hr trip to the bridge will cost about $95.

Bridge to Nowhere Jetboat Tours, Pipiriki, T0800-480308/T06-3854622, www.bridgeto nowhere.co.nz. 4 hrs, $115. All trips depart from Pipiriki (see page 380).

Wade's Landing Outdoors, Whakahoro, T06-895 5995. Canoe, kayak and jet-boat trips. Flexible itineraries.

Whanganui River Adventures, T06-385 3246/T0800-862743, www.riverspirit.co.nz. Trips from Pipiriki to Bridge to Nowhere, from $115.

Tramping
From 1 Oct-30 Apr you must buy a hut and campsite pass from DoC (or VIC and some operators) before staring your journey. This pass costs $45 youth $22.50. In the off-season standard backcountry hut/campsite rates apply. Concessions are available for some canoe and jet boat trips. Campsites provide a water supply, toilets and shelters with benches for cooking. Huts have bunks, stoves, benches, tables and cooking facilities. In winter campsites are free while hut users must have hut tickets or an annual hut pass. The **Teieke Hut** on the eastern riverbank near the Matemateaonga Landing is fairly unusual in that it is also a *marae*, (traditional protocol must be observed).

As well as the **Bridge to Nowhere** track which is accessible only by jet boat canoe or by foot there are 2 main tramps in the park: the Matemateaonga Walkway and the Mangapurua Track, see page 382.

Contents

...ington

★ Don't miss ...
1 Mount Victoria, page 389.
2 Waterfront, page 391.
3 Museum of Wellington, page 391.
4 Te Papa Museum of New Zealand, page 393.
5 Botanic Gardens and Cable Car, page 394.
6 Cuba Street and Courtenay Place, page 401.
7 Kapiti Island, page 408.

N

5 km

5 miles

Although Wellington is the nation's capital it enjoys a s.
atmosphere. And with its surrounding hills, generally cor
layout and well-preserved historical buildings, it has far mo
character than sprawling Auckland or monotonously flat
Christchurch. Wellington is a vibrant, cosmopolitan city, noted
its arts and café culture, with almost as many restaurants and café
per capita as New York. Its most famous visitor attraction, the
multi-million dollar 'Te Papa' Museum, is on the city's recently
revamped and buzzing waterfront. Some of the best shopping in
the country can also be found in the compact city centre. If you
are heading for the South Island by ferry, you will inevitably
encounter Wellington and you are advised to give it more than a
cursory glance before boarding the ferry.

To the east of the city are the rather unremarkable commuter
towns of Upper and Lower Hutt, from where you can reach the
beautiful, off-the-beaten-track region of the Wairarapa, with its
remote coastline. First, though, you must negotiate the Rimutakas
(known as 'the hill'), a natural barrier that has always prevented
the spread and pace of settlement and development. To the north,
major rail and road links hug the scenic Kapiti coastline, with its
pleasant coastal towns and their associated beaches and
attractions – the most noteworthy being the nature reserve of
Kapiti Island looming a short distance offshore.

→ For Sleeping, Eating and other listings see pages 397-406.

...re

...gton airport ① *Miramar, 6 km south of the centre, T04-385 5100, www.well ...port.co.nz*, is highly modern and efficient, handling both international and ...ic flights. It is perhaps the most infamous airport in the country due to its short ...ay, nestled precariously between populated hillsides. During southerly storms the ...s often shows the latest 'interesting' landing from Wellington. The fact you can ...actically make eye contact with the residents in the houses on the hillsides, makes arrival by air rather memorable. Although there are dozens of Trans-Tasman and **Pacific Island** flights per week, Wellington primarily operates a domestic schedule, with regular daily flights from most principal centres. **Air New Zealand**, T0800-737000, www.airnewzealand.co.nz, **Jetstar**, T0800-800995, www.jetstar.com, and **Pacific Blue**, T0800-670000, www.pacificblue.co.nz, are the main carriers. A number of smaller operators fly from upper South Island destinations. These include **Sounds Air**, T0800-505005, www.soundsair.co.nz, which offers regular and very reasonable fares from Picton (from $89 one way) and **Air2there.com**, T0800-777000, which operates from Nelson and Blenheim. The terminal has all the usual facilities including food outlets, shops, left luggage, visitor information and car rental companies. There are plenty of taxis to meet you and the fare into town is about $30. Shuttle buses can be shared for about $15, T04-472 9552. Shuttles and taxis depart from outside the baggage claim area. The **MetlinkAirport Flyer**, T0800-801700, runs a regular bus service between the airport and the city, $8, Mon-Fri 0545-2120, Sat and Sun 0530-2030.

Rail The train station is next to the quay on Bunny Street and has an information centre, T0800-692378. **TranzScenic** operates the daily 'Overlander' service from Auckland, T0800-872467, T04-495 0775, www.tranzscenic.co.nz. **Metlink**, T0800-801700, www.metlink.co.nz, offers regular daily services from the Wairarapa including Martinborough (bus link) and Masterton direct.

Road Wellington is 658 km from Auckland. The principal route is via SH1. SH2 is the principal route to the Wairarapa and the east coast. **Intercity** T04-3850520 and **Nakedbus**, www.nakedbus.com, are the principal bus companies and arrive and depart from the train station. **White Star/Dalroys**, T0508465622, operates services to Palmerston North, Wanganui and New Plymouth. Tickets are available from the VIC (I-Site).

Getting around

Wellington city centre is quite compact and best explored on foot. There is also a wealth of well-marked walking tracks around the city, with some interesting highlights and views (ask at the VIC for details).

Parking can be a nightmare in the city centre. It is heavily metered and mercilessly patrolled. If you struggle to find a spot in the centre, try the 'park and display' areas around the railway station, north and south of the centre, and at the 'Te Papa' Museum; you can walk from there to the centre.

Metlink buses operate throughout greater Wellington daily 0700-2300. For information call T0800-801700, www.metlink.co.nz, and get your hands on the free *Wellington bus and train guide* from the VIC (I-Site). For taxi, car rental and bike hire, see page 406.

Metlink runs regular daily services between Wellington City and Upper
and Paraparaumu. There are also services to the Wairarapa and Palmersto
information call **Metlink**, T0800-801700, www.metlink.co.nz.

Orientation
Wellington is easy to negotiate, unless you are in a car and swept away on its one
systems. However, all roads lead to the centre, which is sandwiched between the hills
the waterfront, and those arriving by road will be delivered right into the heart, within
stone's throw of Lambton Quay, the main business and shopping street. Lambton then
doubles back north to meet Molesworth Street, Thorndon and the Parliament District.
The harbour, with its merging main roads (north to south) of Waterloo and Aotea Quay,
Customhouse, Jervois, Cable Street and Oriental Parade, sweeps back south and east,
encompassing the modern and highly developed waterfront, including the dominant 'Te
Papa' Museum. From the heart of the waterfront south, Willis and Jervois connect with
Victoria, Cuba and Courtenay places, where you'll find many restaurants and cafés.
Behind the CBD are the spacious Botanical Gardens and hillside suburb of Kelburn.
Dominating the view southeast is Mount Victoria, a 'must see' lookout and an ideal place
to get your bearings.

Tourist information
Wellington VIC (I-Site) ① *corner of Wakefield and Victoria sts, T04-802 4860, www.well
ingtonnz.com, Mon-Fri 0830-1800, Sat-Sun 0930-1700.***Upper Hutt VIC (I-Site)** ① *CBD
Towers, 90 Main St, Upper Hutt, T04-527 2141, www.upperhuttcity.com, Mon-Fri 0800-1700,
Sat-Sun 0900-1500.* **Hutt City (Lower Hutt) VIC (I-Site)** ① *The Pavilion, 25 Laings Rd, Lower
Hutt, T04-560 4715, www.huttvalleynz.com, Mon-Fri 0900-1700, Sat-Sun 1000-1600.*
DoC ① *18 Manners St, T04-384 7770, www.doc.govt.nz, Mon-Fri 0900-1630, Sat-Sun
1000-1500.* Useful free guides include: *Wellington Visitors' Guide, What's On Wellington*,
the *Wellington Arts Map, Wellington Wine Food and Shopping* and the *Wellington Fashion
Map*. The weekly newspaper *Capital Times* is also designed for visitors. The main daily
newspaper in the lower North Island is the *Dominion Post*.

Sights

Mount Victoria Lookout
Most of Wellington's major attractions are within walking distance or a short bus ride
from each other. An ideal spot to get your bearings, is the 196-m Mount Victoria Lookout
① *take a No 20 bus (Highbury)*. Although from a distance the wooded sides of the mount
hardly seem in character with the film trilogy *Lord of the Rings*, it proved both a
convenient and aesthetically suitable location for several scenes depicting 'The Shire' in
the first film, the *Fellowship of the Ring*. It was also here that the four Hobbits hid from the
evil Nazgul. Looking southeast from the city centre Mount Victoria is not hard to miss, but,
to the uninitiated, reaching the lookout can be somewhat akin to an expedition up K2.
The best ascent is by car. Head straight for the hill up Majoribanks Road at the bottom of
Courtenay Place. From Majoribanks turn left on to Hawker, carry on up Moeller, Pallister,
and then Thane. The entrance to the lookout is on the right, off Thane. If you get lost in the
web of residential hillside streets, just keep going up and eventually you will reach the
summit. You might like to investigate the **Byrd Memorial**, a rather modernist edifice
pointing south towards the Antarctic, in honour of the American Admiral Richard Byrd.

...ectacular at sunrise and after dark. If you are on foot, the summit is part of ...n Walkway'; leaflets are available from the VIC.

...entary District

...liamentary District is centred on and around Bowen Street, in the Lambton ...er just west of the rather grand looking **railway station** building. Standing on ...bton Quay or Bowen Street you will be immediately struck by the rather odd and ...tly named **Beehive**, which houses the various government offices. Designed by British architect, Sir Basil Spence, and built in 1980, it is either loved or hated. Far more pleasing is the 1922 **Parliament House** ① *T04-471 9503; tours Mon-Fri 1000-1600, Sat 1000-1500, Sun 1200-1500, 1 hr, free*. And next door to that is the **Parliamentary Library**, which is older still. There is an excellent **visitor centre** in the ground floor foyer of Parliament House. Regular tours are available and you can also see parliament in session.

While in the vicinity of Parliament House take a peek or stop for lunch in the **Backbencher Pub**, across the road on Molesworth Street facing the High Court. Adorning the walls are some superb cartoons and *Spitting Image*-style dummies of past and present prime ministers. The best has to be the less than flattering one of Rob Muldoon (perhaps New Zealand's most famous prime minister), which is particularly grotesque, looking for all the world like an alien slug – or 'Jabba the Hut' from *Star Wars*.

Just a short stroll from the **Backbencher Pub** on Lambton Quay is the historic **Old Government Buildings** ① *partially open to visitors, T04-472 7356*, built in 1876 to house the Crown Ministers and public servants of the day. It has an interesting interior with a rather grand staircase and cabinet room, but it is worthy of above average scrutiny externally as well. The building was designed to look like stone but actually constructed of wood and is the second largest wooden building in the world (the largest being the Todaiji Temple in Nara City, Japan). An expensive restoration was completed in 1996 and it now houses the Victoria University's Law Faculty. Also in the Parliamentary District is the **National Library Gallery** ① *5b-7b Molesworth St, T04-474 3000, Mon-Fri 0900-1700, Sat 0900-1300*, with its impressive collection of research books, colonial photographs and in-house gallery. It also has a shop and a café.

From the library, heading towards the water is the **Archives New Zealand** ① *10 Mulgrave St, Thorndon, T04-499 5595, www.archives.govt.nz, Mon-Fri 0900-1700, free*. Within its hallowed walls are a number of important historical documents including the original and controversial 'Treaty of Waitangi'.

Also on Mulgrave Street is the **Old St Paul's Cathedral** ① *T04-473 6722, daily 1000-1700, free*, an 1866 Gothic-style church adapted from traditional stone to native timbers. It is worth a look, not only to see the superb timberwork of the interior, but also the impressive stained-glass windows.

The suburb of **Thorndon**, to which the Parliamentary District essentially belongs, is the oldest and most historic in Wellington. Tinakori Road (www.tinakoriroad.co.nz), Thorndon, is a lovely historic area of Wellington, and has, over the years, been home to many of New Zealand's well known writers, artists and musicians. There's consequently a lovely range of galleries and shops selling antiques, clothing, gifts and books as well as cafés and restaurants. The *Thorndon Heritage Trail* leaflet (available from the VIC) outlines historical sites in the area. Two notable examples are the 1843 **Premier House** (still the official Prime Minister's residence) on Tinakori Road and, further north at 25 Tinakori Road, the **Katherine Mansfield Birthplace** ① *T06-473 7268, www.katherinemansfield.com, Tue-Sun 1000-1600, $5.50*. Mansfield is generally hailed as New Zealand's most famous writer, having penned many

internationally well-known short stories. Some of thos~
Birthday) feature this house, where she lived until she w~
have been faithfully restored and there is an interesting vide~

Civic Square and the waterfront

Civic Square, just behind the VIC (I-Site), was given a major revamp in ~
is blessed with some interesting architectural features. These includ~
striking Nikau Palm columns adorning the modernistic **Public Libr~**
imaginative and beautiful silver fern orb, cleverly suspended above the cen~
square. Civic Square is often used for outdoor events and also houses the **City**
ⓘ *T04-801 3952, www.citygallery.org.nz, daily 1000-1700, $10, child $8; the Nikau ca~*
the ground floor is recommended. With Wellington considered the artistic heart of tr~
nation, the gallery strives (successfully it would seem) to present a regular programme of
the very best of contemporary visual arts. There is an impressive array of media on show
and the gallery also hosts special events, film screenings and performances.

Also in the square is the kids' paradise of **Capital E** ⓘ *T04-913 3740, www.capitale.
org.nz, open during events and exhibitions only.* Described as 'an inner city children's
events centre' it offers an ever-changing agenda of experiences, events and exhibitions.
You won't be surprised to learn that there is a large and expensive toyshop attached.

From Civic Square it is a short walk across the very arty **City to Sea Bridge**, which
connects the square with the waterfront. The bridge sprouts a number of interesting
sculptures that celebrate the arrival of the Maori in New Zealand.

The **waterfront** has become a major focus in the city for its museums, aesthetics and
recreational activities. Stretching from the modern landscaped milieu of '**Waitangi Park**'
east of Te Papa to Queens Wharf, on a sunny weekend it is abuzz with tourists and locals
simply relaxing, sightseeing, inline skating, kayaking or fishing.

At the heart of the waterfront and to the north of Civic Square is **Frank Kitts Park** with
its impressive children's play area complete with model lighthouse and slide. Further
north is the classy revamped **wharf**, with its waterfront cafés and restaurants where you
can relax over a beer and watch the sightseeing helicopter come and go.

The **New Zealand Film Archive** ⓘ *84 Taranaki St, CBD, T04-384 7647, www.film
archive.org.nz, Mon-Fri 0900-1700, Sat from 1200, free, tours by appointment*, houses a
collection of New Zealand and overseas film and TV materials of artistic, social and
historical value dating back to 1897. It runs frequent specialist exhibitions.

Museum of Wellington

ⓘ *T04-472 8904, www.museumofwellington.co.nz, daily 1000-1700, free.*
Housed in the former Bond Store on Queens Wharf is the recently revitalized Museum of
Wellington. Being in such close proximity to Te Papa, you might think its attempts to
compete and woo visitors was an exercise in futility, but this museum is actually superb
and, in its own way, competes favourably with Te Papa. The multi-levelled design of the
interior is modern yet rustic, maintaining the feel of its former function and the modern
dose of sensual bombardment it now houses is very powerful. The emphasis is of course
on more local history than Te Papa with a particular maritime bent. Of note is the **Wahine
Disaster Gallery** and the state-of-the-art holographic display on Maori legends. *The
Wahine* was a passenger ferry that came to grief at the harbour entrance in 1968 with the
loss of 51 lives. Original film footage set to a suitably dramatic score documents the
chilling series of events. The 3D and holographic mix of the Maori legend display is simply

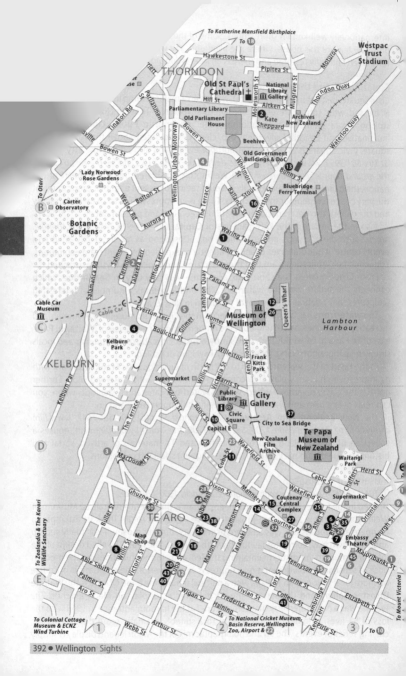

To Katherine Mansfield Birthplace

To 18

Hawkestone St

THORNDON

Pipitea St

Westpac Trust Stadium

Old St Paul's Cathedral

National Library Gallery

Hill St

Molesworth St

Aitken St

Mulgrave St

Thorndon Quay

Kate Sheppard

2

Archives New Zealand

13

Parliamentary Library

Old Parliament House

Bowen St

Beehive

Waterloo Quay

Wellington Urban Motorway

4

Whitmore St

Old Government Buildings & DoC

Bunny St

Bowen St

Ballance St

Stout St

Bluebridge Ferry Terminal

Lady Norwood Rose Gardens

Bolton St

The Terrace

Featherston St

16

To Otari

Carter Observatory

Wesley Rd

Aurora Terr

11

B

Botanic Gardens

Waring Taylor St

1

John St

Clermont

Talavera Terr

Clifton Terr

Lambton Quay

Brandon St

Panama St

Everton Terr

Cable Car

7

Grey St

Customhouse Quay

Queen's Wharf

Cable Car Museum

Gilmer

5

Hunter St

Museum of Wellington

12

26

Lambton Harbour

C

Kelburn Park

4

Boulcott St

Willeston St

Kelburn Par

KELBURN

Frank Kitts Park

Supermarket

Willis St

Harris St

City Gallery

37

Boulcott St

The Terrace

Public Library

Civic Square

10

City to Sea Bridge

Te Papa Museum of New Zealand

D

Bond St

Capital E

New Zealand Film Archive

23

Wakefield St

3

MacDonald St

11

Cuba St

Cable St

Waitangi Park

Herd St

To Zealandia & The Karori Wildlife Sanctuary

Ghuznee St

Dixon St

28

Manners St

Wakefield St

8

Chaffers St

Supermarket

9

Cuba Mall

44

Coutenay Central Complex

27

25

Oriental Par

Butler St

TE ARO

Egmont St

Manners St

15

Courtenay Pl

14

6

35

29

3

Roxburgh St

Map Shop

13

23

38

24

Marion St

Taranaki St

Allen St

7

Embassy Theatre

8

Willis St

9

18

19

39

45

To Mount Victoria

Able Smith St

21

Tory St

Tennyson St

19

6

Victoria St

43

20

12

Cambridge Terr

Palmer St

40

Wigan St

Jessie St

Lorne St

Kent Terr

Levy St

Aro St

Vivian St

College St

Elizabeth St

Frederick St

41

Haining St

Webb St

Arthur St

1

To Colonial Cottage Museum & ECNZ Wind Turbine

2

To National Cricket Museum, Basin Reserve, Wellington Zoo, Airport &

22

3

To 10

Pirie St

392 • Wellington Sights

stunning and is a fantastic
technology has injected
museums as a whole. Recom...

Te Papa Museum of New Zea...
(Te Papa Tongarewa)

ⓘ 55 Cable St, T04-38...
*www.tepapa.govt.nz, daily 1000-1800,
1000-2100, free, (around $15 for temporary
exhibitions). Allow half a day at the museum;
much more and you'll suffer from sensory
overload and go early in the day if you want to
avoid the processions of noisy children. 1-hr
'Introducing Te Papa Tours' available Nov-Apr
daily on the hour 1000-1500, $11; May-Oct 1015
and 1400. Specialist tours (including a Maori
Experience Tour) are available at a cost. There is
an excellent shop on the ground floor but the
café is less than impressive.*

To the south of Civic Square and gracing the
harbour's eastern bank is the unmistakable
Te Papa Museum of New Zealand –
Wellington's biggest tourist attraction. As if
the exterior is not enough, the interior is
also mind-bending. Heavily publicized Te
Papa has faithfully represented the nation's
heritage since 1998, at an initial cost of $317
million. Since then over twice the
population of the nation itself (9.3 million)
have passed through its doors and few have
been disappointed. Of its many temporary
exhibits not surprisingly the most
successful was the *Lord of The Rings* props
exhibition, in 2003.

In Te Papa they say there is something
for everybody and this does seem to hold
true. As expected, there is a heavy emphasis
on Maori heritage, *taonga* (treasures) and
biculturalism, mixed with the inevitable
early settler material, contemporary
displays of all things Kiwi and 'Toi Te Papa' –
an exhibition of 130 New Zealand artworks.

Most recently it was the turn of the
natural history section to grab the
headlines with the arrival and display of
the world's largest specimen of colossal
squid (Mesonychoteuthis hamiltoni, or
'Squid Vicious' as it is known to staff). The

200 metres
200 yards

Sleeping
Apollo Lodge Motel **1** *E3*
Base Backpackers **19** *E3*
Bolton **4** *B2*
Cambridge **15** *E3*
Comfort Wellington **12** *E2*
Copthorne Hotel
  Wellington **9** *D3*
Duxton **23** *D2*
Halswell Lodge **6** *E3*
Intercontinental **7** *C2*
James Cook
  Grand Chancellor **5** *C2*
Lambton Heights
  B&B **2** *B1*
Lighthouse **22** *E2*
Museum **8** *D3*
Ohtel **16** *D3*
Rowena's City
  Lodge **10** *E3*
Top Ten Hutt Park
  Holiday Park **18** *A2*
Victoria Court
  Motor Lodge **13** *E1*
Wellesley **11** *B2*
Wellington YHA **14** *E3*
Wellywood
  Backpackers **16** *E2*
Worldwide
  Backpackers **3** *D1*

Eating
Astoria Café **1** *B2*
Backbencher **2** *A2*
Boulcott Street
  Bistro **4** *C1*
Café Istanbul **9** *E2*
Café Lido **10** *E2*
Caffe L'Affare **41** *E2*
Citron **8** *E1*

Dockside **12** *C2*
Donald's Pie
  Cart **13** *B2*
Espressoholic **15** *D2*
Fidels **40** *E2*
Floriditas **18** *E2*
Hede Café & Bar **11** *D2*
KK Malaysia **23** *E2*
Little India **3** *E3*
Logan Brown **20** *E2*
Midnight Espresso
  & Olive **21** *E2*
Molly Malone's
  Dubliner **14** *E2*
Monsoon Poon **6** *E3*
One Red Dog **35** *E3*
Osteria Del Toro **19** *E2*
Parade Café **42** *D3*
Sakura **16** *B2*
Satay Kampong **25** *E3*
Satay Village **38** *E2*
Shed 5 **26** *C2*
Sweet Mothers
  Kitchen **39** *E3*
Tasting Room **7** *E3*
Trawling Seamarket **43** *E2*
Tugboat on the
  Bay **37** *D2*
Tulsi **24** *E2*
Uncle Changs **27** *E3*

Bars & clubs
Big Kumara **28** *D2*
Blondini's **45** *E3*
Bodega **30** *E1*
Coyote St **32** *E2*
Establishment **29** *E3*
Matterhorn **44** *D2*
Wellington Sports
  Café **36** *E3*

ng specimen arrived at the museum in March 2007, after being captured
waters a month before.

particularly Europeans who are blessed with a long and complex human
apa does leave the impression of the country's relative youth on the grand
world history and events. However, there is no doubt that as a whole it is
ass and provides the usual high-tech sensual bombardment – perhaps too much
ce it's free, it is a good idea to have an initial quick recce and return later for a more
epth investigation to avoid the almost inevitable information overload.

Botanic Gardens, Cable Car and Cable Car Museum

ⓘ *The main entrance is on Glenmore St in Thorndon, on the No 12 bus route (Karori Park), T04-499 1400, www.wellington.govt.nz, free, open dawn till dusk. The Cable Car, T04-472 2199, runs every 10 mins, Mon-Fri 0700-2200, Sat-Sun 0830-2200, $5, child $2 return. Before going anywhere near the gardens you should pick up the free gardens map and leaflet, available from the VIC (I-Site).* Wellington's Botanic Gardens are really quite magnificent, but excruciatingly hilly, and although well worth the visit and a stroll, almost require oxygen and a base camp support team to do so. Gracing its precarious slopes are 26 ha of specialist gardens, radiant flowerbeds, foreign trees and native bush. Its crowning glories are the **Carter Observatory** and the **Lady Norwood Rose Garden**. By far the most sensible and conventional way to visit the gardens is via the **Cable Car**, at 280 Lambton Quay, first built in 1902 and now a tourist attraction in itself. The almost completely subterranean single line has cables that haul the two lovely red carriages up and down, with four stops on the way. When your carriage glides in quietly to the summit (Kelburn) station you step out into the gardens and are immediately rewarded with a fine view across the city. The recently renovated and expanded **Cable Car Museum** ⓘ*T04-475 3578, www.cablecarmuseum.co.nz, daily 0930-1730, free*, houses some lovingly restored cars, as well as audio visual and interpretive displays.

Having arrived in such style you are now in the perfect position to explore the gardens. At the crest of the hill and a short walk from the summit station is the **Carter Observatory** ⓘ *T04-4728167, www.carterobservatory.org*. After recent and major redevelopments it now offers some excellent state of the art displays and planetarium shows. Be sure to see another fine view over the city on the lawn, just in front of the observatory.

Not surprisingly one of the most popular spots in the gardens is the **Lady Norwood Rose Gardens**, where you can muse upon the names and fragrances of more than 300 varieties form a budding pink 'Little Willy' to the rather disheveled 'Nancy Reagan'. It is located at the northern end of the gardens, at the base of the hill and along with the **café** ⓘ *Mon-Fri 1100-1500, Sat-Sun 1000-1600*, should perhaps be your last port of call.

The **Otari Wilton's Bush** ⓘ *160 Wilton Rd, Wilton, northwest of the Botanic Gardens, T04-499 1400, www.wellington.govt.nz, dawn to dusk, free, take bus No 14 (Wilton via Wadestown)*, is another famous garden that is the only botanical garden in the country dedicated solely to native plants.

Zelandia and the Karori Wildlife Sanctuary ⓘ *31 Waiapu Rd, Karori T04-920 9200, www.visitzealandia.com, daily 1000-1700, from $15, child $7; introductory guided tours daily at 1100, from $33, and night tours to view or hear nocturnal wildlife, including kiwi, from $60, child $35, pick-ups from the VIC; take buses No3 or No18 from the city centre;* is a great conservation success story and a tribute to an army of devoted volunteers. In 1994 250 ha of bush in the northern hills neighbouring the suburb of Karori was set aside and protected with a predator-proof fence. This was of course a challenge and an expensive one at that, the idea being to try to repeat the efficacy of New Zealand's offshore islands.

Now, with the eradication of non-native pest species within th[...]
the benefits for both native flora and fauna are plain to see. Re[...]
kaka (native parrot) and the 'living fossil' tuatara are making a [...]
birdsong is returning to native bush that once lay silent. The sanctuary[...]
bush walks to explore its many features from the lake to specialist feed[...]
impressive new visitor centre with state-of-the-art interactive exhibition[...]
story of New Zealand's unique natural history from the day before huma[...]
through to the groundbreaking conservation techniques of today. Recommend[...]

South of the city centre

Wellington Zoo ① *200 Daniell St, Newtown, directly south of the city centre, T04-381 675.*
www.wellingtonzoo.com, daily 0930-1700 (last entry 1615), $18, child $9; take bus No 10 from the
city centre.
Like Auckland and Hamilton, Wellington has embraced the need for the modern-day zoo
to be involved in conservation projects as well as being commercially viable. Wellington
Zoo has just celebrated its centenary and offers some fine exhibits of natives, including
kiwi (housed in a modern nocturnal house), tuatara and a wide variety of non-natives
species, including Sumatran tigers, red panda, Malayan sun bears and troupe of chimps,
the second largest in the southern hemisphere.

An exciting new addition to its activities is the 'Zoo Encounters' programme, which
allows the public to go behind the scenes with keepers and get close up and personal
with some of the more congenial inmates, like the giraffes, red pandas and cheetahs,
from $65 to $800.

The **National Cricket Museum** ① *T04-385 6602, daily 1030-1530, weekends only in*
winter, $5, child $2, is a small but worthy attraction, particularly for the enthusiast. It is
housed in the old grandstand of the Basin Reserve (a ground that has hosted some
famous encounters) and displays a range of national and international memorabilia
dating back to 1743. Inevitably perhaps, particular emphasis seems to be placed on the
team's encounters with the arch-enemy Australia.

The **Colonial Cottage Museum** ① *68 Nairn St, Brooklyn, T04-384 9122, daily*
1200-1800, May-Dec weekends only, $5, children free, is housed in one of the city's oldest
buildings dating back to 1858. Georgian in style, the faithfully restored and furnished
interior takes you back to the early settler days.

While visiting the Colonial Museum you might like to supplement the trip with a city
view and the starkly contrasting **ECNZ Wind Turbine**, which slices the air above Brooklyn.
From Brooklyn Road turn right in to Todman Street and follow the signs.

Around Wellington

There are a number of attractions around Wellington that are worth a visit.

Set in the middle of Wellington harbour is the **Matiu Somes Island Reserve**
① *T04-499 1282, www.eastbywest.co.nz, Dominion Post Ferry $21, child $11.* Once a
quarantine station, the island is now administered by the DoC and is home to a number of
protected native birds. The island can be reached by **ferry** ① *T04-494 3339, with regular*
departures, from Queen's Wharf stopping off at the island on the way to Days Bay near the
coastal resort of Eastbourne.

There are two New Zealand **fur seal colonies** near Wellington. The first and the most
accessible is the Red Rocks colony, which can be reached on foot from Owhiro Bay (see

Safari offers tour options, while **Wellington Rover Tours** can
point you in the right direction (see Activities and tours, page 405).
Turakiae Head to the south east of Pencarrow Lighthouse, requires
the DoC. To get there, take the Coast Road to Baring Head via Petone
and Wainuiomata. Then walk east to the headland (it's a half- to full-day
no public transport to Pencarrow.

beaches in the area, suitable for sunbathing and swimming, can be found to the
the city. From the airport follow the road round the headland to Palmer Head and
ing Bay on the edge of Seatoun.

while in Miramar it is worth calling in at **The Weta Cave** ⓘ *corner of Camperdown Rd and
eka St, Miramar, T04-3809361, www.wetanz.com/cave, open daily 0900-1730, free.* Weta
Workshops was founded in part by Peter Jackson and was responsible for the characters,
props and special effects for films like *Lord of the Rings*, *King Kong* and most recently *The
Hobbit*. The Weta Cave is a small museum that takes a detailed look at the Weta Workshops
phenomenon including screened interviews with its founders and artists. There are also
some of the famous – and infamous – characters, props and displays from the movies and a
shop selling general merchandise and Weta designed clothing, jewellery and mementos.

If you take a scenic drive around the bays, also try to take in the eclectic metal and junk
creations of **Carl Gifford's Carlucci Land** ⓘ *281 Happy Valley Rd, T04-971 8618,
www.carlucciland.co.nz.* Following a work accident, the Italian found himself with lots of
spare time, which acted like a fertile growbag from which the his latent creative talent has
exploded in to life. From miniature metal kiwis to squashed cars, his quirky installations
now consume the valley. Call at the house for sales and permission to view at close hand.

🔺 Walks
There are a number of great walks in and around the city and details and free leaflets that
cover these are available from the VIC (I-Site) or DoC. The *Heritage Trail* leaflet takes in
many of the sights within the city above. There are **Northern**, **Southern**, **Eastern** and
Waterfront walkways. These range from one or two hours covering just a few kilometres
to a full day's jaunt. They take in a range of city, suburb, waterfront, coastal and country
scenery with both historic, contemporary or natural sights outlined. **Mount Kaukau**
(430 m), to the northwest of the city, is a good climb and offers a rewarding view of the
region. It can be accessed from Simla Crescent in Khandallah (two hours). One of the most
popular walks near the city is the walk to **Red Rocks** and the fur seal colony (see above),
which is accessed via the quarry track at the western end of Owhiro Bay (4 km). Owhiro
Bay is reached via Brooklyn and Happy Valley Road (take bus Nos 1 or 4, then 9).

Hutt Valley 🔵🔺 ➤➤ *pp397-406.*

To the east of Wellington, sitting obstinately right on a major fault-line and split by the
Hutt River, are the fairly unremarkable Wellington dormitory towns of Lower and Upper
Hutt, or 'Hutt City'. There isn't much to draw in the visitors, but if you can drag yourself
away from Wellington or just happen to be passing, there are a few sights and activities
that may appeal.

Sights
In Lower Hutt, the **Petone Settlers Museum** ⓘ *waterfront, T04-568 8373, Tue-Fri
1200-1600, Sat-Sun 1300-1700, donation,* highlights the early historical significance of the

area in an effective way. The **New Dowse** ⓘ *corner of* T04-570 6500, www.dowse.org.nz, Mon-Fri 1000-1630, Sat-Sun. underwent an extensive $6,000,000 makeover by Wellingto Architects (Ian Athfield is the well respected kiwi architect who desi and the Wellington Public Library among other things) and has been re hub, with an eclectic display that includes fashion, jewellery, multi-medi finely crafted ceramics.

In Upper Hutt, the **Silverstream Railway Museum** ⓘ *Reynold Bach Dr, Si* T04-971 5747, www.silverstreamrailway.org.nz, Sun only 1100-1600, $10, child $5, r. large collection of steam locomotives, some of which operate on a short track on Su. between 1100-1600. A bit of a trek but still worth it is the **Staglands Wild** Reserve ⓘ *Akatarawa Rd, T04-526 7529, www.staglands.co.nz, daily 1000-1700, $16, child $8,* capable steward and advocate of native New Zealand wildlife conservation. There is a very pleasant café on site with an open fire in winter. The **Kaitoke Regional Park** (12 km north of Upper Hutt) is a popular spot which, since the release of the *Lord of the Rings* trilogy, has attracted a stream of loyal fans. It was here amid the native forest glades and alongside the riverbank that the set of 'Rivendell' was created. During filming over 300 crew were on site – hard to imagine now since, like all the other film locations, little remains except the memory, the atmosphere and little *Rivendell* signs directing you to the right spot. To get there enter the northern entrance to the park off SH2 down Waterworks Road and follow the signs.

The **Hutt River** also featured in the film as the 'Great River Anduin' that flowed through Middle Earth from the 'Misty Mountains' and 'Mirkwood'. Locations used for filming were between **Moonshine** and **Totara Park**. Access is left off SH2 across Moonshine Bridge, just beyond Poets Park.

Upper Hutt also gives access to some short and more challenging walks in the **Akatarawa Forest** and **Rimutaka Forest Park** (camping available).

◉ Wellington listings

For Sleeping and Eating price codes and other relevant information, see Essentials pages 44-50.

◓ Sleeping

Wellington *p389, map p392*
Unlike Auckland, Wellington has the advantage that all types of accommodation are centrally located and within walking distance of most attractions. During festivals and in summer book ahead. Upper-range hotels seem to dominate but, given the emphasis on weekday business, prices are usually halved at weekends.
LL-L Lambton Heights B&B, 20 Talavera Terr, Kelburn, T04-472 4710, www.lambton heights.co.nz. Elegant, heritage home with 2 classy king-sized en suites, garden with spa and city views, all within a short walk of the

city centre. Charming hosts.
LL-L The Bolton Hotel, corner of Bolton and Mowbray sts, Thorndon, T04-472 9966, www.boltonhotel.co.nz. A stylish and contemporary 5-star hotel located within easy walking distance of the city centre offering a wide range of studios and suites, all the standard facilities and an award-winning restaurant specializing in Mediterranean cuisine. Off-street valet parking.
LL-AL Duxton, 170 Wakefield St, T04-473 3900, www.amorahotels.com.au/ duxtonwellington. Right in the heart of the city and a stone's throw from the waterfront and Te Papa, this is one of the best of the hotel chains. It has all the usual amenities including a surprisingly affordable restaurant/ bar. Ask for a room on an upper floor with views across the city and harbour.

...ngton, 2 Grey
...otelsgroup. com.
...e action, it offers the
...ilities including an
...estaurants – the
...ng contemporary NZ
...e well-established **Arizona Bar**
...quintessential Tex-Mex.

**...mes Cook Hotel Grand
...ellor**, 147 The Terrace, T04-499 9500,
...w.ghihotels.com. All mod cons, a fine
...ano bar and in an ideal spot to climb the
steps down to Lambton Quay.

L Ohtel, 14 Hobson St, T04-803 0600,
www.ohtel.com. New designer 10-room
boutique hotel. Rooms are large, spacious
and very well priced. Good location at the
higher end of Cuba St.

L The Lighthouse, 326 The Esplanade, Island
Bay, T04-472 4177, www.thelight
house.net.nz. Your chance to stay in a
lighthouse (built in 1993). Offers suitably
impressive views across the harbour entrance
and oozes character. Small kitchen and
bathroom, with living and sleeping areas (2
rooms with 1 main bedroom with spa) above.
Breakfast included.

L-AL Museum Hotel, 90 Cable St,
T04-802 8900, www.museum hotel.co.nz. A
modern establishment ideally located across
the road from Te Papa and in the heart of the
café, bar and restaurant areas. It oozes class,
both inside and out, and a recently added
apartment complex including single studios
may also prove an attractive proposition.

L-AL Wellesley Hotel, 2-8 Maginnity St,
T04-474 1308, www.wellesleyboutique
hotel.co.nz. A 1920s neo-Georgian-style hotel
offering tastefully appointed period furnished
suites right in the heart of the Lambton
Quarter. In-house facilities include a sauna
and a popular English-style restaurant
featuring an open fire and regular live
entertainment (mainly jazz).

AL Copthorne Hotel Wellington Bay, 73
Roxburgh St, T04-385 0279, www.millennium
hotels.com. On the waterfront with wonderful
views across the harbour and CBD, it's worth

staying here for that reason alone. With a
recent $10 million upgrade it also boasts some
fine facilities including an indoor pool and
popular licensed restaurant. Good value.

AL-C Cambridge Hotel, corner of Alpha St
and Cambridge Terr, T04-385 8829,
www.cambridgehotel.co.nz. Impressive
establishment on the edge of the Courtenay
Quarter that feels more like a grand hotel
than a mid-budget option. Full range of
rooms from shared backpacker-style, to tidy
doubles with en suite bathroom, standard
in-house facilities, Sky TV and a quite
remarkable bathroom section. Quality budget
meals are also a feature. The only drawbacks
are the lack of atmosphere and off-street
parking. Otherwise recommended.

A Apollo Lodge Motel, 49 Majoribanks St,
T04-385 1849, www.apollolodge.co.nz.
Standard modern unit interiors, most with
kitchen facilities. Conveniently placed within
walking distance of Te Papa and Courtenay Pl.

A Comfort Hotel Wellington, 213 Cuba St,
T04-385 2153, www.hotelwellington.co.nz.
Located right in the heart of the Cuba
Quarter. Fine facilities and good value rooms.
In-house café and 'charge-back'
arrangements with local restaurants,
off-street parking.

A Halswell Lodge, 21 Kent Terr, T04-385
0196, www.halswell.co.nz. Comfortable hotel,
sited well off the main street. Walking
distance from Te Papa and Courtenay Pl
restaurants and cafés.

A Moana Lodge, 49 Moana Rd, Plimmerton,
(24kms north of the city), T04-2336628,
www.moanalodge.co.nz. One of very few
backpackers to earn a 5-star rating and an
excellent alternative to the busier and more
commercial hostels in the city, free parking is
also an advantage. Transport into the city is
also easy by train or bus. Very cosy,
comfortable rooms from family and double
through to twins and 3 to 4 share, with
shared bathrooms. The property has views
across the harbour and has well above
average facilities throughout, including
internet and kayak hire.

A The Victoria Court Motor Lodge, 201 Victoria St, T04-385 7120, www.victoria court.co.nz. Nicely appointed motel in a perfect location for the café/restaurant districts of Cuba and Courtenay. Standard range of rooms and apartments, some with spa and kitchen. Sky TV.

C-D Base Backpackers, 21-23 Cambridge Terr, T04-801 5666, www.stayatbase.com. Part of a national chain with modern, spacious accommodation (including en suites and a girls-only level) close to the Cuba Quarter. In-house bar, but no off-street parking.

C-D Rowena's City Lodge, 115 Brougham St, Mt Victoria, T0800-801414/T04-385 7872, www.wellingtonbackpackers.co.nz. Pleasant, friendly hostel in a large rambling house, far more intimate than many of the larger backpacker hostels. Good value single rooms and tent sites available. Also has the advantage of off-street parking.

C-D Wellington YHA, 292 Wakefield St, T04-801 7280, www.yha.org.nz. Deservedly popular with a wide range of rooms (some with en suite bathrooms and TV), excellent facilities and helpful friendly staff. All this just a stone's throw from Courtenay Quarter's cafés and restaurants, a major supermarket and Te Papa. The only drawback is the lack of off-street parking. Daily coupon ticketed parking ($5) is available 200 m away. Recommended.

C-D Wellywood Backpackers, 58 Tory St, Courtenay Quarter, T04-381 3899, www.wellywoodbackpackers.co.nz. Famous for its zebra-stripe exterior, the purpose-built interior is even more notable both aesthetically and functionally. Large living areas, full range of rooms from motel-style double en suites to dorms, large open-plan kitchen, Sky TV room and a 24-hr internet suite and spa. Off-street parking also available.

C-D Worldwide Backpackers, 291 The Terrace, T0508-888555/T04-802 5590, www.worldwidenz.co.nz. Small, homely option offers cosy shared, double and twins.

Spotless throu... also offers attrac... breakfast and ferry...

Hutt Valley *p396*
Motorcamps and camp...
There are no motorcamps in W...
B-D 'Top-Ten' Hutt Park Holida...
Hutt Park Rd, Lower Hutt, T04-568 5...
www.huttpark.co.nz. The best and clos... the centre. Standard 'Top Ten' facilities w... full range of accommodation options, from 2-bedroom motel-style units, to non-powered campsites. Camp kitchen, spa and internet.

❼ Eating

Wellington *p389, map p392*
Wellington prides itself on its thriving café and restaurant scene and is often dubbed 'the café-crazy capital'. More than 100 new establishments have opened up in the last seven years and the choice is vast, which means you are almost guaranteed good quality. The **Courtenay Quarter** is where most are located (Blair St, off Courtenay Pl, is practically wall-to-wall restaurants), with a number of classy pubs offering fine, reliable and mainly international or Pacific Rim cuisine. **Cuba St** has numerous inexpensive restaurants, funky cafés and takeaways. **Queen's Wharf** on the waterfront is also a favourite haunt. For the more expensive restaurants booking is advised.

Finally, if it is late at night, you are near the railway station and desperate, there is always the 24-hr **Donald's Pie Cart**.
ⅲ Boulcott Street Bistro, 99 Boulcott St, T04-499 4199, www.boulcottstbistro.co.nz. Mon-Fri from 1200, Sat from 1800. A top restaurant in the historic surroundings of a period wooden villa. The cuisine is mainly French, with some international dishes.
ⅲ Citron, 270 Willis St, T04-801 6263, www.citronrestaurant.co.nz. Daily from 1000, licensed. Consistently lauded as one of the

...aginative
... 3- and

...harf, T04-499 9900,
... n. Daily from 1100. Very
... a fine evening venue. Al
... ainly Mediterranean or
... es. A great place to watch the
... y with a cold beer.

... **an Brown**, corner of Cuba and Vivian
... 04-801 5114, www.loganbrown.co.nz.
... unch Mon-Fri, dinner daily. A
well-established, multi award-winning
establishment, offering international cuisine
in the old historic and spacious banking
chambers. The spectacular interior sports a
huge chandelier.

Shed 5, Queen's Wharf, T04-499 9069,
www.shed5.co.nz. Daily from 1100. A fine
evening venue, but particularly popular
during the day and at weekends. Al fresco
atmosphere is great for people-watching. The
menu is mainly seafood or Mediterranean.

Café Istanbul, 156 Cuba St, T04-385 4998,
www.istanbul.co.nz. Daily from 1730. A
Turkish-style restaurant with a very congenial
atmosphere, a loyal following and the
occasional belly-dancer.

Floriditas, 161 Cuba St, T04-381 2212,
www.floriditas.co.nz. Daily from 0700. Stylish
option, popular with locals, with good value,
imaginative contemporary menu and great
coffee. Breakfasts are highly recommended,
but you won't be alone.

Little India, 18 Blair St, T04-384 9989, and
115 Cuba Mall, T04-384 2535, www.little
india.co.nz. Lunch Mon-Fri, dinner daily from
1730. One of the city's best Indian offerings.

Matterhorn, 106 Cuba St, T04-384 3359,
www.matterhorn.co.nz. Mon-Fri 1100-0300,
Sat-Sun 1000-0300. A large and popular pub
restaurant option that has won consistent
awards for its casual dining.

Monsoon Poon, 12 Blair St, T04-803 3555,
www.monsoonpoon.co.nz. Mon-Thu
1100-2300, Fri 1100-2400, Sat 1700-2400, Sun
from 1700 until the chefs get sleepy.
Considered the pick of the Asian restaurants,

offering a wide range of dishes from Thai to
Vietnamese. The chefs do their thing in full
view of the spacious dining floor. Lively bar,
great atmosphere.

One Red Dog, 9-11 Blair St, T04-384 9777,
www.onereddog.co.nz. Daily 1000-2400. A
bar-cum-restaurant offering some of the best
gourmet pizza in town. Fine wine list. The
only drawback is its popularity as both
restaurant and bar can get a little too busy at
times.

Osteria Del Toro, 60 Tory St,
T04-381 2299. Mediterranean restaurant/bar,
offering authentic tastes from Italy, Spain,
Morocco, Turkey and Greece. Beautiful décor,
pig on the spit nights on Wed.

Sakura, corner of Featherston and
Whitmore sts, T04-499 6912. Mon-Fri 1130-
1400 and Mon-Sat from 1730. In the heart of
the city, for excellent traditional Japanese
fare.

Sweet Mothers Kitchen, 5 Courtney Pl,
T04-3854444, www.sweetmothers
kitchen.co.nz. Sun-Thu 0800-1030, Fri-Sat
0800-late. Cute wee place and a great
alternative to the large high profile city
restaurants. Offers tastes of New Orleans and
South America all imaginatively presented.
Licensed with great décor, music and service.

Tasting Room, 2 Courtenay Pl, T04-384
1159, www.thetastingroom.co.nz. Mon-Fri
1100-late, Sat-Sun 1000-late. Touts itself as a
premium 'gastro pub'.

Trawling Seamarket, 220 Cuba St. Mon-Sat
0700-2030, Sun 0800-2000. Fine fish and
chips or fresh seafood.

Tugboat on the Bay, in an old tugboat in
Oriental Bay, T04-384 8884. Lunch from 1130,
dinner from 1730. If you prefer waterscapes
to cityscapes and really want to get intimate
with the harbour, this place offers the seafood
dishes with traditional Kiwi backups.

Tulsi, 135 Cuba St, T04-802 4144,
www.tulsirestaurant.co.nz. Daily for lunch and
dinner. An Indian restaurant with a very classy
modern interior, known for its highly
contemporary cuisine and friendly service.
Voted 'Best Butter Chicken in the city'.

Uncle Changs, 72 Courtenay Pl, at the other end of Courtenay, T04-801 9568. One of the better Chinese restaurants, it specializes in Taiwanese and Szechuan.

Backbencher, 34 Molesworth St, T04-472 3065. Popular pub opposite the Beehive, famous for its *Spitting Image*-style political 3-D caricatures. Good pub lunches.

KK Malaysia, 54 Ghuznee St. Good value and good quality Malaysian fare.

Molly Malone's Dubliner Restaurant (upstairs), corner of Courtenay and Taranaki sts, T04-384 2896. Daily from 1100. You can't go wrong with a traditional pub lunch here.

Satay Kampong, 16-24 Allen St. Lunch and dinner. Basic and immensely popular Malaysian restaurant.

Satay Village, 58 Ghuznee St, T04-801 8538. Will not disappoint in either price or quality.

Cafés

Cuba St is the focus of the café scene where 'funky' **Fidels** (No 234), late-night **Midnight Espresso** (No 178), **Espressoholic** (No 136) and **Olive** (No 170) all stand out.
Also on Cuba St is:

Hede Café and Bar, upstairs at No 43 Cuba St, T04-472 5249. Daily from 0700. A Japanese restaurant, offering set menus and tapas-like options. Tasty, well priced food. BYO.
Elsewhere, others include:

Astoria Café, 159 Lambton Quay, T04-473 8500, Mon-Thu 0700-1930, Fri 0700-2030, Sat-Sun 0900-1600. A modern, popular Euro-style café that fills with suits at lunchtime; it is famous for the weird water sculpture outside that looks for all the world like a stand off between a group of rival sperm – something to mull over while you drink your coffee.

Café L'Affare, 27 College St, T04-385 9748. Mon-Fri 0700-1630, Sat 0800-1600. Well worth the extra walk. It is a thriving coffee business as well as an excellent café, full of atmosphere. As you might expect the coffee (and even the smell of the place) is sublime.

Café Lido, right in the heart of town, just opposite the VIC, T04-499 6666. Mon 0730-1500, Tue-Fri 0730-late, Sat-Sun 0730-late.

One of the mos... always busy. A fine... Wellingtonians and ...

Espressoholic, 128 Cou... 7790. Sun-Thu 0730-late, ... Laid-back base for the seriou...

Parade Café, 148 Oriental Parad... 3925. A popular award-winning ca... overlooking the harbour and CBD.

Pubs, bars and clubs

Wellington *p389, map p392*
The main hot spots in the city are **Courtenay Pl** and its off-shoots **Blair St** and **Allen St** with the odd reputable drinking hole in **Cuba St**, **Willis St** and the **Central Business District** (CBD). With the vast range of cafés and restaurants, many of which are licensed, the main pubs tend to remain quiet until late, at which point they fill with young and old alike into the small hours, especially at weekends. For details see www.wellingtonnz.com.

Backbencher, 34 Molesworth St, Thorndon, T04-472 3065, is worth a look just out of interest, with its *Spitting Image*-type dummies and cartoons decking the walls, keeping the country's politicians in check. It also is a good venue to watch sports, has live bands at the weekend and is a hugely popular venue on Fri nights.

Queen's Wharf is a great daytime drinking venue with a number of fine waterfront cafés providing the ideal spot for a relaxing afternoon libation. These include **Dockside** and **Shed 5** (see Eating, page 400); **The Bodega**, 101 Ghuznee St, T04-384 8212, a laid-back, live music venue; and **Big Kumara**, 80 Cuba St, T04-803 3380, a similar venue, especially good for cheesy 1980s music.

The selection on Courtenay and its off-shoot streets of Blair and Allen are vast but the following are a few of the most popular: **Molly Malone's**, corner of Taranaki St and Courtney Pl, T04-384 2896, the city's most popular Irish offering and hosts bands both

. beer too is
 ‥‥g and the
 ‥‥sa, both on Blair St,
 ‥‥you're jolly' venues.
 ‥‥ook out for include
 ‥‥, **Vivo** and **Gogo**.

 ‥‥n enjoys a lively club scene
 ‥‥gh the popularity of individual places
 ‥‥es and wanes. As usual it always pays to
 ‥‥lk to the locals. See also
www.wellingtonnz.com.
Big Kumara, 60 Dixon St, T04-384 8441. A
laid-back low-key place playing lots of 1980s
music. Has a loyal and friendly local clientele.
Coyote St Bar, 63 Courtenay Pl,
T04-385 6665, www.coyotebar.com. Takes
itself less seriously than **The Establishment**.
The Establishment, Courtenay Pl, T04-382
8654. Rather trendy and uptight but popular
dance music venue.
Good Luck Bar, 126 Cuba St. Often referred
to as the 'Chinese Opium den revisited' and
the best place to be in this part of town.
     Other places to look out for include: **The
Last Supper Club**, Blair St; **The San
Francisco Bathhouse**, 171 Cuba St; and
Sandwiches, 8 Kent Terr.

Gay and lesbian
Good venues include: **S&M's (Scotty and
Mal's Cocktail Bar)**, 176 Cuba St,
T04-8025335, www.scottyandmals.co.nz; and
Club Ivy, 13 Dixon St, www.clubivy.co.nz,
with its regular 'Best Butt Competitions'.

⊙ Entertainment

Wellington p389, map p392
Although Aucklanders would disagree,
Wellington probably has the edge when it
comes to a good night out. As well as a large
number of pubs and clubs, there are
numerous venues including large concert
halls such as the **Michael Fowler Centre**,
offering rock and classical, and noted theatres

such as the **Westpac St James** and **Circa**,
offering contemporary drama, dance and
comedy.
     For listings ask at the VIC or check the
daily newspaper *The Dominion Post*, or the
tourist paper *Capital Times*. Useful websites
are: www.feelinggreat.co.nz or
www.wellington nz.com. Tickets for major
events can be bought from **Ticketmaster**,
Westpac St James Theatre, 77-87 Courtenay
Place, T04-3843840, www.ticket ek.co.nz.
The VIC sometimes offers discounts on
theatre tickets.

Art galleries
Wellington is a major national venue for the
visual arts and there are some fine galleries.
Dealers in contemporary New Zealand art
include: **The Bowen Galleries**, 35 Ghuznee
St, T04-381 0351, www.bowengalleries.com,
Mon-Fri 1000-1730, Sat 1000-1500; and **Ora
Design Gallery**, 23 Allen St, T04-384 4157,
Mon-Fri 0830-1800, Sat 1100-1700, Sun
1100-1600.

Cinemas
Tue night is cheap ticket night.
The Embassy Theatre, 10 Kent Terr, at the
bottom of Courtenay Pl, T04-384 7657,
www.deluxe.co.nz. This deserves special
mention due to its giant screen (one of the
largest in the southern hemisphere). It was
also used to host the premieres of Kiwi
director Peter Jackson's *Lord of the Rings*
trilogy.
Paramount, 25 Courtenay Pl, T04-384 4080,
www.paramount.co.nz. Considered the
town's best, most characterful cinema. Also
has an in-house bar.
     Mainstream cinemas include: **Reading
Theatres**, in the Courtenay Central
Complex, 100 Courtenay Pl, T04-801 4601,
www.readingcinemas .co.nz; and **Hoyts**,
Manners St, T04-384 3567.

Comedy
Bathhouse, 171 Cuba St, T04-801 6797. Well
known for its laid-back comedy nights.

Concert halls

The Michael Fowler Centre, 111 Wakefield St, T04-801 4242; and the **Wellington Town Hall**, T04-801 4231, combine to form the **Events Centre**, T04-801 4242, www.wellingtonconvention centre.com. The city's largest concert venue, hosting a mix of rock and classical concerts. Tickets sold on-site by Ticketek.

Theatres

Bats Theatre, 1 Kent Terr, T04-802 4175, www.bats.co.nz. A small characterful venue offering live professional theatre focusing on alternative works and New Zealand drama.
Circa Theatre, 1 Taranaki St, T04-801 7992, www.circa.co.nz. Next to Te Papa, this well-established theatre offers lively international drama, comedy and music. In-house café.
Downstage Theatre, 12 Cambridge Terr, T04-801 6946, www.downstage.co.nz. One of New Zealand's leading professional theatres presenting touring shows of classic contemporary drama, dance and comedy.
Opera House, 111 Manners St, T04-802 4060. Another favourite venue for touring shows.
Westpac St James Theatre, Courtenay Pl, T04-802 4060, www.stjames.co.nz. Originally built in 1912, after a multi-million dollar refurbishment in 1998 it is now considered a premier venue and a central focus to the performing arts. The James is also home to the Royal New Zealand Ballet.

Live music

Occasional **classical** concerts are staged at University School of Music; Conservatorium of Music (Polytechnic) and St Andrews on the Terrace. See VIC (I-Site) for further details.

For **folk music**, check out **Molly Malone's**, corner of Taranaki St and Courtenay Pl, T04-384 2896, which can usually get the toes tapping most nights; and **Kitty O'Sheas**, T04-384 7392, a few doors down, less traditional but comes a close second.

Jazz fans should head to **Blondini's Café and Bar**, at the Embassy Theatre on Kent Terr, which offers a dynamic jazz programme at weeken... till late.

There are numerous pub... mainly weekend **rock** gigs in... Bodega, 101 Ghuznee St, T04-... Backbencher, 34 Molesworth St, ... 3065; Indigo, 171 Cuba St, T04-801 ... Matterhorn, 106 Cuba St, T04-384 33... Shooters, 69-71 Courtenay Pl, T04-801 ... Starlight Ballroom, 235 Willis St, T04-802 1310; and **Wellington Sports Café**, corner of Tory St and Courtenay Pl, T04-801 5515.

⊛ Festivals and events

Wellington *p389, map p392*
It seems that Wellington is happy and proud to host more 'events' than any other town or city in New Zealand and there is always something going on. The jazz and arts festivals are particularly well celebrated.
Jan Wellington Cup Carnival, T04-528 9611, www.trentham.co.nz. A major social and sporting event, and the region's high point on the annual racing calendar. Usually held in the last week of the month.
Feb-Mar Wellington Fringe Festival, T04-495 8015, www.fringe.org.nz. An exciting month-long event that begins in the last week of Feb and celebrates modern and contemporary theatre, music and dance.
Cuba Street Carnival, www.cubastcarnival.co.nz, takes over the entire downtown of Wellington every other year (next 2011). The growth in popularity over the last 10 years now sees the event attract national and international interest, and audiences of 150,000, while keeping the eccentricity of Cuba St at its core. It is dedicated to delivering the most extraordinary, diverse, and creative inner-city celebrations in New Zealand and transforming Wellington's streets into a free explosion of colour, music and performance.
Mar International Rugby Sevens Tournament, T04-389 0020, www.sevens. co.nz. The world's best rugby sevens teams

at the Westpac
...nd International Arts
...)149, www.nzfestival.
...s is a biennial event (next in
...lington's most celebrated. It
...eeks and is currently the country's
...ntural event with a rich and varied
...t of music performers, drama, street
...re, traditional Maori dance, modern
...nce and visual arts.
Wellington International Jazz Festival,
www.jazzfestival.co.nz. An increasingly
popular celebration of national and
international jazz talent.
May NZ International Comedy Festival,
www.laugh.co.nz. A popular event open to
local, national and international talent.
Jul Wellington Film Festival, T04-385 0162,
www.enzedff.co.nz. A showcase of nationally
and internationally celebrated films.
Sep Rugby World Cup, www.rugbyworld
cup.com. In 2011 Wellington will play a major
part in hosting fixtures at the Wellington
Regional Stadium.
World of Wearable Art Awards, T03-
548 9299, www.worldofwearableart.com. A
unique Kiwi arts affair that has grown from
strength to strength from humble beginnings
in the country's arts capital, Nelson. This is
your once in a lifetime chance to see models
dress as a banana, or a boat, or in something
made of copious sticky back plastic and toilet
roll holders. Anything is possible and even
ex-PM Helen Clark once hit the catwalk
donned in a fetching kind of paua shell
number. Delightful and recommended.

O Shopping

Wellington *p389, map p392*
Wellington is a fine city for shopaholics. The
main shopping areas are Lambton Quay,
Willis, Cuba and Courtenay sts. For quality
souvenirs try the shop at Te Papa.
Cuba St With a distinctly funky flair, the
bohemian Cuba quarter in downtown is
worth a muse. It has trendy stores, high

quality second-hand boutiques, and a wealth
of fantastic cafés. Here you can discover
upcoming designers of fashion, food and
attitude all in a fascinating environment of
old-meets-new.
Courtenay Place A little more upmarket
than Cuba but still has a variety of interesting
shops.
Featherston St Try Robyn Mathieson, 183
Featherston St, for menswear.
Lambton Quay Nicknamed 'The Golden
Mile', the highlights here are the boutique
shops of the Old Bank and Kirkcaldie and
Stains. Sommerfields, 296 Lambton Quay, is
perfect for New Zealand souvenir hunters.
Dymocks, 366 Lambton, and Whitcoulls, 312
Lambton, the major bookshops, are also
based here.
Willis St Well-known for its sheer variety
with a number of popular clothing stores
including Starfish, 128 Willis St; and Unity
Books, 57 Willis St. An excellent bookshop
specializing in New Zealand titles.

▲ Activities and tours

Wellington *p389, map p392*
Cruising
Charter boats are available at Queen's Wharf,
see www.wellingtonwaterfront.co.nz.
Dominion Post Ferry, T04-499 1282,
www.eastbywest.co.nz. For day trips around
the harbour and the eastern harbour seaside
resorts of Days Bay and Eastbourne via Somes
Island ($10, child $5 one way, Somes Island
return $20). It operates a regular sailing
schedule daily from Queen's Wharf.

Golf
Karori Golf Club, on the outskirts, T04-476
7337. Quite a challenging course.
Miramar Links Golf Course, next to the
airport, T04-801 7651. Average.
Paraparaumu Beach Golf Club, just north of
Wellington, T04-902 8200. An international
standard links ranked 73rd in the world and
still benefitting from the fact. Tiger Woods

played here in the New Zealand Open in 2001.

Inline skating

Hugely popular along the waterfront.
Cheapskates, 60 Cuba St, T04-499 0455. Skate hire from $15, 1 hr.
Ferg's Kayaks, Shed 6 on Queen's Wharf, T04-499 8898, www.fergskayaks.co.nz. Blade hire $10 per hr, tuition also available.

Kayaking

Ferg's Rock 'n' Kayak, see Inline skating, above. Hugely popular at weekends hiring out a range of single or double kayaks for self-guided or organized trips on the harbour. Hire from $15 for 1 hr, Basic Skills Course (Sun mornings) from $75. There is also a climbing wall on the premises reputed to be the highest in the country, from $15.

Mountain biking

There are a number of good tracks around Wellington including the **Karori Wildlife Sanctuary** perimeter fence (from Brooklyn Hill), **Karori Reservoir**, parts of the **Southern Walkway**, **Tinakori Hill** and **Mount Kaukau**.
Mud Cycles, 338 Karori Rd, T04-476 4961, www.mud cycles.co.nz. Cycle hire and tours from $30 for a half-day, $45 full-day.

Rugby

Westpac Stadium, Waterloo Quay, T04-473 3881, www.westpactruststadium.co.nz. Rugby fans should try to catch a Wellington Lions game at this world-class venue.

Scenic flights

Helipro, Queen's Wharf, T0800-4354776/ T04-472 1550, www.helipro.co.nz. Helicopter flights over the city, harbour or beyond, $95 for 10 mins.

Swimming

The best beaches are east of the city around the coast at Seatoun. The invitingly named **Scorching Bay**, 3 km north of Seatoun, is a favourite. If the beach holds no appeal, head

for the **Freyberg Pool**, 139 Oriental Parade, T04-801 4530, daily 0600-2100.

Tour operators

There are a number of specialist sightseeing operators offering a range of city (and further afield) tours as well as specialist operators and an attractive option for kids.
Experience Stansborough, 100 Hutt Park Road, Seaview, T04-566 5591, www.stans borough.com. Unique 1½-hr tours to look at Stansborough Greys, a very rare sheep that produce a hallmark quality grey wool. The wool has become a highly regarded fashion accessory and the fascinating tour takes in the history and successes of this local cottage industry. From $22, child $15.
Flat Earth, T0800-775805/T04-977 5805, www.flatearth.co.nz. A well-established tour company offering an exciting range of tours, from the half- to full-day 'Wellington Tour'; a 'Wild Wellington' Eco-tour that focuses on local native wildlife; a 'Classic Wine Tour' to the Wairarapa; a 'Maori Treasures' tour that offers demonstrations of art and crafts; and, of course, the inevitable *Lord of the Rings* tour. Tours cost around $145-325. Recommended.
Seal Coast Safari, T0800-7325277/T0274-534880, www.sealcoast.com. Departs from the VIC at 1030 and 1330 and offers 3-hr tours of the seal colony and Red Rocks often taking in the ECNZ Wind Turbine on the way from $85.
Walk Wellington, T04-802 4860, www.walk.wellington.net.nz. For informative and entertaining guided walks, from $20, child $10 (2 hrs). Try to book at least 3 days ahead.
Wally Hammond's Tours, T04-472 0869, www.wellingtonsightseeingtours.com. Scheduled daily sightseeing trips for the more mature traveller with a well-established and entertaining operator, 2½ hrs, $50.
Wellington Rover Tours, T021-426211, www.wellingtonrover.co.nz. Good value hop-on, hop-off tour schedules taking in a range of venues from the seal colony at Red Rocks and Scorching Bay Beach to Te Papa and the Zealandia Karori Wildlife Sanctuary

(from \$45). They also offer half- or full-day *Lord of the Rings* tours taking in city and film locations from \$90.

Wild About Wellington, T027-441 9010, www.wildaboutwellington.co.nz. The small group flexible tours do a fine job of combining the city's sights and culinary specialities, and a special 'Wellington for Kids Tour' is a convenient adjunct, taking the kids off your hands while you enjoy one of the other tours. From \$95.

Zest, T04-801 9198, www.zestfoodtours.co.nz. This operator offers an attractive package for small groups of self-confessed gourmands, whipping up the ingredients of local knowledge and fascinating ventures behind the scenes to create a fine tour experience from \$230,

Windsurfing/surfing

Wild Winds Sail and Surf, at the Overseas Terminal near Te Papa, T04-384 1010, www.wildwinds.co.nz (summer only). Windsurf hire and tuition.

Hutt Valley *p396*

H20Xtream Aquatic Adventure Centre, corner of Blenheim and Brown sts, Upper Hutt, T04-527 2113. Daily. Water slides, wave machine and all manner of water activities.

HangDog Climbing Centre, 453 Hutt Rd, Alicetown, Lower Hutt, T04-589 9181. Mon-Thu 1300-2130, Fri 1300-1830, Sat-Sun 1000-1830. From \$16, child \$13 (includes harness, shoes and chalk). 14-m walls with over 70 routes as well as a bouldering room, abseiling tower and climbing shop. All in all, for the vertically unchallenged, it's well worth a visit.

⊖ Transport

Wellington *p389, map p392*

For travel to South Island, see box, page 409.
Bicycle hire Mud Cycles Karori, 1 Allington Rd, Karori, T04-476 4961. **Penny Farthing**, 89 Courtenay Pl, T04-385 2279. **Car hire** At the airport, also: **Ace**, 150 Hutt Rd, T04-471 1176; **Budget**, 81 Ghuznee St, T04-802 4548; **Pegasus**, 51 Martin Sq, T04-384 4883.
Taxi Wellington Combined, T0800-384444/T04-384 4444.

ⒸDirectory

Wellington *p389, map p392*

Embassies and consulates See Essentials (page 54). **Foreign exchange** Travelex, 120 Lambton Quay, T04- 472 8346.

Internet Available at the VIC. Otherwise, Manners, Cuba and Courtney sts are your best bet. **Cyber City**, 97 Courtenay Pl; Cyber Spot, Lambton Sq, 180 Lambton Quay; and IPlay, 49 Manners St. **Library** Victoria St (Civic Sq), T04-801 4040, Mon-Thu 0930-2030, Fri 0930-2100, Sat 0930-1700, Sun 1300-1600.

Medical services Wellington Hospital, Riddiford St, T04-385 5999. A&E Centre (and After Hours Pharmacy), 17 Adelaide Rd, T04-384 4944. Urgent Pharmacies, Medical Centre Building, 729 High St, T04-939 6777.

Police Corner of Victoria and Harris sts, T04-381 2000. **Post office** 94-98 Lambton Quay, T04-472 3301. Mon-Fri 0830-1700. **Post Restante**, 43 Manners St, T04-473 5922. Mon-Fri 0800-1730.

Kapiti Coast → *Colour map 3, C2.*

Just north of Wellington, SH1 slices its way through the hills of a major fault-line and passes the rather dull town of Porirua before joining the picturesque Kapiti coastline. For the next 30 km the small coast and inland settlements of Paekakariki, Waikanae and Otaki are shadowed by Kapiti Island on one side and the Tararua Forest Park on the other. Kapiti Island is well worth a visit while Paekakariki, Paraparaumu and Waikanae offer a number of interesting local sights and activities. Otaki is the principal access point to the Tararua Forest Park. ▶▶ *For Sleeping, Eating and other listings, see page 410.*

Ins and outs

Getting there
Paekakariki, Paraparaumu, Waikanae and Otaki are all on SH1 and the main rail line. The main bus companies and **Metlink**, T0800-801700, www.metlink.co.nz, trains stop at these centres. The regional trains to and from Paraparaumu run frequent day and evening services and are relatively cheap.

Tourist information
Paraparaumu VIC (I-Site) ① *Coastlands shopping centre, off SH1, T04-298 8195, www.naturecoast.co.nz, Mon-Fri 0900-1700, Sat-Sun 1000-1500.* **DoC** ① *10 Parata St, Waikanae, T04-296 1112.* **Kapiti Coast VIC (I-Site)** ① *Centennial Park, SH1, Otaki, T06-364 7620, www.naturecoast.co.nz, Mon-Fri 0900-1700, Sat-Sun 1000-1500.*

Paekakariki

Paekakariki is a tiny seaside village (population 1,600), popular with train enthusiasts, still recovering from some of the worst flooding in recent history, which occurred in February 2004. The first thing to do is take a 3-km diversion up to the **viewpoint** on Paekakariki Hill Road. On a clear day there are great views of Kapiti Island and the coast right up to Wanganui. At the village railway station is the **Steam Inc Engine Shed** ① *T0800-783264, Wed, Thu, Sat (evenings)*, where devoted enthusiasts have restored a number of vintage trains, some of which still huff and puff along the tracks. A few kilometres further north is the **Wellington Tramway Museum** ① *Queen Elizabeth Park, T04-292 8361, weekends 1100-1630*, where historical displays look back at one of Wellington's former modes of transport. Several trams are currently in operation and rides are available.

Paraparaumu and Waikanae

Paraparaumu, with a population of about 30,000, is the principal township on the Kapiti Coast and has close ties with Wellington both as commuter town and as a seaside resort popular during the summer months. There are two main beaches, **Raumati** to the south and **Paraparaumu Beach** to the north. All the usual facilities are here and the town also serves as the gateway to Kapiti Island. A little further north on SH1 is the small satellite town of **Waikanae**, which also prides itself on its fine beach. Paraparaumu's main claim to fame came in 2001 when Tiger Woods was lured with a rather attractive $2 million to play at the New Zealand Open golf challenge on its world-class golf course, T04-902 8200.

Other than the beach, the main attractions are scattered along SH1 just to the north of Paraparaumu and around Waikanae. The **Lindale Centre** ① *2 km north of town, T04-297 0916, daily 0900-1700*, is essentially a kitsch coffee stop for coach tours, but there is also a farm park for kids with weekend farm shows ($13, child $8).

Just a little further north still on SH1 is the **Southward Car Museum** ① *T04- 297 1221, www.southward.org.nz, daily 0900-1630, $10, child $3*. It has a huge collection of 250 vehicles dating from 1895. In addition to cars there are traction engines, motorcycles, bicycles and a model railway, shop and café.

On the outskirts of the village of **Waikanae**, 5 km north of Paraparaumu is the **Nga Manu Nature Reserve** ① *T04-293 4131, www.ngamanu.co.nz, daily 1000- 1700, $12, child $4; it is quite hard to find but signposted from SH1.* Although mainly for educational purposes, this reserve is worth the detour. Everything is well presented and this is one of the few establishments in the country that is not ashamed to display non-native pests. There is a wonderful (well enclosed) display of rats, some possums and the less well advertised mallard ducks on the lawn, eyeing up your picnic. There are the usual collections of native birds, geckos, tuatara and a nocturnal kiwi house. Eel feeding takes place at 1400. At some point along the coast it is well worth taking at least a look at the beach. This can be done at a number of access points, one of which is **Te Horo Beach** just north of Waikanae. The coast is piled high with amazingly sculpted pieces of driftwood.

Kapiti Island

ⓘ *All access and landing permits must be pre-booked well in advance with DoC. Only 50 people can land per day; permits cost $11, child $5. No overnight stays are allowed. The useful booklet Kapiti Island Nature Reserve, is available from the Wellington DoC, see page 389. Private boats are not allowed to land but two principal permitted private operators run day-trips: Kapiti Tours Ltd, T04-237 7965, www.kapititours.co.nz; and Kapiti Marine Charter, T0800-433779/T04-297 2585, www.kapitimarinecharter.co.nz; both $55, child $30. Boats depart from Paraparaumu Beach in front of the Kapiti Boating Club at 0900-0930 and return 1500-1530. Kapiti Island Alive, T06-362 6606, www.kapitiislandalive.co.nz, departs at 0900 or 1430 for 1-hr guided walks ($20) on the island. Night-time kiwi-spotting trips are also a possibility. For the latter Flat Earth Company, T04-977 5805, www.flatearth.co.nz, offers transport from Wellington as part of a package.*

Sights

Kapiti Island is a very special place; not only is it a delight to visit but it's like going back in time to when New Zealand was an unspoiled paradise. Lying 5 km offshore from Paraparaumu, it is 10 km long, 2 km wide and has a total land area of 1965 ha. Its highest point is Tuteremoana at 520 m. The island is now one of the most important reserves in the country and has an adjunct marine reserve, all of which is administered, protected and nurtured by DoC. It took a huge budget and six years of hunting and poisoning in the 1980s to rid the island of 22,500 possums, while further exhaustive helicopter poison drops in the 1990s have been successful in keeping rats at bay. After numerous plant and animal re-introductions, the results are the first signs of regeneration and hints of what once was. Here you are in nature's territory – not human. You can walk on a number of well-kept tracks through proper New Zealand bush. Inquisitive birds like robin, saddleback and stitchbird flit about your head, while weka and takahe poke about for insects disturbed by your feet. At night you can hear kiwi, or share the coastal path with little blue penguins. And at dawn, if you are very lucky, you can hear one of the most beautiful bird songs ever to grace human ears – that of the endangered kokako.

Otaki

Otaki (population 5,600) is the last (or first) settlement within the Wellington Regional Boundary. Steeped in Maori history, there are a number of *marae* canoe including the **Te Pou O Tainui Marae**, dating from 1910, on Te Rauparaha Street. The **Rangiatea Church** was one of the finest restored Maori churches in the country, but was destroyed by fire in 1995; restoration is now complete. Otaki is the main eastern gateway to the **Tararua Forest Park**. Otaki Gorge Road, 2 km south of town, takes you 19 km to Otaki Forks where a number of tracks lead into the mountains. Information about the park, local sights and accommodation options can be obtained from the VIC (see page 407).

Getting to the South Island

The scenic 85 km journey across Cook Strait takes three hours. The service is offered by two companies: the long-established **Interislander** T0800-802802/T04-498 3302, www.interislander.co.nz, has three vessels in its fleet. **Bluebridge**, T0800-844844, T04-471 6188, www.bluebridge.co.nz, offers a single vessel, which is older and offers more basic facilities, but is also cheaper (standard fare from $55, child $25, vehicles including campervans cost $150-350 including driver).

In adverse weather conditions the crossing can be a bit of an ordeal with one crossing in 2006 taking a nauseating 10 hours. Sailings will be cancelled if conditions are considered too dangerous, but this is rare. If you can, schedule your trip so that it is daylight during the one- hour scenic approach through the 'sounds' to Picton. Advance booking is advised at all times, but especially in December/January. Most major VICs (I-Sites) and travel agents can organize bookings and tickets.

The three vehicle/passenger ferries in the Interislander fleet consist of the newly upgraded *Arahura* (meaning 'Pathway to Dawn'), the *Aratere* (meaning 'Quick Path') and, the newest acquisition, the *Kaitaki* (meaning 'Challenger'). Facilities include a range of bars, food courts, cafés, a movie theatre and information point. There is also a children's play area and nursery and private work desks, although negotiating a laptop on stormy seas can prove entertaining in itself.

Club class tickets will allow you access to a private lounge, complimentary tea and coffee, magazines, newspapers (and a slightly better class of sick bag?).

A free shuttle bus to the terminal (2 km) is available from the Wellington railway station (Platform 9), 30 minutes before each scheduled ferry departure. At the Picton end, a free shuttle is available to the railway station connecting Picton with Christchurch.

Various day/limited-excursion, family and group fares and standard discounted fares are available but must be booked in advance and are subject to availability. Like most travel bookings these days the internet will secure the best deals. At peak periods (particularly December/January) discounts are rarely available; discounts are offered mainly in winter and for very late or early sailings. Fares for passengers range from the standard $73 (child $43), to the web saver $63 (child $33). Vehicles, including campervans, cost $200-300 including the driver and depending on time of departure. Motorcycles cost $100-120 including passenger, bicycles $15 on top of passenger charge.

◉ Kapiti listings

For Sleeping and Eating price codes and other relevant information, see Essentials pages 44-50.

● Sleeping

Paekakariki *p407*
A Killara Homestay, 70 Ames St, T04- 905 5544, www.killarahomestay.co.nz. 2 rooms in a large comfortable beachfront villa within walking distance of the village. Spa and internet.

C-D Paekakariki Backpackers, 11 Wellington Rd, T04-902 5967, paekakbackpack@ paradise.net.nz. Very pleasant, comfortable little place set on the hillside above the village. Doubles, twins, singles and dorms.
C-D Paekakariki Holiday Park, Wellington Rd, T04-292 8292. Above average rooms and amenities in a sheltered position near the beach.

Paraparaumu and Waikanae *p407*

AL Te Horo Luxury Lodge, 109 Arcus Rd, Te Horo, T0800-483467/T06-364 3393, www.tehorolodge.co.nz. Luxuriously homestay with 4 rooms inear the driftwood beach.

AL Te Nikau Forest Retreat, Kakariki Grove, Waikanae, T04-299 2587, www.tenikau.co.nz. Contemporary house set in coastal forest, 2 doubles, treehouse spa. Multiple nights only.

A Copperfield Seaside Motel, 13 Seaview Rd, Paraparaumu Beach, T04-902 6414, www.seasidemotel.co.nz. Modern motel, 2 mins' walk from the beach, offering a convenient stop on the Kapiti Coast. Studio units and 1- to 2- bedroom apartments (some with double spa baths), Sky TV. Licensed restaurant.

A Sand Castle, Paetawa Rd (off Peka Rd), Peka Peka, Waikanae, T04-293 6072, sandmotel@kapiti.co.nz. An aptly named motel right next to the beach.

Motorcamps and campsites

C-D Lindale Motor Park, Main Rd North, SH1, Paraparaumu, T04-298 8046. Ideally located next to all Lindale tourist amenities. Good value basic doubles with cooking facilities.

D Ngatiawa Campsite, Terrace Rd, Waikanae, T04-293 5036. A lovely quiet campsite set in bush by the Ngatiawa stream.

Otaki *p408*

A Byron Resort, 20 Tasman Rd, Otaki Beach, T04-364 8121, www.byrons resort.co.nz. Quality motel units with resort amenities including restaurant, pool, spa and sports facilities. Camping is also available.

🍴 Eating

Paekakariki *p407*

Paekakariki Cafe, 7 Beach Rd, T04-292 8860. Open breakfast and lunch Wed-Mon, dinner Thu-Sat. Relaxed and pleasant café with quality Kiwi cuisine and good coffee.

Paraparaumu *p407*

Farmyard Cafe, Lindale Tourist Centre just north of Paraparaumu, T04-297 0911. Right in the heart of the tourist complex.

Otaki *p408*

Brown Sugar Café, corner of SH1 and Riverbank Rd, T06-364 6359. Lots of delicious home cooking in a garden setting.

▲ Activities and tours

Paraparaumu and Waikanae *p407*

Kapiti 4x4 Adventures, Maungakotukutuku Rd, T04-299 0020, www.kapitifourX4.co.nz. Trailblazing bike trips near Paraparaumu. 1-hr all day and overnight trips.

Kapiti Island Alive, T06-362 6606, www.kapitiislandalive.co.nz. Maori owned and operated offering excellent day trips to the island, departing 0900 or 1430 with 1-hr guided walks ($20). Overnight kiwi spotting trips are also a possibility but book well ahead.

Kapiti Tours and Kapiti Island Nature Reserve, T0800-527484, www.kapititours. co.nz. Also runs day trips to the island, departing Paraparaumu 0900 from $55.

Contents

Footprint features

Nelson & Marlborough

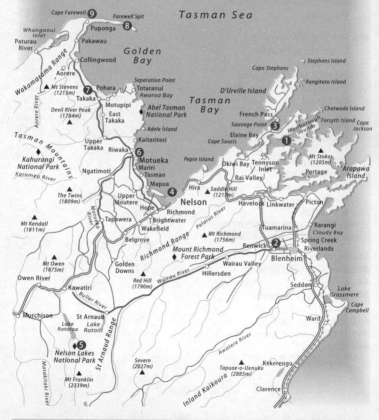

Tasman Sea

Cape Farewell ⑨ Farewell Spit
Whanganui Inlet   ⑧
Paturau River   Puponga
    Pakawau
Collingwood   Golden
Aorere   Bay
Wakamarama Range   Pohara ⑦ Separation Point   Cape Stephens   Stephens Island
Mt Stevens (1213m)   Takaka   Totaranui   D'Urville Island   Rangitoto Island
    Motupipi   Awaroa Bay
Aorere River   Devil River Peak (1784m)   East Takaka   Abel Tasman National Park   Tasman   French Pass
    Bay   Sauvage Point ③   Chetwode Island
Tasman Mountains   Adele Island   Elaine Bay   Marlborough   Forsyth Island   Cape Jackson
    Upper Takaka   Kaiteriteri   Cape Soucis   Sounds ①
Kahurangi National Park   Riwaka ⑥   Pepin Island   Okiwi Bay   Tennyson Inlet   Mt Stokes (1205m)
Karamea River   Motueka   Rai Valley   Portage   Arapawa Island
The Twins (1809m)   Ngatimoti   Mariri   Hira   Saddle Hill (1211m)   Havelock   Linkwater   Picton
    Tasman
Mt Kendall (1811m)   Mapua ④   Nelson   Pelorus River
    Upper Moutere   Hope   Richmond   Tuamarina   Rarangi
Mt Owen (1875m)   Tapawera   Brightwater   Mt Richmond (1756m)   Cloudy Bay
    Belgrove   Wakefield   Mount Richmond   Renwick ②   Spring Creek
Owen River   Golden Downs   Forest Park   Blenheim   Riverlands
    Red Hill (1790m)   Wairau Valley   Wairau River
Murchison   Kawatiri   Hillersden   Seddon   Lake Grassmere
    Buller River   St Arnaud Range   Awatere River   Cape Campbell
    Lake Rotoroa   Lake Rotoiti   Ward
Matakitaki River   St Arnaud   Severn (2027m)   Tapuae-o-Uenuku (2885m)   Kekerengu
    Nelson Lakes National Park ⑤   Inland Kaikoura
    Mt Franklin (2339m)   Clarence

N
20 km
20 miles

The regions of Marlborough and Nelson have all the classic New Zealand ingredients – mountains, lakes, golden beaches and great tramping tracks – all safe within the boundaries of its national parks and warmed by the sunniest climate in the country. And, as if that wasn't enough, they also have a relatively low population density to boot.

Those who do live here are a diverse bunch: from the farmers, fruit growers and winemakers in the valleys, to the artists and writers in the quiet creative havens of the Marlborough Sounds and smaller rural towns, like Motueka or Takaka. Despite the appealing lifestyle and obvious attractions, few foreigners have heard of this 'secret region'. Most simply pass through on their way to the tourist honey pots further south, stopping only briefly in Picton, the main ferry port on the South Island.

Marlborough Sounds → Colour map 4, A5.

The Marlborough Sounds is like the South Island's giant foyer. This vast, convoluted system of drowned river valleys, peninsulas and islets – often dubbed New Zealand's 'little slice of Norway' – is the picturesque introduction to the South Island where you can enjoy stunning scenery, cruising, tramping, kayaking, wildlife watching or just a few days' peaceful relaxation. The port of Picton is the gateway to the sounds. From here it is then only a short journey to Blenheim, the region's capital. Although the town itself is fairly unremarkable, the area produces some of the best wines in New Zealand. A visit to some of the top vineyards is recommended. South of Blenheim is the pretty coastal settlement of Kaikoura, famous for its whales, dolphins and seabirds (see page 501).

On the map, it may look like the Marlborough Sounds takes up a relatively small area of the South Island, but its myriad 'sounds' (drowned glacial river valleys as opposed to fjords) create an astonishing 1500 km of coastline. Although the endless inlets and bays are not bound by snow-capped peaks as they are in Norway, the topography is just as intriguing and very picturesque. Wildlife flourishes and the area is particularly well known for its seabirds and dolphins. The two main inlets are the Queen Charlotte and Pelorus Sounds, the former being plied several times daily by the inter-island ferry between North and South Islands. ►► *For Sleeping, Eating and other listings, see pages 424-434.*

Tramping in the sounds ● ►► pp424-434.

Although most of what the sounds has to offer is easily accessed by boat, it is also possible to explore much of it on foot. There are two popular tramping tracks, the **Queen Charlotte Track** and the **Nydia Track**.

Ins and outs

Marlborough Sounds Adventure Company, based in Picton T0800-283283/ T03-5736078, www.marlboroughsounds.co.nz, offer guided walks (4-day $1310, 5-day $1750) and self-guided walks (4- or 5-day, including food, transport and accommodation, from $610). It also offers kayaking trips and an increasingly popular 4-day walk/mountain bike or walk/kayak adventure all on the Queen Charlotte Track, from $1380. **Wilderness Guides**, T0800-266266/T03-573 5432, www.queencharlottetracknz.com, (Queen Charlotte and Nydia Tracks) and **Natural Ecounters**, T021-2688879, www.natural-encounters.com (Queen Charlotte Track) offer similar services.

There are plenty of water-based operators who will drop off or pick up from a number of points along the track, with most offering day-walk options. Unbiased information can be secured from the VIC (I-Site). Sea access is possible at Ship Cove, Resolution Bay, Endeavour Inlet, Camp Bay (Punga Cove), Bay of Many Coves, Torea Bay (the Portage), Lochmara Bay, Mistletoe Bay (Te Mahia) and Anakiwa. **Picton Water Taxis**, T03-573 7853, www.pictonwatertaxis.co.nz, and **Arrow Water Taxis**, also based in Picton, T03-573 8226, www.arrowwatertaxis.co.nz, offer flexibility and will go to anywhere in Queen Charlotte Sound or Tory Channel for about the same price. A typical single fare to Anakiwa is $35. **Beachcomber Fun Cruises**, based in Picton, T0800-624526/T03-573 6175, www.beachcombercruises.co.nz, also offers a wide range of daily cruise/walk packages or simple drop-off/pick-up transport options, with a flexible 'Track and Pack' pass, costing from $95. **The Cougar Line**, based on the Waterfront in Picton, T0800-504090/T03-573 7925, www.queenchar lottetrack.co.nz, is the most modern and comfortable. It offers one way transfers from $35; multi-day walk packages; mountain biking packages; and a daily scheduled 'Track Pass' that will drop you off at Ship Cove (departs Picton 0800, 1000 and 1330) and pick up at Anakiwa (Tirimoana, 1430 and 1645) from $95. It can also deliver your pack to your accommodation and offers half- or full-day cruise walks from $68. **Endeavour Express**, based in both Endeavour Inlet and at the Waterfront in Picton, T03-573 5456, www.boatrides.co.nz, offers similar wide-ranging services, with drop-offs and pick-ups from various strategic points on the track (including Ship Cove and Anakiwa) as well as a regular daily services to Ship Cove and Endeavour Inlet, from $90 return. Basic single drop-off fares start from $35. **Picton Floatplane Service**, based at the Ferry Terminal in Picton, T03-573 6866, www.nz-scenic-flights.co.nz, can also deliver you just about anywhere in the sounds with the emphasis on the larger and/or luxury resorts and accommodations. They also offer scenic flights from 20-mins $190.

The Marlborough Sounds

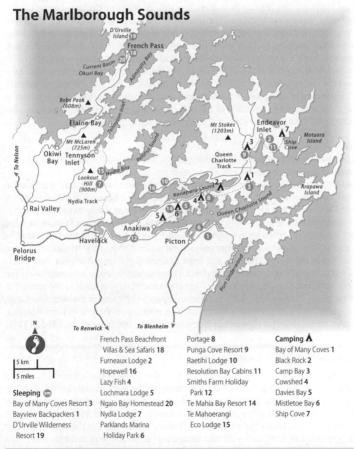

N

5 km
5 miles

Sleeping
Bay of Many Coves Resort **3**
Bayview Backpackers **1**
D'Urville Wilderness
  Resort **19**
French Pass Beachfront
  Villas & Sea Safaris **18**
Furneaux Lodge **2**
Hopewell **16**
Lazy Fish **4**
Lochmara Lodge **5**
Ngaio Bay Homestead **20**
Nydia Lodge **7**
Parklands Marina
  Holiday Park **6**

Portage **8**
Punga Cove Resort **9**
Raetihi Lodge **10**
Resolution Bay Cabins **11**
Smiths Farm Holiday
  Park **12**
Te Mahia Bay Resort **14**
Te Mahoerangi
  Eco Lodge **15**

Camping Λ
Bay of Many Coves **1**
Black Rock **2**
Camp Bay **3**
Cowshed **4**
Davies Bay **5**
Mistletoe Bay **6**
Ship Cove **7**

There are also general road tours and options by road from Picton to Anakiwa. **Beachcomber Cruise's Rural Mail Run,** T0800-624526/T03-573 6175, www.beachcombercruises.co.nz, from $85, is one option. This and other road trips can be booked and pre-paid via the VIC (I-Site). If you have your own wheels, road access is also possible at Camp Bay (Punga Cove), Torea Bay (The Portage) and Mistletoe Bay (Te Mahia).

Queen Charlotte Track

ⓘ *Details of the track are outlined in DoC leaflets available from the VIC (I-Site); DoC in Picton provides information and maps. The website www.qctrack.co.nz is also useful.*

The Queen Charlotte Track is a 71-km (three- to five-day) well-formed track from **Ship Cove** (Captain Cook's New Zealand base, 1770-1777) to **Anakiwa**. It is suitable for most people of average fitness and sections of the track are also popular for mountain biking. The track makes its way around sheltered coves, over skyline ridges and through native forest fringing a vast network of sunken river valleys. Although the track can be tackled from either Anakiwa or Ship Cove, conventionally the start is at Ship Cove and all written information describes the track in this direction (east to west). The track is becoming increasingly popular, so plan and book well in advance. There are numerous DoC campsites along the route and independent accommodation establishments cater for all budgets. Boat access is also well organized and readily available. Water taxis and cruise operators regularly stop not only at Ship Cove, but also at many of the accommodation establishments or campsites en route so it is possible to do part of the track, or to stay in one place and simply chill out. For the real cheats you can also arrange to have your backpack transported on to your next accommodation or port of call.

Nydia Track

ⓘ *Details of the track are outlined in the relevant DoC leaflets. The VIC (I-Site) and DoC offices in Picton and Havelock can provide comprehensive information and maps.*

The Nydia Track is the lesser known and shorter of the two tramping tracks. It is 27 km in length and takes two days. The track, which is essentially a network of old bridle paths, begins at Kaiuma Bay (near Havelock) and traverses the Kaiuma and Nydia saddles, taking in the sheltered, historic timber-milling site at **Nydia Bay**, before ending at **Duncan Bay**. The track is particularly noted for its magnificent forest, much of which is untouched and a fine example of the native bush that once covered the region. Although the Nydia Track is more difficult than the Queen Charlotte and requires detailed planning, it offers a shorter, less busy, alternative. However, bear in mind that it is not so well served by accommodation and public transport. From Havelock it is 12 km (45 minutes) drive via SH6 to the turn-off at Dalton's Road, then another 21 km to Kaiuma car park and the start of the track. Given that, you are far better off catching a water taxi (five minutes) to Shag Point from Havelock. Contact the VIC (I-Site) in Havelock or Picton for the latest operator listings, T03-520 3113.

Picton ⊜❼▲⊜❻ ▸▸ *pp424-434.*

Once you cross the Cook Strait and enter the 'The Sounds', you arrive in the pretty township of Picton (population 4,000), gateway to the Marlborough Sounds and the South Island. In summer Picton is a buzz of activity with visitors coming and going by ferry, car or train, but in winter it reverts to its more familiar role as a sleepy port.

Despite its size, Picton has an interesting history. It was once the site of an important Maori *pa* called Waitohi before the first Europeans settled and renamed it Newton. For a while Newton was the proud capital of Marlborough (before Blenheim stole the honours) and later, after being renamed Picton, became a candidate for the country's capital. In more recent times controversy has affected the town. For almost a decade the issue of relocating the ferry port south closer to Blenheim has been hotly debated. Thankfully for 'the Picts' that option was dismissed by the government, who claim it is not financially viable. So, thankfully, as the gateway to both the South Island and the sounds, pretty Picton looks set to remain.

Ins and outs

Getting there Picton airport ① *10 km south of town*, is served by **Soundsair**, T0800-505005/T03-520 3080, www.soundsair.com, eight times daily from Wellington, $89 one way. Scenic flights and a range of flight/activity combos are also available. ▸▸ *See Activities and tours, page 430.*

There are numerous bus companies that network their way to Picton from the south or west including **Intercity**, T03-573 7025, www.intercitycoach.co.nz; **Nakedbus**,

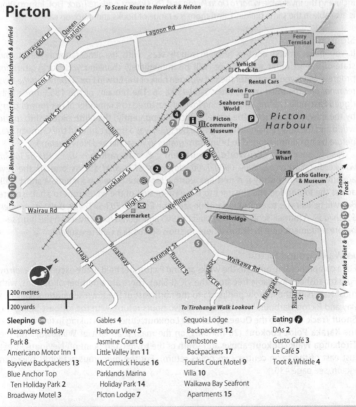

Picton

To Scenic Route to Havelock & Nelson

Lagoon Rd
Queen Charlotte Dr
Gravesend Pl
Kent St
York St
Devon St
Dublin St
Market St
Auckland St
High St
Wairau Rd
Otago St
Broadway
Taranaki St
Russell St
Wellington St
London Quay
Waikawa Rd
Sayers Cres
Newgate St
Rutland St

To 8 11 12, Blenheim, Nelson (Direct Route), Christchurch & Airfield
To Tirohanga Walk Lookout
To Karaka Point & 16 18 19 10
To Snout Track

Ferry Terminal
Vehicle Check-In
Rental Cars
Edwin Fox
Seahorse World
Picton Community Museum
Picton Harbour
Town Wharf
Echo Gallery & Museum
Supermarket
Footbridge

200 metres
200 yards
N

Sleeping 🛏
Alexanders Holiday Park **8**
Americano Motor Inn **1**
Bayview Backpackers **13**
Blue Anchor Top Ten Holiday Park **2**
Broadway Motel **3**

Gables **4**
Harbour View **5**
Jasmine Court **6**
Little Valley Inn **11**
McCormick House **16**
Parklands Marina Holiday Park **14**
Picton Lodge **7**

Sequoia Lodge Backpackers **12**
Tombstone Backpackers **17**
Tourist Court Motel **9**
Villa **10**
Waikawa Bay Seafront Apartments **15**

Eating 🍴
DAs **2**
Gusto Café **3**
Le Café **5**
Toot & Whistle **4**

www.nakedbus.com; **Atomic Shuttles**, T03-349 0697, www.atomictravel.co.nz; and **Southern Link**, T0508-458835, www.southernlinkkbus.co.nz. A single fare from Blenheim is $10-12, Nelson $20-25 and Christchurch around $40. Buses drop off or pick up at the railway station, ferry terminal or outside the VIC (I-Site). The main intercity coach agent is the VIC (I-Site), but the **Picton Travel Centre** ① *in the ferry terminal building, T03-573 7025*, can also assist with onward travel.

The **Interislander** and **Bluebridge** ferries dock in the rather plush **ferry terminal** ① *500 m north of town centre*. There are at least four sailings daily, see box page 409, or contact T0800-802802/T04-498 3302, www.interislander.co.nz/www.ferrytickets.co.nz.

The **train station** ① *Auckland St, T0800-872467/T04-495 0775, 0900-1700*, is the terminus for the daily **TranzCoastal** service from Christchurch, T0800-872467/T04-495 0775, www.tranzscenic.co.nz. It arrives daily at 1213 and departs at 1300, from $118. This trip is famous for its coastal scenery.

Tourist information **Picton VIC (I-Site)** ① *on the foreshore, T03-520 3113, www.destinationmarlborough.com, daily 0830-1800 (1700 winter)*, has many useful leaflets including the invaluable *What to Do In Picton* and *The Queen Charlotte Track*. **DoC** information is available in the same building, and there is a range of books and maps on sale.

Sights

If you have arrived on the ferry in rough seas, with its almost comfy seats and state-of-the-art radar screens, you will be immediately thanking your lucky stars for progress when you encounter the old wooden hulk of the **Edwin Fox** ① *between the ferry terminal and the town centre, daily 0900-1700, $6*. The remains of the 1853, once fully rigged East India Trading ship is being lovingly restored to a reminder of her former glory by the Edwin Fox Society. The vessel, which is (apparently) the ninth oldest ship in the world and the only remaining example of her type, was a troop carrier in the Crimean War before being commissioned to bring immigrants to Australia and New Zealand.

Next door is **EcoWorld Aquarium & Terrarium** ① *T03-5736030, www.ecoworldnz.co.nz, daily 0900-1700, day pass $17, child $9*. As one of the few aquariums in the country it is perhaps worth a look, but more fun for kids. A short walk across the footbridge and the inlet to the eastern side of the waterfront to Shakespeare Bay will deliver you to another maritime relic, the **Echo** ① *T03-5737498, daily in summer, $3, child $1*. A former 'scow' she was built in 1905 and served for 60 years on the high seas before retirement here in Picton where she now serves as a café/restaurant.

▲▲ Walks around Picton

For a comprehensive guide to the walks around Picton, get hold of the excellent *Picton by Foot* broadsheet, available free from the VIC (I-Site). There are a number of options, with most traversing the narrow peninsula to the northeast of the town separating Waikawa Bay and Picton Harbour. Most are around two hours return, with the longest being the **Snout Track**, taking in the **Queen Charlotte Lookout**. Other walks taking in fine views are the **Karaka Point Lookout** (20 minutes, on the main road east of Waikawa) and the **Tirohanga Walk Lookout**, above and south of the town (start point off Newgate Street just east of the town centre, two hours return). For the numerous activities based in Picton, see page 430.

Blenheim ⊜⊘⊗▲⊜⊙ ▶▶ pp424-434.

Although it is depressingly flat and unremarkable looking, Blenheim – Marlborough's largest town with a population of 27,000 – is a popular tourist base, primarily for those intent on sampling the region's fine wines. Most of the wineries lie just to the west of town and around the satellite village of Renwick 12 km west, on the fertile soils of the Wairau Plains. Marlborough is New Zealand's largest wine-growing region and forms the start (or finish) of the Classic New Zealand Wine Trail that tipples its way through Wellington and the Wairarapa to the Hawes Bay, www.classicwinetrail.co.nz.

Ins and outs

Getting there **Blenheim airport** ① *Middle Renwick Rd, 7 km west of town*, is serviced by **Air New Zealand Link**, T0800-737000, www.airnewzealand.co.nz. Flights are met by the **Airport Super Shuttle**, T03-572 9910; or **Neal's Shuttles**, T03-577 5277, $18.

Blenheim sits on both the main road (SH1) and rail links south, via Kaikoura (129 km) to Christchurch (308 km). An interesting alternative route by car to Blenheim from Picton is via the coast road, Port Underwood and the scenic bluffs of Rarangi. There are many bus services heading south. There are also services that head northwest via SH6 to Nelson, the Abel Tasman National Park and Golden Bay and west to St Arnaud and the Nelson Lakes National Park. See Picton Ins and outs, page 417, for details.

The **TranzCoastal** train service north to Picton or south to Christchurch passes through Blenheim once a day, T0800-872467, www.tranzscenic.co.nz.

Tourist information **Marlborough VIC (I-Site)** ① *railway station on Grove Rd (SH1), T03-577 8080, www.destinationmarlborough.com/www.winemarlborough.net.nz, daily 0830-1830; winter Mon-Fri 0830-1800, Sat-Sun 0900-1600*, has information about the town, region and, of course, the wineries. The free *Marlborough Visitor Guide* is useful.

Sights

Being primarily a service town, Blenheim has little to offer the tourist in the way of sights, with most visitors simply joining the various winery tours based in town, or picking up the information to tour the vineyards. However, of some historical interest is the provincial museum and archives complex at the **Brayshaw Museum Park** ① *New Renwick Rd, T03-5781712, 3 km south of the town, daily 1000-1600, free entry with a small charge for some attractions*. The museum is a mainly open-air affair, featuring an interesting reconstruction of an early settlers' village along with the inevitable farm machinery and ancient vehicles. Right in the centre of town is **Seymour Square** with its landmark clock tower. It also hosts the **Marlborough Millennium Gallery** ① *T03-579 2001, Mon-Fri 1030-1630, Sat-Sun 1300-1600, donation*, which is the main focus for the arts in the region. If you are interested in more regional detail surrounding arts and crafts pick up the free *Art and Craft Trail* leaflet from the VIC (I-Site).

Wineries

The biggest attractions around Blenheim – and arguably the entire region – are the world-class wineries. Sun-baked Marlborough is New Zealand's largest wine-growing region, with over 50 wineries producing highly acclaimed Chardonnay, Riesling, Cabernet Sauvignon, Merlot, Pinot Noir, sparkling Methode Champenoise and some of best Sauvignon Blanc in the world. Of all the varieties in recent times it is the Sauvignon Blanc

Blenheim

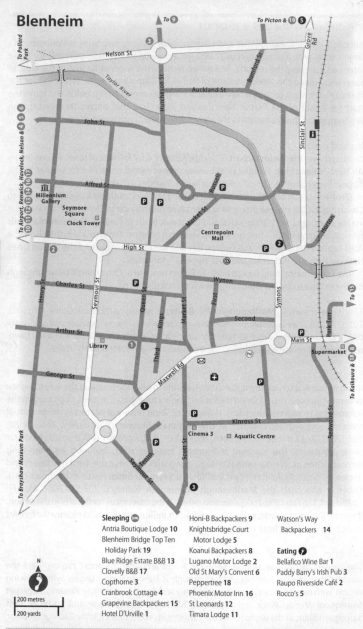

Sleeping
Antria Boutique Lodge **10**
Blenheim Bridge Top Ten
 Holiday Park **19**
Blue Ridge Estate B&B **13**
Clovelly B&B **17**
Copthorne **3**
Cranbrook Cottage **4**
Grapevine Backpackers **15**
Hotel D'Urville **1**

Honi-B Backpackers **9**
Knightsbridge Court
 Motor Lodge **5**
Koanui Backpackers **8**
Lugano Motor Lodge **2**
Old St Mary's Convent **6**
Peppertree **18**
Phoenix Motor Inn **16**
St Leonards **12**
Timara Lodge **11**

Watson's Way
 Backpackers **14**

Eating
Bellafico Wine Bar **1**
Paddy Barry's Irish Pub **3**
Raupo Riverside Café **2**
Rocco's **5**

that has become the most popular. Montana sowed the first seeds of success in the early 1970s and is now the largest winery in the country. Three decades on, Montana has been joined by other world-famous names and has become a major national export industry.

Like Hawke's Bay in the North Island, the wineries have been quick to take advantage of the tourist dollar, with most offering tours, tastings (free or small charge) and good restaurants. Although the competition in Marlborough is fierce, the region's vineyards lack the architectural splendour or variety of Hawke's Bay. Perhaps they just leave the wine to do the talking.

If you are a complete novice it's a good idea to join one of the many excellent tours on offer. They generally last a full- or half-day, taking in the pick of the crop and the widest variety of wine types. There is always an informative commentary, often a lunch stop and, of course, numerous tastings included in the package. If you know a bit about wines and have particular tastes, many tour operators will create a personal itinerary. If you wish to explore by yourself, there are plenty of maps and leaflets at the VIC (I-Site).

Most of the wineries are located off SH6 around the small village of **Renwick**, 10 km west of Blenheim. Should you tire of all this viniculture there are other distilleries, breweries, vineyards and orchards in the area producing everything from liqueurs and fruit wines to olive oil. There is even an English-style pub and brewery, **The Cork and Keg** ① *Inkerman St, Renwick, T03-572 9328*, which produces its own beer.

Some excellent and detailed information about the region and New Zealand wines generally can be found in the magazine *Campbell's Wine Annual*, which can be bought in most leading bookshops and magazine outlets. The VIC (I-Site) also produces *The Wines and Wineries of Marlborough – Wine Trail Map* and *The Marlborough Wine Region* broadsheet. With all of these you cannot go wrong. For web information visit www.winemarlborough.net.nz.

Havelock ●❼▲❸ ➤➤ *pp424-434*.

From Blenheim SH6 passes through the small village of Renwick before winding its way through the rolling hills of the Inner Marlborough Sounds to Nelson. About a third of the way (41 km), at the head of the expansive Pelorus Sound, is the enchanting little village of Havelock. Blink and you will miss it, but if you have time, a stop here is well worth it.

Ins and outs
Getting there and around Havelock is 41 km from Blenheim and 75 km from Nelson on SH6. By bus, **Intercity**, **Atomic Shuttles** and **Nakedbus**, www.nakedbus.com, all service Havelock (Main Road) on their way back and forth to Nelson. For full service listings, see Picton Ins and outs, page 417. For track transport, **Kenepuru Water Taxi**, T03-573 4344, www.kenepuru.co.nz, offers a water taxi service.

Tourist information There are several independent visitor centres in the main street that serve as a source of local information and local activity booking agents. Internet is also available. The **Havelock Information Centre** ① *46 Main Rd, T03-574 2104, www.havelockinfocentre.co.nz*, is a reliable option.

Sights
The village itself has little to offer except a friendly welcome, a fine café, restaurant, art and craft galleries, some rugby-playing mussel shells (honest), a small but interesting

Wineries around Blenheim

A comprehensive list of the wineries is beyond the scope of this guide, but some wineries of particular note are listed below. The best time to visit the vineyards is in April when the heavily laden vines are ripe for the picking. See also Winery tours listings, page 433.

Allan Scott Estate, Jackson's Rd, T03-5729054, www.allanscott.com, daily 0900-1700, lunch from 0900. Established in 1973, producing fine Sauvignon, Chardonnay and Riesling wines. Twelve Trees restaurant is deservedly popular.

Wairau River, 264 Rapaura Rd, T03-572 9800, www.wairauriverwines.com, daily 0900-1700 (lunch 1200-1500). Family owned and producing fine, hand-tended, fruity vintages. Lovely aesthetics and a popular restaurant as well.

Cloudy Bay, Jackson's Rd, T03-520 9197, www.cloudybay.co.nz, tastings and tours daily 1000-1700. An internationally famous label.

Herzog, 81 Jeffries Rd, T03-572 8770, www.herzog.co.nz, daily 1100-1500. Not only fine wine (particularly Pinot Noir) but one of the best winery restaurants in the country, open Oct-mid May. Exceptional international wine list.

Highfield Estate, Brookby Rd, T03-572 9244, www.highfield.co.nz, daily 1030-1700. Fine wine, architecture and the best view of the lot from its rampart tower. Reputable restaurant open daily for lunch 1130-1530.

Hunters Wines, Rapaura Rd, T03-5728489, www.hunters.co.nz. Another of the larger, most popular labels producing a wide variety of wines. Also home to a fine restaurant open for lunch (1130-1430) and dinner Thu-Sat, from 1800.

Johanneshof Cellars, SH1, Koromiko, 20 km north of Blenheim, T03-573 7035, www.johanneshof.co.nz, summer Tue-Sun 1000-1600. Cellar tours. Famous for underground 'rock cellars', lined with both barrel and bottle.

Montana Brancott Winery, Main South Rd (SH1), just to the south of Blenheim, T03-578 2099, www.montana.co.nz, daily 0900-1700. It is almost rude not to visit this, the largest wine-producer in the country. The visitor centre is very impressive and there are half-hourly tours (1000-1500), tastings, a restaurant with outdoor seating and a classy shop. This is also the venue for the now world-famous **Marlborough Food and Wine Festival** in February (see Festivals and events, page 430).

Prenzel Distillery, Sheffield St, Riverlands Estate, T03-520 8215, www.prenzel.com. New Zealand's first commercial fruit distillery producing a range of fruit liqueurs, schnapps, and brandies.

Seresin, Bedford Rd, Renwick, T03-5729408, www.seresin.co.nz, summer daily 1000-1630, winter Mon-Fri 1000-1630. Noted not only for its wine, but also its artwork.

museum ① *Main Rd, T03-574 2176, daily (seasonal) 0900-1700, entry by donation*, and a fine Scottish pub, but it is an ideal base from which to explore the glorious Pelorus and other 'outer sounds'. As the quiet neighbour to the much-hyped Queen Charlotte Sound, the Pelorus does not receive as much attention, but it is no less impressive and, in summer, provides a much quieter alternative. Havelock was once a thriving gold-mining town and also the boyhood home of one of New Zealand's most famous sons, Ernest Rutherford – the man who 'split' the atom. His former home is now the busy youth hostel. Havelock was also the latter-day home of another famous New Zealander, the writer Barry Crump, whose humorous accounts of hunting and life in the bush has had many a proud

Kiwi smiling in recognition. These days Havelock's gold is the green-lipped mussel, a major export industry within the sounds.

If you intend to explore the sounds by road you can do this along the **Kenepuru Road**, which starts just past Linkwater (east of Havelock on Queen Charlotte Drive), or the **Tennyson Inlet** and **French Pass** roads, just north of Rai valley, west of Havelock (see below). Maps are available at the Picton or Havelock VICs (I-Sites).

▲▲ Walks

Havelock is the principal base from which to embark on the increasingly popular **Nydia Track** (see page 416); **Rutherford Travel**, T03-574 2104, can advise. About 18 km west of Havelock is the **Pelorus Bridge Scenic Reserve**. This is a pretty little spot where the azure waters of the Rai and Pelorus rivers carve their way through the surrounding bush-clad hills. There are a number of walks from 30 minutes to three hours. A number of DoC information boards or the tearooms near the car park will keep you right. At the very least, stop and have a look at the river from the bridge.

Closer to Havelock itself is the climb to **Takorika Hill**. Located behind the town, its ascent will be rewarded by fine views. The lazy, or pushed-for-time, can reach the transmission tower by car via forest tracks (6 km). The entrance via Wilsons Road is about 5 km west of Havelock on SH6.

Tennyson Inlet, French Pass and D'Urville Island ⊜⊙ ❱❱ pp424-434.

The Ronga and Opouri roads which connect the remote corners of the outer sounds are worthy of investigation, offering some stunning coastal scenery of a type that is unsurpassed elsewhere in the country. Both roads can be accessed just beyond the small settlement of Rai Valley, 48 km east of Nelson and 27 km west of Havelock. To explore the roads properly you should stock up with food and petrol and give yourself at least two days: one to take in Opouri Road and Tennyson Inlet (40 km), then back to Ronga Road to French Pass (70 km); and the second to spend some time in French Pass before returning to SH6. From French Pass it is possible to explore the most remote and largest of the sounds' islands, D'Urville Island, named after the intrepid French explorer who discovered it in 1827. If you don't have your own transport, you could try the local **Mail Run** but times and schedules vary, or contact **Havelock Information Centre**, T03-574 2114.

Tennyson Inlet

About 1 km from SH6, Opouri Road shadows the Opouri River and cuts through paddock upon paddock full of sleepy stock lying in the shade of sheds that have seen better days. Then it suddenly and dramatically straddles **Lookout Hill** (900 m) before falling like a stone to Tennyson Inlet. The view at the crest of the hill is almost as impressive as the hairpin bends which must be negotiated to reach the inlet. But once there, the peace and tranquillity seem reward enough. If you are feeling energetic you might like to walk part of the Nydia Track to **Nydia Bay** where there is camping and accommodation available (see pages 416 and 425).

French Pass

Back on Ronga Road, the route cuts through the paddocks of a river valley before climbing through attractive native bush to reach the first stunning views of Croisilles Harbour and out to the west coast of **D'Urville Island**. The first settlement of any consequence is **Okiwi Bay**, a secret little haunt of many a boatie Nelsonite. Okiwi provides a great base from which to go sailing or fishing in the quiet undisturbed bays of the Sounds westernmost coastline.

Just past Okiwi Bay the road passes through some beautiful tracts of beech forest before becoming unsealed. It is another 40 km to French Pass but after just a few kilometres the views of the sounds really open up and damage to your hire car will be the last thing on your mind. From **Elaine Bay** the road clings precariously to bush-clad ridges giving you a glimpse of the scenic splendour, before the trees peter out and D'Urville Island comes into view. You then head along the western side of the now bare ridge to French Pass. On the way, take the short detour to the top of the hill with the transmitters. From there you can soak up another stunning vista of Tennyson Inlet.

French Pass is really nothing more than a row of houses and a DoC campsite in a small sheltered bay at the very tip of the mainland. It takes its name from the nautical nightmare that is just around the corner. The best view of this alarmingly slim channel of water can be seen from a path that leads down to a viewing point from the road (about 1 km before the settlement). At anytime, but particularly mid-tide, the chaotic currents can be seen forcing their way between the mainland and D'Urville Island. First discovered by D'Urville in 1827, this passage is a very important point on the nautical map because it offers an enticing short cut between Wellington and Nelson. If you are lucky you can time your visit to coincide with the passage of a ship.

◉ Marlborough Sounds listings

For Sleeping and Eating price codes and other relevant information, see Essentials pages 44-50.

● Sleeping

Queen Charlotte Track *p416, map p415*
The Queen Charlotte Track is well served with accommodation options with a broad range from DoC campsites (from $3-$14) to privately owned backpacker hostels, self-contained units and luxury lodges. The VIC (I-Site) has full listings and will help you plan your itinerary and book your accommodation, but in summer you are advised to do this well in advance. There are also ample accommodation options elsewhere throughout the sounds with most offering meals and some having in-house restaurants or at the very least adequate cooking facilities. Some can be reached by water taxi, others by road, or even by air. Again the VIC (I-Site) will advise. Some of the more noteworthy establishments are listed below.
LL-L Lazy Fish, about 12 km from Picton, Queen Charlotte Sound, T03-573 5291, www.lazyfish.co.nz. A superb luxury option set in its own bay, only accessible by boat. Its

motto is '*Ubi Dies Omnis Festus*' ('where every day is Sunday'). The homestead, beautifully appointed and renovated, is only a few metres from the water with guest bungalows set in bush. Contemporary artworks and antiques dominate the decor and each bungalow has a 4-poster bed. The old UK telephone box on the jetty adds to the character and charm. Meals included. Outdoor bathtub, excellent kitchen, windsurfer/canoe/fishing tackle hire.
LL-L Raetihi Lodge, Kenepuru Sound, T03-573 4300, www.raetihi.co.nz. Modern, luxury lodge over looking Double Bay in Kenepuru Sound noted for its architecture, secluded location and cuisine. 14 themed rooms reflect a variety of topics from the colours of the Sounds, to nautical or Egyptian, stunning views, licensed à la carte restaurant. Dinner, B&B packages available. Accessible by road, boat or by air (direct from Wellington with **Soundsair**). Boat recommended.
LL-A Bay of Many Coves Resort, Queen Charlotte Sound, T03-579 9771, www.bayof manycovesresort.co.nz. Comes recommended and represents the area at its best. Remote seclusion yet all the comforts of

a modern award-winning resort. Classy studio units and apartments with memorable views across the sound, café, restaurant and a wide range of activities from kayaking to heli-fishing.

L-AL Te Mahia Bay Resort, Kenepuru Sound, T03-573 4089, www.temahia.co.nz. Compact and in a peaceful location. Self-catering waterfront apartment and motel-style accommodation. No restaurant. Fishing trips a speciality.

L-C Punga Cove Resort, Punga Cove, Endeavour Inlet, T03-579 8561, www.pungacove.co.nz. Wide range of options from private chalets and self-contained studios to a backpacker lodge with twin bunkrooms ($40pp) and one double ($85). Facilities and services include a licensed restaurant, shop, laundry, spa and canoe hire. The resort is a 500-m walk from the road. Water taxi recommended.

AL-D Portage Hotel, Kenepuru Sound, T03-573 4309, www.portage.co.nz. A wide range of accommodation from luxury spa rooms to bunkrooms. Restaurant, well-stocked shop, pool and DoC campsite nearby. Kayak and bike hire available.

A-D Furneaux Lodge, Endeavour Inlet, T03-579 8259, www.furneaux.co.nz. Historic lodge set in idyllic gardens near a waterfall. Self-contained chalets and backpacker accommodation in a lovely stone 'croft'. Campsite available. Restaurant and bar. Ideal for a night stopover from Ship Cove.

A-D Lochmara Lodge (Backpackers), Lochmara Bay, T03-573 4554, www.lochmara lodge.co.nz. Closed Jun-Oct. A deservedly popular eco- and arts-oriented backpacker hostel with a great, laid-back atmosphere. Dorm and private studio chalets (some en suite). If you can remove yourself from a hammock there is a spa (in the bush where the Punga People live), open fire, free kayak and windsurf hire. Excellent art gallery, a small wildlife reabilitation facility and in-house eco-trips to Motuara Island. Recommended.

A-D Resolution Bay Cabins, Resolution Bay, T03-579 9411, www.resolutionbay cabins.co.nz. Accommodation ranges from

cabins to self-contained cottages. Good atmosphere and fine café. Shop on site.

B-D Hopewell, Kenepuru Sound, T03-573 4341, www.hopewell.co.nz. Excellent establishment in a remote location on Kenepuru Sound, providing the perfect blend of value and comfort. Although accessible by road from Havelock North or Picton it is a tortuous drive. A water taxi is recommended and adds the overall experience, or you can fly direct from Wellington (**Soundsair**) to the local airfield from where you can be picked up. A range of options from a self-contained cottage to doubles and 4-shares. Attractive grounds right down to the water's edge. Outdoor spa overlooking the sound, internet, kayaks and plenty of water-based activities, with fishing trips a speciality. Friendly, caring hosts. One night is not enough. The secret is out so book well ahead. Recommended.

C-D Smiths Farm Holiday Park, Queen Charlotte Drive, Linkwater, T03-574 2806. Spotless self-contained motel units, cabins, powered and tent sites close to the track start at Anakiwa to which there is courtesy transport. Bike hire and lots of friendly animals. Recommended.

Campsites

D DoC campsites are available at Ship Cove, Camp Bay, Bay of Many Coves, Black Rock, Cowshed, Mistletoe Bay and Davies Bay.

Nydia Track *p416, map p415*
C-D Te Mahoerangi Eco Lodge, Nydia Bay, T03- 579 8411, www.nydiatrack.org.nz. Private Double Cabins upstairs in a cosy wooden cabin. Twin Cabins all sharing funky bathrooms and a large well-equipped kitchen. There is also a Dorm Room and camping. Basic vegetarian meals are available as well as organic coffee, or herbal tea.
D Nydia Lodge, on the south coast of Nydia Bay, T03-520 3002. Sleeps 50 in 9 bunk rooms, kitchen and hot showers.

Campsites

DoC campsites (from $5) available in the

northwestern corner of Nydia Bay: 2 in Tennyson Inlet and 1 in Duncan Bay.

Picton *p416, map p417*
There are few modern hotels but plenty of motels to choose from.
LL McCormick House, 21 Leicester St, T03-573 5253, www.mccormickhouse.co.nz. A modern, friendly and luxury B&B in a quiet location. 3 lovely en suites. Courtesy car.
AL Waikawa Bay Seafront Apartments, 45 Beach Rd, T03-573 5220, www.Apartments OnTheWaterfront.co.nz. A modern establishment located beside the Waikawa Bay marina complex, east of Picton. Offers luxury self-contained apartments, pool, spa, and café/restaurant/bar nearby.
AL-A The Broadway Motel, 113 High St, T03-573 6563, www.broadwaymotel.co.nz. Centrally located and handy for the ferry terminal the Broadway is one of the most modern motels in the town. Spotless standard units, some with spa and balcony.
A Americano Motor Inn, 32 High St, T0800-104104/T03-573 6398, www.americano.co.nz. Right in the heart of town this is a large motel with a popular licensed restaurant attached.
A The Jasmine Court, 78 Wellington St, T03-573 7110, www.jasminecourt.co.nz. Another good motel offering a fine range of well-appointed, modern units. Good location.
A Little Valley Inn, 21 Garden Terr, T03-573 7600, www.littlevalleyinn.co.nz.co.nz. Set in a quiet location on the edge of the town Little Valley offers a cosy en suite self contained studio with queen bed, small log fire and private courtyard with outside bath.
A-B The Gables, 20 Waikawa Rd, T03-573 6772, www.thegables.co.nz. Enjoys a good reputation and in an ideal location with 3 rooms and 2 self-contained cottages on site plus another cottage option in Waikawa Bay.
B The Harbour View, 30 Waikawa Rd, T03-573 6259, www.harbourviewpicton. co.nz. 12 fully self-contained studio units and fine views across the harbour.
A Tourist Court Motel, 45 High St, T03-573

6331, www.tourist-court.co.nz. One of the better, long-established mid-budget motels, near the centre.
B-D Tombstone Backpackers, 16 Gravesend Pl, T03-573 7116, www.tomb stonebp.co.nz. A century-old villa in an elevated position overlooking the harbour, yet within walking distance of the ferry terminal. Fully renovated with all modern fittings and décor. Tidy, cosy doubles, twin and shared en suites. Facilities include Sky TV, fast internet and a spacious lounge. Overall a fine start to the South Island experience. Deservedly popular so book ahead. Recommended.
B-D Bayview Backpackers, 318 Waikawa Rd, T03-573 7668, www.truenz.co.nz/ bayviewbackpackers. A modern, friendly and spacious place in Waikawa Bay, just east of Picton. Good value dorm beds, single, twin and double rooms some with en suite bath and TV. It offers the peace and quiet absent at the bustling hostels in the town centre. Free pick-up/drop-off to the ferry. Free bikes, kayaks and sailing trips arranged. Internet. Recommended.
B-D Picton Lodge, 9 Auckland St, T0800-223367/T03-573 7788, www.pictonlodge. co.nz. The closest hostel to the ferry terminal and close to the VIC (I-Site) and town centre, pub next door. Singles, doubles/ twins and small dorms. Large open plan living area. Free breakfast and bike hire.
B-D Sequoia Lodge Backpackers, 3A Nelson Sq, T0800-222257/T03-573 8399, www.sequoialodge.co.nz. Although about 500 m from the town centre and 1 km from the ferry terminal, this is an excellent hostel run by enthusiastic staff. Modern facilities with secure parking. Dorms, private singles, twin and double rooms, some en suite. Spa, log fire, free breakfast, tea and coffee. Free pick-up/drop-off to ferry. Internet.
B-D The Villa, 32 Auckland St, T03-573 6598, www.thevilla.co.nz. A deservedly popular, well-established and lively backpacker hostel in a century-old villa. Dorms, twins and doubles. Fine facilities and a great outdoor area with spa. The managers are a hive of information on

local activities and can assist with plans and bookings. Free 'all you can eat' breakfast, tea, coffee, duvets, bike hire and shuttle service. Internet. Pre-booking advisable.

Motorcamps
B-D Blue Anchor Top Ten Holiday Park, 78 Waikawa Rd, T0800-277444. An excellent award-winning holiday park and very popular. It is well located within walking distance of the town, has tidy cabins and tourist flats and great facilities. It gets a little crowded at times, especially if you are camping, so try to arrive early in the day.

B-D Alexanders Holiday Park, T0800-474286/T03-573 6378, www.accommodationz.co.nz/pages/alexanderspark. A spacious park, located at the southern edge of the town and about 1500 m from the ferry, with ageing but adequate facilities, including a large well-equipped camp kitchen.

B-D Parklands Marina Holiday Park, T03-573 6343 on Beach Rd, Waikawa, close to the marina. This is another large, but older and less salubrious holiday park.

Blenheim p419, map p420
There is no shortage of beds in Blenheim with plenty of hotels, motels and backpacker hostels. The emphasis, however, is on the many excellent boutique-style lodges, B&Bs and homestays outside the town, often in the vineyards. The VIC (I-Site) has comprehensive listings and can book on your behalf. During the picking season (Apr/May) it's advisable to pre-book backpacker hostels in the region.

Blenheim Township
LL Hotel D'Urville, 52 Queen St, T03-577 9945, www.durville.co.nz. Quality boutique hotel in a former bank in the heart of the town centre. Individually themed rooms, from the 'New Zealand' or 'Merlot' room; to the African or 'Retro', ensures something for everyone. Classy restaurant attached.

L The Copthorne Hotel Marlborough, 20 Nelson St, T03-577 7333, www.marlborough hotel.co.nz. A modern option with a wide range of rooms and suites, heated pool, internet and the quality Nikau restaurant.

AL-A Lugano Motor Lodge, corner of High and Henry sts, T03-577 8808, www.lugano. co.nz. A modern and popular luxury motel, close to the centre of town. Ever tried a 'thermo-mattress'? Well, now is your chance.

AL-A Phoenix Motor Inn, 174 Middle Renwick Rd, T03-577 9002, www.phoenixmotor inn.co.nz. Modern, with a good reputation. 12 studios and 3 luxury units with spa.

A Knightsbridge Court Motor Lodge, 112 Middle Renwick Rd, T03-578 0818, www.knightsbridgecourt.co.nz. Considered one of the better motels in town. Spa suites available. Shopping centre opposite.

A-D Blenheim Bridge Top Ten Holiday Park, 78 Grove Rd, T03-578 3667, www.blenheimtop10.co.nz. Located to the north of the town beside SH1, the main railway line and the river. Close to the main road and railway line so a bit noisy but otherwise well equipped and functional.

B-D Grapevine Backpackers, 29 Park Terr, T03-578 6062, www.thegrapevine.co.nz. Another large suburban single-storey villa on the riverbank. Full range of rooms, free canoe and bike hire. Assistance finding seasonal work.

B-D The Koanui Backpackers, 33 Main St, T03-578 7487, www.koanui.co.nz. A rambling single-storey refurbished villa and a purpose-built lodge close to town. The villa serves as the traditional backpacker hostel while the lodge offers studio style en suites with TV. Both offer spacious lounges and well-equipped kitchens. Internet, bike hire and off-street parking.

C-D Honi-B Backpackers, corner of Hutcheson and Parker sts, T03-577 8441, www.honi-b.com. Centrally located hostel that is revitalizing the town's backpacking scene. Standard modern facilities and wide range of rooms, parking and internet. Recommended.

Around Blenheim
LL Antria Boutique Lodge, 276 Old Renwick Rd, T03-579 2191, www.antria.co.nz.

Described as a modern European castle, Antria is certainly aesthetically different. But don't expect ramparts or moats. This is a truly modern concept, more Mediterranean in design, with large Gothic timber doors opening up into an open-air courtyard. Stylish, well-appointed Italian-style rooms and contemporary artwork throughout adds to the overall class and atmosphere. The tariff is reasonable in comparison to many other top-range establishments.

LL Old Saint Mary's Convent, Rapaura Rd, T03-570 5700, www.convent.co.nz. One of the most popular places to stay in the region. A century-old, renovated and relocated 2-storey convent set in expansive gardens and surrounded by vineyards. Spacious modern en suites vary according to price, but all have great views across the vineyards, Sky TV, access to the balcony or garden. Even if you are not in the honeymoon suite ask to see it, it is positively angelic. Library, billiard room, authentic chapel and free bike hire.

LL Timara Lodge, Dog Point Rd, T03-572 8276, www.timara.co.nz. Luxury by the lake. 1920s homestead amid 73 ha of beautiful gardens. Superb rooms, facilities and fine cuisine, but it all comes at a cost.

LL-L The Peppertree, SH1, Riverlands, T03-520 9200, www.thepeppertree.co.nz. Historic villa set amid an extensive country garden, boutique vineyard and olive grove with a choice of five sumptious en suites. Fine breakfast.

L Cranbrook Cottage, Giffords Rd, T03-572 8606, www.cranbrook.co.nz. Without doubt one of the most characterful self-contained cottage B&Bs in the region. Set among the vines and fruit trees, the 135-year-old renovated cottage provides plenty of privacy and is very romantic, with breakfast delivered to the door each morning.

AL Blue Ridge Estate B&B, 50 O'Dwyers Rd, T03-5702198, www.blueridge.co.nz. Very classy purpose-designed homestay in an 8-ha rural setting, with fine views across some of the best-known vineyards. Well-appointed rooms with earthy colours and an almost minimalist feel. Good value, recommended.

AL Clovelly B&B, 2a Nelson Pl, Renwick, T03-572 9593, www.clovelly.co.nz. A more affordable B&B option in the sleepy village of Renwick 10 km west of Blenheim. Good value and only 2 mins from **The Cork and Keg** English-style country pub and brewery.

AL St Leonards, 18 St Leonards Rd, T03-577 8328, www.stleonards.co.nz. Beautifully appointed self-contained accommodation sleeping up to 6, in 3 vineyard cottages (one of which is a former stables) and a homestead annexe. Open fires, potbelly stoves and claw-foot baths add to a cosy, homely atmosphere. Good value.

B-D Watson's Way Backpackers, 56 High St, Renwick, T03-572 8228, www.watsonsway backpackers.co.nz. The most popular hostel in the Blenheim region. Lots of character, relaxed and well-equipped, and within walking distance of numerous vineyards and **The Cork and Keg** English pub and brewery.

Havelock *p421*

There is little in the way of accommodation in Havelock itself, most is out in the sounds.

B Havelock Garden Motel, 71 Main St, T03-574 2387, www.gardenmotels.com. Set in large gardens close to all amenities.

C-D Rutherford Lodge Havelock YHA, 46 Main Rd, T03-574 2104, www.yha.co.nz. Spacious YHA, the former home of world-famous scientist Ernest Rutherford. Double, twin and bunks. Camping available. Internet. Activity specialists.

Motorcamps and campsites

C-D Chartridge Holiday Park, SH6 (3 km south of Havelock), T03-574 2129. A superb peaceful and low-key little motorpark with 2 great value cabins and a bunkroom. Small camp kitchen and games lounge with TV. Recommended. Book ahead.

C-D DoC campsite, Pelorus Bridge, T03-571 6019. Cabins and powered sites. Café nearby with good homemade fare.

C-D Havelock Motor Camp, 24 Inglis St, T03-574 2339, www.havelockmotorcamp.

co.nz. Powered/tent sites and only a few basic cabins close to the harbour.

French Pass p423

There are lots of places to stay and a surprising amount of activities in or around French Pass.

L Ngaio Bay Homestead, on the western side of the peninsula, T03-576 5287, www.ngaiobay.co.nz. Idyllic B&B with its own private beach. Home-grown organic produce a speciality.

AL French Pass Beachfront Villas and Sea Safaris, T03-576 5204, www.seasafaris.co.nz. Here in this remote and fascinating corner of the Marlborough Sounds, this is the main focus for activities and offers delightful motel accommodation. The modern 3-star units are fully self- contained and have balconies looking out across the bay. Meals provided on request. Trips are flexible, half- to multi-day adventures including diving, fishing, walking or wildlife watching, with dolphins a regular sight. Booking essential.

A-B D'Urville Wilderness Resort, T03- 576 5268, www.durvilleisland.co.nz. It doesn't get much more remote than this. Comfortable rooms and a waterfront café and bar accessible only by boat. Ideal for that total getaway experience or for exploring D'Urville Island.

Motorcamps and campsites

B-D Okiwi Bay Holiday Park, T03-576 5006, www.okiwi.co.nz. A small homestay lodge, powered and tent sites, petrol and a store.
D DoC Campsite French Pass. Small and basic but, not surprisingly, popular ($6).

❶ Eating

Picton p416, map p417

Despite (or perhaps because of) competition from so many fine vineyard restaurants around Blenheim and resort restaurants in the sounds, Picton seems lacking in fine dining options. There is a supermarket, **Supervalue**, in the Mariners Mall on High St, 0730-1930.

¶¶ DAs, 53 High St, T03-573 5223. Daily 0900-2200. A reliable mid-range option with a café-style menu, specializing in gourmet pizza but it cannot seem to decide if it is a pokie (slot machine) parlour or a café.
¶¶ Gusto Café, 33 High St, T03-573 7171. Sun-Fri 0800-1500, Thu-Sat 1700-late. Imaginative menu, good coffee and service to match.
¶¶ Le Café, on London Quay, T03-573 5588. Daily for breakfast, lunch and dinner. Perhaps the best bet, it has a good atmosphere and is well placed on the waterfront.
¶ Toot and Whistle, Auckland St, near the ferry terminal, T03-573 6086. Daily 0900-late. The best pub grub and beer to be found in town. A lively place that has no doubt seen its fair share of clients miss the ferry.

Blenheim p419, map p420

With the influence of the wineries and the many gourmet travellers, the choice and quality are excellent. The **New World** supermarket is on Main St, daily 0800-2100.
¶¶¶Hotel D'Urville, 52 Queen St, T03-577 9945. Daily 0600-2400. The place for fine dining in Blenheim.
¶¶¶Nikau, Nikau Copthorne Hotel Marlborough, 20 Nelson St, T03-577 9821. Recommended poolside dining.
¶¶Bellafico Wine Bar, 17 Maxwell Rd, T03-577 6072, www.bellafico.co.nz. Mon-Sat 1000 until late. European offerings and a huge wine list, even by Blenheim standards.
¶¶ Kekerengu Store, Kekerengu (halfway between Blenheim and Kaikoura), T03-575 8600. 0700-late. Set overlooking the ocean with fine café-style cuisine. Crayfish is a speciality, but stop for a coffee at the very least. Recommended.
¶¶ Paddy Barry's Irish Pub, 51 Scott St, T03-578 7470. Good for pub grub.
¶¶Rocco's, 5 Dodson St, T03-578 6940, evenings only. A fine Italian restaurant.
¶¶Raupo Riverside Café , 2 Symons St, T03-577 8822. Fairly new and earning a good reputation and not just for its prime position overlooking the Taylor River.

Wineries p419 and p422

Some of the larger wineries have fine restaurants or cafés offering indoor/outdoor seating and lunch and/or dinner. Some of the best can be found at: **Allan Scott**, T03-572 7123, www.allanscott.com (restaurant lunch only); **Hunters**, T03-572 8489 (café serving lunch daily and dinner Wed-Sat); **Highfield**, T03-572 9244 (lunch only); **Montana Brancott**, T03-520 6975, www.montana.co.nz (cafe lunch only); and **Wairau River Wines**, T03-572 9800, www.wairauriver wines.com (restaurant lunch only).

Havelock p421

♙♙♙ **The Mussel Pot Restaurant**, 73 Main Rd, T03-574 2824. Daily 1100-2130. A stay in Havelock would not be complete without sampling the green-lipped mussels at this award winning restaurant. A bowl of seafood chowder will cost a value $12 and steamed mussels from $18.

♙♙ **Clansman Scots Pub**, Main Rd, T03-574 2495, www.theclansman.co.nz. Great for a pint and some fine pub grub.

♙♙ **Slip Inn Café and Wine Bar**, by the main marina, T03-574 2345. Mon-Thu 1000-2000, Fri-Sun 1000-2300. Small but lively place worth checking out if you are planning a trip out on the sound.

French Pass p423

The only place to eat is at the **D'Urville Wilderness Resort**, see Sleeping. There's also a small store and a petrol station.

☻ Festivals and events

For further information on other annual events and specific dates contact the VIC (I-Site) or look up the regional website www.marlborough4fun.co.nz.

Blenheim p419, map p420

The **Marlborough Centre**, Arthur St, T03-520 8558, www.mctt.co.nz, is the region's principal entertainment venue with a variety of shows, exhibitions and performances on offer throughout the year. However, most of the Blenheim and Marlborough events revolve around fine wine and food.

Feb Blues, Brews and Barbecues annual festival (1st week), T03-578 9457, www.blues brews.co.nz, entry fee. This is the breweries' answer to their wine-making neighbours. Tents are raised and all kinds of ales demolished to accompanying live music. **Marlborough Wine Festival** (2nd Sat), T03-5579299, www.wine-marlborough-festival.co.nz. The principal event of the year and now world famous, is the lively and very alcoholic celebration of the region's gourmet food and wines. Live music provided.

Apr Easter Airshow (end of month), www.classicfighters.co.nz. Heads are raised from wine glasses for this show which stages some mock dog fights between classic fighter planes from both world wars. Wine and food included of course.

▲ Activities and tours

Picton p416, map p417

Most activities are based around cruising, tramping (see page 414) or kayaking, with the odd bit of dolphin and birdspotting thrown in. The VIC (I-Site) in Picton has a comprehensive list of activities, which are helpfully listed by time of day, not operator, and well worth a look. It can also advise on horse trekking, winery tours (see page 433), diving, tandem paragliding, scenic flights, fishing and independent boat charters. With so many choices and choices within choices it pays to take your time and shop around.

Cruises

There are endless bays, coves and islands to explore in the sounds, with a rich variety of wildlife including dolphins and rare seabirds. As you might expect, there is a mind-boggling range of cruise options available with fiercely competitive operators. Most are based on the waterfront in Picton. It's a good idea to check at the VIC (I-Site) before parting with your cash.

Beachcomber Fun Cruises, on the waterfront, T0800-624526/T03-573 6175, www.beachcombercruises.co.nz. Offers a range of cruise options, including a popular half-day 'Mail Boat' cruise: the *Queen Charlotte Mail Boat* explores the Queen Charlotte Sound, with a stop at Ship Cove, from $85. The 2-hr 'Round the Bays' cruise takes in a number of Queen Charlotte Sound bays, including Double Cove where you stop briefly to feed tame fish; departs daily at 1130 and 1400; from $57. The 6-hr luncheon cruise to the **Portage Resort Hotel** and Torea Bay, departs daily at 0930, from $61 (transport only). There are also a range of half- or full-day cruise-and-walk options from $51, Queen Charlotte Track transfers pass (with pack transfers) from $95 and an eco-tour of Motuara Island Bird Sanctuary, from $73.

The Cougar Line, on the waterfront, T0800-504090/T03-573 7925, www.cougar linecruises.co.nz. Offers a similar series of cruises. The most popular is the day trip to Ship Cove where you have the option of a 5-hr bush walk to **Furneaux Lodge** where you are picked up later in the afternoon. It departs at 0800 and 1000. Various short cruises are also available taking in up to 80 km of coastline in 3 hrs with an informative commentary on the way. These depart at 1000 and 1330. Cougar also offer a luncheon cruise to the **Punga Cove Resort** that leaves at 1000 and a 3-hr twilight tour that departs at 1800. Cruises cost from $68.

Endeavour Express, on the waterfront, T03-573 5456, www.boatrides.co.nz. Are the best bet for independent travellers offering flexible tramping track and accommodation transfers as well as a range of day walking options from $35.

Water Taxis, T03-573 8229, www.arrow watertaxis.co.nz. Flexible water taxi service.
Picton Water Taxis, T03-573 7853, www.pictonwatertaxis.co.nz. As above.

Day walks
Most operators offer half- or full- day walking trips. Popular trips include Ship Cove to Furneaux Lodge (with **Endeavour Express** and **Cougar**, from $68), which takes in the Captain Cook monument and some lovely native bush and views. Also popular is the eco-based trip to Motuara Island Bird Sanctuary (with **Beachcomber Cruises** and **Endeavour Express**, from $73) but the choices and options are endless. The VIC can advise. Cougar has the best boats and tends to offer the most modern, comfortable service, but competition is fierce so shop around.

Eco-tours
The Sounds are not only home to seals and dolphins but also some rare birdlife such as the king shag (found only in the sounds), New Zealand robins, little blue penguins and saddlebacks. Many of the land-based birds are typically fearless and will constantly check your route for disturbed insects.
Dolphin Watch Marlborough, 14 Auckland St, 200 m east of the VIC (I-Site), T03-573 8040, www.naturetours.co.nz. Offers a range of trips including dolphin swimming (when the dusky dolphins allow); an excellent jaunt to the Motuara Island bird sanctuary (departs 0830/1330, from $100) and a 'Birdwatchers' Special' (departs daily in winter and twice daily in summer at 1330, from $120).
Sea Safaris, based in French Pass, T03-576 5204, www.seasafaris.co.nz. Also offers some superb, flexible wildlife trips to see dolphins and seabirds in the outer Marlborough Sounds. Recommended.

Fishing
Sounds Connection, 10 London Quay, T0800-742866/T03-573 8843, www.sounds connection.co.nz. Scheduled half-day trips or charters to the vineyards with expert local guides departing daily from Picton and Blenheim. They also offer art, garden and fishing options.

Flightseeing
Soundsair, based across the road from the VIC (I-Site) in the old railway station, T0800-505005, www.soundsair.com. Offers an

extraordinary number of flight combinations and options that include one night's lodging, lunch, day walks and cruises from $150-400. Standard flightseeing trips range from a 20-min flight over Kenepuru Sound from $120, 45 mins taking all the main sounds for $180, and a 1 hr 15 mins that includes both the Sounds and vineyards of the Wairau Valley from $240. The standard single fare to Wellington costs from $89, child $77.

Picton Floatplane Service, based at the Ferry Terminal in Picton, T03-573 6866, www.nz-scenic-flights.co.nz, also offer scenic flights from 20-mins $190 with the added advantage of course of a water landing.

Sailing

The VIC (I-Site) has full charter and cruise listings.

Compass Charters, T0800-101332, www.compass-charters.co.nz. Skippered and self-drive cruise and charters.

Sail Marlborough, T03-575 7312, www.sailmarlborough.co.nz. Geared up for group charter, more luxury orientated.

Scuba diving

Dive Marlborough, Beach Rd, T0800-463483, www.godive.co.nz. Given the location it is no surprise that this company specializes in wreck diving with the 155-m *Mikhail Lermontov* (1986) the highlight, guided from $255.

Sea kayaking

Most travellers save their kayaking experience for the Abel Tasman National Park (see page 451), the most famous sea-kayaking venue in the country. However, Abel Tasman is now getting very crowded in summer and the idea of having a beautiful golden bay to yourself is a near impossibility. What the sounds can offer that the Abel Tasman often cannot, is almost guaranteed shelter and relative peace and quiet. Also note that Abel Tasman has about 50 km of coastline, whereas the sounds has 1500 km.

Marlborough Sounds Adventure Company, on the waterfront, T0800-283283/T03-573

6078, www.marlboroughsounds.co.nz. The principal operator in Picton, it offers a wide variety of highly professional trips including kayaking, walking and mountain biking. The excellent options vary from a few hours (including a twilight trip), to the 4-day paddle/ walk or 6-day specialist itineraries. It is also possible to hire mountain bikes (from $60; one to three-day guided trips from $123) or kayaks (from $40 per day decreasing to $35 after 3 days). The excellent and increasingly popular 3-day 'Ultimate Sounds Adventure', is a guided 1-day hiking, 1-day sea kayaking, 1-day mountain biking adventure, with an overnight stay at **Portage Resort Hotel**. The trip departs every Wed from 1 Nov-30 Apr, and costs from $585.. Note there is no other track in New Zealand where you can walk and mountain bike on the same track. Recommended.

Sea Kayaking Adventure Tours, based in Anakiwa, T03-574 2765, www.nzsea kayaking.com. 1- to 5-day trips on both Queen Charlotte and Pelorus Sounds.

Wilderness Guides, Railway Station, 3 Auckland St, T0800-266266/T03-573 5432, www.wildernessguides.co.nz. Day trips from $50, independent bike hire from $50 and good guided kayak/walk and kayak/ cycle options on the Queen Charlotte Track from $145.

Self-drive

If you are looking for an alternative method of exploring the sounds you can do so in part by road. Note, however, that the roads throughout the Sounds are tortuous, mostly unsealed and not entirely suitable for campervans, or indeed sightseeing. Perhaps this is the time to have a break from driving and take a boat? The **Queen Charlotte Drive** is (for the passenger) a scenic 35-km drive from Picton to Havelock taking in a number of sheltered bays, campsites and viewpoints on the way. From Linkwater it is possible to then traverse the ridge between Queen Charlotte and Kenepuru Sounds by road (close to the route of the Queen Charlotte Track) before the road joins the main landmass of the sounds. The intrepid explorer can reach the outermost bays from this road and combine some walking on parts of the Queen Charlotte Track, including the most popular day walk – the **Endeavour Inlet to Ship Cove Track**. On a clear day the half-day to full-day walk to the summit of **Mount Stokes** (at 1203 m the highest point in the sounds) is recommended for the view. The walk is a moderate expedition involving 500 m of ascent.

Campsites are available at Mistletoe Bay, Cowshed Bay, Punga Cove (Endeavour Inlet) and at Titirangi Bay. Note that some accommodation establishments are also accessible by road, including **Punga Cove**, **The Portage**, **Te Mahia**, **St Omer House** and **Raetihi Lodge**. For another fine and remote exploratory drive into the sounds see the French Pass section, page 423.

Blenheim *p419, map p420*

The wilderness of the Marlborough back-country and the remote Molesworth Station (New Zealand's largest cattle station) can be explored with **Molesworth Tour Company**, T03-577 9897, www.molesworthtours.co.nz. 1- to 5-day excursions from $235.

Horse trekking

High Country Horse Treks, Ardnadam, Taylor's Pass Rd, Redwood Village, T03-577 9424, www.high-horse.co.nz. 1-4 hrs.

River trips

Marlborough River Queen, T0800-266322/T03-577 5510, www.theriverqueen.co.nz. If you fancy a trip along the Opawa River on board a paddleboat, try this very gracious trip. Both lunch and dinner trips from Tue-Sun.

Walking

There are some fine walking venues in the region, particularly around the Richmond Ranges, the **Withers Farm Park** and on the coast road, via Rarangi, to Picton. The ascent of **Mt Richmond** (1760 m) with its memorable views is recommended. For self-guided trips consult DoC or the VIC (I-Site) for their free leaflets.

Winery tours

There is a broad range of tour operator, all of whom will look after your every whim. Some offer more formal scheduled trips, while others can design a trip around your personal tastes or take in arts and crafts and garden visits. You can even go by bicycle.

Highlight Tours, T03-577 9046, www.highlight-tours.co.nz. Both full-day or half-day (morning or afternoon). Flexibility with venues (including craft and garden) and lunch (extra cost) included, from $65.

Marlborough Travel Centre Winery Tours and Wine Line, T0800-990800/ T03-577 9997, www.marlboroughtravel.co.nz. Quality half-day tours from $89.

Marlborough Wine Tours, T03-579 5038, www.marlboroughwinetours.co.nz. Personalized tour of up to 8 wineries. Flexible itinerary depending on taste, from $43.

Sounds Connection, T03-573 8843, www.soundsconnection.co.nz. Scheduled and private half- to full-day tours. Based in Picton. Half day from $65, full $89, gourmet (includes food and wine matching, underground cellar tour, olive grove and lunch stop), from $199 (lunch not included).

Wine-Tours-By-Bike, T03-577 6954 www.winetoursbybike.co.nz. A delightfully common sense method of visiting the wineries. The drawback obviously is the steady deterioration of the senses as the day wears on and the inability to pedal after 10 glasses of wine. You can join a guided tour or hire your own bikes with accessories (a map being pivotal) and have them delivered to your door. Half day from $40, full $55, guided tour $25 per hour.

Havelock *p421*

Most of what Havelock has to offer and almost all of its services will be found on Main Rd or down at the harbour, which is a short walk from centre of the village.

Cruises

Pelorus Sound can be explored by boat or by road. There are numerous opportunities to

get on the water from scheduled cruises to charter boats and kayak trips. Note that water taxis are available from Havelock and you can be flexible with your intentions and itinerary (see Ins and outs, page 421). There are also fishing and diving charters available.
Affinity Cruises, T03-572 7223, www.affinitycruises.co.nz. Day charters or overnight cruises from 2-7 days. The 63-ft vessel has 8 private cabins, all meals are included and activities range from fishing to bush walking.
All Season Cruises, based in Havelock, T0274-300 5226, www.allseasoncruises.co.nz. Sedate and popular range of trips on board the 58-ft launch *Foxy Lady*. A choice of morning, evening (BBQ) or overnight cruises all taking in the beautiful scenery of the sounds with an added insight into how the famous mussels are bred and harvested.
Marlborough Travel, T0800-990800/ T03-5779997, www.greenshellmussel cruise.co.nz. Offers the 'Greenshell Mussel Cruise': an afternoon cruise through the Pelorus and Kenepuru Sounds. Daily departures from Havelock at 1330 (Nov-Mar) including a visit to a mussel farm where you can enjoy freshly steamed mussels with a glass of Sauvignon Blanc, from $110.
Pelorus Mail Run Cruises, T03-574 1088, www.mail-boat.co.nz, leaves Havelock at 0930 on Tue, Thu and Fri, costing from $120, child free. The Mail Run delivers supplies and mail to a number of the isolated settlements and visits one of the many mussel farms before returning at about 1730.

Fishing
Captain Clays, T03-574 2911. Half- or full-day cruise/fishing charters with local guru Clayton after snapper and the feisty kingfish. Optional lunch or overnight stops, from $125.

Sea kayaking
If this is your thing or you would like to try it, the sounds provides excellent opportunities.
Sea Kayaking Adventure Tours, Anakiwa, T03-574 2765, www.nzseakayaking.com. Trips

are half-day from $85, full- or multi-day $200-500. Independent hire available from $40.
Sounds Natural, 46 Main Rd, Havelock, T275-382203, www.soundsnatural.co.nz. Full or multi-day 'clothing optional' guided trips to remote private locations from $95.

⊖ Transport

Picton *p416, map p417*
Car hire Lots of companies just outside the ferry terminal, with a few others on High St in the centre of town: **A2B**, T0800-222929; **Ace**, T0800-422373; **Apex**, T0800-939597; **Budget**, T03-573 6081; **Pegasus**, T03-5737759. **Petrol** (24 hrs) Shell Picton, 101 High St, T03-573 7949. **Taxi** T03-573 7662 or T03- 5772072.

Blenheim *p419, map p420*
Bicycle hire Bikes for winery tours can be hired from Wine-Tours-By-Bike, T03-577 6954.
Taxi Marlborough Taxis, T03-577 5511.

⊙ Directory

Picton *p416, map p417*
Internet United Video, corner of High and Dublin sts, 0900-2100. **Police** High St, T03-520 3120. **Post office** Mariners Mall, 72 High St, T03-573 6900, Mon-Fri 0830-1700. **Storage** Sounds Storage, 7 Market St, T021-335136, soundsstorage@xtra.co.nz. Offers secure car and boat storage.

Blenheim *p419, map p420*
Internet Travel Stop Cyber Centre, corner of Market and Alfred sts, T03-5791902, www.travelstop.co.nz, open Mon-Sat 1000-2100 and Sun 1000-1600 and the I-Site.
Post office 1 Main St, T03-578 3904, Mon-Fri 0830-1715, Sat 0930-1230.

Havelock *p421*
Internet Available in the Havelock Information and Travel Centre and the YHA both on the Main Rd.

Nelson and around → Colour map 4, A4 Population: 50,000.

Nelson is known as the sunniest place in the country, though this label could equally be applied to its atmosphere, its people and its surroundings because, in addition to a Mediterranean climate, Nelson has a great deal going for it. It is lively and modern, yet steeped in history. Surrounding it, all within 100 km, are some of the most beautiful coastal scenery and beaches in New Zealand, not to mention three diverse and stunning national parks, where you can experience some of the most exciting tramping tracks in the South Island, plus a host of other activities. Little wonder that Nelson is one of the top holiday destinations in the country as well being considered the best place to live in New Zealand. ▶▶ *For Sleeping, Eating and other listings, see pages 442-449.*

Ins and outs

Getting there
By car Nelson is 144 km from Picton via SH6, 424 km to Christchurch via SH6, SH65 (Lewis Pass) and then SH1 and 226 km to Westport via SH6. **Nelson airport** ① *6 km southwest of the town centre on SH6, in the suburb of Nayland*, is small but efficient. **Air New Zealand Link**, T0800-737000, www.airnew zealand.co.nz, offers regular scheduled flights from Auckland, Wellington and Christchurch. Also worth noting is **Abel Tasman Air**, T0800-304560/T03-528 8290, www.abeltasmanair.co.nz, which runs a good service with small fixed-wing aircraft throughout the region. **Super Shuttle**, T03-547 5782, or **Nelson Bays Cabs**, T03-5418294, both operate to and from the airport; about $20.

The following companies provide regular bus services to Nelson and the region as a whole: **Intercity**, T03-5737025, www.intercity.co.nz; **Atomic Shuttles**, T03-322 8883, www.atomictravel.co.nz and **Nakedbus**, www.nakedbus.com.

Operators servicing Motueka and the Abel Tasman National Park include: **Atomic Shuttles** and **Abel Tasman Coachlines**, T03-548 0285, www.abeltasmantravel.co.nz. **Abel Tasman Coachlines** also run further northwest to Takaka and Golden Bay.

Buses heading south to St Arnaud and the Nelson Lakes National Park and the Rainbow ski area include: **Nelson Lakes Shuttles**, T03-521 1900, www.nelsonlakesshuttles.co.nz. The VIC (I-Site) can assist with bookings.

Average fares to Christchurch are $60, Greymouth $40, Takaka $35, Heaphy Track $55 and Blenheim $30. Most of the bus services stop right outside the VIC (I-Site) on the corner of Trafalgar and Halifax streets. **Intercity** drop off at the bus terminal on Bridge Street.

Getting around
The local suburban bus company is **Nelson SBL**, T03-548 3290, www.nelsoncoaches.co.nz, based at the **bus terminal** ① *Lower Bridge St*. SBL runs a 'summertime bus', which does a circuit of the city's major attractions on the hour departing the VIC (I-Site) from 1000-1600. The standard fare starts at $2.

Tourist information
Nelson VIC (I-Site) ① *corner of Trafalgar and Halifax sts*, T03-548 2304, www.nelsonnz.com, *Mon-Fri 0830-1700, Sat-Sun 0900-1600*. The booklet *Nelson – Live the Day* is informative and there is a range of other brochures available. **DoC** information is also held at this office. The website www.backpacknelson.com has lots of useful information.

Sights

Sadly the appearance of central Nelson is spoiled by one thins you cannot miss. The **Civic Tower**, across the road from the VIC, dominates the skyline and is without doubt the most hideous looking building in the country. An utter mess of concrete and steel, covered with aerials and radar, it looks like something that is about to take off. That aside, however, there are many attractive sights to see around Nelson.

A fine place to start is a short climb (one hour return) to the **viewpoint** above the **Botanical Gardens**, which can be accessed off Milton or Maitai roads. This site is claimed as the geographical centre of New Zealand, but other than offering a fine view of the town and giving you a sense of location, it is also the regular target for some delightful expressions of daring and protest. It recently staged a flag proclaiming disgust at the use of GM (genetically modified) foodstuffs; and it is not at all unusual to see some wonderfully colourful and frilly lingerie fluttering from the flagpole. Sadly, after that, the attractive botanical gardens, though admirable, are far less remarkable. Other green havens in Nelson include the very attractive **Queens Gardens** off Bridge Street, complete with the city's fair share of ducks, and the vibrant flowerbeds of **Anzac Park** at the end of Rutherford Street. The **Miyazu Japanese Park** ① *Atawhai Dr, dawn to dusk, free*, has a traditional 'stroll' garden built to celebrate Nelson's links with sister city Miyazu in Japan. There are numerous other fine gardens to visit in the region and the VIC (I-Site) can provide further information, including the handy leaflet *Gardens of the Nelson Region*.

The most lauded tourist attraction in the Nelson area is perhaps the **World of Wearable Art and Collectable Cars** ① *95 Quarantine Rd, Annesbrook, just north of the airport, T03-547 4573, www.wowcars.co.nz, daily 1000-1830 (1700 in winter), from $20, child $8*. Set in a 1-ha site the complex has two galleries. The first is the Wearable Art Gallery showcasing the historic Wearable Art Garment collection. There is a fully scripted show that uses mannequins rather than live models but with all the usual elements of sound and lighting. The original concept was first initiated in 1987 as a gallery promotion by local sculptor Suzie Moncrieff and is easy to describe. Choose a theme, make the most remarkable and creative costume imaginable, from any material or media and get a bonny lass to show it off. But such a basic description could never do justice to the results, the story of how it all came about, or, indeed, how it has all developed since. This is a remarkable synergy of art and fashion and a true tribute to the creative imagination.

The second gallery – perhaps almost inevitably a disappointment after the first – has an impressive collection of classic cars that were formerly on view in the town centre.

Although Nelson was one of New Zealand's earliest and largest settlements, there is little architectural evidence. Of obvious notoriety, but hardly historical (having being finally completed in 1965), is the **Nelson Cathedral** ① *T03-548 1008, daily in summer 0800-1900 (winter 0800-1700), tour guides are on duty most days, entry by donation*, which dominates the southern end of town. Although its exterior barely matches the view of Trafalgar Street from the steps that lead up to it, the interior contains some fine stained-glass windows and a 2000-pipe organ.

Also worth a quick look is **Broadgreen Historic House** ① *276 Nayland Rd, Stoke, 6 km southwest of town via the coast road, T03-547 0403, summer daily 1030-1630, $4, child $1*. It is an 11-room 1855 Victorian 'cob' house furnished accordingly and set amongst pleasant gardens.

A far better sense of history can be found at the new **Nelson Provincial Museum: Town Acre 445** ① *corner Hardy and Trafalgar sts, T03-548 9588, www.museumnp.org.nz, exhibitions Mon-Fri 1000-1700, Sat-Sun 1000-1630 and Sat-Sun 1200-1600, $5, child $2,* which serves as the region's principal museum and contains all the usual suspects including exhibits on life in a Maori settlement using an imaginative and dynamic range of well presented displays. The free leaflet *Nelson City of History – Trevor Horne Heritage Trail* is available from the VIC (I-Site).

With over 300 artists resident in the town arts and crafts feature heavily in the list of attractions. A copy of the *Nelson Regional Guide Book – Art in its Own Place* is a great guide

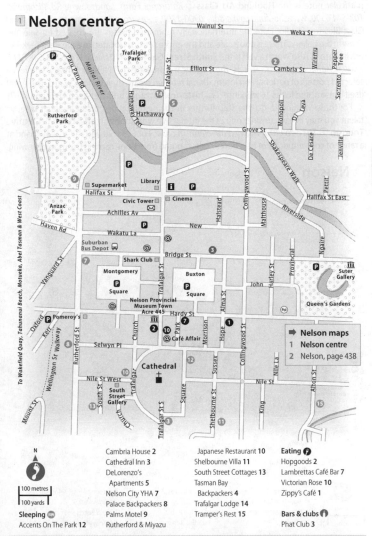

Nelson centre

N

100 metres
100 yards

Sleeping
Accents On The Park **12**

Cambria House **2**
Cathedral Inn **3**
DeLorenzo's
Apartments **5**
Nelson City YHA **7**
Palace Backpackers **8**
Palms Motel **9**
Rutherford & Miyazu

Japanese Restaurant **10**
Shelbourne Villa **11**
South Street Cottages **13**
Tasman Bay
Backpackers **4**
Trafalgar Lodge **14**
Tramper's Rest **15**

Eating
Hopgoods **2**
Lambrettas Café Bar **7**
Victorian Rose **10**
Zippy's Café **1**

Bars & clubs
Phat Club **3**

and available from most bookshops. The Te Aratoi-o-Whakatu or **Suter Gallery** ① *208 Bridge St, T03-548 4699, www.thesuter.org.nz, daily 1030-1630, $3*, heads the list of major art galleries. Located next to Queen's Gardens, it boasts four exhibition spaces that showcase both permanent and temporary historical and contemporary collections. There is also a café, cinema and theatre on site that runs a programme of musical and theatrical performances.

There are many other galleries in the area displaying a vast array of creative talent. Of particular note is the **Höglund Art Glass** ① *Korurangi Farm, Landsdowne Rd, Richmond, T03-544 6500, www.hoglund.co.nz, daily 0900-1700, tours from $15*, home to the Hoglund Glass Blowing Studio. Here the internationally renowned pieces are created for sale and show in the gallery. There is also a café and the entire set-up is located in a pleasant park-like environment. Also worth a visit is the **South Street Gallery** ① *10 Nile St West, T03-548 8117, www.nelsonpottery.co.nz*. This is the historical home of the Nelson Pottery where 25 selected potters of national and international renown create their various wares. The street itself is also noted for its 16 working-class **historical cottages** built between 1863 and 1867.

For those wishing to go one step further in their explorations of the region's creative talent you may like to consider one of the interactive workshops on offer through **Creative Tourism** ① *T03-526 8812, www.creativetourism.co.nz*. For $65-120 you can try your hand at a range of contemporary or traditional crafts ranging from bone carving to organic brewing.

② Nelson

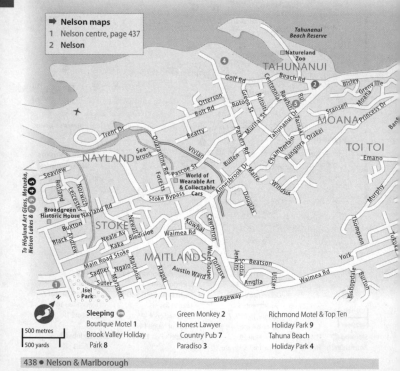

➡ **Nelson maps**
1 Nelson centre, page 437
2 Nelson

Sleeping 🛏
Boutique Motel 1
Brook Valley Holiday
Park 8

Green Monkey 2
Honest Lawyer
Country Pub 7
Paradiso 3

Richmond Motel & Top Ten
Holiday Park 9
Tahuna Beach
Holiday Park 4

Around Nelson ● ▸▸ p445.

Beaches

No visit to Nelson would be complete without a trip to the beach. The most popular stretch of golden sand is to be found at the **Tahunanui Beach Reserve**, just a few kilometres southwest of the town centre. Although you will not find the same scenic beauty and certainly not the solitude of the other, more remote beaches in the region, it is a convenient place to lay back and soak up the rays, swim or fly a kite. It is a great spot for kids with the small **Natureland Zoo** ① *T03-548 6166, 0930-1600, $7, child $4*, and a large fun park nearby. Slightly further afield (20 km) towards Motueka (SH60) are the beaches and forest swathe of **Rabbit Island**. This seemingly never-ending beach offers a far quieter and expansive alternative. It is worth checking with the DoC, however, to confirm that it is not closed due to fire risk. With recent droughts this is becoming a more frequent occurrence.

Wineries

Wineries around Nelson are also a big attraction. Although the region and its fine winemakers perhaps suffer from the reputation and sheer scale of their much-hyped neighbours in Marlborough, the wine they produce can be of a very fine quality. For more information on

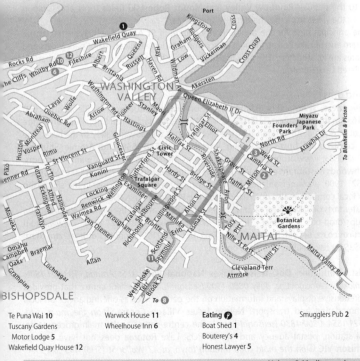

Te Puna Wai **10**
Tuscany Gardens
  Motor Lodge **5**
Wakefield Quay House **12**

Warwick House **11**
Wheelhouse Inn **6**

Eating ●
Boat Shed **1**
Bouterey's **4**
Honest Lawyer **5**

Smugglers Pub **2**

Nelson Region wineries consult www.nelsonwines.co.nz. For a list of some of the better-known wineries, which all offer (at the very least) tastings, see box, page 443.

Breweries

Lovers of beer will be relieved to learn that some local brewing talent is hot on the heels of the winemakers and the region now has its own Brewery Trail. The VIC (I-Site) can provide all the detail and the major players are listed in the box on page 443. While it is hardly on a par with Australia's legendary Bundaberg, from small seeds great things can grow.

Nelson Lakes National Park and Murchison ⊜🕖🔺 ›› pp442-449.

The slightly under-rated Nelson Lakes National Park protects 102,000 ha of the northernmost Southern Alps range. The park is dominated by its long, scenic and trout-filled lakes – **Rotoroa** and **Rotoiti** – cradled in beech-clad alpine ranges, hiding beautiful tussock valleys and wildflower-strewn meadows. Although a quick look at the lakes are all that most people see of this park, the ranges and river valleys offer some superb walking. The two most noted tramps are the 80-km, four- to seven-day **Traverse-Sabine Circuit** and the excellent two- to three-day **Robert Ridge/Lake Angelus Track**. There are a number of very pleasant short walks from 20 minutes to two hours that extend into the park from St Arnaud or Lake Rotoroa. Nelson Lakes also plays host to the popular **Rainbow Valley** and **Mount Robertski fields** (only accessible in winter); the views from the chairlifts are spectacular.

The principal base for the park is pretty village of **St Arnaud**, which nestles at the northern end of Lake Rotoiti. Almost all accommodation, services, major park access and activities are located here. The park is also accessible from the more remote and sparsely populated Lake Rotoroa.

Ins and outs

Getting there St Arnaud is 90 km from Nelson (via SH6), 100 km from Blenheim (SH63) and 163 km from Westport (SH6/63). To visit Lake Rotoroa, turn off SH6 at Gowan Bridge west of St Arnaud. An 11-km side road takes you up the Gowan Valley to the lakes. The west coast-bound buses (including **Intercity**, T03-548 1538 and **Atomic Shuttles**, T03-322 8883, www.atomictravel.co.nz) stop in Murchison outside **Collins Tearooms**, **Beechwoods Restaurant** or the VIC (I-Site). St Arnaud is served by **Nelson Lakes Shuttles**, T03-521 1900, www.nelsonlakesshuttles.co.nz, on a year-round basis. In the ski season other local companies also operate; consult the VIC (I-Site) in Nelson.

Water taxis on lakes Rotoroa and Rotoiti offer scenic and/or fishing trips and tramping pick-ups/drop-offs. Contact **Rotoiti Water Taxis**, T03-521 1894, www.rotoiti watertaxis.co.nz, or **Lake Rotoroa Water Taxi**, T03-523 9199, simpson.r otoroa@xtra.co.nz; from $35 for two people, lake's end one way.

Tourist information DoC Nelson Lakes National Park ⓘ *St Arnaud, T03-521 1806, nelsonlakesvc@doc.govt.nz, daily 0800-1900 (seasonal)*. An excellent centre that provides comprehensive displays and information on the park, as well as offering advice on local accommodation and transport. **Nelson Lakes Village Centre** ⓘ *on the main road, T03-521 1854, 0800-1830 (seasonal hours)*. The centre serves as the main grocery store, petrol station, postal agency and has EFTPOS. Lake Rotoroa does not have a shop. **Murchison VIC** ⓘ*on the main road through town, at 47 Wallar St (SH6), T03-523 9350,*

Let's split

New Zealand's most eminent scientist, Ernest Rutherford, is best known for being the first person to split the atom. He was born at Spring Grove near Nelson in 1876 and after being awarded several scholarships, graduated with a Bachelor of Arts at the age of 17, and a Bachelor of Science two years later. By the age of 22 he was a professor at McGill University in Montreal and was already deeply involved in to research surrounding radioactivity. Within a decade he had discovered the natural transmutation of elements, the development of techniques that allowed the radioactive dating of geological samples and also made the first deduction of the nuclear model of the atom. All this brought him to world prominence and earned him several prestigious awards, including the Nobel Prize for Chemistry in 1908 and a knighthood in 1914. But despite all this, his best work was yet to come, and at the end of the First World War he conducted an experiment which split the atom – something which had far reaching consequences for mankind. Rutherford died in Cambridge, England at the age of 61.

www.murchisonnz.com, 1000-1700 (seasonal). **Ski-ing information** ① *T03-521 1861, www.skirainbow.co.nz, www.snow.co.nz.*

▲▲ Mount Robert to Lake Angelus Basin walk → *2-3 days, 30 km.*

If you are short of time this walk is touted as one of the best in the park. The destination (and highlight) is the beautiful Lake Angelus Basin and an overnight stay at the Mount Angelus Hut (\$10) from which to take it all in. It is a walk that should only be considered by those of reasonable fitness, in good weather conditions. Go prepared and pre-book your hut accommodation (and fill in an intentions sheet) at the DoC visitor centre.

From the Upper Mount Robert car park (accessed from West Bay, 5 km from St Arnaud) climb the steep zigzag track up the face of Mount Robert to the bushline shelter near the summit (two hours). From there follow the marked route along the ridge and around the **Mount Robert ski field** to **Flagtop Summit** (1690 m). Then descend and continue on the saddle beneath **Julius Summit** (1794 m). The route now leaves the ridge briefly, crossing rocky ground before rejoining the ridge. At a small saddle marked by a metal pole, the route drops again to the west side and crosses a steep, rocky slope to another broad saddle at the head of **Speargrass Creek**. From here a short climb to the ridge reveals the beautiful **Angelus Basin** (five hours).

Stay the night at the Angelus Hut (book at DoC, \$15) and get up for sunrise. To return you can either retrace your steps, or descend in to the **Hukere Valley** to join the **Cascade Track** to **Coldwater Hut** at the southern end of the lake. From there the Lakeside Track will deliver you back to the lower Mount Robert car park. If you have no vehicle and have been dropped off, you may consider booking a water taxi from the southern end of the lake and reward yourself with a scenic cruise back to St Arnaud.

Murchison

Murchison (population just 750), 65 km further along SH6 from St Arnaud, at the head of the Buller Gorge and junction of the Matakitaki and Buller rivers, is a service centre for the local farming community and for many, the gateway to the west coast from the north. Although once an important gold mining town (and famous for being nearly wiped out by a violent earthquake in 1929), it is today a quiet place, primarily of interest to the tourist as the base for a number of interesting activities. It is also the haunt of the odd serious tramper intent on exploring the remote southern wilderness of the Kahurangi National Park. *The small* **Murchison Museum** ① *Fairfax St, daily 1000- 1600, donation*, has interesting exhibits on gold mining and the town's somewhat shaky past.

◉ Nelson and around listings

For Sleeping and Eating price codes and other relevant information, see Essentials pages 44-50.

◉ Sleeping

Nelson *p435, maps p437 and p438*
Being such a popular holiday destination there is no shortage of beds in Nelson with a few good hotels, numerous B&Bs and homestays, the usual rash of motels and more backpacker hostels than almost anywhere else in New Zealand. Despite this, mid-summer is very busy and you are advised to book ahead.
LL-L Cambria House, 7 Cambria St, T03-548 4681, www.cambria.co.nz. An established, beautifully appointed and well- located B&B in a 130-year-old homestead.
LL-L Cathedral Inn, 369 Trafalgar St South, T03-548 7369, www.cathedralinn.co.nz. Well-located, historic option with a fine reputation.
LL-L DeLorenzo's Apartments, 43-55 Trafalgar St, T0508-335673/T03-548 9774, www.de lorenzos.co.nz. Modern, well-appointed fully self-contained block of 5-star rated apartments in a central location.
LL-L Shelbourne Villa, 21 Shelbourne St, T03-545 9059, www.shelbournevilla.co.nz. Right next to the cathedral, offering 3 king size suites and 1 loft with 2 twins. Beautiful garden.
LL-L Te Puna Wai, 24 Richardson St, Port Hills, T04-548 7621, www.tepunawai.co.nz. An immaculate villa-style B&B set overlooking the bay in the Port Hills area. 3 luxury en suite rooms, 2 of which can be combined to form a spacious apartment. Great views, open fire, classy decor and hosts that go the extra mile to ensure a truly memorable stay. Recommended.
LL Wakefield Quay House, 385 Wakefield Quay, T03-546 7275,

www.wakefieldquay.co.nz. Heritage villa offering luxury B&B in a superb position overlooking the harbour. Two classy queen sea view rooms with en suites, antiques and original artworks by local artisans. The house features an impressive rimu staircase, polished native timber floors and the obligatory open fire. Excellent breakfast and personally guided sailing trips a speciality from $100 per hour.
LL-L Warwick House, 64 Brougham St, T0800-022233/T03-548 3164, www.warwick house.co.nz. Built in 1854, and used as a major venue for lavish entertainment by early New Zealand politicians and leading merchants, 'the castle' as it is affectionately known has been transformed into an elegant boutique hotel, complete with ballroom and spiral tower staircase. There are 3 beautifully appointed Victorian heritage-style en suites replete with native Kauri and claw-foot baths. Excellent cuisine, attractive gardens and a warm welcome also add to its considerable appeal. Recommended.
LL-AL The Rutherford Hotel, Trafalgar Sq, T03-548 2299, www.heritagehotels.co.nz. The principal hotel in the city, centrally located and now part of the nationwide Heritage Hotels group. It has all the usual mod cons including a pool, sauna and health centre. Rooms range from spacious standard doubles to executive suites. There are 2 restaurants and a café, one being **Miyazu** – a very good Japanese option. Secure parking.
L The Honest Lawyer Country Pub, 1 Point Rd, Monaco, T03-547 8850, www.honestlawyer.co.nz. Although out of town (near the airport) this is well worth the effort. Rustic en suite rooms above a characterful English-style pub. Cosy restaurant/bar downstairs where you are

Wineries and breweries around Nelson

Wineries

Glovers Vineyard, Gardner Valley Rd, T03-543 2698, www.glovers-vineyard.co.nz. Owned by the very congenial David Glover, who is considered something of an institution when it comes to producing fine wines and sampling others. The great 'sorcerer' will be delighted to give you a taste, but best pre-book, since there may be a great tasting party raging. If you get lost, just head for the sound of classical music.

Greenhough Vineyard, Hope (Patons Rd) T03-542 3868, www.greenhough.co.nz. Now 11 ha, with a small block of much valued Riesling, Pinot Noir and Pinot Blanc vines, now over 30 years old.

Kahurangi Estate, Sunrise Rd, T03-543 2980, www.kahurangiwine.com. Open daily summer 1030-1630. Boutique vineyard specialising in hand-made wines with some of the oldest vines in the South Island. Café and Cellar Door.

Seifried Estate Vineyard, Redwood Rd, Appleby, T03-544 5599, www.seifried.co.nz. The largest and oldest in the region. Offers tours and tastings with a fine restaurant.

Waimea Estate, 22 Appleby Highway, Hope, T03-544 6385, www.waimeaestates. co.nz. Which also has a café and is open daily from 1000-1700. Live local music Sun 1230-1530.

Moutere Hills, Sunrise Valley, T03-543 2288, www.moutere hills.co.nz. Noted not only for its wine but its café, open daily 1100-1800 (weekends only in winter).

Neudorf, Neudorf Rd, T03-5432643, www.neudorf.co.nz. Daily 1100-1700. Offers tastings.

Ruby Bay Wines, Korepo Rd, T03-540 2825, www.rubybaylodge.co.nz. Very scenic. Cellar door is by appointment only.

Spencer Hill Estate, Best Rd, T03-543 2031, www.spencerhillwine.com. Popular and well-established.

Breweries

Founders Brewery, Founders Historic Park, 87 Atawhai Drive, T03-548 4638, www.biobrew.co.nz, open daily 1000-1630. A certified organic brewery offering a range of heady organic brews. Good café.

McCashin's Brewery, 660 Main Rd, Stoke, T03-547 5357, www.mccashins.co.nz. Home to the popular Mac's Ales.

South Pacific Distillery, 258 Wakefield Quay, T03-546 6822, www.roaringforties.co.nz, open Mon-Sat 1000-1630, tours available in season. If spirits are more your thing, this is a good one to try.

---

invited to relax and 'tell little white lies with the locals'. Off-street parking.

L South Street Cottages, 1, 3 & 12 South St, T03-540 2769, www.cottage accommodation. co.nz. Compact, self-contained historic cottages in Nelson's most historic street.

L-AL Palms Motel, 5 Paru Paru Rd, T03-546 7770, www.palmsnelson.co.nz. One of the best upper-range motels in the centre.

L-AL Tuscany Gardens Motor Lodge, 80 Tahunanui Drive, Tahunanui , T03-548 5522, www.tuscanygardens.co.nz. Luxury motel with a good reputation, close to the beach.

L-AL Wheelhouse Inn, 41 Whitby Rd, T03-546 8391, www.wheelhouse.nelson.co.nz. A spacious, timber-style establishment, with self-contained accommodation suited to larger groups and loner stays. Quiet bush setting with a superb view.

A Boutique Motel, 7 Bail St, Stoke, T03-547 1439, www.boutiquemotel.co.nz. A new and well-appointed establishment located in the quiet suburb of Stoke and near the airport.

AL-A Trafalgar Lodge, 46 Trafalgar St, T03-548 3980, www.trafalgarlodge.co.nz. A fine and well-located budget option with 2 en suites and 2 shared rooms in the lodge and 4 studio motel style units.

Backpacker hostels

The choice of budget accommodation is vast with over 15 to choose from. The following are recommended.

B-D Accents on the Park, 335 Trafalgar Sq, T0800-888335/T03-548 4335, www.accents onthepark.com. In a word: exceptional. A beautifully renovated Victorian villa with a distinct air of class. A full range of well-appointed rooms from en suite to shared dorms and a lovingly constructed basement lounge bar with open fire and plenty of character. Camping also an option and parking available. Recommended.

B-D The Green Monkey, 129 Milton St, T03-545 7421, www.thegreenmonkey.co.nz. A small, modern and quiet option with great doubles and fine facilities.

B-D Nelson City YHA, 59 Rutherford St, T03-545 9988, www.yha.org.nz. A large, modern, purpose-built YHA in the heart of the town. Mainly twin and doubles but ask to see them first as some are very small. A little lacking in atmosphere. Internet and plenty of local advice. Parking is a problem.

B-D Palace Backpackers, 114 Rutherford St, T03-548 4691, www.thepalace.co.nz. Another popular place set in a spacious historic villa overlooking the town. Wide variety of rooms including separate en suites. Great view, free breakfast/coffee, spa and a nice friendly atmosphere. Internet.

B-D Paradiso, 42 Weka St, T0800-269667/ T03-546 6703, www.backpacker nelson.co.nz. Club-Med in Nelson. A bit of a walk from the centre of town but very popular with a pool, spa and sauna. Wide range of rooms, conservatory kitchen, Sky TV and internet. Busy so book ahead.

B-D Tasman Bay Backpackers, 10 Weka St, T0800-222572/T03-548 7950, www.tasmanbaybackpackers.co.nz. A relaxing, homely and friendly backpacker hostel with the full range of rooms and good facilities including an open fire. Free bike hire, breakfast and

homemade bread. The owners also have their finger on the pulse regarding local information and activities so you will be well looked after.

B-D Tramper's Rest, 31 Alton St, T03-545 7477. This is a small, homely backpacker hostel with plenty of character, set in a suburban house in a quiet location near the centre of Nelson. Accommodation is in a small dorms and double rooms with proper beds. The atmosphere is relaxed and friendly and the owner is something of a guru when it comes to tramping locally and throughout the South Island. Perfect for the single, active, independent traveller. No off-street parking. Book well ahead. Recommended.

Motorcamps and holiday parks

AL-D Richmond Motel and Top Ten Holiday Park, 29 Gladstone Rd, Richmond, T0800-250218/T03-544 5281, www.nelsontop10.co.nz. Pick of the bunch. 14 km from Nelson but worth it. Full facilities.

AL-D Tahuna Beach Holiday Park, 70 Beach Rd, Tahunanui, T0800-500501/ T03-548 5159, www.tahunabeachholiday park.co.nz. Close to the most popular beach in town. Shop on site.

B-D Brook Valley Holiday Park, 2 km south town centre on Brook St, T03-548 0399, www.brookholidaypark.co.nz. The closest motorcamp to the town in a pleasant position in the valley beside the river but it is basic and the sandflies can be a menace.

Nelson Lakes National Park *p440*

LL Kikiwa Lodge, Korere, Tophouse Rd, T03-521 1020, www.kikiwalodge.co.nz. Reputable luxury B&B with quality fishin.

LL Lake Rotoroa Lodge, T03-523 9121, www.lakerotoroalodge.com. Exclusive fishing retreat.

AL-D Alpine Lodge and Chalet, St Arnaud, T03-521 1869, www.alpinelodge.co.nz. The mainstay of accommodation and eating in the village. A wide range of options from self-contained studio units in the main lodge to twin, family or dorms in the chalet. Licensed à la carte restaurant, café, bar and spa. Bike hire.

A St Arnaud Log Chalets, T03-521 1887, www.nelsonlakes.co.nz. Offers very pleasant modern self-contained log chalet-style units.
A Tophouse, Tophouse Rd, 9 km north of St Arnaud, T0800-867468/T03-521 1848, www.tophouse.co.nz. A very animal-friendly, historic farm guesthouse. It has 4 self-contained units and 5 comfortable B&B rooms all good value. At one time it also boasted New Zealand's smallest bar. Café on site, open daily to non-guests 0930-1700.
A Woodrow Cottage, Tophouse Junction (5 km), T03-521 1212. Pretty and self-contained.
C-D Travers Sabine Lodge, T03-521 1887, www.nelsonlakes.co.nz. Modern purpose-built lodge. Family double twin share and dorm rooms all with heaters. Spacious dining room and commercial kitchen, cosy lounge with fire.

Campsites
D DoC campsite, sites with power, at the edge of the lake in West and Kerr bays, T03-521 1806. Deposit fees at DoC visitor centre. Beware: the sandflies will eat you alive.

Murchison *p441*
LL Maruia River Lodge, Shenandoah, Maruia River Valley, T03-523 9323, www.maruiariverlodge.co.nz. The most luxurious option in the immediate area offering all mod cons, in a pleasant bush setting next to the river.
AL-A Murchison Lodge B&B, 15 Grey St, T03-523 9196, www.murchisonlodge.co.nz. Pretty B&B with 4 comfortable, well-appointed rooms. Fishing trips are a speciality.
C-D Lazy Cow Homestyle Accommodation, 37 Walker St, T0800-5299269/T03-523 9451, laxycow@xnet.co.nz. A warm welcome at this 18-bed backpacker hostel right in the heart of the village.

Motorcamps and campsites
AL-B Kiwi Park Motel and Holiday Park, 170 Fairfax St, T03-523 9248, www.kiwipark.co.nz. Offers some tidy, modern motel units.
AL-D Riverview Holiday Park, 2 km north of

town, T03-523 9591, www.holidayparks.co.nz/riverview. Standard facilities beside the river.

❷ Eating

Nelson *p435, maps p437 and p438*
There are over 50 cafés and restaurants in Nelson, the centre of town and the waterfront being the prime locations. Ask for the free and comprehensive *Eat, Drink Nelson guide* from the VIC (I-Site). Supermarkets include: **Woolworths**, corner of Paru Paru Rd and Halifax St, T03-546 6466; and **Countdown**, 35 St Vincent St, T03-546 7443.
⫴⫴⫴ The Boat Shed, 350 Wakefield Quay, T03-546 9783, www.boatshedcafe.co.nz. Daily for breakfast, lunch and dinner. There is no denying the quality of the food or the location. Fresh, local seafood is a speciality.
⫴⫴⫴ Miyazu Japanese Restaurant, Rutherford Hotel, Trafalgar Sq, T03-548 2299. Mon-Sat from 1800. An excellent but expensive Japanese restaurant with a loyal following.
⫴⫴ Bouterey's, 294 Queen St, Richmond, T03-5441114. Tue-Sat from 1600. The pick of the eateries in Richmond should you be staying out in that direction. Specializes in local cuisine.
⫴⫴ Hopgoods Restaurant and Bar, 284 Trafalgar St, T03-545 7191, www.hopgoods.co.nz. Lunch Thu-Fri 1100-1400, dinner Mon-Sat from 1730. Quality handcrafted locally sourced cuisine, with much of it – including the beer and wine – proudly organic. Recommended.
⫴⫴ Lambrettas Café Bar, 204 Hardy St, T03-545 8555, www.lambrettascafe.co.nz. 0900-late. Another popular, good value café specializing in all things Italian, including scooters. Excellent pizzas.
⫴⫴The Honest Lawyer, 1 Point Rd, Monaco, near the airport. Fine pub worthy of the ale and steak lover's attention.
⫴The Smugglers Pub, 8 Muritai St, T03-546 4084, Tahunanui. An Olde English-style pub with good value 'villainous' menu. Worth the extra effort to get there.

Ψ-ΨΨ Zippys, 276 Hardy St, T03-546 6348. Mon-Fri 0900-1600, Sat 1000-1400. Excellent funky vegetarian cafe.

Wineries *p439*
There are a number of winery restaurants out of town but worth the trip for a leisurely lunch. They include:
ΨSeifrieds, corner of SH60 and Redwood Rd, Appleby, Richmond, T03-544 5599, www.seifried.co.nz. A popular restaurant at the biggest winery.
ΨWaimea Estates, 22 Appleby Highway, Hope, T03-544 4963, www.waimeaestates.co.nz.

Murchison *p441*
ΨΨ Commercial Hotel, next to the VIC, T03-523 9696. Ironically, a far less commercial atmosphere here than in many other places.
Ψ Beechwoods Café, on SH6 where all the buses stop at SH6 southern end of town, T03-523 9571. Daily 0630-2130. Highly commercial, with a wide range of light meals and snacks available.
Ψ Rivers Café, at the Adventure Centre, 51 Fairfax St, T03-523 9009, www.rivers.co.nz. Good for a quick coffee and check of the email. But, beware, you will be hard pushed to walk out without being lured for a trip down the river. And why not?

⏾ Pubs, bars and clubs

Nelson *p435, maps p437 and p438*
When it comes to nightlife, most of the action in Nelson (and it can be considerable) takes place on or around Bridge St.
Honest Lawyer, Monaco and **The Smugglers Pub** (see eating), are both Olde English-style pubs worth the extra effort to get there.
Phat Club, 137 Bridge St, T03-548 3311. The place to go in the wee hours to shake your pants – presumably big ones?
The Shark Club, 132 Bridge St, T03-546 6630. Not, as the name suggests, a haunt for second-hand car salesmen or lawyers but

perhaps the town's most popular pool parlour and backpacker hangout. Free pool 1700-1900.
Victoria Rose, Trafalgar St, the place to go if you like jazz or blues, or if you're fed up with the noise of Bridge St and just want to watch some sport on the big screen. The good stuff (Irish and English beer) is expensive.

☺ Entertainment

Nelson *p435, maps p437 and p438*
Cinema and theatre
State Cinema Centre, opposite the VIC (I-Site), T03-548 3885. Also has a café upstairs.
Suter Gallery, 208 Bridge St, T03-548 4699, www.suter.org.nz. Occasionally the focus for more cultural events including theatre, dance and non-mainstream films.

❀ Festivals and events

Nelson *p435, maps p437 and p438*
For up-to-date events listings consult the website www.nelsonnz.com/events. The most famous event in the region used to be the iconic **Wearable Arts Festival** but thanks to its resounding success it has now been relocated to the country's capital, Wellington. This has of course caused ripples of controversy among the locals but it should perhaps be seen as a tribute to the region's considerable creative talent, a talent that thankfully is, despite the loss, still showcased through many other events throughout the year.
March Festival of Opportunities (late Feb). Typically unusual, this festival explores and contemplates the mind, the body, the spirit and probably even your navel, www.nelsonhealthfest.co.nz.
Oct Nelson Arts Festival. The biggest event of the year, with a week-long celebration showcasing the region's many colourful forms of artistic expression.
Dec-Feb Sealord Summer Festival. Various highlights including a lantern festival and Opera in the Park all aimed mainly at families.

O Shopping

Nelson *p435, maps p437 and p438*
For detailed information on arts and crafts outlets get a copy of the *Nelson Regional Guide Book – Art in its Own Place*, available from most bookshops.
Bead Gallery, 18 Parere St, T03-546 7807, www.beads.co.nz. Excellent.
Höglund Art Glass Gallery, Korurangi Farm, Landsdowne Rd, Richmond, T03-544 6500.
Monty's Market, Montgomery Sq, T03-546 6454. Sun 0900-1300. Popular with a crafts edge.
Nelson Market, Montgomery Sq, Sat 0800-1300. Local arts and crafts.
Pomeroys Coffee and Tea Co, 80 Hardy St, T03-546 6944. Stock up on filter coffee or tea.

▲ Activities and tours

Nelson *p435, maps p437 and p438*
The Nelson Region offers a wide range of activities from the crazy to the traditional.

4WD quad biking and the skywire
4WD quad biking is a speciality in the region with one of the oldest and best operators in the country based nearby.
Happy Valley Adventures, 194 Cable Bay Rd, Hira T03-545 0304, www.happyvalley adventures.co.nz. Back-country guided rides, taking in a mighty maitai tree and some superb views. Interesting eco-based commentary. Kids' fun rides in an 8WD also available, and there's a café on site. An excellent wet weather option. From 1-4 hrs $80-150, standard tour $110 for 2½ hrs.
Skywire is a novel addition to the adrenaline cocktail and is essentially a 4-person flying-fox that runs 1.6 km across the valley, reputedly at 120 kph. A 'Granny Run' is available for the faint-hearted. From $85. Horse trekking from $65. Transportation available.

Arts and crafts workshops
Creative Tourism, T03-526 8812, www.creativetourism.co.nz. An excellent creative workshop programme where you can try your hand at an amazing range of contemporary or traditional crafts from bone carving to organic brewing for $65-120. Visit the website or VIC (I-Site) for more details.
Nelson Bone Carving, 87 Green St, T03-546 4275, www.carvingbone.co.nz. Has a studio at Tahura Beach and offers a day traditional bone carving workshop from $65.

Cruising and sailing
Cat Sailing Charters, 46 Martin St, Monaco, T03-547 6666, www.sailingcharters.co.nz. Offers an excellent range of affordable sailing and launch cruise options, from evening racing, fishing or the exploration of local nautical sights, to half or full-day and overnight/multi-day trips to the Abel Tasman National Park. Recommended.

Flightseeing and aerobatics
U-Fly Extreme, Motueka Airfield, College St, T0800-360180/T03-5288290, www.uflyextreme.co.nz. Fun to the extreme aboard a Pitts-Special Biplane. A once-in-a-lifetime opportunity to fly an aerobatic aircraft yourself, from $285 (20-min flight). Remarkably easy, safe, good value for money and without doubt one of the most exhilarating activities available in NZ. Highly recommended
Abel Tasman Air, Nelson Airport, T03-528 8290, www.abeltasmanair.co.nz. An excellent and friendly outfit offering both transportation and flightseeing options. A flight around Abel Tasman and Kahurangi national parks is recommended.
Nelson Helicopters, T0800-450350/T03-547 1177, www.nelsonhelicopters.co.nz. Scenic helicopter flights. Used extensively during the filming of *Lord of the Rings* for shuttling cast and crew into the depths of the Kahurangi National Park.

Golf

Nelson is not short of quality courses, including: **Golf Range**, 453 Nayland Rd, Stoke, T03-547 2227; **Greenacres**, Richmond, T03-544 8420; and **Nelson Golf Club**, Bolt Rd, T03-548 5029.

Horse trekking

Stonehurst Farm Horse Treks, Stonehurst Farm, Clover Rd, T03-542 4121, www.stonehurstfarm.co.nz. Excellent variety of treks to suit all levels from 1-4 hrs and from $65.
Thorndale Horse Treks, north of Nelson (near **Happy Valley Adventures**), on Cable Valley Rd, T03-545 1191. Recommended, 1 hr to overnight from $65.
Western Ranges Horse Treks, Wakefield, T03-522 4178, www.thehorsetrek.co.nz. A good outfit well suited to both beginners and the experienced. Treks in the Kahurangi National Park and Northwest Nelson ranges from full-day to 10 days, from $200-3500.

Rock climbing

Vertical Limits, 34 Vanguard St, T03-545 7511, www.verticallimits.co.nz. Offers some excellent half- or full-day rock climbing trips to some notable venues in Golden Bay, $65-130. It also has an indoor climbing wall for instruction or independent use, from $16. Open Mon-Thu 1200-2100, Fri-Sun 1000-1800.

Skydiving, paragliding, kiteboarding and hang-gliding

Adventure Paragliding, 18A Marybank Rd, Atawai, T0800-212359, www.skyout.co.nz. Tandem paragliding and kiteboarding from $150, courses also available.
Nelson Hang-gliding Adventures, T03-548 9151, www.flynelson.co.nz. From $165. Tandem and solo introductory hang-gliding courses are also available.
Nelson Paragliding, T0508-359669/ T03-544 1182, www.nelsonparagliding.co.nz. Tandem paragliding from $110, courses from $180.
Skydive Abel Tasman, 16 College St, Mouteka, T0800-422899/T03-528 4091,

www.skydive.co.nz. If the weather is in your favour you can do your obligatory tandem skydive,12,000 ft ($279).

Walking

For a short walk the viewpoint above the Botanical Gardens is recommended (see page 436), while for longer excursions and expansive views try the **Dun Mountain Walkway**, which is accessible via the Broom Valley. From Brook St take a left on to Tantragee Rd.

Water-skiing, wakeboarding and kitesurfing

Kitesurfing is huge in Nelson with the winds over Tahunanui Beach often creating the perfect conditions.
Kitescool, based in Marahau, T021-354837, www.kitescool.co.nz. 'Discovery' Lessons to advanced courses from $170.

Winery tours and sightseeing

There are numerous sightseeing and wine tour operators available. See also box page 443. Recommended operators include:
Bay Tours, 48 Brougham St, T03-548 6486, www.baytoursnelson.co.nz. Flexible with wine tours a speciality from $78.
JJ's Quality Tours, T0800-229868/ T03-546 5470, www.jjs.co.nz. A well-established operator offering a brewery tour as well as the standard vineyard tours, half- or full-day from $78.

Nelson Lakes National Park *p440* Mountaineering

For all tramping and mountaineering information in the Nelson Lakes National Park contact the DoC Nelson Lakes Visitor Centre, View Rd, St Arnaud, T03-521 1806, www.doc.govt.nz.

Murchison *p441*

The principal activities in the area include fishing, whitewater rafting, kayaking, caving, mountaineering and walking. If you feel lucky and want to try **gold-panning**, the VIC hires Out Pans And Shovels For $6 ($20 Bond) And

Will Point You In The Right Direction. The Vic Can Also Provide Details And Directions Of The Numerous Short And Long Walking Options In The Area. The View From The **Skyline Walk** (1½ Hrs, 6 Km) Is Recommended. If A Walk Seems Too Much, It's Worth Visiting The **Ariki Falls** Which Are Located 3 Km From O'sullivan's Bridge Heading West Down Sh6 (Turn Left Down The Track 1 Km After The Statue Of 3 People Hugging). The Pink Rocks Are Even More Attractive Than The Falls. But Beware, Take Insect Repellent.

Buller Gorge, Buller Gorge Swingbridge, beside SH6, 14 kms west of Murchison, T03-523 9809, www.bullergorge.co.nz. Jet-boat trips down the Buller from $75 (hourly, Sep-Apr). The infamous swingbridge crossing from $5, the 'Cometline' and 'Supaman' Rides (a form of flying fox) from $30 and goldpanning from $13.

New Zealand Kayak School, 111 Waller St, T03-352 5786, www.nzkayakschool.com. Offers a 4-day introductory, intermediate, advanced and women-only whitewater kayaking courses and multi-day trips (with helicopter drop-off) from $175 per day. Price includes accommodation.

Ultimate Descents Murchison Adventure Centre, 51 Fairfax St, T03-5239899, www.rivers.co.nz. An attractive range of rafting and kayaking trips, with the local Buller River (Grade 3-4) being the main focus. A 4½-hr blat down the Buller followed by a soak in the hot tub costs from $120. There is also a shop and a café on-site.

⊖ Transport

Nelson *p435, maps p437 and p438*
Bicycle hire Coppins Great Outdoors Centre, 255 High St, Motueka, T03-528 7296.
Car hire Avis, Nelson Airport, T03-547 2727; Pegasus, 83 Haven Rd, T03-548 0884; **Hardy Cars**, 31 Bolt Rd, T03-548 1618. **Taxi** Sun City Taxis, T0800-422666, and **Nelson City Taxis**, T03-548 8225.

❶ Directory

Nelson *p435, maps p437 and p438*
Banks You will find all the main branches in or around Trafalgar St. **Internet** Boots Off, 53 Bridge St; **New Endeavour**, 93 Hardy St. **Medical services** Nelson Hospital, Tipahi St, T03-546 1800. Pharmacy, 131 Hardy St T03-548 4366. **Police** T03-548 8309. **Post office** Post Restante, 209 Hardy St, T03-546 7818, Mon-Fri 0800-1700, Sat 0930-1230.

North of Nelson → *Colour map 4, A4.*

For many international visitors (perhaps too many) Nelson and the small township of Motueka, 54 km to the north, act merely as a convenient staging post to the main focus of tourism in the region, the Abel Tasman National Park. This small stretch of coastline, with its picturesque sandy bays, well-worn coastal walking track and world-class kayaking trips, is one of the most popular natural attractions in the country. As such, it seldom disappoints, but don't expect to find much solitude here. For that you should leave the crowds behind and head further north on SH60, traversing Takaka Hill to the quieter, far more laid-back realms of Golden Bay.

Beyond the great hill, the small arty township of Takaka offers a fine introduction to the region, while the nearby Pupu springs possess an almost palpable sense of peace, and an extraordinary clarity. Then, skirting the shores of Golden Bay, via the former gold rush town of Collingwood, SH60 finally terminates at the surreal sandy sweep of Farewell Spit, with the unforgettable beauty of Whararuki Beach within walking distance. All in all, in can prove a memorable diversion and the scenery and general atmosphere of this little corner of the South Island can act like a natural tranquillizer well worth taking. ▸▸ *For Sleeping, Eating and other listings, see pages 455-459.*

Nelson to Motueka

From Richmond, 14 km southwest of Nelson, SH60 follows the fringe of Nelson Bay west to Motueka. This route – often labelled as 'Nelson's Coastal Way' – is the realm of vineyards, orchards, arts and crafts outlets and some pleasant seaside spots. One such spot worth a look, particularly around lunch or dinnertime, is **Mapua**. A congenial little settlement at the mouth of the **Waimea Inlet** (and just a short diversion off SH60), it boasts one of the best restaurants in the region, **The Smokehouse**, see page 457.

Across the road is the fairly unremarkable **Touch the Sea Aquarium and Gift Shop** ① *T03-540 3557, daily, $8.50, child $5*, which is maybe worth a look if you love seahorses or have kids. Far more impressive is the quality work of local artisans showcased nextdoor in the **Cool Store Art Gallery** ① *T03-540 3778.*

Motueka ⬤❼❶▲ ▸▸ *pp455-459.*

Motueka (population 12,000) itself is a rather unremarkable little place of little note, but set amidst all the sun-bathed vineyards and orchards and within a short distance from some of the most beautiful beaches in the country, it seems to radiate a sense of smug satisfaction. Once a thriving Maori settlement, the first residents were quickly displaced by the early Europeans, who were also intent on utilizing the area's rich natural resources. Today Motueka is principally a service centre for the numerous vineyards, orchards and market gardens that surround it, or for the many transitory tourists on route to the Abel Tasman National Park and Golden Bay. With such a seasonal influx of visitors Motueka is also a place of contrast, bustling in summer and sleepy in winter. One thing you will immediately notice on arrival is its almost ludicrously long main street – so long you could land a 747 on it and still have room for error. See also Abel Tasman National Park, page 451.

Ins and outs
Getting there The **Motueka airport** ① *College St, SH61, 2 km west of the town centre*, has no scheduled air services but **Abel Tasman Air**, T03-528 8290, www.abeltasmanair.co.nz, can get you there from within the region if you want to arrive in style. By road, Motueka is 51 km from Nelson on SH60 (Coastal Highway). Several bus companies offer regular services to Mouteka and beyond including, **Abel Tasman Coachlines** and **Atomic Shuttles**. See Nelson Ins and outs, page 435.

Tourist information Motueka VIC (I-Site) ① *Wallace St, in the town centre, T03-528 6543, www.abeltasmangreenrush.co.nz, daily 0800-1800 (0800-1630 winter)*, is a busy centre that prides itself on providing the best and most up-to-date information on the Abel Tasman National Park. **DoC field centre** ① *corner of King Edward and High sts, T03-528 1810, motuekaao@doc.govt.nz, Mon-Fri 0800-1630*, has maps and leaflets for the entire region and can book huts for the Abel Tasman Coastal Walkway, Kahurangi National Park and Heaphy Tracks. You could also call into **Abel Tasman Wilson's Experiences** ① *265 High St (main road into town, next to the New World supermarket), T0800-223582/T03-528 2027, www.abeltasmanco.nz*, which operates beachfront lodges, launch cruises, water taxi, guided/non-guided sea kayaking and walking; it can provide maps, tide information and help with itinerary planning.

Sights

The best beaches near Motueka (and before the national park) are in **Kaiteriteri**. For a local short walk try the Motueka Quay accessed via the waterfront west of the town centre. For other walks in the area contact the DoC. There's also the small and fairly unremarkable **Motueka Museum** ① *High St, T03-528 7660, Mon-Fri 1000-1500 (also weekends in summer), donation.* ▸▸ *For activities in the Abel Tasman National Park see page 458.*

Kaiteriteri and Marahau

Kaiteriteri and Marahau are both on the dead-end road to the southern boundary of the Abel Tasman National Park, which is accessed from SH60 just north of Motueka. **Kaiteriteri** (13 km) is a very pretty village with two exquisite beaches of its own and is a popular holiday spot. The main beach is the departure point for scenic launch trips, water taxis and kayak adventures into the Abel Tasman National Park. If you do nothing else in Kaiteriteri, allow yourself time to take in the view from the **Kaka Pa Point Lookout** at the eastern end of the beach. There is a signpost with destinations and distances that will remind you how far you are from home – and how close to paradise. **Breakers Beach** below, looking east towards the park, is truly idyllic.

    Marahau, a further 6 km east of Kaiteriteri, is principally an accommodation and activity base at the main access point to the national park. There is a good range of accommodation options, a number of water taxi and activity operators and a café to satisfy the needs of exhausted, hungry trampers. There is much controversy surrounding a $15 million resort development on environmentally sensitive wetlands, right at the entrance to the national park that has been given building consent but as yet (thankfully) remains on the drawing table. Should it go ahead (which it inevitably will), sadly this sums up the fears of many conservationists that it may be the beginning of the end for the unspoilt beauty of the Abel Tasman.

Abel Tasman National Park ⊜▲ ▸▸ *pp455-459.*

The Abel Tasman is the smallest and most popular national park in New Zealand, and one of the most beautiful, protecting 23,000 ha of some of the finest coastal scenery and beaches in the country. Rolling hills of native bush fall to azure-coloured clear waters and a 91-km coastline, indented with over 50 beaches of golden sand. It is a paradise for trampers and sea kayakers and boasts the famous and increasingly popular 51-km **Coastal Walkway**; while the **Inland Track** offers a quieter and more energetic tramp away from both the coast and the hordes of people. The park is also home to the Tonga Island Marine Reserve.

    The park was opened in 1942 after the tireless efforts of conservationist and resident Perrine Moncrieff; it was named after the Dutch navigator Abel Tasman who first sighted New Zealand in 1642. Many of the place names are accredited to the explorations and subsequent mappings in 1827 by the French explorer Jules Sebastien Cesar Dumont d'Urville.

Ins and outs

Getting there Marahau, at the park's southern entrance, is the principal gateway to the park. Access from this point is by foot, water taxi, kayak or launch. The northern (walk) gateway to the park is via Takaka (Golden Bay) at the road terminus on the eastern edge of Wainui Bay. There is access by unsealed road into the northern sector of the park terminating at Totaranui and Awaroa Bay. You can also fly into Awaroa Bay from Nelson or Motueka, with **Abel Tasman Air**, T03-528 8290.

Abel Tasman Track

A rough outline of the recommended route, distances and times (from south to north) is as follows:

Marahau to Anchorage: 11½ km, 4 hours

Anchorage Bark Bay: 9½ km, 3 hours

Bark Bay to Awaroa: 11½ km, 4 hours

Awaroa to Totaranui: 5½ km, 1½ hours

Totaranui to Wharwharangi: 7½ km, 3 hours

Wharwharangi to Wainui: 5½ km, 1½ hours

Kaiteriteri, Marahau and Takaka are served via Motueka by **Abel Tasman Coachlines**, T03-548 0285, www.abeltasmantravel.co.nz.

All the major water taxi and/or water-based transportation and tour operators are based in Kaiteriteri or Marahau which are both considered the gateways to the park. Other than pure sightseeing trips the various services and schedules offer casual walkers or day-trippers the option of being dropped off at one beach to be picked up later at the same, or at another. For trampers this can also provide numerous options to walk some of the **Coastal Walkway** or to retire early in the attempt to walk its whole length. Note also that some operators will tow kayaks, giving you the option to kayak and walk or again retire early. Bags and backpacks can also be carried independently, but this tends to be in conjunction with organized trips. Alas, in the Abel Tasman these days it is actually possible to 'hail' a water taxi, or at least gesticulate wildly, to catch one, even though you are not pre-booked. Also note that most water-taxi companies can pick up or help arrange bus transport from Nelson and Motueka to coincide with departures and of course they also offer a huge range of 'suggested' itineraries for a set price. In Kaiteriteri the principal operator is **Abel Tasman Sea Shuttles**, T0800-732748, www.abeltasmanseashuttles.co.nz, a return fare to Tonga Bay will cost from $70 return. In Kaiteriteri the principal beachfront operators are, again, **Sea Shuttles**, www.abeltasmanseashuttles.co.nz, and **Abel Tasman Wilson's Experiences**, T0800-223582, www.abeltasman.co.nz. In Marahau **Abel Tasman Aqua Taxi**, T0800-278282/T03-527 8083, www.aquataxis.co.nz, has an office and café (where you also board your boat-n-first leg by tractor-trailer). Prices are reasonable and competitive. An average fare to Totaranui at the top end of the park will cost from $32-55 one way. Most water taxis depart between 0830 and 1030 from Motueka, Kaiteriteri and Marahau with additional sailings in the early afternoon (1200 and 1330), depending on the tides.

Tourist information VIC (I-Site) and DoC offices in Motueka (see Motueka Ins and outs, page 450) are the principal sources of information on the park. They can assist with accommodation bookings and passes, transportation and activities; they can also provide tide times. DoC can also assist with general information, hut bookings, maps, and leaflets. Unmanned DoC information stations and intentions sheets are available at Marahau and Totaranui (seasonal).

▲▲ Abel Tasman Coastal Track

This two- to five-day, 51-km walk requires medium fitness and the track itself is well maintained (and certainly well trod). The only obstacle and sections that can cause difficulty are the two estuary crossings at Awaroa Inlet and Torrent Bay; these two stretches must be negotiated at low tide, otherwise it is your swimming skills that will be tested, rather than your walking.

Abel Tasman National Park

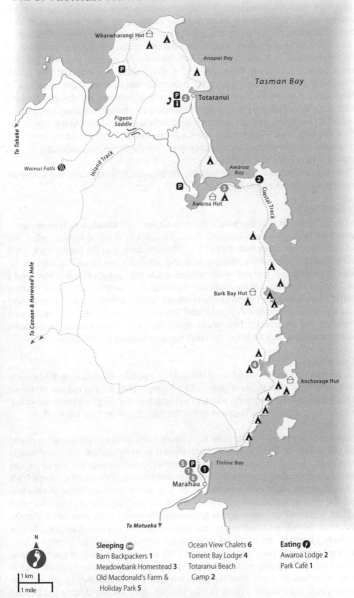

Sleeping 🛏
Barn Backpackers **1**
Meadowbank Homestead **3**
Old Macdonald's Farm &
Holiday Park **5**

Ocean View Chalets **6**
Torrent Bay Lodge **4**
Totaranui Beach
Camp **2**

Eating 🍴
Awaroa Lodge **2**
Park Café **1**

There are a number of ways to tackle the track in whole or in part. The most popular route is from south (Marahau) to north (Wainui), or commonly from Totaranui in the north (by water taxi from Marahau) back to Marahau in the south. There are plenty of DoC campsites and huts along the way and a few other, more salubrious, independent lodges should you choose the luxury option. Detailed information about the track can be obtained from DoC in Motueka and the website www.doc.govt.nz; its leaflet *The Abel Tasman Coast Track* ($1) is invaluable and it can provide the essential tide tables. Although the walk takes in many attractive bays, inlets and beaches, it does involve a lot of bush walking, where the view of the sea, never mind beaches, are obscured for long periods of time. So if you are not a seasoned tramper a combination of water taxi/walking over part of the route is perhaps recommended. Although the whole trip is a delight, the most scenic beaches are **Torrent Bay** and the **Awaroa Inlet**. These should not be missed and have the added novelty of the tidal crossing – which will give you a mild taste of what tramping in New Zealand is all about.

There are DoC huts at Anchorage, Bark Bay, Awaroa and Wharwharangi and numerous campsites along the way (see below).

▲▲ Inland Track

The Inland Track is for obvious reasons less popular and links **Marahau** to **Wainui** via the **Pigeon Saddle** on the Takaka-Totaranui Road. It is a 37-km, three- to five-day effort. The main attraction here, other than the fact it is far less trodden than the coastal track, is the beautiful undisturbed and regenerating bush and occasional fine views. The track can be tackled in whole or part and one recommendation is to start at the car park at **Harwood's Hole**. This way you can take in the impressive Harwood's Hole before tackling the remaining 20-km track north over the Pigeon Saddle to Wainui. Note that the track can also be tackled in part with the access point at Pigeon Saddle (Totaranui Road via Takaka). DoC can provide information and an essential broadsheet about the track. There are four huts but no separate campsites. They are not of the same standard as those on the Coastal Track.

▲▲ Day walks

If you are short of time or cannot stand the sight of a paddle, the following are two-day walks that will provide a pleasant taste to Abel Tasman. They are also not too strenuous and have the added fun of getting your feet wet and then stopping for a lovely cup of tea. The first is accessed from the southern end of the park, the other from the north.

Torrent Bay to Marahau (14 km, three to six hours) From Marahau take an early morning water taxi to **Torrent Bay**, $30-38. Although there is an alternate high tide route around Torrent Bay try to make sure your arrival at Torrent Bay coincides with low tide so you can make the direct crossing. Take in the immediate delights here, then take the Coastal Track heading south, for which you need to take off your boots and then follow the markers across the estuary. Return boots to feet and find the track again that climbs the small headland before falling to the exquisite **Anchorage Bay** Beach. Then, from halfway up the beach, climb the hill, not forgetting to look back at the stunning view. Take the sidetrack (15 minutes) from the top of the hill down to the incredibly cute (and hopefully quiet) **Watering Cove**. Climb back up to the coastal track and continue south. If you have time check out **Stillwell Bay** and certainly walk along **Appletree Bay** (re-access to main track at far end of the beach). From there complete the walk past **Tinline Bay** to the Marahau entrance point. If the tide is in your favour, you can cross the bay directly just beyond

Tinline Bay (where the path descends to beach level). Fall exhausted and happy in to the **Park Café**, reward yourself with a pint of beer, a glass of wine or the full seafood fettuccine. While there use the email facility to make friends jealous back home.

Awaroa Bay (6 km, three to six hours) From Takaka take the Totaranui Road via **Pohara**, **Wainui Inlet** and the **Pigeon Saddle**, enjoying the views on the way. From the Totaranui Road take a right on the Awaroa Road to the **Awaroa** car park. Make sure once again that your arrival coincides with an outgoing tide. Digest the view across the inlet and the walk you are about to do. Descend to the beach and remove footwear. Cross the inlet in a direct line towards the sea, ignoring the especially muddy bit for the first 100 m. Enjoy the paddle and negotiate the deepest part (should be no more than knee deep) to **Sawpit Point** and the DoC Awaroa Hut. Follow the bay around and if possible extend your walk to the tip of the sand spit. From there walk along Awaroa beach to the far end. Follow the signs to **Awaroa Lodge**. Enjoy this oasis in paradise and sample the beer, a coffee or a refreshing cup of tea. Then retrace your steps to the Awaroa car park, keeping an eye on the tide.

◉ North of Nelson listings

For Sleeping and Eating price codes and other relevant information, see Essentials pages 44-50.

◉ Sleeping

Nelson to Motueka *p450*
LL Jester House, 15 km south of Motueka on the Coastal Highway (SH60), T03-526 6742, www.jesterhouse.co.nz. Something totally different and without doubt the most original accommodation in the region. Quite simply, this could be (and probably will be) your only opportunity to stay in a giant boot.
LL-L Bronte Lodge, Bronte Rd East, T03- 540 2422, www.brontelodge.co.nz. A luxury option set in beautiful gardens. 2 suites and self-contained villas over looking the bay and with all mod cons.
LL-L Kina Colada Holiday and Health Retreat, Kina Peninsula, T03-526 6700, www.kinacolada.co.nz. Enjoy the congenial surroundings, a massage, sauna or an oxygen, hydro- and moor-mud therapy.
AL Istana Coastal Cottage, located just south of Mapua on the Coastal Highway (SH60), T03-544 1979, www.istana.co.nz. Self-contained rammed earth cottage in a superb position overlooking the coastal inlet, very peaceful and tastefully appointed with Asian antiques and modern furnishings. Swimming pool and free kayaks.

B-D Mapua Leisure Park (clothing optional), 33 Toru St, T03-540 2666, www.nelsonholiday. co.nz. An excellent camp, set amid pine trees and sheltered surroundings, at the river mouth. It has numerous pretty areas to camp in, powered sites, cabins, chalets, sauna, pool and spa. There is also a small café and bar on the beach and internet. If the holiday park is not to your taste, there are a number of good B&Bs in the area.

Motueka *p450*
The area has many fine lodges, B&Bs and homestays, most of which are located out of town. The VIC (I-Site) has full listings. Given the proximity to the Abel Tasman National Park you are advised to book well ahead in summer.
LL Kahurangi Estate, Sunrise Rd, T03-543 2980, www.kahurangiwine.com. Luxury self-contained cottage set in a working vineyard.
LL Motueka River Lodge, Motueka Valley Highway, Ngatimoti, T03-526 8668, www.motuekalodge.co.nz. A small, luxury boutique fishing lodge designed in French provincial style and located in the picturesque Motueka River Valley. Whether you're an angling fanatic or not you will be given a warm welcome and you cannot fail to be impressed with the aesthetics. Modern, country-style decor and open fires create a warm and homely feel and cordon bleu cuisine is offered.

In-house fishing guides with an intimate knowledge of the best local and regional fishing spots. Minimum 2-night stay.

AL Gingerbread House, Neudorf Rd, Upper Moutere, T03-543 2472, www.cottage stays.co.nz/neudorfs_gingerbread_house/. Tidy little self-contained eco-friendly chalet (sleeps 4) set in a peaceful rural property with 2.8 ha of land. Breakfasts available. Caring Swiss/Kiwi hosts with lots of local knowledge.

AL-A Blue Moon, 57 School Rd, T03-528 6996, www.thebluemoon.co.nz. Self-contained, spacious guest room. Tastefully decorated and good value.

AL-A The Estuary B&B, 543 High St, T03-528 6391, www.hauplains.co.nz. Good value, modern with good facilities.

A Rowan Cottage Organic B&B, 27 Fearon St, T03-528 6492, www.rowancottage.net. Studio with good facilities and character amid a proudly nurtured organic garden.

Motels

L-A Nautilus Lodge Motel, 67 High St, T03-528 4658, www.nautiluslodge.co.nz. A possible exception to the generally unimpressive options available.

Backpackers

B-D Bakers Lodge , 4 Poole St, T03-528 0102, www.bakerslodge.co.nz. A modern and well-maintained establishment with a wide variety of rooms, purpose-built facilities and a nice atmosphere. Internet and off-street parking. Very popular so book well in advance.

B-D Hat Trick Lodge, 25 Wallace St (opposite VIC), T03-528 5353, www.hattricklodge.co.nz. Purpose-built and conveniently located.

B-D White Elephant, 55 Whakarewa St, T03-528 6208, www.whiteelephant.co.nz. Deservingly popular and spacious backpacker hostel. Excellent en suites. Tent sites available.

Motorcamps

B-D Fernwood Holiday Park, 519 High St (SH60), T03-528 7488, www.fernwoodholidaypark.co.nz . Beside the

roundabout at the start of the never-ending main road through the town (2 km). Usual facilities including camp kitchen.

B-D Motueka Top Ten Holiday Park, 10 Fearon St, at the other end of the town, T0800-668835/T03-528 7189, www.motuekatop10.co.nz.

Kaiteriteri p451

LL-L Kimi Ora Holiday and Health Resort, Martin Farm Rd, T03-527 8027, www.kim iora.com. 22 modern Swiss-style chalets, pool, spa and a health centre offering a range of treatments. In-house vegetarian restaurant (open to non-guests) and courtesy pick-up.

L Bayview, Kaiteriteri Heights, Little Kaiteriteri, T03-527 8090, www.kaiteriteri bandb.co.nz. Offers exactly what the name suggests from 2 lovely rooms. Enjoy breakfast on the deck outside.

AL-A Torlesse Coastal Motels, Kotare Pl, Little Kaiteriteri Beach, T03-527 8063, www.torlesse motels.co.nz. The best motel option with a choice of studio or 2-bedroom units.

Motorcamps and campsites

C-D Kaiteriteri Motor Camp, across the road from the beach on Sandy Bay Rd, T03-527 8010, www.kaiteriteribeach.co.nz. Has tent and powered sites and cabins. Given its location it is hugely popular so very busy in the high season, especially over domestic holiday periods. Book well ahead.

Marahau p451

L Ocean View Chalets, T03-527 8232, www.accommodationabeltasman.co.nz. Neat, self-contained 1- to 2-bedroom cottages and studio units set on the hillside overlooking the bay, about 500 m from the main village.

L-B Abel Tasman Aqua Packers, Anchorage Bay, T0800-430744, www.aquapackers.co.nz. A rather unusual option worth considering with accommodation on board a small ex-Second World War naval patrol vessel. Standard, dinner or B&B options. Private doubles or dorm-style rooms. It isn't cheap but then you don't get an ever-changing view like that very often. Plenty of activities and a good base from which to explore the park.

AL Abel Tasman Marahau Lodge, T03-527 8250, www.abeltasmanmarahau lodge.co.nz. Purpose-built establishment conveniently located between Kaiteriteri Beach and the start of the Abel Tasman Coastal Track. Modern studios and self- contained units, pool, sauna and spa. Breakfast and room service evening meals on request.

C-D Barn Backpackers, Harvey Rd, T03-527 8043, www.barn.co.nz. A smaller but similar set up to Old McDonald's, below. Can assist in park accommodation and activity bookings.

C-D Old McDonald's Farm and Holiday Park, Harvey Rd, at the entrance to the Abel Tasman Park, T03-527 8288, www.oldmacs. co.nz. A large but sheltered, well-equipped holiday camp complete with various animals, including 2 friendly and extremely dozy kune pigs. There are plenty of sheltered tent and powered sites and a range of well-appointed self-contained units, cabins and a backpacker's dormitory. Small café and shop on site and internet. Within walking distance of the Park Café, see page 458.

Abel Tasman National Park *p 451, map p453*

LL Meadowbank Homestead, on the beachfront at Awaroa, with **Abel Tasman Wilson's Experiences** (see pages 450 and 459). A replica of the original settler's home. It is a relaxed holiday home on the beachfront, providing accommodation primarily for guided walkers and kayakers. Price includes twin/double accommodation, en suite bathroom, meals and launch transfers.

LL Torrent Bay Lodge, further south, also owned and operated by Abel Tasman Wilson's Experiences, T03-528 7801, www.abeltasman.co.nz. Offers an excellent standard of modern, mid- to upper-range accommodation as part of a walks or kayaking package from 2-days/1-night to 5-days/ 4-nights. The lodge in Torrent Bay has a relaxed atmosphere, with natural wood decor

reflecting a nautical theme. It is only metres from the beach and Abel Tasman coastal track. All equipment, meals and transport by water taxi are included in the package.

Campsites and huts

There are 4 DoC huts and 21 campsites on the Coastal Track plus a number of private B&Bs and lodges. DoC huts have heating, toilets, bunks, mattresses and a water supply (all water should be boiled). Campsites have water and toilets. From Oct-Apr, DoC huts must be booked in advance and a summer season hut pass ($30 per hut per night depending on season) purchased. Campsites cost $12 per night.

D Totaranui Beach Camp, T03-5288083. Popular budget camp next to the beach. It is accessed from the north by road, or from the south by water taxi. It is basic (no power) with limited facilities and is administered by DoC ($12). Bookings are essential Oct-Apr.

● Eating

Nelson to Motueka *p450*

¶¶ **The Smokehouse Restaurant**, a few doors down from Flax, Mapua, T03-540 2280, www.smokehouse.co.nz. Daily for lunch and dinner. Well known for its fine smoked fish and other seafood delicacies. The restaurant is set overlooking the river with a very pleasant outdoor eating area where you can sample a glass of local wine while taking in the view. Attached is a very popular fish and chip shop.

¶¶ **Wharfside Bar and Restaurant (Shed 1)**, Mapua, T03-540 2028. Daily for lunch and dinner, from 1100. Has plenty of class and enjoys a fine reputation.

Motueka *p450*

¶¶¶ **Gothic Gourmet Restaurant**, 208 High St, T03-528 6699. Daily 0730-late. Interesting concept, but lacks atmosphere and is too expensive for what it is.

¶¶ **Hot Mama's Café**, 105 High St, T03-528 7039. Attracts a younger crowd, great coffee.

The Moorings, 218 High St, T03-528 6103. Open daily 'ate' till late. Along with Hot Mama's Café, above, has a loyal local following, good coffee and inviting blackboard menus.

Riverside Café, just out of town on the way to Lower Moutere (Inland Highway 7 km), T03-526 7447. Thu-Sun 0930-1700. A fine option, especially if you have kids. Spacious grounds, great staff.

Up the Garden Path, 473 High St, T03-528 9588. Daily 0900-1900 (winter 0900-1700). Also a good bet for a quality caffeine hit amid an attractive art garden. Good for vegetarian.

Kaiteriteri and Marahau *p451*

Hooked on Marahau Café and Restaurant, Marahau Waterfront, T03-527 8576. Daily for breakfast, lunch and dinner (closed Jun-Sep). A new establishment in a prime location offering outdoor and indoor dining, licensed.

Park Café, just at the entrance to the park on Harvey Rd, T03-527 8270. Daily from 0800 (closed May-Aug). Fine blackboard fare, a bar, good coffee and internet. Great atmosphere.

Pubs, bars and clubs

Motueka *p450*

Dodgy Ref, 121 High St, T03-528 4101. The best place for a beer in town.

Hot Mama's Café and Bar (see Eating, above). A popular spot, especially with the younger set. Regular DJ's and 'Jam' sessions.

Activities and tours

Motueka *p450*

For other activities see Nelson, page 447, and Kaiteriteri, below.

Skydive Abel Tasman, 16 College St, Mouteka, T0800-422899/T03-528 4091, www.skydive.co.nz. If the weather is in your favour you can do your obligatory tandem skydive, 12,000 ft ($279).

U-Fly Extreme, see page 447.

Abel Tasman Wilson's Experiences, see page 450. Offers a wide range of guided/non-guided sea kayaking, and walking trips to the Abel Tasman National Park.

Bush and Beyond, 35 School Rd, T03-528 9054, www.naturetreks.co.nz. Offers a variety of conservation-based walks from 1-8 days, mainly in the Kahurangi National Park, from around $195 a day.

Kaiteriteri and Marahau *p451*

Cat Sailing Charters, 46 Martin St, Monaco, T03-547 6666, www.sailingcharters.co.nz. Offer an excellent range of affordable sailing and launch cruise options, from evening racing, fishing or the exploration of local nautical sights, to half or full-day and overnight/ multi-day trips in the Abel Tasman. Recommended.

Abel Tasman National Park *p451, map p453*

The choice is so vast that it is all very confusing to start with. You can tramp, walk, kayak, walk/kayak, cruise or even swim with seals, but working out exactly how you do it and how much you pay for it is a headache. Give yourself plenty of time to pre-plan and don't jump at the first option with which you are presented.

Organized trips and cruises

For other water taxi operators, see page 452. There are a bewildering number of organized trips on offer designed to help make the decisions for you, but they can, if you are indecisive, make it very difficult to choose. All the water taxi operators offer a range of cruises and half- to full-day trips, with combinations of cruising and walking.

Abel Tasman Seal Swim, Main Rd, Kaiteriteri, T0800-732529/T03-5278022, www.sealswim.com. Swim with the seals at the Tonga Island Marine Reserve (within the park boundary). It is the only operator that has a DoC concession to do so. From $169 (spectator from $90). Most water taxis depart between 0830 and 1030 from Kaiteriteri and

1200 and 1330 from Marahau. In summer wherever you are in the park it is basically a 0900-1700 operation with water taxis plying the coast and various stops constantly between those times.

Abel Tasman Wilson's Experiences, 265 High St, Motueka, T03-5287801, www.abeltasman.co.nz. A professional and reliable outfit. It offers half- to 5-day guided/non-guided options based from the only beachfront lodges in the park, including transport on water taxi or comfortable launch. A transport-only fare can be as little as $32 and a day-cruise from $70, while a 5-day guided walking/sea kayaking trip weighs in at around $1700, all inclusive.

Sea kayaking

The Abel Tasman offers a world-class sea kayaking experience and it is, without doubt, the top venue in New Zealand. But it is very busy. On a midsummer's morning the colourful flotilla of kayaks departing from Kaiteriteri and Marahau are a sight to behold and something that would probably even have had the early Maori paddling their *waka* for cover. There is an army of operators offering a wide range of options from simple independent day hire and self-guided day-trips, to multi-day, guided kayak/walking combinations. The choice is yours and the decision difficult.

If walking is not your thing, then a kayak only trip is obviously recommended. But to get the overall essence of the Abel Tasman, a guided combination of both kayaking and walking is recommended. The beauty of the Abel Tasman, other than the scenery, crystal clear waters and the wildlife, is the layout of its myriad bays and beaches, which makes a staged trip and the logistics eminently surmountable. Even if you have never been sea kayaking before, it is relatively safe and easy. The modern day sea kayak is very stable and all the major operators provide training, guidance and have adequate safety standards. Serious sea kayakers tend to leave the Abel Tasman to the novice flotillas and are to be found hiding in the serenity of the Marlborough Sounds or Fiordland. Competition is fierce so the best advice is to shop about and research thoroughly before deciding. Prices range from about $45 independent hire per day, $95-185 for a guided day trip, to around $450 for a 3-day trip (camping) with food provided. The principal and reputable companies include the following.

Abel Tasman Kayaks, Marahau Beach, T03-5278022/T0800-732529, www.abel tasmankayaks.co.nz. Offers a range of trips from half- to multi-day. The 1-day guided trips with walks or seal swim combos from $100-$220.

Abel Tasman Sea Kayak Company, 506 High St, Motueka, T0508-252925/T03-528 7251, www.seakayaknz.co.nz.

Abel Tasman Wilson's Experiences, 265 High St, Motueka, T03-528 2027 www.abeltasman.co.nz. Offers civilized adventures staying at the only beachfront lodges, chef-prepared meals and private rooms with en suite bathrooms. A 3-day guided kayak/walk costs around $1200.

Golden Bay Kayaks, Pohara, Golden Bay, T03-525 9095, www.goldenbaykayaks.co.nz. Popular and slightly different with trips in both the Abel Tasman National Park and Golden Bay region. The quieter end of the park!.

Kaiteriteri Sea Kayak, Kaiteriteri Beachfront, T0800-252925/T03-5278383, www.seakayak.co.nz.

Ocean River Adventure Company, Motueka, T0800-732529/T03-5278022, www.seakayaking.co.nz. Specializes in independent freedom rentals from $65 a day.

Kahu Kayaks, Sandy BayRd, Marahau, T0800-300101/T03-527 8300, www.kahukayaks.co.nz. A small, fun crowd offering freedom hire and entertaining guided trips.

Golden Bay → *Colour map 4, A4.*

From the pretty township of Takaka SH60 continues northwest, eventually reaching the coast and the tiny village of Collingwood, the gateway to Kahurangi National Park, the Heaphy Track and Whararíki Beach, one of the most beautiful beaches in the country. From the end of terra firma, 22 km north of Collingwood, the huge 35-km Farewell Spit extends like a golden rainbow out into ocean to envelop the vast mud flats of Golden Bay. ▶▶ *For Sleeping, Eating and other listings, see pages 465-468.*

Ins and outs

Getting there **Takaka airfield** ① *6 km west of town on SH60*, is served by **Abel Tasman Air**, T03-528 8290, www.abeltasmanair.co.nz, from Nelson. This operator also provides excellent scenic flights and air transport from the southern end of the Heaphy Track. By road (SH60), Takaka is 109 km from Nelson and 50 km to Farewell Spit. Bus companies include **Abel Tasman Coachlines**, T03-548 0285, www.abeltasmantravel.co.nz and **Golden Bay Coachlines**, T03-525 8352, www.goldenbaycoachlines.co.nz buses stop outside the VIC (I-Site).

If you do not have your own transport you might consider the various adventure tours on offer to the region with **Golden Bay Connections**, T0800-752232/T03-5257678, www.goldenbayconnections.com. All tours start in Kaiterteri.

Tourist information and orientation Almost all the services the visitor requires can be found along Commercial Street, the main street through Takaka. **Golden Bay VIC** ① *Willow St, at the southern entrance to Takaka, T03-525 9136, goldenbay@nelsonnz.com, www.goldenbay.net.nz, www.nelsonnz.com, daily 0900-1700,* stocks the full range of information for the entire Golden Bay area, including Collingwood and Farewell Spit. The free *Golden Bay Heart of the Parks Guide* is useful. **DoC** ① *62 Commercial St, Takaka, T03-525 8026, goldenbayao@doc.govt.nz, Mon-Fri 0800-1600,* has detailed information on both the Abel Tasman and Kahurangi national parks (including the Heaphy and Abel Tasman Coastal Tracks).

Motueka to Takaka

From Motueka the **Takaka Hill Highway** (SH60) climbs its 800-m namesake offering spectacular views back towards Nelson and across Golden Bay. It is this physical barrier that gives Golden Bay a very special quality, almost like a natural gatekeeper to a more peaceful place and subtle protection from the hype surrounding Motueka and the Abel Tasman National Park. But before descending the hill it is well worth taking a look at **Harwood's Hole**, which at 176 m is the deepest open and vertical sinkhole in the country.

To access it you must travel 11 km along the unsealed Canaan Road that heads north back towards the Abel Tasman National Park off SH60 (on the right, just before the summit of the Takaka Hill). Almost immediately you will see the distinct karst (limestone) scenery that gave rise to Harwood's Hole and many far smaller and more subtle rock features and developing sinkholes. From the terminus of the road it is a very pleasant 45-min walk through mountain beach forest and more limestone features to reach the sinkhole. A word of warning here: upon reaching it you cannot see the base of the hole and there are no barriers. The water-enlarged (but now dry) sinkhole, drops to an

Te Waikoropupu Springs

Borne of the Takaka Marble Aquifer, the turquoise waters of the 'Pupu Springs' bubbles out at an average rate of 13.2 cubic metres per second, creating a lake that is the clearest of any freshwater body outside Antarctica. To the scientific community they are of interest not only as an unusual landform, but also for the resident aquatic plants and animals. If these springs were in North America and Europe there would be no way casual divers would be able to enter the waters given the sheer demand and subsequent environmental impact but here in the 'clean and green' as long as you adhere to the stringent criteria you can dive casually providing the experience of a lifetime. To the Maori, the springs are considered *taonga* – a treasure, and *wahi tapu* – a sacred place to be revered. It is a peaceful, beautiful place that has a palpable and rare sense of purity lost in the parks and reserves in the more populous nations of the world. If you are in the area a visit here is highly recommended.

underground river that emerges below and flows into Gorge Creek and then into the Takaka River. Just before Harwood's Hole a right-hand branch leads to Gorge Creek Lookout with its expansive views over the Takaka Valley and Gorge Creek.

Takaka ⬤🅟🅐🅒 ⏩ *pp465-468*.

Takaka (population around 1,200) was founded in 1854 and is the principal business and shopping area for Golden Bay. In summer it is a bustling little place and year round the residence of a colourful and cosmopolitan palette of arts and crafts people. It is also home to a large dairy factory. There are a number of interesting attractions around the town including the intriguing 'Pupu' Springs and Rawhiti Cave. The township also serves as the gateway to the northern sector of the Abel Tasman National Park, the vast Kahurangi National Park and the remote 35-km Farewell Spit. The small seaside village of **Pohara**, about 10 km north east of Takaka on the road to the northern boundary of the Abel Tasman National Park, boasts the best local beach and provides safe swimming.

In the town itself, the **Golden Bay Museum and Gallery** ⓘ *T03-525 6268, daily 1000-1600, closed Sun in winter, free*, displays the usual local treasures and a special feature on early explorer Abel Tasman's unfortunate first encounter with the local Maori. Of further interest is the gallery next door, which showcases the cream of local arts and crafts talent. There are many other independent galleries in the area for which the VIC's free *Arts of Golden Bay* leaflet can point you in the right direction.

The biggest attraction in the immediate area are the beautiful and crystal-clear **Te Waikoropupu or Pupu Springs** ⓘ *administered by DoC, open daily; to get there follow SH60 north of Takaka, turning left just after the bridge over the Takaka River, follow Pupu Valley and Pupu Springs Rd to the car park*. There are well-maintained paths and the reserve can be explored thoroughly in about 45 minutes. Nearby the **Pupu Walkway**, which starts at the end of Pupu Valley Road, retraces an old gold-mining water race, taking in some interesting features and lovely bush. It is one of the best short walks in the region and takes about two to three hours.

Of the two limestone cave systems in the area, Te Anaroa and Rawhiti, it is the **Rawhiti Cave** that is the most impressive. It is, however, the least accessible. This ancient cave, with its enormous entrance laden with thousands of coloured stalactites, can be accessed independently, but a guided tour with **Kahurangi Walks** ① *T03-525 7177, www.kahurangiwalks.co.nz, 3 hrs $35, child $15*, is recommended. Closer to Takaka are the weird and wonderful limestone (karst) formations of the **Labyrinth Rocks** ① *3 km outside town, Labyrinth Lane, Three Oaks, T03-525 8434, daily 1200-dusk, small admission charge*, which will keep the kids occupied for hours.

Also of note, and accessed where Motupipi meets the Clifton Crossroads, is the **Grove Scenic Reserve**. A short 10-minute walk will bring you to an intriguing spot where massive rata trees grow out of curiously shaped karst rocks. Nearby those with green fingers and the love of a fine view will enjoy the **Begonia House and gardens** ① *Richmond Rd, Pohara, T03-525 9058, flower house open Mon-Fri1000-1530, free*.

While in the area, take a look at the **Abel Tasman Memorial** on the headland just beyond Tarakohe (Totaranui Road) and the pretty **Wainui Falls** (Wainui Bay); an easy 40-minute walk. This road can also take you to the northern beaches and tramping access points of the **Abel Tasman National Park**. Of some novelty are the famous Anatoki eels at **Bencarri Farm** ① *6 km south of Takaka, signposted off SH60 on McCallum Rd, T03-525 8261, www.bencarri.co.nz, daily 1000-1700, $12, child $6*. The eels are reputed to be the oldest tame eels in the country with some individuals still enjoying a daily snack after 80 years of residence. There is a good café on site (open 1000-late).

Collingwood ⊜🕖▲ ▸▸ *pp465-468*.

Collingwood was formerly known as Gibbstown and was (believe it or not) once a booming gold-mining town that was promoted as an eminently suitable capital for the nation. But that dream turned to dust when the gold reserves were laid waste and a fire almost destroyed the entire village. Rebuilt and renamed Collingwood in honour of Nelson's second-in-command, fire struck again in 1904 and yet again as recently as 1967 when the town hall, hotel and two shops were reduced to ashes. Despite its fiery past, Collingwood still retains a few historical buildings, including the characterful **courthouse**, which is now a café where you can sentence yourself to a lengthy tea break. Collingwood itself also has a small and unpretentious **museum** ① *Tasman St, T03-524 8131, daily 0900-1800, donation $2, child $1*.

The area has a few other notable attractions worth visiting. South of Collingwood, in the attractive **Aorere River Valley** and back on the limestone theme, are the privately owned **Te Anaroa and Rebecca Caves** ① *Caves Rd, near Rockville, T03-524 8131, 1-hr guided tours of the Te Anaroa Caves available in summer at 1030, 1230, 1430 and 1630 (in winter by arrangement); dual cave tours of 2-3 hrs are also available $25*. The Te Anaroa Caves are 350 m in length and include the usual stalactite and stalagmite formations and fossilized shells, while the Rebecca Caves are best known for their glow-worms. At the end of Cave Road are two limestone rock monoliths known as the **Devil's Boots** (presumably because they are upside-down). The walks and mountain bike tracks of the **Aorere Goldfields**, which were New Zealand's first, are accessed from the road end and are of far more interest. The free DoC leaflet provides information. For something longer and more challenging, the three- to four-day hike to **Boulder Lake** is recommended.

If you have time, an exploration of the pretty **Aorere River Valley** (Heaphy Track Road) is recommended. Beyond the pleasures of the drive itself, a stop at the river **gorge** at Salisbury Bridge (Quartz Range Road) and the old **Bainham Store** will both have the camera clicking. Access down to the river is possible, to the left just beyond Salisbury Bridge, while the Bainham Store is an original, store that has changed little in decades and is still open for business.

Farewell Spit

ⓘ *Access on the spit is restricted so an organized tour is the only way to truly experience this weird and wonderful place. You can also book and join the Farewell Spit tour en route to the spit at the visitor centre, or see tour operators, page 467.*

The spit is formed entirely from countless tons of sand ejected into the northerly ocean currents from the numerous river mouths scattered all the way up the west coast. It is a dynamic, almost desert-like landscape, with sparse vegetation struggling to take root in the dry and constantly shifting sand. The majority of the spit is a DoC nature reserve and the vast mud flats that it creates along its landward edge are one of New Zealand's most important wading-bird habitats. Over 100 species have been recorded around the spit, but it is the sheer numbers of each species that are most notable. Migrating flocks of godwit and knot can run well in to the thousands, providing a memorable sight. **Black swans** use the food-rich mud flats of Golden Bay, and when the tide is in they gracefully tread the water in huge flocks. There is also a small colony of rapacious **gannets** at the very end of the spit.

Both Cape Farewell and Farewell Spit were noted by Tasman in 1642 (no doubt a little shorter than it is now) and named by Cook when he left the shores of New Zealand in 1770. The lighthouse, at the very tip of the spit, was first erected in 1870. It has an interesting history and was replaced due to rotting timber.

The spit is a remarkable and memorable landscape if only for its powerful sense of isolation, but to see it from afar and from sea level is a strangely unremarkable experience. With its vast dune system, no more than 20 m in height, its sheer length and the omnipresent coastal haze, its very presence is, to say the least, muted. At best only a small grove of pine trees near its tip can be seen, like some tiny far off island. If you cannot afford to go out on the spit or simply want to get a better impression of its scale from afar, the best place to view it is from the elevated hills around the Pillar Point Light Beacon, accessed from Wharariki Road and Puponga.

At the base of the spit and just beyond the last small settlement of Puponga is the **Farewell Spit Visitor Centre and Paddlecrab Kitchen** ⓘ *T03-524 8454, daily 0900-1700 (seasonal).* It stocks a range of informative leaflets and has a number of interesting displays surrounding the spit, its wildlife and the rather sad and repetitive whale strandings in Golden Bay. The café sells a range of refreshments and snacks and has a fine deck overlooking the bay and the spit itself. Most of the established walking tracks leave directly from the centre.

Wharariki Beach

Wharariki Beach has to be one of the most beautiful beaches in the country. Perhaps it is its very remoteness that makes it so special, but add to that its classic features – including caves, arches and dunes – and you have near perfection. It is so beautiful you almost find yourself feeling a corrupting sense of guilt at leaving your lone footprints on its swathes of golden sand. You can access the beach by road from Puponga via Wharariki Road (20-minute walk) or make it the highlight on a longer and stunning coastal walk from **Pillar Point Lighthouse** (see Activities and tours, page 467). Note that swimming here on Wharariki Beach is very dangerous.

Pillar Point to Wharariki Beach coastal walk → *13 km, 6-8 hrs.*
From **Puponga**, follow Wharariki Beach Road to the turn-off (right) up to **Pillar Point Light Beacon** ('Blinking Billy'). Note this is a rough non-signposted road. Park your vehicle

at the base of the hill below the light beacon. Climb the hill to Pillar Point and enjoy your first proper view of Farewell Spit before heading further north towards the **Old Man Rock** (155 m) along the crest of the hill. Take in the views of the spit and Golden Bay before retracing your steps to Pillar Point. From Pillar Point follow the sporadic orange markers south through a small tract of manuka trees. From there follow the markers and the cliffs taking in all the cliff-top views to **Cape Farewell**. Keep your eyes peeled for fur seals, whose plaintive cries will probably reach the senses first. Continue south along the cliffs before descending to Wharariki Beach. If the tide is in your favour, walk its entire length and investigate the many caves and rock corridors along its length. Once at the base of **Pilch Point** (at the very end of all the beaches) retrace your steps to Pillar Point. If you cannot afford to go out on the spit and do not have time to walk to Wharariki Beach, or simply want to get a better impression of its scale from afar, the best place to view it is from the elevated hills around the Pillar Point Light Beacon, accessed by foot from Wharariki Road and Puponga.

Kahurangi National Park ⊜▲▲ ↠ pp465-468.

Opened in 1996, Kahurangi is New Zealand's second newest national park (Stewart Island was opened in 2001) and also the second largest, after Fiordland. It is a vast and remote landscape of rugged alpine ranges and river valleys, the most notable being the Heaphy, which meets, in part, the park's most famous tramping route, the Heaphy Track. One of the most interesting features of the park is its ancient geology. It contains some of the country's oldest rock landforms, with spectacular limestone caves, plateaux, arches and outcrops. Kahurangi is home to over half of New Zealand's native plant species (over 80% of all alpine species) and over 18 native bird species, including the New Zealand falcon, the great spotted kiwi and the huge New Zealand land snail.

The **Heaphy Track** is usually the visitor's first and only acquaintance with the park but the **Cobb Valley**, **Mount Arthur** and the **Tablelands** (accessed from the Cobb River Valley, 50 km south of Takaka and from the Flora car park, 30 km south of Motueka) offer some shorter walking options. The view from Mount Arthur (four hours, 8 km), which is accessed from Motueka, is particularly recommended.

Ins and outs

Getting there Transport to the various trailheads is available from Nelson, Motueka, Takaka, Collingwood and Karamea (west coast). **Kahurangi Bus**, Nelson, T0800- 881188, T03-525 9434, www.kahurangi.co.nz, and **Abel Tasman Coachlines**, Nelson, T03-528 8805, www.abelttasmantravel.co.nz, and **Golden Bay Coachlines**, Takaka, T03-525 8352, www.goldenbaycoachlines.co.nz, are the main inter-town operators. **Golden Bay Coachlines** and **Trek Express**, Upper Moutere, T0800-128735/T03-5402042, www.trekexpress.co.nz, can get you to the various trailheads. **The Heaphy Bus**, T0800-128735/T03-5402042, wwww.theheaphybus.co.nz, serves both ends of the Heaphy Track.

Wadsworth Motors, T03-522 4248, wadsworthmotors@xtra.co.nz, runs from Nelson to the Whangapeka Track. **Karamea Express**, west coast/Karamea, T03-782 6757/T03-7826718 , serves the Heaphy from the south (west coast). The average fare from Takaka is $35 and from Karamea $15. **Abel Tasman Air**, Nelson, T03-528 8290, www.abeltasmanair.co.nz, offers flights to Karamea and Takaka.

Getting around They say it takes a long time and many walks to acquaint yourself properly with Kahurangi and for many this is its main appeal. One of the best ways to see

Heaphy Track

The approximate walking times are as follows – west to east:

    Kohaihai River Mouth to Heaphy Hut: 16 ½ km, five hours

    Heaphy Hut to Lewis Hut: 8 km, 2½ hours

    Lewis Hut to Mackay Hut: 13 ½ km, 3½ hours

    Mackay Hut to Saxon Hut: 14 km, three hours

    Saxon Hut to Gouland Downs Hut: 5 km, 1½ hours

    Gouland Downs Hut to Perry Saddle Hut: 8 km, two hours

    Perry Saddle Hut to Brown Hut: 17 km, five hours

the park is from the sky (see Activities and tours, page 468). The eastern Heaphy Track trailhead is accessed via Collingwood (28 km) and Bainham (Aorere River Valley) at the end of the Heaphy Track Road. The route is signposted from Collingwood. The eastern trailhead is served daily (see Getting there, above) in summer and on demand in winter.

Tourist information The DoC field centres in Nelson (see page 435), Motueka (see page 450) and Takaka (see page 461) can provide detailed information on the park, including access, walking and tramping. On longer walks or tramps you are advised to go well prepared and, in summer, book the huts and passes ahead – especially on the popular Heaphy Track. The DoC administer hut tickets and bookings.

Heaphy Track

The Heaphy Track is one of New Zealand's most popular 'Great Walks' and the most popular tramp in the Kahurangi National Park. It is a low-level tramp of 82 km taking four to six days. The Heaphy is named after Major Charles Heaphy, a noted soldier, who was the first to traverse the coastal portion of the modern track in 1846. Although not famed for its mountainous vistas, the track does provide a wide range of habitats and a superb coastal section. It is also noted for being 'open' for much of its length, offering a fine sense of space and wilderness. **Flannigan's Corner** (915 m), near Mount Perry (880 m), is the highest point on the track and provides memorable views. The Heaphy is usually negotiated from west to east. The western trailhead starts about 15 km north of Karamea, while the eastern, starts 28 km south of Collingwood. Take insect repellent with you.

◉ Golden Bay listings

For Sleeping and Eating price codes and other relevant information, see Essentials pages 44-50.

● Sleeping

Takaka *p461*

The VIC has a full list of B&Bs and homestays, most of which are near the beaches at Pohara.
L-D The Nook Guesthouse, 8 km from Pohara on Abel Tasman Dr, T0800-806665/ T03-525 850, www.thenookguesthouse. co.nz. Comfortable, self-contained doubles in a straw-bale cottage, or guesthouse doubles, twins, shared rooms and tent sites. Free bike hire, cosy log fire, organic produce.
AL Mohua Motels, Willow St, T0800-664826/T03-525 7222, www.mohuamotels.com. Modern motel in town located next to the VIC.
AL Para Para Beachfront Holiday Home, Para Para, Takaka South, T03-524 8175,

www.homepages.paradise.net.nz/
whitaker.family/. A self-contained cottage
sleeping 4 in a private setting right next to
the beach. Full kitchen facilities and wood
fire. Three-night stay minimum.

AL-A Sans Souci Inn, Richmond Rd, Pohara,
T03-525 8663, www.sanssouci inn.co.nz. A
mud-brick Mediterranean-style establishment
with lovely bedrooms and a great licensed
in-house restaurant.

A Anatoki Lodge Motel, 87 Commercial St,
T0800-262333/T03-525 8047, www.anatoki
motels.co.nz. Modern facilities, well located.

B-D Annie's Nirvana Lodge, 25 Motupipi St,
T03-525 8766/T0800-266937, www.nirvana
lodge.co.nz. Well-established and cosy
backpacker lodge. Bike hire and internet.

B-D Barefoot Backpackers, 114 Commercial
St, T03-525 7005, www.bare-foot.co.nz. Offers
free trips to the Pupu Springs, has a spa and
terrific homemade bread.

B-D Kiwiana, 73 Motupipi St, T03-525 7676.
Another alternative with a good reputation in
a spacious, well-kept suburban villa, free
bikes, internet. Log fire and hot tub.

C-D River Inn, Waitapu Rd, at the other end
of town, T03-525 9425, www.riverinn.co.nz.
Closest to the Pupu Springs, a century-old
pub-style place. Has a wide range of rooms
and cheap singles. Kayak hire, free bike hire,
Sky TV and internet.

Motorcamps
**B-D Pohara Beach Top Ten Holiday Park
and Motels**, Abel Tasman Dr, Pohara,
T0800-764272/T03-525 9500,
www.poharabeach.com. The best motorcamp
with tent, powered sites, modern kitchen
cabins and facilities, next to the beach.

Collingwood *p462*
LL Collingwood Homestead B&B, Elizabeth
St, in Collingwood itself, T03-524 8079,
www.collingwoodhomestead.co.nz. It gets
the vote as the best B&B in the region.

A Station House Motel, 7 Elizabeth St,
T0800-752722/T03-524 8464,
www.accommodationcollingwood.co.nz.

Immaculate units in a quiet and peaceful,
garden setting.

C-D Innlet and Cottages, Main Rd, Pakawau,
on the road to Farewell Spit, T03-524 8040,
www.goldenbayindex. co.nz/theinnlet. Oozes
character and is in a lovely bush setting
offering dorms, twins and doubles and 2
charming self-contained cottages that sleep
3-6. The owners are friendly, dedicated
long-term residents. Bike hire available and
excellent harbour/ rainforest kayak trips.

C-D Somerset House Backpackers, Gibbs
Rd (signposted off the main road in the
village), T03-524 8624, www.backpackers
collingwood.co.nz. Top-quality 16-bed place
with good facilities, including internet, kayak
and bike hire, a very congenial deck
overlooking the village. There is also a 4WD
vehicle for hire at $40 per day.

Motorcamps
B-D Collingwood Motor Camp, in the
centre of the village at the end of William St,
T03-524 8149. Unremarkable self-contained
cabins, basic cabins and sites.

Heaphy Track *p465*
The 7 huts along the track are supplied with
bunks, heating, water (must be boiled) and
toilets. Hut passes are $25 in peak season
(Oct-May), $15 non-peak. Note a pass does
not guarantee a bunk. Camping is $12/$8. For
more information and bookings contact DoC
or the major VICs. You can also book direct
with DoC greatwalksbooking@doc.govt.nz.

🍴 Eating

Takaka *p461*
🍴 **The Brigand Café Bar**, 90 Commercial St,
T03-525 9636. Daily from 1000. A good choice
with an imaginative menu and pleasant
outdoor eating area. Local mussels a speciality.
🍴 **Dangerous Kitchen**, 48 Commercial St,
T03-525 8686. Daily 1000-late. Fine pizza.
🍴 **Sans Souci**, Richmond Rd, Pohara, T03-525
8663. A pleasant mud-brick Mediterranean

Inn with a reputable licensed restaurant, open for lunch and dinner (seasonal).

🍴 **Wholemeal Café**, Commercial St, T03-525 9426, www.wholemealcafe.co.nz. Daily 0730-late. A bit of an institution in Takaka and the main haunt for the locals. It has good coffee, breakfasts, health-conscious blackboard menu and excellent service.

🍴 **Bencarri Farm** (south off SH60), T03-525 8261. Daily 1000-late. For a café experience surrounded by a veritable menagerie.

Collingwood p462

🍴 **Collingwood Tavern**, Tasman St, T03-524 8160. Serves pub/bistro style food.

🍴 **Mussel Inn Bush Café**, Onekaka, half way between Takaka and Collingwood on SH60, T03-525 9241, www.musselinn.co.nz. 1100-late. Good pub grub, great value mussels, the best beer around and a toilet to remember.

🍴 **Courthouse Café**, corner of Gibbs and Elizabeth sts, T03-524 8025. Daily 0830-late (seasonal). The best bet in Collingwood.

🍴 **Paddlecrab Kitchen**, at the end of the road at Farewell Spit, T03-524 8454. Daily 0900-1730 (seasonal). Café with basic menu.

▲ Activities and tours

Takaka p461

Barefoot Guided Tours, 114 Commercial St, Takaka, T03-524 8624, www.bare-foot.co.nz. Local, regional or park guided tours from $40-200.

Bencarri Farm, T03-525 8261, www.ben carri.co.nz. Eel farm, see page 462.

Golden Bay Kayaks, Pohara, Golden Bay, T03-525 9095, www.goldenbaykayaks.co.nz. Popular operator with trips in both the Abel Tasman National Park and Golden Bay region from $75. Independent hire from $40-100.

Collingwood p462

Kahurangi Guided Walks, T03-525 7177, www.kahurangiwalks.co.nz. Guided half-, full- and muti-day trips from $35. 3-day Boulder Lake for $200; 5-day Wangapeka Track from $1300.

Tours to Farewell Spit

Farewell Spit Tours, 6 Tasman St, T03-524 8257, T0800-808257, www.farewellspit.com. The original tour operator and has been taking people out on to the spit for over 60 years.

The most popular tour is the 'Lighthouse Safari' which is a 4½-hr excursion to the end of the spit and the lighthouse. Transportation takes the form of robust but comfortable RL Bedford trucks. You will meet the spit's wildlife (which can include the occasional bleary-eyed fur seal) and be allowed stops to take in the special atmosphere of the spit, before arriving at the lighthouse. There you can climb it to see the rather unremarkable view from the top, before learning a little of its interesting history over a welcome cup of tea. This tour costs a very reasonable $100, child $50.

The 'Gannet Colony Eco Tour' (6½ hrs, $135, child $55) is an extended trip that takes in the above and the gannet colony at the end of the spit (this company are the only operators with DoC concession to get up close).

The 'Cape Farewell Eco Tour' (6 hrs) is basically the same trip as the Lighthouse Safari with a diversion to the dramatic cliffs at Cape Farewell, the most northerly point of the South Island, from $120, child $55.

The 'Wader Watch Safari' (3-4 hrs, $100) is a specialist and fascinating trip to see the wading birds on the spit often numbering into the thousands. Although most suited to birdwatchers and somewhat seasonal (summer only), it would be of considerable interest to any nature lover, especially given the limited access to the spit.

Whariki Beach p463

Cape Farewell Horse Treks, Puponga, T03-524 8031, www.horsetreksnz.com. Cover some of the most scenic routes in the region including Wharariki Beach, 1 hr to overnight, from $55, (Wharariki Beach 3-hr $105). Recommended.

Kahurangi National Park *p464*
Guided walks
Barefoot Guided Tours, also in Motueka,
T03-5248624, www.bare-foot.co.nz.
Kahurangi Guided Walks, Takaka, T03-525
7177, www.kahurangiwalks.co.nz.

Rock climbing
Vertical Limits, Nelson, T03-545 7511,
www.verticallimits.com. Offers some excellent
rock climbing trips to Kahurangi, from $130.

Scenic flights
Abel Tasman Air, Nelson, T03-528 8290,
www.abeltasmanair.co.nz. Offers flights to
Karamea and Takaka, as well as flights across
the bare mountain tops and remote valleys. A
truly memorable experience.

⊙ Directory

Takaka *p461*
Internet Cyberworld (178) or Kiwi
Konnection, 113 High St, Motueka.

Contents

Footprint features

Canterbury

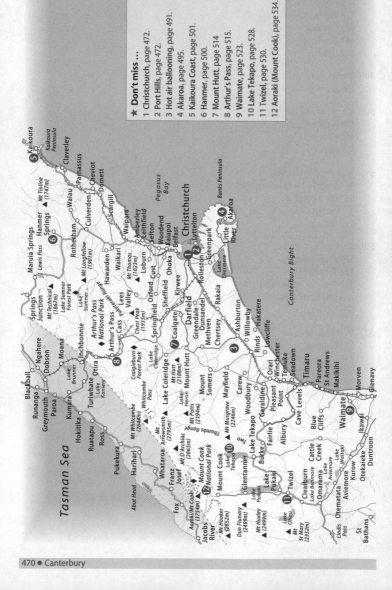

N

20 km
20 miles

Tasman Sea

Kaikoura

Kaikoura Peninsula

Claverley

Parnassus

Cheviot

Domett

Waiau

Mt Tinline (1747m)

Mt Longfellow (1901m)

Hanmer Springs

Waipara

Sergill

Culverden

Rotherham

Springs Junction

Lewis Pass

Maruia Springs

Mt Technical (1867m)

Lake Sumner Forest Park

Lees Valley

Mt Thomas (1023m)

Hawarden

Waikari

Amberley

Leithfield

Sefton

Woodend

Pegasus Bay

Blackball

Runanga

Ngahere

Dobson

Inchbonnie

Moana

Lake Brunner

Greymouth

Paroa

Kumara

Turiwhate

Otira

Lake Kaniere

Arthur's Pass

Arthur's Pass National Park

Otira Pass

Cass

Lake Sumner

Chest Peak (1935m)

Craigieburn Forest Park

Lake Coleridge

Oxford

Cust

Loburn

Kaiapoi

Belfast

Christchurch

Lyttelton

Banks Peninsula

Little River

Akaroa

Governors Bay

Lake Ellesmere

Rolleston

Rakaia

Kirwee

Sheffield

Darfield

Coalgate

Springfield

Hokitika

Ruatapu

Ross

Pukekura

Harihari

Mt Whitcombe (2644m)

Whataroa

Whitcombe Pass

Mt Evans

Mt Arrowsmith (2795m)

Mt D'Archiac (2865m)

Lake Heron

Mt Potts (2194m)

Mt Hutt (2188m)

Mount Hutt

Mount Somers

Lake Coleridge

Greendale

Dunsandel

Methven

Chertsey

Rakaia

Ashburton

Hakatere

Willowby

Rinds

Lowcliffe

Canterbury Bight

Franz Josef

Fox

Jacobs River

Abut Head

Aoraki/Mt Cook (3754m)

Mt Hooker (2652m)

Mt Cook

Aoraki (Mount Cook) National Park

Dun Fiunary (2499m)

Mt Huxley (2499m)

Mt St Mary (2332m)

Lake Ohau

Lindis Pass

St Bathans

Thumbs Range

Mt Musgrave (2246m)

Two

Lake Tekapo

Carew

Woodbury

Mayfield

Geraldine

Winchester

Orari

Temuka

Seadown

Timaru

Pleasant Point

Cave

Levels

Fairlie

Fairlie

Albury

Burke

Glentanner

Mount Cook

Lake Tekapo

Twizel

Lake Pukaki

Clearburn

Omarama

Otematata

Lake Benmore

Lake Aviemore

Lake Waitaki

Kurow

Otekaieke

Duntroon

Makikihi

Morven

Glenavy

Waimate

Ikawai

Cattle Creek

Blue Cliffs

Pareora

St Andrews

Aorangi

Tekapo

Lake Pukaki

Twizel

Whichever way you arrive in Canterbury, by air or by road, the Canterbury Plains dominate, giving an impression of a broad and vast expanse. And yet, despite appearances, much of Canterbury is mountainous and home to New Zealand's highest peak, Aoraki, or Mount Cook (3754 m). Canterbury is the largest region in the South Island, extending from the Pacific Ocean and the Canterbury Plains in the east to the Great Divide and Southern Alps in the west, and from the Kaikoura Ranges in the north, to the braided Waitaki River in the south.

Central Canterbury is the hub of the South Island and its capital, Christchurch, is the country's second largest city. Dubbed 'The Garden City', it is very pretty in parts, although it lacks the impressive architecture and remarkable friendliness of Dunedin. North Canterbury is home to the South Island's 'little piece of Rotorua' in the form of the Hanmer Springs thermal resort, providing just one of many good reasons to stop en route to the west coast via the beautiful Lewis Pass. Along with Arthur's Pass to the south, these form the region's two main portals from the east coast to the west and are also the focus for skiers in winter.

In South Canterbury the pleasant coastal port of Timaru provides a starting point from where to head west, via Fairlie and Burke's Pass to the MacKenzie Country. Here you will find the region's most stunning and diverse scenery, culminating in Lake Tekapo, Pukaki Lake and Mount Cook Village.

A 7.0-magnitude earthquake struck South Island on 4 September 2010. The epicentre was 35 miles northwest of Christchurch and the city experienced widespread damage with over two thirds of homes affected. Despite the damage, only two serious injuries were reported and no one was killed.

Christchurch → *Colour map 5, A/B6 Population: 350,000.*

Dubbed 'The Garden City', Christchurch is casting off its label as the most English of New Zealand's cities and forming its own contemporary and vibrant identity. It's true that reminders of these roots are everywhere from the formal blazers and straw hats of the city's school children to the punts on the river and the distant chorus of 'howzatt' from its myriad cricket pitches on lazy summer Sunday afternoons. And without doubt the key to its charm is the immense, tree-lined Hagley Park and Botanical Gardens that border its centre and have, over the decades, remained remarkably intact. But, natural aesthetics and its obvious English colonial feel aside, Christchurch has developed its own very Kiwi-orientated atmosphere. It has the buzz and vitality of Auckland, the cosmopolitan 'town' feel of Wellington and it shares a pride in its heritage and architecture that only Dunedin can beat. ▸▸ *For Sleeping, Eating and other listings, see pages 482-493.*

Ins and outs

Getting there

By air **Christchurch airport** ① *12 km northwest of the city via Fendalton Rd and Memorial Av, T03-358 5029, www.christchurch-airport.co.nz,* receives direct flights from Australia, Singapore and Japan, as well as all national provincial airports. **Air New** Zealand, T0800-737000, www.airnewzealand.co.nz; **Qantas**, T03-379 6504/T0800-808767, www.qantas.co.nz; **Jetstar**, T0800-800995, www.jetstar.com; **Emirates**, T0508-364728, www.emirates.com; and **Pacific Blue**, T0800-670000, www.pacificblue.co.nz, cover most long-haul destinations and Australia; while **Air New Zealand** is the principal domestic carrier, with **Jetstar** and **Pacific Blue** also providing regional services. Combined they offer flights from Wellington and Auckland almost every hour.

The international and domestic terminals are located in a single building and are easily negotiated. There are information centres in both terminals, and city transport is to be found outside the building. **Metro buses**, T03-366 8855, www.metroinfo.org.nz, offer a regular service to Cathedral Square (20 mins) hourly, Mon-Fri 0600-2300, Sat-Sun 0800-2300, $7.50. **Red Bus City Flyer**, T03-379 4260/T0800-733287, www.redbus.co.nz, also offers services hourly Mon-Fri 0600-2300, Sat-Sun 0730-2230. Various shuttles, including **Super Shuttle** (door to door), T03-357 9950/T0800-748885, or **Airport Shuttle Services**, T03-351 2481, will take you into town for around $20. A taxi from the airport costs around $40. ▸▸ *See Transport, page 492.*

By road Christchurch is 336 km south of Picton (Kaikoura 183 km) via SH1; and 579 km north of Invercargill (Dunedin 362 km/Timaru 163 km) on SH1. Queenstown is 486 km southwest via SH1/SH8, and Greymouth, 258 km via Arthur's Pass and SH73. **Intercity**, T03-365 1113, www.intercitycoach.co.nz, is the main bus company, with daily services from most major towns in the South Island including Picton (5½ hrs), Dunedin (6 hrs), Mount Cook (5½ hrs), Wanaka (9 hrs) and Queenstown (10 hrs). In Christchurch its agent is the **Christchurch Travel Centre**, 123 Worcester St, T03-377 0951. **Atomic Shuttles**, T03-349 0697, www.atomic travel.co.nz, is the main Christchurch-based company offering services across the South Island. **Nakedbus**, www.nakedbus.com, also offers services nationwide and as an online-oriented agency is often the cheapest. There are many smaller shuttle services listed in 'Getting there' sections of intended destinations. **West Coast Shuttles**, T03-7680028, www.westcoastshuttle.co.nz, offers daily services to Greymouth;

while the **Hanmer Shuttle**, T0800-800575, www.akaroabus.co.nz, offers a daily service to Hanmer Springs. **The Cook Connection**, T0800-266526, www.cookconnect.co.nz, offers a daily shuttle between Tekapo, Mount Cook and Oamaru. It links with the Wanaka/Queenstown **Intercity**, and **Atomic** services. For special deals, including the Intercity **Travelpass** which offers a combination of train, ferry and coach travel, see the Getting around section of Essentials, page 37.

Most coach companies including Intercity and Atomic Shuttles stop in or around Cathedral Square. Check specific drop-off or pick-up points with each company. The VIC (I-Site) has full details on national bus travel and can make bookings on your behalf. Typical return prices are: Dunedin $35, Queenstown $40, Invercargill $65, Tekapo $30, Kaikoura $29, Picton $50, and Greymouth $40.

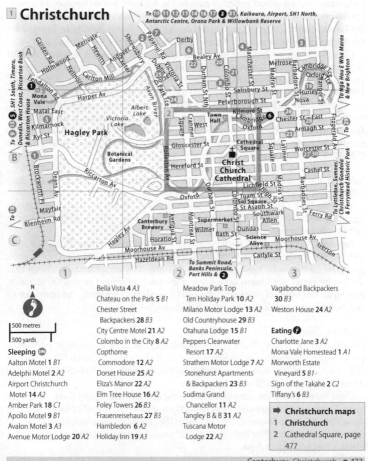

Christchurch

Bella Vista **4** A3
Chateau on the Park **5** B1
Chester Street
   Backpackers **28** B3
City Centre Motel **21** A2
Colombo in the City **8** A2
Copthorne
   Commodore **12** A2
Dorset House **25** A2
Eliza's Manor **22** A2
Elm Tree House **16** A2
Foley Towers **26** B3
Frauenreisehaus **27** B3
Hambledon **6** A2
Holiday Inn **19** A3

Meadow Park Top
   Ten Holiday Park **10** A2
Milano Motor Lodge **13** A2
Old Countryhouse **29** B3
Otahuna Lodge **15** B1
Peppers Clearwater
   Resort **17** A2
Strathern Motor Lodge **7** A2
Stonehurst Apartments
   & Backpackers **23** B3
Sudima Grand
   Chancellor **11** A2
Tangley B & B **31** A2
Tuscana Motor
   Lodge **22** A2

Vagabond Backpackers
   30 B3
Weston House **24** A2

Eating
Charlotte Jane **3** A2
Mona Vale Homestead **1** A1
Morworth Estate
   Vineyard **5** B1
Sign of the Takahe **2** C2
Tiffany's **6** B3

➡ **Christchurch maps**
1 Christchurch
2 Cathedral Square, page
   477

Sleeping
Aalton Motel **1** B1
Adelphi Motel **2** A2
Airport Christchurch
   Motel **14** A2
Amber Park **18** C1
Apollo Motel **9** B1
Avalon Motel **3** A3
Avenue Motor Lodge **20** A2

By train Christchurch's **train station** ① *Addington St, 3 km from the city centre at the southwestern tip of Hagley Park*, is the departure point for two of New Zealand's major railway journeys. **TranzScenic**, T0800-872467, www.tranzscenic.co.nz, operates the northbound 'TranzCoastal' service (departs 0730; to Kaikoura- Blenheim-Picton, $40-120); and the deservingly popular 'TranzAlpine' (departs 0815; to Greymouth $161). For details and fares get the 'times and fares' booklet from the train station or the VIC (I-Site). The **Travelpass** offers a combination of train, ferry and coach travel (see Essentials, page 43). A shuttle from the station to the centre costs from $12; taxi $18.

Getting around

Christchurch is best explored on foot or by public transport. If you do have a car, note that the one-way road system can be confusing, and although there are plenty of parking lots and meters they are almost as tightly patrolled as Auckland and Wellington. An hour in the city centre will cost about $4. You can park for free south of Moorhouse Avenue (the Old Train Station and Hoyts 8 Cinema) and catch the free shuttle from there. Being so flat the city makes for easy cycling. ▶▶ *For bike, motorcycle and car hire, see Transport, page 492.*

Christchurch has an excellent public bus system with a modern terminal, the **Bus Exchange** ① *corner of Lichfield and Colombo sts.* For all bus information contact T03-366 8855, www.metroinfo.org.nz, Mon-Fri 0630-2230, Sun 0900-2100, or **Red Buses**, T0800-733287, www.redbus.co.nz. The buses run on a two-zone system; Zone 1 costs $2.80; Zone 2 costs from $4. Monthly passes and **Metrocards** (electronic top-up cards from $10 minimum) are available and you can purchase cash fares from the driver as you board the bus. The **Free Yellow Shuttle** takes in a north-south route from the casino, through Cathedral Square and down Colombo St and back, every 10-15 mins (Mon-Fri 0730-2230, Sat 0800-2230, Sun 1000-2000). It's worth jumping on to get your bearings.

The **The Grand Tour and associated shuttles** takes in the main city attractions including the Antarctic Centre and the Gondola, departing Cathedral Square, daily 0900-1800. Enquire at the VIC for details and tickets.

The **Midnight Express**, offers late selected night services to the outer suburbs departing on the hour from 0100-0500 from Oxford Terrace, $6. For shuttle services to Lyttleton and Akaroa see the Bank's Peninsula section, page 493.

Between 1905 and 1954 Christchurch had a thriving **tram system** ① *T03-366 7830, trams operate Apr-Oct 0900-1800 and Nov-Mar 0900-2100, from $15, child $5.* There is also a restaurant car that hosts a daily dining tour, T03-366 7511, www.tram.co.nz. Since 1995 the beautifully restored trams now follow a 2½-km loop around central Christchurch, passing various sights of interest on the way (commentary provided). The trams can be boarded at many stops including Cathedral Square.

Tourist information

Christchurch VIC (i-Site) ① *Old Post Office Building, Cathedral Sq (West), T03-379 9629, www.christchurchnz.com, www.localeye.co.nz, daily Mon-Fri 0830-1700, Sat-Sun 0830-1600.* There are also VICs (I-Sites) in the international (T03-353 7783/4) and domestic (T03-353 7774/5) airport terminals.

There is a wealth of free material including the useful *Official Visitors Guide*, which is a must. There are also numerous city attractions and 'drive' maps including the *Top Attractions, A Guide to Christchurch's City Centre; The Avon River Drive; The Garden Drive; The Antarctic Heritage Trail; Wine Trail;* and *Arts Trail* maps. The daily paper in the Central South Island is the *Christchurch Press.*

DoC ①*Level 4, Torrens House, 195 Hereford St, T03-341 9102, www.doc.govt.co.nz, Mon-Fri 0830-1630*, can provide local, regional and South Island walks and tramping information.

Maps Get hold of the *Christchurch Mini-map*. The major bookshops (see Shopping page 489) also stock Christchurch city map books, and **Mapworld** ① *corner of Manchester and Gloucester sts, T03-374 5399, www.map world.co.nz*, is an excellent source of city, town, provincial and national maps.

City centre

The heart of Christchurch lies just to the east of **Hagley Park**, with **Cathedral Square** being the focus. The borders of the city centre are known as the 'Four Avenues': **Deans Avenue**, which borders the western fringe of Hagley Park and the Botanical Gardens, **Moorhouse Avenue** to the south, **Fitzgerald Avenue** to the east and **Bealey Avenue** to the north. One of the most attractive features of the city is the **Avon River**, which winds its way through Hagley Park and the city centre from west to east. The city is essentially flat and has a basic grid system of streets extending in all directions from Cathedral Square, with the north/south **Colombo Street** being the main shopping street. The city centre is easily negotiable by foot using the cathedral and high-rises around Cathedral Square as a reference point.

Within the '**Four Avenues**' there are a number of sights and attractions that could easily take up a day of your time. Ask at the VIC (i-Site) about the **Grand Tour**, which can combine transport and entry to a number of major venues.

Cathedral Square

Dominated by the Gothic-revival Anglican **Christ Church Cathedral** ① *T03-366 0046, 1-hr tours Mon-Fri 1100 and 1400, Sat 1100, Sun 1130, free*, Cathedral Square is considered the heart of the city and its main focus point, but it is not without contention. An expensive redevelopment of the square in the late 1990s resulted in most Cantabrians feeling the development was an aesthetic disaster and a crass waste of money. Certainly, it does seem hopelessly out of character with the rest of Christchurch, with its sharp angles and dull façades of steel and concrete, but as time has passed some character has crept back in with the market stalls and buskers. And once again it seems to suffer from a severe disregard for trees. However, current aesthetics aside, the main feature worth looking at in the square is of course the cathedral itself. It houses a number of interesting memorials and boasts an interior design that is an interesting and eclectic mix of Maori and European. The spire can be climbed in part, offering a panoramic and memorable view of the city. There is also an audio-visual presentation and a good café attached.

The square also hosts a statue of **John Robert Godley**, the founder of the Canterbury Association and essentially Christchurch itself.

Nearby the '**Four Ships Court**', a memorial to the 'first four ships', stands outside the 1879 **Old Post Office** (which now houses the Christchurch VIC). Accessed through the VIC (I-Site) is the **Southern Encounter Aquarium and Kiwi House** ① *T03-359 7109, www.southernencounter.co.nz, daily 0900-1630, from $17, child $7; trout and salmon feeding 1300, marine tank dive and feeding 1500*, which seems remarkably out of place but is still worth a look for its interesting collection of local sea creatures and obligatory kiwi exhibit.

Avon River

Heading west from Cathedral Square along Worcester Boulevard, you immediately encounter (and not for the first time) the pretty Avon River. This is one of the city's greatest assets. The river meanders like a snake from the northwest tip of the 'four avenues' through Hagley Park and the Botanical Gardens, through the city centre, before finally continuing its journey through the city's eastern suburbs to the sea. The river is very attractive in spring when daffodils decorate its banks and also in autumn when poplar and weeping willows are radiant with golden hues. It offers some lovely city walks, which are outlined in the free *River Walks of Christchurch* available from the VIC (I-Site). The *Avon River Drive* is another alternative. On the eastern bank of the river, just beyond Cathedral Square and beside the Worcester Street Bridge, is a base for **punting** ① *T03-366 0337, daily 0900-1800, winter 1000-1600, 30 mins, $20, child $10*, on the river. Note also the 1917 statue of **Scott of the Antarctic** beside the river – a reminder that Christchurch is a principal gateway to the Antarctic.

The Cultural Precinct

Across the bridge and on the right, further up Worcester Street, is the **Christchurch Art Gallery (Te Puna O Waiwhetu)** ① *T03-941 7300, www.christchurchartgallery.org.nz, daily 1000-1700 (Wed 2100), free with a charge for major exhibitions*. Immediately christened by some cynics as 'a warehouse in a tutu' it is actually supposed to evoke 'the sinuous form of the koru and the River Avon that flows through Christchurch'. With over 3000 sq m of exhibition space, it is over four times the size of the Robert McDougall Gallery that for years struggled to showcase its formidable 5,500 permanent works. So whether you see the building as a tutu or not is up to you – what cannot be denied, however, is the quality of its content. One is immediately struck by the mesmerizing multicoloured staircase and within the various galleries many famous New Zealand artists are represented, including Charles Goldie, Colin McCahon and Ralph Hotere. But there is also an emphasis on contemporary works and a dynamic schedule of national and international exhibitions. There is a quality retail outlet that specializes in contemporary art and crafts and a café/bistro.

The **Centre for Contemporary Art** ① *66 Gloucester St, T03-366 7261, www.coca.org.nz, Tue-Fri 1000-1700, Sat-Sun 1200-1600, free*, is also worth visiting. There are five galleries and over 50 exhibitions per annum; much of the art is for sale.

Nearby, **The Arts Centre** ① *2 Worcester Boulevard, T03-363 2836, www.artscentre.org.nz*, was once the site of the original University of Canterbury. The old Gothic revival buildings now house an excellent and dynamic array of arts and crafts, workshops, galleries and sales outlets, as well as theatres, cinemas, cafés, restaurants and bars. It is well worth a visit, particularly at the weekend when it hosts a lively arts and crafts market. It becomes very much the focus of attention for tourists with an international food fair and top local entertainment, from a local town crier to city buskers. There are also some notable historical features including the 'Den' of scientist Ernest Rutherford (see box, page 441), the Great Hall with its stained-glass windows and the Townsend Observatory with its working telescope. Free guided tours are available and depart from the information centre in the clocktower foyer and for the best coffee go to the **Backstage Bakery** in the heart of the complex behind the Court Theatre. The free *What's on at The Arts Centre* and *Christchurch City Arts Trail* booklets are very useful.

Hagley Park

At the western edge of The Arts Centre, Worcester Street meets Rolleston Avenue and the eastern fringe of Hagley Park. Amazingly intact after all the years of development, Hagley Park (over 200 ha) is divided into two portions by Riccarton Avenue and comprises pleasant

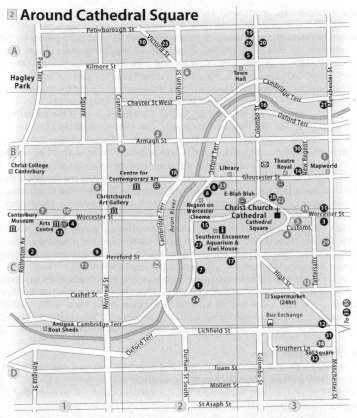

2 Around Cathedral Square

N

200 metres
200 yards

➡ **Christchurch maps**
1 Christchurch, page 473
2 Cathedral Square

tree-lined walkways, sports fields and, in its central reaches, the **Botanical Gardens** ① *0700-dusk, Conservatory Complex 1015-1600*, enclosed by a loop of the Avon River. Well maintained and with a huge variety of gardens from 'herb' to 'rose', these provide a great escape from the buzz of the city year round. Autumn sees the gardens at their most colourful. There is an **information centre and café** ① *T03-941 8999, daily Sep-Apr Mon-Fri 0900-1600, Sat-Sun 1015-1600*, adjacent to the Armagh car park (off Rolleston Av), which showcases the social and natural history of the gardens. Guided tours depart daily from the Canterbury Museum entrance at 1330, returning at 1500, from $5.

At the entrance to the Botanical Gardens on Rolleston Avenue is the **Canterbury Museum** ① *T03-366 5000 www.cantmus.govt.nz, daily 0900-1730 (winter 1700), general entry is free but there are charges for the Exhibition Court and Discovery Centre ($2); guided tours are also available.* Housed in a grand 1870 neo-Gothic building and founded in 1867, it is well worth a visit, the undoubted highlights being its impressive Maori collection and the Hall of Antarctic Discovery. In keeping with other museums in the country, it also hosts a dynamic Discovery Centre for kids and big kids alike. The Exhibition Court displays a changing programme of travelling national and international exhibitions. There is also a fine in-house shop and a café overlooking the Botanical Gardens.

Just north of the museum is **Christ College Canterbury** ① *guided tours at 1000 on Mon, Wed and Thu in summer, T03-366 8705 for information*, which is without doubt New Zealand's most famous historic school. Built in 1850 it is an aesthetic and architectural delight, and in the late afternoon spills forth suitably clad scholars.

At the southern end of Rolleston Avenue are the **Antigua Boat Sheds**, which were built in 1882, making them one of the oldest buildings in Christchurch. The former boat-builders' premises now host a café and are the base for **Punting in the Park**, ① *T03-366 0337 www.punting.co.nz, 30-min punting trips daily 1000-dusk, from $20.* You can also hire canoes, paddleboats and rowing boats ① *T03-366 5885, 0930-1730 (winter 1600).*

Canterbury Brewery

① *Near the junction of Riccarton and Hagley avenues (Hagley Park), 36 St Asphalt St, T03-477 7697. Tours (1½ hrs) and tastings Mon-Thu, from $20, bookings essential.*
Founded in 1854, its long established 'CD' (Canterbury Draught) is something of an institution round these parts. The brewery has a good museum and tours are available.

City North and West

Mona Vale

① *Just beyond the northwest corner of the 'Four Avenues' at 63 Fendalton Rd, T03-348 9660, May-Sep Wed-Sun 1000-1530, Oct-Apr 1000-1900.*
Heading out towards the airport is Mona Vale, a beautiful Elizabethan-style homestead and gardens, built in 1905 on the land first settled by the Scots Dean brothers in 1843. While the Homestead itself is now a fine restaurant and café, the 5½-ha grounds are a spectacular array of features including a lily pond, rhododendrons, azaleas and exotic trees, all set in reverence to the lovely River Avon. The gardens can be reached by punt, and guided tours are available. Phone for details.

International Antarctic Centre and Hagglund Ride

① *At the airport (signposted), Orchard Rd, T03-353 7798, www.iceberg.co.nz, daily Oct-Mar 0900-1900, Apr-Sep 0900-1730; All-day Pass, that includes all attractions, from $55, child $36.*

Guided tours are available from officers who have lived and worked on the ice or you can self-guide with the help of 'snow-phones' ($6). The centre runs its own shuttles regularly from Cathedral Square (from $5), or take the city airport bus (also from Cathedral Sq) that runs every 30 mins.

Since the turn of the 20th century and the days of Scott and Shackleton, Christchurch has been a principal 'gateway to the Antarctic'. Today, the Antarctic Centre is a working campus and formidable array of buildings. In its entirety, it is home to **Antarctica New Zealand** (managers of New Zealand's activities in the Antarctic), the **Antarctic Heritage Trust**, the US and Italian Antarctic programmes, the **International Centre for Antarctic Information and Research**, and the Antarctic passenger terminal and aircraft hangers, where you can often see the Hercules that head off into the wild blue and very cold yonder. The **visitor centre**, which was opened in 1992, is an excellent introduction to the great white continent and a place from which would-be world travellers will emerge dreaming. Overall it is both informative and fun, with an excellent array of displays from the historic to the modern-day.

One of the first displays you will encounter are the current Antarctic weather statistics, which send a shiver down your spine and your hands plunging into your pockets. Then, to get an even better idea of the real thing, you can don jackets and overshoes and enter the **Snow and Ice Experience**, a room kept at -5°C, replete with manufactured snow and ice. The **Antarctic Storm** room promises to take you into 'another world of wind and extreme cold'; visitors must attempt to endure an indoor blizzard replete with howling wind, plummeting temperatures and a general sense of severe meteorological extremes. (Naturally, if you are from warmer climes this is a new and fascinating experience, but if you are from the UK it is a bit like popping out for a pint of milk.) Once back to normal temperatures, you can sit in a comfy seat and be treated to a superb audio-visual presentation, which beautifully marries images from the ice with inspiring music.

Another almost obligatory attraction at the Antarctic Centre is the **Penguin Encounter** a small group of mainly rehabilitated and permanently disabled little blue penguins – a species that is, ironically, far more at home around the golden beaches of Australasia than the icebergs of Antarctica. From the displays you then emerge into the well and unusually stocked Antarctic shop and the **South Café and Bar**.

In addition to the centre's indoor activities is the **Antarctic Hagglund Ride**. The Hagglund is a tracked vehicle that was originally used by the USA and New Zealand Antarctic programmes in Scott and McMurdo bases. During the 15-minute ride you can experience the all-terrain abilities of the vehicle on a man-made adventure course. The centre also forms part of the interesting '**Antarctic Heritage Trail**' (free leaflet from the VIC/I-Site). Note that the Canterbury Museum (see page 478) also hosts an excellent Antarctic display.

Orana Wildlife Park and the Willowbank Wildlife Reserve

While out in the vicinity of the airport it is worth visiting one (or preferably both) of Christchurch's main wildlife attractions. **Orana Park** ⓘ *743 McLeans Island Rd (10 mins from the airport), T03-359 7109, www.oranawildlifepark.co.nz, daily 1000-1700, from $24, child $8*, is New Zealand's largest captive wildlife reserve, set in 80 ha of parkland. It has a good mix of native and international wildlife with an emphasis on African animals. All the usual suspects are there from the lofty giraffes and horny rhinos to the ever-popular, inquisitive meerkats.

Also near the airport (five minutes' drive), is the **Willowbank Wildlife Reserve** ⓘ *60 Hussey Rd (off Gardiners Rd), T03-359 6226, www.willowbank.co.nz, daily 1000-2200, $25, child $10; for transport, book at the city VIC (I-Site) or T0800-484485*, which focuses primarily on native wildlife and farm animals. The reserve has a very successful kiwi

The road to Edoras

For *Lord of the Rings* fans or indeed anyone who wants to see some classic Southern Alpine scenery, then the trip to **Mount Sunday** (Potts Station) in the Rangitata Valley is a great day out. Mount Sunday, which sits predominantly in the Rangitata River Valley and in stark contrast against the mountainous skyline of Southern Alps, became the perfect filming location and set for Edoras and King Theoden's grand hall in The Two Towers, the second film in the *Lord of the Rings* trilogy. From Mount Somers take the road west through the Ashburton Gorge towards Hakatere and **Lakes Camp and Clearwater**. At Hakatere the road splits (turn left). From here the countryside opens up in to the wide tussock valley giving an almost surreal sense of space. The lakes and their scattering of holiday baches are favourite haunts for windsurfers and waterskiers. Keep heading west towards the end of the valley. There, at the western edge of the Mount Harper Range (Harpers Knob), is a sudden and dramatic view down into the Rangitata Valley and in the far distance, the prominent outcrop known as Mount Sunday (611 m). In geological terms Mount Sunday is known as a 'rochemoutone' which, roughly translated, means a low, round hill shaped by a glacier. It was (apparently) named 'Mount Sunday'

by high country station boundary riders who used to meet there on Sundays. As you get ever nearer you can see why it was the perfect film location and although nothing remains of the set itself, it still has plenty of impact. The best place for photos is just past the Mount Potts Station or looking back down the valley as the road climbs the hill towards the Erewhon Station.

If you don't have your own transport you can join a day or multi-day tour with **Hassle-free Holidays**, T0800-427753/T03-385 5775, www.hasslefree.co.nz, and **Tussock and Beach Tours**, T03-303 0880, www.nature.net.nz, both based in Christchurch, (see Activities and tours, page 492) or, if you are feeling flush, even charter a light aircraft and fly into the valley and the airstrip at Mount Potts. Mid-range accommodation is available at **Mount Potts Alpine Lodge**, T03-303 9060, www.mtpotts.co.nz.
Travel notes The road is unsealed from Hakatere, 24 km from Erewhon. The last petrol stop station on the journey is the Mount Somers Store, T03-303 9831, open daily till 1800. For breakdown assistance call Methven Motor Services, Main Rd, T03-302 8201. There is limited cell phone coverage west of Mount Somers.

breeding programme and one of the better kiwi exhibits in the country. Weekends are best avoided, however, when it can seem more like a human kindergarten than a wildlife reserve. The reserve is also base for the **KoTane Maori Experience** ⓘ *daily at 1730, 1830 (1830 winter), $48, child $24 (performance only); $65, child $30 (performance and tour); $110, child $55 (performance and traditional New Zealand dinner).*

Riccarton Bush and Riccarton House (Putaringamotu)

ⓘ *3½ km west of the city centre on the banks of the Avon River, the main entrance to the reserve is at 16 Kahu Rd, T03-341 1018, www.riccartonhouse.co.nz. Deans Cottage is open daily, the homestead is open Mon-Fri 1300-1600. Tours Sun-Fri at 1400, $15 child $6.*

Set in 12 ha of parkland, the historic Riccarton Estate was once the home of the Scots pioneers and brothers William and John Deans (the first European settlers on the Canterbury Plains). It features the faithfully restored and furnished original 1843 **Deans**

Cottage in which they first lived, and the grand Victorian/Edwardian **homestead** that was built by the next generation from 1856-1874. Within the house, which has been restored and redecorated in period style, you will find the detailed brochure *The Story of Riccarton House* which gives more details about the family and the lives they led. There is a restaurant/café on site.

City East

East of the city centre the River Avon negotiates suburbia before emptying its contents into the Pacific. There is a **wildlife reserve** on the estuary that offers good birdwatching, opportunities for short walks and a number of fine beaches. New Brighton is the main focus of activity, with beachside cafés and a pier that attracts hopeful anglers. New Brighton can be reached from the centre of the city, via Cashel Street, then Buckleys Pages Road (8 km). South of the estuary via Ferry Rd (SH74) is the coastal resort of Sumner (12 km) which also has some fine beaches with safe swimming and plenty of cafés. The scenic drive to Lyttleton and the **Lyttleton Harbour** from Sumner (Evans Pass Road) is recommended.

City South

The Tamaki Heritage Village → *See also page 245.*
ⓘ *Ferrymead Park Dr, Ferrymead, T03-3667333, www.maoriculture.co.nz. From $126, child $73.*
Set within an era of dramatic change in New Zealand's history, this is an excellent interactive evening experience called, 'Lost in our Own Land'. It re-lives the impact of colonization upon the Maori people from 1820 onwards. A Maori village, fortified *pa* and colonial village come to life with performances and you then feast upon a selection of traditional Maori hangi and colonial banquet food. The evening is capped off with a short journey by steam train.

Science Alive
ⓘ *392 Moorhouse Av (Old Train Station), T03-365 5199, www.sciencealive.co.nz. Sun-Thu 1000-1700, Fri-Sat 1000-1800, all-day pass from $14, child $8.*
Although the Discovery Centre in the museum, the Antarctic Centre and wildlife parks are all obvious draws for kids, the Science Alive centre is a great wet weather attraction. It is very much a hands-on place that could even see your kids waiting outside for you.

Christchurch (Port Hills) Gondola
ⓘ *T03-384 0700, www.gondola.co.nz, daily 1000-2130, $24, child $10. The Best Attractions Shuttle Bus leaves from the visitor centre at 1000, 1400 and 1600 ($6 all-day pass) or the No 28 bus from the Bus Exchange, from $2.80.*
If only for the stunning views, the Christchurch Gondola is well worth the trip. The base terminal is in the Heathcote Valley 10 km southeast of the city via Ferry Road. From there gondolas whisk you 945 m to the top of the Port Hills (1500 m) and the Summit Complex. The complex has all the expected shops and a café but also offers viewpoints from which you can gaze down to Lyttleton and across the Banks Peninsula. Northwards, the view across the city is equally stunning, and on a clear day, beyond the Canterbury Plains, is the distant line of the Southern Alps. You can embark on a number of walks from the complex that explore the crater rim, including the Bridle Path which was once used by the early pioneers as the main route to Lyttleton. An attractive way of descending is by mountain bike (see page 491).

On the way or coming back from the gondola you might like to stop off at the **Ferrymead Historic Park** ① *in the suburb of Ferrymead (Ferrymead Park Dr), T03-384 1970, www.ferrymead.org.nz, daily 1000-1630, $6, child $3 ($15/5 at weekends when trams are operating)*. It's an entertaining mock-1920s Edwardian township and a working museum with a wide array of period memorabilia including transport displays, Clydesdale horse-drawn carts and a working bakery. Trams and trains operate at weekends.

◉ Christchurch listings

For Sleeping and Eating price codes and other relevant information, see Essentials pages 44-50.

● Sleeping

As you would expect, Christchurch has plenty of accommodation catering for all tastes and budgets. Almost all the national chain hotels are in evidence in the city centre, with the majority being located in or around Victoria and Cathedral Sq. A few independent boutique-style options surround Hagley Park and overlook the River Avon. Likewise there are many B&Bs both in the city centre and a little further out, with some set in historic and spacious villas. There are literally dozens of motels, offering affordable prices, within walking distance of the city; many are northwest of the city centre along Papanui Rd and Bealey Av west (to SH1), or on Riccarton Rd heading south. Hostels abound in the city centre, from the small purpose-built, or old hotel/pub-style, to the large and modern. All the motorparks are on the city fringes in all directions, but mainly close to SH1 north and south. Overall you will find prices above average for the South Island, but winter can see a drop in rates and some very reasonable deals, especially with the many competing hotels. Since Christchurch is the starting point for so many South Island travellers you are advised to pre-book in mid summer.

City centre *p475, maps p473 and p477*
LL The George Hotel, 50 Park Terr, T03-371 0256, www.thegeorge.com. Overlooking the river and handy for the Arts Centre, The George has a solid reputation with excellent, well-appointed suites, facilities and award-winning cuisine.

LL Heritage Hotel, Cathedral Sq, T0800-368888/T03-377 9722, www.heritagehotels.co.nz. Modern, well-appointed with good facilities, this is perhaps the best of the chain hotels. The restaurant and bar is popular with non-clients due to the ideal location.
LL Weston House, 62 Park Terr, T03-366 0234, www.westonhouse.co.nz. This listed neo-Georgian mansion offers luxurious suites and elegant surroundings opposite Hagley Park and the Avon River. Private guest entrance, very helpful, friendly hosts and a legendary breakfast.
LL-A The Classic Villa, 17 Worcester Boulevard, T03-377 7905, www.theclassicvilla.co.nz. Very classy Italian-style boutique B&B/hotel in an ideal position opposite the Arts Centre.
LL-L Copthorne Hotel, corner of Kilmore and Durham sts, T03-365 4699, www.milleniumhotels.com. A large, high-profile chain hotel conveniently located on the fringe of the CBD, alongside the Avon River and opposite the casino. Renovated rooms with standard facilities and city views.
LL-AL Hotel off the Square, 115 Worcester St, T03-374 9980, www.offthesquare.co.nz. Central and modern but a pleasant change from the standard chain hotels. Labelled as 'highly individual' with 'new-age modernism' it offers a variety of classy, character rooms from standard (yet far from it) to 'superior loft apartments', all generously adorned with contemporary art. The city trams pass through the entrance level, which adds that memorable and quintessential Christchurch touch. Recommended.
LL-AL Millennium Hotel, Cathedral Sq, T0800-227006/T03-365 1111,

www.millenniumhotels.co.nz. Central, modern and well-appointed with all the usual facilities. The popular restaurant is open to non-clients.

L-AL Hotel So, 165 Cashel St, Christchurch, T0508-165165/T03-9685050, www.hotelso.co.nz. 'Funky', 'hip' and 'cool' are the predominant adjectives used in the guestbook of this ultra-modern hotel conveniently located in the centre of the city. Causing a bit of a stir in the industry, its interior design and functionality makes for an experience beyond the norm. Fresh colours, sweeping curves and clean lines throughout and it has all the facilities of a 5-star including gym, sauna, guest lounge and balcony, computer facilities, laundry and café/bar, yet at a fraction of the price. Off-street parking is also available at $15 per day.

L-AL Orari Bed and Breakfast, 42 Gloucester St, T03-365 6569, www.orari.net.nz. Former heritage house, fully renovated with modern decor and in a convenient location close to the Arts Centre. Ten elegant suites and shared lounge with private entrance.

L-A City Centre Motel, 876 Colombo St T03-372 9294, www.citycentremotel.co.nz.

AL Chateau on the Park, 189 Deans Av, T0800-808999/T03-348 8999, www.chateau-park.co.nz. Near the river and retaining that 'Garden City' feel at the northwestern edge of Hagley Park. A little further from the action but that is part of its appeal. Its gardens – complete with vineyard – are excellent and the restaurant and bar have a nice cosy atmosphere.

AL Windsor B&B Hotel, 52 Armagh St, T03-366 1503, www.windsorhotel.co.nz. A good-value B&B in the heart of the city. Although nothing remarkable, the century-old 2-storey house provides some character and the trams that pass right by the property.

AL-A Colombo in the City, 863 Colombo St, T03-366 8775, www.colombointhe city.co.nz. Convenient for the town centre.

AL-A Croydon House, 63 Armagh St, T03-366 5111, www.croydon.co.nz. A fine choice, friendly and well located. Rooms are

en suite. It's a pleasant spot for watching the trams rattle past outside. Good breakfast.

A Stonehurst Apartments, 241 Gloucester St, T0508-786633/T03-379 4620, www.stonehurst.co.nz.

Backpacker hostels

AL-D Chester Street Backpackers, 148 Chester St, T03-377 1897, www.chesterst.co.nz. Classic,small 'home from home' hostel. Cosy, with plenty of character and well-equipped. Double, twin and share rooms and a fully self-contained cottage nearby. Recommended. Also affiliated with a reliable second-hand campervan dealership for those new arrivals hoping to hit the road.

B-D Stonehurst Backpackers, 241 Gloucester St, Latimer Sq, T0508-786633/ T03-379 4620, www.stonehurst.co.nz. Without doubt one of the best backpacker hostel in the city, with the added appeal of a modern motel annexe and campervan facilities. It is centrally located and has just about everything: a wide range of good single, double, twin and dorm rooms (some are self-contained and en suite), clean facilities, a pool, pizza bar, internet, travel shop and off-street parking. It is deservedly popular so book in advance.

C Christchurch City YHA, 273 Manchester St, T03-379 9535, www.yha.org.nz. The more modern of the 2 YHA options. It is purpose-built, well located and spacious with all the usual facilities and services. Limited off-street parking is available.

C Foley Towers, 208 Kilmore St, T03-366 9720, foley.towers@backpack.co.nz. Has a great range of rooms and facilities, internet. Friendly and peaceful.

C-D Old Countryhouse, 437. Gloucester St, T03-381 5504, www.oldcountryhousenz.com. 2 renovated well-equipped villas, similar in style, with doubles and shared rooms. Internet, off-street parking. Recommended.

C-D Rolleston House YHA, 5 Worcester Blvd, across the road from the Arts Centre, T03-366 6564, www.yha.org.nz. A little tired but still popular and has a good atmosphere.

C-D Thomas's Hotel, 36 Hereford St, T03-379 9536, www.thomashotel.co.nz. Ideally located (on the other side of the Arts Centre), well-equipped and spotless. Ideal for couples looking for a good-value double and some peace and quiet, but perhaps lacking atmosphere if you are alone.

C-D Vagabond Backpackers, 232 Worcester St, T03-379 9677, vagabondbackpackers@hotmail.com. Very tidy, peaceful and friendly with off-street parking.

Motorcamps and campsites
B-D Stonehurst Backpackers, see above. The only establishment in the city centre catering for campervans offering a small number of powered sites with full amenities.

City North and West *p478*
LL Elm Tree House, 236 Papanui Rd, Merivale, T03-355 9731, www.elmtree house.co.nz. Further out and quieter location. Characterful 1920s colonial-style homestead with 6 luxury suites and fine cuisine. Recommended.

LL Hambledon, 103 Bealey Av, T03-379 0723, www.hambledon.co.nz. A large and well-appointed 1856 mansion with 4 lovely luxury suites (with bath), 1 self-contained apartment, 3 self-contained historic cottages (close to Hambeldon), a large collection of antiques and a peaceful garden.

LL Peppers Clearwater Resort Hotel, Clearwater Av, Harewood, T03-360 1000, www.peppers.co.nz. Home to the popular (and highly aquatic) Bob Charles 72-hole championship golf course. The hotel provides luxury lakeside villas and suites, spas and a quality restaurant. Discount B&B or golfing packages are often available.

LL-L Tangley on Clyde Boutique B&B, 193 Clyde Rd, T03-351 8940, www.tangley. co.nz. Fine boutique B&B in a quiet and convenient location close to both the city and airport. The large Edwardian home offers two luxury suites sleeping two and one sleeping four. Beautifully appointed throughout. Recommended.

LL-L Eliza's Manor on Bealey, 82 Bealey Av, T03-366 8584, www.themanor.co.nz. A vast,

historic, well-appointed mansion with 12 rooms, 10 of which are en suite. The wooden façades and staircase of the ground floor are superb and the open fire gives a lovely atmosphere. Off-street parking.

LL-AL Copthorne Hotel Commodore, at the end of Memorial Av, 5 mins from the airport and the Antarctic Centre, T03-358 8129, www.commodore.net.nz. Set in 3 ha of land with award-winning gardens.

L-AL Sudima Hotel Grand Chancellor, end of Memorial Av, 700 m from airport, T03-358 3139, www.sudimahotel.co.nz. Comfortable and convenient for that early morning flight or late night arrival.

B-D Dorset House, 1 Dorset St, T03-366 8268, www.dorsethouse.co.nz. A historic, friendly place pitched somewhere between a backpacker hostel and a B&B, with good doubles, twins and singles. It also has Sky TV, Wi-Fi and provides pick-ups.

Motels
L-A Airport Christchurch Motel, 55 Roydvale Av, T0800-800631/T03-9774970, www.airportchristchurch.co.nz.

AL-A Avenue Motor Lodge, 136 Bealey Av, T0800-500283/T03-366 0582, www.avenue motorlodge.co.nz. Standard facilities.

AL-A Bella Vista, 193 Bealey Av, T03-377 3363, www.bellavistamotel.co.nz.

AL-A Milano Motor Lodge, 87 Papanui Rd, T0800-878766/T03-3552800, www.milanomotorlodge.co.nz.

AL-A Strathern Motor Lodge, 54 Papanui Rd, T03-355 4411, www.strathern.co.nz.

AL-A Tuscana Motor Lodge, 74 Bealey Av, T03-377 4485, www.tuscana.co.nz.

A Adelphi Motel, 49 Papanui Rd, T03-355 6037, www.adelphimotel.co.nz.

A Avalon Motel, 301 Bealey Av, T03-379 9681, www.avalonmotel.co.nz. Near the centre. Standard facilities.

Motorcamps and campsites
A-D Meadow Park Top Ten Holiday Park, 39 Meadow St (off Papanui Rd at the northwestern end of the city),

T0800-396323/T03-352 9176,
www.meadowpark.co.nz. Has a great range
of options from self-contained motels, lodges
and flats to chalets, cottages and standard
cabins, powered/tent sites. That said, you pay
more for its location and the facilities, which
include a spa pool, sauna and weight training
room. Keep your eyes peeled for the sign off
Papanui Rd – it is quite hard to spot.
B-D Amber Park, 308 Blenheim Rd,
southwest of the city centre , T03-348 3327,
www.amberpark.co.nz. Older but tidy, it
offers flats, cabins, powered/tent sites in a
quiet garden setting.

City East p481
D Frauenreisehaus, 272 Barbadoes St,
T03-366 2585. Bohemian, health-promoting
backpackers for women only. It prides itself
on offering beds not bunks and has internet.

City South p481
LL Otahuna Lodge, RD2, Rhodes Rd, Tai Tapu
(30 km), T03-329 6333, www.ota huna.co.nz.
A characterful historic homestead with 7
immaculate luxury suites and a day spa, all set
amid spectacular century-old gardens. There
is also a horse-trekking operation on site.
AL-A Apollo Motel, 288 Riccarton Rd,
T03-348 8786, www.apollomotel.co.nz.
A Aalton Motel, 19 Riccarton Rd,
T03-348 6700, www.aalton.co.nz. Central.

❶ Eating

While Christchurch can't quite match
Auckland or Wellington in its range of fine
eateries, it is by no means wanting. Generally
you will find a wide range of options to suit all
budgets. Most of the modern places are to be
found along the trendy 'Strip' overlooking the
river from Oxford Terrace or in the fast
developing Sol Square, off Lichfield Street.
Both offer great choice and are convenient
for the city centre. Colombo St and
Manchester St also offer a wide choice.
   Note Christchurch has several rather

unique dining options. Romantic couples
can arrive at the **Retour Restaurant** by punt
and other unusual options include the
Tramway Restaurant, the Maori
performance at the **Tamaki Heritage Village**,
page 481, the **Octagon Live** dining
experience, and the **Willowbank Wildlife
Reserve**, page 479.

City centre p475, maps p473 and p477
A number of the better restaurants are within
hotels, including **Pescatore** in the George;
The Piko Piko in The Millennium; or the
Maddison's in the Heritage, are all popular
(see Sleeping, above).
¶¶¶ **The Charlotte Jane Restaurant**,
Charlotte Jane Hotel, 110 Papanui Rd,
T03-355 1028, www.charlotte-jane.co.nz.
Offers an intimate and congenial atmosphere
with the added attraction of outdoor seating
with an open fire.
¶¶¶ **St Germaine**, 121 Worcester St, T03-
366 9046, www.lebonbolli.co.nz. A good
French option, rather too modern in aesthetics,
but more than makes up for it with the cuisine.
¶¶¶ **Mona Vale Homestead**, 63 Fendalton Rd,
T03-348 9660. The daytime menu (0930-
1530) offers the best chance to appreciate the
surroundings, but it is also open for dinner.
¶¶¶ **Octagon Live**, 124 Worcester St (corner
Manchester and Worcester), T03-366 6171,
www.octagonlive.co.nz. Tue-Sun for dinner
(winter Wed-Sun). Dubbed the 'shrine to fine
dining' the Octagon is a former 1873 Trinity
Anglican Church built by renowned local
architect Benjamin Mountfort and using
Oamaru stone. The interior has been fully
refurbished right down to the 1871 Pipe Organ,
stained glass and vaulted timber ceilings. The
space creates a wonderful ambience and near
perfect acoustics, which led almost inevitably to
the concept of providing top quality live music
to enhance the dining experience. The à la carte
menu features traditional Canterbury fare with a
subtle modern twist. All in all really quite
memorable. Recommended.
¶¶¶ **Pescatore in the George**, T03-371 0278.
An award-winning hotel option (see page 482)

offering fine Pacific Rim cuisine amid minimalist décor and in a very pleasant setting.

Retour Restaurant, in the rotunda, corner of Cambridge Terr and Manchester St, T03-365 2888, www.retour.co.nz. Lunch Thu-Fri 1130-1400, dinner Tue-Sun from 1730. A romantic option, it is very unusual aesthetically, offering an imaginative, mainly kiwi menu and, most importantly perhaps, it can be reached by punt from the city centre. To book a punt, see Avon River page 476 or Hagley Park, page 476.

Annie's Wine Bar and Restaurant, corner Rolleston Av and Hereford St, T03-365 0566, www.annieswinebar.co.nz. Daily from 1100-2300. Good for light lunches and has a decent wine list.

Coyote Street Bar and Restaurant, 126 Oxford Terr, T03-366 6055. Imaginative Kiwi/ Mexican combos, from seafood to pasta. Vegetarians should try the 'Tortilla Twosome'.

Dux de Lux, 41 Hereford St, T03-366 6919, www.thedux.co.nz. A Christchurch institution, perhaps the best thing is its position on the fringe of the Arts Centre complex. It is busiest at the weekend when the markets are in full swing, but remains popular well after dark. Attracting a mixed crowd, a lively atmosphere is virtually guaranteed and there is a fine choice of beer.

Fat Eddie's, Unit 10, Sol Sq, 179 Tuam St, T03-9432833. Tue-Sun from 1800. One of a handful of fine drinking (and eating) venues in the city's latest hip precinct, Sol Square. Eddie's is a cool jazz bar with live entertainment six nights a week, a pub-style menu, a good wine list and speciality cocktails. Try a kiwi 'Wondering Eye'.

Hay's, 63 Victoria St, T03-379 7501. Tue-Sat from 1700 and Mon evenings in summer. Great New Zealand Lamb.

The Little India Bistro and Tandoori, corner of Gloucester and New Regent sts, T03-377 7997. Mon-Fri for lunch from 1200 and daily for dinner from 1700.

Palazzo del Marinaio, 108 Hereford St, T03-365 4640. Daily for lunch and dinner. For seafood it would be rude not to mention this Italian-style restaurant. Try the 'Piatto combo'.

The Sala Sala Japanese Restaurant, 184 Oxford Terr, T03-366 6755, daily from 1730 and Mon-Fri 1200-1400 for lunch.

Santorini, corner of Gloucester St and Cambridge Terr, T03-379 6975, www.santorini. co.nz. A good and very colourful Greek option with live entertainment most nights.

Strawberry Fare Restaurant, 114 Peterborough St, T03-365 4897. Mon-Fri 0700-late, Sat-Sun 0900-late. Lovers of weight-gaining and creative desserts should throw caution to the wind here.

Tandoori Palace 56 Cathedral Sq, T03-365 7816, www.tandooripalace.co.nz. Mon-Fri 1130-1700 for lunch and daily for dinner from 1700.

Tap Room Bar and Restaurant, 124 Oxford Terr, T03-365 0547. Breakfast, lunch and dinner. One of the best and most popular overlooking the Avon River.

Thai Smile, 818 Colombo St, T03-366 2246. Any Thai restaurant that proclaims that 'your satisfaction is our happiness' and is one of only 3 in New Zealand to be awarded the Thai Government's very own 'Thai cuisine to the World' award surely has to be tried.

Tiffany's Restaurant, 95 Oxford Terr, T03-379 1350. A great choice for NZ cuisine and often offers good value three course set menu.

Tramway Restaurant, T03-366 7511, www.tram.co.nz. An unusual and romantic dining option. In the evening you can join the popular dining tour that adds a very pleasant convivial edge to the usual sightseeing trip.

Casino, Victoria St (see Entertainment, page 488). Has several good-value eateries.

The Oxford on Avon, 794 Colombo St, T03-379 7148. A Christchurch institution offering huge, great-value lunch and dinner from $20, or set-price meals, from 0700.

The Fish and Chip Shop, Sol Sq, 96 Lichfield St, T03-9432994. More up-market chippy in the heart of the happening Sol Square precinct.

Thai Tasty, in the Gloucester Arcade, 129 Gloucester St, T03-3653508, daily until 2200.

Wagamama, 152 Oxford Terr, T03-377 6819, daily from 1130 until late. The award-winning Asian inspired noodle restaurant chain.

City North and West p478
🍴 **Willowbank Wildlife Reserve**, on the city fringe, T03-359 6226 (see page 479). A unique dining option encompassing a heavy emphasis on Kiwi culture and nature. Dine next to a variety of tame native animals.

City South p481
🍴 **The Sign of the Takahe**, 200 Hackthorne Rd, in the Port Hills (south via Colombo St then straight up Dyers Pass Rd), T03-332 4052, www.signofthetakahe.co.nz. Tue-Sat from 1800. Historic country house and restaurant with award-winning cuisine. The views are better than anything in the city. Bookings essential.

Cafés
Boulevard Bakehouse, below the Arts Centre, T03-377 2162. Daily 0800-2400. Popular, especially at lunchtime.
Café Metro, corner of Colombo and Kilmore sts, T03-374 4242. Has a loyal following and a good atmosphere.
Caffe Roma, 176 Oxford Terr, T03-379 3879. Very popular breakfast/brunch hangout, especially at the weekend.
Java, corner of High and Lichfield sts, T03-366 0195. Funky and a popular hangout with the younger and more alternative crowd.
Le Café, Arts Centre, Worcester St, T03-366 7722. Sun-Thu 0700-2400, Fri-Sat open 24 hrs. Based in the heart of the city, this is a popular hangout for both locals and tourists. It is especially popular at the weekends when the colourful markets and street performers provide an added attraction to the permanent arts and craft outlets, architecture, theatre and cinema. There is an extensive menu of traditional Kiwi fare; brunch is a speciality.
Mitchelli's, Ash St (near Sol Sq), T03-377 4574. Tue-Fri 0900-1700, Sat 1000-1700. Excellent family owned Italian café/deli combo and some of the best coffee in town.
Underground, 791 Colombo St, T03-982

8394. Daily 1000-late. Home of champion baristas.
The Yellow Rocket Bagel and Coffee Company, southwest corner of Cathedral Sq, T03-365 6061. Daily from 0900. Although not one of the city's most celebrated cafés, the Yellow Rocket, tucked in the corner of Cathedral Sq and next door to the 1879 Old Post Office building (which now houses the VIC), is a very pleasant option in a fine location. It's is a great place to escape the traffic and watch the tourist world go by, particularly in fine weather. Here you can muse over your various information centre leaflets and plan your sightseeing agenda with a choice of sweet or savoury bagels and a fine cup of coffee.

🍷 Pubs, bars and clubs

Christchurch p475, maps p473 and p477
Pubs and bars
Christchurch's main drinking venues are a conglomerate of modern, well-appointed and lively restaurant/bars on Oxford Terr or 'The Strip', the new Sol Square Precinct off Lichfield St and around Poplar St. The Strip is a good spot to be both in the evening and more especially during the day, when you can sup on your libation while watching the world (and the river) go by, while Sol Square is predominantly an evening venue. Most pubs/bars stay open to at least 2300 with some on The Strip and Sol Square remaining open at weekends until 0230.
Bailies Irish Bar, Cathedral Sq, T03-366 5159. The largest and most popular in the Square.
The Bard on Avon, corner of Oxford and Gloucester sts, T03-377 1493. An old English favourite.
The Bog, across the road from the **Tap Room**, at the top of Cashel Mall, T03- 379 7141. Will satisfy the Irish pub fans.
Dux de Lux, in the Arts Centre, corner of Hereford and Montreal sts, T03-366 6919. Daily from 1100, particularly popular at weekends. A spacious long-established pub

with an old English feel. It attracts a daytime clientele as well as night revellers. Also has a microbrewery on site producing a range of potent beers, and regular live music.

His Lordships, Sol Sq, Lichfield St, T03-366 3225. Another English-style venue with a good atmosphere and range of traditional and import beers.

Twisted Hop, 6 Poplar St, T03-962 3688, www.thetwistedhop.co.nz. Real ale brew pub again with a good atmosphere and great range of beers. They offer tours daily at 1600 from $6 and this is an ideal opportunity to taste 6 of the beers alongside each other in custom made tasting glasses, $8 extra with the tour (usual price $17). No doubt you will then stay! Recommended.

205 Cocktail Bar, 205 Manchester St, T03-961 0359. Offers the biggest cocktail list in the city, great décor and dance music.

Tap Room Bar and Restaurant, 124 Oxford Terr, T03-365 0547. Currently the most popular place, serving the full range of South Island brews and also serves great food.

Clubs

For listings of local gigs and visiting acts consult *The Press* newspaper. The website www.bethere.org.nz and www.realgroove.co.nz can also be useful. There are plenty of pubs hosting live music, especially at weekends, and overall there is a lively and modern dance/club scene in the city centre. The best bet, if you can stand all the mobile phones, is to gather with the city slickers in the pre-club pubs along The Strip on Oxford Terr, then just tag along. Many of the late-night clubs are on Lichfield St.

Base, 92 Struthers Lane, T03-377 7149. Good venue for base and house.

Illusions, corner of Chancery Lane and Gloucester St. The best bet for 'trendy-phobics', with disco classics from the 1960s and 1980s.

Ministry, 88-90 Lichfield St. Popular and large dance venue.

⊙ Entertainment

Christchurch *p475, maps p473 and p477*
For performance and cinema listings consult *The Press* newspaper. The free leaflet *The Package* available from the VIC (I-Site) is also useful, www.thepackage.co.nz.

Casino

Christchurch Casino, 30 Victoria St, T03-365 9999. A well-established institution and naturally a popular entertainment venue. There are also various bars and good-value food outlets. Dress code is smart casual, the minimum age limit is 20, and it is open 24 hrs. The free yellow shuttle stops right outside, T0800-227466.

Cinema

The following are mainstream cinemas.
Cinema 3 Hornby, Hornby Mall, T03-349 2365.
Hoyts, 392 Moorhouse Av (Old Train Station), T03-366 3791.
Hoyts 6, Northlands Mall, T03-366 6367.
Metro 105 Worcester St, T03-377 5705, www.artfilms.co.nz. Quality art house cinema.

Theatre

If you missed out on the Maori performances and *hangis* (feasts) in the North Island, Christchurch provides one of the few opportunities in the South Island (see Tamaki Heritage Village page 481, and Willowbank Wildlife Reserve page 479). A good source of information for performance dates and venues is www.artists.co.nz/concerts.html.
The Arts Centre, Worcester Blvd, is home to the **Court Theatre**, T03-963 0870, www.courttheatre.org.nz; the **University Free Theatre**, T03-374 5483; the **Southern Ballet and Dance Theatre**, T03-379 7219; and the **Academy Cinema**, T03-366 0167. There is a dynamic programme of events year-round listed at the information centre, T03-363 2836, www.artscentre.org.nz. The 'Friday Lunchtime Concert Series' featuring local, national and international musicians is held in the **Great Hall of the Arts Centre**.

Theatre Royal, 145 Gloucester St, T03-377 8899, www.isaactheatreroyale.co.nz. The other major events venue featuring everything from rock to jazz.
Town Hall, 86 Kilmore St, T03-377 8899, www.convention.co.nz. Includes the in-house **James Hay Theatre**.

⊛ Festivals and events

Christchurch *p475, maps p473 and p477*
For details on events have a look at the useful website www.bethere.co.nz and www.christchurchnz.com.

The 'Summertimes' programme, www.summertimes.org.nz, includes summer theatre and retro events, twilight concerts and even a teddy bears' picnic. The culminating outdoor **Motors Classical Sparks** in Mar is the highlight, with a classical concert and fireworks in Hagley Park.

National and international rugby **Super Twelve** and **Tri-Nations** (Mar-Oct) and Test matches at Christchurch's AMI Stadium in the south of the city is a top spot and still wet with the tears of British Lions supporters after the 2005 tour. Christchurch and the AMI will serve as a major venue for the **Rugby World Cup** in Sep/Oct 2011, www.rugbyworldcup.com.
Jan World Busker's Festival (15-24), www.worldbuskersfestival.com. A lively event attracting artists of all shapes and sizes.
Feb Coast to Coast (6-7), www.coastto coast.co.nz, a classic South Island event with a gruelling combination of running, kayaking and cycling to the west coast. **Festival of Romance**, dancing and jazz in Victoria Sq. **International Garden City Festival of Flowers**, www.festivalofflowers.co.nz, over 30 events from garden tours to floral carpet displays. This event coincides with the **Jade Wine and Food Festival**, a celebration of local produce held in Hagley Park.
Mar Ellerslie International Flower Show Formerly held in Auckland this has steadily grown into a major annual gardening

and lifestyle event showcasing the best of garden design, garden trends and new products. It attracts a global audience of garden designers and garden lovers.
Festival of Asia A day of Asian celebration at The Arts Centre.
Le Race, www.lerace.co.nz, South Island's largest cycling event.
April NZ International Jazz and Blues Festival, the country's biggest, www.jazzfestivalnz.com.
Jul Kidsfest (3-16), www.kidsfest.org.nz. This is a fun annual festival of events, workshops and performances for children.
Jul/Aug Christchurch Arts Festival, www.artsfestival.co.nz. Includes theatre, dance, classical and jazz concerts, cabaret and exhibitions of the visual arts.

⊙ Shopping

Christchurch *p475, maps p473 and p477*
Arts, crafts and souvenirs
There is a rash of souvenir shops in and around Cathedral Sq selling everything from furry kiwis in rugby shirts to sheepskin slippers. **The Arts Centre**, Worcester Blvd, is an excellent place to pick up arts and crafts, as is the weekend market. Rugby shirts are always a great buy in New Zealand and Christchurch is home to **Canterbury Clothing Company (CCC)**. The have a clearance store at Dress Smart, main South Rd, Hornby, T03-3490667, www.canterburyofnz.com. You can also find a wide selection at **Champions of the World**, outlets at 767 Colombo St, T03-377 4100.

Bookshops and maps
Whitcoulls and **Dymocks** are in the Cashel Street Mall, just south of Cathedral Sq.
Mapworld, corner of Manchester and Gloucester sts, T03-374 5399, www.mapworld.co.nz.
Scorpios, 79 Hereford St, T03-379 2882. An excellent modern independent bookstore.
Smiths Bookshop, 133 Manchester St, T03-379 7976, www.smiths.bookshop.co.nz.

A good second-hand bookshop in a multi-storey building.

Outdoor and camping equipment
Kiwi Disposals, 611 Colombo St, T03-365 3381, www.kiwidisposals.co.nz. An excellent place for all manner of outdoor equipment and supplies without all the designer labels. Excellent value.
Other more traditional stores include:
Mountain Designs, 656 Colombo St, T03-377 8522, and **Snowgum**, 637 Colombo St, T03-365 4336.

Second-hand shops
Toffs, 141 Gloucester St, just off Cathedral Sq. An innocuous looking place that gives no indication of the marvels inside. Stocks all manner of second-hand clothing and accessories, from snow chains and Nikon photo jackets to Armani business shirts and silk ties.
Tete a Tete, 88 Hereford St, T03-3665442. A fine vintage clothing store that's also worth a muse.

▲ Activities and tours

Christchurch *p475, maps p473 and p477*
There is a huge range of tours operating out of Christchurch, encompassing everything from sightseeing, activity combos, wineries, gardens, walking and motorcycling. The VIC (I-Site) has brochures and full listings.
Adventure Canterbury, T03-351 2658, www.adventurecanterbury.com. One of the main activity operators in Christchurch. It offers a wide array of trips and activities including jet boating on the Waimakariri (2-2½ hrs, $80-110); horse trekking (15 hrs, $80-155); fishing (5-6 hrs $715); farm visits (3-4 hrs, $75, with lunch $110); winery tours half-day including 20 tastings, from $120; and day trips to Hanmer and Akaroa from $215.

Bone carving
The Bone Dude, 229B Fitzgerald Av, T03-379 7530, www.thebonedude.co.nz. A carving studio where you can carve your own Maori-style pendants (tiki) from $55. Excellent value.

Climbing Walls and Obstacle Courses
The Roxx, corner Waltham Rd and Byron St, T03-377 3000, www.theroxx.co.nz. Mon-Fri 1200-2200, Sat-Sun 1000-1830. Has a world class climbing wall that is open to the public for casual use. Equipment hire and instruction is available at extra cost.
Adrenaline Forest, 105 A Heyders Rd, Spencerville, T03-329 8717, www.adrenalin-forest.co.nz. Daily 1000, last start time at 1400. A great test of gravity, balance and agility on a multi-level aerial obstacle course set in the forest. There are 6 pathways more than 2 km in length, with features from 1 m to 20 m high, 100 challenges taking an average of 2-3 hrs to complete, from $35, child $23. Pick-ups from the city available from $10.

Cruising
For wildlife and historic/scenic cruises on the Lyttleton Harbour see page 498. For punting, see River Avon, page 476, and Hagley Park, page 476.

Fishing
There are a number of operators offering half-day to full-day trips or tailor-made options from $700. The VIC (I-Site) has listings.

Horse trekking and harness racing
Waimak River Horse Treks, T0800-873577/ T03-323 9064, www.gohorsetrekking.co.nz. Offers interesting 30-min or 1½-hr horse trek/ jetboat combos, or trekking-only trips from 1 hr to full-day, from $50.
Otahuna Horse Riding, based in Tai Tapu, T03-329 0160, www.otahuna.co.nz. An upmarket operation offering intensive riding lessons as well as trekking.
Horsepower Experience, 59 Russley Rd, Avonhead, T03-342 9246, www.horsepower.co.nz. A unique opportunity to partake in full speed harness or 'sulky' racing, from $250.

Hot air ballooning

Ballooning over the Canterbury Plains is perhaps Christchurch's classic activity. Both of these companies offer early morning flights of about 1 hr, with champagne breakfast from $330. Recommended.

Aoraki Balloon Safaris, Methven, T03-302 8172, www.nzballooning.com.
Up Up and Away, T03-381 4600, www.ballooning.co.nz.

Jet boating

Both companies offer jet-boating trips on the eastern Southern Alps rivers from $85-230, including transport.

Jet Stream Tours, T03-3851478, www.jetstreamtours.co.nz. Offers 30 min blasts down the Waimakariri from $75 and also offers a heli-jet boat option with 10-min heli and 20-min jet boat, from $295.
Waimak Alpine Jet, T0800-263626/T03-318 4881, www.waimakalpinejet.co.nz. Again a wide range of options from $105.

Mountain biking and cycling tours

There are some attractive options around Christchurch, with the Port Hills and Banks Peninsula being the main venues. See also Transport, page 492, for hire companies.

Adventure South, T03-942 1222, www.adv south.co.nz. Offers more far-flung options.
Christchurch Bike Tours, T0800-733257, www.chchbiketours.co.nz. An old-fashioned cycling experience touring the local parks and historical sites in typical Christchurch English fashion – on a bike with a basket and a bell. Tours from 2 to 4 hrs and from $35 (departs 1400 from the VIC/i-Site).
Mountain Bike Adventure Company, T0800-424534/T03-339 4020, www.cyclehire-tours.co.nz. Offers a good trip that goes up the Port Hills via the gondola to then descend by bike, from $60, plus longer tours from 3-5 days and independent hire from $35 per day.

Paragliding

Paragliding is big in Christchurch, with a number of companies vying for the tourist dollar. All are safe and pretty similar in price.
Nimbus, T03-389 1999/T0800-111611, www.nimbusparagliding.cjb.net. Offers a 2-hr trip and flights daily at 1000 and 1300 for $160. Introductory courses from $240.

Rafting

Rangitata Rafts, T0800-251251/T03-696 3534, www.rafts.co.nz. Offers day excursions down the scenic Rangitata River, south of Methven (Grade IV-V), from $185 including transport from Christchurch. Also offers gentler family oriented trips from $165, child $120.

Swimming

Atlantis Pool, QEII Park, Travis Rd, New Brighton, T03-941 6849, www.qeiipark.co.nz. Mon-Fri 0600-2100, Sat-Sun 0700-2000. A modern themed attraction that has the largest wave pool in the country. It is a great place to take the kids and has spas, sauna, steam room and café, from $5, child $2.50.

Tandem skydiving

The Christchurch Parachute School, Methven, T03- 302 9143, www.skydiving.co.nz. Operates out of the Pudding Hill Airfield in Methven 100 km west of the city. 10,000 ft, from $329.

Tank driving

Tanks for Everything, 985 Mcleans Island Rd, T03-359 1007, www.tanksforeverything.co.nz. Yes, you read right: experience authentic military vehicles (guided driving) from classic jeeps to the full 52-tonne battle tank. Its certainly not cheap, but it is the full 'Armour Geddon' and no 'big Jessies' allowed.

Tours including eco-tours

Hassle-free Tours, T0800-427753/T03-385 5775, www.hasslefree.co.nz, from $215, departs 0900. *Lord of the Rings* fans or indeed anyone who wants to see some classic Southern Alpine scenery could try a trip to Mt Sunday (Potts Station) in the

Raingitata Valley. Day or multi-day tours available.

TranzAlpine High Country Explorer Tour, T0800-863975/T03-377 1391, www.high-country.co.nz. An interesting full-day trip that combines 1-hr transfer by coach across the Canterbury Plains, morning tea, a 15-km jet-boat trip, a 65-km 4WD safari lunch and then a 2-hr trip back to Christchurch from Arthur's Pass on the famous **TranzAlpine** railway line, from $375.

Tussock and Beach Ecotours, T03-303 0880, www.nature.net.nz. Several eco-tour options including 2 nights' accommodation, all meals and a fully guided eco-tour through a spectacular glaciated landscape, culminating in Mt Sunday with the opportunity to explore the site of 'Edoras' from *The Two Towers*. A beech forest walk along a mountain stream and a champagne lunch beside a sub-alpine lake are also included. Accommodation is in the historic Ross Cottage, a peaceful, carefully restored building registered with the New Zealand Historic Places Trust, from $320.

Heritage Expeditions, 53B Montreal St, Christchurch, T03-365 3500, www.heritage-expeditions.com. Guided birdwatching trips and expeditions throughout New Zealand and the sub-Antarctic Islands.

Walking

In town, a stroll along the River Avon is recommended, as are the 'city walks' (self-guided or guided, brochures from the VIC/I-Site). Further afield the 'Port Hills Bridle Path' and 'Crater Rim Walks' provide great views and can be tackled in part with the gondola. The VIC (I-Site) has details, or see page 481. The beaches of New Brighton and Sumner offer good and easygoing beach walks. DoC has details and leaflets covering walks throughout the Banks Peninsula (see Tourist information, page 474).

Banks Peninsula Track, T03-304 7612, www.bankstrack.co.nz. Main portal for doing the 2-4 day track.

Tuatara Tours, T0800-377378/ T03-962 3280, www.tuatara tours.co.nz (see Akaroa

Activities, page 499). Offers the all inclusive 3-day, 39-km Christchurch-Akaroa walk, from $1486.

⊖ Transport

Christchurch *p475, maps p473 and p477*
Airline offices
Air New Zealand, 549 Colombo St, T03-363 0600 (after hours T0800-737000). **Mount Cook**, T0800-730000. **Qantas**, T03-374 7100 (after hours T0800-808767).

Bicycle hire
Mountain Bike Adventure Company, T03-339 4020/T0800-424534, www.cyclehire-tours.co.nz.

Car hire
All the major national companies have offices at the airport and in town. Prices average about $70 per day with unlimited mileage. **Scotties**, 189 Blenheim Rd, T03-3482002/ T0800-736825. Also has offices in Auckland, is recommended and can offer good hire rates and buy back sales.

Others include: **Apex**, 160 Lichfield St, T0800-939597/T03-3796897; **Hertz**, T0800-654321; **KiwiCar**, T0800-5494227; **Omega**, T0800-112121; **Pegasus**, T0800-803580.

For cheaper deals try: **Cut Price**, T03-366 3800; **Mac's**, T0800-154155; **Rent-A-Dent**, T0800-736823; **Shoestring Rentals**, T03-385 3647; and **Trusty**, T03-366 6329.

Motorcycle hire
Motorcycle Rentals and Tours, 32 Allen St, T03-377 0663, www.nzbike.com.
Rental Motorcycles, 28B Byron St, T03-372 3537, www.motorcycle-hire.co.nz.

Motorhome hire
Adventure Kiwi, T0800-113131, www.adventurekiwi.co.nz; **Backpacker Campervan Rentals**, T0800-288699 / T03-3575610; the arty colourful vans of

Escape Independent Car Rentals, T0800-216171, www.escape rentals.co.nz; Maui, T0800-651080; or Tomlinson Campers, T03-374 5254.
Chester Street Backpacker Campers, 148 Chester St, T03-377 1897, www.chesterst.co.nz.

Taxi
Blue Star, T03-353 1200/379 9799, 24 hrs.
First Direct, T03-377 5555.
Gold Band, T03-3795795.

❶ Directory

Christchurch *p475, maps p473 and p477*
Banks ANZ, ASB, BNZ, National and Westpac are around Cathedral Sq. Banking hours Mon-Fri 0900-1630. **Currency exchange** Most of the major bank branches offer exchange services. **Interforex**, 65 Cathedral Sq, T03-377 1233. **Travelex**, at the VIC or Harvey World Travel, corner of Armagh and Colombo sts, T03-366 2087, www.travelex.co.nz. **Disabled services** Disability Information Service, 314 Worcester St, T03-3666189, dis@disinfo.co.nz, 0900-1630; Kiwiable, T03-941 8774.
Internet There are numerous places around Cathedral Sq: **Cyber Nutz Café**, 266 High St, T03-379 6688; **E Blah Blah**, 77 Cathedral Sq (bus info corner), T03-377 2381, daily 0800-2230. **Laundry** 247 Armagh St, T03-379 6622, Mon-Fri 0730-1730, Sat 0900-1600. **Library** Gloucester St, Mon-Fri 1000-2100, Sat 1000-1600, Sun 1300-1600.
Medical services 24 hr surgery corner of Bealey Av and Colombo St, T03-365 7777; Christchurch Hospital, Riccarton Av, T03-364 0640; Dentist, T03-366 6644 (ext 3002); Urgent pharmacy, 931 Colombo St, T03-366 4439, until 2300. **Police** Central Station, corner of Hereford and Cambridge Terr, T03-363 7400. **Post office** (Post Restante) Cathedral Square North Postshop, 736 Colombo St, T03-3775414, Mon-Fri 0830-1730, Sat-Sun 1000-1400. **Useful addresses** Emergencies, T111.

Banks Peninsula → *Colour map 5, B6.*

Jutting out into the Pacific Ocean from Christchurch, like the bulb on a jigsaw piece, is the Banks Peninsula. Distinctly out of character with the (now) connected and monotonously flat alluvial Canterbury Plains, it is a refreshing and rugged landscape of hills and flooded harbours formed by two violent volcanic eruptions. The two largest harbours, which now fill the craters and shelter their namesake settlements, are Lyttleton to the north and Akaroa to the south. These settlements provide an interesting excursion from Christchurch, with Lyttleton – 12 km away via the Lyttleton Tunnel – being by far the most accessible.

Other than the refreshing hill and harbour scenery, both places offer some historic sites, and activities such as dolphin and penguin watching. The bays and waters that surround the peninsula are home to the world's smallest and rarest dolphin, the Hector's dolphin. The two- or four-day trek on the Banks Peninsula Track from Akaroa is also a popular attraction. ▶▶ *For Sleeping, Eating and other listings, see pages 496-499.*

Ins and outs
Getting there If you can afford it, hiring a car is the best way to explore the peninsula (see Christchurch Transport, page 492, for hire companies). By road, Lyttelton is 12 km from the centre of Christchurch via the tunnel or about 20 km via the windy roads above Sumner. Both Sumner and Lyttelton are well signposted from Ferry Rd at the

southeastern corner of the city. The scenic Port Hills road is accessed via Colombo St via the Cashmere Hills. Akaroa is 84 km southeast of Christchurch via SH75, which skirts past Lake Ellesmere, before turning inland into the heart of the peninsula. Just past the small settlement of Little River the road climbs, offering great views from the **Hilltop Hotel**, before falling to the head of Akaroa Harbour and into Akaroa itself. An alternative route is via Lyttelton but it is no shorter.

By bus, Lyttelton is served by the No 28, which leaves regularly from the casino or Cathedral Square in Christchurch. The **Akaroa Shuttle**, T0800-500929, www.akaroashuttle.co.nz, provides day tours and shuttle services. Shuttles depart from the Christchurch VIC (I-Site) daily Nov-Apr at 0830 and 1400, returning from Akaroa at 1030, 1535 and 1630, from $45, return; in winter daily from Christchurch at 1000 returning at 1600. Day tour shuttles depart at 1000 and 1030 and return at 1535 or 1630, from $55, $110 with lunch. Similarly, **Akaroa French Connection**, T03-366 4556, T0800-800575, www.akaroabus.co.nz, offers a scenic day-tour and shuttle services to Akaroa and other places of interest on the peninsula, departing daily from the Christchurch VIC (I-Site) at 0845 (shuttle), 0930 (tour), 1300 (additional service at 1645 on Fri), with the last shuttle returning from Akaroa at 1545 (Apr-Aug) and 1615 (Sep-Mar), from $20 return, tour from $35; transport only.

Tourist information **Lyttelton VIC (I-Site)** ⓘ *20 Oxford St, T03-328 9093, www.lytteltonharbour.co.nz, daily 0900-1700*, has enthusiastic staff who can provide leaflets on all the relevant walks and activities; of particular interest is the self-guided historical walks leaflet. It also has full accommodation listings and internet access. **Akaroa VIC (I-Site)** ⓘ *Akaroa District Promotions, 80 Rue Lavaud, T03-304 8600, www.akaroa.com, daily 0900-1700*, is an independent information office, with very helpful staff, who will share their knowledge regarding the village and the peninsula's more out-of-the-way places.

Lyttelton

Whichever way you arrive in Lyttelton, by the Port Hills scenic route via Sumner, or through the road tunnel, it is quite an exciting delivery and will, along with the deeply contrasting scenery, provide a pleasant sense of escape from the city buzz and the flat vistas of Christchurch. Lying on the northern shores of the volcanic crater that now forms the Lyttleton Harbour, this busy characterful port (population 3,100) has an air of history, befitting its stature as the place where the 'first four ships' arrived in 1850. It was also the port that Captain Scott and Lieutenant Shackleton used as their base to explore the Antarctic.

Relics from these times and its fascinating past can be found in the **Lyttelton Museum** ⓘ *Gladstone Quay, T03-328 8972, Tue, Thu, Sat-Sun 1400-1600, donation*. Also of historical interest is the **Lyttelton Timeball Station** ⓘ *high on the hillside off Sumner Rd, T03-328 7311, www.historic.org.nz, daily 1000-1730 (winter Wed-Sun), $7, child $2*. After years of disuse the station building, which is very grand both inside and out, was fully restored and is now open to visitors. Built in 1876, it is the only survivor of three such contraptions ever constructed in New Zealand, and was used as an essential timing device to keep mariners accurate in their calculations of longitude. From 1876 to 1934 the large ball, clearly visible at the top of a mast on the building's turret, would drop at precisely 1300 in accordance with Greenwich Mean Time.

Ripapa Island was originally a Maori *pa* before it became home to Fort Jervois, once declared 'the strongest port fortress in the Empire'. It was built originally in 1886 to repel the 'Great Russian Scare'. Jervois later held the notorious First World War prisoner of war, Count

Felix Von Luckner, who sunk 14 allied vessels before being captured and imprisoned.

In contrast, **Quail Island** was a former leper colony but now, devoid of both lepers and introduced predators, it is a safe haven abounding with native birds. Both Islands feature on the **BlackCat Wildlife Cruise**, T03-304 7641, www.blackcat.co.nz, which departs daily from Lyttelton at 1330, from $60, child $25. The **Lyttelton Farmers Market** is held every Saturday 1000-1300 at Lyttelton Main School, Oxford St.

Akaroa

Background The name Akaroa, which is a variant on the Maori word 'hakaroa'– meaning 'Long Harbour', gives no impression of Akaroa's French roots. In 1835 French whaler Jean Langlois established a whaling station in the harbour at French Bay and, seeing its potential for settlement and as an ideal shipping port, made a down payment on the land with the local Maori. Once he had secured the deal he returned to France to organize the colonization of the newly acquired territory. Knowing nothing of the Treaty of Waitangi, which had effectively placed New Zealand under British sovereignty only 13 days before, a group of French settlers set sail on board *L'Aube* on 19 February 1840. When the French arrived there was a fractious period of political 'growling, lamp post sniffing and marking' before the French eventually agreed to accept the situation, sell their claims and integrate. Thankfully, perhaps through their long association and history of dealing with such situations, this integration was successful and before long Akaroa had become a pleasant and cosmopolitan European community. They brought with them the rich culture that gives Akaroa its modern-day legacy of fine architecture, place names and a wonderful sense of community and friendship.

Banks Peninsula

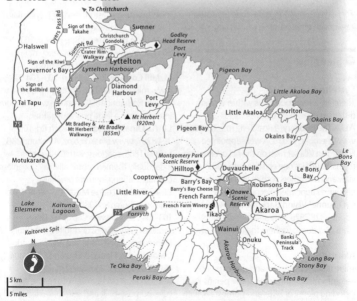

Sights Akaroa is a very pretty little place with a lovely atmosphere, made even more intriguing by its French names. But perhaps before getting properly acquainted with the place you should take in the superb view of the locality from the hill to the south, via Rue Jolie and then Onuku Road (lighthouse road). Given the village's rich history it's worth paying a visit to **Akaroa Museum** ① *corner of Rue Lavaud and Rue Balguerie, T03-304 1013, daily Nov-Apr 1030-1630, May-Oct 1030-1600, $4, child $1.* A 20-minute film provides a fine introduction backed up with collections focusing on early Maori, whaling, the French connection and the British succession. The **Custom House** at Daly's Wharf that dates from 1852, the old **Court House** and the **Langlois-Eteveneaux House** nearby, are three fine remnants that are an adjunct to the main museum.

Given the fact it is little dolphins wearing smiley faces and not 'old Europeans' wearing berets that are equally (if not more) popular around these parts it is no surprise to find an attraction dedicated solely to them. In late 2005 the Blackcat Group (see page 498) opened the **Dolphin Discovery Centre** ① *Main Wharf, T03-304 7641, www.blackcat.co.nz,* in tune with most modern eco-centres the emphasis is on interactive, state-of-the-art displays with, in this instance, a particular focus on the rare and endangered Hector's dolphins, which are only found around the South Island of New Zealand.

Of more convivial and contemporary interest is **Barry's Bay Cheese** ① *Main Rd, Barry's Bay (at the head of Akaroa Harbour), T03-304 5809, www.barrysbaycheese.co.nz.* This small family-owned operation makes a fine array of cheeses between October and May, and visitors are welcome to watch the process (alternate days between October and April) and sample the varieties, before purchasing their favourites in the shop.

⊙ Banks Peninsula listings

For Sleeping and Eating price codes and other relevant information, see Essentials pages 44-50.

⊖ Sleeping

Lyttelton *p494*
There are a few good B&Bs within walking distance of the town centre.
AL-A The Rookery, 9 Ross Terr, T03-328 8038, www.therookery.co.nz. A well- appointed Edwardian villa set high on the hill overlooking the harbour. Has one en suite with harbour view and two others with shared bathroom, all beautifully appointed. Recommended.
C-D Tunnel Vision Backpackers, 44 London Rd, T03-328 7576. Tidy and friendly, doubles, twins and dorms, right in the heart of town.

Akaroa *p495*
There is some attractive and more remote accommodation throughout the peninsula, including plenty of B&Bs and homestays, with most boasting a historic and/or French flair. The VIC has full listings.
LL Maison de la Mer, 1 Rue Benoit, T03-304 8907, www.maisondelamer.co.nz. Elegant 5-star B&B on the waterfront.
LL Mill Cottage, Rue Grehan, T03-304 8007, www.millcottage.co.nz. Another good 5-star option. Romantic 1850s cottage with modern interior, set in a large peaceful garden.
LL-AL Oinako Lodge, 99 Beach Rd, T03-304 8787, www.oinako.co.nz. A historic B&B, built in 1865, spacious, with 6 elegant individually themed rooms all in a convenient central location. Gourmet breakfast.
LL-AL Tresori Lodge Motel, corner of Rue Jolie and Church St, T0800-273747/ T03-304 7500, www.tresori.co.nz. Offers spotless classy studios and suites, in a distinctly French style. Good value and recommended.
L Maison des Fleurs, 6 Church St, T03-304 7804/T0800-6952000, www.maisonde fleurs.co.nz. A stark contrast to the others: cute, purpose-built and self-contained.

L Wilderness House, 42 Rue Grehan T03-304 7517, www.wildernesshouse.co.nz. Historic B&B set in a beautiful garden, all 4 rooms are en suite.

L-A Akaroa Village Inn, opposite the main Wharf at 81 Beach Rd, T0800-695 2000/ T03-304 7421, www.akaroavillageinn.co.nz. In a central position, this French-influenced hotel offers standard rooms or self-catering luxury apartments, most with views over the harbour. Swimming pool, spa and bike hire.

AL Linton (Giant's House), 68 Rue Balguerie, T03-304 7501, www.linton.co.nz. Decorated with quirky artworks by local Josie Martin and complete with artists' garden, this residence offers 2 spacious, comfortable doubles, one with conservatory, the other with a 'boat bed'. A memorable stay is guaranteed. Recommended.

AL-A Akaroa Criterion Motel, 75 Rue Jolie, T03-3047775, www.holidayakaroa.com. Spacious luxury studios and rooms close to the village centre.

A L'Hotel Motel, 75 Beach Rd (wharf end), T03-304 7559, www.lhotel.co.nz. Good units overlooking the harbour and a licensed restaurant downstairs.

Backpacker hostels

C-D Bon Accord Backpackers, 57 Rue Lavaud, T03-304 7782, www.bon-accord.co.nz. Tidy dorms and cosy, good-value doubles. Well located and peaceful. Ask about the house's interesting history. Bookings advised.

C-D Chez-la-Mer Backpackers, 50 Rue Lavaud, T03-304 7024, www.chezlamer.co.nz. Equally well placed and a pleasant historic house with a secluded garden. It offers dorms, doubles, twins and singles, is well-equipped throughout and has its own backpacker boat for fishing trips and 4WD tours.

C-D Double Dutch, 32 Chorlton Rd, Okains Bay, T03-304 7229, www.doubledutch.co.nz. An absolute gem of a place in a rural location 20-min from Akaroa. Small, modern 7-bed hostel on a 8-ha farm. Shared, twin and doubles, one with en suite. Excellent hosts. If

you want a few days of peace and quiet, look no further. Recommended.

C-D Pohatu Penguin Reserve Batch, Pohatu-Flea Bay, T03-304 8552, www.pohatu.co.nz. In keeping with the nature of the peninsula and owned by **Pohatu Adventure Tours**, this a self-contained bach in a sublimely peaceful setting near the beach. Part of their nature tour package. Recommended.

Motorcamps and campsites

B-D Akaroa Top Ten Holiday Park, off Morgan Rd at entrance to village, T0800-727525/T03-304 7471, www.akaroa-holidaypark.co.nz. It is the best-equipped motorcamp with flats, cabins, powered/tent sites and views across the harbour. The camp kitchen is very small.

⊙ Eating

Lyttelton *p494*
There are plenty of places to eat in Lyttelton, with most on Norwich Quay or London Rd.

♈ **Volcano Café and Lava Bar**, corner of London and Canterbury sts, T03-328 7077, www.volcano.co.nz. Brightly coloured, good traditional blackboard menu and good coffee.

♈ **Satchmos**, 8 London St, T03-328 8348. Daily 1000-2100. Wide-ranging good-value menu, attractive courtyard garden and, as the name suggests, some mellow sounds. Even the pizzas are named after music legends.

♈ **Lyttelton Coffee Company**, 29 London St, T03-328 8096. Boutique café with excellent coffee and value all day menu.

Akaroa *p495*
Given the French influence, Akaroa offers some fine restaurants and cafés, but many are subject to seasonal hours.

♈ **Bully Hayes Restaurant and Bar**, 57 Beach Rd, T03-304 7533, www.bullyhayes.co.nz. Daily 0800-2100. Enjoys a fine reputation particularly for its seafood.

₦₦ **Le Hotel, Le Restaurant Le Bar**, 75 Beach Rd (wharf end), T03-304 7559, www.lhotel.co.nz. Conveniently located on the waterfront, open fire in winter.
₦₦ **Harbour 71**, 71 Beach Rd, T03-304 7659. Open for lunch and dinner, licensed. Traditional option with fine harbour views. Fresh fish recommended.
₦₦ **Ma Maison**, 2 Rue Jolie, T03-304 7668. Traditional food, again with harbour views.
₦₦ **L'Escargot Rouge Deli to Go**, 67 Beach Rd, T03-304 8774. Excellent French style breakfasts and a large selection of all the favourite French sweet and savoury items. Recommended.
₦ **Turenne Coffee Shop**, corner of Rue Balguerie and Rue Lavaud, T03-304 7005. Daily 0700-1800. Seems to be the most popular daytime café and has good coffee, light snacks, legendary muffins and internet.

● Pubs, bars and clubs

Lyttelton *p494*
There is no shortage of pubs – it is a port after all. London Rd is the focus.
Wunderbar 19, T03-328 8818. Aesthetically the most memorable, it offers regular live acts and is deservingly popular.
Monster Bar, 29 London St, T03-328 9166, www.monsterbar.co.nz. Good atmosphere, cocktail specials and also 'Yakitori' cuisine, which in essence is meat, seafood and vegetables on bamboo skewers with salt and sweet yakitori sauce and seasoning.

▲ Activities and tours

Lyttelton *p494*
Cruises
Several cruises leave from the port from vessels both old and new.
Black Cat Group, T03-3047641, www.black cat.co.nz. Offers an interesting array of catamaran harbour trips. The 2-hr 'Wildlife Cruise' takes in both sides of the harbour and

out just beyond its entrance, passes some interesting sites on the way including an old whaling station, a shipwreck and the Godley Head Lighthouse. There is usually plenty in the way of wildlife, with the highlight being the tiny and rare Hector's dolphin. Departures are from B Jetty, Lyttelton, at 1330 , from $60, child $25. Note that there is a free shuttle that departs from the Christchurch VIC (I-Site) 35 mins before departure.
Tug Lyttelton Preservation Society, T03-322 8911, www.nzmaritime.co.nz/tug.htm. The 1907 steam tug *Lyttelton*, lovingly restored, has been taking passengers for historical cruises for 28 years. Contact the VIC for details.

Walking and scenic drives
As well as the historical walks around town and those up to the Christchurch (Port Hills) Gondola, the **Crater Rim Walkway** (19 km, 4 hrs) provides a longer and spectacular walk with memorable views across the Banks Peninsula and the Canterbury Plains to the Southern Alps. The VIC (I-Site) can provide directions and all the relevant leaflets. At the very least return to Christchurch via the Summit Road.

Akaroa *p495*
The **Akaroa Adventure Centre** (see Kayaking, below) rents out kayaks, surf boards and mountain bikes.
   If you fancy exploring the many bays of the peninsula yourself perhaps a smart scooter is another option, with hire available from the **La Rochelle Motel**, T03-304 8762, 2 hrs from $40, full-day $90. Mountain bikes from $15 per day.

Harbour/wildlife cruises and nature tours
BlackCat Cruises, T03-304 7641, www.blackcat.co.nz, offer two Akaroa based cruises: **Dolphins up Close** a 3-hr excursion to encounter the rare Hector's dolphin, from $130, child $110 (viewing only $70/35), trips depart the main wharf at 0600, 0830, 1130 and 1330; and **Nature Cruise**, a 2-hr scenic/ wildlife cruise. While the highlight is the

probable sighting of Hector's dolphin, you can also see little blue penguins, spotted shags and fur seals, from $65, child $25.

Akaroa Seal Colony Safari, T03-304 7255, www.sealtours.co.nz. An interesting 2½-hr road trip via the rim of the crater to a fur seal colony on the eastern bays, from $70, child $50. Trips leave from the VIC twice daily.

Pohatu Adventure Tours (Shireen Helps), T03-304 8552, www.pohatu.co.nz. Offers 2 tours: a full day-tour of historical and scenic sites with a sea kayaking and snorkelling option, from $75; or a 3-hr specialist tour of the Penguin Reserve, from $66. For $99 you can combine the above with a 4WD tour and one nights accommodation in a great beachside setting. Recommended.

Kayaking

For independent kayak hire consult the VIC.
Pohatu Adventure Tours, (above) offers guided sea kayaking and snorkelling from $75.
Mafi's Kayak Trips, Onuku Farm Hostel, T03-304 7066, www.onukufarm.com. Entertaining trips with possible encounters of Hectors dolphin, daily from $45. Also offers excellent accommodation.

Walking

The 2- or 4-day, 35-km **Banks Peninsula Track**, T03-304 7612, www.bankstrack.co.nz, is a popular tramp across private farmland, the hills and outer bays, and is recommended. It is very much an off-the-beaten-track experience, with great huts provided for accommodation. The track is open from 31 Oct-Apr and costs from $230 for the 4-day trip and $150 for the 2-day. Cost includes an introductory talk, booklet,

transport to the first hut and accommodation. You must take your own food. For other day-walk options on the peninsula contact the VIC in Akaroa.

Tuatara Tours, T0800-377378/ T03-962 3280, www.tuatara tours.co.nz. Offers a 39-km walk from Christchurch to Akaroa. You take the gondola to the crater rim, then walk 9 km along the summit track before descending into Lyttelton to visit the Timeball Station. The first night is then spent in Diamond Harbour. Day 2 sees you negotiating 19 km of ridge trails with expansive views and another comfortable night at the private Pentrip Lodge. Day 3 takes in a further 11 km of track before you are delivered by boat to Akaroa. The 3-day/ night package costs $1486 all-inclusive.

Eastern Bays Scenic Mail Run, T03-304 8600. The Eastern Bays Scenic mail run combines an authentic mail delivery with a scenic drive covering 100 km through some of the most beautiful scenery on Banks Peninsula and visiting local attractions like the Barrys Bay Cheese factory and French Farm Winery. Departs Christchurch daily at 0900 and arrives in Akaroa at 1330, from $50.

❶ Directory

Akaroa *p495*

Banks BNZ Bank, opposite the VIC, Mon-Fri 0900-1630, has an ATM. **Internet** Akaroa Library, 141 Rue Jolie, T03-304 8782, Mon-Fri 1030-1600, Sat 1030-1300. **Turenne Coffee Shop**, corner of Rue Balguerie and Rue Lavaud, T03-304 7005. **Useful numbers** Police, T03-304 1030. Doctor, T03-304 7004.

North of Christchurch → Colour map 4, B4/5.

From Christchurch SH1 heads north through the unremarkable settlement of Amberley before reaching the junction with SH7 and the Waipara Valley. The Waipara Valley is one of the country's fastest growing wine regions and now attracts visitors in its own right. From the Waipara SH7 heads northeast, through the Hurunui District to Hanmer Springs and the west coast via the Lewis Pass, while SH1 heads north to Kaikoura and eventually Blenheim. Another road, SH70, leaves SH7 just north of Culverden, offering a scenic short cut from Hanmer Springs to Kaikoura. These routes are known collectively as the (signposted) Alpine Pacific Triangle, which is designed to combine the lesser attraction of the Waipara Valley vineyards with its two star destinations, Hanmer Springs and Kaikoura. Although many people visit Kaikoura (which actually lies in Marlborough, not Canterbury) on their way to Christchurch from the north, this 'triangle' offers an attractive multi-day trip from Christchurch. There is much to see and do in both Hanmer Springs and Kaikoura, but they are very different. In landlocked Hanmer the wealth of activities includes skiing, rafting, horse trekking and, perhaps its speciality, mountain biking. All these activities of course are in addition to the more obvious and soporific attraction of its hot pools in the thermal resort. Kaikoura, in contrast, set on the spectacular northeast coastline and almost miniaturized in the shadow of the Kaikoura mountain ranges, is equally abuzz with activity. But here the emphasis is most definitely in the colder waters of the ocean and its inhabitants. At Kaikoura you can see, and even swim with, an impressive list of the ocean's 'who's who', including albatrosses, seals, dolphins and of course Kaikoura's very own whales. ⏵⏵ *For Sleeping, Eating and other listings, see pages 505-513.*

Hanmer Springs ⬤❷▲❸ ⏵⏵ *pp505-513.*

Hanmer (population 900) has long been popular with Kiwi holiday-seekers, and has only recently come into its own as a top national tourist venue. Its biggest attraction is of course its impressive **Thermal Reserve**, but it is also very popular as a base for mountain biking and walking in the **Hanmer Forest Park** nearby and, in winter, as a base for the **Hanmer** and **Mount Lyford ski fields**. When winter snows lie on the ground or spring rain plays on the puddles, the hot pools are the perfect place to be. Hanmer offers a wide range of modern accommodation, some good restaurants and numerous activities from bungee jumping to horse trekking. The town is particularly beautiful in autumn when the forest and tree-lined streets are flush with golden hues and falling leaves. The name Hanmer derives from the name of Canterbury pioneer Thomas Hanmer, often misspelt.

Ins and outs

Getting there Hanmer Springs is 136 km north of Christchurch and 214 km east of Greymouth. The **Hanmer Shuttle**, T0800-800575, www.akaroabus.co.nz, offers a daily bus service to Hanmer Springs departing Christchurch daily at 0945, from $45. Springs Junction is 95 km west of Hanmer Springs via SH7. There is a service station at Springs Junction with 24-hour EFTPOS.

Tourist information Hanmer Springs VIC (I-Site) ⓘ *in front of the Thermal Reserve off Amuri Av in the centre of the village, T0800-442663/T03-315 7128, www.hanmersprings.co.nz, www.hurunui.com, daily 1000-1700,* has information on DoC walks.

Sights

With all the other activities on offer, a visit to the **Hanmer Springs Thermal Reserve**

① *Amuri Av, T0800-442663/T03-315 7511, daily 1000-2100, $14, child $7 (return pass $18, child $9)*, may not be high on your agenda. However, the reserve is undoubtedly the top attraction. The springs were first discovered by the Europeans in 1859 and later became a commercial venture and public attraction; in 1907, the first facilities and a hotel formed the beginnings of the resort and, subsequently, the town as a whole. The resort has enjoyed an impressive expansion and improvement in recent years, and has various pools including open and landscaped, freshwater, swimming and a children's play pool – all connected by steaming boulder streams. The mineral-rich waters range in temperature from a lukewarm 32°C to a balmy 42°C. Also on site are a massage and beauty clinic, private pools, saunas, a steam room, a licensed café and a picnic area.

Hanmer Springs to the west coast

From Hanmer Springs SH7 crosses the northern ranges of the Great Divide (Southern Alps) to the west coast via the **Lewis Pass, Maruia Springs, Springs Junction** and **Reefton**. Although not as dramatic as Arthur's Pass further to the south (see page 515), it offers some lovely scenery and a few good walking opportunities on the way. It also boasts a mountain with one of the most unusual names in the country. There are many with wonderful names, but frankly **Mons Sex Millia** has to take the prize.

At the top of the Hope River Valley from Hanmer, the road skirts the borders of the **Lake Sumner Forest Park** and begins to follow the Lewis River to its headwaters and the saddle known as Lewis Pass (864 m). In pre-European times the Ngai Tahu Maori of Canterbury used this route to access the west coast in search of greenstone (*pounamu*). Having negotiated the pass on their return, they are said to have dispensed with their slaves – alas not with a 'thanks lads, see you next year', but a brutal death followed by a feast of their various bodily parts. A valley known as **Cannibal Gorge** remains testament to this rather grim form of the early 'transport café'.

The pass itself was named in 1860 after pioneer surveyor Henry Lewis. Ironically, Henry's daughter Eleanor married Arthur Dudley Dobson who surveyed 'Arthur's' Pass. But it doesn't end there. Arthur's sister then married the geologist and surveyor Julian Von Haast who is accredited with much of the exploration, survey work and many place names on the west coast.

Lake Sumner Forest Park and the Lewis Pass offer some excellent walks, which are outlined in various DoC leaflets, including the *Lewis Pass Region* broadsheet, which is available from the Hanmer VIC (I-Site). The lichen-covered beech forests are particularly superb in this region and well worth further investigation.

The five-day **St James Walkway** that begins near the Lewis Pass summit car park (and infamous Cannibal Gorge) is particularly good. There is a network of DoC huts, and the moderate track is best negotiated in summer or autumn. Just beyond the Lewis Pass, heading west, is the oasis of **Maruia Springs**, a small thermal resort with hot pools, accommodation, a restaurant and a bar. It is a perfect stop for tired trampers. A further 21 km west is **Springs Junction**, the only significant settlement between Hanmer and Reefton, with accommodation, a café, and also a petrol station.

Kaikoura ☺️❼🅰️😊🅲 ➻ *pp505-513*.

So you want to see Moby Dick and friends? Well, you have certainly come to the right spot. Kaikoura is a place that is not only aesthetically stunning but one that has some of the best sea creatures in the world. They are all here: Moby, Flipper, Keiko, Jaws – you might

Modern-day whaling in Kaikoura

The whale-watching experience is a wonderful mix of expectation, unpredictability and awe. Kaikoura is home to its own pod of **sperm whales** – the species you are most likely to see. Although it is a complex social set up and much is still not known, it is probably one or two of the young males from these resident bachelor pods that you will see. A bull male can weigh as much as 50 tonnes and be up to 20 m in length. Other whale species that are seen regularly include **humpbacks, rights** and orcas. If you are exceptionally lucky you may also see the endangered and truly industrial-sized **blue whale**.

Your boat trip to 'hunt down' and 'encounter' the whales is a fascinating and well-orchestrated performance of hydrophonics and simple 'eye-spy'. However, before all the action takes place you are invited to watch a new and very clever state-of-the-art computer graphic that shows the incredible depths of the Kaikoura Trench and explains why the whales are so drawn to it. Once out in the bay proper, a combination of local knowledge and hydrophonics is used to locate the whales. It is very exciting and timing is all-important as they are known to surface for around three minutes. This is your big and brief chance. With such unpredictability and in such a frenzy of expectation people-watching can be as much fun as watching the whales. When the great leviathan is spotted and the word is given, everybody jumps from their seat and clambers to get that illusive National Geographic shot from the decks. On rough days this can be quite riotous, with copious bouts of unintentional head-butting and hair-pulling. Only a few poor souls are left strapped to their seat, their vision of a whale long lost at the bottom of a sick-bag. On calm days it is much more orderly and you will get a better view of the whale's vast bulk. Whales are a bit like icebergs: for all you can see above the surface, there is an awful lot more beneath. However, regardless of conditions, what you are guaranteed to see is the point when the whales dive, flipping their tail in the air and descending gracefully like a hot knife through butter, back into the depths. It is this vision that is so engrained in our imagination. You can expect to see up to three whales on each trip, however, there is of course no guarantee and you will receive a refund if the trip is unsuccessful.

even bump into Marine Boy having a beer in the local boozer or a mermaid on the bus. Okay, not quite. But for the wildlife enthusiast the Kaikoura Coast is second only to the Otago Peninsula for richness and accessibility to some of New Zealand's biggest and most famous wildlife icons. This is due to the topography and depth of the ocean floor: just south of Kaikoura, a trough comes unusually close to the coastline creating an upsurge of nutritious plankton soup, giving rise to the many creatures with which we are more familiar further up the food chain. At the very top of course, on the ocean throne, is the majestic and much victimized king of them all – the whale.

But even if you came to Kaikoura thinking that whales was a small and fine rugby-playing nation somewhere in Britain, or indeed that seals clap and throw beach balls to each other, you cannot fail to be impressed. From the azure waters that surround the beautiful Kaikoura Peninsula, backed by the snow-capped peaks of the Kaikoura Ranges, you can get up close and personal with them all, from whales and dolphins to seals, albatrosses and even sharks. So the place is very special and even before you arrive there is a sense of excitement.

Ins and outs

Getting there Kaikoura is 187 km north of Christchurch, 129 km south of Blenheim (154 km Picton) on SH1, and 133 km northwest of Hanmer Springs via SH70. By bus, Kaikoura is served from Christchurch-Blenheim-Picton by **Intercity**, 123 Worcester St, T03-319 5641 (book at the VIC); **Nakedbus**, www.nakedbus, daily; **Atomic Shuttles**, T03-322 8883, www.atomictravel.co.nz, daily; and **K-Bus**, T03-358 8355, www.southernlinkbus.co.nz. The fare to Christchurch or Blenheim costs from $25.

By train, Kaikoura is served by **TranzCoastal**, T0800-872467, www.tranzscenic.co.nz, daily (Christchurch 1528, from $68; Blenheim-Picton 0954, from $108). The train station is on Clarence St. The VIC (I-Site) caters for all transport bookings and enquiries.

Getting around Kaikoura Shuttle, T03-319 6166/T0800-766962, offers 1- or 2-hr tours of the region. There are scheduled or on-demand shuttles to both the Hanmer and Lyford ski fields, for $20-30. For details contact the VIC (I-Site).

Tourist information Kaikoura VIC (I-Site) ① *West End, T03-319 5641, www.kaikoura.co.nz, daily 0800-1800 (Jun-Aug 0900-1700)*, provides information and arranges bookings for accommodation and transport. There is also a 20-min precursory audio-visual presentation about the local environment and wildlife shown every hour or on demand, $3, child $1. All DoC information is also held here. Trees for Travellers, www.treesfortravellers.co.nz, is a Kaikoura based incentive that allows visitors to help with local native bush restoration. You can plant your own natural memento from $20. T03-3197148, ask for details at the I SITE Visitor Centre.

Sights

Of course most of what you have probably come to see lies beneath the waves and has flippers, but Kaikoura also offers a number of land-based features worthy of investigation. Paramount is the **Kaikoura Peninsula** that juts out into the ocean like a well-weathered head. The cliff-top and shoreline walkways, which link the northern and southern settlements of Kaikoura, cross the head of the peninsula and offer superb coastal scenery (see page 512). A good spot to get an overall impression of the town, the peninsula and its mountain backdrop is from the **lookout** just off Scarborough Terrace (off SH1 between the northern and southern settlements).

There are three historical venues of note. The first is the **Kaikoura District Museum** ① *14 Ludstone Rd, T03-319 7440, Mon-Fri 1230-1600, Sat-Sun 1400-1600, $3, child $0.50*, was established in 1971 and offers an interesting insight into the early Maori and whaling activities. If the weather closes in and you cannot get out on to the water it can provide a good activity option and help pass the time. **Fyffe House** ① *62 Avoca St, near the Old Wharf, T03-319 5835, 30-min guided tours Thu-Mon 1000-1700, $7*, is the remnants of the Waiopuka whaling station dating from 1842. The **'Maori Leap' Cave'** ① *2 km south, T03-319 5023, from $12, child $5*, was only discovered this century and is a sea-formed limestone cave featuring all the usual karst scenery. It can be visited on a 40-minute guided tour.

While in the area of the cave you might like to visit the **Kaikoura Winery** ① *just south of town, T03-319 7966, www.kaikourawinery.co.nz*. There are hourly tours (from $15), underground cellars and tastings ($25 with transport from the VIC/I-Site).

Kaikoura

To 22 23

To 2 17 21, Blenheim & Picton

6

7

Ludstone Rd

Rorrisons Rd

Lyell Creek

Kaikoura Helicopters

11

Whale Watch Kaikoura

Beach Rd (Hwy 1)

3

8

Kiwi St

Gray St

Davidson

Kaikoura District Museum

To Airport, Christchurch, Hammer Springs, Maori Leap Cave, Kaikoura Winery & 19 20

Fyffe Chance Haven

Bayview St

Adelphi Terr

West End

3

@ Kodak Express

Supermarket

6

2

Dolphin Encounter

Hastings St

Churchill St

13

Deal St

4 5

i

12

Takahanga

(Hwy 1)

Killarney

18

Torquay St

Esplanade

14

Yarmouth

Pacific Ocean

South Bay Parade

Scenic Reserve

Scarborough St

Brighton

Torquay St

Ramsgate

Kotare Pl

Takahe

Peninsula Walkway

Nga Niho Park

Margate

1

5

South Bay

Scenic Reserve

Konuku Rd

Kea

Lookout

24

Inari

Dover St

10

9

4 1

Wakatu

Avoca St

16

Tui

Waka

Austin St

Cromer

Endeavour

Looters on

Ward St

Peninsula Walkway

Lower Ward

Fyffe House

8

Kaikoura Peninsula

Peninsula Walkway

To Point Kearn Car Park

25

🛏 Sleeping

Hanmer Springs *p500*

There is plenty of choice in Hanmer to suit all budgets, with most of the options being modern, well-appointed and within walking distance of the town centre. You are advised to book ahead in mid-summer and at weekends in the winter ski-season.

LL Braemar Lodge and Spa, T03-315 7555, www.selectbraemarlodge.com. A fine modern luxury lodge on a hillside 9 km from the town that has recently undergone a $16 million redevelopment and been labelled perhaps rather pretentiously as a 'super luxury lodge'. The result is nevertheless impressive with beautifully appointed rooms, spa, holistic healing centre and excellent cuisine.

LL-L Cheltenham House B&B, 13 Cheltenham St, T03-315 7545, www.cheltenham.co.nz. Well-located, with 6 spacious suites from super king to queen with en suite bath.

LL-AL Heritage Hotel and Resort, 1 Conical Hill Rd, T0800-368888/T03-315 0060, www.heritage hotels.co.nz. Modern and ideally located overlooking the town centre. Rooms range from the honeymoon suite to standard, with self-contained stand-alone villas also available. It has all the usual facilities including a good restaurant, bar and a swimming pool. 2 mins from the hot pools.

L Hanmer View B&B, 8 Oregon Heights (very end of Conical Hill Rd), T03-315 7947, www.hanmerview.co.nz. Set high on Conical Hill above the town this place offers memorable views to complement a warm welcome and 3 tidy en suites.

AL-A Glenalvon Lodge Motels and B&B, 29 Amuri Av, T03-315 7475, www.glenalvon.com. A cheaper and friendly option. It has pleasant rooms with private bath. Self-contained modern units are also available.

200 metres
200 yards

Sleeping 🛏

Admiral Court Motel **16**
Albatross
 Backpackers **18**
Alpine Pacific
 Holiday Park **3**
Anchor Inn **1**
Bay Cottages **25**
Blue Seas **5**
Campsites **20**
Clifftop Apartment **9**
Dolphin Lodge **4**
Donegal House **23**
Dusky Lodge **7**
Fyffe Country Lodge **19**
Hapuku Lodge **2**
Kaikoura (Maui) YHA **10**
Kaikoura Top Ten
 Holiday Park **11**
Lemon Tree Lodge **15**
Lyell Creek Lodge **17**
Mediterranean **21**
Miharotia **24**
Nikau Lodge **12**
Old Convent **22**
Sunrise Lodge **6**
The Point B&B **8**
Topspot Backpackers **13**
White Morph **14**

Eating 🍽

Adelphi Bar &
 Restaurant **3**
Craypot Café & Bar **2**
Green Dolphin **4**
Hislop's Café **8**
Pier Hotel Pub & Café **1**
Sonic on the Rocks
 Bar & Café **5**
Why Not Café **6**

Motels

Motels here are generally of a high standard.
AL Clear Ridge, corner of Chisholm Cres and Jacks Pass Rd, T0800-555596/ T03-315 5144, www.clearridge.co.nz. Modern luxury motel offering classy spa bath suites, all a short walk from the town centre.

AL Tussock Peak Motor Lodge, corner of Amuri and Leamington sts, T0800-8877625/ T03-315 5191, www.tussockpeak.co.nz. Another modern luxury option in the heart of town, a stone's throw from the thermal reserve.

AL-A Alpine Lodge, 1 Harrogate St, T0800-993377/T03-315 7311, www.alpinelodge motel.co.nz. Modern lodge-style, again well-placed.

AL-A Greenacres Chalets and Apartments, 84 Conical Hill Rd, T03-315 7125, www.green acresmotel.co.nz. Modern, with self-contained chalets/apartments overlooking the town. Spa.

AL-A Scenic Views, 10 Amuri Av, T03-315 7419, www.hanmerscenicviews.co.nz. Just at the entrance to the town, this place offers peace and quiet, and mountain views.

B-D Kakapo Lodge YHA, 14 Amuri Av, just as you come in to the village on the left, T03-315 7472, www.kakapolodge.co.nz. Modern and spacious hostel but lacking in atmosphere. It offers the full range of rooms including motel-style en suites and has good kitchen facilities, internet and parking.

B-D Le Gite Backpackers, 3 Devon St, to the west off Jacks Pass Rd, T03-315 5111, www.legite.co.nz. Described as a boutique backpacker hostel, it is indeed cosy with tidy doubles in separate garden chalets, dorms, polished wood floors, TV lounge with log burner, internet and off-street parking.

C-D Hanmer Backpackers, 41 Conical Hill Rd, T03-315 7196, www.hanmerbackpackers.co.nz. Well-established backpacker hostel, just north of the town centre. Friendly, with dorms and good-value doubles. Open fire, high-speed internet and off-street parking.

Motorcamps and campsites

Both places have flats, cabins, powered/tent sites and clean modern facilities.

B-D Alpine Adventure Tourist Park, 200 Jacks Pass Rd, south of the thermal resort, T03-315 7112, www.aatouristpark.co.nz. A good walk from the town centre but nonetheless an excellent choice with spacious sheltered sites, excellent value cabins and good facilities. Recommended.

B-D Mountain View Top Ten, at the entrance to town, T03-315 7113, www.mountain viewtop10.co.nz. All the usual Top Ten quality and about 500m from the hot pools.

Hanmer Springs to the west coast *p501*

L-AL Maruia Springs Thermal Resort, T03-523 8840, www.maruia.co.nz. Has lovely luxury/standard studio and family units. 2 licensed restaurants, one of which is traditional/Kiwi, the other Japanese. The tariff includes unlimited access to the thermal pools. Public access to the hot pools daily 0900-2100, from $18, child $8. Private pools available 1100-1700, from $25 per 45-mins.

A Lewis Pass Motels, SH7, 16 km from Maruia Springs Thermal Resort, T03-523 8863, www.lewis-pass.co.nz. Modern self-contained units in a pleasant country setting.

B-C Alpine Motor Inn and Café, Springs Junction, T03-523 8813, www.alpine motorinn.co.nz. Offers studio units and a separate budget chalet for backpackers. Attached is a café and shop selling light snacks, daily 0800-1930. Internet.

Kaikoura *p501, map p504*

There is plenty of choice in Kaikoura, with motels being the dominant force, but there are also plenty of fine B&Bs. Local farmstays are another option often overlooked. You are advised to book ahead in mid-summer; the VIC (I-Site) has full listings.

LL-L Fyffe Country Lodge, SH1 (south), T03-319 6869, www.fyffecountrylodge.com. Luxury accommodation in mud-brick, native timber lodge surrounded by English-style gardens. There is a range of studio en suites and a romantic in-house gourmet licensed restaurant with open fire, specializing in seafood, beef, lamb and Pacific Rim cuisine.

LL-L Hapuku Lodge and Tree Houses, Hapuku Rd (12 km north of Kaikoura), T03-319 6559, www.hapukulodge.com. A contemporary complex offering 4 elegant en suites and 5 luxury 'tree houses' with ocean views. The emphasis is very much on natural materials and a scattering of original New Zealand art. There is also an in-house restaurant with a focus on local produce. All in all it equates to a memorable stay and something quite unique. Recommended.

L-A Old Convent, Mt Fyffe Rd, T03-319 6603, www.theoldconvent.co.nz. In a quiet setting and full of character. This former convent, built for French nuns in 1911, now offers an unusual B&B option. Here you can imagine yourself as Mother Superior taking up her former quarters, or try behaving yourself in a choice of former nuns' cells. The chapel is now a cosy guest lounge with log fire. Although a French-style dinner is available you would do better to sample the eateries in town. Internet, off-street parking.

AL-A Donegal House, Schoolhouse Rd, T03-319 5083, www.donegalhouse.co.nz. Has a strong Irish influence and 13 tidy en suites. However, what makes the place special are the grounds and the Irish bar/restaurant.

AL-A The Point B&B, 85 Fyffe Quay, T03-319 5422, www.pointbnb.co.nz. A deservingly popular B&B on a working sheep farm and within a short walk of the peninsula. In spring and summer you can even get involved with lamb feeding and take part in the daily sheep shearing show ($10). Accommodation consists of two nicely appointed queen en suites.

B&Bs and apartments

There is a scattering of fine B&Bs and self-contained apartments on the peninsula itself, all offering spectacular views.

L-AL Lemon Tree Lodge 31 Adelphi Terr, T03-319 7464, www.lemontree.co.nz. A boutique B&B that caters especially for couples or single independent travellers. Renovated 2-storey house with 4 tidy rooms, all with private deck or balcony and good

attention to detail. Outdoor hot tub. Caring, experienced and well-travelled owners.

L-AL Miharotia, 274 Scarborough St, T03-319 7497, www.miharotia.co.nz. Modern boutique B&B set overlooking the town and Kaikoura Range. There are 4 contemporary guestrooms, one king en suite with a 4-poster and 3 queen en suites all with private patios. The long-term resident owners also possess a wealth of local information especially regarding the area's fishy residents.

L-AL Nikau Lodge, 53 Deal St, T03-319 6973, www.nikaulodge.com. Has 5 en suites and a room with private bathroom. Internet, Sky TV and good views across town.

AL Clifftop Apartment 5 Dover Terr, T03-319 6649. A modern, spacious timber home with a magnificent outlook. Value twins and doubles.

B Bay Cottages, 29 South Bay Parade, South Bay, T03-319 5506, baycottages@xtra.co.nz. Tidy modern and good-value self-contained cottages sleeping up to 4.

Motels

There are almost 20 motels to choose from, with most being along the Esplanade or heading north out of town on Beach St, SH1.

LL-L White Morph, 92-94 Esplanade, T03-319 5014, www.whitemorph.co.nz.

L-AL Admiral Court Motel, 16 Avoca St, near the wharf, T03-319 5525, www.kaikoura motel.co.nz. A good choice, a short walk from the start of the coastal track.

L-AL Anchor Inn, 208 Esplanade, T03-319 5426, www.anchor-inn.co.nz. Recommended.

AL Mediterranean, 239 Beach Rd, T03-319 6776, medmotel@xtra.co.nz. Slightly cheaper option north of the town centre.

AL-A Blue Seas, 222 Esplanade, T03-319 5441, blue.seas@xtra.co.nz.

Backpacker hostels

There is no shortage of hostels in the town. In fact there are so many quality establishments it's a hard choice.

B Lyell Creek Lodge, at the northern end of town, 193 Beach Rd, T03-319 6277, lyellcreeklodge@yahoo.co.nz. A great place for couples looking for value and peace. It has 5 modern tidy rooms, a twin and double with en suite and 3 rooms with shared bathroom. All have TV and there is a cosy lounge.

C-D Sunrise Lodge, 74 Beach Rd, T03-319 7444. Small hostel near the centre of town secluded and comfortable. Well known for its warm welcome and early morning cray fishing trips with the owner. Definitely one of those places where one night can quickly turn to three. Free pick-ups and bike hire.

B-D Dusky Lodge, 67 Beach Rd, 3 mins to the West End, T03-319 5959, www.dusky lodge.com. Recently expanded, it is modern, spacious and friendly with dorms, twins and good-value en suite doubles with TV. Facilities include internet, spa, heated pool, sauna, open fire, off-street parking and bike hire. Another nice touch is the authentic Thai cuisine served al fresco beside the pool daily from 1700.

B-D Kaikoura (Maui) YHA, 270 Esplanade, T03-319 5931. The best sea and mountain views, it has dorms, twins and doubles and a good atmosphere, and is worth the 10-min walk from the West End.

B-D Dolphin Lodge Backpackers, 15 Deal St, T03-319 5842, www.dolphinlodge.co.nz. Another small, homely option with full compliment of rooms including one double en suite. A deck overlooking the ranges, spa, log fire and the odd hammock add to the appeal and relaxing atmosphere.

B-D Topspot Backpackers, 22 Deal St, T03-319 5540, topspot@xtra.co.nz. Very tidy, with dorms and doubles. It runs good-value $60 seal-swimming trips.

C-D Albatross Backpackers, 1 Torquay St, T03-319 6090, www.albatross-kaikoura.co.nz. A little further west in the old telephone exchange on a quiet suburban street. Good attention to detail and a warm welcome for guests. Wide range of spotless, themed rooms (including a self-contained option) and good facilities, not to mention some cool music that complements a laid-back atmosphere. Internet and off-street parking.

Motorcamps and campsites
There are also a number of basic beachside campsites (**D**) on the coastal roads south of Kaikoura. For information call the local council on T03-319 5348.

AL-D Alpine Pacific Holiday Park, 69 Beach Rd, T03-319 6275, www.alpine- pacific.co.nz. If the **Top Ten** is full, or for a quieter option, try this very friendly place.

A-D Kaikoura Top Ten Holiday Park, 34 Beach Rd, T03-319 5362, www.kaikoura holidaypark.co.nz. The best motorpark, only 3 mins from the town centre and the beach. Modern facilities, motel units, en suite units, cabins and powered/tent sites.

❼ Eating

Hanmer Springs *p500*
There is a scattering of cafés along Amuri Av, Conical Hill Rd and in the Mall, all of which are quite similar in fare and value. ₹₹₹-₹₹ **Heritage Hotel**, see Sleeping, above, T03-315 7021. Breakfast 0730, lunch 1200- 1430 and dinner from 1800. A la carte and buffet breakfast, lunch and dinner in elegant surroundings.

₹₹ **Alpine Village Inn**, Jack's Pass Rd, T03-315 7005. Mon-Fri 1100-2130, Sat-Sun 0900-2130. The local pub. Hearty, value pub food.

₹₹ **Malabar**, Alpine Pacific Centre, 5 Conical Hill Rd, T03-315 7745. Daily from 1800. A fine mix of Indian and Malaysian in a casual setting. Takeaway service.

₹₹ **Robbie's Restaurant and Bar**, near the Thermal Resort at 2 Jack's Pass Rd, T03-315 7631. Daily from 1730. Lots of character, it specializes in affordable pub-style cuisine.

₹₹ **Wai Ariki Nature Park Cafe**, 108 Rippingale Rd (off Argelins Rd that bisects the golf course) T03-315 7772, www.waiariki-naturepark.co.nz. Tue-Sat 1000-1700. While adults can indulge in a coffee or light snack the kids can come face to face with a llama or highland cow.

₹ **Powerhouse**, 8 Jack's Pass Rd, T03-3155252. Best of the café options.

Kaikoura *p501, map p504*

There are plenty of affordable options for both lunch and dinner, with most specializing in seafood.

There are 2 supermarkets: **Dreaver's Four Square**, West End, T03-319 5332; and further out (north) **New World**, 124 Beach Rd.

Craypot Café and Bar, 70 West End, T03-319 6027, www.craypot.co.nz. A good place to try crayfish at an affordable price.

Donegal House, Mt Fyffe Rd, T03-319 5083. Daily 1100-1400 and 1800-2100. In a lovely setting, with an Irish touch.

Fyffe Country Lodge, south on SH1, T03-319 6869. Daily for lunch and dinner. Good seafood and a fine view (especially after a late whale-watch). Cosy evening dining.

The Green Dolphin, 12 Avoca St, at the far end of the Esplanade, T03-519 6666. Daily in summer lunch and dinner, Tue-Sun dinner only in winter. A firm seafood favourite serving such delights as scallops on kumara mash.

Adelphi Bar and Restaurant, 26 Westend, T03-319 6555. Recently refurbished pub/restaurant. Sit al fresco under the giant whale mural – a great photo opportunity.

Hislop's Café, 33 Beach Rd, T03-319 6971. Daily for lunch and dinner, closed Tue evenings in winter. The place to find wholefoods and the best vegetarian dishes.

Pier Hotel Pub and Café, 1 Avoca St, T03-319 5037. Daily from 1700. Combine a coastal walk to the wharf (1 km) with good pub-style grub, a fine atmosphere and views. Indoor and outdoor seating. Local seafood recommended.

Sonic on the Rocks Bar and Café, 93 West End, T03-319 6414. Daily 1000-late. The best place for evening entertainment, with live bands; the main backpacker hostel hangout. It also serves a fine value meal.

Why Not Café, 66 West End, T03-319 6486. 0600-2100 in summer and 0600-1800 in winter. Recommended for its coffee.

▲ Activities and tours

Hanmer Springs *p500*

There's plenty to choose from, with mountain biking and skiing being the most prominent. **Hanmer Springs Adventure Centre (HSAC)**, 20 Conical Hill Rd, T03-315 7233, www.hanmeradventure.co.nz. Daily. Wide range of activities, mountain biking a speciality. Independent hire of mountain bikes, scooters, motorbikes (ATV adventures from $99), fishing tackle, inline skates and ski equipment, also available. **Thrillseekers Adventure Centre (TAC)**, 9 km south of the town at the Waiau River Bridge, T03-315 7046, www.thrillseeker.co.nz. Offers a 35-m bridge bungee, which is a 'light taster' for the higher jumps in Queenstown (from $145), as well as jet boating and rafting.

Fishing

There is excellent local fishing, and the VIC (I-Site) sells licences ($21 per day) and lists local venues and guides. A half-day will cost about $300.

Flightseeing

Hanmer Springs Helicopters, T0800-888308, www.hanmerhelicopters.co.nz. Offers 8-min to 1-hr trips over the forest park and surrounding mountains, $175-400.

Four-wheel drive trips

Backtrax, T0800-422678/T03-315 7073, www.backtrax.co.nz. A 2-hr trip across farmland and the hills bordering the Waiau River will cost $90.

Molesworth Tours, T03-315 7401, www.molesworth.co.nz. Day trips by 4WD to the largest and one of the most remote cattle stations in New Zealand, from $225.

Horse trekking

Hanmer Forest Park and the surrounding countryside is superb horse riding country. **Alpine Horse Safaris**, Hawarden, T03-314 4293, www.alpinehorse.co.nz. Standard treks and some excellent multi-day trips in the region from $185 (1 day) to $4250 (12 days).

Hanmer Horses, T03-315 7444/T0800-873546, www.hanmerhorses.co.nz. Offers 1-hr to full-day rides from $45.
Hurunui Horse Treks, T03-314 4500, www.horseback.co.nz. Entertaining 1- to 8-day options from 'Station to Station' or 'Mountain to Sea', from $225-3595, Oct-May.

Massage
If you are exhausted even reading this list, or fancy some pampering after your activities, then a massage can be secured at the new **Hanmer Springs Pools and Spa** therapy centre (30 mins from $60), see page 500.
Wisteria Cottage Day Spa, 34 Conical Hill Rd, T03-315 7026, www.nzhotsprings.com/dayspa. Numerous treatments with a 1-hr run-in with some seaweed costing from $120.

Maze
Kids might like to lose themselves (or adults might like to lose their kids) in the fairly unremarkable **Hurunui Jones and the 'Lost Temple of Indra' Maze**, on the roadside as you come into town, 1000-1730. It's great if you want to get lost, but you cannot help wondering if it was only ever a rock garden project gone horribly wrong. From $9, child $6.

Mountain biking
Mountain biking is a major reason why many come to Hanmer Springs, and the **Forest Park** offers some superb tracks from easy and moderate to the wonderfully muddy. **HSAC** (see page 509) offers bike hire from around $19 for 1 hr to $45 for a full day.

Skiing
Skiing is another major reason why many flock to Hanmer in winter. Ski equipment can be hired from **HSAC** (see page 509). Lift passes start at about $55 and shuttle transport from Hanmer from $22. For more information contact the VIC (I-Site) or visit the website, www.nzski.com, or www.snow.co.nz. The 2 ski fields are:
Hanmer Springs Ski Area, 45 mins from town, T027-4341806, has 2 rope tows, poma

and lodge and accommodation facilities.
Mount Lyford, off SH70 (75 mins), T03-315 6178, has some challenging runs for both intermediates and the advanced as well as a good learners' area, ski hire, lodge and a restaurant.

Walking
There are plenty of good walking tracks around Hanmer, particularly in the **Forest Park** offering both short/long and easy/moderate options. The 1-hr **Conical Hill Lookout Walk**, with its views south across the town, is accessed from the top of Conical Hill Rd and continues through the forest to link up with Jollies Pass Rd and back into town. For more walks information contact the VIC (I-Site).

Kaikoura *p501, map p504*
There are 2 things you need to bear in mind with the boat-based activities in Kaikoura. The first is simple: in mid-summer book the whale-watching and dolphin-swimming well in advance. Even the other less popular activities are worth pre-booking to avoid disappointment. The second is the notoriously fickle weather. Given its position on the Southern Ocean, Kaikoura is subject to the vagaries of wind and wave, and trips can be cancelled at a moment's notice. Again to avoid disappointment allow yourself at least 2 days, just in case your trip is rescheduled. Also be sure to request your inclusion on another trip on cancellation, since this will not be done as a matter of course.

4WD
Glenstrae Farm 4 Wheeler Adventures, T0800-004009/T03-319 7021, www.4wheeladventures.co.nz. Offers 4WD and quad-bike adventures. Based about 25 km south of the town it offers 3-hr trips in the coastal hinterland with great views. Departs 0900, 1330 and at dusk, from $120. Courtesy pick-ups from Kaikoura.

Birdwatching

New Zealand is considered the seabird capital of the world and a remarkable 70% of its bird list are pelagic species. Kaikoura offers a world-class opportunity to see many that would otherwise involve long excursions far offshore. Of particular interest are the albatross, mollymawks, and numerous petrel species. The many notable regulars include the giant petrel, which is as big as a goose, the Westland petrel, which is endemic to New Zealand, and the cape pigeon that could not be more aptly named. The birds are attracted to the boat using a block of 'chum' (fish guts) and almost the instant it hits the water the show begins.

Albatross Encounter with Ocean Wings, 96 Esplanade, Kaikoura, T0800-733365/ T03-319 6777, www.oceanwings.co.nz. Boat trips to see a wide variety of rare seabirds.
Ocean Wings, 96 Esplanade, T0800-733365/ T03-319 6777, www.oceanwings.co.nz. Run by the Dolphin Encounter outfit (see below), 2-3-hr trips on demand, from $100, child $55. Recommended.

Dolphin swimming/watching

The coastal waters around Kaikoura abound with dolphins, and not just 1 species. They range from the common and bottlenose dolphins to the smaller dusky and rare Hector's dolphin. It is the dusky dolphin you are most likely to encounter (or swim with), and pods running into their hundreds, even thousands, are not uncommon. The duskies are also well known for breaching, and will jump out of the water or even somersault in an almost choreographed display of 'being'. Depending on their mood they may show great interest in the boat or swimmers or, on other days, show complete indifference.
Dolphin Encounter, 96 The Esplanade, T0800-733365/T03-319 6777, www.dolphinencounter.co.nz. The main operator. In summer the 3-hr trips leave from West End at 0530, 0830 and 1230, in winter 0830 and 1230, from $165, child $150 (viewing-only $80, child $40). If you swim,

and provided a pod is found (which is highly likely, you'll get a refund if not), you will have plenty of time in the water frolicking around with the dolphins. You will be given a safety briefing and will be encouraged to make high-pitched bagpipe-like noises to attract them. This will keep the 'viewing-only' passengers highly entertained. Take a towel and warm clothing, and book well in advance.

Fishing

Top Catch, T03-319 6306, www.kaikoura fishingcharter.co.nz. 3 hrs from $90.

Flightseeing

See also Kaikoura Helicopters page 513.
Pilot A Plane, based at Peketa Airfield, south of town, T03-319 6579, www.airkaikoura.co.nz. Offers the chance to take the controls on a 30-min scenic flight.

Horse trekking

Fyffe Horse Treks, T03-319 5069, www.kaikourahorsetrekking.co.nz. 2 hrs, $65.

Scenic and cultural tours

Maori Tours, T03-319 5567, www.maori tours.co.nz. Offers plenty of local cultural insight and protocol with visits to local *pa* sites and a walk amid native bush to see how the plants were traditionally used by the Maori. Entertaining with plenty of participation, half-day from $115, child $65.

For a more conventional tour option contact **Kaikoura Shuttles**, T0800-766962.

Skydiving

Skydive Kaikoura, Kaikoura Airport, T1800 843 759/T03-319 3309, www.skydivekaikoura.co.nz. Given the scenery Kaikoura presents a superb venue for skydiving. Tandem jumps start at 9,000ft from $259 to 13,000 at $359.

Scuba diving

Dive Kaikoura, 94 West End, T03-319 6622, www.divekaikoura.co.nz. The main operator offering a wide range of options with the emphasis on seal encounters. Hire and tank fills available.

Seal watching and swimming

With whales and dolphins being the main oceanic stars, the New Zealand fur seals are often overlooked. But encounters with these inquisitive 'fat-bodies' can be a memorable experience. On land they are undisputed 'beach-bum couch-potatoes', but underwater they display an ease and grace in motion that would put any ballet dancer to shame. In Kaikoura there is the choice of observing them from land, boat, kayak, or getting up close and personal in the water.

Dive Kaikoura, 94 West End, T03-319 6622, www.divekaikoura.co.nz. The main dive operator with an emphasis on sub-aqua seal encounters.

Kaikoura Kayaks, T0800-452456/ T021-462889, www.seakayakkaikoura.co.nz. A kayak can provide a great way to get up close and personal to the seals. This outfit has half-day guided tours taking in the lovely scenery of the peninsula, and also offers the opportunity to dive and snorkel with the seals. Trips depart from the VIC (I-Site) daily at 0830, 1230 and 1630 (winter 0900/1300), from $85, child $70. Freedom hire costs from $50 for a half-day, $65 for a full-day.

Seal Swim Kaikoura, T03-319 6182, www.sealswimkaikoura.co.nz. 2-hr shore and boat based snorkelling tours daily 0900, 1030, 1230 and 1400 (Oct-Nov, Apr-May 0900-1230), from $90, child $70.

Star gazing

Kaikoura Night Sky, T03-319 6635, www.kaikouranightsky.co.nz, from $50, child $40. For a fine close-up of the moon and a little insight into nebulae, allow 2 hrs.

Tree planting

Trees for Travellers, T03-319 7148, ask for details at the VIC (I-Site), www.treesfor travellers.co.nz. A programme that allows visitors to help with local native bush restoration. You can plant your own natural memento from $20.

Walks around Kaikoura

The 2-hr return 'Peninsula Walk', which links the 2 settlements is excellent and recommended. You can either walk along the clifftop or the shoreline (depending on the tide) and start at the Point Kearn car park (at the end of Avoca St), or alternatively at the South Bay car park. You will encounter seals, lots of interesting rock pools, and some superb coastal scenery.

A much longer jaunt is the celebrated 3-day, 45-km 'Kaikoura Coast Track', which combines sights inland and along the coast. **Sally and David Handyside**, T03-319 2715, www.kaikouratrack.co.nz, offers this as a package from $185.

Mount Fyffe (1602 m), directly behind Kaikoura, offers spectacular views and can be accessed (15 km) from the end of Postman's Rd (junction Athelney Rd/SH1 north of Beach Rd) or Grange Rd (SH1 north); 8-hr return, DoC huts en route ($5, book at the VIC/I-Site).

There is also a good lookout and short walk, 'Fyffe Palmer Track', at the end of Mount Fyffe Rd (8 km). To get there, drive out of town on Ludstone Rd (north) then turn right onto Mount Fyffe Rd and follow it to its terminus. The VIC (I-Site) has DoC broadsheets on all these walks and others.

Whale watching

The first commercial whale-watching operation in New Zealand was started in 1987 by the Maori-owned and operated **Whale Watch Kaikoura** (see below). The company now has 4 purpose-built vessels and can accommodate about 100,000 visitors annually. You can expect to see at least one whale on your trip as well as dolphins, seals, albatrosses and other unusual seabirds. If no whales are seen at all there is an 80% refund.

A recent addition to the on-board entertainment is an excellent computer generated animation entitled 'World of the

Whales' which provides an imaginative view of the geography and remarkable depth of the Kaikoura Canyon. Trips are weather-dependent and can be cancelled at any time. Note that your inclusion on a later trip is not automatic and needs to be requested. **Kaikoura Helicopters**, based at the 'Whale-way Station', T03-319 6609, www.worldofwhales.co.nz. Offers 30- to 40-min flights from $195-455. If you don't like the idea of a boat trip, or just fancy seeing the whales from a different (and better) perspective, then you should go whale watching from the air. This can be particularly good in calmer sea conditions when you can see the whole whale from above rather than just the tail end and flukes. At just over 150 m you can also spot dolphins and enjoy the added bonus of spectacular aerial views across the peninsula and the coast. Photographers will need a good telephoto lens, fast film and a polarizing filter.
Whale Watch Kaikoura, T0800-655121/T03-319 6767, www.whalewatch.co.nz. Based at the 'Whaleway Station' (next to the Railway Station), accessed off Beach Rd (SH1) just beyond West End. It offers several 2- to 3½-hr trips daily (seasonal departures) from $145, child $60. The boats all leave from South Bay, 10 mins from the Whaleway Station.
Wings Over Whales, based at the Peketa

Airfield 6 km south of Kaikoura, T0800-226629/T03-319 6580, www.whales.co.nz. Entertaining and personable flightseeing trips from 30-45 mins at 0900, 1100, 1300 and 1500, from $165, child $75. Recommended.

⊕ Directory

Hanmer Springs *p500*
Banks There is an ATM at the **Four Square** foodmarket, in the main shopping centre on Conical Hill Rd. TCs are also accepted and exchanged there. **Internet** Mountain View **Top Ten**, at the entrance to the town, T03-315 7113. **Medical services** Medical centre, 20 Amuri Av, T03-315 7503.
Police 43 Conical Hill Rd, T03-315 7117.
Post office Four Square foodmarket, T03-315 5112.

Kaikoura *p501, map p504*
Banks BNZ, 42 West End with an ATM.
Internet Internet Outpost, 19 West End, slower, but stays open later (until 2100).
Kodak Express, on West End, daily 0900-1730. **Police** T03-319 5038. **Post office** 41 West End, T03-319 6808, Mon-Fri 0830-1700, Sat 0900-1200.

West of Christchurch → Colour map 5, A/B 5/4.

Until recently there were basically two main reasons tourists 'headed for the hills' west of Christchurch. The most obvious reason was to reach the west coast via The Great Alpine Highway (SH73), the Craigieburn Forest Park and Arthur's Pass, while the other was to ski the popular Mount Hutt ski fields near Methven. However, since the release of the Lord of the Rings trilogy, there is now another very good reason in the surprising form of a large and conspicuous lump of rock. Mount Sunday, which sits predominantly in the Rangitata River Valley and in stark contrast against the mountainous skyline of Southern Alps, became the perfect filming location and set for Edoras and Meduseld, King Theoden's grand hall in the realm of Rohan. Although the set is long gone, it remains one of the most scenic drives in the country and, even without all the hype, was always a great place to visit. ►► For Sleeping, Eating and other listings, see pages 516-520.

Ins and outs

Getting there Methven is 90 km southwest of Christchurch via the celebrated 'Inland Scenic Route' (SH73) and SH72. **Intercity**, T03-377 0951, operates buses from Christchurch. For winter shuttles to Mount Hutt and Christchurch, contact **Methven Travel**, T03-302 8106, which offers Methven-Christchurch from around $59 return. Contact the VIC for shuttle bookings. From Christchurch it is 240 km to the west coast; Arthur's Pass is 158 km. **Atomic Shuttles**, T03-349 0697, www.atomictravel.co.nz, offer daily services to Greymouth via Arthurs Pass. **West Coast Shuttles**, T03-7680028, www.westcoastshuttle.co.nz, also offer daily services to Greymouth.

TranzScenic's, T0800-872467, www.tranzscenic.co.nz, daily rail service *Tranz Alpine* is touted as one of the most scenic rail journeys in the world and is a popular way to get from Christchurch to Greymouth. It leaves Christchurch at 0815, arriving Arthur's Pass 1042 and the Greymouth at 1245. It makes the return journey from Greymouth at 1345, to Arthur's Pass at 1557, arriving in Christchurch at 1805. A standard one-way fare is around $160.

Getting around **Methven Travel** (see above) offers taxi services and a ski bus to the slopes in winter. It also provides transportation to the Mount Somers Walkway, T03-302 8106. Several companies offer shuttles to the Mount Hutt ski field from around $30 return including: **Ride Snow Shuttles**, T0800-339433, www.ridesnowshuttles.co.nz, and **Mount Hutt Express**, T0800-808070. Mountain bikes can be hired from **Big Al's** in The Square, T03-302 8003, from $45 per day.

Tourist information **Methven VIC (I-Site)** ① *121 Main St, T03-302 8955, www.methveninfo.co.nz, daily 0830-1730 (winter 0800-1800),* can provide free town maps and information about the ski fields. It also stocks DoC information covering regional walks, has internet, and administers transport and activity bookings. For other specific ski information and online snow reports contact the **Mount Hutt Ski Area** ① *T03-302 8811,* or www.snow.co.nz, www.nzski.com. **Arthur's Pass VIC (DoC)** ① *in the heart of the village on the southern side of SH73, T03-318 9211, www.doc.govt.nz, daily 0900-1600,* has various displays about the national park, a video ($1), walks information and all local accommodation and service details. Ask for the *Village Information* broadsheet and map. Before embarking on any long walks or tramps check the weather forecast and ask about up to date track conditions.

Methven and Mount Hutt ⊖⊘⋔⊙⋏⊙ ►► *pp516-520.*

The biggest attraction to the small, but congenial agricultural town of Methven is its location close to the **Mount Hutt Ski Area**. At an elevation of 2075 m and covering an area of 365 ha, 'The Hutt' is highly regarded within the skiing fraternity. The reason for this is not only its proximity to Christchurch, but also because of its reputation for having some of the best snow in the country and the longest and most consistent season in the southern hemisphere (mid-June to October). It also has modern base lodge with brasserie, bar, cafés, shops and snowboarding facilities.

In summer, although the town is quiet, it still offers an escape from the city or the tourist hype and various activities including balloon flights, mountain biking, whitewater rafting, golfand walking. The region is also noted for its farmstays.

West coast via Arthur's Pass ⚫🚌🚂 ↦ *pp516-520.*

The route to the west coast via The Great Alpine Highway (SH73) from Christchurch across the Great Divide and the northern ranges of the Southern Alps is one of the most celebrated scenic drives and rail journeys in the country. It is most notable perhaps for its sheer range of dramatic South Island landscapes from the flatlands of the Canterbury Plains to the east, through the rugged mountain peaks and river gorges in its centre, to the lush coastal valleys and lakes to the west. On the way, other than its aesthetics, are the **Craigieburn Forest** and **Arthur's Pass National Park**, which offer some excellent walking, tramping, rock climbing and skiing opportunities.

Sights

From Christchurch, with the almost constant sight of the mountains looming ever larger, you pass through the small and aptly named rural settlements of **Darfield** and **Springfield** to reach the foot of the Torlesse Range. Just beyond Springfield the road climbs steeply through **Porters Pass** before falling once again into the valleys and unusual karst landscapes that border the **Craigieburn Forest Park** (100 km). The area offers a small flurry of ski fields including **Porter Heights**, **Mount Olympus**, **Mount Cheeseman**, **Broken Rivers**, **Craigieburn** and **Temple Basin**. The majority are 'club fields', offering a wide range of slopes and conditions. Porters is the only commercial field and is the closest ski area to Christchurch. For information contact the VIC (I-Site) in Christchurch or the Arthur's Pass Visitor Centre, or consult the excellent websites www.selwyndistrict.co.nz and www.nzski.com. There are also plenty of walking opportunities. The DoC leaflet the *Craigieburn Forest Park Day Walks* is very useful and available from the VICs (I-Sites) above. The rugged karst landscape of **Kura Tawhiti** or **Castle Hill Reserve** (30 km west of Springfield) provides more interesting walks and also some excellent rock climbing.

Six kilometres further west is the **Cave Stream Scenic Reserve** which is easily accessible from The Great Alpine Highway (SH73). Here you will find the rather unique opportunity of a self-guided blackwater hike in a limestone cave system that has been created over the millennia by the Waimakariri River and its tributaries. The cave system was used for centuries by Maori on their transmigration west to the coast and still contains some examples of rock art and bones. The one-hour underground hike is of course more of a 'wade', but is worth the soaking. Just be sure to take a good torch and dry clothing. The DoC panels in the car park will keep you right; leaflets are available from the VICs (I-Sites).

At the northern border of the Forest Park, and just beyond the tiny settlement of Cass, both road and rail penetrate the vast open-braided **Waimakariri River Valley** before entering the Arthur's Pass National Park. From there it is only a short drive to the enveloped outpost village of **Arthur's Pass**.

Arthur's Pass

It was one Arthur Dudley Dobson, a pioneer surveyor, who first explored the route to the west coast via the east Waimakariri and west Otira River Valleys in 1864. Although at the time Arthur was merely on a routine trip, his observations became an integral part of securing road access to the west coast during the gold boom of the 1860s. Remarkably, or perhaps not, given the motivation, a basic road was built within a year, but the rail link that later served the coal and timber trade took a further 60 years to complete. Now, long after all the gold has gone, the railway remains a monument to patience, while the road continues to need constant maintenance and improvement. These modern feats of road engineering and construction become obvious just beyond Arthur's Pass in the form of the impressive, and only recently opened, **Otira Viaduct.**

Even before the rail link to Arthur's Pass was complete, the area was proving popular for tramping and skiing, and by 1930 Arthur's Pass was gazetted as a National Park. The tiny settlement of Arthur's Pass is 924 m above sea level and is used as the base for activities in the park, or as a welcome halfway stop en route to the west coast.

Arthur's Pass National Park →*Colour map 5, A5.*
The Arthur's Pass National Park was designated in 1929 and is 114,500 ha in area. It extends from the vicinity of Harper's Pass in the northern Southern Alps to the mountains around the head of the Waimakariri and Otira rivers. The park is essentially made up of high mountain ranges, gorges and expansive braided river valleys. One of the highest and most attractive mountains is **Mount Rolleston** (2270 m), which lies just to the southwest of the Arthur's Pass. Its impressive **'Bealey Face'** can be seen from the road just west of the village.

The mountain ranges are 'alpine' in nature, containing a broad range of vegetation which varies greatly from east to west in accordance with the varying climatic conditions and rainfall. To the east the forests are almost entirely made up of mountain beech, while to the west, on the other side of the 'Great Divide', it is more complex with a variety of podocarp species, beech, kamahi and kaiakawaka. The park is rich in alpine plant species, many of which thrive above the tree line and are endemic to New Zealand. Many native birds are also present, the most notable being the notoriously inquisitive and destructive native mountain parrot, the kea. If this is your first trip across to the west coast you may also notice one other creature, one that will make its presence known in no uncertain terms: the sandfly.

The park offers a network of tramping tracks that are equipped with over 30 DoC backcountry huts. Two of the best day walks are the seven- to eight-hour ascent of **Avalanche Peak**, directly behind the village on its southern side, or, further west still, the more difficult (mainly summer) climb to the summit of **Mount Rolleston**. The Avalanche Peak track begins from behind the DoC information centre, which can offer detailed information and advice on these tracks and others. Note that braided rivers and the small tributaries that feed them are notorious for flash floods, so extra care is required. History buffs might like to negotiate the 1½-hour **Arthur's Pass Village Historic Walk**; a leaflet is available from the VIC (I-Site).

◉ West of Christchurch listings

For Sleeping and Eating price codes and other relevant information, see Essentials pages 44-50.

● Sleeping

Methven and Mount Hutt *p514*
Given its popularity as a ski resort there is no shortage of beds in the town, with the majority being upper- and mid-range self- contained lodges, with spas, open fires and drying rooms. There are also a good number of backpacker lodges and, again, these have a 'ski-lodge' feel

with all the facilities. The VIC (I-Site) has full listings; advanced bookings are advised in winter. Prices drop dramatically in summer.
LL Terrace Downs High Country Resort, Coleridge Rd, Rakaia Gorge, Darfield, T03-318 6943, www.terracedowns.co.nz. Classy golf course resort in the Canterbury foothills, offering excellent modern villas and luxury chalets and in-house restaurants, café and bar.
L Beluga, 40 Allen St, T03-302 8290, www.beluga.co.nz. Excellent high-end B&B and self-contained cottage option.

L Powderhouse Country Lodge, 3 Cameron St, T03-302 9105, www.powderhouse.co.nz. Restored villa with a glass-atrium hot tub.

L-AL Glenthorne Station, Harper Rd, Lake Coleridge, T0800-926868, www.glenthorne.co.nz. The largest and best equipped, modern en suite chalets and self-contained lodges a restaurant and in-house 4WD tours all in wonderfully remote (yet accessible) location.

AL Brinkley Village Resort, Barkers Rd, T03-302 8885, www.brinkleyvillage.co.nz. Modern option, a little lacking in atmosphere, which specializes in self-contained studios and apartments. It has a restaurant, bar, hot tubs, pool and the welcoming open fire.

AL-A Mount Taylor Lodge, 32 Lampard St, T03-302 9699, www.mounttaylorlodge.co.nz. Modern, well-facilitated alpine-style lodge and a good mid-range option.

AL Whitestone Cottages, 3020 Methven Hwy, T03-302 9271, www.whitestonecottages .co.nz. Modern 2-bedroom fully self-contained cottages near the centre of the village.

AL-A Lodge on Chertsey, 1 Chertsey Rd, T03-303 2000, www.thelodgenz.com. Right in the heart of the town, this purpose-built lodge has some excellent luxury spa rooms, en suites, and good modern facilities including a licensed restaurant, bar and internet. Off-street parking. Often has special rates in summer.

AL-D Abisko Lodge and Campground, 74 Main St, Methven, T03-302 8875, www.abisko.co.nz. Friendly place with modern tidy en suites, apartments (with log fires) and powered sites for campervans or tents. Restaurant, bar, spa/sauna and a comfortable lounge with obligatory open fire.

A-D Pudding Hill Lodge, on the Inland Scenic Hwy, 12 km west of Methven, T0800-783445/T03-302 9627, www.pudding hilllodge.co.nz. A 3-star rated establishment close to Mt Hutt and the ski-field. It has 1- and 2-bedroom studio units, budget lodge rooms, powered/tent sites, sauna and spas.

C-D Alpenhorn Chalet, 44 Allen St, T03- 302 8779, www.alpenhorn.co.nz. A cosy

bungalow with new facilities, dorms and doubles and a spa. Recommended.

C-D Redwood Lodges, 5 Wayne Pl, T03-302 8964, www.snowboardnz.com. Provides 2 good-value purpose-built self-catering lodges, one with shared facilities and one with great-value en suites. All ski facilities are provided, and it has a cosy log fire.

C-D Kowhai House Lodge and Backpackers, 17 McMillan St, T03-302 8863, www.kowhaihouse.co.nz. In a convenient location in the town. Well-established, friendly and very comfortable with well-heated rooms and spa.

Motorcamps and campsites

The Abisko Lodge and Campground, see above, has powered sites and is recommended.

D Methven Camping Ground, Barkers Rd, T03-302 8005. An older option also located in town with basic but adequate facilities.

West coast via Arthur's Pass *p515*

There are a number of good places to stay before you reach Arthur's Pass. In winter these are very popular with skiers, while in summer it is walking boots that sit on the steps.

LL Grasmere Lodge High Country Retreat, SH73, Cass, T03-3188407, www.grasmere.co.nz. All mod cons in luxury suites; dinner and activities as part of the package. It can also be reached on the *TranzAlpine* which stops at the edge of the property on request.

AL-D Flock Hill Lodge, a further 40 km east of Arthur's Pass, T03-318 8196, www.flock hill.co.nz. Part of the expansive Flock Hill Station, has tidy motel units, backpacker lodge and a restaurant. Activities arranged. Ideally located close to the ski fields and the Craigieburn Forest Park walks.

C-D Smylie's YHA, Springfield, on Main Rd in the centre of the village, T03-318 4740, www.smylies.co.nz. Cosy dorms and doubles, with modern facilities and motel units. The ideal base for both winter and summer activities. In winter it rents skis and arranges transport to the slopes. In summer rock climbing, horse trekking and hiking can be arranged.

Arthur's Pass p515

Arthur's Pass village offers a small range of accommodation options ranging from self-contained, backpackers and chalet-style to basic DoC camp sites. The dining options include a fully licenced restaurant and two cafés.

AL Arthurs, at the western end of the village, T0800-676884/T03-318 9236, www.arthurs pass.co.nz. The most expensive, with comfortable chalets, 8 of which are en suite. There is an outdoor spa, an in-house à la carte and a bistro/restaurant.

A Alpine Motels, just beyond the bridge on the right at the eastern end of the village, T03-318 9233, www.apam.co.nz. Has self-contained doubles. It also offers a 'car minding' service.

C-D Mountain House Backpackers YHA, T03-318 9258, www.trampers.co.nz. A spacious lodge offering good private and shared rooms with shared bathroom, some excellent self-contained cottages on the grounds with open fires and tent sites. Recommended.

Campsites

The **Mountain House Backpackers YHA** is the best bet for tent sites while the **Arthurs** offers a few powered sites using lodge facilities. Doc also administer several basic campsites in the area. For details contact the VIC or refer www.doc.govt.nz.

🍴 Eating

Methven p514

There are 2 supermarkets: **Supervalue** and **Topnotch**, both on McMillan St. The former is open until 2100 in winter.

♔♔ **The Last Post Restaurant**, Main St, T03-3028259. Another reliable option, licensed and one of the most popular après ski venues.

♔♔ **Ski Time Restaurant**, Racecourse Av, T03-302 8398, www.skitime.co.nz. Popular lodge restaurant bar with cosy atmosphere and open fire 5 mins from town by car. Courtesy vehicle available for groups.

♔♔ **Steel-Worx Restaurant and Bar**, 36 Forest Drive, T03-302 9900.The 'Worx' enjoys a good reputation. It is stylish, full of character with a cosy, log-burning stove.

♔♔ **Stronechrubie Restaurant**, Mt Somers, 30 km from Methven, T03-303 9814, www.stronechrubie.co.nz. Open for lunch 1200-1400, dinner Wed-Sat from 1830. One of the best fine-dining restaurants in the region.

♔ **Café 131**, Main St, T03-302 9131. 0900-1600. Good coffee, recommended for breakfast.

♔ **Primo Café**, McMillan St, T03-302 9060. 0730-1830. In the second-hand shop, **Secundo**, and well worth a visit

Arthur's Pass p515

The only licensed restaurant is at **Arthurs** (see Sleeping, above).

♔ **Wobbly Kea Café and Bar**, T03-318 9101, in the centre of town. The best bet for a meal and good home baking.

🍸 Pubs, bars and clubs

Methven p514

The colourful pubs, **The Blue**, on Barkers Rd, and **The Brown**, just opposite, are both traditional favourites, with the former the most popular for après-ski.

Steel-Worx Restaurant and Bar, 36 Forest Dr, T03-302 9900. Smaller and already earning a good reputation for its lively party nights in winter. All offer good pub lunches.

🎭 Entertainment

Methven p514

Cinema Paradiso, 112 Main St, T03-302 1957. Specializes in art house movies.

⛰ Activities and tours

Methven p514

Flightseeing and heli-skiing
Mount Hutt Heliskiing, Alford Forest

(15 mins from town), T03-3028401, www.mthuthelicopters.co.nz. Flightseeing trips from $98 and heli-taxi ski/board trips and service to the ski slopes, from $175. Heli-skiing runs from $175, full day $675.

Golf
Clubs can be hired from **Big Al's** in The Square, Methven.
Methven Golf Course, Hobbs Rd, T03-302 8438. Quality 18-hole course with fine mountain views.
Terrace Downs, Lake Coleridge Rd, T0800-465373, www.terracedowns.co.nz.

Horse trekking
High Country Horse Adventures, T0800-386336, www.horsetrek.co.nz. Adventurous excursions from $75.

Hot air ballooning
Even outside the ski season Methven offers a good range of activities year round.
Aoraki Hot Air Balloon Safaris, T0800-256837/T03-302 8172, www.nzballooning.com. Relaxing flights with a champagne breakfast, from $330.

Jet boating
Rakaia Gorge River Tours, T03-3186574, www.rivertours.co.nz, offer scenic trips and heli-jet options on the Rakaia River from $75.

Rafting
Rangitata Rafts, T0800-251251/T03-696 3534, www.rafts.co.nz. Offers excellent day excursions down the scenic Rangitata River, south of Methven (Grade IV-V), from $185 ($195 includes return transport from Christchurch). To keep up the adrenaline, you might also consider a spot of mountain biking for which the VIC (I-Site) can provide all the details.

Skiing
Day lift passes cost $89, child under 6 free. A 3-day lift pass costs from $259, child $143. Ski equipment hire is available at the field itself or in various outlets in Methven, including **Big Al's**, The Square, T03-302 8003, www.bigals.co.nz. For more information regarding the Mt Hutt field visit www.nzski.com. For transport to the field see Getting around, page 514.

Tours (Lord of the Rings 4WD tours)
The following companies offer 4WD trips to Erewhon and Mt Sunday (Edoras); both can be booked at the VIC.
Hassle Free Holidays, T03-385 5775, www.hasslefree.co.nz. Trips depart Methven at 1045, returning 1600 and include driving on Mt Sunday. Includes a champagne picnic lunch, from $215.
Ride Snow Shuttles, T0800-121414, www.ridesnowshuttles.co.nz. Offers similar trips.

Walks
There are numerous walks or longer hikes on offer in the Mt Hutt Forest (14 km west) including the Mount Somers Conservation Area including the Sharplin Falls and the climb to the summit of Mt Somers (1687 m). The new Hakatere Conservation Park also offers some excellent walks. Ask at the VIC (I-Site) for details.

Arthur's Pass *p515*
Skiing
The Arthur's Pass region has 5 ski fields; Porters, Mt Cheeseman, Broken River, Craigieburn and **Temple Basin**. Ski equipment is available at Porters, Mt Cheeseman and Temple Basin. All the ski fields have accommodation available but bookings are essential. For more information refer www.selwyndistrict.co.nz.

Walking
There are many walking and hiking options in and around Arthur's Pass from strenuous summit climbs to 30-min strolls through native beech forest. Ask at the VIC for maps and details.

❶ Directory

Methven *p514*
Banks BNZ (ATM), Main St. **Medical facilities** Medical Centre, The Square, T03-302 8105; **Pharmacy**, Main St, T03-302 8103. **Police** T03-302 8200. **Postal agent** Methven Post, Main St, T03-302 8463.

Arthur's Pass *p515*
Internet Available at the I-Site. **Post office** Main St, limited opening hours. **Useful addresses** There is a petrol station and a police station in the village, T03-318 9212. For breakdown, **Springfield Service Centre**, T03-318 4845, or the **Otira Recovery Service**, T03-7382890.

South Canterbury → *Colour map 5, B4/5.*

From Christchurch SH1 heads south through the flat heartland of the Canterbury Plains to Timaru. With so much seemingly omnipresent and stunning scenery elsewhere in New Zealand, aesthetically it is often labelled as the least exciting drive in the country; only the occasional glimpse of the distant Southern Alps far to the west and the odd wide pebble-strewn riverbed crossing, breaks the monotony of the endless roadside windbreaks and expansive fields. Even the cows look bored to death. Roughly half way between Christchurch and Timaru is the only major settlement, Ashburton. ▶▶ For Sleeping, Eating and other listings, see pages 524-527.

Ins and outs

Getting there **Timaru airport** ① *12 km north of town via SH1*, is served by **Air New Zealand Link**, T0800-737000, daily from Christchurch and Wellington. For taxi from the airport contact **Timaru Taxis**, T03-688 8899, from $18. For car hire and taxi services see page 527. The VIC (I-Site) holds local suburban bus (CRC) timetables.

Ashburton is 87 km south of Christchurch and 76 km north of Timaru on SH1. All the major bus companies heading south can stop in Ashburton and Timaru including **Intercity**, T03-688 6497; **Naked Bus**, www.nakedbus.com; and **Atomic Shuttles**, T03-349 0697. Buses stop outside the VIC (I-Site) in Ashburton and the station in Timaru. The VIC (I-Site) can help book tickets.

Tourist information **Ashburton VIC (I-Site)** ① *corner of East and Burnett sts, T03-308 1050, www.ashburtontourism.co.nz, Mon-Fri 0830-1700, Sat 1000-1500, Sun 1000-1300,* has a free town map and full accommodation and local activity listings. **Timaru VIC (I-Site)** ① *in the former Landing Service Building, 2 George St, T03-6886163, www.southisland.org.nz, Mon-Fri 0830-1700, Sat-Sun 1000-1500,* also has DoC information. **Geraldine VIC (I-Site)** ① *corner of Talbot and Cox sts, T03-693 1006, www.southisland.org.nz, Mon-Fri 0830-1700, Sat-Sun 1000-1600,* has full listings for local accommodation and DoC information. The free leaflet *Geraldine* includes comprehensive listings including the varied arts and crafts outlets. **Temuka VIC (I-Site)** ① *72-74 King St, T03-615 9537, temlibrary@xtra.co.nz,* has full accommodation listings. **Waimate VIC (I-Site)** ① *75 Queen St, T03-689 7771, www.waimate.org.nz,* has detailed accommodation and local activity listings.

Ashburton ⬤❼▲ ▶▶ *pp524-527.*

Due to its surrounding topography and perhaps its very location right on SH1, as well as being so near Christchurch and so far from the principal tourist attractions to the south, Ashburton (population 13,400) seldom lures tourists to stop for anything other than a hurried toilet break, quick snack and cup of coffee. But having said that, it is not a bad little place and if you take a little time (especially on Sundays), it will reveal a few worthy attractions and tempting activities to complement the warm welcome offered by its friendly residents.

The main attractions are its small museums and craft outlets. The **Ashburton Art Gallery and Museum** ⓘ *Baring Sq East, T03-308 1133, Tue-Fri 1000-1600, Sat-Sun 1300-1600, donation,* has the obvious focus on local history but is particularly noted for its displays of local and contemporary arts and crafts.

Also of note, though seldom open, is the **Plains Vintage Railway and Historical Museum**, which is just over the Manoran Road level crossing (off SH1) in the **Tinwald Domain and Recreation Park** ⓘ *south of the town centre, T03-308 9600, www.plainsrailway.co.nz, Jul-Sep Sun only, Oct-Jun every second Sun of the month*. It offers short rides on some of its fine array of restored locos and traction engines, from $6, child $2.50. Also in the Domain is the **Vintage Car Museum** ⓘ *T03-308 7025, Sun only*, which has a collection dating back to 1905. For crafts, the **Ashford Craft Village** ⓘ *415 West St, T03-308 9087*, is worth a look and can double as a good place for lunch.

Timaru ●●❋▲●● ▸▸ *pp524-527.*

The port city of Timaru (population 27,300), halfway between Christchurch and Dunedin, provides a refreshing stopover on SH1, or a convenient starting point from which to head west, via SH8, to the 'MacKenzie Country', Mount Cook and Queenstown. The city is pleasant, boasting the popular **Caroline Bay beach** near the town centre, a few good parks, the region's main museum, a reputable art gallery and a few unique attractions, including some ancient seventh-century **Maori rock art**.

Background
With the existence of over 500 sites featuring Maori rock art, particularly in the caves and rock overhangs of the Opihi and Opuha rivers, west of Timaru, historians have estimated that the Maori settled in the area as early as AD 1400. During the 17th century the warring Ngati Tahu, from the north of the South Island, drove the descendants of these people, the Ngati Mamoe, south into Fiordland. European settlement began in 1837 with the establishment of a whaling station at Patiti Point, close to the present town. This was followed by the purchase and creation of a sheep station known as 'The Levels' in 1852 by the influential Rhodes brothers from England. For over two decades disputes arose between the brothers and the government surrounding land ownership and development, but this was eventually settled and the two communities merged to form Timaru. With the reclamation of land in 1877 and the creation of the harbour at Caroline Bay, the town quickly developed as a major port. Today, Timaru boasts the second largest fishing port in New Zealand and is even visited by the occasional cruise liner. The name Timaru is thought to be derived from the Maori *te maru* meaning 'place of shelter'. However, some authorities dispute this and suggest the literal translation of *ti*, meaning 'cabbage tree', and *maru*, meaning 'shady' is the correct one.

Sights
At the VIC (I-Site) you are immediately confronted by the original 'bluestone' façade of

the **Landing Service Building** which was built in 1870 to facilitate the export of wool and other goods from the surrounding district. This building now forms the starting point for the town's three main heritage trails.

South Canterbury Museum ① *Perth St, T03-687 7212, Tue-Fri 1000-1630, Sat-Sun 1330-1630, free,* is the main regional museum and contains some interesting exhibits on local maritime history, Maori rock art and the exploits of aviator Richard Pearse (1877-1953). In 1903 Pearse is said to have made the first manned flight, nine months before the Wright Brothers of America (see Temuka, page 523). A full replica of the impressive contraption that allowed him to do so is on display. Other relics of Pearse's various flying inventions are held at the Pleasant Point Railway Museum (see page 523).

The **Aigantighe** (pronounced 'egg and tie' and meaning 'at home' in Scots Gaelic) **Art Gallery** ① *49 Wai-iti Rd, T03-688 4424, Tue-Fri 1000-1600, Mon, Sat-Sun 1200- 1600, gardens open dawn to dusk, free,* is one of the best art galleries in the country. Founded in 1956, and set in a 1908 historic home surrounded by a sculpture garden, its hallowed walls feature exhibitions from a substantial permanent exhibition dating back to the 16th century, as well as contemporary works by Colin McCahon and C F Goldie. The gallery also hosts regional and national exhibitions.

After experiencing these three-dimensional works you may like to see a very different craft in action in the form of Gareth James at the **Artisan Forge** ① *40 Fraser St, Timaru Port, T03-684 8872, www.iron.co.nz, daily 1000-1700.* Gareth is one of New Zealand's few remaining working blacksmiths and offers a fascinating 40-minute show, with all sparks flying, from $7.50.

Timaru has some pleasant parks and beaches. The beach at **Caroline Bay**, north of the town centre, was formed as a result of land reclamation and original harbour development in 1877. Although in close proximity to the busy port, and not aesthetically remarkable, the beach still remains a popular and safe haven for swimming.

The park alongside the beach has a number of attractions including a roller-skating rink, a mini-golf course, a maze and an open-air concert soundshell. Every summer, just after Christmas, this area is the focus for the **Summer Carnival** (see Festivals and events, page 526). The **piazza** (built in 1997) leads from Bay Hill down to Caroline Bay and adds to the relaxed seaside café, restaurant and wine bar scene. More traditional are the **Timaru Botanical Gardens** ① *T03-688 6163, daily 0800-dusk,* which were established in 1864. They are especially noted for their collection of rose species and are located just south of the town centre; they are best accessed on the corner of King and Queen Streets. **Centennial Park** follows the course of the Otipua Creek and also offers a peaceful escape and a lovely 3½-km, one-hour (one way) walk that begins from the old 'bluestone' Gleniti School on Clearmont Street, west of the town centre.

Around Timaru and south to Oamaru ⊕⊘⊛▲ ›› *pp524-527.*

If you have given yourself plenty of time in the immediate area and find yourself at a loose end, the small rural communities that surround Timaru, namely, **Geraldine**, **Temuka**, **Pleasant Point** or **Waimate**, off SH1 to the south, provide some unusual attractions that may lure you off the beaten track.

Geraldine

The Anglicized country town of Geraldine, nestled amid the Four Peaks and Peel Forest Mountain ranges, is home to a thriving arts and crafts community providing an attractive, if brief, diversion off SH1 (15 km). Other than a scattering of arts and craft galleries and shops, the town has two museums. The **Vintage Car Club and Machinery Museum** ⓘ *178 Talbot St, T03-693 1006, daily 1000-1600, $7,* has a collection of cars and tractors dating back to 1900, as well some notable aircraft, including its star attraction, the 'Spartan'. The small but lovingly maintained **town museum** ⓘ*Cox St, T03-693 8082, Mon-Sat 1000-1200, 1330-1530, Sun 1400-1600, donations,* is housed in the former Civic Centre (1885).

The best way to negotiate the arts and crafts outlets is with the guidance and maps available at the VIC (I-Site). Of particular note is **Barkers Berry Barn** ⓘ *Talbot St, T03-693 9727, www.barkers.co.nz,* which offers tastings and sales from its fine range of fruity products. **The Giant Jersey** ⓘ *10 Wilson St,* is also worth a look; it reputedly displays the largest jersey in the world.

There are a number of good walks in the vicinity, particularly in the **Talbot Forest Scenic Reserve**, next to the town, and the **Peel Forest**, 19 km northwest via SH79 (Peel Forest Road). The VIC has details or call in at the **Peel Forest Outdoor Pursuits Centre** ⓘ *at the OPC office, T03-696 3832, www.peelforestopc.org.nz, Mon-Fri 0900-1630.*

Temuka

This small agricultural service town (population 4,000), 19 km north of Timaru, is the former home of farmer and eccentric inventor Richard Pearse (1877-1953). In April 1903, at the tender age of 26, Pearse created history by making the first-ever powered flight in a 'heavier-than-air-man-carrying airplane'. His flight, though neither long nor spectacular, was a world first and was completed nine months before the better-known and much-celebrated flight by the American pioneer aviator Orville Wright of the famous Wright brothers. A **memorial** to his achievement can be seen at Waitohi (signposted off SH1), which was the site of his brief and historic flight. In 2003 – on the 100th anniversary – locals attempted to rebuild his plane and get airborne; sadly, on the day, inclement weather meant nothing except umbrellas were airborne. Pearse died an unrecognized recluse in a psychiatric hospital in Christchurch.

Besides the memorial to its most famous son, Temuka is noted for its modern-day crafts outlets, particularly the **Temuka Pottery** ⓘ*Thomas St (Factory Shop), T03-615 0085, open Mon, Wed and Fri 1300-1600.* Its location is fitting given the fact that the town's name derived from the Maori Te-Umu-Kaha, meaning 'The Place of the Hot Ovens'.

Pleasant Point

Eighteen kilometres northwest of Timaru (SH8), Pleasant Point offers a few brief diversions including the **Pleasant Point Museum and Railway** ⓘ *T03-686 2269, www.pleasantpointtrail.org.nz.* It is home to the world's only remaining 1925 *Model T Ford* Railcar. There are regular scheduled rides on the glistening restored loco hourly ($8, child $4), and kids will further delight at others that feature faces akin to 'Thomas the Tank Engine' and friends. Although additional rides are offered on most weekends (1030-1630) you are advised to phone for specific dates and details.

Near Pleasant Point is one of the finest examples of **Maori** rock art in the country. The weathered 14-ft drawing known as the Opihi 'Taniwha' (Maori for 'monster') is considered to be the oldest, having been created sometime in the 16th century. It is in a shallow limestone shelter on private farmland and is best viewed lying on your back. To visit the site you will need to be accompanied by a guide, which can be organized through the Timaru VIC (I-Site).

Waimate

Although noted as being an atypical New Zealand rural township, Waimate (population

3,000), 47 km south of Timaru, is perhaps better known as a 'little bit of Aussie abroad', with its very furry resident population of cuddly marsupials. Known rather unfortunately perhaps as 'red necked' or bush **wallabies**, these appealing plump and bouncy little characters were originally introduced to the area in 1875 for fur and sport. But, like so many other intellectually wanting acts of 'wildlife familiarization', it has resulted in a resident population of rapacious native plant-eaters that are now considered a major pest. Given this, the activities surrounding the wallabies are in complete contrast with most folks taking delight in hunting them down. But it doesn't end there (Lord no!). In Waimate one eminent bright spark recently came up with the idea of making **wallaby meat pies**. Who knows, it might just prove to be a major tourist drawcard.

You can either take the indirect, sympathetic and close-range option, with copious amounts of petting and feeding, at the wallaby-friendly **EnkleDooVery Korna** ① *Bathgates Rd, T03-689 7197, www.waimate.org.nz/tamewallabies, Oct-May daily 1000-1700, $6, child $3*, or alternatively the more distant and direct approach, with a bullet (hunting details from the VIC). If you do take the former option you can cuddle the irresistible pouch babies. Wallabies can also be seen, petted and fed at the **Kelcey's Bush Holiday and Animal Park** ① *Mill Rd, 7 km west of the town (signposted), T03-689 8057, kelceysbush@xtra.co.nz.*

Of a more historical nature is the less cuddly but very smart **Waimate Historical Museum** ① *in the former 1879 Waimate Courthouse, 28 Shearman St, T03-689 7832, Tue-Fri 1330-1600, Sat 1300-1500 (mid-Dec to end Mar), Sun 1400-1600, donation*. It houses a small but significant array of memorabilia and forms part of the town's 'Strawberry Heritage Trail'.

Also of historical interest, but of very different structural aesthetics, is the Te Waimate historic thatched **'cuddy'**, which is almost as cute as the wallabies. Built in 1854 from a single totara tree, it was the home of Michael Studholme, the first European settler in the town. Waimate is often used as a short cut to the Waimate River and **Benmore/Aviemore Lakes**, which are famous for their watersports and superb fishing. The huge and very uncuddly Quinnant salmon are the prime target. The VIC (I-Site) has details and listings of local guides.

◉ South of Canterbury listings

For Sleeping and Eating price codes and other relevant information, see Essentials pages 44-50.

◉ Sleeping

Ashburton *p520*

AL-A Ashburton Motor Lodge, 507 West St, T03-307 0399/T0800-427428, www.ashburton motorlodge.co.nz. Modern and upmarket.

AL-A Hotel Ashburton, 11 Racecourse Rd, T0800-330880/T03-307 8887, www.hotelash.co.nz. Modern units with in-house restaurant, bar and spas.

A-B Taylors Lodge, 770 East St, T03-308 9119, www.taylorslodgemotel.co.nz. 11 units, standard facilities.

AL-D Coronation Holiday Park, 780 East St, T0800-101965/T03-308 6603,

www.coronationpark.co.nz. Ideally placed with full range of accommodations and camp kitchen. Bookings advised.

C-D Ashburton Holiday Park, Tinwald Domain, Moronan Rd, T03-3086805. 2 km south of town but recommended, offering 2 great value spacious cabins, powered/tent sites, and camp kitchen.

Timaru *p521, map p525*

The piazza overlooking Caroline Bay is a fine place to be based.

LL Kingsdown Manor, 10 Bristol Rd, T03-684 9612, www.kingsdownmanor.co.nz. A 4-star rated boutique B&B in a former Anglican chapel located 7 km south of the town centre. Three luxurious en suites, a guest lounge with open fire and a private courtyard, all maintaining their former ecclesiastical character. Dinner on request.

AL-A Aspen on King, 51-53 King St, close to the Botanic Gardens, T03-688 3054, www.aspenonking.co.nz. Units with spa.

AL-A Benvenue Hotel and Motor Inn, 16-22 Evans St, T0800-104049/T03-688 4049, www.benvenue.co.nz. Good restaurant, heated pool and spa.

A-B Panorama Motor Lodge, 50-52 Bay Hill, T0800-103310/T03-688 0097, www.panorama.net.nz. Handy for restaurants on the piazza, and Caroline Bay.

B-D 1873 Wanderer Backpackers, 24 Evans St, T03-688 8795, wandererbackpackers@xtra.co.nz. All types of room, including good spacious doubles. Homely atmosphere with open fires, free bike hire. Pick-ups available.

Motorcamps

B-D Timaru Top Ten Holiday Park, 154a Selwyn St, T0800-242121/T03-684 7690, www.timaruholiday park.co.nz. In a suburban setting, a good walk from the centre, quiet, spacious, and modern.

Geraldine *p522*

L The Crossing, 124 Woodbury Rd, Geraldine, T03-693 9689, www.thecrossingbnb.co.nz. A former old 'gentleman's residence' in the town itself, with sunny, spacious en suites, pleasant gardens, open fire and in-house restaurant.

A-B Crown Hotel, 31 Talbot St, T03-693 8458, Geraldine-crown@xtra.co.nz. Has ood-value en suites. Cheap pub meals.

A-B Four Peaks, 28 MacKenzie St, T03-693

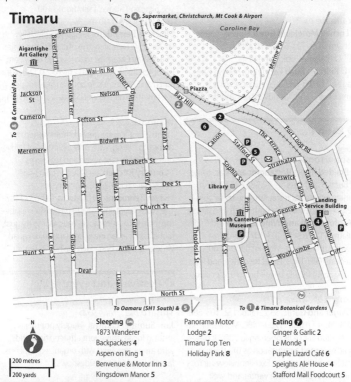

Timaru

To ④, Supermarket, Christchurch, Mt Cook & Airport

Caroline Bay

Beverley Rd

Aigantighe Art Gallery 🏛

Beverley Hill

Wai-Iti Rd

Albert

Jackson St

Seaview Terr

Nelson

Hewling

Bay Hill

Piazza

Cameron

Sefton St

Sarah St

Canon

Stafford St

The Terrace

Port Loop Rd

Strathalan

Beswick

Meremere

Bidwill St

Elizabeth St

Grey Rd

Dee St

Matilda St

Sophia St

Library □

Station

Clyde

York St

Brunswick St

Church St

Sutter

Perth

King George St

Landing Service Building

South Canterbury Museum 🏛

Barnard St

Stafford St

Turnbull

Le Cren St

Gibson St

Arthur St

Theodosia St

Bank St

Butler

Latrel St

Woollcombe

Cliff

Hunt St

Deal

Lisava

North St

Pol

To Oamaru (SH1 South) & ⑤

To ① & Timaru Botanical Gardens

N

200 metres
200 yards

Sleeping 🛏
1873 Wanderer Backpackers **4**
Aspen on King **1**
Benvenue & Motor Inn **3**
Kingsdown Manor **5**

Panorama Motor Lodge **2**
Timaru Top Ten Holiday Park **8**

Eating 🍴
Ginger & Garlic **2**
Le Monde **1**
Purple Lizard Café **6**
Speights Ale House **4**
Stafford Mall Foodcourt **5**

8339, www.fourpeaksmotel.co.nz. Modern and good value.

A-B Rawhiti Backpackers, 27 Hewlings St, T03-693 8252, www.rawhitibackpackers.co.nz. Pleasant backpackers in a peaceful position, yet just a short walk from the town centre. All room types and off-street parking.

Motorcamps
B-D Geraldine Holiday Park, 39 Hislop St, T03-693 8147, www.geraldine holidaypark.co.nz. In a central location adjacent to the park. Cabins and powered/tent sites.
C-D Peel Forest Motor Camp, 1202 Peel Forest Rd, T03-696 3567, www.peel forest.co.nz. Basic but tidy, it offers cabins, powered/tent sites and pleasant walks nearby. On-site café and characterful bar.

Waimate *p523*
B Locheil Motel and Guest House, 100 Shearman St, T03-689 7570. Offers self-contained studios and units.
B-D Kelcey's Bush Farmyard, Mill Rd (see page 524), T03-689 8057. Good for campervans and has tidy cabins and flats.

🍴 Eating

Ashburton *p520*
🍴🍴 **Braided Rivers Restaurant and Bar**, corner of Burnett and Cass Sts, T03-307 2540. New contemporary bar restaurant and by far the best bet in the town for both lunch and dinner.
🍴 **Ashford Café and Wine Bar**, Ashford Craft Village, 415 West St, T03-307 7664, www.ashford.co.nz. Mon-Fri 0900-1600, Sat-Sun 1000-1600. Great for coffee and light snacks, with freshly baked bread a speciality.

Timaru *p521, map p525*
🍴 **Ginger and Garlic**, 335 Stafford St, T03-688 3981. Mon-Fri from 1200-1400, Mon-Sat from 1700-2200. Since its opening in 2005 it has steadily earned a reputation as the town's best fine dining venue. Excellent views across the bay, an open fire in winter and well

above average service all add to the experience.

The piazza and Bay Hill Rd that overlook Caroline Bay have 2 good affordable eateries:
🍴🍴 **Le Monde**, T03-688 8550. A good mix of Euro and Pacific Rim cuisine, lunch and dinner.
🍴🍴 **Speights Ale House**, George St, T03-686 6030. As ever, a good option.
🍴 **The Purple Lizard Café**, 332 Stafford St, T03-688 8890. Mon-Fri 0730-1700, Sat 0900-1700, Sun 1000-1700. For homesick Scottish people there is porridge on the breakfast menu. It might not be as good as Granny's but it will do and the coffee is grand.

Geraldine *p522*
🍴🍴 **Totara Bar and Restaurant**, Crown Hotel, see Sleeping above. Daily from 1100. Traditional kiwi pub meals.
🍴 **Barkers Berry Barn**, see page 523. Daily 0900-1730. Definitely the place for smoothies.
🍴 **Easy Way Café**, next to the Barkers Berry Barn Complex, 76F Talbot St, T03-693 8090. Daily for lunch and dinner. A safe bet with fine cuisine, live entertainment (especially jazz) and internet.

Waimate *p523*
There is not a great deal of choice when it comes to eating, with only a handful of fairly unremarkable takeaways and tearooms.
🍴 **Country Kitchen**, on Queen St, T03-689 8222. Daily 0500-2100. Light snacks.
🍴 **Savoy Tearooms**, 59 Queen St, T03-689 7147. The place to get your gnashers round a wallaby meat pie with plum sauce. You can also try goat, rabbit and thar (an introduced mountain goat). Vegetarians had best catch the bus to Timaru.

🎉 Festivals and events

Timaru *p521, map p525*
Jan Summer Carnival Hugely popular among locals, this event attracts thousands who are entertained with organized concerts, fairground rides and sideshows.

▲ Activities and tours

Ashburton p520
For local activities consult the VIC. Pick-ups are provided for other activities to the west including rafting and ballooning. There are also some interesting day tours available to the Foothills and Mt Somers.

Timaru p521, map p525
Fishing
Timaru is noted not only for its sand and surf but also for its inland rivers, which come complete with monster trout. The VIC can advise on locations and guides.

Walking
There are plenty of good short walks in the town, with 3 heritage trails, and the 1-hr **Dashing Rocks**, the 45-min **Caroline Bay Walks**, and the **Centennial Park Walk** (see page 522). The VIC has details.

Geraldine p522
Geraldine is the base for activity operators. **Wilderness Adventures**, T03-693 7254, www.4x4newzealand.co.nz. Full- or half-day excursions to remote stations in a 4WD truck and perhaps the inevitable but deservedly popular *Lord of the Rings* tour to the stunning Erewhon Station and Mt Sunday (Edoras). **Rangitata Rafts**, T03-696 3534, T0800-251251, www.rafts.co.nz. Day excursions on the scenic Rangitata River (Grade IV-V), $195.

◉ Transport

Timaru p521, map p525
Car hire Avis, 9 Heaton St, T03-688 6240/ T0800-655111. **First Choice Rental Vehicles Ltd**, 207 Evans St, T03-688 5560.
Taxi Timaru Taxis, T03-6888 899.

❶ Directory

Timaru p521, map p525
Banks All the main branches have ATMs and are in the town centre around Stafford St. **Internet** VIC (I-Site); Library, King George Pl, T03-684 8199. **Police** North St, T03-688 4199. **Post office** 19 Strathallan St, T03-686 6040, Mon-Fri 0830-1730, Sat 0900-1300.

MacKenzie Country → Colour map 5, B3/4

The area known as the MacKenzie Country refers mainly to the flat expanse of tussock grasslands that make up the watersheds of the Tekapo and Gray rivers. It is a strange barren landscape, devoid of trees and almost analogous to the plains of heartland USA. There is nowhere else like it in New Zealand and it bears little semblance to the lofty peaks that rise from around its edge. The name MacKenzie was bestowed upon it through the near-legendary activities of Scottish pioneer and sheep drover James 'Jock' MacKenzie. ➤ *For Sleeping, Eating and other listings, see pages 531-534.*

Ins and outs
Getting there All the daily west-east buses from Christchurch and Queenstown pass through Fairlie, Lake Tekapo and Twizel including **Intercity**, T03-365 1113, and **Atomic Shuttles**, T03-349 0697. Only **Intercity** stop in Mount Cook. **Cook Connection**, T0800-266526/T021-583211, www.cookconnect.co.nz, offers daily services between Mount Cook, Tekapo and Twizel, $30 one way. Transport bookings can at the VIC on Main St, Tekapo, T03-680 6686 and the Twizel VIC, T03-4353124.

Tourist information The closest you find to a VIC in Fairlie is the **Resource Centre** ⓘ *64 Main St, T03-685 8496, www.fairlie.co.nz, daily 0900-1700*. The independent **Lake Tekapo VIC** ⓘ *is on the main street, T03-680 6686, www.mtcooknz.com, daily 0800-2000*, is very small but has free town maps, information about lodging and local activities. **Twizel VIC (Events** Centre) ⓘ *Market Pl, centre of the village, T03-435 3124, www.twizel.com, daily 0900-1800 (winter Mon-Sat 1000-1600)*. The free leaflet *Twizel – Town of Trees* has a detailed map and is useful. The **DoC area office** ⓘ *Wairepo Rd, Twizel, T03-435 0802, kakivisitorhide@doc.govt.nz, Mon-Fri 0830-1730*, can provide specialist tramping and mountain bike track information. The best website is www.mtcooknz.com.

Fairlie

Lying relatively out on its own at the foot of the Hunter and Two Thumbs Ranges, the small rural settlement of Fairlie is often labelled as the rather dull gateway to the MacKenzie Country that lies just to the west through the portal of the **Burke's Pass**.

While it is unlikely that Fairlie will ever set the world alight, it seems perfectly happy with its pretty autumn colours and quiet existence. Quiet, that is, until winter when it is used as a base for the **Mount Dobson Ski-field** ⓘ *T03-685 8039, www.dobson.co.nz*.

If you look a little closer you will find considerable evidence that contradicts Fairlie's reputation for being just another dull rural town. It has in fact been home to some rather innovative folk. One such resident, Rodolph Wigley, for example, drove from Timaru to Mount Cook in 1906 in a De Dion Bouton single-cylinder car, taking three days and encountering atrocious conditions (and few roads) to do so. Not satisfied with this rather impressive mechanical feat, he then went on to develop a motor-coach service and later an air transport service to Mount Cook, thereby creating the **Mount Cook Company**. Still not satisfied with this thriving enterprise, he then added a threshing mill business to his list of achievements and a traction engine that could do the work of 16 bullocks at twice the speed. And it doesn't end there. Rodolph's son, Harry, went on to design a landing gear that allowed his aircraft to land on the snow and ice of the Tasman Glacier. This gear was later to become the precursor to the landing gear used today. So, you see, it is interesting after all.

Other little insights can be procured from the two small museums in town: the **1875 Mabel Binney Cottage** and the **Vintage Machinery Museum** ⓘ *on the main highway west of the town centre, daily 0830-1700, seasonal, $2*. Five kilometres west of here is the historic 1879 limestone **Woolshed** ⓘ *on the privately owned Three Springs Station, T03-685 8174, daily 1000-1600, seasonal*.

Lake Tekapo

Between Lake Tekapo and Twizel is the heart of the MacKenzie Country. If you have come north from the heady heights of Mount Cook there could hardly be a greater contrast in scenery. Lakes and mountains quickly give way to the vast expanse of featureless tussock grasslands of the Tekapo River basin. Suddenly it seems you have been magically transported from the Swiss Alps to Mid-West USA, and on less than a litre of petrol. From whichever direction you have approach, SH8 delivers you to the southern shores of Lake Tekapo and the settlement of the same name.

Tekapo is a pretty place, famous for its lakeside church and an ever-watchful little collie dog. However, over the last five years or so Tekapo has suffered somewhat from the rapacious development so evident throughout the central South Island. Already parts of the village are looking horribly like a Christchurch suburb, which is enough to have a little collie dog heading for the hills with its tail between its legs.

The legend of 'Jock' McKenzie

The story goes that in 1855 James was caught in the Burke Pass, east of Lake Tekapo, with 1000 sheep, which belonged to the Rhodes brothers from the large Levels Station near Timaru. The Rhodes boys had sent out a small party to look for the flock and found James happily droving them to pastures new. James managed to escape but was later recaptured in Lyttleton near Christchurch, found guilty of sheep rustling and sentenced to five years in jail, despite professing his innocence, claiming the sheep had in fact been bought and that he was taking his 'legally purchased' flock to a new claim in Otago. A determined James escaped, not once, but two (some say three) times, by which time the powers that be were beginning to believe his story. Remarkably, after only nine months he was given a full pardon and released. He is immortalized by a monument and stone cairn on the roadside, just west of the pass. On the monument you can read the immortal words: 'In this spot James MacKenzie (sic) freebooter, was captured by John Sidebottom and Maoris, Taiko and Seventeen and escaped the same night, 4th March 1855'.

Just about everybody who visits Lake Tekapo pays homage to the **Church of the Good Shepherd**, which sits alone, overlooking the lake. Even on closer inspection it could not look more perfect, with an open door revealing a cross on the altar backed by a large stained-glass window. It was built in 1935, primarily as a functional place of worship, but also as a memorial to the lives of the MacKenzie Country pioneers. Sadly though, its modern-day function is almost entirely aesthetic, and the minister, who is in attendance almost daily, must tend a very superficial and transitory flock (the vast majority of whom fall out of tour buses). Whatever you do, go early in the morning or late in the day to avoid the hordes.

A few pew lengths from the church is a statue of a collie **sheepdog**; a simple tribute to the shepherd's best friend. It's a lovely statue, with the dog facing the lake with an alert and loyal expression as if waiting for his master to appear from its mists. He has waited a long time, and may wait forever, his little nose covered in ice in winter, wet with rain in spring and bleached by the sun in summer.

Dominating the scene at the western end of Tekapo Village is **Mount John**, which at 300 m offers great views and a suitable home for the University of Canterbury's **Observatory** ① *T03-6806960, www.earthandsky.co.nz, Observatory tours 1100-1500, 40-mins from $30, child $15; stargazing summer 2200 (winter 2000), 2hrs from $75, child $45, café open 0900-1700*. Open to the public, its popular Earth and Sky operation offers daytime guided tours and night stargazing. Weather permitting, the stargazing tour is fascinating and offers a great opportunity to see such 'heavenly bodies' as the Alpha-Centuri and the Southern Cross. Even if you cannot join the tours the café is well worth a visit for the views.

Back down to earth and at the base of Mount John is Tekapo's latest attraction the **Alpine Springs, Spa & Winter Park** ① *6 Lakeside Dr, T03-6806550/T0800 23538283, www.alpinesprings.co.nz, open daily 1000-2100. Hot pools from $16, child $9; ice-skating $14, child $11; snow tubing $15, child $11; combo deals available.*

The Springs facility offers 3 hot pools and several private hot tubs that look out over the lake and range in temperature from 36-40°C. The day spa offers the standard facilities and treatments including sauna, steam room and massage. The Winter Park comprises an ice rink for skating, ice hockey and curling events and outside a snow tubing run (in effect a 100-m long artificial snow slope with purpose built contours for snow tubing).

If you have time (and a rugged vehicle) the unsealed roads on either side of Lake Tekapo are well worth exploring. The road to the west passes **Lake Alexandria** and **Lake McGregor**, both of which are very peaceful (and full of trout), before winding its way north to terminate at the Godley Peak Station. On the eastern side the road travels along the lakes edge past the Mount Hay and Richmond Stations and the junction to the **Roundhill Ski Area** before continuing up in to the wilds of Macaulay and Godley River basins. On a map you will see just how far the glacier formed Godley River Basin goes before submitting inevitably to the peaks of the Mount Cook National Park and Mt D'Archiac (2865 m). This is the realm of the serious tramper and climber; without a helicopter it takes days to reach.

Twizel

Right in the heart of the MacKenzie Basin, near the river after which it was named, is Twizel, a former hydroelectric scheme construction town built in the 1970s. Pioneer surveyor John Thompson bestowed the name Twizel upon the town after the Twizel Bridge that crosses the River Tweed on the border between England and Scotland. Twizel's most famous residents are the critically endangered and endemic khaki, or black stilt, which, along with the village's proximity to the Mount Cook National Park and mountain biking, are its biggest tourist draw.

Twizel also presents an excellent opportunity to see cutting-edge conservation in action. The DoC's efforts to maintain the wild populations of the **black stilt** – one of the rarest wading birds in the world – have been internationally recognized. Known as 'khaki' by the Maori and considered to be a *taonga* species (living treasure), these birds were once common in the heartlands and braided-river beds throughout New Zealand. Thanks primarily to man's indirect introduction of non-native predatory species, like the weasel and stoat, numbers have been decimated and currently total less than 100 wild birds. A guided visit to the **viewing hide** ⓘ *3 km south of the village, tours daily late Oct-mid Apr (weekdays only in winter), $12.50, child $5, contact Twizel DoC, T03-435 0802*, allows the public to see some of the stalwart survivors. The captive population of 66 are bred in enclosed aviaries and used to replenish the wild population. Bookings are essential and visits are by prior arrangement only.

Lake Ohau

Largely unbeaten by the commercial stick, Lake Ohau provides a pleasant diversion off SH8 between Omarama and Twizel, and in winter a popular skiing venue. The **ski field** ⓘ *for skiing information, T03-438 9885, www.snow.co.nz*, is best known for its scenic views, less frenzied atmosphere and the longest T-bar in New Zealand (1033 m). Most of the activity centres around **Lake Ohau Alpine Village** which is above the southern shores of Lake Ohau, just west of **Lake Middleton**, a small sub-lake separated from Lake Ohau by a narrow strip of land.

In summer the lake and its surroundings are popular for walking, fishing and mountain biking. It has six forests around its shores, with a number of tracks, access points and campsites. The best information is contained in the DoC brochure *Ohau Conservation Area*, available from the VIC in Twizel.

For Sleeping and Eating price codes and other relevant information, see Essentials pages 44-50.

● Sleeping

Fairlie *p528*

AL-A Dobson Lodge, Burke's Pass, T03-685 8316, www.dobsonlodge.co.nz. Halfway between Fairlie and Tekapo (5 mins from Mt Dobson ski field), this B&B has standard double and single en suites and a self-contained converted railway carriage. Dinner available.

A McKenzie Motel, 16 School Rd, T0800-685001/T03-685 8452. Basic but very clean and comfortable.

B Possum Cottage, McLeans Rd, Bedeshurst, T03-685 8075, www.possumcottage.co.nz. Self-contained, farm-based and very cosy.

B Rimuwhare, 53 Mt Cook Rd, T03-685 8058, rimuwhare@xtra.co.nz. Four self-contained units in a garden setting. In-house restaurant.

Motorcamps and campsites

B-D Fairlie Gateway Top Ten Holiday Park, Allandale Rd, northwest of the town centre, T03-685 8375, www.fairlietop10.co.nz. Usual reliable Top 10 facilities.

Lake Tekapo *p528*

In Maori the name Tekapo means 'sleeping mat', but thankfully the village can offer far more than a bivvy beside the lake. Contact the VIC for full listings.

LL-L Tekapo Lodge, 24 Aorangi Cres, above the main street, T03-680 6566, www.lake tekapolodge.co.nz. Spacious, purpose-built B&B overlooking Lake Tekapo, a short stroll from the village centre. 4 luxury en suites, one with spa. Large guest lounge with open fire.

L-AL Godley Resort Hotel, SH8, T03-680 6848, www.tekapo.co.nz/The-Godley-Resort-Hotel. The main hotel in town. Although getting a little tired it is in prime position in the centre of the village overlooking the lake. It has comfortable suites with great views, and restaurant serving a seasonal buffet and à la carte menu. It gets busy with tour groups in summer, but in winter when rates are reduced, it is worth considering.

L-AL Glacier Rock B&B, 35 Lochinver Av, T03-680 669, www.glacierrock.co.nz. Just 2 mins from the centre of the village a new and impressive two-storey timber frame home offering 2 immaculate en suites with fine lake and mountain views.

L-A Chalet Boutique Motel, T03-680 6774, www.thechalet.co.nz. A fine lodge-style boutique motel. In a great location by the lake (near the church) and with plenty of activities.

AL-A Lake Tekapo Scenic Resort Motel, T0800-118666/T03-680 6808, www.laketekapo.com. In the heart of the action. Modern studio units with views and spas and also budget rooms (sleeping 4) or dorms with shared facilities.

B-D Tailor-Made-Tekapo Backpackers, 9-11 Aorangi Cres, T03-680 6700, www.tailor-made-backpackers.co.nz. Friendly and efficient. An activity-oriented place, with a good range of rooms, some en suite.

C-D Lake Tekapo YHA, 3 Simpson Lane, T03-680 6857, yhatekapo@yha.org.nz. Lakeside location at the western end of the village, offering great views. Doubles, twins and dorms, cosy lounge with log fire, bike hire. There is even a hostel cat to cuddle if you are missing your own.

Motorcamps and campsites

A-D Lake Tekapo Motels, Motor Camp and Backpackers, western end of the village, Lakeside Dr, T0800-853853 T03-680 6825, www.laketekapo-accommodation.co.nz. Spacious and peaceful in a fine lakeside spot and just metres from the new Alpine Springs, Spa & Winter Park. Self-contained motels, flats, cabins and sheltered powered/tent sites. The purpose-built backpacker lodge has earned a 4-star rating and faces the lake. It offers the full compliment of rooms and a spacious lounge.

Twizel p530

L-AL MacKenzie Country Inn, corner of Ostler and Wairepo rds, T03-435 0869, www.mackenzie.co.nz. Very plush, with good facilities and close to the town centre.

AL Aoraki Lodge, 32 MacKenzie Dr, T03-435 0300, www.aorakilodge.co.nz. A reliable option.

AL Artemis B&B, 33 North West Arch, T03-435 0388, atremistwizel@paradise.net.nz. A central modern home with very welcoming hosts and fine views.

AL Heartland Lodge, 19 North West Arm, T03-435 0008, www.heartland-lodge.co.nz. Has some pleasant en suite rooms and a self-contained loft, good value for up to 6.

AL-A Aspen Court Motel, 10 MacKenzie Drive, T03-435 0274, www.aspencourt.co.nz. 15 units with good facilities.

AL-A Lake Ruataniwha Homestay, 9 Max Smith Dr, T03-435 0532, robinandlester@xtra.co.nz. A spacious modern home overlooking the lake, southwest of the centre.

A Mountain Chalets Motel, Wairepo Rd, T03-435 0785, www.mountainchalets.co.nz. Standard units, mountain chalets and a lodge with budget accommodation.

A-D High Country Holiday Lodge and Motel, 23 MacKenzie Dr, T03-435 0671, www.highcountrylodge.co.nz. A huge motel with backpacker facilities, including cheap en suites, doubles, singles and dorms. There is also a restaurant and bar on site and it is a stone's throw from Market Place.

Motorcamps

B-D Parklands Alpine Tourist Park, 122 MacKenzie Dr, T03-435 0507. Sheltered with self-contained and budget accommodation.

C-D Lake Ruataniwha Holiday Park, 4 km south of the village, T03-435 0613. In a pleasant setting near the lake.

Lake Ohau p530

L-AL Lake Ohau Lodge, T03-438 9885, www.ohau.co.nz. Set by the lake, it has 72 standard self-contained studio and luxury units, a restaurant, bar, cosy open fire and hot outdoor spa pools. Of course it is most popular in winter as a base for the local skifield but in summer is the perfect place to get off the beaten track.

● Eating

Fairlie p528

♥ **Old Library Café**, in the centre of town, T03-685 8999. Daily 1000-late. Recommended, offering snacks to dinners including a great 2-course 'skiers' menu for under $15.

Lake Tekapo p528

There are many café/bars and takeaways in the main street; many have views across the lake, but the best view is to be had from the **Astro Café** at the summit of Mt John (see below). There is a **Four Square** supermarket at the service station, open until 2100.

♥♥ **Astro Cafe**, Mt John Observatory, (follow signs west end of the village). Daily 0900-1700. An excellent venue for good coffee and light meals. Recommended.

♥♥ **Godley Resort Hotel**, T03-680 6688. Daily for breakfast, lunch and dinner. Convenient with a choice of buffet or à la carte.

♥♥-♥ **Pepes Pizza and Pasta**, T03-6806677. Mon-Fri 1800-late, Sat-Sun from 1200-late.

♥♥-♥ **Reflections Restaurant**, T03-680 6234. Daily from 1000. Suitable for light lunches and formal dinner, with good views across the lake.

Twizel p530

The limited options are centred in Market Pl.

♥♥ **The Hunter's Bar and Café**, T03-435 0303. The local's choice for lunch, dinner and entertainment. It can serve up a decent coffee.

♥♥ **MacKenzie Country Inn**, see above. Daily from 1100. Also offers fine dining.

♥♥-♥ **Shawty's Cafe**, 4A Market Pl, T03-435 3155. Daily from 0830. Reliable option, reasonably priced and with good coffee.

▲ Activities and tours

Lake Tekapo p528
Although Lake Tekapo is a small place there is plenty to do. Being the first major stop for the east-west tour buses and independent tourist traffic, there is an instant lure to leave the car parked and head for the skies on an exciting scenic flight or, more recently, with the new stargazing and daytime tours of the Mt John Astronomical Observatory. Various operators also vie to offer the best deals. For the latest deals contact the VIC.

Astronomical observatory tours and star gazing
Earth and Sky, T03-680 6960, www.newzealandsky.com/earthandsky. Observatory tours 1100-1500, 1 hr from $30, child $15; stargazing summer 2200 (winter 2000), 2 hrs from $80, child $45. Family tours on request. See page 529.

Cruising and fishing
Cruise Tekapo, T027-479 7675, www.cruise tekapo.co.nz. Offers lake cruising from 20 mins to 2 hrs and half or full-day trout fishing excursions.

Flightseeing
There are a number of flightseeing options. The airfield in Tekapo is the starting point for 2 main operators that also pick up passengers in Mt Cook, before embarking on world-class scenic flights across the Great Divide.
Air Safaris, Main St, T0800-806880, www.airsafaris.co.nz. The popular 'Grand Traverse' is a memorable 50-min (200 km) trip that takes in Mt Cook and the glaciers on both sides of the divide. It is an unusual combination that you would be hard-pressed to find anywhere else. There will also be plenty of other options in Wanaka and Queenstown, but this trip (beyond a flight to Milford Sound) is one of the best and, at $295, child $195, is good value for money.
Tekapo Helicopters, T0800-359835/ T03-680 6229, www.tekapohelicopters.co.nz.

Helicopter trips are a little more expensive, but provide a different kind of experience. Note that the choppers based here do not land on the snow unlike those flying from Mt Cook, but, what you lose in that experience, you will gain in flight time.

Horse trekking
McKenzie Alpine Trekking, Godley Rd (north), below Mt John, T0800-628269, www.maht.co.nz. Horse trekking from 1 hr to overnight, suitable for all levels.

Mountain climbing and trekking
Alpine Recreation, T0800-006096/ T03-680 6736, www.alpinerecreation.co.nz. Highly experienced guided mountain climbing and trekking trips from the 3-day 'Ball Pass Trek' in the Tasman Glacier Valley, to the serious 6-day ascent of Mt Cook, which will set you back $4000.

Skiing
Roundhill Ski Area, T03-680 6977, www.roundhill.co.nz. Lift pass from $70, with gear hire from $38 per day.

Twizel p530
The VIC also lists over 60 things Twizel can offer in the way of activities, ranging from frisbee golf to ice skating. There are also some excellent fishing venues.
Discovery Tours, T03-435 0114, www.discoverytours.co.nz. Run by ex-park rangers, it offers a wide variety of options in Glentanner Park (see page 535) including hiking (glacier and mountain), mountain and heli-biking and even the inevitable *Lord of the Rings Tour*, start from $55. Recommended.

Climbing
Twizel Events Centre, Market Pl (just opposite the VIC), T03-435 0496. Wall open Mon, Wed, Fri 1900-2100, Sat 1700-1900, Sun 1600-1800. New and impressive complex with climbing wall as well as squash courts and a gym, all open for casual use. A session on the wall costs from $12.

Eco-tours
Khaki (Black Stilt) Visitor Hide Guided Tours, Wairepo Rd, T03-435 0802, kakivisitorhide@doc.govt.nz. Guided trips to see one of the rarest waders in the world.

Flightseeing
A number of scenic heli-flightseeing trips leave from beside the MacKenzie Country Inn on Wairepo Rd, but you are advised to look at the numerous other choices available from elsewhere before parting with your cash (see Mt Cook National Park, page 538).

Mountain biking
Of particular note are the heli-biking trips to several locations including Benmore and Lake Ohau. The numerous canals and their associated tracks that connect the waterways and hydroelectric schemes provide ideal biking opportunities. For more information consult the VIC or the DoC leaflet *Ohau Conservation Area*. Bike hire is available. **Heli-bike Twizel**, T0800- 435424/ T03-435 0626, www.helibike.com. Rides

(helicopter and non-helicopter) range from 1½-3½ hrs and cost $55-449.

Mountaineering
High Country Expeditions, T03-435 0622, www.highcountrynz.com. World-class mountain guide Shaun Norman offers climbing, mountaineering and abseiling.

⊖ Transport

Lake Tekapo *p528*
Bicycle hire From the mini golf office behind the main shopping complex, T03-680 6961.

❶ Directory

Lake Tekapo *p528*
Banks There is only one ATM in Tekapo, next to the petrol station. **Internet** Reflections Restaurant, top end of the village and **Helicopter Flights Office** on Main St.

Mount Cook National Park → *Colour map 5, B3.*

This 70,696-ha park has to be one of the most spectacular in New Zealand, and a natural 'cathedral' second only to Milford Sound. With the 3754 m peak of Mount Cook as its altar, its robust ministers include Tasman (3498 m) and Mount Sefton (3158 m), surrounded by a supportive choir of 19 peaks all over 3000 m. Rising up to this great chancel are the vast and impressive Hooker and Tasman glaciers, which not only created the long nave but once blocked the very porch. All this natural architecture makes for world-class scenery and mountaineering. Indeed, it was here that Sir Edmund Hillary first started a career that was to reach its 'peak' on the summit of Everest in 1953. The park is connected to the Westland National Park by the Great (east-west) Divide and peaks of the Liebeg Range, yet the two parks are significantly different. With such a dramatic upheaval of rock so close to the sea, the western side sees most rain and snow, creating slopes draped in dense rainforest and, higher up, huge snowfields, spawning the great Franz and Fox glaciers (to name but two). In the Mount Cook National Park, on the other hand, there is virtually no forest, with around one-third of it being permanent snow and ice. In among the rock beds and valley floors rare alpine plants flourish, some endemic and rare, and rummaging around in this heady garden are endemic bird species, like the mountain parrot and resident vandal – the kea.

The area is considered sacred by the Maori who see Aoraki (Mount Cook) as a symbol of being, an ancestor from whom the Tangata Whenua (the Ngai Tahu people) are descended, and a link between the supernatural and natural world. ▸▸ *For Sleeping, Eating and other listings, see pages 538-540.*

Ins and outs

Getting there Mount Cook village is 63 km from Twizel. **Intercity**, T03-365 1113, buses offer a daily service from Christchurch (Queenstown-bound) departing at 1415 and Queenstown (Christchurch-bound) departing at 1350 from the Hermitage Hotel. Several tour buses, including **Great Sights**, T0800-744487, www.greatsights.com, also ply the Christchurch/Queenstown route daily, arriving from Christchurch at 1255 and departing early afternoon. **The Cook Connection**, T021-583211/T0800-252666, www.cookconnect.co.nz, offers a daily service between Mount Cook and Glentanner/Tekapo/Twizel from $15 one-way. All the bus services stop at the YHA and the Hermitage, both of which act as booking agents.

Tourist information There is a VIC at the head of Lake Pukaki, SH 8, Lake Pukaki, T03-4353280.The **DoC information centre** ① *just below the Hermitage Hotel, Bowen Drive, T03-435 1186/1818, www.mtcooknz.com, daily 0830-1800 (winter 0830-1700),* has displays, an audio-visual presentation and information surrounding the park and its obvious attractions. There are leaflets on walks, tramping information and an up-to-date weather forecast. All hut bookings are administered here and intentions forms are provided. Of immediate use is a map of the village contained in the handy leaflet *Aoraki, Mount Cook Alpine Village.*

The road to Mount Cook

Some 8 km north of Twizel, the famed SH80 skirts the western banks and azure waters of **Lake Pukaki** to pay homage to Aoraki (Mount Cook). Before entering the chancel you are first advised to admire the cathedral from afar from the southern banks of the lake. There is a car park, information centre and **lookout point** from which, on a clear day, the mountain beckons. Unless you are really pressed for time, or the weather is foul, it really is sacrilege not to make the scenic 55-km drive to **Mount Cook Village** (see below). Located so close to the base of the mountains and Hooker and **Tasman Glacier** valleys, it is like a miniature toy-town which acts as the gateway to national park. And once here, it seems a terrible waste to move on without exploring the park from even closer quarters.

Glentanner Park

For the first 32 km towards the mountain valleys, your excitement grows in parallel with the vista before you, as the great snow-capped edifices get larger and larger and, more poignantly, you get smaller and smaller. It really is a bit like entering the gaping mouth of Moby Dick. Before reaching Mount Cook Village, and just beyond the water terminus of Lake Pukaki, you will encounter the motorpark and scenic flightseeing base of **Glentanner Park** ① *T03-435 1855, www.glentanner.co.nz.* You are strongly advised to stop here and muse at the scenic flights and other activities on offer, perhaps over a coffee, in its café overlooking the mountain. If you are in a campervan and intend to stay in the valley overnight, this will be home – there is good basic DoC campsite but no fully facilitated motorpark in the national park or Mount Cook Village.

Mount Cook Village ⊜❼▲⊖ ▶▶ *pp538-540.*

From Glentanner you begin to enter the 'chancel' of the mountains and the national park proper. In Mount Cook, about 23 km further towards the mountains and 63 km from Twizel, you will find yourself climbing out of your 'dinky-toy' car feeling like a termite. It's easy to get neck ache round here.

Sights

After you have recovered from the incredible surrounding views, you will be immediately struck at how ordered and dull in colour Mount Cook Village is. This is not an accident, since the settlement comes within the boundary of the **Mount Cook National Park** and is therefore strictly controlled. The only real exception to this is the **Hermitage Hotel** ① *T0800-686800 /T03-435 1809 www.mount-cook.com*, which many claim to be the most famous in New Zealand (while others hail it merely as a blot on the landscape). Of course it is the setting that makes the hotel special, with its boast of 'mountain views' taking on far more than mere honest credibility. But although the Hermitage has been blessed by location it has also been cursed with misfortune. What you see today is not the original, in fact it is essentially the third. The original that was built in 1884 was located further down the valley and destroyed by flash floods in 1913. Relocated and rebuilt in its present position it was then gutted by fire 44 years later. It has now, once more, been fully renovated. From the hotel's interior, or from its well-manicured lawns, you will no doubt find yourself continuously staring up at Mount Cook along with a statue of Sir Edmund Hillary who is arguably New Zealand's favourite son.

The Hermitage also houses the **Sir Edmund Hillary Alpine Centre Museum** where the Hillary Gallery depicts Sir Edmund's connection with the region and reflects upon his achievements, expeditions and life's work.

While around the hotel also keep your eyes and ears open for kea, the cheeky green mountain parrots that hang about with the sole intention of harrying anything with legs and dismantling all they possess. The DoC campsite at White Horse Hill (see Sleeping, page 539) is another good place to look for them.

As well as the gargantuan vista of Mount Cook and **Mount Sefton** (3158 m), the associate glacier valleys are well worthy of investigation. Directly north of the **Hermitage** is the **Hooker Valley**, and east, over the dwarfed **Wakefield Range**, the vast **Tasman Valley** with its own massive glacier – the longest in New Zealand. Both valleys act as the watersheds, which feed Lake Pukaki and were once full of ice, hence the incredible expanse of boulder-fields that precede the lake's azure waters. It is, incidentally, the presence of fine glacial moraine ('rock flour') that gives the glacial lakes their exotic colour. (It is the presence this flour that is also the reason, thankfully, that you will see no boats on the lake as the flour ruins boat propellers.) There are a number of activities that focus on the glacier valleys and lakes which have already been mentioned (see Glentanner Park, page 535), but they can of course also be explored by foot (see Walking, below).

▲ Tramping

Mount Cook village is the gateway to the **Copeland Pass Track** ① *given the popularity of this hike you will need to book a few days in advance, T03-435 1186*, which is a four- to five-day tramp to the west coast across the Great Divide. As attractive as this may seem, the tramp requires considerable experience and proper mountaineering experience and specialist equipment. It is also ill advised at present due to rock falls at the higher altitudes. Conditions are expected to improve, however, especially with the planned relocation of the Hooker Hut. Although you are still currently permitted to attempt the crossing you are advised to seek advice and check with up-to-date conditions with DoC.

A far more realistic option is the overnight tramp to the new **Mueller Hut**, which sits in a superb position (1768 m) on the ridge of **Mount Oliver** (1933 m) behind Mount Cook Village. Although a strenuous climb requiring a fair level of fitness, proper planning and equipment, it is a classic excursion. If you stay overnight in the vastly improved Mueller Hut, the views at sunset and sunrise over the Hooker and Mount Cook especially are

Sir Edmund Hillary

Sir Edmund Hillary is one of New Zealand's most famous sons, and although best known as the man who first conquered Mount Everest, he is also a noted Antarctic explorer and, in more recent times, well known for his welfare work in Nepal. Born in Auckland in 1919, he worked as an apiarist, before serving with the air force in the Pacific during the Second World War.

It was after the war that Hillary was drawn, time and again, to the mountains of the Southern Alps in New Zealand. Being a committed mountaineer and having immense stamina and ability, it was not long before his obsession took him to the Himalaya. He immediately joined expeditions in 1951 and 1952, but it was on the 29 May 1953 as a member of John Hunt's British team that Hillary and sherpaTenzing Norgay made the first known successful ascent to the summit of Everest – a feat that brought instant fame.

After further expeditions to Nepal in 1954 and 1955, Hillary turned his attentions to another of nature's last frontiers – the Antarctic. From 1956 to 1958 he was a member of a team that completed the first tractor journey from Scott Base to the South Pole. After this successful expedition he returned once again to Everest where he led several expeditions between 1961and 1965, before embarking on another journey to Antarctica to lead the first successful ascent of Mount Herschel.

It is refreshing perhaps that Hillary has gone well beyond the mere desire of climbing, or ego of summit- bagging, and has worked very hard to 'pay back' something to his much- loved Nepal. There is no doubt he has developed a great respect for its people and worked over the years to help raise funds for the creation of schools and hospitals in the region. The first hospital was built in 1966 and he went on to form the Himalayan Trust. His work led to his appointment as New Zealand's High Commissioner to India in 1985.

Still drawn to both Nepal and Antarctica and with an ever-present desire to explore, Hillary served as a tour guide on commercial flights over Antarctica in the 1970s. With a love of nature added to his love of people, Hillary was also, for a time, the proud director of the World Wildlife Fund, adding conservation to his list of interests and activities. He has published several books about his expeditions and two autobiographies. As a small nation New Zealand is proud of Hillary, perhaps because he stands for much of what the country is all about: a oneness with nature and the courage to venture where others have not.

In January 2008, Hillary died of heart failure in Auckland at the age of 88. His death was recognised by the lowering of flags to half-mast on all Government and public buildings and at Scott Base in Antarctic. A state funeral was held later that month. Surprisingly perhaps Hillary's ashes were scattered not from a mountain summit but at sea level on Auckland's Hauraki Gulf as he had desired. He is constantly in the minds of his fellow New Zealanders, not least because his face features on the nation's $5 banknote.

Tip: If you are in the Mount Cook region do not miss the Sir Edmund Hillary Alpine Centre Museum in the Hermitage Hotel, where his life and achievements are showcased.

simply world class. In total it is a stiff four-hour climb each way. A further one-hour return will see you at the top of Mount Oliver, which, rumour has it, was the first peak in the region that Sir Edmund Hillary climbed. For more information and bookings contact DoC and the *Mueller Hut Route* leaflet, $1.

▲▲ Walking

There are some very appealing walks in the vicinity that offer fine views and insights into the local hardy flora and fauna, with most beginning from the village. The shortest is the **Bowen Bush Walk**, which is only 10 minutes but takes you through some classic totara forest. It starts from behind the **Alpine Guides (Aoraki)** ① *Mount Cook Village, T03-435 1834, www.alpineguides.co.nz.* A similar 30-minute walk, the **Glencoe Walk**, starts from behind the **Hermitage Hotel** and another, the one-hour **Governor's Bush Walk**, begins from the public shelter, just to the south of the Alpine Guides Centre. The latter also offers a good viewpoint. Two longer options are the two-hour **Red Tarns Track** (which again begins from the public shelter) and the two- to three-hour **Sealy Tarns Track**, which is part of the Mueller Hut ascent and begins from the Kea Point Track from the **Hermitage**. Both of these walks offer spectacular views from higher altitudes.

The **Kea Point Track** can be tackled from the Hermitage (two hours) or from the White Horse Hill campsite car park (one hour), which is accessed north via the Hooker Valley Road (beside the Kitchener Stream Bridge just at the entrance to the village complex). At the terminus of the Kea Walk is a lookout deck that offers memorable views of Mount Sefton, Footstool, the Hooker Valley, Mueller Glacier and of course Mount Cook. If you want to investigate the Hooker Valley you can do this from the village or from the White Horse Hill car park. In addition to the spectacular views of Mount Cook towering above, the four-hour **Hooker Valley Track** takes you all the way to the ice and melt-water features of the **Hooker Glacier terminal lake**.

The **Tasman Valley** also offers some interesting walks that take in the snout of the vast, advancing glacier. From the village you will need to travel by car or mountain bike to the end of the Tasman Glacier Road (8 km) which is accessed off SH80 south of the village. There are two walks: the three- to four-hour **Ball Shelter Walk**, which skirts the side of the glacier, and the more remarkable one-hour **Glacier Walk**, which investigates the terminal lake and head of the glacier. Both walks start from the car park.

◉ Mount Cook National Park listings

For Sleeping and Eating price codes and other relevant information, see Essentials pages 44-50.

● Sleeping

Glentanner Park *p535*
A-D Glentanner Park, SH80, 15 mins' before Mt Cook, T03-435 1855, www.glen tanner.co.nz. Glentanner Park is the only motorpark in the valley, and the base for several fixed-wing and helicopter scenic flight operators. This certainly creates some noise but surrounded by such scenery it only adds to the buzz of excitement and desire to join in. The accommodation is excellent with surprisingly well-sheltered tent sites as well as self-contained cabins, bunk cabins, backpacker dorms and powered campsites.

The amenities block is also very good with a fully equipped kitchen and a spacious lounge with TV, open fire and a detailed map of the region. The reception and scenic flight terminal also has a full activities booking service and a café open during the day.

Mount Cook Village *p535*
LL-AL Hermitage Hotel, T03-435 1809, www.mount-cook.com. Book ahead in high season. The Hermitage offers something for everyone, from traditional rooms, to a luxury wing with views and modern decor, or self-contained motel doubles, studios and chalets with basic facilities. Bear in mind that the price reflects the location, not necessarily the quality of accommodation. Both the hotel and the motel complex have restaurants and bars

and offer buffet-style lunch and dinner. The café in the hotel serves a range of light snacks and good coffee. There is also a small but expensive store and souvenir shop.

B-D Mount Cook YHA, corner of Bowen Drive and Kitchener Dr, T03-435 1820, yha.mtcook@yha.co.nz. Even if it had competition, this YHA would compete very favourably. It has tidy double, twin and shared rooms, modern ski-lodge style facilities including a log fire, sauna and internet. Book your bed well in advance in summer.

Motorcamps and campsites
Camping is also available at **Glentanner Park**, see above.

D White Horse Hill Campsite, at the end of the Hooker Valley Rd, 2 km from the village (see Walking, page 538). Sheltered DoC campsite.

🍴 Eating

Mount Cook Village *p535*
₩₩₩-₩₩ Hermitage Hotel (see above). There are 2 restaurants, the Alpine Restaurant (buffet), and the à la carte Panorama Restaurant serving traditional New Zealand fare including seafood and game.
₩₩ Old Mountaineers Café Bar, just below the DoC visitor centre, T03-4351890. Daily for lunch and dinner. A fine alternative, offering a wholesome menu. It has a congenial atmosphere with open fire and a room with a pool table and internet.

▲ Activities and tours

Glentanner Park *p535*
Flightseeing
The biggest draw at Glentanner are the fixed-wing and helicopter flightseeing trips. The choices are vast. Fixed-wing trips are also available from Lake Tekapo, see page 533. For all options, bookings are advised and payment is taken shortly before any flights in case of inclement weather.

Cloud 9, T03-4351077. Offers some very appealing heli-hiking trips, from $300.
Helicopter Line, T0800-650651/T03-435 1801, www.helicopter.co.nz. Its Mt Cook (East) operations are based at the park. It offers 3 trips: a 20-min trip with landing to the slopes of the Mt Ohau Range ($210); a 30-min option over the Mt Ohau Range with a landing on the Richardson Glacier (from $295); and a 45-min 'Mountains High' adventure (from $390). The latter is truly memorable: you are flown up and over the Tasman Valley Glacier, before making a snow landing at over 2000 m to sample the view of Mt Cook. Then, back in the air, you cross the Great Divide. From here you encounter the views of the west coast and the fractured bed of the upper Franz and Fox glaciers, before skirting just below Cook's awesome summit and dropping down the Hooker Valley, over Mt Cook Village and back to base.
Mount Cook Ski Planes, Mt Cook Airport just a few kilometres south of Mt Cook Village, T0800-800702/T03-430 8034, www.skiplanes. co.nz. This flightseeing option offers the exciting prospect of a snow-landing high up amid the peaks on the Tasman Glacier. As if the scenery in transit is not spectacular enough, you will experience a very different world at high altitude. As you reluctantly climb back into the aircraft after about 10 mins, you do so in the knowledge that the conditions up there are frequently very different. Trips on offer range from 25-min 'Mini Tasman' with no glacier landing (from $255) to the 40-min 'Glacier Highlights' with glacier landing (from $375), to the 55-min 'Grand Circle', with a landing and a close up of Mt Cook (from $495). Recommended.

Kayaking
Guided kayak trips exploring the ice walls of the glacier lakes, T03-435 1890, 3hrs from $98. Kayak and hike options also available.
Glacier Explorer Trips, T0800-686800/ T03-435 1641, www.glacierexplorers.com. 30-min walk to the terminus of the Tasman Lake, followed by a fascinating 2-hr boat trip to the edge of the ice. From $130, child $65. Recommended.

Other activities
Glentanner has its own horse trekking
operation, T03-435 1855, from 30 mins ($40)
to 3 hrs ($130). It also offers mountain bike
and fishing tackle hire (fishing licence $21).
See also **Discovery Tours** in Twizel (see page
533) for tours within the park.

Mount Cook Village *p535*
Note that all the activities already mentioned
above (Glentanner Park) are also available
from Mt Cook Village. Do not risk any climb
without proper experience or equipment. Mt
Cook National Park is serious business.
Alpine Guides, T03-435 1834, www.alpine
guides.co.nz. The only resident guiding
company in the park and, given the terrain,
the potential challenges and hazards at hand,
its presence is welcome. It offers an excellent
range of multi-day mountaineering and
trekking trips as well as half- to full-day (8-km)
walks. In winter full-day skiing and heliskiing
trips are available on the upper Tasman

Glacier and other equally remote locations.
Although these trips are expensive, they
provide the rare opportunity to ski on virgin
snow in areas simply inaccessible to the
masses. For the latest details and prices visit
their HQ in the village. Open daily 0800-1700.

❶ Directory

Mount Cook Village *p535*
Hermitage Hotel forms the hub of all activity
and services in the village, housing 2 restaurants,
bars, a small and expensive grocery store, and a
café. The hotel also offers internet, currency
exchange, a post office, EFTPOS and activity
bookings. The only thing it does not provide is
petrol which can be purchased (24-hr credit
card and EFTPOS) near the **Alpine Guides
Centre** just to the south (unmanned).
Breakdown assistance T03-435 0214.
Police T03-4350719.

Waitaki Valley → *Colour map 5, B/C 3/4.*

*From Oamaru you have the option of turning inland via SH83 through the picturesque Waitaki Valley
to Omarama, the MacKenzie Country and Mount Cook. It is a pleasant drive, best negotiated in
autumn when the poplar and lakeside weeping willows are draped in gold. Many of the orchards on
the way also offer a palette of autumnal hues. The valley is best known for its lakes and the Waitaki
River, which are regulated by an extensive system of hydroelectric dams that begin to dominate the
waterways of the southwestern Canterbury Region. Fishing for both trout and salmon is one of the
more obvious leisure activities in the area. ►► For Sleeping, Eating and other listings, see page 542.*

Ins and outs
Tourist information **Oamaru VIC (I-Site)** ① *1 Thames St, Oamaru, T03-434 1656,
www.tourismwaitaki.co.nz, Mon-Fri 0800-1800 (1700 in winter), Sat-Sun 1000-1700 (1600 in
winter).* Although in Otago it is the main source of information for the Waitaki Valley to
Omarama.

Omarama
Located at the head of the Waitaki Valley and north of the scenic **Lindis Pass** (from
Wanaka and Queenstown), Omarama provides a convenient overnight stop and starting
point from which to explore the MacKenzie Country (see page 527). There are a number of
local activities that may detain you, including fishing and water sports on lakes Benmore
and Aviemore, gliding from Omarama airfield and skiing at Lake Ohau.

Other than the obvious appeal of the local lakes, the **Clay Cliffs** between Omarama and Twizel are worthy of investigation, and echo the bizarre eroded rock and gravel formations of the Pinnacles in the Wairarapa, North Island. To reach them turn off SH8 west towards the mountains on Quailburn Road, 3 km north of the village (signposted), 15 km. There is a small charge at the gate to the cliffs. Omarama is world-renowned for gliding, with the huge expanses of thermal-rich grasslands and mountain offering world-class conditions and scenic flights that are virtually unparalleled. ▶ *See Activities and tours, page 542.*

The newest attraction in the village is the **Hot Tubs complex** ① *2 Omarama Av, T03-4389703, www.hottubsomarama.co.nz,* offering eight private tubs (from $40), two private wellness 'pods' (with private sauna, outdoor private hot tub, shower and changing room, from $125) and a public sauna (from $25). Massages are also available.

Duntroon

From east to west the first settlement of any significance is Duntroon. With the discovery of gold in 1868 the town enjoyed a brief boom, before the diggings proved a failure, earning them the label of the 'poor man's field'. After a return to relative obscurity, there was more excitement with the discovery of a quartz reef between the Maerewhenua and Otekaike rivers in 1870, but once again, this was short-lived.

Now a small farming settlement, it offers a number of amenities, activities and scenic attractions. There is a petrol station, and visitor information can obtained from the **Flying Pig Café** ① *Campbell St, T03-431 2717.* The **Elephant Rocks**, accessed from Livingstone Road, near the Maerewhenua River Bridge, are an unusual set of limestone outcrops that are worth investigating and also provide good rock climbing possibilities, T03-432 6855. There are **Maori rock drawings** at Takiroa on the other side of the Maerewhenua River Valley dating back over 1000 years (ask at the café for directions).

Kurow to Omarama

Some 23 km west of Duntroon is **Kurow**, which nestles at the confluence of the Hakataramea and Waitaki rivers. Most of the residents work on the hydroelectric dams of lakes Benmore and Aviemore to the west, but for leisure they say there is one activity that stands head and shoulders above the rest – fishing. For insider information and guided trips contact **Waitaki Jet**, Oamaru, T027-221 1069. South of Kurow is another potential distraction in the form of the former **1871 homestead** of the Hon Robert Campbell now open to the public by arrangement, T03-431 1111. West of Kurow you soon encounter **Lake Aviemore** and the higher, more extensive and truncated **Lake Benmore**. Both have dams. The Aviemore Dam has a 1-km-long fish spawning race that is used by up to 3000 adult trout at a time. The dam at the head of Benmore is the largest in New Zealand and can also be investigated though the lakeside picnic grounds. Safe swimming and water sports in both lakes may prove more attractive. For more information contact the **Benmore Power Station and Visitor Centre** ① *T03-438 9212, daily 1030-1630, tours 1100, 1300, 1500, $6.*

For Sleeping and Eating price codes and other relevant information, see Essentials pages 44-50.

● Sleeping

Omarama *p540*
AL-A Heritage Gateway Hotel,
T0800-809805/T03-438 9805,
www.heritagegateway.co.nz. 3-star hotel in a convenient location at the junction of SH8 to Wanaka and Queenstown, with SH83 to the east coast. Modern standard rooms and self-contained apartments. Bar and à la carte restaurant. Can arrange tours.
AL-D Ahuriri Motel, SH 83, T03-438 9451, www.ahuririmotels.co.nz. 14 comfortable, modern self-contained units and powered tent sites
D Buscot Station, 8 km north of the village, T03-438 9646, www.buscotstn@xtra.co.nz. Backpacker dorms, en suite rooms and tent sites on a working cattle/sheep station. Friendly hosts, good views. Quintessential Kiwi experience guaranteed. Recommended.

Motorcamps and campsites
B-D Omarama Top Ten Holiday Park,
T0800-662726/T03-438 9875, www.omarama top10.co.nz. Spacious and sheltered flats, cabins and powered/tent sites. Good facilities.

Duntroon p541
LL-L Tokarahi Homestead, 2 km down Dip Hill Rd (47), 11 km south of Duntroon on the Dansey's Pass Rd, T03-431 2500, www.homestead.co.nz. Luxurious, beautifully appointed accommodation in 19th-century Victorian style. A perfect peaceful, historic retreat.

Motorcamps and campsites
D Dansey's Pass Holiday Camp, end of Dansey's Pass Rd, T03-431 2564, www.danseyspass.com. Cheaper and less salubrious but no less peaceful. Offers an interesting range of scenic tours.

Kurow *p541*
Motorcamps and campsites
B-D Kurow Holiday Park, 76 Bledisloe St, T03-436 0725. If you are tired and cannot reach the **Top Ten** motorpark in Omarama then this is not a bad place.

❶ Eating

Omarama *p540*
There is a good restaurant in the **Heritage Gateway Hotel**, see Sleeping above.

Duntroon *p541*
Food is available at **Duntroon Tavern**, Main St, T03-431 2850, or the **Flying Pig Café**, Campbell St, T03-431 2717.

▲ Activities and tours

Omarama *p540*
Flightseeing
Alpine Soaring, T0800-762746/T027-248 8800, www.soaring.co.nz. Offers a range of options from the airfield in the village, from $235 for 20-25 mins during which you can – briefly – take the controls.

Fishing
Recommended local guides are **Doug Horton**, T03-438 9808, and **Max Irons**, T03-438 9468.

Contents

West Coast

N

30 km
30 miles

Tasman Sea

Wekakura Point

Oparara
Karamea
Karamra Bight
Little Wanganui
Seddonville
Granity   Hector
Westport   Lyell
Buller River
Charleston   Inangahua
Wainta
Mt Victoria (1640m)
Perpendicular Point
Punakaiki   Reefton
Pancake Rocks & Blowholes
Paparoa National Park
Barrytown
Blackball   Waiuta
Runanga
Greymouth   Ngahere
Shantytown
Moana
Mt Ajax (1834m)
Lake Brunner   Inchbonnie
Hokitika
Lake Mahinapua   Lake Kaniere
Lake Kaniere   Otira
Ross   Arthur's Pass   *Esk River*
Lake Ianthe   Cass
Pukekura   Craigieburn Forest Park
Abut Head
Okarito Lagoon   Mt Whitcombe (2644m)
Okarito   Harihari
Whataroa   Mt Arrowsmith (2795m)   Springfield
Franz Josef   *Rakaia River*
Gillespies Beach   Fox   Franz Josef Glacier   Mt Potts (2194m)   Lake Coleridge   Coalgate
Fox Glacier
Heretaniwha Point   The Thumbs (2545m)   Mount Hutt
Copeland Track   Mount Cook   Mount Somers
Lake Moeraki   Bruce Bay   *Lake Tekapo*   Mayfield   Ashburton
Lake Paringa
Mt Macfarlane (2057m)   Mt Musgrave (2246m)   Woodbury   Hakatere
Okuru   Haast   *Lake Pukaki*
Jackson's Bay
Cascade Point

The west coast of the South Island is a land of extremes: extreme climate, extreme geography, extreme ecosystems. It is a place of majestic beauty. Bounded on one side by the Tasman Sea and on the other by the heady peaks of the Southern Alps, it encompasses a narrow stretch of land that accounts for only eight percent of the total landmass of New Zealand. Between these boundaries lies a quarter of all New Zealand's native forest, a lush and predominantly impenetrable landscape copiously watered by an average annual rainfall of more than 5 m. The boundaries of five of the country's 14 national parks breach the west coast region. Two of these, Paparoa National Park and the Westland National Park, it can call its very own, with the latter boasting the huge Fox and Franz Josef glaciers.

The settlements in the region, strung along the 600 km length of SH6, from Karamea in the north to Jackson's Bay in the south, are not attractive places and stand in stark contrast to the beauty surrounding them. Nature, thankfully, has never made it easy for man to live here nor plunder its resources. The modern-day west coast is sparsely populated, housing less than one percent of the country's total population. Indeed, there are less people living here now than there were in the late 19th century.

Westport and around →

Westport, the west coast's oldest town, is not a pretty place. On first acquaintance, its long main street, fed by a flat expanse of unimaginative orderly blocks and overly wide roads, is uninspiring to say the least. Whether under clear blue skies or, more often, a veil of rain, its drabness is all the more exposed by the beautiful surroundings. But if the place lacks spirit, its people do not. They retain the proud and stoic traditions of the old pioneers and coal miners: the down-to-earth working-class attitude, the warm welcome and the humour. Westport is often used as an overnight base before heading north to Karamea and the Heaphy Track or south towards Greymouth. There, however, are a few attractions and activities that may detain you, including rafting on the Buller River and a large seal colony at Cape Foulwind. ⟫ *For Sleeping, Eating and other listings, see pages 551-555.*

Ins and outs

Getting there Westport airport ① *8 km south*, is served daily by **Air New Zealand Link**, T0800-737000. A taxi into town costs around $18, T03-789 6900. The airstrip at Karamea is often used (from the north) for pick-ups/drop-offs for the Heaphy Track. For more information contact the VIC in Karamea T03-7826652, www.karameainfo.co.nz. **Abel Tasman Air**, T03-528 8290, runs a quality service with fixed-wing aircraft from Nelson to Karamea.

Bus companies serving the area include: **Intercity** (from Nelson), T03-7896658, www.intercity.co.nz; **Atomic Shuttles** (from Nelson), T03-3490697, www.atomictravel.co.nz, and **West Coast Shuttles**, T03-7680028, www.westcoastshuttle.co.nz, which offers daily services from Christchurch to Greymouth (but not Westport). Most buses stop just outside the VIC (I-Site). **Intercity** stops at Craddock's Energy Centre, Caltex, 197 Palmerston St. For all services north to Karamea (and the Heaphy Track) call **Karamea Express**, T03-782 6757, or the VIC in Westport.

Tourist information Westport VIC (I-Site) ① *1 Brougham St, T03-789 6658, www.westport.org.nz, daily 0900-1800, winter 0900-1600*, handles DoC information and enquiries. **Karamea VIC (I-Site) and Resource Centre** ① *Bridge St, just as you come into the village, T03-782 6652, www.karamea.info.co.nz, daily 0900-1700*, has helpful staff who can provide plenty of information on local attractions and all the latest on the Heaphy Track. It also has internet, can organize activities and issues DoC hut passes.

Before heading over to the West Coast and certainly before booking a flight over the glaciers, it is worth looking at the detailed weather resource at **www.metservice.co.nz** and the forecast charts at **www.metvuw.com** for the latest synopsis.

Westport ⊜❼🛆🕓 ⟫ *pp551-555.*

With such a tradition of gold and coal mining in the area it is almost rude not to visit the excellent **Coaltown Museum** ① *Queen St South, T03-789 8204, daily 0900-1630, $12, child $5*. It has an extensive range of displays, with an emphasis on coal mining, but also gold, pioneer and maritime exhibitions. Of particular note is the interesting presentation covering the history of coal mining in the region, the simulated walk-through mine and the massive 20-ton brake drum from the Denniston Incline. Pitched at a 47° angle the brake drum creates a fearful sight. The sheer feats of engineering cannot fail to impress.

In contrast, yet related, is the **West Coast Brewery** ① *Lyndhurst St, T03-789 6201, www.westcoastbrewing.com, free tastings Mon-Sat*, where various heady brews are created to quench the thirst of the modern-day miner, including a fine pint of 'Good Bastards'. Pick up a free copy of the *Buller Coalfields Heritage Trail* leaflet from the VIC (I-Site).

North to Karamea ⊜⊘▲ℂ ►► pp551-555.

From Westport, SH67 heads north to Karamea (100 km) and an eventual dead-end at the trailhead of the Heaphy Track (111 km). If you have time there are a few places of interest and several good walks on offer along the way. Of particular note is the former mining township of **Denniston**. Perched high (900 m) on the Rochford Plateau and accessed via Waimangaroa (15 km north of Westport), Denniston was once the largest producer of coal in the country and the surrounding area was a hive of industrial activity. The **Denniston Walkway** (two hours, 1 km, 520 m ascent), which follows the former supply route, is the best way to explore the area and eventually leads to the former settlement. Little remains except a few rusting pieces of machinery, but there are great views of the impressive **Denniston Incline** (1878-1967) on which 20-ton brake drums brought millions of tonnes of coal down over 500 m to the railhead at terrific speeds. There is a small **museum** ⓘ *old schoolhouse, open weekends and public holidays.*

Back on SH67 and 6 km north is the once bustling township of **Granity**. The **Drifters' Café** on the main street is worth a stop and has some interesting artwork and mining remnants on display. Inland from Granity a road sweeps up the ranges to 'Porridge Hill' and two more former coal towns, **Millerton** and **Stockton**. Little remains of either, but again they are still worthy of some investigation. The short **Millerton Incline Walkway** (40 minutes) takes in a number of features and, as the name suggests, another incline, although it's a far less impressive affair than the one at Denniston. Approximately 1 km north of Granity is the very pleasant **Charming Creek Walkway** (two hours, 4 km one way), which follows the old coal line through the Ngakawau River Gorge, taking in various old tunnels and other mining features along the way.

At the mouth of the Mokihinui River the SH67 turns inland and climbs precariously around the bush-clad and scenic **Karamea Bluff**, before falling again to the coast towards Karamea.

Karamea

After the rather bleak nature of the former coal mining towns, encountered on its approach, you might expect Karamea to be similarly afflicted. However, this former 'frontier' settlement, perched on its namesake river mouth and overshadowed by the rising peaks of the **Kahurangi National Park**, is a far more pleasing sight and has a peaceful (as opposed to dead) atmosphere. Although most often used as a base for the famed **Heaphy Track** (which begins at the road terminus 15 km north) Karamea also has some lesser-known sights nearby that are quite simply superb, in particular the limestone caves and arches of the Oparara Basin.

Oparara Basin → For Kahurangi National Park, see page 464.

ⓘ From Karamea take the main road north for 10 km, then turn right at Break Creek Bridge (signposted) and head for the hills. Access to the basin is 16 km of narrow, unsealed road. The basin is split into areas with both open and restricted public access. This is a magical place that offers the most interesting concentration of karst (limestone) topography in the **Kahurangi National Park**, and some of the most spectacular in the South Island. Although the karst features will keep you spellbound, the thick veil of ancient rainforest that covers it all creates a wonderful atmosphere all of its own like some 'lost world'. Some fantastical animals have been found here: ancient moa bones have been discovered in the caves along with others belonging to the now extinct New Zealand eagle with a 3-m wingspan. Today, you may still stumble across the huge carnivorous snail (*Powelliphanta*). Also of note is the wonderfully named gradungula spider, the largest in New Zealand with a leg span of 10 cm. But, even if the prospect of such creatures leaves you cold, the Oparara Basin is still a 'must see'.

At the very end of the track is the access point to the main feature of the basin – the **Honeycomb Caves** ⓘ *Oparara Guided Tours at the VIC, T03-782 6652, 2½ hrs, $85*, can only be visited on a guided tour because of their delicate nature and fragile ecosystem. They are a 15-km underground labyrinth only discovered 30-odd years ago, revealing all the usual limestone cave features plus the bones of several moa and other extinct species.

Nearby is the **Honeycomb Arch** ⓘ *contact Oparara Tours at the VIC, from $85*, the first of three spectacular arches that have been formed by the age-old meanderings of the Oparara River. Although this arch is indeed impressive, access is again restricted and is by kayak only. The **Oparara Arch** ⓘ *free public access*, is equally if not more impressive and is reached from a path (signposted) beside the road. A pleasant 20-minute (one way) walk alongside the intriguing tannin coloured river, and through beautiful forest, will bring you to the awesome arch entrance. Once you have marvelled at the main entrance it is then worth exploring the other end through the 140-m passage. This will involve getting your feet wet and crossing the river so care is required.

On a far smaller scale, but in a way more beautiful, is the **Moria (Little) Arch**, accessed from the other side of the road. Again it is reached on a well-formed track (40 minutes). What it lacks in grandeur, the Moria makes up for in serenity. Perhaps before or after the arches you can visit the **Crazy Paving** and **Box Canyon Caves**, which are a five-minute walk from the road. Beyond their unnerving darkness (take a torch), they are the least impressive of all the features. The river itself is also beautiful and well worthy of investigation, particularly around the track to the small and self-explanatory **Mirror Tarn**. A small map of the Oparara Basin is available free from the VIC (I-Site).

▲▲ Walks
ⓘ *The VIC (I-Site) has detailed information on these walks and others.*

Karamea is a fine base for walking, particularly along the coastal stretch of the **Heaphy Track**. From the Kohaihai River (trailhead), cross the swing bridge and walk through the forest to **Scotts Beach** (1½ hours return). From there you have the option of continuing along the coastline to **Kapito Shelter** (six hours return) or going the whole hog with an overnight stop at the **Heaphy Hut** (five hours one way) before retracing your steps. This stretch of coast is noted not only for its wild unspoilt beaches but also for its nikau palms, which give it an almost tropical feel. Other tracks and expeditions include the **Fenian Track** (three to five hours) which takes in a small cave system and a former gold mining settlement and **Mount Stormy** (1084 m, six to eight hours return) with its magnificent views.

South of Westport ●▲▲ ►► *pp551-555*.

Cape Foulwind
ⓘ *11 km south of Westport; easily accessible and signposted.*

Cape Foulwind is a buttress of land, apparently named by James Cook in 1770, after his ship was beset by gales and rain. It was formerly called Clyppygen Hoek - or Rocky Corner - by Abel Tasman in 1642 and, before that, Tauranga by the Maori, which meant 'a sheltered anchorage or landing place'. The main attraction on the cape is the thriving **fur** seal colony at the very beautiful **Tauranga Bay**. You are guaranteed to see seals here at any time of year (be it from a lookout situated quite far above the rocks) but summer, when the pups are born, is the best time to see them with over 500 in residence. The colony is best accessed from the Tauranga Bay car park. Before you set off, keep your eyes open for the rather comical and cheeky **weka** around the car park itself. Weka are a flightless, endemic, brown game-like bird about the size of a chicken. Although you are not supposed to feed them it is hard to resist.

From the seal colony, the **Cape Foulwind Walkway** also takes in the lighthouse and offers great views (1½ hours, 4 km one way). At the southern end of Tauranga Bay there is the fine **Bay House Restaurant**. It offers outdoor seating overlooking the bay and is a great place to sup a cup of coffee, or tuck into a cooked breakfast, while watching the surfers beyond.

Buller Gorge

There are actually two gorges on the Buller River: the Upper Gorge and the Lower Gorge. They are separated by an area of relatively flat farmland around the small settlement of Inangahua, which lies roughly halfway between Murchison and Westport. Following the river is the northernmost arterial to the west coast, SH6. This 100-km road journey from Murchison to the coast is a scenic, and at times dramatic experience, where you descend with the river through mountains and valleys draped in an ever-increasing veil of green. The drive to the coast is, in itself, pleasant enough but also holds a number of interesting attractions and stops along the way.

Just beyond the junction of SH6 and SH65 the road crosses O'Sullivan's Bridge and the **Upper Gorge** begins proper. Almost immediately you come to the **Buller Gorge Swingbridge** ① *Swingbridge Centre, next to SH6, T03-523 9809, www.bullergorge.co.nz, daily 0800-1900 (0900-1730 in winter), café*, which at 110 m is New Zealand's longest. You can walk across by foot ($5, child $2), or fly beside it, strapped to a small chair ($35/$15). The sensible can watch with great amusement from afar, the fit go for a guided walk and the hopeful go **gold panning** (guided $13). There are also jet boating trips from $75.

A little further on, just before **Newton Livery Hotel**, is the **Lookout** (Earthquake White Creek Fault Slip) where the violent (7.8 on the Richter scale) earthquake of 1929 was centred. Some 8 km on is the **Brunner Memorial**, which is a small metal plaque attached to the rock, commemorating the epic journeys of Thomas Brunner. The intrepid Mr Brunner took three months to negotiate the gorge in 1846.

After a long bend in the river the road then passes through the former gold mining town of **Lyell** – now very much a village. Relics of the great but brief gold rush days, including an old stamper battery, can be seen on the **Lyell Walkway** (two hours return). A further 17 km on will bring you to the rather unremarkable settlement of **Inangahua**. It has little more than a petrol pump and the rather dubious claim to fame of nearly being destroyed by an earthquake in 1968.

Just beyond Inangahua, the **Lower Gorge** begins its dramatic descent to the sea. At **Hawk's Crag** the rock has been gouged out to form a dramatic overhang. Its negotiation is really very interesting provided there is not a large petrol tanker coming the other way.

Punakaiki and the Paparoa National Park ⬤🅕🅐🅒 ▸▸ *pp551-555.*

From Westport SH6 begins its relentless 600-km journey south, down the length of the west coast. Once past the small, and at one time booming, gold mining settlement of Charleston, the road hits the coast proper and then skirts the northern boundary of the

A hard rain's a-gonna fall

The west coast of the South Island, especially Fiordland, is one of the wettest places on earth. Moist, prevailing, westerly air streams fan across the Tasman Sea and on encountering the mountain ranges of the Great Divide condense and dump rain or snow in huge quantities. At lower levels the annual rainfall is a rather aquatic 1.5 m but at higher levels this can rise to staggering 5 m. Most of the rain falls on the seaward side. The eastern slopes are in the 'rain shadow' and receive only 750 mm.

On a more positive note, although it frequently rains on the west coast, it often clears quickly and the sun is never too far away. Besides, west coast rain is real rain, industrial strength rain, so perhaps for once in your life get out there and enjoy it.

Paparoa National Park. Designated in 1987, Paparoa covers a relatively small area (by New Zealand standards) of 30,000 ha and features a predominantly karst (limestone) topography. From mountain to coast, the park has everything from limestone bluffs to dramatic overhangs and caves. The most famous feature in the park are the pancake rocks and blowholes of Dolomite Point at the small coastal settlement of **Punakaiki**, which is in the main commercial centre. The park also offers some notable walks inland, including the popular Inland Pack Track.

Ins and outs

Getting there Punakaiki is 60 km south of Westport and 50 km north of Greymouth. **Intercity**, T03-789 6658, and **Atomic Shuttles** (Greymouth-Nelson), T03-349 0697, pass through the village daily and stop briefly for passengers to grab a snack and take a quick look at the pancake rocks and blowholes.

Note: Whether heading north or south be sure to fill up your tank in Greymouth or Westport as there is no petrol station in Punakaiki.

Tourist information DoC Paparoa National Park Visitor Centre ① SH6, *Punakaiki, T03-731 1895, www.doc.govt.nz, www.punakaiki.co.nz, daily 0900-1800, winter 0900-1630,* has interesting displays and information on activities and walking conditions.

Sights

Immediately across the road from the visitor centre is **Dolomite Point** with its oddly shaped **pancake rocks** and crowd-pleasing **blowholes**. The fluted vertical columns are a lime/mudstone feature known as 'karren', which develop their layered appearance as a result of erosion by rain and sea spray. The track (20 minutes return) takes the form of a loop, offering various lookout points across the rocks and blowholes, and down into the surge pools. On a high tide and especially during a strong westerly, the 'show' can be amazing, with the ground physically shaking to the thunderous pounding of the waves and the sea-spray hissing from the cracks. But note that when the tide is out, or there is little swell, the blowholes can be quiet and idle, leaving many visitors disappointed. Regardless of conditions, the rocks are certainly intriguing and the views are stunning. Keep your eye out for **hector's dolphins**; it is not unusual to see pods or individuals mingling with surfers with the mutual intent to catch the best wave.

If you have time there is also some stunning coastal scenery, easily accessed via the

Truman Track, which begins beside SH6, 3 km north of Punakaiki. A 15-minute walk through coastal rainforest and nikau palms delivers you on the sands and rocky outcrops of **Perpendicular Point**. The rock formations here are fascinating with fissures, holes and mosaics, and although it is quite hard going and should only be attempted at low tide, a thorough investigation of the point (northwards), is well worthwhile.

Turning your attention inland, the river valleys lead to some fine scenery and a number of other dramatic limestone features such as caves and overhangs. At **Tiromoana**, 13 km north of Punakaiki, the Fox River finds the sea, and a small car park north of the bridge acts as the northern trailhead for the **Inland Pack Track**. The entire track (which is usually walked from the southern trailhead in Punakaiki) is a 27-km, two- to three-day affair that takes in many limestone features, and inland valleys. Its main highlights – the **Fox River Gorge**, **caves** and **Ballroom Overhang** – can all be accessed from the mouth of the Fox River on an exciting four- to six-hour return walk. The track is well-formed for much of its length, but also involves crossing the river a number of times guided only by orange markers, so be prepared to get your feet wet. The Fox River caves can be accessed with a short diversion before the first major river crossing. The main cave is over 100 m in length and decorated with the usual calcite formations. Once across the river, the track follows the base of the dramatic gorge before terminating at the confluence of the Fox and Dilemma creeks. Here you can leave the Inland Pack Track, cross the river, and then continue alongside the main Fox tributary to the **Ballroom Overhang** (1 km). Sitting like half an umbrella embedded in the riverbed, its 100 m by 30 m overhang is impressive, but spoilt somewhat by graffiti.

Closer to Punakaiki are the **Bullock Creek** and **Pororari River** valleys. The Pororari acts as the southern access of the Inland Pack Track which can be walked in part to join the Bullock Creek Valley and to access **Cave Creek**, a deeply incised limestone gorge and another karst feature worthy of investigation. It is also one that now serves more as a tragic memorial than a tourist attraction: in 1995 a viewing platform set high above the cavern collapsed sending 15 students to their deaths. As a result of the incident there was a complete review of all similar DoC structures countrywide and revised safety standards and protocols were subsequently put in place. Cave Creek can also be accessed via the Bullock Creek Valley, which is generally fun to explore by car, bike, or on foot. All walks in the area are subject to flooding so check with DoC before setting off.

The area is also home to some rare wildlife. Of particular note is the **Westland black petrel** (teiko) – a gull-sized, black seabird, which nests in burrows on the bush-clad slopes of Paparoa's mountains. They do not breed anywhere else in the world. Tours are available in season (March to December); contact the VIC for details.

⊚ Westport and around listings

For Sleeping and Eating price codes and other relevant information, see Essentials pages 44-50.

⊜ Sleeping

Westport *p546*
AL Archer House B&B, 75 Queens St, T03-789 8778, www.archerhouse.co.nz. A classy boutique B&B set in a heritage villa and a half acre in the centre of town. Well-

appointed, good value en suites with all the comforts you'd expect. Recommended.
AL-A Chelsea Gateway Motor Lodge, 330 Palmerston St, T0800-660033/ T03-789 6835, www.chelseagateway.co.nz. Opposite Westport Spa, also with spa units.
AL-A Westport Motor Hotel, 207 Palmerston St, T03-789 7889, www.westportmotorhotel.co.nz. Popular, well-located and well-established, with the

added attraction of a good in-house restaurant and internet.

AL-A Wesport Spa Motel, 239 Palmerston St, T0800-375273/T03-789 5273, www.west portspa.co.nz. Modern and spacious spa units.

B-D Bazils, T03-789 6410, www.yha.co.nz. A vast establishment and YHA affiliate close to the town centre with a wide range of units, self-contained dorm apartments, powered/tent sites. Good facilities, internet.

C-D The Trip Inn, 72 Queen St, T03-789 7367, www.tripinn.co.nz. A grand, spacious villa, kept squeaky clean. Good value with a wide range of rooms and good facilities.

Motorcamps

A-D Westport Holiday Park, 37 Domett St, T03-789 7043, www.westportholiday park.co.nz. A short walk from town. Motel units, flats, en suites and standard chalets, on-site vans, powered/tent sites.

North to Karamea p547

AL Rough and Tumble Bush Lodge, Mokihinui River, 5 mins from Seddonville Pub, T03-732 1337, www.roughandtumble.co.nz. Classic and affordable bush lodge accommodation overlooking the Mokihinui River. 5 cosy en suites with memorable views. Furnishings of native timber abound and an outdoor campfire, swimming hole and bush bath all add to the appeal. Excellent in-house cuisine. It is remote but well worth the effort.

B-D Gentle Annie's Coastal Enclave and Cowshed Café, on the far side of the mouth of the Mokihinui River, Gentle Annie's Beach, T03-782 1826, www.gentleannie.co.nz. A great spot for food and accommodation with quiet, dorms or self-contained lodges and camping sites. The café is imaginatively housed in a former milking shed. It has information about activities including kayaking on the river nearby.

C-D Old Slaughterhouse Backpackers, 35 km north of Westport at Dean Creek, Hector, T03-782 8333. A top-notch purpose-built lodge overlooking the ocean, reached by a 10-min bush walk. It offers tidy doubles

and shared rooms. A good place to break the journey north to Karamea and the Heaphy Track. Recommended.

Karamea p547

AL-A Bridge Farm Motels, Bridge St, T0800-527263/T03-782 6955, www.karameamotels.co.nz. With a riverside location, offers 1- to 2-bedroom self-contained suites.

AL-A Karamea Lodge, 4589 Karamea Highway (4 km south of the village), T03-782 6033, www.karamealodge.co.nz. Modern lodge overlooking the ocean with 3 spacious, well-appointed en suites. Shared kitchen and lounge with fireplace. The lack of TV or internet makes a refreshing change and adds to the sense of retreat. The property is set in 3 ha of native bush with an attractive walkway. Excellent hosts. Recommended.

AL-D Last Resort, 71 Waverley St, T0800-505042/T03-782 6617, www.lastresort.co.nz. A modern and imaginatively designed complex with lodge-style accommodation and a large adjunct bar/café. Rooms include dorms, self-contained en suites and cottages. There are also tent sites with communal kitchen facilities. Internet is available.

A Karamea Village Hotel, T03-782 6800, corner of Wharf Rd and Waverley St. Has comfortable units separate to the hotel which is itself a historic and lovingly restored building. It is also renowned for its fine cuisine.

C-D Rongo Backpackers, 130 Waverley St, T03-782 6667, www.rongobackpackers.com. Colourful (to say the least), cosy and laid-back hostel that lives up to its name – 'rongo' is Maori for peace. Spacious doubles and dorms, open fire, fire bath, in-house gallery, internet and fresh homegrown vegetables and free range eggs.

C-D Wangapeka Backpackers Retreat, Atawhai Farm, Wangapeka Valley (15 mins south of Karamea at the end of the Wangapeka Track, T03-782 6663, www.wangapeka.co.nz. Simple but delightful budget farmstay accommodation. Barn loft with 4 backpacker beds and a separate double. Meals by request (included with farmstay tariff). A fire-bath set in native bush offers an added attraction for trampers coming off the track. Recommended.

Motorcamps and campsites
B-D Karamea Holiday Park, Maori Point Rd, just south of the village, T03-782 6758, www.karamea.com. Offers a range of motel units, cabins and powered/tent sites.
D DoC campsite, at the mouth of the Kohaihai River (15 km north), at the trailhead of the Heaphy Track, T03-782 6652.

South of Westport p548
L River View Lodge, 7 km east of town, SH6, Lower Buller Gorge Rd, T03-789 6037, www.rurallodge.co.nz. A good out-of-town B&B option with 4 tidy en suites, set in pleasant gardens overlooking the Buller River.
C-D Beaconstone Backpackers, 17 km south of town on SH6, T027-431 0491, www.beaconstone.co.nz. An 'alternative', environmentally friendly lodge in a bush/coastal setting with solar power and futon beds. Local caving activities arranged. One of the best hostels on the coast. Recommended.
D BerlinsCafe and Lodgings, Inangahua, Buller Gorge, T03-789 0295. On the banks of the Buller River near the Lower Buller Gorge. Just 11km from Inangahua Junction and 35 km from Westport. Comfortable option if you are in the area.

Motorcamps and campsites
A-D Seal Colony Top Ten Tourist Park, Marine Parade, Carter's Beach (6 km on Cape Foulwind/Carter's Beach Rd), T03-789 8002, www.top10westport.co.nz. Popular with all the usual Top 10 facilities and just 6 km from the seal colony.

Punakaiki p549
Almost all the accommodation is just off SH6. The most upmarket accommodation is at the southern end of the village.
L-AL Punakaiki Rocks Hotel and Villas, T03-731 1168, www.punakaiki-resort.co.nz.

Separate but affiliated establishments both close to the beach with fine ocean views. The hotel is tidy and the individual units are very good, but have a rather clinical air. The restaurant boasts great views over the beach. Across the road, the villa complex offers luxurious options, from studio units with private decks to 12 eco-designed rooms set further back from the highway in native bush.
L Treetops Hideaway, T03-731 1140, www.punakaiki-nz.co.nz. Excellent Scandinavian styled self-contained option set 100 m above sea level 9 km south of the village. Three doubles or two doubles and a twin single, ideal for a family or couple. Modern facilities throughout and the obligatory 'bush bath'. Recommended.
AL-A Paparoa Park Motel, north of the main centre, just off the main road, T03-7311883, www.paparoa.co.nz. Tidy and congenial, offering studio and family units.
A Punakaiki Tavern Accommodation and Bistro, northern sector of the village, T03-731 1188. Tidy modern en suite studio units situated near the tavern/bistro (the focus of social activity in the village) and only a short stroll from the beach.
B Hydrangea Cottages, north of the centre, T03-731 1839, www.pancake-rocks.co.nz. Very cute and reasonably priced self-contained cottages in a peaceful location and with great ocean views.
C-D Punakaiki Beach Hostel, Webb St, T03-731 1852, www.punakaikibeach hostel.co.nz. 2 compact houses near the beach and pub. Outdoor spa, internet.
C-D Te Nikau Retreat, in Te Miko, just north of the Truman Track (look for homestay/backpacker sign pointing out Hartmount Place), T03-731 1111, www.tenikauretreat.co.nz. A superb retreat with stand-alone cottages set in the bush, and a very special atmosphere. Also good for families and some units have wheelchair access. Enthusiastic manager. Excellent facilities throughout. Internet and pick-ups from the village centre also available. Recommended.

Motorcamps and campsites

C-D Punakaiki Beach Camp, T03-731 1894, www.holidayparks.co.nz/punakaiki. Set next to the beach and only a short walk from the main village. It offers spacious grounds, cabins and powered/tent sites.

🍴 Eating

Westport and around *p546*
There is a **Fresh Choice** supermarket at 18 Fonblanque St, T03-789 8546.
🍴 **Bay House Café**, southern end of Tauranga Bay, Cape Foulwind (near the seal colony), T03-789 7133, www.thebayhouse.co.nz. The best local restaurant, offering breakfast, lunch and an imaginative à la carte menu for dinner and in a superb setting overlooking the bay.
🍴 **Berlin's Café**, Lower Buller Gorge, T03-789 0295.
🍴 **Freckles**, 216 Palmerston St, 0900-1700. A daytime café with good coffee.
🍴 **Denniston Dog Café and Bar**, 18 Wakefield St, T03-789 5030. Daily Mon-Fri from 1100 and Sat-Sun from 0900. A casual bar/café with lots of character and a good all-rounder for either brunch, lunch or dinner. Vegetarian options.

Karamea *p547*
The **Last Resort** and the **Karamea Village Hotel** have licensed restaurants, see Sleeping, above.
🍴 **LR Bar and Café**, Last Resort. Daily. Cheap pub-style menu and a good atmosphere.
🍴 **Saracens Café**, 99 Bridge St, T03-7826600. Daily from 0800. Fully licensed, good for light meals and coffee.

Punakaiki *p549*
🍴 **Waterline Restaurant**, Punakaiki Resort Hotel, T03-7311168. Daily from 0700. For fine dining this is the best option in the village. Perfectly acceptable food and excellent views.
🍴 **Punakaiki Tavern Bistro Café and Bar**, next to the motorcamp (SH6), T03-7311188. The main hub of entertainment offering palatable beer and the usual value pub grub.

🍴 **Wild Coast Café**, Main Rd (across the road from Dolomite Point and the pancake rocks), T03-731 1873. Daily 0800-2100 (winter 0800-1700). Good coffee and an eclectic menu. There is also a small grocery shop attached and several internet terminals at $3 per hr.

⛰ Activities and tours

Westport and Buller Gorge *p546 and p549*
Buller Adventures, east of Westport on SH6 (Buller Gorge Rd), T03-789 7286, www.adventuretours.co.nz. Offers rafting trips (half-day from $120); jet boating (1½ hrs from $79); quad bikingtours (1½ hrs from $140) and horse trekking (2½ hrs from $80).
Out West Tours, T0800-688937/ T03-7898626, www.outwest.co.nz. An interesting range of trips by 4WD Unimog to the former Denniston coal mines, down the coast or inland to Buller Gorge. Call for latest schedules and prices.
Underworld Adventures, 182 Queen St, Westport, T0800-116686/T03-788 8168, www.caverafting.com. Offers tours, caving and underground rafting trips to the Te Tahi and Metro limestone caves in Paparoa National Park. Trips leave twice daily from Westport and include a short trip by miniature rail (ride-only $20). 'Glowworm Cave Tour' (3 hrs from $90), 'Underworld Rafting' (4 hrs from $145), and 'Adventure Caving' with 130-ft abseil (5 hrs from $295).

Karamea *p547*
Heli Charter Karamea, 79 Waverly St, Karamea, T03-782 6111, www.karamea helicharter.co.nz. A quality, personable company offering a flexible range of local and regional flight options, from local flightseeing, to fishing expeditions, or transportation to the track-heads of the Wangapeka or Heaphy.
Oparara Kahurangi National Park Guided Tours, Karamea, T03-782 6652, www.oparara.co.nz. The principal operator

offering guided walking (cave tours) and kayaking trips to the Honeycomb Hill Caves from \$85–\$230. Recommended.

Punakaiki *p549*
Green Kiwi Tours, T03-731 1843, www.greenkiwitours.co.nz. Small group eco-tours and caving trips from \$60.
Punakaiki Canoe Hire, T03-731 1870, www.riverkayaking.co.nz. Independent hire 2 hrs from \$35, all day from \$55 and guided trips from \$70.
Punakaiki Horse Treks, T03-731 1839, www.pancake-rocks.co.nz. Along the beach or into Punakaiki River Valley, 2½ hrs \$125.

⊙ Directory

Westport *p546*
Banks Palmerston St. **Internet** Web Shed,

204 Palmerston St, T03-7888002, Mon-Fri 0830-1700, Sat 0930-1230. **Library**, 87 Palmerston St, Mon-Thu 1000-1700, Fri 1000-1830, Sat 1030-1300. **Post office** Palmerston St, T03-7888193, Mon-Fri 0830-1700, Sat 1000-1230.

Karamea *p547*
Banks There is no bank or ATM in the village. **Internet** VIC, see page 546.
Medical services Doctor's surgery, Waverley St, T03-782 6737. **Postal services** Karamea Hardware Store, opposite the VIC.

Punakaiki *p549*
Banks There are no banks but EFTPOS is available in the retail and food outlets.
Internet Wild Coast Café (see Eating, above) or both the local backpacker hostels (see Sleeping above).

Greymouth and around → *Colour map 4, B2 Population: 10,000*

From Punakaiki the coast road continues its relentless route south, treating you to some fine coastal scenery, before turning inland through Runanga to meet the Grey River and the west coast's largest commercial centre – Greymouth. On initial acquaintance Greymouth seems to share the drab aesthetics of most northern west coast towns and certainly lives up to its uninspiring name. That said, the people of Greymouth are welcoming, friendly and certainly not short of heart or colour. Today, the bustling town is mostly used by tourists as a short stopover point or supply base for further investigations of the coast. It does, however, have a few local attractions and some exciting activities on offer. Inland from Greymouth, the small satellite towns of Blackball and Reefton are the main highlights along the watershed of the Grey River Valley and provide further evidence of the regions gold and coal mining past. It was in Blackball in the early 1900s that the Labour and Trade Union movements were first formed in New Zealand. Further south the peaceful surroundings of Lake Brunner are a stark contrast to the highly commercial 'Shantytown' a working replica of an 1880s gold mining settlement. ▸▸ *For Sleeping, Eating and other listings, see pages 559-562.*

Ins and outs
Getting there **Air New Zealand Link**, T0800-737000, flies to **Hokitika airport** ① *40 km south of Greymouth*. The town is 258 km west of Christchurch via SH73 and Arthur's Pass, 290 km south of Nelson via SH6, and 583 km north of Queenstown, also via SH6. The major bus companies serving the Greymouth include: **Intercity**, T03-768 5101 (Nelson-Westport); **West Coast Shuttles**, T03-7680028, www.westcoastshuttle.co.nz, which offers daily services from Christchurch to Greymouth; and **Atomic Shuttles**, T03-349 0697, www.atomictravel.co.nz (Christchurch). Most buses stop at the VIC or at the **Travel Centre** ① *in the railway station, 164 Mackay St, T03-768 7080*, greymouthtravel@snap.net.nz, Mon-Fri 0900-1700, Sat-Sun

1000-1500. By train, Greymouth is the western terminus of the famous **TranzAlpine**, T0800-872467, www.tranzscenic.co.nz, from Christchurch, which is considered a world-class scenic journey. The train arrives daily at Mackay St at 1245 and departs Greymouth again at 1345 from $161 one way. Moana (on Lake Brunner) is also on the TranzAlpine line (westbound 1221, eastbound 1405).

Tourist information Greymouth VIC (I-Site) ⓘ *corner of Mackay and Herbert sts, T03-768 5101, www.greydistrict.co.nz, www.west-coast.co.nz, Mon-Fri 0830-1900, Sat 0900-1800, Sun 1000-1700*, also provides DoC information. **Reefton VIC (I-Site)** ⓘ *67 Broadway, T03-732 8391, www.reefton.co.nz, daily 0830-1800 (1630 in winter)*, has eco-based displays and lots of information on walking and tramping.

Greymouth ▶▶ pp559-562.

Greymouth enjoyed the former colonial names of Crescent City and Blaketown, before its present name (given in honour of the former New Zealand Governor, Sir George Grey) finally stuck. Not surprisingly its creation centred principally on gold prospecting and mining, but unlike so many of the other west coast settlements that diminished with its exhaustion, Greymouth continued to thrive. This was due to the coal and timber industries, sound communication links and its status as the region's principal port. But its watery affairs have not all been smooth sailing. The Grey River Valley receives some of the heaviest rainfall in the country and on more than one occasion the town has been badly flooded.

One of Greymouth's most famous sights is the **Montieth's Brewery** ⓘ *corner of Turamaha and Herbert sts, T03-768 4149, www.monteiths.co.nz, tours Mon-Sun 1130, 1400, 1600 and 1800, $15*. Considered locally as a place of sanctity, its brands of 'Original', 'Black' and 'Celtic Red', are considered by most Kiwis to be the country's greatest brews. Although not in the same league, nor enjoying the same reputation as Guinness or many other European beers, it is indeed a fine drop. A few years ago there was a major controversy when the powers that be decided suddenly to announce that operations were to be moved to Auckland (of all places). This act of insanity resulted in an outcry of such proportions that the owners wisely changed their minds.

If you are more culturally inclined you should head for the small, but effective, **History House Museum** ⓘ *Gresson St, T03-768 4028, www.history-house.co.nz, Mon-Fri 1000-1600, small admission charge*. Its emphasis is on the region's mining and nautical past with a copious collection of old photographs. Creative souls will particularly enjoy the **Jade Country** ⓘ *1 Guinness St, T03-768 0700, www.jadeboulder.co.nz, daily 0830-2100, winter 1700*. It is one of the better jade galleries showcasing a range of crafted jewellery and sculptures with the added attraction of a 'Jade Discovery Walk', master sculptors at work, a huge river-polished jade boulder and a good café. **Shades of Jade** ⓘ *16 Tainui St, T03-768 0794, www.westcoastjade.co.nz, open daily*, is a smaller gallery and shop where you can watch a jade carver fastidiously crafting the 'green gold'. Also worth a look is the **Left Bank Art Gallery** ⓘ *Tainui St, T03-768 0038, www.leftbankatrs.org.nz, Mon-Fri 1000-1700, Sat-Sun 1000-1400, small entry charge*, which displays some finely crafted examples of the west coast ancient *poanamu* (greenstone/jade) pieces.

▲▲ Walks around Greymouth

The **Point Elizabeth Track** (three hours return) follows an old gold-miners trail along the Rapahoe Range and provides a good local jaunt. Access is north of Greymouth via Bright Street, then Domett Esplanade and North Beach Road (6 km) or via Rapahoe, Seven Mile

Greymouth

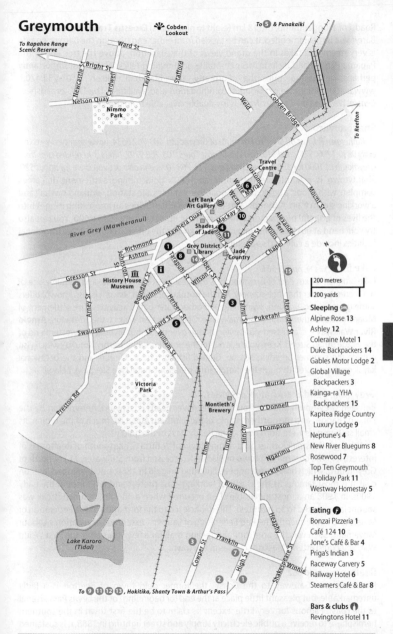

To ⑤ & Punakaiki

Cobden Lookout

To Rapahoe Range Scenic Reserve

Ward St

Bright St

Newcastle St

Cardwell

Taylor

Stafford

Nelson Quay

Nimmo Park

Cobden Bridge

Weld

To Reefton

Mount St

Travel Centre

Custom St

Werita St

Weld Marian

⑥

Left Bank Art Gallery @

Mackay St

⑩

Mawhera Quay

Alexander Terr

Willis St

Shades of Jade

④

⑪

River Grey (Mawheranui)

Richmond

Ashton

Johnston St

①

Grey District Library

⑧

Jade Country

Chapel St

Tarapuhi St

Albert St

Whall St

Gresson St

ℹ

⑭

History House Museum

Boundary St

Guinness St

Witson St

Isport

⑮

Tainui St

Puketahi

N

200 metres
200 yards

Arney St

Swainson

Herbert St

Leonard St

William St

③

⑤

Sleeping 🛏

Alpine Rose **13**
Ashley **12**
Coleraine Motel **1**
Duke Backpackers **14**
Gables Motor Lodge **2**
Global Village
 Backpackers **3**
Kainga-ra YHA
 Backpackers **15**
Kapitea Ridge Country
 Luxury Lodge **9**
Neptune's **4**
New River Bluegums **8**
Rosewood **7**
Top Ten Greymouth
 Holiday Park **11**
Westway Homestay **5**

Preston Rd

Victoria Park

Montieth's Brewery

Murray

O'Donnell

Thompson

Ngarimu

Frickleton

Elme St

Tunnuhana

Hinchy

Lake Karoro (Tidal)

Brunner

Heaphy

Eating 🍴

Bonzai Pizzeria **1**
Café 124 **10**
Jone's Café & Bar **4**
Priga's Indian **3**
Raceway Carvery **5**
Railway Hotel **6**
Steamers Café & Bar **8**

③

Cowper St

Franklin

⑦

②

High St

①

Shakespeare St

Winnie

To ⑨ ⑪ ⑫ ⑬, Hokitika, Shanty Town & Arthur's Pass

Bars & clubs 🍷

Revingtons Hotel **11**

Road. For a longer tramp, the 18 km (eight to nine hours) **Croesus Track** from Blackball to Barrytown is recommended. It can be tackled from either end (though the Barrytown side is very steep) and takes in the grand views of the coast from above the tree line of the Paparoa Ranges and includes some notable gold-mining relics. Also, most importantly perhaps, it has a pub the 'Formerly the Blackball Hilton', T03-732 4705, www.blackballhilton.co.nz. Good accommodation also available. The DoC broadsheet *Central West Coast – Croesus Track* is invaluable; available from the VIC.

Shantytown

ⓘ *Rutherglen Rd, just off SH6, 10 km south of Greymouth, T03-762 6634, www.shantytown.co.nz, daily 0830-1700, $25, child $10. Kea West Coast Tours, T03-768 9292, offers 3-hr guided trips from Greymouth at 1000 for $70. Greymouth Taxis, T03-768 7078, can also get you there for about $20.*

Shantytown is a faithful recreation of an 1880's gold mining settlement. It comes complete with shops, a bank, saloon, goal, livery stables, fire station, working sawmill and a working steam train. Although a little commercial, it provides an interesting insight into the lives of hopeful prospectors. The steam train operates daily 0945-1600. You can also try your hand at gold panning, or even tie the knot in the original church. More traditional facilities include a café and souvenir shop.

Lake Brunner ›› pp560-561.

Lake Brunner, 37 km east of Greymouth, is the west coast's largest lake and certainly one of the prettiest. Other than fine scenery, **Moana Kotuku** (or Heron Sea as it is also known) offers some great fishing, walking, swimming and other water-based activities. The settlement of **Moana** on its northern bank is the main base. One of the best walks – the 20-minute **Arnold River Walkway** – is accessed via a swing bridge over the Arthur River at the western end of the village (Ahau Street). Keep your eye out for the beautiful **white heron** (Kotuku), which visit outside the summer breeding season. Guided fishing trips, tackle hire and the occasional kayak can be secured through the motorcamp, motel and hotel (see Sleeping, below).

Grey Valley and Blackball ›› pp560-561.

Between Greymouth and Reefton, the Grey River heads coastward, hemmed in by the Paparoa Ranges and the northern flanks of the Southern Alps. Like much of the region, its small settlements were born during the heady days of the gold rush.

Although the small former gold mining town of **Waiuta** (21 km south of Reefton) is of interest, it is the coal mining town of Blackball (accessed from Stillwater, 11 km north of Greymouth), which holds most appeal. Founded on gold in 1866, but developed later on coal, it is most famous as the cradle of working-class protest and unionism in the early 1900s. In 1908 an almost inevitable clash occurred when a 30-minute lunch break was sought (as opposed to 15 minutes). This debacle led to the formation of the Federation of Miners and subsequently the Red Federation of Labour – essentially the nation's Labour Movement. Such was the anti-capitalist feeling that, for a few years after the First World War, you could attend Marxism classes in the town.

Reefton ›› pp560-562.

Known as the 'Gateway to the Coast', the former gold town of Reefton is a fairly unremarkable, but pleasant little place at the end (or beginning) of the Lewis Pass arterial to the coast. Famous for very little, except its claim to be the first town in the southern hemisphere to receive a public electricity supply and street lighting in 1888, it is sustained by coal, forestry, farming and gold. The nice thing about Reefton is its unpretentious atmosphere. It seems very real. Although underrated and rarely on the tourist agenda, Reefton offers some fine fishing in the local rivers as well as a wealth of walking, tramping and mountain biking opportunities, primarily in the vast and local 180,000 ha Victoria Conservation Park – the largest forest park in the country.

The two most noted walks in town are the 'Reefton Heritage Walk' and the 'Powerhouse Walk'. The Heritage Walk takes in a number of interesting historical buildings including the renovated **Courthouse**, the beautifully decorated **Masonic Lodge**, the former **School of Mines** ($2) and even the odd bearded miner. On the Strand you will find the lovingly restored, former workhorse *R28 Fairlie* locomotive, the sole survivor of its type. The Powerhouse Walk is an easy 40-minute walk across the river to see the former **powerhouse** that once proudly lit up the town. Free leaflets outlining both walks are available from the VIC (I-Site); guided tours are available by arrangement.

Blacks Point Museum ⓘ *just beside SH7 (Lewis Pass Rd) in Blacks Point, T03-732 8835, summer Wed-Fri, Sun 0900-1200, 1300-1600, $5,* has extensive displays on the region's goldfields history. For a fine view of the town and the Inangahua Valley head south on SH7, turn left after 1 km into Soldier Flat Road and left again shortly afterwards. Follow this road to the lookout point in the pine forest.

◉ Greymouth and around listings

For Sleeping and Eating price codes and other relevant information, see Essentials pages 44-50.

◉ Sleeping

Greymouth *p555, map p557*
LL Kapitea Ridge Country Luxury Lodge, Chesterfield Rd (out of town, off SH6, 20 km south), T03-755 6805, www.kapitea.co.nz. Intriguing architectural aesthetics, stylish with some excellent artwork and cuisine. Well worth the journey, but comes at a price.
L-AL Hotel Ashley, 74 Tasman St, T0800-807787/T03-768 5135, www.hotelashley.co.nz. Comfortable with good facilities and a fine restaurant.
L-AL New River Bluegums, 985 Main South Rd (12 km south), T03-762 6678, www.bluegumsnz.com. A very characterful but out of town farmstay offering B&B and luxury self-contained cabins.
L-AL Rosewood, 20 High St, T03-768 4674, www.rosewoodnz.co.nz. Charming, beautifully preserved 1920s villa built by Greymouth's 'bookie' at the time. Excellent hosts. Recommended.
AL-A Westway Homestay, Herd St, Dunollie

(10 mins north of Greymouth), near Runanga, T03-762 7077, www.westway.co.nz. Well worth the effort with friendly hosts and excellent value en suite queen, twin with shared bathroom and an en suite twin with singles for families. Continental breakfast included and dinner on request.

Motels
Most of the motels are on the main drag (High St/SH6) heading south out of town. The following are recommended.
L-AL Coleraine Motel, 61 High St, T03-768 0077, www.coleerainemotel.co.nz. Relatively new 5-star rated with luxury serviced and self-contained units and about 4 mins' drive from the town centre.
L-A Alpine Rose, 139 High St, T0800-266835/T03-768 7586, www.alpinerose.co.nz.
L-A Gables Motor Lodge, 84 High St, T0800-809991/T03-768 9991, www.nzmotels.co.nz/gables.

Backpacker hostels
B-D Kainga-ra YHA Backpackers, 15 Alexander St, T03-768 4951, yha.greymouth@ yha.co.nz. A former Marist Brothers' residence, set overlooking the town, this place retains an

ecclesiastical theme that certainly extends to an innately peaceful atmosphere. Full range of rooms (some en suite), well-facilitated throughout and plenty of assistance with local activities.

C-D Duke Backpackers and Bar, 27 Guinness St, T03-768 9470, www.duke.co.nz. Fully renovated, it is well located in the heart of the town and offers value doubles, twins and dorm beds with free DVD movies, tea/ coffee, an internet café (free with coffee purchase) and, of course, a bar.

C-D Global Village Backpackers, 42-54 Cowper St, T03-768 7272, www.globalvillagebackpackers.co.nz. The best of the bunch with a good range of rooms and excellent facilities including a spa and sauna, its only downfall is its location from the centre of town. Kayaking is available in the creek that runs alongside it. Recommended.

C-D Neptune's, 43 Gresson St, T0800-003768/T03-768 4425, www.neptunesbackpackers.co.nz. All things fishy is the emphasis this time, with the wide range of comfortable rooms and facilities (including baths) decorated accordingly, Sky TV and free spa pool in case the weather does its worst, internet and off-street parking. Neptune's is good value and particularly good for couples. The owners also have plenty of local knowledge.

Motorcamps

A-D Top Ten Greymouth Holiday Park, 2 Chesterfield St, T03-768 6618/T0800-867104, www.top10greymouth.co.nz. A spacious, well-managed place located alongside the beach, with self-contained units, cabins and powered/tent sites with excellent facilities.

Lake Brunner *p558*

LL Lake Brunner Lodge, Mitchell's, Kumara-Inchbonnie Rd (at the southern end of the lake), T03-738 0163, www.lakebrunner.com. A historic fishing retreat with 11 luxury rooms and fine cuisine.
L-C Moana Hotel, 34 Ahau St, T03-7380083, www.moanahotelmotel.co.nz. Basic but value

double rooms, cabins, motel units and a restaurant.
AL-D Lake Brunner Country Motel, 2014 Arnold Valley Rd, at the outskirts of the village towards Greymouth, T03-738 0144, www.lakebrunnermotel.co.nz. Some excellent modern self-contained chalets, 1 motel unit, cabins, campervan sites and can arrange fishing and bush-walking excursions.

Blackball *p558*

B 'Formerly the Blackball Hilton', Hart St, T03-732 4705, www.blackballhilton.co.nz. Now a comfortable, friendly and very affordable B&B. Can arrange a number of local activities including gold panning, horse trekking and walking.

Reefton *p558*

AL-A Historic Reef Cottage B&B and café, 51 Broadway, T0800-770440/T03-732 8440, www.reefcottage.co.nz. Cosy restored 1880s cottage, self-contained, centrally located with a café. Fine full cooked breakfast.
AL-A Lantern Court Motels, corner of Broadway and Smith St, T0800-526837/ T03-732 8574, www.lanterncourtmotel.co.nz. One of the most modern in the town with 12 standard and fully self-contained units, Sky TV, spas.
AL-A Reefton Auto Lodge (Dawsons on Broadway), 74 Broadway, T03-732 8406. Modern self-contained studio and motel units. Spa and café/bar with a lovely open fire. Fishing trips and packages a speciality.
A Quartz Lodge B&B, 78 Sheil St, T03-732 8383, www.quartzlodge.co.nz. Perfectly comfortable with 3 tidy rooms.
B Bellbird Motel, 93 Broadway, T03-732 8444, www.nzmotel.co.nz. A cheaper motel option.
C-D The Old Bread Shop Backpackers,157 Buller Rd, T03-7328420, breadshopbackpackers@gmail.com. Small, homely and colourful set in the heart of the Victoria Conservation Park. The caring owners live next door and know the best fishing spots. Doubles and a dorm. Good value.

C-D Old Nurses Home Accommodation and Backpackers, 104 Shiel St, T03-732 8881, reeftonretreat@hotmail.com. Spacious establishment offering self-contained units, family double, twin and singles with all the usual facilities. Massage therapies are an added attraction. Recommended.

Motorcamps and campsites
C-D Reefton Domain Motorcamp, at the edge of town at the top of Broadway, T03-732 8477. Basic. Has powered/tent sites and cabins and a kitchen and amenities block.

● Eating

Greymouth *p555, map p557*
♦♦♦ **Ashley's Hotel**, 74 Tasman St, T0800-807787. Daily for dinner. A la carte restaurant with a good reputation.
♦♦ **Bonzai Pizzeria**, 31 Mackay St, T03-768 4170. 0700-late. Won't let you down.
♦♦ **Café 124**, Mackay St, T03-768 7503. Mon-Fri 0900-late, Sat-Sun 1000-late. Classy option, popular for lunch and dinner and also for breakfast or brunch at the weekend.
♦♦ **Jone's Café and Bar**, 37 Tainui St, T03-768 6468. A good alternative and open late, offers a traditional-style menu with a few good vegetarian options and has occasional live jazz and blues. Good breakfast.
♦♦ **Raceway Carvery**, Union Hotel, 20 Herbert St, T03-768 4013. Value pub meals.
♦♦ **Priga Indian Restaurant**, 84 Tainui St, T03-768 7377. Mon-Sat 0800-1700. Good hot option when the rain stops play.
♦♦ **Steamers Café and Bar**, corner of Mackay and Tarapuhi sts, T03-768 4193. Daily 1200-1400 and 1700-2000. Does a good Sun roast and pub grub.
♦ **Railway Hotel**, Mawhera Quay, T03-768 7023. Daily from 1830. For the real 'fill your face' deal.

Lake Brunner *p558*
For the more budget conscious based in Moana your only eatery options are:

♦♦ **Moana Hotel**, see Sleeping above; and
♦ **Stationhouse Café**, overlooking the lake and train station, T03-738 0158, seasonal hours. Recommended.

Blackball *p558*
♦ **Blackball Salami Company**, 11 Hilton St, T03-732 4111. Mon-Sat. Award-winning sausages for your picnic basket.

Reefton *p558*
♦♦ **Alfresco**, across the road from the Domain Motor Camp, 16 Broadway, T03-732 8513. Daily in summer for lunch and dinner. Lives up to its name with takeaway pizzas and good coffee.
♦♦ **Hotel Reefton**, Broadway, T03-7328447. Traditional pub-style meals.
♦♦ **Reefton Auto Lodge (Dawsons)**, see Sleeping above. Pub grub, known for its roasts.
♦ **Reef Cottage Café**, 51 Broadway, T0800-770440. Daily 1000-late. Cosy café serving good coffee and light snacks.

● Pubs, bars and clubs

Greymouth *p555, map p557*
Greymouth has several traditional hotels which are the focus of the town's nightlife with **Revingtons Hotel**, 47 Tainui St, T03-768 7055, perhaps being the most popular and certainly a good starting point.

● Entertainment

Greymouth *p555, map p557*
The cinema is the **Regent Theatre**, corner of Mackay and Herbert sts, T03-768 0920, www.regentgreymouth.co.nz.

▲ Activities and tours

Greymouth *p555, map p557*
Kea West Tours, T03-768 9292, www.keatours.co.nz. Range of road trips to

Punakaiki, Hokitika, the Glaciers, the Grey Valley and Shantytown, from $70.

On Yer Bike, T0800-669372/T03-762 7438, www.onyerbike.co.nz. Off-road adventures with 4WD, 8WD, motorbikes and go-karts, 1hr to full-day, $95-395.

Rafting Adventures, T0508-669675, www.ecorafting.co.nz. Quality half- or multi-day trips on one of the many west coast rivers from $185. Helicopter option also available from $450.

Wild West Adventures, 8 Whall St, T0508-286877/T03-768 6649, www.fun-nz.com. A major activity operator in the region offering a wide range of trips. An exhilarating half-day blackwater rafting in the Taniwha cave system from $160. Jungle Boat Rainforest Cruise, on board an imaginative range of traditional Maori craft and more conventional rafts with a distinct 'Tarzan' edge; the 3-hr trips are certainly different and offer a fine opportunity to learn more about the rich Maori culture and traditions of the west coast, from $135. 3-hr rafting trip (Grade II, suitable for families), from $145. 4-hr scenic guided tours to glow-worm caves (with some gold panning the way), to Shantytown and to Pancake Rocks, from $95. Multi-day guided walks on application.

Reefton *p558*

Spend some time in the VIC looking at the very attractive walking, tramping and mountain biking opportunities in the highly underrated and quiet **Victoria Forest Park**.

There are numerous routes and half- to multi-day walking/tramping options that take in a wealth of former gold-mining relics. An excellent 'helicopter in/mountain bike out' trip to Big River can be arranged by the VIC. Prices on application. The DoC leaflet *Reefton-Victoria Conservation Park* is useful.

The local fishing is superb (information about local guides available from the VIC). **Reefton Sports Centre**, 56 Broadway, T03-732 8593. Fishing licences and tackle hire.

◉ Transport

Greymouth *p555, map p557*
Car hire Alpine West Rentals, 11 Shelly St, T0800-257736. **Avis**, Mackay St, T03-768 0902. **NZ Rent-a-Car**, 170 Tainui St, T03-768 0379. Older, cheaper models.
Taxi Greymouth Taxis, T03-768 7078.

◉ Directory

Greymouth *p555, map p557*
Banks All bank branches can be found on or around Mackay St. **Internet** Grey District Library, Mackay St. **VIC (I-Site)**, see page 556.

Reefton *p558*
Internet VIC (I-Site), see page 556.
Library/post office, across the road, Mon-Fri 1030-1230, 1330-1630.

Hokitika and around → *Colour map 5, A4 Population: 4,000.*

Hokitika, or 'Hoki' as it is known, offers the same warm welcome and has the proud, healthy heartbeat felt all along the west coast. An important port until 1954, the town is also steeped in gold mining history; more of the precious metal passed through Hoki in the 1860s than any other town on the coast. Between 1865 and 1867, over 37,000 hopefuls arrived from Australia, America and Britain, requiring a staggering 84 hotels to put them all up in. In 1865, pioneer surveyor Julius von Haast described Hokitika as 'a scene of almost indescribable bustle and activity'. In those heady days it seemed only the river itself could hold the town back. At one point during the gold rush there was at least one grounding every 10 weeks – and 21 in 1865 alone. Like everywhere else the gold ran out and old 'Hoki' slipped into decline. But today gold has been replaced by that other precious resource –

Greenstone (Pounamu)

It would take several PhDs in geology to describe the make up, formation and various types of greenstone (nephrite), but suffice it to say it is old, uncommon and as the name suggests, coloured with almost transparent olive green shades. Greenstone, or jade – as it is better known – is precious (taonga) to the Maori and has been revered for centuries. The Maori called it *pounamu*. In New Zealand greenstone is found in the South Island, predominantly in Westland. The Maori called the South Island *Te Wahi Pounamu* (The Place of Greenstone). They went to great lengths to find and transport the precious stone, before carving it into a range of items, both practical and ornamental. Foremost among these was the mere (a flat hand-held weapon): highly treasured and in the hands of a warrior was lethal. Heitiki (pendants), were also painstakingly carved, often in the form of mythical spirits and monsters. These tiki were passed on from generation to generation and in doing so, increased in mana (prestige or spiritual power). Today greenstone is mainly used to create ornaments and tiki for the tourist market. Hokitika, on the west coast of the South Island is the best place to buy it and see it being made.

tourism. It is now the craft capital of the west coast and summer sees crowds of visitors arrive by the bus load, to watch glass-blowing and greenstone carving and to browse in its numerous galleries.

South from Hokitika the influence of humanity decreases dramatically and the aesthetics begin to reflect the sheer dominance of nature. Mountain ranges climb steadily on the eastern horizon, ascending in ever-increasing beauty towards the heady peaks of the Westland National Park and to Mount Cook itself. Small villages like Ross and Hari Hari cling precariously to a history of gold mining and demonstrate in size alone how much nature rules these parts, and hopefully always will. This is where the 'real' west coast begins. ▸▸ *For Sleeping, Eating and other listings, see pages 569-571.*

Ins and outs

Getting there Hoki boasts the west coast's main **airport** ⓘ *1 km east of the town centre*, served up to four times daily by **Air New Zealand Link**, T0800-737000. By road Hoki is 40 km south of Greymouth and 429 km north of Wanaka. Principal bus services are provided by **Intercity**, T03-7556166 (points south to Greymouth-Christchurch); **Atomic Shuttles**, T03-349 0697 (Queenstown/Greymouth/Christchurch, stops outside the VIC/I-Site) and **West Coast Shuttles**, T03-7680028, www.westcoastshuttle.co.nz, that offers daily services from Christchurch to Greymouth. Buses stop outside the **Travel Centre**, 60 Tancred St, T03-755 8557.

Tourist information **Westland VIC (I-Site)** ⓘ *Carnegie Building, corner of Hamilton and Tancred sts, T03-755 6166, www.hokitika.org.nz, www.west-coast.co.nz.nz, daily in summer 0830-1800, winter Mon-Fri 0830-1700, Sat-Sun 1000-1600*, stocks most of what you need. **DoC** ⓘ *10 Sewell St, Hokitika, T03-756 9100, www.doc.govt.nz, Mon-Fri 0800-1700*. **Ross VIC (I-Site)** ⓘ *4 Aylmer St, T03-755 4077, www.ross.org.nz, daily 0900-1700 (seasonal)*.

Hokitika ▸▸ *pp569-571.*

Hokitika is famous for its arts and crafts, particularly **greenstone** carving and **glass-blowing**. Tancred Street is the hub of the many artisan outlets and factory shops. Not to be missed is the **Hokitika Glass Studio** ① *9 Weld St, T03-755 7775, www.hokitikaglass.co.nz, daily 0900-1730 (longer in summer)*, where you can see the glass being blown and crafted into rather lurid ornaments and objets d'art. There are a number of other Jade factory shops and craft outlets including **Westland Greenstone** ① *34 Tancred St, T03-755 8713, daily 0800-1700*, where you can see the beautiful and spiritual stone being cut and handcrafted into an array of jewellery, ornaments and traditional Maori pendants (*tiki*).

Also worthy of investigation is the **Gold Room** and **House of Wood**, both on Tancred Street. The huge natural nugget pendants in the Gold Room (at a hefty $8,000) would delight the critical eye of Jimmy Saville or even Mr T.

If you fancy a go at jade carving yourself, then try **Bonz and Stonz** ① *16 Hamilton St, T03-755 6504*. This outfit will give you tuition and you get to keep your masterpiece – or disaster. The full jade package costs from $125 (bone $85).

Once crafted out and replete with souvenirs, you might like to absorb some Maori heritage and history at the new **Te Waipounamu Maori Heritage Centre** ① *39 Weld St, T03-7558304, www.maoriheritage.co.nz, daily 0830-1700, free*. The importance and legacy of Pounamu (Greenstone) is of course a major feature.

For general local history there is also the **West Coast Historical Museum** ① *Carnegie Building (accessed through the VIC), 7 Tancred St, T03-755 6898, daily 0830-1700 (seasonal), $5, child $1*. Again there is a heavy emphasis jade, but the troubled history of the port during the gold boom and its numerous shipwrecks offshore provides some added excitement.

The **Quay**, near the museum, is worth a stroll with its centrepiece, the 1897 Custom House, now housing a small gallery. The free *Hokitika Heritage Walk* leaflet available from the VIC outlines all places of historical interest.

Far removed from both craft and history is the small, but effective, **New Zealand Kiwi Centre** ① *64 Tancred St, T03-755 5251, 0900-1630, $14, child $8*. It is a small complex with a variety of native and non-native species, the stars of which are the New Zealand kiwi, tuatara and eels – big eels, in fact the biggest eel species in the world. These unfeasibly large, ugly and lethargic octogenarians are fed daily at 1000, 1200, and 1500.

The town also has its very own **Glow-worm Dell** at the northern entrance to town. If you have not seen them yet and missed out on the spectacular displays in Waitomo, then this is your chance to see how amazing a glowing bottom can be.

Around Hokitika

Lake Kaniere

Inland from Hokitika (14 km) is the picturesque Lake Kaniere, a popular haven in summer for swimming, watersports, picnicking and walking. The lake can be explored by foot, car, boat or bicycle and has many pleasant features. At the entrance to the **Lake Kaniere Scenic Reserve** is an information kiosk outlining the options. The two best short walks, both of which include lovely beaches, are the **Kahikatea Walk**, at Sunny Bight (10 minutes), and the **Canoe Cove Walk** (15 minutes). If you are feeling energetic the **Lake Kaniere Walkway** (four hours one way), which also starts at Sunny Bight, follows the western shore of the lake to Slip Bay at its southern edge. The road on the eastern edge will give you access to the ascent of **Mount Tuhua** (1125 m, seven hours return). Further south are the **Dorothy Falls** (64 m) near Big Bay. There is a basic campsite at Hans Bay. The DoC leaflet *Central West Coast – Hokitika* outlines all the options ($1).

Hokitika Gorge

Accessed directly from Hokitika (33 km) via the settlements of Kaniere and Kokatahi (end of Kowhitirangi and Whitcombe Road) or, alternatively, via Lake Kaniere (loop road to Kokatahi) is the picturesque and moody Hokitika Gorge. Other than the impressive scenery the highlight here is the **swing bridge**. Most of the time the river slides gracefully

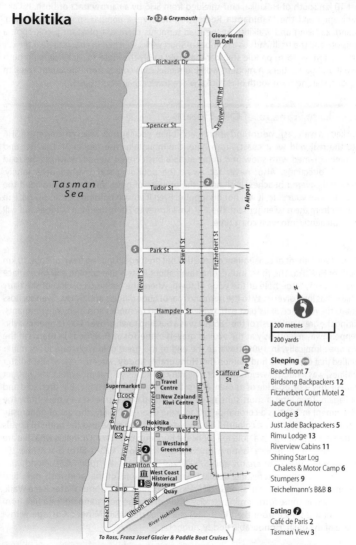

Hokitika

Sleeping 🛏
Beachfront **7**
Birdsong Backpackers **12**
Fitzherbert Court Motel **2**
Jade Court Motor
  Lodge **3**
Just Jade Backpackers **5**
Rimu Lodge **13**
Riverview Cabins **11**
Shining Star Log
  Chalets & Motor Camp **6**
Stumpers **9**
Teichelmann's B&B **8**

Eating 🍴
Café de Paris **2**
Tasman View **3**

below, however, it can become a raging torrent after heavy rains, making the crossing an exciting prospect. Once across, you can continue through the bush for another 100 m to emerge at a rock wall that offers an even better view of the gorge.

Lake Mahinapua

Just 10 km south of Hokitika, and shielded from SH6 by a narrow tract of bush, is Lake Mahinapua and the **Mahinapua Recreation Reserve**, a popular spot for swimming, fishing, kayaking and walking. At the road terminus there is a pleasant picnic spot, a campsite and the trailheads to a number of short walks. Perched in concrete near the car park is a former 15-m paddle steamer that used to ply the route to 'Hoki' carrying both freight and passengers. A modern working model runs cruises from the outlet creek to the lake, starting 6 km south of Hokitika. ⟫ *See Activities and tours, page 571.*

Hokitika to Franz Josef 🚌🌐🏔 ⟫ *pp569-571.*

Stocked up with cash, petrol and photographic film, you can now follow the artery of SH6 into the real wild west coast. From here, the mountains rise higher and higher and become crowned with snow and impenetrable bush creeps steadily towards the road from all directions. Also, never far away, the pounding surf crashes onto lonely, driftwood-covered beaches. It all holds the promise of great things and, provided the weather is on your side, it will not disappoint. Even if you do nothing but simply gaze in wonder from the passenger seat, the 137-km journey to Franz Josef is a stunner and will ease you gently into west coast time.

Ross

The first settlement of consequence is the tiny but pretty gold mining town of Ross, 30 km south of Hokitika. The most interesting thing about Ross is that mining still takes place here, in a very large hole at the edge of town, where the gentle chip, chip of the early pickaxe has long given way to the hum and roar of huge diggers and trucks. Even so, Ross retains the romance of its past with evidence of fond memories and many old remnants. During the great gold rush of the 1860s it was a bustling town of over 3,000 hopefuls, who chipped away relentlessly at the alluvial gravels of the Totara Riverbeds in search of the 'big one'. Ironically, in 1909, towards the end of the great gold rush, one lucky miner fulfilled that dream. His find, named the '**Honourable Roddy**', after the erstwhile Minister of Mines, was a nugget weighing in at a healthy 3.1 kg. As you might expect, the nugget immediately took on a life of its own, at first being paraded from bar to bar then sold and sold again. Then after a short stint as a doorstop (apparently true) it was bought by the government in 1911 as a coronation gift for King George V. Sadly, this act of generosity proved its demise. After a colourful life above ground, the good and the grateful Royals melted it down for use as a gold tea service at Buckingham Palace. Or that is what we are led to believe. A replica is now on view at the **Ross VIC (I-Site)** ① *4 Aylmer St, T03-755 4077, www.ross.org.nz, daily 0900-1700, guided walks 1000-1400.* Along with Roddy it has some interesting displays and photographs of the gold rush days and information on a number of short local walks, including the one-hour **Water Race Walk**, which takes in some former mining relics. You can also go gold panning (pan hire from $6). A short distance from the VIC (I-Site) is a renovated 1885 **Miner's Cottage** with a replica of the great 'Honourable Roddy' nugget.

Pukekura

About 18 km further south of Ross is the small settlement of Pukekura and the **Bushman's Centre** ⓘ *T03-755 4144, www.pukekura.co.nz*. This place is instantly recognizable and notorious for the **giant sandfly** (*Renderus insanitus*) that hangs with menace from its walls (don't panic: despite local gossip, they could never grow that big). The Bushman's Centre is the ongoing project of local west coaster and extrovert Peter Salter and his partner Justine Giddy. As well as a fine café (with its superb 'road kill soup of the day') and shop it has a great little interactive **museum** ($4), where you can learn about bushcraft, meet live possums, stroke a pig, baulk at ugly eels, then wantonly throw sharp knives and axes at the wall. It's brilliant. Other activities based at the centre include horse trekking and gold panning.

Harihari

From Pukekura the bush continues to envelope you and you are blessed with your first occasional views of Mount Cook's snowy peak. At **Lake Ianthe** there are opportunities to stop and take in the views, enjoy a picnic on its bush-clad bank. From the car park you can take a short walk to visit a large **maitai tree**, the South Island's equivalent to the North Island's mighty kauri.

Harihari, 20 km south of Lake Ianthe and 80 km from Hokitika, is a small farming settlement nestled on the open alluvial plains of the Wanganui and Poerua rivers. It is famous due to the unexpected visitation by a 21-year-old Australian aviator called Guy Menzies in January 1931. Young Guy had set off unannounced and alone from Sydney in his Avro-Avian plane called the *Southern Cross* armed with little except a lot of courage and a good sense of direction. Just under 12 hours and an awful lot of sea later he crash-landed in a swamp near the town. The interesting thing is that bold Guy had not officially told anybody of his attempt to cross the ocean to New Zealand and he completed it in 2½ hours less than the much publicized success of Sir Charles Kingsford Smith, in a three-engine plane, with crew, three years earlier.

If you fancy some thorough exploration of the coastline, the **Harihari Coastal Walkway** (three hours) utilizes part of the old Wanganui River pack track and is a fine walk. It traverses kahikatea and rimu forest and essentially links the two river mouths. The car park and trailhead is accessed via La Fontaine Road at the southern end of Harihari (19 km). One of the many highlights of the walk is the lookout at the top of **Mount Doughboy** (or to use its more attractive name – Mount Oneone). Although not especially high it does afford a great view up and down the coast. The DoC leaflet *Harihari Coastal Walk* provides detailed information.

Whataroa

It is little wonder that the Maori have long revered the **white heron** (**kotuku**). Although a non-native and essentially an Australian import, its presence here on the west coast seems utterly befitting of the place. Somehow, with its colour echoing the snow of the mountaintops and its graceful unhurried flight in rhythm with west coast time, there could be no better mascot. Whataroa, 35 km south of Harihari, provides your only opportunity to see these majestic birds congregated at their sole New Zealand breeding rookery. The birds are only in residence from mid-October to mid-March.

White Heron Sanctuary Tours ⓘ *T0800-523-456/T03-753 4120, www.whiteherontours. co.nz*, tours $110, child $45, daily at 0900, 1100, 1300 and 1500, in season, offers a 2½-hour tour by jet boat to access the hide that overlooks the colony. All tours are guided and the colony cannot be visited independently without a permit. Outside the breeding season there is still an enjoyable 2½-hour 'Rainforest Nature Tour' available, again by jet boat, to view the ancient Kahikatea forest and whatever birdlife that decides to show (costs as above).

While in Whataroa don't miss the **Kotuku Gallery** ① *Main St, T03-753 4249, kotuku.gallery@xtra.co.nz*, Regarded as one of the best Maori galleries in the country the Kotuku showcases some superb work, including pieces carved from ancient whalebone and aotea stone, the latter being found in only two rivers in the world: one on the West Coast the other, surprisingly, in Germany. *Poanamu* (Greenstone), the signature stone of the West Coast, also features heavily.

Okarito

Okarito, a small coastal settlement and former goldfields port, is 13 km off SH6 and 15 km south of Whataroa. This beautiful little paradise, set beachside next to the vast 3240-ha Okarito Lagoon backed by stunning views of the Southern Alps, is not surprisingly the favourite haunt of many a New Zealander. Thankfully most people shoot past the road junction from SH6 in their rush to see their first glacier – Franz Josef – 29 km to the south. But for those who take the time and the diversion, they will be rewarded not only with Okarito's simple do-nothing appeal, but also some excellent walking, kayaking and birdwatching opportunities. There is no public transport to Okarito and no shops in Okarito so take your own supplies.

There are few remnants of Okarito's once bustling gold mining past when the population remarkably ran into the thousands. It's hard to believe there were once 25 hotels, two banks, several stores, a busy school (now the YHA) and three theatres. Across the road from the obviously historic and incredibly cute YHA is the almost unsightly **obelisk** commemorating Abel Tasman's first sighting of New Zealand, somewhere off Okarito in 1642.

The best walk is the steady climb (1½ hours) via an old, but well-formed, pack track through native bush to the **Okarito Trig**. On a clear day it affords a stunning view across the bush-clad hills to the Southern Alps and the peak of Mount Cook and its associates. As if that weren't enough, you can then turn to take in the expansive views back towards the Okarito Lagoon and north up the coast. The **Trig Track** starts from the Strand at the southern end of the village. Once you have negotiated the Trig you can then consider carrying on along the main pack track for about an hour to reach **Three Mile Lagoon**. It is a lovely spot with a quiet beach and more coastal views. If the tide is right, you can then walk back to Okarito via the beach where huge white-veined schist rocks that have been eroded from the Kohuamarua Bluff litter the beach. Look out for dolphins playing just off shore.

The great expanse of **Okarito Lagoon** is a birdwatchers' paradise with almost every mainland bird species in New Zealand visiting at some point. Over 70 species have so far been recorded. The best way to view the birds and other fauna and flora of the lagoon is by kayak or boat tour. It's a great opportunity to go deep in to kiwi habitat to listen to (or possibly see) the great avian national icon in the wild. ▶▶ *See Activities and tours, page 571.*

For Sleeping and Eating price codes and other relevant information, see Essentials pages 44-50.

⊚ Sleeping

Hokitika *p563, map p565*
Hokitika is blessed with good accommodation but in summer, like everywhere else on the west coast, be sure to book well in advance.
LL Rimu Lodge, 33 Seddons Terr, T03-755 5255, www.rimulodge.co.nz. Purpose-built luxury lodge in a peaceful location and commanding memorable views over both river and mountain. 4 fine, spacious en suites from super-king to queen. 2-course dinner on request and full cooked breakfast included. All in all, a good-value option. Recommended.
L Teichelmann's B&B, 20 Hamilton St, T03-755 8232, www.teichelmanns.co.nz. Large heritage building, centrally located, with an arts and crafts edge. 6 en suites both double and single and a delightful cottage with spa in the garden. The hosts have a great knowledge of the town and region. Recommended.
L-AL Beachfront Hotel, 111 Revell St, T0800-400344/T03-755 8344, www.beachfronthotel.co.nz. The most high-profile hotel in town. Well-equipped and comfortable with 53 rooms from standard to luxury, most en suite and some with ocean views. A reputable restaurant/bar overlooking the beach being its best point. Off-street parking available.
AL-A Fitzherbert Court Motel, 191 Fitzherbert St, T03-755 5342, www.fitzherbertcourt.co.nz. 1- to 2- bedroom suites (some with spa bath), studios, Sky TV.
AL-A Jade Court Motor Lodge, 85 Fitzherbert St, T0800-755885/T03-755 8855, www.jadecourt.co.nz. Self-contained studios and 1- to 2-bedroom units in a spacious garden setting.

AL-D Shining Star Log Chalets and Motor Camp, 11 Richards Dr, T03-755 8921, www.accommodationwestcoast.co.nz. A superb motel/motorpark with tidy self-contained lodges designed and built by the owners. It is close to the beach in a quiet location and also takes campervans and tents. The facilities are excellent.
B-D Riverview Cabins, 154 Kaniere Rd, 3.5 km east of town, T03-755 7440, www.hokitika.com/riverviewcabins. Set amid a heritage homestead and gardens this 4-unit complex is very peaceful, well-equipped and good value. Recommended.
C-D Birdsong Backpackers, SH6 (4 km north), T03-755 7179, www.birdsong.co.nz. Small beachside backpacker hostel, just north of the town, offering dorms, doubles and a large dose of peace and quiet. Outdoor bath for navel and galaxy contemplation. Recommended.
B-D Stumpers, 2 Weld St, T03-7556154, www.stumpers.co.nz. Pitched somewhere between a budget motel and a backpacker hostel, it offers tidy en suite and standard doubles, singles and dorms. Its central location and in-house bar and café are an added attraction. In-house dining is encouraged so there are no kitchen facilities.

Ross *p566*
B-D The Old Church, SH6 Kakapotahi River, 16kms south of Ross, T03-755 4000. This converted church sits on the banks of the river and offers a great budget option. Six doubles, twins and a dorm. Plenty of character and huge open fire. No shop so take supplies. Recommended.

Pukekura *p567*
Across the road from the Bushman's Centre (see page 567) there is a fine array of accommodation options (**AL-D**) from tent sites and budget dorms to motel units 'under canvas' with all facilities and even hot pools.

Harihari p567
AL-D Harihari Motor Inn, Main Rd, T0800-833026. Tidy en suites, backpacker rooms, powered/tent sites and a licensed restaurant.

Whataroa p567
A Sanctuary Tours Motel, T0800-523456/T03-753 4120, www.whiteherontours.co.nz. Self-contained units, studio units and cabins.
A-C Whataroa Hotel, T03-753 4076. Rooms, a motel unit, a cabin and powered sites. In-house restaurant.

Okarito p568
D Okarito YHA Hostel, Palmerston St, T03-379 9970, www.yha.co.nz. Something of a novelty set in the former 1870's 'bijou' schoolhouse. Bookings can be made via the Franz Josef VIC or payment made at the warden's house close to the hostel. Coin-operated showers at the campground.

Campsites
D DoC campground, opposite the hostel. A very pleasant, sheltered and basic campsite facilities are adequate. Fires are permitted. Beware of sandflies and take insect repellent. No bookings necessary.

❶ Eating

Hokitika p563, map p565
There is a supermarket: **New World**, 116 Revell St. Mon-Fri until 2000, Sat 1900, Sun 1900.
♥♥♥ Café de Paris, 19 Tancred St, T03-755 8933. Daily from 0730. Award-winning restaurant with imaginative French-style à la carte dinner and changing blackboard menu for breakfast and lunch. Good coffee.
♥♥♥ Tasman View Restaurant, attached to the Beachfront Hotel, Revell St, T03-755 8344. Dinner daily from 1800. Popular not only for the views of the crashing waves and the sunset, but also for its seafood.
♥ Stumpers Café & Bar, 2 Weld St, T03-755 6154. Daily 0700-2200. A more conventional menu and aesthetics.

Ross p566
There is a supermarket on Main Rd, open until 2000.
♥ Roddy Nugget Café, 5 Moorhouse St, T03-755 4245, on the Main Rd. Daily from 0800-1900.
♥ Empire Hotel, Aylmer St, T03-755 4005. Offers pub-style breakfast, lunch and dinners.

Pukekura p567
♥ Puke Pub, on the main road, T03-755 4144, www.pukekura.co.nz. Without doubt one of the finest drinking establishments on the west coast. Full of character with pub-style grub.

Harihari p567
♥♥♥ Harihari Motor Inn, see Sleeping above. Basic restaurant.
♥ Glenalmond Tearooms, on the main road through the town.

Whataroa p567
The only eateries are both on the main road:
♥ Whataroa Hotel, see Sleeping, above.
♥ White Heron Store and Tearooms.

❶ Pubs, bars and clubs

Hokitika p563, map p565
Stumpers Bar, see Eating, above. The main hub of entertainment and attracts a diverse crowd and stages live bands most weekends.

Pukekura p567
Puke Pub, see Eating, above. Not to be missed. It's pronounced 'pookie'.

❸ Festivals and events

Hokitika p563, map p565
Mar Hokitika Wildfoods Festival, T03-7569084, www.wildfoods.co.nz. Hokitika goes mad each Mar and enjoys such a human influx that it can jog the memories of the gold rush days. The attraction is not gold but good food and lots and lots of beer and wine. This

is a celebration of the west coast's unique lifestyle and hospitality (not to mention drinking capacity). On offer is a vast array of culinary delights from BBQ possum, or witchetty bug to the famed local whitebait fritter. There's even the odd testicle – yum! A number of lesser events over the 2- to 3-day event (which includes diverse activities as a basketball exhibition match and a Monteiths Beer tasting) leads up the main festival and dance on the Sat.

▲ Activities and tours

Hokitika p563, map p565
The VIC can advise on local kayaking and rafting operations.
Kokatahi Helicopters, T03-7557912, www.kokatahihelicopters.com. Offer whitewater kayaking via helicopter.
Wilderness Wings, T0800-755 8118, www.wildernesswings.co.nz. Flightseeing trips following the Main Divide to Mt Cook and the glaciers, then back over the wild and remote beaches. Personable service, from 45 mins to 3½ hrs, from $320.

Whataroa p567
White Heron Sanctuary Tours, PO Box 19, Whataroa, T0800-523456, www.whiteheron tours.co.nz. Guided boat trips to New Zealand's only White heron breeding site. See also page 567.

Okariko p568
For details, see Franz Josef Activities and tours, page 578.

Okarito Kiwi Tours, T03-753 4330, www.okaritokiwitours.co.nz. Offers the chance to go deep into kiwi habitat to listen to (or possibly see) the great avian national icon in the wild. Low impact guiding is backed up by good local knowledge. 2-3 hrs from$75. Recommended.
Okarito Nature Tours, T03-753 4014, www.okarito.co.nz. Offers independent kayak rental (2 hrs, $40) and a range of excellent guided trips to explore the scenery and natural history of the lagoon and its many secluded channels, from $75 (overnight from $80). Recommended.

⊖ Transport

Hokitika p563, map p565
Bicycle hire Hokitika Cycles and Sportsworld, 33 Tancred St, T03-755 8662.
Taxi Hokitika Taxis, T03-755 5075.

① Directory

Hokitika p563, map p565
Banks Most branches and ATMs are in the town centre. If heading south, there are no further banks, or ATMs until Wanaka.
Internet Kodak Shop, 15 Weld St, T03-755 7768. **Medical services** Westland Medical Centre, 54 Sewell St, T03-755 8180. **Post office** 93 Revell St, T03-756 8034, Mon-Fri 0830-1700.

Glacier Region → *Colour map 5, A/B3.*

To add to New Zealand's majestic scenery and ecological surprises, the two gigantic and dynamic monoliths of ice – Franz Josef and Fox Glaciers – provide a dramatic sight. They are the brightest jewels in the highly decorated crown of the Westland and Mount Cook national parks, joined, yet separated on the map, by the jagged summits and peaks of the Southern Alps and the Great Dividing Range. Descending from a height of 3000 m to 300 m at the remarkable speed of over 1 m a day, the glaciers create one of the best examples of glaciology in the world.

In summer there are two moods to the neighbouring villages of Franz and Fox. When the sun shines they are a frenetic buzz of activity: from the moment the sun peeks over the mountains, the skies fill with the sound of aircraft, the roads swarm with tour buses and the streets fill with expectant tourists, consumed with the desire to get to the glaciers, walk on them and photograph them. And yet, when the clouds gather (which is often) and the rain descends (or rather crashes down), the pace of everything slows, dramatically: the air hangs heavy with silence, the streets fill with puddles and the tourists' glum faces stare out from behind café windows. At Franz and Fox it's amazing just how much the weather and two multi-million ton blocks of ice can dictate. ▸▸ *For Sleeping, Eating and other listings, see pages 576-582.*

Ins and outs

Getting there There are no scheduled air services to Franz Josef. By road Franz Josef is 177 km south of Greymouth, 404 km north of Queenstown and 25 km north of Fox Glacier on SH6. Fox Glacier is 177 km north of Haast. By bus, **Intercity**, T03-752 0754, and **Atomic Shuttles**, T03-349 0697, north and southbound services all stop at Franz Josef and Fox. The **YHA**, T03-752 0754 (see Sleeping, page 576) act as the local Intercity agents.

Getting around Most of Franz Josef's amenities are on the SH6 (Main Road) with everything, except the glacier, within easy walking distance. **Glacier Valley Eco-tours**, T03-752 0699, www.glaciervalley.co.nz, provides transport to the glacier every 2 hrs 0845-2100 (1800 in winter), $13 return. It also offers road and walking tours to Lake Matheson, Franz and Fox glaciers from $65. Hitching to the glacier and back is rarely a problem. Note that there is no petrol available between Fox Glacier and Haast.

Tourist information DoC Franz Josef Glacier VIC (I-Site) ① *southern end of town (seaward side), T03-752 0796, www.glaciercountry.co.nz, 0830-1800 (winter 0830-1630)*, is the best place for non biased information and has plenty of displays, information on walks and up-to-date weather forecasts. **DoC Fox Glacier VIC (Area Office)** ① *SH6, at the northern end (seaward side) of the village, T03-751 0807, Mon-Fri 0900-1630*, also offers information but the Franz office is far more comprehensive.

Franz Josef ⊝❼▲⊜❶ ▸▸ *pp576-582.*

Franz Josef owes its existence and its name, to the block of ice that sits 5 km south of the village. Of the two principally tourist-based settlements (Franz and Fox), Franz is the larger and better serviced. As you might expect it is a seasonal destination, crowded in summer, quiet in winter. Although the glacier can of course be visited in the rain and the guided glacier walks are rarely cancelled, the scenic flights, and essentially, an overall impression of the glaciers from above and below, are completely dependent on favourable conditions. Plan to give yourself at least two days in the area. If you have scenic flights booked, these can be forwarded if it's cloudy. While you wait there are a few things to keep you occupied, even in the rain (see Wet weather activities, page 580). The average annual rainfall in the area is 5 m over 180 rain days. In summer always book your accommodation well in advance.

Franz Josef Glacier

Franz Josef was first sighted and officially documented by both Abel Tasman in 1642 and Cook in 1770, but first properly explored and named by geologist and explorer Julius von Haast in 1865. When he first explored its lower reaches it was almost 3 km nearer the coast than it is today. The official title of 'Francis Joseph Glacier' was given in honour of the Emperor Franz Josef of Austria. The spelling was later changed to Franz Josef in accordance with the internationally accepted version – as in Franz Josef Land in the Arctic and Franz Josef Fjord in Greenland. Until 1985, and apart from a few sporadic advances last century, the glacier had actually been receding steadily since 1865. As it stands, it is unclear what it will do next. After advancing almost 1 km, at almost 1 m a day over the last 17 years, it is now slowing down. Many are worried that global warming will see the glaciers recede at an unnatural rate due to a lack of snow at the summits.

The glacier is 5 km south of town and accessed by the Glacier Access Road which runs alongside the cold, grey Waiho River, which dramatically appears from beneath its face. From the car park it is a 1½-hour return walk along the wide rocky river bed to within 500 m of the glacier. Unless properly equipped you cannot walk on the glacier itself; to do that you are strongly advised to join one of the many guided trips. By far the best way to view the glacier is from the air; there are numerous options available. From the ground, the 280 m-high viewpoint on **Sentinel Rock** (a remnant of previous glacial erosion) is perhaps the best place; it is easily accessed from near the main car park (20 minutes). ▶▶ *See Activities and tours, page 578.*

Fox Glacier ⊜❼▲⊜❻ ▶▶ *pp577-582.*

Many people visiting the Glacier Region only visit one of the great monoliths, with Franz Josef being the most favoured. However, if you have time, Fox Glacier (25 km south of Franz and a further 8 km southeast) is no less dramatic. The **Fox Glacier Valley** and the chilly **Fox River**, which surges from the glacier terminus, provide a significantly different atmosphere, with the precipitous, ice-carved cliffs near the car park being particularly remarkable. The Fox Glacier was originally called the Victoria Glacier and was renamed in honour of former New Zealand prime minister, Sir William Fox, on a visit in 1872. The small village of Fox Glacier is the main service centre and sits on a site that was, as recently as 5000 years ago, covered by the present glacier.

Although less commercial, Fox, like its neighbour Franz, can be explored independently at its terminus, but you will need a guide to walk or climbed on it. Once again, however, the recommendation is to admire it from the air. There are a number of interesting walks within the valley, at the coast and around the reflective **Lake Matheson**, which lies 4 km west of the village. ▸▸*See Activities and tours, page 580.*

South to Haast ⊜❼▲▸▸ *pp577-582.*

From Fox Glacier you leave the great glaciers and towering peaks of the national parks behind and SH6 winds its scenic way ever southwards to Haast a World Heritage Area and to the most remote region of the west coast: South Westland. For many years Fox was as far south as any tourist ventured, the road from there becoming rough and eventually non-existent at Paringa. With the opening of the great Haast Pass Highway in 1965 the two roads were linked making the continuous journey possible. Given the terrain in South Westland, it is not hard to understand why such a link was so late in coming. Despite the intrusion, much of South Westland remains remote, unspoilt and remarkably beautiful.

Copeland Pass

The heavily forested **Copeland Valley**, 26 km south of Fox, heralds the trailhead of the **Copeland Track** ⓘ *details on the 'Copeland Track' broadsheet from DoC.* Hut fees are $15 per night and there is a resident warden at Welcome Flat from November to April. Although the complete three- to four-day tramp makes a spectacular high-alpine crossing into the Hooker Valley and, eventually, the haven of Mount Cook Village, recent rock falls have made the route very difficult and one only suited to the experienced mountaineer. Nevertheless, the 17-km overnight tramp up the Copeland Valley to the **Welcome Flat Hut** is recommended. This tramp acquaints you with some superb forest, river and mountain scenery and includes the natural hot pools at Welcome Flat. The one-way tramp to the hut takes about six hours. From Welcome Flat you then have the option of an overnight stay and a return, or the extra (three hours one way) excursion higher up the valley to the **Douglas Rock Hut** ($5).

Bruce Bay

From the Copeland Valley, a further 20 km will see you rejoining the coast at Bruce Bay, a quiet, scenic spot, once famous for a false gold claim made during the rush of 1865. Apparently, three miners in Hokitika initiated the story that they had secured a hundred-weight of gold in Bruce Bay and, as a result, over 2000 hopeful souls made the long and difficult journey south. Frustrated and angry after realizing it was a hoax, they then went on the rampage looting and destroying the makeshift stores and shanties. Although it is very pretty in itself, one of the most beautiful and scenic bays and beaches of the west coast lies just over the headland, to the south. The much-photographed (from the air) **Heretaniwha Bay**'s golden curve of sand and rim of windshorn rimu epitomize the west coast wilderness. With the Mahitahi River and trackless headland preventing easy access it is very difficult to reach, which is perhaps what makes it so special.

Paringa

Turning inland again, the SH6 continues south to cross the Paringa River before arriving at **Lake Paringa**. The river is noted as the furthest point south that the intrepid early explorer Thomas Brunner reached in his epic 18-month journey from Nelson and the

Buller Gorge in 1848. Considering it would be another 100 years before the road even reached this point, his 'feat' can only be admired. A plaque by the river honours it. At Lake Paringa you will find accommodation and a café. The lake is noted for its good trout fishing and the **Jamie Creek Walkway** (15 minutes), which negotiates a fine tract of beech and rimu, 1 km south of the café near the DoC campsite.

Lake Moeraki and Munroe Beach

The reflective waters of **Lake Moeraki** are a further 18 km south of Lake Paringa and 30 km north of Haast. Although popular for swimming, kayaking and birdwatching most people are in an understandable rush to share the intent of its outlet river and head straight for the beach. The car park and trailhead to **Munroe Beach** is 200 m north of Moeraki River bridge. An easy, well-formed path leads through some beautiful coastal forest to the pounding surf. It is a typical west coast stunner and a place where wildlife abounds. In the breeding season (July to December), or during their moult in late summer, it is a great place to see the rare and beautiful **Fiordland crested penguin**. If you are lucky, and provided you are quiet, you can watch them fighting their way through the crashing waves to waddle uneasily up the beach before disappearing into the bush. It really is a wonderful spectator sport.

If the tide is well out try to investigate the beach and the Moeraki River mouth to the south of Munroe. It's even better. Note that there is one other species that is present in its thousands and are far less interesting or welcome – sandflies. Apply lots of repellent or you will re-emerge at the car park looking like you have had a serious road accident.

Knight Point

South of Moeraki SH6 rejoins the coast and climbs to Knight Point with its spectacular views of sea stacks and near inaccessible beaches. Just south of the viewpoint you should be able to see **fur seals** dozing on the beach. It was just south of Knight Point that the Haast Highway was officially opened in 1965, thereby connecting Otago with south Westland and the west coast proper. At the base of the hill, about 3 km south, is a small car park allowing unadvertised access to **Murphy's Beach**. This is a superb spot for a beach walk. If the tide is out you can explore this beautiful sweep of sand and the rugged coast north or south. The rock outcrops and pinnacles to the south of the beach provide some superb photo opportunities, especially at sunset.

Ship Creek

A little further south is the more popular access to the beach at Ship Creek. Here you can choose from a number of excellent short walks to explore the beach, coastal forest and a small lake held captive by the dunes. If the tide is out you can make the easy river crossing, negotiate the headland and explore the beaches heading north. In summer it is not unusual to see **Fiordland crested penguins** coming ashore to their breeding areas hidden in the coastal fringe. When it comes to an archetypal wild and remote coast it does not get much better than this. Ship Creek was named after a wreck that ironically occurred on the Australian coast at Cape Otway in Victoria in 1854. On her maiden voyage, the 2600-ton *Schomberg* ran aground and several years later, pieces of the ill-fated vessel were washed up where over 1500 km away. From Ship Creek SH6 hugs the coast and passes some spectacular examples of coastal rimu, rata and kahikatea forest on its approach to Haast and the Haast River crossing.

For Sleeping and Eating price codes and other relevant information, see Essentials pages 44-50.

⊙ Sleeping

Franz Josef *p572*

Given the amount of tourist traffic in summer and the fickle weather, you are advised to book your accommodation well in advance and add an additional night, just in case.

LL Franz Josef Glacier Country Retreat, off SH6, 6 km north of the village, T0800-372956733/T03-752 0012, www.glacier-retreat.co.nz. A replica of a traditional west coast homestead in a peaceful farmland setting, owned by a fourth-generation west coast family. 12 beautifully appointed luxury en suite rooms with a historical edge. 4-poster beds and claw-foot or spa baths add to the appeal. In-house café and bar. Activities and massage therapies can be arranged. Recommended.

LL Westwood Lodge, SH6, 1 km north of the village, T0800-200209/T03-752 0112, www.westwood-lodge.co.nz. A modern, well-appointed single-storey B&B, with 9 luxury en suite rooms.

LL-L Te Waonui Forest Retreat, SH6, T03-752 0555, www.sceniccircle.co.nz. New and environmentally conscious 5-star complex operated by the Scenic Circle Hotel Group. 100 luxurious guest rooms with every imaginable comfort – including a 'pillow menu'. Restaurant, café and bar. Recommended.

LL-L Franz Josef Glacier Hotels, Main Rd, T03-752 0729, www.sceniccircle.co.nz. Catering mainly to tour groups, with a restaurant, a café and 3 bars, plus a spa. It is showing its age, but the decor is modern.

LL-L Holly Homestead B&B, off SH6, 1½ km north of the village, T03-752 0299, www.hollyhomestead.co.nz. Gracious old homestead with native timbers throughout. 4 en suites, some with wheelchair access, children welcome. Internet, full cooked breakfast included.

LL-L Punga Grove Motel and Suites, northern end of Cron St, just east of Main Rd, T03-752 0001, www.pungagrove.co.nz. Modern stylish studios and units from standard to luxury all backing on to native punga fern gardens, with premium rooms incorporating your very own 'punga grove'.

AL-A Alpine Glacier Motor Lodge, 17 Cron St the village centre, T03-752 0226, www.alpineglaciermotel.com.

AL-A Bella Vista, northern end of Cron St, just to the east of Main Rd, T03-752 0008, www.bellavistamotels.co.nz.

AL-A The Glacier Gateway Motor Lodge, T03-752 0776, www.franzjosef motels.co.nz. Quieter and on the southern edge of town (nearest the glacier).

L-AL Glenfern Villas, T0800-453633/T03-752 0054, www.glenfern.co.nz. This modern place offers self-contained and serviced apartments and is in a peaceful location near the Tatare River 3 km north of the village.

AL-D Rainforest Retreat, 46 Cron St, T0800-873346/T03-752 0220, www.rainforest retreat.co.nz. Affordable eco-based log cabins in a quiet bush setting, yet still close to the village centre. The various options include studios, self-contained suites and family units. There are also campervan facilities and tent sites, with modern facilities including a camp kitchen. Spa and internet. Recommended.

Backpacker hostels

There are many backpacker hostels available in the village, most being on Cron St.

A-D Glow Worm Cottages, 27 Cron St, T0800-151027/T03-752 0172, www.glow wormcottages.co.nz. The favourite, along with **Chateau Franz**, below. Both offer the best in facilities, character and atmosphere.

A-D Franz Josef YHA, 4 Cron St, T03-752 0754, www.yha.org.nz. Modern, spacious hostel with all the usual reliable YHA facilities including some very tidy en suite doubles and a heavy and refreshing emphasis on

eco-awareness and recycling.
Recommended. Book well ahead.
A-D Chateau Franz, 8 Cron St, T03-752 0738, www.chateaufranz.co.nz. Well equipped and deservedly popular, with free soup, spa and video library to ease the rain fall blues.

Motorcamps and campsites

Camping (**D**) is available at the **Rainforest Retreat**, see above.
L-D Mountain View Top Ten, SH6, 5 km north of the village, T0800-467897/ T03-7520735, www.mountain-view.co.nz. Great views of the mountains. Full range of options and standard **Top Ten** facilities.

Fox Glacier p573

LL Te Weheka Inn, opposite the DoC/VIC, Main Rd, T0800-313414/T03-751 0730, www.teweheka.co.nz. A recent addition to the village and pitched somewhere between a motel and a boutique hotel. It has a striking design and offers modern luxury suites. Facilities include a library and internet. Tariff includes breakfast.
L Heartland Hotel Glacier Country , Main Rd, T03-751 0847, www.scenichotelgroup.co.nz. An old hotel that has been refurbished in recent years. It has a wide range of fairly unremarkable rooms from studio to single. Restaurant and bar with large open fire. Internet.
L-AL High Peaks Hotel, 163 Cook Flat Rd, T03-751 0131, www.highpeakshotel.co.nz. A new establishment offering a good range of suites and units (some with spa) and an in-house restaurant.
AL-A Homestead Farm B&B, Cook Flat Rd, T03-751 0835, foxhomstd@xtra.co.nz. One of the few B&Bs in the village offering all the comforts of home in a century- old farmhouse.
A-D Fox Glacier Inn, Sullivan's Rd, T03-751 0022, www.foxglacierinn.co.nz. Tidy family, double or shared rooms, a café, restaurant and bar. Tents also welcome.
C-D Ivory Towers, Sullivan's Rd, T03-751 0838, www.ivorytowerslodge.co.nz. An old

favourite with a cosy atmosphere and great facilities, including a small cinema, sauna, bike hire and internet. Its double rooms are especially good value and the copious flowerbeds and hanging baskets are a memorable, attractive feature. Recommended.

Motels

Many motels in Fox are on Cooks Flat Rd.
L-AL Mount Cook View Motel, T03-751 0814, www.mtcookview.co.nz.
L-AL The Westhaven Motel, Main Rd, T0800-369452/T03-751 0084, www.the westhaven.co.nz. Offers a wide range of rooms, some with spa.
AL-A Lake Matheson Motel, T03-751 0830, www.lakematheson.co.nz. Recently refurbished. Recommended.
AL-A Rainforest Motel, T03-751 0140, www.rainforestmotel.co.nz.

Motorcamps

L-C Fox Glacier Holiday Park, Cooks Flat Rd, T0800-154366/T03-7510821, www.foxglacierholidaypark.co.nz. The main motorpark in the village. Very spacious, it has all the usual facilities including cabins, lodge rooms, flats, powered/tent sites and a backpacker dorm. Good facilities, but it can get a bit over-crowded.

Bruce Bay p574

LL Mahitahi Lodge, off SH6 in Bruce Bay, T03-7510095, www.mahitahilodge.co.nz. Purpose-built luxury homestay accommodation named after the river that meets the ocean at Bruce Bay. 3 well-appointed en-suites with native timbers throughout, open fire and some fine in-house cuisine (breakfast included in tariff but dinner $65 extra). The exceptional hosts will also take you on an informative and entertaining local tour.

Lake Moeraki p575

LL-L Moeraki Wilderness Lodge, beside SH6 at the Moeraki River outlet, T03-750 0881, www.wildernesslodge.co.nz. An exclusive eco-based B&B establishment. The lodge has 22 rooms all with private facilities and an in-house restaurant. Guided nature/ history walks and canoe trips are also available, with some being part of the package.

🍴 Eating and drinking

Franz Josef *p572*
Grocery supplies are available from **Fern Grove Food Centre**, Main Rd, 0800-2200 (seasonal). Well-stocked but expensive.

🍴 **Alice May Bar and Restaurant**, Cron St, T03-752 0740. Daily from 1500. English pub-style, with arguably more atmosphere and better value food. Noted for its fine ales.

🍴 **Beeches Café, Restaurant and Bar**, Main Rd, T03-752 0721. Daily from 0800- 2100 (seasonal). Standard fare for breakfast, lunch and dinner.

🍴 **The Blue Ice Café & Pub**, Main Rd, T03-752 0707. Serves up a good pizza upstairs and à la carte dining on the ground level. All-out war on the free pool table is its other speciality. Recommended.

🍴 **Franz Josef Glacier Hotel and Te Waonui Forest Retreat restaurants**, T03-752 0729. A la carte, but often busy with bus tours. Bookings are recommended.

🍴 **The Landing**, Main Rd, T03-752 0229. Daily 1000-late, breakfast, lunch and dinner. Fine pizzas and currently the base in Franz for après-rain or after-hours entertainment.

Fox Glacier *p573*
Grocery supplies are available at the **General Store**, Main Rd, T03-751 0829, daily 0800-2030 (1900 in winter) at inevitably elevated prices.

🍴 **Café Neve**, Main Rd, opposite the Alpine Guides Centre, T03-751 0110. 0800-late (seasonal). Quite expensive, but still a pleasant place for breakfast, light snacks, home baking and coffee with outdoor seating that offers a good spot from which to watch the world go by.

🍴 **Cook Saddle Café and Saloon**, Main Rd,

T03-751 0700. From 1200. It offers a good meat-lover's menu and has a bar.

🍴 **Hobnail Café**, in the Alpine Guides Centre, T03-751 0005. Daily 0700-1700 (seasonal). Offers a hearty, good-value breakfast and some fine home baking.

🍴 **The Plateau**, Sullivan Rd, T03-751 0058. Daily 0900-late (seasonal). Earning a good reputation in the village, the menu is imaginative enough but more attractive still is the open fire and the wine list.

🍴-🍴 **Fox Glacier Inn**, see Sleeping, above. Good for a beer and a chat.

🍴 **Café at Lake Matheson**, at the car park at the entrance to the lake, T03-7510878. Open for breakfast lunch and dinner. A good option if you plan to go walking there, it is especially welcome after the popular sunrise photo opportunities. Cheap breakfasts.

Paringa *p574*
🍴 **Salmon Farm Café**, just north of the Paringa River, T03-751 0837. Daily 0730-1700 (winter 0830-1600). A popular 'quick-stop' eatery. Either feed the salmon in the tanks below or eat one in the café.

⛰ Activities and tours

Franz Josef *p572*
There are many operators based in Franz Josef offering a range of options for acquainting yourself with the great glacier. Competition is fierce so shop around. Most people do one of 3 things: they walk to the glacier's terminal face independently, they take a guided walk on to the glacier, or they take to the air. A glacier walk is both exciting and very informative, however, if you can possibly afford it, take an extended scenic flight around Mt Cook and down the face of the glacier, landing briefly on the snow at its crown. The atmosphere up there, and the silence on a calm, clear day, is simply unforgettable. When the rain shows who's boss, you might like to try a spot of indoor, all-weather ice climbing (followed by a hot

bath of course) at the new and impressive **Hukawai Glacier Centre and Ice Climbing Wall** (see below). Alternatively, if ice for you is something that belongs in several small blocks deep in a gin and tonic, you can sit and watch from the comfort of the café.

Glacier Country Tours and Kayaks (Ferg's Kayaks), 20 Cron St, T0800-423262/ T03-752 0230, www.glacierkayaks.com. 2½-hr kayaking trips in the area including Lake Mapourika (similar to Lake Matheson). Also offers a full-day heli-hike and kayak combo.
Glacier Valley Ecotours, T03-752 0690, www.glaciervalley.co.nz. Conventional road and walking tours of both glaciers and Lake Matheson, 1-3 hrs, from $65.
Skydive Glacier Country, T0800-7510080, www.skydivingnz.co.nz. Offers 9000-12,000 ft tandem skydives amid some of the country's most stunning scenery, from $245-295.
South Westland Horse Treks, Wahio Flat Rd, just south of Franz, T0800-187357/ T03-752 0223, www.horsetreknz.com. Offers 1- to 3-hr horse treks including some great beach rides, from $60.

Flightseeing
There are 2 companies offering fixed-wing flights over the glaciers: **Air Safaris** and **Mount Cook Ski Plane Adventures** (Aoraki Mt Cook). The latter offers the only opportunity in New Zealand to land on a glacier in a fixed-wing aircraft. Both companies are based in Fox (see page 580) but can provide pick-ups from Franz.
    Helicopter flightseeing is also available with all flights offering a glacier landing. Again, the companies are based in Fox:
Fox and Franz Josef Heli-services, T0800-800793/T03-7520793, www.newzealandnz.co.nz/helicopters. From 20-40 mins, snow landings.
Glacier Helicopters, Main Rd, T0800-800732/T03-7520755, www.glacier helicopters.co.nz. 10- to 40-min flights with snow landing, from $195-385.
Helicopter Line, Main Rd, T0800-807767, www.helicopter.co.nz. Flights from 20-40

mins and a 3-hr heli-hike option. Its helicopters are twin-engine.
Mountain Helicopters, T03-7510045, www.mountainhelicopters.co.nz. Flights from both Franz and Fox from 10-40 mins. It offers competitive charter prices for independent climbers.

Glacier walking and ice climbing
Glacier walking is an extraordinary experience and a magical way to explore a glacier. By climbing across the surface and descending into small crevasses you get a better feel of how they work and can witness the beautiful blue colour of the ice. The tours are also very informative. Fox is generally accepted as the better glacier for ice climbing, while Franz is steeper and more heavily crevassed which makes for better glacier walking.
Alpine Guides, see Fox Glacier, page 581. Offers ice-climbing and heli-hiking.
Franz Josef Glacier Guides, Main Rd, T0800-484337/T03-752 0763, www.franz josefglacier.com. A highly experienced and professional outfit offering 4- to 8-hr excursions as well as heli-hike and high-level alpine trips. The 8-hr trip takes you to the impressive icefalls, while the 2- to 3-hr tour takes in the lower parts of the glacier face. For tours on the glacier, the famous 'Ice-Talonz' crampons and thermal, waterproof boots make for comfortable walking. Prices are from $65 (glacier face walk); half-day glacier trip $105 (4 hrs), full-day $160 (8 hrs); ice climbing $250 (8 hrs).

Heli-hiking
For the keen tramper, being at the base of all these stunning mountains and the 2 glaciers is almost too much to bear and with time a premium you might like to consider heli-hiking. Although inevitably expensive the combination of the views and exploring the upper reaches of the glaciers makes it well worth it. All the companies listed below offer heli-hiking options from 2-3 hrs with about 10 mins in the air from around $300
Alpine Guides, see Fox Glacier, page 581.

Franz Josef Heli-Hike, Main South Rd, T0800-807767, www.helicopter.co.nz.
Glacier Guides, T0800-484337, www.nzguides.com.
The Helicopter Line, see Helicopter flightseeing, above.

Hot pools

Glacier Hot Pools, Cron St, T0800-044044, www.glacierhotpools.co.nz. Daily 1200-2200, from $23, child $16. Massage is available from $80 (book ahead).

Walking

Other than the glacier terminal walk there are a number of other walking options in the glacier valley. The wonderfully named **Lake Wombat** (after a gold miner's nickname) and another, **Alex Knob** (don't ask), can be accessed 350 m down the Glacier Access Rd. The route, which traverses the valley wall, takes you through classic rata and kamahi forest, rich in birdlife. The 'kettle' lake, Lake Wombat can be reached in 45 mins, while the stunning view of the glacier from Alex Knob will take another fairly strenuous 3 hrs.

A little further along the Glacier Access Rd is the access point to the **Douglas Walk** and Peter's Pool. Named after a young camper who set up his tent there in 1894, it is an easy walk and the lake can be reached in 10 mins. The track continues to reunite with the road further up the valley (1 hr). Located 1 km from the junction of the Glacier Access Rd and SH6 is **Canavan's Knob Walk** (40 mins return), which, like Sentinel Rock in the glacier valley, withstood the actions of the ice that completely covered it until about 10,000 years ago. Now covered only in rimu trees it offers views of the glacier and the mountains.
Glacier Valley Eco-Tours, T03-752 0690/ T0800-999739, www.glaciervalley.co.nz. Runs shuttles to Franz Josef Glacier for $13 return, as well as trips to Lake Matheson and Fox Glacier.

Wet weather activities

Should the heavens open and the hot pools not appeal try:
Across Country Quad Bikes, T0800-234288/T03-7520123, www.acrosscountryquadbikes.co.nz. A good wet-weather activity, with 4 trips daily in summer, 2-3 in winter, on 2-seater ATVs from $150 (passenger $75). Safe professional outfit and of course fine scenery.

Fox Glacier *p573*
Flightseeing

Both companies offer pick-ups from Franz.
Air Safaris, Main Rd, T03-680 6880, www.airsafaris.co.nz. A 50-min 'Grand Traverse' flight over 10 glaciers and the upper peaks of both national parks from $295, child $195. This flight has no snow landing.
Mount Cook Ski Plane Adventures (Aoraki Mt Cook), Kew Building , Main Rd, T0800-800702, www.mtcookskiplanes.com. Offering the only fixed-wing glacier landing in New Zealand, this company has been in business over 35 years. The 30-60 min flights offer a memorable experience and the engines are switched off once on the glacier so you can experience the silence. Should the romance of it all be overwhelming, Alex (a marriage celebrant) can oblige, anywhere from 6000-8000 ft. Flights start at $230.

Glacier walks

The closest short walk is the (25 mins return) **Minnehaha Walk**, which starts beside the road just south of the village. It is a pretty rainforest walk that takes in a small **glow worm dell** ($2); best viewed with a torch at night. The glacier valley walks and the glacier itself is accessed via Glacier Rd, which leaves SH6 about 1 km south of the village. The **Glacier terminus** can be accessed from the car park (1 hr return) which is about 8 km from Fox village. About 3 km down Glacier Road is a small car park on the left which is the trailhead for the River (1 km, 30 mins return) and **Chalet Lookout Walk** (4 km, 2 hrs return). The very pleasant **River Walk** begins with a swing bridge crossing over the

Flightseeing options

Fixed wing or helicopter? Twin engine or single? Snow landing or no landing? Weather permitting, these are the questions to ask yourself. Generally speaking fixed-wing aircraft will allow longer in the air for the price and cover more 'air', but you miss out on that unique feel of a helicopter. Helicopters have twin or single engines. Most helicopters offer 10-minute snow landings whereas most fixed-wing planes do not. All modes are intrinsically safe and all companies are accommodating regarding weather cancellations (payment takes place pre-flight and post-booking) even offering alternative flights at sister locations.

cold, grey Fox River. Once across the river the track then climbs through the rainforest, with occasional views of the glacier, before reaching the car park and terminus of the Glacier View Rd (which runs along the southern bank of the river). From here it is a steady climb through forest and across crystal clear streams to reach the lookout point. The walk itself is as good as the view. However, do not expect to get good photographs of the glacier from here as there is too much bush in the way. The walk around **Lake Matheson** (4 km west from Cook Flat, then Lake Matheson Rd, 1½ hrs return) and to the **seal colony** at **Gillespies Beach** (20 km west via Cook Flat Rd) are other excellent options. The marked route (6 hrs return) up **Mt Fox** (1021 m), 3 km south of the village, provides great views across the higher peaks and forest.

Helicopter flightseeing

Helicopter flights cost $195 for 20 mins; $270 for 30-40 mins. Snow landings are offered on all flights. There are 4 helicopter companies: **Fox and Franz Josef Heli-services**, Alpine Adventure Centre, T0800-800793/ T03-752 0793, www.scenic-flights.co.nz. Flights from 20-40 mins. The helicopters are small but comfortable. Being perhaps the most competitive in price they better suit the budget traveller. Charters are also available. **Glacier Helicopters**, Fox Glacier Guiding Building, Main Rd, T03-752 0755/T0800-800732, www.glacierhelicopters.co.nz. 10- to 40-min flights all with snow landing, from $195-$385.

The Helicopter Line, Main Rd, T03-751 0767, www.helicopter.co.nz. Flights from 20-40 mins, with snow landings and a 3-hr heli-hike option.
Mountain Helicopters, T03-751 0045, www.mountainhelicopters.co.nz. A small, local company, offering competitive prices, suitable for the budget traveller. Charters also available. Flights cost $95-180 for 10-20 mins and $240-340 for 30-40 mins.

Ice climbing

Fox is generally accepted as the better glacier for ice climbing.
Fox Glacier Guiding, Alpine Guides Building, Main Rd, T0800-111600/ T03-751 0825, www.foxguides.co.nz. With 30 years of experience, this is a highly professional outfit offering 2- to 8-hr excursions as well as heli-hike, ice climbing, multi-day mountaineering and high level (overnight) alpine-hut trips. Trips leave throughout the day and include a guided excursion to the glacier terminus ($49). Heli-hike, from $395 (4 hrs) and heli-hike and Chancellor Hut experience (8 hrs), from $599 (overnight $850). Ice-climbing instruction days are also a speciality ($235).

Lake Moeraki p575

Moeraki Wilderness Lodge, PB Bag 772, T03-750 0881, lakemoeraki@wilderness lodge.co.nz. Accommodation, guided nature walks and kayak trips in World Heritage park. See Sleeping, above.

Franz Josef *p572*
Bicycle and scooter hire
Chateau Franz or Glow Worm Cottages (see Sleeping, above) both offer bikes for hire.

Fox Glacier *p573*
Bicycle hire
Ivory Towers Backpackers (see Sleeping, above). Full day hire $30.

Franz Josef *p572*
Banks There are no banks in the village but there is an ATM outside the **Blue Ice Pub** at the southern end of main St. The **Mobil Service Station** (Glacier Motors Ltd), T03-752 0725, open from 0800, nearby has EFTPOS. Foreign exchange is available at **Fern Grove** Souvenirs, Main Rd (across the road from Alpine Adventures), T03-752 0731.
Internet Franz Josef Glacier Guides/ Helicopter Line on Main Rd. Also in most backpacker hostels and **Glacier Country Tours and Kayaks (Ferg's Kayaks)**, 20 Cron St, T0800-423262. **Medical services** Doctor, Whataroa, T03-756 1080. **Police** Whataroa, T03-756 1070. **Postal agent** Mobil Service station, see Banks.

Fox Glacier *p573*
Banks There are no banks or ATMs but EFTPOS is accepted in most places. Foreign currency exchange available at **Fox Glacier Guiding**, Main Rd, T03-751 0825, daily 0800- 2100 (winter 0830-1730). **Internet** Glacier Country Hotel or Ivory Towers Backpackers, see Sleeping page 577. **Postal agents** Fox Glacier Guiding, Main Rd, T03-751 0825, daily 0800-2100 (winter 0830-1730).

Haast Region → *Colour map 5, B1/2.*

The Haast Region of South Westland contains some of the most unspoiled ecosystems in New Zealand and is a lauded World Heritage Area. The stunning scenery, from mountaintop to coastal plain, includes pristine streams that flow into vast river mouths fringed with dense tracts of ancient coastal (Kahikatea) forests. Within the forest lie swamps and hidden lakes and all along their fringe are endless swathes of beach covered in sculpted driftwood. Wildlife, too, abounds, from the playful keas on the mountains to the sleepy fur seals on the coast. Few tourists stop long enough in the Haast Region to truly appreciate or explore properly. But if you do, Haast itself is an ideal base and gateway to a timeless environment. ▸▸ *For Sleeping, Eating and other listings, see pages 585-586.*

Ins and outs
Getting there By road Haast is 120 km south of Fox Glacier and 145 km northwest of Wanaka. North and southbound **Intercity** and **Atomic Shuttle** services stop in Haast Township and/or the DoC visitor centre.

Tourist information **DoC visitor centre** ① *next to SH6, 300 m past the Haast River Bridge,* T03-750 0809, www.haastnz.com, www.west-coast.co.nz, *daily 0900-1800 (1630 in winter).* As if the water features outside were not impressive enough, the interior displays are memorable and plenty of information on walks and natural attractions is provided. Ask to see the *Edge of Wilderness* video, which is a fine introduction to the local landscape ($3, children free).

Haast

From the north, a lush corridor of coastal forest and the 750-m Haast River Bridge brings you to the rather splintered settlement of Haast. The Haast River is a fitting introduction to the village and the stunning wilderness that surrounds it. On the coastal plain the annual rainfall, at 5 m, is similar to that of much of the west coast. But above 1500 m, the average can be over three times that and, after a deluge, the great river can turn into a menacing torrent. Haast is the epitome of a west coast village: remote and unobtrusive, with residents who are full of pride and moulded by the wild, rugged and harsh environment that surrounds them.

Haast is named after the geologist/explorer/surveyor Julius von Haast who first explored the then almost inaccessible coast in 1863. He did so via the pass to the east, which now bears his name and provides the modern-day road access. Locals, however, will pull your leg and tell you the name derived from a misquotation by Captain James Cook. On sailing past he was, by all accounts, so appalled at the sight and inhospitable nature of the place, he ordered all the ships flags to be flown at half-mast. He entered 'Half-mast' in his log. A century later, when the log was reopened, the fold in the page disguised the full name and it became known as Haast.

On initial acquaintance Haast (the 'settlement') is a bit confusing. Immediately on the southern side of the bridge is a huddle of buildings that form **Haast Junction**. This is home to the DoC visitor centre, a petrol station and the **World Heritage Hotel**. A further 4 km south of Haast Junction, on the Jackson's Bay Road, is **Haast Beach**, another small conglomerate, including another petrol station, a motel, food store and some private homes. From there the road continues for 50 km before reaching a dead end and the remote village of **Jackson's Bay**. East of there an unsealed road accesses the Arawata River and the **Cascade Saddle**, a memorable day trip. The main settlement of Haast – or **Haast Township** – is 4 km inland and east of Haast Junction on SH6. Here you will find the major residential area, shops and most of the accommodation.

Jackson's Bay Road

Other than the obvious attractions of the coast to the north, the true wilderness of the Arawata and Cascade River valleys south of Haast via the Jackson's Bay Road, is considered legendary. Though this stunning landscape is well worthy of some thorough investigation, the tiny pioneering settlement of **Jackson's Bay** is the main attraction.

From Haast Junction and Haast Beach, Jackson's Bay Road hosts the tiny settlement of **Okuru**, set on the Okuru River and principally based on whitebaiting. The road then carves a straight 20-km path through native forest to the Arawata River; on the way the covert streams crossing the road have some intriguing names including 'Dizzy', 'Dancing' and 'Dismal'. In the heart of this forest is the stubborn plug of bedrock known as **Mount McLean**, which, like Mosquito Hill near Haast, withstood the assaults of old glaciers. At the **Arawata Bridge** you are afforded a grand view up the valley before the road forks inland to the **Cascade River Valley**, or west along the coast to Jackson's Bay.

The unsealed Cascade Road follows the beautiful **Jackson River Valley** (a tributary of the Awawata). The river provides a wonderful place to go fishing or simply kick back and admire the scenery. But perhaps your first stop should be the walk to the hidden **Lake Ellery**. Beginning just beside the Ellery River Bridge, a well-disguised track follows the river to the lake edge. It is neither well signposted nor well maintained so expect to get muddy and lost. However, the beautiful reflections of the forest on the river and the tranquil atmosphere of the lake itself, makes the one-hour return walk well worthwhile. Once you reach the lake head you can go no further and must back track.

From Lake Ellery River the Cascade Road rises steadily crossing the Martyr River and the evocatively named **Monkey Puzzle Gorge**, before reaching a high point in the valley and the road terminus. From here you are afforded an expansive view down to the **Cascade Valley** and the dramatic glacial sculpted sweep of the hills to the coast. Inland the Olivine Range and Red Hills herald the boundary of the **Mount Aspiring National Park**. The **Red Hills** are a particularly interesting and noted geological feature. The colouration is caused by high concentrations of magnesium and iron in the rock that has been forced up by the actions of the Austral and Pacific tectonic plates. What makes this mountain range of special interest is that their other half (Dun Mountain) now lies in the Nelson Region.

Jackson's Bay

Fighting hard to survive its wild remoteness, is the historic little village of Jackson's Bay at the end of Jackson's Bay Road. Jackson's Bay has an interesting and troubled history. Now a small fishing settlement with about 20 registered vessels moored in what is the nearest thing to a natural harbour the length of the west coast, it was first settled by a hardy group of 400 in 1875. A cosmopolitan bunch of Scandinavians, Germans, Poles, Italians, Irish, Scots and English, they set about trying to establish agriculture and the small port. However, due to the weather, poor soils and a general lack of interest from beyond, the project was a catastrophic failure. Within weeks whole families fell ill, or simply gave up and moved out. Only three years after landing the community shrank from 400 to a mere handful. Only a few of the most prosperous survivors managed to stay by founding large cattle runs.

The iron-framed grave of pioneer settler Claude Morton Ollivier, who died of pneumonia only weeks after his arrival, is a fitting testament to the Europeans' failed attempts. It is the oldest known European grave on the west coast and is next to the main road above the beach.

Other than a wander around Jackson's Bay itself you might like to try the 1½ hour return **Smoothwater Track**. Beginning about 500 m north of the village it climbs the forested hill to take in the fine views north, before crossing a saddle and dropping down again to the Smoothwater River Valley and neighbouring Smoothwater Bay. One attraction not to miss in Jackson's Bay is the **Cray Pot Café**, on the waterfront (see Eating, page 586).

Haast Pass

From Haast Township SH6 turns inland and follows the bank of the Haast River before being enveloped by mountains and surmounting what was, until 1960, the insurmountable. The Haast Pass at 563 m is an ancient Maori greenstone trail known as Tiori-patea, which means 'the way ahead is clear'. Ironically, being the principal water catchment of the Haast River and plagued by frequent floods and landslips, the name is one of misplaced optimism as the modern-day road can testify. However, although sometimes treacherous and difficult to negotiate, the crossing captures the mood of the place, with names such as the **Valley of Darkness** and **Mount Awful**. Even beside the road there is suggestion of this, with other evocative titles like **Solitary Creek No 2** and the first of three waterfalls, **Roaring Billy**, 28 km inland from Haast. Best viewed on a short (signposted) loop walk, Roaring Billy plunges down mountain slopes on the opposite side of the river, and although it's only a steady flow most of the time, after heavy rains it most certainly lives up to its name.

A further 25 km, just before the 'Gates of Haast', another waterfall – the competitively named **Thunder Creek Falls** – drop a vertical 28 m into the Haast River. They too can be accessed and photographed from a short loop track beside the road.

The gorge, known as the **Gates of Haast**, is just a little further on and you can see the boulders and precipitous rock walls that proved such a barrier to road construction for so many years. Above the Gates the road and the river level off and the mountains take on a less menacing appearance, as do the waterfalls, with **Fantail Falls** (signposted and accessed next to the road) proving far less threatening, with moderate plumes of whitewater tumbling over a series of rocky steps. From Fantail Falls it is only a short distance before the Haast Pass itself and the boundary of Westland and Otago. From here the scenery dramatically changes and you leave the west coast behind.

◉ Haast Region listings

For Sleeping and Eating price codes and other relevant information, see Essentials pages 44-50.

▣ Sleeping

Haast and Jackson's Bay Road *p583 and p583*
L Hannah's Homestead, Jackson's Bay Rd, T0800-538723/T03-750 0708, www.hannahs homestead.co.nz. Great new B&B offering one double unit, double king and a queen. Great location and local activities arranged.
L Collyer House B&B, Jackson's Bay Rd, further south on the banks of the Okuru River, T03-750 0022, www.collyerhouse.co.nz. Wonderfully peaceful and offers 4 luxury en suite rooms with views. Open fire and antiques abound. Activities are arranged.
L-A McGuires Lodge, between Haast Junction and Haast Township, T03-750 0020, www.mcguireslodge.co.nz. Has a fine range of en suite units and can arrange activities.
AL-C Heartland World Heritage Hotel, corner of SH6 and Jacksons Bay Rd, Haast Junction, T0800-502444/T03-750 0828, www.world-heritage-hotel.com. Long-established and recently refurbished, it has 54 en suite units from standard to family, but is best known for its restaurant and bar. Activities arranged.
AL-D Aspiring Court Motel and Haast Lodge, T03-750 0703, www.aspiringcourt motel.com. Has a range of units, cabins, powered/tent sites. Close to all amenities.
A-B Acacia and Erewhon Motel, Jackson's Bay Rd, 4 km from junction, Haast Beach, T03-750 0803. Modern and friendly, it has 3

elite, 4 studio and 5 standard units all self-contained.
A-B Heritage Park Lodge, Marks Rd, Haast Township, T0800-526252/T03-750 0868, www.heritage parklodge.co.nz. Cheaper option with a range of modern units and en suites.
A-C Wilderness Backpackers Motel, Pauareka Rd, T03-7500029, www.wildernessa ccommodation.co.nz. The favoured backpacker hostel. Single-storey building with good value en suite doubles, twins and family units. Bike and scooter hire and internet access.

Motorcamps and campsites
Camping is also available at Haast Lodge, see Sleeping, above.
A-D Haast Beach Holiday Park, Okuru (15 km south), Jackson's Bay Rd, T0800-843226/ T03-750 0860, haastpark@xtra.co.nz. Excellent. It offers a number of motel units, self-contained and standard cabins, but is mainly noted for its location, friendliness and fine modern kitchen and lounge facilities.

❶ Eating

Haast *p583*
There is a supermarket on Pauareka Rd in Haast Township. 0800-1930 . There's a general store next to the motel in Haast Beach, T03-750 0825.
❢❢ **Fantail Café and Restaurant**, Haast Township, T03-750 0055, 0730-2200. Basic meals served all day.

¶ Heartland World Heritage Hotel Café and Bar, Haast Junction, T0800-502444. Daily 1100-1000. The best (and only) option at the junction. Hearty, good value and quality meals.

¶ Hard Antler Bar and Restaurant, Marks Rd, Haast Township, T03-750 0034. Daily from 1100, dinner from 1800. Bar with good pub grub.

Jackson's Bay *p584*
¶ Cray Pot Café, T03-750 0877, Jackson's Bay. Daily 1030-1900. A quirky cross between a rail carriage and a barge serving average fish and chips. You can eat in (recommended) or take away, but beware of the sandflies.

yourself with the area, its history and folklore. The tours last from 3-4 hrs.

Waiatoto River Safaris and Beach Comber Quads, T0800-538723, www.riversafaris.co.nz. As the name suggests, provides an opportunity to explore the Waiatoto River south of Haast. The 2½-hr trips depart at 1000, 1300 and 1600, from $199, child $129. Also you can have a blast down the beach on a 2-hr trip from $140, two on one bike $210 (minimum age 8 years).

Wanna Go Fishing, T03-750 0134. Offers guided trips from half-day $750 to full-day at $1050. There is some superb fishing on offer especially south of Haast on the Arawata River.

▲ Activities and tours

Haast *p583*
Haast River Safaris, in the 'Red Barn' between Haast Junction and Haast Township, T0800-865382/T03-7500101, www.haastriver.co.nz. Reputedly offers a scenic river safari up the Haast River Valley. The 1½-hr trips on its purpose-built (covered) jet boat depart daily at 0900, 1100 and 1400 and cost from $132, child $95. Recommended.

Round About Haast Tours, Jackson's Bay Rd, T03-750 0890, www.roundabout haast.co.nz. Operated by locals Mauryne and Bob Cannell, the tours are an ideal way to acquaint

---

① Directory

Haast *p583*
Internet Wilderness Backpackers, Pauareka Rd, Haast Township and **McGuires Lodge**. **Police** T03-750 0850. **Telephone** There is no cell phone coverage in Haast. **Useful addresses** Johnston Motors (Caltex), in Haast Junction, beside the VIC, T03-750 0846, has EFTPOS and provides AA recovery and an independent breakdown recovery service. Petrol is available 24 hrs with EFTPOS and credit cards. **Mobil Service Centre**, Haast Beach, T03-750 0802, also provides the same services and acts as car hire and postal agents.

Contents

Footprint features

Otago

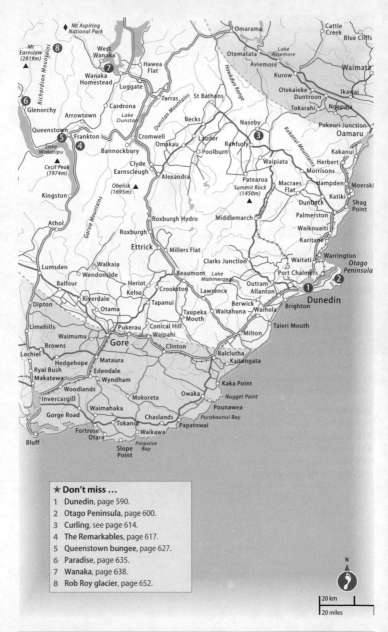

N

20 km
20 miles

If the Otago Region was a girl she would be a very engaging sort from a good Scottish background and good-looking. Her height and build can be likened both to the towering peaks of Fiordland and Mount Aspiring national parks in the west, and to the gently rolling hills, harbours and golden beaches of the Otago Peninsula in the east. Her two large blue eyes would be Lakes Wakatipu and Wanaka. And down her entire length carves the vein of New Zealand's second longest river, the Clutha. Her personality varies too: from the student city buzz of Dunedin to the quiet whispers of Glenorchy or Clyde. Otago is also down-to-earth and wears her heart on her sleeve. She has distinct moods which change with the seasons: cold and snowy in winter; miserable with rain in spring; and boasting beautiful golden hues in autumn. Otago owes her considerable pedigree to her predominantly Scottish heritage and the discovery of gold, a resource that was once her lifeblood. Now, though, Otago pumps fast and furious with sheer adrenaline. Although her head is in Dunedin, her heart is in Queenstown – the adventure sports capital of the world. Otago is not only pretty, she also knows how to have a good time.

Dunedin → *Colour map 6, B6 Population: 100,000.*

There is perhaps nowhere else in the world – and certainly nowhere so far from its roots – that boasts a Scottish heritage like Dunedin, the South Island's second largest city. For those who have walked the centuries-old streets of Edinburgh in Scotland, let alone lived there, a trip to Dunedin (which actually means 'Edin on the hill') is somewhat disconcerting. Immediately, you will notice the echo of Scottish architecture – grand buildings of stone, built to last, that go far beyond the merely functional and, in true Scottish tradition, defy inclement weather. The streets are blatant in their similarity, even sharing the names of Edinburgh's most famous – Princes Street, George Street and Moray Place – and presiding over the scene, in its very heart, a statue of one of Scotland's greatest sons, the poet Robert Burns.

Although a lively and attractive city, Dunedin has seen better days. In the 1860s, thanks to the great Otago gold boom, it enjoyed prosperity and considerable standing. But as ever, the gold ran out, decline set in and very quickly Dunedin, like so many other places in the South Island, had to learn how to survive. Having said that, modern-day Dunedin has many assets, of which its university and rare wildlife are perhaps the best known. In term-time the city boasts a population of 18,000 students who study at Otago University, New Zealand's oldest seat of learning. While the Otago Peninsula – Dunedin's beautiful backyard – is home to another form of wildlife: the only mainland breeding colony of albatross, the rare yellow-eyed penguins and Hooker's sea lions. There is also one other undeniable asset to Dunedin, and one that can perhaps also be attributed to its Scottish heritage: without doubt it has the friendliest people and offers the warmest welcome in New Zealand. ▶▶ *For Sleeping, Eating and other listings, see pages 595-600.*

Ins and outs

Getting there
Dunedin airport ① *T03-4862879, www.flydunedin.com is 27 km south of the city*, is served daily by **Air New Zealand Link**, T0800-737000, www.airnewzealand.co.nz, from Christchurch, Wellington, Auckland and Rotorua. **Air New Zealand** and **Pacific Blue**, T0800-670000, www.pacificblue.com, both provide trans-Tasman flights daily from eastern Australia. Several companies offer airport shuttles including **Dunedin Airport Shuttles**, T0800-748885. Expect to pay from $25 for the shuttle and $75 for a taxi (one way).

Dunedin is 362 km south of Christchurch and 217 km north of Invercargill via SH1. Queenstown is 283 km south then west via SH8. By bus Dunedin is served by several national companies including **Intercity**, book at the VIC (I-Site), T03-474 3300 (Christchurch/Invercargill/ Queenstown/Wanaka) stopping on St Andrews St.

Nakedbus.com, www.nakedbus.com, also offers services throughout South Island as far south as Dunedin, book online. Several shuttle companies offer regional services and stop outside the railway station on Anzac Av. They include: **Atomic Shuttles**, T03-349 0697, www.atomictravel.co.nz (Christchurch/Invercargill/Wanaka/Queenstown); **Time2 (Wanaka Connexions)**, www.time2.co.nz (Queenstown/Wanaka); **Catch-A-Bus**, T03-449 2024, www.catchabus.co.nz, which serves Queenstown, Wanaka and The Otago Central Rail Trail; **Catlins Coaster**, T03-4779083, www.travelheadfirst.com, and **Bottom Bus**, T03-4779083, www.travelheadfirst.com, which serves the Southern Scenic Route (to Te Anau) via Catlins and Invercargill and provides pick-ups and drop-offs along the way.

Getting around

Citibus, T0800-474082/T03-477 5577, www.orc.govt.nz, www.citibus.co.nz, serves Dunedin and its surrounds. The VIC (I-Site) has timetables. City buses stop in the Octagon, the distinctive heart of the city. For bus services to the Otago Peninsula, see page 600.

Tourist information

Dunedin VIC (I-Site) ① *Octagon, No 48, below the Municipal Chambers Building, T03-474 3300, www.dunedinnz.com, www.dunedin.govt.nz.com, Mon-Fri 0800-1800, Sat-Sun 08450-1800*, is an efficient centre that provides free city maps and advice on local tours and activities, particularly to the Otago Peninsula; it also acts as a transport booking agent and has internet. **DoC** ① *77 Lower Stuart St, T03-477 0677, www.doc.govt.nz, Mon-Fri 0800-1700*.

Sights

Princes Street and **George Street** combine to form the main thoroughfare through the city centre, with the **Octagon** forming its heart. The Central Business District (CBD) is easily negotiated on foot, and you'll find most restaurants and cafés at the northern end of George Street or around the Octagon.

The Octagon

Presiding over the Octagon, is the **statue of Robert Burns**, the Scottish poet, whose nephew, the Reverend Thomas Burns, was a religious leader of the early settlers. There are many fine examples of the city's architecture, including the grand **Municipal Chambers buildings**, which house the VIC (I-Site).

The city's churches are worth more than just a passing glance, particularly the **First Church of Otago** ① *Moray Pl, T03-477 7150, daily 0800-1800*, which is one of Dunedin's famous landmarks, and **St Paul's Cathedral**, which houses the only stone-vaulted ceiling in the country. Just west of here, **St Joseph's Cathedral**, on the corner of Rattray and Smith Street, is noted for its robust architectural aesthetics. The **Dunedin Public Art Gallery** ① *Octagon, T03-477 4000, www.dunedin.art.museum.co.nz, daily 1000-1700, free*, provides a grand and stable platform from which to display a fine collection of traditional and contemporary art. It is the oldest art gallery in the country and of special note is its collection of New Zealand works that dates from 1860 to the present day. There are also some works by the more familiar names like Turner, Gainsborough and Monet.

South and east of the Octagon

A five-minute walk east of the Octagon, at the end of Lower Stuart Street, is Dunedin's **train station**. Built in 1906, its grand towered exterior cannot fail to impress, but the interior too is rather splendid, complete with stained-glass windows, Royal Doulton tiles, mosaics and brass fittings. Upstairs, the **New Zealand Sports Hall of Fame** ① *1st floor, T03-477 7775, www.nzhalloffame.co.nz, daily 1000-1600, from $6, child $3*, celebrates the legacy of more than a century of New Zealand champions and is a worthy attraction for any avid sports fan.

Just a few hundred metres from the train station, and boasting a couple of monstrous historic steam trains, is the **Otago Settlers Museum** ① *31 Queens Gardens, T03-477 5052, www.otago.settlers.museum, daily 1000-1700, $4, child free; guided tours daily at 1100, from $5, and 1½-hr city heritage walks departing daily at 1400, from $8*. The emphasis is placed firmly on people and transport, with many fine temporary and permanent displays. Recent additions include the 'Across the Ocean Waves' exhibit, which highlights the ocean crossings that the early settlers had to endure. Various interactive elements incorporated into a recreation of the steerage quarters (including free reign to climb into bunks and sit at tables) adds some authenticity and a firm reminder of the relative luxury of modern-day travel. There are also two fine old locos including the 1872 *Josephine* and a fine collection of archives and over 20,000 photographic portraits of the early pioneers.

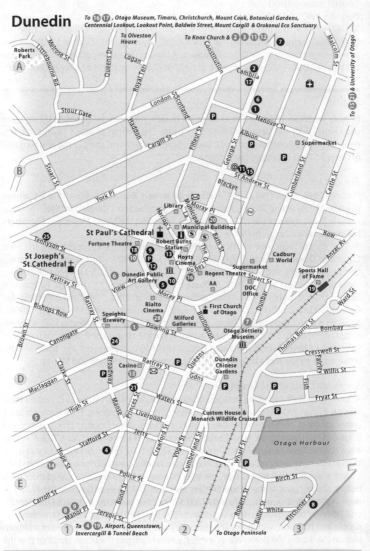

Dunedin

To ⑯ ⑰ , Otago Museum, Timaru, Christchurch, Mount Cook, Botanical Gardens, Centennial Lookout, Lookout Point, Baldwin Street, Mount Cargill & Orokonui Eco Sanctuary

To Olveston House

To Knox Church & ② ③ ⑪ ⑫ ⑦

To ⑬ ㉑ & University of Otago

Next door to the Settlers Museum is the new **Dunedin Chinese Garden** ① *(T03-4773248, open daily 1000-1700 and Wed 1900-2100, $9, children free)*. Completed in 2008 using authentic Chinese materials crafted by a team of artisans/craftsmen for Dunedin's sister city of Shanghai it is a fine example and a great place to escape the buzz of the city.

On Dowling Street, the **Milford Galleries** ① *18 Dowling St, T03-477 7727, www.milfordgalleries.co.nz, Mon-Fri 0900-1700, Sat 1000-1600*, are considered to be one of the country's leading dealer galleries and represent more than 130 artists.

While in the area, chocaholics should head straight to **Cadbury World** ① *280 Cumberland St, T0800-223287, www.cadburyworld.co.nz; regular tours 0900-1515, $18, child $12*. The interactive tours offer an interesting and mouth-watering insight into its production. There is also a well-stocked shop.

Those who prefer something a bit stronger should sample South Island's iconic **Speights Ale** at the surprisingly small **Speights Brewery** ① *200 Rattray St, T03-477 7697, www.speights.co.nz; heritage tours and tastings Mon-Thu 1000, 1200, 1400, 1900, Fri-Sun 1000, 1200, 1400, 1600, from $20, child $8; also worth considering is the 'tour and meal' option lunch from $49, dinner $65, bookings essential*.

North and west of the Octagon

About 1 km north of the Octagon, is the 1906 'Edwardian time capsule' of **Olveston House** ① *42 Royal Terr, T03-477 3320, www.olveston.co.nz; guided 1-hr tours recommended, $16, child $7*. Bequeathed to the city in 1966 by the last surviving member of the wealthy and much-travelled Theomin family, the 35-room mansion comes complete with an impressive 'collection of collections', containing many items from the Edwardian era. It gives an interesting insight into Dunedin of old and the lives of the more prosperous pioneer.

A few minutes' east of Olveston, the **Otago Museum** ① *419 Great King St, T03-474 7474, www.otagomuseum.govt.nz, daily 1000-1700, $5 donation; 'Discovery World' $10, child $5; café on site; guided*

N

⊙

|—————
200 metres
|—————
200 yards

tours daily at 1530, $10, was established in 1868 and is one of the oldest in the country, with a staggering 1.7 million items. The museum's primary themes are culture, nature and science, all housed in newly renovated surroundings. The 'Southern Land – Southern People' exhibit is particularly good and has been designed to become the museum centrepiece. The traditional Maori and Pacific heritage, maritime, natural history and archaeology displays are also impressive and there is (of course) a hands-on 'Discovery World' to keep the kids engrossed for hours. The latest edition to the permanent exhibits is **Discovery World Tropical Forest – Live Butterfly Experience**, featuring around 1000 imported tropical butterflies. The museum also has a café on site.

A short stroll from the museum is the sprawling campus of the **University of Otago**. Founded in 1869, it was New Zealand's first university and is famous for its architecture as well as its contributions to medical science. The grand edifice of the original **Administration building and clock tower** ① *Leith St*, is perhaps the most photographed building in the city.

Another New Zealand 'first' in Dunedin are the **Botanical Gardens** ①*north of the university campus, corner of Great King St and Opoho Rd, T03-477 4000, dawn to dusk*. Nurtured since 1914, the 28-ha site is split into upper and lower gardens that straddle Signal Hill. Combined they form an interesting topography and include all the usual suspects, with a particular focus on rhododendrons (at their best in October), as well as plants from the Americas, Asia and Australia, native species, and winter and wetland gardens. If you tire of the flora there is also a modern aviary complex, housing many exotic and native birds including the 'cheeky' kea and kaka parrots. Also on site are information points, a café and a small shop, all in the Lower Garden. Access to the Lower Garden is from Cumberland Street while the Upper Garden is reached via Lovelock Lane. The **Centennial Lookout** (6-km, 1½ hours' walk) and **Lookout Point** offer grand views of the harbour and the city, and are accessed via Signal Hill Road (beyond Lovelock Avenue).

While in the north of the city, you might also like to visit the famed **Baldwin Street** ① *5 km north of the centre, head north via Great King St then veer right at the Botanical Gardens on to North Rd; Baldwin is about 1 km (10th street) on the right*, which at a gradient of nearly one in three, is reputed to be the steepest street in the world.

Taieri Gorge Railway and the Otago Central Rail Trail

① *Details available at the train station or T03-477 4449, www.taieri.co.nz. Trips to Pukerangi/Middlemarch depart daily Oct-Mar at 1430 (additional trip on Sun at 0930), Pukerangi $76 return; extended trip to Middlemarch $87, one child free, one-way $51 (Middlemarch $58); train and coach connection to Queenstown $115. Licensed snack bar on board.*

The Taieri Gorge Railway is considered a world-class train trip encompassing the scenic splendour and history of Otago's hinterland. The former goldfields supply line was completed in 1891 and, as one negotiates the **Taieri Gorge** with the aid of 12 viaducts and numerous tunnels, it very quickly becomes apparent why it took over 12 years to build. The four-hour trip gets off to a fine start amidst the splendour of Dunedin's grand train station before heading inland to the gorge and Pukerangi. An informative commentary is provided along the way and you are allowed to disembark at certain points of interest. Also, if you ask really nicely, you may also be able to ride alongside the locomotive engineer. If you wish, you can extend the rail journey by coach across the rugged **Maniototo Plateau** to **Queenstown** (6½ hours), from $115. Another popular alternative is to take a mountain bike (no extra charge) and disembark at **Middlemarch** (only selected trains, but one-way fares available). From there you can negotiate the

150-km **Otago Central Rail Trail** (the former goldfields railway from Middlemarch to Clyde). It is a wonderful bike ride that includes over 60 bridges, viaducts and tunnels and much of Central Otago's classic scenery. The VIC (I-Site) can supply all the relevant details. Horse trekking is also an option. DoC, in conjunction with the Otago Central Rail Trail Trust, produces an excellent leaflet *Otago Central Rail Trail Middlemarch-Clyde*, available from the DoC or the VIC (I-Site).

Taieri Gorge Railway also offer a trip to experience the new **Orokunui Ecosanctuary** (see below). Called the **Orokonui Express**, it hugs the coastline north to Waitati and is very pleasant scenic trip in itself. Call for the latest schedules and prices. Recommended.

Tunnel Beach

ⓘ *South of the city centre near Blackhead, 1 km, 1 hr return; car park seaward end of Green Island Bush Rd off Blackhead Rd.*

Tunnel Beach is a popular spot and a precursor to the splendid coastal scenery of the Otago Peninsula. A steep path through some bush delivers you to some impressive weathered sandstone cliffs and arches. For details see DoC's *Tunnel Beach Walk* broadsheet. If you do not have your own wheels take the Corstorphine bus from the city centre to Stenhope Crescent (start of Blackhead Road) and walk from there.

Orokunui Ecosanctuary

ⓘ *600 Blueskin Rd, Waitati (20 mins north of the city or via train, see Taieri Gorge Railway above), T03-4821755, www.orokonui.org.nz. Open daily 0930-1630, from $15, child $7.50, guided tours 1030 and 1330, from $38, child $19.*

The Orokonui Ecosanctuary was a project initiated in 2007 when 307 ha of protected habitat was encircled by 9 km of pest-proof fencing at a cost of $2.2 million. Once introduced mammals like rats, stoats and feral cats were eradicated and endangered native species were reintroduced. These species included birds like the Haast tokoeka kiwi, the kaka (a native parrot), the tom tit (piropiro) and rifleman (titpounamu). Many native fish and reptiles have also found sanctuary and thriving. There is a impressive visitor and information centre with interpretive displays as well as a small shop and café.

◉ Dunedin listings

For Sleeping and Eating price codes and other relevant information, see Essentials pages 44-50.

● Sleeping

Dunedin *p590, map p592*
Dunedin has a good range of options, but you might like to consider those available on the Otago Peninsula (see page 600). For both, pre-booking in summer is advised.
LL-AL Brothers Boutique Hotel, 295 Rattray St, T0800-477004/T03-477 0043, www.brothershotel.co.nz. European-style boutique hotel in a central location offering a range of 15 well appointed en suites (with

one in a former chapel). There is a spacious guest lounge with fast internet, and great views across the city. Off-street parking.
LL Mandeno House, 667 George St, T03-471 9595, www.mandenohouse.com. Within walking distance of the city centre its interior design has a strong hint of Glasgow's most famous architect Charles Rennie Mackintosh and as such has a distinct air of class and sophistication. 2 queen suites and a twin, Sky TV, breakfast, off-street parking.
LL-L St Clair Beach Resort, 24 Esplanade, St Clair Beach, T03-4560555, www.stclair beachresort.com. New beachfront resort hotel quickly earning a fine reputation,

offering top notch rooms, suites and apartments with LCD TVs, iPods and fast broadband. Quality in-house restaurant/bar all overlooking the ocean. Recommended.

L Fletcher Lodge, 276 High St, T03-477 5552, www.fletcherlodge.co.nz. Another fully renovated luxury establishment set in an elegant historic mansion. There are 6 en suites all richly furnished with antiques.

L-AL Southern Cross Hotel, corner of Princes and High sts, T03-477 0752, www.scenic-circle.co.nz. Dunedin's premier hotel, well located in the heart of the city, with standard rooms and suites. Its history dates back to 1883 when it was the original **Grand Hotel**, but it now boasts all the mod cons of the Scenic Circle Chain with an in-house bar/restaurant.

L Nisbet Cottage, 6A Eliffe Pl, Sheil Hill (east of the city centre), T03-454 5169, www.natureguidesotago.co.nz. At the base of the Otago Peninsula, a short drive to the city centre. A choice of 2 tidy en suites sleeping 2-3, a guest lounge with open fire, great hospitality. Minimum two night package deal in conjunction with the host's nature-based tours **Otago Nature Guides** (see Activities and tours, page 607). Your stay includes dawn and dusk trips to see the peninsula penguin colonies. Recommended.

AL-A Hulmes Court, 52 Tennyson St, T0800-448563/T03-477 5319, www.hulmes.co.nz. A well-established, slightly cheaper option set in an 1860s Victorian mansion close to the city centre. Comes complete with a friendly ex-stray cat called Solstice who, in keeping with all IT savvy felines, even has his own Facebook page. (Interest in 'Twitter', however, is reserved for the birds in the garden.) Having expanded to include an adjoining property Hulmes now offers 8 en suites, as well as doubles, twins and singles. The caring owners have plenty of local knowledge and can offer valuable advice on activities and tours.

AL-B Leviathan Hotel, 27 Queens Gardens, T0800-773773/T03-477 3160, www.dunedin hotel.co.nz. An older and good-value establishment with character located near the train station and a short walk from the Octagon. It has a wide range of rooms from self-contained suites (with spas) to budget rooms. In-house bar/restaurant, internet, off-street parking and above average service and hospitality. Recommended.

B Albatross Inn, 770 George St, T03-477 2727, www.albatross.inn.co.nz. A pleasant and spacious budget B&B with 13 rooms, well located close to the city centre.

Motels

There are plenty of motels to choose from, with most on the main drags in and out of town, particularly George St.

AL-A 97 Motel, hidden away at 97 Moray Pl, T03-477 2050, www.97motel.co.nz. Modern motel offering a wide variety of standard and executive units that are quiet, well appointed, and all within a stone's throw of the Octagon. Off-street parking.

A 858 George St, no prizes for guessing the location, T03-474 0047, www.858george streetmotel.co.nz. Modern, and an aesthetic award winner. Recommended.

A Allan Court Motel, 590 George St, T03-477 7526, allan.court@earthlight.co.nz.

A Commodore Luxury, 932 Cumberland St, T03-477 7766, www.commodoremotel.co.nz.

A Regal Court, 755 George St, T03-477 7729.

B Manor Motel, 22 Manor Pl, T03-477 6729, manormotel@earthlight.co.nz.

Backpacker hostels

There is no shortage of choice when it comes to backpacker hostels and vast majority are housed in traditional suburban villas.

C-D Billy Brown's Backpackers, 423 Aramoana Rd, Hamilton Bay (across the harbour, just outside Port Chalmers, 15 mins north of Dunedin), T03-472 8323, billybrowns@actrix.co.nz. If you fancy a day or two away from the city centre, you would do well to consider this small, relaxing, rural hostel with friendly owners and fine views. Also offers free bike hire. Recommended.

C-D Hogwartz Backpackers, 37 Dowling St, close to the Octagon, T03-474 1487, hogwartz@actrix.co.nz. Set in a spacious, historic villa, this is a popular choice with the log fires keeping it very cosy. Dorms, singles, twins and doubles. Internet, no TV. Recommended.

C-D Manor House, 28 Manor Pl, T0800-4770484/T03-477 0484, www.manorhouse backpackers.co.nz. Another historic colonial villa, with modern kitchen and dining areas, dorms, twins and doubles. Quiet location, bike hire, off-street parking and organized wildlife tours.

C-D Stafford Gables YHA, 71 Stafford St, T03-474 1919. A rambling old villa with lots of character, offering a good range of rooms including a particularly attractive double on the top floor with a view across the harbour. Parking, rooftop garden, internet and an emphasis on recycling.

Motorcamps and campsites

B-D Dunedin Holiday Park, 41 Victoria Rd, alongside St Kilda Beach at the southern end of town, T03-455 4690, www.dunedinholiday park.co.nz. Modern facilities, en suite units, standard cabins, flats and powered/tent sites.

B-D Leith Valley Touring Park, 103 Malvern St (towards the northern end of town), T03-467 9936. In a sheltered setting next to the Leith Stream. It has modern motel units, self-contained cabins, powered/tent sites and a vast cosy guest lounge.

❷ Eating

Dunedin *p590, map p592*

There is lots of choice in Dunedin, with over 140 restaurants and cafés, most of which are along George St or around the Octagon. On George St you will also find plenty of cheap Asian eateries and takeaways designed to keep poverty-stricken students mildly plump and chirpy, with numerous Thai and Chinese options particularly between St Andrew and Fredrick sts. You will also find 2 **Star 24 hour** shops in George St.

♥♥♥ Bell Pepper Blues, 474 Princes St, T03-4740973. Lunch Wed-Fri, dinner Mon-Sat from 1830. A few mins' walk from the Octagon but worth it. The menu is highly imaginative and the service and presentation is excellent.

♥♥ Etrusco at the Savoy, 8a Moray Pl (1st floor), T03-477 3737, www.etrusco.co.nz. Daily from 1730. Very grand and a fine Italian choice that is good value despite the plush surroundings.

♥♥ High Tide, 29 Kitchener St, T03-477 9784. Tue-Sun from 1800. Provides a convenient escape from the city centre and overlooks the harbour. It has a mainly seafood but can cater for those looking for traditional New Zealand and European dishes.

♥♥ Indian Summer, corner of Upper Stuart and Moray Pl, T03-477 8880. Affordable and enjoys a good reputation.

♥♥ Little India, 308 Moray Pl, T03-477 6559. Similar to **Indian Summer**. Good reputation.

♥ Ananada Indian Café and Takeaway, 365 George St, T03-477 1120. Lunch Mon-Sat 1130-1430 and dinner daily 1700-2100. Noted for vegetarian dishes.

♥♥ Table Se7en, 1st floor, corner of George and Hanover sts, T03-477 6877. Mon-Thu 1200-2400, Fri 1200-0300, Sat 1700-0300. A chic and well-established traditional choice.

♥ Ale House at the Speights Brewery, 200 Rattray St, T03-471 9050. Daily from 1130. Traditional pub grub, generous in both choice and servings. Tour and meal option from $55.

♥ Joseph Mellor Restaurant, Tennyson St, T03-479 6172. Mar-Nov daily 1200-1400 and 1800-2130. Well worth considering with very affordable and imaginative dishes created by trainee chefs. Lunch $9.50 and dinner $19.50. Where else would you get seared Cervena Medallions Baden-Baden for that price? Recommended.

♥ Reef Seafood Restaurant and Bar, 333 George St, T03-471 7185. For fish and chips.

♥ Scotia Whiskey Restaurant and Bar, Dunedin Railway Station, T03-477770, www.scotiadunedin.co.nz. Mon-Fri 1100-late,

Sat 1500-late. Fine Scottish themed restaurant/bar housed in the historic railway station. Scots classics like haggis and black pudding are of course on offer, yet there are other tastes to suit everyone, from venison, smoked beef, steak, salmon or salads and for sweet bread & butter pudding-'just like Mum used to make'. After dinner sample one or two of the 300-odd whiskies proudly showcased in the bar.

Cafés

Many of the cafés are around the Octagon. **Circadian Rhythm Vegan Café**, 72 St Andrew St, T03-474 9994. Mon-Wed 0800-1800, Thu-Sat 0800-2330, Sun 0800-2330. Great value buffet style vegetarian, vegan and gluten-free dishes, relaxed atmosphere and live music at weekends. Licensed.
Governors Café, 438 George St, T03-477 6871. Daily 0800-late. No great shakes aesthetically but is very popular, with a cosmopolitan clientele, good-value meals (especially breakfasts) and an internet suite next door.
Jizo, 56 Princes St, T03-479 2692. Mon-Sat 1130-2100. A pleasant Japanese café offering standard and affordable sushi.
Mazagran Espresso, 36 Moray Pl, T03-477 9959. Recommended specialist coffee house.
The Nova, 29 The Octagon, next to the Dunedin Art Gallery, T03-479 0808. Mon-Wed 0800-late, Thu-Fri 0700-late, Sat 0900-late, Sun 1000-2300. A good place for brunch, breakfast and even sells porridge.
Nector, 286 Princes St, T03-4778976. Mon-Fri 0700-1600, Sat-Sun 0830-1430. Quality coffee and another good breakfast venue.
Tangente, 111 Moray Pl, T03-477 0232. Mon-Tue, Sun 0800-1530, Wed-Sat 0800-late. Designer café/restaurant that is pretty faultless. Specializes in organic fare and offers a wide-ranging blackboard menu with some great vegetarian dishes and brunch options. It also has a great atmosphere, wine list and service, all making a return trip likely.

♠ Pubs, bars and clubs

Dunedin p590, map p592
There are a number of café/bars around the Octagon; they are especially popular at the weekends.
The Bog, corner of George and London sts. Popular Irish-style drinking establishment, at the north end of George St and it often stages live gigs at weekends.
Bath St, 1 Bath St, T03-477 6750. For the full 'shake of the pants'.
Bennu Restaurant and Bar, 12 Moray Pl, T03-474 5055. Aesthetically one of the best and also offers good food.
Di Lusso, 12 The Octagon, T03-477 3776. One of the newest and most frequented. The name means 'of luxury' in Italian.
K World Karaoke Bar, 142 Princes St, T03-477 2008. At the end of a good night out this place can be a riot.
The Ra Café and Bar, 21, T03-477 6080. Also popular, with good food.
Scotia Whiskey Bar, Dunedin Railway Station, T03-477770, www.scotiadunedin. co.nz. Mon-Fri 1100-late, Sat 1500-late. Fine Scottish themed bar where you can sample one or two of the 300-odd whiskies in stock.

♣ Entertainment

Dunedin p590, map p592
There is a healthy music, arts and cultural scene in Dunedin, and the best place to view current event and gig listings is in the *Otago Daily Times* or the free weekly *Fink* magazine available free from the VIC (I-Site).

Casino

Dunedin Casino, 118 High St, T03-477 4545, www.dunedincasino.co.nz. Daily 1000-0300.

Cinema

Hoyts, on the Octagon, T03-477 7019.
Metro, in the town hall, T03-471 9635, www.metrocinema.co.nz. A venue that boasts 'No raincoats, no popcorn, no

dinosaurs – just the finest films'. Hosts the best in Euro-arthouse film.
Rialto, Moray Pl, T03-474 2200, www.rialto.co.nz. Mon-Tue cheap night, $9.

Theatres
Fortune Theatre Company, corner of Moray Pl and Stuart St, T03-477 8323, www.fortunetheatre.co.nz. Offers performances in both the **Mainstage** and **Studio Theatres**, Feb-Dec, Tue-Sun.
Regent Theatre, on the Octagon, T03-477 8597. Hosts the annual film festival as well as touring international and national shows.

⊕ Festivals and events

Dunedin *p590, map p592*
For more information on these or other annual events contact the VIC (I-Site) or log on to www.dunedinnz.com.
Feb Dunedin Summer Festival. Annual festival celebrating the region and its lifestyle.
Mar Dunedin Fashion Show. Dunedin fashion designers showcase their collections in the City's premier fashion show.
Jul/Aug Dunedin International Film Festival. For 2 weeks international films are shown at the Regent Theatre.
Cadbury Chocolate Carnival. Events include the Choc Art Awards, a 'Bake-off' and Jaffa (iconic New Zealand, small, round orange coated chocolates). Race down the steep gradient of Baldwin St.
Sep-Nov Rhododendron Festival. With a climate and soil well suited to growing rhododendrons, the whole city blossoms during these month.

▲ Activities and tours

Dunedin *p590, map p592*
For the highly popular attractions and tours beyond Dunedin to the Otago Peninsula see Activities and tours, page 607.

Flightseeing
Helicopters Otago, T03-489 7322, www.helicoptersotago.co.nz. A flexible flightseeing schedule locally and throughout Otago from $400.
Mainland Air, Dunedin airport, T03-486 2200, www.mainlandair.com. Flights throughout the southern South Island and off-shore to see the occasional passing iceberg.

Golf
Dunedin claims yet another first, having created the first Golf Club in the southern hemisphere in 1871.
Otago Golf Club, 125 Balmacewen Rd, T03-467 2096, www.otagogolfclub.co.nz. From humble beginnings the club was officially formed in 1892 and is regarded as one of the best 18-hole courses in the country. The clubhouse also has an interesting collection of early memorabilia, cups and medals. Green fees from $75.

Horse trekking
Hare Hill, based in Port Chalmers, north of the city, T03-472 8496, www.horseriding-dunedin.co.nz. Standard and overnight adventures with harbour views, half- or full-day from $75.

Mountain biking
Other than the obvious attraction of the Otago Central Rail Trail (see page 594), there are a number of other shorter tracks available in the area. These are outlined in *Mountain Bike Rides in Dunedin*, available free from the VIC (I-Site).

Surfing
Esplanade Surf School, T03-455 8655, www.espsurfschool.co.nz. Lessons available at St Clair beach from $45.

Sightseeing tours
Given the region's colourful history it is not surprising to find ghosts lurking somewhere on the heritage walks agenda and should you be interested in the alleged facts you can join 'The Hair Raiser' ghost walks, departing from

the VIC (I-Site) at 1800 on Wed and Fri, from $25, T0800-428683.

Arthur's Tours, T03-4877853, www.arthurs tours.co.nz. Long-established operator offering a entertaining and flexible range of local tours ranging from gardens to architecture.

Dunedin Heritage Tours (Citibus), T03-477 5577. Offers a 1-hr tour around the major city sights with pick-ups at the Octagon at 0900, 1015, 1300, 1415 and 1530 from $20, child $10. It also runs 2- to 4-hr tours to the wildlife attractions on the Otago Peninsula departing at 1430, from $90, child $30, and Olveston (adjunct to city tour from $35, child $18).

Passion for Fashion, T03-4780610, www.walkthetalk.co.nz. The perfect local catalyst for shopaholics. Retail enthusiast Jeannie Hayden takes the search out of shopping. 2-hr to half-day trips, with coffee breaks and lunch included, from $30.

Walking

Other than the **Centennial Lookout** (Signal Hill) and **Tunnel Beach** (see page 595), another recommended local walk is to the summit of **Mt Cargill** with its wonderful views across the city and the Otago Peninsula. It can be accessed by foot (4 km, 3½ hrs return) from Bethunes Gully (Norwood St off North Rd past the Botanical Gardens), or via Cowan Rd (off Pine Hill Rd, off SH1 heading north). For details see the DoC broadsheet *Mt Cargill and Organ Pipes Walk*, available from the DoC or the VIC.

⊜ Transport

Dunedin *p590, map p592*
Bicycle hire Cycle Surgery, 67 Stuart St, T03-477 7473, www.cyclesurgery.co.nz. **Car hire** Jackie's Rent-a-Car, 23 Cumberland St, T03-477 7848. **Pegasus**, 1 King Edward St, T03-477 6296. **Dunedin Car Hire**, 531 Kaikorai Valley Rd, T0800-505051. **Taxi** City Taxis, T0800-771771. **Dunedin Taxis**, T03-477 7777. Southern Taxis, T03-476 6300.

❶ Directory

Dunedin *p590, map p592*
Banks Represented along Princes and George sts, with many accommodating currency exchange services. Travelex, 346 George St, T03-477 3383, Mon-Fri 0830-1700, Sat 1000-1230. **Internet** Dunedin Library, Moray Pl, Mon-Fri 0930-2100, Sat 1000-1600, Sun 1400-1800. NetPlanet, 78 St Andrew St, T03-479 2424, open daily till late. **Medical services** Dunedin Hospital, 201 Great King St, T03-474 0999; Urgent doctor, Otago Peninsula, 95 Hanover St, T03-479 2900 (pharmacy next door). **Police** 25 Great King St, T03-471 4800. **Post office** 243 Princes St, T03-477 3517, Mon-Fri 0830-1730. Post restante services. **Useful addresses** AA, 450 Moray Pl, T03-477 5945.

Otago Peninsula → *Colour map 6, B6.*

The beautiful Otago Peninsula, which stretches 33 km northeast from Dunedin out into the Pacific Ocean, is as synonymous with wildlife as Dunedin is with Scotland. If there were any place that could honour the title of being the wildlife capital of the country, this would be it. It is home to an array of particularly rare species including the enchanting yellow-eyed penguin and the soporific Hooker's sea lion, as well the more common New Zealand fur seals. But without doubt the peninsula's star attraction is the breeding colony of royal albatross on Taiaroa Head, at the very tip of the peninsula. This colony is the only mainland breeding albatross colony in the world and offers an extraordinary opportunity to observe these supremely beautiful masters of flight and long-haul travel. A day trip to see all these wildlife delights is highly recommended and will leave a precious and lasting memory. Besides wildlife, the principal attractions on the Otago Peninsula are historic Larnach Castle and the stunning vista of Sandfly Bay, as well as sea kayaking, cruising and walking. ▸▸ For Sleeping, Eating, and other listings, see pages 606-608.

Ins and outs

Getting there The best way to see the peninsula is by car, but if you have no wheels of your own or you are not familiar with the wildlife, an organized tour is recommended. Some of the tours on offer can take you to several wildlife sites (and sights) that are out of bounds to the general public. By road there are two main routes that penetrate the peninsula. On the western side, hugging the numerous small bays and inlets of the Otago Harbour, is the Portobello Road which serves the peninsula's main village, Portobello. From Portobello this road then continues past the small settlement of Harington Point to terminate at Taiaroa Head and the albatross colony. An alternative route to Portobello via Highcliff Road accesses two of the peninsula's major physical attractions, Larnach Castle and Sandfly Bay, and straddles the hilltops of the peninsula offering some memorable views. Note that both roads are sealed but very windy and dangerous. It is important to slow down and not maintain the pace and buzz of Dunedin's city streets. Both Highcliff Road and Portobello Road are easily accessed via Cumberland Street (city) across the railway line and then by skirting the Otago Harbour on Wharf Street and Portsmouth Drive. For a free map of the Otago Peninsula ask at the VIC (I-Site). ▸▸ See Activities and tours, page 607.

Tourist information One of the principal *raisons d'être* of the **Dunedin VIC (I-Site)** (see page 591) is arranging half- to full-day trips out to the peninsula. There are a number of options regarding the length of time of visit, the route and the sight itinerary, so it pays to study the options carefully before parting with your cash. The DoC office in Dunedin can provide further information on walks and wildlife.

Albatrosses

Although **Taiaroa Head** is an interesting historic site in its own right, it is the colony of royal albatross that has really put the small, rocky headland on the map. Ever since the first egg was laid in 1920, the site, which is the only mainland-breeding colony in the world, has become an almost sacred preserve of these magnificent seabirds. The colony, now numbering almost 100, is fully protected and managed by the DoC and the Otago Peninsula Trust. With the opening of the **Royal Albatross Centre** ⓘ *T0800-528767/T03-478 0499, www.albatross.org.nz, daily 0830-2100 (seasonal)*, in 1972, thousands of people have been given the opportunity to view the birds from an observatory and to learn about their fascinating lifestyle and the threats we place upon them. Even before you enter the centre, if the conditions are right, you can see the great birds wheeling in from the ocean on wings that span over 3 m (the largest of any bird) and with a grace that defies the effort. If there is such a thing as airborne ballet this is it.

The albatross centre has some superb exhibits that include static and audio-visual displays and even a live TV feed from the occupied nests in the breeding season. It takes about eight months for the parent birds to rear one of these avian B52s so your chances of seeing the industrial size carpet-slipper chicks are high. The activity of the adults varies, depending on courting, mating, incubating and feeding, with the best viewing times generally being between late-November and April. Having said that you would be fairly unlucky not to see at least one on any given visit at any time of year. The centre also has a café and a shop. ▸▸ *See Activities and tours, page 607, for details of the different tours available.*

There is plenty of other wildlife to see on and around Taiaroa Head. Of particular note are the rare **Stewart Island shags**, which also breed on the headland. They are beautiful birds but when it comes to flight they are the complete antithesis of the albatross. Also known as 'the flying brick', on a very windy day, it is not completely out of the ordinary for

Otago Peninsula

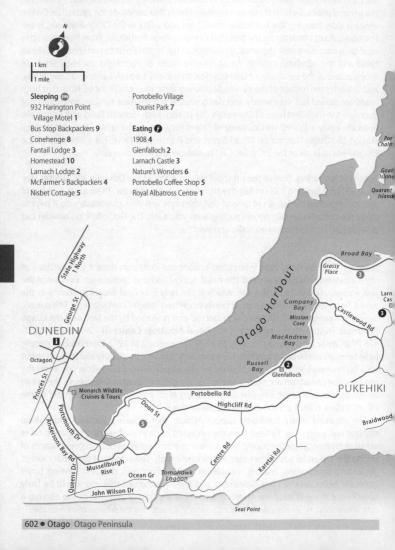

Sleeping 🛏️
932 Harington Point
 Village Motel **1**
Bus Stop Backpackers **9**
Conehenge **8**
Fantail Lodge **3**
Homestead **10**
Larnach Lodge **2**
McFarmer's Backpackers **4**
Nisbet Cottage **5**

Portobello Village
 Tourist Park **7**

Eating 🍴
1908 **4**
Glenfalloch **2**
Larnach Castle **3**
Nature's Wonders **6**
Portobello Coffee Shop **5**
Royal Albatross Centre **1**

one to 'take out' you, your child and your ice cream from the viewing area near the centre. Around the base of the headland, **fur seals** and **little blue penguins** can regularly be seen and, if you have binoculars, the ocean will reveal a plethora of petrels and other seabirds.

The coast and headlands immediately south of Taiaroa Head are private land, however, **Nature's Wonders** offers wildlife-watching tours of the area by ATV, see page 607.

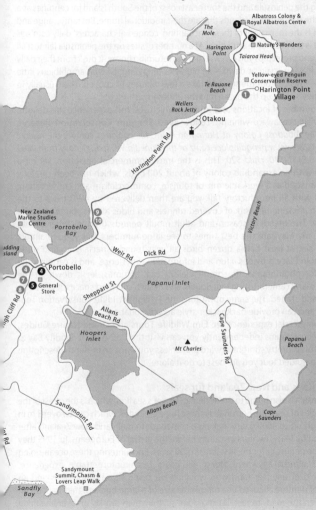

Albatross Colony &
Royal Albatross Centre

The Mole

Harington Point

Nature's Wonders

Taiaroa Head

Te Rauone Beach

Yellow-eyed Penguin Conservation Reserve

Harington Point Village

Wellers Rock Jetty

Otakou

Harington Point Rd

New Zealand Marine Studies Centre

Portobello Bay

Victory Beach

Pudding Island

Portobello

Weir Rd

Dick Rd

General Store

Sheppard St

Papanui Inlet

Cape Saunders Rd

High Cliff Rd

Allans Beach Rd

Hoopers Inlet

Mt Charles

Papanui Beach

Sandymount Rd

Allans Beach

Cape Saunders

son Rd

Sandymount Summit, Chasm & Lovers Leap Walk

Sandfly Bay

Yellow-eyed penguins

The Otago Peninsula is a haven and breeding site for the yellow-eyed penguin, one of the rarest penguin species in the world. For many, the conditioning we have of the penguin/ice relationship and their near symbiosis is shattered amidst the golden sands and grasses of the peninsula's bays and inlets. The 'yellow eyes' or *hoiho* (to give them their Maori name) have been using the peninsula and the southeast coast of the South Island for centuries as a spill over from the sub-Antarctic islands that are their traditional home. But rarity, range and biology aside, it is the mere sight of these enchanting, congenial characters' daily comings and goings that is the irresistible attraction. At a number of sites on the peninsula (almost all on private land and protected) you can watch them returning home at dusk from their daily fishing trips or leaving again at dawn – all highly entertaining. Like fat amphibious little surfboards they emerge from the surf and take a few minutes to cool off. Then, usually in small groups, they scuttle up the beach into the undergrowth.

There are a number of locations and tours on which you can experience this delight. Most people visit the award-winning **Yellow-eyed Penguin Conservation Reserve** ⓘ *just before the Albatross Colony at Harington Point; for bookings contact the reserve direct, T03-478 0286, www.penguinplace.co.nz or the Dunedin VIC (I-Site), daily from 0800 (May-Sep from 1515), $40, child $20*. This is the most commercial operation, set on a private reserve with an expanding colony of about 200 birds, which has been carefully created and managed as a workable mix of tourism, commercialism and conservation. Once provided with an introductory talk you are then delivered by 4WD truck to the beach where an amazing network of covered tunnels and hides allows you to view the birds discreetly. The breeding season and adult moult periods (mid- October to late February and early May) are the best times to see large numbers, but you are almost guaranteed to see at least half a dozen birds all year round especially around dusk. Although Penguin Place provides a fun and informative experience, and is certainly the best location for photographs, its commercialism can, at times, let it down. In the company of so many camera-toting individuals, and in such confined spaces, it can all be a bit too busy and staged. The same outfit runs the Twilight Wildlife Conservation Tour (see page 607) and can provide backpacker-style accommodation.

For a less commercial experience see **Elm Wildlife Tours** and **Otago Nature Guides**, page 607. To see penguins independently you can visit the DoC hide at Sandfly Bay at dawn or dusk. This is pretty straightforward and unless you want an in-depth description of the birds on a guided tour you are best to go it alone.

Hooker's sea lions and New Zealand fur seals

The Otago Peninsula is also home to the endemic Hooker's sea lion, which is the rarest of the world's five species of sea lions. Fortunately these huge creatures, which can be over 3 m in length and weigh up to 400 kg, are making a comeback to mainland New Zealand after being eliminated by Maori hunters centuries before the arrival of Europeans. In 1995 they bred again on the peninsula for the first time in 700 years. Encountering these ocean-going couch potatoes almost anywhere along the coast is an unforgettable experience. Seemingly devoid of any fear (and who wouldn't be, given those proportions and an impressive set of dentures housed in a mouth the size of a large bucket), they haul up on beaches and even the roads to rest. Having done so, they then display an overwhelming desire to do very little, except sleep, break wind, scratch, or eye you up occasionally with an expression of complete indifference. If you are lucky enough to see one, do not go any nearer than 10 m and never get between the said 'Jabba the Hut' and the water, since they are hardly going to say 'excuse me' as they head for home. Despite their looks, they can move like a slug from a slingshot and you would certainly lose the argument. Otago also has a number of **fur seal colonies**, the most accessible of which is around Taiaroa Head. Below the main car park you can usually find one or two hauled up in an almost enviable soporific state. Again, you can take a closer look but do not approach within 10 m.

Larnach Castle

ⓘ *Signposted off Castlewood Rd (from Portobello Rd), T03-476 1616, www.larnach castle.co.nz, daily 0900-1900 (1700 in winter), $25, child $10 (gardens only $10, child $3). The castle provides some of the best accommodation and views in the region.*

Perched on the highest point of the peninsula, 16 km from Dunedin, is Larnach Castle, the former residence of Australian William Larnach (1833-1898). As a minister of the Crown, banker, financier and merchant baron of the prosperous late 1880s, there is no doubt Larnach was a man of wealth and title, but he was far more renowned for his personal life and excesses – which finally lead to his tragic suicide surrounded by the very monument of his desires. Only the best would do for Larnach, who had both the will and the wherewithal to live up to the saying 'a man's home is his castle'. He employed 200 workmen for three years to build the exterior, and another 12 years was spent by master craftsmen embellishing the interior with 32 different woods, marble from Italy, tiles from England, glass from Venice and France, and even slate from Wales. Both Larnach and his castle have a fascinating history. After his death, the castle changed hands a number of times before falling into a state of disrepair. Then in 1967 the remains were purchased by the Barker family who have since lovingly renovated the place to something very close to its former glory and opened it to the public. Both the castle and its 6 ha of gracious grounds now remain open for self-guided tours and give a fascinating insight into the period and the man. There is a licensed café on site in the very Scottish ballroom, which comes complete with stag's head and open fire. Most of the peninsula tour operators visit Larnach Castle as a matter of course.

Other sights

There are many scenic bays and walks on the peninsula, with perhaps the most dramatic and accessible being the idyllic, and at times wild, **Sandfly Bay**, on its eastern shore. From Highcliff Road take Seal Point Road to the reserve car park. From there the beach can then be accessed by foot (20 minutes). At the far end of the beach there is a small public hide overlooking the only free, or publicly accessible, **yellow-eyed penguin colony** on the peninsula (40 minutes return). The best times for viewing are just before dawn and dusk. Do not be tempted to go down to the beach when the penguins are there – remember you are looking at one of the rarest birds in the world.

Beyond Sandfly Bay, and either accessible by foot (poled route) or via Sandymount Road (also off Highcliff Road), is the **Sandymount Summit**, **Chasm** and **Lover's Leap** Walk (one hour). The Chasm and Lover's Leap are impressive coastal cliff features formed when the sea eroded the soft, lower layers of volcanic rock. For details about these walks and others on the peninsula get the *Otago Peninsula Tracks* leaflet from the Dunedin VIC (I-Site) and the peninsula walks broadsheets, available from the DoC. **Glenfalloch** (Gaelic for 'hidden valley') ⓘ *9 km from Dunedin, 430 Portobello Rd, T03-476 1006, www.glenfalloch.co.nz, daily, donation,* is a pleasant wooded garden and historic estate. The gardens are particularly noted for their rhododendrons, azaleas and camellias, which are at their bloomin' best between mid-September and mid-October. There is a popular restaurant on site.

Near Portobello, on the shores of Otago Harbour, is the **New Zealand Marine Studies Centre** ⓘ *Hatchery Rd, T03-479 5826, www.otago.ac.nz/marinestudies, daily 1000-1630, $24, child $12; guided tours $48, child $21.* On display there are a number of aquariums and 'touch tanks', with a range of native New Zealand sea creatures from sea horses to the octopus. There is even the opportunity to taste nutritious seaweed, and knowledgeable and friendly staff are on hand to answer any questions.

◉ Otago Peninsula listings

For Sleeping and Eating price codes and other relevant information, see Essentials pages 44-50.

● Sleeping

Otago Peninsula *p600, map p602*
L-A Larnach Lodge, T03-4761616, www.larnachcastle.co.nz. Accommodation at Larnach Castle is some of the best in the region. The lodge offers beautifully appointed themed rooms from the 'Scottish Room' with its tartan attire, to the 'Goldrush Room' which comes complete with a king-size 'cart bed' made out of an original old cart found on the property. The views across the harbour and peninsula from every room are simply superb. Breakfast is served in the old stables; dinner is optional in the salubrious interior of the castle. Cheaper 'Stable Stay' rooms with shared bathrooms in the former coach house are also available. Book well in advance. Recommended.
AL Conehenge, High Cliff Rd, T03-478 0911, kolig@ihug.co.nz. A modern purpose-built property set above Portobello village among an intriguing rock sculpture garden. The well-travelled hosts ensure a warm welcome and lost of good local advice regarding sights and activities. Cosy private en suite.
AL Homestead, 238 Harington Point Rd (2 km north of Portobello), T03-478 0384, www.the-homestead.co.nz. Set in a lovely position near the water's edge overlooking Portobello Bay, 3 modern self-contained units with Sky TV. Includes breakfast.
AL-A 932 Harington Point Village Motel, Harington Point, T03-478 0287, www.haringtonpointmotels.co.nz. Further out on the peninsula and conveniently placed for both the albatross and Penguin Place yellow-eyed penguin colonies. Small, modern and comfortable.
A Fantail Lodge, 682 Portobello Rd, Broad Bay, T03-478 0110, www.visit-dunedin.co.nz/fantail.html. Two charming, rustic, self-contained cottages in a peaceful setting, one with spa. Ideal for couples. Free kayak hire.
A Nisbet Cottage, 6A Eliffe Pl, T03-454 5169, www.natureguidesotago.co.nz. Located at the base of the Otago Peninsula and only a short drive to the city centre. The German hosts operate **Otago Nature Guides** (see page 607) and organize accommodation packages that include dawn and dusk trips to see the peninsula penguin colonies, or multi-day trips to the Catlins and Stewart Island. A choice of 2 tidy en suites sleeping 2-3, a guest lounge with open fire and great hospitality.
C-D Bus Stop Backpackers, 252 Harington Point Rd, Portobello, T03-478 0330, www.bus-stop.co.nz. Peaceful waterside house close to the major wildlife attractions, with 2 rooms and additional beds in a house bus or caravan. A log fire adds to the appeal and character.
C-D McFarmer's Backpackers, 774 Portobello Rd, T03-478 0389, www.otago-peninsula.co.nz/mcfarmers.html. Homely farmstay with dorms and doubles. Close to village amenities. Recommended.

Motorcamps and campsites
C-D Portobello Village Tourist Park, 27 Hereweka St, Portobello, T03-478 0359, www.portobellopark.co.nz. Self-contained tourist flats, powered/tent sites and a bunkroom. Bike hire is available.

🍴 Eating

Otago Peninsula *p600, map p602*
There are only 2 restaurants and a scattering of cafés on the peninsula. **Larnach Castle** (see Sleeping, above), **The Royal Albatross Centre** and **Natures Wonders** have cafés. There is a well-stocked general store on the main street in Portobello, T03-478 0555.

🍴 **1908 Café/Restaurant**, 7 Harington Point Rd, Portobello, T03-478 0801. Daily for lunch and dinner. Pleasant but a little expensive. European/NZ menu with a seafood edge.

🍴 **Glenfalloch Restaurant**, 430 Portobello Rd, T03-476 1006. Daily from 1100. A licensed café-style establishment set in the pleasant Glenfalloch Gardens.

🍴 **Portobello Coffee Shop**, 699 Highcliff Rd, T03-478 1055. 0900-1700. Has snacks, breakfast, acceptable coffee and internet.

▲ Activities and tours

Otago Peninsula *p600, map p602*
Cruising
Monarch Wildlife Cruises and Tours, corner of Wharf and Fryatt sts, T0800-666272/ T03-477 4276, www.wildlife.co.nz. Award-winning outfit offering a variety of trips from 1-7 hrs taking in all the main harbour and peninsula sights. The main highlights are the Marine Studies Centre Aquarium at Portobello and the wildlife of Taiaroa Head; Larnach Castle, the Albatross and penguin reserves can also be included. For a short trip you can join the boat at the Wellers Rock Jetty near Taiaroa Head. Regular daily departures, 1-hr cruise (Wellers Rock) $45; tour combining bus tour of the peninsula and cruise half-day $85, full package including entry to main sights $210.

Sea kayaking
Otago Harbour and Taiaroa Head provide some of the best sea kayaking in the country with the added attraction of viewing and accessing wildlife in a manner simply not possible by land. Where else in the world can you kayak while viewing albatross?
Wild Earth Adventures, T03-489 1951, www.wildearth.co.nz. Provides an excellent range of tours, some in combination with the land-based attractions, the most popular being the 4- to 5-hr 'Taiaroa Ocean Tour' around the heads and its Albatross colony, from $95 (connections available with **Elm Wildlife Tours**). Recommended.

Wildlife
Citibus, T03-477 5577, www.transport place.co.nz. A well-established sightseeing operation by bus to the peninsula providing packages to all the major sights including Larnach Castle, the albatross centre and the Penguin Place Yellow-eyed penguin colony. It can also drop off at the Monarch Wildlife Cruise jetty. Regular daily departures from the city, From $90.
Elm Wildlife Tours, 19 Irvine Rd, Dunedin, T0800-356563/T03-454 4121, www.elmwildlifetours.co.nz. Provides a wide range of excellent award-winning eco-tours of the peninsula and the region. Its 5- to 6-hr peninsula trip takes in the Albatross Centre, a New Zealand fur seal colony and their its yellow-eyed penguin-breeding beach at the remote Cape Saunders. The tour is fun and informative, yet non-commercial, and gives you access to some of the most scenic private land on the peninsula. From $89 (albatross observatory and additional activities extra). Pick-ups available. Recommended.
Nature's Wonders, near Taiaroa Head, T0800-246446/T03-478 1150, www.natures wondersnaturally.com. Features a cross-country '8x8 Argo tour' and walk to the penguin colonies on private land. Albatross sightings, fur seals and occasionally sea lions are also encountered. The main tour is 1-hr minimum and costs $50, child $45. Coach packages available from Dunedin. Café on site.
Otago Nature Guides, T03-454 5169, www.nznatureguides.com. Personalized, small group tours at dawn to see the Yellow-eyed penguin colony at the beautiful Sandfly

Bay. Tours in conjunction with its fine B&B accommodation in Nisbet Cottage (see Sleeping, above) are recommended. Extended trips to the Catlins and Stewart Island are also available. German spoken.

Royal Albatross Centre, see page 601. There are a number of tours available. The 1½-hr 'Unique Taiaroa' tour includes an introductory video, a viewing of the colony from the hilltop observatory, and a look at the remains of Fort Taiaroa. This is a series of underground tunnels, fortifications and a 'disappearing gun' that were originally built in 1885 in response to a perceived threat of invasion from Tsarist Russia. From $45, child $23. Also on offer is the 1-hr 'Royal Albatross' which includes all the above except the fort. From $40, child $20. For those with an interest in forts, paranoia and guns you may like to join the 30-min 'Fort Taiaroa Tour'

($20, child $10). You can also combine the centre and its tour options as part of the Elm Wildlife Tours (see above). Note that the observatory is closed 17 Sep-23 Nov each year, to allow the new season's birds to renew their pair bonds.

Sam's 4x4 Adventures, T03-4780878, www.samsoffroadtours.com. A small group oriented operation offering personalized 4WD road tours of the peninsula. 2½-hr evening tour ($50). Peninsula accommodation package also available.

Twilight Wildlife Experience Tours, T03-454 4121, www.wilddunedin.co.nz. A relaxed and friendly 5- to 6-hr tour of the albatross colony (entry optional), various wildlife sites and peninsula beaches. Tours depart from Dunedin Mar-Oct 1330 (Nov-Feb 1430). From $91.

Central Otago → *Colour map 6, A/B5.*

The barren, rugged and almost treeless landscapes of Central Otago have a dramatic sense of space and loneliness. Looking at these vistas now and passing through the quiet, unassuming towns of its back roads and river valleys, it is hard to imagine the immensity of the chaotic gold boom years that once made Otago the most populous region in the land. After gold was first discovered in 1861 by Gabriel Read, an Australian prospector, near Lawrence in the Clutha River Valley, Central Otago erupted into a gold fever that spread like wildfire across its barren landscape. It was a boom and a resource that would last until the turn of the 20th century. This period saw the establishment of many towns including Alexandra, Clyde, Cromwell, Roxburgh, Ranfurly and St Bathans and the construction of the impressive Taieri Gorge Railway and what is now the Otago Central Rail Trail which both formed vital communication links with Dunedin.

With the lure of Wanaka and Queenstown to the west, Central Otago sees little but transitory tourist traffic. However, if you have a couple of days to kill, a more thorough exploration of this historic gold-mining region can be rewarding and provide some respite from the crowds elsewhere. Attractions of particular note include the Taieri Gorge Railway trips, a walk around historic St Bathans or Clyde, and the 150-km Otago Central Rail Trail. The latter is becoming increasingly popular, with its 68 bridges, and numerous tunnels and viaducts to add to the pleasant scenery. The trail also offers some of the best mountain biking in the region. Other equally less gold-orientated activities include fishing, walking and horse trekking. ▸▸ *For Sleeping, Eating and other listings, see pages 612-615.*

Ins and outs

Getting there There are three main roads into Central Otago which converge to form a loop. From Palmerston, 55 km north of Dunedin (via SH1 and the coast), SH85 turns inland to follow the 'Pig Root' to Ranfurly and Alexandra, with a small diversion to St Bathans. At Alexandra SH85 joins SH8 that follows the Clutha River Valley, south through Roxburgh, Raes Junction and Lawrence, before rejoining SH1 near Milton, 60 km south of Dunedin.

At Mosgiel, 15 km south of Dunedin, SH87 follows close to the Taieri George Railway and Otago Central Rail Trail to merge with SH85 just east of Ranfurly.

One of the best ways to get a taste of Central Otago is by train via the Taieri Gorge Railway and then by mountain bike from Middlemarch to Clyde on the now disused line that forms the Otago Central Rail Trail (see page 594). Alternatively you can combine train and bus to Queenstown. Roxburgh, Alexandra, Clyde and Cromwell are all on the main highway to Queenstown (SH8) and are served by **Intercity**, book at the VIC (I-Sites), (Christchurch/Invercargill/Queenstown/Wanaka). Several shuttle companies offer regional services including: **Nakedbus.com** (throughout the South Island as far south as Dunedin); Atomic Shuttles, T03-349 0697, www.atomictravel.co.nz (Christchurch/Invercargill/ Queenstown/Wanaka) and **Time2 (Wanaka Connexions)**, www.time2.co.nz (Queenstown/ Wanaka). **Catch-a-Bus (Wanaka)**, T03-449 2024, www.catchabus.co.nz, offers the only public transport from Wanaka to Middlemarch along the Otago Central Rail Trail.

Tourist information Alexandra VIC (I-Site) ① *22 Centennial Av, T03-448 9515, www.centralotagonz.com, Mon-Fri 0900-1700, Sat-Sun 1000-1700 (1600 winter)*, is an excellent centre and is an adjunct to the Central Stories Museum and Art Gallery. It is almost as full of information as the staff are with enthusiasm for the region. There are free maps, leaflets and displays outlining the many historical aspects of the region and its most popular activities, including mountain biking, fishing and horse trekking. **DoC Central Otago Regional Office** ① *43 Dunstan Rd, T03-440 2040*. **Cromwell and Districts VIC (I-Site) and Museum** ① *47 The Mall, T03-445 0212, www.cromwell.org.nz, Mon-Fri 0900-1700, Sat-Sun 1000-1600*. The staff here are very enthusiastic and helpful and will do their best to make sure you see the financial and health benefits of staying in Cromwell as opposed to Queenstown. The website is excellent and full of useful information. **Ranfurly VIC (I-Site)** ① *3 Charlemont St, T03-444 1005, www.centralotagonz.com, Mon-Fri 0900-1700, Sat-Sun 1000-1600*. Can advise on local accommodation.

For **ski information** contact: **Cardrona**, T03-443 7341; **Coronet Peak**, T03-442 4620; **The Remarkables**, T03-442 4615; **Treble Cone**, T03-443 7443; and **Waiorau**, T03-443 7542; or www.nzski.com. The *Time for Real Adventure – Cromwell and Lake Dunstan* is an excellent leaflet that is available from the VIC (I-Site) listing everything from climate statistics to local walks.

The **Otago Goldfields Heritage Trust** ① *T03-445 0111, www.nzsouth.co.nz/ goldfields*, has a useful website. Many of the region's towns and goldfields heritage sites come within the boundaries of the Otago Goldfields Park administered by DoC. For the serious historian the *Otago Goldfields Heritage Trail* booklet, available free from all of the region's VICs (I-Sites), provides a solid route guide from which to explore the diverse historical sites scattered throughout the region. The websites www.centralotagonz.com and www.tco.org.nz may also prove useful. The **Otago Central Rail Trail** has its own website, www.otagocentralrailtrail.co.nz.

Dunedin to Alexandra via the Mainiototo and the 'Pig Root'

From Palmerston, 55 km north of Dunedin (via SH1 and the coast), SH85 turns inland to follow the 'Pig Root' (the old coach road between the coast and the goldfields) to Ranfurly and Alexandra, with a small diversion to St Bathans. A diversion from the conventional route south or west, it is seldom taken by tourists, who instead head straight for Dunedin.

Like the MacKenzie Country to the north it has a mood all of its own. Five mountain ranges encompass the region and within their embrace lies the expansive **Maniototo Plain** that became the mainstay of the region's economy once the 1860s gold boom was over. Highlights along the way include the art deco buildings of **Ranfurly** (the largest town in the region), curling in **Naseby** (this ancient Scottish game has been a central feature of the Maniototo since the late 1870s – see page 614) and the historic buildings and **Blue Lake** in the quaint former gold boom town (now village) of **St Bathans**.

🌙 *The coldest village in New Zealand, Ophir, lies just outside the Maniototo's western boundary. Ophir set a teeth-chattering record of –21.6° C in July 1995.*

Alexandra

At the junction of the Clutha and Manuherikia Rivers, Alexandra was one of the first gold mining towns to be established in Central Otago. Its creation was due to the first strikes made in 1862 by Horatio Hartley and Christopher Reilly in the once rich Dunstan fields, in what is now the neighbouring town of Clyde. The river junction became known as Lower Dunstan and later became the settlement of Alexandra. Once the gold ran out at the end of the 1800s the orchardists moved in, making fruit growing Alexandra's modern-day industry. The town is at its best in autumn. Alexandra serves as the principal gateway to the **Otago Central Rail** and **Dunstan gold mining heritage trails**, which are a major attraction for mountain bikers and 4WD enthusiasts.

Almost instantly noticeable and visible from almost everywhere is the 11-m diameter **clock** on part of the **Knobbies Range** to the east of Alexandra, built by one Alexander Jaycee in 1968. Besides the clock and its simple riverside aesthetics, the main attraction in town is the **Central Stories Museum and Art Gallery** ⓘ *21 Centennial Av, T03-448 6230, daily 1000-1700 donation*. It concentrates on gold mining, but also includes some interesting displays on the role of the early Chinese settlers and sheep farmers as well as the work of local artisans. Wildlife also features with an interesting insight into the endangered Otago Skinks of which only around 1,400 are thought to remain. There is a live display of the cryptic little lizards and feeding time is around 1100.

A short walk from the centre of town will take you to **Shaky Bridge**, which crosses the Manuherikia River on Fox Street (just below the clock). Originally built in 1879, it was once used by wagons and horses. Now purely a footbridge, the smart **Shaky Bridge Vineyard Café and Restaurant** on the far side provides an incentive to cross.

As well as orchards, the area has its fair share of vineyards including the **Black Ridge** ⓘ *76 Conroys Rd, T03-449 2059, daily 1000-1700*, which claims to be the most southerly winery in the world. Ask the VIC (I-Site) for the free *Central Otago Wine Map*.

If you are a *Lord of the Rings* fanatic, Alexandra will no doubt provide the launching pad to visit the remote **Poolburn Reservoir**, which sits on the Rough Ridge Range 40 minutes east of the town. There, an expansive area of rocky outcrops (tors) and tussock surrounding the reservoir, provided the perfect backdrop for the realm of '**Rohan**'. Note that the area is by no means easy to reach and you are advised to seek detailed directions from the VIC (I-Site) before venturing out independently. If you do not have a reliable vehicle of your own then you can always join one of the local tours, perhaps taking in the former gold mining village of **Ophir** on the way. Contact the VIC (I-Site) in Alexandra for the latest details.

Clyde

Just 10 km west of Alexandra is the pretty and historic village of Clyde. Backed by the concrete edifice of the Clyde Dam, which incarcerates **Lake Dunstan**, it offers a pleasant stop on the way to Queenstown or Wanaka. Originally called Dunstan and the hub of the rich Dunstan Goldfields, it assumed its present name in the late 1860s. Clyde in Scottish

Gaelic is *Clutha* – which is the river that once flowed freely through the Cromwell Gorge and is the longest in the South Island. The village boasts a number of historic old buildings including the **Town Hall** (1868), various pioneer cottages and a handful of its once 70 hotels. The **Old Courthouse** on Blyth Street is another fine building, built in 1864 but sadly no longer open to the public. Nearby, are the **Clyde Historical Museum**5 Blyth St and The **Briar Herb Factory** ① *12 Fraser St, T03-449 2092, museum $3, herb factory $3 (both $5), Tue-Sun 1400-1600 or at other times by arrangement*. The herb factory originally began operations in the 1930s processing local thyme, but has since grown into a museum housing not only the original herb-processing machinery, but also a variety of exhibits illustrating the life of the early settlers. These include the workshops of blacksmith, farrier and wheelwrights, and stables with various horse-drawn vehicles.

The trilogy of historical sites is completed by the **Clyde Station Museum** ① *at the former railway station on Fraser St, T03-449 2400, Sun 1400-1600 or by appointment, donation*. It houses some lovingly restored locos.

Although perhaps a bit morbid, the **cemetery** in Clyde (Springvale Road) can be an interesting place for reflection. Having been in use since the 1850s, the headstones provide fascinating reading, particularly the ages, surnames and origins of the former settlers. Once you have enjoyed the atmosphere and historical aspects of the village, you might like to take the 30-minute walk to the **Clyde Lookout hill** (signposted) above the town and enjoy the views.

Cromwell

From Clyde, SH8 negotiates the Cromwell Gorge and plays tag with a section of Lake Dunstan, which on the map looks like the antenna of a large blue sea creature. At its head, 23 km to the north, is the tidy little town of Cromwell, ideally situated between Wanaka, Queenstown, the Lindis Pass to Mount Cook and SH8 to Dunedin. The accommodation here is much cheaper than Queenstown and the place is far less stressful. It is also in a great position to access five ski fields (see Tourist information, page 609). Those who like peace and quiet should base themselves here.

A former gold town, Cromwell was originally called 'The Junction' due to its position at the confluence of the Clutha and Kawarau rivers. These important bodies of water, which are now masked with the creation of Lake Dunstan, form an integral part of the South Island's hydropower scheme. The **museum**① *attached to the VIC (I-Site), donation*, focuses on the early history and building of the dam and is worth a look. The decision to build the **Clyde Dam** in the 1980s, using Cromwell as the accommodation base, brought many changes to the town and gave rise to a mix of old-world charm and modern, tidy aesthetics. With the dam now established they say Cromwell's future lies in tourism, and its status as the 'Fruit Bowl of the South'.

The main attraction in the town itself is the **Old Cromwell Town Precinct** ① *at the end of Melmore Terr, at the point where the 2 rivers merge, 1000-1630, free*. Since the 1980s and encouraged by the disruption of the dam work, many of the former buildings have been restored or reconstructed and now house local cafés and craft shops. The precinct boasts several restored buildings that are open for viewing and the VIC (I-Site) has various free leaflets. *In Search of the Main Street* is particularly useful.

As you might expect, there are also numerous former gold mining sites and relics surrounding Cromwell. **Bannockburn**, **Bendigo** and the **Carrick Goldfields** are of particular interest. The VIC (I-Site) has details and maps. The **Goldfields Mining Centre** ① *Kawarau Gorge (SH6 west), 6 km towards Queenstown, T03-445 1038, www.goldfieldsmining.co.nz, daily*

0900-1700, $20, child $8; guided tours $25, child $10, provides the opportunity to explore historic gold workings, a Chinese settlers' village, gold stamper batteries and a sluice gun. You can also pan for gold, go horse trekking or jet boating ($90, child $49).

Vineyards

As well as its many orchards, the immediate area is also home to a number of vineyards. In **Bannockburn**, just to the south of Cromwell, you will find the **Felton Road Winery** ⓘ *Felton Rd, T03-445 0885, www.feltonroad.com, by appointment, May-Oct*; **Akarua** ⓘ *Cairnmuir Rd, T03-445 0897, www.akarua.com, café/bar daily 1100-1600*; **Carrick** ⓘ *Cairnmuir Rd, T03-445 3480, www.carrick.co.nz, daily 1100-1700*; and the **Olssen's Garden Vineyard** ⓘ *306 Felton Rd, T03-445 1716, www.olssens.co.nz, tastings daily 1000-1700, closed Sat and Sun May-Sep*. The intriguingly named **Mount Difficulty Vineyard** ⓘ *Felton Rd, Bannockburn, T03-445 3445, www.mtdifficulty.co.nz, daily 1030-1700 (1030- 1600 Apr-Oct)*, is a small boutique winery that is fast contributing to the region's reputation for fine Pinot Noir, if not its expansive views.

If time is short and you have only a vague interest in wine, the **Wine Adventures Big Picture Complex** ⓘ *corner of Sandflat Rd and SH6 (towards Queenstown), T03-445 4052, daily 0900-2000*, offers an interactive experience through a film, an 'Aroma Room', the obligatory tastings and, of course, the chance to buy a bottle or six in the shop or sample with a spot of lunch or dinner at the restaurant/café.

⊚ Central Otago listings

For Sleeping and Eating price codes and other relevant information, see Essentials pages 44-50.

⬤ Sleeping

Alexandra *p610*

The VIC (I-Site) has full accommodation listings and can book on your behalf. There are a number of motels, most on the main drag north, towards Clyde.

L Rocky Range, Half Mile, T03-448 6150, www.rockyrange.co.nz. Luxury B&B with 4 well appointed en suites, excellent hosts, spa treatments and good views. Recommended.

AL-A Iversen B&B, 47 Blackman Rd, T03-449 2520, www.otagocentral.com. For a lovely orchard stay.

A Centennial Court Motor Inn, 96 Centennial Av, T03-448 6482, www.nzsouth.co.nz/centennial court. A la carte restaurant and bar, luxury spa suites, fully-equipped family units.

A-B Alexandra Heights Motel, 125 Centennial Av, T03-448 6366, www.manz.co.nz/alexandra. All units have

cooking facilities. Spa baths available.

B Alexandra Garden Court Motel, Manuherikia Rd, T03-448 8295. Recommended. Standard amenities and pleasant gardens.

C-D Alexandra Backpackers, 8-12 Skird St, T03-448 7170, www.alxbackpackers. zoomshare.com. The main budget hostel in town, centrally located and well geared up for cyclists and advice about the Rail Trail.

C-D Two Bobs Flashpackers, 30 Marshall Rd, T03-449 3188, twobobs@xtra.co.nz. A rural alternative 4 kms out of town with one double and two twins. Free bike hire and tailor-made 3-5-day cycle tour packages

AL-C Flannery Lodge, in the historic village of Ophir (28 km north), T03-447 4256, www.ophir.co.nz. A fine alternative with 2 double en suites, bunk rooms and tent sites. The added attractions here, other than the peaceful and friendly atmosphere of the village, are the local walks, bike trails and fishing and the local pub. Flannery Lodge also offers its own 'The Best Bits Tour', a 2-day package, which includes the Poolburn

Viaduct. You stay your first night at the lodge, then the next morning, you ride (or walk) back to Ophir (approx 30 km) the total cost is a very reasonable $120.

Motorcamps and campsites
B-D Alexandra Holiday Camp, on the Manuherikia Rd, T03-448 8297. A little lacking in character but still has perfectly acceptable cabins, backpacker rooms, powered/tent sites, camp kitchen and hires kayaks and mountain bikes.

Clyde p610
LL-AL Oliver's Lodge, 34 Sunderland St, T03-449 2860, www.olivers.co.nz. Equally lauded for the quality of its accommodation and its restaurant, Oliver's offers a classic mix of old-world character and fine cuisine. Choose from one of 12 individually styled en suites ranging from the 'stable' and 'homestead' rooms, to the individual 'smokehouse' room with its charming old shower and sunken bath. The restaurant, which also exudes character with its cobblestone fireplace and red brick floor, has been a focus for quality fine dining in the region for years.
A Antique Lodge Motel, 56 Sunderland St, T03-449 2709, www.antiquelodge motel.co.nz. A good motel option.
A Dunstan House, Sunderland St, T03-449 2295, www.dunstanhouse.co.nz. This historic former hotel has been well refurbished and offers elegant en suites decorated in turn of the 20th century style.

Cromwell p611
There is a surprisingly good range of accommodation in Cromwell and, given its popularity as a base close to (but cheaper) than Queenstown, the number of beds is increasing. The VIC (I-Site) has a full list of options and can book on your behalf. In summer it would still be wise to book ahead.
L-AL Villa Amo, Shine Lane, Pisa Moorings on Lake Dunstan, T03-445 0788, www.villa amo.co.nz. A modern spacious villa built in neoclassical Roman style and a good option

in the upper B&B range. Located on the shores of Lake Dunstan and commanding fine views of the mountains, it offers 1 room with shared bathroom with an adjunct double if required. There is also an outdoor spa and in-house eco-experience tours of the region (see Activities and tours, below).
AL-A Carrick Lodge Motel, 10 Barry Av, T03-445 4519, www.carricklodge.co.nz. New motel with studios and units (some with spa) all with broadband internet.
AL-A Golden Gate Lodge, Barry Av, T0800-104451/T03-445 1777, www.goldengate. co.nz. The closest thing to a hotel in town. Smart and spacious, it is designed to reflect the region's gold-mining heritage and offers well-appointed studios, suites (some with spa) and units and restaurant.
AL-B Lake Dunstan Lodge, Cromwell Rd, SH8, 5 km north of Cromwell, T03-445 1107, www.lakedunstanlodge.co.nz. A smart, modern home in a peaceful location on the shores of Lake Dunstan, offering tidy twin and queen rooms, with balconies, a spa pool and some great home cooking.
A-B Cottage Gardens B&B, 80 Neplusultra Street, T03- 445 0628, cottage.gardens @ihug. co.nz. Good self-contained units .
B Anderson Park Lodge, 9 Gair Av, T0800-220550/T03-4450321, www.andersonpark motel.co.nz. A cheaper option with spa pool.
B Colonial Manor corner of Barry and Mead Aves, T0800-428648, T03-445 0184, www.colonial manor.co.nz. Quality motel accommodation.

Motorcamps and campsites
B-D Cromwell Top Ten Holiday Park, 1 Alpha St, T0800-107275/T03-445 0164, www.cromwellholidaypark.co.nz. A wide range of modern motel, en suite/standard cabins and powered/tent sites in a quiet setting beside the golf course.
C-D Chalets and Holiday Park, 102 Barry Av, T03-445 1260, www.thechalets.co.nz. Former revamped dam workers' residences. It has bunkrooms and cheap but comfortable singles and doubles with shared facilities.

🍴 Eating

Alexandra *p610*

Clyde, see below, provides far better dining options than Alexandra.

🍴 **Red Brick Café**, just off Ennis St, T03-448 9174. Mon-Sat for lunch or dinner. The exception to the plethora of unremarkable cafés and takeaways in the centre of town.

🍴 **The Shaky Bridge Café**, near Shaky Bridge, Graveyard Gully Rd, T03-448 5111. Sun-Thu 0900-1600, Fri-Sat 0900-1730. A fine venue for an al fresco lunch or a coffee all year and for dinner in summer.

Clyde *p610*

🍴 **Dunstan House**, 29 Sunderland St, T03-449 2295. Mon-Wed 1800-late, Thu-Sun 1200-1400 and 1800-late. Offers café-style cuisine that focuses mainly on local produce in an equally historic setting.

🍴 **Oliver's Restaurant**, 34 Sunderland St (in the former 1863 general store) T03-449 2860, www.olivers.co.nz. Daily for lunch and dinner (bookings advised). The award-winning food is complemented by the pleasant surroundings.

🍴 **The Post Office Café and Bar**, 2 Blyth St, T03-449 2488. Daily from 1000. Pleasant aesthetics and light meals.

Cromwell *p611*

🍴 **Bannockburn Hotel**, 420 Bannockburn Rd, 8 km from Cromwell, Bannockburn, T03-445 0615. Daily for lunch and dinner. Boasts a pleasant setting and good selection of local wines. Recommended.

🍴 **Feast**, in theMall, T03-445 3020. Daily 0700-2100. Good gourmet pizza indoor or out.

🍴 **Cromwell Town and Country Club**, Melmore Terr, T03-445 1169. Fri-Sat. Provides a good cheap feed.

🍴 **Grain and Seed Café**, 63 Melmore Terr (in the original 1880 Grain and Seed store), T03-445 1077. Daily from 1000-1630. The best coffee in town and light meals.

⛏ Activities and tours

Maniototo (Naseby) *p610*
Curling
Maniototo Curling International, 1057 Channel Road, Naseby, T03-4449878, www.curling.co.nz. A state of the art indoor curling rink that now serves as the hub for the ancient sport in New Zealand. It is great fun even for beginners and you can give it a go from $14 per hour.

Alexandra *p610*

Fishing permits and a list of local guides are available from the VIC (I-Site).

Alexandra is a principal starting point for the **Otago Central Rail Trail** and **Dunstan Trails**. The VIC (I-Site) can provide information and leaflets on the methods and negotiation of both, mainly by mountain bike or 4WD. The **Otago Central Rail Trail** has its own website, www.otagocentral railtrail.co.nz, which is very useful. Various transport operators provide luggage and bike pick-up or drop-offs and bike hire (and/or guided tours) for both trails.

Altitude Adventures, 88 Centennial Av, Alexandra, T03-448 8917, www.altitude adventures.co.nz. Offers a whole host of ride options from 2- to 3-hr, fast single track ride to a full-day trip for a very reasonable $95, various customized multi-day 'Rail Trail' packages and a full-day backcountry biking tours. Full rental service.

Other companies worth looking at include:
Trail Journeys, corner of SH8 and Springvale Rd, T0800-724587/T03-449 2150, www.trail journeys.co.nz.

Off The Rails, T027-3633724, www.offtherails.co.nz.

Etours, T03-464 3353, www.etours.net.nz.

Rail Trail Active, T0508-724587/ T021-942613, www.railtrailactive.co.nz.

Rabbit Range Horse Trekking, T03-448 5423, www.rabbitrange.com. Local trekking operator.

Cromwell *p611*

There are plenty of good walks in the area, described in the *Walk Cromwell* brochure available free from the VIC (I-Site). The area also has some excellent fishing, mountain biking, motorcycle touring and 4WD opportunities, again, contact the VIC (I-Site).

Vineyard tours

There are also several orchard and vineyard tour operators including:
Freeway Orchards, T03-445 1500, www.freewayorchard.co.nz.
Jackson Orchards Tours, T03-445 0596, www.jacksonorchard.co.nz. From $10.

Queenstown → *Colour map 6, A4 Population: 10,000.*

Ladies and gentlemen, fasten your seat belts and welcome to Queenstown – Adrenaline Central, Thrillsville, New Zealand – the adventure capital of the world. You are perhaps studying this guide in your hotel room, or perched in your hostel bunk, with a pained expression trying to decide which of the 150-odd activities to try and, more importantly, how your wallet can possibly cope? But first things first: look out of the window. Where else in the world do you have such accessible scenery? And all that is free.

Queenstown has come a long way since gold secured its destiny in the 1860s. It is now the biggest tourist draw in New Zealand and considered one of the top (and almost certainly the most scenic) adventure venues in the world. It simply has so much to offer. Amidst the stunning setting of mountain and lake, over one million visitors a year partake in a staggering range of activities from a sedate steamboat cruise to the heart-stopping bungee jump. You can do almost anything here, from a gentle round of golf to paddling down a river in what looks like a blow-up carrot. Add to that a superb range of accommodation, services, restaurants and cafés and you simply won't know where to turn. And it goes on year-round, day and night. In winter the hiking boots are simply replaced by skis, the T-shirt with a jumper and, after sunset, the activity guide with the wine glass, knife and fork. It just goes on and on. ►► *For Sleeping, Eating and other listings, see pages 620-633.*

Ins and outs

Getting there

Queenstown airport ⓘ *8 km east of the town in Frankton, www.queenstownairport.co.nz,* receives direct daily flights from Auckland, Christchurch, Wellington and Dunedin with **Air New Zealand**, T03-441 4870. **Qantas**, T0800-808767, **Jetstar**, T0800-800995, www.jetstar.com, and **Pacific Blue**, T0800-670000, www.pacificblue.com, also offer domestic and international services, and in winter there are some direct services from eastern Australia. Several small domestic operators offer flights to Milford, including **Air Fiordland**, T0800-107505/T03-442 3404, www.airfiordland.com, and **Milford Sound**

Scenic Flights, T03-442 3065, see Activities and tours, page 629. From the airport, **Connectabus**, T03-441 4471, www.connectabus.com costs $6 into town. **Kiwi Shuttle**, T03-442 2107, or **Super Shuttle**, T0800-748885/T03-442 3640, serve the airport door to door. A taxi will set you back about $35.

By road, Queenstown is 486 km from Christchurch, 283 km from Dunedin, 68 km from Wanaka and 170 km from Te Anau (Milford Sound 291 km). The town is served daily by **Intercity**, T03-379 9020/T03-442 4100, www.intercitycoach.co.nz (Dunedin/Christchurch via Mount Cook/Te Anau/Franz Josef); **Atomic Shuttles**, T03-349 0697, www.atomic travel.co.nz (Dunedin/Christchurch/Invercargill/Greymouth); **Southern Link**, T0508-458835, www.southernlinkcoaches.co.nz (Dunedin/Christchurch via Wanaka and Tekapo); **Nakedbus.com** offers cheap internet fares to Christchurch and Dunedin; **Mount Cook Landline**, T0800-800904, serves Christchurch via Mount Cook. Fares to Dunedin start from $40, Christchurch $65. The backpacker-orientated **Bottom Bus**, T03-477 9083, www.bottombus.co.nz, offers several packages to Dunedin via the Southern Scenic Route, Te Anau and Invercargill. **Intercity**, **Atomic Shuttles**, and the recommended **Wanaka Connextions**, www.time2.co.nz, offer services to Wanaka/Dunedin/ Middlemarch and Invercargill from $25. The smaller shuttle operators **Topline Tours**, T03-249 8059, www.toplinetours.co.nz, offer services to Te Anau between Nov-April, while **Tracknet**, T03-249 7777, www.tracknet.net, also go to Te Anau from $43 and the Routeburn Track from $32. For bus trips to Milford Sound, see pages 666 and 670.

Getting around

The **Connectabus**, T03-441 4471, www.connectabus.com, stops at most major hotels and accommodation establishments. It offers a day pass for $19, which can be a good way to negotiate the town (timetable from the VIC/I-Site).

Alpine Taxis, T03-442 6666, serve the skifields of Cardrona, Coronet Peak, the Remarkables and Treble Cone, from $35. But during the winter season you are advised to check on the latest operators at the VIC (I-Site). **Connectabus** offers standard bus services and a 'Double-Decker Bus Tour', T03-441 4471, from top of the Mall at 0930 and 1330 to Arrowtown via several attractions, from $48 return, standard fare from $6. **Backpacker Express**, T03-409 2049, www.glenorchyinfocentre.co.nz, runs daily buses to Glenorchy. For taxis, car rental and bike hire see Transport, page 633. You are advised to book car rental well in advance in summer.

For detailed information on tramping track transport and trailhead bookings contact the **Information and Track Centre** (see Tourist information below). **Tracknet**, T03-2497 777, www.tracknet.net, are the specialist tramping track operators to Te Anau (Kepler/ Milford/Dusky). For Glenorchy and beyond (Routeburn/Greenstone-Caples/Rees-Dart) contact **Backpacker Express**, T03-442 9939, info@glenorchyinfocentre.co.nz or **Buckley Transport**, T03-4428215, www.buckleytransport.co.nz. For water taxi transport contact **Queenstown Water Taxis**, T03-4411116, www.queenstownwatertaxis.co.nz.

Tourist information

There is total information overload in Queenstown. For impartial advice head straight to the very efficient and busy **Queenstown Travel and Visitor Centre** ① *below the Clock Tower, corner of Shotover and Camp sts, T0800-668888, T03-442 4100, www.queenstown-vacation.com and www.queenstown-nz.co.nz, open 0700-1900 (winter 1800).* **DoC** ① *38 Shotover St, T03-442 7935, queenstownvc @doc.govt.nz,* is next to the **Information and Track Centre** ① *37 Shotover St, T03-442 9708, www.infotrack.co.nz, daily 0700-2100, winter*

The best view in Queenstown

Although it takes a rugged drive and a fair scramble (in summer) to get there, the view of Lake Wakatipu and Queenstown from the **Remarkables Lookout** is worth every rut and step of the journey. Before considering this trip make sure the weather is clear and settled, since you will be more than 2000 m above sea level. Assure that you are well prepared, with warm clothing and proper walking boots and that your car will survive the 1500-m climb up the unsealed road to the ski fields (in winter you may need chains). The ski field road is accessed off SH6 about 2 km south of Frankton. If the ski field is open you might consider taking a shuttle from Queenstown, T03-442 6534. From the Remarkables ski field buildings you are basically trying to reach the top of the Shadow Basin Chair Lift, the base of which is in the main car park. If the lift is open you have the option of using it, but in summer (or if you fancy the climb) then follow the path that zigzags up the slopes behind the main building to the 'Mid- Station'. From the Mid-Station continue on the path in a rough line with the chairlift until you reach its terminus. The lookout is about 200m directly behind and further up from this point. On a clear day surrounded by snow, you won't forget it!

From the lookout (2½ hours return) it is then possible to climb and scramble with care, further south along the ridge to the weather station. From here you will have even greater views including Lake Alta, the entire ski field below and north, to Mount Aspiring. On an exceptional day you may even see Mount Cook almost 200 km away.

0730-2000, which provides up-to-date information on local walks and major tramps, and deals with transportation and hut bookings. It also offers gear hire and has the latest weather forecasts. The DoC office closes in winter. The **Real Journeys Visitors'** Centre ① *Steamer Wharf, Lakefront Drive, T0800-656501/T03-249 7416, www.realjourneys. co.nz,* deals with a multitude of pleasures and trips to Milford and the Fiordland National Park. It also owns the *TSS Earnslaw Steamship.* ▶▶ *For details, see Activities and tours, pages 618 and 627.*

Sights

Queenstown is compact and easily negotiable by foot. The main street for information and activity bookings is Shotover Street while the **Mall**, bordered by Camp Street to the east and Marine Parade on the waterfront, is the principal shopping and restaurant centre. The **Esplanade** (lakeside) and **Steamer Wharf** also have retail, information and activity outlets. **Queenstown Gardens**, on the southern edge of Queenstown Bay, offers sanctuary from the chaotic town centre.

Perhaps the best place to start is the **Skyline Gondola** ① *Brecon St, T03-441 0101, www.skyline.co.nz, 0900-dusk, gondola $23, child $12; gondola and luge (5 rides) $45, child $35.* Perched on **Bob's Peak**, 450 m above the town, it boasts a world-class view and has a host of activities including The Ledge Bungee, The Luge, The Sky-Swing, paragliding and helicopter flightseeing. The **Kiwi Haka Maori performance** ① *T03- 442 7063,* is also based at Skyline with 30-minute shows nightly from $53 (including gondola) and the option of an all-inclusive dinner from $104. Other on-site amenities include shops, a café

(0930-2100) and a restaurant (see Eating, page 624). A good time to go up is just before sunset when the golden rays slowly creep up the **Remarkables Range** and the town's lights come on. Then you could perhaps enjoy a meal before watching the bungee jumpers and the novel 'Sky-Swing' below the main building. At night it is quite hard to believe such a place and such activities exist. You can also walk (one hour one way) up to the Skyline Complex via the **Ben Lomond Track** which starts on Lomond Crescent (via Brunswick Street off the Lake Esplanade).

While at the base of the gondola you might like to see the obligatory kiwi and friends in the **Kiwi and Birdlife Park** ⓘ *Brecon St, T03-442 8059, www.kiwibird.co.nz, daily 0900-2100 (winter 0900-1700), $35, child $15*. Set in 8 ha of quiet(ish) pine forest it displays all the usual suspects, including kiwi, morepork (owl), parakeets, tui and of course the 'cheeky kea'. Of the 16 endangered species, the rarest is the delicate black stilt, sadly, one of only about 150 remaining. Added attractions include a free 20-minute conservation show held at 1100 and 1500.

Also in Brecon Street is **Caddy Shack City Mini-Golf** ⓘ *T03-442 6642, 1000-dusk, $19, child $15*, where a plethora of weird and wonderful holes will keep small kids (and big kids) amused for hours on rainy days or evenings. Beside the town centre on the waterfront the **Queenstown Gardens** are well worth a visit and offer some respite from the crowds. There are oaks, some stunning sequoias and 1500 roses planted in 26 named rose beds. On the way you might like to pop into the historic 1865 **Williams Cottage**, on Marine Parade, which has been restored and now serves as a shop selling quality homeware.

There are also a number of **wineries** around Queenstown that boast surprisingly fine wines (especially Pinot Noir) and claim to be the most southerly vineyards in the world. The most notable include: **Peregrine** ⓘ *T03-442 4000, www.peregrine wines.co.nz*; **Chard Farm** ⓘ *T03-442 6110, www.chardfarm.co.nz*; **Amisfield Lake Hayes** ⓘ *T03-442 0556, www.amisfield.co.nz*; and **Gibbston Valley** ⓘ *T03-442 6910, www.gvwines.co.nz*, which are on or just off SH6 on the way in to Queenstown. The VIC (I-Site) has details and tours are available. ▶▶ *See Activities and tours, page 633.*

Finally, if you have run out of money or simply want a good laugh, head for the **Kawarau Bungee** (23 km east on SH6) and watch the jumpers. It is a fascinating mix of fear and fun and watching the spectators is just as entertaining.

Activities

The choice is of course vast. There are over 150 activities to choose from, with everything from the tipples of a wine tour to the ripples of jet boating. And Queenstown is not just geared up for the young and the mad. There are activities to suit all ages, from infant to octogenarian and from the able to the disabled. If a 91-year-old can do a bungee jump, surely the possibilities are endless? Of course it is the bungee that made Queenstown famous. If you are prepared to make 'the jump' and have been saving your pennies to do so, then it is here that you must finally pluck up the courage. Heights vary from 40 m to 134 m, and if there is any advice to give (other than psychological and financial counselling) it is: do it in style and go high.

The 'big four' activities in Queenstown are considered to be the **bungee**, **jet boating**, **rafting** and **flightseeing**. Try to consider a variety of pursuits according to the budget at hand. For example, consider something that costs nothing and is rather sedate, like taking a walk to appreciate the stunning views (see box, page 617), since this as just as much 'Queenstown' as anything else. Then by all means get the pulse racing with something high

Walks around Queenstown

Remarkables ski field If you have half a day, reliable wheels and walking boots, the walk to the lookout above the ski field is highly recommended, see box page 617.

Queenstown Hill Accessed from York Street (look for DoC sign), this is a two- to three-hour moderate walk up to a scenic lookout above the town. The millennium gate on the way up is a nice and unusual piece of craftsmanship.

Ben Lomond (1747 m) dominates the scene above Bob's Peak and the Gondola and provides stunning views of the town and Lake Wakatipu. The full walk can be negotiated through forest from Lomond Street (from the Esplanade), but the best bet is to take the Gondola and join the track from there, six to eight hours return. Details available from DoC. Ben Lomond Guided Walks, T03-442 9434, www.benlomond.co.nz, offers a two-day fully guided walk to Ben Lomond with the added attraction of an exhilarating 4WD trip through Skippers Canyon, a night in a high country station lodge and meals from $495, child $395. Recommended.

Cecil Peak The peak dominates the southern shore opposite Queenstown and is another challenging option. A hike to the summit can be combined with a scenic helicopter flight and/or boat trip across Lake Wakatipu to get there and back. The ridgeline offers some fantastic views back across to Queenstown, and on the way up you can always throw in a picnic beside the dubiously named 'Fanny Falls'. It would be a full-day trip and you would need to organize either charter boat transportation, or better still, a boat there and helicopter pick-up, but it will be expensive. Getting a group together will reduce costs and it does present a great opportunity for a self-organized trip in a town (let's face it) that just loves to offer the opposite. Bear in mind it can get mighty cold up there and the weather can close in rapidly, so go well kitted out and if you can, take a mobile phone. For boat charter try Fishing Boat Trips (Stu Dever), T03-442 6371 www.fishing-queenstown.co.nz, and for helicopter Over the Top, T03-442 2233, www.flynz.co.nz.

Twelve-Mile Delta to Bob's Cove Far more conventional and an easy two-hour jaunt on the shores of Lake Wakatipu. It is accessed from the main Glenorchy Road (12 km).

Mount Crichton Scenic Reserve Inland and just a bit further along the road also offers good options. DoC can provide details and leaflets.

on the 'adren-o-meter', like a bungee, then perhaps something easy-going or an activity you can do nowhere else like a cruise on the *TSS Earnslaw* (see Cruising, page 628). Above all, don't only consider what you are 'supposed' to do, but also what most others do not. Queenstown is special and deserves far more of your attention and imagination.

The moment you arrive you will be confronted with sales and promotional outlets that can sniff your dollars in a dead calm, so be careful. Do not be swayed by reputations or the Las Vegas-style marketing. The big players are **A J Hackett** (Lord of the Bungee) and **Shotover Jet**. A J Hackett has its high-profile office in 'The Station', conveniently located right where the buses stop, at the corner of Shotover and Camp streets, with numerous others surrounding it and biting at their heels. Bookings can be made direct, but most accommodation establishments, especially backpacker hostels, will book on your behalf. The station is also the main pick-up and drop-off point for activities. The best advice is to head to the unbiased **Queenstown Travel and Visitor Centre** (see page 616), have a chat and avail yourself of the leaflets and information, then retire quietly to a coffee shop for a small nervous breakdown.

Activity combos There are a huge number of combo packages available from the main players like **A J Hackett** and **Shotover** to independents like **Adventure Marathon**. Most gravitate (no pun intended) between the 'big four' activities, with the odd 'luge' or movie thrown in. Others offer fishing, trekking, heli-skiing or hiking. If you are short of time a combo is probably the best way to go, and with prices ranging from about $250-550 the savings can be substantial. One of the best, but most demanding combos, is the **Awesome** Foursome ① *Queenstown Combos, T03-442 7318, www.combos.co.nz*, which includes the Nevis Bungee, Shotover jet-boat, rafting and a helicopter flight over Skippers Canyon for $575.

A slightly less demanding package is the **High Five** ① *from $255*, which includes a 3½-hour jet-boat, helicopter, skyline and luge. The half-day (five-hour) helicopter-raft and jet-boat **Shotover Trio** ① *is also good value at $345*. If you are still intent on a bungee this could perhaps be combined with one of the Hackett multiple jumps. ▶▶ *For all Activities and tours, see page 627.*

◉ Queenstown listings

For Sleeping and Eating price codes and other relevant information, see Essentials pages 44-50.

◉ Sleeping

Queenstown *p615, map p621*
Despite a healthy range of accommodation and around 10,000 beds, it is essential to book 2 or 3 days in advance in mid-summer or during the height of the ski season (especially during the Winter Festival in mid-Jul). This particularly applies to backpacker accommodation. To browse the options check out www.queenstown accommodation.co.nz or visit the **Queenstown Accommodation Centre**, First Floor Chester Building, Corner Camp and Shotover sts, T03-442 7518, www.qac.co.nz. **LL Eichardt's Private Hotel**, Marine Parade, T03-441 0450, www.eichardtshotel.co.nz. Grand yet discreet, catering to the luxury boutique market, Eichardt's has accrued some lauded international awards and offers all the décor, lavish furnishings and amenities one might expect for the exorbitant price. That said, however, it does have the edge when it comes to a caring, personable service.

LL Millbrook Resort, T0800-800604/ T03-441 7000, www.millbrook.co.nz. Sumptuous out-of-town choice with a world-class golf course and luxury facilities. It has suites, villas and cottages, 2 restaurants (one Japanese), a bar, and a health and fitness complex and day spa. **LL Sofitel**, 8 Duke St, T03-450 0045, www.sofitelqueenstown.com. One of the newest and most celebrated hotels sitting in prime position just above the town centre. Luxury rooms, suites and penthouses furnished in European style and in warm shades of beige and brown marry well with the views. The class extends to the facilities and the in-house restaurant. But perhaps, just perhaps, your abiding memory will be of its famous 'little boy's' room in the lobby (go on girls – have a peek!). **LL-L Millennium Hotel**, corner of Frankton Rd and Stanley St, T03-441 8888 www.millenniumhotels.co.nz. Well positioned and close to town. Also has a wide range of suites and all the usual modern well-appointed facilities. **LL-AL Heritage Hotel**, 91 Fernhill Rd, T03-442 4988, www.heritagehotels.co.nz. One of the town's most popular chain hotels, located at the western edge of town in a

Queenstown

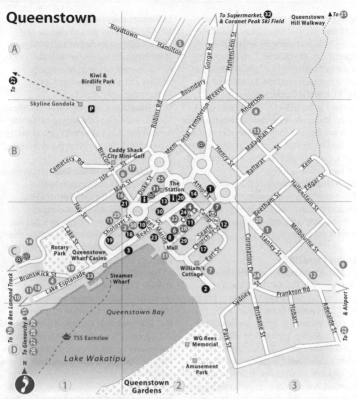

100 metres		
100 yards		

Sleeping 🛏️
Base Queenstown **30** *C2*
Blue Peaks Lodge &
 Apartments **3** *C3*
Bumbles Backpackers **4** *C1*
Chalet Queenstown
 B&B **22** *D3*
Coronation Lodge **24** *C3*
Creeksyde Campervan
 Park **5** *A2*
Dairy **6** *B2*
Eichardt's **31** *C2*
Glebe Luxury
 Apartments **20** *C3*
Heartland **1** *C3*
Heritage **28** *D1*
Hippo Lodge **8** *B3*
Hurleys **9** *C3*

Lakefront Apartments **18** *C1*
Lakeside Motel **10** *C1*
Lodges **11** *C1*
Matakauri Lodge **26** *D1*
Millennium **12** *C3*
Novotel Gardens **7** *C2*
Point Luxury
 Apartments **21** *A3*
Punatapu **27** *D1*
Queenstown
 House B&B **13** *B3*
Queenstown Lakeview
 Motor Park **14** *C1*
Queenstown Lodge &
 Fernhill Apartments **29** *D1*
Queenstown YHA
 Central **2** *C2*
Queenstown YHA
 Lakefront **15** *D1*
Scallywags **16** *D1*

Sofitel **25** *C1*
Southern Laughter;
 Sir Cedrics **17** *B2*
Waterfront **19** *C1*

Eating 🍴
Bathhouse **2** *C2*
Bella Cucina **21** *C2*
Boardwalk **3** *C2*
Bob's Weigh **13** *B2*
Brazz on the Green **1** *B2*
Cow **8** *C2*
Dux de Lux & McNeill's
 Cottage Brewery **17** *C2*
Fergburgers **24** *C2*
Freiya's Indian **14** *B2*
Gantley's **32** *A3*
Habebes **10** *C2*
HMS Brittannia **11** *C2*
Joe's Garage **12** *C2*

Minami Jujisei **18** *C2*
Naff Caff **19** *C1*
O'Connells Food
 Hall **20** *B2*
Pog Mahone's **23** *C2*
Skyline **27** *A1*
Tatler **29** *C2*
Vudu Café **30** *C2*

Bars & clubs 🍸
Altitude **15** *C1*
Bunker **4** *C2*
Chico's **6** *C2*
Lone Star **16** *B1*
Minus 5C **33** *C1*
Morrison's **22** *C2*
Pig & Whistle **7** *C2*
Red Rock **25** *B2*
Tardis **28** *C2*
World **31** *B2*

quiet position and commanding fine views back towards the town. Luxury rooms and suites from 1-3 bedrooms with all the standard, quality facilities. Cosy in-house restaurant with open fire, and a health club with pool, sauna and spa. Excellent service.

LL-AL Novotel Gardens, corner of Earl St and Marine Parade, T03-442 7750, h5308-re01@accor-hotels.com. Recently refurbished exterior with spacious and contemporary rooms ideally situated on the waterfront by the town centre, and a stone's throw from the peace and quiet of Queenstown Gardens.

AL-A Heartland Hotel, 27 Stanley St, T03-442 7700, www.scenic-circle.co.nz. A cheaper option that offers well-appointed A-frame-style units with great views within 2 mins of the town centre.

Lodges and B&Bs

LL Matakauri Lodge, Farrycroft Row (off Glenorchy Rd), T03-441 1008, www.matakauri.co.nz. A magnificent B&B set in private bush 5 km west of Queenstown, with uninterrupted views across Lake Wakatipu. Accommodation is in modern villas and fully self-contained suites. The spacious lodge offers a library and 4 fireplaces, while within the grounds a spa pavilion is perfect for that après-ski. A la carte dinners prepared by an in-house executive chef plus top local wines are all part of the experience.

LL Pear Tree Cottage, 51 Mountain View Rd, T03-442 9340, www.peartree.co.nz. Enchanting B&B at the base of the Coronet Peak ski field. A quiet, tastefully restored 1870s cottage, fully self-contained with 2 bedrooms. In summer, flowers abound.

LL Punatapu, 1113 Rapid Gate (7 km from town on Glenorchy Rd), T03-4426624, www.punatapu.co.nz. A sumptuous B&B with an individually styled 'hamlet' of suites around a central courtyard. The views are stunning and there is a swimming pool, spa and sauna. Contemporary New Zealand art features heavily and in summer there is usually an artist in residence.

LL Remarkables Lodge, south along SH6, T03-4422720, www.remarkables.co.nz. A well-established renovated luxury lodge set at the base of its namesake mountain range, with a fine reputation. It offers modern facilities and great cuisine but it is the location that really appeals.

LL-L The Dairy, Corner of Brecon and Isle sts, T03-442 5164, www.thedairy.co.nz. Central newly renovated B&B with 13 cosy en suites in period-style house restored and modelled on a 1920s dairy.

LL-L Queenstown House B&B, 69 Hallenstein St, T03-442 9043, www.queenstownhouse.co.nz. A well-established modern upper-range B&B in a central location overlooking the town. Elegant en suites and villa suites complete with fireside sitting rooms. Excellent full cooked or continental breakfast. Internet and off-street parking.

L Chalet Queenstown B&B, 1 Dublin St, T03-442 7117, chaletqueenstown.co.nz. Swiss-style chalet in a quiet location, with 7 cosy and tastefully furnished en suites.

B-C Scallywags, 27A Lomond Cres, T03-442 7083. A cross between a budget B&B and a backpacker hostel, this is good value, friendly, slow paced and quiet. Dorms, twins and doubles.

Self-contained apartments

Like the main cities, Queenstown has realized the preference for luxury, fully self-contained and serviced apartments. Just a few of the recommended examples are:

LL-AL Glebe Luxury Apartments, corner of Stanley and Beetham sts, T03-441 0310, www.theglebe.co.nz. 5 star and central with off-street parking.

LL-AL Point Luxury Apartments, 239 Frankton Rd, T0800-222239/T03-4411899, www.thepoint.net.nz.

L-AL Lakefront Apartments, 26 The Esplanade, T03-441 8800, www.queenstownaccommodation.co.nz. Long established and waterside.

Motels

There are over 75 to choose from, so shop around. The VIC (I-Site) has full listings. Prices are generally more expensive than elsewhere, especially in mid-summer, so do not necessarily expect the value for money that you are used to. Those on the waterfront offer superb views, but this is reflected in the price.

LL-AL Coronation Lodge, 10 Coronation Dr, T03-441 0860, www.coronationlodge.nz. Spacious rooms with natural wood abounding, well placed close to both the town centre and the sanctuary of the botanical gardens

L-AL Blue Peaks Lodge and Apartments, corner of Stanley and Sydney sts, T03-442 9224, www.bluepeaks.co.nz. In an elevated position and conveniently located a short distance from the town centre, the motel complex offers standard units, while a sister property located opposite Queenstown Gardens offers very tidy self-contained apartments, again a very short distance from the town centre. Off-street parking.

L-AL Hurleys, T0800-589879/T03-4425999, www.hurleys.co.nz. Has tasteful fully self-contained studios supported with great facilities, centrally located.

L-AL Lodges, 8 Lake Esplanade, T03-442 7552, www.thelodges.co.nz. Suites and apartments on the lakefront.

AL Lakeside Motel, 18 The Esplanade, T03-442 8976, www.queenstownaccommodation. co.nz. 15 no-nonsense units, all with views.

AL Waterfront, 109 Beach Rd, T0800-889889/T03-4425123, www.thewaterfront.co.nz. As the name suggests, it's in prime position.

C-D Queenstown Lakeview Motor Park, Off Brecon St, T03-442 7252, www.holiday park.net.nz. Although not a motel the modern units here are often very good value, especially for small groups. It is also centrally located and has facilities on a par with any standard mid-range motel.

Budget options/backpacker hostels

As you can imagine Queenstown is not short of backpacker hostels and with around 20 establishments both old and new, staid or funky, there is plenty to choose from. This is not the complete listing, just those that we recommend or that stand out. In summer you should book at least 5 days in advance.

AL -C Queenstown Lodge and Fernhill Apartments, Sainsbury Rd (a little further out at the west end of town), Fernhill, T03-442 7107/T0800-756343, www.qlodge.co.nz. Reasonably priced ski lodge-style property located at the western fringe of town. It is quiet, has off-street parking, a pizza restaurant, spa, sauna and most of the rooms offer excellent views across Lake Wakatipu. The lodge also administers a new, self-contained apartment complex and clients have full use of lodge facilities.

AL-D Base Queenstown, 47-49 Shotover St, T03-441 1185, www.stayatbase.com. A purpose-built chain backpackers. Set in the heart of town it is pitched somewhere between a budget hotel and backpacker hostel with tidy en suite doubles with TV and bath and shower to dorms with shared facilities. Well-equipped and has a travel and job search centre, good security, high-speed internet café and nightclub. Being right in the heart of town it is a happening place and not one for quiet sanctuary. As ever, parking is also a problem.

B-D Bumbles Backpackers, corner of Brunswick St and Lake Esplanade, T0800-2862537/T03-442 6298, www.bumbles backpackers.co.nz. Well-rounded 50-bed hostel, spotlessly clean and efficient. Has a good range of well-heated dorms, singles, twins, doubles and a few tent sites, all with modern facilities and views. Storage, drying rooms, internet and – importantly – off-street parking.

B-D Hippo Lodge, 4 Anderson Heights, T03-442 5785, www.hippolodge.co.nz. A fine place with the best backpackers' view in town. It is modern, friendly, clean and well equipped, with dorms, twins and doubles (1 en suite), making it worth every step of the climb to get there. Parking can be a problem.

B-D Queenstown YHA Lakefront, 80 Lake Esplanade (at the western end of town), T03-

4428413, yhaqutn@yha.org.nz. Deservedly popular and with a wide range of comfortable shared, twin and double rooms and modern facilities. Internet. Limited off-street parking. Recommended. There is also a second YHA, the **Queenstown YHA Central**, 48A Shotover St, T03-4427400, should the central location and its convenience be an issue.

B-D Southern Laughter: Sir Cedrics, 4 Isle St (towards the gondola, but still well positioned for town), T03-441 8828, www.southernlaughter.co.nz. Small, but well established, has a good atmosphere and facilities including en suite dorms, a spa, Sky TV, 24-internet and off-street parking. The Larson cartoon theme will keep you chuckling on rainy days.

Motorcamps and campsites

A-D Creeksyde Campervan Park, 54 Robins Rd, T03-4429447, www.camp.co.nz. Centrally located and has modern motel units, flats, cabins, lodge rooms and good facilities including spa. It perhaps takes too much advantage of its position with charges and gets busy in summer, so pre-book. Supermarket very close by.

AL-D Queenstown Lakeview Motor Park, off Brecon St, T03-442 7252, www.holidaypark.net.nz. After a complete revamp this park has increased dramatically in popularity and stature. The complex is the closest park to the town centre (2 mins) and includes tidy and good-value studio units, en suite cabins, luxury flats, as well as the standard powered/tent sites. There is a spacious kitchen block with internet and lockable food cupboards. Note that the showers take 2 x 50c pieces. Also good for information and activity bookings.

❶ Eating

Queenstown *p615, map p621*
There are over 100 eateries in Queenstown with a choice and quality to compete with any

of the larger cities in New Zealand. There are Chinese, Mexican, Indian, Korean, Lebanese and Italian restaurants alongside those serving traditional New Zealand fare with many doubling as bars and nightspots. Again, although prices can be slightly elevated, there are restaurants to suit all budgets as well as 2 unique eating options in the form of the Gondola restaurant which can be combined with a Maori cultural performance and the *TSS Earnslaw*, see Activities and tours, page 628.

₸₸₸ The Boardwalk, 1st floor, Steamer Wharf, T03-442 5630. Daily from 1200. Well known for its superb seafood and great views. They are still dining out on the fact that it was Bill Clinton's choice when he visited in 1999.

₸₸₸ Gantley's, Arthur's Point Rd, T03-442 8999, www.gantleys.co.nz. Daily from 1830. A very romantic affair set in a historic stone building 7 km out of town towards Arrowtown. Award winning, the equal of the others above and its wine list, like its cuisine, is superb.

₸₸₸ Skyline Restaurant, at the Skyline Gondola Complex, Brecon St, T03-441 0101. Daily, lunch buffet 1200-1400, dinner from 1800. Offers a 6-course 'Taste of New Zealand' buffet which includes roast meats, seafood, local produce and salads followed by dessert and cheeseboard from $47 (lunch), $72 (dinner). The views are exceptional, even at night. You can also combine your visit and meal with the Kiwi Haka Maori cultural performance from $104, child $50.

₸₸₸-₸₸ Tatler, at the west end of the Mall, T03-442 8372. Daily 1000-late. Modern, stylish and popular not only for traditional New Zealand fare including lamb but also seafood with chowder a speciality.

₸₸ Bathhouse, T03-442 5625, www.bathhouse.co.nz. Daily from 1000. Perched on the edge of the beach, next to Queenstown Gardens is this very romantic place. With an imaginative menu, it is a lovely spot for both lunch and dinner.

₸₸ Brazz On the Green, 1 Athol St, T03-442 4444. Daily from 1100. Modern and classy, and given its open fires, especially popular with the après-ski crowd in winter. Traditional

New Zealand/European menu and a fine place to watch the world go by.

The Cow, Cow Lane, T03-442 8588. Daily 1200-2300. Also popular, though more for its exterior aesthetics and atmosphere than its food. Set in a former stone milking shed it is a little cramped but full of character. Pizza and pasta are the specialities.

McNeill's Cottage Brewery, 14 Church St, T03-4429 688. Daily from 1130. A nice mix of heritage and atmosphere, it's another award-winner with a good selection of gourmet pizzas, open fire outside, live bands at the weekend and, of course, some fine home brewed ales.

HMS Britannia in The Mall, T03-442 9600. Good if you have kids or simply enjoy good seafood. It is a wee bit on the expensive side but the portions are huge and the walls are something of a museum exhibit.

Freiya's Indian Restaurant, 33 Camp St, T03-442 7979. Daily 1100-2300. Good Indian food. Sit-in or takeaway.

Pig and Whistle, 41 Ballarat St, T03-442 9055. English-style pub offering standard pub grub and a good range of tap beers.

Minami Jujisei, 45 Beach St, T03-442 9854. Decent Japanese choice.

Bella Cucina, 6 Brecon St, T03-442 6762. Daily from 1800. A popular pizza place.

Pog Mahone's, 14 Rees St, T03-4425382. Irish pub with good food and atmosphere.

Fergburger, 42A Shotover St. The late-night munchy option.

O'Connell's Food Hall, Camp St. Daily from 0800. The usual cheap buffet lunch outlets.

Cafés

Bobs Weigh, further up towards town next to the VIC (I-Site), T03-442 8542. It's small but in a perfect position for that essential caffeine hit after arriving back from all the activities based at the 'The Station'.

Joe's Garage, originally in Camp St and now it seems successfully relocated to Searle Lane nearby Joe's. The secret hang out for locals and noted for its great coffee and light meals. Recommended.

Naff Caff, 1/66 Shotover St, T03-4428211. Daily from 0730. One of Queenstown's best, with light snacks, coffee and a value breakfast.

Vudu Café, 23 Beach St, T03-4425357. Has a loyal local following and is good for breakfast.

Supermarkets

Alpine Food Centre, Upper Shotover St. Mon-Sat 0800-2000, Sun 0900-2000. Handy for groceries and tramping food supplies.

Fresh Choice, 1 km out along Gorge Rd (Skippers and Coronet Peak Rd), T03-441 1252. Mon-Sun 0800-2100. The most convenient.

New World, Franktown (6 km), T03-442 3045. This is the biggest and cheapest.

⊙ Pubs, bars and clubs

Queenstown *p615, map p621*
Queenstown is very much a party town and, particularly at New Year, it goes off like a firecracker. It can all be a lot of fun, but at its busiest don't go out looking for refined culture and conversation. With so much adrenaline and testosterone flying around it doesn't go far beyond the standard yelps about the 'awesome' bungee jumping, or the double-flip-half-hernia on the snowboard, maaaan. The well-established favourites known for a good beer and atmosphere are the **Dux de Lux**, Church St; the Irish offerings **Pog Mahone's**, Rees St; the smaller more sedate **Morrison's**, Level 1, Stratton House, Beach St; and the quaint **Bardeaux**, Eureka Arcade.

That said, the latest hype surrounds the intriguing sculpted ice bar called **Minus 5C**, Steamer Wharf, T03-442 6050, daily from 1030. Of course it depends where you come from really. If you are just off the plane from Texas or Australia, or if you have had a hot day on the ski slopes or are coming down from a bungee jump, the thought of a cocktail in a beautifully sculpted ice cavern may be very appealing. But for the average European, particularly the Irish or the Scots, a bar made of ice? It's just like being back home in mid-Feb. Besides, the pub is exactly where Europeans go to get away from the stuff. That said it is the unusual experience that counts and it is indeed impressive. Entry costs $30 includes the first drink and you are of course kitted out with warm jackets and gloves. Naturally this is more a tourist attraction than a conventional bar, so don't expect to settle in for a session or a game of darts.

More conventional and popular with the upwardly mobile is the **Boiler Room** in the Steamer Wharf; **The Tatler**; **The Mall**; and the hard-to-find **The Bunker**, Cow Lane. **The Lone Star**, Brecon St, and **Altitude**, Shotover St, are well-known places to acquaint oneself with the opposite sex. They all provide regular live music and DJ and are the favoured haunts of the younger set.

Clubs
As far as late-night drinking and dancing goes, try **Chico's**, at the bottom of the Mall (open until 0230); **The Tardis**; and **The Bunker**, Cow Lane. **Sub Culture**, Church St, is a new and popular nightclub.

If you fancy some 70s, 80s and 90s music try the new **12 Bar** on Church Lane. Despite the music, it is contemporary and sophisticated. **The World**, Shotover St, and bars on Brecon St are the most commercial chat-up (or throw-up) venues with regular happy hours. Most stay open until about 0230.
Kiwi Crawl, T021-994139, www.kiwicrawl.co.nz, is a Queenstown-based operator that offers organized nights out visiting 6 bars with a free drink in each, from $25. There also a cruise option from $35.

☻ Entertainment

Queenstown *p615, map p621*
Cinema
Reading Cinema, The Mall, T03-442 9990.
Queenstown Wharf Casino, Steamer Wharf, T03-441 1495. 1100- 0300.

☻ Festivals and events

Queenstown *p615, map p621*
Throughout the year there are many multi-sport events from triathlons to mountain traverses, peak to peaks, jet-boat races, marathons and even horse cavalcades. For more details visit www.queenstown-nz.co.nz.
Jan Glenorchy Races (1st Sat in Jan). A local affair regarded as reflecting Glenorchy's true colours as a wild west frontier town.
Mar Gibbston Harvest Festival is a food and wine festival with a little barrel rolling thrown in, www.gibbstonharvestfestival.com.
Arrowtown Autumn Festival (late Mar) and the **Ben Lomond Assault** (late Mar). Colourful and exhausting race to the town's famous 1747 m lookout.
Jun/Jul Lindauer Queenstown Winter Festival, www.winterfestival.co.nz. Queenstown's most famous and popular event (10 days), which of course has its focus on skiing, but also involves many other forms of entertainment from live concerts, arts and fashion events to madcap races.
Sep Spring Carnival (mid-Sep). More extreme and zany ski competitions at the Remarkables Ski Area.
Oct Queenstown Jazz Festival (Labour weekend), www.asbjazzfest.co.nz.
Dec Christmas and particularly New Year see the town a-buzz with Kiwis and foreigners.

☻ Shopping

Queenstown *p615, map p621*
Outside Sports, Shotover St, T03-442 8883, www.outdoorsports.co.nz. 0700-2200. For new sports/outdoor/ski equipment.
Small Planet Recycling Co, 17 Shotover St, T03-442 6393. For second-hand outdoor and ski equipment.
Whitcoulls, Beach St, T03-442 9739. The principal bookshop and stationer in town.

Queenstown *p615, map p621*

Quirky Queenstown Historical Walking Tours, T03-4420572. In the town itself you can learn something of its interesting past on the 1-hr historical perambulation followed by a welcome libation in McNeill's Cottage Brewery. Trips depart from the west end of the Mall at 1130, 1330 and 1530. The immediate Queenstown area offers many excellent walks from 1-hr to ½-day. The **DoC Visitor Centre** on Shotover St has displays and can advise on the local alternatives.
Remarkable Experience, T03-4098578, www.remarkableexperience.co.nz. Operates a fully restored open-topped 1937 Chevrolet convertible bus on a 3-hr tour visiting local sights including Arrowtown (see page 634) and Lake Hayes among others and the al fresco factor just adds to the experience. Departs daily 0930 and 1330, $145, child $78.
Skyline (Gondola) Complex, T03-441 0101, www.skyline.co.nz. Among the multitude of activities available at the Skyline above the town is the **Luge**, the rather tame cousin of the famous course in Rotorua. The gondola trip and 5 rides will cost $45, child $35 (0930-dusk). Also based at the Skyline, is one of the few opportunities to enjoy a **Maori Concert and Feast**. If you missed out in Rotorua this is your chance. The performance alone costs from $53, child $27 (includes gondola) while the performance and dinner costs from $104, child $50.
Sunrise Balloons, T03-442 0781, www.ballooningnz.com. Offers a 3-hr flight with champagne breakfast for $375, child $245. It is expensive, but given the scenery it is a great venue (0530 summer/0830 winter).

Bungee jumping
The first commercial bungee jump in the world was created at **Kawarau Bridge**, about 12 km east of Queenstown, by A J Hackett and associates in 1988. Although perhaps the most famous spot and certainly the most

accessible, at 43 m it is now dwarfed by most of the others. Since 1988 Hackett has created several other sites in and around Queenstown. The 47-m urban **Ledge Bungee**, beside the Skyline complex above Queenstown is the baby of the set while the mightiest and certainly the best, is the awesome 134-m **Nevis Highwire**. Jump prices range from $175 for the Kawarau and a cool $250 for the Nevis. This includes a T-shirt, but videos are usually extra. Given the prices and the fact you may only ever do it once the best advice is to 'go high' – the Nevis – it is simply rude not to.
A J Hackett, at 'The Station', corner of Shotover and Camp sts, T0800-2864958/ T03-442 4008, www.ajhackett.com. Daily 0700-2100, winter 0800-2000. For all bungee bookings.

Bungee variations
It hasn't taken long for the Great Adrenaline Professors to realize that wetting your pants at high speed need not necessarily occur at vertical angles alone, so the fiendishly clever and rich chappies have now come up with various cunning 'swing' contraptions. These are also wonderful fun and require the same hefty dry cleaning bills.
Ledge Sky Swing, Skyline Complex, book through A J Hackett (see Bungee jumping, above). At 47 m high, this is the more sedate option, from $120 including gondola.
Shotover Canyon Swing, T0800-279464/ T03-4426990, www.canyonswing.co.nz. This is the real monster. We won't get into the technical details, suffice to say that's it's a 109-m-high, 60-m freefall, 200-m arc using various jump styles from the 'Backwards', 'Forwards', the 'Elvis Cutaway' and even the 'Gimp Boy Goes to Hollywood'. Prices start at $199, spectators $20.

Canyoning
Note: canyoning is not for the agoraphobic or the 'damn it darling, my shoes are wet' type.
Routeburn Canyoning, T03-441 3003, www.gycanyoning.co.nz. Offers an attractive package that involves a part walk and

canyoning session on the Routeburn Track near Glenorchy. As well as the great 30-min walk and scenery along the initial stage of the track the trip involves abseiling, scrambling, rappelling and plunging your way down a mountain river. Routeburn trip from $195.

Children's activities

If you have kids and want to do the family thing, or conversely leave them in somebody else's capable hands, try one of the companies below. A fine resource for sourcing other activities for children is the *Kidz Go* magazine, available free from the VIC (I-Site), www.kidzgo.co.nz.

Activecare Childcare Agency, T03-442 0409, www.activecarenz.com. Can organize qualified care around Queenstown.

Family Adventures, T03-442 8836, www.familyadventures.co.nz. Offers full- or half-day 'sedate' rafting trips for families from $155, child $110.

Climbing, abseiling and mountaineering

The possibilities are endless, and the Mt Aspiring National Park provides world-class venues. Most of the facilities and operators are based in Wanaka.

Queenstown Events Centre, Joe O'Connell Dr, Frankton, T03-442 3664, www.qt events.co.nz. Has a 12-m climbing wall, $13, child $10, Mon-Fri 0900-2100, Sat-Sun 0900-1700. There are also instructor supervised nights Mon-Thu 1900-2100.

Summits Mountain Guiding, T03-442 9551, www.summits.co.nz. Offers a wide variety of trips from day-walks to expeditions and instruction courses. It also guides on Mt Aspiring, Mt Cook and Mt Tasman. Prices range from about $250 for a full-day of rock climbing with instruction (depending on numbers) to about $4,750 for a 6-day ascent of Mount Cook.

Cruising

MV Yvalda, T027-434 5555. Offers 2-hr or overnight lake cruises aboard the lovingly restored 1936 ketch. Call for schedules/prices.

Real Journeys, beside the Steamer Wharf, T0800-656503, www.realjourneys.co.nz. It won't take you long to spot the delightful **TSS Earnslaw** (TSS stands for Two Screw Steamer), plying the waters of Lake Wakatipu from the Steamer Wharf in Queenstown Bay. The **TSS Earnslaw**, named after the highest peak in the region, Mt Earnslaw (2819 m), was launched at the most southerly end of Lake Wakatipu, Kingston, in 1912 and burns 1 ton of coal per hour. Despite her propensity to belch half of New Zealand's carbon emissions quota into the air she is a lovely sight indeed and there are a number of cruising options available. A standard 1 hr 35-min cruise heads west across the lake to its southern edge to the Walter Peak Station. It departs from the Steamer Wharf, Oct-Apr every 2 hrs from 1000-2000 (reduced winter schedule), from $48, child $20. A 3½-hr cruise, plus a farm tour of the Walter Peak Station which is designed to give an insight into typical Kiwi farming life (and to access lots of affectionate animals), costs $68, child $20. With a BBQ it's $93/$45. A 4-hr evening dinner cruise costs $115, child $57.50.

There are also 40-min horse trekking and wagon rides available at Walter Peak from $105 (all inclusive). Numerous cruise/bus and cruise/fly options on Milford and Doubtful Sounds operate out of Queenstown (see Milford and Doubtful Sound, page 668 and page 673).

Fishing

The region provides some excellent trout and salmon fishing, and there are numerous guides offering simple half-day to full-day heli-fishing trips. Prices vary from around $130 per person for a 2-hr trip, to $450-650 for the full day. Heli trips range from half-day for $850 to a full day for $3,500, both for 2 people. A compulsory fishing licence costs $21per day.

Trout Stalkers, T0275-226966, www.trout-stalkers.co.nz.

Over the Top Helicopters, T03-442 2233, www.flynz.co.nz.

Queenstown Fishing Guides, T03-442 5363, www.wakatipu.co.nz.

Stu Dever, T03-442 6371,
www.fishing-queenstown.co.nz.

Flightseeing

There are numerous options available and
you are advised to shop around. If you don't
have time to reach **Milford Sound** by road
then a scenic flight is highly recommended.
Note that there are numerous fly-cruise-fly
and bus-cruise-fly options on offer to Milford.
Other flightseeing options include **Mt Cook**
and the glaciers, **Mt Aspiring National Park**
and the **Catlins Coast**. Prices range from a
30-min local flight costing from $195 to the
full 4-hr Milford Sound and Mt Cook
experience, from $395; shop around. Fixed-
wing operators offering flights to Milford and
Fiordland are listed below. See also helicopter
flights, and *Lord of the Rings* flights, below.
Air Fiordland, T03-442 3404,
www.airfiordland.com.
Air Milford, T03-442 2351, www.airmilford.
co.nz. A small personable company with lots
of local knowledge and a flexible itinerary.
Air Wakatipu, T03-442 3148,
www.airwakatipu.com.
Glenorchy Air, T03-442 2207,
www.glenorchy.net.nz.
Milford Sound Scenic Flights, T03-442
3065, www.milfordflights.co.nz.

Helicopter flights

Prices range from a 20-min local flight across
the Remarkables from $200, to the full 'Milford
Extravaganza' from around $700. For more
information on flightseeing trips to Milford
Sound and Fiordland see Milford page 664.
Glacier Southern Lakes, T03-442 3016/
T0800-801616, www.heli-flights.co.nz.
The Helicopter Line, T03-442 3034/
T0800-500575 www.helicopter.co.nz.
Heliworks, T03-441 4011/T0800-464354,
www.heliworks.co.nz.
Over The Top Helicopters, T0800-123359/
T03-442 2233, www.flynz.co.nz . Provides a
great range of Milford-Queenstown
heli-fishing and heli-skiing options.

Golf

Arrowtown (see page 634) has a nice course
at Centennial Av, T03-442 1719, from $45.
Frisbee Golf Course, Queenstown Gardens.
Of course Queenstown would have one of
these, but don't be surprised if a dog
disappears with your frisbee. Contact **Outside
Sports**, Shotover St, T03-442 8883, $2, who
sell frisbees, but no dog treats.
Millbrook Resort, Malaghan's Rd,
Arrowtown, T03-441 7010,
proshop@millbrook.co.nz. One of the best
courses in New Zealand. It was designed by
former Kiwi ace Bob Charles and opened in
1993. It is renowned for its long fairways,
water hazards and, of course, its views. Green
fees from $135.

Horse trekking

For other operators see Glenorchy, page 637.
Moonlight Stables, 15 mins from
Queenstown near Lake Hayes, T03-442 1240,
www.moonlightcountry.co.nz. A 2½-hr ride
costs from $99, child $65. Full day treks,
fishing trips also available.

There are other options at Glenorchy (see
page 637) or a trip in combination with a
lake cruise (*TSS Earnslaw*) and a visit to
Walter Peak from $105 (see Cruising above).

Horse and carriage rides are available in
town from $25; depart Steamer Wharf
1200-1600 and 1800-late (seasonal).

Jet boating

Jet boating is one of the 'Big 4' activities in
Queenstown and, other than the thrills of the
precipitous Shotover Gorge, there are also
independent operations on the Kawarau and
the superb aesthetics of the Dart River.
Shotover Jet, The Station, Shotover St,
T03-442 8570/T0800-SHOTOVER, www.shot
overjet.com. The original company, having
been in existence for over 30 years, offers the
almost 'must-do' operation on the Shotover
River – the only folks permitted to do so on
the lower reaches. It's an efficient, safe and
thrilling 30-min, 70-kph 'blat' down the river
– and intermittently shocking as you are

given the impression of coming perilously close to rock walls and jagged logs. The highlights of all the trips are the superb 360° turns that always soak some poor soul in the boat. Shotover Jet picks up from town several times a day for the 15-min ride to the riverside. From $109, child $69.

Other companies include: **Kawarau Jet**, Marine Parade (lakeside), T0800-529272/ T03-442 6142, www.kjet.co.nz in combination with **Twin River Jet**. Both zoom out across Queenstown Bay and down the Kawarau and up the lower reaches of the Shotover; 1 hr from $95, child $55. **Dart River Safaris** (recommended) in Glenorchy (see page 635) offer one of the best scenic jet-boating trips in the world; 3-6 hrs from $199, child $99 to $279, child $179 (includes transport).

Kayaking

Some superb day to multi-day sea kayaking is offered on Milford (see page 669) and Doubtful Sounds (see page 672). Locally kayaks can usually be hired on the waterfront. **Funyak Trips**, on the Dart River, see page 638. Offers the very enjoyable 'blow-up carrot'; full-day costs from $279 including transport.

Lord of the Rings flights

An addition to the many local flightseeing options is the *Lord of the Rings* 'Trilogy Trail' offered by the personable owners and staff of **Glenorchy Air**, Queenstown Airport, T03-442 2207, www.glenorchy.net.nz, www.trilogytrail.com, POA. This down to earth company has been around for many years and were regularly utilized by the *Rings* cast and crew during extensive filming in the region. The 2½-hr Trilogy Trail takes in the mountains and valleys of Skippers Canyon and the Rees-Dart, with a landing near Paradise (quite literally), and then a journey south to Mavora Lakes with plenty of informative commentary and behind the scenes stories as you go. Given the aesthetics one cannot fail to be awestruck, even if such

fictional location names as Isengard, Lothlorien, Amon Hen and Fanghorn Forest mean very little. Even without the complex world of Tolkien to fuel your imagination this has to be one of the most spectacular and affordable scenic flight experiences in the world. There is also an extended 7-hr Trilogy Trail offered, taking in other locations including the spectacular Rangitata Valley-Mt Sunday ('Edoras') from $820.

Massage

If you simply can't take any more action, try a soothing massage or a beauty treatment with **Body Sanctum**, 12 Man St, T03-4428006, www.bodysanctum.co.nz, or **Hush Spa**, Level 2, corner of Gorge and Robins Rds, T03-4090901, www.hushspa.co.nz. Massage treatments start at 30 min from $70. Also worth considering are the **Onsen Hot Pools**, 9351/160 Arthur's Point Rd, Arthur's Point, T03-4425707, www.onsen.co.nz.

Mountain biking

There are many options, from the manic heli-bike to the low level mundane. One increasingly popular option is to cycle around the lake stopping for a night at Kinloch Lodge (see page 636). Note that permission needs to be sought from Greenstone Elfin Bay station, T027-442 9901, to transit through their property, though it is possible to circuit the head of the lake and take the Earnslaw back to Queenstown. For bike rentals see Transport, page 633.

Fat Tyre Adventures, T0800-328897/ T027-2262822, www.fat-tyre.co.nz. Offers a range of local trips and tracks from 4-hr easy to moderate, $195, and heli-biking from $449. **Vertigo Mountain Biking**, 4 Brecon St, T0800-837846/T03-442 8378, www.vertigobikes.co.nz. Offers various track adventures from the local Gondola Downhill Tour from $149 to heli/bike combo adventures taking in backcountry farm tracks and the Remarkables, from $349.

Snow business

Queenstown is as much a winter ski resort as it is a summer madhouse. From June to September the two local ski fields of Coronet Peak and the Remarkables spring into action.

Coronet Peak (1649 m) is the larger of the two and the more accessible (25 minutes via SH6 west and Lower Shotover Road). It also has a longer season, night skiing (Friday and Saturday 1600-2200), and a brasserie, bar, café and crèche. Slopes are suitable for all levels, with intermediate skiers being the best catered for. A day lift pass costs $95, youth (7-17) $52, under 7's free, T03-442 4620.

The Remarkables ski field is higher (1935 m) and accessed from SH6, south of Frankton (45 minutes). The road is steep and often requires snow chains. Shuttle buses from Queenstown are recommended. Being the highest in the region, the snow conditions are often superior, and then, of course, there are the stunning views. Slopes cater for all levels of skier and snowboarder as well as cross-country. A day lift pass costs $89, youth (7-17) $49, under 10s, free, T03-442 4615.

Also within range of Queenstown are the **Cardrona** (45 km), T03-443 7411, www.cardrona.com, and **Treble Cone**, T03-4437443, www.treblecone.co.nz (95 km).

Getting there From Queenstown the standard fares toCoronet are around $21, Remarkables $21 and Cardrona $41return. See Ins and outs, page 615, for transport options. For detailed information on both ski fields get your hands on the *Queenstown Winter Resort Guide* from the VIC (I-Site), or visit the website www.nzski.com or www.snow.co.nz.

Rental equipment One-day ski or snowboard and boots $47, youth $36. Group lessons: 2 hrs from $58, youth $43; personal lessons from $95 per hr. For hire shops, see Directory, page 633.

Snow reports For snow reports, T0900-99766 ($0.99/min), www.met service.co.nz, or the resort websites.

Off-road, rallying, trial-bike and snowmobile adventures

Cardrona Adventure Park, Cardrona (Highway 89) near Wanaka, T03-443 6363, www.adventurepark.co.nz. Here you can try conventional ATV tours of 1-3 hrs from $95 or choose to ride in a range of overly rubber-endowed, customized vehicles from trucks to buses. Guided tours from $175 (10 mins), self-drive from $250 (10 mins), family rides from $80 (15 mins). Kids and families are well catered for.

Nevis Snowmobile Adventures, T03-445 0843, ww.snowmobilenz.co.nz. Self-drive or guided heli/snowmobile adventures available in winter. Expensive but great fun (mid Jun-Oct), 3 hrs costs from $560.

New Zealand Nomad Safaris, T0800-688222/T03-442 6699, www.nomadsafaris.co.nz. Offers an excellent range of 4WD tours taking in some of the stunning scenery used in *LOTR*, including the stunning scenery around Glenorchy and the Dart River Valley, which was used as the backdrop to Isengard and Lothlorien; departs 0830 and 1330, from $149, child $75. The 'Wakatipu Tour', concentrates on local sites from the stunning vistas over Deer Park Heights (used as the dramatic backdrop to the scene depicting the escaping refugees of Rohan) and a number of other locations used in the trilogy; departs 0830 and 1330, prices from $149, child $75. The tours are very relaxed with entertaining knowledgeable guides some of whom were extras during filming. Other non-*LOTR* orientated trips include a 4-hr tour taking in the former gold-mining remnants along the 'entertaining' Skippers Canyon Rd from $149and quad bike tours from $220.

Off Road Adventures, 61A Shotover St, T03-442 7858, www.offroad.co.nz. Conventional 4WD or Quad tours self-drive or guided from $140. Kids welcome. Trail bike hire also available.

Parapenting, paraflying and hang-gliding

When you arrive in Queenstown it won't be long before you see the colourful chutes of the tandem paragliders descending gracefully down into the town from Bob's Peak and the Skyline Complex. It's a wonderful way to see the views, but all a bit 'Queenstown' when your instructor answers his mobile phone mid-flight. Flights are also available from Coronet Peak.

Coronet Peak Tandem Paragliding and Hang Gliding, T0800-467325/T03-442 2988, www.tandemhangliding.com. Tandems from Coronet (15 mins) from $179, hang-gliding from $189.

Paraflights Queenstown, T03-441 2242, www.paraflights.co.nz. If you would rather be alone and feel safer over water, then you might like to try paraflying across the lake. 20 mins tandem from $95, child $75, solo from $129.

Queenstown Commercial Paragliders, T0800-759688/T03-4418581, www.para glide.net.nz. 8-12 minute flights from the Skyline (gondola) Complex above the town, from $185.

Extreme Air, T0800-727245. If the tandem flight has you hooked you might then like to have lessons here. Day (5-hr) course from $195.

Sky Trek, T0800-759873/T03-409 0625, www.skytrek.co.nz. Similar hang gliding trips with the highest locations, from $210.

Rafting

There is a glut of rafting operators, all trying to lure you with their ineluctable inflatables. Shop around for the best deal.

Challenge Rafting, T0800- 423836/ T03-442 7318, www.raft.co.nz. Offers half-day or raft combo trips, again on the Shotover and

Kawarau from $175. Minimum age 13.

Extreme Green Rafting, T03-442 8517, www.nzraft.com. Offers similar options.

Family Adventures, T03-442 8836, is a family and children's rafting adventure specialist, see Children's activities, above.

Queenstown Rafting, T03-442 9792, www.rafting.co.nz. Plies the rapids of the Shotover, Kawarau and a 3-day Landsborough with such enchanting highlights as 'The Toilet' and 'The Sharks Fin'. Departs Queenstown 0815 and 1315, half- to full-day conventional, heli or in combination with other 'Big 4 Activity Combos', $175-1495.

River sledging and surfing

River surfing is the cunningly simple concept of replacing a raft with your own personal body board. It is great fun and provides a far more intimate experience with the water. River sledging involves more drifting as opposed to surfing and provides more buoyancy. Companies include:

Frogz Have More Fun, Wanaka, see page 652, T0800-437649/T03-443 8244, www.frogz.co.nz. Pick-up from Queenstown twice daily. 4-5 hrs (2 hrs on the water) from $149 and a full day dunking from $370.

Mad Dog, T03-442 7797, www.riverboarding.co.nz. Also offer jet ski and rock jumping adventures.

Serious Fun, T0800-737468/T03-442 5262, www.riversurfing.co.nz.

Tandem skydiving

Queenstown offers one of the most scenic venues on earth, for the 'bungee without the bounce' – or the elastic rope for that matter. **Nzone** 35 Shotover St, T0800-376796/ T03-442 5867, www.nzone.biz. This slick high-profile operator offers jumps from 9-15,000 ft from $249. Allow 3 hrs.

Tramping

Queenstown is a principal departure point for the **Routeburn, Greenstone-Caples** and **Rees-Dart Tracks**. For detailed information, hut and transportation bookings visit the Information and Track Centre (see Tourist information, page 616). Another attractive local option is the **Ben Lomond trek** or **Cecil Peak** (see box, page 619).

Guided Walks New Zealand, T03-442 7126, www.nzwalks.com. A very professional outfit, again offering a flexible range of guided options from 2-hr local nature walks (from $103) to 3- to 9-hr 'samplers' of the 'Great Walks' from $230.

Ultimate Hikes (Encounter Guided Day Walks), T0800-659255/T03-4501940, www.ultimate hikes.co.nz. A good company and offers guided walks on the Routeburn, Greenstone and Milford tracks from 1-6 days. A 3-day/2-night package on the Routeburn will cost from $1100 low season, $1240 high; Milford high season from $1950. It also offers a wide range of 10-hr day 'encounter' or multi-day options both locally on the Routeburn or further afield on the Milford or Mt Cook from $190, child $120.

Wine tours

Vineyard, garden and general sightseeing tours offer a more sedate diversion from the mainstream adrenaline activities.
Appellation Wine Tours, T03-442 0246, www.appellationcentral.co.nz. Takes you to local vineyards and further afield to the Cromwell vineyards. Half- to full-day from $155.
Queenstown Wine Trail, T03-441 3990, www.queenstownwinetrail.co.nz. Visits all the main Kawarau Valley vineyards, 3-5 hrs from $118. Also offers local garden tours, from $90.
Wine Time, T0508-946384, www.wine time.co.nz. Full- or half-day lunch and dinner tours, from $150, child $100.

❸ Transport

Queenstown *p615, map p621*
Airlines Air NZ, Queenstown Travel and Visitor Centre, Clocktower Shotover St,

T03-442 4100. **Bicycle hire** Vertigo, 4 Brecon St, T03-442 8378. **Car hire** There are a number of operators at the airport. In town Budget, Chester Building, corner of Shotover and Camp sts, T03-442 9274; Hertz, 1 Earl St, T03-442 4106; NZ Rent-A-Car, corner of Shotover and Camp sts, T03-442 7465; Pegasus, The Mall, T03-442 7176; Queenstown Rental Cars, Lucas Pl, Frankton, T03-441 4614; Thrifty, Queenstown Airport, T03-442 8100. **Taxi** AA Taxis, T03-441 8222; Alpine Taxi, T0800-442 6666; Queenstown Taxis, T03-442 7788; Prestige Tourist Services, T03-442 9803.

❸ Directory

Queenstown *p615, map p621*
Banks All the major banks are represented and ATMs are available in the Mall, Shotover St, Beach St, Rees St, Steamer Wharf and the O'Connell's Shopping Centre. **Currency exchange** There is a Travelex in the VIC (I-Site) and additional outlets at the BNZ, Rees St (daily 1000-2000); Travelex, corner of Camp St and The Mall; ANZ Postbank, Beach St. Travelex, at the airport, daily until 1900. **Internet** The E Café, 50 Shotover St. Internet Outpost, 27 Shotover St. Most outlets open 0900-2300. **Library** 10 Gorge Rd. **Medical services** Hospital, Douglas St, Frankton, T03-441 0015. No Accident and Emergency Department. Doctor, Athol St Surgery, T03-442 7566; Queenstown Medical Centre, 9 Isle St, T03-441 0500. **Outdoor equipment hire** Information and Track Centre, 37 Shotover St, T03-442 9708. **Police** Non-emergency, 11 Camp St, T03-441 1600. Emergency, T111. **Post office** 13 Camp St, T03-442 7670, Mon-Fri 0830-1730, Sat 0900-1600; post restante. **Ski and snowboard hire** Browns , 39 Shotover St, T03-442 4003; Snow Rental, 39 Camp St, T03-442 4187; Green Toad, 48 Camp St, T03-442 5311.

With time usually so short the vast majority of visitors to Queenstown tends to focus on the activities themselves, but if you have a day or two to spare and your own transport it is well worth Queenstown"s hinterland. To the north, at the head of Lake Wakatipu, the small and far less developed settlement of Glenorchy is the gateway to some of the country's most impressive scenery and several of its best tramping tracks, including the Routeburn, the Greenstone, Caples and Rees-Dart. But without even needing to don boots and gaiters you can explore the immediate area or partake in several activities including jet-boat trips, canoeing or horse trekking. The Dart River Basin reached almost legendary status when it was used as a set for the Lord of the Rings trilogy, but you don't need to know your Orcs from your Nazguls to appreciate its innate natural beauty.

The small former goldrush settlement of Arrowtown, which sits tucked away in the corner of the Wakatipu Basin, 23 km south of Queenstown, has a fascinating history that is now well presented in the village museum and complemented nicely with a main street that boasts a surprising number of fine shops, cafés, restaurants and pubs . ▸▸ For Sleeping, Eating and other listings, see pages 635-638.

Ins and outs

Getting there and around The Arrowtown **Double Decker Bus Tour** departs from the top of the Mall in Queenstown daily at 0930 and 1330, allowing one hour in Arrowtown and returning from outside the museum. It visits Lake Hayes and the Kawarau Bungee Bridge on the way, T03-441 4421, $48, child $20. **Backpacker Express**, 2 Oban St, T03-442 9939, info@glenorchyinfocentre.co.nz and **Buckley Transport**, T03-4428215, www.buckleytransport.co.nz, both offer a comprehensive transport system between Queenstown, Glenorchy and the major tramping track trailheads by road ($25 one way).

Tourist information **Arrowtown VIC (I-Site)** ⓘ *49 Buckingham St, Lakes District Museum building, T03-442 1824, www.museumqueenstown.com, daily 0900-1700.* The free brochures *Welcome to Historic Arrowtown* and *Historic Arrowtown* are comprehensive guides to the history and historic sites of the village and the surrounding area. If your intentions are merely to pass through Glenorchy on your way to one of the major tracks, you are advised to avail yourself of the information, and secure hut bookings, options at the Queenstown offices. Otherwise, for accommodation and activities, the **Glenorchy Store** in the Holiday Park on Oban St, can provide information. For general pre-visit information on Glenorchy, the VIC (I-Site) in Queenstown is your best bet, as well as the website, www.glenorchy.com. For information on the Routeburn, Greenstone and Caples Tracks, see Walking, page 638.

Arrowtown

Arrowtown provides some respite from the stress and adrenaline highs of Queenstown. Yet another former gold mining settlement, its pleasant tree-lined streets with their old historic buildings lie nestled below the foothills of the Crown Range. The origins of Arrowtown go back to 1862 when prospector William Fox made the first rich strike in the Arrow River Valley – a find that soon brought over 7000 other hopefuls to the area. The first few weeks of mining produced 90 kg alone. Although first called Fox's, once the settlement was firmly established it was renamed Arrowtown after the river that revealed its riches. Once the gold was exhausted, the town's economy was centred first on agriculture and, in more recent years, the more lucrative resource of tourism. Autumn (end of March) sees the village at its most colourful both in scenery and spirit when the hugely popular **Arrowtown Autumn Festival** takes place.

Sights The **Lakes District Museum and Gallery** ① *49 Buckingham St, T03-4421824, www.museumqueenstown.com, 0830-1700, $6, child $1,* offers plenty of insight into the 'calm before the storm', and then depicts the area's rather chaotic and feverish gold mining boom. For a small fee you can also hire out gold pans (with instruction sheet).

Outside the museum the tree-lined avenue of **Buckingham Street** reveals several old historic cottages. At the far end the **Chinese Settlement** offers further insight with several mud-walled huts, and a reconstruction of a general store. The Chinese were subjected to much prejudice and derision by the European miners and, much of the time, instead of seeking claims of their own, would sift through the tailings looking for fine gold undetected or simply left by the other miners. In the hills upriver from Arrowtown, and accessed via a difficult 13-km track, is the former mining settlement of **Macetown**. Its remnants are the focus for a number of interesting tours by foot, 4WD or on horseback.

Glenorchy

North of Queenstown (48 km) via the superb **Wakatipu Lake** scenic drive Is the tiny former frontier village of Glenorchy. Backed and surrounded on both sides by the rugged peaks of the **Fiordland** and **Aspiring National Park**, the glacier-fed **Rees** and **Dart Rivers** and ancient beech forests, it is little wonder it has been labelled the 'Gateway to Paradise'. Indeed, part of the attraction here, other than the pure scenic delights or activities is a visit to **Paradise** itself – an aptly named little farming settlement 20 km further north. So stunning are the mountain backdrops around here and so lacking in any signs of human habitation that the Dart River Valley became a principal filming venue for the *Lord of the Rings* trilogy as Isengard, home of the evil wizard Saruman, and the forests of Lothlorien.

Activities available in Glenorchy include jet boating and horse trekking. The village also serves as the main access point to the **Routeburn**, **Greenstone/Caples** and **Rees-Dart** tramping tracks. Both 4WD and scenic flight tours from Queenstown explore the *Lord of the Rings* film locations (see Queenstown Activities and tours, page 627).

◉ Around Queenstown listings

For Sleeping and Eating price codes and other relevant information, see Essentials pages 44-50.

● Sleeping

Arrowtown *p634*
The VIC has full listings of the many charming B&Bs in the village and its surrounds.
LL Arrowtown House Boutique Hotel, 10 Caernarvon St, T03-441 6008, www.arrowtownhouse.co.nz. In the original church grounds, this very smart boutique luxury hotel has 5 well-appointed en suites each with a private garden or balcony.
AL Pittaway's Cottage, 69 Buckingham St, T03-442 0441, www.romantic-cottages.co.nz/html/pittaway_s_cottage.html. A fully self-contained and refurbished 1875 miners cottage

with wood fire and double spa bath. Good value and within a short walk of the village centre.
AL-A Arrowtown Lodge , 7 Anglesea St, T03-442 1101, www.arrowtownlodge.co.nz. 4 cottage-style en suites all designed in keeping with the village's historic past.
AL-A Settlers Cottage Motel, 22 Hertford St, T0800-803801/T03-4421734, www.settlerscottage motel.co.nz. Characterful units and again good value.
AL-A Viking Lodge Motel, 21 Inverness Cres, T0800-181900/T03-442 1765, www.viking lodge.co.nz. Self-contained A-frame units and a pool. Good for small groups.
B New Orleans Hotel, 27 Buckingham St, T03-442 1745, www.neworleanshotel.co.nz. 9 comfortable en suites, right on the main street and with views across the river.

B-D Poplar Lodge Backpackers, 4 Merioneth St, T03-442 1466, www.poplarlodge.co.nz. Cosy and homely. Shared, doubles and twins, two double ensuites. Only a short stroll from the village centre, bike hire, WiFi and specialist camping and 4WD trips.

Motorcamps and campsites
B-D Arrowtown Holiday Park, 12 Centennial Av, T03-442 1876, www.arrowtownholiday park.co.nz. Recently redeveloped and only 600 m from the town centre offering full range of accommodation including flats, cabins, shared lodge, powered/tent sites and camp kitchen.

Glenorchy p635
LL Blanket Bay, T03-441 0115, www.blanketbay.com. One of the most celebrated luxury lodges in the region and with undoubtedly some of the best amenities and aesthetics in the country. International celebs are said to be frequently flown in here.
LL Glenorchy Lakehouse, corner Mull and Jetty sts, T03-442 7084, www.glenorchylake house.co.nz. If you are looking for a B&B look no further. This is a new 4-star rated luxury B&B and sister operation to the much lauded Kinloch Lodge. Lavish king and superking/ twin ensuites with deep bathtubs. Outdoor spa and uninterrupted views across the lake and mountains. There is also a small shop and café at the Lakehouse, serving great soup and snack foods as well as fair trade coffee.
AL-A Mount Earnslaw Motels, 87 Oban St, T03-442 6993, www.mtearnslawmotel. co.nz. Glenorchy's most modern motel offers tidy en suite units.
A Glenorchy Lodge, corner of Argyle and Mull sts, T03-442 9968, www.wakatipu.com. Offers 8 ski lodge-style en suites or standard rooms all with a shared lounge and open fire. There is also an in-house cafeand bar.
A-B Kinloch Lodge, T03-442 4900, www.kinlochlodge.co.nz. Historic lakeside lodge and the perfect base from which to explore the area before (and especially after) tramping the Routeburn or Greenstone

tracks. Tidy doubles (the heritage doubles are very small), twins and shared dorms, all the usual facilities as well as an outdoor hot tub, a café/restaurant and a small shop. Road or water taxi transport is available from Glenorchy and local activities arranged. Really well managed and a memorable stay is just about guaranteed.
A-D Glenorchy Hotel and Backpackers, across the road from Glenorchy Lodge on Mull St, T03-4429902, www.glenorchynz.com. Traditional New Zealand-style hotel doubles, en suites or a self-contained cottage. Also has backpacker dorms. The cheap in-house restaurant and bar is popular, with the outdoor upper-deck views proving a top spot.

② Eating

Arrowtown p634
Ψ Café Mondo, Ballarat Arcade, Buckingham St, T03-442 0227. Mon 1000-1730, Tue-Wed 0800-1730, Thu-Sun 0800-late. Popular for its traditional café-style breakfast or lunch and seems to attract a diverse crowd. The coffee is some of the best in the village and there is internet and occasional live music.
Ψ Saffron, 18 Buckingham St, T03-442 0131, www.saffronrestaurant.co.nz. Daily 1130- 2130. A very congenial atmosphere and an excellent reputation for its Pacific Rim menu.
Ψ Stables Café and Restaurant, 28 Buckingham St, T03-442 1818. Daily 1100-late. Older and more historic but especially popular for alfresco dining.
Ψ Arrowtown Bakery, 11 Ballarat Av, Buckingham St. Light snacks and great pies.
Ψ The Blue Door, 18 Buckingham St. Excellent little pub in the old European style, with cosy open fire and large leather settees.
Ψ New Orleans Hotel, Buckingham St. Recently renovated with cheap pub grub.
Ψ The Tap , 51 Buckingham St, T03-4421860. A resurrection of the Royal Oak Hotel with contemporary cuisine and a good ambience.
Ψ Wind in the Willows Bookshop Café, Ramshaw Lane (turn right at the top of

Buckingham St), near the river, T03-442 0055. Daily. For something more peaceful.

Glenorchy p635
♥ **Glenorchy Café**, Mull St, T03-442 9958. A funky little place that offers light snacks and a good breakfast – all of which can be enjoyed to the dulcet tones of 1980s hits, played on an ageing record player.
♥ **Kinloch Lodge**, (refer accommodation above), T03-442 4900, www.kinlochlodge.co.nz. Another fine choice and they offer water taxi transport across the lake from Glenorchy. Book ahead.

⊛ Festivals and events

Arrowtown p634
Apr/May Autumn Festival, T03-442 1570, www.arrowtownautumnfestival.org.nz. Brings locals and visitors together to celebrate autumn with various shows, arts and events.

O Shopping

Glenorchy p635
Made in Glenorchy Fur Products, Main St, www.glenorchy-fur.co.nz. Have you been wanting to get your dear mother or girlfriend that special homecoming present? Well, if so you have found ideal-presents-utopia. Of particular appeal is the fine range of possum fur nipple warmers. They are the genuine article and come in a fine array of colours. And should your mother or dearest not feel the urge to accept or indeed model them on a regular basis, then they will make a wonderful pair of eyeshades for the next flight back to New Zealand after the fall out. Just don't expect to make friends with the person sitting next to you.

▲ Activities and tours

Arrowtown p634
Gone Potty, 4 Norfolk St, T03-442 1085,

www.gonepotty.co.nz. If it is raining you might like to consider madly colouring your own ceramic. The finished product is fired for you and can be picked up within a few days.
New Zealand Nomad Safaris, T03-442 6699, www.nomadsafaris.co.nz. An exhilarating 2-hr (4½ hrs from Queenstown) 4WD trip to Macetown. There are over 25 river crossings and a stop for a spot of gold panning in the Arrow River (summer only), from $149. Also popular 'Safari of the Rings Tours' $149 (see Queenstown Activities and tours, page 618).

Glenorchy p635
Flightseeing
Glenorchy Air, T03-442 2207, www.glenorchy.net.nz. Flightseeing trips around both national parks and to Milford Sound, as well as the popular *Lord of the Rings* 'Trilogy Trail Trip'.

Horse trekking
Dart Stables, Glenorchy, T0800-4743464/ T03-442 5688, www.dartstables.com. Several attractive options including 2-hr trek ($100), 5-hr 'Ride of the Rings' ($165), and 2-day/ 1-night ($595) horse-trekking trips through scenic forest trails near the Rees and Dart rivers. This is a great way to really experience the *Lord of the Rings* locations.
High Country Horses, T03-442 9915, www.high-country-horses.co.nz. Based in the Rees Valley offering a range of options amid the stunning aesthetics of the Paradise Station. Good for small groups, 2 hrs from $95.

Jet boating
Other than the stunning scenery and the services on offer to the tramping fraternity, the big attraction in Glenorchy is the jet-boating operations that ply the **Dart River**. Unlike the highly commercial rides of the Shotover and Kawarau in Queenstown, the Dart penetrates parts of the **Mt Aspiring National Park** not accessible by road, and provides one of the most scenic jet-boat trips in the world. Combos are worth considering including reductions on a Milford Sound

fly/cruise/fly; horse trekking; 3-hr guided walk and a 4WD gold mining heritage trip to the ghost town of Sefferton. Note there is a bad weather refund policy on all trips.

Dart River Safaris, Mull St, T0800-327853/ T03-442 9992, www.dartriver.co.nz, transport provided from Queenstown. There are 2 excursions on offer: the 6-hr 'Safari' involves a wonderfully scenic ride to Glenorchy by bus, then a 1½ hr fun-filled jet-boat trip upriver followed by a short stroll through native beech forest at the start of the Rees/Dart Track. From there you transfer to 4WD to negotiate the back roads past the settlement of Paradise taking in the 2 main *Lord of the Rings* film locations on the way back, from $229, child $129 including transport.

The 'Wilderness Adventure Trip' is 2½ hrs of pure jet-boating going higher up the Dart River, from $199, child $99 including transport from Queenstown. Departs Queenstown daily 0740 and 1140; Glenorchy 0900 and 1330.

Also on offer is the wilderness **'Funyak'** (www.funyaks.co.nz), which is part jet boat (32 km, 1¼-hrs), part paddle (2 hrs) on a blow-up carrot (actually a kayak), $279, child $179, including transport from Queenstown. It's a great day out and the scenery is very memorable. Lunch is included (departs Queenstown 0800; Glenorchy 0900).

Walking
If you wish to explore the area under your own steam there are several short walks on offer immediately around Glenorchy, with the 2-km wetlands boardwalk (**Glenorchy Walkway**) just at the northern outskirts of the town (accessed from Islay St) being particularly recommended. The reflections and views of **Mt Earnslaw** are superb and there is an abundance of birdlife. By road you can head north of Glenorchy and explore the **Rees** or **Dart River (Routeburn) valleys**, or better still visit **Paradise** (the surrounding fields were the film location for Isengard and Lothorien) and head to the western trailhead of the **Rees-Dart Tramping Track**. From the trailhead, you can also take a short walk through the beech forest on the tramping track's first section. Again the views of Mt Earnslaw from the Paradise Rd are excellent and you can also have some fun with silly photos at the Paradise Road sign. For more information on walking in the area contact the DoC visitor centre in Queenstown.

● Directory

Internet Café Mondo, see Eating, page 636. Also at the library, Buckingham St, Mon-Fri 1000-1700, Sat 1030-1230.

Internet Glenorchy Café, Mull St. **Postal agent** Mobil Station, Mull St.

Wanaka and around → *Colour map 5, B/C2 Population: 4,500.*

Wanaka is almost unfeasibly pleasant and has to rank as one of the most desirable places in New Zealand. With the lake of the same name lapping rhythmically at its heels and its picture-postcard mountain backdrops – bordering as it does the Mount Aspiring National Park – it is easy to understand why Wanaka is such a superb place to visit, or indeed live. In recent years Wanaka has seen a boom in both real estate sales and tourism, but it is reassuring that its manic neighbour, Queenstown, will always keep growth in check. As it is, Wanaka is just perfect: not too busy, not too quiet; developed but not spoilt, and a place for all to enjoy. Although now you would never guess it, Wanaka's history goes back to the 1860s when it played an important role as a service centre for the region's itinerant gold miners. Today, its principal resources are activities and its miners are tourists. Year-round, there is a multitude of things to do from watersports and tramping in summer to skiing in winter. But it can also be the perfect place to relax and recharge your batteries beside the lake. Wanaka is that kind of town. ▸▸ *For Sleeping, Eating and other listings, see pages 644-654.*

Ins and outs

Getting there
Wanaka is accessed via Queenstown airport, which is served twice daily by **Air New Zealand Link**, T0800-737000. The airfield for the Wanaka Region is 11 km east of the town via SH6. **Aspiring Air**, T03-443 7943, www.nz-flights.com, flies between Queenstown and Wanaka.
Wanaka is 424 km southwest of Christchurch via SH1 and SH8; 276 km northwest of Dunedin via SH8; and 117 km north of Queenstown via SH8 and SH6. Alternatively, it's 70 km from Queenstown via the Cardrona Valley Road. Wanaka is served daily by **Intercity**, T03-443 1233 (Christchurch/Dunedin); **Atomic Shuttles**, T03-349 0697 (Christchurch/Dunedin/Queenstown), and **Southern Link**, T0508-458835, www.southernlinkcoaches.co.nz (Dunedin/Christchurch via Wanaka and Tekapo). **Nakedbus.com** offers cheap internet fares to Christchurch and Dunedin. **Wanaka Connextions**, www.time2.co.nz, offer services to Queenstown /Dunedin/Middlemarch and Invercargill from $25. **Intercity** services can be booked at the VIC (I-Site).
All the major bus companies heading up or down the west coast pass through Makarora. **Mount Cook Landline**, T0800-800904, serves Christchurch via Mount Cook linking with intercity services.

Getting around
Local shuttle services are available to Wanaka airfield ($12), the ski fields (from $35 return), local sights (Puzzling World from $6) and the Mount Aspiring trailheads (from $55). **Alpine Coachlines Wanaka** (Outside), 17 Dunmore St, T03-443 7966, www.alpinecoachlines.co.nz, have ski field and trailhead connections (Raspberry Creek, twice daily 0915 and 1400 from $35, Mount Roy $15, Diamond Lake $20) and offers a drive up–bike back option.

Tourist information
Wanaka VIC (I-Site) ① *in the Log Cabin on the lakefront, 100 Ardmore St, T03-443 1233, www.lakewanaka.co.nz, daily 0830-1830 (winter 0930-1630)*. This office also administers most of the local activity and adventure bookings through **Lakeland Adventures**, T0508-525352/T03-443 7495, www.lakelandadventures.co.nz. There is also a café on site that overlooks the lake. The **DoC VIC (Wanaka)** ① *Upper Ardmore St at the junction with McPherson St, T03-443 7660, www.doc.govt.nz, daily 0830-1630*, deals with all national park/tramping hut bookings and local walks information. An up-to-date weather forecast is also available. **DoC VIC (Makarora)** ① *T03-443 8365, daily 0800-1700 (closed weekends in winter)*, has information on the northern sector of Mount Aspiring National Park, Haast Pass, local short walks, and also issues hut passes. Given the isolation and the potential for very wet weather conditions in the area you are advised to consult DoC before embarking on any of the major walks or tramps. Intentions sheets are provided. **Oamaru VIC (I-Site)** ① *corner of Itchen and Thames sts, T03-434 1656, www.visitoamaru.co.nz, Mon-Fri 0900-1800 (1700 Easter-Nov), Sat-Sun 1000-1700 (1600 Easter-Nov)*. The centre has town maps and a wealth of information surrounding the historical buildings, local tours and things to see and do. The leaflet *Historic Oamaru* is useful, and local DoC walks leaflets are available. Note the penguin colony has its own **Information Centre** ① *base of MacAndrew Wharf (Waterfront Rd), T03-433 1195, www.penguins.co.nz*, can supply general information after hours.

Wanaka ⬤🐟🏠⚘▲⬤🏕 *pp644-654*.

One of the most immediate ways to get acquainted with the area is to make the short 45-minute climb up **Mount Iron** (240 m), just 2 km before the township on the main road. A stubborn lump of rock left by the glaciers, its 360° views are very impressive and provide an ideal way to get your bearings. The track is well marked and there is a car park by the roadside. Wanaka town centre borders the very pretty **Roy's Bay** that opens out beyond Ruby Island into the southern and indented bays of **Lake Wanaka**. The lake, which is 274 m above sea level and over 45 km long, occupies an ancient glacier bed. The aesthetics speak for themselves, but the glistening waters are also a prime attraction for boaties, water-skiers, kayakers and windsurfers. Even before you consider these activities you will find yourself simply admiring its beauty from Wanaka's attractive lakefront.

On the way into town you cannot fail to miss New Zealand's 'Leaning Tower of Wanaka', the centrepiece of **Stuart Landsborough's Puzzling World** ① *T03-443 7489, www.puzzlingworld.com, 0830-1730, $13, child $9, shop and café*. This is a madcap and puzzling conglomerate of mazes, illusions and holograms that is worth a muse. The toilets and 'Hall of Following Faces' are particularly engaging.

Some 8 km east on SH6, surrounding Wanaka airfield, are a couple of interesting museums. The **New Zealand Fighter Pilots Museum** ① *T03-443 7010, www.nzfpm.co.nz, daily 0900-1600, $10, child $5*, honours the lives (and deaths) of New Zealand Fighter Pilots, and provides a fascinating insight into wartime aviation. Immerse yourself in history through moving stories, view personal objects, and interactive and audio visual displays. The aircraft on display are rotated on a regular basis. The museum is the historical annexe of Wanaka's main biennial event, the 'Warbirds Over Wanaka International Air Show', which attracts thousands of spectators.

Also on site is the **Wanaka Transport and Toy Museum** ① *T03-443 8765, www.nttmuseum.co.nz, daily 0830-1700, $10, child $4*. It provides a good wet-weather option and is the largest privately owed vehicle and toy collection in New Zealand. There are over 15,000 items on display, including a staggering 9000 toys and 200 vehicles, comprising a tank, fire engines, trucks and the obligatory tractors. There is even a collection of spark plugs. Within the museum is **Wanaka Beerworks** ① *T03-443 1865, www.wanakabeerworks.co.nz, daily 0900- 1800, $5, child, free*. It is a craft brewery producing very palatable award-winning beers for many Central Otago outlets. There are daily tours at 1400, tastings and, of course, sales.

Near the airfield is the **Have a Shot complex** ① *T03-443 6656*, with its range of 'smack it or shoot it' activities from clay-birds to archery to golf. Prices range from $5-32.

North of Wanaka ⬤🐟▲ ›› *pp646-654*.

Hawea → *Colour map 5, B/C2*.

North of Wanaka on SH6 towards the west coast is **Lake Hawea** and the small holiday settlement of Hawea. Lake Hawea, like its neighbour Lake Wanaka, occupies an ancient glacier valley, and only a narrow strip of moraine known as 'The Neck' separates the two. Lake Hawea is noted for its fishing and beautiful scenery, with mountain reflections that disappear towards its remote upper reaches, 35 km north of Hawea settlement. The lake level was raised by 18 m in 1958 as part of the Clutha River hydropower system. Hawea itself nestles on its southern shore and, although a fairly new settlement, was formerly the site of an important and strategic Maori *pa*.

Makarora → *Colour map 5, B2.*

From Lake Hawea and the narrow Neck you revisit Lake Wanaka and head north through some beautiful 'Scottish' scenery to its northern edge and the small settlement of Makarora. At about 67 km from Wanaka, and almost on the border of the Otago and west coast regions, Makarora acts as the portal to the northern tramps and activities within the **Mount Aspiring National Park**. The village itself offers little except a small conglomerate

Wanaka

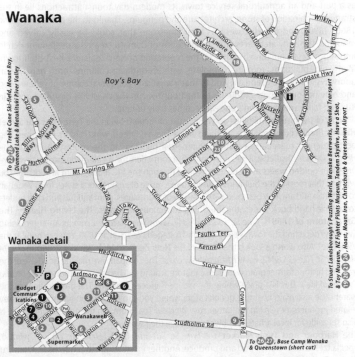

N

400 metres

400 yards

Sleeping
Aoturoa Lodge **20**
Aspiring Campervan
Park **1**
Aspiring Lodge Motel **2**
Brookvale Manor **3**
Cardrona **26**
Cardrona Alpine
Resort **27**

Clearbrook **6**
Edgewater Resort **5**
Glendhu Bay Motor
Camp **28**
Grand Mercure Oak
Ridge **9**
Holly's **23**
Lakeside Apartments **18**
Lake Wanaka Lodge **12**
Lime Tree Lodge **24**
Minaret Lodge **19**
Moorings **7**
Mt Aspiring **15**
Pleasant Lodge Top 10
Holiday Park **22**

River Run **21**
Te Wanaka Lodge **11**
Wanaka **14**
Wanaka Bakpaka **17**
Wanaka Lakeview
Holiday Park **16**
Wanaka Stonehouse **4**
YHA Purple Cow **10**

Eating
Ashrafs **6**
Bombay Palace **4**
Kai Whakapai **1**
Muzza's Bar **2**
Reef **7**

Relishes &
Apartment One **3**
Soulfood **12**
White House Café
& Bar **4**

Bars & clubs
Barluga **8**
Finchy's Restaurant
& Bar **5**
Paradiso Cinema
& Café **11**
Shooters **9**
Slainte **10**

of tourist services reflecting the desires of most visitors who either pass through quickly or head for the hills.

Oamaru ☺❷❶❽❸ » pp647-654.

Oamaru is an unusual and appealing coastal town on the South Island's east coast, somehow befitting its position gracing the shores of 'Friendly' Bay. Primarily functioning as a port and an agricultural service town, its modern-day tourist attractions lie in the strange combination of stone, architecture and penguins. Thanks to the prosperity of the 1860s-1890s, and the discovery of local limestone that could be easily carved and moulded, the early architects and stonemasons of Oamaru created a settlement rich in imposing, classic buildings, earning it the reputation of New Zealand's best-built town. Many old buildings remain, complete with Corinthian columns and gargantuan doorways, giving it a grand air. Add to that a small and congenial colony of yellow-eyed and blue penguins that waddle up to their burrows on the coast like dignified gents in 'tux and tails', and the town's appeal becomes truly unique.

Most of the historic buildings and associated attractions are in the **Tyne-Harbour Street Historic Precinct** (begins at the southern end of Thames Street), which boasts the largest and best-preserved collection of historic commercial buildings in the country. Although the *Historic Oamaru* leaflet will provide enough information for a self-guided tour, there are one-hour **guided walks** available on demand through the VIC (I-Site), from around $5. You will find that most of the buildings demonstrate a range of architectural styles from Venetian to Victorian and are now occupied with a variety of tourist lures, from antique and craft outlets to second-hand book stores, theatres, auto collections and cafés. The **Living History-The Great Storm of 1868** ⓘ *Tyne St, T0800-548344, www.livinghistorynz.com*, is an entertaining live show depicting the town's early days and is staged Wed-Sun at 1800. You can book at the Vic (I-Site). Also worth a look is the home of the **New Zealand Malt Whisky Company** ⓘ *14 Harbour St, T03-434 8842, www.nzmaltwhisky.co.nz*. The company are making good use of the vast and historic former grain warehouse to store around 600 barrels of maturing *uisge beatha* ('water of life'). This is a place where the silence is indeed 'golden'. The ground floor of the warehouse also plays host to a general store where you can muse upon a range of whiskey related products, or relax in the rather cosy Whiskey Tea Room. On the upper levels space is also set aside for local artists to showcase and sell their work.

The **Harbour and Tyne Market** ⓘ *2 Tyne St, Sat-Sun 1000-1600 (Sun only in winter)*, specializes in local crafts, food and produce. Another interesting attraction is the **Oamaru Steam Train** ⓘ *T03-434 7525, www.oamaru-steam.org.nz*, which is lovingly owned and operated by the local and very enthusiastic Steam and Rail Society. The shiny engine comes complete with a proud conductor in period uniform and hisses into action from beside the VIC (I-Site) to the Harbour on Sundays, 1100-1600, from $8, child $4. As if there were not enough history on the streets, the town is also home to the **North Otago Museum** ⓘ *58-60 Thames St, T03-434 1652, www.northotagomuseum.co.nz, Mon-Fri 1030-1630, Sat/Sun 1300-1630, donation*, which has a modest collection, focusing on Maori history and the early settlers. Of special interest are the information and displays about 'Oamaru Stone', the white limestone for which the town is so famous.

In one of Oamaru's original banks is the **Forrester Art Gallery** ⓘ *9 Thames St, T03-434 1653, www.forrestergallery.com, daily 1030-1630, donation*. It features local contemporary works as well as national and international touring exhibitions. The VIC (I-Site) has listings of other notable galleries in the area.

There are a number of historic homesteads that are open to the public, including the Victorian country mansion, **Burnside** ⓘ *T03-432 4194*; the **Tokarahi** ⓘ *T03-431 2500*, and the Oamaru stone buildings of the **Totara Estate** ⓘ*T03-434 7169*, *www.totaraestate.co.nz, daily 0900-1700, $7 child $2*. Most offer regular self guided or guided tours. Ring for details and opening times.

If you get fed up with stone then head for the very pleasant **Oamaru Public Gardens** ⓘ *off Severn St, dawn-dusk, free*. Rated as one of the top 10 public gardens in the country, and first set aside in 1876, its 12 ha boast rose and Chinese gardens, fountains, statues and, of course, the ubiquitous duck pond. The area also has a number of private gardens open to the public; the VIC (I-Site) can provide the details.

No visit to Oamaru would be complete without visiting its penguin colonies. The town has two very different species in residence – the enchanting little blue penguin (the smallest in the world) and the rare, larger, yellow-eyed penguin. There are two colonies and observation points, one at Bushy Beach (see below), where you can watch the yellow-eyed penguins from a hide for free, or the official harbour-side **Oamaru Blue Penguin** Colony ⓘ *T03-443 1195, www.penguins.co.nz, $18, child $8*, which you must pay to access. Obviously the free option is an attractive one, but if you do not know anything about penguins and were always under the impression they lived on icebergs and wore bow ties, then you are advised to join a tour, or visit the official colony before venturing out alone. The only time to view the penguins is from dusk (specific times are posted at the colony reception). There is a large covered stand from which you are given a brief talk before the penguins come ashore and waddle intently towards their burrows. During the day 'behind the scenes tours are available', which can be done in combo with the 'evening viewing' from $28, child $13.The colony is accessed via Waterfront Road past the Historic Precinct.

The **Bushy Beach** yellow-eyed penguin colony and viewing hide is accessed on foot via the walkway at the end of Waterfront Road (30 minutes), or alternatively by car via Bushy Beach Road (end of Tyne Street from the Historic Precinct). The best time to view the birds is an hour or so before dawn and dusk when they come and go from their fishing expeditions. If you want a closer, more informative experience you are advised to join Jim Caldwell's walking tours during the summer. Tours last 40 minutes and depart at 1800 and 1900, from $10. Book at the VIC (I-Site). The **Penguin Express**, T03-439 5265, offers transport and tours to both colonies from $28, child $12.

As well as its historical aspects and penguin-watching, Oamaru has a number of other activities on offer including fresh and salt-water fishing, kayaking, heritage and fossil trails, gold mining and farm tours, jet boating, horse trekking and glider flights. The VIC (I-Site) has all the details.

Oamaru to Dunedin→ *Colour map 5, C4/3.*

If you are heading south and have time, take the quiet and scenic coast road from Oamaru, through Kakanui to rejoin SH1 at Waianakarua. The area hosts a number of market gardens so keep your eyes open for fresh, good value produce at roadside stalls. Kayak hire is also available for the lower reaches of the **Kakanui River**, T03-439 5404. About 10 km south of Waianakarua are the **Moeraki Boulders**, a strange and much-photographed collection of spherical boulders that litter the beach. Although Maori legend has it that these boulders are *te kai hinaki*, or food baskets and sweet potatoes, science has determined that they are in fact 'septarian concretions', a rather classy name for 'darn big rock gob-stoppers' left behind from the eroded coastal cliffs. To understand exactly how they are formed requires several PhDs in geology and physics, but you will find something near a layman's explanation at the **Moeraki Boulderpark Visitor Centre and Café**, T03-439 4827, which is signposted just off SH1. The centre is, rather predictably, shaped like the boulders themselves and is open daily for lunch and dinner. The path to the boulders starts at the car park, where an interpretative panel provides information for the geologically wanting. You are requested to provide a donation of $2. **Coastline Tours**, T0800-216 5651/T03-434 7744, www.coastline-tours.co.nz, operates from Oamaru and includes the boulders on their range of itineraries.

There are other, smaller boulders to be seen at **Katiki Beach** and **Shag Point** a few kilometres south, beyond the village of Moeraki. Sadly, there used to be many more, with most having been pilfered as souvenirs, prompting the protection of the larger boulders at Moeraki. The small fishing village of **Moeraki**, 3 km from the boulders, can be reached along the beach by foot (three hours return) or by car via SH1. Once a whaling settlement, first settled as long ago as 1836, it now offers far more acceptable forms of fishing, as well as swimming, wildlife cruises (to try to see the rare Hector's dolphin) and some very pleasant coastal walks. The historic **lighthouse** is also worth a visit and for seafood don't miss **Fleur's Place** (see Eating, page 649). The coastline at **Shag Point**, south of Moeraki, is a good spot to observe New Zealand fur seals but do not go too close.

With the boulders still fresh in your mind your imagination can really run wild a further 20 km south on SH1 in **Palmerston**. Dominating the scene above the town is the rather spectacular phallus adorning **Puketapu Hill** (343 m). A monument to the late John McKenzie, a Scottish runholder who rose to high office and pushed through the Land Settlement Act in the 1890s; the monument and its accompanying views can be reached from the northern end of town (signposted). If you resist closer inspection perhaps you can gaze from afar while sampling the almost legendary mutton pies from the **McGregor's Tearooms**, T03-465 1124. From Palmerston it is a further 55 km through gently rolling hills to Dunedin.

◉ Wanaka and around listings

For Sleeping and Eating price codes and other relevant information, see Essentials pages 44-50.

● Sleeping

Wanaka *p638, map p641*
Although Wanaka has plenty of beds you are advised to book at least 3 days in advance in summer (especially at New Year) and during the winter ski season. As well as hotels, there are many B&Bs and homestays available, from the luxury lodge or self-contained cottage to the basic B&B. You may also like to consider Lake Hawea, which offers a very pleasant and peaceful alternative to Wanaka and is only 15 mins away. The VIC (I-Site) has full listings.
LL Aoturoa Lodge, 17 km from Wanaka on the banks of the Clutha River, T03-443 5000, www.aoturoa.co.nz. 4 excellent, very private suites on offer amid spacious grounds.

LL Minaret Lodge, 34 Eely Point Rd, T03-443 1856, www.minaretlodge.co.nz. Set in a peaceful 1-ha park-like setting a short walk from the town centre. The modern mud-brick lodge has 4 en suite guest rooms in chalets behind the property and a 2-room suite. Sauna and spa.
LL River Run, Halliday Rd, T03-443 9049, www.riverrun.co.nz. Set on an escarpment with sweeping views across the mountains, this huge 120-ha property provides a perfect retreat with imaginatively appointed rooms and furnishings, often using recycled materials in traditional New Zealand style. There are 5 excellent en suites. Fine dining is offered but given the price you would be better off sampling some of the good eateries and congenial atmosphere in town.
LL Wanaka Stonehouse, 21 Sargood Dr, T03-443 1933, www.wanakastonehouse.com.

Mount Aspiring National Park

Like most of New Zealand's majestic national parks, Mount Aspiring has an impressive list of vital statistics. First designated in 1964 the park has been extended to now cover 3500 sq km, making it New Zealand's third largest. It stretches for about 140 km from the Haast Pass to the Humbolt Range at the head of Lake Wakatipu and it is 40 km at its widest. It contains five peaks over 2600 m, including Aspiring itself – at 3027 m, the highest outside the Mount Cook range. It contains over 100 glaciers, including the Bonar, Therma and Volta. It enjoys an annual rainfall of between 1000-6000 mm a year. It is home to some unique wildlife like the New Zealand falcon, the kea and the giant weta. It is part of a World Heritage Area of international significance – the list just goes on. For more information contact the DoC Information Centre in Wanaka or Makarora (see page 639) or visit the website www.doc.govt.nz.

A top-quality country house 'boutique' lodge within Wanaka township, a short stroll from the lake. Has 4 well-appointed double en suites, pleasant gardens, spa and sauna.

LL-AL Edgewater Resort, Sargood Dr, T03-443 0011, www.edgewater.co.nz. Set in spacious grounds overlooking Roy's Bay and within a short stroll of the town centre. Modern rooms and apartments with standard facilities including Sky TV and internet access. Lots of activities can be arranged in-house and there is a spa, sauna and in-house à la carte restaurant.

LL-AL Grand Mercure Oak Ridge Resort, corner of Cardrona Valley and Studholme rds, T03-443 7707, www.oakridge.co.nz. Purpose-built luxurious resort with well-appointed units (some with spa) and smart self-contained apartments that look out across spacious lawns and a swimming and spa pool complex to the mountains. Living areas are very spacious and comfortable with a large log fire. Restaurant/bar on site.

L Lime Tree Lodge, Ballantyne Rd, T03-443 7305, www.limetreelodge.co.nz. A modern, spacious, single-storey place with 2 luxury suites and four guest rooms (all en suite), pool, spa and 5-hole golf course, set in 4 ha of farmland near Wanaka Airport. Very impressive.

L Te Wanaka Lodge, 23 Brownston St, T03-443 9224, www.tewanaka.co.nz. Excellent centrally located alpine-style lodge complex with en suites, self-contained cottage, garden spa (with in-house massage service), open fire, wine cellar and library. Internet and off-street parking.

L-AL Cardrona Hotel, Crown Range (Cardrona) Rd, 26 km from Wanaka, T03-443 8153, www.cardronahotel.co.nz. A little way out but well worth the journey, especially in winter when fires are lit in the gardens from dusk to welcome those coming off the ski field. The hotel is over 140 years old and still retains much of its former character. As it is, the 16 comfortable en suite double rooms in the old stables are charming and front a beautiful enclosed garden and courtyard. There is a great rustic restaurant and bar attached and a spa. Bookings are essential.

L-AL Lake Wanaka Lodge, 24 Tenby St, T03-443 9294, www.lakewanakalodge.co.nz. Backs on to the golf course and offers 10 quiet, well-appointed en suites.

L-A Wanaka Hotel, 71 Ardmore St, T03-443 7826, www.wanakahotel.co.nz. Not an aesthetic stunner by any means but well located and equipped. Good value en suites (some with spa) and budget rooms. In-house restaurant and a good restaurant/bar next door.

AL Mt Aspiring Hotel, Mt Aspiring Rd, T03-443 0025, www.wanakanz.com. Within walking distance of the town centre. A popular choice, with comfortable, good-value studios and suites, some with spa. Restaurant, bar and internet.

Motels and apartments

Apartment complexes are very much an increasing feature in Wanaka.

LL Lakeside Apartments, 9 Lakeside Rd, T03-443 0188, www.lakesidewanaka.co.nz. 4- to 5-star fully serviced apartments in a central position with lake views, pool and spa.

LL-AL Clearbrook, corner of Helwick and Upton sts, T03-443 4413, www.clear brook.co.nz. Well-appointed motel units. Right in the heart of the town centre.

LL-AL Moorings, 17 Lakeside Rd, T0800-843666/T03-443 8479, www.themoorings. co.nz. Modern and classy boutique apartment and motel block overlooking the lake and only metres from the lakeshore and town centre. Stylish motel rooms with good views from the balconies, and spacious apartments with log burners and individual carports. Sky TV.

AL-A Aspiring Lodge Motel, corner of Dunmore and Dungarvon sts, T0800-269367/ T03-443 7816, www.aspiringlodge.co.nz. Offers good standard and executive suites and a spa.

A Brookvale Manor, 35 Brownston St, T0800-438333/T03-443 8333, www.brookvale.co.nz. 1-bedroom and studio suites, pool, spa.

A Cardrona Alpine Resort, T03-443 7411, www.cardrona.com. Units actually within the ski field complex, sleeping 1-8 from $230.

Backpacker hostels

The hostels in Wanaka are all generally of a high standard. The following are three of the best.

C-D Holly's, 71 Upton St, T03-443 8187, www.hollys-backpacker.co.nz. Ideal if you want to avoid the crowds and heavy social scene of most of the other hostels. It is homely, well-equipped and the staff make you very welcome and will make sure you make the most of what the area has to offer. It has dorms, doubles and twins, internet, a good video library and is close to the town centre.

C-D YHA Purple Cow, 94 Brownston St, T03-443 1880, www.purplecow.co.nz. A large place with stunning views across the lake. YHA affiliate with a wide range of comfortable dorms, twins and doubles all

with en suites. Great facilities, Sky TV, internet, walks information and a friendly atmosphere.

C-D Wanaka Bakpaka, 117 Lakeside Rd, T03-443 7837, www.wanakabakpaka.co.nz. 5 mins' walk from the centre of town. It has great views and clean, modern facilities. It is very much a tramper's retreat with great walking advice and information. Kayaks for hire and internet. Recommended.

Motorcamps and campsites

There are several choices here from the convenient to the luxurious and the stylish.

AL-C Aspiring Campervan Park, Studholme Rd, T0800-229843/T03-443 7766, www.campervanpark.co.nz. An entirely different and new concept in motorcamps. Charges a hefty $35 for a powered site, but has all mod cons including a spa (included in tariff) that looks out towards Mt Aspiring. Modern lodge, motel and tourist flats are also available.

AL-D Pleasant Lodge Top 10 Holiday Park, 217 Mt Aspiring Rd, at the western end of the town 3 km towards Glendhu, T03-443 7360, www.wanakatop10.co.nz. In an elevated position overlooking the lake and with all the usual facilities including spa, bike and fishing rod hire.

A-D Wanaka Lakeview Holiday Park, 212 Brownston St, T03-443 7883, www.wanakalakeview.co.nz. Closest to town and rather unremarkable, it has adequate facilities, cabins and powered/tent sites.

C-D Glendhu Bay Motor Camp, Mt Aspiring Rd, 11 km from town, T03-443 7243, www.glendhubaymotorcamp.co.nz. For the best aesthetics, offers lakeside sites with views up to Mt Aspiring. Facilities are too basic given its popularity and it is in need of an upgrade. However, the location is superb location and the prices reasonable. Gets very busy in mid-summer and in the ski season (book ahead). It has petrol, a small store and boat hire.

Hawea p640

AL Bellbird Cottage, 121 Noema Terr, Lake Hawea, T03-443 7056, www.bellbird cottage.co.nz. A fine and good-value

self-contained option in Hawea Village offering an ideal escape from the bustle of Wanaka. Fully self-contained can sleep up to five, log burner. Minimum 2-night stay.
AL Lake Hawea Station, Rapid 22, Timaru River Rd, Lake Hawea, T03-443 1744, www.lakehaweastation.co.nz. With 2 fully self-contained former packhorse cottages sleeping 4-8. Wood burners, a peaceful setting and good value.
AL-A Lake Hawea Motor Inn, 1 Capell Av, T0800-429324/T03-443 1224, www.lakehawea.co.nz.

Makaroa *p641*
AL-A Larrivee Homestay, near the VIC (I-Site), T03-443 9177, www.larrivee homestay.co.nz. Comfortable and offers a spacious en suite room or self-contained cottage. Dinner on request. Good value.
B-D Makarora Wilderness Resort, T03-443 8372, www.makarora.co.nz. Motel, cabin, backpacker and camping facilities.

Oamaru *p642*
There is an ever-increasing number of fine B&Bs and homestays on offer, many set in historic surroundings. Motels tend to be on Thames Highway, heading out of town. There are several hostels in and around town, all comfortable, clean and friendly. The VIC (I-Site) has full listings.
LL Pen-Y-Bryn Lodge, 41 Towey St, T03-434 7939, www.penybryn.co.nz. A vast and lovely Victorian villa, which is actually the largest single-storey timber dwelling in the South Island. It offers luxury en suites and a sumptuous 4-course dinner (and breakfast) included in the price.
AL Homestead 271, T03-434 2610, www.globalife.co.nz. If you fancy a break from all things Kiwi, this modern, well-appointed and good-value B&B just outside Oamaru, is owned by a Japanese couple (ex-Christchurch chefs), who combine the conventional B&B experience with Japanese cooking (tariff includes Japanese breakfast, with dinner from $60). Double, twin and single rooms with lounge and loft with open fire.

AL-A Bella Vista Motel, 206 Thames St, T03-434 2400, www.bellavistamotels.co.nz. Centrally located.
AL-A Heritage Court Motor Lodge, 346 Thames Highway, T03-437 2200, www.heritagecourtlodge.co.nz. Tidy and modern accommodation.
AL-A Kingsgate Hotel Brydone, 115 Thames St, T03-433 0480, www.millennium hotels.com. Centrally located and built of the locally ubiquitous Oamaru stone in 1881, it has standard doubles or suites. The popular 'T' Bar and restaurant housed in the hotel is the biggest attraction.
AL Oamaru Creek B&B, 24 Reed St, T03-434 1190, www.oamarucreek.co.nz. Centrally located, historic double storey villa with contemporary décor and three stylish en suites. Great value and dinner on request.
AL- Alpine Motel, 285 Thames St, T03-434 5038, www.alpineoamaru.co.nz.
D Kakanui Old Bones Backpackers, Beach Rd, T03-434 8115, www.oldbones.co.nz. A gem of a hostel situated right on the coast 4 km south of Oamaru. Purpose built and in a rural setting, it has spacious and immaculate open plan communal areas, two doubles and six twins. Wonderfully peaceful and an open fire. Free internet. Recommended.
C-D Empire Hotel Backpackers, 13 Thames St, T03-434 3446, www.empire backpackersoamaru.co.nz. Cosy, centrally located, Victorian-style house that has the added attraction of free internet and even penny farthings. All room types.
C-D Red Kettle YHA, corner of Reed and Cross sts, T03-434 5008, yhaoamaru@ yha.org.nz. Traditional villa offering dorms or doubles/twins and a welcoming open fire.
C-D Swaggers, 25 Wansbeck St, T03-434 9999, www.swaggersbackpackers.co.nz. A large suburban house doubles/twins dorms and 1 single. Small and homely.

Motorcamps and campsites
B-D Oamaru Gardens Top Ten Holiday Park, Chelmer St (signposted off Severn St, SH1), T03-434 7666, www.oamarutop10. co.nz.

Backs onto the Oamaru Public Gardens and has generally overpriced flats, cabins, units, powered/tent sites and standard facilities.

Oamaru to Dunedin p643
L Noah's, 2 Coronation St, Moeraki, T03-439 4998, noahs.boutique@xtra.co.nz. Fine B&B in an elevated position overlooking the bay. Two en suites and fully equipped kitchen.
AL-C Moeraki Village Holiday Park, 114 Haven St, T03-4394759. Excellent spacious park overlooking the bay. Motel units, flats, cabins and sheltered powered/tent sites. Shop on site. Recommended.
B-D Olive Grove Lodge, SH1, just before the settlement of Waianakarua (28 km south of Oamaru), T03-439 5830, www.olive branch.co.nz. An excellent eco-friendly organic lodge near the river offering tidy doubles, twins and dorms, spa and sauna, log fire, free local tours and plenty of resident farm animals. It is so relaxing you probably won't want to leave.

● Eating

Wanaka p638, map p641
The **New World** supermarket is on Dunmore St, daily 0800-2030.
♥♥♥ **White House Café and Bar**, corner of Dunmore and Dungarvon sts, T03-443 9595. Daily from 1100. Deservedly popular with an imaginative Mediterranean/Middle Eastern menu with vegetarian options. Fine wine list, outdoor eating.
♥♥ **Bombay Palace**, upstairs in Pembroke Mall, T03-443 6086. A good Indian choice.
♥♥ **Cardrona Hotel**, see Sleeping above, T03-443 8153. Daily from 1100. Historic and cosy and well worth the 26-km journey for lunch or dinner.
♥♥ **Kai Whakapai**, Lakefront, T03-443 7795. Daily from 0700. A good spot for daytime eating. Has freshly baked bread, pies, pastas, pizzas and a good vegetarian selection. Breakfasts are good value, the coffee is great and there is outside seating from which to watch the world go by on the waterfront.

♥♥ **Reef**, 145 Ardmore St, T03-443 1188. Daily. Modern seafood specialists, good lake views.
♥♥ **Relishes**, 1/99 Ardmore St, T03-443 9018. 0800-1500 and 1800-late. A decent option with a good-value blackboard menu, outdoor dining in summer and fireside dining in winter. Good coffee and breakfasts.
♥♥-♥ **Ashraf's**, 2 Brownston St, T03-443 1073. Run by 2 brothers who offer great service and quality Indian and Kashmiri food. Good value. Recommended.
♥♥-♥ **Soulfood**, 74 Ardmore, T03-443 7885. Daily from 0700. Offers an excellent range of organic produce in a relaxed and friendly atmosphere. Recommended.
♥ **Muzza's Bar**, corner of Brownston and Helwick sts, T03-443 7296. Good pub food.

Hawea p640
♥ **Sailz**, Capell Av, T03-443 1696. Serves light meals and refreshments.

Oamaru p642
Oamaru has a surprisingly good range of eateries offering everything from seafood to Thai. Most are on or around Thames St. The town also has quite a high Chinese population which has a noticeable influence on the standard of the Chinese restaurants.
♥♥♥ **T'Bar Restaurant**, Kingsgate Hotel, 115 Thames St, T03-434 0011. Pleasant ambience and good traditional NZ/European menu.
♥♥ **Golden Dragon**, 36 Ribble St, T03-434 8670. The most noted Chinese restaurant, along with **Golden Island**, below.
♥♥ **Golden Island**, 243 Thames Highway, T03-434 8840.
♥♥ **Last Post Bar and Restaurant**, 12 Thames St, in the former Oamaru Stone-built Post Office, T03-434 8080. Casual dining at reasonable prices.
♥ **Criterion Hotel**, in the Tyne St precinct. Pub grub and good beer in historic hotel.
♥ **Whisky Tea Rooms**, 14 Harbour St, T03-434 8842. Traditional café fare with the added attraction of whisky sampling.
♥ **Whitestone Cheese Factory**, corner of Torridge and Humber sts, T03-434 8098. Daily

0900-1700. As well as the innovative blackboard menu in the café, you can of course sample and purchase their impressive range of cheeses.

Oamaru to Dunedin *p643*
♂ **Fleur's Place**, 169 Haven St (Old Jetty), Moeraki, T03-439 4480. Excellent seafood in a great setting. Recommended.

● Pubs, bars and clubs

Wanaka *p638, map p641*
Apartment One, above **Relishes Restaurant**, 99 Ardmore St, T03-443 4911. Especially popular for its laid-back atmosphere, balcony overlooking the lake and its cocktails, après ski and open fire in winter.
Finchy's Restaurant and Bar, 2 Dunmore St, T03-443 6262. A more sedate atmosphere.
Paradiso Cinema and Café, 1 Ardmore St, T03-443 1505, www.paradiso.net.nz. Famous for its 1-of-a-kind movie offerings, complete with easy chairs and homemade ice cream. Front man (and Scot) Calum McLeod often provides an entertaining introduction. The café is just as laid back. Recommended.
Shooters Bar. Highly commercial and seems very much aimed at the young and rapacious. Its saving grace is its fine position.
Slainte Irish Bar, 21 Helwick St, T03-443 7663. Proving popular and offers live music.
 Barluga, Post Office Lane off Armore, T03-4435400. New and contemporary with large open fire.

Oamaru *p642*
Penguin Entertainers Club, Sea Side, Harbour St, T025-373922, www.thepenguin club.co.nz. A little-known spot for occasional visiting live acts. Check the website for dates and directions.
Armada Motor Inn Bowling Complex, 500 Thames Highway, T03-437 9040. Also popular. Serves takeaway pizzas.

❀ Festivals and events

Wanaka *p638, map p641*
April Warbirds Over Wanaka, T03-443 8619, www.warbirdsoverwanaka.com. New Zealand's premier air show is held biannually (next in 2012). The airfield, which hosts a wide variety of visiting 'birds', but also blows the dust off the New Zealand Fighter Pilots Museum's very own Spitfire. Entry is from $45-$70, child $10 (3-day $165).
Festival of Colour, www.festivalofcolour. co.nz. Launched in 2005, this is a 5-day biennial arts and music festival featuring both artists from New Zealand and across the globe including sculptors, contemporary dancers, jazz musicians and photographers. The next is in 2011.

Oamaru *p642*
Nov Oamaru Victorian Heritage Celebrations. This annual event takes place in the Historic Precinct on the 3rd weekend in Nov. It's all fun, top hats and penny-farthings.

▲ Activities and tours

Wanaka *p638, map p641*
Most activities can be booked at the VIC (I-Site) or the Lakeland Adventures office. There are obviously many options but if Wanaka is known for one thing it is perhaps rock climbing, scenic flights, fishing, skydiving and paragliding (off Roy's Peak).The principal operators are as follows.
OutsideSports, 17 Dunmore St, T03-443 7966, www.outsidesports.co.nz. Hires out bikes, kayaks, 'funyaks', 'sit-on kayaks', fishing rods and tackle, plus the full range of ski and snow-sports equipment.
Lakeland Adventures, T03-443 7495, www.lakelandadventures.co.nz. Offers fishing, jet boating and cruising.

Canyoning
Most of the activities available in Wanaka you can also do elsewhere, but canyoning is a

local speciality and recommended. It basically involves negotiating a mountain river with the assistance of gravity and in suitable attire. Methods of descent include scrambling, abseiling or just plain jumping. All great fun. Heli and jet boat combos are also available. **Deep Canyon**, T03-4437922, www.deep canyon.co.nz. 'Do' the Emerald Creek, Niger Stream and others (6-7 hrs) from $225 (min age 16). Transport and lunch included.

Cruising
Lakeland Adventures, see above. Scenic cruises of varying duration explore the waters and islands of Lake Wanaka from 2½-3½ hrs, $75-100.

Fishing
The local fishing is excellent and there are many operators and guides. Most of the companies listed below can also organize more adventurous heli-fishing trips throughout the region. Prices start at about $100 per person per hr and about $350-750 for a privately guided half-day trip. **Lakeland Adventures** and **Outside Sports**, Dunmore St, offer independent rod hire from $35 per day and licences from $21.
Alpine Fishing Guides, Hawea, T03-443 1023, www.driftfishingnz.com. Specializes in drift trout fishing ($625 per boat per day).
Southern Lakes Fishing Safaris, T03-443 4486, www.southernlakesfishing.co.nz. Full day $650 (1-2 people).
Wanaka Fishing Safaris, T03-443 7748, www.trout.net.nz. From $350 half-day.

Flightseeing
Wanaka is a superb base from which to reach Milford Sound by air, with the bonus of the stunning aesthetics of the **Mt Aspiring National Park** on the way. Most flights from Queenstown and other centres (which cost about the same) do not follow the same spectacular flight path. Given its museum it also hosts other exciting flight options.
Aspiring Air, at the airfield, T0800-100943/ T03-443 7943, www.aspiringair.com. Offers a range of flights from a 20-min local flight for

$140 to its highly recommended 4-hr 'Majestic Milford Sound' flight. Leaving at 0845 or 1345 and arriving back at 1300 or 1800 this epic involves a superb flight over Wanaka, up the Matukituki River Valley, past Mt Aspiring and then out across the national park and out to sea, before flying up the chancel of Milford Sound and Milford Sound Village. Included in the trip is a 45-min cruise on the Sound. It is a truly memorable experience and well worth the $435, child $260. Other alluring options include a scenic flight over Mt Cook (from $395) or several activity combos from jet boating in the Haast Region to west coast glacier landings (from $710).
Vintage Tigermoth Flights, Wanaka Airport, T0508-4359464/T03-4434043, www.classicflights.co.nz. This offers something a little bit different. Don a leather flying helmet, goggles, silk scarf and *tally ho!* yourself back to a bygone era aboard a 1941 Tigermoth. Several flight options ($225-375) with the more adventurous involving aerobatic stunts. There is even a sunrise/ sunset option for the real romantics.
Wanaka Flightseeing, at the airfield, T03-443 8787, www.flightseeing.co.nz. Offers similar trips to **Aspiring Air**, from $195.

Golf
Wanaka's very scenic course is on Ballantyne Rd, just behind the town, and welcomes visitors, T03-443 7888. Green fees are a very reasonable $35, club hire full set $35.

Horse trekking
The Wanaka region offers some superb horse-trekking possibilities.
NZ Backcountry Saddle Expeditions, near Cardrona, T03-4438151, www.ride nz.com. Offers 2-hr to 4-day treks, from $70, child $50 (transport from Wanaka $10).

Jet boating
Lake Wanaka and its surrounding scenic rivers almost has to incorporate a jet-boat trip somewhere. There are a number of operators. **Clutha River Jet** (Lakeland Adventures), on

the Lakefront, T03-443 7495. Offers 1-hr trips down the Clutha for $95, child $45.

Wilkin River Jets, Makarora, T03-4438351, www.wilkinriverjets.co.nz. Plies the Makarora and Wilkin rivers.

Kayaking

Lakeland Adventures and Outside Sports see above, offers independent kayak hire.

Alpine Kayak Guides, T0800-KAYAK1/ T03-443 9023, www.alpinekayaks.co.nz. Daily guided whitewater trips on the Clutha, Matukituki and Hawea rivers, suitable for beginners. Transport and free pick-ups included, from $195 full day, $149 half day.

Mountaineering and rock climbing

With Mt Aspiring and so many attractive mountain climbs so close to Wanaka it is not surprising to find a number of quality companies offering a range of packages.

Adventure Consultants, T03-443 8711, www.adventure.co.nz. Mt Aspiring $4100, 1:1 client-guide ratio, with flights. Very good for mountaineering and ice-climbing courses.

Alpinism and Ski Ltd, 11 Rimu Lane, T03-443 6593, www.alpinismski.co.nz. Offers guided trekking excursions throughout the region, and year-round to a number of peaks including Mt Aspiring and further afield to Mt Cook and the Westland National Park. Once you have flown over Aspiring you will appreciate that having a guide makes a lot of sense! The price of a guided climb of Aspiring on a 2:1 client:guide ratio is around $2300 (5 days without flights). Mountaineering courses, snow tours and trekking also offered.

Base Camp Wanaka, 50 Cardrona Valley Rd, T03-4431110, www.basecampwanaka. co.nz. This new camp is described as an 'all weather mountain adventure centre' boasting a sate of the art 500 sq m climbing space/wall for all levels. The complex houses a café, map room, library, shop and even a micro-brewery. They also offer organized indoor tuition and outdoor climbing trips and hire out a wide range of outdoor gear for climbing, trekking etc. Casual free-climbing from $15, child $5,

harness hire $5.45 mins tuition from $45.

Mount Aspiring Guides, T03-443 9422, www.aspiringguides.com. Offers a range of trips and packages all year round. Mt Aspiring $3750, 1:1 client-guide ration, with flights.

Wanaka Rock, T03-443 6411, www.wanakarock.co.nz. A reputable company. Courses include introductory (1 day from $190), abseil (half-day from $120) and multi-day technical courses, from $510.

Mountain biking

Mountain bike hire is also available from Lakeland Adventures, see above.

Cardrona Alpine Resort, T03-443 7341, www.cardrona.com. Stays open in summer to allow climbers, trampers and bikers to access the mountains. The chairlift operates daily 1000-1600 and there are 2 purpose-built downhill bike tracks. Cardrona is 34 km southeast of Wanaka on the Crown Range Rd.

Off-road, 4WD and rallying

See also Queenstown Activities, page 631.

Cardrona Adventure Park, SH89, Cardrona Valley Rd, T03-443 6363, www.adventurepark.co.nz. The principal ATV 4WD quad bike specialists, offering guided half to 3-hr trips on farm and hill trails with great views, $95-190. Also offers a 'Monster Trucks' option, with ludicrously deformed and bouncy vehicles from $140.

EWA Adventures, T03-443 8422, www.adventure.net.nz. Offers a range of local excursions on land and water including a trip to Rob Roy Glacier from $235 (includes lunch).

Paragliding

Paragliding is huge around Wanaka with the slopes of Mt Roy in particular providing ideal terrain and conditions. On a fine day it is not unusual to see over 20 colourful chutes drifting across the skyline.

Wanaka Paragliding, T0800-359754/ T027-469 7685, www.wanakaparagliding. co.nz. 15-25 min tandem from Treble Cone (800 m), $180.

The Rob Roy glacier walk

If you haven't time or the energy for any of the major tramps, there is one day-walk in the Mount Aspiring National Park that is accessible from Wanaka and quite simply a 'must do'. From Wanaka drive (or arrange transportation) to the **Raspberry Creek** Car Park in the West Matukituki Valley (1 hr). From there follow the river, west to the footbridge over the river and up in to the **Rob Roy Valley**. From here the track gradually climbs, following the chaotic Rob Roy River, through beautiful rainforest, revealing the odd view of the glacier above. After about 1½ hrs you will reach the tree line and enter a superb hidden valley rimmed with solid rock walls of **waterfall** and **ice**. It is simply stunning and well deserving of the label 'The Jewel of the Park'. Keep your eyes (and ears) open for kea and in the forest for the tiny rifleman. After some thorough investigation of the area, you can then retrace your steps back down the valley to the Matukituki River and the car park (five hours return). **Alpine Coachlines Wanaka** (Outside), 17 Dunmore St, T03-443 7966, www.alpinecoaclines.co.nz offer trailhead connections (Raspberry Creek, twice daily 0915 and 1400 from \$35).

River sledging

Whitewater sledging is growing in popularity and provides a far more intimate experience with the water on a modified boogie board. **Frogz Have More Fun**, T0800-437649/T03-4412318, www.frogz.co.nz. 4- to 9-hr trips on the Kawarau River, from \$149 (minimum age 10-14 years depending on the river).

Skiing

Wanaka has several great ski fields within 50 km of the town and encompassing standard ski and board slopes, cross-country and even a specialist snowboard freestyle park at the new Snow Park. Cardrona, Snow Park and Snow Farm are to the south, while Treble Cone is to the northwest. For general information and snow reports check out www.snow.co.nz; www.nzski.com; www.snowparknz.com; www.snowfarmnz.com or www.skilakewanaka.com.

Daily transport from Wanaka is available with **Alpine Snow Shuttles** (transport and lift day-packages available), T03-443 7966. Other shuttle operators are listed in Getting around, page 639.

Equipment can be hired from: **Base**, corner of Helwick and Dunmore sts, T03-443 6699, www.base.net.nz; **OutsideSports**, Dunmore St, T03-4437966, also arranges transport; and **Racer's Edge Planet Snow**, 99 Ardmore St, T03-443 7882, www.racers edge.co.nz. Average prices are skis/boots \$38, child \$19. Snowboard and boots from \$46, child \$23. **Harris Mountain Heli-skiing**, 99 Ardmore St, T03-442 6672, www.heliski. co.nz, offers 3-7 days from \$775.

Cardrona, 34 km from Wanaka on the Crown Range (Cardrona) Rd, T03-4437411, www.cardrona.com. It has a base area at 1670 m, and ski and board runs suitable for all levels, with the intermediates being especially well catered for. Facilities include bars and restaurants and, unusually, apartment accommodation. The ski season runs from 23 Jun-7 Oct but the resort (and some lifts) remain open in summer for trampers and mountain bikers. Lift passes from \$89, child (6-17) \$44, with hire of ski/snowboard (day) from \$44, child \$34

Treble Cone Ski field, 20 km northwest of Wanaka via Glendhu, T03-4437443, www.treblecone.co.nz. Well known for its good snow and interesting terrain, not to mention its stunning views. It also offers more skiable terrain than any other ski or board area in the South Island and has the longest vertical rise in the Southern Lakes Region.

Little wonder it is considered one of the best fields in the country. It is open from 0900-1600 late Jun-early Oct (no access in summer). Lift passes are from $91, youth $46. 'First Timer' package including lift/hire and lesson from $100. Full clothing, ski and board hire are available on the mountain with hire of ski/snowboard (day) from $47, youth $37. There is also a café, bar, childcare centre and ski/board schools.

Snow Farm, on the other side of the valley to Cardrona, summer T03-4439729, winter T03-4437542, www.snowfarmnz.com. A base for cross-country skiing with international standard tracks. It is open mid-Jun to the end of Sep and a pass costs from $40, child $15.

Snow Park, Cardrona, T03-443 0300 www.snowparknz.com. A base for freestyle snowboarding with international standard 'pipes'. It is open mid-Jun to the end of Sep and a pass costs around $75.

Tandem skydiving

The Wanaka Region is one of the most scenic in the country, which gives that added edge to any jump.

Tandem Skydive Wanaka, T0800-786877/ T03-443 7207, www.skydivenz.com. Operates out of the airfield from heights of 12,000 ft ($295), 15,000 ft ($395) allowing 30-60 seconds of freefall at around 200 kph, followed by a gentle and peaceful 6-min parachute ride to earth. Weight limit 100 kg/ age limit 7 years. The scenery both on the way up and down are superb and many

people in the business recommend Wanaka – as we do. Pick-ups from Wanaka are free.

Tours

Ridgeline, T0800-234000/T027-6024018, www.ridgelinenz.com. Offers full-day wine tours, and heli-hikes, from $179.

Southern Lakes Sightseeing, T03-338 0982, www.lordoftheringstours.co.nz. Offers very pleasant 2- to 5-hr sightseeing tours of the region and has added half-, full- and multi-day *Lord of the Rings* tours. The full-day takes in 20 filming locations from $299.

Walking

Other than the **Mt Iron Walk** (see page 640) and the walk to **Rob Roy Glacier** (highly recommended, see box, opposite), there are many other possibilities. Popular alternatives are the ascent of Mt Roy or the easier, but still quite demanding, climb to the top of **Rocky Mountain past Diamond Lake**. From lakeside, Mt Roy (1585m) dominates the western edge of Roy's Bay, but its ascent can reward you with some tremendous views. A well- formed path zigzags its way to the summit from a car park 6 km north of Wanaka towards Glendhu Bay. The walk takes about 5 hrs return (return transfer to the car park $15 with Alpine Coachlines Wanaka, T03-443 7966, www.alpinecoaclines.co.nz).

Further up this road, past Glendhu and before the entrance to the Treble Cone Ski field, is the **Rocky Mountain and Diamond Lake Walk**. The appeal here is the view of Mt Aspiring and the Matukituki River Valley, as

well as Lake Wanaka itself. The geology is also fascinating, with rocks that form unusual mounds and folds across the landscape. It is a stiff climb, but the path is marked and it is definitely worth the effort. At the end of Hospital Flat you will see the signposted car park. From there it is 20 mins to the fairly unremarkable lake before the track skirts around the slopes to the top. On the descent be careful not to stray off the path far from the lower lookout. You need to double back here to rejoin the track. The walk takes about 3 hrs return (transfer $45 with Alpine Coachlines Wanaka, T03-443 7966, www.alpinecoaclines.co.nz).

For detailed walks information see the numerous walks leaflets available from the DoC Visitors Information Centre (see information above).

Eco Wanaka Adventures, T03-4432869, www.ecowanaka.nz and **Mount Aspiring Guides**, 99 Ardmore St, T03-443 9422, www.mountaspiring guides.com, both offer an extensive range of guided day and multi-day options. The latter also offers transfers for both of the walks detailed above.

Watersports

Lake Wanaka is the perfect place for waterskiing and wakeboarding and big enough for you to be able to find a quiet spot. Ask at the VIC for detail regarding equipment hire.

Makarora *p641*
Walking

Of special note in this area is the superb 3-day **Gillespie Pass Tramp** and 'The Siberia Experience'. This evocatively named jaunt is a combination of scenic flight, tramp and jet boat, which gets consistently good reviews. You are first flown (25 mins) into the beautiful and remote Siberia Valley, from where you tramp for about 3 hrs to the Wilkin River to be picked up by jet boat with a 30-min scenic ride back to Makarora. At $310, it is good value. It also offers scenic flights to Milford, Mt Cook or over Aspiring National Park (Mt Aspiring) from 20 mins to 2-4 hrs ($210-680).

Trips are run by **Southern Alps Air**, T0800-345666/T03-443 8666, www.siberia experience.co.nz, www.southernalps air.co.nz, in conjunction with **Wilkin River Jet Boats**, T03-443 8351, www.wilkinriver jets.co.nz. The latter also offers 1-hr trips on the scenic Wilkin from $95, child $45, as well as water taxi services for trampers from $75.

⊖ Transport

Wanaka *p638, map p641*
Bicycle hire Outside Sports, Dunmore St, T03-443 7966, www.good-sports.co.nz, $25-50 per day. Lakeland Adventures, lakefront, T03-443 7495. **Car hire** Adventure Rentals, 20 Ardmore St, T03-443 6050. Wanaka Rent-a-car, T03-443 6641. **Taxi** T03-4455954

❶ Directory

Wanaka *p638, map p641*
Banks National, T03-443 7521. Westpac, T03-443 7857. They also have ATMs. **Internet** Bits & Bytes, 48 Helwick St, T03-443 7078, daily 1000-2200. Wanaka Web, 3 Helwick St, T03-443 7429, daily 0900-2100. **Medical services** Aspiring Medical Centre, 28 Dungarvon St, T03-443 1226. Wanaka Medical Centre, 21 Russell St, T03-443 7811. **Police** 28 Helwick St, T03-443 7272. **Post office** 39 Ardmore St, T03-443 8211, Mon-Fri 0830-1730, Sat 0900-1200.

Oamaru *p642*
Banks Most of the major bank branches and ATMs are on Thames St, with some housed in grand historic buildings. The National Bank, in the former 1871 Bank of Otago building, is the best example. **Internet** VIC (I-Site), see page 639. Small Bytes Computing, 187 Thames St, T03-434 8490. Lagonda Coach Travel tearooms, 191 Thames St, T03-434 8716. **Post office** Severn St, near the intersection with Thames.

Contents

Footprint features

Southland

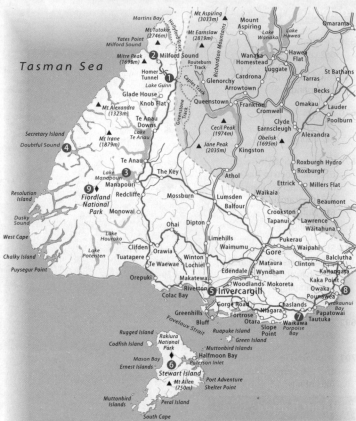

Tasman Sea

Martins Bay

Mt Aspiring (3033m)

Mount Aspiring

Lake Wanaka

Lake Hawea

Omarama

Yates Point
Milford Sound

Mt Tutoko (2746m)

Mt Earnslaw (2819m)

Richardson Mountains

Mitre Peak (1695m)

2 Milford Sound

Routeburn Track

Wanaka

Hawea Flat

Homer Tunnel

1

Lake Gunn

Glenorchy

Arrowtown

Cardrona

Luggate

St Bathans

Tarras

Becks

Glade House

Knob Flat

Queenstown

Frankton

Cromwell

Omakau

Lauder

Mt Alexandra (1323m)

Te Anau Downs

Earnscleugh

Clyde

Poolburn

Secretary Island

Lake Te Anau

Cecil Peak (1974m)

Obelisk (1695m)

Alexandra

Doubtful Sound 4

Mt Irane (1879m)

Jane Peak (2035m)

Kingston

Te Anau

Roxburgh Hydro

Roxburgh

Lake Manapouri

3

The Key

Athol

Ettrick

Millers Flat

Resolution Island

Manapouri

Redcliffe

Mossburn

Lumsden

Waikaia

Beaumont

Fiordland National Park

Monowai

Balfour

Crookston

Tapanui

Lawrence

Waitahuna

Dusky Sound

Lake Hauroko

Ohai

Dipton

Limehills

Pukerau

West Cape

Clifden

Orawia

Winton

Waimumu

Gore

Waipahi

Chalky Island

Lake Poteriteri

Tuatapere

Te Waewae

Lochiel

Mataura

Clinton

Balclutha

Puysegur Point

Orepuki

Makatewa

Edendale

Wyndham

Mokoreta

Kaitangata

Kaka Point

Riverton

Woodlands

Owaka 8

Colac Bay

5 Invercargill

Gorge Road

Niagara

Chaslands

Pounawea

Purakaunui Bay

Greenhills

Fortrose

Otara

Catlins

Papatowai

Tautuka

Bluff

Fortrose

Slope Point

Waikawa 7

Foveaux Strait

Ruapuke Island

Porpoise Bay

Rugged Island

Rakiura National Park

Green Island

Codfish Island

Muttonbird Islands

Mason Bay

Halfmoon Bay

Ernest Islands

Paterson Inlet

6

Stewart Island

Port Adventure

Shelter Point

Muttonbird Islands

Mt Allen (750m)

Peral Island

South Cape

Pacific Ocean

★ Don't miss ...

1 Milford Road, page 660.
2 Milford Sound, page 666.
3 Lake Manapouri, page 671.
4 Doubtful Sound, page 672.
5 Invercargill, page 677.
6 Stewart Island park, page 684.
7 Catlins Coast, page 692.
8 Nugget Point, page 696.

N

30 km
30 miles

Southland is a region of stark differences. It is one of the most spectacular yet inaccessible landscapes on earth. Even its boundaries are contrasting, stretching roughly in a straight line from the unremarkable and flat coastal town of Balclutha in the east, to the towering peaks and fiord of Milford Sound to the west. Half of its coast is mountainous, remote and inhospitable – virtually unchanged since Cook first landed (briefly) in 1770. The other half is home to Southland's largest town, Invercargill, the beautiful coastal holiday haunts of the Catlins and Riverton and an unsightly aluminium smelter. Amid this, knocking at its backdoor, is New Zealand's third island and newest national park: Stewart Island.

Most visitors head for the hills, and who can blame them? The Fiordland National Park, which is part of the internationally acclaimed Te Wahipounamu World Heritage Area, is a staggering 2.6 million hectares of some of the world's most magnificent scenery; it covers 10 percent of the country as a whole. And, although the vast majority of it is wonderfully inaccessible, it contains over 5000 km of walking tracks. But don't be fooled into thinking the less spectacular parts are not worth a look. There, too, you will find a warm welcome and some pleasant surprises. Where else on earth, for example, can you meet a 120-year-old tuatara, a reptile that has outlived the fiords themselves? Or see, unusually in daylight hours, the weird and wonderful kiwi, that flightless national icon.

Te Anau → *Colour map 6, B3 Population: 3500.*

On the shores of New Zealand's second largest lake and at the edge of the magnificent wilderness of the Fiordland National Park is the 'walking capital of the world', Te Anau. Pretty isn't it? But, as they say... 'You ain't seen nothing yet'. In summer it is like a busy gatehouse with crowds of eager trampers, intent on and excited by the prospect of visiting its enormous garden. In winter it is like an unused holiday house, with only its resident caretaker, quietly waiting and wanting to turn the heating on again. Ironically, as you drive into Te Anau, often wedged between a convoy of tour buses, it can initially seem a rather dull little town, but once you acquaint yourself with its bustling centre, spacious open areas and beautiful lake views, your desire to move on will quickly fade. And although what lies beyond the town is what you have really come to see, it is worth giving Te Anau a little time. And, given the fickle weather in these parts, you my have little choice.▸▸ *For Sleeping, Eating and other listings, see pages 662-666.*

Ins and outs

Getting there By air **Te Anau airfield** ① *between Te Anau and Manapouri*, is served from Queenstown using unscheduled services with **Air Fiordland**, T03-249 6720, www.airfiordland.co.nz, though the vast majority of visitors arrive by road. For airfield transport contact **Te Anau Taxis**, T03-249 7777. By car, Te Anau is 177 km southwest of Queenstown via SH6, 152 km from Invercargill via SH99 (Southern Scenic Route) and 290 km west of Dunedin via Gore and SH94. The town is served by **Intercity**, T03-249 7516 (Christchurch/Invercargill/Dunedin daily); **Topline Tours**, T03-249 8059, www.toplinetours. co.nz (Queenstown from $38); **Tracknet**, T0800-483262/T03-249 7777, www.tracknet. co.nz (Queenstown daily, from $43); **Bottom Bus and Scenic Shuttle**, T03-4779083, www.bottombus.co.nz, www.scenicshuttle.co.nz cover the Southern Scenic Route between Queenstown/Dunedin/Invercargill and The Catlins. All buses stop in the town centre. **Back Road Transport (Tracknet)**, T03-249 7777, offers a rather unique way to get to Te Anau via Lake Wakatipu (Queenstown) and the steamer *TSS Earnslaw*. Once ashore at the remote Walter Peak Station you can then travel by coach via the pretty Von Valley and Mavora Lakes to Te Anau, from $90 including cruise.

Getting around Local fixed-wing and helicopter companies offer chartered transportation (or packages) for tramping to Milford and beyond, see Activities and tours, page 664. **Air Fiordland**, Town Centre, T03-249 6720 (Hollyford/Milford); **Wings and Water**, Lake Front (Milford/Dusky), T03-249 7405, www.wingsandwater.co.nz; **South-West Helicopters**, T03-249 7402, www.southwesthelicopters.co.nz, offer helicopter charters throughout the region. **Tracknet**, based at Te Anau Lake View Holiday Park, Te Anau-Manapouri Highway, T03-249 7777, www.tracknet.co.nz, offers shuttle bus services and packages to Queenstown ($43 one way); Milford-Te Anau Downs ($22); Routeburn/Greenstone/Hollyford turning ($37); Kepler control gates ($6). All shuttle services run from Oct-May except the Milford Track service which is year-round, T03-249 7777, www.greatwalksnz.com. **Topline Tours** (see Getting there, above) also offers shuttle services to tramping trailheads.

By boat, **Real Journeys**, based on the lakefront, T03-249 7416, www.realjourneys.co.nz, offers a water shuttle service to the start of the Milford Track, from $65, child from $20. **Kepler Water Taxi**, Te Anau, T03-249 8364, stevesaunders@xtra.co.nz, runs a water taxi service to Brod Bay and the Kepler Track daily at 0830 and 0930, from $18 one way.

Tourist information Te Anau has a disconcerting number of information centres and booking offices. The most unbiased information is available from **Fiordland VIC (I-Site)** ⓘ *Lakefront Dr, T03-249 8900, fiordland@i-site.org, daily 0830-1800 (winter 0830- 1700)*. It deals with all local information and serves as the agents for domestic air and bus bookings. **Real Journeys** ⓘ *downstairs from VIC (I-Site), daily summer 0830-2100*, deals with its own considerable scope of transport, sights and activity bookings including local sightseeing trips on Lake Te Anau (including the Te Anau Caves) and to Milford and Doubtful Sounds. **DoC Fiordland National Park Visitor Centre** ⓘ *southern end of lakefront, T03-249 7924, fiordlandvc@doc.govt.nz, daily 0830-1800 (seasonal)*, is the principal source for track information, track bookings office (T03-2498514) and up-to-date weather forecasts. There is also a small museum and audio-visual theatre ($3).

Te Anau

To ④ ⑭ ⑮ , Te Anau Downs (27 km) & Milford Sound (120 km)

Lake Te Anau

To Queenstown

To Ivon Wilson Park, Kepler Track, Airfield & Manapouri (20 km)

400 metres
400 yards

Sleeping 🛌
Anchorage **1**
Arran **2**
Bob & Maxine's
  Backpackers **15**
Cat's Whiskers B&B **3**
Croft B&B **4**
Fiordland Lodge **14**
Lake Front Lodge **6**
Lakeside Motel **8**
Radfords Motel **9**
Red Tussock Motel **11**
Steamers Beach
  Backpackers **12**

Te Anau & Villas **5**
Te Anau Lakefront
  Backpackers **7**
Te Anau Lake View
  Holiday Park **12**
Te Anau Top Ten
  Holiday Park **10**
Te Anau YHA **13**

Eating 🍴
Kingsgate Hotel **4**
La Toscana Pizzeria **1**
Moose & Bar **2**
Naturally Fiordland **6**
Olive Tree Café **3**
Redcliff Café & Bar **5**
Sandfly Café **7**

Sights

Once settled in to your accommodation, without doubt the first thing to do is book a ticket to see the 35-minute film *Ata Whenua or Shadowland*, at the contemporary **Fiordland Cinema** ⓘ *The Lane, T03-249 8812, www.fiordlandcinema.co.nz, daily 1300 and 1730, from $10*. The film is a stunning visual exploration of the Fiordland National Park and the vast wilderness area that extends almost beyond the imagination to the west of Lake Te Anau. Dubbed with evocative music and filmed using state-of-the-art photographic techniques (mostly from the air) it visits areas you would never be able to, it will leave you in no doubt about the purity and awe of the Te Wahipounamu World Heritage area. In this invasive and frantic technological age and given current world events it is more than a mere tonic, some fleeting entertainment or a promotional activities video. In essence it is a refreshing and stark reminder that nature will, despite us, always be 'the boss'.

The cinema itself has been causing something of a stir in the town since it is 'very Queenstown' with contemporary design, a log fire and a wine bar attached (you are encouraged to take a glass in to the film with you). It is an example and an indication of where the town is inevitably going, which in a way is exciting and welcome, but if you take a trip to the outskirts of town and see the suburban eyesore and the real estate eating away the countryside, you will also see the more insidious 'dark side'.

Lake Te Anau → *Colour map 6, B3.*

At 61 km long, 10 km at its widest point and a total of 344 sq km in area, Lake Te Anau is the largest lake in the South Island and second largest in New Zealand. Looking from the lakeside up its length to the Earl Mountains it certainly seems worthy of those dimensions and perhaps the label of prettiest in the country. Directly opposite Te Anau, unseen in the bush, is the meandering **Kepler Track** which begins at the southern end of the lake and skirts its southwestern edge, before climbing steadily towards the Kepler Mountains and the spectacular views from the **Luxmore Hut**. Also along the western edge between the Middle and South Fiords are the 200-m **Te Ana-au Caves**. Long revered by Maori, but only rediscovered by the Europeans in 1948, they provide the usual spectacular rock formations, fossils, whirlpools, waterfalls and glow-worms. The caves can only be accessed by boat, and 2½-hour guided trips leave from the wharf at Te Anau up to six times daily. After arriving by launch, there is a video presentation. The caves themselves are then explored by foot and on the water by punt. The 2015 (summer) or 1845 (winter) evening trips are recommended. Book with **Real Journeys**, Lakefront Drive, T03-249 7416; tours cost from $63, child $20.

On the southern shores of the lake on the road to Manapouri, is the **DoC Te Anau Wildlife Centre** ⓘ *T03-249 7921, entry by donation*, an important breeding centre for **takahe** and other rare native species. The story of the takahe is a fascinating one. Thought to be extinct for over 50 years, a small group were rediscovered in the Murchison Mountains above Lake Te Anau in 1948, by ornithologist and medical practitioner Dr Geoffrey Orbell. Although much of what goes on at the centre (in their efforts to maintain the new breeding colony in the Murchison Ranges) is off-limits, the open-air aviaries and grounds are very appealing. It is very refreshing to see such efforts being made in wildlife conservation in New Zealand and to witness unique species in such a relaxed atmosphere. There are takahe, kea, morepork and kaka to name but a few. Across the road from the wildlife centre is the 35-ha **Ivor Wilson Park** (open dawn to dusk), which offers a number of pleasant tracks and picnic spots amongst native bush and surrounding Lake Henry. For children or urbanites **Glen Monarch Farm Tours** ⓘ *off SH94 (17 km), T03-249 7041*, offers an entertaining three-hour introductory Kiwi farm tour with the obligatory sheep shearing and working dog demonstrations as well as plenty of animal petting, from around $60 (vehicle transport from Te Anau extra).

Milford Road → *Colour map 6, A3.*

The 119-km trip into the heart of the **Fiordland National Park** and **Milford Sound** is all part of the world-class Milford Sound experience. In essence it is a bit like walking down the aisle, past the interior walls of a great cathedral, to stand aghast at the chancel and the stunning stained-glass windows above. This may sound like an exaggeration but if nature is your religion, then the trip to Milford is really nothing short of divine. Of course much depends on the weather. Ideally it should be of either extreme – cloudless, or absolutely thumping it down. Under clear blue skies it is of course magnificent, but many say that the trip through the mountains is better during very heavy rain. It is an incredibly moody place so don't be put off by foul weather.

From Te Anau you skirt the shores and enjoy the congenial scenery of Lake Te Anau before heading inland at **Te Anau Downs** (30 minutes). This is principally a boat access point to the Milford Track; there is a motel, T0800-500706, and a hostel, T03-249 7811, www.teanau-milfordsound.co.nz. Another 30 minutes will see you through some low-lying alluvial flats and meadows as the Earl Mountains begin to loom large. After penetrating some beech forest you suddenly emerge into the expanse of the **Eglinton River Valley** with its stunning views towards the mountains. This is known as the 'Avenue of the Disappearing Mountain' and it speaks for itself.

Fiordland National Park

Fiordland National Park is 1.25 million ha and the largest of New Zealand's 14 national parks. It is twice the size of Singapore with 0.06% of the population. In 1986 it was declared a World Heritage Area on account of its outstanding natural features, exceptional beauty and its important demonstration of the world's evolutionary history. Four years later, in 1990, Fiordland National Park was further linked with three others – **Mount Aspiring**, **Westland** and **Mount Cook (Aoraki)** to form the World Heritage Area of South West New Zealand. It was given the Maori name **Te Waipounamu** (Te 'the'/ Wai 'waters'/ Pounamu 'greenstone' or 'jade'). Hopefully we can rest assured, that with such official labels and protection it will remain the stunning wilderness it is.

At the northern end of the valley you then re-enter the shade of the beech forests and encounter **Mirror Lake**, a small body of water overlooking the Earl Mountain Range. The lookout point is a short walk from the road. On a clear day you can, as the name suggests, capture the mood and the scene twice in the same shot.

Several kilometres further on is **Knobs Flat** where there is a DoC shelter and information/display centre and toilet facilities. For much of the next 25 minutes you negotiate the dappled shadows on a near constant tunnel of beautiful beech forest before reaching **Lake Gunn**, which offers some fine fishing and a very pleasant 45-minute nature walk through the forest. The copious growth of mosses and lichens here provide the rather unsubtle hint that the place can get very wet, very often!

From Lake Gunn you are really beginning to enter 'tiger country' as the road climbs to **The Divide**, one of the lowest passes along the length of the Southern Alps. Here a shelter and an assortment of discarded boots marks the start of the **Routeburn** and **Greenstone/Caples Tracks**. The car park also serves as the starting point to a classic, recommended (three hours return) walk to **Key Summit** which looks over the Humboldt and Darran Ranges. Round the corner there is the **Falls Creek (Pop's View) Lookout**, which looks down the **Hollyford Valley**. Depending on the weather this will be a scene of fairly quiet serenity or one of near epic proportions as the swollen Hollyford River rips its way down to the valley fed by a million fingers of whitewater.

Following the river is the **Lower Hollyford Road** and access to **Lake Marian** (1 km), a superb (three hours return) walk up through forest and past waterfalls into a glacial hanging valley that holds the lake captive. A further 7 km on is the charming **Hollyford (Gun's) Camp**, and the Hollyford Airfield, important access and accommodation points for the **Hollyford Track** (see page 705), the trailhead for which is at the road terminus 6 km further on. The short 30-minute return walk to the **Humboldt Falls**, which again are spectacular after heavy rain, starts just before the car park.

Back on the main Milford Road the mountains begin to close in on both sides as you make the ascent up to the **Homer Tunnel**, an incredible feat of engineering, and a bizarre and exciting experience, like being swallowed by a giant drain. It seems to have changed little since the last bit of rubble was cleared and is only lit by road markers. This simply adds to the appeal as long as you are not claustrophobic, or indeed on a bike! (If you are, you'd better pedal like mad for its entire 1200 m length.)

However, keep your eyes open for kea (native mountain parrots) that frequent the main stopping areas at either end of the tunnel. If they are not there, it is worth stopping a while to see if they turn up. Watching these incredibly intelligent birds go about their business of creating general mayhem in the name of food and sheer vandalism is highly entertaining. There will be plenty of photo opportunities and despite the obvious temptation DO NOT feed them. A parrot fed on white bread, crisps and chocolate is, obviously, a very sick parrot.

Once out of the tunnel you are now in the spectacular **Cleddau Canyon** and nearing Milford Sound. Instantly you will see the incredibly precipitous aspect of the mountains and bare valley walls. The rainfall is so high and rock and mudslides so frequent that the vegetation has little chance to establish itself. As a result the rainwater just cascades rapidly into the valleys. Note the creeks that cross under the road. There are so many they don't have names, but numbers. These all count up steadily to form the **Cleddau River**, which, at **The Chasm** (20 minutes return), is really more waterfall than river, and has, over the millennia, sculpted round shapes and basins in the rock. From The Chasm it is five minutes before you see the tip of the altar of **Mitre Peak** (1692 m) and spire of **Mount Tutoko** (2746 m), Fiordland's highest peak. It's now only five minutes before your appointment with the Minister of Awe at the Chancel of **Milford Sound**.

◉ Te Anau listings

For Sleeping and Eating price codes and other relevant information, see Essentials pages 44-50.

● Sleeping

Te Anau *p658, map p659*
Bear in mind that there are some excellent overnight cruise options on both Milford and Doubtful sounds see page 668 and page 673. There are a generous number of B&Bs and homestays, many of which are out in the country. There are also plenty of motels around town, the best and most expensive being on Lakefront Dr heading south from the centre, and the older and cheaper tending to be elsewhere, with many on Quintin Dr.
LL Te Anau Hotel and Villas, 64 Lakefront Dr, T03-249 9700, www.teanauhotel.co.nz. Lakeside, and the most high-profile hotel in town. It has had a number of name changes and renovations and offers good rooms, self-contained villas and 4 de luxe suites. A la carte restaurant, spa pool and sauna.
LL-L Fiordland Lodge, 472 Te Anau- Milford Highway (5 km north of Te Anau), T03-249 7832, www.fiordlandlodge.co.nz. A purpose-built luxury lodge, built in the classic lodge style and commanding stunning views across the lake and mountains. Smart en suite guest rooms, 2 self-contained log cabins, quality restaurant and

a large open fire. The owners also offer a wide range of guided excursions.
L-A Lake Front Lodge, 58 Lakefront Dr, T03-249 7728, www.lakefrontlodgeteanau. co.nz. Modern upmarket motel close to the lake, 13 units, some with spa bath.
AL Cat's Whiskers B&B, 2 Lakefront Dr, T03-249 8112, www.catswhiskers.co.nz. Conveniently placed town B&B.
AL Croft B&B, Milford Rd (on the edge of town, 3 km north), T03-249 7393, www.thecroft.co.nz. With 2 self-contained cottages set in private gardens on a farm with memorable views across the lake. Very peaceful and plenty of pets dying to make your acquaintance including Dolly the pet sheep (but not *that* Dolly).
AL-A Radfords Motel 56 Lakefront Dr, T03-249 9186, www.radfordslakeview motel.co.nz. Standard facilities.
A Arran, 64 Quintin Dr, T03-249 8826, www.arranmotel.co.nz.
A Lakeside Motel 36 Lakefront Dr, T03-249 7435, www.lakesideteanau.com. Set among pleasant gardens overlooking the lake.
A Red Tussock Motel, 10 Lakefront Dr (at the southern end), T03-249 9110, www.redtussockmotels.co.nz.
A-B Anchorage, 47 Quintin Dr, T03-249 7256, www.teanaumotel.co.nz.

Backpacker hostels

There are lots of backpacker hostels, most of which are geared up to cater for trampers and muddy boots. There are also options on the road north to Milford or south to Manapouri.

A-D Fiordland National Park Lodge, Te Anau Downs (30 km north), T0800-500805/ T03-249 7753, www.teanau-milfordsound. co.nz. Lakeside on SH94, 600 m from the Milford Track departure point (water taxi). 11 rooms with en suite, TV and fridge. Share kitchen, lounge and log fire.

C-D Bob and Maxine's Backpackers, 20 Paton Pl, T03-9313161, bob.anderson@ woosh.co.nz. New purpose-built establishment on the edge of town with a rural outlook. Very homely, well managed and equipped, offering 2 twin rooms and dorms. WiFi and free bike hire.

B-D Te Anau YHA, 29 Mokonui St, T03-249 7847, yhatanau@yha.org.nz. After years out of town it was relocated right in the centre. It is the most popular backpacker option (deservedly so) with a wide range of rooms and a very comfortable lounge. There is also a fully self-contained cottage available.

C-D Barnyard Backpackers, 80 Mt York Rd (south off SH95, 9 km), T03-249 8006, www.barnyardbackpackers.com. Tidy log cabins, van or campsites on a deer farm, open fire, horse trekking, internet and transport.

C-D Steamers Beach Backpackers, across the road from the DoC visitor centre, T03- 249 7457, www.teanauholidaypark.co.nz. The strangest looking hostel in town, owned and operated by the Te Anau Lake View Holiday Park. Perhaps looks a little over the top but you'll find perfectly comfortable and fine facilities on deck.

C-D Te Anau Lakefront Backpackers, 48-50 Lakefront Dr, T0800-200074/T03-249 7713, www.teanaubackpackers.co.nz. A large bustling place with all the usual facilities plus some excellent double or quad ex-motel units and fully self-contained units at reasonable prices. Tent sites. Spa, TV theatre and internet. Bike hire.

Motorcamps and campsites

See also backpacker hostels, above.

AL-D Te Anau Lake View Holiday Park, 1 Te Anau-Manapouri Highway (overlooking the lake on SH95), T03-249 7457, www.teanauholiday park.co.nz. Spacious with a lots of options from new motel units, to cabins, powered sites and tent sites. Internet café, sauna and spa, Sky TV. The added attraction is the ease of tramping track transportation in conjunction with the in-house **Tracknet** company.

A-D Te Anau Top Ten Holiday Park, 128 Te Anau Terr, T03-249 7462, www.teanau top10.co.nz. A proud multi-award winner and one of the best holiday parks in the country. The facilities are excellent and kept exceptionally clean and well maintained. You are even personally escorted to your site. It lives up to its name as having a 'bed for every budget'.

● Eating

Te Anau *p658, map p659*
There are 2 supermarkets: **Fresh Choice**, 5 Milford Cres; and **Four Square**, town centre, 0830-2100, seasonal.

♥♥♥ Kingsgate Hotel (Bluestone), T03-249 7421. Daily. Provides fine à la carte dining.

♥♥♥ Redcliff Café and Bar, 12 Mokonui St, T03-249 7431. Daily 1800-late. Intimate and congenial, and offers some particularly good lamb and venison dishes.

♥♥♥ Te Anau Hotel and Villas (McKinnon Room), T03-249 9700. Daily. Fine à la carte dining in this hotel restaurant.

♥♥ La Toscana Pizzeria, 108 Town Centre, T03-249 7756. 1730-2200. Good for pizza.

♥♥ Moose Restaurant and Bar, Lakeside Dr, T03-249 7100. Daily from 1100 for lunch and dinner. It has lost a little of its former atmosphere but can still serve up a good meal and has the town's most popular bar attached.

♥♥ Naturally Fiordland , 62 Town Centre, T03-249 7111. Daily 0900-2100. Good value, excellent pizza and recommended.

♥ Olive Tree Café, 52 Town Centre, T03-249 8496. Daily 0800-2130. Good coffee.

♥ Sandfly Café, 9 The Lane, T03-249 9529. Daily 0800-1630. Local's favourite.

▲▲ Activities and tours

Te Anau *p658, map p659*
The vast majority of visitors to Te Anau use it as a portal to Milford and Doubtful sounds and the major tramping tracks. Note that there are other activity operators in Milford Sound, Manapouri and Queenstown offering a wide range of other trips in the region (see page 627and page 673).

Cruising
Real Journeys, lakefront, T03-249 7416, www.realjourneys.co.nz. Although, as yet, no specific lake cruises are available, taking the shuttle to the start of the Milford track is an attractive option, you can then organize your own transport back (see **Tracknet** above) from Te Anau Downs. Another option is to join their Milford Track Guided Day Walk.

Fishing
As you might imagine the fishing in the region is superb, provided you can take your eyes off the stunning backdrops.
Fiordland Lodge Guides, T03-249 7832, www.fiordlandguides.co.nz. More specialist services. Charges about $800 for a full day trip. Overnight camping trips are also an option.
Fish Fiordland, T03-249 6855, www.fish fiordland.co.nz. Full-day trips from $95 per hr.
Fish and Trips, T03-249 7656, www.fiordland-flyfishing.com. Very reasonable at $300 for a half-day and $550 for a full day for 2 including snacks.

Flightseeing (fixed wing)
Without doubt the best way to see the Fiordland National Park is from the air. See also helicopter flightseeing, below.
Air Fiordland, Town Centre, T03-249 6720, www.airfiordland.com. Fixed-wing flights to Milford and Doubtful sounds with numerous options and combinations with sounds cruising and coach, ex Te Anau. Also available for private charter.
Wings and Water, Lakefront Dr, T03-249 7405, www.wingsandwater.co.nz. A fixed- wing floatplane that operates from the lake shore.

Offers a range of options principally to Milford and Doubtful sounds including flight only to flight/cruise and coach in/fly out, from 1-4½ hrs, $210-510. Also offer flights with kayaking and hiking options and can be chartered to see some of the remote locations used for filming in the *Lord of the Rings* trilogy.

4WD
High Ride 4 Wheeler Adventures, T03-249 8591, www.highride.co.nz. Offers scenic (3-4 hr) backcountry safaris on 4WD ATVs from $145. Recommended in any weather conditions but an ideal option if you booked a more weather dependent activity that has been cancelled.

Helicopter flightseeing
All the companies below offer a range of flights and packages from 10 mins (from around $160) to 1½ hrs ($700). Again the principal locations are **Milford** and **Doubtful sounds** though a trip to see the remote wilderness of the **Dusky Sound**, a heli-hike-cruise trip to the Mt Luxmore Hut on the **Kepler Track** or a scenic flight and jet-boat combo are all available (at a price). See also Flightseeing, above.
Fiordland Helicopters, T03-249 7575, www.fiordlandhelicopters.co.nz.
South West Helicopters, T03-249 7402, www.southwesthelicopters.co.nz.
Southern Lakes Helicopters, Lakefront Dr, T03-249 7167, www.southernlakes helicoptersco.nz. The principal helicopter operator in Te Anau.

Golf
Te Anau Golf Club, T03-249 7474. Green fee from $60, clubs from $30. Quite a hefty price for the scenery compared to many other better courses.

Horse trekking
High Ride, see 4WD, above, T03-2498591, www.highride.co.nz. Horse treks with transport from Te Anau, 2½ hrs, from $80.
Westray, 55 Ramparts Rd, T03-249 9079, www.fiordlandhorsetreks.com.

Jet boating

Luxmore Jet, T0800-253826/T03-249 6951, www.luxmore jet.co.nz. Offers a wide range of memorable trips with very personable guides down the Upper Waiau River, which connects Lake Te Anau and Lake Manapouri, from $95, child $45. The trip is also suitable for kids and more scenic oriented rather than the 'Queenstown style' thrills and spills. It also offers a '*Lord of the Rings*' heli/jet option (1 hr 40 mins) taking in local film locations, from $470.

Kayaking

Other spectacular kayaking options are available in Milford and Doubtful sounds from Manapouri (see page 668 and page 673).
Fiordland Wilderness Experiences, T0800-200434/T03- 249 7700, www.fiordland seakayak.co.nz. Full-day excursions on Milford from $155, multi-day trips to Doubtful Sound from $380. The Milford trip is especially good, taking in the scenery of the Milford Road.
Milford Sound (Rosco's) Sea Kayaks, see page 669. A long-established company based in Milford Sound, offering similar trips.

Scuba diving

Tawaki Dive (Dive Milford), T0800-829254/T03-249 9006, www.tawakidive.co.nz. Full-day diving trips to view the unique species of the fiords including the rare black coral from $189 (ex Te Anau). Open Water courses from $525.

Sightseeing tours

All the highly commercial Queenstown-based scenic day coach tours (see page 618) pass through Te Anau and you can join these to reach Milford or Doubtful sounds. The VIC (I-Site) has details and you are advised to book in advance.
Trips and Tramps, T0800-305807/ T03-249 7081, www.tripsandtramps.co.nz. Locally orientated, personable day-trips to Milford Sound (including cruise and walking options) from $165, child $100.

Walking

The biggest local attraction here is of course the 67-km (2- to 3-day), **Kepler Track** which can be walked in whole or part. One of the most popular day or overnight walks is to capture the view from the **Luxmore Hut**, which is the first DoC hut on the track (in the traditional anticlockwise direction). To access the hut by foot, walk along the southern edge of the lake to the control gates. From there it is a fairly strenuous 11-km (6 hrs) one-way walk along the lake edge and up above the tree line to the hut. A very appealing way to cut out much of the strain is to get a water taxi (T03-249 8364, $40 return) or to join a walk/cruise trip (see Cruising above) from Te Anau to **Brod Bay**. It is then a 16 km (8 hrs) return trip.
Bev's Tramping Gear, 16 Homer St, T03-249 7389, www.bevs-hire.co.nz. Rents out a range of walking, tramping and camping equipment at competitive prices. Open daily 0900-1200 and 1730-1900, closed Sun morning.
Kiwi Camping Centre, 38-40 Town Centre, T03-249 8195, www.kiwicamping.co.nz. Has a vast range of walking, tramping and camping equipment for hire.
Trips and Tramps, T03-249 7081, www.tripsandtramps.co.nz. Locally orientated, personable day-trips to Milford Sound (including cruise and walking options to Lake Marian and Key Summit) from $165, child $100.

● Transport

Te Anau *p658, map p659*
Bicycle and scooter hire
Fiordland Bike Hire, 7 Mokonui St, T03-249 7211, bikes and scooters.

Car hire
Rent-a-Dent, Manapouri T03-249 8576. **Te Anau Taxi and Tours**, T03-249 7777. For breakdown services contact **Mobil**, town centre, T03-249 7247 (24 hr) and **Caltex**, 33 Luxmore Dr, T03-2497140.

Taxi
Te Anau Taxi and Tours, T03-249 7777.

❶ Directory

Te Anau *p658, map p659*
Banks There are 2 banks (Westpac/BNZ) in the town centre both have ATMs and offer currency exchange services. **Internet** Te Anau Photocentre, 62 Town Centre, T03-249 7620.

E-stop, Jailhouse Mall, town centre, 0900-2100, seasonal. **Air Fiordland (tic-it Te Anau)**, town centre, 0900-1900, seasonal. Mountain View Holiday Park, Te Anau Terr. Lake Te Anau Backpackers, 48 Lakefront Dr. Fiordland Electrical, 19 Luxmore Drive, (24 hr). **Medical services** Doctor Luxmore Dr, T03-249 7007, Mon-Fri 0800-1800, Sat 0900-1200. **Police** Milford Rd, T03-249 7600. **Post office** 'Paper Plus', town centre.

Milford Sound → *Colour map 6, A3 Population: 300 (seasonal).*

There are simply no words in a thesaurus to describe the sight of Milford Sound; let alone its moods. Come rain or shine, calm or storm, dawn or dusk, it is ever-changing, always dramatic, and never dull. In every sense Milford Sound is quite simply New Zealand at its glorious and unparalleled best. Given the enormity (quite literally) of the attraction you will be immediately struck by how under-developed Milford Sound is. With its conservative scatter of low-key buildings it seems only the boat terminal stands out like a sore thumb. This is quite deliberate. The fact that Milford is the jewel in the crown of the Fiordland National Park and administered by the DoC, means that further development is strictly controlled, hence the lack of accommodation. How utterly refreshing it is to see a place of such outstanding natural beauty so unspoilt and not completely over-run with rapacious developers out to make a buck, or the well-heeled building their dream homes, eating up the acres and then calling in the 'Animal Control' man. In Milford only nature (and that includes sandflies) rule and you had better respect it.

    However, that said, this is still one of New Zealand's biggest tourist attractions and our physical presence there is, sadly, predominantly money-driven and places a huge burden on the environment. Despite the limits on building in Milford Sound, those that already exist are in desperate need of a facelift, if not a complete transplant. Other than the recently upgraded yet completely sterile cruise terminal, the waterfront buildings are nothing short of a national disgrace and surely an embarrassment to the image of tourism in New Zealand. Also, the big corporates that exist there are no less rapacious and profit driven than they are in money-mad Queenstown. In mid-summer the place is a hum of propeller and diesel engines, as the masses are brought in to 'take the cruise'. On any given day in the high season there are scores of coaches and campervans doing the trip from Queenstown and Te Anau which, against a backdrop of such enormity, can be a surreal sight in itself. This is one place where 'Ant Travel' or 'Humblin Coaches' would seem entirely appropriate. Without proper investigation Milford can almost be too much for the senses, so it's best to arrive independently, or indeed go in winter. By all means take a cruise, and more especially a scenic flight, but if you can linger a while, and wait until the buses have left, you can appreciate this incredible place even more. ▸▸ *For Sleeping, Eating and other listings, see pages 668-670.*

Ins and outs
Getting there You can reach Milford Sound by air, bus, road, or by foot, via the Milford Track. But the best way to arrive, if you can afford it, is to take a scenic flight/cruise combination from Wanaka or Queenstown. Then, if you do not have your own wheels, hire a car from Queenstown or Te Anau and give yourself at least two days to explore the

area properly. Your arrival by air will almost certainly be in combination with a scenic flight or tour option from Wanaka, Queenstown or Te Anau (see Flightseeing, page 669). The landing and take-off from the airfield in Milford, 1 km from the visitor centre, is a memorable experience.

There is a vast array of bus and coach operators serving Milford Sound, with an equal number of tour options, from simple bus-in/bus-out, to bus/cruise/bus or bus-in/cruise/fly-out and even bus/overnight cruise options. Most operators are based in Queenstown, from where they make the 12-hr, 291-km day trip by road, picking up passengers from Te Anau on the way. This is one of the most spectacular bus trips in the world, provided the weather is favourable. However, if dark clouds are gathering, or the forecast is for heavy rain (which it frequently is) do not despair. Even if it is pouring down this can actually add to the drama and spectacle of the Milford Road as channels of water fall from the precipitous outcrops and in all directions like a some sort of surreal giant's car wash. In fact, the heavier the better. Many people actually prefer Milford in awful weather and quite right too – with an average of about 7 m annually it really knows how to rain here.
▶▶ See also Tour operators, page 670.

Tourist information If you have arrived independently and not yet pre-booked any activities you can choose from the array of options at the **Milford Sound Visitor Centre** ① *boat terminal, 0900-1700*. You are, however, advised to research the huge number of options prior to your visit. The VICs (I-Sites) in Queenstown and Te Anau will assist.

Sights

Milford Sound is in itself, of course, just one huge sight but there are individual aspects worth noting. The centrepiece of the Sound is **Mitre Peak**. At 1692 m it is not that high by New Zealand standards but, as with the entire corridor of Milford Sound, it is the sheer rate of ascent created by the actions of the glaciers that creates such an impact. Opposite Mitre Peak is **The Lion** (1302 m) and further up the ridge behind it **Mount Pembroke** (2045 m). Milford Sound itself is 15 km in length and about 290 m at its deepest. The mouth of the fiord is only about 120 m wide, due to melt action and the terminal moraines of the former glaciers. In heavy rains the fiord can seem like one great waterfall but by far the most impressive at any time are the 160-m **Bowen Falls**, which was until recently reached by a boardwalk from beside the boat terminal. Sadly, due to unstable rock conditions on the slopes above, this is now closed until further notice. Similarly, about midway along the eastern well of the fiord are the **Stirling Falls** (154 m) whose mist and rainbows can only be visited by boat or kayak.

The fiords are home to some fairly unusual and hardy wildlife. Fur seals are commonly seen lazing about on the rocks on almost every cruise, but it is below the water's surface that the most noted species are found. Milford Sound is home to the unusual **Milford Deep Underwater Observatory** ① *T0800-264536/T03-441 1137, www.southerndiscoveries.co.nz*, which was no mean engineering feat. In the sheltered waters of **Harrison Cove**, about a third of the way out of the sound on its eastern edge, the observatory can be visited in combination with a Red Boats cruise from $24 on top of the cruise price. From the observatory's interesting interpretative centre you can descend 8 m into a circular viewing chamber where a wide array of sea creatures can be seen at close quarters. There are many rare species in Milford including the very rare black coral (which is actually white), a species that can live for over 300 years. Another white resident you may encounter is 'Charlie' the kotuku (white heron). Charlie has been using Milford Sound as his winter residence for over 12 years. In summer Charlie reunites with his mate in Okarito on the west coast, which is New Zealand's only breeding colony. The best place to spot Charlie is around the boat harbour or on the beach where he will probably be busy fishing or just watching the tourists go by. ►► *See also Activities and tours, see page 668.*

◉ Milford Sound listings

For Sleeping and Eating price codes and other relevant information, see Essentials pages 44-50.

◉ Sleeping

Milford Sound *p666*
A-D Milford Sound Lodge, just off the Milford Rd about 1 km east of the airfield, T03-249 8071, www.milfordlodge.com. For the independent traveller this really is the only place to stay in Milford Sound and, in mid-summer outside the Milford pub opening hours, forms the hub of Milford's leisure activity. Here you can mix with all types, from rich tourists to locals and trampers. Despite the inevitable 'damned biting things', it has a comfortable range of chalet-style en suites, double/twins, dorms and hard, sheltered and very pricey tent sites. Beyond the chalets the bathroom facilities are shared. All in all surrounded by such splendour it's a great place to be. The staff are good fun, there is a small guest kitchen, large comfortable lounge, small grocery store and satellite internet. You can also get a continental breakfast. A word of warning about the kitchen, however: in summer it can be like catching the last train to Rawalpindi from 1700 onwards, so get in there at 1600 and spend the rest of the evening relaxing in the lounge and feeling smug as the tempers fray next door. One other thing – the resident keas. Several individuals regularly visit the lodge to cause the standard mayhem and your car and possessions are naturally a prime target. These guys are more switched on than you could ever imagine. So, beware for example the heinous photo on the rock trick. It's simple genius really. While one grabs your undivided attention posing for you on a rock another family member will be eating your dinner, chatting up your girlfriend or downloading the contents of your iPod behind you. Marvellous stuff.

B-D Mitre Peak Lodge, T03-441 1138, near the boat terminal. More salubrious, yet a blot on the landscape, that caters only for clients of Milford Track guided walks.

◉ Eating

Milford Sound *p666*
Blue Duck Pub and Café, next to the main car park on the waterfront T03-249 7657. Summer 0830-1700, bar 1100 till 'close' (local jargon for when most of the punters have all left and the local operators have had their fill); winter 0900-1630, bar 1630 till 'close'. Owned by Red Boats, this is your only option for eating, other than the **Milford Lodge**. It serves a full range of pub-style food from generous breakfasts to toasted sandwiches. There are also lunch options on some cruises. When the rain is relentless the renovated bar, with its open fire and widescreen TV, provides sanctuary. Milford attracts a multifarious bunch of characters both long-term and transitory and you can almost be assured of an entertaining night out. But be careful: drop your defences, drink too much and partake in idle bets and you may find yourself enlisted as 'lead runner' in the annual naked Milford Tunnel dash.

▲ Activities and tours

Milford Sound *p666*
Cruising
The majority of day cruises explore the entire 15-km length of the sound to the Tasman Sea, taking in all the sights on the way, including the waterfalls, precipitous rock overhangs, seal colonies and the underwater observatory (optional). On the overnight cruises (see **Real Journeys**, below) you take in

all the usual sights, but can enjoy an extended trip, meals, accommodation and other activities including boat-based kayaking. Given the fact you are not joined on the water by the fleets of day cruise ships you are more likely to see the local wildlife, including dolphins. All prices listed are ex Milford but there are also numerous options that include air or bus transportation from Wanaka, Queenstown or Te Anau.

Mitre Peak Cruises, T03-249 8110, www.mitrepeak.com. One of the smaller cruise operators offering a low passenger number (smaller boat), nature-orientated day cruise, from $64 (Underwater Observatory from $28)

Southern Discoveries (Milford Sound Red Boat Cruises), T0800-264536/T03- 441 1137, www.southerndiscoveries.co.nz. A major operator, offering similar cruises and rates to **Real Journeys**, but they have no overnight cruises. They also own and operate the Underwater Observatory (see page 667), which can alsobe visited as an adjunct to other operators' cruises.

Real Journeys, T03-249 7416/T0800- 656501, www.fiordlandtravel.co.nz. Offers a 'Small Boat Daytime Cruise', a standard (larger boat) 'Scenic Cruise' and a longer 'Nature Cruise'. Prices range from $62(child $20) to $84. There is an interesting commentary, with free tea or coffee, and you are encouraged to ask the crew questions. Free access is allowed all around the boat with the most hardy souls and budding National Geographic photographers braving the wind on the upper decks. Additional lunch options are also available.

Overnight cruises are available on 2 vessels: the *MV Milford Wanderer*, which has quad-share bunk style cabins (1645-0915; from $161-$230, child $80-$115); and the top of the range *MV Milford Mariner* Overnight Cruise (16 hrs; from $161-470, child $80-$235) which has quad-share to double cabins and includes dinner and breakfast. All prices are for twin share but sole occupancy is available from $576.

Flightseeing

Flightseeing trips to Milford are readily and principally available from Wanaka, Te Anau and Queenstown. The most popular option is the combination fly/cruise trip, which combines an extended scenic flight with one of the regular daytime cruises. Expect to pay $350-400 (Queenstown/Wanaka). Note, however, this only allows about 2 hrs in Milford itself. Another popular trip, missing out the long bus journey back, is the bus-in/ cruise/fly-back option, which costs from $500 (Queenstown). The flight into and around Milford Sound is right up there with the glacier and Mt Cook flights of the west coast.

The principal operators based in Milford, Queenstown and Te Anau are listed below. They offer an array of options, with some flights taking in the Sutherland Falls on the Milford Track and Doubtful Sound. **Air Fiordland**, T0800-107505/T03-249 6720, www.airfiordland.com; **Air Milford**, T03-442 2351, www.airmilford.co.nz; **Fiordland Helicopters**, T03-249 7575, www.fiordland helicopters.co.nz; and **Milford Helicopters**, T03-249 8384.

Kayaking

A far more serene and atmospheric way to see the sound is by kayak, giving you an incredible sense of scale and intimacy. **Fiordland Wilderness Experiences**, Te Anau, T03-249 7700, www.fiordland seakayak.co.nz. Offers a day excursion on the Sound from $125 ($155 ex Te Anau), taking in the scenery of the Milford Rd. Summer only. **Milford Sound (Rosco's) Sea Kayaks**, based at Deep Water Basin (just east of the airfield), T03-249 8500, www.roscosmilford kayaks.com. Operated by the intrepid Rosco Gaudin and offers a range of day safaris, fly/kayak, paddle/walk (part of the Milford Track) from 4-7 hrs (flight options are also available from Queenstown). The standard paddle costs $149 from Te Anau, $115 from Milford. This is the only company that operates year round.

Scuba diving

Tawaki Dive (Milford Dive), Te Anau, T0800-829254, www.tawakidive.co.nz.

Full-day fiord diving trips to view the varied species of this unique habitat including rare black coral and the odd sea dragon, from $189 ex Te Anau and $159 ex Milford (gear hire from $45).

Tour operators
From Queenstown the principal upmarket operators serving Milford Sound can be booked through **Real Journeys**, see below. There are a few other companies operating out of Queenstown (via Te Anau) that cater for smaller groups, thereby offering a more personable experience.
BBQ Bus, T0800-421045/T03-442 1045, www.milford.net.nz. A reputable company and recommended. Its day trip from Queenstown (departs 0715, pick-ups in Te Anau, return to Queenstown at 1900), includes lunch in the Hollyford Valley, a cruise on the Sound and a visit to the wildlife centre in Te Anau, all from $174. You can also join the tour from Te Anau (from $144) and there is also a coach/cruise and return flight option, from $484.
Kiwi Discovery, Camp St, Queenstown, T03-442 7340, www.kiwidiscovery.com, and

Kiwi Experience, 37 Shotover St, Queenstown, T03-442 9708, www.kiwiexperience.com, are backpacker-orientated outfits offering similar coach/cruise options from $175. They will also pick up in Te Anau.
Real Journeys, 74 Shotover St, Queenstown, T03-442 7509, www.realjourneys.co.nz; or at the VIC (I-Site) in Te Anau, T0800-656501/T03-249 7416. Expect to pay around $225 for a coach/cruise day trip, from $340 for a coach/overnight cruise combo (from $235-1000) and around $320 for the bus/cruise/fly option.
There are also many options available by bus from Te Anau, many linking up with the Queenstown tours. Again **Real Journeys**, above, is the principal operator. The VIC (I-Site) lists others. From Te Anau expect to pay $195 for a day coach/cruise option, or $250-560 for an overnight trip.
Trips and Tramps, T03-2497081, www.tripsandtramps.co.nz. Locally orientated, personable day-trips to Milford Sound (including cruise and walking options to Lake Marian and Key Summit) from $165, child $100.

Manapouri and Doubtful Sound → Colour map 6, B3.

As you drive into Manapouri with its stunning vistas across the eponymous lake, you are immediately struck by how unobtrusive it is. If it were anywhere else in the developed world, it would probably be an unsightly mass of exclusive real estate and tourist developments. Thankfully it is not, though perhaps the recent history of this pretty little village, the main gateway and access point to activities on Lake Manapouri, Doubtful Sound and the incredible and challenging Dusky Track, has something to do with that. Though you would never guess it, Manapouri has been the sight of some major altercations between the advocates of economics and conservation. Hidden away at the West Arm of the lake, and smack-bang in the heart of Fiordland National Park, is the country's largest hydroelectric power station, which has, over the years, created much controversy. Yet it is the very development of the power station that allows the tourist and conservationist access to some of the most remote parts of the park. Now it is home to an uneasy mix of power station workers and eco-friendly tourist operators and service providers. ▸▸ *For Sleeping, Eating and other listings, see pages 672-674.*

Ins and outs
Getting there Manapouri is 20 km south of Te Anau via SH95. Several bus companies pass through Manapouri on their way south via SH99 to Invercargill, including **Scenic Shuttles**, T0800-277483/T03-249 7654 (Invercargill, daily Nov-Apr, Mon-Fri May-Oct);

Bottom Bus, T03-442 9708; and Topline Tours, T03-249 8059/T0508-832628, www.toplinetours.co.nz. Real Journeys, T03-249 7416, also offers regular shuttles back and forth to Te Anau.

Getting around   Real Journeys, Pearl Harbour, Manapouri, T0800-656501/T03-249 7416, www.realjourneys.co.nz, offers excellent day (8-hr) and overnight (24-hr) excursions to Doubtful Sound via Lake Manapouri and the Wilmot Pass.

Tourist information   There is no information centre in Manapouri, but Real Journeys① on the wharf (Pearl harbour), T03-249 7416, www.realjourneys.co.nz, is the base for all water activity on the lake and Doubtful Sound tour operations. For further information contact the VIC (I-Site) ① T03-249 8900, or DoC ① T03-249 7924, in Te Anau.

Lake Manapouri

Lake Manapouri is stunning not only because of its backdrop of bush and mountain but also its moods. From the beach beside the village the whole scene echoes the constant change of Milford Sound. It is of course not so dramatic in its topography, but no less dynamic. There are 35 islands which disguise its boundaries and, at a forbidding 420 m deep, is the second deepest lake in the country (the deepest is Lake Hauroko in southwestern Fiordland). To really appreciate the size and complex nature of Lake Manapouri it is necessary to get out on the water, which, thankfully, is a matter of course on the route to Doubtful Sound.

Manapouri Underground Power Station

At the terminus of West Arm, and forming the main access point via Wilmot Pass to Doubtful Sound, is the Manapouri Underground Power Station. Although an unwelcome development to the conservationist, one cannot fail to admire the environmentally sympathetic way in which this incredible feat of engineering has been achieved and is maintained. Started in 1963 and completed eight years later, now only a few unsightly pylons connected to a switchyard, a control building and water intakes, belie the mammoth constructions underground – all supplied by a fairly unobtrusive barge that goes back and forth across the lake to Supply Bay near Manapouri. A 2040 m (1:10) tunnel set in the hillside allows access to the main centre of operations – a large machine hall housing seven turbines and generators, fed by the water penstocks from 170 m above. What is most impressive is the 9.2 m diameter tailrace tunnel, which outputs the used water at the head of Doubtful Sound – an amazing 10 km from Lake Manapouri and 178 m below its surface. Started in 1964 the tailrace took four years to build. Real Journeys (see Activities and tours, page 673) make three-hour trips to the power station (it is also a port of call on the Doubtful Sound day-excursion, see below); the bus drives down the dank and forbidding access tunnel and makes a very tight turn at the bottom where passengers are decanted out to look at the interior of the machine hall. Even the worst luddite will be impressed.

Wilmot Pass

① *The road can be explored independently by mountain bike (provided you are fit enough) and acts as the northern trailhead to the Dusky Track.*

The 22-km road from West Arm to Doubtful Sound across the Wilmot Pass is spectacular. Encompassing remote mountain and beech and podocarp forest scenery, lookout points and waterfalls, the unsealed road, which took two years to complete, was built as part of the hydropower project. At a cost of nearly $5 for every 2.5 cm, it is easily the most expensive road in the country. With its numerous twists and turns and heady topography, together with an annual rainfall of over 7 m, it is also a very hard road to maintain. Like the power station, the road forms part of **Real Journeys**' Doubtful Sound day trip (see page 673).

Doubtful Sound

Doubt nothing, this fiord, like Milford Sound, is all it is cracked up to be – and more. Many who have made the trip to Milford feel it may be very similar and therefore not worthy of the time or expense to get there. But Doubtful Sound has a very different atmosphere to Milford. With the mountain topography in Fiordland getting generally lower the further south you go, and the fiords becoming longer and more indented with coves, arms and islands, Doubtful Sound offers the sense of space and wilderness that Milford does not.

Doubtful is, after Dusky, the second largest fiord and has 10 times the surface area of Milford and, at 40 km, is also more than twice as long. It is also the deepest of the fiords at 421 m. There are three distinct arms and several outstanding waterfalls including the heady 619-m **Browne Falls** near Hall Arm. This is only marginally less than the near-vertical Sutherland Falls on the famed Milford Track. At the entrance to Hall Arm is the impressive 900-m cliff of **Commander Peak** (1274 m), the only true echo of Milford's dramatic corridor.

Doubtful Sound hosts its own pod of about 60 bottlenose dolphins that are regularly seen by visitors as well as fur seals and fiordland crested penguins. It is also noted for its very lack of activity; on a calm night the silence is deafening.

Captain Cook originally named it Doubtful Harbour during his voyage of 1770. He decided not to explore past the entrance, fearful that the prevailing winds would not allow him to get back out; hence the name. It was not until 23 years later that Italian explorer Don Alessandro Malaspina, leading a Spanish expedition, dropped anchor and sent a small crew on a whaleboat into the fiord to make observations. Although a brief excursion it was both brave and meticulous and left a number of present-day names in its wake – Malaspina Reach being the most obvious.

◉ Manapori & Doubtful Sound listings

For Sleeping and Eating price codes and other relevant information, see Essentials pages 44-50.

● Sleeping

Doubtful Sound *p672*
Real Journeys, T03-249 6602, www.real journeys.co.nz, offers overnight packages in season on Doubtful Sound, from $265 quad-share to $700 single occupancy.
LL Beechwood Lodge, 40 Cathedral Dr, T03-249 6993, www.beechwoodlodge.com. A modern, deservedly popular boutique B&B that sits overlooking the lake and mountains. Guests are accommodated on the ground floor, which has 2 spacious en suites, a private entrance and a guest kitchen. From the lounge you can sit and muse upon the ever-changing moods of the lake. Internet

and off-street parking. No children.
LL Murrell's Grand View House, 7 Murrell Av, T03-249 6642, www.murrells.co.nz. A rambling house near the mouth of the outlet and surrounded by spacious gardens. It offers 4 spacious double en suites and fine cuisine, just a short walk from the cruise terminal.
A-D Manapouri Motels and Holiday Park, 86 Cathedral Dr, T03-249 6624, www.manapourimotels.co.nz. Wonderfully quirky place with a range of 'disney-esque' cottages, old Morris Minors and even a period costume collection. It has the cottages of course, which are a delight plus more conventional cabins, powered sites and good facilities. The lakeshore is just across the road.
A-D Manapouri Lakeview Motor Inn, 68 Manapouri-Te Anau Highway, T03-249 6652, www.manapouri.com. This older place

overlooks the lake and has serviced rooms and units and budget rooms, a bar and café.

B-D Freestone Backpackers, 3 km east of Manapouri on Hillside Rd, T03-249 6893, freestone@xtra.co.nz. 5 tidy self-contained timber chalets with wood burners in a 4-ha rural setting. Singles, doubles, twins and shared rooms. Recommended.

B-D Manapouri Glade and Possum Lodge, at the end of Murrell Av and right on the headland at the Waiau River mouth, T03-249 6623, possumlodge@xtra.co.nz. Self-contained cottages, backpacker cabins and powered/tent sites. Peaceful place with lovely short walks.

D Deep Cove Hostel, very remote, at the head of Doubtful Sound, T03-249 6602, www.deep covehostel.co.nz. A possibility outside school term-time but phone first for details.

❶ Eating

Doubtful Sound *p672*
There are few options in Manapouri and you would be better to head back to Te Anau for evening dining.

♥ **Beehive**, in the Lakeview Motor Inn, T03-249 6652. Mon-Sat 1100-2130 (seasonal). Has a licensed café and bar, serving acceptable pub-style grub into the evening.

♥ **Cathedral Café**, Cathedral Dr (next to the general store and petrol station). Serves coffee and snacks during the day.

▲ Activities and tours

Doubtful Sound *p672*
Eco-tours
Adventure Kayak and Cruise, Waiau St, T0800-324966/T03-249 6626, www.fiordland adventure.co.nz. Offers day or overnight rental or fully equipped kayaks on Lake Manapouri (from $50 per day) as well as full-day guided and guided overnight trips to Doubtful Sound, from $225 (overnight $255, 2-day $365).

Fiordland Ecology Holidays (Real Journeys), based on the main road in Manapouri, T03-249 6600, www.fiordland.gen.nz. Offers an excellent range of holiday options from 3 days to 2 weeks on board its 12 passenger, 65-ft yacht *Breaksea Girl*. The yacht is very comfortable and well equipped and the tours offer a very sensitive insight into Fiordland's unique wildlife. Trips cost from $215 per day.

Fiordland Wilderness Experiences, based in Te Anau (see page 665). Offers 2- to 5-day trips to Doubtful, Breaksea and Dusky Sounds from $285. It also offers independent rental for the experienced, from $55 a day.

Mountain biking
The **Wilmot Pass** is a superb (but challenging 500 m ascent) road to explore by mountain bike. For bike hire see Te Anau page 665.

Tours of the sound
This trip is recommended not only because of the stunning natural scenery and the wildlife but because of the novelty of entering into the very bowels of the earth.

Deep Cove Charters, Manapouri, T03-249 6828, www.doubtful-sound.com. Offers a small-scale craft and a personalized laid-back operation. It is perfect if you want to spend a night out on the sound and avoid the big commercial operations. An overnight cruise costs from $440. Departs 0900.

Fiordland Explorer Charters, T0800-434673/T03-249 6616, www.doubtfulsound cruise.com, also offers a smaller scale, personalized operation and day excursion (7½ hrs) daily at 0930, from $250, child $80.

Real Journeys Pearl Harbour, T03-249 6602, www.realjourneys.co.nz. The main commercial tour operator to the Manapouri Power Station and Doubtful Sound. It offers a Wilderness Day Cruise (10 hrs) from $275, child $60; and the popular Overnight Cruise.

Wilderness Day Cruise After boarding a modern launch at Manapouri you cross the lake to West Arm (interesting commentary and free tea/coffee). From West Arm you then board a bus and negotiate the Wilmot Pass, stopping at a viewpoint over Doubtful Sound before descending past rivers, waterfalls and the hydropower tailrace outlet to the Doubtful Sound wharf. From there you board another launch for a superbly scenic and informative cruise through the Sound to the Tasman Sea. If time allows, you negotiate one or 2 of the fiords 'arms' and throughout the cruise can often see the resident dolphins. Once returned to the wharf, reunited with the bus and Lake Manapouri's West Arm, you then leave the dramatic scenery and daylight behind and negotiate the underground access tunnel to the machine hall of the hydropower station. There you stop for 30 mins to learn how it all works before re-emerging into daylight and catching the launch back to Manapouri. Trips depart daily at 0930 (Te Anau at 0815) and cost from $275, child $60 (Te Anau $296, child $53).

Overnight Cruise This trip involves all of the above, plus an overnight stay on the Sound, aboard the comfortable Fiordland Navigator. Designed along the lines of a traditional New Zealand trading scow, it comes complete with sails and offers private en suite cabins or quad-share bunks. There are friendly nature guides on board and also

kayaks with which you can do your own scheduled exploring. Trips depart daily Nov-Apr at 1230 from $128 quad-share, double $237, and $827 single occupancy. Both these trips link in with Queenstown and Te Anau departures.

Walking and tramping
The Wilmot Pass is the principal access point to the northern trailhead of the **Dusky Track** (see page 701). There are also a number of walks available around Manapouri most of which negotiate the **Garnock Burn** catchment and start on the southern bank of the Lake Manapouri outlet at Pearl Harbour. The most popular walk is the (3 hrs) **Pearl Harbour Circle Track**, which follows the riverbank, upstream, before negotiating the forest ascent to a lookout point, then descending back to Pearl Harbour. The Circle Track also allows access to the longer **Back Valley** and **Hope Arm Hut** tracks that explore Hope Arm (Lake Manapouri) and the inland **Lake Rakatu**. For details pick up the Manapouri Walks leaflet ($1) from the DoC VIC in Te Anau. For dinghy hire across the river (call at the post centre next to the petrol station and café) or contact **Adventure Kayak and Cruise**, T03-249 6626, www.fiordlandadventure.co.nz.

Southern Scenic Route → *Colour map 6, C4.*

From Manapouri SH99 leaves the vast majority of tourist traffic behind, as most retrace their steps to Queenstown or cross-country east, to Dunedin. The Southern Scenic Route, which first heads south to the coast via Tuatapere and Invercargill, then north via the beautiful and underrated Catlins coast to Dunedin, provides an attractive alternative. The highlights of this trip, other than the sheer peace and quiet, are the potential stops in Tuatapere to walk the relatively new and celebrated Hump Ridge Track, an overnight stay in the pleasant seaside resort of Riverton, a day or two in Invercargill, before a trip to Stewart Island (see page 684) and then a thorough exploration of the Catlins Coast (see page 692). ▸▸ *For Sleeping, Eating and other listings, see pages 681-684.*

Ins and outs
Getting there and around The Southern Scenic Route which is sometimes advertised as encompassing the entire journey from Dunedin to Milford Sound is a total of 440 km. By bus, the route is served by **Scenic Shuttle**, T0800-277483/T03-249 9083, www.scenicshuttle.co.nz

(Invercargill, daily Nov-Apr, Mon-Fri May-Oct), and the backpacker orientated **Bottom Bus**, T03-434 7370, www.travelheadfirst.com (Queenstown/Dunedin/Invercargill). Local shuttle services and transport to and from Invercargill are listed in the places below.

Tourist information Tuatapere VIC ① *31 Orawia Rd, T0800-HUMPRIDGE/ T03-226 6399, info@humpridgetrack.co.nz, daily 0900-1700 (winter Mon-Fri 0900-1700)*, has enthusiastic and helpful staff who can provide infinite detail about the Hump Ridge Track, www.humpridgetrack.co.nz, www.southernscenicroute.co.nz. They also administer all track bookings and have internet. **DoC** has an office in Tuatapere but you will find all the relevant administration at the VIC. **Riverton VIC (I-Site)** ① *across the river (from the west) and housed in the new Te Hikoi Museum, 172 Palmerston St, T03-234 8260, www.riverton-aparima.co.nz, daily 0900-1700*. **Invercargill VIC (I-Site)** ① *Southland Museum & Art Gallery, 108 Gala St, T03-211 0895, www.southlandnz.com, daily Oct-Apr 0900-1900, May-Sep 0900-1700*, has listings of local activities, transport, accommodation and attractions. **DoC** ① *regional office, 7th floor, State Insurance Building, 33 Don St, T03-211 2400, www.doc.govt.nz, Mon-Fri 0800-1700*, can also organize hut bookings for Stewart Island tramps.

Manapouri to Tuatapere ⬤⭘▲ ↠ *pp681-684.*

Still reeling from the highs of Fiordland's stunning scenery, your journey south could include the main drag of Vegas and still seem boring, so just accept that fact and sit back and enjoy the peace and quiet of the road. SH99 has to be one of the quietest main roads in the country and between Manapouri and Milford it's unusual to pass more than half a dozen cars even in summer. Generally speaking you will encounter very little with two legs. Instead what you will see is paddock upon paddock of sheep.

Although birdwatchers can find considerable pleasure at the **Redcliffe Wetland Reserve** just north of Blackmount (38 km) there is little to justify a stop until **Clifden** (66 km). As well as its limestone caves, Clifden boasts one of the oldest and longest suspension bridges in the country (built in 1899). Though a little disappointing in global terms, it is still worth a look and makes a nice picnic spot by the river. Near Clifden (signposted off Clifden Gorge Road to Winton) are its non-commercial and undeveloped limestone caves, which can be explored carefully with a good torch.

Just south of Clifden is the 30-km unsealed road to **Lake Hauroko**, the deepest body of water in New Zealand. Its remoteness is undoubtedly appealing and there is an interesting walk up a precipitous bluff to a lookout point. The area is also known for its many Maori (Ngai Tahu) burial sites. Lake Hauroko provides jet-boat access to the **Dusky Track**, one of the country's most challenging and remote tramps. **Lake Hauroko Tours**, based in Tuatapere, T03-226 6681, www.duskytrack.co.nz, can provide access. On your way back from Lake Hauroko you may consider the short diversion north (off the Hauroko Road just before SH99) to sample the delights of **Dean Forest**. There, a pleasant short walk takes in its most famous native, a 1000-year-old totara tree. Once back on SH99 it is a further 13 km to Tuatapere, considered the gateway to the southeast corner of the Fiordland National Park (not that there are any roads).

Tuatapere → *Colour map 6, B3 Population: 800.*

Tuatapere is a quiet little town that wants to start making a big noise. The reason for this and the town's intended 'raison d'être tourisme', is the 53-km **Hump Ridge Track**, New Zealand's newest 'Great Walk' and one that is advertised as being on a par with any of the others in Fiordland, or indeed the country (see page 702). The track starts at the western end of **Bluecliffs Beach**, which, in itself, is a nice spot to spend a couple of hours. Nearby, on the first section of the Hump Ridge Track is the 36-m-high, 125-m- long **Percy Burn Viaduct**, the largest wooden viaduct in the world. But even as it stood, this former saw-milling and farming town and (mysteriously) self-proclaimed 'sausage capital' of the country, had a few other notable local attractions, including some fine jet-boating operations down the **Wairaurahiri River**. **Lake Hauroko Tours**, T03-226 6681, offers transport and trips to and from the tracks.

Tuatapere to Invercargill ⊜🅗🅞🅐 ▲ ↦ *pp681-684*.

A further 10 km south and SH99 reaches the coast at the evocatively named **Te Waewae Bay**. Here you can stop at **McCraken's Rest** to admire the beach and the views west over southern Fiordland, or east, to **Monkey Island**. Monkey Island was the anchor site of the great Maori *waka* (canoe) Takitimu which, as legend tells, was wrecked on the bar of the Waiau River. Te Waewae Bay itself is quite a serene sight in fine weather and often the playground for Hector's dolphin and the odd whale, but in winter the wind can come sweeping in from the Antarctic with a vengeance.

This phenomenon is starkly highlighted in the next port of call – the intriguing village of **Orepuki** – where the macrocarpa trees have been sculpted into amazing, tangled shapes by the wind. Apparently, it is not in fact the wind that is directly responsible for this but the tree's aversion to sea salt in the air. The tiny former gold rush village is worth investigating, not only for its trees, but because it looks like the village that time forgot. The buildings seem to have changed little in decades. Also, 500 m north of the village is the **Orepuki Gemstone Beach**, which may reveal garnets, jasper, quartz, nephrite as well as the odd worm fossil or even sapphires.

From Orepuki the road garrotes the Wakaputa Point before rejoining the coast again at the beachside settlement of **Colac Bay**. A place rich in Maori history, it is now mainly frequented by surfers. Unless you have a board, you are best moving on to the far more ample amenities and sights of Riverton, a further 11 km east.

Riverton →*Colour map 6, C3 Population: 1900.*

Riverton – or Aparima, to use its former Maori name – is the oldest permanent European settlement in Southland and one of the oldest in the country. Located on the banks of the common estuary formed by the Aparima and Purakino rivers, it was formerly a safe haven for whalers and sealers and was first established as early as the 1830s. Now having gradually developed into a popular coastal holiday resort Riverton is a fine place to stop for lunch, a short walk on the beach, or even to consider as a quieter alternative base to Invercargill, now only 42 km to the east.

Given the rich history of the area the **Te Hikoi 'Southern Journey' Museum** ⓘ *172 Palmerston St, T03-234 8260,www.tehikoi.co.nz, daily 1030-1630, donation*, is worth a look. It is a new complex with modern displays and a small art gallery focusing on the early Maori, whaling and gold mining days. It also provides genealogical research assistance. Nearby, the **South Coast Environment Centre** ⓘ *T03-234 8717, daily 1330-1630*, promotes the local environment and wildlife with displays and information.

The **Riverton Rocks** and **Howell's Point**, at the southern edge of Taramea Bay, provide safe swimming, fishing, short walks and fine views across to Stewart Island. If you are looking for a good place for lunch then try the excellent **Beachhouse Café and Bar** (see Eating, page 682). Other local walks are outlined in the free *Riverton Scenic Walks* leaflet; available free from the VIC (I-Site).

Invercargill ⬤❶❷❸⬤▲⬤❸ ➤ pp681-684.

When it comes to aesthetics a lot has been said about Invercargill (population 53,209) over the years and sadly (and undeservingly) much of it has been negative. Invercargill is not pretty. Let's be honest. Stuck at the very rear end of New Zealand and sandblasted by the worst extremes of the southern weather, even its climate and geography are against it. This is nothing new or unusual, after all Scotland (to which Invercargill and the region as a whole is so closely linked) is an entire country that suffers the same affliction. But for Invercargill there is one added problem. For most tourists the city features late on the travel schedule and by the time they get here they are almost drunk on stunning world-class scenery. No remedy there of course, it's an inevitable 'coming back down to earth', but were it not for the geography and the climate one cannot help wonder if the problem could all be addressed with one weekend of frenzied mass tree-planting.

However, that said, Invercargill has many good points, and although you will hear different, it is certainly not the underdog it Is reputed to be. For a start, it is the capital of the richest agricultural region in the South Island and so far in to the new millennium has had the strongest economic growth in the country. As the commercial hub of the region the 'City of Water and Light' (as it has been labelled) often buzzes (yes buzzes!) with the prosperity of that thriving economy, the vivacity of student life (the city is the regional focus for further education) and of course boasts a rich and fascinating history that marries the strong Maori and Celtic influence that pioneered the region. It is also a fine base from which to explore the delights of Southland and the 'Southern Scenic Route'. Within a two-hour radius are a wealth of internationally acclaimed experiences of which Stewart Island, the Catlins Coast and southern Fiordland are the most obvious and the most lauded. So, by all means linger for a while – you won't regret it – and before you leave (while no one is looking) plant a tree!

Ins and outs

Getting there **Invercargill airport** ① *2½ km south of the city*, is served predominantly by **Air New Zealand Link**, T0800-737000, www.airnewzealand.co.nz. There are direct flights daily from Christchurch and Dunedin. **Stewart Island Flights** (Southern Air), T03-218 9129, www.stewartislandflights.com, and **Southeast Air**, T03-214 5522, southeast.air@xtra.co.nz, also serve Oban and Mason Bay on Stewart Island.

By bus, Invercargill is 579 km from Christchurch and 217 km from Dunedin via SH1; and 187 km from Queenstown via SH6 and 168 km from Te Anau via SH99 Southern Scenic Route. It is served by **Intercity**, T03-211 0895(Christchurch/Dunedin); **Atomic Shuttles**, T03-211 0895 (Queenstown/Christchurch/Dunedin); **Wanaka Connexions**, T03-216 0717/T0800-244844, www.time2.co.nz (Queenstown/Wanaka daily); **Knightrider** T03-342 8055, www.knightrider.co.nz (Christchurch/Dunedin, every night except Saturday); **Scenic Shuttle**, T03-4779083, www.scenicshuttle.co.nz (Invercargill, daily Nov-Apr, Mon-Fri May-Oct); and the backpacker-orientated **Bottom Bus**, T03-477 9083, www.travelheadfirst.com (Queenstown/Dunedin). Also plying the Southern Scenic Route is the **Catlins Coaster** (Catlins/Dunedin), T03-4779083, www.travelheadfirst.com. Most buses arrive at and leave from the VIC (I-Site). Note there is now no train service south of Dunedin. For ferry services from Bluff (Stewart Island), see page 684.

Getting around **Scenic Shuttle**, T03-4779083, www.scenicshuttle.co.nz, connects with Invercargill airport flights and will pick-up from your accommodation ($6). **Invercargill**

The Tuatara

To describe the noble and endemic tuatara as the most ancient reptile on earth is impressive enough, but when you consider that these 'living fossils' are even older than the landscape itself, it seems truly remarkable that they exist at all. They belong to a very singular order of reptiles known as beakheads that once roamed the earth (be it very slowly) over 225 million years ago. Once common throughout the country, but subject to predation and a widespread loss of habitat, the tuatara, has sadly joined the long list of New Zealand creatures in decline and now exists on only 30 offshore islands. They grow to a maximum of 610 mm, live in burrows and feed mainly on ground-dwelling insects. Given their status and natural habitat, your best chance of seeing a tuatara is in one of the country's zoos or museums. The Southland Museum in Invercargill is without doubt the most famous venue, having the most successful breeding and research programme in the world. It also boasts perhaps the most famous tuatara in the land – 'Henry'.

Passenger Transport, 100 Leven St, T03-218 7108, provides local suburban bus services $1.50-3.50. **Stewart Island Experience**, T03-212 7660/T0800-000511, www.stewartisland experience.co.nz, provides shuttle services to Bluff and the Stewart Island ferry ($20, child $10 one way). For taxis, car and bike rental, see Transport, page 684. **Lynette Jack Tours**, T03-215 7741, is a noted local and regional sightseeing tour operator.

Background

Although the south coast was settled by European sealers and whalers as early as 1835, it was not until 1857, that the Chief Surveyor for Otago, John Turnbull Thompson, was ordered by Governor Sir Thomas Gore Browne, to choose a site and take responsibility for the planning of what is now the country's most southerly city. When Southland seceded from Otago in 1861 to become a separate province, Invercargill became its capital. Named in honour of Captain William Cargill (1784-1860), the first superintendent of Otago, 'Inver' is Scottish Gaelic for 'at the mouth of' and refers to the city's proximity to the Waihopai River. Note the many street names dedicated to Scottish rivers.

Sights

The main highlight in the town is the excellent **Southland Museum and Art Gallery** ① *edge of Queen's Park, Victoria Av, T03-219 9069, www.southlandmuseum.co.nz, Mon-Fri 0900-1700 Sat-Sun 1000-1700, donation.* Housed in the largest pyramid in the southern hemisphere (27 m), it boasts all the usual fine Maori Taonga and early settler exhibits and national and international art exhibitions, but is particularly noted for its 'Roaring Forties Antarctic and Sub-Antarctic Island' display and audio-visual (25 minutes, $2) shown several times daily. Also excellent is the museum's **tuatara** display and breeding programme. The 'Tuatarium' is an utter delight and an opportunity to come face to face with a reptilian species older than the land on which you stand. Henry, the oldest resident at an estimated 120 years plus, usually sits only a foot or two away from the glass. You can try to stare the old fella out, but you will fail, because Henry has had plenty of practice. At the age of around 110 and after decades of abstinence Henry New Zealand's most famous Tuatara is (apparently) back in action. Yes, that kind of action – and with Mildred, age 80! What is more, it appears he has live ammunition. By late 2009 all eleven eggs hatched and the babies are doing well.

Beyond the museum is **Queen's Park**, the city's saving grace. Its 80 ha of trees, flowerbeds and duck ponds provide a lovely setting for a walk, a picnic or a quiet doze. **Anderson Park**① *McIvor Rd, 7 km north of the city centre (signposted off SH6), T03-215 7432; gallery open daily 1030-1700*, is another 24 ha of beautiful parkland, with an interesting public art gallery. The VIC (I-Site) has a very useful free *Parks and Gardens* and *Heritage Trail* leaflets.

If beaches and sand are your thing, then the huge 30-km expanse of **Oreti Beach**, 10 km west of the city (past the airport) will not disappoint. It has the added attraction of allowing vehicles (with sensible drivers) on the sand and safe swimming. Nearby **Sandy Point**, on Sandy Point Road, offers a range of short walks and other recreation activities. There is an unmanned information point at the entrance to the park. For a fine view of the city head for the very unusual 1889 **Water Tower** ① *corner of Gala St and Queen Drive, Sun only, 1330-1630*.

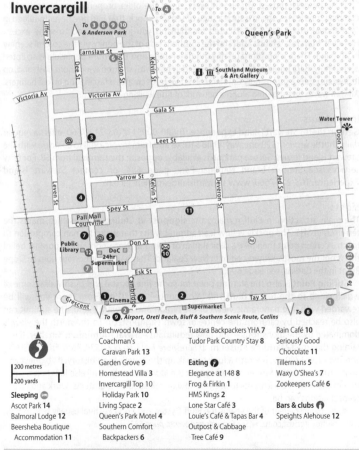

Invercargill

Sleeping 🛏
Ascot Park **14**
Balmoral Lodge **12**
Beersheba Boutique
  Accommodation **11**
Birchwood Manor **1**
Coachman's
  Caravan Park **13**
Garden Grove **9**
Homestead Villa **3**
Invercargill Top 10
  Holiday Park **10**
Living Space **2**
Queen's Park Motel **4**
Southern Comfort
  Backpackers **6**
Tuatara Backpackers YHA **7**
Tudor Park Country Stay **8**

Eating 🍴
Elegance at 148 **8**
Frog & Firkin **1**
HMS Kings **2**
Lone Star Café **3**
Louie's Café & Tapas Bar **4**
Outpost & Cabbage
  Tree Café **9**
Rain Café **10**
Seriously Good
  Chocolate **11**
Tillermans **5**
Waxy O'Shea's **7**
Zookeepers Café **6**

Bars & clubs 🍸
Speights Alehouse **12**

Bluff ⊖🄿🄵🄸 ▸▸ *pp681-684.*

Some 27 km south of Invercargill, the small port of Bluff heralds the end of the road in the South Island. Most visitors to Bluff are either on their way or returning from Stewart Island, or come to stand and gawk at a wind blasted signpost at the terminus of SH1, which tells them they are several thousand miles from anywhere: next stop Antarctica.

The town itself is as strange as it is intriguing. As a result of a dying oyster-fishing industry and protracted general social decline, there is a very palpable sense of decay in Bluff. While the vast majority of New Zealand's other towns progress and grow at a healthy pace, here, it is as if the clocks have stopped and no-one's home. The place is like some long forgotten, withered pot plant in desperate need of a drink. Worse still, the architectural aesthetics leave a lot to be desired. Here, the tastelessness and kitsch of many of the older properties and their facades is so awful it's almost an attraction in itself – as the late and iconic Paua Shell House once proved. Up almost every street the older property designs and colour combinations leaves one in a such a state of sensory shock, that had one never indulged in recreational drugs you'd be excused for thinking you just did – and to some excess. However, human creations aside, on the southern side of the peninsula the coastal scenery is stunning. There is no shortage of wind down here and the entire peninsula is sculpted accordingly. Bare boulder-clad hills shrouded in part with stunted wind shorn bush and, on its leeward side, a surprisingly tall stand of native trees creates a fascinating mix of habitats. All well worth investigating along a network of fine walking tracks.

Ins and outs
Getting there Stewart Island Experience, T0800-000511/T03-212 7660, offers a regular daily shuttle service ($20 one way, child $10) to and from Invercargill to coincide with the Stewart Island ferries. Secure parking is available opposite the terminal from $8. For ferry services see Stewart Island National Park, page 684, or contact **Stewart Island Experience**, T03-212 7660, www.stewartislandexperience.co.nz.

Sights
The main attraction in Bluff remains the **signpost** at Stirling Point, which marks the terminus of SH1. The prickly yellow icon admirably fits that weird human compulsion to reach a certain point then take a digital snap of doing so. Note, contrary to popular belief this is not the most southerly point in New Zealand. That particular honour goes to Slope Point in the Catlins, see page 694.

Stirling Point is also the starting point for some fine coastal and bush walks, some of which climb to the top of **Bluff Hill** (Motupohue) at 270 m. From there you will be rewarded with fine panoramic views of the region and Stewart Island. The summit can also be reached by car from the centre of town (signposted). To the north the view is dominated by the monstrous – and now redundant – **Tiwai Aluminium Smelter**. If it is raining the small **Maritime Museum** ① *Foreshore Rd, T03-212 7534, Mon-Fri 1000-1630, Sat-Sun 1300-1700, $2,* is worth a look to soak up the town's long history. Its biggest and main attraction is the former oystering boat the *Monica*. Finally, if all else fails take a small tour of the town's backstreets to see just how tasteless some architects' work and colour co-ordinations can be.

Bluff's biggest event of the year is the **Bluff Oyster and Food Festival** usually held in May, www.bluffoysterfest.co.nz. ▸▸ *See Festivals and events, page 683.*

◉ Southern Scenic route listings

For Sleeping and Eating price codes and other relevant information, see Essentials pages 44-50.

◉ Sleeping

Tuatapere *p675*

B Wicked Wee Dump near the Hump, Papatotara Rd (about 2 km southwest), T03-226 6238. With a name like that how can you resist! Wicked yes, but a dump? Far from it. Excellent fully self-contained unit, caring hosts and very reasonably priced. Recommended.

A-D Shooters Backpackers and Holiday Park, 73 Main St, T03-226 6250. The main backpackers in town, with powered and unpowered sites.

B Waiau Hotel, 47 Main St, T03-226 6409, www.waiauhotel.co.nz. Basic B&B and budget accommodation, some en suites.

Riverton *p676*

AL Abalone Beach House, 230 Colac Foreshore Rd (12 km west of Riverton), T03-234 8149. Excellent open-plan beachfront bach overlooking the bay in Colac,. Perfect peace and quiet.

AL-A Riverton Rock, 136 Palmerston St, T03-234 8886, www.riverton.co.nz. An excellent mid-budget establishment in a restored historic villa. It offers a range of very well-appointed, themed rooms including one with a superb original Victorian bath. There is also an open fire in one room. Modern facilities and good value.

C-D The Globe Backpackers, 144 Palmerston St, T03-234 8527, www.theglobe.co.nz. Centrally located in the town's oldest hotel offering doubles, twins and dorms. Pizzas available from the bar. Also offers 2 self-contained units near the beach, from $105.

C-D Longwood Holiday Park, 43 Richard St, Riverton, T0800-234813/T03-234 8132, lex.wylie@xtra.co.nz. 2 ensuite units, powered and tent sites all with ocean views. Basic camp kitchen.

Invercargill *p677, map p679*

For farmstay options contact the very helpful Western Southland Farm Hosting Group, T03-225 8608, www.nzcountry.co.nz/farmhost.

LL-A Ascot Park Hotel, corner of Tay St and Racecourse Rd, T03-217 6195, www.ascotparkhotel.co.nz. The city's top hotel and a large modern establishment offering a wide range of rooms and fine facilities in a quiet setting. Spa, pool and in-house restaurant and bar.

L Beersheba Boutique Accommodation, 58 Milton Park Rd, T03-216 3677, www.beersheba.co.nz. A modern B&B with 2 well-appointed en suites, or a self-contained cottage in peaceful setting on the outskirts of the city. Outside fireplace.

L-AL Tudor Park Country Stay, 21 Lawrence Rd, Royal Bush, T03-221 7150, www.tudorpark.co.nz. Fine B&B in a rural setting 15 mins' north of the city. Set in 4 ha of beautiful garden it is a neo-Tudor home with comfortable en suite rooms. Meals available.

AL-A Living Space,15 Tay St, T050-8454 846/T03-2113800, www.livingspace.net. Excellent value modern studio rooms and 2- to 3-bedroom apartments right in the heart of the town. Facilities include a comfy movie theatre, full kitchen facilities and off-street parking. Recommended.

B-D Tuatara Lodge Backpackers, 30-32 Dee St, T0800-8828272/T03-214 0956, www.tuataralodge.co.nz. A modern hostel ideally located in the centre of town. It offers a full range of rooms with some very tidy shared standard double/twins and a few luxurious and value double en suites. Good kitchen, popular street-side café with fast internet and value meals and breakfasts, Sky TV and off-street parking.

C-D Southern Comfort Backpackers, 30 Thomson St, T03-218 3838. An old, spacious villa near the museum and Queen's Park. It is a Southland favourite and offers dorms, doubles and free bike hire. Recommended.

Motels

There are plenty of motels, some upmarket and modern, others older and cheaper.
AL-A Birchwood Manor, 189 Tay St, T03-218 8881, www.birchwoodmanor.co.nz.
A Balmoral Lodge, 265 Tay St, T03-219 9050, www.ilt.co.nz/balmoral. Recommended.
A Homestead Villa, corner Avenal and Dee sts, T03-214 0408, www.lit.co.nz/homestead.
A Queen's Park Motel, 85 Alice St, T03-214 4504, www.queensparkmotels.co.nz. Good motel within a short walk of Queen's Park.
B Garden Grove, 161 North Rd, T03-215 9555, www.gardengrovemotel.co.nz.

Motorcamps and campsites

C-D Coachman's Caravan Park, 705 Tay St, T03-217 6046, www.coachmans.co.nz. The only reputable central option.
D Invercargill Top 10 Holiday Park, 77 McIvor Rd (northern edge of town off SH6), T03-215 9032, www.invercargilltop10.co.nz. Small, peaceful and friendly. Recommended.

Bluff *p680*

Bluff has a few good accommodation choices but, given the regular shuttle service and lack of general services most Stewart Island bound choose to stay in Invercargill.
AL Land's End Hotel, at the very end of SH1, T03-212 7575, www.landsend.net.nz. A boutique hotel with comfortable, well-appointed en suite rooms and a wine bar/café with open fire. Good views.
AL-A Lazy Fish, 35 Burrows St, T03-212 7245, www.thelazyfish.nz. A pleasant B&B in a traditional villa. Separate self-contained option and private room in the house, both cosy and comfortable. Good value and close to ferry terminal. Also has tent sites.
B-D Argyle Park Camping Ground, Gregory St (off marine Parade), T027-6262018. Recently redeveloped with good facilities. Units, powered and non-powered sites.

❶ Eating

Tuatapere *p675*

❖ **Highway 99 Café/Bar and Takeaway**, 73 Main St, T03-226 6898. Fine for a quick daytime snack. But its biggest attraction is 'Brandy', the spectacularly conceited cockatoo. As you enter the shop you will be told in no uncertain terms that 'Brandy is a very (very) pretty boy'.

Riverton *p676*

❖ **Beachhouse Café and Bar**, 126 Rocks Highway, T03-234 8274. 1000-late. Overlooks the bay and understandably popular. Internet.

Invercargill *p677, map p679*

Not a huge amount of choice. There is a supermarket on the eastern fringe of the city centre on Tay St, open until 2100 or 2200.
❖❖❖ **Elegance at 148 On Elles**, 148 Elles St, T03-216 1000. Closed Sun. Both are recommended.
❖❖❖ **Emberz Restaurant**, Ascot Hotel, T03-2176195. Lunch Mon-Sat 1200-1400, dinner Mon-Sun from 1800.
❖❖ **HMS Kings**, 80 Tay St, T03-2183443. Daily lunch and dinner. Serves up a great seafood chowder amidst the nets and anchors.
❖❖❖ **Lone Star Café**, corner of Leet and Dee sts, T03-214 6225, daily from 1730. Recommended Tex-Mex.
❖❖ **Louie's Café and Tapas Bar**, 142 Dee St, T03-214 2913. Tue-Sun from 1800. Affordable evening dining.
❖❖ **Waxy O'Sheas**, 90 Dee St, T03-214 0313. Invercargill's obligatory serving reasonably priced pub meals.
❖❖-❖ **Rain Café**, 35 Kelvin St, T03-2183561. Arguably the best coffee in town.
❖ **Frog and Firkin**, Dee St, next to the cinema, T03-214 4001. Lunch 1200-1400, dinner Mon-Sat from 1700. Pub grub.
❖ **Outpost and Cabbage Tree Café**, 379 Dunns Rd (west, out towards Otatara and Oreti Beach), T03-213 1443. 1100-late. Lunch or dinner in a relaxed rural setting.

¶ **The Seriously Good Chocolate Company Cafe & Concept Store**, 147 Spey St, T03 218 8060. Say no more!
¶ **Zookeeper's Café**, 50 Tay St, T03-218 3373. Daily from 1000-late. The best café in town with has a nice atmosphere, good coffee and good-value evening meals.

Bluff *p680*
¶¶-¶ **Land's End** (see Sleeping, above). Serves breakfast, lunch and dinner and will happily serve up the famous oysters Mar-Aug.
¶ **Drunken Sailor**, Stirling Point, T03-212 8855. Mon-Thu 1130-1600, Fri-Sat 1130-2100. A recent addition offering traditional fare and good views. Sporadic opening hours.

❶ Pubs, bars and clubs

Invercargill *p677, map p679*
The *Southland Times* is the best source of local events and entertainment information. **Zookeeper's Café**, **Speights Alehouse**, 38 Dee St, and **Waxy O'Sheas**, see above, are popular spots and often have live gigs at the weekend.
Invercargill Brewery, 8 Wood St, T03-214 5070. Mon-Sat 1100-1800, Fri 1100-1900. While visiting Invercargill it would perhaps be rude not to sample its finest beer. The very tasty brews on offer from the including 'Pitch Black' and 'Stanley Green' are really very good, as the evening queues outside the small outlet can attest.

❻ Entertainment

Invercargill *p677, map p679*
Reading Cinema, 29 Dee St, T03-211 1555.
Ten Pin Bowling Centre, corner of Kelvin and Leet sts (licensed bar), T03-214 4944.

❻ Festivals and events

Invercargill
Nov Burt Munro Challenge. Following the

success of the 2005 movie *The World's Fastest Indian* about Invercargill resident Burt Munro's inspirational life, the Southland Motorcycle Club created the 'Burt Munro Challenge' to honour him, his ingenuity, determination, and love of speed and motorcycles. The inaugural event was held in 2006, and has now become one of New Zealand's major motorsport events. It attracts top New Zealand riders as well as all the weekend warriors, all provided with a variety of events from beach racing to street races all enhanced by that famous southern hospitality.

Bluff *p680*
Apr Bluff Oyster and Food Festival, www.bluffoysterfest.co.nz. A celebration of the diminishing world-class Bluff oysters and other seafood delights, with lots of fine wine to wash it down and plenty of entertainment, including live bands and oyster opening and eating competitions. The festival's raucous finale is the Southern Seas Ball.

▲ Activities and tours

Tuatapere *p675*
Jet boating
Jet boating on Lake Hauroko and the Wairaurahiri River are the big attractions. Exciting full-day jet boat trips down a 10-km section of Lake Hauroko, before negotiating its 27-km 'outlet' river to the coast. It is a Grade III river and boasts the steepest lake-to-coast river fall in the country. Recommended. Half-day from $150, full from $190, heli-jet (from $320), 2-day trips (Hump Ridge Jet, from $190). Water taxi services to both Dusky and Hump Ridge Tracks are also available. There are 2 main companies, both offer a safe and personable service.
Hump Ridge Jet, Otautau, T03-225 8174, www.humpridgejet.co.nz.
W Jet, Clifden, T0800-376174/T03-225 5677, www.wjet.co.nz.

Riverton *p676*

Adventure Southland, close to town, T03-215 4221, www.adventuresouthland.com. High ropes activities and course.
Kiwi Wilderness Walks, T021-359592, www.nzwalk.com. A popular operator that provides guided eco-walks of Stewart Island (5 days, 4 nights, from $1795) Raikura Track (also on Stewart Island) the Hump Ridge Track and the Dusky Track. The all-inclusive guided trips are best suited to the less independent traveller but are no less exciting. The highlight of the Stewart Island trip is the chance to observe kiwi in daylight, an unforgettable experience. Recommended.

⊖ Transport

Invercargill *p677, map p679*
Bicycle hire Wensley's Cycles, corner of Tay and Nith sts, T03-218 6206. **Car hire** The airport has branches of most major players.

Others include **Riverside Rentals**, corner of Deeand Fox sts, T03-214 1030. Rent-a-Dent, T03-214 4820. **Taxi** Blue Star, T03-217 7777. City Cabs, T03-214 4444.

❶ Directory

Invercargill *p677, map p679*
Banks The main banks (most of which offer currency exchange) are around Don St in the city centre. **Internet** VIC, see page 675. **Library**, Mon-Fri 0900-2000, Sat 1000-1300. **Tuatara Backpackers YHA**, 30-32 Dee St. **Com zone**, just opposite Tuatara, T03-214 0007, daily 0930-late. **Global Byte Café**, 150 Dee St, T03-214 4724, Mon-Fri 0800-1700, Sat-Sun 0900-1600. **Medical services** Doctor, 103 Don St, T03-218 8821, Mon-Fri from 1700, 24-hr Sat-Sun. **Police** 51 Don St, T03-214 4039. **Post office** 51 Don St, T03-214 7700, Mon-Fri 0830-1700, Sat 1000-1230.

Stewart Island (Rakiura National Park)

➜ *Colour map 6, C3 Population: 390.*
Lying 20 km southwest off Bluff, across the antsy waters of Foveaux Strait, is the 'land of the glowing skies' (Rakiura) or Stewart Island. Often called New Zealand's third island (making up 10% of its total area), Stewart Island was described over a century ago by pioneer botanist Leo Cockayne, as 'having a superabundance of superlatives'. There is much truth in that. It can be considered one of the country's most unspoilt and ecologically important areas. Such are its treasures that only the country's national parks can compare, which is why it was only a matter of time before it entered the fold in 2001, with 85% of the island now enjoying the limelight as the newest of New Zealand's 14 national parks. ▶▶ *For Sleeping, Eating and other listings, see pages 690-691.*

Ins and outs

Getting there
Stewart Island can be reached by air (20 mins) from Invercargill to Halfmoon Bay or the western bays of Mason, Doughboy, West Ruggedy or Little Hellfire (trampers) with **Stewart Island Flights**, T03-218 9129, www.stewartisland flights.com, from $185 return ($105 one way). There are scheduled flights three times daily. Only 15 kg of personal baggage can be flown over on a full flight (additional gear can be flown over on subsequent flights). A shuttle to/from the airfield is included in the fare.

The principal ferry operator, **Stewart Island Experience**, T0800-000511/T03-212 7660, www.stewartislandexperience.co.nz, operates regular sailings from the port of Bluff. The crossing by fast catamaran takes about one hour and costs $63/$31.50 one way). The company offers a regular daily shuttle service to and from Invercargill to coincide with the Stewart Island ferries ($20, child $10 one way). Contact direct for latest schedules, bookings advised, T0800-000511. Secure outdoor vehicle storage is available at Bluff.

Getting around

Once on the island you will find that most things are within walking distance, but many hotels will provide pick-ups. **Stewart Island Experience** (see above) also offers car hire (from $70 per day) and scooters from $30 per hour. **The Stewart Island Experience Terminal**, on the Wharf, T03-219 1439/T0800-000511, info@sie.co.nz, can also arrange tours, boat trips and water taxis. **Stewart Island Flights**, has a depot on the waterfront, T03-219 1090.

There are numerous water taxi operators including **Stewart Island Water Taxi**, T03-219 1394, www.portofcall.co.nz; **Seaview Water Taxi**, T03-219 1014, www.seaviewwatertaxi.co.nz; **Aihe Eco Charters and Water Taxis**, T03-219 1066, www.aihe.co.nz. Fares cost about $25-return to Ulva Island.

Stewart Island

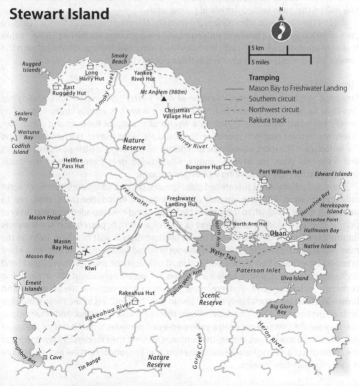

Tourist information

Stewart Island VIC (I-Site) ① *12 Elgin Terr, T03-219 0056, www.stewartisland.co.nz*, is the principal source of non-biased information on the island. For detailed walks/tramping information and bookings contact the **DoC Visitor Information and Field** Centre ① *Main Rd, T03-219 0009, www.doc.govt.nz, Mon-Fri 0800-1700, Sat-Sun 0900-1600*. It also provides storage lockers, sells maps and hires personal locator beacons.

Background

According to Maori legend, Stewart Island is the anchor stone of the canoe of the mythological hero and explorer Maui and is therefore known as 'Te Puka-o-te-waka-a-Maui'. As early as the 13th century there is evidence that the island's rich natural resources were being utilized by the Maori, with the particular attraction being attributed to the vast numbers of muttonbirds (sooty shearwater) or 'Titi'. The first European visitor (no prizes for guessing), in 1770 sailed past and mistook the island to be the mainland, calling it Cape South. Thirty-nine years after Captain Cook, it took one William Stewart, the first officer aboard the whaling ship *Pegasus*, to get it right and bless the island with its modern name. In the first half of the 18th century, whalers and sealers were beginning to establish themselves in the region and they were soon followed by fishermen and saw-millers that soon settled the island permanently.

In 1864 the island was officially bought from the Maori by the British, for the standard price of £6000. Besides a brief and sudden increase in population in the late 1800s, thanks to a very unproductive gold rush, the island has remained fairly uninhabited, with the current 390 residents mainly involved in fishing or tourism.

Flora and fauna

Stewart Island has an indented coastline of river inlets, bays and offshore islands not dissimilar to parts of southern Fiordland. In many ways it is equally unspoiled and its heavily bush-clad landmass is host to a wealth of ecological habitats and a rich bio-diversity. The most common species on the island are sadly, as ever, the non-natives and the introduced. The most unwelcome and destructive of these are the possums, the rats and feral cats. Also, for over a century, white-tailed deer have roamed the bush, introduced to occupy the hunting interests of humans.

The island is home to 21 threatened plant species, some of which are endemic or occur only on the island. With the absence of dominant and introduced trout, there are 15 native fish species and, when it comes to birds, the island is surrounded by a vast array of pelagic species, including **mollymawks** (a kind of albatross), **petrels** and **shearwaters** (muttonbirds), many of which breed on the offshore islets in vast numbers. Even on the main island (and fighting to survive the ravages of introduced vermin), its impressive bird breeding list includes two of the rarest and most unique in the world: a distinctly odd and enchanting, flightless parrot called a **kakapo** (of which only about 80 remain) and perhaps most famous of all – *Apteryx australis lawryi* – better known as the **Stewart Island brown kiwi**, the largest and only diurnal kiwi in New Zealand. It is to see these whimsical birds on the beach or a bush track by daylight that many visit the island. And what's more, you may see the kiwi sidestepping a **yellowed-eyed penguin**, which is one of the rarest penguins in the world. And, in turn, the penguins may get their flippers in a twist to avoid the attentions of a dosing **New Zealand sea lion**. You've probably got the picture; Rakiura is a very special place indeed.

Oban and around

The pleasant little village of Oban on Halfmoon Bay is the island's main settlement. It is connected to several smaller settlements including Golden Bay, Horseshoe Bay, Leask Bay and Butterfield Bay, by about 28 km of mainly sealed road. Almost all of Oban's amenities and (non-B&B) accommodation can be reached easily by foot from the wharf. The principal streets are Elgin Terrace (the waterfront) and Main Road.

Other than to see kiwi, the boat trips and kayaking, people visit Stewart Island for two main reasons: either to bask in its tranquility and do very little in Oban; or attempt one of its challenging, very long and very wet tramping tracks. Yes, it rains a lot here.

Sights

Perhaps the best place to start is by foot with a short, steady climb to **Observation Rock** (southern end of Oban village, up Ayr Street). From here you get a grand view of **Paterson Inlet** and the impenetrable forests that deck its southern shores and disappear beyond the horizon. This vista gives an idea of the rest of the island's wild and unspoilt make-up. In Oban itself, the **Rakiura Museum**① *9 Ayr St, T03-2191221, Mon-Sat 1000-1200, Sun 1200-1400, $2*, can entertain between rain showers, showcasing many aspects of the island's interesting history, including the early Maori and their continued harvesting of muttonbirds (titi), to whaling, saw-milling, gold mining and fishing. The beach on the waterfront (Elgin Terrace) is a fine place to simply sit and watch the world go by, play industrial size chess, or decide on one of the many water-based trips that are available.

You could head north of Oban towards Horseshoe Bay, which is a very pleasant walk in itself. On the way you can spend some time exploring or swimming at **Bathing Bay**, a lovely sheltered beach accessed via Kamahi Road off Horseshoe Bay Road. This walk can be extended to **Horseshoe Point** (three to four hours), accessed from the southern end of

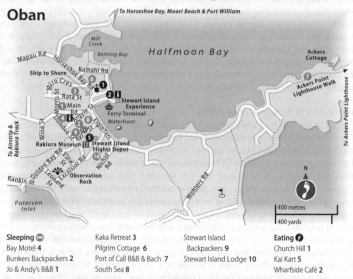

Oban

To Horseshoe Bay, Maori Beach & Port William

Sleeping 😴
Bay Motel **4**
Bunkers Backpackers **2**
Jo & Andy's B&B **1**

Kaka Retreat **3**
Pilgrim Cottage **6**
Port of Call B&B & Bach **7**
South Sea **8**

Stewart Island
  Backpackers **9**
Stewart Island Lodge **10**

Eating 🍴
Church Hill **1**
Kai Kart **5**
Wharfside Café **2**

Horseshoe Bay. On the southern entrance to Halfmoon Bay the three-hour **Harrold Bay to Ackers Point Lighthouse Walk**, accessed at the end of the southern bay road (Elgin Terrace), is another fine alternative. Harrold Bay is the site of **Ackers cottage** (1835), one of the oldest stone cottages in New Zealand. DoC produces a very useful *Day Walks* leaflet available from the VIC ($1).

Ulva Island

Guarding the entrance of Paterson Inlet is Ulva Island, a nature reserve criss-crossed with trails and home to abundant and extremely tame and exuberant birdlife. The island's profile was further enhanced in 2006, when DoC trialed the public viewing of a Kakapo (one of the rarest birds in the world), which proved immensely popular both domestically and internationally. Hopefully it will be repeated in the future, but Kakapo or not, the island provides the most popular day or half-day trip from Golden Bay, with a number of water taxi operators offering organized trips taking in the mussel and salmon farms in **Big Glory Bay**, as well as seal and shag colonies (four-hour guided trips costing around $95). Most companies also offer independent transportation from $25 return. A trip to Ulva is recommended. Ulva and Paterson Inlet also provide one of the many excellent sea-kayaking venues. You could also consider a paddle/tramp option with the trip up to the DoC Freshwater Hut and access from there to Mason Bay.

▲ Tramping

With 245 km of walking tracks, Stewart Island is a popular venue for trampers. These tracks range from the many short 'warm-up' walks around Oban, to the Northwest Circuit, a mammoth 125-km, 10- to 12-day tramp around the island's northern coast. Some other, far more remote routes are sometimes negotiated, including the fascinating **'Tin Range'** route on the island's southwestern corner, but these require expert planning, logistics and a high level of fitness. Overall, tramping on Stewart Island presents its own challenges, not only because the island is so underdeveloped, remote and rugged, but also because it is particularly wet underfoot. There are numerous basic DoC huts that vary in size and standard. Hut details and bookings, maps and detailed track information is available with the DoC and it is highly recommended that you obtain all the details and fill in an intentions form for the longer or more remote tramps. ▶▶*For guided walk operators, see page 691.*

Mason Bay to Freshwater Landing

This is a 14-km four-hour walk with no road access. It can be approached in various ways. You can walk to Mason Bay from Oban (37 km, three days one way), taking in part of the Rakiura Track, then reach Mason Bay via Freshwater Landing. Once at Mason Bay you can then walk or fly back to Oban. Or take a water taxi or kayak to Freshwater Landing then make the return walk to Mason Bay (28 km, two days return). The recommended alternative is to fly into Mason Bay, then make the leisurely return walk to Freshwater Landing (14 km, four hours) giving yourself an extra day to explore Mason Bay (and give yourself the best chance of seeing kiwi). You can then get a water taxi from Freshwater landing to Golden Bay and Oban. The track is low-level all the way, with a pleasant mix of open flax and tussock country and intriguing corridors of enclosed manuka tree. You will not manage to negotiate this trip without getting your feet wet and it is notoriously muddy, but there are boardwalks in the worst sections. The DoC Mason Bay hut has 20 bunks but is popular and runs on a first come first served basis, so take a tent if you can.

Rakiura Track

The Rakiura is one of New Zealand's 'Great Walks' immediately accessible by foot from Oban and is a 29- to 36-km track requiring two to three days. The appeal of the Rakiura, other than ease of access, is the mainly rimu and kamahi forest scenery, and views and secluded beaches of **Paterson Inlet**. There is also an abundance of bird life. In the forest this includes kaka, tomtit, bellbirds, tui and shining cuckoo, while wading birds including New Zealand dotterel and seabirds, including shags and little blue penguins, that can be seen on the coast. The track can be negotiated clockwise or anti-clockwise from Oban. In a clockwise direction the walking distances and times are as follows: Halfmoon Bay–Port William Hut, 12 km, four to five hours; Port William Hut–North Arm Hut, 12 km, six hours; North Arm–Halfmoon Bay 12 km, four to five hours. Port William and North Arm huts are well equipped and have 24 bunks each. There are designated campsites with water and toilets at Maori Beach, Port William and Sawdust Bay. Note huts and sites come at a first come first served basis but the VIC (I-Site) can give an indication of the anticipated numbers.

Northwest Circuit

At 125 km and requiring at least 10 days, this is one of the longest tramps in the country and is not for the faint-hearted. The appeal, other than the sense of achievement and feeling of complete solitude, is the remote and rugged coastal scenery with its stunning bays and features, some with such evocative names as Hellfire Pass and West Ruggedy Beach. The side trip to climb **Mount Anglem** (980 m), the island's highest peak, is also a recommended highlight. The track is also noted for its wildlife. The track is notoriously muddy and wet at times but don't let that put you off. There are 10 DoC huts on the route with 12-20 bunks.

The track distances and minimum times are as follows: Halfmoon Bay–Port William, 12 km, four hours; Port William– Bungaree Hut, 6 km, three hours; Bungaree Hut–Christmas Village Hut, 11½ km, six hours; Mount Anglem side trip, 11 km, six hours; Christmas Village Hut–Yankee River Hut 12 km, six hours; Yankee River Hut–Long Harry Hut, 8½ km, five to six hours; Long Harry Hut–East Ruggedy Hut, 9½ km, five hours; East Ruggedy Hut–Hellfire Pass, 14 km, seven to eight hours; Hellfire Pass Hut–Mason Bay Hut, 15 km, seven hours; Mason Bay Hut–Freshwater Landing Hut, 14 km, three hours; Freshwater Landing Hut–North Arm Hut, 11 km, six to seven hours; North Arm Hut–Halfmoon Bay, 12 km, four hours.

Southern Circuit

The Southern Circuit is a 74-km six- to seven-day tramp suitable for the experienced and well-equipped tramper. It takes in many similar (but more remote) aspects of the Rakiura Track and the delights of the rugged wilderness coastline from Doughboy Bay to Mason Bay and Mason Bay itself. Access to the start and finish point of Freshwater Landing is by water taxi. Four DoC huts and an interesting bivvy at Doughboy Bay provide accommodation. The DoC can provide detailed information about the tramp.

For Sleeping and Eating price codes and other relevant information, see Essentials pages 44-50.

⊜ Sleeping

Stewart Island *p684, maps p685 and p687*
Most of the accommodation on the island takes the form of comfortable upper- to mid-range B&Bs and homestays, cottages and budget options but there is one hotel and a handful of motels. Note that some of the budget hostels do not take advance bookings in summer and beds must be secured on the day of departure from Bluff or Invercargill airport. Note also that there is much gossip surrounding certain bachelor-owned/operated hostels and the 'comfort' of single women travellers. The best advice is ask the VIC about the latest vacancies and maybe check out a few places on arrival (particularly those recommended below), then decide for yourself.
LL Stewart Island Lodge, 14 Nichol Rd, Halfmoon Bay, T0800-656501/T03-219 1085, www.stewart islandlodge.co.nz. Well established as one of the best upper-range B&Bs on the island. It provides 5 luxury en suites and is famous for its good cuisine, amidst the perfect peaceful setting.
L Port of Call B&B and Bach, Jensen Bay, T03-219 1394, www.portofcall.co.nz. Set in an idyllic spot overlooking the entrance to Halfmoon Bay, very cosy and friendly. It offers a charming en suite double and great breakfasts and views from the deck. There is also a fully self-contained bach (holiday house) offering plenty of privacy. In-house water taxi and eco-guiding operation, including kiwi-spotting.
L-AL Kaka Retreat, 7 Miro St, T0800-500252/T03-219 1252, www.stewartisland.net. Set in native bush overlooking the bay offering well appointed B&B luxury suites with flat-screen LCD televisions and a kitchenette. Also available are 2 or 3 bedroom, fully self-contained

bungalow units. 2-night packages with ferry or flight. WiFi, bike hire and occasional visitations of the enchanting kakas (native parrots) on the deck.
AL Bay Motel, 9 Dundee St, Halfmoon Bay, T03-219 1119, www.baymotel.co.nz. Tidy units, good facilities, views across the bay and within a short walk of all amenities.
A Pilgrim Cottage, T03-219 1144, philldismith@xtra.co.nz. Neat and affordable self-contained option, kiwi trips are a speciality.
A South Sea Hotel, corner of Elgin Terr and Main Rd, Oban, T03-219 1059, www.stewart-island.co.nz. A fine place to stay if you want to mix with the locals and experience Stewart Island life. A mix of traditional hotel rooms (some with sea views) and self-contained motel units on an adjacent property. Obviously there is an in-house bar where all the action (or lack of it) takes place and a restaurant where you can sample the local delicacy – muttonbird.
B-C Jo and Andy's Bed and Breakfast, Main Rd, T03-219 1230, jariksem@clearnet.net.nz. Small and personable, sleeping 5 and with the added attraction of massage therapies – ideal for tired trampers.
C-D Stewart Island Backpackers, Ayr St, T03-219 1114, www.stewart-island.co.nz. In town this is a sprawling but highly functional place, with a wide range of dorms and units.
C-D Bunkers Backpackers, 13 Argyle St, T03-219 1160, www.bunkersbackpackers. co.nz. Smaller option, again centrally located.

❼ Eating

Stewart Island *p684, maps p685 and p687*
Stewart Island has only a few eateries, with the famed muttonbird (*titi*) being the speciality dish round these parts. By all accounts it is very tasty, being a bit like venison and certainly more oily than chicken. But if you see these seabirds up close, never

mind the chicks (which resemble fluffy brown slippers), you'll be picketing these establishments with a placard round your neck! The only place for groceries is Ship to Shore general store, on the waterfront.

Church Hill Café Bar and Restaurant next to the church on the headland above the wharf, T03-219 1323. Daily from 1030 (seasonal). The best bet for fine dining.

South Sea Hotel, see Sleeping, above. 0800-0930, 1200-1400 and 1800-2100, seasonal. Provides fine no-nonsense lunch and dinner options including the unique muttonbird for around $23.

Wharfside Café, Ferry Terminal, Oban, T03-219 1470. Daily from 0900. All-day breakfasts, café-style light meals, licensed.

Kai Kart, Ayr St, T03-219 1442. Class fish and chips for lunch or dinner.

O Pubs, bars and clubs

Stewart Island *p684, maps p685 and p687*
South Sea Hotel, Elgin Terr. Without doubt the place to be for a beer and unpredictable entertainment. But what kind of night will depend on who you bump into and whether they are in good spirits or bad. They are a welcoming bunch most of the time, so just place your cards on the table and give as good as you get.

▲ Activities and tours

Stewart Island *p684, maps p685 and p687*
As you can imagine there is a wide range of possibilities from fishing and diving to simple daytime sightseeing, overnight or luxury multi-day adventures. The VIC (I-Site) lists all the operators and charter possibilities.
Aihe Eco Charters and Water Taxis, T03-219 1066, www.aihe.co.nz. Small group cruises, sightseeing, sea bird watching, wildlife viewing and guided tours with natural history and cultural history interpretation, from $95

Raikura Kayaks, T03-219 1160, www.raikura.co.nz; and **Ruggedy Range Wilderness Experience**, Oban, T03-219 1066, www.ruggedyrange.com, both provide a range of guided single to multi-day sea kayaking trips around Ulva and Paterson Inlet and independent hire.
Stewart Island Experience, T03-212 7660/T0800-000511, www.stewartisland experience.co.nz. Offers a 2½-hr scenic cruise to Paterson Inlet with a stop and guided walks on Ulva Island departing daily 1230 from $80, child $20. Picnic lunch $15 extra. It also operates a semi-submersible and given the water clarity this is usually worthwhile. Tours daily (45 mins), from $35, child $20.

Walking and ecotours
There are a couple of good companies offering guided walks, including the recommended and unique 'kiwi experience': **Kiwi Wilderness Walks**, based in Tuatapere, T021-359592, www.nzwalk.com; and **Ruggedy Range Wilderness Experience**, Oban, T03-219 1066, www.ruggedy range.com, both offer multi-day walking trips in which you have the unique opportunity to encounter kiwi during daylight hours. The latter also offer half- to 5-day kayaking options from $100.
Ulva's Guided Walks, T03-219 1216, www.ulva.co.nz. Offers an informative 3 to 4-hr trips to Ulva Island, from $110. Recommended.

O Directory

Stewart Island *p684, maps p685 and p687*
Banks Most businesses accept credit cards, New Zealand TCs and have EFTPOS. There are no banks on the island. **Internet** Stewart Island Backpackers, Ayr St and the South Sea Hotel, Main Rd. **Medical centre** Argyle St, T03-219 1098. **Police** T03-219 0020. **Postal agents** Stewart Island Flights depot, waterfront (Elgin Terr), T03-219 1090.

The Catlins → *Colour map 6, C4/5.*

If you like remote and scenic coastlines you are going to love the Catlins; the added bonus here is their location. Like the Wairarapa in the southwest of the North Island, the area is generally off the beaten track and certainly underrated. You can negotiate the Catlins from the north or the south via the publicized Southern Scenic Route, encompassing a 187-km network of minor now fully sealed roads. The journey between Invercargill and Dunedin (or in reverse) is often attempted in one day, which is definitely a mistake. A more thorough, comfortable and less frustrating investigation will take at least two days, preferably three. But, if you can really only afford one day, the highlights not to be missed are – from the north – Nugget Point (for sunrise); the opportunity to see the seductively named Hookers sea lions at Cannibals Bay (morning); the Purakaunui Falls and Purakaunui Bay (for lunch); then Curio Bay and Slope Point in the afternoon.

The Catlins is also noted for its rich wildlife and vegetation. Of particular note are the pinnipeds, or seals. The Catlins is the only mainland region where you can observe New Zealand fur seals, Hookers sea lions and Southern elephant seals in the same location. The region is also within the very limited breeding range of the rarest penguin on the planet – the yellow-eyed penguin (hoiho) – and the rare and tiny Hector's dolphin. Incredibly, with a little luck, all these species can be observed quite easily, independently and at relatively close range. The tracts of dense coastal forest that still remain are made up predominantly of podocarp and silver beech (but Curio Bay is home to a scattering of petrified fossil trees that are over 180 million years old) and are home to native birds like native pigeon (kereru), yellowhead (mohua) and fernbird. The forests also hide a number of attractive waterfalls. ▸▸ *For Sleeping, Eating and other listings, see pages 697-700.*

The Catlins - Invercargill to Papatowai

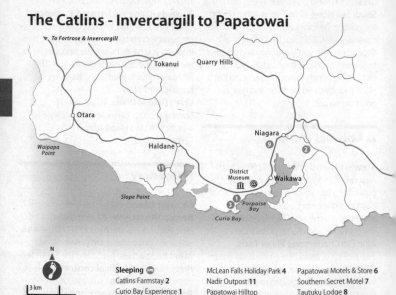

Sleeping
Catlins Farmstay **2**
Curio Bay Experience **1**
Curio Bay Salthouse **3**

McLean Falls Holiday Park **4**
Nadir Outpost **11**
Papatowai Hilltop
 Backpackers **5**

Papatowai Motels & Store **6**
Southern Secret Motel **7**
Tautuku Lodge **8**
Waikawa Holiday Lodge **9**

Ins and outs

Getting there **Bottom Bus**, T03-442 9083, www.travelheadfirst.com, provide transport and tour options via Queenstown, Invercargill and Te Anau. A typical 2-day trip between Dunedin and Invercargill (or vice versa) via the Catlins will cost $155 including tour, ex accommodation. Being on SH1 Balclutha and Gore are serviced by all the major north–south or east–west bus companies. Petrol is available at Owaka and Papatowai. ▸▸ *See also Activities and tours, page 700.*

Tourist information The VIC (I-Site) in Invercargill can also supply information about the Catlins. The free *The Catlins* booklet and the websites www.catlins.org.nz, www.catlins.co.nz and www.catlins-nz.com, are all useful. **Owaka Museum and VIC (I-Site)** ① *10 CampbellSt, T03-415 8323, www.catlins-nz.com, summer Nov-Jun Mon-Fri 0930-1300 and 1330-1630, Sat/Sun 1000-1600.* **Balclutha VIC (I-Site)** ① *4 Clyde St, T03-418 0388, vin@cluthaadc.govt.nz, Mon-Fri 0830-1700, Sat-Sun 0930- 1400.* The latter can provide all the northbound information surrounding the Catlins and Southern Scenic Route. DoC information is also available here, including leaflets ($1) on Catlin's walks and ecological highlights. **Gore VIC (I-Site)** ① *Norfolk St, T03-208 9288, www.gorenz.com Mon-Fri 0830-1700 Sat-Sun 0930-1600.* Has a list of local walks including the popular 1½-hr Whisky Falls Track.

Background

The first human settlers in the region were the South Island Maori who used the abundant coastal resources and hunted the flightless moa as long ago as AD 1350. Within 200 years most of the moa had been plundered and the settlers turned their attentions to the fur seals, fish and other seafood. The thick almost impenetrable coastal forests of the region prevented easy access inland so the population waxed and waned but was never substantial. The forbidding forests were also thought by the Maori to be the home of a race of hairy giants known as *Maeroero* (a group of early Scottish settlers looking for a pub?). The Maori were joined, first by small groups of European whalers, then timber millers who began their relentless rape of the forest from the 1860s. Once depleted, as with most other parts of New Zealand, it was the farmers who moved in. Thankfully a few tracts of the original coastal forest escaped the axe.

Invercargill to Papatowai

From Invercargill the Southern Scenic Route (SH92) crosses the Southland Plains to join the coast and the Mataura River mouth at the former coastal whaling station of **Fortrose** (42 km). At Fortrose you leave SH92 and begin to negotiate the coastal road networks of the Catlins towards **Otara** and Waikawa. The first potential diversion is to **Waipapa Point**. From just beyond Otara take the signposted road cross-country to a car park beside the lighthouse. The gently sloping beach is backed by dunes and decked with rock pools and offshore reefs. These reefs were the cause of New Zealand's second worst shipping disaster in 1881, when the *SS Tararua* ran aground with the loss of 131 lives. It was this tragedy that prompted the erection of the **lighthouse**. Completed in 1884, it was the last wooden lighthouse built in New Zealand. Keep your eyes open for Hookers sea lions, which sometimes haul up on the beaches here for a doze.

Once back on the main route near Otara continue to Haldane and follow signs for **Slope Point**, which is actually the southernmost point in New Zealand, contrary to what most visitors believe. The real geographical point and obligatory signpost can be reached here via a short 10-minute walk from a roadside car park. From the car park there are views of the dramatic headlands that herald a distinct change from Waipapa's lowly dunescapes. Also of note are the macrocarpa trees.

From Haldane the road skirts the Haldane Estuary before delivering you at the beautiful **Porpoise Bay**, a popular spot for swimming and surfing. From the junction it is a short drive (right) to the headland and Curio Bay.

The headland overlooking both bays is a superb spot to simply admire the coastal scenery, crashing waves and try to spot the tiny **Hector's dolphins**. Some patience may be required for this but eventually you may see a pod (especially near the rocks that protect Porpoise Bay). They are a delight to observe as they breach the surface in exuberant playfulness.

At **Curio Bay**, about 500 m west, is the fossil forest. At first glance it is difficult to make out the petrified stumps and logs that scatter the rock platform, but a more thorough investigation by foot reveals the distinct features of these Jurassic ancestors.

Although it is hard to drag yourself away from Curio Bay, the road now turns briefly inland to rejoin the Waikawa River Estuary at **Waikawa**. Here you will find a small **District Museum** ① *daily 1300-1600 (seasonal)*, which contains some relics from the whaling and saw-milling years.

From Waikawa the road heads north past the former saw-milling village of **Niagara**. A few hundred metres past the village you then join the main SH92 Catlins road (from Tokanui and Fortrose) and turn right through more dramatic topography and coastal forest towards **Chaslands** and Papatowai. The **Chasland Scenic Reserve** boasts some of the best forest in the area with large rimu and kamahi. Look out for the left turn to **McLean Falls** (1 km north of the Cathedral Caves turning). The falls car park is reached via the Rewcastle Road (3 km). The picturesque three-stepped falls (often said to be the most beautiful in the Catlins) are reached easily on foot (40 minutes return).

The 30-m-high **Cathedral Caves** at the north end of Waipati Beach are accessible only at low tide (posted at the road junction or available from the local VICs). The 2-km access road will deliver you to a car park where the caves are accessed via a short (30 minutes) forest and beach walk. Although the forest is part of **Waipati Scenic Reserve**, note that part of the area is Maori owned. After several land claim disputes a small fee is now requested to access the caves.

Just before the beautiful **Tautuku Bay** is the **Lenz Reserve** and the **Traill's Tractor Historic Walk** (10 minutes). Tautuku was a prolific logging area and the walk takes you to a former milling site and an original 'Traill's Tractor' logging machine, that took over from horse-drawn trams in the steeper country. The walk starts from the Flemming River

Bridge. Nearby is the hidden delight of **Lake Wilkie**. Formed in a dune hollow and surrounded by lush bush, it can be viewed from a lookout a mere five minutes' walk from the car park. You can then complete a 30-minute circuit of the lake's scenic coastal edge. The boardwalk provides another view across the lake and comes complete with interpretative signs that outline the botanical features of the unique habitat. Note there is no access to the beach from this point.

About 1½ km south of Lake Wilkie is the new **Tautuku Estuary Walk** (30 minutes return), which offers access to the estuary and coastal forest. The beautiful beach is best accessed via the **Tautuku Dune/Forest Walk** (15 minutes) which is just opposite the Tautuku Outdoor Education Centre on SH92. A stunning view of the whole bay and its thick fringe of coastal forest can be seen from the road as you climb **Florence Hill** at its eastern edge. Just offshore are the **Rainbow Isles**, which owe their name to the effects of the sun on sea-spray, squirted skywards by a small blowhole on the main island. The Maori call it *rerekohu*, meaning 'flying mist'. From Florence Hill it is a 2-km drive to **Papatowai** – the Catlins 'mid-point' and base for services and accommodation.

Papatowai to Owaka

There are a number of notable walks around Papatowai, the most popular of which is the **Picnic Point Track** (40 minutes), which takes in both coast and forest and with a short diversion to the unusual **Kings Rock** formation. From McLennan and the river of the same name you can access both the **Maitai** (north) and **Purakaunui Falls** (east). They are both easily reached from the road (Maitai first via SH92), and significantly different and worthy of investigation.

About 4 km east of the Purakaunui Falls is the access road to **Purakaunui Bay**. This is one of the most beautiful and supremely quiet spots on the Catlins Coast and is excellent for a short walk, surfing, a picnic or an overnight stay at the basic campsite. Be careful on this road, it is very narrow and winding.

If you want a change from all the coastal scenery the Catlins River Track (five hours one way) provides an excellent opportunity. Access is about 3 km south of Catlins Lake via **Tawanui** where there is a DoC campsite. Follow the road to **The Wisp** (farm lease) and the picnic site trailhead. The section between Wallis Stream and Franks Creek (1½ hours) is recommended.

Back on the coast many visitors are drawn along the western bank of the Catlins Lake and the Owaka Heads to see **Jack's Bay** and blowhole. At 55 m deep, with an opening of 140 m by 70 m, it is quite an impressive sight, even when it's not stormy.

Owaka and around

Returning back to Catlins Lake and SH92 it is then a short drive to the Catlins' largest settlement and supply centre, Owaka, which offers a host of basic facilities including a good information centre and museum combo, a restaurant, petrol, a grocery store, accommodation, visitor centre and internet. But if the weather is fine and you still have time on your hands before sunset, don't hang around. Instead, head back to the coast. **Pounawea**, 4 km south of Owaka, offers a very pleasant (45 minutes) nature walk through podocarp forest and salt marsh.

Just east of Pounawea is **Surat Bay**, which is reached across other side of the Owaka River (the bridge is 2 km south of Owaka). Its golden swathes of sand and those of its neighbour, **Cannibals Bay** (access from SH92, a few kilometres north of Owaka), provide the reasonable likelihood of encountering some dozing Hookers sea lions.

Cannibals Bay was mistakenly named in the late 1800s by geologist James Hector, who took the human remains from a Maori burial site to be something far more sinister. A pleasant walk from here negotiates the length of Cannibals Bay (from the car park) to the **False Islet** headlands. Then, once you have taken in the views, from the west to Jack's Bay and then east, to the rocky outcrops of the **Nugget Point**, continue on to Surat Bay, before returning across the neck of the headland to Cannibals Bay (two hours).

Nugget Point, Roaring Bay and Kaka Point
Back on SH92 the road turns inland again towards Balclutha. About 3 km east of Owaka is **Tunnel Hill**, which is a historic reserve featuring the 246-m-long tunnel, once the most southerly railway tunnel in New Zealand. Completed in 1915 it was the most prominent feature on the Catlins branch railway line that ran between Balclutha and Tahakopa near McLennan. The line closed in 1971.

Just beyond the hill is the turn-off to Nugget Point, without doubt the highlight of the Catlins Coast. To get a proper feel for 'The Nuggets' they are best visited at sunrise, when the spectacular rock pillars and outcrops take on the orange glow of the sun. The track to the 1870 **lighthouse** starts at the terminus of a delightful road that skirts the beach and rock platforms of Molyneux Bay. It takes about 10 minutes to reach the lighthouse and its associated lookout point, but by far the best view is to be had from the hill, about 100 m short of it. Care must be taken here, but the views from the top are outstanding. The islets and rocky, inaccessible coastline offer an important haven for wildlife, and is home to seals (all three species: fur, Hookers and elephant), yellow-eyed and blue penguins, sooty shearwaters, gannets and occasionally royal spoonbills. Even below the waves life abounds and the area boasts a wide diversity of underwater habitats. Keep your ears open for the plaintive wails of fur seal pups playing in and around the rock pools below the track and look out for squadrons of shearwaters, skimming the waves in search of food. It really is a magical place.

Just inland from the Point is **Roaring Bay** that has a small public hide where yellow-eyed penguins can be seen coming ashore at dusk, or leaving again for their routine fishing trips at dawn. If you are lucky enough to see one, remember you are looking at the rarest penguin in the world so be discreet and do not approach them. Back along the edge of Molyneux Bay is **Kaka Point** (8 km), a charming little coastal settlement that, along with Owaka, provides the necessary visitor amenities and accommodation. From Kaka Point it is about 22 km to Balclutha and SH1 to Dunedin.

Balclutha
Balclutha (which is actually in South Otago) is 80 km southwest of Dunedin on the banks of the Clutha River, which, with its origins at Lake Wanaka, is the South Island's longest (322 km). Known as 'Big River Town' its name actually refers to the Scottish Gaelic for 'town on the Clyde' after Glasgow's great river. The town's first known white resident was Scot Jim McNeill who used to run a ferry service across the river between 1853 and 1857. The modern-day concrete bridge that provides the vital road link with Southland is not the original bridge. The first effort, which was constructed in 1866, was washed away in floods. Fishing is of course a popular local pursuit and the VIC (I-Site) has details of this and other local activities. The **South Otago Museum** ① *1 Renfrew St, T03-418 2382, Mon-Fri 1000-1600 Sun 1300-1600, free*, is particularly noted for its collection of bottles and displays surrounding the history of the local **Kaitangata Coal Mine**.

Gore

Gore (population, 9,000), on the banks of the Mataura River, is Southland's second largest town and most famous for its unusual mix of trout fishing, country music and formerly (we can only presume) illegal whisky distilling. So although you might think the place to be a just another quiet backwater, beware. At times, particularly during the 10-day annual **New Zealand Gold Guitar Awards** (see Festivals and events, page 700), sleepy Gore can go off like Dolly Parton in a lingerie shop. During the festival both amateur and professional artists compete, while the true fanatics get the chance to dust off their cowboy boots and line dance the night away.

Other local attractions include the **Hokonui Moonshine Museum** and the **Gore Historical Museum** ① *Hokonui Heritage Centre, next to the VIC, T03-203 9288, $5, Tue-Fri 1300-1630, Sat-Sun 1300-1600*. There, the heady days of Gore district's insobriety and chaos, alongside its times of prohibition and prudence, are revealed. Just opposite the VIC (I-Site) is the recently renovated **Eastern Southland Gallery** ① *14 Hokonui Dr, T03-208 9907, Mon-Fri 1000-1630, Sun 1300-1600*, showcasing the impressive private collection of expatriate Kiwi John Money, and donated works by one of New Zealand's most well-known contemporaries Ralph Hotere. Still in the planning is a **Fishing Museum** where the monster brown trout and the fishermen that come from around the globe to catch them will be celebrated. Should you fancy a spot of fishing yourself, you'll get a licence at the VIC ($21 for a day). The VIC (I-Site) also has an extensive list of local guides.

Also of note in the region is **Moth Restaurant and Bar** and the new museum complex of the **Croydon Aircraft Company** ① *SH94, Mandeville, west of Gore on SH94, T03-208 9755/T03-208 9662, www.themoth.co.nz/www.croydonaircraft.com*. Not only does it provide good food but also the opportunity to combine your visit with a look at aviation history.

If you have animal-loving children, the **Reservation** ① *at the top of Coutts Rd, T03-208 1200, Tue-Sun 1200-1630, $6, child $3*, has a small menagerie of warm, cuddly animals from windless bovines to chinchillas and Clydesdale horses, all of whom are available for copious stroking and generous feeding. Café on site.

◉ The Catlins listings

For Sleeping and Eating price codes and other relevant information, see Essentials pages 44-50.

◉ Sleeping

Invercargill to Papatowai *p693, map p692*
L Catlins Farmstay, midway between Cathedral Caves and Curio Bay, T03-246 8843, www.catlinsfarmstay.co.nz. Set on a 400-ha working farm, offers 3 rooms one self-contained, queen and twin.
AL-A Curio Bay Salthouse Motel, 517 Waikawa-Curio Bay Rd, T03-246 8598, www.curiobaysalthouse.co.nz. New motel with 2 self-catering open-plan studio units right on the beach.

A-C Papatowai Hilltop Accommodation and Backpackers, Papatowai, T03-415 8028, www.hilltopbackpackers.co.nz. An excellent place offering doubles (with a great view) and dorm beds. Log fire, modern facilities, hot tub, bikes, canoes, internet and much more. Recommended.
AL Southern Secret Motel, Papatowai, T03-415 8600, www.southcatlins.co.nz. A stylish modern place with 4 studio units, all with balcony. Close to amenities and coastal walks.
AL-D Curio Bay Experience, Curio Bay Rd, Waikawa, T03-246 8552. 4 self-contained beachfront holiday houses sleeping up to 8 and a budget option with comfortable doubles and dorms in a spacious house.

Dolphin trips and surf lessons can be arranged.

B Papatowai Motels and Store, T03-415 8147, b.bevin@paradise.net.nz. Has 3 spacious self-contained units.

C-D Nadir Outpost, 174 Slope Point Rd, T03-246 8544, nadir.outpost@ihug.co.nz. Peaceful and friendly this 14-bed hostel offers a fine option as a first or last night stop if taking your time and in possession of your own transport. Good standard backpackers' facilities as well as tent and van sites, shop and information centre.

D Tautuku Lodge, set in the Lenz Reserve at Tautuku, T03-415 8024, diana.keith@ruralzone.net. Owned by the Forest and Bird Society. The lodge sleeps 10 but there is also a smaller cabin sleeping 4. Supply your own bedding.

Motorcamps and campsites
See also Nadir Outpost, above.

L-D McLean Falls HolidayPark, 29 Rewcastle Rd, Chaslands Hwy, Chaslands, T03-415 8338, www.catlinsnz.com. The most modern (and expensive) holiday park in the Catlins. Full range of accommodation options from 2 bedroom cottages to tent sites, full facilities including a caféand shop. The falls are a short drive away.

C-D Papatowai Motor Camp, behind the motel, T03-415 8565. Holiday home, basic cabins, backpacker rooms, powered and non-powered sites, camp kitchen.

Papatowai to Owaka p695
C-D Falls Backpackers, Purakaunui Falls, T03-4158724, www.catlins-nz.com/falls-backpackers/. Offers 4 doubles and shared twin rooms and a lovely homely atmosphere. Walking distance from the falls. Recommended.

Campsites
D DoC campsite, Purakaunui Bay. Basic but in a superb setting – worth buying a tent for.

Owaka and around p695
AL Kepplestone-by-the-sea, 9 Surat Bay Rd, T03-415 8134/T0800-105134, kepplestone@xtra.co.nz. Tucked away near the coast and Surat Bay. A delightful B&B with a range of en suite rooms and fine cuisine.

A Catlins Area Motels, 34 Ryley St, T03-415 8821. Recommended motel option.

A Catlins Gateway Motel, corner of Main Rd and Royal Terr, T03-415 8592. Has some nice new 1-bedroom units. Recommended.

B-C Catlins Blowhole Backpackers, 24 Main Rd, T03-454 5635, www.catlinsbackpackers.co.nz. Something of a hit, this conveniently located backpacker hostel offers 2 lovely cottages each with nicely decorated double, twin and triples and above average facilities. Recommended.

C-D Mohua Park Eco-Cottages, Tawanui, T03-415 8613, www.catlinsmohuapark.co.nz. Self-contained 4-star rated cottages in a peaceful rural setting with great views. Ideal for couples and just a short drive from Owaka.

C-D Surat Bay Lodge Backpackers, Surat Bay Rd, T03-415 8099, www.suratbay.co.nz. A small, peaceful backpacker lodge a stone's throw from the beach. It also runs its own nature, farm, walking and canoe tours (2-3 hrs) from $40.

Motorcamps and campsites
C-D Pounawea Camp Ground, Park Lane, Pounawea, Owaka, T03-415 8483, www.catlins-nz.com/pomoca.html. Basic motorpark.

Nugget Point, Roaring Bay and Kaka Point p696
L-B Nugget View and Kaka Point Motels, 11 Rata St, Kaka Point, T03-412 8602, www.catlins.co.nz. 15 comfortable studio units, some with spa. Free kayak hire and also offers boat-based eco-tours to the Nuggets.

AL-A Cardno's, 8 Marine Terr, Kaka Point, T03-412 8181, www.cardnosaccommodation.co.nz. Stylish and modern, offering a choice of a self-contained or a studio unit overlooking the beach. Excellent hosts and all round good value. Recommended.

A Nugget Lodge Motels, 2 km from Nugget Point right on the beach, T03-412 8783, www.nuggetlodge.co.nz. Run by a former honorary DoC field officer with plenty of local knowledge. On offer are 2 modern units, one overlooking the bay.

C-D Fernlea Backpackers, Moana St, Kaka Point, T03-412 8834. Small, homely and well-established. Wonderful view from the balcony.

Motorcamps and campsites

C-D Kaka Point Motor Park, on the edge of the town on Tarata St, T03-412 8803, kakapoint@hotmail.com. Quiet place offering 2 modern cabins, sheltered sites and a spacious camp kitchen.

Balclutha p696

AL-A Lesmahagow, Main Rd, Benhar, T03-418 2507, www.lesmahagow.co.nz. You will find a warm Irish welcome and all the comforts at this B&B. 2 en suites and 2 rooms with shared bathroom. It is located just north of the town in a peaceful setting.

A Highway Lodge Motel, 165 Clyde St, T03-418 2363. A modern motel option that sits at the start of the Southern Scenic Route and the Catlins coast.

A Rosebank Lodge Motor Hotel, 265 Clyde St, T03-419 0021, www.rosebanklodge.co.nz. Comfortable chalet-style units, with spa, sauna and an in-house restaurant/bistro.

Motorcamps and campsites

C-D Balclutha Motor Camp, 56 Charlotte St, T03-418 0088. The only option for camper-vans. It has a few cabins, an excellent campground and camp kitchen.

Gore p697

A RiverleaMotel, 46 Hokonui Dr, T03-208 3130, www.riverleamotel.co.nz. Modern 4-star motel.

A Scenic Circle Croydon Lodge, corner of SH94 and Waimea St, T03-208 9029, www.scenic-circle.co.nz. A large motel set in extensive grounds with a 9-hole golf course, à la carte restaurant and bar and Sky TV.

C-D Old Fire Station Backpackers, 19 Hokonui Dr (across the road from the VIC), T03-208 1925. Small backpacker hostel with double/twin, singles and dorms.

Motorcamps and campsites

B-D Gore Motor Camp, 35 Broughton St, T03-208 4919. Basic cabins, on-site vans, powered/tent sites and camp kitchen.

● Eating

Invercargill to Papatowai p693, map p692

If you are not in a B&B or self-contained place then eating out in the South Catlins really takes the form of a stove or a BBQ with the sandflies. There is a general store in Papatowai, daily 0830-2200, winter Sun-Thu 0900-1800, Fri-Sat 0900-1830, which sells BBQs and basic takeaway food.

♦♦ **Niagara Falls Café**, Main Rd, Niagara, T03-246 8577. Popular highway café and gift shop combo offering a good selection of light meals and a fair caffeine fix.

Owaka p695

♦♦ **Lumber Jack Bar and Café**, Main St, T03-415 8747. Daily from 1200 (1600 in winter). A fairly classy place, with a traditional Kiwi menu and good coffee.

Kaka Point p696

♦♦-♦ **Point Café and Bar**, on the Esplanade, T03-412 8800, www.kakapoint.co.nz. Daily 0800-2000. The most popular eatery/bar in the area with the obligatory ocean views. It also has a grocery store attached.

Balclutha p696

♦♦ **Rosebank Lodge**, see Sleeping, above. Daily for breakfast, lunch and dinner. The restaurant here is recommended.

Gore *p697*

¶ **Howl at the Moon**, 2 Main St, T03-208 3851. Daily from 1200. A café/bar with a reasonable blackboard menu.

¶ **Moth Restaurant and Bar**, see page 697. Tue-Sun from 1100-2100.

¶ **Table Talk Café**, 70 Main St, T03-208 7110. Has a modern New Zealand menu and serves a good all-day breakfast.

⊕ Festivals and events

Gore *p697*

June New Zealand Gold Guitar Awards, T03-208 1978, www.goldguitars.co.nz. A 10-day annual event on the Queen's birthday weekend (end of the month). Up to 5,000 people come for the southern hospitality and country music atmosphere.

▲ Activities and tours

The Catlins *p692, map p692*
Bottom Bus, based in Dunedin, T03-4479083, www. travelheadfirst.com. Regional transport provider offering packages taking in the Catlins en route from or to Dunedin, Invercargill, Queenstown and Te Anau.

Catlins Encounters is an adjunct to the already very successful **Elm Wildlife Tours**in Dunedin, T0800-356563/T03-4544121, www.elmwildlife tours.co.nz. The entertaining full-day takes in all the best sights, including a good chance to see yellow-eyed penguins and Hooker's sea lions, from $132. Can organize

onward travel to Stewart Island.

Catlins Natural Wonders, Balclutha, T0800-304333/T03-4779083, www.catlinsnatural.co.nz. Another eco-based tour operator offering day trips (from $130 Dunedin/$85 Balclutha return) 4 times a week (departing Dunedin 0830/Balclutha 1000), and 2-day stop over trips (from $200) from Dunedin or Balclutha, which includes a choice of accommodation at extra cost.

Catlins Wildlife Trackers Eco-tours, Papatowai, T03-415 8613, www.catlins-ecotours.co.nz. Has been operating for over 12 years and offers award-winning 2- to 7-day eco-tours ($600-1500), which explore the region's forest, coast, natural features and wildlife. Very informative with a range of comfortable accommodation options.

Curio Bay Experience, based in Waikawa, T03-2468552, dolphinsurf@xtra.co.nz. Trips to see general marine life with the chance of spotting the rare Hector's dolphin and surf lessons.

Nugget View Charters, Kaka Point, T03-412 8602, www.catlins.co.nz. Offers water-based wildlife spotting and fishing trips around Molyneux Bay and Nugget Point.

❶ Directory

The Catlins *p692, map p692*
Banks There are no banks in the Catlins but EFTPOS is available at the general stores and petrol stations. **Internet** VIC, Owaka. **Lumberjack Café and Bar**, Owaka. **Table Talk Café**, Gore.

Tramping in Southland and the Fiords

Fiordland National Park offers some of the best tramping (hiking) tracks in the world ranging from the relatively straightforward Kepler and Humpridge tracks to the more demanding Dusky and Hollyford. Then of course there is the Milford Track considered by many (deservingly) as the best walk in the world. All the tracks are administered by DoC, are well facilitated and must be booked well in advance. Before embarking on any trip do your homework and make sure you are well prepared. The weather in this region is notorious with the higher elevations receiving over 6 m (yes, metres) of rain a year. Of course you may strike it lucky and have a clear run with omnipresent and stunning views making it a truly memorable experience, but to avoid disappointment count on about half the trip being head down, wet and cold. ▸▸ For Sleeping, Eating and other listings, see pages 705-706.

Ins and outs

For information (including the DoC self-guided leaflet), the latest conditions on all the tracks listed below and hut bookings contact the **DoC** at the VIC (I-Site) in Te Anau (see page 658) and the VIC (I-Site) in Tuatapere (see page 675). The following websites are also useful: www.doc.govt.nz, www.hollyfordtrack.co.nz, www.humpridgetrack.co.nz (for online bookings). Most mainstream bookshops stock specialist guides on the Milford or Fiordland tracks. DoC also stock maps.

Dusky Track → *Colour map 6, B2 Grade of difficulty 9/10.*

Now this is a track for 'real trampers': the sort with tree trunk legs, well-worn boots and facial hair. The Dusky offers the widest range of 'experiences' of any track in Fiordland from stunning glacial valley and mountain scenery, to the possibility of complete immersion in icy water. It really is magnificent and thoroughly recommended. Perhaps the true attraction, other than the relative peace, is the sense of awe at the remote **Dusky Sound**, at the very heart of the Fiordland National Park. It is a true wilderness that has changed little since Captain Cook first set foot there over 200 years ago.

The Dusky attracts less than 1000 trampers a year, which is a reflection of its remote and difficult nature. Both its location and grade of difficulty make it a true challenge and one that should only be attempted in summer. Note the track is subject to bad flooding year round. Always consult with the DoC before any attempt and fill in an intention sheet (Te Anau). Locator beacons are also recommended.

Walking times and distances The track is 84 km in total. Allow 8-10 days from Lake Hauroko to Supper Cove to West Arm (Lake Manapouri), or four days one way to Supper Cove: Hauroko (Hauroko Burn Hut)–Halfway Hut: 12 km, four to six hours. Halfway Hut–Lake Roe Hut: 7 km, three to five hours. Lake Roe Hut–Loch Maree Hut: 10 km, four to six hours. Loch Maree Hut–Supper Cove: 12 km, six to eight hours. North Access (Wilmot Pass Road Access Point to Loch Maree): Wilmot Pass Road Access Point–Upper Spey Hut, 8 km, four to five hours (add 45 minutes to West Arm Wharf and Hut). Upper Spey Hut–Kintail Hut: 7 km, six hours. Kintail Hut–Loch Maree Hut: 11 km, four to seven hours.

Trailhead transport and access The Dusky Track can be accessed from the south via Lake Hauroko (64 km west of Tuatapere) or from the Wilmot Pass Road (40 minutes from West Arm Wharf), or via boat from Lake Manapouri. By road, Lake Manapouri is reached from Manapouri (SH95), 21 km south of Te Anau. **Scenic Shuttles**, T03-477 9083, www.scenicshuttle.co.nz, provides transport to Manapouri and Tuatapere (departs Te Anau daily at 0815; November to May Monday to Friday only). **Lake Hauroko Tours**, Tuatapere, T03-226 6681, www.duskytrack.co.nz, offers road and jetboat access to the southern trailhead via Lake Hauroko (departs November to May Monday and Thursday at 0900, \$70). **Real Journeys**, T0800-656501/T03-249 7416, and **Fiordland Explorer Charters**, T0800-434673, www.doubtfulsoundcruise.com, both based in Pearl Harbour, Manapouri, provide daily boat transport to and from West Arm and Wilmot Pass Road. You can fly in or out of Supper Cove or Lake Hauroko by floatplane with **Wings and Water**, Te Anau, T03-249 7405, www.wingsandwater.co.nz. Or by helicopter with **Southern Lakes Helicopters**, T03-249 7167, www.southernlakes helicopters.co.nz, or **South West Helicopters**, Te Anau/Tuatapere, T03-249 7402, www.southwesthelicopters.co.nz. For more trailhead transport and trailhead access details, see Te Anau, Getting around, page 658.

Hump Ridge Track → *Colour map 6, B2/3 Grade of difficulty 5/10.*
The Hump Ridge Track opened in late 2000 and is New Zealand's newest tramping track. It is a 53-km three-day 'moderate' circuit track at the southeastern end of the Fiordland National Park. Although it remains low-profile in relation to the excellent older tracks to the north, there is no doubt it offers a great tramping experience. As well as the mix of both coastal and podocarp/beech forest landscapes, the main attraction is the historic appeal of its four viaducts. The 125-m **Percy Burn Viaduct** is reputed to be the largest wooden viaduct in the world. Wildlife to look out for include kea and bellbirds. Fur seals and the endangered Hector's dolphins can be seen on the coast. The track is boardwalk through the areas most subject to any flooding, but you are still advised to check on track conditions before departure.

Walking times and distances The track is 53 km in full. Allow three days: Bluecliffs Beach car park–Okaka Hut: 18 km, eight to nine hours. Okaka Hut–Port Craig Village Hut: 18 km, seven hours. Port Craig Village Hut–Bluecliffs Beach: 17 km, six to seven hours.

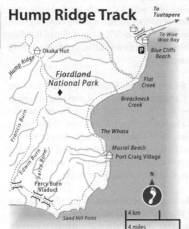

Hump Ridge Track

Trailhead transport and access The Hump Ridge Track starts and finishes at the western end of Blue Cliffs Beach on Te Wae Wae Bay (signposted from Tuatapere). An anticlockwise approach is generally recommended. Road transportation to the trailhead can be arranged through **Lake Hauroko Tours**, Tuatapere, T03-226 6681, www.duskytrack.co.nz, or the VIC in Tuatapere (see page 675). Independent vehicles can be left at the Tuatapere Hump Ridge Track office in Tuatapere, 31 Orawia Rd, T03- 226 6739, www.humpridgetrack.co.nz.

Kepler Track → *Colour map 6, B3 Grade of difficulty 6/10.*
The Kepler Track is a 60-km, three- to four-day 'Great Walk', which is accessible from Te Anau, providing a convenient and viable alternative to the Milford Track. It

traverses the edge of the beautiful **Lake Te Anau** before ascending to the **Luxmore Hut** – reputed to offer one of the best 'hut views' in Fiordland. From the Luxmore Hut the track negotiates the scenic, open tops of the **Luxmore Range**, before falling through forest in to the **Iris Burn Valley** and back to civilization via Shallow Bay on **Lake Manapouri**. The highlights are of course the views from the Luxmore Hut and the scenic combination of lake, mountain and river valley scenery. The forest is classic silver beech and podocarp, which at night often echoes with the cry of kiwi. New Zealand robin and blue duck are also seen occasionally. This track attracts over 10,000 trampers a year so book well in advance and expect company. The Kepler offers an excellent two-day (return) part-track walk to the Luxmore Hut and back.

Walking times and distances It's a 60-km full circuit from Te Anau. Allow four days: Control Gates–Luxmore Hut: 14 km, six hours (Brod Bay campsite 1½ hours). Luxmore Hut–Iris Burn Hut: 18½ km, five to six hours. Irish Burn Hut–Moturau Hut: 17 km; five to six hours. Moturau Hut–Rainbow Reach: 6 km, 1½ hours.

Trailhead transport and access The Kepler Track starts at the Lake Te Anau outlet control gates, 5 km south of Te Anau and finishes at **Rainbow Reach**, 11 km south of Te Anau near SH95. By road, **Tracknet**, T03-249 7777, www.tracknet.co.nz, offers transportation from Te Anau town to the control gates ($6) or Rainbow Reach ($10), departs Te Anau 0830, 0930, 1445 ($6). It also provides transport from Queenstown.

Kepler Track

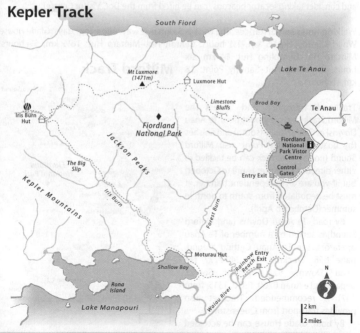

By boat, the Kepler can be accessed opposite Te Anau at Brod Bay (missing out first the 5½-km lakeside section of track), contact **Kepler water taxi**, T03-249 8364, from $25 (one way). The Luxmore Hut can be reached by helicopter with **Southern Lakes Helicopters**, T03-249 7167, www.southernlakeshelicopters.co.nz. For more trailhead transport details, see Te Anau, Getting around, page 658.

Milford Track → Colour map 6, A/B3 Grade of difficulty 6/10.

Ever since the *National Geographic* magazine hailed the mighty, 53-km, four-day, Milford Track as the 'World's Greatest Walk' in the early 1980s, it has become a victim of its own reputation. Of its utter scenic splendour there is no doubt, but there is also human traffic and commercialism. That of course does not mean that it cannot be treated as a challenge. It is essentially a difficult tramp and should be tackled with enthusiasm, but more importantly, also, a sense of realism.

Highlights on the Milford are many, including the stunning vista of the **McKinnon Pass** (1073 m) and the 580-m **Sutherland Falls**. Then, of course, at the track's end is the stunning and unforgettable **Milford Sound**. The Milford Track attracts up to 20,000 trampers a year so book well in advance (at least two months) and expect company. Bookings are on a first-come-first-served basis and start on 1 July for the following summer. Trampers should be of a suitable fitness level and be able to carry a heavy pack for four days. The track is very well-maintained but is still steep and rough in places. In winter the McKinnon Pass can be impassable due to snow and ice and there can be a severe avalanche danger. In winter always consult the DoC before setting off, check weather forecasts, fill in an intentions sheet and consider taking locator beacons (can be hired from the DoC Visitor Centre).

Walking times and distances The track is 53 km one way. Allow four days: Glade House Wharf–Clinton Hut: 5 km, 1½ hours. Clinton Hut–Mintaro Hut: 16½ km, 5½ hours. Mintaro Hut–Dumpling Hut: 14 km, six hours. Dumpling Hut–Sandfly Point: 18 km, six hours.

Trailhead transport and access The Milford Track starts (by boat from Te Anau Downs) at Glade House (south) and finishes (by boat) at Sandfly Point near Milford Sound (north). The track can be tackled in either direction in winter (April to October) but, if you are an independent tramper, it must be negotiated from south to north in summer (October to April).

By road, Te Anau Downs (and Milford Sound) is served by a number of Te Anau operators, see Te Anau Getting around, page 658. **Tracknet**, T03-249 7777 (Te Anau Downs $22; Milford Sound, departing Te Anau 0700, 0930, 1315, from $47) is recommended. Tracknet also provides transport from Queenstown.

By boat, Glade House can be accessed

Milford Track

from Te Anau with **Real Journeys**, T03-249 7416 (1030, 1400; from $65). **Wings and Water**, T03-249 7405, can deliver you to Glade House by floatplane. From Milford Sound, the **DoC**, T03-249 8514 (1400, 1515; $30) and **Rosco's Sea Kayaks** provide pick-ups and drop-offs to Sandfly Point.**Tracknet** (see above) offer complete road and water transport package deals from $160.

Hollyford Track → *Colour map 6, A3 Grade of difficulty 6/10.*
The Hollyford Track is essentially a low-level (bush) 56-km four-day (one way) tramp that negotiates the **Hollyford River Valley** and bank of **Lake McKerrow** to the remote **Martins Bay**. It is not a tramp for those expecting spectacular high-level views, but does offer fine scenery and a superb sense of wilderness. The undeniable highlight is the **Martins Bay Hut** at the mouth of the Hollyford River. Two days at Martins Bay taking in the coast and seal colony is a fine remote west coast experience. The tramp is most often tackled in conjunction with jet-boat returns/shortcuts via Lake McKerrow and a flight out from Martins Bay Lodge to Milford or Hollyford Valley airfield is highly recommended. Note that guided walks are available. Also note that the Hollyford can be extended or combined to include the long (9-10 day) and arduous **Pyke-Big Bay Track**. Martins Bay to Big Bay Hut offers a good day trip but the route is vague.

This is not a tramp to be tackled after heavy rain. The sections between the Trailhead car park and the Hidden Falls Hut (first hut) are tricky in wet weather; some river crossings have **three-wire bridges**. The sandflies at Martins Bay Hut are legendary.

Walking times and distances The track is 56 km one way. Allow four to five days to Martins Bay Hut, one way. Road End–Hidden Falls Hut: 9 km, two to three hours. Hidden Falls Hut–Alabaster Hut: 10½ km, three to four hours. Alabaster Hut–Demon Trail Hut: 14½ km, four to five hours. Demon Trail Hut–Hokuri Hut: 9½ km, five to six hours. Hokuri Hut–Martins Bay Hut: 13½ km, four to five hours.

Trailhead transport and access For air transportation contact **Air Fiordland**, T03-249 6720, www.airfiordland.com. For jet-boat transfers contact **Hollyford Track**, T0800-832226 (T03-442 3000), www.hollyfordtrack.com. **Tracknet**, T03-249 7777 ($47), runs buses departing Te Anau Mon/Wed/Fri only1130. **Trips and Tramps**, T0800-305807/T03-2497081, www.tripsadntramps.co.nz, also offers road transfers. For more trailhead transport and trailhead access details see Getting around, in the Te Anau section, page 658.

◉ Southland and The Fiords listings

For Sleeping and Eating price codes and other relevant information, see Essentials pages 44-50.

● Sleeping

Dusky Track *p701*
All 7 huts (Halfway, Lake Roe, Loch Maree, Supper Cove, Kintail, Upper Spey and West Arm Hut) are 'serviced' ranging from 12-20 bunks with mattresses and toilet facilities.

There are no gas cookers but there are potbelly stoves in each hut. Huts must be booked through DoC and cost $15, per night. For post-walk accommodation see Manapouri/Te Anau and Tuatapere sections. For more booking information see the DoC website, www.doc.govt.nz.

Hump Ridge Track *p702, map p702*
Both huts (Okaka and Port Craig Village) are

maintained and managed by the Hump Ridge Track Trust. Wardens are seconded to each hut from Oct-Apr. The huts are very modern with 40 bunks, mattresses, lighting, cooking, heating and toilet facilities (limited hot water). Huts must be booked through the Track Trust direct, or through the VIC in Tuatapere. Various walk/accommodation packages are available from the 'Freedom Walk' to the 'Guided' from $90 to $1395. For post walk accommodation see Tuatapere sections.

Hollyford track *p705*

All the DoC huts are 'Serviced' ($15) from 12-20 bunks with wood fires but no gas cookers. **Martins Bay Lodge** (between Hokuri and Martins Bay Huts, accessible by jet boat and administered by Hollyford Track as part of tramping package), much higher standard than the DoC Huts. Guided trips, fully catered and fly-in/walk-out or walk-in/walk-out tramps available with **Hollyford Track**, T0800-832226/T03-442 3000, www.hollyfordtrack.co.nz. From Te Anau a 3-day (fly out) adventure costs from $1,655.

Kepler Track *p702, map p703*

Another of the country's premier walks and administered as one of the DoC's 'Great Walks', www.greatwalks.co.nz. All 3 huts (Luxmore, Iris Burn and Moturau) are of a good standard ranging from 40-60 bunks with mattresses and cooking facilities. Note that huts do not have heating or cooking facilities in winter (May to mid-Oct). They cost $45 per night.
D Campsite at Brod Bay, $15, child $6. All bookings should be made with the DoC in advance, especially in mid summer. For trailhead accommodation see Te Anau, page 662. For more booking information, www.doc.govt.nz.

Milford Track *p704, map p704*

The 3 DoC huts (Clinton, Mintaro and Dumpling) are of a good standard with 40 bunks and cooking, heating and toilet facilities. Wardens are seconded to all huts in summer. The cost of the 3 nights' accommodation is $135 (14 or under, $75). In winter Apr-Oct the huts revert to backcountry hut standard/category (no heating or cooking facilities) and cost $15. The 'Guided Walks' companies have separate huts (Glade House, Quintin Hut and Milford Lodge). Given the popularity of the Milford, as an independent tramper you cannot stay consecutive nights in one hut and must move on. No camping is allowed. All bookings should be made with the DoC's Great Walks booking office (Te Anau) well in advance (preferably the year before), especially during mid-summer.

▲ Activities and tours

Hump Ridge Track *p702, map p702*
Hump Ridge Track, T0800-486774, www.humpridgetrack.co.nz. All inclusive multi-day package deals with a 4-day/3-night 'Freedom Plus' package from $300 and a 4-day/3-night guided option from $1,395.

Kepler Track *p702, map p703*
Trips and Tramps, Te Anau, T03-249 7081, www.tripsandtramps.co.nz, offer guided walks on the Kepler. Prices on application.

Hollyford Track *p705*
Hollyford Track, T0800-832226/T03-442 3000, www.hollyfordtrack.co.nz. Guided trips, fully catered and guided fly in/walk out or walk in/walk out tramps. From Te Anau a 3-day (fly out) adventure costs from $1,655.

Milford Track *p704, map p704*
Ultimate Hikes, T03-450 1940, www.ultimatehikes.co.nz. Offers excellent full guided walk packages, from $1,740 low season and $1,900 high season (Dec-Mar). **Trips 'n' Tramps**, Te Anau, T03-249 7081, www.tripsandtramps.co.nz. Offers similar trips.

Contents

Footprint features

Background

History

Maori legends

According to Maori legend New Zealand was created by the great Polynesian demigod **'Maui-Tikitiki-a Taranga'** who hailed from the original Polynesian homeland of **Hawaiki**. Maui was well known for his trickery and guile and through the magical powers of a magic jawbone given to him by his 'sorcerer' grandmother, he was blessed with many god-like powers, with which to confront the world around him. Once, while out fishing with his five brothers, Maui used a piece of his magic jawbone as a fishhook and his own blood as bait. Soon he caught an almighty fish and struggling to pull it to the surface placed a spell upon it to subdue it forever. This great fish became **Te-Ika-a- Maui** (the Fish of Maui) and in essence the North Island of New Zealand: the shape is said to resemble the body of the fish with the mouth being Palliser Bay at its southernmost tip, the fins Taranaki and the East Cape and its tail Northland. The mountains and valleys were created when Maui's jealous brothers hacked hungrily at the fish with their greenstone *mere* (clubs). The South Island is **'Te-Waka-a-Maui'** (the Waka of Maui) and Stewart Island **'Te-Punga-o-te-Waka-a-Maui'** (the anchor)

Maori trace their ancestry to the homelands of 'Hawaiki' and the great Polynesian navigator **Kupe**. On a brave scouting mission, across the uncharted oceans to the southeast, Kupe made landfall on a new and as yet undiscovered land (Maui's fish) at a spot now called the Hokianga in Northland, around AD 800. Finding the new land viable for settlement, Kupe named it **Aotearoa – The Land of the Long White Cloud**. Leaving his crew to colonize, Kupe then returned to Hawaiki to encourage further emigration. A century later the first fleet of *waka* left Hawaiki on the great migration to settle Aotearoa permanently. It was the crew of these great canoes that formed the first *iwi* (tribes) of a new race of people called the **Maori**.

Early beginnings

Due to its geographic isolation New Zealand was one of the last 'viable' lands to be settled by humans. Although it is a matter of debate, most modern historians speculate that the first peoples to discover and settle permanently in New Zealand were the ancestors of early Polynesians, who gradually spread southeast to the Pacific Islands from Indonesia around AD 1000. The ancestral land called Hawaiki is thought to be Tahiti and the Society Islands. This late ocean-going migration is quite incredible if you consider that just across the Tasman, in Australia, the aborigines had already been happily ensconced for over 50,000 years. Again, exactly when and how these early Polynesians arrived and how they actually lived is in doubt. What is known is that they arrived sporadically in **double-hulled canoes** and initially struggled with the colder climate of New Zealand. Finding their traditional root crops like yam and **kumara** (sweet potato) hard to establish, they had to change their principal diet and methods of hunting. Fishing and seafood gathering took precedence over cultivation, and seals and abundant flightless land birds (mainly moa) became principal food items. With such plentiful food, for many decades the early Maori thrived, but like the first aboriginal settlers of Australia they made the fatal mistake of plundering the environment without thought for the future or sustainability. They also brought with them **dogs** and **kiore** (rats) which, in the absence of predators, and along with hunting, reaped havoc on the flightless native birds.

Before long, especially in the South Island, much of the native bush had been burnt down and the hapless moa, along with a number of other species, were hunted to extinction. This period of colonization was to become known as the **Archaic Period**. Facing starvation, many of the tribes that had ventured south returned to the warmer environment of the North Island

Maori values

To the Maori everything has a mauri, an essence that gives everything its special character and everything is viewed as a living entity. Mauri infuses everything: things living and non- living, earth and sky. Sometimes a sacred stone, which is placed at a secret location in a forest or river, represents it and sometimes it has no tangible presence at all, but always the mauri must be nurtured, cared for and respected. When kia moana (seafood) is taken from the sea, a tree is felled, or any other thing is harvested, a karakia should be said beforehand and thanks given afterwards.

The concept of mauri leads to a sense of unity between man and nature. The unity extends to the opposing principles that make up the cosmos, as is expressed in the creation tradition. The tradition expounds how Rangi, the sky father, and Papa, the earth mother, were once united and how Tane Mahuta, the god of the forest, tore them apart to let in the daylight. The separation brought great sorrow to Rangi and Papa. This sorrow continues in the clinging mists and falling rain,and rising of the dew.

Water is therefore fundamental to the Maori world view. It is considered a basic essence, a part of every living thing, the linking medium between individuals and their environment. The water of a hapu or iwi is a crucial source of their mana and plays a central role in many rituals. (Department of Conservation).

where traditional crops could still be grown and seafood could easily be gathered. By the time the first European explorers arrived the Maori had developed their own culture, based on the tight-knit family unit and a tribal system not dissimilar to the Celts and Scots. In a desire to protect family, food resources and land the Maori, like the Scots, saw their fair share of brutal inter-tribal conflict. The Maori developed a highly effective community and defence system built within fortified villages or *pa* and cannibalism was also common. By the 16th century they had developed into a successful, fairly healthy, robust race, free from European diseases or intercontinental greed and were, by this time, like the aborigines millennia before them, beginning to develop a sustainable future in tune with the environment around them. This period is known as the **Classic Period**.

However despite the Maori successes in colonization, in many ways, when the first human footprint was made on New Zealand shores, the subsequent environmental damage was inevitable and irreversible. A 'classic' dynamic of cause and effect was set in place that would compromise the land forever. The Maori had proved the nemesis of the unspoiled and isolated biodiversity of the land. Now, with the sails of European ships appearing above the horizon and the first European shoe-print – it was, effectively, to become the turn of the Maori themselves to be facing threat.

European exploration

Although there is a vicious rumour that the French or Spanish were actually the first Europeans to sight New Zealand, the first documented discovery was made in 1642 by Dutch explorer **Abel Tasman**. Commissioned by the Dutch East India Company, Tasman was sent to confirm or otherwise the existence of the hotly rumoured Great Southern Continent (**Terra Australis Incognita**) and if discovered, to investigate its viability for trade. Doubtless with great satisfaction, he first set eyes on the new continent (Aotearoa) off what is now Okarito in Westland, on 13 December 1642, before heading north and anchoring in **Golden Bay** at the northern tip of the South Island. However, the excitement turned to despair when the first encounter with the Maori proved hostile, with a loss of life on both sides. Without setting foot on land Tasman turned tail and fled up the west coast of the North Island en route to Tonga and Fiji. He christened the land 'Staten Landt', which was later renamed **'Nieuw Zeeland'**. It was Tasman's first and last encounter with the new land, but his visit led to New Zealand being put on the world map.

The next recorded European visit occurred with the arrival of the ubiquitous British explorer **Captain Cook** on board the **'Endeavour'** in 1769. It would be the first of three voyages to New Zealand. Cook's first landing, on 7 October in **Poverty Bay** was eventful to say the least, with what proved to be a classic culture clash with the resident Maori. Ignorance and fear on both sides led to a mutual loss of life, but unlike Tasman, Cook persevered with his public relations efforts and after further encounters managed to establish a 'friendly' relationship with the new people he called *tangata* Maori (the 'ordinary people').

Cook spent a further six months in New Zealand coastal waters mapping and naming the geographical features as he went. From Poverty Bay he first sailed south via the Bay of Plenty and Cape Kidnappers to Cape Turnagain (on the border of modern day Southern Hawke's Bay and the Wairarapa), before heading back north, around the North Island, then south again to the Cook Strait and **Ship Cove** in the Queen Charlotte Sound. Ship Cove was clearly a favourite of Cook's and would be revisited on every subsequent voyage. After refitting the *Endeavour* in Ship Cove, Cook returned to Cape Turnagain (via Cape Palliser), before sailing down the eastern coast of the South Island, passing Stewart Island (which he mapped as a headland), sighting the entrance to Dusky Sound in Fiordland, before returning via the west coast back to Cook Strait. Perhaps reluctantly he then left for Australia, but not before naming Cape Farewell, just south of Farewell Spit.

Cook's second voyage in 1773 on board the **'Resolution'** saw him land briefly in Dusky Sound (virtually unchanged to this day) before returning to Ship Cove via the west coast of the South Island and from there on to South America. On his third and last voyage, three years later, he returned to Ship Cove and his beloved 'Sounds', before heading for Hawaii (**Sandwich Islands**), where he was killed by the natives. Modern-day New Zealand owes a great deal to Captain Cook; not least the long list of place names that he bestowed upon what was perhaps his favourite destination. There are at least six statues around the country that now immortalize the great man.

European settlement and the clash of cultures

After news spread of the Cook voyages, and perhaps more so due to the observations of his colleague and ship's naturalist Joseph Banks, it did not take long for European **sealers** and **whalers** to reach New Zealand and rape the rich marine resources. Many set up stations around the south coast and Sub-Antarctic Islands and by the 1820s the New Zealand fur seal and numerous species of whale had been brought to the verge of extinction. As the industries subsequently declined they were quickly joined or replaced with a limited but still repetition of timber and flax **traders**. Others including adventurers, ex-convicts from Australia and some very determined (and some would say, much needed) missionaries joined the steady influx in. **Samuel Marsden** gave the first Anglican sermon in the Bay of Islands on Christmas Day, 1814.

Inevitably, perhaps, an uneasy and fractious integration occurred between the Maori and the new settlers and, in the familiar stories of colonized peoples the world over, the consequences for the native people were disastrous. Western diseases quickly ravaged over 25% of the Maori population and the trade of food, land or even preserved heads for the vastly more powerful and deadly European weapons resulted in the **Maori Musket War**s of 1820-1835, a swift and almost genocidal era of inter-tribal warfare. With such a melting pot of divergent cultures, greed and religion simmering on a fire of lawlessness and stateless disorganization, contrary to the glowing reports being given back in Europe, New Zealand was initially an awful place to be. Crime and corruption was rife. The Maori were conned into ridiculously unfavourable land for weapons deals and, along with the spread of Christianity and disease, their culture and tribal way of life was gradually being undermined. Such were the realities of early settlement that Kororareka (now known as Russell) in the Bay of Islands, which was the largest European settlement in the 1830s, earned itself the name and reputation as the 'Hellhole of the Pacific'. Amidst all the chaos the settlers began to appeal to their governments for protection.

Treaty of Waitangi

By 1838 there were about 2,000 British subjects in New Zealand and by this time the country was under the nominal jurisdiction of New South Wales in Australia. In 1833 **James Busby** was sent to Waitangi in the Bay of Islands as the official 'British Resident'. He was given the responsibility of law and order, but without the means to enforce it. Matters were made worse with the arrival of boatloads of new British immigrants sent under the banner of the privately owned and non-government supported **New Zealand Company**. Four years after Busby's arrival British settlers petitioned William IV for protection, citing the fact that Frenchman Baron de Thierry was threatening to pre-empt any British attempt to claim sovereignty of New Zealand. Fearful of losing any possibility of control, Britain appointed **Captain William Hobson** as Lieutenant Governor to replace Busby in New Zealand. His remit was to effect the transfer of sovereignty over the land from the Maori chiefs to the British Crown. In many ways the circumstances bore an uncanny resemblance to the situation in Britain before it became a United Kingdom. In essence the fact that the Maori were, like the Scots, a culture based on family (clan or tribe) and fought ferociously to protect *that* rather than a whole nation, would undoubtedly be in their favour. The lure for the Maori would of course be material gain in return for land and 'full protection' as British citizens. For many Maori *iwi* (tribes) whose power was inferior to that of others, this would of course be an attractive proposition. With the help of Busby who was now familiar with the ways and desires of the Maori, Hobson created what was to become the most important and controversial document in New Zealand history, the Treaty of Waitangi.

In the hastily-compiled document there were three main provisions. The first was the complete cession of sovereignty by the Maori to the Queen of England. The second was the promise of full rights and possession of Maori lands and resources (but with the right to sell, of course). The third, and perhaps the greatest, attraction, given the chaotic environment, was the full rights and protection of Maori as British citizens. After two days of discussions, a few amendments and amidst much pomp and ceremony, over 40 Maori chiefs eventually signed the Treaty on 5 February 1840. With these first few signatures from the predominantly Northland tribes, Hobson went on a tour of the country to secure others.

To this day the Treaty of Waitangi remains a very contentious document. From its very inception it was inevitably going to be a fragile bridge between two very different cultures. Given the many differences in communication, translation and meaning, at best it was spurious or vague but worse still could, as a result, be easily manipulated in both actual meaning and subsequent enactment. In essence the best politician, public relations consultant or rabid optimist could only have sold it as a 'beginning' or a 'start' on the 'difficult road to stable biculturalism', while many a realist would have (and still would) declare it an unworkable 'scam'.

By the September of 1840 Hobson had gathered over 500 signatures, all in the North Island. Feeling this was enough to claim sovereignty over New Zealand he did so, and declaring the right of discovery over the South Island, made New Zealand a Crown Colony, independent of New South Wales. But the refusal and subsequent omission of several key (and powerful) Maori chiefs paved the way for regional disharmony and eventually war.

Maori (Land) Wars

In 1840 Hobson established Kororareka (the hell-hole of the Pacific') as the first capital of New Zealand, but given its reputation and history, he moved the seat of government to Auckland within a year. With the increased influx of settlers, all greedy for land and resources, human nature very quickly superseded the legal niceties and undermined the fragile bridge of the new bicultural colony. In a frenzy of very dubious land deals between Maori and *Pakeha* (white settlers), as well as misunderstandings in methods of land use and ownership, resentment between the two was rife. This, plus the heavy taxes that were being raised by the financially strapped government, strained the bridge to breaking point. The Maori were beginning to feel disenfranchised and began to rebel against British authority.

One of the first disputes was initiated by a particularly fractious and persistent chief called **Hone Heke** who was one of the original chiefs to sign the treaty in the Bay of Islands. In 1844 he protested in a way that he knew would hit hard at the British psyche by cutting down the flagpole that so proudly flew the Union Jack in Kororareka (later renamed Russell). He did this not once, but (almost admirably) four times. Hone Heke's actions led to a bloody war with the British that was to last two years. Sadly, this clash was just the beginning. In 1852 the **Constitution Act** was created and in 1853 the country was divided into six provinces, each with a Provincial Council exercising the functions of local government which included land purchases and sales.

At the same time, immigration was increasing and with the spread of disease, the Maori were becoming well outnumbered. As with many native peoples around the world, they were becoming a resented minority and a displaced people. Exacerbated by the provincial administration, the continued greed of the settlers and inter-tribal conflicts, the Maori continued to lose land at an alarming rate and often in return for only meager material gains.

Some of the more savvy Maori chiefs became reluctant to sell land and, in 1858, several Waikato tribes went a step further by electing their own Maori king. This became known as the **King Movement**. Although initially designed to preserve cultural identity and serve as a land policy maker, supporters were encouraged to resist all land sales and *Pakeha* settlement. The British reacted with complete derision, seeing the movement only as a barrier to further colonization. The Land Wars (or Maori Wars) inevitably ensued. Troops from both Britain and Australia were sent to aid the New Zealand militia in an attempt to quash the uprising, which spread outside the Waikato to Northland and Taranaki. The east coast later joined the fold with the formation of a Maori 'Hauhau' religious movement. One of the most noted Maori rebels was **Te Kooti** who for a time became the most wanted man in the land (see page 225).

It proved to be a bloody time in New Zealand's early history with the fierce and fearless Maori warriors putting up a determined and courageous fight. Their traditional methods of fighting from a fortified *pa*, with trenches, proved so effective (and later, so admired by the British) it became the chosen method of defence and attack in ground warfare until after the Second World War.

With far superior weaponry and organization the British quickly subdued the rebels. In return for their disobedience, and despite the treaty, they confiscated huge tracts of land.

This land was then sold to new or already established settlers. By 1900 over 90% of the land was outside Maori ownership or control. They were a defeated people and, with little or no power and with continued integration, their culture was rapidly crumbling.

Natural resources, consolidation and social reform

Although development in the North Island suffered as a result of the conflicts, both timber, agriculture and gold came to the rescue. On an already solid base of productive agriculture, and with the lucrative rape of the upper North Island's **kauri forest** already in full swing, the discovery of **gold** in the Coromandel in 1852 sealed the economic boom. The South Island too, which had been a relatively peaceful haven compared to the North, joined the party, with the discovery of gold from 1857 in the Nelson, Otago and west coast regions.

With much of the economic focus being on the South Island, the seat of a new central (as opposed to provincial) government was moved to Wellington which became the capital in 1876. With gold fever the prime attraction, the *Pakeha* population grew dramatically. With so much good fortune in the south, Dunedin's headcount alone grew from 2000 in 1861 to 10,000 four years later, making it the largest town in the land. Although the gold boom lasted only a decade, the infrastructures that the boom set in place paved the way for agricultural, timber and coal industries to take over.

In the agriculture sector alone, especially through sheep and dairy cattle, New Zealand was becoming an internationally significant export nation and prosperity continued. Towards the end of the 19th century led by the enigmatic Liberal Party leader **Richard 'King Dick' Seddon**, New Zealand's colonial settlers went through a dramatic and sweeping phase of **social reforms**. Well ahead of Britain, the USA and most other Western nations, women secured the vote and pioneering legislation was enacted, introducing old-age pensions, minimum wage structures and arbitration courts.

But while the *Pakeha* prospered the Maori continued to suffer. The **Native Lands Act** of 1865 was established to investigate Maori land ownership and distribute land titles, but again, thanks mainly to Maori tribal structure and the split of land to individual as opposed to communal blocks, this only exacerbated the disintegration of the Maori culture and undermined its cohesion. Maori were given the vote in 1867 but only held four out of 95 seats in the parliamentary House of Representatives. By 1900 the Maori population had decreased to less than 50,000 and with the integration of Maori and *Pakeha* and many Maori/*Pakeha* marriages, the pure Maori were becoming even more of a minority.

Prosperity and the world wars

By 1907 New Zealand progressed to the title of '**Dominion**' of Britain rather than merely a 'colony' and by the 1920s was in control of most of its own affairs. By virtue of its close links with Britain, New Zealand and the newly formed (trans-Tasman) **Australia and New Zealand Army Corps (ANZAC)** became heavily embroiled in the Boer War of 1899-1902 and again in the First World War, at Gallipoli and the Western Front. Although noted for their steadfast loyalty, courage and bravery, the ANZACs suffered huge losses. Over 17,000 never returned with one in three men aged between 20 and 40 being killed or wounded. Almost a century on there remains a palpable sense of pride in both Australia and New Zealand for those lives lost and quite rightly so; their First World War casualties remain the greatest of any combat nation.

New Zealand joined the Western world in the **Great Depression** of the 1920s but it recovered steadily and independently progressed in an increasing atmosphere of optimism. Again from a solid base of agricultural production it prospered and immigration, particularly from Britain, grew steadily. The population had now passed one million. In 1935 New Zealand became the fist nation to enact a social welfare system, which included free health care and low-rental council properties. These pioneering acts of social reform, along with the economy, resources and common attitude, secured one of the highest standards of living in the world and New Zealand was an envied, prime 'new-life' destination.

However, along with the rest of the world, water was temporarily thrown on the fires of progress and prosperity with the outbreak of the Second World War. Once again, New Zealand and the loyal ANZACs answered the call. This time, in both Europe and Asia, it was the turn of the **28th Maori Battalion** to earn a widespread admiration and respect for their tenacity and courage. It seemed their warrior spirit, if not their culture, was still alive and well. Like most warring nations the war effort extended to the home shores where women replaced men in the vast majority of industrial and social practices. With the spread of the conflict across the Pacific, it proved a nervous time for the nation and although many would be correct in saying it was not for the first time, the people of New Zealand were under a renewed threat of invasion. However, with the dropping of the atomic bomb in Japan the threat ceased and the war was over.

Post 1945

Shortly after the war, in 1947, New Zealand was declared an independent nation but thanks to the war and its important agricultural exports, it maintained close defence and trade links with the Great Britain, the USA and Australia. In 1945 it became one of the original member states of the **United Nations** (UN) and later joined the **ANZUS Defence Pact** with the USA and Australia. Domestically, the country again prospered but the nagging problems of race relations, land and resource disputes between Maori and *Pakeha* still had to be addressed.

By the early 1970s the vast majority of Maori had moved to urban areas in search of work but with many being unsuccessful, social problems proved inevitable. In an attempt to spawn a new sense of spirit, the government passed the **Waitangi Day Act** in 1960 making 6 February a day of thanksgiving in celebration of the treaty and the cohesive bicultural society it was supposed to have created. This was further emphasized with an official public holiday in 1973. But some Maori (and *Pakeha*) merely saw the day as an opportunity for protest and although the public holiday remains, the traditional pomp and ceremony annually enacted at Waitangi in the Bay of Islands, was scrapped for much more low-key governmental diplomatic posturing. In 1975 more significant progress was made with the formation of the **Waitangi Tribunal** which was established to legally and officially hear Maori claims against the Crown. This method of addressing the problems continues to this day, but as ever, the misinterpretations of the treaty and its translation remain a major stumbling block.

New Zealand joined most of the developed world in the economic slump of the '70s and '80s. The traditionally strong agricultural exports to Europe declined, the price of oil and manufacturing imports rose and it was hit hard by the stock market crash of 1987. In response to the economic decline, the government of the day – under **Robert Muldoon's** National Party – deregulated the country's economy, paving the way for free trade. The most important and lasting trade agreement was the **Closer Economic Relations Trade Agreement** made with Australia in 1983, but New Zealand was beginning to see itself playing a far more significant role in the Asian markets as opposed to the traditional European ones.

In 1984 the Labour government, under its charismatic leader **David Lange**, took control and made further sweeping and radical changes to the economy. These were dubbed **'Rogernomics'** after the then finance minister Roger Douglas. Although the policies of privatization, free enterprise and the deregulation of the labour market improved the situation, unemployment rose and the policies began to prove unpopular with the voting public. Fearful of losing re-election votes Lange sacked Douglas, but the party reinstated him, and this resulted in his own shock resignation in 1989, leaving the party in disarray. Subsequently, the National Party led by the far less charismatic **Jim Bolger** swept to power in 1990.

One of the most important landmark decisions made on foreign policy in the 1980s was New Zealand's staunch **anti-nuclear** stand. In 1984 Lange refused entry to any foreign nuclear-powered ships in its coastal waters. This soured its relationship with the US who reacted by suspending defence obligations to New Zealand made under the ANZUS pact in the 1950s. This anti-nuclear stance is still maintained with considerable pride and is one that was only strengthened when the French Secret Service bombed the Greenpeace vessel **Rainbow Warrior** in 1985, causing national and international outrage. Relations with France were further soured in 1995 with the rather arrogant and insensitive testing of nuclear weapons in French Polynesia.

Throughout the 1990s the National Party continued successfully to nurture the free market economic policies first initiated by Labour. In 1993 a national referendum voted unanimously in favour of a mixed-member proportional representation (**MMP**) system of government. This system, which has proved successful in Germany, gives electors two votes: one for a candidate in their own electorate and the second for their favoured political party. Maori can choose to vote in either a general or Maori electorate. There is a 120-seat parliament with 60 general electorate seats, five Maori and 55 allocated to parties according to the percentage of party votes received.

Whether this system of government has been good for the country is debatable, but what did result, through internal politics and fragile power-sharing agreements, were two women prime ministers. The first in New Zealand's history was **Jenny Shipley** of the National Party who engineered a 'coup' to seize party leadership from Jim Bolger in 1997 and currently in power is **Helen Clark** of the 1999-elected Labour Party. Her success as Prime Minister is almost unprecedented. The new system can hardly be accused of restricting a diverse representation. One Green Party MP, Nandor Tanczos, is a Rastafarian and a Labour Party MP, Georgina Beyer, is transgender.

A highly significant event outside politics in 1995 was New Zealand's win in the coveted **America's Cup** yachting race. It was the first time the cup had been won by any nation other than the US and, given the country's love of yachting, it was the cause of unprecedented national celebration and pride. Over 300,000 people lined Queen Street in Auckland to congratulate the heroic yachties' return. With the successful defence of the cup again in 2000 it seemed yachting would join – or some would say replace – rugby as the nation's world-dominating sport. Amidst much hype and after considerable amounts of money were spent to transform Auckland's waterfront into a state-of-the-art sailing arena, the Kiwi populace prepared themselves for what would surely be another convincing win in 2002/2003. But it was a dream that turned, quite dramatically, into a nightmare as amidst tactical errors, design faults and even the mast snapping, former Kiwi team member Russell Coutts led a far superior outfit in the form of the Swiss *Alinghi* team to a highly embarrassing 5-0 whitewash. In the 2007 campaign, this time in Europe, Team New Zealand fought courageously to reach the final, but again despite valiant efforts, they lost to Alinghi for a second time and once again-for now-all hopes went out with the tide.

Modern New Zealand

Given its size and isolation New Zealand enjoyed its 15 minutes of international fame on 1 January 2000 when it was the first country to see the dawn of the new millennium.

Since the infamous terrorist attacks of 11 September 2001 and more recently the US-led military interventions in Afghanistan and Iraq that were, we are told, such a fundamental part of its ongoing, self-styled global **'War Against Terrorism'**, it seems New Zealand, through its steadfast determination (unlike the Howard government of Australia) not to align itself with that US policy, will almost certainly pay a heavy price, both in recognition and the nuts and bolts of trade agreements and economics. Ask the average Kiwi what they think of all this global politicking however and they will say that for them and their country little has changed. New Zealand is a great country, easily forgotten on the world stage and too easily mocked. Most are very proud of Helen Clark's intelligent and (some say) truly democratic leadership, courageously demonstrated in her stoic stance against war in Iraq and reaction to US and UK policy and its ramifications in current world affairs. The majority of Kiwis did not want to join the campaign in Iraq and its government rightfully and steadfastly exercised that voice. Kiwis are proud of their country and by their very nature and number are traditionally more concerned about community and the environment than misguided patriotism, rhetoric ad populum, power and politics. Surely, if you look at the bigger picture, through history and to the long term, it is just as wise to be as concerned about non-native species getting through customs as explosives and drugs?

So returning to the shadows (bar the considerable and ongoing hype surrounding the filming of *Lord of the Rings*) New Zealand remains an essentially 'low-key' nation largely left to its own devices, blessed by an outstanding natural environment, healthy independence and the huge asset of a low and cosmopolitan population. Its current economic struggles lie in a poor exchange rate and that has only been exacerbated by the recent global financial crisis. At least, however, on that front one could argue that it is not alone. Beyond economics New Zealand's biggest social challenge is the continued and difficult journey down the road of biculturalism as well, perhaps, as the need for some sensible long-term decisions about the future levels of immigration.

But perhaps New Zealand's greatest challenge lies in the conservation and protection of its environment, for which it is most famous and much loved. Dubbed the 'Clean Green Land' it remains to be seen whether its government and people can truly embrace the reality that its relatively healthy ecological condition is mainly due to its lack of population, as opposed to the common and traditional human attitudes that have proved to be so ruinous elsewhere. One can only hope that this wise and determined attitude can blossom, even though it is very much against the international grain. Without doubt, New Zealand is a premier tourist destination with a great deal to offer. Like its much larger neighbour Australia, tourism is fast becoming the biggest and most important growth industry. Encompassed within that industry is the sensible, desirable and sustainable realm of eco-tourism, which it is hoped can assist in the country's efforts to conserve its many unique and vulnerable species. At the forefront of these conservation efforts is the ongoing programme to conserve the iconic kiwi as well as the country's impressive position on international whaling and the creation of a South Pacific Whale Sanctuary. So, from the creation of the great fish by the Maori demigod Maui, to its current efforts to protect them, the land and the people remain on an inextricable and co-dependent voyage into the new millennium.

Culture

People and population

The population of New Zealand currently stands at about four million. The population densities are unevenly spread between the two islands, with the North Island home to about three million and the South Island about one million. Greater Auckland alone is home to just over one million, almost a third of the total population. New Zealand is essentially a bicultural society made up of Maori and Europeans, and many Caucasian (*Pakeha*) nationalities are present. Maori make up about 15% of the total population, with the vast majority living in the North Island. Pacific Islanders make up the second largest non-Caucasian group at around 6% with almost all living in Greater Auckland. Asians make up 3% of the total population and are the fastest-growing minority group. Again, the vast majority of Asians choose to live in Greater Auckland. New Zealanders are famous for being 'the world's greatest travellers' and at any one time a large proportion of citizens are absent or living abroad. Over 400,000 live and work in Australia alone. Through their close trans-Tasman ties Australian and New Zealand citizens are free to live and work in both countries.

Religion

The dominant religion is **Christianity**, with Anglican, Presbyterian and Roman Catholic denominations the most prominent. Other minority religions include Hinduism, Islam, Judaism and Buddhism. The Maori developed two of their own minority Christian-based faiths; Ratana and Ringatu, both of which were formed in the late 19th to early 20th centuries. Reflecting the increasing trend in most developed nations, at least a quarter of the total population are atheists or have no religion and this number is growing.

Music

For such a small country New Zealand has a thriving **rock** scene with **Dunedin** considered the hotbed of talent. In the '70s and '80s **Split Enz** was New Zealand's best-known group, reaching international recognition. Other notable bands include **Crowded House** and the **Exponents**. In the late 1990s **OMC** (Otara Millionaires Club) shot to fame with their catchy hit 'How Bizarre', but despite their success have since broken up. Many alternative bands and singers like **Bic Runga** and **DJ Amanda**, who are fast developing a unique Kiwi or rap sound, mixed with mainly Polynesian influences, thrive within the mainstream. **Neil Finn**, formerly of Crowded House, and **Dave Dobbyn**, spearhead the most successful ageing-rocker solo careers. In the classical arena **Dame Kiri Te Kanawa** has for many years been New Zealand's most noted international opera star. Traditional domestic or world music – outside of Maori performances and Irish pubs – is quite hard to find, however the **Pacific Festival** held in Auckland in March is one notable exception.

Film

Even before Kiwi Peter Jackson, director of *Lord of the Rings* changed the face of New Zealand film making, the nation had produced a number of notable feature films andwas home to internationally recognized actors and directors. Perhaps the most famous film (though an alarming and uncomfortable experience) is *Once Were Warriors* (1994) – an adaptation of Kiwi writer Alan Duff's portrayal of a highly dysfunctional urban Maori family, directed by Lee Tamahori. For those looking for a reality check of the worst social aspects of the advertised, pleasant 'clean green land' it is a must-see, superbly

Rugby Union – sport or obsession?

Like Australia, New Zealand finds much of its national identity in sport. Paramount among these is the game of Rugby Union. It is the focus of a public devotion that verges on the obsessive. Although invented in England, New Zealand has adopted rugby as if it were its own, making it the most played and most publicly supported national sport.

Over the years the world famous national team known as the All Blacks (due to their iconic black strip) have added a particular 'Southern Hemisphere' flair and style to the game, which, to the layman, is epitomized by the fearsome haka (Maori dance or challenge) that is performed in front of the opposition before every match.

The New Zealand Rugby Union was formed in 1892 and the All Blacks very quickly became a dominant force on the world stage. For decades the All Blacks were practically invincible and greatly feared by any opposition.

Drawn from a rich array of national provincial teams the 15 players are considered idols, many becoming almost legendary household names, like Colin Meads, who played 55 tests; George Nepia, a Maori who played 32 times; Grant Fox, an awesome goal kicker; Sean Fitzpatrick, perhaps the best captain in the game's history and, of course, the unstoppable Jonah Lomu (although Jonah is in fact Tongan by nationality).

But in many ways, the All Blacks have become victims of their own success. With the creation of the Rugby World Cup in 1987 (held every four years) the All Blacks were naturally expected to win and did so, comfortably. But in 1991 they lost to Australia in the semi-finals, a cause of some despair, but felt to be merely an aberration. Then in 1995, in South Africa, the bough broke, when a team still considered to be unbeatable lost to the South African 'Springboks' in the dying moments of the final. Back home in New Zealand there was a period of palpable national depression and anger directed upon both players and the coach. Losing was a new experience.

It did not end there. Once again salt was rubbed in the wound when in the World Cup of 1999 the French (considered underdogs) in the semi-finals trounced the All Black team. Australia went on to beat France. It seemed the unthinkable was happening – Australia was taking over the mantle of the world's best team.

In the run up to the 2003 Rugby World Cup, the All Blacks were still struggling. With the usual hype and pressure placed on both players and coach came another humiliating defeat to the host nation and archenemy – Australia. The coach John Mitchell was sacked and the nation mourned.

The team has consolidated under the wing of veteran coach Graham Henry. And after the post-World Cup hype surrounding England's win, the stage was set for a mighty contest during the Lions tour in 2005. As it happened the All Blacks took the test series 3-0 with considerable ease. For many this was a solid sign that the All Blacks were back in business. Surely, this time, the great ABs would lift the 2007 World Cup? But, quite remarkably, it wasn't to be. Facing hosts France in the semi finals, they lost again, albeit by a narrow margin.

Somehow, Graham Henry survived as coach and has steered the team back to its regular winning ways in recent years. But although the nation's fanatical supporters would – despite their humbling – still never admit it, storm clouds are again brewing. After 24 long years it will once again be New Zealand's turn to host the tournament in 2011. Can they possibly loose again? And – for better, or for worse, glory or abiding shame – could it really come down to a final in Auckland against 'Les Bleus' (France)?

demonstrating that New Zealand is not immune to the death of traditional cultures, poverty, alcoholism and domestic abuse.

On a lighter note, yet still depicting harsh times, is the romantic classic *The Piano* (1993) directed by New Zealand's most noted director **Jane Campion**. Starring Holly Hunter, Sam Neill and Hollywood tough guy, Harvey Keitel, it tells the haunting story of a Scottish immigrant (Hunter) and her daughter (Anna Paquin) who are brought to New Zealand in the early 19th century in an arranged marriage to troubled colonial landowner (Neill). Finding Neill to be as romantic and warm-hearted as the mud they seem to spend all their time trudging through, she turns to the brooding, yet caring employee (Keitel) for love and affection. Part of the attraction is also his willingness to transport her prized possession – a grand piano – inland from the beach where she and her daughter were so unceremoniously off-loaded. It is a deserving multi-award winner that is well acted and has a superb musical score. However, it may leave you thinking New Zealand is a very harsh, wet place of little more than tangled bush and mud – which essentially it once was. Although actor **Sam Neill** was not born in New Zealand, he grew up in the South Island and now lives in Queenstown, so is considered by many to be an adopted son. Another actor who was born in New Zealand, but grew up in Australia, is **Russell Crowe**, who shot to fame for his macho role in *Gladiator* and has been in the public eye ever since.

But it was the creative talent and determination of North Islander **Peter Jackson** that put the country firmly on the movie-making map in 1999-2000 with the filming and release of the much lauded *Lord of the Rings* trilogy. At a cost of over $300 million it was a far cry from Jackson's other lesser-known projects, which including the New Zealand classic *Heavenly Creatures*, an intriguing tale of two troubled teenage girls. Perhaps it was his talent, his passion and his unflappability that made what was for him a childhood dream – a film version of JRR Tolkien's *Lord of the Rings* (LOTR) – into such a success, but ask any Kiwi and they will add two other essential ingredients with pride and alacrity to what was a mammoth technical and logistical filming project. The first is the very nature and variety of the Kiwi landscape, from its foreboding volcanoes to classic snow-capped mountain ranges that were so suited to Tolkien's realm of 'Middle Earth' and the collective global imagination of what it would really look like. The other essential ingredient for the film's technical success is the famed Kiwi ingenuity and down-to-earth enthusiasm – traits so obvious and refreshing in Jackson's own rather plump persona. In tune perhaps with the fictional characters he so brilliantly portrayed on film, you would not catch the boffin-like Jackson posing in tux and tails at an award ceremony or emerging from some stretch limo with a vacuous, leggy model by his side. Whether on set or in Tinsel Town he is far more likely to be discussing scenes with an equally down-to-earth actor or technician, in a pair of training shoes and munching on a ham sandwich.

There is no doubt that Jackson is now seen as the true founding father of film in New Zealand and many more films and directors have followed suit in a bid to utilize the landscape and boundless, innate Kiwi skills. In 2002/2003 *The Last Samurai*, starring Tom Cruise, was filmed in the shadow of Mount Taranaki and in 2005/2006 Jackson directed his next big project – another childhood passion – *King Kong*. In 2006 *The World's fastest Indian* starring Anthony Hopkins and directed by Roger Donaldson also received international acclaim. Based on a true life story of New Zealander Burt Munro, who spent years building a 1920 Indian motorcycle with which he set the land speed world record at Utah's Bonneville Salt Flats in 1967.

In 2010, after much legal wrangling surrounding production rights, filming was due to start on the two-part LOTR film *The Hobbit* when director Guillermo del Toro suddenly pulled out of the project. It has been rumoured that Peter Jackson, who also serves as the film's executive producer and co-writer, will now also direct it. The release date is set for 2012, but as the book went to press this was beginning to look a little unlikely.

But whether you are an avid fan of *LOTR* and are still desperately keen to pay homage to the many film locations, or don't know a *Hobbit* from an *Uruk-Hai*, one thing is for sure: despite all the hype and the massively increased profile of the New Zealand landscape, in reality and aesthetically nothing has changed and the country exists as it always has – undeniably in your face and breathtakingly beautiful.

Maori culture and traditions

The Maori are essentially a tribal race consisting of the *whanau* (family unit), extending to the **hapu** (sub-tribe) and then the **iwi** (full tribe). Together they are referred to as the **tangata whenua**, which directly translated means 'people of the land'. The Maori relationship with their ancestors (or *tipuna*) is considered to exist through their genetic inheritance, and an individual's own genealogy (or **whakapapa**) can be traced right back to the gods via one of the original migratory canoes (or **waka**). There are over 40 **iwi** in New Zealand with the largest being the **Ngapuhi** (descendants of Puhi) in Northland who have over 100,000 members, to one of the smallest, the **Ngai Tahu** (descendants of Tahu) in the South Island, who have only about 30,000 members. The Maori's family based social structure is in many ways remarkably similar to the early Scottish clan system, which developed almost in parallel on the other side of the planet. Like the Scots, the Maori culture have a love of music, song (**waiata**), dance (**haka**), oration (particularly storytelling), socializing and unfortunately, fighting amongst themselves and against outside invaders with fearless courage and determination. The word **Maori** does in itself not denote a common background but derives from a term of differentiation used between the ordinary people (natives) and the European explorers.

Traditional Maori life is bounded by the customs, concepts or conducts of **tapu** (meaning taboo, or sacred) and **noa** (meaning mundane, or the opposite of *tapu*). If something is *tapu* – whether an object, place, action or person – it must be given the accordant respect. To do otherwise can result in ostracism, bad luck or sickness. A good example would be a burial place that is forever *tapu*, or a food resource that is given seasonal *tapu* to encourage sustainability. One good example for the visiting tourist is the summit of **Moehau**, the Coromandel Peninsula's highest peak. It is currently *tapu* which means that despite the views or absence of any guard (beyond the spiritual that is) it would be very culturally insensitive to go clambering all over it. Another is **Green Lake** (Rotokakahi) near Rotorua; the island on the lake is an ancient Maori burial ground and the lake is therefore *tapu*. As such you cannot use it for any recreational activity and you must not set foot on the island.

Noa is a term heard less often, but plays an important role in the balance or cancellation of *tapu*. For example, at some point the summit of Moehau may, through ceremony, have its *tapu* rendered *noa*. Once *noa* you can clamber away to your little heart's content! Of course in the modern day your average 'Maori Joe' cannot just place a *tapu* on anything he chooses – his beer for example, or the Visa bill! If this were the case there would be social mayhem! Placing a *tapu* is a matter that requires deliberation by the *iwi* and enactment by the **elders**, very often after a meeting or **hui**. All things whether living or otherwise possess **mauri** (see next page), **wairau** (spirit) and **mana**. The meaning of *mana* goes well beyond words, but in essence means prestige, standing, integrity or respectability. It is a term that is often used by both Maori and *Pakeha*, and is even sometimes heard outside New Zealand. If a Maori warrior won a fight or a battle this would increase his *mana*, if he lost it would undermine it, and so on. Objects too have *mana*. The pendants (or **tiki**) that you buy, for others never yourself, can hold spiritual *mana* or can increase in *mana* as they are passed on to others. It is a lovely term and perhaps the one most tourists remember once they leave.

Maoritanga (the Way of the Maori)

The Maori language, lifestyle, social structure, customs, spirituality, legends, arts and crafts are all enjoying something of a revival in modern-day New Zealand. The unique Maori culture and history are all very well represented in museums throughout the country, with both **Auckland Museum** and the state-of-the-art **Museum of New Zealand (Te Papa)** in Wellington, in particular, offering a fascinating insight. Although there are thought to be no 'true' full-blooded Maori left in New Zealand, the majority of those of undisputed Maori descent remain staunchly and rightly proud of their ancestry and cultural identity. It is a sad fact that their cultural journey in the face of what many would call a 'European invasion' has been, and continues to be, a difficult and troubled one. To that end it is important for the visitor to be aware of the basics and to realize that New Zealand culture, in total, goes a lot deeper than the practice or development of a cosmopolitan mix of cultures imported from elsewhere. In a country that essentially has a very short human history and one that some critics declare as 'historically wanting', Maoritanga is, in essence, as old as it gets.

The Marae

The *marae* is essentially the sacred 'place of meeting', or of simply 'being', that exist around a **wharae tupuna** (or ancestral meetinghouse). It is traditionally used as a communal centre, meeting place or sometimes a retreat. Strict customs and protocols (or **kawa**) surrounds the *marae* and for any tourist who wishes to visit or stay it is important to be aware of these customs and the protocols. It is akin to taking your shoes off in a Japanese house, offering the correct welcome, introduction and so on. Visitors are welcomed on to the *marae* with a **powhiri** (a welcome), which is multi-faceted. First, a warrior will greet you (or all visitors – **manuhiri**) with a **haka**, which is a traditional dance that can look decidedly threatening. In essence this is a challenge (or **wero**). Do not return the gestures, unless you want to be considered uncouth, culturally ignorant or have the desire to get your head removed. At the end of the *wero* there is a peace offering (or **teka**), which is placed on the ground between you and the warrior. Once accepted, a female elder will then initiate the **karanga** (a chant), that both welcomes and addresses the visitor and their ancestors.

On moving forward you must bow to acknowledge the ancestors. At the entrance to the *whare* the chief will then offer a **whaikorero** or *mihi* (a welcoming speech). If you can, you, or traditionally the leader (chief) elect of your group, are supposed to respond accordingly. You, or your chief, then perform the **hongi** – the touching (not rubbing) of noses unique to Maori. The *hongi* is an action which is equivalent to a hug or a kiss, and is often accompanied with a handshake. The equivalent of English 'hello' is the Maori **'kiaora'**.

Once this protocol is enacted you are then a welcome guest in the *marae* and free to talk, stay or feast. The feast (or **hangi**) is a superb experience of earth-oven, steamed meat and vegetables with a very distinctive, succulent taste. A **karakia** (or prayer) is traditionally said beforehand.

The Pa

The *pa* (traditional **fortified settlements**) built by the Maori are worth special mention.

Built predominantly on a headland or hill and from wood and often networked by trenches, they were used to protect against invasion by hostile tribes and also the *Pakeha* during the **Maori Land Wars**. Within the *pa* boundary are the *marae*, *whare* and food storage facilities. So effective was this system defence and so impressed were the colonial British forces, that the design was echoed in the First World War in the trenches of the Western Front. There are many subtle remains around the country with one of the best being the distinct earthworks and *kumara* (sweet potato storage) pits on **One Tree Hill** in Auckland. The volcanic plugs of the Auckland area made ideal *pa* sites.

Song and dance

Like the aborigine of Australia the Maori did not keep a written history, but rather passed down the essence of their culture and historical journey by song – **waiata** – and chants – **karakai**. The two most common song types are **waiata tangi** (songs of mourning) and **waiata aroha** (songs of love).

Maori dance is known as **haka**. The most famous form of this has been given somewhat false iconic status in the modern day by the sporting rugby legends the **All Blacks** before the start of each game. This particular form of *haka* is a war chant made as a challenge to all opposition and is quite a sight to behold. Whether you were Captain Cook or a 120-kg lock forward in the English rugby team, to be confronted with a Maori doing a *haka* is to know you're in for quite a battle!

There are other far less threatening forms of dance called **taparahi**. These include the **poi** dance, commonly seen in traditional Maori performances; the *poi* being balls of strings that are swung or twirled in harmony and synchronicity to the music. Traditional musical instruments are the flute or **putorino**. The beat is kept by the stamping of feet.

Arts and crafts

The artistic styles used by the Maori were already well developed on their arrival in New Zealand and influenced heavily by Polynesian tradition. in the absence of clay for pottery and metals with which to fashion rock or wood, they developed a unique style.

Wood or greenstone (pounamu) **carving** was the commonest form of craft both for functional purposes (like **waka**) or for decoration, on panels, **pou** (equivalent to Native American totem poles) or adorning **whare whakairo** (meeting houses). **Kauri** or **totara** were the commonest native wood types and it was fashioned into highly distinctive patterns using **greenstone (pounamu)**, shells or sharp stones. Sadly the early Christian missionaries often discouraged the Maori from producing their carvings, which they saw as containing obscene or inappropriate imagery. This is especially the case in Northland where elaborate carving is far less commonly seem on the *marae*. Other forms of carving were the creation of pendants or **tiki**, which were made predominantly from whalebone or pounamu. These pendants often depict spiritual ancestors – or **hei tiki** – as well as legendary or sacred animals. Weapons like **taiaha pouwhenua** (long clubs) and **patu** (short clubs) were fashioned from wood, while **mere** (short, close- combat clubs) were traditionally fashioned from greenstone.

One of the best places to see traditional and contemporary Maori arts and crafts in creation is at the **Maori Arts and Crafts Institute**, at the Whakarewarewa Thermal Reserve in Rotorua. Aside from carving and other three-dimensional works, Maori rock art is in evidence, particularly around Timaru in the South Island. There are also some very interesting contemporary Maori artworks showpieced in the Rotorua Museum.

Moko

The Maori facial tattoo (or **moko**) was traditionally applied using bone chisels, a mallet and blue pigment. The moko was predominantly the decoration of the higher classes with men covering their entire face (and sometimes their buttocks) while the women were decorated on the chin. Today, Maori (especially those in the Maori gangs like the Mongrel Mob and Black Power) still apply *moko* but this is done of course using modern tattooing techniques. To get the best idea of its design and permanence (let alone to imagine the pain), take a look at the superb realist paintings of the Maori elders done in the late 1800s by renowned New Zealand painters **Gottfried Lindauer** and **Charles F Goldie**. Examples are on display in major art galleries throughout the country, with the Auckland Art Gallery being especially good.

Language

The Maori language is still spoken throughout New Zealand and generally encouraged and spoken with pride within the *whanau* and *iwi* (Maori family and tribes), but has never been given the respect it deserves In mixed (*Pakeha*/Maori) schools over the years, hence its general decline. To the layperson who cannot understand a word, it is an intriguing language to listen to, unusually repetitive in sound and hardly melodic. There is much accentuation and repetition of vowels and the 'w' and it is wise to be aware of a few basic rules before arriving in the country. Perhaps the most important feature is the pronunciation of 'wh' as the English 'f'. For example Whanau above is not pronounced 'Wha-now' , but 'Fha-now' and Whangarei is not pronounced 'Wangarei', but 'Fhongarei'. Likewise Whakapapa, or Whakarewarewa gets similar treatment and the 'a' is pronounced more like a 'u'. Other than that it's a bit like pronouncing your vowels like the Scots twins and folk-rockers *The Proclaimers* with songs like *Letter From America* – with lots of power and opening your mouth as wide as the Homer Tunnel. A limited Maori word glossary can be found on page 738.

Land and environment

Geography

New Zealand consists of three main islands – **North Island**, **South Island** and **Stewart Island** – with a handful of other small far-flung subtropical and **sub-Antarctic islands** (the largest being a group called the **Chathams**, which lie 853 km east of South Island) completing the family. The total land area is 268,704 sq km (slightly larger than the UK).

New Zealand's boundaries extend from 33° to 53° south latitude and from 162° east longitude, to 173° west longitude, which results in a broad climatic range from north to south. It is bounded north and east by the **South Pacific Ocean**, on the west by the **Tasman Sea** and on the south by the great **Southern Ocean**. The nearest mainland is Australia, 1,600 km west, which is roughly the same distance as New Zealand is in length.

Geographical features Although compact in size, New Zealand's landscape is rich and varied: glaciers, braided rivers, lakes, fiords (flooded glacial valleys), sounds (flooded riverbeds) – found predominantly in the South Island – lowlands, alluvial plains, wetlands, large natural coastal harbours and a rash of offshore islands. Given the fact New Zealand is located at the meeting point of the Pacific and Indo-Australian Plates, it is also a distinctly 'shaky' land of frequent earthquakes and constant **volcanic activity**. The **Taupo Volcanic Zone** in central North Island is one of the most active in the world. A string of volcanoes stretches from the currently active

White Island in the Bay of Plenty, to the moody Mount Ruapehu in the heart of North Island. The area also has numerous **thermal features** including geysers, mineral springs, blowholes and mud pools, most of which can be found around Rotorua and Taupo. One of the largest **volcanic eruptions** in human history occurred in New Zealand in AD 186, the remnants of which is the country's largest lake – Lake Taupo. The most recent eruption occurred in 1995 (and again in 1996), when Mount Ruapehu – North Island's highest peak – had a moderate stomach upset. The country's most dramatic **earthquake** in recent history occurred in Napier on North Island's east coast in 1931.

Due to the 'uplift' created by the clash of the two tectonic plates, the South Island has many more mountain ranges than the North Island and boasts the country's highest peak, **Mount Cook**. *Aoraki*, as the Maori call it, stands less than 40 km from the west coast at a height of 3,753 m. The country's longest river is the **Waikato**, which stretches 425 km from Lake Taupo to the Tasman Sea.

Geology

New Zealand is an ancient land that has been so isolated from any other land mass for so long that its biodiversity is described by some scientists as the closest one can get to studying life on another planet. The oldest rocks, which make up part of the New Zealand we know today, were first rafted away from the great Gondwana landmass over 100 million years ago by a process called continental drift. The modern landscape is the dramatic result of geological uplift and volcanic activity created by New Zealand's location on the boundary of the Pacific and Indo-Australian Plates. Further 'sculpturing' occurred as a result of natural erosion, particularly the glacial erosion of numerous ice ages in the last two million years. Thanks to its long isolation, much of New Zealand's biodiversity is not only ancient, but also highly unique, with such incredible oddities as the kiwi, tuatara and weta still in evidence today. A useful comparison is with the endemic biodiversity of Great Britain: having been separated from continental Europe for a mere 10,000 years it has only one endemic plant and one endemic animal species. In contrast, as a result of over 80 million years of isolation, the vast majority of New Zealand species are endemic. Around 90% of its insects and marine molluscs, 80% of its trees, ferns and flowering plants and 25% of it bird species, all 60 reptiles, four remaining frogs, two species of bat and eel are found nowhere else on earth. But on the tragic day that man arrived, a mere 1000 years ago, it was not only 'paradise found', but was to become 'paradise lost'. Our arrival has caused more devastation to this 'clean green land' than anything else in 80 million years of evolution.

Wildlife

Urban

Birds It is a tribute to the little bird itself to start with the humble, clever and ubiquitous **house sparrow**. As you emerge bleary-eyed from the airport terminal, the chances are you will see one before you do a taxi. Whether on high or at your feet, they are waiting and watching, and have your bag contents under close observation. After humans and, in essence, thanks to them, these master scavengers are one of the most successful and omnipresent species on earth. In New Zealand, the humble sparrow was introduced in 1867 and like anywhere else the land provides a happy hunting ground.

New Zealand's urban landscape is home to many introduced plants and animals and Europeans especially will notice many familiar species. In the average garden these include birds like the **song thrush**, the **blackbird**, the **starling** and the **chaffinch**. Almost all of these were, of course, introduced. One notable exception that is absent is the European **robin**. However, old habits die hard and they are still seen in two dimensions, annually, on the front of New Zealand Christmas cards.

Elsewhere, in the parks and open spaces, you will see (or more likely hear) the **Australasian magpie**, as well as the comical **pukeko**, and on the urban waterways, the obligatory **mallard duck** and **black swan**. The Australasian magpie is the size of a crow. He's dressed in black and white – like a butler – and is melodious and very intelligent. They are, as the name suggests, an Australian import and very unpopular in New Zealand. While nesting they are fiercely territorial and every year newspapers are full of Hitchcockian tales of people being attacked. The **pukeko** is a much more amicable import from Australia, where it is known as the swamphen. They look like a cross between a chicken and a spider, with outrageously long feet, with which they walk on water. They are a gorgeous blue/purple colour and sport a robust red beak. Get used to the 'pookie', as you will see them everywhere.

Often mistaken for the similar-looking pukeko, the **takahe** is much larger (and certainly much rarer). The black swan takes the place of the mute swan in Europe and is common throughout. They are smaller than the mute variety, but just as daft and just as delighted to share your sandwiches. The most common urban 'seagull' is the antsy and stern-looking **red-billed gull**. They are also encountered on the coast and will show up at your feet before your stomach even grumbles. The same applies of course to the **feral pigeon**. They too are commonplace, especially in sight of flat-whites and menus. Out and about almost anywhere in the North Island you will also see the street-wise **Indian myna**, a chestnut coloured, medium-sized passerine that, like the sparrow, is an introduced, almost human-reliant 'opportunist'. Their speciality is dodging traffic, which they can do with precision while catching dead insects on the road.

Mammals When it comes to mammals in suburbia you will find that Mrs Tiggywinkle (alias the **hedgehog**) moved in long ago. By all accounts 'she' paid a visit, liked both the climate and the menu and decided to stay. While the hedgehog at least adds slugs and other such unwelcome garden pests to its menu of native bird's eggs, the notorious **cat** is just the wanton, careless and prolific killer of old. Domestic and feral cats maul literally millions of native and non-native birds every year and next to **humans**, the **stoat**, the **possum** and the **rat**, they are native wildlife's worst enemy.

Coastal

Seabirds Of course the coast is never far away in New Zealand and it is home to some of New Zealand's 'wildlife royalty', specifically the world's only mainland colony of **royal albatross**, found only on the Otago Peninsula near Dunedin. If you are from the northern hemisphere this is simply a must-see, since without an expensive trip to Antarctica, this is perhaps your only chance. To watch them in flight or see their fat, infant chicks awaiting their next inter-continental meal (looking like large, bemused, fluffy white slippers) is simply unforgettable. It is amazing to think that said 'slippers' must grow wings that will span over 3 m and that those wings will then subsequently take them around the world more times than Michael Palin or Richard Branson.

New Zealand is actually known as the seabird capital of the world and a remarkable 70% of its total avian 'who's who' is pelagic (the world average is 3%). The list is long. Numerous types of **mollymawk**, which are similar to albatrosses, are common, especially off the southern tip of the South Island, where another family of seabirds, the **shearwaters**, also abound. If you go to **Stewart Island** you may see many of them, but

The mystical kiwi

New Zealands national symbol, the kiwi, deserves a special mention. Along with the platypus of Australia, or perhaps the peacock, it has to be one of the most curious and endearing creatures on earth – one, perhaps, that even Charles Darwin, given a party pack of recreational drugs, a bottle of vodka and a considerable bet, could still not devise. Almost half-bird half-mammal it evolved over millions of years of isolation to fill a specific niche free of any predators. Although related to the ostrich of Africa, the emu of Australia and the extinct native New Zealand moa, it is unsual in many ways and in some ways absolutely unique.

Flightless of course; they have no wings and their feathers are more like hairs. They are nocturnal and live in burrows. They have long whiskers almost like those of a cat, which, along with an acute sense of hearing and smell, are its ammunition in the hunt for food. It is the only bird with nostrils at the end of its beak and its egg-to-body weight ratio is legendary. The egg of a kiwi averages 15% of the female's body weight, compared to 2% for the ostrich. Females tend to be larger than males and when it comes to the brown kiwi, the male tends to do most of the incubating. They mate for life, sleep for almost 20 hours a day and live as long as 30 years.

There are four identified species of kiwi.

The **brown kiwi**, is the most common species and the one you are most likely to see in captivity. Although relatively widespread in central and northern North Island there is only an isolated popul**little spotted kiwi** is extinct on the mainland and survives only as 1000 birds on Kapiti Island and 200 on four smaller islands. The **great spotted kiwi** is only found on the South Island and an estimated 20,000 remain. Lastly the **tokoeka** is found on Stewart Island, Fiordland and around Haast. The tokoekas of **Stewart Island** are the only kiwi that can be seen during the day, which creates something of a tourist pilgrimage to try to see them (see page 686).

The best and only chance the vast majority of visitors get to observe these quirky characters in one of the many darkened '**kiwi houses**' scattered around the country. Some of the best are to be found at the Whangarei Museum, 'Kiwi Encounter' in Rotorua, the DoC Wildlife Centre at Mount Bruce in the Wairarapa, Wellington Zoo, Orana Park in Christchurch and in Queenstown. Like so many New Zealand species, even the kiwi is not immune from the tragic threat of extinction and it is feared that they too will no longer be found anywhere in the wild on mainland New Zealand within two decades. For more information on kiwi and the efforts being made to conserve them, consult www.kiwirecovery.org.nz.

you are more likely to find one boiled, next to your ketchup and chips. The prolific **sooty shearwater (or Titi)** has been hunted by the Maori for centuries and is still harvested today for food. Other seabirds include numerous species of **petrel**, including the Westland, Pycroft's and Cook's, all of which are found nowhere else in the world. One, the **taiko**, which was collected during Captain Cook's voyages, was not encountered again for nearly two centuries, when it was finally tracked down to its sole breeding site on the Chatham Islands. Most petrels and shearwaters nest in burrows and in huge numbers on the many offshore islands. They come ashore mainly at night, so your best chance to see them is offshore from boats or promontories, especially in Otago and Southland. Sometimes you will see huge rafts of petrels or shearwaters surface feeding, looking from a distance like a huge brown oil spill. One member of the petrel family you may bump into while out sea fishing is the **giant petrel**. He's big (about the size of a goose), uniform brown, and looks like an industrial-strength mole-grip on wings. So don't mess! Throw out your fish scraps and smile politely.

Another huge treat for any visitor from the northern hemisphere are New Zealand's **penguin**. Believe it or not, there are in fact three species perfectly at home in New Zealand and without an iceberg in sight! The **little blue** is the most common, being found all round the coast. It is also the smallest of the penguin species and probably the cutest. They come ashore to their burrows at dusk, and there are many places where you can observe them doing this. Oamaru in Otago is one of the most noted sites. Some reserves, like **Tiritiri Matangi** Island near Auckland have nest boxes in which you can take a quick peek at little blues during the day. This can be highly entertaining as the enchanting little souls will merely look up at you with a pained expression as if to say 'Oh god, go away, you mustn't see me this fat'. Sometimes, if you encounter them on a path at night, by torchlight, they will look utterly bemused, stick their heads in the grass and point their bums in the air.

Almost as enchanting are the endangered **yellow-eyed penguins** of the Otago and Southland coasts. Enough is said about them in the preceding chapters, but like the albatross they are a must-see. Less easily encountered is the rarest penguin in the world, the **Fiordland crested penguin**. Your best chance to see one of these is on the west coast between Fox Glacier and Haast, as they come ashore at dusk or leave again at dawn.

Other notable seabird attractions include the colonies of greedy **gannets** at Murawai (near Auckland), Cape Kidnappers (near Napier, in Hawke's Bay) and on Farewell Spit, off the northern tip of the South Island. Several species of **shag** (cormorant) are also present in New Zealand. The most common are the large **black shag**, the black and white **pied shag** and again, as the name suggests, the petite (and again black and white) **little shag**. Some very rare, endemic and more colourful cousins include the **spotted shag**, the **Stewart Island shag** and **king shag**. Many other rare birds also inhabit the coastline including the **New Zealand dotterel** and one of the world's rarest birds, the **fairy tern**, of which tragically only around 30 remain.

Marine mammals When it comes to **whales** the word 'common' can only be used with extreme caution, with many species being more prevalent around the New Zealand coast than most countries worldwide. **Kaikoura** is, of course, synonymous with the whale and presents one of the best whale-watching opportunities in the world. As well as its resident pods of **sperm whale**, it plays host to humpback whales, **southern right whales**, **orca** and occasionally, even the endangered and massive **blue whale**. New Zealand is a world leader in promoting the conservation of whales and certainly does not share the view that these awesome creatures that have been around for millions of years are – as one Japanese minister at the International Whaling Commission conference recently put it – 'cockroaches of the sea'. Now there's a man who needs a shark encounter without the cage! New Zealand is also a world leader in dealing with mass **whale strandings**, which are all too common, particularly in the natural trap of **Golden Bay**, at the northern tip of the South Island.

Still in the XXL department are the three sub-Antarctic pinniped species (or seal). The **hooker's sea lion** (or New Zealand sea lion), the **leopard seal** and the **southern elephant seal**. Although actual breeding is rare on the mainland, all three regularly visit the southern coast. The best place to see these soporific barrels of bad breath and wind (gas) are the Otago and Southland coasts. Indeed, the Catlins coast in Southland often presents the opportunity to see all three species in one day – which is unheard of out of the sub-Antarctic Islands.

Given plenty of mention throughout the text is the **New Zealand fur seal**, which is a character of infinite charm and one that you will almost certainly encounter at close range. Out of the water, their ability to look fat and lazy, break wind and scratch their privates (all at the same time), while looking at you through one eye as if you are a complete waste of space, is frankly legendary. Quite right too – having had their brains battered to near extinction around New Zealand's waters throughout the 19th century perhaps we deserve such derision. A little word of warning: do not go within 10 m of any seal that you encounter on the beach. In the water they are even more agile and can swim faster and with more grace than anything in Speedos. Underwater or on the surface is also the best place to encounter **seals**. Whether diving independently or on an organized seal swim, they will often check you out like a dog in the park.

Dolphins are also a major feature of New Zealand's coastal wildlife, with dolphin watching and swimming being one of the country's many world-class activities. Apart from New Zealand's 'speciality' species, the tiny and endemic **Hector's dolphin** (one of the rarest in the world), and at least four others are regularly seen, including the **dusky dolphin**, **common dolphin**, **striped dolphin** and **bottlenose dolphin**.

Offshore islands

The New Zealand coast features literally thousands of offshore islands that are proving crucial to the conservation of the country's native wildlife. Many combine to form an invaluable flotilla of 'arks'; ultimately the only hope for many species. Once the Department of Conservation has eradicated formerly introduced predators, for example cats, rats and possums, which involves an expensive and time-consuming poisoning or capture programme, the remaining small pockets of resident birds, plants and animals are encouraged to re-colonize, and captive endemic breeds can be re-released. Some of the species that are now reliant on the 'arks' include birds like the kakapo, the kokako and takahe. Other non-avian species include the precious tuatara.

The most crucial of the island's reintroduction programmes concerns the ancient flightless parrot, the **kakapo**; the flagship of New Zealand's conservation efforts. Only about 62 named individuals remain and each is closely monitored. The vast majority are kept on three island reserves, **Codfish Island** (off Stewart Island), **Maud Island** in the Marlborough Sounds and **Little Barrier Island**, near Auckland in the Hauraki Gulf. But the intense efforts being made to save the kakapo is merely plugging up the holes. Many species are often their own worst enemies, taking years and very specific environmental requirements to breed successfully. Many say it is only a matter of time.

However, to visit one of these vital reserves is to at least get a taste of the New Zealand of old and to experience the 'paradise lost'. On one of these islands you enter a world of unique and ancient wildlife that shows little fear of humans, creating a near bombardment of the senses. To encounter a kiwi at night or listen to the sublime dawn chorus of the near flightless **kokako** is one of the greatest wildlife experiences in the world. While most of the offshore islands are, understandably off-limits to visitors, New Zealand is very refreshing in its attitudes towards the education and access to its endangered wildlife for the average person. The islands of **Tiritiri Matangi** (see page 118) and **Kapiti Island** off the Wellington coast (see page 408) are just two examples.

Rivers, lakes and wetlands

New Zealand is riddled with rivers, lakes and low-lying wetlands all of which are home to both common, rare and unique species of animals and plants. From the rafts of mallard and black swan on **Lake Taupo** to the endangered **brown teal** on the quiet backwaters of **Great Barrier Island**, there is much to hold your interest. Other than the brown teal, other waterfowl of particular note include the beautiful **New Zealand shoveler** and the unique **blue duck**. A resident of remote and fast-flowing forest and mountain rivers, the blue duck uses highly specialized feeding methods to find algae and river insects and it is so unique it has no close relatives anywhere else in the world. Called the *whio* by Maori, which is an apt pronunciation of its call, they can sometimes be seen (or heard) from a kayak or raft, or even on the more remote tramps near mountain rivers. The rivers that feed **Lake Waikaremoana** in the **Te Urewera National Park** are just some good places to search.

Although not strictly confined to areas of wetland, another far more common duck you will almost certainly encounter in New Zealand is the **paradise shelduck**. Most often seen in pairs the male is relatively dark in colour, while the female is unmistakable with a predominantly chestnut plumage and a white head. In city parks and publicly utilized lakes they can often be approached with little protest, but in less urban areas they are shy and notoriously loud, often circling continuously overhead issuing a repetitive, high-pitched call until you have left their territory.

On the lower reaches of glacial rivers, where they become vast braided beds of moraine, there are two '**waders**' that are very unique and special. The first is the **black stilt**, or khaki, of which only about 80 individuals remain, making it one of the rarest waders in the world. You can see these beautiful and fragile-looking 'birds in black' on a guided tour of the DoC's captive breeding hides in **Twizel**, Canterbury. These are part of the excellent conservation programme put in place to protect them.

The black stilt's close cousin the **pied stilt** is much more common and a regular sight in the shallows of lakes, estuaries and natural harbours. Again they are very delicate in stature and boast a smart, almost formal-looking plumage of black and white. Also, like their pure black relative they have legs like busy knitting needles. Another unique wader with unusual appendages is the endemic **wrybill**, which has a bill bent to one side. This remarkable adaptation assists this small bird in its search for insects under small stones and driftwood. In winter they can be seen along with huge numbers of migratory waders at the **Miranda Naturalist's Trust Reserve** on the **Firth of Thames**, south of Auckland, while in summer they join the stilts, breeding 'incognito' and well camouflaged among the moraines of the braided rivers of the South Island.

Very common in both the urban environment and especially around water is the non-native **sacred kingfisher**. Like its European counterpart it is a shy bird but does not share quite the same bright iridescent colours. Far less prevalent is the un- mistakable **white heron** or Kokutu. Although relatively common worldwide, there is only one colony in New Zealand, near Okarito in Westland, South Island. Around 200 birds gather between September and November to breed, before scattering throughout the country during the winter months. You can see these magnificent birds on one of the tours that visit the Okarito breeding colony from Whataroa, north of Franz Josef. In winter, if you find yourself in Milford Sound, look out for 'Charlie', a famous heron that has spent the last 12 winters around the boat terminal. Little wonder the Maori have always held the white heron in such high esteem. The other far more common and smaller heron you will certainly see throughout New Zealand is the non-native **white-faced heron**.

Of course New Zealand's waterways are also home to many endemic fish and insects. Two native **eels**, the short-finned eel and the long-finned eel, have been sacred to the Maori for generations and once provided an important food source. They are huge, reaching up to 2 m in length and are thought to live up to 100 years old. You can see them in many nature reserves and animal parks. The DoC **Mount Bruce Wildlife Centre** in the Wairarapa and **Rainbow Springs** in Rotorua are just two good examples.

Lowlands and forest

Less than 25% of New Zealand is under 200 m so, despite appearances there is not as much room as you think. When man arrived and set to with his short-sighted slash and burn policy, New Zealand's landscape was irrevocably altered and has now lost over 85% of its natural forest cover. The impact on the whole ecosystem has been immense; most of the native forest that remains is confined to inaccessible areas and mountain slopes, with almost a quarter of that being in South Island's west coast region alone.

One of the most evident yet hardly common species of the forests and low lying bush is the native **New Zealand pigeon** or **kereru**; a large, handsome, colourful character, with a signature plumage of almost iridescent greens, browns, purples and white, with bright red eyes. Often heard crashing about in the leaf canopies, they exhibit the congenial air of one who is over-fed and bring new meaning to the word plump. Little wonder the Maori prized the kereru as an important source of food. Today, despite being protected, their numbers are declining, mainly due to habitat loss and illegal hunting. The kereru can be seen in gardens and parks, but if it remains illusive you can see them at most animal parks. 'Pig', a rather daft Kereru residing in **Wellington Zoo**, is amenable to visitors and nearly died once after swallowing a pencil!

The stitchbird, bellbird and tui are also found in the lowland and forest habitats and are New Zealand's three representatives of the **honeyeaters**. A New Zealand endemic, the **tui** is quite common throughout the country and you are bound to see, and certainly hear them. From a distance they look a dull-black colour with a distinctive white bib (that also earned it the name of the 'parson's bird'), but on closer inspection their plumage is a superb mix of iridescent blues and greens. Their song is almost legendary, a delight to listen to, but almost impossible to describe. In essence they boast a remarkable range of audible whistles, grunts and knocks. Much of the tui's repertoire is beyond our audible range which is why they often look as if someone kept the camera rolling but momentarily pressed the 'mute' button. One of the best places to see tui in large numbers is during spring in the blooming cherry trees behind the **Wairakei Golf Club**, near Taupo. There, up to 30-odd birds can be seen in action, which is quite a sight and sound. The **stitchbird** and **bellbird** are not as common as the tui but are equally colourful and just marginally less melodic. They are best seen on the offshore island reserves.

Of all the smaller birds encountered most folk's favourite is the enchanting little **fantail**. These charming little birds are a bit like butterflies on speed and your visit to New Zealand will more than once be enhanced by their inquisitive nature. While walking down any bush or forest park they will often appear from nowhere and with manic audible 'peeps' fly about your person as if interested in making your acquaint- ance. They do this not once but for some time, flitting about and fanning their tails manically. In actuality, fantails are only interested in the insects you are disturbing within their individual territories, which is why, after a while, they suddenly seem to lose interest. Another little charmer, that is less common and shares this behaviour, is the **tom tit**: a small, native black-and-white character that in many ways resembles the European robin. Trampers will become familiar with the tom tit, especially in the South Island. New

Zealand does also have its own robin, the dull-coloured **New Zealand robin** which can often be seen in the forests of both North, South and Stewart Islands.

The **morepork** is New Zealand's only native owl species. It is a small owl that feeds mainly on insects but is not impartial to the odd lesser-sized avian. Being very illusive and nocturnal, they are most often heard rather than seen and it is their distinctive butcher's shop request – 'more pork, more pork' – that earned them the name. The only other raptors (birds of prey) present in New Zealand are the native New Zealand falcon and the 'imported' **Australasian harrier**. Commonly seen soaring above hillsides and fields in the countryside, the harrier is often mistaken by the amateur to be an eagle. But eagles are much larger; the **Haast eagle**, which is now extinct but once ruled the skies in New Zealand, was over 26 times the harrier's weight and had a wing span of over 3 m, so large it would probably have been able to tackle a child.

Also with a curvaceous beak, the adorable **kaka** is one of New Zealand's three native parrot species. Once common throughout the country they are now confined mainly to old-growth beech and podocarp forests. Although unmistakable in both call and plumage the average visitor would be lucky to see one in the wild, making your best bet the zoos or DoC wildlife centres at **Mount Bruce** in the Wairarapa or Te Anau in Fiordland. At Mount Bruce, a small group has been successfully captive-bred and were released locally. Now, although essentially wild, they remain in the vicinity, returning to the same spot at the same time each day to be fed. This daily spectacle provides the kind of quality entertainment for which parrots can always be relied upon and also offers a superb photo opportunity.

Even tamer than the kaka but sharing its love for a free lunch is the **weka**, a sort of flightless brown rail. Again, without any predators, the weka evolved to dispense with the need for flight and focused its hunting activity entirely on the forest floor. In modern times it is not just the forest, but the human car park and campground, that offers rich pickings. If you are joined at any point by this appealing albeit uninvited guest, bear in mind they can be very persistent and notoriously quick with the steal.

Of course the lowlands and forests are also home to many non-avian species, but most of the true endemics are either reptiles or insects. Two notable exceptions are the much celebrated and impressively sounding **peripatus** and **powelliphanta**, both of which are as old as the land itself. Peripatus is like a cross between a worm and a centipede, while powelliphanta is a carnivorous land snail with a shell the size of a saucer. Both are remarkable creatures and were around millions of years before man.

Mammals It is remarkable to think that New Zealand played host to only one mammal before we arrived, a small bat, of which two species evolved. The **long-tailed bat** and the **short-tailed bat** are rarely seen by the casual observer, living in small local populations, and even then mainly on only a few remote offshore islands. Of course in New Zealand today, besides the bat, there is now a thoroughly cosmopolitan and unsavoury list of mammalian guests. This extraordinary list of reprobates includes possums (an estimated 70 million – 20 to every person), stoats, weasels, rabbits, hares, wallabies, ferrets, rats, mice, pigs, cats, horses, deer, goats and the infamous Paul Holmes (watch New Zealand television any weeknight at 1900).

Highlands

With over 75% of the country being above 200 m, this is a vast, yet inhospitable habitat. However, New Zealand's mountains and glacial valleys, like the rest of its ecosystem, boast a fair number of endemic animals and many unique plants that can often be spotted by the casual observer.

Most noted of the birds is of course, the notorious **kea** – the only alpine parrot in the world. This highly intelligent, entertaining 'avian thug' lives high above the tree line, where it nests amongst rocks and feeds on just about anything edible. Although you may only ever hear them, if lucky you may encounter them at close range. Nicknamed the 'cheeky kea' – thanks to their inherently inquisitive nature and extrovert behaviour – they are particularly fascinated by cars, rucksacks and shoelaces, or anything that can be dismantled, demolished or eaten. To have a flock descend in the middle of your picnic is a bit like an encounter with a class of unsupervised infants with severe behavioural disorders – out of control. I say children because that is truly how they behave and it certainly relates best to your subsequent reaction. They are so appalling, carefree and fun-loving that it is almost impossible not to just let them get on with it.

Another creature of the slopes and mountain valleys is the equally clever, but far less frivolous, **New Zealand falcon**. Quite elusive and capable of demolishing its prey like a surface-to-air missile you would be lucky to see one, but once spotted they are unmistakable. Nothing else in New Zealand flies with such stealth or purpose, nor when it arrests momentarily (most probably still grasping its latest victim) is so stern in looks. Even keas don't mess with a falcon's lunch!

Another bird of the mountains and remote glacial valleys is the remarkable and flightless **takahe**. They are the most appealing of birds and look like some congenial, almost 'clueless', prehistoric, purple chicken. Another ancient species once thought to be extinct, they were dramatically rediscovered deep in the Murchison Mountains of Fiordland in 1948. There is now an intensive breeding programme to attempt to secure their conservation, with only about 100 birds remaining in the wild and about the same again kept in captivity or on predator-free islands. The best place to see them is **Tiritiri Matangi** Island near Auckland, where several families (about 20 birds) are allowed to roam free. Being incredibly tame and inquisitive it is both memorable and remarkable to sit amongst them. But, as with so many of the species on the brink, you do so with perhaps a sense of guilt and the worrying question – but for how much longer?

Insects

New Zealand has an impressive range of creepy-crawlies, ranging from the noisy and the colourful to one that is the size of mouse. Although lacking in butterflies and far more replete with moths, one large and perhaps familiar butterfly that you will see, especially in Auckland and the upper North Island, is the **monarch butterfly**. Famous the world over as a migratory species, these tawny-red and black-striped beauties, with a wingspan of 10 cm first arrived in New Zealand around 1840 (some say much earlier). It is very common in the urban and suburban habitats, but rarely seen in the bush or south of Christchurch. Although well known in the Americas for their swarming and long inter-state migrations, the butterflies found in New Zealand infrequently demonstrate these behaviours. However, like their American cousins and unlike most butterfly species, they often over-winter and live for several months.

One moth species that has a remarkable tendency to commit suicide by flying into any artificial light source at night is the large, native **puriri moth**. A beautiful lime-green colour with a wingspan of up to 15 cm, it is the country's largest moth species but is only found in the native forests of the North Island. Although the adults only live for a few days the caterpillars spend several years in tunnels bored in to trees.

By far the noisiest insect in the country is the **cicada**, which in summer and en masse can create an ear-splitting din in almost any area of bush or forest throughout the country. There are many species in New Zealand with one of the most common being the clapping cicada which was one of the first insects noted by Joseph Banks, the naturalist accompanying Captain Cook on his first new Zealand voyage in 1769-1770. They are fascinating creatures, about 30 mm in length with a wingspan up to 80 mm. The larvae of the very vocal adults can live in the ground for many years before aspiring to split eardrums. It is only the males that sing and the noise is created by the vibration of a unique ribbed structure called a 'tymbal' which resonates the sound in the almost hollow abdomen. Despite their being so many, try to take some time to focus on one song and try to locate the insect on the tree trunk branch or underside of leaves.

There are a number of spider species in New Zealand with the two most notable being the **katipo** and the **avondale**. The **katipo spider** is about 10 mm in length and, along with the average politician, is the only poisonous creature in the land. Looking the part, with a shiny black body, long legs and a red spot on its abdomen, it is a relative of the famous black widow and can deliver a nasty bite that can be incapacitating, but rarely fatal. You will doubtless be relieved to learn that they are a coastal species that frequent the undersides of logs rather than toilet seats!

The **Avondale spider** is a sub-species of the well known Australian huntsman. It is relatively harmless, but very large at over 10 cm in length. A unique, localized sub-species, found only in the suburb of Avondale in Auckland, it is an amenable easily-handled species that was bred in captivity and used in the film *Arachnophobia*.

Perhaps the most remarkable native insect in New Zealand is the **glow-worm**. Although essentially a gnat, it is the worm-like larvae that frequent the damp limestone caves and sheltered cavities on both the North and South islands that are most famous. The sight of an ethereal 'galaxy' of glow-worms (often called 'grottoes') on the roof of a cave in the darkness, particularly at Waitomo in the Waikato, is a truly memorable sight. What you are actually seeing are the shiny bottoms of the larvae, which emit a bright blue/green light. It is a clever and remarkable mechanism and a chemical reaction known as bioluminescence used to attract insect prey; the prey flies towards the light and is caught in sticky threads that the worm hangs from like a row of fishing lines from the roof of the cave. To enter a grotto at night then emerge into a clear starlit sky is a firm reminder of the incredible world in which we live.

Not to be outdone by a glowing bottom, the New Zealand weta is perhaps the king of all the New Zealand insects. They are an ancient creature that has been around for millions of years. A number of species are found in gardens, forests caves and rock crevices throughout the country ranging from the common tree weta to the cave weta. But without doubt the most impressive is the giant weta. At up to 9 cm in length and weighing up to 80 g they are about the size of a mouse and the largest insect in the world. With their huge abdomens, beady black eyes, long antenna and 'alien' like legs you will either love or hate the weta. Your best bet to see one is in the country's zoos. Weta are not dangerous despite a fine set of mandibles used to crunch up leaves, shoots and small insects.

Of course, if you go anywhere near the west coast of the South Island you will become very intimate with the infamous New Zealand sandfly.

Fern species

Like the country's animal life, much of New Zealand's plant life is very beautiful, very ancient and very unique, making it a veritable paradise for any 'budding' botanist. Over 80% of the country's flowering plants are not endemic to any other land. But like the fauna, much of the country's plant life is in a worrying state of decline, not as a result of predation, but by the clear felling and burning that has taken place since the arrival of man. Tragically, only about 15% of the New Zealand's original forest remains. Even a brief description of New Zealand's plant species is beyond the scope of this guide, but the following are some of the most notable species that you are likely to see.

Fern species
Alongside the iconic kiwi, the ponga or silver fern is New Zealand's other great national emblem and just one of a vast array of over 80 fern species. Depicted on everything from the national rugby jersey to the side of America's Cup yachts, the silver fern is a common sight in both the natural and commercial world. It is found throughout the mainly subtropical bush landscape, forming stands of almost prehistoric-looking umbrellas. A lush green colour on top, it is the silver underside that has created their notoriety, and not just in pure aesthetics. One well-known aspect of 'bush survival and rescue' is to lay out the fronds upside down in a clearing so as to capture the attention of a helicopter from above. Ferns generally have always been a very significant and sacred symbol of the Maori culture, especially in their tendency to 'unfurl' into 'being'. Often alongside the ponga, you will find the taller and more classic desert island-type nikau palm, the cabbage tree, as well as creepers, palm lilies, tree ferns and mosses.

Forest trees
The ancient New Zealand forest is traditionally one of **podocarp** and **beech trees**. Without doubt the most celebrated, yet overly utilized of the 100-odd forest tree species is the **kauri**. Occurring predominantly in the north of the North Island and a member of the podocarp family, it was once the dominant tree of the Auckland province and the Coromandel Peninsula. With vast trunks often over 15 m in diameter, and 30 m tall, free from knots and blemishes, the kauri was prized by both the Maori for canoe building and by the early Europeans for masts and other ship-building materials. The tree's resin ('kauri gum') was used as a derivative of varnishes and paint products and also as medium suitable for carving into elaborate ornaments. Sadly, over 90% of the trees were harvested and only a few ancient individuals remain. Most noted of these is the impressive 1,200-year old **'Tane Mahuta'** ('Lord of the Forest') which stands proudly in the **Waipoua Forest** in Northland. Other notable podocarp species, used for canoes and boat building, are the native **matai** (black pine), **rimu** (red pine), **totara**, **miro** and New Zealand's tallest tree – the **kahikatea** (white pine). The kahikatea can grow to 60 m.

Another plant heavily utilized by the Maori is the tough-stemmed **flax** plant, found predominantly in wetlands the length and breadth of the country. It was used for everything from footwear to building.

Flowering trees
Two very colourful flowering trees, well known throughout the country, are the yellow flowering **kowhai** (New Zealand's national flower) and the red flowering **rata**, a climber that literally strangles its host tree to death. New Zealand's best known flowering tree is the beautiful **pohutukawa**; a gnarled-looking coastal evergreen that bursts into bright crimson flower for three weeks in December, earning it the affectionate label as New Zealand's Christmas tree.

Endemic flowers
Of the many endemic flowers in New Zealand a large number are found in the high alpine

areas, including the **Mount Cook lily**, the largest of all the buttercups. With flowers as big as its leaves it is an impressive sight provided, that is, you can find it amongst the 60-odd species of mountain daisy!

Conservation

Describing New Zealand's rich and unusual animal and plant species is an act of celebration, but it is also a sorry tale. Although the country is often dubbed '**clean and green**', many agree that it is far more a result of low population than attitude. Since the arrival of man we have had a dramatic and tragic effect on the landscape and biodiversity of New Zealand. As a result of our presence 32% of indigenous land and freshwater birds and 18% of seabirds are now extinct. The most recent extinction occurred in 1907 with the last sighting of the beautiful huia, a relative of the kakako, which is now also endangered. The loss of the huia occurred not only as a result of a decline in habitat, but man's ridiculous desire to adorn himself with its feathers. Many other unique and well-known species have also disappeared, like the legendary moa, which was hunted to extinction by the Maori. In the present day many others currently sit quietly on the brink. As it stands, with endemic bird species alone, there are only 36 fairy terns remaining, 62 kakapo, about 70 Campbell Island teal, 70 taiko, 80 black stilt and 200 takahe, to name but a few. Even the kiwi, the very emblem of the nation and its people is severely under threat and without more financing, it too is expected to be completely absent on mainland New Zealand within the next two decades. To lose the kiwi itself – the very bird after which its native humans are named – seems unimaginable. One can only hope, that given its prestige, it may stir people into action.

Government initiatives

Sterling efforts are being made in the war of conservation by governmental departments, for example the Department of Conservation, as well as independent organizations and individuals. Numerous captive breeding and predator eradication programmes have been initiated to stop, or at the very least slow down, the decline of so many species. Indeed, New Zealand is on the 'front line' of the global conservation war and thankfully there have been some fine and victorious battles. The **black robin**, an endemic little bird found only on the Chatham Islands, is one such example and one of the most famous conservation successes in human history. From a population of only nine individuals in the mid 1970s, it has essentially been saved and now numbers around 250. But these battles all defy the short-sighted, financial and technologically driven society of the modern day. Since the very act of conservation is a drain on funds rather than a source, the DoC is always under-funded and under-researched and it seems, tragically, a war that can perhaps never be won. Eco-tourism offers a viable path in some areas but it is just part of a long and difficult climb towards salvation.

Paradise lost

In the New Zealand of today, the great clean, green land – the paradise, but really the paradise lost – it almost makes the heart cry to experience the deathly hush of forests once alive to the sound of birds. At times it really is like standing in an ancient church that has been sacked of all its contents and robbed of both congregation and choir. Instead of a heads held high in celebration, the whispers of prayer and beautiful arias of worship, the pose is one of despair, the atmosphere one of remorseful reflection and the sound, one of eternal silence. To lose the kakapo, the kokako or the kiwi itself, all species that have been around for millions of years is too tragic to contemplate.

Books

For detailed information on the full range of New Zealand titles, subjects and authors contact the **Book Publishers' Association of New Zealand**, T09-4802711, www.bpanz.org.nz.

Non-fiction, pictorial, natural history

There is a vast array of pictorial books celebrating New Zealand's stunning scenery. The best known photographers are **Craig Potton**, **Andris Apse** and **Robin Morrison**. Their books are of a very high quality and contain some exquisite photographs. There are a few good wildlife guidebooks and field guides. **Geoff Moon's** *New Zealand Birds* is an old favourite while the new *Field Guide to New Zealand Wildlife* by **Rod Morris** and **Terence Linsey** (Collins) is recommended. From afar the pictorial websites of www.photonewzealand.com; www.andrisapse.co.nz; and www.craigpotton.co.nz, are all excellent.

History, politics and culture

The History of New Zealand by **Keith Sinclair** is a dated but celebrated historical work, starting from before the arrival of Europeans. *Maori: A Photographic and Social Study* and *Being Pakeha*, both by **Michael King**; *The Old-Time Maori* by **Makereti**; *The Treaty of Waitangi* by **Claudia Orange**; and *The New Zealand Land Wars* by **James Belich** are all equally celebrated works covering the often contentious historical issues of the Maori and Pakeha. For an overall insight *The New Zealand Historical Atlas: Ko Papatuanuku e Takoto Nei* is highly visual, easy to read and generally recommended.

Biographies and travelogues

For tramping, the *Moirs Guides* (NZ Alpine Club) and *New Zealand's Great Walks* by **Pearl Hewson** (Hodders) are recommended. Also check out titles by **Craig Potton**, www.craigpotton.co.nz. For cycling, **Bruce Ringer's** *New Zealand by Bike* (Mountaineers) is excellent. For skiing try the annual *Ski and Snowboard Guide* available free from Brown Bear Publications, www.brownbear.co.nz.

Guidebooks and reference

The Mobil New Zealand Travel Guide by **Diana and Jeremy Pope** offers a general place-orientated guide, with interesting background reading and historical insights. *Wise's New Zealand Guide*, available in most second-hand bookshops, is excellent. For B&B guides the *New Zealand Bed and Breakfast Guide* by J **Thomas** (Moonshine) and the *Friar's B&B Guide* are recommended. For fans, *The Lord of the Rings Location Guidebook* by **Ian Brodie**, ($50), provides details the film locations around the country and how to get there (with GPS references). The book is only available in New Zealand, www.harpercollins.co.nz.

Fiction

The **New Zealand Book Council**, PO Box 11-377, Wellington, T04-4991596, www.bookcouncil.org.nz. Excellent source of listings of books, places of literary interest and events. When **Keri Hulme** won the Booker Prize in 1985 for *The Bone People*, and children's writer **Margaret Mahy** won the Carnegie Medal twice for *The Haunting* and *The Changeover*, New Zealand writing was put on the map. Previously, only the celebrated short stories by **Katherine Mansfield** (1888-1923) received international acclaim. *The Collected Stories of Katherine Mansfield* is her best-known title. Other works of note include: **Maurice Shadbolt's** *Season of the Jew*, a tale about dispossessed Maori identifying with the Jews of ancient Israel; **Maurice Gee's** *Going West*, a story of unravelling relationships amidst the backdrop of Auckland and Wellington; **Witi Ihimaera's** *Bulibasha*, an affectionate look at Maori sheep shearing gangs in Eastland; and **Alan Duff's** much acclaimed *Once Were Warriors*, a disturbing and powerful insight into Maori domestic life. The film of it provides a reality check and is the complete antithesis of New Zealand's clean green, peaceful image.

Contents

Footnotes

Maori words and phrases

Aotearoa New Zealand
Ariki tribal leader
Atua spiritual Being
Harakeke flax plant, leaves
Hawaiki ancestral Polynesian homeland
He Ao a land or a world
He tangata the people
Iwi tribe
Kaikaiawaro a dolphin (Pelorus Jack) who cruised the Sounds and became a guardian for iwi
Kaitiaki protector, caretaker
Kapa haka group of Maori performers
Kiaora welcome
Kaumatua elders
Kawa protocols
Maori words & phrases
Kete basket
Kowhaiwhai rafter patterns
Mana integrity, prestige, control
Manawhenua people with tribal affiliations with the area
Maoritanga Maori 'ness'
Marae sacred courtyard or plaza
Mauri life essence
Moana large body of water, sea
Moko tattoo

Muka flax fibre
Ngati people of
Pa a fortified residential area
Paheka white European
Poi ball attached to flax string
Pounamu sacred greenstone
Rangatira Tribal leader
Taiaha A fighting staff
Tangata people/person
Tangihanga death ritual
Taonga treasure, prized object (often passed down by ancestors)
Tapu sacred, out of bounds
Te Ika-a-Maui North Island
Tipuna ancestor
Tukutuku wall panels
Utu cost
Wahakatauki proverb or saying
Waiata song, flute music
Wairua soul
Waka canoe
Whakairo carvings
Whakapapa origins of genealogy
Whanau extended family/to give birth
Whare house
Whenua land

Index → Entries in bold refer to maps

Credits

Footprint credits

Project Editor: Jen Haddington
Editor: Sarah Thorowgood
Layout and production: Davina Rungasamy, Patrick Dawson
Cover design: Rob Lunn
Colour section: Rob Lunn
Maps: Kevin Feeney
Proofreader: Jen Haddington

Managing Director: Andy Riddle
Commercial Director: Patrick Dawson
Publisher: Alan Murphy
Publishing managers: Jo Williams, Felicity Laughton
Marketing: Liz Harper
Sales: Diane McEntee
Advertising: Renu Sibal
Finance and administration: Elizabeth Taylor

Photography credits
Front cover: Darroch Donald
Back cover: Darroch Donald
Colour section: All photographs are by Darroch Donald except whale breaching on page 7, Koekeloer/Shutterstock.

Printed in India by Nutech Print Services

Footprint feedback

We try as hard as we can to make each Footprint guide as up to date as possible but, of course, things always change. If you want to let us know about your experiences – good, bad or ugly – then don't delay, go to **footprinttravelguides.com** and send in your comments.

Publishing information

Footprint New Zealand Handbook
5th edition
© Footprint Handbooks Ltd
October 2010

ISBN: 978 1 907263 10 1
CIP DATA: A catalogue record for this book is available from the British Library

® Footprint Handbooks and the Footprint mark are a registered trademark of Footprint Handbooks Ltd

Published by Footprint
6 Riverside Court
Lower Bristol Road
Bath BA2 3DZ, UK
T +44 (0)1225 469141
F +44 (0)1225 469461
footprinttravelguides.com

Distributed in the USA by Globe Pequot Press, Guilford, Connecticut

Footprint Mini Atlas
New Zealand

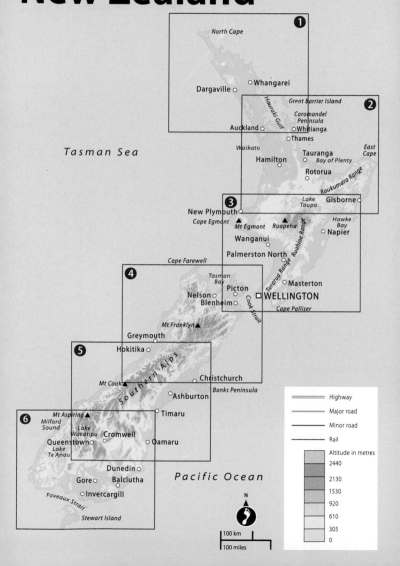

Tasman Sea

❶
North Cape
Dargaville ○ ○ Whangarei

❷
Great Barrier Island
Hauraki Gulf
Coromandel Peninsula
Auckland ○ ○ Whitianga
Waikato ○ Thames
East Cape
Bay of Plenty
Hamilton ○ Tauranga ○
Rotorua ○
Raukumara Range

❸
Lake Taupo
Gisborne ○
New Plymouth ○
Cape Egmont ▲ Mt Egmont ▲ Ruapehu
Hawke Bay
Wanganui ○ Napier ○
Ruahine Range
Palmerston North ○

❹
Cape Farewell
Tasman Bay
Picton ○
Tararua Range
Nelson ○ Masterton ○
Blenheim ○ □ WELLINGTON
Cook Strait
Cape Palliser

❺
Mt Franklyn ▲
Greymouth ○
Hokitika ○
Southern Alps
Mt Cook ▲ Christchurch ○
Ashburton ○
Banks Peninsula
Timaru ○

❻
Mt Aspiring ▲
Milford Sound
Lake Wakatipu
Cromwell ○
Queenstown ○ ○ Oamaru
Lake Te Anau
Dunedin ○
Gore ○ ○ Balclutha
Invercargill ○
Foveaux Strait
Stewart Island

Pacific Ocean

	Highway
	Major road
	Minor road
	Rail

Altitude in metres
2440
2130
1530
920
610
305
0

N

100 km
100 miles

Map 1 North Island

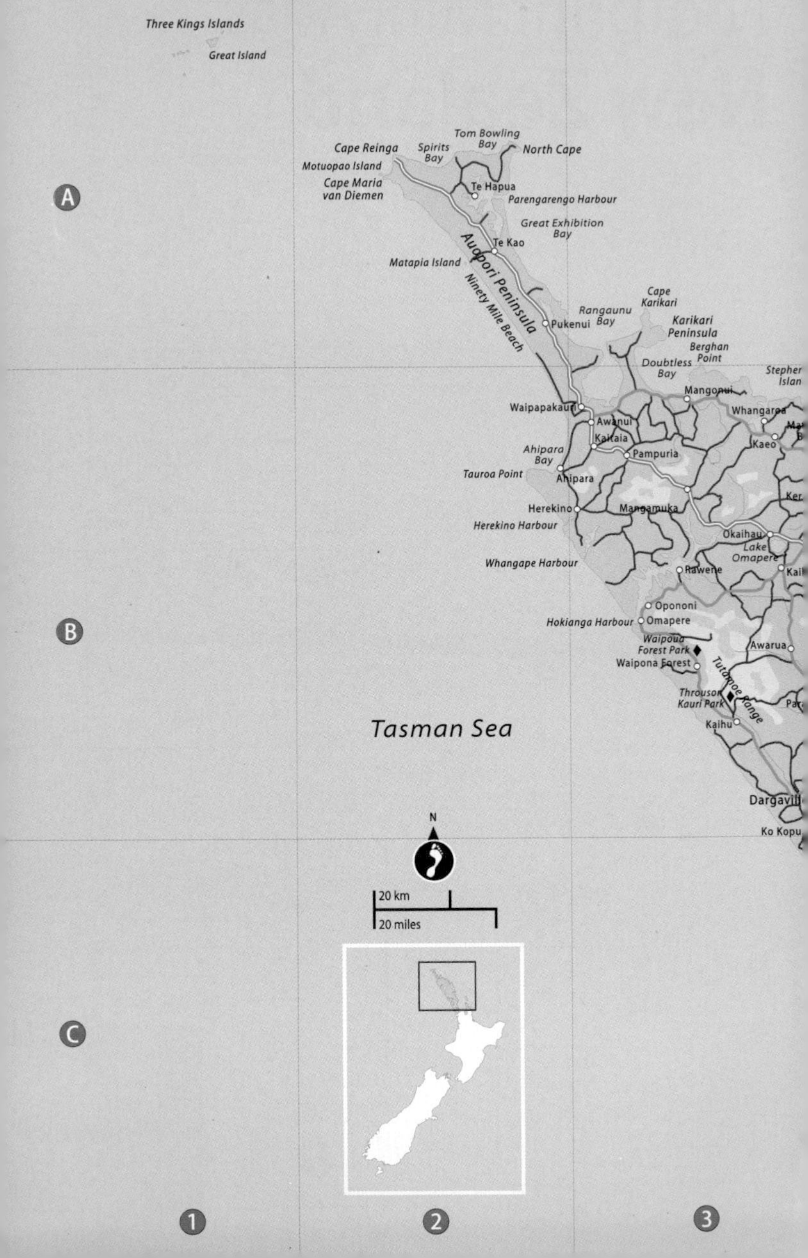

Three Kings Islands

Great Island

A

Cape Reinga
Motuopao Island
Cape Maria
van Diemen

Spirits
Bay

Tom Bowling
Bay

North Cape

Te Hapua

Parengarengo Harbour

Great Exhibition
Bay

Te Kao

Auōpori Peninsula

Matapia Island

Ninety Mile Beach

Cape
Karikari

Rangaunu
Bay

Pukenui

Karikari
Peninsula

Berghan
Point

Doubtless
Bay

Stepher
Islan

Mangonui

Waipapakaur

Awanui

Whangare

Kaitaia

Pampuria

Kaeo

Ma

Ahipara
Bay

Ker

Tauroa Point

Ahipara

Mangamuka

Okaihau
Lake
Omapere

Herekino

B

Herekino Harbour

Rawene

Kai

Whangape Harbour

Opononi

Hokianga Harbour

Omapere

Waipoua
Forest Park

Awarua

Waipona Forest

Tuthiwai Tonge

Tasman Sea

Throuson
Kauri Park

Par

Kaihu

N

Dargavill

Ko Kopu

20 km

20 miles

C

① **②** **③**

South Pacific Ocean

A

B

C

Bay of Islands · Cape Brett
ngi · Russell
Dia
erewa
awakawa
Home Point
Whangaruru Harbour
Helena Bay
Poor Knight Islands
wai
Hikurangi
Tutukaka
Ngunguru
Ngunguru Bay
Whakapara
Whangarei
Onerahi
Whangarei Heads
Portland
Bream Head
Ruakaka
Bream Bay
Hen & Chickens
Waipu
Waipu Cove
Bream Trail
Waiotira
Taipuha
Maungaturoto
Papara
atakohe
Mangawhai
Kaiwaka
Port Albert
Tomarata
Pakiri
Wellsford
Cape Rodney
Leigh
ato
Tapore
Matakana
Takatu Point
South Head
Warkworth
Kawau Island
Channel Island
th ad
Shelly Beach
Ahuroa
Weiterholm
Motuora Island
Cape Colville
Port Jackson
Colville Channel
Cape Barrier
Kaukapakapa
Waiwera
Orewa
Tiritiri Matangi Island
Hauraki Gulf
Mt Moehau (892m)
Port Charles
Kennedy Bay
Helensville
Coatsville
Whangaparaoa
North Shore
Albany
Motutapu Island
Rangitoto Island
Waiheke Island
Oneroa
Onetangi
Amodeo Bay
Papaaroha
Whangapoua
Coromandel
Matarangi
Te Rerenga
Opito Bay
Opito
Kuaotunu
Waimauku
Kumeu
Muriwai
Waitekere
Swanson
Piha
Mt Eden
Devonport
Howick
Omiha
Maraetai
Ponui I
Whitianga
Mercury Bay
Hotwater Bay
Hahei
Waitekere
Huia
Mangere
Manurewa
Papatoetoe
Takanini
Auckland
Orere Point
Tapu
Coromandel
Tairua
Shoe Island
The Alderman Islands

Little Barrier Island
Port Fitzroy
Rakitu I
Great Barrier Island
Tryphena
Cuvier Island
Great Mercury Island
Red Mercury Island

2

4 · **5** · **6**

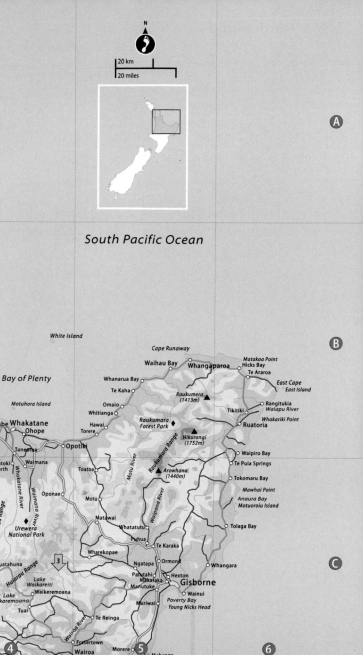

South Pacific Ocean

A

B

C

20 km
20 miles

N

White Island

Bay of Plenty

Cape Runaway

Motuhora Island

Matakoa Point
Hicks Bay
Te Araroa

Waihau Bay

Whangaparaoa

Whanarua Bay

Te Kaha

East Cape
East Island

Raukumera
(1413m)

Omaio

Matata

Whitianga

Raukumara
Forest Park

Rangitukia
Waiapu River

Tikitiki

Edgecumbe

Whakatane

Ohope

Hawai

Torere

Whakariki Point

Te Teko

Taneatua

Opotiki

Hikurangi
(1752m)

Ruatoria

Raukumara Range

Waimana

Ruatoki
North

Waipiro Bay

werau

Te Pula Springs

Rangitaiki River

Toatoa

Arowhana
(1440m)

Tokomaru Bay

Galatea

Whakatane River

Waimana River

Motu River

Oponae

Murupara

Mawhai Point

Anaura Bay
Motuoroiu Island

Ikawhenua Range

Motu

Urewera
National Park

Matawai

Whatatutu

Tolaga Bay

Puhua

Wharekopae

Te Karaka

Ruatahuna

Huiarau Range

Ngatapa

Whangara

inginui

3

Lake
Waikareiti

Parutahi

Ormond

Hexton

hirinaki
est Park

Lake
Waikaremoana

Waikaremoana

Makaraka

Manutuke

Gisborne

ungataniwha
(1375m)

Tuai

Wainui

Muriwai

Poverty Bay
Young Nicks Head

Te Reinga

Wairoa River

ka River

4

Raupanga

Frasertown

Wairoa

Morere

5

Mahanga

6

Nuhaka

Opoutama

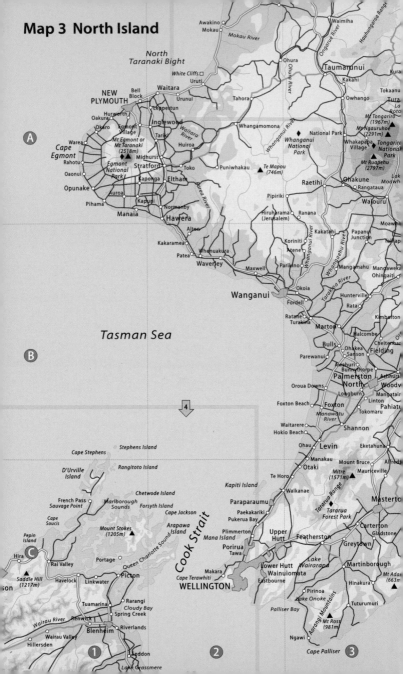

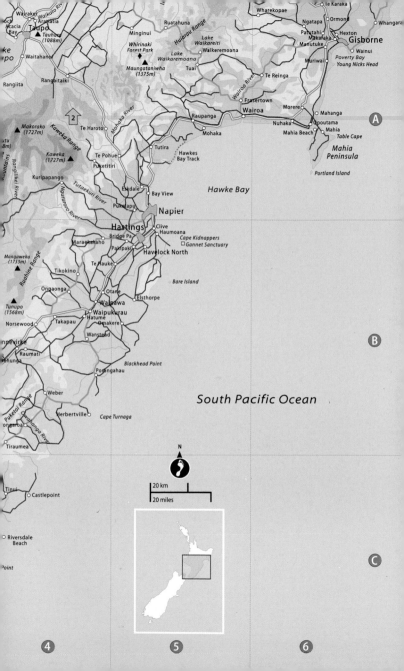

Map 4 South Island

Paturau Ri

Mount (162

Wekakura Point

Wakamar

Aorere R

Mount Domett (1623m)

Kahura Natior Park

A

Oparara

Karamea

Karamea River

Karamra Bight

Little Wanganui

Mokihinui River

Seddonville

Hector

Granity

Stockton

Millerton

Matiri Range

Owen R

Carters Beach

Westport

Waimangaroa

Denniston

Lyell

Buller River

Buller River

Murchi

Charleston

Inangahua

Paenga

Mount Fardday (1485m)

Mount Victoria (1640m)

Marua River

Victoria Range

B

Perpendicular Point

Punakaiki

Pancake Rocks & blowholes

Paparoa National Park

Paparoa Range

Reefton

Maruia

Barrytown

Ikamatua

Waiuta

Inangahua River

Springs Junction

Mar Sprin

Lewis Pas

Runanga

Blackball

Ahaura River

Ngahere

Mount Technica (1867m)

Greymouth

Shantytown

Paroa

Dobson

Moana

Kopara

Mount Ajax (1834m)

Lake Sumner Forest Park

Kumara

Lake Brunner

Lake Sumner

Mount Longfelle (1901

Hokitika

Lake Kaniere

Inchbonnie

Lake Mahinepua

Turiwhate

Ruatapu

Lake Kaniere

Otira

Arthur's Pass National Park

Esk River

Ross

Kowhitirangi

Arthur's Pass

Arthur's Pass

Pukeeroki Range

C

Pukekura

Browning Pass

Cass

Chest Peak (1935m)

Lees Valley

Abut Head

Wanganui River

Craigieburn Forest Park

Mount Thomas (1023m)

Rotokino

Okarito

Okarito Lagoon

Harihari

Mount Whitcombe (2644m)

Whitcombe Pass

Wilberforce River

Lake Coleridge

Porters Pass

Oxford

Whataroa

Mount Arrowsmith (2795m)

Rakaia River

Springfield

Franz

Josef Glacier

Mount D'Archiac (2865m)

Mount Potts (2194m)

Lake Heron

Lake Coleridge

Sheffield

Waimakariri Rive

Gillespies Beach

Waiho River

Fox Glacier

Fox Glacier

Franz Josef Glacier

South B

Coalgate

Darfield

Kirwee

Rolleste

Westland National Park

1

Mount Cook National Park

The Thumbs (2545m)

2

Mount Hutt (2188m)

Mount Hutt

3

Hororata

North

Greendale

5

Map 5 South Island

Tasman Sea

Ⓐ

Puk
*Wange
River*

Abut Head

*Okarito
Lagoon* Rotokino Ha

Okarito

Whataroa

Gillespies
Beach Fox Glacier Franz
Josef Glacier Mount
D'Arch
(2865m)

Fox Glacier Fox Glacier *Franz
Josef
Glacier*

Westland
National Park Mount Cook
National Park Go

Heretaniwha Point Jacobs River Copland Track Mount Cook
(3754m)
Bruce Bay

*Poringa
River* Mount
Cook,

Lake Moeraki

Lake Paringa

*Mount Hooker
(2652m)* Mount Ward
(2644m) Lᵉ
Te

Okuru Haast Dun Fiunary
(2499m) Glentanner

Hannahs
Clearing *Mackenzie
Country* Lᵉ
Te

Jackson Head *Mount Brewster
(2423m)* *Lake
Pukaki*

Jackson's Bay

Cascade Point *Haast Pass* Mount Huxley
(2499m) Lake
Ohau Lake
Pukaki Twizel

Makarora ▽ 6 Lᵉ
Te

Awarua Point *Hunter River* Mount St Mary
(2332m) Ohau
River Lake
Benmore

Big Bay *Olivine Range* Clearburn

Martins Bay Mount Aspiring
(3033m) Mount Melina
(1905m) Omarama

Lake
McKerrow Mount Aspiring
National Park *Lake
Wanaka* *Lindis
Pass*

Mount Aha
(2347m) Lake
Hawea Lake
Aviemore Lake
Wait

Mount Tutoko
(2746m) Mount
Earnslaw
(2819m) Otematata

ᵗᵉ Peak
(695m) West
Wanaka *Lindis River* Aviemore Kurow

Milford
Sound Wanaka
Homestead St Bathans Otel

Homer
Tunnel Mount
Bonpland
(2348m) Hawea
Flat *Duntan Mountains*

Lake Gunn Glenorchy Luggate Becks Naseby

Cascade Creek *Caples Track* Cardrona *Lake
Dunstan* Lauder Ranfurly Waipiata

lade House Arrowtown Omakau *Menuheriki River* Poolburn

Knob Flat Ⓒ *Greenstone Track* Cromwell Patearoa Morrisor

Queenstown Frankton Clyde

Bannockbury *Kakanui*

ns *Livingston Mountains* Lake
Wakatipu Cecil Peak
(1974m) Alexandra Summit Rock
(1450m) Macra
Flat

Te Anau
Downs Obelisk
(1695m)

Eyre Mountains Jane Peak
(2035m) *Taieri River*

Lake
Anau Kingston *Garvie Mountains* Middlemarch ③

Te Anau ① Roxburgh Hydro ②

The Key *Mararoa River* Athol Roxburgh

Mo *ia River*

Map 6 South Island

Awarua Point
Big Bay
Martins Bay
Lake McKerrow
Yates Point
Milford Sound
Mount Tutoko
(2746m)
Milford
Sound
Seabreeze Point
Mitre Peak
(1695m)
Homer
Tunnel
Mount Gor
(2348
Sutherland Sound
Bligh Sound
Mackinnon
Pass
Lake Gunn
Cascade Creek
George Sound
Glade House
Round Head
Fiordland
National
Park
Knob
Coswell Sound
Charles Sound
Mount Alexandra
(1323m)
Nancy Sound
Thompson Sound
Mount Irene
(1879m)
Lake
Te Anau
Te Anau
Downs
Secretary Island
Doubtful Sound
Febreo Point
Te Anau
Dagg Sound
Lake
Manapouri
Manapouri
The Key
Breaksea Sound
Mount
Crowfoot
(1695m)
Fiordland
National
Park
World
Heritage Site
Redcliffe
Resolution Island
Monowai
Ohai
Cooper Island
Long Island
Lake
Monowai
Anchor Island
Dusky Sound
Birchwood
West Cape
Cameron Mountains
Caroline Peak
(1722m)
Lake
Houroko
Clifden
Orawia
Great Island
Chalky Inlet
Chalky Island
Preservation Inlet
Coal Island
The Hump
(1067m)
Tuatapere
Otautau
Lake
Hakapoua
Te Waewae
Puysegur Point
Te Waewae Bay
Thorn
Orepuki
Pahia Point
Colac Bay
Ri
Centre
Island
Tasman Sea
Fove
Str
Rugged Island
Mount An
(980m
Codfish Island
Mason Bay
Rakiura
National
Park
Halfr
Ernest Islands
Doughboy Bay
Stewart I
Mount
(750
Muttonbird
Islands
Peral Islan
Port Pegasus
South West Cape
South Cape

N

20 km
20 miles

Franklin Mountains
Stuart Mountains
Morano River
Hunter Mountains
Waiau River
Takitimu Mountains
Holyford Track

A
B
C
1
2
3

Map symbols

□	Capital city	▭	Building
○	Other city, town	▪	Sight
⌁	International border	✝ ✝	Cathedral, church
⌁	Regional border	☎	Chinese temple
⊖	Customs	🛕	Hindu temple
⬭	Contours (approx)	🛕	Meru
▲	Mountain, volcano	🕌	Mosque
⥺	Mountain pass	△	Stupa
⏜	Escarpment	✡	Synagogue
⬭	Glacier	🛈	Tourist office
⬚	Salt flat	🏛	Museum
⬚	Rocks	✉	Post office
❦	Seasonal marshland	℗	Police
⬚	Beach, sandbank	⑤	Bank
⟋⟋	Waterfall	@	Internet
⌒	Reef	☏	Telephone
═══	National highway	🏠	Market
───	Paved road	✚	Medical services
───	Unpaved or *ripio* (gravel) road	🅿	Parking
⁃⁃⁃	Track	🅖	Petrol
⋯⋯	Footpath	⛳	Golf
───	Railway	⚒	Archaeological site
▬■	Railway with station	◆	National park,
✈	Airport		wildlife reserve
🚌	Bus station	✾	Viewing point
Ⓜ	Metro station	⛺	Campsite
⁃ ⁃ ⁃	Cable car	⌂	Refuge, lodge
⧓	Funicular	🏰	Castle, fort
⛴	Ferry	🤿	Diving
▭▭▭	Pedestrianized street	✝🌲	Deciduous, coniferous,
Σ Ⅼ	Tunnel		palm trees
→	One way-street	🌿	Mangrove
⫼⫼⫼	Steps	⌂	Hide
⋈	Bridge	🍷	Vineyard, winery
⎯⎯	Fortified wall	⚗	Distillery
⬚	Park, garden, stadium	⚓	Shipwreck
●	Sleeping	✕	Historic battlefield
❼	Eating	▷	Related map
❶	Bars & clubs		